REPORTS OF CASES IN THE COURT OF CHANCERY IN THE TIME OF KING GEORGE I

English Law Reports of the Early Modern Period

Volume One: *Equity Cases in the Court of Exchequer, 1660–1714*, Edited by W. H. Bryson, 2007. [This volume can be cited as Eq. Cases Exch.]

Volume Two: *Robert Paynell's Exchequer Reports (1627–1631),* Edited by W. H. Bryson, 2009. [This volume can be cited as Paynell Exch.]

Volume Three: *Robert Paynell's King's Bench Reports (1625–1627),* Edited by W. H. Bryson, 2010. [This volume can be cited as Paynell K.B.]

Volume Four: *Reports of Cases in the Court of Exchequer in the Time of King George I (1714–1727),* Edited by W. H. Bryson, 2013. [This volume can be cited as Exch. Cases *temp.* Geo. I.]

Volume Five: *Reports of Cases in the Court of Exchequer in the Time of King Charles II,* Edited by W. H. Bryson, 2017. [This volume can be cited as Exch. Cases *temp.* Char. II.]

Medieval and Renaissance
Texts and Studies

Volume 507

Center for Law Reporting

Volume 6

REPORTS OF CASES IN THE COURT OF CHANCERY IN THE TIME OF KING GEORGE I

(1714 TO 1727)

EDITED BY

W. H. BRYSON

ACMRS Arizona Center for Medieval & Renaissance Studies

Tempe, Arizona
2019

Arizona Center
for Medieval &
Renaissance Studies

Published by ACMRS (Arizona Center for Medieval and Renaissance Studies)
Tempe, Arizona

∞
This book is made to last. It is set in Adobe Caslon Pro,
smyth-sewn and printed on acid-free paper to library specifications.
Printed in the United States of America

Introduction

This is a collection of miscellaneous manuscript reports from the Court of Chancery from 1714 to 1727, the reign of King George I. There can be no pretension to completeness as there is no way of knowing what manuscripts are presently lurking in private libraries. These manuscripts are in no way glamorous, nor are they very old, and thus they go unnoticed however useful they may be to lawyers and to legal scholars. A few out of the way cases and some short printed reports are also included. Among the larger manuscript collections used are the following.

Lincoln's Inn MS. Misc. 506

Lincoln's Inn MS. Misc. 506, 'Cases Argued and Adjudged in the High Court of Chancery and in the Court of Exchequer'. This is a collection of Chancery reports, the first of which, *Brown v. Barkham* (Ch. 1717), was copied from 1 Strange 35, 93 E.R. 368, and is not included here. There are only two Exchequer cases, *Joscelyn v. Brewet* (Ex. 1722) and *Marriot v. Marriot* (Ex. 1725–1726), and these have been recently printed elsewhere,[1] but they are not included here. These reports were 'probably collected by Mr. Emlyn', according to a note at 2 Merivale 440, 35 E.R. 1008, where one of these cases, *Burnett v. Chetwood* (Ch. 1721), Case No. 509 herein, is printed. Sollom Emlyn (1697–1754) was a barrister of Lincoln's Inn.[2] However, it is also possible that only this single case was copied from Emlyn's now lost reports and/or that John Herman Merivale (1779–1844) was generally mistaken.

This set of reports was printed in *Miscellaneous Chancery Reports (1714–1730)* (2009); they are included here with the kind permission of William S. Hein & Co., Inc.

---

[1] *Reports of Cases in the Court of Exchequer in the Time of King George I (1714 to 1727)* (W. H. Bryson, ed., 2013), pp. 218, 860.

[2] N. G. Jones, 'Emlyn, Sollom', *Oxford Dictionary of National Biography*, vol. 18, p. 409.

Lincoln's Inn MS. Misc. 384

Lincoln's Inn MS. Misc. 384 is a very extensive collection of Chancery reports. It appears to have been copied from thirteen other books; these books may have been the rough notes taken in court by the same person who put this volume together or they may have been independent collections. This is an anonymous set of Chancery cases dating from 1713 to 1747. The reports are not in chronological order. Only a selection of these cases are published here.

British Library MS. Hargrave 81

British Library MS. Hargrave 81 is an eighteenth century professional copy. The text was copied on the rectos only, leaving the versos blank except for one case, *Cope v. Futor* (Ch. 1714), which the copyist omitted in the copying and then went back and added at the correct place, but on the facing verso. There is no internal or external evidence of the reporter's identification. The book was bought by Francis Hargrave (d. 1821) from Mrs. Elizabeth Lynch (d. 1794), a Dublin bookseller, along with a number of other legal manuscripts. Hargrave's manuscripts were sold to the British Museum (now the British Library) in 1813.[3] This manuscript has 287 folios at the present; the following folios in the original foliation are now missing, 89, 94, 107–124, 193–194. They were missing when the British Museum acquired the book, and most probably also when Hargrave received it. The cases date from 1710 to 1724. They are not in chronological order. These cases all come from the Court of Chancery except for one case from the Court of Exchequer, *Bean v. Lee* (Ex. 1713). This manuscript is a combination of two separate sets of Chancery reports: part 1, ff. 2–163 (1710–1718); part 2, ff. 164–286 (1722–1724). Note that each has a different version of the case of *Duke of Rutland v. Duchess of Rutland* (Ch. 1724), Case No. 629, herein.

British Library MS. Hargrave 82 is another copy of the set of reports found in British Library MS. Hargrave 81. The copying is not as careful as British Library MS. Hargrave 81. It also was acquired by Hargrave from Lynch and, no doubt, in the same shipment. It also is a professional copy in a very similar hand, and the versos are left blank. One may suppose that they were both made for Mrs. Lynch for her stock of books for sale.

British Library MS. Hargrave 77, ff. 1–42v, is another copy of the reports that comprise the first part of British Library MS. Hargrave 81, ff. 2–163, and British Library MS. Hargrave 82, ff. 1–173, with some additional cases at ff. 43–55 dating from 1714 to 1716. It came from Mrs. Lynch also.

---

[3] H. Ellis, *A Catalogue of Manuscripts . . . of Francis Hargrave, Esq.* (1818), pp. [v], 21; J. H. Baker, 'Hargrave, Francis', *Oxford Dictionary of National Biography*, vol. 25, pp. 270–271.

British Library MS. Hargrave 303, ff. 1–75, is another copy of the cases in British Library MS. Hargrave 77, ff. 1–42v. The same additional cases at the end of Hargrave 77 are at ff. 75v-94 here. This was formerly Lynch MS. 28.

Hargrave 77 and Hargrave 303 are the same. These two collections are very close to Hargrave 81 and Hargrave 82, but there are substantial differences.

Lincoln's Inn MS. Misc. 107, ff. 91–141, includes some of the reports towards the end of this set of cases. This manuscript is a long notebook; however, the reports are not notes made in court, but, rather, it is a carefully made copy of another manuscript. This book was owned by Charles Abbot, baron Colchester, (1757–1829) and was presented to Lincoln's Inn in November 1848.[4]

Lincoln's Inn MS. Hill 73 (Thomas Bold's reports)

Lincoln's Inn MS. Hill 73 is a short manuscript in a long notebook signed by Thomas Bold, the text being in the same handwriting as the signature. The cases date from 1717 to 1719 and are from the Court of Chancery except for *Gregg v. Raymond* (K.B. c. 1719), at p. 114, and three common law cases from 1719, *Copden v. Vancittera* (1719), *Wright v. Pope* (1719), and *Anonymous* (1719), at the end of the book, reversing. All of these reports are well reported though very brief. This manuscript was sold by Thomas Osborne (d. 1767), a bookseller at Gray's Inn Gateway, London, to George Hill (1716–1808), King's Serjeant; it was bought by Lincoln's Inn in 1808.[5]

Thomas Bold was born in 1695, the son of William Bold of St. Bride's Parish, London. He entered Westminster School in 1708 and Christ Church, Oxford, on 23 June 1713. Bold received his B.A. in 1718 and an M.A. in 1721. He was admitted as a law student at the Middle Temple on 15 June 1711 and called to the bar on 31 May 1717. He was admitted *ad eundem* at Lincoln's Inn on 23 November 1717.[6]

[4] J. H. Baker, *English Legal Manuscripts* (1978), vol. 2, p. 98.

[5] J. H. Baker, *English Legal Manuscripts* (1978), vol. 2, pp. 80–84.

[6] G. F. R. Barker and A. H. Stenning, *The Record of Old Westminster* (1928), vol. 1, p. 101; J. Foster, *Alumni Oxonienses* (1891), part 1, vol. 1, p. 145; H. A. C. Sturgess, *Register of Admission to the . . . Middle Temple* (1949), vol. 1, p. 269; *Records . . . of Lincoln's Inn, Admissions* (1896), vol. 1, p. 380.

Lincoln's Inn MSS. Misc. 10–12

Lincoln's Inn MSS. Misc. 10–12 were compiled and partly written by William Melmoth, Sr. (1665–1743), a bencher of Lincoln's Inn. They cover the period 1695 to 1742. After a contentious will dispute, these books were acquired by Lincoln's Inn in 1835.[7] The cases are not in chronological order.

William Melmoth was born in 1665. He was admitted to Clifford's Inn on 15 April 1686 and to the Inner Temple on 30 May 1689; he was called to the bar on 29 May 1693. He moved to Lincoln's Inn on 25 April 1699 and was called to the bench in 1719; he was Treasurer of Lincoln's Inn in 1730. Melmoth was a co-editor of the first edition of Vernon's reports. He died on 6 April 1743 and was buried under the cloister of Lincoln's Inn chapel.[8]

We acknowledge our great appreciation to Lincoln's Inn, the British Library, and the King's Inns, Dublin, for collecting and preserving these manuscripts and for giving permission to publish the reports that are printed herein.

[7] J. H. Baker, *English Legal Manuscripts*, vol. 2, pp. 91–92 (1978).

[8] E. Major and N. Pohl, 'Melmoth, William, the elder', *Oxford Dictionary of National Biography*, vol. 37, pp. 757–758.

Table of Cases Reported

[These references are to case numbers, not page numbers.]

1

Serle v. Smith

(Ch. 1714)

A person held in strict custody for a contempt of court cannot have the liberty of the rules of the prison.

British Library MS. Hargrave 81, f. 118, pl. 1

10 August 1714.

Where a person, for contempt, is ordered into *arcta custodia*, he cannot have the liberty of the rules nor go out of the prison gate. Such contemners must be distressed and made as uneasy as may be to force them to submission and to do right.

[Other copies of this report: British Library MS. Hargrave 82, f. 131.]

[Other reports of this case: British Library MS. Hargrave 77, f. 32v, pl. 1, British Library MS. Hargrave 303, f. 59, pl. 2.]

2

Champney v. Champney

(Ch. 1714–1715)

The words 'equally to be divided' make the grantees tenants in common.

The words 'dying without issue male' mean a failure of issue male.

Lincoln's Inn MS. Misc. 380, pt. 3, p. 138

Michaelmas Term 1714.

The bill was to have lands exonerated of some annuities and sums of money charged upon them and to have possession. Among other points were these three.

First, lands are by a marriage settlement limited to the use of the husband for life then to trustees for 200 years to raise £1200 for the younger child or children of the marriage, if but one, then all to that one, if more than one, then in such proportion as the husband should appoint and, for want of such appointment, then among them equally to be divided between them. I think there was no time of payment limited.

The husband dies leaving a son and two daughters, one whereof died unmarried. The question was what became of the share of the daughter so dying.

Sir Joseph Jekyll urged that it being a provision for children arising out of lands and the child dying who should have had it, it shall sink into the estate for the benefit of the heir.

Serjeant *Hooper* insisted that the daughters were joint tenants and provision being by deed and the survivor therefore should have the whole.

The other counsel on the same side insisted only on the other daughter's having her distribution part, which happened to be a third part only.

The Lord Chancellor [Lord Cowper] said he thought is a vested provision which should not sink into the estate but be distributed and that, by reason of the words 'equally to be divided', the two daughters should take as tenants in common and not as joint tenant so that the daughter should only have her distribution share or part.

I observed that there had been an account made up sometime before wherein the surviving daughter had computed only a distribution part to be due to her and was allowed by the heir, for which reason (or for what other I know not) that point seemed not much to be contended; else it seems to be contrary to a resolution given by this very Chancellor about five years ago, *viz.* Hilary [term] 1709, between Carington and Tournay, where lands were limited by a marriage settlement (besides the jointure) to the husband for life, then to trustees for ninety-nine years for raising £400 apiece for his younger son and three daughters at their respective ages of twenty-one or marriage, which should first happen. The father died, then one of the three daughters died intestate under the age of twenty-one unmarried. The other daughter with her husband brought their bill to have the wife's portions and particularly to have the distributive part of the sister's share who died intestate. It was urged that the provision of £400 vested immediately and that the time of payment only was [in the] future so that it should go to the administrator of the daughter who died and be distributed. The Lord Chancellor said so it should had it been a pecuniary legacy and no more, but, this being a provision for children arising out of the estate of the heir and the child who should have had it being dead and therefore having no occasion for it, the estate of the heir should not be burdened only to make a distribution. So he decreed it to sink into the estate for the benefit of the heir.

The second point was lands were limited to the husband for life, then a small part of them only (among other lands) to the wife for life, then the whole to trustees for 210 years, then to the first and every other son in tail male etc. The term of 210 years was upon trust that, if the husband and wife died without any issue male, that then the trustees should raise £3000 for daughters' portion etc. The husband and wife had issue, a son who died without issue in his mother's lifetime (who was still living) and two [. . .] in the lifetime of his sisters, who brought her bill (which in truth was a cross-bill) to have the money. It was insisted, and so the Lord Chancellor said, that the son dying without issue in the construction of a court of equity as well as law, the father and mother dying without issue especially since it happens in the lifetime of the party to whom the money was to come upon the contingency and that the portion should vest and carry interest from the death of the heir.

But *Sir Joseph Jekyll* urged very strongly that the portion could not vest until the death of the mother. And he made a difference between the words 'and in case of failure of issue' [and] the words 'and if they too die, *viz.*, the father and mother die without issue', for that may be said to be a failure of issue when as soon as one of the tenants in special tail dies without issue. But it cannot be said that they two are dead without issue so long as either of them are living. He cited the case of the Duke of Southampton, in the House of Lords;[1] an estate was limited to a man for life (without any estate to the wife), remainder to his first and every other sons etc. and, if the husband and wife died without issue of their body, then over to Sir [*blank*]; the husband died, and the wife was living. The question was whether the lands should immediately go over to him in remainder or not. And it was decreed that they should not, for it could not be said that they two were dead without issue so long as one of them was living so that the lands should not remain over until the wife was dead also, but they should descend to the heirs at law in the meantime.

The Lord Chancellor [Lord Cowper] said he would consider of this point. But [he was] sure this difference was never thought of by any conveyancer at the time of his drawing the deed.

Vide postea, the same case, fol. 142.

Lincoln's Inn MS. Misc. 380, pt. 3, p. 142, pl. 1

The 21st of May 1715, the Lord Chancellor Cowper made his decree. The Case of the Duke of Southampton was a case in point. And [he held] that, by the authority of that case, the words must be literally taken so that there must not be only an impossibility of the condition's being performed, but the parties must be actually dead too (and upon the authority of that case), which words he used so often as if he were rather governed by no authority than reason be said he thought the money ought not to be raised until the wife's death payable at the respective days of marriage or twenty-one which should first happen. But it must not be intended that the money should be paid at those times if it happened after the death of the parties but, if those days should happen before the death of the parties, then the money must be paid when the party dies. He also said that the annuity to be paid in the meantime did (though it was hard) depend upon the same

[1] *Duke of Southampton v. Cramborne* (1692), 2 Freeman 186, 22 E.R. 1151, 1 Vernon 338, 23 E.R. 506, Shower P.C. 83, 1 E.R. 58.

conditional precedent and it was not to be raised until the mother's death, for the words 'in the meantime' signified only after the money was not raisable until after the death of both father and mother. The annuity cannot begin until then.

There followed other words, namely 'and also in the meantime the raising the £3000 and, after the days of payment, the trustees to put it out for their benefit'. But those words he looked upon as nonsense and not duly considered and so to signify nothing in the case.

British Library MS. Hargrave 80, f. 198

By a settlement, part of the freehold lands were limited to the husband for life, remainder to the wife for life, remainder to trustees to preserve contingent remainders, remainder to the first son etc. in tail male, remainder to trustees for 200 years, with several remainders over and the other was limited to the husband for life, remainder to trustees for 210 years, remainder to the first son etc. in tail male, remainder to trustees for 200 years, with remainders over. The trust of the 210 years term was declared to raise a £1500 for the younger child or children equally to be divided between them. And, afterwards, the trust of the 200 years term and of the 210 years term and of a subsidiary term carved out of the leasehold estate [was] declared to be to the intent that, if the husband and wife should die without issue male, that then the further sum of £3000 should be raised for the daughters or daughter if but one. The husband died, leaving but one son, who lived to suffer a recovery and died without issue male, and two daughters, one of whom was since dead, the other and the wife being *yet al*ive.

The first question was concerning the £1500.

Jekyll: No time being limited for raising it, the proper time is when portions are wanted, marriage or twenty-one, and one of the daughters dying unmarried and under age, her share sinks into the estate in ease and favor of the inheritance.

Chesshyre, of the same side, [said] that the words 'equally to be divided' make the daughters tenants in common and that, one dying, the survivor could have no more than her own share and such part of her sister's as she was entitled to by the Statute of Distribution.[1]

Hooper: It is a joint interest in its creation, and the words 'equally to be divided' being in a deed make no tenancy in common. The share of the dead survives therefore to the other. Had there been but one at first, she would undoubtedly have had the whole £1500. It is the same thing now they are reduced to one by death.

Lord Chancellor [Lord Cowper]: The portions vested immediately, and they were tenants in common.

The next question was whether the £3000 could be raised at all.

[1] Stat. 22 & 23 Car. II, c. 10 (*SR*, V, 719–720).

Jekyll, Chesshyre, and *Mead* [said] that that was to rise upon the contingency of the husband and wife dying without issue male. And though, at law, a man might be said to be dead without issue male whenever his male descendants failed at any distance of time, such a construction in this case would be unreasonable, that it could not be the intent of the parties to create a contingent charge which might be continually riding upon the estate as long as there were any issue male and not within the power of the tenants in tail to bar, that, therefore, the words of the contingency ought to expect no longer than the death of the husband or, at least, ought to determine when any issue male came of age and thereby had a power over the estate, that the term is principally intended to be a fund for the £3000 now limited after the estate tail and, therefore, in the power of the tenant in tail to bar (which he had done accordingly) which showed the parties to have meant a failure of issue male before any of them should come of age, that the 210 years term was principally designed to raise the £1500 and come in only in aid of the 200 years term, and not to be singly charged.

Lord Chancellor [Lord Cowper] [held] *e contra* that the common signification of 'dying without issue male' is failure of issue male and, since that happened in a reasonable time in the life of the person that is entitled to demand the portion, there can be no objection to the raising of it. The bringing in the 210 years term in aid of the 200 years term, which lay behind an estate tail and were therefore liable to be defeated was an agreement of the intent of the parties to provide against such an event and that the inference from their being barred was not that the other ought not to be charged, but that it ought, that, though the law allowed a tenant in tail the liberty of barring such terms, it was a hardship and, therefore, not to be carried further in equity. He, therefore, declared that the daughter was well entitled to this additional £3000 and that it ought to be raised out of the 210 years term and the term of the leasehold estate.

The next question was whether it should be raised immediately or expect until the death of the mother. It was made payable at twenty-one, and which the daughter was, or marriage, but it being upon a condition precedent, if the father and mother should die without issue male of their two bodies.

Jekyll insisted that it ought to be strictly accomplished and that it was certain there could be no issue male between them, yet the death of the mother must of necessity precede the raising of the portion, as in the case upon Sir Harry Wood's [estate] between Cranmer and Sir Caesar Child.[1] And, though the 210 years term was fallen into possession, it ought to attend the inheritance, as terms created for a special purpose do when that purpose is satisfied, until the contingency should happen and that, the rest being charged with a jointure, it was probably

[1] *Duke of Southampton v. Cranmer* (1685), 1 Vernon 338, 23 E.R. 506, 2 Freeman 186, 22 E.R. 1151, Shower P.C. 83, 1 E.R. 58, also discussed in *Kirk v. Webb* (1698), Precedents in Chancery 84, 24 E.R. 41.

the intent of the parties that the profits of this should be enjoyed by the person entitled to the inheritance until the jointure fall in.

Of this point, Lord Chancellor [LORD COWPER] took time to consider.

[Other copies of this report: Lincoln's Inn MS. Misc. 383, p. 315, pl. 2, Lincoln's Inn MS. Misc. 107, f. 39.]

10 Modern 314, 88 E.R. 743

Easter 1 Geo. I [1715].

In a marriage settlement, a power was lodged in trustees to raise £3000 for a daughter to be paid to her at the age of twenty-one years or day of marriage, which should first happen, when Champney and his wife should die without issue male and, in the meantime, £100 a year to be paid her for her maintenance.

COWPER, Lord Chancellor, resolved upon the authority of The Duke of Southampton's Case[1] that the words 'when Champney and his wife should die without issue male' amounted to a condition precedent and that the time of raising the portion did not commence when one of them should be dead without issue male and so the other be tenant in tail after a possibility of issue extinct but where both of them should be dead without issue male.

[It was] resolved that 'the meantime' in which the £100 a year was payable for a maintenance must necessarily relate to the intermediate time between the raising the money and her attaining the age of twenty-one or day of marriage.

[Other copies of this report: 2 Eq. Cas. Abr. 640, 22 E.R. 537.]

3

Rawlinson v. Rawlinson

(Ch. 1714)

A court of equity will enforce a power that gives a discretion as to its exercise.

Where a London freeman's wife has compounded for her customary share, a moiety of his estate will go after his death to his children.

The widow of a knight can retain her paraphernalia though she cannot by the custom of London.

British Library MS. Hargrave 80, f. 186v

Sir Thomas Rawlinson [1647–1708], an alderman of London, gave several jewels and other things of value to his lady for her life [and] desired her by his will to distribute them after her death among such of their children as should be then living and be most dutiful to her.

---

[1] *Duke of Southampton v. Cramborne* (1692), 2 Freeman 186, 22 E.R. 1151, 1 Vernon 338, 23 E.R. 506, Shower P.C. 83, 1 E.R. 58.

The Attorney General [*Northey*] pressed for directions that the children living at her decease should have them equally and allowed that My Lord Jeffreys was of opinion in Sir Thomas Croke's Case[1] that, where a power was given to a person to distribute according to his discretion, equity would control an unequal distribution.

Vernon: It is contrary to the intent of the will, which was to secure to My Lady the duty of her children, as well as to the words to have an order made now that she shall distribute equally at his death. If she make an inequality hereafter without a sufficient reason, then will be your time to complain.

Jekyll: In Peter Warburton's Case,[2] the court controlled an unequal disposition, but it was because the trustee disposed of a considerable share to himself.

The Chancellor [Harcourt] desiring it to be equal to a devise, but he seemed to think that she had a discretionary power and directed in general terms that they should be distributed after her death as the will directs. But in regard that she had married twice improvidently since Sir Thomas's death, he directed that security should be given that they should be delivered accordingly at her death or, in default of such security, that they should be immediately deposited with a master.

In this case, *Vernon* said that, if a freeman have ten children and fully advance nine of them, that he shall have no power of disposing of what would otherwise belong to them by the custom, but the tenth shall have the whole orphanage part.

And the widow here having by her jointure before marriage compounded for her customary part, My Lord [Harcourt] directed the estate to be divided into moieties and declared the children entitled to one moiety by the custom.

Some of them chose what was given them by their father's will [and] waived their share of the orphanage part. Others *e contra* and had it.

My Lord [Harcourt] directed the paraphernalia, though not merely due by the custom, she being the wife of a knight and not to be brought into the account of the personal estate.

The *Attorney General* insisted that a father might devise the orphanage part of a child upon a contingency of his death under age.

Mead [argued] *contra*, that the custom had been certified to be otherwise in several cases in this court and that it survived, to which the court agreed.

[Other copies of this report: Lincoln's Inn MS. Misc. 383, p. 306, pl. 1, Lincoln's Inn MS. Misc. 107, p. 24, Misc. Chancery Reports (1714–1730), p. 2.]

---

1 *Wall v. Thurbane* (1686), 1 Vernon 355, 414, 23 E.R. 519, 555.

2 *Warburton v. Warburton* (1702), 4 Brown P.C. 1, 2 E.R. 1.

Lincoln's Inn MS. Misc. 506, p. 100 (a loose sheet)

The Lady Rawlinson, on her marriage with Sir Thomas,[1] had a jointure settled upon her for her life in lieu of dower and her customary part. And it was decreed that the testator had power by his will to dispose of one moiety and that the other moiety was the orphanage part and to be divided among the children. Sir Thomas left eleven children. Two of them died [before] the age of twenty-one. And Thomas,[2] who insisted on his customary share and was not content with his legacy, was ordered to have one-ninth of the moiety for his customary share if no regard is had of those two who died.

Sir Thomas, by his will, devised to the Lady Rawlinson all his plate, jewels, a pearl, coach and horses, and household goods which he should died possessed of, requesting her to dispose of the same among such of her children as should be living at her decease who should be most obedient and dutiful to her, which he doubted not she would do according to her promise. She submitted to the court by her answer what power she had over them. And it was decreed that they should be brought before a master, who should cause an appraisement to be made thereof and she to give security that she will dispose thereof among the children according to the trust reposed in her by the said will and that the same should be delivered upon her decease according to such disposition or to or for the benefit of such of the children or their representative[3] who, in default of such disposition, shall then claim any interest therein.

British Library MS. Hargrave 81, f. 125

8 July 1714.

Sir Thomas Rawlinson [1647–1708], father of the plaintiff and a freeman of London, before his marriage in the year 1684, in consideration of £3000 portion and of the intended marriage, settled a jointure upon the defendant, the Lady Rawlinson, in full satisfaction and bar of dower and thirds at common law or which she might claim by the custom of London. And subject to that jointure and his own estate, he limits the remainder to his first and every other son in tail male with remainders over and, by another deed, covenants to pay her £40 *per annum* during her life for her separate use and that, for securing the same, a house in Fenchurch Street, the rent of which was £40 *per annum*, should stand charged to pay it clear of all taxes. The marriage is had, and he had several children, *viz.* the plaintiff in the original cause, his younger children, and the plaintiff in the cross-cause, his eldest son.

[1] C. Welch and P. Gauci, 'Rawlinson, Sir Thomas (bap. 1647, d. 1708)', *Oxford Dictionary of National Biography*, vol. 46, pp. 165–166.

[2] T. Harmsen, 'Rawlinson, Thomas (1681–1725)', *Oxford Dictionary of National Biography*, vol. 46, pp. 166–168.

[3] representation *MS.*

Sir Thomas, by his will, devises to his lady all his plate, jewels, coach horses, china, and household goods to her use during her life and desires that, at her death, she would give the same at her discretion among such of his children as should be then living and carried themselves most dutiful to her. And he gives his eldest son £4000 and to each of his younger children £3000. And, by a codicil, he gives his wife £1000 and to three of his daughters £1000 apiece over and above what he had given them before. And he makes his wife sole executrix and dies leaving nine children, all infants, except the eldest son. He was seised of some freehold estate of about £30 *per annum* in Lancashire not comprised in the settlement and of some freeholds and copyhold and a house at Fulham purchased after the settlement. The copy, by the custom, descended to the youngest son, and the freehold here and in Lancashire descended to the eldest.

Sir Thomas, in his lifetime, had a book kept for entering the separate estate of his wife and the payments made her of the £40 *per annum* and of the interest of East India bonds and other things purchased with her separate money. These entries were made in the book with his own hand, but, for about eight years before his death, he ceased paying the £40 *per annum*. After his decease, the wife possessed herself of the estate, entered on her jointure, takes the rents and profits, and, for several years, maintains and educates the younger children and not only advances to her eldest son the £400 legacy but pays other sums to a considerable value and, afterwards, improvidently, marries. The younger children, thereupon, brought their bill against her and her husband for an account of their father's personal estate and to have their parts of it according to his will and codicil and for securing to each of them an equal part and portion of the jewels, plate, etc. And the eldest son, by his cross-bill, prays an account of his father's personal estate and to have the will set aside and that he might have his orphan's part, insisting that his customary right could not be altered by a will.

For the plaintiff in the original cause, it was said that a desire or recommendation in a will to do anything amounts to a devise of the thing or to a command to do the thing and, where money, goods, etc. were left to be distributed at the discretion of a wife, executors, or trustees, the court usually regulates and ascertains that discretion and decrees a distribution, especially among children of the party, in equal proportions, for they are all in equal consideration with him and his office or obligation by nature was equal to all, and the person to distribute was not intended to have any benefit of the thing distributed in case there were no distribution made. And so they hoped it should be here and the rather because the lady had departed with the discretion or power by the marrying of a second husband.

For the lady, it was insisted that her discretion or power remained notwithstanding the second marriage and that she did not claim the jewels by the custom or will but by common law as her paraphernalia.

Curia [Lord Harcourt]: The intent of the party is to be here considered, and that plainly appears not to be generally that the lady should at her death in all events make an equal distribution among all her children but that, though she should distribute the whole, yet the proportion should be at her pleasure as a means to secure, encourage, and reward the children's dutiful carriage towards her. And this judgment of their dutifulness and the power of distinguishing and rewarding it was not transferred or altered by the marriage but remained still in the mother as before; those jewels are not taken as paraphernalia. Sir Thomas left so great an estate and no debts.

And [it was] decreed accordingly that an account and inventory should be taken of the plate, jewels, and household goods [and] the lady to have the use of them according to the will and give security to leave them at her death among such of her children as should have behaved themselves most dutifully to her and the settlement and jointure being made before marriage and the lady expressly excluded thereby from any customary part and having acquiesced under it and taken the rents according to the settlement is effectually excluded from any customary part. And, in the distribution of it, the testator is to be considered as if dead without a wife and what is specifically devised to her or to any of the children or to others by the will or codicil is to be taken out of his moiety or testamentary part. And, as the eldest son insists on his customary part, the will *quoad* his single demand must be set aside. And, as there is a clause in the will that, if any of the children should have recourse to the customs or call the will in question, he should lose what was given him by the will, the £400 legacy, and the other money advanced by the lady to the eldest son must be taken in part of his orphanage share.

[Other copies of this report: British Library MS. Hargrave 82, f. 138.]

[Other reports of this case: British Library MS. Hargrave 77, f. 34v; British Library MS. Hargrave 303, f. 62.]

4

Stanhope v. Nott

(Ch. 1714)

Deeds cannot be protected from discovery by giving them to a lawyer.

British Library MS. Hargrave 80, f. 190

To a bill for discovery of deeds, the defendant pleaded that he knew nothing of them otherwise than as counsel and that he had them not.

The court held that it was not sufficient to plead that he knew nothing but as counsel without divesting himself of them and disclosing to whom he had delivered them, for, otherwise, deeds by being placed into the hands of a counsel might be suppressed and the party injured left without a remedy.

The plea was, therefore, ordered by Lord Chancellor [Harcourt] to stand for an answer but with liberty to except as to when and to whom he had delivered the deeds.

[Other copies of this report: Lincoln's Inn MS. Misc. 383, p. 308, Lincoln's Inn MS. Misc. 107, f. 29.]

5

Christ's Hospital v. Gallway

(Ch. c. 1714)

The personal estate of a decedent is liable for the payment of his debts though devised to the widow and executrix.

British Library MS. Hargrave 81, f. 122, pl. 1

[Where there was] a devise to a widow and executrix, there it was decreed the personal estate devised to her shall go to pay the debts notwithstanding the devise.

[Other copies of this report: British Library MS. Hargrave 82, f. 135, British Library MS. Hargrave 77, f. 33v, pl. 4, *sub nom.* Christ's Hospital v. Garway, British Library MS. Hargrave 303, f. 61.]

[Related cases: *sub nom.* Christ's Hospital v. Budgin (1712), 2 Vernon 683, 23 E.R. 1043, 1 Eq. Cas. Abr. 70, 21 E.R. 883.]

6

Jones v. Hiccock

(Ch. 1714)

Where a plaintiff could have joined several causes of action in one single action but did not do so, the unsuccessful defendant is liable to pay court costs for only a single action.

British Library MS. Hargrave 77, f. 32v, pl. 2

14 August 1714.

Jones and one Hoar were jointly and severally bound in a bond of £100 penalty to maintain all his children lawfully begotten. This being neglected, he puts the bond in suit, and Jones agrees with him and pays him £50 to be discharged. And the bill being brought against Hoar and Hiccocks, Hoar is in contempt to an attachment for want of an answer. Hiccocks was bound in a bail bond for Hoare's appearance, and, after the time for appearing was out and before the bail bond was put in suit, Hoar dies. Then actions were brought on the bail bond against the sureties, who demurred to the plaint. And on argument, the demurrers were allowed.

Hiccocks was likewise in contempt to an attachment and was arrested. And Jones was bail for him. And being in contempt for want of a further answer and arrested, Jones and Vere were bound for him in another bail. And, afterwards, the several actions were brought against Jones, Hiccocks, and his bail. And upon an order referred to the Master to tax the costs, the plaintiff in law insisted on about £50 for the charges of these actions.

The Master would allow costs but in one action only, being of opinion that bringing so many actions was vexations.

On a petition to the Lord Chancellor, it was insisted on by *Sir Joseph Jekyll* and *Sir N. Hooper* for [*blank*] that all the demands brought against Hoar and his sureties might and ought to have been brought and included in one action only and so, if a man be a creditor by several bonds, he may bring an action of debt for them all and the splitting of matters into so many actions even at law would not be endured and that costs would not be allowed at law in more than one of those actions.

Curia [LORD HARCOURT]: They might have been so included. But he may bring several actions on the five bonds. They are several as well as joint. However, as this is not for a duty to be paid but for a contempt only and that the action whereby Hiccocks is principal could not have been joined in that wherein he was not, so let the costs taxed by the Master in one action only stand, and let him tax costs in one of the actions only on the bond wherein Hiccocks is the principal and in which plaints are of Trinity term 1713, *viz.*, the term when the five declarations were of.

[Other copies of this report: British Library MS. Hargrave 303, f. 59.]

7

Halsey v. Anonymous

(Ch. 1714)

An outroper is not a merchant and cannot be a bankrupt.

British Library MS. Hargrave 81, f. 117

19 August 1714.

A commission of bankruptcy [was] sued out by Halsey against J.S., who kept an outroper's office at the Exchange.

And Mr. *Cooper*, in support of the commission, insisted that the way of trade or business of outropers was not only to sell at a public auction or outcry other people's goods, but that they constantly mixed among them goods of their own, which they sold among the rest, which he apprehended to be a buying and selling within the words and meaning of the Statute concerning Bankrupts[1] and that, in the Case of one Gibbons, an outroper who had this very office before, a commission issued against him and it was held by this court that it lay.

E contra, Sir Joseph Jekyll and Mr. Common Serjeant [*Duncan Dee*] [said] that an outroper is merely an officer of the City and not a trader or dealer within the meaning of the Statute and as in the nature of an auctioneer or an Exchange broker and his selling is [as] an agent for others and not for his own benefit or account and the statutes of bankruptcy were made with regard to and for the advantage of trade. And, as to the Case of Gibbons, he was a linen draper and kept on that trade with his office, and it was in respect of his trade and out of his office the commission lay.

Curia [Lord Harcourt]: A commission of bankruptcy does not lie against an outroper merely as such. I will supersede the commission.

[Other copies of this report: British Library MS. Hargrave 82, f. 130.]

[Other reports of this case: British Library MS. Hargrave 77, f. 32, pl. 2, British Library MS. Hargrave 303, f. 59, pl. 1.]

8

Attorney General v. Cust

(Ch. 1714)

A devise of a specific fund does not become a general charge on the decedent's estate where a codicil changes the time of its payment.

British Library MS. Hargrave 77, f. 43v, pl. 2

19 August.

Jane Proby, by her will, devises to her executors £3000 out of the money remaining of the purchase money for lands sold by her husband, John Proby, and she devises generally out of her estate several money legacies and, *inter alia*, £2000 to Frances Mather to be put out at interest by her executors for her benefit. She mentions no time when the money should be paid. And, by her codicil, she directs that her debts, legacies, and funerals should be paid before any of her charities and that her executors should have two years' time to raise the legacies.

One point was whether the £3000 given by the will out of the purchase money were not by the codicil made a general charge upon the personal estate by reason of the time given for the raising of the legacies generally without any destruction.

1 Stat. 10 Ann., c. 25 (*SR*, IX, 685–686).

Curia [LORD HARCOURT]: It was not and that, as, by the will, more time is limited for the payment of the legacies whereby they become payable immediately. Now, a certain time was limited, *viz.* two years.

The second [point] was whether the int[erest] of the personal estate should during the two years [go] to increase the bulk of the personal estate.

Lord Chancellor [LORD HARCOURT]: If there be sufficient [assets] to pay all the debts, legacies, and funerals, the executors will be entitled; else it must go to enlarge the fund.

The third [point] was as to the £2000 legacy whether, by this clause in the condition, interest should be only for the two years or from the death of the testator.

It was said for the legatee that interest should be reckoned from the time of the death of the testatrix because the will directed the money to be put only by her executors which was immediately for the infant's benefit and, in the case of infants, matters were to be construed favorably and, though a codicil may revoke or control a preceding part, yet that is where the latter is repugnant to the former and they are both inconsistent together. But there is nothing of that here; both stand well together, for the testatrix's intent is express that interest should be paid for the infant's benefit and having any limited time for the payment of the principal, there was a seeming inconsistency that interest, which implies time and forbearance, should be paid for what was to be paid immediately, for, by construction of law, the legacies were immediately due and payable, for the time for payment was limited. And, therefore, she cures all this by the codicil appointing two years for the payment of the legacy itself without revoking or altering the devise touching interest and, by this construction, interest being to be paid in the meantime, both the will and the codicil will very well concert together.

Curia [LORD HARCOURT]: I will consider this when the report touching the estate is made.

[Other copies of this report: British Library MS. Hargrave 303, f. 76v, pl. 2.]

9

Mackerness v. Pongett

(Ch. 1714)

A creditor for less than £100 cannot sue out a commission of bankruptcy.

British Library MS. Hargrave 77, f. 45, pl. 4

7 September.

Mackaness bought goods of [*blank*] to £103 value, and, at the same time, he gives two notes, one for £50 payable in six months, the other for £53 payable in nine months. After the first note became payable and before the second was payable, Mackaness failed, and Pongett alone sued out a commission of bankruptcy against him. The commissioners sat [and] found him a bankrupt. Several of the creditors came in and proved their debts to upwards of £200 and paid their contribution, and an assignee was chosen. Mackaness and some others of the creditors preferred a petition alleging a commission was unduly sued out, for this Pongett was not such a creditor for £100 as within the Statute 5 *anno* Car., 22,[1] and, therefore, they prayed that the commission be superseded and the bond assigned.

Lord Chancellor [Lord Harcourt] declared his opinion that Pongett was not such a creditor for £100 as is within the said Statute because he could not sue at [common] law or recover by virtue of any of those notes but what were actually payable, *viz.* the first note only, and that he had asked the opinion of the Lord Chief Justice Parker and Trevor, who were both of the same opinion. And Lord Parker declared he had tried a cause on the like point at the Guildhall since that last Trinity term.

[It was] ordered that the commission be superseded but that the bond should not be assigned nor any costs given and that such creditors as were proper were at liberty to sue out a new commission if they thought fit.

[Other copies of this report: British Library MS. Hargrave 303, f. 79, pl. 1.]

[Other reports of this case: 1 Peere Williams 260, 24 E.R. 379, 2 Eq. Cas. Abr. 96, 22 E.R. 82.]

10

Ekins v. Vernon

(Ch. 1714)

A warrant from the crown passes no interest in common law or equity in anything before it is carried into execution by an actual grant.

British Library MS. Hargrave 77, f. 45v

14 September 1714.

King William, being entitled to some stocks that were the late king's, promises them to the earl of Romney, who, thereupon, agrees with Ekins to let him have them paying to His Lordship £4000. Ekins pays him £2500 in money and gives his bond for the rest. And the earl delivered him two warrants signed by His Majesty whereby he directs the persons in whose names the stocks stood to transfer them to Abraham Williams, a servant of Ekins, or his order or to the

[1] Stat. 21 Jac. I, c. 19, s. 2 (*SR*, IV, 1227).

bearer thereof. These are afterwards delivered to Mr. Vernon, Secretary of State,[1] in order to the passing the privy seal for the stocks. And the king, being unacquainted with it, orders Mr. Secretary to keep the warrants and not part with them without his further order. And, soon [?] afterwards, the earl and, then, the king die.

No transfer being made, Ekins brings his bill against Vernon and the Attorney General to have them delivered to him. And he, afterwards, amends the bill by making the administrators of Williams a party but not any representative of the earl. And, afterwards, he obtains an order from the Master of the Rolls for a commission to Bordeaux to examine one Lebille, which, by a subsequent order of Chancery, was discharged unless cause that day.

Attorney General [*Northey*]: A warrant from the crown passes no interest in [common] law or equity in any estate, either real or personal, before it is carried into execution by an actual grant. Until then, it is always liable to be countermanded, revoked, cancelled, or altered. And it is entirely under the power and control of the crown. And the late king having ordered them to be kept and not delivered up is a countermand or in the nature of a repeal of those warrants. And a bill will not lie to compel a Secretary of State to act contrary to his order from the crown or to compel the crown actually to give what once in kindness it intended to do.

Williams, contra: We are purchasers of those warrants and stock for a valuable consideration in money, which we have paid. We delivered the warrants to the Secretary and only desire then to have them returned to us as to have our own again. We desire no money from the crown or Mr. Vernon by the commission. It is only to prove the payment of the purchase money.

Curia [Lord Harcourt]: This is a very new bill. The plaintiff can never have any decree against the crown in this case or against Mr. Vernon, who has acted pursuant to the late king's order. Nor can the bill be maintained against the successor for a matter which was the promise or bountiful intention of his predecessor. He cannot be bound by any such thing. If the party have really paid any money in this case, it was his own fault to part with it for a promise or a thing which was wholly at the pleasure of the crown to perform or not or to vary or determine as he pleased. Perhaps if the payment be fully proved, it may serve him for a pretense to go abegging to the crown for something. But his remedy, if any, is against the representative of the earl to have the money refunded.

So he was ordered to amend accordingly and procure an answer in a fortnight, the commission to stand but to examine only J.S. only to the payment of the money.

[Other copies of this report: British Library MS. Hargrave 303, f. 79, pl. 2.]

---

[1] A. Marshall, 'Vernon, James (bap. 1646, d. 1727), *Oxford Dictionary of National Biography*, vol. 56, pp. 369–371.

11

Tate v. Austin

(Ch. 1714)

A testator's debts must be paid before his specific legacies.

Where a married woman allows her husband to borrow money using her land as a security, after his death, the land will be exonerated out of his estate.

British Library MS. Hargrave 77, f. 46

25 October 1714.

The plaintiff was seised of lands in fee and marries. Afterwards, her husband, in order to pay his debts and buy a commission in the Army, prevails with her to join with him in a mortgage of the lands, which was done accordingly. And, in the mortgage, the husband covenants for the title and to pay the mortgage money and interest. He buys a commission and goes into the service in Spain and dies, the mortgage remaining unsatisfied. He, by will, devises a £600 legacy to the defendant and makes the plaintiff sole executrix.

She brings her bill setting forth the whole matter and that her late husband had all the money and that it was his own proper debt and her estate was only a pledge by her consent for the money in case it was not paid and that her husband did not pay it or leave an estate sufficient but, the having done so, his estate ought to be applied to pay his debts and, as her estate and pledge, be discharged and, therefore, that his personal estate thus specially devised might be applied to discharge the mortgage.

Mr. *Vernon*, for the defendant, insisted that, in a court of equity, the intent of the parties was to be observed and pursued, that the plaintiff, notwithstanding her marriage might have sold the estate absolutely and, since the mortgage is but a conditional qualified sale and the mortgagee is but a purchaser for a valuable consideration, the money being received and disposed of by the husband with the privity of the wife, it was to be considered as a gift in law of the wife to the husband which she raised out of her own estate and not to be repaid again by the same estate and not by the husband out of his own estate for which there was not any agreement by the husband. And if none such, then a court of equity would not intend or presume there was any such thing and that the covenants by the husband was only because the wife could not covenant or contract in a sale but she might depart with a charge or subject her estate for doing what she could not covenant to do and so here. And, therefore, the defendants ought to enjoy their specific legacies according to the will.

Curia [Lord Cowper]: The intent of the parties is to be observed, but that must be collected from what appears to the court. Now, no more appears but that the wife, at the desire of her husband, in whose power she is, does pawn or pledge her own estate to furnish him with money and to be a fund for securing the repayment of it with interest if he did not pay it. And it was to be a security in aid and for the benefit of the mortgagee only, not to ease the mortgagor by taking the burden of the debt entirely on the plaintiff and her estate and exempt the husband's estate and that he would presume and intend as most likely and natural that this was the intent and design of the parties unless the defendants could show a special agreement between the husband and wife to the contrary. And, accordingly, he decreed an account of the personal estate and thereout the mortgage is to be discharged and then the rest is to go to satisfy the quantum of the specific legacies.

[Other copies of this report: British Library MS. Hargrave 303, f. 80.]

British Library MS. Add. 35990, f. 49v

Michaelmas term 1 Geo.

One Austin married the plaintiff, who had an estate of inheritance of £80 *per annum*. And she, by the persuasion of her husband, levies a fine of it to enable her husband to borrow £500 by a mortgage on it, which her accordingly did. And with the money so borrowed, he bought a commission. And, some years after, he died, leaving a personal estate of £600, which, by will, he devised to the defendant.

But the widow exhibited her bill to have her land exonerated of the £500 out of this personal estate, which was, in truth, nothing but the produce of the £500 borrowed by virtue of the mortgage.

And Lord Chancellor Cowper decreed that the land should be accordingly discharged by the personal estate.

British Library MS. Hargrave 80, f. 192v

The plaintiff joined with her former husband in mortgaging her own estate for £400, which was received by the husband. And he covenanted in the deed of mortgage to pay the money. But he dying before the money was paid off, the wife and her second husband brought his bill to have her estate exonerated by the personal estate of her first husband, which he had specifically bequeathed to the defendant.

Vernon, for the defendant: The question depends upon the intent of the parties at the time of levying the fine. If there had been any agreement at that time between the husband and wife that he should discharge the mortgage out of his own estate, if he had given a bond to or covenanted with any trustee of the wife for that purpose, he must have discharged it. But since no such contract appears, it must be presumed to have been intended by the wife as a gift to the husband. The covenant from the husband in the mortgage was not for the sake of the wife but for the security of the mortgagee had the land been entirely sold and the money received by the wife, yet it would have belonged to the husband. This is in effect a partial sale. In the common cases of a mortgage, the land is the principal debtor and though the covenant makes the personal estate liable, yet it does not subject it so far as to disappoint the ancestor's will in favor of the heir, from whence he concluded that a specific legacy ought not to be taken from the defendant to exonerate the plaintiff's estate.

Jekyll: The calling this a gift is begging the question. The wife's making the mortgage implies no such thing nor anything more than that she was willing to pledge her land to raise money for her husband, who is the original debtor. And a covenant from him differs widely from the common case. where the land is the mortgagor's.

Lord Chancellor [Harcourt]: A specific legacy cannot take place of a debt. If this be to be considered as a debt of the husband, the evidence that the money was borrowed for the husband's use is probable. And when a wife is induced to pledge her lands to borrow money for the husband, which he has not credit to take up without it, it ought to be taken with the greatest strictness in favor of the wife and against the husband and all claiming under him. What was done here in pursuance of the fine imports the substance of the agreement between the husband and wife. And it is no more than that her land should be pledged for him subject to a proviso of redemption and with a covenant from him that he would redeem. In all cases of mortgages, the land in strictness is only a pledge and the person the debtor. And here, the wife accommodates the husband with a pledge. If he is ever able to redeem it, there is all the reason in the world that he should exonerate her estate. He cited Lord Huntington's Case,[1] who got his wife to join with him in a mortgage of her estate to raise money to buy a post of Captain of the Band of Pensioners and afterwards got money enough to pay off the mortgage and procured it to be assigned in trust for himself and would have kept it on foot as his own personal estate; the Court of Chancery decreed against My Lady. But the House of Lords reversed the decree. The Lord Chancellor was of counsel upon the appeal and said he never was more satisfied with any judgment than that of the House of Lords in that case.

He decreed here for the plaintiff.

[Other copies of this report: Lincoln's Inn MS. Misc. 383, p. 311.]

[Other reports of this case: 2 Vernon 689, 23 E.R. 1047, 1 Peere Williams 264, 24 E.R. 382, 1 Eq. Cas. Abr. 62, 21 E.R. 876.]

[1] *Earl of Huntingdon v. Countess of Huntingdon* (1702), 2 Vernon 437, 23 E.R. 881, 2 Brown P.C. 1, 1 E.R. 753, 1 Eq. Cas. Abr. 62, 316, 21 E.R. 876, 1071, 2 Eq. Cas. Abr. 672, 22 E.R. 564.

12
Knight v. O'Hara
(Ch. 1714)

A writ of ne exeat regno *should be discharged after the defendant has answered.*

British Library MS. Hargrave 81, f. 130, pl. 2

27 October 1714. Lord Chancellor.

Curia [Lord Cowper]: A [writ of] *ne exeat regno* is in the nature of an injunction until answer and further order and, therefore, when the party has put in a full and sufficient answer, the writ ought to be discharged.

[Other copies of this report: British Library MS. Hargrave 82, f. 143, pl. 2.]

[Other reports of this case: British Library MS. Hargrave 77, f. 35v, pl. 1, British Library MS. Hargrave 303, f. 64, pl. 1.]

13
Bredon v. Blagrave
(Ch. 1714)

A deed of settlement entered into through fraud is void and unenforceable.

British Library MS. Hargrave 80, f. 194

The bill was brought by a remainderman to be relieved against an endorsement, by which there was a power given to the tenant for life to revoke all or any of the uses in the deed of settlement and to limit new ones either to raise portions for younger children in such manner or to such other uses as the tenant for life should think fit, as obtained by fraud. And it appearing that there had been a previous treaty about the settlement, which was prepared by Peere Williams and was more beneficial to the tenant for life than a former settlement, which was broken through to make this, and there being no evidence of any treaty or agreement about the endorsement, the preamble of which imported no more than an intent of the parties to enable the tenant for life to provide for younger children and yet the operating part gave him a power to control all the uses of the settlement but was worded so intricately as not to appear at first view, especially to one that was no lawyer, to import more than the preamble it appearing not, that, on the day the deed was to be executed, the tenant for life, at whose house they were, postponed the execution until the evening and, in the meantime, got the plaintiff in to drink hard, though not so far as entirely to lose his understanding, and that it was the usual way of the tenant for life to draw people into drink and then make hard bargains with them and that, at the execution of the deed, the plaintiff showed a reluctance even in the condition he was and the tenant for life pressed the execution at that time.

Lord Chancellor [HARCOURT] declared himself satisfied from the whole that it was a plain fraud and that, though the plaintiff might possibly have agreed to let the tenant for life have a power of providing for younger children, yet he never designed to give him an absolute power over the whole settlement. And, therefore, he relieved him against that part of the endorsement which gave that general power to the tenant for life and which he had executed by his will.

It was in effect equivalent to a relief against the whole endorsement, the tenant for life being dead without issue.

[Other copies of this report: Lincoln's Inn MS. Misc. 383, p. 312, Lincoln's Inn MS. Misc. 107, f. 33.]

Lincoln's Inn MS. Misc. 384, p. 23, pl. 2

30 October.

A bill [was brought] to set aside an endorsement obtained by fraud. In Fowler and Fowler's Case, [it was] adjudged parol evidence may not be admitted to set aside a deed by the Statute of Frauds unless in a case of imposition.

Curia: Here is endorsed a general power of revocation, whereas the power was intended only to enable him to make a provision for his daughters. Therefore, it ought not to extend further.

14

Sayer v. Sayer

(Ch. 1714)

A pecuniary legacy is not to be paid before a specific legacy, especially where there are sufficient assets in the estate to pay the pecuniary legacy.

The amount of a bequest is fixed as of the date of the testator's death, not the date of the making of the will.

British Library MS. Hargrave 80, f. 194v

Dr. Sayer bequeathed all his personal estate at Wonston to the defendant and a legacy of £300 to the plaintiff to be paid out of his personal estate and out of some houses in London. Upon this, two question arose, first, whether the personal estate thus specifically bequeathed to the defendant should be part of the fund for the money legacy.

And Lord Chancellor [LORD COWPER] declared that it should not, the words 'out of' etc. are general and it is not said 'all my personal estate wheresoever', nor are they any terms of that extent and the testator appears to have left other personal estate besides that at Wonston of the value of £300 or more and, if that were deficient, has provided another fund in aid.

Secondly, what should pass by the devise of all his personal estate at Wonston.

Lord Chancellor [Lord Cowper] decreed that whatever personal estate had there at the instant of his death should pass. A personal estate is fluctuating and, therefore, not to be confined to the personal estate there at the time of the devise, and should it not be limited to the instant of death, no other period could be fixed. The argument whether its being there one, two, or three weeks before would suffice would run upon you. Arrears of rent due to the testator for lands in Wonston he declared would pass. They are personal estate and there, in all respects, they are demandable there etc. And this court will follow the construction which the law makes in all cases where it does not appear from the will that the testator's intent was otherwise.

[Other copies of this report: Lincoln's Inn MS. Misc. 383, p. 313, pl. 1.]

Lincoln's Inn MS. Misc. 11, p. 20, pl. 1

3 November 1714.

A man gives 'all his personal estate at W.' to his wife. The question was what passed by this bequest.

[Lord Cowper] decreed that all the personal estate which was there at the death of the testator and not what was there either at the time of the making of the will or at any time between that time and his death passed by these words, and, therefore, a coach and horses which used to be there backwards and forwards but were not there at the testator's death did not pass.

He decreed also that arrears of rent which were due at the testator's death for lands in W. did also pass as part of his estate in W.

[Other reports of this case: Precedents in Chancery 392, 24 E.R. 176, Gilbert Rep. 87, 25 E.R. 60, 2 Vernon 688, 23 E.R. 1046, 1 Eq. Cas. Abr. 200, 298, 21 E.R. 989, 1058, 2 Eq. Cas. Abr. 553, 22 E.R. 465.]

15

Atkins v. Dawbury

(Ch. 1714)

A wife's legacy can be assigned by her husband.

Interest is due from a testator's death on a legacy that is in praesenti.

British Library MS. Hargrave 80, f. 195v

A legacy of £300 was left to a woman charged equitably upon a reversion of a term for years. Her husband had afterwards assigned all his right in the land charged to J.S. by a deed for particular purposes. And, by his will made a few days after, he devised the £300 to the same uses. After the husband's death, the executor of the first testator having no notice of the deed (I think he had of the will) compounded with the wife for £120, which he paid her, and took a general release from her. The bill was brought by the plaintiff as assignee of the husband for the £300 and interest.

Vernon, for the executors, [argued] that the will of the husband could not bind or transfer a legacy due to the wife, which was agreed, and that the deed did not do it in this case, that choses in action were not assignable at common law and the assignment of them was supported in equity in favor of purchasers, that they were not always in favor of volunteers, that in the Case of Kinaston v. Burnett,[1] where the defendant had married a woman who was entitled to a mortgage in fee which was forfeited and had taken upon him to limit it in the common way of settlements to himself for life, then to the wife for life, remainder to the issue etc. and died, though a mortgage in fee be looked upon in equity as money, yet it ruled here.

Wright [argued] that the disposition by the husband alone would not bind the wife surviving.

Lord Chancellor [Harcourt]: That case seems to have turned upon its being a mortgage in fee and the disposition by the husband therefore void at law, to which *Vernon* agreed. But here, the disposition of the husband of his right in the term, which is the security for the £300, is good at law, and equity will but follow the law in affirming it.

The rule that equity would not support assignments of choses in action in favor of volunteers was decreed by Cowper.

Lord Chancellor [Harcourt] took time to consider. And at another day, he decreed the legacy to have been well assigned by the deed and the will, which explained his intention in making the deed, but that the executor having paid £120 to the wife without notice of the assignment, her release was a good discharge to

---

[1] *Burnett v. Kinnaston* (1700), 2 Vernon 401, 23 E.R. 860, Precedents in Chancery 118, 24 E.R. 57, 2 Freeman 239, 22 E.R. 1183, 1 Eq. Cas. Abr. 69, 21 E.R. 882.

him at law and in equity *pro tanto* and that the executors should pay the plaintiff the residue and that the wife should refund to the plaintiff. Interest was decreed from the testator's death, it being a legacy *in praesenti*.

[Other copies of this report: Lincoln's Inn MS. Misc. 383, p. 313, pl. 2, Lincoln's Inn MS. Misc. 107, f. 35.]

[Other reports of this case: Gilbert Rep. 88, 25 E.R. 61, 1 Eq. Cas. Abr. 45, 21 E.R. 862.]

16

Ballet v. Powle

(Ch. 1714)

There is no determinate time limitation in equity for a redemption of a mortgage. An assignee of a lease can redeem a mortgage of the leasehold.

British Library MS. Hargrave 77, f. 46v

6 November.

The plaintiff [a pauper], in the right of his wife as co-heir and next of kin to George and Thomas Histon, father and son, claims to redeem a freehold estate and also some houses held by lease from the bishop of Winchester. The first was mortgaged for £800 in 1682. In 1682, the latter were made a collateral security for the same sum upon the mortgage of the first. The equity of redemption was limited for want of issue of Histon to his wife in fee. Thomas Histon died without issue. The defendant claimed under the mortgagee and a release of the equity of redemption in 1693, which was a flat bar to the plaintiffs' claim.

As to the leasehold, the plaintiffs had lately gotten administration to Thomas in whom the term was first vested, and so they claimed the redemption both ways.

The estate was £70 *per annum*, and they paid the bishop £2 3s. *per annum* and two turkeys. This lease Histon had first mortgaged to [*blank*] for £50, and he, as it was said, assigned to one Briggs, a scrivener. But, as no money was proved paid nor assignment produced but it appeared that Briggs had surrendered the lease and gotten a new one from the bishop and had so done a second time, which second lease the defendant had purchased in at £400 and, for him, it was insisted that, after so great a length of time, as above thirty years possession, there ought not any redemption to be admitted.

For the pauper, it was insisted that both the securities being for one sum and the party that claimed them had his liberty of recourse for satisfaction to which of them he pleased but must have but one satisfaction and, having taken a release of the equity of redemption of the freehold, had made his election to take his satisfaction by that estate and that acceptance of the lease was a satisfaction for the debt and, if not and a redemption be decreed, it would necessarily decree an account of the profits of the freehold as well as the leasehold, else there would be a double satisfaction, *quod fuit concessum*.

Curia [Lord Cowper]: As to the length of time, there is no determinate time in equity for a redemption. As to the first mortgage of the term, the estate being of so great value and the first mortgage money so little as £50 and no money paid by the assignee, it must be intended that it was satisfied by the profits and the rather for that the mortgagee had delivered the mortgage and assignment to the mortgagor of the freehold. The renewal of leases follows always the interest, and the party stands in the place and circumstance of the assignee and so it continues redeemable in equity. An account and redemption was decreed.

[Other copies of this report: British Library MS. Hargrave 303, f. 81.]

17

Greenhouse v. Leech

(Ch. 1714)

A motion for a preliminary injunction to prevent waste should be supported by an affidavit.

The question in this case was whether a reversioner of a leasehold can prevent the current leaseholder from committing waste of the leased premises.

British Library MS. Hargrave 77, f. 47, pl. 1

11 November 1714.

The defendant was the lessee for years of a house of the earl of Exeter. The plaintiff was a lessee for them of the same from the earl in reversion after the defendant's lease. And the house being well fitted up with wainscot etc. and the defendant threatening to pull it down and carry it away, the plaintiff brings his bill to stay waste and spoil.

The defendant, by an answer, owned the threatening, and he insists it was what, by law, he might do. And he did threaten and intend to do more than the law would justify him in.

Now, the plaintiff moved on the answer without an affidavit to stay the defendant from the waste or spoil.

Curia [Lord Cowper]: In strictness, it is irregular for want of an affidavit. And, at [common] law, it being in the case of a lessee for years, no action at law could lie against the preceding lessee. But the lessee in reversion has in him for the time the interest of the reversion in fee and perhaps paid a greater fine and is to pay a greater rent in consideration of the house at the time of his taking the lease and so is a purchaser of it in these circumstances for a valuable consideration and that taking away those things would be depriving him in a great measure of the benefit of his purchase.

N.B. The plaintiff covenanted to pay the defendant what the things he insisted not to have removed should be worth if, at the hearing, it appeared the defendant had a right to take them away and also consent not to dismiss his bill and to revive in case of abatement else and especially for want of an affidavit.

The court seemed at last inclinable to deny an injunction.

[Other copies of this report: British Library MS. Hargrave 303, f. 81v.]

18

Watts v. Creswell

(Ch. 1714)

Where an infant knowingly perpetrates a fraud, he will be held liable for it when he comes of age.

British Library MS. Hargrave 80, f. 196v

The defendant's father was tenant for life, remainder to the defendant in tail under an old settlement. The defendant solicited the borrowing of money for his father, carried a deed to the scrivener importing his father was tenant in fee, and was a witness to the mortgage from his father as tenant in fee to the plaintiff. The defendant was then under age, as it was alleged, but knew or at least had a general notice of his own title. And, after he came of age, he procured his father a further sum upon the said security. The bill was against the defendant, his father being dead, to have the estate made effectually liable to the mortgage.

Jekyll, for the plaintiff, [argued] that an infant, though he is not bound by his contract, is answerable for torts, as trespass etc., at law and, therefore, ought to be so here. He cited the case of Standish and Shein, *coram* Somers, where an infant, clerk to an attorney, wrote a bond, the condition of which created a charge upon an estate which he purchased after he came of age; and he was decreed to be bound by this notice.

Lord Chancellor [Harcourt]: The notice he received within age remained with him when he purchased, and then he was of full age, and, in that respect, that case differs from this. I do not think that, if an infant in remainder be barely witness to a deed, it would make him liable because, in a stronger case, if he joined in the deed, provided it was without fraud, he would not, the law protecting him. In this case, it is doubtful whether the defendant was an infant or not at the time that he transacted and solicited this affair. It is certain he was very near his age, and it appears from his answer that he knew at least in general of his title and, knowing it, he produces a forged deed to the scrivener, by which his father should appear to be tenant in fee, and is a witness to the mortgage. If he was old enough to commit a cheat and to use a forged deed to impose upon another, equity will oblige him to make satisfaction after he comes of age. Here, after he came of age, he was privy and consenting to further loans upon the same security; that is a continuation and ratification of what he had done before. Therefore, I decree him to suffer a recovery and do such other acts to make good the party's security as the party's counsel shall direct and to pay costs.

[Other copies of this report: Lincoln's Inn MS. Misc. 383, p. 314, Lincoln's Inn MS. Misc. 107, f. 36.]

Lincoln's Inn MS. Misc. 384, p. 23, pl. 1

12 November.

The defendant's father, being a tenant for life with remainder to the defendant in tail, made a mortgage to the plaintiff for £600. The defendant, then an infant about twenty years of age, was a witness to the mortgage deed. The query was whether the defendant, the infant, should be bound by this mortgage.

Jekyll, for the plaintiff: An infant may be punished for a fraud or tort though he cannot contract by law.

Lord Chancellor [Lord Cowper]: If an infant son in remainder agree to a mortgage deed made by his father, tenant for life, he will not be bound if there be no fraud in him. But here is manifest fraud, for the son knew that there was a settlement whereby his father was but a tenant for life and he was privy to this whole transaction and concealed this settlement from the plaintiff, the mortgagee, but he produced a forged deed whereby it appeared his father was seised in fee. I think, if a man is of age to contrive a cheat, he is old enough to be punished for it. But the cheat was carried on after he came of age, whereby he ratifies the whole fraud from the beginning. Therefore, the defendant must make good to the plaintiff the whole mortgage with interest, and he must pay costs.

[Other reports of this case: 2 Eq. Cas. Abr. 515, 22 E.R. 435.]

19

Manning v. Norcott

(Ch. 1714)

A bill lies in equity to redeem a mortgage of government annuities.

British Library MS. Hargrave 80, f. 197v

The bill was for a redemption of Exchequer annuities which had been pledged to the defendant, a goldsmith, in 1711. And My Lord Chancellor [Cowper] decreed the plaintiff a redemption though the sum for which they had been pledged was not a great deal less than the value and probably the plaintiff would never have thought of redeeming had not the stocks risen in value.

Lord Chancellor [Cowper] said that it was by the first agreement a mortgage and that no act of the parties afterwards had varied it. He distinguished it from the case of Tooker v. Wilson,[1] where, upon failure of payment, the mortgagee had sent notice to the administrator of the mortgagor that he would sell such a day and then, at his request, respited the sale a few days and then sold, and this where the annuity still continued in the defendant's hands.

The defendant insisted in case of redemption to have an allowance for the cost sustained by him in disposing of £500 Bank stock at the low rate it was at in 1711 to enable him to advance the money to the plaintiff who, by redeeming, had the advantage of the rise of the annuities.

But Lord Chancellor [Cowper] declared he could not make any allowance for those consequential damages, there being no special agreement between the parties for that propose. But, there being some debts due from the plaintiff to the defendant, who was a goldsmith in the way of his trade, he thought they ought to come into an account and that the defendant's pledge ought not to be taken from him without a satisfaction for them. He gave but a month's time to redeem after the report in respect of the variable nature of those securities, but he gave the master a power of selling it in the meantime.

[Other copies of this report: Lincoln's Inn MS. Misc. 383, p. 315, pl. 1, Lincoln's Inn MS. Misc. 107, f. 38.]

Lincoln's Inn MS. Misc. 384, p. 6, pl. 2

13 November 1714.

After Tooker v. Wilson was reversed, [it was] decreed by Lord Cowper that annuities in the Exchequer were redeemable after forfeiture unless there were an express agreement that the mortgagee might sell after forfeiture.

20

Bright v. Bright

(Ch. 1714)

In this case, a promise made by an executor to the decedent was enforced so that there would be assets in the estate to pay a legacy.

British Library MS. Hargrave 80, f. 200v

The defendant's sister died intestate in the life of her father. The defendant possessed her personal estate, the father being ignorant of his right, and wrote to his brother that he thought it proper that his father's right should be concealed from him and promised him a share. The father, sometime after, was acquainted with

[1] *Tooker v. Wilson* (Ch. 1713), British Library MS. Hargrave 80, f. 147v, Lincoln's Inn MS. Misc. 384, p. 6, pl. 1, 1 Peere Williams 261, 24 E.R. 379, 5 Brown P.C. 193, 2 E.R. 622, 2 Eq. Cas. Abr. 597, 608, 634, 22 E.R. 502, 511, 532.

it and released to the defendant and made him his executor. The brother too died and made the defendant his executor and gave a legacy of £100 to the plaintiff, there being a deficiency of assets without it.

Lord Chancellor [Cowper] decreed the defendant to be bound by this promise and that the share promised by him to his brother and which he should make good should be intended a distributable share. If A., being in pursuit of a place, tell B. of it and promises him £100 to be quiet and not to press for it himself, he said it is a good ground for an [action of] *assumpsit* at law. In this case, the defendant had a sufficient motive to promise a share, the acquiescence of his brother who might otherwise have informed their father of his right and have made application to him for a part. And men ought not to play with promises made deliberately and upon reasonable inducements.

[Other copies of this report: Lincoln's Inn MS. Misc. 383, p. 318, pl. 1, Lincoln's Inn MS. Misc. 107, f. 43.]

21

Anonymous

(Ch. 1714)

A suit for an account of a joint venture where all of the partners are not before the court can proceed if the missing parties cannot be served with process.

British Library MS. Hargrave 80, f. 201

A bill was brought for an account of the profits of a joint undertaking in trade. Some of the partners not being before the court, the defendants objected to the plaintiffs' going on, that those not brought before the court are equally entitled to an account against the defendant with the plaintiffs, that an account taken between the plaintiffs and defendants would not conclude them and, therefore, to prevent multiplicity of suits and, which might happen, repugnant decrees and orders, they ought to be before the court. Before the plaintiffs could proceed on the account. To this, it was replied that the other partners lived beyond the sea and were not amenable by the process of the court and, if the objection should take place in this instance, there must be a failure of justice, the plaintiffs' not being prepared to make out this fact.

Lord Chancellor [Cowper] decreed the Master to inquire whether the other partners were amenable by the process of the court or not and, if he found they were not, to proceed in making the account.

[Other copies of this report: Lincoln's Inn MS. Misc. 383, p. 318, pl. 2.]

22

Phillips v. Cary

(Ch. 1714)

The question in this case was whether interest should be payable out of a trust fund before the beneficiary of it could be determined.

British Library MS. Hargrave 80, f. 201v

A woman gave £2000 by her will unto her niece and to be paid to her at twenty-one or marriage and, if she died before twenty-one and unmarried, she gave it over to D. and directed that the £2000 should be deposited within a year after her decease in the hands of two trustees named in the will to be applied according to the directions of the will. As to the interest of it from the time of its being so deposited until it became payable over to A. or B., the will was silent. Some cases were cited where legacies being given but payable at a future day, interest had been given in the meantime for maintenance. And, in this case, the testatrix, having directed the £2000 to be deposited in the hands of trustees, could not intend that the produce of it from thence to the time it should become payable should belong to her executrix. It was, therefore, urged that it should be paid to A. for her maintenance.

Lord Chancellor [Cowper]: It is uncertain whether the principal will ever be payable to A. or not. The fruit must follow the tree, and the interest attend the contingency. It would be absurd to give the interest from the person who, upon the contingency happening, will be entitled to the principal or to the person that will not. Upon the instance of the counsel for A., he directed them to attend him with precedents.

[Other copies of this report: Lincoln's Inn MS. Misc. 383, p. 318, pl. 3.]

23

Dale v. Moysey

(Ch. 1714)

A writ of sequestration does not create a lien on any specific property before it is executed.

British Library MS. Hargrave 77, f. 47, pl. 2

16 November.

The plaintiff had obtained a decree in this court against one Mitchell, who being arrested for debt at the suit of another person, the defendant Moysey was his bail. And he was also a creditor to him for money. Mitchell was possessed of a leasehold estate, and, for non-performance of the decree, he was prosecuted on contempt. Then, Moysey prevailed on him to sell his estate to discharge the debt and that for which he was bail.

The defendant Liddington buys it for a valuable consideration and retains of the purchase money so much as the encumbrances came to, and he pays off Moysey's debts and pays him the quantum of the debt for which he was bail, and he paid the residue to Mitchell.

And now, the plaintiff, having gotten a [writ of] sequestration but not executed or returned, brings his bill in order to affect the estate or the moneys in the defendant's hands suggesting that the debt was fraudulent and collusive to elude the decree and the justice of the court and that Liddington purchased with notice of the decree against Mitchell.

It was said for the plaintiff that the decree was personal yet the sequestration laid a lien upon the party's estate and effects against whom the duty is decreed and, though there was a sale, yet it being by fraud and collusion, it ought not to deprive the plaintiff of the fund for satisfaction and that, however the overplus being then paid to Mitchell after the notice of the decree, it ought to be answered over again.

On the other side, it was said that this was carrying things farther than ever had been done in this court and was introducing a new sort of process and multiplying suits, for, had the sequestration been executed or returned, then the purchaser, according to the course and practice of the court, must have come in and been examined *pro interesse suo* and, if he did not make a good title against the plaintiff, the estate would be liable against this demand. But, if this suit should be countenanced, then, after every decree, there would be a new bill for discovering every person's right that had any dealing with the party decreed and so draw the matter of the original suits over again and so *ad infinitum*. Besides, a decree lies not on a man's estate or effects but he might notwithstanding dispose of them as he thought fit. But a [writ of] sequestration, when served, did indeed lay a lien because it was the ultimate process and remedy of the court to compel obedience to its decree.

Curia [Lord Cowper]: Until the [writ of] sequestration was served, Mitchell's estate remained entirely in his own disposal. Moysey had done nothing in this case but what was very proper and prudent for him to do. He was bail for Mitchell. He found he was involved and going to rack and ruin. Then, he steps in to save him while it was yet time before the sequestration came to attach or affect his estate. Nothing [is] more natural than for a man to do. And the better to secure himself, he procures Liddington to be the purchaser. This is very just. And it is no matter whether either of them had any notice of the decree or not, though it is very likely they had. And the notice is not clearly denied or the answers so candid as they ought to have been.

And as to detaining the money to satisfy encumbrances he was informed of, nothing is more proper and usual to protect his purchase by having encumbrances assigned.

And, for the surplus money, it was nobody's but Mitchell's, and neither of the defendants could justify the detaining it, though it is very likely they had a greater kindness for Mitchell than the [plaintiff] and had rather he should have the money than the plaintiff. Therefore, I can give no relief against either of them but dismiss the bill only with 10s. for the costs of this day in regard the plaintiff is in possession of a decree and has a just demand. But the defendants for the manner of answering having given some grounds to suspect there had not been such fair dealings as there ought.

[Other copies of this report: British Library MS. Hargrave 303, f. 82.]

24
Gaudy v. Bill
(Ch. 1714)

A nomination to be exercised by the heirs of the donor that is part of the creation of a charity is not alienable by the heirs.

British Library MS. Hargrave 80, f. 203

An impropriation was vested by a will in trustees and their heirs upon trust to apply the profits for the maintenance of a curate at a certain place, which curate should be nominated from time to time by the testator and his heirs.

Serjeant *Jekyll*: This curacy is not presentative nor a donative nor any lay fee, but he is a mere stipendiary curate.

Lord Chancellor [Cowper]: The nomination is part of the appointment of the charity and, therefore, not alienable by the heir, even by express words. The reserving the nomination to the heir of the donor might be with intent that it might be known by that in after ages who was the donor. And it is of the greatest consequence to charities to support the will of the donors, even where they appear to have something of humor in them. He, therefore, declared that the right of nomination was in the heirs of the donor notwithstanding any act done by them and that it would remain in them unalienable.

[Other copies of this report: Lincoln's Inn MS. Misc. 383, p. 319, pl. 2, Lincoln's Inn MS. Misc. 107, f. 44, pl. 2.]

British Library MS. Hargrave 77, f. 47v

Gawdy v. Pett.

Sir Charles Gawdy [was] seised in fee of the manor of Cronshall and was the rector and impropriator of Ipsall.

Lord Cowper: If a person seised in fee impropriate settle the impropriation on a charitable use, as for the benefit of the curate for the time being and that his heirs and assigns, lords of the manor of [*blank*] shall under their hands and seals nominate and appoint the curate, this nomination and appointment relating to a charity is unalterable and in the first case none but the heir or owner of the manor for the time being.

[Other copies of this report: British Library MS. Hargrave 303, f. 83, pl. 1.]

25

Keen v. Cooke

(Ch. 1714)

A reasonable time is allowed for registering deeds, and a subsequent purchaser cannot jump ahead where there has not been a reasonable time for the earlier purchaser to register.

The Registry Act extends to executory contracts to sell real estate.

In this case for specific performance of a contract to sell real estate, one of the owners did not join in the agreement to sell and thus the suit was dismissed.

British Library MS. Hargrave 80, f. 203v

A woman was tenant for life, remainder to her son in tail, remainder to her in fee of a parcel of tithes in Middlesex. And the son covenanted with the plaintiff by articles sealed that he and his mother and their trustees would in consideration of £360 convey the tithes to the plaintiff in fee and received ten guineas in part [payment]. The defendant, Cooke, soon after and with a general notice of the articles, bought the same tithes of the woman and her son for £380 and took an absolute conveyance from both. His conveyance was registered after[wards] according to the late Act of Parliament,[1] but the plaintiff's articles were not. The plaintiff brought his bill against the woman, her son, and Cooke to have a conveyance pursuant to his articles. The woman pleaded the Statute of Frauds[2] and that the articles were not signed by her or any authorized by her. And her plea was allowed. Cooke, at the hearing, insisted upon the Statute for registering deeds and the articles, not been registered, were void.

Sir Joseph Jekyll, for the plaintiff: The Statute for registering deeds was intended for the security of the purchasers without notice, not of purchasers with notice. Conveyances of legal or equitable interests are within the Act, but not mere executory agreements, such as articles, which cannot injure a subsequent purchaser without notice and, therefore, are not of necessity to be registered. The sealing of those articles will not vary the case. They would have been equally valued had they been only signed. Therefore, they are not such a deed as is de-

1 Stat. 7 Ann., c. 20 (*SR*, IX, 89–93).

2 Stat. 29 Car. II, c. 3 (*SR*, V, 839–842).

scribed in the Act, nor are they a conveyance, they being only an agreement to convey.

Sir Thomas Powys denied the distinction made by *Sir J. Jekyll* between purchasers with or without notice and cited Cooke's Case, 5th Report.[1] There, the purchaser had notice of a prior voluntary conveyance, and it was urged that it could not be fraudulent against him because *non decipitur qui scit se decipi*,[2] but it was overruled, that, here, the Statute had settled the rules of notice, that such as could affect a purchaser must be one that arises from the register.

Lord Chancellor [Cowper]: The time appointed by the Act for registering conveyances is before the subsequent conveyance is registered. If a subsequent purchaser with notice of a former purchase and within two or three days after it should hastily get his conveyance registered in order to avoid the former, should that prevail, there must be a reasonable time allowed for registering deeds. But the difficulty is whether the Act extends to agreements executory.

Serjeant *Powys*: The articles are sealed and are a deed. Articles affect the land against the vendor and against a subsequent purchaser with notice. The party that claims under them is looked upon in equity as a purchaser from the time of the articles, and the plaintiff founds his demand to have our conveyance set aside upon the estate's being affected by his articles.

Serjeant *Hooper*: The articles, as to the legal interest, are executory; as to the equitable, executed, that passes by them immediately. They are, therefore, a deed that conveys an equitable title.

Lord Chancellor [Cowper]: Several things have been urged by *Sir Thomas Powys* and Serjeant *Hooper* very plausibly, which it may not be easy to untie. An arrangement that is intended to be final, though it affect only an equitable interest, must be registered. But, if an agreement be made (though under seal) only in order to have a conveyance two or three days after and another slip in in the meantime with notice of the agreement and to defeat it gets his deed registered immediately, this court cannot reach such a practice upon the head of fraud, as it might in such a case. Even in the first, were there an actual conveyance, there would otherwise be a great room for fraud. A conveyance might be prepared at the same time and that which is last executed supplant the first by being immediately registered and, in the case of articles, it is to be presumed that the party articling intends to pursue the law and to enroll his conveyance when made. The provision made by the Act in relation to the equitable interest must be taken with some distinctions. If articles are intended to be final or, if to avoid the Act, they are made for a conveyance to be executed several years after or, if being for a present conveyance, they are rested upon for an unreasonable time, they will be within the Act.

---

[1] *Chaloner v. Cook* (1599), 5 Coke Rep. 46, 77 E.R. 125.

[2] He is not deceived who knows himself to be deceived. *Rous v. Gooch* (1590), 5 Coke Rep. 60, 77 E.R. 146, 147.

But another point having been insisted upon, *viz.* that the son had no authority from the mother to enter into or sign the articles, that now was proved and by Serjeant *Hooper*, that the mother's plea of that being allowed and not replied to (though the cause be brought on against the other defendants and not against her) stands *pro confesso*, the bill and plea remaining upon record, after a plea allowed, though, in the case of a demurrer allowed, the bill is out of court as to the party demurring, which distinction seemed to be allowed *per* CURIAM.

Lord Chancellor [COWPER]: That part of the Statute of Frauds which relates to signing the others lawfully authorized must be taken in the strictest sense. There will otherwise be a gap left for fraud upon that head. Therefore, 'lawfully authorized' must be intended for that special purpose, *viz.* to sign, not to treat or agree. In this case, the right of the mother is not bound by the articles and though the plaintiff as to the son's interest has a good title, yet the agreement being mixed, it cannot be entirely executed nor can it be severed, for which reason he was of opinion that the bill should be dismissed but without costs.

[Other copies of this report: Lincoln's Inn MS. Misc. 383, p. 319, pl. 3, Lincoln's Inn MS. Misc. 107, f. 45.]

26

Langton v. Hall

(Ch. 1714)

A plaintiff's debtor cannot voluntarily and fraudulently allow the debt in issue to be attached by the plaintiff's creditor and thus defeat the debt.

A party to litigation cannot use an offer to settle the case out of court to defeat the other party's right.

British Library MS. Hargrave 80, f. 207v

The plaintiff was a builder, and the defendant Hall was indebted to him in £200 upon a building contract. Two of the other defendants had been employed by the plaintiff in the work and were creditors of the plaintiff upon that head. The defendant, to defeat the plaintiff of the £200 contrived that the other defendants should attach it in his hands for their debt, prevailed with them to do so and went on purpose within London, where it was accordingly attached and condemned. The plaintiff, upon this, brought his bill for relief against all the defendants.

Lord Chancellor [COWPER]: As between the defendants, let the attachment stand. But, nevertheless, in respect of the fraud of the defendant Hall, he decreed the plaintiff a satisfaction for the £200 against him. He cited a like case (I think Langton and Langton) where a debtor came purposely within Holborn Bar to a tavern by appointment and recited with impatience until the money was attached in his hands, but he burnt his fingers.

In this case, overtures had been made by the plaintiff for an agreement, but so as all might be concluded at once and he might have no further trouble. The defendant would have taken advantage of this overture of the plaintiff at the hearing.

Lord Chancellor [Cowper]: While I have attended courts, I have been sorry to see those overtures laid hold of and decrees founded upon them. It is a discouragement to all kind of fairness. They are made *sub modo* that they may have no further trouble or expense and yet you would have a decree founded upon one, though the plaintiff has had a further trouble and expense.

[Other copies of this report: Lincoln's Inn MS. Misc. 383, f. 323, Lincoln's Inn MS. Misc. 107, f. 51.]

[Other reports of this case: 2 Eq. Cas. Abr. 108, 22 E.R. 92.]

27

Sansom v. Ogle

(Ch. 1714)

A court of equity can order an account taken upon a contract and can determine the extent of the agreement between the parties to it.

British Library MS. Hargrave 80, f. 208

The plaintiff's testator, Captain Sansom, being captain of the *Merry Gally*, and the defendant Captain Ogle[1] of the *Tarter*, both fifth rates, made an agreement in writing mutually signed the 4th November 1708 that, whatever prizes should be taken by either of them in the ship they then commanded or in any other ship they might happen to command, all the shares of such prizes that should become due to either of them by any capture or recapture from the date of the agreement during that war with France or Spain should be equally divided between them after the agreement. Ogle, by orders of the Admiralty, sailed to Newfoundland and, from thence, to the Straights, where he took several prizes of value and continued there until after the death of Sansom, who was ordered and did cruise at home until October 1709, at which time, he got the command of the *Bonaventure*, a fourth rate, and made a winter cruise in her, But she, striking upon a sand, was ordered into dock in February 1709 to be refitted, and Sansom was then paid off and discharged. But before she was laid up, he applied for another ship and continued his application until May 1711, when he was appointed captain of the *Moor*, a fourth rate, in which command, he died. In November following, the plaintiff's executor brought this bill for an account of the prizes taken by Ogle.

[1] J. K. Laughton and R. Harding, 'Ogle, Sir Chaloner (1680/81–1750)', *Oxford Dictionary of National Biography*, vol. 41, pp. 593–594.

The chief questions were whether the discharge of Captain Sansom in February 1709 determined the agreement entirely and, if not, whether it suspended it until he got a new commission.

It was urged for the plaintiff that the words of the agreement had fixed the time from whence it was to commence and during which it was to continue, that, during that space of time, all the profit to be taken by Ogle were to be divided and *e converso* that no provision was made for exempting prizes taken by one while the other was out of commission, and that the court, therefore, ought not to exempt them, that there was no reason either to make any provision of that kind in the agreement, that, at the time of the agreement (at which time the intent of the parties was to be considered), their prospects were equal, but that their continuing at sea or in commission, being appointed to one station or another, or being more or less successful depending upon the will of others and various accidents made it probable that one might be more successful than the other and that probability and the uncertainty on whom the success would fall were the foundation of their agreement for sharing each other's good fortune, and though Captain Ogle had the fortune to continue longer in commission than Sansom, that being one of the contingents which at the time of the agreement was foreseen might happen and it is presumed was one of the motives for making it, especially since the party did not except that case, it ought not to be turned into a reason for breaking it, especially since Sansom, being discharged, was involuntary and without any default. Had he thrown himself out of service willfully or by any demerit, it might have laid a foundation for the court to have set Ogle free from his part of the agreement from that time, that though they had not any equal chance while Sansom was out of commission, their chance was equal at the time of making the agreement, and the inequality, afterwards arising without any default of Sansom, ought not to deprive him of the benefit of any part of the agreement.

Of the other side, it was insisted that the foundation of the agreement was the mutual hazard they were to run and the assistance they were to give each other, that, when Sansom was discharged, he ran no hazard nor was he capable of giving any assistance to the other nor was there at that time within the intent of the agreement that, by the words, they were to share what they took as captains, that Sansom, at that time, was no captain and, therefore, not within the words and that the agreement being once determined could not be revived.

The Master of the Rolls [TREVOR] was of opinion that the agreement ought to be confined to the time during which they were both in commission, that, while Sansom was out, he was in effect dead, but that, upon his gaining a new commission, the agreement revived. And he decreed an account of the prizes taken before Sansom was discharged and after he got another ship, but not of those in the meantime.

[Other copies of this report: Lincoln's Inn MS. Misc. 383, p. 324, Lincoln's Inn MS. Misc. 107, f. 52.]

[Affirmed on appeal: 1 Brown P.C. 149, 1 E.R. 477.]

28
Mitchell v. Thorowgood

(Ch. 1714)

The words in a will 'and other goods whatsoever' includes all the surplus of the personal estate which was not disposed of by the will.

Lincoln's Inn MS. Misc. 11, p. 9

12 November 1714.

Alice Wingfield, having a son and a daughter, gives £100 to her son and £150 to her daughter, and she also gives them equally several pieces of household goods therein particularly enumerated and all other her household goods and other goods whatsoever except a chest of drawers and her wearing apparel, which she gives to her daughter. And then she gives £3 to the defendant, her brother, and £4 to one Dennet, and she makes them executors.

The defendant Thorowgood, at the death of the testator, was indebted to her in two bonds, one for the payment of £30 and the other for the payment of £50.

The plaintiff marries the daughter and receives her legacy and share of the household goods. The brother dies, and administration is granted to the plaintiff's wife, who also dies. The plaintiff takes administration to his wife and administration *de bonis non* to the brother. And now, he brings his bill to have satisfaction of the sums of £50 due from the executor on bond to the testatrix as part of the surplus, which he alleged was given by the will to the children, the defendant having paid the £30 bond before to the plaintiff.

The defendant, by answer, admitted the payment of the £30 bond to the plaintiff, but he said he did it ignorantly, not knowing he had any right to the money, but now he insisted that the £50 was extinguished by his being made executor.

It was insisted on for the plaintiff that, by the words 'all other my goods', the bond passed or, if not, the surplus did not belong to the executor, he being excluded by having a legacy given him.

On the other hand, it was said for the defendant that the bond did not pass, that the words 'all other my goods whatsoever' must be restrained to the particulars mentioned before and must be something of the same nature. But, however, if the general words did carry the bond, yet being extinguished by law, according to Dorchester and Webb's Case, in Cro. Charles,[1] the general words could only extend to such surplus as was not thereby disposed by express words or by construction of law.

---

1 *Dorchester v. Webb* (1634), Croke Car. 372, 79 E.R. 924, also W. Jones 345, 82 E.R. 182, Hutton 128, 123 E.R. 1150.

In the next place, this could not belong to the plaintiff as a surplus undisposed of, for the executors were entitled to the surplus notwithstanding they had small legacies given them, according to the Duchess of Beaufort's Case and the Case of Buckley and Littlebury, in the House of Lords.[1]

Lord Keeper [Lord Cowper] was of opinion that the words 'and other goods whatsoever' carried all the surplus of the personal estate which was not disposed of by the will. Had the words, for instance, been 'I give my cabinet, bed, scrutore, and all other my goods whatsoever', the general words perhaps would have been restrained by the particular. But the words here go farther. It is 'all other my household goods and other goods whatsoever'. And he, therefore, decreed the defendant to pay the £50 with interest and costs.

29

Pierpoint v. Neville

(Ch. 1714)

In the case of an infant, accounts that have been approved by a master in Chancery can be ordered to be reviewed.

British Library MS. Hargrave 81, f. 131

16 November. Master of the Rolls. Petition.

The plaintiff was an infant of a considerable estate, and the defendant had been a great while steward in the family and was by the court appointed receiver of the estate with a salary. And, accordingly, he passed his accounts from time to time before a Master. And, afterwards, it was discovered that, in passing them, he had produced as vouchers several acquittances for money as paid by him which had been paid by tradesmen and allowed by the plaintiff's father but no receipt taken and others which, in fact, remained unpaid or that they had compounded in the whole to the amount of £200. It was, therefore, prayed that the plaintiff might not be concluded by accounts thus passed but that the master might review the same and the defendant Neville attend the review and be examined upon oath as to the payments.

Curia [Trevor]: This being in the case of an infant, he cannot be barred by the account passed, especially where it is to his prejudice and there is a fraud. Therefore, [it was] ordered as prayed, and Neville, the defendant, to procure a new report by Christmas or stand committed.

[Other copies of this report: British Library MS. Hargrave 82, f. 143, pl. 3.]

---

[1] *Duke of Beaufort v. Lord Dundonald* (Ch. 1716–1717), see below, Case No. 131; *Buckley v. Littlebury* (1711), 3 Brown P.C. 43, 1 E.R. 1165, 1 Eq. Cas. Abr. 245, 21 E.R. 1021, also 2 Vernon 677, 23 E.R. 1040, Lincoln's Inn MS. Misc. 10, p. 86.

[Other reports of this case: British Library MS. Hargrave 77, f. 35v, pl. 2, British Library MS. Hargrave 303, f. 64, pl. 2.]

30
Gill v. Jennings
(Ch. 1714)

Court costs are first taxed by the Master in Chancery, but the taxing can be reviewed by the court.

British Library MS. Hargrave 81, f. 132

26 November.

Where a duty is recovered, the party is not only entitled to costs of suit in this court but at law also and for all collateral matters necessary to have the fruit and benefit of the decree, so as the proceedings are not erroneous else he must lose those costs though he were a mortgagee or had never so plain a right. Where the exceptions to a master's report relate to several sums not allowed, they must be particularized and may be so in the body of that exception or in a schedule thereto annexed, but, if they relate to bills not allowed which contain divers items, those bills must not be so annexed but the titles with the sums total of them may, for the court is not originally to tax. That is the proper business of the master in ease of the court. But, afterwards, it may be brought into court, who will direct upon the matter. And there is cause. So the matter was sent back to allow those collateral and incidental costs, but, if any erroneous proceedings were, to be at liberty to disallow them.

[Other copies of this report: British Library MS. Hargrave 82, f. 144.]

[Other reports of this case: British Library MS. Hargrave 77, f. 35v, pl. 3, British Library MS. Hargrave 303, f. 64, pl. 3.]

31

Green v. Eversfield

(Ch. 1714)

Where an estate charged with a portion is small and no provision is made for interest or for maintenance of the person entitled to the portion, a court of equity will not decree payment of either.

British Library MS. Hargrave 80, f. 202

In this case, which was heard immediately after the former, a father had charged his real estate with a portion for his daughter to be paid at twenty-one or marriage and, if she died before, to go over. And he made no provision at all for interest or maintenance in the meantime. The estate charged, and which was all the eldest son had, was small.

And, though it was a provision from a father for a child who had no other maintenance provided for her, Lord Chancellor [Cowper] would not load the estate with interest or maintenance.

[Other copies of this report: Lincoln's Inn MS. Misc. 383, p. 319, pl. 1, Lincoln's Inn MS. Misc. 107, f. 44, pl. 1.]

Lincoln's Inn MS. Misc. 13, p. 42, pl. 2

27 November 1 Georgii primi.

Nicholas Gilbert, having one son and two daughters, he, by will, gave a rent charge of £80 *per annum* to his wife for life, clear of all taxes, she taking particular care of the breeding, clothing, and educating of his children. He gave £500 apiece to his two daughters to be paid at their ages of twenty-one or marriage, and, for the securing the payment of his debts and legacies, he devised certain lands to Mr. Eversfield and others and their heirs, whom he made executors upon trust to sell etc. and with the money so raised and with his personal estate to pay his debts and legacies. And, if both fell short, then he charged the legacies upon the residue of his lands.

The two daughters brought their bill to have the interest of their portions for their maintenance until the portions became payable. And the son and heir made his case that the debts by mortgage etc. would reduce the real estate from £500 *per annum* to £160, out of which the £80 *per annum* clear of taxes to his mother was to be paid so that little would be left for his maintenance. And he insisted that the £80 *per annum* was given to his mother upon trust and under a sort of a condition to maintain the daughters.

Lord Chancellor Cowper decreed that no sale should be made until the portions became payable and that no interest should be allowed for maintenance.

32

Wallis v. Newcomen

(Ch. 1714)

The plaintiff in a suit to perpetuate testimony is liable for court costs.

Lincoln's Inn MS. Misc. 11, p. 20, pl. 2

30 November 1714.

The plaintiff brings a bill to perpetuate testimony to prove a will and prays no relief.

The defendant insisted he was the heir at law and that there was no will or, if there was, he was the issue in tail under a settlement.

The plaintiff examines his witnesses, and the defendant joins in the commission. And then, the plaintiff lies still. And, after three terms, the defendant moves for his costs, which were ordered to be paid him upon hearing counsel on both sides.

And now, the plaintiff comes to move to discharge this order, but [it was] denied, the Lord Chancellor [Lord Cowper] saying that there was no reason an heir at law should be put to any costs for supporting a title against himself.

33

Bond v. Harrison

(Ch. 1714)

A mortgage can be paid off by giving the creditor a legacy.

Lincoln's Inn MS. Misc. 11, p. 6

1 December 1714. Lord Cowper.

Henry Fry, being indebted to the defendant in a sum of money for which he had made him a mortgage, devises other lands to him and his heirs, of which the testator was seised in fee in reversion after the death of his mother, upon trust to sell and, out of the money arising thereby, to pay £150 to the plaintiff's wife, which sale was to be made as soon as conveniently might be, and, out of the remainder, to lay out £500 in lands which were to be settled on the plaintiff's wife, remainder to her children, with a remainder to the defendant in fee. And he gives the defendant the residue of the money.

[It was] decreed that the surplus of the money was a satisfaction of the mortgage.

In this case was cited the case of Davy and Hooper, in Lord Harcourt's time,[1] which was affirmed in the House of Lords. A tenant in tail of lands does not suffer a recovery as he might, but he leaves the estate to come to the remainderman in fee, to whom he was indebted. The questions was if, having not done so, it should not be presumed he did so with an intent to make satisfaction of the debt he owed the remainderman. [It was] decreed it should not be a satisfaction, for it was purely contingent. The tenant in tail might have had issue and that would have defeated his intention if he had any such as was contended for, and a contingent interest shall never be a satisfaction of a certain debt.

34

Bassett v. Manlove

(Ch. 1714)

A Master in Chancery can be directed generally to settle the accounts in issue between the parties.

British Library MS. Hargrave 81, f. 133

2 December.

The plaintiff married the widow of Sir Samuel Gerrard, who had mortgaged his estate and, afterwards, created a trust for the payment of his debts. And his widow, after his decease, advanced £2000 of her own money towards the payment of the debts, which £2000 the plaintiff, as administrator to his wife, claimed prior to the defendant, Manlove, and several other puisne encumbrances.

And he brought a bill to have the estate sold to discharge the encumbrances in their order. The estate was accordingly decreed to be sold and the debts paid according to their priority, the Master to see and certify what was due to each of them.

This was done as to all the encumbrances prior to the plaintiff, the estate [was] sold, and they [were] paid out of the purchase money. The plaintiff, after the trust [was] created, was by virtue of his marriage in possession of the estate and received the rents and profits. And being to account and afterwards examined upon interrogatories accordingly the puisne encumbrances estreat[2] out of his examination all his receipts and therewith make a charge upon him and insist that all his payments and disbursements shall be made out by proper vouchers and proofs and that he should be charged with the rents and profits before

[1] *Davy v. Hooper* (1710–1711), 2 Vernon 665, 23 E.R. 1032, 1 Eq. Cas. Abr. 336, 344, 21 E.R. 1085, 1091, 6 Brown P.C. 51, 2 E.R. 926.

[2] Sic in MS.

the decree, to which the plaintiff objecting as not being expressed in the decree and so not warranted by it, the creditors petitioned for the direction of the court.

Curia [Lord Cowper]: Here [they] need no special direction. The difference between the parties is as to the manner or method of accounting, of which the Master is the proper judge, and the plaintiff must account according to the course of the court. And where a Master is to see what is due for a creditor, there he must of course see what the creditor has received or has had out of the estate liable to his demands or towards satisfaction of his debts without any particular direction for that purpose. It is implied in the general for whatever has been received must be deducted out of what was due, and nothing remains due but what is over and above what he has had.

[Other copies of this report: British Library MS. Hargrave 82, f. 145.]

[Other reports of this case: British Library MS. Hargrave 77, f. 36, pl. 1, British Library MS. Hargrave 303, f. 64, pl. 4.]

35

Tayspill v. Tayspill

(Ch. 1714–1715)

An order to pay money can be enforced by a writ of sequestration.

British Library MS. Hargrave 81, f. 134

4 December 1714.

In an examination [upon] an affidavit touching the credit of witnesses or parties, particular facts must not be mentioned because that would create a charge or scandal upon a man which he cannot possibly clear himself from, for that he cannot have an opportunity of doing without trial. The general character, therefore, or reputation of the persons ought only to be given.

British Library MS. Hargrave 81, f. 139, pl. 2

One Hall, an attorney, was committed for the suborning of witnesses and other foul practices in this cause. Upon his application to the Lord Chancellor, it was ordered that, upon his paying costs and damages, which were to be ascertained by the Master, he should be discharged. The Master settled it, and Hall had notice of the sum but did not pay it. Then, a positive order was made to pay it at a certain time. And, it not being paid, a [writ of] sequestration was moved for and granted by the Master of the Rolls [Trevor].

For Hall, it was insisted that it was irregular, for no sequestration could be on the first order; that was only an election to remain in custody or pay the money. The order for payment ought to be followed with proper processes of contempt, *viz.* subpoena, attachment, etc., before sequestration.

But, of the other side, it was said that here were two contempts. It was in vain to serve a subpoena or sue out an attachment against a man in prison, for he could not be arrested or taken upon it. And [there is] no inconvenience because here was full notice what he had to do, which was a contempt of the order and, therefore, as no process against his person could bring satisfaction to the party injured, process against his estate must do it.

[The court] so ordered sequestration to go.

[Other copies of this report: British Library MS. Hargrave 82, f. 151, pl. 2.]

[Other reports of this case: British Library MS. Hargrave 77, f. 37, pl. 2, British Library MS. Hargrave 303, f. 66v, pl. 2.]

36

Sandford v. Sandford

(Ch. c. 1714)

In this case, the purchaser of land from the decedent was allowed to complete the purchase or to abandon it.

British Library MS. Hargrave 81, f. 135

Sandford, the father of the plaintiff and defendant, being seised in fee of lands in Devon in lease for one remaining life, agrees with one Fry to sell him the reversion. And, before anything further was done, *viz.* in three weeks after, Sandford died. And, by will, he devised the said lands to trustees to raise by leasing, mortgage, or sale thereof money for payment of his debts and younger children's portions. And after his death, a decree is had for executing this trust by sale etc. And Fry goes before the Master and, according to his agreement with Sandford, is reported the best purchaser and obtains on his own motion an order to confirm it and then neglects to proceed. And, in the interim, the life drops, and then the estate to be sold is worth £350 more than Fry had agreed to give.

It was, thereupon, moved, that in regard here were infants and creditors concerned in whose favor the court usually was indulgent, to enlarge the fund for their benefit, however, not to diminish it that he might be discharged from being the purchaser, but it was denied.

It was now moved by Fry that he may proceed and the heir be directed to convey.

For the heir, it was said that Fry had no decree nor so much as a bill against him to compel him to convey and this court had never carried it so far against an heir as upon that agreement with the father to compel the heir to convey or Fry to have perfected the purchase. And, therefore, in the Case of Sir William Browne, who contracted for the Cobham estate, though he signed the book, yet, upon his death, the heir was not required to proceed in the purchase. And here, if Fry must have a conveyance, the infants and creditors will be prejudiced.

CURIA: There is no reason why a construction made by the direction or intervention of this court should not be as effectual and binding to all parties as if it had been in writing and signed by the parties and why the court should not take care to see them executed. If the intended purchaser will neglect for any considerable time to proceed, then, for his laches, he is punished by being discharged. But here, there has not been in any laches in him. In the Case of Sir William Brown, he ran away; so there was no person to compel and his signing the book did not make a contract between him and the court, but it is done for the greater notoriety and manifestation of the fact. If Fry does not bring in all his money in three weeks, let him be discharged from the purchase without motion.

[Other copies of this report: British Library MS. Hargrave 82, f. 147, pl. 2.]

[Other reports of this case: British Library MS. Hargrave 77, f. 36, pl. 3, British Library MS. Hargrave 303, f. 65, pl. 2.]

37

Smith v. Dean

(Ch. c. 1714)

A devise of a 'dwelling house' includes all outbuildings that are usually belonging to or convenient for the dwelling house.

British Library MS. Hargrave 81, f. 137

Sir Thomas Doleman, having a seat with fountains, gardens, canals, and a park near Newberry, devises them by the name of the dwelling house and park and the use of the goods to the plaintiff Smyth until his heir attained his age of twenty-five years. And she being to prove and have the benefit of the will, a question was made whether by 'dwelling house' the outhouses, stables, barns, fountains, and waters to the house should pass.

On the hearing, it was declared by the court that, by 'dwelling house', all outhouses etc. usually belonging to or convenient for a dwelling house pass as appurtenance and included in these words. The earl of Radnor by approbation of [*blank*] takes a lease of twenty-one years of this house. But it was doubted whether he was thereby entitled to have the conduits, canals for water to the house, the use of the new way, and wood for fuel to preserve the goods left by Sir Thomas Doleman.

And the court declared that, by the words in the will, all passed which Sir Thomas Doleman used with the house or park, either for necessity, pleasure, or convenience, and so the gardens, fountains, canals, and waters and the new way made by him over his own grounds passed and should accordingly be held by the earl during the term.

Petitions to reargue exceptions must be signed by counsel. [. . .][1] by witnesses to interrogatories need not be signed by counsel. The party must demur for himself because nobody but the executor and witnesses are present at the examination nor, as supposed, he knew the interrogatories.

[Other copies of this report: British Library MS. Hargrave 82, f. 149.]

[Other reports of this case: British Library MS. Hargrave 77, f. 36v, British Library MS. Hargrave 303, f. 66.]

38

Spendlove v. Aldrich

(Ch. 1714)

No action of a person under age will act as a prejudice or estoppel.

Accepting a dividend from a bankruptcy proceeding does not bar a claim against a third party.

British Library MS. Hargrave 77, f. 48, pl. 1

6 December 1714. Rehearing.

Though, on an appeal or rehearing, some errors be assigned, yet the cause is open and any other error may be assigned at the rehearing from the Rolls. Particular errors need not be assigned.

[Other copies of this report: British Library MS. Hargrave 303, f. 83, pl. 2.]

2 Lord Raymond 1320, 92 E.R. 362

6 December 1714. Chancery. Mary Spendlove, daughter of Charles Spendlove, and Mary, his wife, who was sister of John Lambert, deceased, plaintiffs; John Aldrich and Mary, his wife, Henry Capps, Samuel Hartly, Samuel Wade, and John Wade, defendants.

On an appeal from a decree of the Master of the Rolls on a bill brought by the plaintiff Mary Spendlove for the recovery of a legacy of £200 devised to her by her uncle, John Lambert, the case was this. John Lambert, being seised in fee of lands etc. in Norfolk and possessed of a considerable personal estate, 8 June 1696, by his last will, devised to the plaintiff £200 at her age of fifteen years, if she should so long live, and, in the meantime, to be put out by his executors for her best advantage until she attained her said age, and he gave by his said will several other legacies, and particularly £100 to the defendant John Wade, then

[1] admr.

an infant, and he devised all the rest of his real and personal estate after debts and funeral charges to the defendants, Henry Capps and Samuel Wade, who was then an infant, and he made them joint executors of his said will.

John Lambert died soon after. Henry Capps alone proved the will, the other executor, the defendant Samuel Wade, being then and long after an infant, *viz.* born 20 September 1692.

The plaintiff Mary Spendlove was born the 6th of March 1685, and she came to the age of fifteen the 6th of March 1700, when the £200 legacy became payable to her, which she applied to Capps for, but, he not paying, she received interest of him for part of the time before he became a bankrupt.

In 1704, Henry Bonett, being admitted by the ecclesiastical court at Norwich guardian and curator to the defendant Samuel Wade, settled accounts with Capps on behalf of Samuel Wade in relation to John Lambert's personal estate, and £200 was left in Capps's hands to pay the plaintiff. And the defendant Samuel Wade's share of the surplus of Lambert's estate came to £824 16s. 1d., which was left in Capps's hand, and he agreed to pay interest for it, after which Bonett received of Capps £198 10s. 1d., of which £29 13s. was for interest.

Capps, in July 1707, became a bankrupt, and, in August 1707, a commission issued out against him, and he was found a bankrupt. The plaintiff came into the commission and proved this £200 legacy as her debt and £16 due for interest 6 July 1707, and she received her dividend of 5s. in the pound.

Bonett, also as guardian to Wade, came into the commission for £744 1s., part of the said £824 16s. 1d., and received his dividend, £186 2s. 6d., which added to the £189 10s. made £384 12s. 6d., out of which he had made considerable disbursements for the defendant Wade.

After this, in June 1708, the plaintiff Mary Spendlove filed her bill against Capps, Samuel Wade and John Wade, and Bonett, and the assignees of the commission against Capps for a satisfaction of the £200 legacy given her by John Lambert's will. Capps put in his answer, confessed assets of Lambert came to his hands sufficient to pay all his debts, legacies, etc., his own bankruptcy, a certificate and confirmation of it by the Lord Chancellor etc., and he insisted on that as a discharge of his debts. The defendant Wade, by Bonett, his guardian, put in his answer, setting out the facts above alleged. And Bonett put in his answer and thereto annexed a particular of the writings and securities sent to him by Capps belonging to Lambert's estate and a copy of the account he made up with Capps.

Bonett, having made his will and thereby having subjected his real and personal estate to the payment of his debts etc. and having appointed Samuel Hartly executor, died soon after his answer was put in. Hartly refusing to act, administration with the will annexed of Henry Bonett was granted to Mary, his only daughter, wife of the defendant John Aldrich.

The plaintiff brought a bill of revivor against Aldrich and his wife, Hartly, and Samuel Wade, praying a discovery of Bonett's estate from Hartly and Aldrich and his wife. Aldrich and his wife, in their answer, set forth that they had accounted for Bonett's estate before Mr. Orlebar, one of the masters of this court, pursuant to a decree in a cause wherein the creditors of Bonett were plaintiffs against Hartly and Aldrich and his wife and that, by the Master's report, it appeared the whole real and personal estate of Bonett was not sufficient to pay his debts by mortgages and bonds by £675.

The plaintiff having replied and witnesses having been examined, the cause was heard before the Master of the Rolls [Trevor] the 24th of November 1713, who decreed, that it should be referred to Sir Thomas Gery to take an account of the personal estate of the testator John Lambert come to the hands of Henry Capps and Samuel Wade, the residuary legatees, or to the hands of Henry Bonett, as curator of Samuel Wade, His Honor declaring that what money was paid by Capps to Bonett of Lambert's estate on the account of Samuel Wade before Capps became a bankrupt and what money was received by Bonett for interest of Samuel Wade's residuary part of Lambert's estate and also what money was received by Mr. Bonett under the commission of bankruptcy for Samuel Wade's dividend or any dividend to Bonett on account of Samuel Wade in respect of the money which Capps owed Samuel Wade on the balance of his said account made up between Bonett and Capps was still the estate of Lambert and liable to the payment of the said plaintiff Spendlove's demands in regard the said residuary legatees could take nothing by the will of Lambert until all his debts and legacies were paid. And the Master was to distinguish what of Lambert's estate remained in specie and what upon the account should appear to have been received by Bonett as aforesaid; the same was to be made good out of the real and personal estate of Bonett. And Aldrich's wife and Hartly were to account for his estate etc. And what remained due of the £200 legacy with interest from her age of fifteen and her costs were to be paid the plaintiff out of what had been received by Bonett and made out of his estate and out of the assets of Lambert that should appear to be remaining in specie in Aldrich, his wife's, or Hartly's hands. And Aldrich, his wife, and Hartly were to have no costs.

From this decree, Aldrich and his wife, Hartly, and Samuel Wade appealed, which appeal was heard before the Lord Chancellor Cowper December 6, 1714, at which time, it was insisted on for the appellants that the plaintiff after she was entitled to her legacy had accepted Capps as her paymaster by letting the money lie in his hands and receiving interest of him for it some years before he became a bankrupt, secondly, by coming into the commission of bankruptcy, proving her debt, and receiving her dividend after he had failed out of his estate, thirdly, that Capps had accounted with Samuel Wade's guardian only for the surplus and had retained money in his hands on that account to satisfy the plaintiffs legacy, fourthly, that what the guardian Bonett had received of Capps for interest or upon the dividend was received as out of the surplus belonging to Samuel Wade and applied for his maintenance and education, fifthly, that Hartly, having never acted as executor to Bonett, and Aldrich and his wife, having accounted before the Master pursuant to a decree of this Court, ought to have had their costs.

But the Lord Chancellor [Lord Cowper] declared he was of opinion that the decree was right, for, it appearing by the proofs that the plaintiff had often applied to Capps for her legacy, but could not get it out of his hands, she was in the right to get the interest when she could not get the principal; besides, during the time she received the interest, she was under twenty-one, and, therefore, her accepting of interest could not prejudice her. And her coming into the commission and receiving a dividend would be no obstruction to her following Lambert's assets until she had a full satisfaction. And what was received by Bonett of Capps must be looked on as the estate of Lambert and could not be a surplus until all the debts and legacies of Lambert were paid, that the account settled between the guardian and Capps and the leaving money in Capps' hands to pay the plaintiff could not possibly bind her, she not being party or consenting to that transaction, nor could the application of the money received by Bonett any way affect her interest, it remaining, as to her, Lambert's estate still and liable to her legacy. He thought likewise the appellants ought not to have costs, and he affirmed the decree.

Mr. *Vernon* and *Robert Raymond* [were] with the appellants.

39
Whiston v. Partridge

(Ch. 1714)

An executor of a decedent's estate, in a suit for a legacy, cannot receive court costs, but he can charge them against the estate.

British Library MS. Hargrave 77, f. 48, pl. 2

Eodem die [6 December 1714].

Where a person comes against an executor for a legacy, it is not the course [of the court] to decree to the executor costs but only decree payment of the legacy, for the executor will have his costs allowed him in the general account of the estate.

[Other copies of this report: British Library MS. Hargrave 303, f. 83, pl. 3.]

40

Cliffe v. Gibbons

(Ch. 1714)

In this case, the court found that the intent of the testator was to devise his real as well as his personal estate.

British Library MS. Hargrave 80, f. 205v

The testator, being seised in fee of lands in Jamaica, gave a power by his will to his wife to sell if need should be his estate, Negroes, goods, chattels, and shipping there for payment of the debts and of the portions and legacies given by his will. And there he gave his wife £1000 to be retained by her out of the first money arising by profits or sale and several legacies to other persons, which, in case of a deficiency, he directed should abate in proportion except the £1000 to his wife. Then followed these words 'all the rest, residue, and remainder of my estate, goods, and chattels I give to my wife, whom I make my sole executrix'. The wife paid the debts, legacies, and portions out of the profits without a sale and died. And the question was whether the estate in Jamaica passed to the wife by this devise and for what interest.

It was alleged by Serjeant *Jekyll* and the Attorney General [*Northey*] that, if it rested on the power to sell, it would descend in the meantime and that nothing vested in the wife by that but a bare power without any interest and upon the clause of devise that the word 'estate' being blended with 'goods and chattels' ought to be understood of a personal estate only. And cases were cited on that head and the rather for that the devise is to the executrix.

The *Attorney* [*General*] mentioned the case of Cooke and Gwavis,[1] where a man settled his real estate in trust to pay debts, and, by a will of the same date with the settlement, bequeathed all his personal estate to Gwavis and J.S. to their own use, and then made them his executors. It was ruled in the Exchequer (and I think he said in the House of Lords) that, notwithstanding the words 'to their own use', they should take it to their own use as executors.

But this case Lord Chancellor [Lord Cowper] seemed not to lay any weight upon.

The *Attorney* [*General*] said that, in all the cases where lands of inheritance had been ruled to pass by the words 'all the rest of my estate', some part of the estate had been before devised by the same will for life or otherwise, that in the case of Lady Bridgewater and the Duke of Bolton,[2] the reason why the words 'all

[1] *Coke v. Gwavas* (Ex. 1683), Georgetown Law School MS. B88–7, p. 380 (Edward Ward's reports).

[2] *Countess of Bridgewater v. Duke of Bolton* (1704), 6 Modern 106, 87 E.R. 866, Holt K.B. 281, 90 E.R. 1054, 1 Salkeld 236, 91 E.R. 209, 1 Eq. Cas. Abr. 177, 21 E.R. 970,

the residue of my estate real and personal not before disposed of' were held to pass the inheritance of a fee farm rent not before mentioned was that there had been a devise of a real estate in the beginning of the will and the word 'estate' was looked upon as the genus real and personal as the species. And, to make the division perfect, the whole interest ought to pass in one as well as the other. It was said too that an heir at law cannot be disinherited by a will but by express words or a necessary implication, and there was neither in the present case.

Lord Chancellor [LORD COWPER]: It appears plainly to have been the testator's intent to dispose of the inheritance of the estate in Jamaica. If it stood in general 'all my estate, goods, and chattels' without any words of relation, 'estate' being coupled with 'goods and chattels' without any words of relation and all given to the executrix, the reason as well as the authorities would be very strong for retaining the signification of the word 'estate'. But, here, the real and personal estates are mixed together throughout the will; both are made the fund for debts, portions, and legacies. No greater care was taken to preserve one than the other. The sale if need should be equally relates to both. The words 'rest, residue, and remainder' are proper words of relation to what was before mentioned. And the words 'estate, goods, and chattels' are proper to sum that up.

Mr Attorney [General, *Northey*] said that they would carry lands before devised in part. There is no charm in the word 'devise'. If they are before treated of or any way made the subject of the will, these words will relate to them as much as if they had been devised. The wife of the first testator by her will gave all her Jamaica estate and the produce of it to J.S. and all her estate in England to J.N. and made them executors at the time of her death. A parcel of sugars were upon the high sea. The question was whether they should belong to J.S. as the produce of the Jamaica estate or to J.N. as her estate in England, they being consigned hither, or whether they should be looked upon as undevised and go to them as executors equally.

Lord Chancellor [LORD COWPER]: The testatrix intended to make a complete disposition of her estate and the *membra dividentia* were designed to take in the whole. A construction that would let the sugars fall between would be contrary to the will, the devise to J.N. being confined to the estate in England cannot reach them, but the former devise will, they being properly the produce of the Jamaica estate, though, if they had reached England in the life of the testatrix and so fall in under the other devise, the word 'produce' would not have reached them so as to carry them to J.S.

[Other copies of this report: Lincoln's Inn MS. Misc. 383, p. 321, Lincoln's Inn MS. Misc. 107, f. 48.]

2 Eq. Cas. Abr. 299, 22 E.R. 252.

2 Lord Raymond 1324, 92 E.R. 364

8 December 1714. Cliffe *et al*ii versus Gibbons, Kadwell, *et al*ios.

Upon the hearing this day, the case appeared to be this, *viz.* Ranceford Waterhouse, being seised in fee simple of a plantation and several lands etc. in Jamaica the 15th of November 1688, made his will in writing, and he, thereby, directed that all his debts should be paid as soon as conveniently could be after his decease together with his funeral and other charges, and he, thereby, gave power to Elizabeth Waterhouse, his wife, if need should be, to sell his lands, tenements, servants, goods, and chattels in Jamaica, and his leases, shipping, and goods in England to raise money to pay the same and then to pay such legacies as are given by his will, among which he gave his said wife £1000 to be by her detained out of the first money that could be raised by the profits or sale of his estate after payment of his debts and the residue of his estate, after debts and legacies paid, he gave to his said wife, whom he made sole executrix. And soon after, he died. She proved the will and entered upon and possessed herself of the real and personal estate, both in Jamaica and England, and, by perception of the profits thereof, she paid all his debts, funeral charges, and legacies and so did not sell the Jamaica estate.

Elizabeth Waterhouse, the 13th of April 1711, made her will, and she gave all her estate in Jamaica to the defendant John Gibbons and his heirs upon trust to pay the plaintiff Cliffe £1000 by yearly payments out of the neat produce (after all charges deducted) and then to pay several other legacies. And after payment of all the said legacies, she gave that estate to the defendant John Gibbons and his heirs. She being also seised and possessed of both real and personal estate in England, she charged it with the payment of several legacies and among others with £30 to the defendant John Kadwell and £250 apiece to the defendants, Mary and Anne Kadwell, his daughters. And the residuum of her estate in England she gave to the plaintiff Cliffe, and she made the plaintiff Cliffe and the defendant John Gibbons executors.

November 30, 1712, Elizabeth Waterhouse, the testatrix, signed a note as follows, *viz.*:

> London, November 30, 1712. Cousin John Gibbons, in case I die, pay unto my cousins Mary and Ann Kadwell £250 apiece and £70 more to my cousin John Kadwell for mourning and place it to my account, and it shall be allowed you. X The mark of Elizabeth Waterhouse.

she then not being able to write her name as usual, which note. Upon a contest in Doctors' Commons, it was made a codicil to the said will. And the plaintiff Cliffe and the defendant Gibbons joined in the probate.

The testatrix, at her death, had about eighty hogsheads of sugar upon the high seas coming from Jamaica for England, of which thirty-two were lost; the rest, afterwards, came to England and were possessed by the defendant John Gibbons.

This being the fact, Mary Cliffe, the plaintiff, brought her bill against John Gibbons and the Kadwells to have an account of the personal estate of Elizabeth Waterhouse, of which the defendant Gibbons possessed himself, to have her £1000 legacy charged on the Jamaica estate, to have the £250 and £250 and £70 legacies given the Kadwells paid out of the Jamaica estate, and to have an account of the sugars as part of the English estate, to which all the defendants put in their answers, and witnesses were examined, etc.

The Kadwells brought a cross-bill against Cliffe and Gibbons, the executors of the will of Elizabeth Waterhouse, for their legacies given by the will and codicil, etc.

And on the hearing of both causes this day before the Lord Chancellor Cowper, the first question was whether Elizabeth Waterhouse was seised in fee of the Jamaica estate so as to have a power to charge it or not, for the defendant Gibbons, whose mother was heir at law to Ranceford Waterhouse and who had conveyed the Jamaica estate to her son the defendant, insisted that she only had a power given her by her husband's will to sell, which she never executed, but, by perception of the profits, paid his debts, etc., that, by the words, the rest of his estate, which he devised to her, only an estate for life passed, and that the reversion descended to his heir at law, under whom he claimed, and, consequently, that Elizabeth Waterhouse could not charge the £1000 upon that estate for the plaintiff's benefit.

But the Lord Chancellor Cowper was clear of opinion that a fee passed by the devise of all the rest of his estate to his wife Elizabeth, subject to the payment of his debts etc. And he decreed the £1000 to be paid to the plaintiff.

See 3 Mod. 45, Reeves v. Winnington; [where] A. devises all his estate to J.S., a fee passes; 1 Ro. Ab. 834; Stile 193, 281, Johnson v. Kerman; 3 Keble 245, Wilson v. Robinson; 3 Mod. 228, Hyley v. Hyley.[1]

And the Lord Chancellor [Lord Cowper] held that, where a man devises all his estate, goods, and chattels and no mention had been made before in the will of lands of which the testator was seised in fee, a fee simple will not pass; but, where a real estate is mentioned before in the will and then such words follow, a fee passes.

---

[1] *Reeves v. Winnington* (1684), 3 Modern 45, 87 E.R. 28, also 2 Shower K.B. 249, 89 E.R. 920, 2 Eq. Cas. Abr. 299, 22 E.R. 251, Dodd 51; *Garret v. Blisard* (1649), Style 192, 82 E.R. 638; *Kerman v. Johnson* (1651), Style 281, 293, 82 E.R. 711, 721, 1 Rolle, Abr., *Estate*, pl. N, 12, p. 834; *Wilson v. Robinson* (1673), 3 Keble 180, 245, 84 E.R. 663, 701, also 1 Modern 100, 86 E.R. 763, 2 Levinz 91, 83 E.R. 464, 1 Freeman 112, 89 E.R. 83; *Hyley v. Hyley* (1688), 3 Modern 288, 87 E.R. 147, also Comberbach 93, 90 E.R. 364, 1 Eq. Cas. Abr. 210, 21 E.R. 996, 2 Eq. Cas. Abr. 302, 22 E.R. 254.

The next question was whether the Kadwells should have each of them two sums of £250, one by the will and the other by the order. And upon reading witnesses, who deposed that the testatrix took notice she had given them £250 by the will and said she would make it up £500, both sums were decreed them, and also that it should be paid out of the English estate, which appeared to be her intent by the deposition of witnesses.

The third question was whether the sugars that were on the seas at the testatrix's death should be esteemed as a part of her Jamaica or English estate. And [it was] decreed that, it not being arrived in England before her death and the trusts being to be performed by the will out of the neat produce of the Jamaica estate, it should be taken as part of the Jamaica estate.

[Other reports of this case: 2 Eq. Cas. Abr. 301, 328, 22 E.R. 253, 280.]

41

Lord Coningsby v. Anonymous

(Ch. 1714)

A motion for a preliminary injunction to prevent waste must be supported by an affidavit regardless of the allegations of the bill of complaint.

British Library MS. Hargrave 77, f. 48, pl. 3

9 December.

Filing a bill to stay waste and charging the inheritance to be in the plaintiff is not enough to found an injunction to stay waste without an affidavit at least of the plaintiff of his title and seisin.

[Other copies of this report: British Library MS. Hargrave 303, f. 83v, pl. 1.]

42

Noble v. Brewster

(Ch. 1714)

After a foreclosure is absolute and the decree is signed and enrolled, it is too late to have a redemption of the mortgage.

British Library MS. Hargrave 77, f. 48, pl. 4

Eodem die [9 December].

The plaintiff had a decree to foreclose the defendant absolutely which was signed and enrolled. And he now agrees with the person for the sale of the estate and tells the defendant that what the overplus came to above the principal and interest and costs the defendant should have it. Upon this, the defendant moves that he may have some time to redeem, offering to pay the principal, interest, and costs and interest for the costs in four days. And in the Case of Norris and Blake, cited, where, after a decree of foreclosure was absolute and it was too late to come to redeem and the party has sold the estate and, if not, the defendant could not have time enough without opening the enrollment and after two years, it was too late, and that, in the Case of Fielding and Lewis, Lord Keeper Wright had signed the docket at 11 and the Master of the Rolls at 12, [*blank*] at 2 and [there was a] *caveat* at 6 the same day, yet the Lord Keeper would not open that enrollment, but he discharged the *caveat*.

Curia [Lord Cowper]: If time be given by a decree to redeem and, before the time is lapsed, the decree be signed and enrolled, there, the party may have an enlargement, for that is still open and under the power of the court. But where the time is lapsed and the foreclosure is absolute and then the decree is signed and enrolled, then, it is otherwise, else it would make all foreclosures endless and that method of proceeding fruitless. And however it might have been in the case of a rent application, it would be unreasonable after any time to do it. If a man be so very honest after a foreclosure as to promise his mortgagor what he shall make more of his estate than what is strictly due to him, which he is not obliged to let him have, to take advantage of that kind offer and entangle him with a new suit or a continuance of the old by color of that promise would discharge all good nature and charity. And he, therefore, denied the motion.

[Other copies of this report: British Library MS. Hargrave 303, f. 83v, pl. 2.]

43

Redshaw v. Duck

(Ch. 1714–1715)

Any loss of a London freeman's estate due to the insolvency of his executor will fall upon the testamentary part of his estate only.

Lincoln's Inn MS. Misc. 11, p. 10

15 December 1714. Redshaw v. Duck and Greenhill.

Joseph Anderson, a freeman of London, by his will, directed that an inventory should be taken of his personal estate by his executors and that Barbara, his wife, should have her widow's chamber, and, after his debts and funerals paid, he gave her a third part of his personal estate. Another third he gave equally amongst his children Juliana, Hannah, Joseph, and William and Jane, who died in the testator's lifetime. And the remaining third part, he gave as follows, *viz.* £740 to the said Hannah, £40 in small legacies, £200 apiece to the said Joseph, William, and Jane, and the overplus, if any, to be equally divided amongst four of his children. And, if the third part of his personal estate in his disposal should by bad debts or other accidents fall short and not be sufficient to pay all his said legacies, he willed each of his said legatees should bear such loss, whatever it amounted to, in proportion according to their legacies. And he made James Duck, Joseph Chandler, Samuel Greenhill, and Thomas Greenhill executors.

Mr. Duck, Mr. Chandler, and Thomas Greenhill only proved the said will. And they exhibited an inventory of their testator's personal estate into the Chamber of London. And they paid Barbara, the widow, and Mr. Redshaw, who married Juliana, several sums on account of their customary shares.

Thomas Greenhill died. And, Mr. Duck having taken administration to him, a bill was exhibited against Mr. Duck and Mr. Greenhill, the two surviving acting executors, for an account of the testator's personal estate and to have a distribution thereof according to the custom [of London] and the will.

On 13 May 1707, the cause was heard and an account directed. And the Master to whom the cause was referred, by his report, charged the defendant Duck, who was become insolvent, with £163 1s. 10d. as the balance of his own account and with £279 19s. received by his intestate Thomas Greenhill out of the testator's estate, making together £443 0s. 10d. And, upon arguing exceptions taken to the Master's report before the Lord Chancellor, a question arose upon what part of the testator's estate the loss of this money, in case it should not be recovered, was to fall, whereupon it was ordered that the Master should state a case touching such loss and send it to the Recorder of the City of London to certify to the court the custom of the City of London upon the case so to be stated, *viz.* whether, by the said custom, the loss of the said freeman's estate by the insolvency of his executors ought to be borne out of the testamentary part of his estate only or out of his whole personal estate, as well customary as testamentary.

Vide Precedents in Ch. 409.[1] The certificate in this case. And it was there decreed the loss to fall on the testamentary part.

British Library MS. Hargrave 77, f. 51, pl. 1

23 June. Redshaw v. Brasier.

The plaintiff's father was a freeman of London. The bill was to have an orphanage part. The father had made a will and J.S. the executor, who took upon him the executorship and possessed part of the estate. And, afterwards, he proved insolvent, by which part of the estate was lost.

It came to be a question in the cause upon exceptions taken to the Master's report touching the account of the estate how that loss should be born, whether out of the orphanage or the testamentary part of the estate or out of the whole.

And the court referred it to the Lord Mayor etc. to certify the custom in that case. The record came now into court, and it certified there was no custom in this

[1] *Read v. Duck* (1715), Precedents in Chancery 409, 24 E.R. 183.

case either way. But it was considered as a case merely for equity to determine. And the certificate was ordered to be filed.

Query what decree [was made] at the hearing.

[Other copies of this report: British Library MS. Hargrave 303, f. 88, pl. 1.]

British Library MS. Hargrave 81, f. 93

18 October.

Anderson, a freeman of London having a wife and seven children by different venters makes his will and devises one third part of his estate to his wife, one other third to his children, and, as to the residue, devises specific legacies to two of them, and the remainder thereof to four other of them, but gives no part thereof to his daughter Juliana, who was by the first venter. And he appoints four executors and dies. One of the executors renounces, and the others prove the will. The plaintiff marries Juliana and, she dying, he marries Barbara, the mother-in-law to Juliana and widow to the testator, and being administrator to his first wife and so entitled to both his wives' customary parts, he received the greatest part thereof. But, afterwards, one of the executors, who had £400 of the testator's estate in his hands, failed, by which the estate falling short so much, the question was whether that loss should be borne out of the whole estate of the testator or out of the testamentary part only.

The plaintiff and his wife bring their bill to have the residue of the second said customary part and the defendants, who were the surviving executors and the husbands of the other children, insist that this loss ought to be borne out of the whole estate and not the testamentary part only and then the plaintiffs will have received more than the said second customary parts amounted to. And it was referred to the Lord Mayor etc. to certify the custom in this case, whether the loss should be borne out of the whole estate or the testamentary part only, the court taking notice that this case must have so often happened that probably there was some custom one way or the other, the Lord Mayor etc., having heard counsel on both sides, certified that there was no custom of the City in this case.

And the matter coming on to be heard this day on the said certificate and on exceptions to the Master's report touching accounts of the testator's estate decreed at the hearing, it was argued by the counsel for the plaintiff that, there being no custom of the City in this case, the matter must be determined according to the rules of equity and that, in the case of Mitford and Webster,[1] in the Lord Chancellor Harcourt's time, Mitford, on his marriage, covenanted to lease his intended wife a moiety of all his clear personal estate after debts and funeral expenses paid and borne, the marriage took effect, and he, afterwards, made his will and devised a moiety to his wife according to his covenant and made executors and, afterwards, a loss happened. And, in that case, it was decreed that the

1 *Webster v. Milford* (1708), 2 Eq. Cas. Abr. 363, 22 E.R. 308.

widow should have the value of the moiety according to the worth of the estate at the time of the testator's death and that the loss should be borne out of the residue, for the executors by whom the loss happened were but trustees of the husband's own creating to perform his obligations and distribute his estate according to law and, therefore, as they represent him and are of his appointment, it is but reasonable that that part of the estate which he has power over should bear the loss which happens by a trust of his own creating, for the other part was bound by the covenant for the benefit of his wife and so not properly his own estate nor subject to his disposition. So here, the customary part did immediately upon his decease vest in the wife and children and he had power over one-third only and, if a loss happens by the persons whom he appoints, that part only over which he had power ought to answer it.

Sir Robert Raymond, for the defendant: The case cited does not come up to this case. There, the decree was very just because it was founded upon an express covenant preceding the marriage by virtue of which the wife was a real creditor to her husband's estate and no disposition of that estate by the will or by the custom could be good until all debts were satisfied. But here is no covenant, nor are the plaintiffs creditors, as in that case. But it is objected to us that the loss arises by the act of the testator in making such an executor as did the wrong by wasting or running away with part of the estate. Therefore, that part only, over which he had power, ought to make good the loss. Had the testator by appointing those persons done what, by law, he was not authorized or had it appeared in the case that he had appointed them with intention to defraud the plaintiffs of their customary part, there would be some color of reason in that argument. But, as the testator did nothing by such appointment but what the law empowers him to do and that he is entrusted by law to name persons to make such distribution of his estate as the law directs, it is very hard that, if an accident happens that he could not possibly foresee, that his estate only must bear that loss when the trust was regularly and fairly created for the benefit of the whole.

Curia [Lord Cowper]: He had a power by the law to appoint executors, that is one or more trustees to make a legal distribution of his estate. That is according to custom and according to common law but not prejudicial to the custom, for the will of a freeman who did so were a nullity and void. One third part only is properly liable to his control or disposition. The custom cannot prejudice his right in the third part, nor his right over that third effect or lessen the customary part. By virtue of the custom, the widow's and orphans' parts did immediately upon the freeman's death actually vest in those entitled to it by the custom and, therefore, called customary parts, and the rest, as being disposable by will of the freeman as he think fit, is called the testamentary part. And the custom attaching instantly upon the freeman's decease, the wife and children have a right under the custom as creditors for their parts without any diminution and are not to suffer by any contingent or casual subsequent loss or diminution that may happen to the estate more than other creditors. The loss thereof must be borne out of the testamentary part only.

[Other copies of this report: British Library MS. Hargrave 82, f. 89, pl. 2, British Library MS. Hargrave 77, f. 23v, pl. 2, British Library MS. Hargrave 303, f. 45v.]

2 Lord Raymond 1328, 92 E.R. 367

18 October 1715. Chancery. Redshaw versus Brasier *et ux*orem *et al*ios.

Upon exceptions to Mr. Lovibond, the Master's, report, the case was this. Joseph Anderson, a freeman of London, having issue by his first wife, Juliana, who was the first wife to the plaintiff Redshaw and to whom he had took out administration, and Hannah, wife of Brasier, and by Barbara, his second wife, who after Anderson's death married also the plaintiff Redshaw and to whom, after her death, he also took out administration, Joseph, William, and Jane, who died in her father's lifetime, 15th of September 1701, made his will, and, thereby, he directed that an inventory should be taken of his personal estate by his executors and that Barbara, his wife, should have her widow's chamber, and, after his debts and funerals paid, he gave her a third part of his personal estate. Another third part he gave equally amongst his children, Juliana, Hannah, Joseph, William, and Jane. And the remaining third part, he gave as follows, *viz.* £740 to Hannah, £200 apiece to Joseph, William, and Jane, and the overplus, if any, to be equally divided among four of his children and to be paid them by his executors, *viz.* to his sons at the age of twenty-one years and to his daughters at twenty-one or marriage, and, if the third part of his personal estate in his disposal should by bad debts or other accidents fall short and not be sufficient to pay all his said legacies, he willed each of his said legatees should bear such loss, whatever it amounted to, in proportion according to their legacies. And he made James Duck, Joseph Chandler, Samuel Greenhill, and Thomas Greenhill executors, and he died in April following.

Mr. Duck, Mr. Chandler, and Thomas Greenhill only proved the will and exhibited an inventory of their testator's personal estate into the Chamber of London and entered into the usual recognizance and paid Barbara, the widow, and Mr. Redshaw, who had married Juliana, several sums on account of their customary shares.

Thomas Greenhill died, and, Mr. Duck having taken out administration to him, a bill was exhibited against Mr. Duck, Mr. Chandler, and the infants by Redshaw for an account of the personal estate and to have a distribution thereof according to the custom and the will.

May 18, 1707, the cause was heard, and an account was directed. And the Master, by his report, charged the defendant Duck, who was become insolvent, with £163 1s. 10d. as the balance of his account not answered by him and with £279 19s. received by Thomas Greenhill out of the testator's personal estate not answered by him, making together £443 10d. And the Master reported that that

£443 10d. ought to be paid to the defendant in the right of his wife Hannah, who survived both her brothers, Joseph and William, and was entitled to their shares out of the testamentary part, but, if it was lost, it ought to be borne out of the testamentary part, and not out of the customary parts. To which report the defendant Brasier took exceptions, which coming to be argued the 15th of December 1714 before the Lord Chancellor [LORD COWPER], the question arose upon what part of the testator's estate the loss of this money in case it should not be recovered was to fall, whereupon, it was ordered that the said Master should state a case touching the said loss and send it to the Recorder of the City to certify to the court the custom of the City of London upon the case so to be stated, *viz.* whether, by the said custom, the loss of the said freeman's estate by the insolvency of his executors ought to be borne out of the testamentary part of his estate only or out of the whole personal estate, as well customary as testamentary.

The Master stated the case as before, but he sent it to the Recorder. And the Lord Mayor, Aldermen, and Recorder sent a certificate to the court subscribed by them, which, after a recital of the case stated by the Master, was as follows:

> We, the Lord Mayor and Aldermen of the said City of London, whose names are subscribed, do in obedience to the said order by William Thompson, Esquire, Recorder of the said City, *ore tenus*, humbly certify unto your Lordship that, if a freeman of London dies leaving a widow and children, his personal estate (after his debts paid and the customary allowance for his funeral and for the widow's chamber being first deducted thereout) is by the custom of the said City to be divided into three equal parts and disposed of as follows, *viz.* one third part thereof belongs to his widow, another third part belongs to his children unadvanced by him in his lifetime, and the other third part such freeman, by his last will, may devise as he pleases.
>
> But where a loss of a freeman's estate by the insolvency of his executors does happen, there is not any custom of the City of London which directs whether such loss ought to be borne out of the testamentary part of his estate only or out of his whole personal estate, as well customary as testamentary.

Dated the 26th day of April 1715 and subscribed by Sir William Humphreys, Lord Mayor, Sir William Thompson, the Recorder, and fifteen aldermen.

The cause coming on in the paper this day, the certificate being read, it appeared no aid for the determination of this case was to be had from the custom, and, no case being stated as a precedent where this matter had been determined, it stood for the opinion of the court upon the reason of the thing.

And, after hearing the counsel on both sides, the Lord Chancellor COWPER held that the loss was to be borne wholly out of the testamentary part, since it proceeded from the insolvency of the executor, who was appointed by the testator and [was] the nature of his trustee, for whose defaults, it was more just that his legatees etc. should suffer than the persons who claimed a right by the custom, and not under the testator.

Sir Thomas Powys and Mr. *Cowper*, were counsel for the plaintiffs. *Sir Robert Raymond* only was counsel for the defendants, Sir Joseph Jekyll and Mr. Ketlebey, who were the defendants' other counsel, being absent.

Lincoln's Inn MS. Misc. 503, p. 332

Trinity term 1715. By Lord Chancellor Cowper. Readshaw v. Duck

In this cause, there was a freeman's will. And a question arose upon what part of the testator's estate the loss which was occasioned by the failure of the executors should fall. And it was referred to a Master to state a case to be sent to the Recorder of the City to certify to the court the custom of the City of London upon the case so to be stated, *viz.* query whether, by the said custom, the loss of the said freeman's estate by the insolvency of his executors ought to be borne out of the testamentary part of his estate only or out of the whole personal estate, as well customary as testamentary.

> We, the Lord Mayor and aldermen of the said City of London whose names are subscribed, do in obedience to the said order by William Thompson, Esq., Recorder of the said City, *ore tenus*, humbly certify unto your Lordship that, if a freeman of London dies leaving a widow and children, his personal estate, after the debts paid and the customary allowances for his funeral and for the widow's chamber being first deducted thereout, is by the custom of the said City to be divided into three equal parts and disposed of as follows, *viz.* one third part thereof belongs to his widow, another third part belongs to his children unadvanced by him in his lifetime, and the other third part such freeman, by his last will, may devise as he pleases.
>
> But, where a loss of a freeman's estate by the insolvency of his executors does happen, there is not any custom of the City of London which directs whether such loss ought to be borne out of the testamentary part of his estate only or out of his whole personal estate, as well customary as testamentary.

Dated the 26th day of April 1715. William Humphrys, Mayor, Gerard Conyers, William Thompson, Recorder, etc.

This report of the Lord Mayor and Aldermen being returned back to the Lord Chancellor Cowper, the matter was again debated by counsel in Trinity term 1715 before His Lordship, who was of the opinion that the widows and orphans of freemen of London are in the nature of creditors for two-thirds of the personal estate he shall die possessed of and that, if any loss happen by the insolvency of his executors, such loss ought to be borne by the legatee of a freeman entirely out of his death's part. And the same was in this case decreed accordingly so that the widow and orphans had two full thirds of the freeman's estate as if no such loss had been.

[Other copies of this report: Lincoln's Inn MS. Misc. 504, p. 321.]

[Other reports of this case: Precedents in Chancery 409, 24 E.R. 183, 2 Eq. Cas. Abr. 554, 22 E.R. 466.]

44

Overy v. Pope

(Ch. 1714)

Where a widow of a London freeman waives a legacy for life of the interest of a sum of money, this interest will be paid to the residuary legatee of the money during the widow's lifetime unless there be a deficiency of the estate.

Lincoln's Inn MS. Misc. 13, p. 2, pl. 2

18 December 1714.

A freeman of London, without taking any notice of the custom, by will, gives his wife the interest of £800 for her life, and, after her death, he gives the £800 to eight several persons. The wife waives her legacy and insists on her customary share.

It was decreed the estate, there being no child, to be divided in moieties and one moiety to be paid the wife and out of the other moiety £800 to be taken and put out at interest and the interest paid to the residuary legatee during the life of the wife. But, if the moiety did not amount to £800, then the interest of what it amounted to should from time to time be added to the principal until the £800 was made up and, after the death of the wife, the principal to be paid the legatees. If there were any deficiency, they were to abate in proportion.

[Related cases: Overy v. Pope (Ch. 1726), see below, Case No. 750.]

45

Andrews v. Craddock

(Ch. 1714–1715)

Where a married woman disowns a lawsuit brought in her name and for her benefit, the case will be dismissed.

British Library MS. Hargrave 80, f. 182

This bill was brought by Andrews, the defendant Craddock's wife's father, in her name as her next friend and in the name of their infant son and his own against the husband and his father, who was the only acting executor under the will of the wife's grandfather by her mother's side. By that will, £1000 was given to the wife and the residuum, which amounted to several £1000s more. She was likewise devisee of the real estate. And, after her grandfather's death, she, being under the care of the defendant Craddock, married a younger son of his, for whom there was little or no provision made by the father. But he was the person that her grandfather had in his lifetime expressed his desire that she should marry. And her own father, the plaintiff, gave her in marriage to him. And, after they had lived together well for three or four years, he brought this bill without, and even against, the consent of the wife for an account of the personal estate of the grandfather and for the rents and profits of the real estate that had been received by the husband that they might be settled for the benefit of the wife and the issue of the marriage. And he obtained a decree at the Rolls for an account. But how the money that should be coming upon the account should be disposed of, that decree did not provide. It was said to have been founded upon the defendant Craddock's breach of trust in marrying an infant under his care and for whom, as residency legatee, he was executor [and] was a trustee to his younger son.

But upon an appeal to Lord Chancellor [Lord Harcourt], *Sir Joseph Jekyll* and Mr. *Vernon* said, for the defendants, that it was true that a married woman was considered in equity as a *feme sole* and might sue her husband but that, as she might sue, she may dismiss her own bill, that anybody might bring a bill in the name of an infant, who are not thought capable of judging for themselves, even without his consent, but not of a married woman who, in equity, are not thought to be under that incapacity, if they might, it would indeed *ampliare jurisdictionem* but would be attended with many inconveniences, and that no instance could be given of a bill brought in the name of a wife against her will and, where they are brought with their consent, they always sue by a *prochein ami* or a guardian that, if their suit be groundless, there may be somebody liable to costs, but that, in the present case, if the wife was in earnest and consented to the suit, there could be nothing decreed for her, that, if the husband had brought his bill for the legacy and it were a *res integra*, it would be pretty hard to maintain that he should have other terms put upon him here than the ecclesiastical court, which, in that case, has an original and a proper jurisdiction, would put upon him though, in the case of trust money, which is only recoverable here, the court had often interposed as a parent and obliged the husband to make a reasonable settlement, but that this bill was not to have an execution of a trust but to change the law to take what the law gives the husband away from him in equity for asking for that the profit of the real estate which had been received by him he was entitled to by law and that he was decreed to an account even for those profits, that the right to the legacy of £1000 and the residuum vested in the husband by the intermarriage, and he had a power to demand, receive, or release them, that no bill ever was brought before to hinder a husband from disposing of a legacy given to his wife, no husband [was] ever enjoined from releasing such a legacy or suing for it in the spiritual court, no bill [was] ever brought by the wife to set aside a release but that the farthest that the court has ever gone is, where the husband prays the aid of the court to have the benefit of a trust, to grant that aid upon terms and as he would have equity to make him do it, that, though the decree for the defendants to account and the consideration of the disposal of what they have received is reserved, that that is yet a great grievance to be harassed with an account with those who have no right to the balance of it nor can give any legal discharge, that neither the plaintiff Andrews nor the infant had any color of right to anything and the right of the wife was vested in the defendant, her husband.

The wife was in court and was examined by Lord Chancellor [HARCOURT], and she disowned the suit and desired no account might be taken, upon which the former decree was reversed and the bill was dismissed but without costs.

[Other copies of this report: Lincoln's Inn MS. Misc. 383, p. 302.]

Lincoln's Inn MS. Misc. 380, pt. 3, p. 142, pl. 2

Andrews, as *prochein ami* to Elizabeth, the wife of Craddock.

Craddock, the father, and Craddock, the son, appeal from a decree of the Master of the Rolls. The wife was entitled to a real estate and to a legacy of £1000 and to the residue of a personal estate and, by the will of the grandfather, by which will, Craddock, the father, is made guardian to the young woman and executor. Craddock, the son, marries the young woman, then eighteen years old, with the consent of the father, who gave her in marriage. Her father now brings a bill in the wife's name as her *prochein ami* against Craddock, the father, and Craddock the husband, to have an account of the personal estate of the grandfather and of the rents and profits of the real estate and to have some settlement made by the husband upon the wife. The wife was in the court and declared her dissent to the bill and said she was very well satisfied.

It appeared that the wife's real estate was settled upon her by the grandfather's will and the £1000 was laid out in a purchase of lands which were settled, as usual in marriage settlements. The Master of the Rolls had decreed an account but had reserved what should be done with the money.

The Lord Chancellor [LORD COWPER] said it was not to be suffered that a *prochein ami* should thus disturb the peace of a family, there being no previous agreement or trust in the wife as indeed there was not, when [there was] consent of all parties to the marriage and the wife herself was satisfied. And so he reversed the decree. But, as for such part of it as was for bringing the writing into court whereby the purchased lands were settled upon the wife, he confirmed it, but gave no costs. He said it should be without prejudice in case a proper bill was brought and upon a good occasion.

The Master of the Rolls [TREVOR] said here was a manifest breach of trust but nobody could discern wherein.

[Other reports of this case: Gilbert Rep. 36, 25 E.R. 26, Precedents in Chancery 376, 24 E.R. 170, 1 Eq. Cas. Abr. 65, 72, 21 E.R. 879, 884.]

46

Pett v. Lee

(Ch. 1714–1715)

The wife of a London freeman can before marriage contract to take a settlement in lieu of her customary share of his estate.

Lincoln's Inn MS. Misc. 12, p. 190

Mary Pet, the widow of Samuel Pet, a freeman of London, plaintiff, against William Lee and Elizabeth, his wife, John Holton and Mary, his wife, administrators *cum testament annexo* of Samuel Pet and the children and legatees of Samuel Pet, defendants.

The marriage articles upon which the question in this case depended are to the effect following.

On 9 June 1684, by marriage articles, Samuel Pet agreed forthwith to pay or to give such security as the plaintiff should like to pay to trustees £2000 within a year after the date of the articles, and the plaintiff was likewise to pay to the trustees £2000 upon trust that the interest of those two sums should be received by Samuel Pet during his life and, after his death, by the plaintiff for her life and, after both their deaths, the principal and interest to be paid to their children. Fo. 9, 10. And, in case the plaintiff died without issue, her £2000 was to be repaid to such person as she should devise the same and her husband's £2000 was to be repaid to him, his executors, or administrators. Fo. 10, 11. And it was agreed that, in case a convenient purchase of lands could be met with, the money was to be laid out therein and settled to the like trusts. Fo. 12. And it was declared that what was to be settled on Samuel Pet, as above, should be in full [satisfaction] of all profit he was to have out of the plaintiff's estate or in her right, the residue of the plaintiff's estate being declared to be for her sole use. Fo. 14.

On 7 July 7 Ann. [1708], the cause was heard, and the court declared that it appeared that the plaintiff, the widow Pet, and her husband, the deceased Samuel Pet, agreed to take so much and no more out of their respective estates than is expressed in their marriage articles and by necessary implication that the plaintiff Mary Pet did agree to accept out of her husband's estate what is particularly provided for her by the said articles exclusive of any other part thereof. And, therefore, the court ordered the bill as to her demand of her customary share of her husband's estate, as he was a freeman of London, should from thenceforth stand dismissed. And, then, he gave directions as to what was provided for her by the articles and as to what was done by the husband in breach of the articles.

William Lee and his wife and the plaintiffs in the cross-cause being dissatisfied as to some directions in the decree petitioned for a rehearing. And it came on to be reheard, and the decree was confirmed on 28 January 8 Queen Anne [1710].

Then, the Master made a report touching the matters referred to him, and, exceptions being taken thereto, the same, on the 13th May 12 Ann. [1713], came on to be argued and the special matter of the Master's report concerning the estate of her brother, Peter Otgar, to which Mary Pet, the widow, was entitled, as she insisted, distinctly and exclusively from her husband.

The court declared they were not at liberty to make a construction upon the articles of marriage but were to determine the matter of the special report and exceptions according to the construction made of the said articles at the hearing, for that, by the declaration therein mentioned to be made, the plaintiff, Mrs. Pet, was not excluded from her customary share in respect of any composition she is supposed to have made for that purpose by the marriage articles but by virtue of an agreement by which each party was to take so much and no more out of each other's estate, the court did therefore decree that what accrued to the plaintiff Mary out of her brother's estate should be made good to her.

Lincoln's Inn MS. Misc. 11, p. 79

Mary Pett, relict of Samuel Pett, plaintiff; William Lee and several others, defendants.

The plaintiff, being the widow of Samuel Devischer, married Samuel Pett, and before such marriage, articles were entered into dated 9 June 1684 whereby it was agreed that Samuel Pett should deposit £2000 and the plaintiff the like sum in trustees' hands upon the trusts following, *viz.* upon trust to pay the interest thereof to Mr. Pett for his life and, afterwards, to the plaintiff for her life, and then to pay the £4000 to the issue of the marriage in the manner therein mentioned and, if she should die without issue by him, then to pay £2000 to him, his executors etc. and the other £2000 as she should appoint. If a purchase could be found out, then the money was to be laid out in land in trust for Mr. Pett for life, then to the plaintiff for life, remainder to the heirs male of their two bodies, remainder to their issue female, and, for want of such issue, then to pay £2000 as the plaintiff should appoint, and, after payment thereof to Mr. Pett and his heirs. And reciting that the plaintiff, by her marriage agreement with Mr. Devischer, was to have the interest of £5000 or, if laid out in lands, the rents of those lands for a jointure and that the £5000 had not been laid out, it was agreed that Mr. Pett should enjoy all the profits of the said £5000 for and during the life of the plaintiff.

Mr. Pett covenants that he, his executors, and administrators shall pay to the trustees £100 every year during the life of the plaintiff one-half yearly to and for the sole and separate use, expense, and disposing of the plaintiff, the first payment to be made on the first Michaelmas or Lady Day after the marriage, which £100 a year was to be disposed of as the plaintiff should direct by any note or writing under her hand.

It was agreed that, if Abraham Devischer, the plaintiff's son, should die under age whereby his fortune would come to her, that she might make her will and dispose of what should so come to her and might also by her will give away a pearl necklace and some other things therein particularly mentioned and also dispose of by her will any of her personal estate in the hand of Mr. H. and Mr. J. And then follows these words, *viz.*

> And it is further agreed by all the parties that the said Samuel Pett should have the £4000 and the £5000 and the interest and profits thereof only as aforesaid without any other profit or advantage whatsoever and that the residue and overplus of the estate of the plaintiff is to be in the power and disposition of the [plaintiff] by her last will as aforesaid.

The plaintiff paid her £2000 to the trustees, but Mr. Pett did not during his life pay his £2000.

After the marriage, Mr. Otgher, the plaintiff's brother, died, and he bequeathed to the plaintiff a considerable part of his personal estate, which was received by Mr. Pett.

Mr. Pett died [having] made his will. And one of his children by a former wife, the executors renouncing, took administration *cum testamento annexo*. Mr. Pett being a freeman of London, though that was not known when the plaintiff married him, she brought her bill for her customary share of his personal estate and for a satisfaction of what he had received belonging to the plaintiff out of her brother's estate and that she might have the interest of the £2000, which was to have been paid by her husband and the £100 a year paid her for her life out of his estate and her own £2000 repaid her by the trustees.

The defendants insisted that, as to the plaintiff's customary share, she was barred by the articles, there being a particular provision made thereby what she should have if she survived him and that the £100 a year was to continue no longer than during the coverture.

The defendants brought a cross-bill and, amongst other things, insisted that, by virtue of the articles, Mr. Pett's executor was entitled to the interest of the £5000 settled on the plaintiff by her former husband.

On 2 July 7 Anne [1708], [it was] decreed by Lord Cowper that it appeared by the articles that both parties agreed to take so much and no more out of their respective estates than is expressed in the said articles, and, by necessary implication, the plaintiff did agree to accept out of Mr. Pett's estate what was particularly provided for her by the articles exclusive of any other part thereof. And, therefore, he dismissed her bill as to the demand of her customary share of her husband's estate. He decreed her her own £2000 and the interest of the other £2000 and the £100 a year during her life.

And the Master was to enquire what part of the real or personal estate of the plaintiff had been converted by her husband to his own use without her consent, which was to be made good to her out of his assets, and costs of all parties were to be paid out of Mr. Pett's assets.

The defendants petitioned for a rehearing for the following reasons:

That if appeared to be the intention of the parties that the £100 a year should be paid the plaintiff as a separate provision during the coverture and should cease by Mr. Pett's death, for then she would come into her whole estate and the interest of the £2000, as was decreed her;

That it is, as expressly mentioned by the articles, that Mr. Pett should receive the interest of the £5000 during the plaintiff's life as it is that he should pay the £100 a year to her trustees during her life and the defendant's as the representatives of Mr. Pett are equally entitled by the words of the articles to the interest of the £5000 during the plaintiff's life as she is to have the £100 a year after her husband's death;

That this matter was not taken notice of at the hearing, the question then being only concerning the custom of the City of London;

That the plaintiff ought to have had no costs, especially in her own cause by reason her bill was dismissed, for which she ought to have paid costs.

The causes were reheard, and the decree was affirmed by Lord Cowper.

The decree being afterwards signed and enrolled, the defendants brought a bill of review, and they assigned much the same matters for errors as were alleged for a rehearing, with this farther, that Mr. Pett's estate ought not to make satisfaction for what he received out of the plaintiff's brother's estate.

The usual demurrer was put in by the plaintiff. And, upon the arguing of it, the enrollment was set aside. And now, it came on again to be reheard before Lord Cowper.

Serjeant *Hooper*: As to the question whether the articles extended to bar the husband of what came to his wife by her brother's death, he cited the Case of Colton and Launce, before Lord Jeffreys, a man upon his marriage articles was not to intermeddle with is wife's estate nor to take any part of it except what was thereby agreed to be paid him; she dies without making any disposition pursuant to the power thereby given her, and the husband takes administration; [it was] decreed the articles did not extend to bar him of what the law afterwards cast upon him.

Sir Joseph Jekyll: The estate of Peter Otgher was never the estate of the plaintiff. It came to her during the coverture and vested in the husband, who had it in her right. And, as he might, so he did dispose of it. The construction put upon the articles to exclude the husband of this is in derogation of a matrimonial right and, therefore, not to be favored.

The estate of Otgher was not under the consideration of the parties when the articles were entered into. And, therefore, if there had been any words in the articles, as there are not, to exclude the husband of any future right, this court will construe the articles in a limited sense with respect to what the parties had then in contemplation and not in so full and ample a sense as perhaps the [. . .] words in their utmost import might extend to. And so this court has done in many cases of the like nature.

A release of a future right operates nothing, nor can a man grant a future right. And it may be a great question whether a man can by any agreement bar himself of a future right.

As to the customary share, Serjeant *Hooper* said the plaintiff cannot claim that and the benefit of the articles too. In the Case of the Lady Herne, the widow of Sir Joseph Herne,[1] it was decreed by the Lord Keeper she might make her election and either take the benefit of her marriage articles or her share by the custom, but she could not have both.

In the case of dower, suppose an imperfect jointure is made, as if a term for years, for instance, is settled, and the woman brings her writ of dower, this court will, as it has often done, decree that she shall make her election and not take her settlement and her dower too.

Mr. *Vernon*, of the same side: It is now settled that wherever there is any provision made for a wife by articles before marriage, though it is to arise out of land, it is by the custom a bar of the customary part, though there are no words in the articles to exclude the wife, for it is called in the City a composition for the customary part.

Lord Chancellor [Lord Harcourt]: The decree is right. The articles are very express to exclude the husband of everything but what is expressly stipulated for him. The word 'only' in the last clause must be understood to exclude the husband from everything else, and what makes it yet stronger are the following words, which are as strong as words can be, *viz.* 'without any other profit or advantage whatsoever'.

As to the £100 a year, the words are very express that Samuel Pett, his executors, and administrators will pay the wife £100 a year. How long? Why, during her life.

As to the interest of the £5000, this money, in the consideration of equity, must be considered as land. Then, here is a woman who has a jointure; [she] agrees that her husband shall receive the profits of her jointure during her life. Will anyone say that, if the wife survives the husband that made such an agreement, the executors of the husband shall receive these profits during the wife's life? Surely, no. There must be stronger words than what are in these articles to exclude the jointress of the profits of her own freehold.

The decree was affirmed.

British Library MS. Hargrave 80, f. 185

This cause came on upon a demurrer to a bill of review.

Serjeant *Hooper*: We have assigned several errors, but, if we prevail in one, it is sufficient to open the enrollment. The first error assigned was in the foundation

[1] *Herne v. Herne* (1706), 2 Vernon 555, 23 E.R. 959, 1 Eq. Cas. Abr. 203, 21 E.R. 991.

of the decree. The case was thus. Mrs. Pet, being entitled to the interest of £5000 for her life and to £2000 in money and to a contingent interest upon the death of J.S., entered into articles upon her marriage with Mr. Pet, by which part of these interests was limited to him and a power given to her of disposing of all the residue of his estate by her will. On the other hand, £2000 was brought in by Mr. Pet and several limitations [were] made of the interest of that and *inter alia* £100 *per annum* [was] given her for her separate use. After the marriage, she became entitled to a considerable personal estate by the death of her brother.

And, upon the first hearing and rehearing of this cause, I think before My Lord Cowper, the court declared that the articles contained a complete provision how much each party was to take out of the estate of the other and no more, and, therefore, he decreed to the wife what came by her brother's death and dismissed her bill as to any share of her husband's estate upon his death, which she claimed as widow of a freeman of London. The first error assigned was that the husband was not barred by the articles of his title to what accrued to the wife after coverture.

Jekyll: We may give them their choice, either that this interest, which accrued after, was under the consideration of the parties at the time of the articles or that it was not. If it was, then, not being expressly mentioned, it is plain it was not the intention of the parties to include it in the articles. If it was not, then, of necessity, it cannot be directed by them. Even at law and much more in equity, releases and deeds are restrained to the subject matter.

Vernon: The expressing one contingent interest and providing for that *est exclusio alterius*. And, for the customary part demanded by the wife, *Vernon* said that, wherever there is a provision made for the wife by articles made before the marriage, even though it be out of land and that there be no expressions in the articles that it shall exclude her of her customary part, yet it is, in the City language, a compounding for her customary part.

Jekyll: That has been settled so ever since 1641; *a fortiori*, where the provision is out of the husband's personal estate.

Lord Chancellor [Lord Harcourt]: There is a material difference in this case between the wife's claim of her customary share, which, had it been decreed to her, must have been given to her against law, she having compounded for it and thereby barred herself by the custom, and the husband's right to what accrued to the wife during coverture, which, if it be taken away, [is] against law.

He overruled the demurrer.

Vernon, in this case, upon the head of the separate maintenances, said that provisions of that kind were not very ancient and that the court always held a strict hand over them and goes no further in the support of them than is necessary, that, in the Case of Powell, the Master of the Rolls, and Lady Dorset, his wife, she having a separate maintenance and having made a purchase out of it, Lord Jeffreys was of opinion that what she had thus saved and the lands purchased with it belonged to the husband.

But *Vernon* seemed to own that that decree was varied by the House of Lords and said that the cases since have been otherwise and that the court had declared, and with great justice, that the purchase follows the nature of the fund out of which it is made.

[Other copies of this report: Lincoln's Inn MS. Misc. 383, p. 304, pl. 2, Lincoln's Inn MS. Misc. 107, f. 22.]

Lincoln's Inn MS. Misc. 380, pt. 3, p. 141

Hilary term 1714[/15].

In this case, which was long and consisted of many particulars, I observed this point. Upon the plaintiff's marriage, who was a widow and [had] a fortune, with her third husband Pett, he enters into articles whereby it was agreed that he, her intended husband, should enjoy the interest of £5000, which, upon a former marriage, was covenanted to be settled upon the plaintiff for life and, after, upon her issue and to have some other money therein particularly specified and, as to the rest of her fortune or any that may come to her during the coverture, she should have it to her own separate use and dispose it by her will and the husband to be totally excluded from it. The words were agreed to be as full as could be to that purpose. It was further covenanted that she should enjoy £100 *per annum* and the interest of some money that was her husband Pett's for her life without any exclusive words at all. The husband happening to be a freeman of London and dying, the plaintiff brought her bill to have a specific performance of the articles as to what was to be settled upon her by her third husband, Pett, and to have, besides, her customary part as being a widow of a freeman of London, she not being excluded from it by the articles.

The Lord Chancellor [Lord Cowper] decreed twice, for it was upon a bill of review, that, as the husband was totally excluded from having anything farther of the wife's than what was specially mentioned, that, by equity of reason, it should be presumed that the wife should be excluded from claiming anything of her husband's, so she should have no customary part.

British Library MS. Hargrave 81, f. 48, pl. 3

13 May.

Pett, on the marriage with his wife, by deed taking notice of her several estates, agreed that he should have two sums, one of £5000 and another of £4000, and that the wife should have the disposal of the rest by will. It was also agreed that she should have a certain proportion of his estate. The question was whether this agreement should exclude her of a contingency that afterwards happened, that not being under consideration at the time of the agreement.

Mr. *Vernon*: The residue or surplus in all articles is understood and always construed of such estate as the party had at the time of making the articles and not of any future acquisitions. And this was the case of Mr. Powell, so late before

Your Lordship, who was a bencher of Lincoln's Inn. He covenanted that his wife should have her whole estate, and, afterwards, a legacy was given to her. Your Lordship was of the opinion that the covenant could not extend to this legacy and, therefore, decreed it to the husband. And, in that and the present case, the wife would have dower out of lands purchased by the husband afterwards unless there were express words to bar them.

Curia: The parties here have covenanted what to take out of each other's estate and, therefore, by necessary implication, they are excluded from any more that may afterwards accrue.

[Other copies of this report: British Library MS. Hargrave 82, f. 45, pl. 3.]

[Other reports of this case: British Library MS. Hargrave 77, f. 14, pl. 1, British Library MS. Hargrave 303, f. 24v.]

47

Bawdes v. Amhurst

(Ch. 1714–1715)

In this case of specific performance of a contract, the parties had not sufficiently come to an agreement that was enforceable though one of the parties died before the contract was written down.

The signature of a person on a contract only binds that person where it was made with the intention of binding.

British Library MS. Hargrave 80, f. 188v

On a treaty between the plaintiff and the defendant's father for the marriage of the plaintiff to the defendant's sister, the defendant's father went into the country to view the plaintiff's estate and, at his return, dictated instructions to Mr. Minshall for a settlement to be made of the plaintiff's estate and of a portion of £4500 to be given by him to his daughter, the heads of which Mr. Minshall took down in writing. The next day, before anything further was done, the defendant's father died of an apoplexy leaving the defendant his heir and executor. And, in a few hours after his death, the plaintiff and defendant's sister intermarried. And the plaintiff now brought his bill for a specific performance of the agreement and to have the £4500 intended for his wife's fortune, to which the defendant pleaded the Statute of Frauds[1] in bar.

Jekyll, for the defendant, alleged that, before the Statute, such a bare inchoation of an agreement would not have bound the parties much less since when, if it had been a complete agreement, it ought to have been signed by the party or some other by his direction to make it binding and that barely writing it by the

[1] Stat. 29 Car. II, c. 3 (*SR*, V, 839–842).

party's agent was not a signing within the intention of the Act, that, in this case, there was no manner of fraud pretended in the defendant's father much less in the defendant, that the father died before the marriage, which the plaintiff completed with his eyes open.

Vernon, for the plaintiff, [said] that several cases had been exempted from the letter of the Statute of Fraud upon the head of fraud though the agreement were not reduced into writing, that allowance ought to be made for unavoidable accidents, that, in case of Maschall and Cokes,[1] before Lord Somers, where the father encouraged the young couple to proceed upon a parol promise of a portion until their affections were engaged and then fled off, the court decreed him to perform his promise notwithstanding the Statute of Frauds.

Lord Chancellor [HARCOURT] mentioned the Case of Williams, where the father had a power of charging the estate by deed or will and had a will in his pocket by which he intended to charge it. But, before it was duly executed, being traveling with his son and his son's falling into a river, the father want in after him to save him and helped him out but was drowned himself, the son would afterwards have avoided the charge intended by the father to have been laid upon the estate for want of a due signing and attesting the will, but Lord Cowper decreed him to be bound by it.

Lord Chancellor [HARCOURT] said that that case was the furthest that the court had ever gone but yet that everybody that ever heard of the decree approved of it. In the principal case, he only saved the benefit of the plea, but yet he seemed to think the plaintiff not relievable.

Lechmere: It has been frequently adjudged since the Statute of Distributions[2] that a right to a distributable part is an interest vested and shall go to the executors or administrators of the party interested though he die before distribution.

[Other copies of this report: Lincoln's Inn MS. Misc. 383, p. 307, pl. 2, Lincoln's Inn MS. Misc. 107, f. 28.]

British Library MS. Hargrave 80, f. 221

In this case, Lord Chancellor [LORD COWPER] was of opinion the minutes taken by Mr. Minshall were but an inchoation of an agreement and preparatory only to a more solemn act and that, in the meantime, both parties were at liberty to consider and to vary their intentions if they thought fit, and that, consequently, neither was bound. And he, therefore, dismissed the bill. As to the demand of specific performance, he seemed of opinion that the signing by the party to be bound within the Statute of Frauds must be a subscription by him which is an act that imports a resolution to abide by what he subscribes to and that the party writing an agreement with his own hands without subscribing it would not do.

---

1 *Cokes v. Mascal* (1687–1690), 2 Vernon 34, 200, 23 E.R. 631, 730.

2 Stat. 22 & 23 Car. II, c. 10 (*SR*, V, 719–720).

Lincoln's Inn MS. Misc. 11, p. 60

17 May 1715. Bawdes *et ux.* v. Amherst, heir and executor of Jeffery Amherst.

The plaintiff treated with the defendant's father for the marriage of the defendant's sister. And the defendant's father agreed to give with his daughter £4500, and the defendant was to settle his estate in Lincolnshire. This being agreed, they went to Mr. Minshall's chambers together and gave him instructions for drawing the settlement, which instructions he wrote down. And the same was as follows, *viz.* Mr. Amherst to give £4500 with his daughter; Mr. Bawdes to settle his whole estate subject to £450 *per annum* clear of taxes except the manor house etc., which is not to be subject to the £450 a year, for a jointure, then the whole estate to the first etc. in tail male, then a term for daughters upon failer of issue male, if one, to raise £5000, if more, £6000 to be paid at twenty-one or marriage, the £6000 to survive and to be paid in such proportions as Mr. Bawdes and Mrs. Amherst or the survivor shall appoint, and, for want of an appointment, equally, and, if all daughters but one die, she to have only £5000, with a provision for maintenance; Mr. Bawdes to have the power to charge £2000 upon the part excepted that is not to be charged with the jointure, power to charge for younger children, in case of a son, and for Mr. Bawdes to make a twenty-one years lease at the best rents.

About a day or two after these instructions were taken down by Mr. Minshall, which were signed by neither of the parties, Mr. Amherst died suddenly. And the next day, the plaintiffs married, and, now, they bring their bill for an execution of this agreement.

The defendant pleaded the Statute of Frauds etc., and the plea came on before Lord Harcourt, who, at first, allowed it. But, upon the importunity of Mr. Vernon, the benefit of it was saved until the hearing.

And now, the cause came to be heard before Lord Cowper.

And the plaintiff had examined Mr. Minshall, who deposed as follows, *viz.* that, on Saturday before Mr. Amherst's death, he was consulted by Mr. Amherst about a marriage between the plaintiffs and for drawing up articles or proposals of agreement relating thereto, which articles or proposals were intended to be between the said Mr. Amherst and the plaintiff Charles, and, by their mutual dictating, he reduced into writing the minutes or heads of such agreements or proposals and that he was then desired by Mr. Amherst and the plaintiff Charles to draw articles or proposals of agreement pursuant to the said minutes or heads and was desired to perfect the said articles or proposals as soon as he could, but he remembers not that he promised any particular time, that the perfecting thereof was hindered by Mr. Amherst's death, and that Mr. Amherst declared a very great liking of the plaintiff Charles and his estate.

Lord Cowper: I am of opinion that Mr. Minshall's writing down these heads, though dictated to him by Mr. Bawdes and Mr. Amherst, was not a signing within the Statute of Frauds, nor was this a complete agreement; it was only proposals in order to [come to] an agreement, which either party might have receded from or alter upon second thoughts or more mature consideration and, wherever this court has carried on an agreement upon a letter signed by the party or a writing written by the party himself, though not signed, it has been where the agreement was perfect and complete and the marriage has proceeded upon it.

There was a second question which arose upon Mr. Amherst's will. Mr. Amherst had received a legacy of £600 several years ago, which was given to the plaintiff Jane by the will of the Lady Onslow, her grandmother, and Mr. Amherst, by his will, gives the plaintiff Jane £1500, which, says he, with £600 given her by the Lady Onslow makes £2100 and this he directs to be paid her within two years after his death and £80 a year in the meantime.

The question was if the plaintiffs should have interest for this £600 from the time Mr. Amherst received it.

[Lord Cowper] decreed no interest should be paid. It is plain Mr. Amherst intended the £1500 as a full satisfaction for any demand of that kind that could be made upon him.

It was agreed likewise that the defendant, being executor as well as heir of his father, could not apply the personal estate to pay off mortgages on the real estate if that would swallow up the assets and defeat the portions given to his sister.

[Other reports of this case: Precedents in Chancery 402, 24 E.R. 180, 1 Eq. Cas. Abr. 21, 21 E.R. 842.]

48

Maynard v. Wing

(Ch. 1715)

Interest is not payable on a legacy before the legacy itself becomes payable.

Interest does not accrue before the date of payment.

Lincoln's Inn MS. Misc. 380, pt. 3, p. 143

Hilary term 1714[/15]. Maynard v. Minge.

A bill was brought against Minge, surviving executor of Dorothy Jenkins, for legacies. Upon the hearing, there were these points. The testatrix, by her will, gave to the plaintiff £100 to be paid at the age of twenty-one or marriage. And the question was whether the legatee should have interest in the meantime.

The Lord Chancellor [Lord Cowper] stopped the defendant's counsel, saying there was no need to argue it, for interest is no more than damages for nonpayment and, until the time of payment is come, there can be no damage for nonpayment. And so he decreed no interest.

Another point was there was £100 given to A. to be paid by £10 *per annum* and, if A. died before the whole £100 was paid, then so much of it as was unpaid to go to the plaintiff.

The Lord Chancellor [Lord Cowper] decreed that not only what was not become due but also what was actually unpaid, though it was incurred and become due, should go to the plaintiff, the devisee, so that, though there was no representative of A. before the court (which was made an objection), it was well enough.

Lincoln's Inn MS. Misc. 11, p. 12, pl. 1

4 February 1714[/15].

The plaintiff's wife's grandmother having given to her a legacy to be paid at twenty-one or day of marriage and given no direction that any interest should be allowed in the meantime, the question was if the executor should pay this legacy with interest from the death of the testatrix.

The court [Lord Cowper] thought it so plain that interest should not be paid that they would not suffer it to be spoken to on the other side.

49

Rex v. Bradford

(Ch. 1715)

A bond given to a king, his heirs, and executors is given to him in his public capacity and is enforceable by his successors in office.

2 Lord Raymond 1327, 92 E.R. 366

9 February 1714[/15].

In a *scire facias* brought in the Petty Bag, it was set out that the 13th day of March last past at Westminster in the County of Middlesex, Isaac Pyke, the defendant, Bradford, and others, *per quoddam scriptum suum obligatorium sigillis suis sigillatum cognoverunt, et quilibet eorum cognovit, se teneri et firmiter obligari serenissimae dominae Annae nuper reginae Magnae Britanniae etc. defunctae in £500 solvendis dictae nuper reginae executoribus vel administratoribus suis*, which was not paid to the queen in her life, nor yet to the king, therefore, the writ commanded the Sheriff of Middlesex to summon the defendant B. to be in Chancery etc. *in crastino Animarum* next following to show why execution should not be against him etc. *teste 4 Octobris 1 Georgii*. Upon *scire feci* returned, the defendant appeared and demurred to the writ, and the Attorney General joined in demurrer.

And Mr. *Peere Williams* and *Sir Robert Raymond*, for the defendant, took exception, that this bond was not framed according to the Statute of 33 Hen. VIII,

c. 39,[1] and, consequently, it had not the effect of a recognizance, nor could a *scire facias* lie thereon, for the money was made payable to the queen, her executors, and administrators, and, therefore, also was entered into to her in her natural capacity. See Moore 193, pl. 342, Anders. 129, Scroggs v. Lady Gresham,[2] and see the Statute of 33 Hen. VIII, c. 39, s. 50.

Mr. Solicitor General *Lechmere*, for the king.

Of which opinion was the Lord Chancellor [Lord Cowper], and he gave judgment for the king.

See 2 Co. 92; Mich. 35 Hen. VI, 29b, pl. 34.[3]

Dickens 24, 21 E.R. 175

Whereas a writ of *scire facias* issued against the defendant upon his not having performed the condition of a bond entered into by him and one Isaac Pike in the penalty of £500 to her late Majesty Queen Anne, her heirs, executors, and administrators, to which, upon rules given, the defendant appeared and put in a demurrer, and his Majesty's Attorney General [*Northey*] having joined in the same and the proceeding having been made a concilium and coming on this day to be argued before the Lord Chancellor [Lord Cowper] in the presence of counsel on both sides, His Lordship declared, the said bond having been given to her late Majesty in her political capacity, the same subsisted to his present Majesty as her successor, and he did therefore order that the demurrer be overruled.

50

Wellington v. Cotterell

(Ch. 1715)

A devisee is an assignee.

In a will, the words 'the better half' mean a half.

A debt can be paid off by giving a legacy to the creditor.

Lincoln's Inn MS. Misc. 380, pt. 3, p. 140

Hilary term 1714[/15].

In this case, there were these points. A. assigns a term for ninety-nine years if three lives live so long in trust for himself for so many years of the term as the husband live and, if he died within the term, then to the executors, administrators, and assigns of A., the assignor. The assignor devised the term to J.S. And the question was whether the executors of A. or the devisee should have it.

[1] Stat. 33 Hen. VIII, c. 39, s. 50 (*SR*, III, 891).

[2] *Skrogs v. Gresham* (1584), Moore K.B. 193, 72 E.R. 525, 1 Anderson 129, 123 E.R. 391.

[3] *Denis v. Inggam* (1456), YB Mich. 35 Hen. VI, f. 29, pl. 34.

Peere Williams urged that A. could not devise it but his executors should take it as purchasers because it was not limited to him, his executors, etc., but to his executors etc.

The Lord Chancellor [LORD COWPER], without much argument [held] it was clear that, the limitation being in trust for his executors, administrators, and assigns, a devisee was his assignee.

There was this further in it that the testator devised the better half or most part of his goods to S.P.

The Lord Chancellor [LORD COWPER] said, if the goods were sold, the money must be equally divided and the devisee to have an equal half, but, if they were in specie, then to be divided as equally as could be, which was as far as he would carry these words.

Lincoln's Inn MS. Misc. 11, p. 19, pl. 2

A man, by his will, gives 'the better half' of his goods to A.B.

LORD COWPER decreed that the Master should divide the goods as equally as he could and that the legatee choose which half she would take, which is all he could understand by 'the better half'. But, if the goods are sold, let the money be divided equally.

He decreed that a specific legacy was a satisfaction of a debt, which the plaintiff claimed for her labor and pains in looking after the testator during his sickness.

51

Cook v. Oakley

(Ch. 1715)

Where a devisee dies in the lifetime of the testator, the legacy lapses.

A legacy of all things not before bequeathed includes only personal things ejusdem generis *bequeathed but not a leasehold that the testator did not know that he owned.*

1 Peere Williams 302, 24 E.R. 399

Gilbert Cook, one of the five children of Benjamin Cook, went beyond the sea in his father's lifetime, after which, his father, being possessed of a considerable leasehold estate, devised two-thirds of his said estate to his five children equally and one-third to his wife and died. Then, the wife died, having devised her third to her children equally.

Afterwards, Gilbert, the son, having been beyond the sea many years and being on shipboard, made his will, and he gave to his mother, if alive, his gold rings, buttons, and chest of clothes, and to his loving friend, the defendant Francis Goslin, who was on board with him, his red box, arrack, and all things not before bequeathed, and he made him sole executor.

It appeared in the cause (and indeed by Gilbert's will) that he did not know that his mother was actually dead and, consequently, could not know what estate was given him by his mother, and, though he knew his father was dead, yet he was not informed what will his father had made or what his father had left or whether he was entitled to any part of his estate.

And it was insisted on behalf of the testator's brothers and sisters that, here, being an express legacy given to the executor, *viz.*, the testator's red box and arrack, it could not be presumed but that, if the testator had also intended to give him his share in the leasehold premisses, he would have mentioned them and, if he did not know he had any such share in the leasehold estate, then it was plain he could not intend to dispose of it, and the devise of all things not before bequeathed could not be intended to pass the leasehold interest or real chattels, but mere personal things only, such as were on board the ship or things *ejusdem generis* with those above-mentioned; that it was to be intended he did not know that he was entitled to any part of this leasehold estate of his father in regard he would in all probability have given some share thereof to his mother, to whom he gave and for whom he seemed to have designed the most valuable part of his substance, for he gave to her his rings, buttons, and chest of clothes. It was also considerable that Goslin was a mere stranger, and, on the other hand, the testator had so near relations as brothers and sisters, and that the will had been made on shipboard.

The Master of the Rolls [SIR JOHN TREVOR] decreed[1] that Goslin, the executor, should be but a trustee as to the surplus for the testator's brothers and sisters, but that, with respect to the buttons, rings, etc. given to the mother, they were lapsed legacies, by reason of the mother's dying in the testator's lifetime and should therefore fall to the executor.

Also, upon this occasion, His Honor [TREVOR] mentioned a case [*Eyre v. Eyre*] that he remembered to have been adjudged, where a man made a will and appointed J.S., who was no relation, his executor; afterwards, he went beyond the sea, where he became governor of one of the plantations, and sent over for an English woman of his acquaintance, whom he married and had children by, and died without any actual revocation of his will; yet it was determined that this total alteration of the testator's circumstances was an implied revocation of the will.

And, in affirmance of this, *Sir Joseph Jekyll* cited this case from the civil law, *pater credens filium suum esse mortuum alterum instituit haeredem; filio domi redeunte, hujus institutionis vis est nulla. Vide* Cicero, *De Oratore*, Cantab. ed., pp. 69, 102; and Dig., l. *ult.*, *De Haered. Inst.*[2]

[Other reports of this case: 2 Eq. Cas. Abr. 323, 438, 22 E.R. 275, 374.]

1 Reg. Lib. 1715 A, f. 191.

2 *Digesta*, 28, 5, 93.

52

Pearson v. Rowland

(Ch. 1715)

Where the reasons for suppressing evidence are doubtful, the evidence should be given to the court so that the court can weigh it.

British Library MS. Hargrave 80, f. 210

Hilary 1714[/15].

The plaintiff and defendant filed several interrogatories in the office and, afterwards, joined in a commission where the plaintiff exhibited the same interrogatories and the defendant part of his, but omitted, *inter alia*, the interrogatory exhibited to prove a will in question, not having the will at the commission. Several witnesses appeared, who were the defendant's witnesses to the will, and the plaintiff examined them to several matters. And the defendant declined to examine them to any there, not having the will there, but afterwards examined them in the office without the leave of the court.

Upon a motion to suppress these depositions in the office, the regularity of this cross-examination was referred to the two senior masters. Sir Thomas Grey reported it regular; Mr. Rogers, irregular.

And, upon a second motion to suppress, after these reports, it was urged for the plaintiff, that a cross-examination of a witness at the office, who had appeared and been examined at a commission where the other side joined and had interrogatories and an opportunity of cross-examining there, was unprecedented, unless it were to prove an exhibit, and not even that without the leave of the court, that the allowing it would introduce perjury, it being known, that neither the commissioners nor the clerks are sworn to secrecy, and that it is no hard matter for a party to discover what a witness has sworn at a commission, and, when he knows it, if he has time between the witness's examination and cross-examination, be may tamper with him to retract or contradict his first examination upon his second, that, therefore, the examination ought to be perfected *uno flatu* and by the same commissioners, who might refresh his memory if they found him inconsistent with himself, that, if both sides joined in a commission, though the one exhibited no interrogatories, the court, so far regards the probability of that party's being informed of the depositions by the commissioners as not to allow them to examine after without the leave of the court and without referring it to a master to settle the interrogatories.

Vernon, e contra: This is the first time that this was ever made a question. Nobody ever thought but that both parties were at liberty to examine or cross-examine in the office at any time before publication. But, if the doctrine prevails, it will put an end to all second examinations in the office or at commissions. If the supposition of a party's having a means of knowing what a witness has sworn at a commission be a reason to hinder his cross-examining him at a future day, it is equally good against any further examination of any other witnesses, lest they should be drawn in to contradict the first. It is, indeed, a rule of the court that, where a party has examined a witness to some interrogatories, he shall not examine him again to others without the leave of the court. And, for that reason, we declined examining these witnesses at the commission where we had not the will and could not complete their examination. And it is true that, if a party's commissioners have been present at one commission without filing interrogatories, the court, upon application for a second, will direct the pleadings to be laid before a master for him to draw proper interrogatories. But, here, our interrogatories were all exhibited before the commission, and [there is] no room to suppose them adapted to overthrow what had been sworn. The reason given for the necessity for cross-examining by the same commissioners will appear to have nothing in it, if it be considered that the commissioners ask their questions out of the interrogatories, and it is notorious that, in the examiners' office, if a witness be examined, the same examiner does not cross-examine him, but the examiner of the other side. Had we applied for a new commission, the court, perhaps, would have permitted us, for not being provided to examine our witnesses at the commission, by obliging us to bring them to the office. But that we have done voluntarily and regularly.

The Lord Chancellor [Lord Cowper]. Where the reasons for suppressing depositions are doubtful, they ought to be preserved. When they are suppressed, the court has no means to judge upon them. But, when they are preserved, truth has that probability in it, and falsehood is generally attended with some mark or inconsistency that there is no danger of the court's being misled by them. But, in this case, it might be very inconvenient to establish such a rule as the plaintiff desires. One party might by that means trick the other out of his evidence by asking his most material witnesses two or three most immaterial questions, where he finds him not fully provided to examine them, and then telling him you must cross-examine them now or never. Let the depositions stand.

[Other copies of this report: Lincoln's Inn MS. Misc. 383, p. 325, Lincoln's Inn MS. Misc. 107, f. 55, 2 Swanston 266, 36 E.R. 617.]

53

Clopton v. Bernard

(Ch. 1715)

A married woman cannot object to the barring of an entail in which she joined.

A question in this case was whether a child born after a divorce on the ground of adultery is presumed to be a bastard.

British Library MS. Hargrave 80, f. 212

The defendant, upon his marriage with the plaintiff, entered into articles, by which £800 to be brought in of the wife's portion was agreed to be invested in land to be settled to the use of the husband and wife for their lives, with remainder to the issue of the marriage in tail etc. £400 was agreed to be settled on the part of the husband to the husband and wife for their lives, with remainder for the benefit of the issue. The heir of the woman's father settled afterwards £40 *per annum* to the use of the husband and wife for their lives, remainder to the issue in tail etc. in satisfaction of £800, there being no limitation to trustees to preserve the contingent remainders. The husband and wife, before any issue born, joined in a fine and thereby destroyed this settlement. The uses of the fine they declared to themselves for their lives, remainder to the heirs of the survivor. After this, they separated for the misbehavior of the wife. And, during the separation, some years afterwards, the wife had a son and, afterwards, was divorced *a mensa et thoro causa adulterii*, from which sentence, she appealed, but did not prosecute it. By this bill, she and her son sought a specific performance of the articles.

Lord Chancellor [Lord Cowper]: The wife having accepted of a settlement, though not exactly pursuant to the articles and her next relation being a party to it and consenting and she having joined in barring it in the way the law allows before any issue born and the son being born during her elopement and there being little prospect of any future issue between them, the bill as to the £800 must be dismissed. The £400 stands upon a very indifferent foot. No settlement has ever been made of that, but it rests singly upon the articles. The husband has had the full benefit of what was brought in on the part of the wife, and it is reasonable he should be obliged to make good his part of the contract. Let it be settled pursuant to the articles.

Query what is the difference between the infant son's right to the £800 and to the £400 in equity?

Lutwyche cited a case upon a settlement between two parishes where it was ruled about seven years ago upon great debate and producing a like judgment upon a special verdict before that a child born after a divorce in a spiritual court *causa adulterii* is a bastard, contrary, as he said, to the ancient rule of law, while the husband is *infra quatuor maria*.

[Other copies of this report: Lincoln's Inn MS. Misc. 107, f. 58.]

54

Sayer v. Sayer

(Ch. 1715)

Where marriage articles were not performed, a court of equity will order the wife's portion to be given to her after her husband's death, and, for the rest due to her, she will be a creditor of her husband's estate.

Lincoln's Inn MS. Misc. 384, p. 21, pl. 3

24 February.

Lord Chancellor [Lord Cowper]: A court of equity has never gone so far as to bar the issue in tail in equity unless the ancestor had done some act which plainly showed his intent to bar the entail, as by making a feoffment of the entailed lands, but not by a bare covenant which he had not executed in his lifetime.

Vernon: A bargain and sale or other conveyance by a tenant in tail, in equity, has been ruled to be a bar to the issue in tail.

British Library MS. Hargrave 80, f. 215

By articles between the plaintiff and her husband antecedent to their marriage, Mr. Sayer agreed, for every £1000 he should receive of her fortune, to settle lands in fee simple of £100 *per annum* to her for life. And Mr. Sayer was at that time entitled to an estate tail in equity made under his father's will, by which it was limited to three persons in fee in trust to convey to Mr. Sayer and the heirs of his body, remainder to the right heirs of the father. After the marriage, £2000, part of Mr. Sayer's fortune, was placed out upon an assignment of an old mortgage upon Mr. Sayer's estate. Subsequent to the will, upon which that secured remained due, and by the direction of a master in a cause in which Mr. Sayer was a party, £1000, part of the portion of Mrs. Neville, Mrs. Sayer's sister, being lent to Mr. Sayer, the mortgaged term was assigned as a security for that over and above the £2000. Mrs. Sayer, afterwards, eloped and took with her effects of her husband to a great value, in the pursuit of which and of her, he was killed by Mr. Nebble at her lodgings in The Mint. He left an infant. And the legal estate continued at his death in the trustees under the will of his father, no settlement having been made by him pursuant to the articles. The bill was to have the portion refunded, the articles not having been performed.

And though there was no express covenant in the articles to restore the fortune if a settlement should not be made and notwithstanding her conduct to her husband, yet he not having performed his part of the contract, Lord Chancellor [Lord Cowper] decreed her her portion again discounting what she had carried away of her husband's. He directed it to be restored to her *in specie* as far as she could trace it, particularly the £2000 mortgage and some tallies that had been bought with part in the name of her trustees. And, for the rest, he directed that she should come in as a creditor by simple contract.

The infant, by his answer, insisted on his right under the entail in bar of her right against the estate under the articles. But his counsel, at the hearing, thinking a specific performance more for his advantage, pressed to have the articles performed upon the general ground of a tenant in tail in equity, his having a power to bar an entail by a feoffment etc. without the solemnity of a fine or recovery and upon Mr. Sayer's covenant.

But Lord Chancellor [Lord Cowper] would not decree a specific performance, no cause having gone so far as to make a general covenant to settle without naming any particular lands a bar of an equitable estate tail. But, at the same time, he declared Mrs. Newell's additional £1000 well charged upon the estate, Mr. Sayer having expressly agreed to charge it upon this particular estate and having joined in the assignment of the mortgage (though the trustees of the inheritance did not) and it having been lent with the intervention of the court, which, in equitable interest, is adequate to a fine.[1]

55

Masters v. Button

(Ch. 1715)

Only a jury can set a will aside on the ground of fraud.

Lincoln's Inn MS. Misc. 384, p. 15, pl. 1

24 February.

A bill [was exhibited] to set aside a will obtained by fraud and imposition.

Lord Chancellor [Lord Cowper]: Can you show me one precedent where this court has set aside a will upon a pretense of fraud or surprise? It is properly triable at law, and whatever is good evidence here will be so at law. In Bodvile and Robert's Case, cited in Bath and Montague's Case, 2 Ch. Ca. 61,[2] this court could not set aside a will upon the strongest circumstances. There is a great difference between a deed and a will. Where a deed is obtained by fraud, it may properly be determined here, but a will is only triable at law. You may try it in a feigned issue. The plaintiff shall claim as heir at law and the defendant only under the will.

See Mancer's Case, Coke; see Bransby v. Kerrick *contra*.[3]

---

1 Sic in MS.

2 *Roberts v. Wynn* (1664), 1 Chancery Reports 236, 21 E.R. 560; *Earl of Bath v. Earl of Mountague* (1693), 3 Chancery Cases 55, 103, 22 E.R. 963, 992.

3 *Painter v. Manser* (1584), 2 Coke Rep. 1, 76 E.R. 387, also Moore K.B. 182, 72 E.R. 519; *Bransby v. Kerrick* (1718), see below, Case No. 301.

56

Byrd v. Standfast

(Ch. 1715)

A legacy to an infant should be paid into court and not to the infant's father.
An executor must give security for the future payment of contingent legacies.

Library of Congress MS. Jefferson 12, pt. 2, p. 42

A bill was exhibited by several persons under age by their father, their guardian, for legacies bequeathed to them by one Standfast, to whom the defendant is executor. They set forth that the deceased, Standfast, bequeathed to each of them £20 to be paid in twelve months after his decease and £450 to be equally divided among them provided the child with which the defendant, the deceased's wife, was big with should not live to twenty-one years; if it did, then he bequeathed it to the child. And in the close of their bill, they pray a decree for the several £20 and that the defendant may give security for the payment of the £450. The defendant confessed the bill in her answer.

Vernon was of counsel for the defendant and argued that to have paid these several sums to the father would have been entirely wrong because it would be unnatural to sue the father and that the defendant had offered to pay the money into the spiritual court and that there it was refused. And as to giving security for the £450, he conceived that not to be practicable in this case because there was a contingency depending and, in such cases, security was not usual.

Lord Chancellor [Lord Cowper]: The defendant did well in not paying the several £20 to the father of the plaintiffs, and I decree it to be paid to the master [in Chancery] and by him to be put out to interest and paid to the plaintiffs with the interest as they come respectively of age without further trouble. And as to the other point, when there is any contingency that can prevent the payment of a legacy, security is not usually granted. But in this, there is nothing that can excuse the payment of the £450 and, therefore, security must be given. And since, while this contingency is depending, the defendant by the course of law must have the use of the money, I decree that she bring it into court unless she give security within a month.

[Other copies of this report: Randolph K.B. 50.]

57

Anonymous

(Ch. 1715)

A rent can be reserved out of something incorporeal.
A lease need not state the specific days on which the rent is payable.

Library of Congress MS. Jefferson 12, pt. 2, p. 44

An action of debt was commenced for rent in the Petty Bag and before My Lord Chancellor [Lord Cowper], assisted with Sir Robert Eyre, one of the judges of the King's Bench, on a demurrer, exception was taken to the declaration that the rent was reserved out of a room with use of goods and the use of goods was a thing incorporeal and out of which rent could not be reserved and that the rent was made payable at four quarterly payments without mentioning the days, both of which were overruled.

[Other copies of this report: Randolph K.B. 51.]

58

Vane v. Lord Barnard

(Ch. 1715)

The clause 'without impeachment of waste' does not permit the total destruction of the thing.

British Library MS. Hargrave 80, f. 214

Lord Barnard, in consideration of his son's marriage, for a portion, conveyed Raby Castle and a great estate to the use of himself for life without impeachment of waste, remainder to the plaintiff for life without impeachment of waste, remainder to the first son etc. in tail etc. And, after the marriage, conceiving a displeasure at his son, he pulled down a great part of the castle and sold the materials, upon which his son brought this bill for an injunction to stay his destroying the castle and to compel him to put it *in statu quo*. Lord Barnard pleaded the settlement, by which he was tenant for life without impeachment of waste.

The Attorney General [*Northey*], for Lord Barnard, cited the case where that is settled to give an authority to do waste. He said, once, it was usual in settlements after the clause 'without impeachment of waste' to add 'and with full power to do and commit waste', which was intended to exclude the Court of Chancery from interposing, but that it was disused of late as needless, and that it is common still to except voluntary waste in houses where that is intended to be restrained and that Lord Barnard had done no more than the constant exposition of the power warranted. It was added the plaintiff was only tenant for life in remainder, had but a contingency for ever having the possession, it was therefore uncertain whether he would receive any prejudice. And, if Lord Barnard was punishable for waste, yet the plaintiff, not having the inheritance, could not punish him for it, that the account prayed [was] impracticable, what proportion could the plaintiff claim in satisfaction for his precarious interest.

Lord Chancellor [Lord Cowper]: Great care should be taken not to run riot upon the rules of law upon notions of reason. To restrain Lord Barnard from committing any waste would be contrary to the intent of the parties in annexing that privilege to his estate. But that clause ought to be understood of the usual kind of waste, such as felling timber, plowing meadows, and the like, but not extending so far as to give him leave to destroy the seat itself, which is settled by express words, in breach of his contract in the same deed that it shall go according to the limitations in the deed. If a piece of marshland were settled in the same manner and the tenant for life attempted to let in the sea upon it, should not this court stop him? There will be no difficulty in the account. The produce of materials may be again invested in a building and settled to the same use. Let the plea stand for an answer with liberty to except and let the injunction continue.

Afterwards, the plaintiff not excepting, the defendant would have put in a further answer in order to have introduced some new matter of defense. And he applied to the court for leave, resembling it to the case of a demurrer overruled.

But [it was held] by Lord Chancellor [Lord Cowper] the judgment there is *quod respondeat ouster*, and, when the demurrer is overruled, there is no answer remaining in court; here *e contra*. The judgment is that the plea stand for an answer, which it is though it be overruled as a plea. He refused to let them put in a new answer.

[Other reports of this case: 2 Vernon 738, 23 E.R. 1082, Precedents in Chancery 454, 24 E.R. 203, Gilbert Rep. 127, 25 E.R. 89, 1 Salkeld 161, 91 E.R. 150, 1 Eq. Cas. Abr. 399, 21 E.R. 1131, 2 Eq. Cas. Abr. 244, 22 E.R. 208.]

59

Musgrove v. Lord Dunbar

(Ch. 1715)

A witness need not answer a question that is not material to the case, especially where it will be defamatory to a third party.

British Library MS. Hargrave 80, f. 215v

The plaintiff's bill was to have a discovery who was his father and mother, whether dead or alive, and what estate they left, real or personal, on surmises that he had been bred as a gentleman and had been told from time to time sometimes that he was the son of A., other times of B.; sometimes that he had a considerable real estate in this county; sometimes in that; or that he was entitled to a considerable distributive share of his father's or his mother's personal estate.

Lord Dunbar, by answer, admitted him to be his natural son and that he had been at the charge of his education, but he did not disclose by whom.

And the plaintiff attempted to prove who his mother was in expectation of receiving a considerable sum. Rather than that matter should be brought to light, the witnesses demurred to the interrogatories.

And, though they did not ask them to disclose any matter defamatory to themselves, yet Lord Chancellor [Lord Cowper] allowed the demurrer upon this ground, that the matter inquired of would, if disclosed, be defamatory to a third person and it did not appear to be material in the cause.

[Other copies of this report: Lincoln's Inn MS. Misc. 107, f. 60.]

60

Atkyns's Case

(Ch. 1715)

An alteration in a writing will not be given effect unless it is proved to have been made by the maker of the writing himself.

British Library MS. Hargrave 80, f. 216

Sir Robert Atkyns had a power of appointing a sum of money among his children in the proportion he thought fit, which he executed by a deed. And the deed continued many years after in his custody. And being now produced, it appeared upon the face of it that the sum of £300 had been appointed to one of them as the deed was first written, but a line was drawn through the word 'three' and 'two' written over it by another hand.

This being an alteration in a very material part and there being no memorandum that it was done before the execution of the deed nor any proof relating to it, Lord Chancellor [Lord Cowper] decreed £300 to that child, presuming the alteration to have been made after the deed was executed.

It was urged that, if it was, that it must be by Sir Robert, in whose custody the deed was, and that he could not be thought to have done it, having no interest to serve by making that alteration.

But Lord Chancellor [Lord Cowper] said it was too hard for him to inquire into the notion that every person acted upon in doing a wrong thing. And he added it could countenance too slovenly a way of drawing deeds to establish such an alteration without evidence and even put the operation of deeds entirely in the power of the person in whose custody they are.

61

Churchill v. Fitch

(Ch. 1715)

A contract that is indefinite is unenforceable.

British Library MS. Hargrave 77, f. 50, pl. 2

The plaintiff agreed with the defendant for a purchase of lands in Dorsetshire, on which there was a then lease for three lives. The quantum of the purchase money was agreed on, but not the time or manner of payment. Those matters were transacted by letters. Afterwards, one of the lives drops, and the plaintiff not calling for an execution of the agreement, the life was filled.

And, now, he brings his bill to have a specific execution of the agreement and to have the estate without the new life.

The bill was dismissed by reason of the uncertainty of the agreement, there being no time or manner of payment fixed. And, therefore, it is not fit to be carried into execution.

[Other copies of this report: British Library MS. Hargrave 303, f. 86v, pl. 2.]

62

Richmond v. Ady

(Ch. 1715)

Where a mortgagee of a leasehold estate renews the lease, the expenses of such renewal are reimbursable by the mortgagor upon a redemption.

British Library MS. Hargrave 77, f. 50v, pl. 1

26 February. Master of the Rolls.

If a mortgagee of a renewable lease for years determinable on lives enters, afterward, renews the lease or gets any of the lives filled up, the whole charge of this must be repaid him with interest as well as the principal money and interest before the mortgagor shall redeem.

[Other copies of this report: British Library MS. Hargrave 303, f. 87, pl. 1.]

63

Stuart v. Earl of Findlater

(Ch. 1715)

A court has jurisdiction of transitory causes of action which arise in a foreign jurisdiction if it has personal jurisdiction over the parties.

British Library MS. Hargrave 80, f. 216v

The bill was for several sums alleged to be due to the plaintiff for services done to the defendant [James Ogilvy, earl of Findlater (1663–1730)[1]] in Scotland as his steward, and the plaintiff had had offices under the defendant while he was Chancellor and Secretary of Scotland and had been occasionally employed by him in his domestic affairs, for which this bill was brought.

And to it, the defendant pleaded the Scottish Statute of Limitations, which is a bar in three years to debts not due by writ if the defendant denies them to be due upon his oath. And he denies the debt upon oath and likewise pleads the Articles of Union,[2] by which it is provided that laws in Scotland shall not be cognizable in any court of Westminster Hall and that this matter arose wholly within Scotland. The greatest stress of the defense was put upon the last part. And it was insisted the courts were excluded by it from intermeddling either originally or by way of appeal in any causes real or personal arising in Scotland.

The plaintiff's counsel alleged it to be the intent of the Articles of Union only to preserve the jurisdiction of the Scottish courts as they were before the Union and that, before the Union, if two persons made a personal contract in Scotland and came into England, either party might sue the other here and that, even to this day, if two Englishmen contracted in England and went after[wards] into Scotland, they might prosecute there in the courts by whose process they are amerciable[3] and that upon the general ground that actions of that kind are not local, but follow the person.

Lord Chancellor [Lord Cowper]: The words of the Articles are 'causes in Scotland' etc.; in actions transitory, while the parties are here, the cause is here.

Upon the other part of the plea, *Vernon* alleged that the time of a Statute of Limitations in such a case does not run immediately from the services performed, but from such time as the party has made a due application for his reward and has been denied or otherwise despaired of having it and that several allegations of the bill which might amount to a promise by construction were not denied.

---

1 J. R. Young, 'Ogilvy, James, fourth earl of Findlater (1663–1730)', *Oxford Dictionary of National Biography*, vol. 41, pp. 584–586.

2 Stat. 6 Ann., c. 11, art. 19 (*SR*, VIII, 571).

3 Sic in MS. for amenable.

Both which Lord Chancellor [Lord Cowper] gave in to. And upon the whole, he overruled the plea.

Note: The plea seems informal in mixing a plea in bar, which tacitly admits the jurisdiction, with a plea to the jurisdiction. The laws here seem to be the proper measure for the court to govern itself by and not the Scottish law.

Lincoln's Inn MS. Misc. 11, p. 20, pl. 3

5 March 1714[/15].

The plaintiff brought his bill against the defendant to have satisfaction of several personal demands.

The defendant pleaded the Statute of Union and, particularly, the 13th Clause, which says that no causes arising in Scotland shall be cognizable in any court of England.[1]

Curia [Lord Cowper]: The plaintiff's demand is merely personal, and it follows the person wherever he goes. If one man contracts a debt with another in Scotland and both afterwards come into England, the cause of action must be said to arise where the persons are.

And, therefore, the plea was allowed to stand for an answer with liberty to except.

64

Digby v. Mackworth

(Ch. 1715)

The question in this case was whether a testator's personal estate is first liable to the payment of his debts where he devised real property to trustees to sell and pay his debts.

British Library MS. Hargrave 81, f. 91

14 March 1715.

Digby, by will, devises a real estate to trustees to be sold for and towards payment of his debts and the portions thereby given and devises the residue of his personal estate after payment of his debts and legacies etc. to A.

The question was whether the whole real estate should be first sold because first mentioned and so go in aid of the personal estate though there were no words in the will to exempt it. And that it should not, the Case of Garraway and Christ Church Hospital[2] was quoted, where the personal estate was devised to the wife yet, because there were no words of exemption, she was obliged to account for and pay the personal estate for the benefit of the heir at law.

1 Stat. 6 Ann., c. 11, art. 19 (*SR*, VIII, 571).

2 *Christ's Hospital v. Gallway* (Ch. c. 1714), see above, Case No. 5.

Curia [Lord Cowper]: The easing and aiding a real estate is always much favored in this court. If the real had not been first named, here there had been no question, for creditors are as well answered if the real estate be sold after application of the personal estate as if sold first. But in this case, if the real estate be sold first, the devisee will have the residue both of the real and personal estate contrary to the express words of the devise, and though a real estate be devised or appointed to be sold, yet it is the constant justice of this court to save as much of it for the heir as may be and decree no more to be sold than necessary to supply the deficiency of the personal estate where that is not expressly exempted, but not to decree a sale of all the real estate merely to aid the personal or increase the surplus or a residue in favor of a legatee against the heir at law.

Mr. *Vernon*: If the real estate be not first sold, there will be no residue and, consequently, part of the will must be disappointed and made void, and, in the case of a will, this court [would] make a devise to one void and ineffectual for the sake of another.

Curia [Lord Cowper]: See if you can find any precedent of this court's ordering a real estate to be sold in aid or favor of the personal.

[Other copies of this report: British Library MS. Hargrave 82, f. 87.]

[Other reports of this case: British Library MS. Hargrave 77, f. 23, pl. 1, British Library MS. Hargrave 303, f. 44.]

65

Attorney General v. Mayor of Coventry

(Ch. 1715)

Where a party admits an interest in the matter in issue, the other side must reply to it and put the first party to his proof or else be bound by the admission.

British Library MS. Hargrave 80, f. 217v, pl. 1

Mr. Collings had been examined before the Master *pro interesse* and, by his examination, made a title to the thing in question. Instead of replying, the plaintiff brought the matter before the court upon an exception to the report.

And it was insisted for Collings and ruled that they were concluded by the examination, not having replied to it, as they might and put him upon the proof of it, as much as if they had set down a cause upon bill and answer. The rule seems to be the same in all examinations before a master.

[Other copies of this report: Lincoln's Inn MS. Misc. 107, f. 61, pl. 1, 3 Swanston 311, 36 E.R. 876.]

66
Roach v. Hammond
(Ch. 1715)

A devise to 'relations' will be paid according to the Statute of Distributions.

Gilbert Rep. 92, 25 E.R. 64

A man, by his will, in 1704, devises all his real and personal estate to the defendant, to the use of his relations, without specifying any in particular or using any other words. And he makes the defendant his executor, and, in 1706, he died.

And now, the plaintiffs, who were the mother and three sisters of the testator, brought this bill, as his nearest relations, for a discovery and an account of the personal estate.

It appears in the cause that the testator left no real estate; and it was referred to a Master to take an account of the personal estate, and the plaintiffs to come in according to the course of distribution, settled by 1 Jac. II, c. 17.[1]

And it was agreed to be the rule of this court, in construction on such devises to relations that those who, by the Statute of Distributions, would be entitled to the personal estate, in case he had died intestate, should upon such general devises be let into the same proportion.

And My Lord Chancellor [Lord Cowper] said, he thought it the best measure for setting bounds to such general words, and that it had been oftentimes ruled accordingly in this court.

And by this rule I conceive Colonel Norton's Will may be regulated. W.B.

[Other copies of this report: Precedents in Chancery 401, 24 E.R. 180, 2 Eq. Cas. Abr. 438, 22 E.R. 373.]

67
Lord Harley v. Hancock
(Ch. c. 1715)

A bill for discovery and relief in the case of a lost deed must be filed under oath.

Lincoln's Inn MS. Misc. 11, p. 19, pl. 1

The defendant demurred because the plaintiff had not made an oath of the loss of a deed which they sought a discovery of by the bill.

1 Stat. 1 Jac. II, c. 17, s. 7 (*SR*, VI, 19).

The demurrer was allowed though it only went to the discovery and not to the relief because the plaintiffs sought relief by their bill as well as discovery, according to the distinction taken in 1 Ch. Repts., fo. 11.[1]

68

Welch v. Duppa

(Ch. c. 1715)

In the case of an only child, upon the death of his or her father, any advancement will not be brought into hotchpot.

Lincoln's Inn MS. Misc. 11, p. 19, pl. 3

A citizen [of London] having a wife and one child makes his will and takes notice he had advanced that child and given her a £300 portion. She now brings her bill for her share by the custom.

Mr. *Vernon*: It appearing by the will how much her portion was, that is sufficient to let her into her share by the custom according to the Case of Dean and Lord Delawar.[2] Mr. Freeman, being a citizen of London, had entered down in his books what he had given to Lord Delawar as a portion with one of his daughters, and that was decreed by Lord Harcourt to let that child into a share by the custom.

In this case, nothing is to be brought into hotchpot in regard there is no other child so that the plaintiff is entitled to a third of what was the personal estate of the testator at his death, for the child shall not bring into hotchpot in favor of the widow to increase her share. It is true, if there were other children, she should.

Curia [Lord Cowper]: There must be an account taken of the personal estate, and the plaintiff must have a third of what shall remain after payment of the debts and funeral expenses and the widow's chamber without any regard to what she received in part of her advancement, it appearing by writing under the father's hand what the certainty of that advancement was and the law being now settled that the advancement shall not be brought into hotchpot but where there are other children.

---

[1] *Anonymous* (1663), 1 Chancery Cases 11, 22 E.R. 669.

[2] *Dean v. Lord Delaware* (1708), 2 Vernon 628, 23 E.R. 1011, 1 Eq. Cas. Abr. 156, 21 E.R. 955.

69
Bacon v. Eubank

(Ch. 1715)

A purchaser of land who paid off a mortgage is subrogated to the rights of the mortgagor and is entitled to payment for the mortgage and also for an intermediary encumbrance when a prior purchaser sues to redeem.

A court of equity will not allow an innocent purchaser to suffer a loss where he can defend himself at common law.

British Library MS. Hargrave 80, f. 218v

The defendant was a purchaser of parcel of a manor without notice of any encumbrances. The plaintiff was a purchaser of another part of the same manor prior in time to the defendant. The defendant afterwards discovered a mortgage of the whole manor made by the vendor antecedent to both sales and a judgment acknowledged by the vendor after the sale to the plaintiff and before that to the defendant and procured an assignment of the mortgage and judgment. The plaintiff brought his bill to redeem the mortgage only so far as it affected his estate, the judgment not affecting his purchase.

Vernon, for the defendant, insisted that, the defendant having been obliged to take in both to protect his purchase, the plaintiff should not be admitted to take either from him unless he would take both and repay him what he had paid for them and confirm his purchase and that a court of equity would not in any case suffer an innocent purchaser for to be wounded where he could defend himself at law.

The Master of the Rolls [Trevor] was of the same opinion.

Sed adjornatur.

Vernon admitted that, if the mortgage had been standing out in a third person, the prior purchaser would have had the prior right to redeem or, if he had taken in anything subsequent to his title, it had been varied and unnecessary and, therefore, not to be tacked to his prior securities.

Stiles' Case was cited by *Vernon*. Stiles made his will in England, being at that time possessed only of a suit of clothes and a pair of boots, and he then went to Holland where he acquired £200,000 or £300,000. [It was] decreed by Lord Somers, I think, that this new unexpected acquisition should be distributed among his next of kin and not to go to his executors or residuary legatee.

[Other copies of this report: Lincoln's Inn MS. Misc. 107, f. 63.]

Lincoln's Inn MS. Misc. 380, pt. 3, p. 191

Charlton Whitlock mortgages his manor of A. to the bishop of Ely, then grants estates for lives to R., S., and T. Afterwards, R. obtains a judgment against C. Whitlock and afterwards purchases in the bishop of Ely's mortgage. It was decreed that R. should be satisfied his judgment as well as mortgage before the others should be let in.

This was before the Master of the Rolls [Trevor].

70

Buck v. Turner

(Ch. 1715)

A court of equity will not rule against a bona fide *purchaser for value even though the grantor acted in breach of a trust.*

In this case, the purchaser was a mortgagee, and the beneficiaries of the trust were allowed to redeem upon the usual terms.

British Library MS. Hargrave 80, f. 219v

Sir William Bucke and Sir Edward Turner, Sir Thomas Cross, *et al.*

Sir Edward Turner, being in the possession of lands after the death of his father, to which he had no title, mortgaged them to Sir Thomas Cross. The legal interest remained in an infant heir of a trustee under a voluntary settlement made by Joan Eure, who had purchased the lands in trust for Lady Turner, Sir Edward's mother, remainder in trust for the plaintiffs, who sought by their bill, *inter alia*, to have a conveyance from their trustee pursuant to his trust.

Vernon insisted strongly for the plaintiffs that, though they were voluntary, yet they, not claiming under the same person that Sir Thomas Cross did paramount and under a purchaser, ought to have the aid of the court to have a conveyance from their trustee notwithstanding Sir Thomas Cross's purchase of a defective title without notice and that it would be a breach of trust in their trustee not to convey upon request. He cited the case of March v. Gunter and Williams,[1] before the Master of the Rolls, where a second mortgagee without notice procured a prior encumbrance to be assigned to a third person who covenanted to stand seised in trust for him, in which case, it was agreed that, if the prior encumbrance rested in an indifferent hand, equity would give the first mortgagee the redemption of it, but, being in the hands of a trustee for the second mortgagee, who could not dispose of it from him without a breach of covenant, it was decreed to be the same thing as if it were in the hands of the second mortgagee himself.

Lord Chancellor [Lord Cowper] was nevertheless positive in opinion that a court of equity ought not to give any assistance against an innocent purchaser and declared that it appearing to him that Sir Thomas Cross was a purchaser under one in possession without notice of the plaintiff's title, this court ought not

[1] *Brotherton v. Hatt* (1706), 2 Vernon 574, 23 E.R. 973, 2 Freeman 290, 22 E.R. 1217, 1 Eq. Cas. Abr. 330, 21 E.R. 1081.

to aid the plaintiff to evict him, but, as against him, the plaintiff ought to redeem upon the common terms.

Tamen quaere.

[Other copies of this report: Lincoln's Inn MS. Misc. 107, f. 64.]

British Library MS. Hargrave 77, f. 50, pl. 1

Joan Euer, great-grandmother to the defendant, Sir William Buck, by a feoffment in 1650, purchases lands in fee of her daughter, Mary Ashton, and her husband for £500. Afterwards, her daughter, being a widow, marries Mr. Edward Turner, afterwards Lord Chief Baron. Before this marriage, which was in 1652, articles were executed between them and trustees whereby he covenants to set[tle] the lands of £300 *per annum* to the use of Mr. Turner and herself for their lives and, after the death of the survivor, to the use of the issue male of their two bodies, remainder to the issue female, remainder to the heirs of the body of Mr. Turner, remainder to his right heirs. Afterwards, *viz.* in the same month and year, a settlement is made of Mrs. Ashton's estate, to which Turner was a party, reciting that he had agreed to settle £220 *per annum* jointure upon her. This settlement was varying in some of its uses and limitations from what was expressed in the articles. And, by this, the estate for life of Mr. Ashton was to be without impeachment of waste.

[Other copies of this report: British Library MS. Hargrave 303, f. 86v, pl. 1.]

22 Viner, Abr. 21

Easter, 1 Geo. Turner v. Buck *et al. et e contra*.

Turner sold to Cross an estate which he claimed as heir to his father by virtue of a marriage settlement upon the marriage of his father with his mother-in-law M., being the lands of the said M. Buck, as heir under that settlement, brought a bill to discover the title of Turner and Cross and also to compel the surviving trustee in a former settlement in the family to convey to Buck as heir under the settlement.

Cowper, Chancellor, declared he would not decree the trustee to convey the legal estate to the *cestui que trust* to compel him to suffer the *cestui que trust* to bring an ejectment in his name against Cross because he was a purchaser without notice of this former settlement and the *cestui que trust* was a volunteer. And he said it was a constant rule in equity never to aid any person who claims by a volunteer settlement against a fair purchaser without notice, as in the case of a disseisor (as it now appeared that it was) who conveys away the lands upon a valuable consideration. This court will not compel the trustee to convey the legal estate to a *cestui que trust* to enable him to recover the possession at law against the purchaser, but the trustee may do it himself it he think fit. But this court will not compel him to it, though *Sir Joseph Jekyll* and Mr. *Vernon* insisted strongly for it. And he said the possession of the trustee was the possession of the *cestui que trust* and that it was a breach of trust in the trustee not to convey at any time to a *cestui que trust* upon request.

But in this, case Lord Cowper decreed that Turner should account for the profits of the estate from his entry to the time of the conveyance to Cross, for he was a disseisor, though Turner had two verdicts for him in [actions of] ejectment, but this old settlement was discovered after those trials.

[Other copies of this report: 2 Eq. Cas. Abr. 751, 22 E.R. 637.]

71

Lingen v. Sowray

(Ch. 1715)

Money that is required to be invested in land is considered to be a real estate.

A court will not presume that a grantor's intention is based on an ignorance of the law.

Lincoln's Inn MS. Misc. 11, p. 105

William Sowray Lingen and other sons of William Lingen by Sarah, his wife, sister of Dr. Sowray, deceased, and Richard Sowray and others, children of Joseph Sowray, deceased, brother to Dr. Sowray, plaintiffs; Abigail Sowray, widow, relict of the Doctor, and William Blackely, Henry Darley, Thomas Millington, Cornelius Coley, and Richard Denton, defendants.

The defendant Abigail had a portion of £1400 out upon securities, and, by articles on her marriage dated 21 January 1707[/08], her securities and some other of the Doctor's effects of the like nature were assigned to the defendants, the trustees, on trust that they should lay out the £1400 in land and settle the same to the use of the Doctor for life, remainder to trustees to support contingent remainders, remainder to the defendant Abigail for her jointure, remainder to the first and other sons in tail, then to daughters in tail, remainder to the right heirs of the Doctor. And the Doctor covenanted to make good any deficiency.

The trustees never acted and the Doctor took all the securities into his hands and received thereout £625 principal money. And £250, part thereof, he placed on a mortgage in the name of the trustees in trust for himself and his wife. And the residue was standing out on the old securities at his death.

The Doctor died without issue, having made his will. And, after debts and funerals paid, he gives his house wherein he dwelt with all the premises thereto belonging and all his furniture therein to his wife and, after, to the defendant Denton in fee. And he gave the rest of his real estate in the City and County of York or elsewhere in the Kingdom of Great Britain to be equally divided amongst the plaintiffs, and the residue of his personal estate he gave to his wife. And he made his wife executrix.

He left a freehold of £90 a year in the County and City of York, which the plaintiffs enjoy by virtue of the will.

The plaintiffs brought their bill that the defendant, out of her husband's assets, might make good so much of the £1400 as he had made use of or which should prove deficient and that the same might be laid out according to the articles or as near as might be.

The defendant Abigail insisted she was entitled to the whole money.

On 12 October 1712, the cause was heard before Lord Harcourt, who sent it to a master to take an account how much of the £1400 was subsisting at the Doctor's death and what was the value of his personal estate and state his debts. And he reserved the consideration until after the report.

On 11 May 1713, the Master reported there was £785 due subsisting of the £1400 at the Doctor's death and £250 other part had been received by him and put out, as before, that his personal estate over and above the £780 and £250 amounted to £1020 19s. 10d., of which £113 was doubtful, that £421 was the value of the furniture, and his debts amounted to £536 13s. 6d.

On 18 December 1713, the cause as heard on the equity reserved before Lord Harcourt, who declared that so much of the said £1400 as at the time of the devise to the plaintiffs of the said testator's real estate was subsisting on the same securities on which the same was secured at the time of the articles ought to be considered as real estate and that, consequently, the plaintiffs, as devisees of the real estate of the Doctor, are entitled thereto after the death of the defendant Abigail and that £785 appeared to be the sum which remained at the time of the said devise on such securities but that the £250 mentioned in the report having been called in and lent out on a mortgage on a different trust, though in the names of the said trustees, ought not to be taken as part of the real estate, and, therefore, he ordered the securities for the said £780 to be brought before the Master and the defendant Abigail to have the interest for her life and, after her death, the persons who shall be entitled to the money by virtue of the articles and they are at liberty to apply to the court to have the money laid out if they think fit. And, as to all other demands, he dismissed the bill.

The defendant petitioned for a rehearing, for that taking the whole circumstances of the will together with the circumstances of the several estates thereby devised, the said £1400 ought to be taken as personal estate, as well in equity as certainly it was in law, when the Doctor died, or at least the £1400 was intended by the testator to pass by the devise of his personal estate to the defendant, his wife, and the rather for that, if it had been laid out as the articles direct, he would still have had a power of disposing the reversion thereof by his will and the devise of his real estate is confined only to lands in the County or City of York or elsewhere in the Kingdom of Great Britain and there was a real estate sufficient to answer those words and the intention of the testator. And, unless this £1400 do pass as personal estate, the defendant Abigail will be no gainer by her husband's will, which was contrary to his intention. And, if the £1400 be adjudged as real estate to be laid out according to the articles, then ought the same to be made up out of the testator's real and personal estate.

Mr. *Vernon*, for the plaintiff: [There are] several cases where it has been allowed that a man shall be a tenant by curtesy and a woman endowed where money has been agreed to be laid out and all the limitations except the remainder in fee determined. And he cited the Case of Atkins and Atkins.[1] £1500 was brought in by the husband and the like sum by the wife and on the marriage agreed to be laid out in land and settled on the husband and wife and their issue and no remainder was limited over, the articles being silent; the husband died without issue and no purchase was made, and the question was between the heir and the executor of the husband to whom this money should go. It was decreed it should be considered as land and go to the heir.

Lord Chancellor [Lord Cowper] said he thought the decree very nice in declaring the £250 to be personal estate when the Doctor had pursued the trusts so far as to put out the money in the name of the said trustees and to declare it to be in trust for him and his wife. I think the other side have most reason to complain of the decree.

He might have considered it as a real or personal estate and given it accordingly. But here, he has not declared by any words in the will that this should pass, either by the devise of all his real estate or of all his personal estate, so that it stands doubtful what his intention was. And, therefore, it ought to go as the law would say it should in case it had been land. I see no reason to vary the decree.

British Library MS. Hargrave 80, f. 220v

A man, entitled to the remainder in fee of money that was to have been invested in land, devised all his real estate situate in England to J.S. It was argued that it was in the testator's power to dispose this as a realty or a personalty, that it, being money, was, in his apprehension, a mere personalty and could not be supposed to have been designed by him to pass by a devise of all his real estate situate etc., that this was not properly situate anywhere.

Vernon, e contra, [argued] that it was a real estate. He cited the case of Holt and Holt,[2] where a man articled with a builder to build a house upon his inheritance and died; the executor prevailed with him to release the articles, but the heir nevertheless prevailed to have the house built out of the personal estate, and that of Atkins and Atkins, where there were marriage articles for investing £1500 of each side to be settled upon the husband and wife for life and their issue in tail as to the remainder in fee, the articles were silent but the heir nevertheless prevailed against the executor of the husband.

[1] *Knight v. Atkyns* (1687), 2 Chancery Reports 400, 21 E.R. 699, 2 Vernon 20, 23 E.R. 624, 1 Eq. Cas. Abr. 274, 21 E.R. 1041.

[2] *Holt v. Holt* (1694), 2 Vernon 322, 23 E.R. 808, 1 Eq. Cas. Abr. 274, 21 E.R. 1042.

Lord Chancellor [Lord Cowper]: It must be esteemed a real estate unless he who had power over the reversion had declared expressly in his will that he looked upon it as personal. He has left it indifferent, and the court must guide itself by the common rules of construction in the like cases. The argument of his intent founded upon a supposition of his ignorance of the law is no rule of construction in any case; if it were, it would leave everything extremely uncertain.

British Library MS. Hargrave 77, f. 49v, pl. 2

Lingon v. Sewra.

Mr. *Vernon*, for the plaintiff: In the Case of Holt and Holt, where there was on a marriage a covenant to lay out money in rebuilding and the estate to be settled, articles are made with workmen for this purpose. The husband dies. The widow gets a release from the workmen. The heir at law brings his bill founded on the articles to have the benefit of the covenant. It was decreed to the heir notwithstanding the release. And in A. and A., money was laid out in a purchase and settled to the intended husband and wife for life, then to the issue male in tail, silent as to the remainders, it was decreed here to the heir not as money. A person shall be deemed a tenant by curtesy where, by the articles, the wife was to have such an estate as if actually vested by purchase and settled he would have been entitled to. If lands are articled to be purchased, the party, by will, devises all his lands, and then the purchase is made, then the party dies, here these shall not pass by the will because he was then not seised, as mentioned by the Statute of Wills.

Curia [Lord Cowper]: Not at law, but he shall here. [It was] so resolved on great debate here in the Case of Goodyear.

[Other reports of this case: British Library MS. Hargrave 303, f. 86.]

[Other reports of this case: Precedents in Chancery 400, 24 E.R. 179, 1 Peere Williams 172, 24 E.R. 343, Gilbert Rep. 91, 25 E.R. 63, 10 Modern 38, 88 E.R. 615, 1 Eq. Cas. Abr. 175, 21 E.R. 968, 2 Eq. Cas. Abr. 327, 553, 22 E.R. 279, 465.]

72

Shireton v. Hippesley

(Ch. 1715)

A person who benefits from a successful lawsuit should pay the contracted for fees of the lawyer in the case.

Lincoln's Inn MS. Misc. 11, p. 12, pl. 2

30 April 1715.

The plaintiff was employed as a solicitor for the defendant's husband in a suit which was brought in this court in the names of the defendant and her husband for the recovery of a leasehold estate which belonged to the defendant before her marriage. The suit succeeded, and there was a decree for the estate. The defendant's husband, afterwards, died intestate and insolvent. And the term not being disposed of by the husband, upon his death, it came to the defendant, his wife, who refused to take out administration or to pay the plaintiff the costs of the said suit, which were not paid by the husband. And, therefore, he now brought his bill to have satisfaction of these costs from the defendant.

Curia: She having the benefit of the suit and being now in possession of the thing recovered, it is the highest justice that she should pay the costs of the suit. And, therefore, he decreed she should pay what was due to the plaintiff for costs of the said former suit together with the costs of this suit.

73

Aby v. Spencer

(Ch. 1715)

If a jointure be made with respect of any further estate that was to come or might come to the wife, the husband is a purchaser of that future or contingent estate.

British Library MS. Hargrave 77, f. 48v

5 May.

The plaintiffs were creditors of Marmaduke Spencer, who died intestate. The defendant, his widow, renounced administration, which is thereupon granted to the defendant Barrowby, who compounds several of the intestate's debts or pays the whole. And the creditors, on receiving their debts, give the administrator money, which he insists to keep and not be accountable for, as being voluntary to him.

The intestate's wife was to have £500 portion. And, in consideration of it, [he] settles or agrees to settle a jointure upon her. Afterwards, she has a legacy left her by one relation and also a contingency as to a part by another given to her and her brother and sisters and, in cases of any of their dying, the decedents's part to go among the survivors, one of which legatees soon after died, and to another contingency on a legacy of £400 devised to her brother and, if he died before eighteen, then to go among his sisters, which were three in number. And he died before that time. The total of the wife's part of these contingent legacies amounted to £185. Before any of it was received or recovered, her husband, Marmaduke Spencer, died.

And the creditors having brought a bill for the satisfaction of their debts out of his real and personal estate, the question was whether those contingent legacies not recovered should belong to the wife, who survived, or to be taken as part of the intestate's personal assets.

Sir Joseph Jekyll, for the plaintiffs: Where a contingent legacy vests during coverture and the husband had settled a jointure, he is a purchaser of all the wife's estate and interest. And, though he dies before it is recovered, it shall go to his administrator and [not] survive to the wife. [It is] otherwise if no jointure.

Curia [LORD COWPER]: If the jointure was made with respect of any further estate that was to come or might come to the wife, there, the husband might be looked upon a purchaser of that future or contingent estate, not else. If a surety takes counter security, the creditor may pay him and pray to stand in his place and shall do so and have the benefit of the counter security moneys [as] are given by the creditors to an administrator, on receiving their debts. This shall remain and be taken a part of the decedents's assets.

Mr. *Mead*, for the defendant, the infant: Here, where a real estate is not in trust but descends to an infant heir, as the parol must demur at law until infants are of age, so in equity. And it cannot during the infancy be so affected as to have any account of the profits against the infant heir.

[LORD COWPER]: I decree all defendants who have meddled with any of the real or personal estate, either in law or equity, of Marmaduke Spencer to account for them and the administrator to be examined on interrogatories as to what abatements or debts have been made him by creditors or they have refunded him on the payment of their debts. And I reserve consideration how far the plaintiffs shall have satisfaction out of the intestate's real estate until an account be taken of the personal estate. If the whole £500 portion was not paid to the husband, then the creditors are well entitled to the £185 contingency.

[Other copies of this report: British Library MS. Hargrave 303, f. 84.]

74

Barton v. Raskby

(Ch. 1715)

Where a contract is made for a settlement and the party is to be a tenant for life with a remainder in tail by the same deed, a fine and recovery will bar the entail and the remainder.

A court of equity will specifically enforce marriage articles upon a lawsuit of one of the children intended to be benefitted.

A marriage settlement made by a wife in consideration of an equivalent settlement made by the husband is not a purchase of the husband within the Statute of 11 Hen. VII.

British Library MS. Hargrave 77, f. 49

11 May.

The defendant's wife was first married when an infant. Her mother and guardian, before the marriage, enter into articles with the intended husband, by which it was agreed that the infant's estate should be settled to the use of the intended husband and wife for life and to the heirs of their bodies and that the husband should make a settlement of his estate on the intended wife for her life with remainders over. The marriage is had. And the wife being come of full age, a settlement is made of the wife's estate to the use of the husband for life, remainder to trustees to preserve contingent remainders, then to the wife for life, remainder to the first and every other son of that marriage successively in tail male, remainder to the heirs of the body of the husband and wife. Afterwards, the husband dies, leaving only daughters and no issue male of that marriage. The widow married the defendant Raskby and levies a fine and suffers a recovery of that which was her own estate and settles it to the use of her second husband and herself and the issue of that marriage.

The daughters of that marriage by the first husband bring their bill to have the benefit of the marriage articles and the second settlement and the estate settled in strict settlement, *viz.* with remainders to the daughters expressly as well as the sons, supposing the articles not to be performed.

Sir Thomas Powys, for the plaintiff, insisted that the husband, having made a settlement of his own estate in consideration of the settlement agreed to be made of the wife's, was a purchaser of the wife's estate as settled and, therefore, her alienation was of his estate and so within the Statute of Jointures.[1]

Mr. *Vernon*: Articles though solely drawn or corrected in general terms as to settling estates were constantly decreed on bills here to be made good by settlements. And here, it was not the intent of the parties or can be presumed that she, after having accepted the settlement of her husband's estate and enjoyed the benefit of it for many years, should have the power of defeating his issue of his estate he had by that settlement purchased for them.

Curia [Lord Cowper]: If a wife's land be so settled as she is a tenant in tail, though she does not accept a counter consideration from the husband as a settlement of the other part of his estate, whether equal in value to hers is not material. Her alienation of her estate after his death is to be considered not of an estate *ex provisione viri*, and it is not within the Statute Hen. VIII, of jointures. Where articles are for a settlement and the party is to be a tenant for life, remainder in tail by the same deed, a fine and recovery will bar the entail and remainder. A bill will lie on those articles, as too loose in themselves, to have a strict settlement. But, if, afterwards, the parties execute a settlement strictly to the husband and wife for life, then to the first and every other son in tail, remainder in tail general, a bill does not lie to have a strict settlement executed, for the parties have by this determined what is a reasonable settlement and a proper execution of the articles.

The bill was dismissed.

[Other copies of this report: British Library MS. Hargrave 303, f. 84v.]

---

[1] Stat. 27 Hen. VIII, c. 10, ss. 4–7 (*SR*, III, 540–541).

British Library MS. Hargrave 80, f. 217v, pl. 2

Easter term 1715. Burton v. Rasby.

By articles before marriage, the estate of the wife, then an infant, was agreed in consideration of a suitable settlement on the part of the husband to be settled to the use of the husband and wife for their lives, remainder to the heirs of the body of the wife begotten by the husband. After marriage, a settlement was made and the estate was limited to the husband and wife for their lives, remainder to trustees to preserve contingent remainders, remainder to the first son etc. in tail, remainder to the heirs of the body of the wife begotten by the husband etc. The husband died without issue male. The wife enjoyed the lands settled by the husband and levied a fine of her own. And a daughter of the marriage brought her bill to have the benefit of the articles.

Mr. *Vernon*, for the plaintiff: If it had rested upon the articles and a bill had been brought for a specific execution, the court would have executed the articles according to the intent of the parties and in such manner. The estate should in all events come to the issue of the marriage and, though the articles have been carried into an execution by a settlement, the settlement is subsequent to the marriage. Where the settlement, as well as the articles, is precedent, the parties have been allowed to vary from the articles. But, where it is subsequent, it ought to pursue them precisely and to be controlled by them. Where it does not, the limitations in the settlement to the sons are agreeable to the intent of the articles, and the daughters are equally within the words 'heirs of the body of the wife' and ought to have had a limitation for their benefit equally certain.

Lord Chancellor [Lord Cowper] agreed to the case, but upon the articles only. But where a settlement is executed in the words of the articles, though after marriage, he inclined to think it too hard for the court to vary it and make it more strict. But, in this case, where the settlement is much stricter than the articles and the limitations to the sons made certain in all events, he declared he could not carry it any further. The infancy of the wife at the time of the articles he took notice of, but he did not rely chiefly upon that.

Another question was moved by *Sir Thomas Powys*, whether this settlement being made by the wife in consideration of an equivalent settlement made by the husband were not a purchase of the husband within 11 Hen. VII.[1]

But Lord Chancellor [Lord Cowper] ruled it clearly not to be and said it had been so ruled at law.

[Other copies of this report: Lincoln's Inn MS. Misc. 107, f. 61, pl. 2.]

---

[1] Stat. 11 Hen. VII, c. 20 (*SR*, II, 583).

75

Barker v. Robjent

(Ch. 1715)

A court of equity will not give relief to a younger child or to a daughter by supplying a defective conveyance if it will completely disinherit the heir at law.

British Library MS. Hargrave 77, f. 50v, pl. 2

27 May 1715.

The plaintiff's father was seised of freehold lands of about £30 *per annum* and which, on his marriage were settled on the issue male in tail, and he was possessed of some copyhold lands of greater value and a small personal estate. By a will, not having made a surrender, he devises his copyhold lands among his younger children, to each about £17 *per annum*, and he dies. The plaintiff married one of the daughters.

And she brought their bill to have the copyhold lands decreed *prout* the devise.

Sir Joseph Jekyll, for the plaintiff, insisted that the copyhold was entirely in the father's disposal and he was the best and most proper judge of what is most fitting for a portion for his children, that it was the course of this court to supply defective conveyances and want of surrenders in the case of creditors and younger children otherwise unprovided for, and, in the Case of Earing and Earing, the court had done [so], although, by that means, the heir at law was stripped, but, here, the heir at law has a full provision by the settlement.

On the other hand, it was said, if the court should supply the want of a surrender in this case, then the younger children would have a better provision than the heir at law.

Curia: To strip an heir at law and leave him destitute is against reason and the equity of this court. Therefore, let the Master first take an account of the estate, real and personal, that it may appear what provision there is for the heir at law.

[Other copies of this report: British Library MS. Hargrave 303, f. 87, pl. 2.]

76

Pitt v. Willis

(Ch. 1715)

Where a power is revoked before it is exercised, it is void.

British Library MS. Hargrave 81, f. 139, pl. 1

27 May 1715.

If a person be employed to transact a purchase and the question comes to be about notice, his answer, notwithstanding the general rule, shall be read as evidence against the party who employed him and though he is not brought on to hearing and that he be examined as a witness, so it was done in a great debate by Lord Somers in a cause between the Duke of Bolton and Sir Robert Clayton *et al.* Where he, by an answer, confessed the notice, this is a good agreement within the Statute of Frauds[1] and the like here before in the case of Coleman and Upcott.[2]

[Other copies of this report: British Library MS. Hargrave 82, f. 151, pl. 1, British Library MS. Hargrave 77, f. 37, pl. 1, British Library MS. Hargrave 303, f. 66v, pl. 1.]

British Library MS. Hargrave 80, f. 221v, pl. 1

Willys, by a letter to Foyle, recommended it to him to procure a purchaser of an estate at 2000 guineas. Foyle agreed with the plaintiff for it at that sum by parol only, and, by the plaintiff's directions, he wrote Willys word that he had so agreed. Then Willys, by another letter, expressed as earnest a desire not to proceed in the sale, after which Foyle made a memorandum of the agreement in writing upon the back of the first letter. And the plaintiff brought his bill against Willys for a specific performance.

Lord Chancellor [Lord Cowper] was of opinion that the meaning of the words of the Statute of Frauds 'thereunto authorized' is authorized to sign for the parties and that, in this case, Foyle's authority being revoked before he had signed the agreement and while it rested upon parol only, Willys was not bound by it, the parties having time until signing to consider whether they will abide by it or not. And he dismissed the bill.

[Other copies of this report: Lincoln's Inn MS. Misc. 107, f. 65.]

---

1 Stat. 29 Car. II, c. 3 (*SR*, V, 839–842).

2 *Coleman v. Upcot* (1707), 2 Eq. Cas. Abr. 16, 45, 22 E.R. 13, 39, *Upcott v. Coleman* (Ch. 1713), British Library MS. Hargrave 80, f. 147, pl. 1, Lincoln's Inn MS. Misc. 384, p. 7, pl. 1.

Dickens 24, 21 E.R. 175

27 May 1715.

The answer of a defendant, not brought to hearing, was read as evidence against another defendant at the hearing.

77

Williams v. Harstrong

(Ch. 1715)

A person who sues an administrator of a decedent's estate can have discovery of the assets of the decedent.

British Library MS. Hargrave 81, f. 140

28 May.

The plaintiff demanded money of the defendant as administratrix to her son, suggesting that he had employed the plaintiff as solicitor and prayed she might admit assets to satisfy the plaintiff's demands or set forth all the particulars. The defendant, by answer, set forth that her son employed another person in the cause in question as his solicitor and not the plaintiff and had paid him in full and taken his receipt and set it forth and that, upon a fair account, she doubts not to prove she had not assets to pay the plaintiff and the just debts of her intestate of a higher nature and of equal degree with the plaintiff's demands.

On exceptions, the court was of opinion that the answer was insufficient and that assets must be admitted or particulars set forth notwithstanding the bar to the plaintiff's demands and the objection that he ought to verify his demand and that he would not be at any prejudice for want of an admission or discovery, because, if he did verify, the court, at the hearing, would decree an account and the defendant to be examined for a discovery and that, otherwise, any person without any right or claim might bring a bill for vexation and to pry into a man's estate and affairs though he had nothing to do with it and harass and ruin an executor by this means.

[Other copies of this report: British Library MS. Hargrave 82, f. 152.]

[Other reports of this case: British Library MS. Hargrave 77, f. 37v, pl. 1, British Library MS. Hargrave 303, f. 67, pl. 1.]

78

Sutton v. Nightingale

(Ch. 1715)

A devise over is valid where the first devisee died before the testator.

Lincoln's Inn MS. Misc. 11, p. 23, pl. 1

28 May 1715.

Ralph Sheldon, by will, gives a one-third part of his personal estate to his wife and the other two-thirds to his two sons, Ralph and Gilbert, in different proportions, and he declared that, if either died before twenty-one, his share should go and be paid to A.B. Ralph died in his father's lifetime, and Gilbert died soon after the death of his father.

It was agreed by *Sir Joseph Jekyll* and not denied by anyone that, though Ralph died before his father, yet the devise over of his share was good and should take place, and so, he said, it was lately decreed by Lord Cowper in the case of lands, where a devise was to one for life with a remainder over to another; the devisee for life died in the life of the testator, and the estate was decreed to him in remainder.

Lincoln's Inn MS. Misc. 13, p. 31, pl. 1

28 May 1 Georgii. Sutton v. Chitty.

Ralph Sheldon, by will, devises one-third of his estate to his wife and the remaining two-thirds to his two sons, Ralph and Gilbert, and, in case his sons died under age, then he willed that one-half of their shares should go to his wife and the other half thereof to the plaintiffs, his sisters. And Ralph died an infant in the life of his father, and Gilbert, the other son, died an infant soon after his father's death.

The question was whether Ralph's share, he dying in his father's lifetime, was become a lapsed legacy and should be distributed according to the Statute,[1] as being undisposed of by the will or whether it should go over to the testator's wife and sisters, according to the will.

It was decreed the share of Ralph should go over and that the wife was entitled to one moiety and the sisters to the other moiety of the two-thirds devised to the children.

---

[1] Stat. 22 & 23 Car. II, c. 10 (*SR*, V, 719–720).

79

Taunt v. Newman

(Ch. 1715)

Where a defendant's attorney has been examined as a witness for the plaintiff, the defendant can nevertheless thereafter take the depositions of his own witnesses.

British Library MS. Hargrave 81, f. 141

3 June.

The defendant's attorney was examined as a witness for the plaintiff on a commission. The defendant joined in the commission but exhibited no interrogatories and now prayed for a commission to examine one Norris as a witness.

For the plaintiff, it was insisted that, by the rules of the court, where the defendant neglects to exhibit interrogatories, he was not entitled to a commission, that here it would be of dangerous consequence because the defendant's attorney having been examined had an opportunity of seeing the plaintiff's interrogatories and know what the plaintiff aimed at proving so he might instruct his client how to suit his evidence in opposition.

However, the court ordered a commission, the master settling the interrogatories, time, and place.

[Other copies of this report: British Library MS. Hargrave 82, f. 153.]

[Other reports of this case: British Library MS. Hargrave 77, f. 37v, pl. 2, British Library MS. Hargrave 303, f. 67, pl. 2.]

80

Crester v. Meaburn

(Ch. 1715)

An officer of another court who has the custody of a document can be ordered to produce it in court personally or by one of the parties.

British Library MS. Hargrave 81, f. 142

The cause arising in the County Palatine of Durham and a bond, which was the matter in question in the cause, being by order of court there deposited in the court and a bill touching those matters being brought here, Mr. *Mead* now insisted for the defendant that the officer in whose custody the bond was might deliver it to his client upon his security to return it safe.

Curia [Lord Cowper]: [There is] no precedent or example as he knew of for the doing of it, that this was like the case of courts that had the custody of wills, that this court might indeed order the proper officer to attend with the will, being satisfied for his trouble by the party that prayed the order. But he would not order the officer of that court to take security or terms to part with the will in their custody, and so is the court below here as to the bond. But, because of the great charge to have an officer come from Durham hither, he ordered it in the disjunctive and then he said the court there would have it in their own discretion and judgment to do what they should think most fit.

[Other copies of this report: British Library MS. Hargrave 82, f. 154.]

[Other reports of this case: British Library MS. Hargrave 77, f. 37v, pl. 3, British Library MS. Hargrave 303, f. 67v, pl. 1.]

81

Langston v. Langston

(Ch. 1715)

Where a London freeman settles upon his wife her own estate, upon his death, she can claim both her settlement and her customary widow's share.

Lincoln's Inn MS. Misc. 12, p. 192

In a cause depending in the Court of Chancery between Deborah Langston, widow and relict of Francis Langston, a freeman of London, plaintiff, and John Langston, the brother of the said Francis Langston, and others, the defendants, the case appeared to be that, upon a treaty of marriage between the plaintiff and Francis Langston, by an indenture dated the 29th September 2 Will. & Mar. [1690] reciting the intended marriage and that, upon stating the accounts between the plaintiff and the defendant Long, there remained due from him to the plaintiff £2200, it was agreed by the said indenture that the plaintiff should receive the interest of the £2200 to her sole use during her life without the intermeddling of the said Francis Langston, her intended husband, who was after her death to receive the interest of the £2200 during his life and, after his death, the £2200 and the proceeds thereof to go to the issue of that marriage equally and, for want of such issue, in trust for the survivor. Fo. 1 to 5.

On 4 February 1713[/14], the said Francis Langston made his will and thereby gave the plaintiff £1000 and all his plate, jewels, and household goods. And also he gave to the plaintiff for her life an annuity of £400 a year clear of all charges, and he charged all his personal estate with the payment thereof. Fo. 5, 6. The end of the plaintiff's bill was, *inter alia*, that she might have her customary part of his personal estate and also the £1000 and the specific legacies. And, in consideration thereof, she waived the benefit of the said annuity. Fo. 8, 9, and 13, 14.

The defendants put in their answers to this bill and, thereby, insisted that the marriage settlement ought to be taken as a composition for her customary part and that she was thereby debarred from demanding the same. Fo. 19 etc.

On 28 February 1714[/15], the cause was heard before the then Lord Chancellor [Lord Cowper], who declared that the plaintiff was entitled to the £2200, which was her own money before the marriage and the trust thereof kept up since the marriage articles except that the plaintiff permitted the testator to receive the interest thereof and that the same being the plaintiff's own estate, His Lordship [Lord Cowper] could not exclude her from her demand of her share of her husband's customary estate, as he was a citizen of London. And he did therefore order and decree that a clear moiety of the said testator's personal estate, after his debts and costs of suit were paid and all just allowances were made, should be paid to the plaintiff. And he likewise decreed her her widow's chamber and paraphernalia. And proper directions were given touching the accounts to be taken of the personal estate of the testator and touching the other matters in question in the cause.

From this decree, it may be observed that the reason of the plaintiff's having her customary share out of her husband's personal estate was because the settlement, by which the defendants would infer she was barred, was her own estate, whereas it seems pretty plain to be the Lord Chancellor's opinion that, if the estate settled upon the plaintiff had been the husband's, it would have been a bar to her claim of the customary part and, therefore, since, in the present case, the leasehold estate settled upon the widow, the now plaintiff, proceeded from the husband, we think the precedent may be material for us to show the opinion of the then Lord Chancellor in relation to the custom.

Lincoln's Inn MS. Misc. 384, p. 21, pl. 1

28 February.

The plaintiff's husband, being a freeman of London, before the marriage settled the plaintiff's own fortune on her. And, by his will, he gives her some legacies and a real estate. She brings her bill to have her customary share of his personal estate.

Vernon, for the defendant: If the husband had settled on the plaintiff out of his own estate, it had been a composition with her and she had been barred of her customary share.

Curia [Lord Cowper]: In this case, the plaintiff has only her own money settled, and, therefore, it is not the same as if the settlement had been out of her husband's estate. The plaintiff must have her customary share and her widow's chamber and paraphernalia if there be a surplus. But she shall take nothing by the will.

82

Parker v. Harvey

(Ch. 1715)

Where borrowed chattels are given to someone else upon a marriage, the recipient has the ownership of them.

Where a decedent's estate is insufficient to pay the debts of the decedent out of the personal estate, the real estate is chargeable before specific legacies.

A marriage contract is equivalent to a bond contract.

Lincoln's Inn MS. Misc. 384, p. 21, pl. 2

9 May 1715.

Lord Chancellor [Lord Cowper]: If a trustee make a purchase of lands with the trust money in his own name and die not leaving personal assets, the land purchased is not liable to the breach of trust.

If a *cestui que trust* of an estate tail in equity make a bargain and sale or other conveyance whereby he declares his intention to bar the entail, it will bar the issue in tail if the trustee refused to convey so as to make him tenant in possession, but not otherwise, for he ought first to apply to the trustee.

11 Viner, Abr. 181

Easter, 1715.

Where a husband borrowed of his sister jewels to present his wife on his marriage, Cowper, Chancellor, said this giving of them is a change of the property and a kind of sale in market overt, and, on a devise of real and personal estate for payment of debts, if the personal is not sufficient and the real be and the husband devises to her all her jewels etc., she shall have the specific legacy of her jewels.

[Other copies of this report: 2 Eq. Cas. Abr. 627, 22 E.R. 526.]

11 Viner, Abr. 292

Lord Chancellor Cowper: The grantor's covenant in a marriage settlement for him and his heirs that the premises were free from encumbrances shall come in equally with creditors on bond.

[Other copies of this report: 2 Eq. Cas. Abr. 460, 22 E.R. 392.]

83

Atkyns v. Waterson

(Ch. 1715–1716)

A jointure of lands settled on the wife of a London freeman is not a bar of her customary share unless it be so expressly stated.

Lincoln's Inn MS. Misc. 380, pt. 3, p. 145

Easter 1715.

A wife of a freeman of London [had] a jointure before marriage, which was said to be in bar of any dower which she might have a claim out of any land, tenements, or hereditaments, etc., but nothing was said of her customary part. And the question was whether such jointure should exclude her from her customary part.

Serjeant *Jekyll* cited a case of Hancock v. Hancock,[1] where, as he said, it was laid down as a rule by the Common Serjeant as the custom of London that a wife should in such a case be excluded even though the jointure was not said to be in bar of her customary part. And, in the case it was the wife's fortune was all in land and there was a covenant in the marriage settlement that all the personal estate, if there was any issue, should go to the issue and, if none, then over. So it was urged that it was intended the wife should have nothing but her jointure.

Dee, Common Serjeant, [said] he had looked into Coke and found it frequently entered there that the wife was compounded with before marriage so that he thought it was no question but the wife was barred. The only question used to be what should become of the wife's share. And the better authority was that it should be thrown into the estate and that the estate should go in moieties, and as the wife, where there are no children, should have half, so the children, where there is no wife, should have half.

Lord Chancellor [Lord Cowper] asked if it appeared in the books that the wife was compounded withal by having a jointure, which *Dee* could not say, else the composition might be of another kind.

Sir Thomas Powys, on the other side: Having dower is no bar. Why then shall having a jointure, which is but in lieu of a dower?

Lord Chancellor [Lord Cowper] said that the settlement should not bar any right that was consistent with it but, it being alleged to be the custom of London, there was no arguing against it. So he would have the case stated and the custom certified regularly. He said the covenant in the deed was nothing to the point, but it stood upon the single question whether a wife who had a jointure, as above, should be excluded of her customary part.

---

[1] *Hancock v. Hancock* (1707), 2 Vernon 605, 665, 23 E.R. 995, 1033, 1 Eq. Cas. Abr. 153, 21 E.R. 952.

On Friday the ninth of June, it came before the Lord Chancellor at his house upon the certificate of the custom, which was that, where a freeman before marriage settles lands upon his wife and it is said to be in bar of her share or customary part, then it is a bar by the custom, but where it is only in bar of dower out of his lands, tenements, hereditaments, in such case, they had no precedent where it was controverted.

Serjeant *Hooper* urged that, since there was no precedent, there could be no custom and, without a custom, the devise was void by which the personal estate was given away. He cited again the case of Hancock and Hancock. But, in that case, it was said in the decree, which was produced, that it appeared by articles that the wife could not have both, which articles not being there, the Lord Chancellor said nobody could tell how plain it might be by the words of the articles. It seemed to be agreed that a provision out of the personal estate was no bar to dower, but would be a bar of the customary part.

Lord Chancellor [Lord Cowper] declared his opinion that it should be a bar of no more than what it is said to be a bar of, *viz.* dower out of lands, tenements, and hereditaments, and nothing else. And he decreed accordingly.

British Library MS. Hargrave 80, f. 221v, pl. 2

The widow of a freeman of London having a jointure out of a real estate of her husband limited to her by deed before marriage in the usual words in bar of dower and the deed being silent as to her right to the customary part of the personal estate, she brought her bill for that. The single question was whether this jointure was a composition for it. It was said that, in the case of Hancock and Hancock, a jointure before marriage was certified by the Common Serjeant to be a composition, though there was no expression in the deed that it was intended as such.

Dee, the Common Serjeant, added that the reason of the custom was because the wife, by taking a certain provision before marriage in all events, implicitly declines the hazard of the increase or decrease of her husband's fortune. He added that the more difficult question had been what should become of the share of the wife when she was compounded with, that the entry in their books varied somewhere, that her third accrued to the husband's part, he being a kind of a purchaser of it. But the more frequent and the better were that it should go one moiety to the husband, the other to the children. And, in the case of Hancock and Hancock, it was determined that it should go in moieties.

Powys, e contra: The widow, if the deed were laid aside, would have both her dower and third. The jointure is substituted by the deed merely in the place [of it].

Lincoln's Inn MS. Misc. 12, p. 199, pl. 2

On a treaty of marriage between the defendant and her late husband, Edmund Waterson, deceased, indentures of lease and release of the 15th and 16th August 1696 were executed whereby, in consideration of the intended marriage and a £2000 marriage portion, lands to the value of £200 a year were limited to the defendant for life for her jointure and in full [satisfaction] of dower and title of dower to any lands, tenements, or hereditaments whereof or wherein her said intended husband was or should be seised of any estate of inheritance during the coverture between them.

The marriage takes effect. William Waterson dies, whereby some real estate and a considerable personal estate came to Edmund. Then Edmund makes his will, and, having no issue, he devises £500 to his wife and some other legacies the residue of his personal estate to be laid out in a purchase to be settled on the plaintiffs, who were his nephews. And he makes them his executors, and he dies.

This bill was brought against the widow for a discovery and account of the personal estate of Edmund Waterson and that it might be laid out in a purchase and settled pursuant to the directions of the will.

The defendant, by her answer, says that her husband was a freeman of London and that, he dying without issue, she, as widow, was entitled to a moiety of his personal estate as her customary share, there being no child. And whether she was so entitled or not was the single question.

On 23 May 1715, the cause was heard before the Lord Chancellor [Lord Cowper], who sent it to the City to be certified whether the husband's settlement of lands on his wife in bar of dower and thirds out of lands only be a bar to the wife's claim of her part by the custom.

It was certified that, if a freeman dies leaving a wife and no child, the personal estate ought by the custom to be divided into two parts, one whereof the freeman might devise, the other belonged to his widow. But yet, if a freeman makes a settlement of land before marriage declared to be in lieu of her share of the personal estate by the custom, such settlement is a bar of her claim of the personal estate. But, when it is expressed to be only in full [satisfaction] of dower and thirds out of land, whether it shall be a bar to the claim of the customary share of the personal estate is submitted to the court, there [has] been no instance wherein the like case had been controverted.

On 6 June 1716, upon this certificate, the court declared that, of common right, the widow, being entitled to a moiety of the personal estate, had accepted the jointure only in bar of her claim out of the real estate and, accordingly, decreed her a moiety of the personal estate.

Note this settlement was of a real estate only in bar of dower out of lands, on which the custom could not operate, and, therefore, it could not be a bar to the widow's claim to her customary share. But it was admitted at the hearing that a settlement out of the husband's personal estate had been a bar without express words.

British Library MS. Hargrave 81, f. 42

6 June 1716.

The plaintiff's late husband, upon his intermarriage, being a freeman of London, makes a settlement of about £200 *per annum* in lands as jointure upon the plaintiff, which is thereby declared to be in bar of all dower and claim of thirds out of his lands, tenements, and hereditaments. And she, notwithstanding, brings her bill for the widow's part according to the custom.

And, upon the hearing of this cause, the counsel for the defendant insisted that, by such a settlement, the plaintiff barred herself of her customary part of her husband's personal estate and that the same ought to be disposed of according to his will. And he said that such a settlement amounted to a bar by the custom of the City.

The court, therefore, referred it to the Lord Mayor and aldermen to certify whether such a settlement did by custom amount to a bar. And the Lord Mayor and Court of Aldermen, being attended by counsel and long debates thereof, did certify to the Lord Chancellor that, where a freeman died without issue, his widow had a customary right to a moiety of his personal estate unless she had by some act barred herself of that right and that, if a woman marrying a freeman accepts a settlement and it therein declared that the same is in bar of all custom, it is a good bar. But, where lands are settled and declared to be in full of all dower and claim of thirds out of any lands, tenements, or hereditaments, the said court do not find any such point controverted in their books and, therefore, leave it as a matter proper for His Lordship's judgment.

Sir Joseph Jekyll, for the defendant: The reason of the custom is because it is supposed that a freeman's estate is mostly personal and constantly employed in trade and a woman who marries a freeman embarks her fortune, which is sink or swim. But where a woman accepts a jointure in land, she then stipulates or compounds for her customary part and makes sure of her future provision in all events. The certificate leaves it as they found it. They find no such point controverted in their books, i.e. they do not find such custom that, where a wife accepts such a bar as this is, she can yet come and claim her customary part. If no custom stands in our way, as, by this certificate, we apprehend that it is pretty clear there does not, why then the testator by the law had an absolute right to dispose of his personal estate as he thought fit and then the testator's will must stand.

Mr. *Cooper*, for the plaintiff: Upon the hearing of this cause before, Your Lordship seemed to be clearly of opinion for us that the declaration in the settlement, *viz.* in bar of all dower and claim of thirds out of his lands, tenements, and hereditaments did not amount to a bar of the plaintiff's claim to her customary share.

But the counsel of the other side being very positive that, by the customs, it was a bar and that there were precedents for it, Your Lordship did request the Lord Mayor and Court of Aldermen to certify the custom in this case, and they certify they find no such point controverted in their books why then there is no such custom, that is the custom is silent, which is a negative proof for us that it has been always the constant method without any dispute that, in such a case, the widow has a right to her customary share. And, therefore, we are to stand upon the first part of the certificate that, where a freeman of London died without issue, his widow has a customary right to a moiety of his personal estate unless she has done something to bar herself and it not appearing, as indeed it cannot, that such a settlement and declaration as this was ever construed to amount to a bar, by the custom, we are entitled to a moiety of our husband's personal estate by the custom over and besides the said lands settled as aforesaid.

Mr. *Lechmere*, of the same side: Dower is a right every widow has to the thirds of her husband's lands and has no relation at all to the custom of London. Therefore, a bar of all claim of dower out of lands, tenements, and hereditaments can never be supposed to extend to be a bar to her customary right. But we are entitled to a moiety of the personal estate by the custom, we having done nothing to deprive us of it. Besides, were it necessary, which indeed I think it is not, our case being strong enough without it, there are a great many circumstances which would very much corroborate our claim. We brought a very large fortune, though it is not material whether we had any at all, to about £20,000 in money and £300 a year in lands and our late husband felled timber from our estate to almost £4000 value and, for all this, we had settled on us no more than barely £200 *per annum*, but, in that settlement, our husband's father, who was then looked upon to be worth £20,000 in money, expressly covenants that he will leave it all to his son, so that it is plain there was then a very good view and prospect of a considerable personal estate under consideration. But our case is so strong that we had no need of these circumstances. There is a custom in our favor unless barred by some act of ours, and we not having done any which, by the custom, can bear such a construction, we are in the common case and entitled to a moiety of the personal estate.

Mr. *Mead*: I conceive bar of dower and thirds out of lands etc. can no more extend to a bar of the personal estate than a bar of all claims to the personal estate can be construed to extend to the real.

Lord Chancellor [Lord Cowper]: This declaration in the settlement is certainly a very good bar of any claim of thirds which the widow might have had out of the lands of her husband and, if it had said in bar of all dower and claim of thirds and left it there, it might be doubted whether it would not extend to the personal estate too. But, as the words have confined it to the real estate and there being no custom whereby such a declaration was ever construed to extend to a bar of the personal estate, I do not, see any foundation for me to carry farther. And the widow must have a moiety according to the custom.

Note there was a clause in the husband's will whereby he gives his widow £500 and his coach and horses. This legacy her counsel waived at the first hearing. But after the court had pronounced the above decree, *Sir Thomas Powys* said, if they had a mind to go into it, they had a good right to that legacy, to which *Sir Joseph Jekyll* answered that it was the doctrine of this court either to establish a will or defeat it wholly and they, having set it aside as to part, could not now come to claim any benefit thereby.

Lord Chancellor [LORD COWPER] was of that opinion [and] said the plaintiff might have chosen the one or the other, but could not have both.

There was also some plate which the plaintiff's father had given to her mother for life and afterwards to the plaintiff and, they living altogether, the mother gave the plaintiff and her husband leave to use it and the husband without the mother's knowledge had exchanged some of it for new; the plaintiff claimed this now, her mother being dead, as not being any part of her husband's personal estate. But the LORD CHANCELLOR was of opinion that the changing of the plate altered the property and the husband thereby became entitled.

[Other copies of this report: British Library MS. Hargrave 82, f. 39.]

Lincoln's Inn MS. Misc. 384, p. 23, pl. 3

6 June 1716.

A jointure of lands settled on the wife of a freeman of London is not a bar of her customary share unless it be expressly mentioned.

[Other reports of this case: British Library MS. Hargrave 77, f. 12, British Library MS. Hargrave 303, f. 20v, Gilbert Rep. 94, 25 E.R. 65, 1 Eq. Cas. Abr. 157, 21 E.R. 956.]

84

Newling v. Abbott

(Ch. 1715)

Where a mortgagee in possession makes permanent improvements on the land, he is entitled to be reimbursed for two-thirds of their value.

Lincoln's Inn MS. Misc. 380, pt. 3, p. 144

Easter term 1715.

The defendant's testator married an heiress, who had an estate that was in mortgage and to which, having issue, he was entitled as tenant by the curtesy. Ten years after, he paid off the mortgage and took an assignment of it to trustees for himself. It appeared that he had improved the estate by money laid out upon it from £16 to £100 *per annum*, all or most part after the assignment. The testator died having first devised his interest in the premises to the defendant, against whom the heir at law of the wife brings a bill to redeem. And the question was how the defendant should account, i.e. what allowance should be made for these lasting improvements.

The Lord Chancellor [Lord Cowper] was first of an opinion that the defendant testator having two rights in him and being in possession not as mortgagee but in the right of his wife and after as tenant by the curtesy and after the assignment of the mortgage having made no special entry to denote that he even then was possessed as mortgagee that he should naturally have been presumed to have laid out his money for the benefit of the family that might enjoy it and so should have no allowance made. But he, at last, directed that, the defendant testator being entitled to the equity of redemption for life which was to be computed to a third part of the value of the inheritance, one third part of the improvements should sink and that the other two-thirds of the improvements should be allowed to the defendant, the devisee, with interest from the time it arose to a gross sum of £100, but the interest during the life of the tenant by the curtesy to be kept down.

By the Lord Chancellor's first opinion, he gave the defendant his election in which right he would account, either, as mortgagee and, in such case, to be allowed for lasting improvements but then to account as mortgagee for the overplus profits, or else to account as in right of the tenant by the curtesy and, in such case, to have all the overplus profits to himself but to be allowed nothing for improvements. But he decreed as above.

British Library MS. Hargrave 80, f. 220

A man married a woman seised in fee of lands of £16 *per annum* subject to a mortgage of £200, which he, afterwards, took an assignment of, and, by lasting improvements, increased the value of the lands to £100 *per annum*.

In this case, Lord Chancellor [Cowper] decreed that, as tenant for life, he was obliged to keep down the interest, that, for the improvements made before he took an assignment of the mortgage, he was not entitled to any allowance, having acted then as tenant for life only, that, for what sums he expended in lasting improvements after the assignment, he was entitled to be reimbursed two-thirds with interest from the time they were laid out, the remaining third falling upon his estate for life.

British Library MS. Hargrave 77, f. 49v, pl. 1

Newlington, father of the plaintiff and the wife, mortgages the wife's lands, of which she was seised in fee for a term of years. And he dies leaving issue two daughters, the plaintiff and one of the defendants. Afterwards, she marries one Dromwicke. The estate was then but £16 *per annum*. And B. lays out money in improving the estate; afterwards, he takes in the mortgage and, being in possession, lays out very considerably on the estate and improves it to £100 *per annum*. His wife dies. Afterwards, he devises all his estate to the defendant and makes him executor. He proves the will.

The plaintiff, as one of the co-heirs of Newling, the mortgagor, brings her bill to redeem, suggesting that, by the perception of the profits, he was more than satisfied.

The question was how the redemption should be.

The plaintiff insisted that the defendant as representing B. must account for the whole rent and profits from the time of his taking the profits, *viz.* his marriage with the widow in regard it was a forfeited mortgage before or, however, if considered as a tenant for life or by the curtesy, he ought to keep down the interest during the coverture and not have any allowance in respect of his improvements because they were laid out for his own fancy and benefit and for the advantage of his children and family.

Curia: B. had at times two several capacities, one as owner or proprietor as tenant for life or by the curtesy. And, as such, he is only to keep down the interest and not to account for the surplus profits or have an allowance for improvements. They are to be looked upon as done for his own fancy or benefit. And he is compensated by the improvements or surplus profits. The other is as a mortgagee, having taken the mortgage. As such, he shall have an allowance for all necessary repairs and lasting improvements. But he must account for the whole profits.

But he cannot take in both capacities at once. He may have either if the heirs at law would redeem, they must pay two-thirds of the principal, interest, and costs in respect of the improvements and the tenant for life one-third.

[It is] so decreed here the Master to take an account of the whole rents and profits from the time the mortgage was assigned to B. and of the principal and interest and what he laid out in necessary repairs. And as it came at any time to £100, the Master is to carry interest from that time and to tax costs, the plaintiffs, the heirs at law to pay the defendant two-thirds of all his principal and interest and he, as representing the tenant by the curtesy to bear that other third.

[Other copies of this report: British Library MS. Hargrave 303, f. 85v.]

1 Viner, Abr. 185

Easter term 1 Geo. [1715].

A feme sole, seised of lands in fee subject to a mortgage, marries A., who, about ten years after, pays off the mortgage and has it assigned over to B. in trust for himself. And he lays out a considerable sum in improvements upon the estate. And, having issue, two daughters by his wife, he makes his will and devises these lands to his youngest daughter, and dies. The wife survives and holds the lands for her life.

And, after her death, the eldest daughter and her husband bring a bill against her sister and co-heir to redeem a moiety of these lands. The great question was upon what terms and in what manner the plaintiff should redeem, for, if the account was to be taken as between a mortgagor and mortgagee in possession, then the devisee must account for the profits received by the devisor and be allowed for repairs and lasting improvements. But, if, in this case, the devisor should be judged in possession by right of his wife, and not by virtue of the mortgage, then the devisee was not to account for the profits, nor have an allowance for repairs and improvements, but only to have interest allowed from the father's death, for then it would be the common case of a tenant for life of lands in mortgage, who is obliged to keep down the growing interest during the continuance of his estate, and he shall not have any allowance for the improvements.

COWPER, Chancellor, decreed that there should be no allowance for improvements by the husband before he took an assignment of the mortgage, but, from that time, the devisee should have an allowance of the two-thirds of the lasting improvements, but nothing for the other third, because he received the benefit of the improvements during his life, according to the usual proportion between an estate for life and the reversion in fee, and that no interest should be allowed during the devisor's life, for a tenant for life is bound to keep down the interest during his estate.

[Other copies of this report: 2 Eq. Cas. Abr. 596, 22 E.R. 501.]

85

Beal v. Beal

(Ch. 1715)

In this case, the court refused to order lands to be sold in order to support infant children whose father was dead but whose mother was living.

Lincoln's Inn MS. Misc. 380, pt. 3, p. 146

Easter term 1715.

The plaintiff's father was tenant for life, remainder to such woman as he should marry, for life, for her jointure with a power to the father to charge the estate with £2000 for younger children's portions and, after his decease, by deed or will to be paid in such a manner as the father should appoint. The father, by will, appoints the portions to be paid at eighteen or marriage and no interest or maintenance was appointed in the meantime. The bill was brought on the behalf of the younger children in their infancy to have a sale. And the defendant in this case was an infant as well as the plaintiff.

Peere Williams cited the case of Greenhill and Waldo,[1] where, in a marriage settlement, a trust of a term was to raise such a sum of money, with all convenient

[1] *Greenhill v. Waldoe* (Ch. 1713), Precedents in Chancery 367, 24 E.R. 166, Gilbert Rep. 31, 25 E.R. 22, 2 Eq. Cas. Abr. 146, 640, 22 E.R. 125, 537, British Library MS. Hargrave 80, f. 142v.

speed, and to be paid at eighteen, a daughter entitled to the portion applied to the court; no interest was decreed, but some maintenance was allowed.

Lord Chancellor [Lord Cowper]: The charge seems by the words to be precedent to the wife's estate, for it is after the death of the husband, not of the husband and wife. But it being said for the jointure of the wife seems to intend otherwise; else it is not a jointure.

Serjeant *Hooper* urged that the money is not really payable until eighteen or marriage, yet it may be raised sooner that the interest may go for maintenance in the meantime.

The Lord Chancellor [Lord Cowper]: Supposing it was payable at present, how can a sale be decreed against an infant? Without doubt against one of full age, it might. But what foundation have I to decree interest until the portions are payable? It is not an immediate charge so that it shall go to the representatives. But the wife, having the profits of all the estate for life, may afford to maintain the children.

I reserve the consideration whether or no, in case the children should arrive at the age of eighteen, it then should be raised in the lifetime of the mother until that accident happen.

[Other reports of this case: Precedents in Chancery 405, 24 E.R. 182, 1 Peere Williams 244, 24 E.R. 373, Gilbert Rep. 93, 25 E.R. 64, 2 Eq. Cas. Abr. 639, 22 E.R. 536.]

86

Challis v. Casborne

(Ch. 1715)

A court of equity will not supply the lack of a surrender of copyhold lands in favor of a decedent's creditors where there was no express devise of those copyhold lands.

A question in this case was whether, when lands are devised to the testator's executors for the payment of his debts, all the creditors will be paid ratably.

Lincoln's Inn MS. Misc. 11, p. 22

16 June 1715.

A man, by his will, devises all his real and personal estate to his executors for the payment of his debts. And he dies seised both of freehold and copyhold lands, but he had made no surrender to the use of his will. And the question was if the copyhold passed by the will and if the court, in favor of creditors, would not supply the defect of a surrender.

Lord Chancellor [Lord Cowper] would not supply the defect of a surrender as this case was, the copyhold not being expressly devised, but it only passed under general words so that it was not certain whether the testator ever intended his copyhold lands should pass by his will.

Another question was, where lands are devised to the executors to be sold for the payment of debts and the land is sold, whether the money shall be applied to pay the debts in a course of administration according to the nature of such debts or whether all the debts shall be paid ratably, share and share alike, as it was agreed they would be if the lands had been to trustees and not to the executors.

Mr. *Vernon* said the court had always made a distinction between a devise of lands to a stranger for the payment of debts and a devise to the executors, for, when the devise is to the executors and the land is turned into money, even at law, that money is personal assets in the hands of the executors and must be applied as other personal assets.

But Lord Cowper seemed to be pretty clear that there was really no difference and that, in both cases, all the creditors ought to be paid ratably. However, he reserved the consideration of that point until after the Master had made his report.

Lincoln's Inn MS. Misc. 384, p. 22, pl. 2

18 June.

A mortgagee cannot tack his mortgage to a bond against a devisee of the mortgagor for payment of debts as he may against the heir of the mortgagor. Where lands are devised to executors for the payment of debts, they must be paid in the course of administration. But, where they are devised to trustees for the payment of debts, all the creditors must be paid equally. Where there is a devise of all his real and personal estate for the payment of debts, query whether copyhold lands pass without a surrender.

Lord Chancellor [Lord Cowper]: I think they will not unless the intention of the testator appear plainly.

British Library MS. Hargrave 77, f. 50v, pl. 2

18 June. Hinson v. Casborne.

First query, how the money paid the plaintiff should be applied, if to the bond or the mortgage.

Second, whether the bond debt should be tacked to the mortgage.

Third, whether the surviving executor shall be charged for others' account, not because his executor admits assets.

Fourth, bonds paid if [it] will pay the executor's creditors by bond [and] by note.

Sir Joseph Jekyll, for the plaintiff: John Casbern, the mortgagor, by a letter, promises the mortgagee to give what security for his bond debt he was able because, if not, here, in the case of a rent, a devisee is in the same case as the heir at law and must pay the bond as well as the mortgage. In the mortgage, 'all other his lands' are general words. By those general words, leaseholds etc. pass and are parcel of the security.

Curia [LORD COWPER] *e contra quoad* the devisee: In the Statute of Fraudulent Devises,[1] there is a saving clause as to devises for the payment of debts. That is the case here, and the bond cannot be tacked to the mortgage. The letter is no lien.

Mr. *Lutwyche*: As to the mortgage assigned, the party entitled to equity did not join in the assignment. The interest paid cannot carry interest.

Curia [LORD COWPER]: If the Master finds anything difficult, state it specially.

Mr. *Vernon*: By the will, all his real and personal estate is devised to be sold for the payment of debts. By this, the copyhold passes in equity, because a want of a surrender will be supplied in equity in the case of creditors.

Curia [LORD COWPER]: Where a copyhold is expressly devised, the want of a surrender shall be supplied. But to construe general words that are capable of a legal sense should be construed into an illegal sense is too hard. A copyhold is not real or personal. Where there is a devise to executors to sell lands, the moneys by sale are legal assets.

[Other copies if this report: British Library MS. Hargrave 303, f. 87v.]

[Other reports of this case: Precedents in Chancery 407, 24 E.R. 183, Gilbert Rep. 96, 25 E.R. 67, 1 Eq. Cas. Abr. 124, 325, 21 E.R. 930, 1078.]

87

Archer v. Archer

(Ch. 1715)

One defendant's testimony can be used as evidence by a co-defendant.

British Library MS. Hargrave 81, f. 143

22 June.

Dr. Corbett, one of the defendants in the original cause, was examined on interrogatories as a witness for the other defendant, Sir Hewet Archer, by order saving just exceptions. It was now at the hearing said that, though a plaintiff might examine one or more of the defendants for him, yet one defendant could not be examined for the other because that was in a manner swearing for oneself, being both of the same side; it was a precedent of dangerous consequence.

Of the other side, it was said to be usual for that the plaintiff made whom he pleased defendant. And they were passive and could not help being made so. And, though several may be made parties to the same bill, yet their defense may be several and independent one of the other. And, if so, a defendant might by the

[1] Stat. 3 Will. & Mar., c. 14 (*SR*, VI, 320–321).

act and contrivance of the plaintiff be stripped of his defense if another defendant who perhaps is his only witness might not be examined for him.

And the court allowed the doctor's depositions to be read.

[Other copies of this report: British Library MS. Hargrave 82, f. 155.]

[Other reports of this case: British Library MS. Hargrave 77, f. 38, pl. 1, British Library MS. Hargrave 303, f. 67v, pl. 2.]

88

Anonymous

(Ch. 1715)

A common injunction to a plaintiff in an action at common law will be continued in force until the plaintiff at common law responds adequately to a suit in equity for discovery that relates to the action at law.

British Library MS. Hargrave 82, f. 156

The defendant insured with the plaintiff a ship and goods and, afterwards, the ship was lost. And he coming on the insurers and putting their policy in suit and preparing for trial, they brought their bill for relief and to have a discovery what goods with the particulars and values had been put on board that ship at the time of signing those policies and obtain an injunction until answer and further order.

The defendant put in his answer, to which the plaintiff excepts, and the defendant moves for and obtains an order that an injunction should be dissolved unless the plaintiff show the insufficiency for cause and procure a report in a certain time, which they do in time. And now, they pray that the injunction may extend to stay the trial, for so it would have been ordered if the defendant had been in contempt; so an attachment for want of an answer. And here, it being reported insufficient, it was the same as if no answer had been put in, and, then, long before this, he would have been under an attachment, which has been avoided by the contrivance of an insufficient answer and, therefore, ought to be taken as if under that process.

Mr. *Vernon*, for the defendant, [said] that this indeed was good cause to continue the common injunction but not to extend it to stay the trial by which the defendant was to justify his demand.

Baron Price took the plaintiff's objection not to be a general rule but that, in this case, unless the exceptions taken were material to the plaintiff's defense at law, there was no color for extending the injunction to stay the trial. And, therefore, he ordered that, if there were any such execution, it might be opened, which was done, *viz.* that the defendant had not answered whether he had any goods on board nor the particulars nor value, which he allowed to be material, for this was proper for the plaintiff's defense at law and could only come from the defendant's answer and, otherwise, it would be in vain to attempt any defense at law.

[Other copies of this report: British Library MS. Hargrave 81, f. 144, pl. 1.]

[Other reports of this case: British Library MS. Hargrave 77, f. 38, pl. 2, British Library MS. Hargrave 303, f. 68.]

89

Rex v. Bromfield

(Ch. 1715)

When an agent of a defendant is made a co-defendant, his answer cannot be read as evidence against the other defendant, his principal, but he ought to be examined as a witness.

A release of land does not release any encumbrances thereupon.

An oral promise to indemnify a bail is not within the Statute of Frauds.

British Library MS. Hargrave 81, f. 144, pl. 2

18 July.

When the agent of the defendant in a matter in question is made a co-defendant, though he was the agent, his answer cannot be read as evidence against the other defendant, his principal, but he ought to be examined as a witness.

And, if lands be charged with legacies or an annuity or rent charge, a release of the lands will not release the legacy etc. which were collateral to the land and, as it would not do it at law, so neither here at equity.

The plaintiffs were bail at law for the defendant Cullington, and Robert Cullingham verbally promised to indemnify them if they would become bail. This promise is not within the Statute of Frauds and Perjuries[1] and, therefore, is binding.

[Other copies of this report: British Library MS. Hargrave 82, f. 157.]

[Other reports of this case: British Library MS. Hargrave 77, f. 38v, pl. 1, British Library MS. Hargrave 303, f. 68v, pl. 1.]

1 Stat. 29 Car. II, c. 3, s. 5 (*SR*, V, 840).

90

Bagen v. Rogers

(Ch. 1715)

In this case, the devise in issue created a debt to be distributed to the devisee's next of kin.

British Library MS. Hargrave 81, f. 83

18 July 1715.

John Rogers, seised in fee of several lands, had issue two sons, John and Thomas, one daughter, the plaintiff, Mary. And, by his will, he devised part of his lands to his youngest son Thomas, and his heirs forever, provided that, if John paid Thomas £80 at his age of twenty-four years, the said lands shall go to John and his heirs. And he dies leaving both his sons infants. John attains his full age and enjoys the lands devised to Thomas with his own and takes Thomas home and maintains him to the time of his death, which was in the year 1682. He leaves a widow and one child only, which is the present defendant, John, an infant of about two years old in the year 1683. Thomas attains his age of twenty-four. The widow continues the possession of the lands devised to Thomas together with those of her sons and pays Thomas £4 *per annum*, which he constantly accepts. The widow dies, and the infant's guardian continues the possession and the payment of the £4 *per annum* and so did the defendant himself after he came of age until Thomas died, which was in 1712. During all this time, the £80 was not paid or demanded.

And Thomas having died without issue and intestate, the plaintiff, who was his only sister, takes out administration and so brings her bill for the £80 and interest or that the defendant, the heir at law, may be foreclosed and the land sold and she paid principal, interest, and costs out of the money arising thereby, insisting that the £4 *per annum* was paid as interest not as rent for the land, which was the question, the defendant saying that the £4 was a rent only paid for the land and that the devise to Thomas being in fee and he dying without issue, the land descended to him as heir at law.

At the hearing, it was insisted for the plaintiff that the devise to Thomas with condition to be paid a sum of money by the heir at law was in the nature of a mortgage to secure him the payment of so much money as a portion or provision for him and, therefore, the heir at law ought to be compelled to redeem or be foreclosed or the land, at his election, decreed to be sold. And it was said that the £4 *per annum* being paid as a rent was a mere pretense without any foundation, for the land was worth at least £7 *per annum* and the £4 a year was the interest only of the £80, the money intended to be secured by the devise, so that it was evident that the £4 *per annum* was paid as interest and not as rent.

[*blank*] for the defendant: It was said that the lands were devised to Thomas directly in fee and the proviso only gave an option or liberty to John, if he thought fit, to take the lands upon paying £80 to Thomas at his age of twenty-four, and John dying before Thomas had attained that age and the liberty or option, being restrained to John and being personal, determined with him and consequently the fee became absolute in Thomas discharged of the proviso. But suppose it was not but that the liberty of election subsisted after his death, that yet the payment by his widow, who had no interest in the land, cannot bind or be conclusive upon the defendant, who was an infant, and the option or liberty of election while subsisting might have been discharged by bill. Yet Thomas could not have compelled his brother if living to have paid the money and, therefore, there being not a charge subsisting on the land when Thomas died, the plaintiff can have no demand as administrator to Thomas against the defendant, who claims as heir to him.

Curia [Lord Cowper]: While Thomas was living and might have given away the land if it was not in the nature of a mortgage, then the defendant would have it a mortgage, because more worth than the money. But now he is dead, the defendant would have it an absolute estate and that the £4 *per annum* was paid only as a rent that so he may have it as heir and pay nothing. But the witnesses say the payments were for interest not as rent and that the defendant owned he owed his uncle £80 so that he then looked upon it as a mortgage debt. It was then said for the defendant that, if it was a subsisting debt, it must be in a course of administration and subject to a distribution and the defendant, as one of the next of kin to the intestate, is entitled to a moiety of the principle and interest by virtue of the Statute of Distributions[1] and that he was in the nature of a creditor to the estate for what was due to his father for the maintenance of Thomas and that he was to be paid before any distribution, which was allowed.

And the court decreed an account of interest, principal, and costs for the plaintiff, the defendant to have all just allowances and to have a moiety [of] the principal and interest of the distributary part.

[Other copies of this report: British Library MS. Hargrave 82, f. 80.]

[Other reports of this case: British Library MS. Hargrave 77, f. 21v, pl. 2, British Library MS. Hargrave 303, f. 41v.]

1 Stat. 22 & 23 Car. II, c. 10 (*SR*, V, 719–720).

91

Gillingham v. Hopkins

(Ch. 1715–1716)

The question in this case was whether the evidence of a single witness can overcome the contrary evidence of an answer put in under oath in a case of fraud.

British Library MS. Hargrave 77, f. 51, pl. 2

18 July.

The bill was to have satisfaction for money as belonged to one Watkins, the plaintiff's intestate, who was accidentally burnt in his own house, and, particularly, fifty guineas said to be delivered to the defendant the next day after the fire.

She, by an answer, denied having these guineas. One witness only charged her with them contrary to her oath.

But his evidence being very circumstantial and upon probability, the court would not decree upon this single evidence against her answer nor wholly reject it. And, therefore, it retained the bill and ordered the plaintiff to proceed at law and the bill and answer to be made use of at the trial as the bill and answer, not as evidence by [*blank*] of this court.

Memorandum, about the beginning of May 1716, upon an appeal from the Rolls, the appellant's counsel very much insisted and wholly depended upon the rule that a single evidence could not found a decree upon or against an express answer. But it appeared plainly to be a great fraud on the appellant's part. It was overruled, and the decree for the plaintiff was affirmed.

[Other copies of this report: British Library MS. Hargrave 303, f. 88, pl. 2.]

92

Fazackerly v. Hoar

(Ch. 1715)

In this case of a deposit or a trust, the consignment was to have been in England, and the English rate of interest was applicable.

British Library MS. Hargrave 81, f. 88

19 July.

The plaintiff, being in India, delivered to one Harvey, President of Carwart, several parcels of gold and silver specie to invest in goods and consign to the plaintiff's direction, for which Harvey gives the plaintiff a note acknowledging the receipt thereof and promising to invest the same in goods and consign them as the plaintiff should direct. And twenty months after this, Harvey dies in India. And, by his will, he makes the governors of Christchurch Hospital and his sister Lydia his executors. And the defendant Lockington, by order of the Court of Directors of the India Company, proves the will for their interest. And the other defendant, Hoare, is President of the said Hospital. The plaintiff, being now in England and possessed of the said note, brings his bill against the defendants as representatives of Harvey for satisfaction for the value of the gold and silver and for the damage or loss sustained by their not being invested which might have been hundreds per cent or at least to have foreign interest, the transaction being in foreign parts where the interest is greater than here.

For the plaintiff, it was insisted that, if no part of the gold or silver were invested, the plaintiff might have lent or paid it to the India Company and have had £50 per cent advance upon the return without running any hazard and, if invested and consigned were a hazard would have been run if the goods had come home safe, the profits might have [been] treble or more and it was Harvey's fault they were not invested and it would be hard to make the plaintiff suffer for his neglect and that, therefore, he should have the interest of the place where the transaction was since, without all doubt, the plaintiff might have made that of his money. And, for that, they relied on the Case of Lane and Nicholls, in this court and afterwards in an appeal confirmed in the House of Lords, where there was an account current between two merchants, partners in Turkey, and no account settled in their lifetime; after the death of one of the partners, the suit was brought and a balance found and, for that balance, foreign, *viz.* Turkish, interest was decreed here and by the Lords.

For the defendant, [it was said] there was no debt or contract between the parties in India but, at best, a deposit or trust, which remained under the party's own conusance, and for aught the defendants could know or be apprised of might have been executed by Harvey or discharged by the plaintiff in India and, probably, so it was, considering the great length of time that Harvey lived after this deposit in which the plaintiff being all that time in India would certainly have called for his effects again or ordered consignment or remission to him from Carwart if Harvey had not before discharged his trust. Therefore, it were hard they who were strangers and had not the assistance of Harvey's books and papers or an opportunity of enquiring into the truth of the case in order to make their defense should pay foreign interest and that, if Harvey really did make an investment and consignment, they were not answerable for principal or interest, though the whole were lost.

Curia [Lord Cowper]: This differs from the case of Lane and Nicholls for, there, the partnership and dealing were in Turkey. The partnership determined there, and the balance ought to have been paid there, and, then, it would have produced Turkish interest. But, here, the consignment was to have been in England and the party in England comes for satisfaction of money which he should have received there. He must have, therefore, such interest only as is given here and, as the plaintiff may have had the deposit made good to him or the trust may have been executed or discharged and the defendant not being in any condition to make it out, especially before they can inquire into the testator's books and papers, the plaintiff must be examined upon interrogatories whether he has received any satisfaction for the said pieces of gold and silver or any and what part thereof or knows whether the said money or any and what part thereof had been invested or paid out.

[Other copies of this report: British Library MS. Hargrave 82, f. 84.]

[Other reports of this case: British Library MS. Hargrave 77, f. 22v, British Library MS. Hargrave 303, f. 43.]

93

Riely v. Plant

(Ch. 1715)

Where a party refuses to produce evidence which is in his power to produce, it will be presumed to be against him and his interests.

British Library MS. Hargrave 77, f. 23, pl. 2

21 July 1715.

The plaintiff, a poor old woman, was in possession of a cottage built on a waste. The defendant knows it was so [and] purchases it of her and gives one Goodwin a bond in trust for her to pay her 30s. *per annum* during her life. Afterwards, the lord of the manor brings [an action of] ejectment to stop this cottage as being on his waste and erected without his license. And he has a verdict by the consent of the defendant. But no notice of the suit [was given] to the plaintiff to come in and defend the title.

The matter between the lord and the defendant being reserved to arbitration, the defendant is awarded to pay the lord £6 and to take a lease of him of the cottage. And thereupon, Goodwin delivers the defendant his bond, and he stops paying the annuity.

And for the arrears and to compel payment for the future, this bill is brought. The defendant, by an answer, admitted the purchase and the bond was delivered up. And he insists on his eviction as a bar to the annuity. And the counsel alleged that the payment was to be only while he quietly enjoyed and not during the plaintiff's life in all events and that she had not proved the agreement or bond to be so. The defendant, being requested to produce the bond to clear this matter, pretended it was lost, burned, or cancelled.

Curia: If so and you will not produce it and since it is admitted and proved that it was delivered up to you, I will presume the case against you and to be as laid by the bill. Therefore, he decreed an account and payment of the arrears and payment of the annuity *in futuro* and the defendant to pay costs.

[Other copies of this report: British Library MS. Hargrave 303, f. 45, pl. 1.]

94

Guise v. Saunders

(Ch. 1715)

Where two co-executors jointly give a receipt for the testator's estate, they are both chargeable.

British Library MS. Hargrave 81, f. 92

23 July.

If two executors act jointly in giving a receipt for money, part of the testator's estate, and though one only receives it, however they divide it, yet both shall be chargeable. But, if one only gives the receipt and receives or only receives without giving any receipt, that one only shall be charged.

If an executor or administrator has a decree for principal, interest, and costs and, before he receives the whole, assigns the security for or conveys the estate charged with the same, he shall be answerable for the residue, for he is to account for what he did or might have received and he not being compellable to part with the security instead of it, it is at his own peril and he must be answerable for the whole in all events.

[Other copies of this report: British Library MS. Hargrave 82, f. 89, pl. 1.]

[Other reports of this case: British Library MS. Hargrave 77, f. 23v, pl. 1, British Library MS. Hargrave 303, f. 45, pl. 2.]

95

Burgess v. Trinder

(Ch. 1715)

Debts that are contracted before the making of a will are satisfied by the payment of a legacy made by the debtor.

Lincoln's Inn MS. Misc. 11, p. 12, pl. 3

27 July 1715.

Serjeant [Henry] Trinder having received the rents and profits of an estate of his brother charged with £350 and £50 for his daughter Dorothy and having put his son, the defendant, into possession of that estate and covenanted to indemnify him against those two sums and having also received the sum of £80 as her share of the personal estate of one Mr. A.B., her mother's brother, he makes his will and gives his daughter £1000 to be paid at twenty-one with £60 a year maintenance in the meantime. But he takes no notice of his will of these sums.

Dorothy assigns her legacy to the plaintiff and then makes her will and makes the plaintiff executor and residuary legatee, and she dies.

He brings his bill to have satisfaction of the legacy and the other moneys. And if he should have both was the question.

Curia: The debts being contracted before the making of the serjeant's will and the legacy being more than the debts, it merges the debts and must be taken in satisfaction of these debts. But, if the serjeant has not left assets to satisfy the legacy, then the £250 and £50 with interest is to paid out of the trust estate charged with those sums and the plaintiff is to come in as a creditor as to the £80 and have a satisfaction thereof out of the serjeant's estate.

96

Thomson v. Lord Haversham

(Ch. 1715)

Specific performance will not be ordered for a contract that lacks consideration.

Specific performance will not be ordered for a contract to present a candidate to a rectory.

British Library MS. Add. 35990, f. 120v

3 August. At the Lord Chancellor's house upon pleas and demurrers.

The defendant, being heir apparent to his father, the late Lord Haversham, who was seised of the manor of Haversham with the advowson of the parish church appendant, covenanted with the plaintiff for divers good causes and considerations to present the plaintiff's son to that church upon the first avoidance that should happen after the said advowson came to him, either as heir at law to his father, by a settlement, or otherwise. The father died. The defendant became seised of the advowson, and the avoidance happened.

And now the plaintiff brought his bill, setting forth this agreement and that it was made by the defendant of his own free will and accord, that, in confidence thereof, he, the plaintiff, had bred his son to literature and at the university and that he had taken orders, that he had required His Lordship to perform his agreement and he had refused and would present another or suffer a lapse. And so he prays a specific performance.

To this, the defendant demurred.

And the Lord Chancellor Cowper, after consideration, allowed the demurrer for these reasons:

First, for that there was not any valuable consideration for this covenant set out in the bill, but, on the contrary, it was expressly alleged to be entered into 'of the defendant's own accord', so it appeared to be only a voluntary agreement and, therefore, not within the rule of equity to be carried on into a specific execution in this court;

Second, for that it would be dangerous in point of precedent to encourage agreements of this nature for that they are liable to great abuse by tutors over their pupils etc. and, therefore, this court ought not to enforce a specific execution of them, neither ought they to have any other effect than the law of the land gives them, at which the plaintiff may take his remedy by an action on the covenant.

Note Mr. *Vernon*, for the plaintiff, took a difference, that, where a voluntary conveyance without a valuable consideration was made defective, Chancery would never assist to perfect and complete it, but, of a voluntary agreement to do an act, it would enforce a specific execution, e.g. if a voluntary conveyance was made with a covenant for further assurance, the court would oblige to a performance of that covenant.

But, upon this, Lord Chancellor [COWPER] gave no opinion.

Lincoln's Inn MS. Misc. 11, p. 24, pl. 1

3 August 1715.

The plaintiff brought his bill to have a specific performance of an agreement made by the defendant in his father's lifetime, whereby the defendant, for divers good causes and considerations, agreed with the plaintiff that, when an estate which was settled on the defendant after the death of his father and to which an advowson was belonging should come into possession, that he would grant the plaintiff the next presentation of the living, to which bill the defendant demurred.

Lord Chancellor [LORD COWPER] took time to be attended with precedents. But none being produced which came up to this case, he now gave his opinion that the demurrer ought to be allowed, first, for that this was a naked promise without any consideration, second, an agreement of this nature ought not to have the aid and countenance of this court, for it may tend to the encouraging of young gentleman to grant presentations to their tutors and to make other contracts and conveyances of this nature.

97

Anonymous

(Ch. 1715)

A married woman can sue her husband in the Court of Chancery, and the court can order the husband not to hinder such a lawsuit.

British Library MS. Add. 35990, f. 121v

8 August. At the seal at the Lord Chancellor's [house].

H. died whereby an estate came to his sister, who was a married woman. And the husband, under pretense of getting a letter of attorney from her, surreptitiously got some kind of conveyance to himself from her.

And then he brought his bill in Chancery for discovery of the title deeds and to be let into possession without naming his wife a party, whereupon she brought her bill alone, setting forth the whole matter and praying relief. Upon this, the husband used her so ill that she was forced to go and live with her brother. And, upon affidavits that he threatened to seize and confine her wherever he found her and that he had made some attempts of that sort, the court was now moved by Mr. *Cowper* that he might be ordered not to seize or confine his wife, which was opposed by *Sir Joseph Jekyll*, for the husband, for that it would be to enjoin a man from having the consortium of his wife and pronounce a sentence of separation by an order of Chancery.

The Master of the Rolls [TREVOR] (*absente* the Lord Chancellor) declared he could make no order that the husband should not seize his wife, but he would order that he should do nothing to prevent or hinder her from prosecuting this cause, for that, as a suitor to the court, she was under the protection of it. And he said he did it upon this foundation, that Chancery allowed a woman to bring a bill against her husband and would oblige him to pay the charges of that suit in order to enable her to carry it on. And since the court could do that, by parity of reason, it would restrain him from doing any act to disable her from pursuing it.

98

Ellington v. Paggen

(Ch. 1715)

The expenses of mourning clothes given to a decedent's servants who attend the corpse to the grave is very proper part of the funeral expenses.

Where a substantial sum of money is in issue, the matter should be proved by witnesses other than the party himself.

British Library MS. Hargrave 81, f. 98

25 October.

J.S. devises to Ann Motlow, an infant, £50 at her age of twenty-one and, afterwards, by a codicil, directs that interest should be paid her for the £100 given her by the will. And the question was what Ann should have, whether, by the codicil, the legacy should be enlarged into an £100 or only as no interest was to be paid by the will, the legacy being *in futuro* and contingent, now, by the codicil, the interest of £100 should be paid for her benefit towards maintenance.

Sir Joseph Jekyll [said] that the codicil could not enlarge or increase the legacy given by the will, because it was apparently a mistake and might be probably the error of the writer, there being no such legacy in the will as mentioned in the codicil, and the devise by the codicil not being independent of itself, but relative and referring to the will, must either be void entirely or be governed and confined to what is really in the will and so construed interest for the £50 given by the will. And he cited a case in this court, the Lady Warren, daughter of Sir Thomas Middleton, who had £2000 given her by a relation, and Sir Thomas, by his will taking notice of the former devise but not expressly mentioning the sum, devises to her £1000 to make up what was given her £10,000. Here, there was an express devise of £10,000 as the mistake appeared and the testator's intent was plain that, in the whole, she should have £10,000. Yet it was by the court reduced to £80,000.[1]

Curia [Lord Cowper]: I have heard it litigated among the civilians that such a devise or legacy is void because founded on a falsity. But, here, the principal question is not before me. The legatee is not of age, and, therefore, if I order but £50 to be laid by to answer this future legacy, I determine the matter before it is proper and without hearing the party and so do an act that may be injurious. I will rather, therefore, do a cautionary act of justice by ordering £100 to be laid by until the legatee be of age to claim his[2] legacy and litigate the quantum.

There was another question in this cause touching an allowance to executors for funeral charges. The testator, by his will, left it entirely to the discretion of his executors to bury him as they thought fit. The defendant Paggen alone took

[1] Sic in MS.

[2] Sic in MS.

upon himself the management of the funeral and expended £120, part of which charge consisted in three or four items of about £4 each to the testator's servants who attended the funeral for mourning. And the Master refused to allow those as not being funeral charges and because the proof thereof was only the defendant's own oath.

Curia [Lord Cowper]: The allowance of mourning to the decedent's servants, especially such as attend the corpse to the grave, is very proper and decent and much more so than burnt wine and gloves and ought to be allowed, especially where there is such a power and latitude to executors as here. And, though it be done by one of them only, yet it is well done.

But here wants proof of the fact. Here is only the party's oath, and the sums are each above 40s. and so not within the rules of the court to be allowed on the party's oath. He might have made better proof by examining the parties who had the mourning or those who made it up for them. And the rules of the court must be observed as well in a small matter as in a great for the sake of justice. And it is better the defendant should lose some small sums than that the rules of the court should be broken into. And, therefore, he overruled this exception.

[Other copies of this report: British Library MS. Hargrave 82, f. 94.]

[Other reports of this case: British Library MS. Hargrave 77, f. 24, British Library MS. Hargrave 303, f. 47.]

99

Buckwell v. Packer

(Ch. 1715)

It is a contempt of court to marry a lunatic without leave of court.

A wife's personal estate, though never in her husband's possession, belongs to him at common law and can be seized by his creditors.

Lincoln's Inn MS. Misc. 10, p. 234

9 November 2 *Georgii*. Buckwell *et al.*, creditors of Philip Packer v. Isabelle Packer, administratrix of Philip Packer *et al.*

Philip Packer having married Mrs. Anne Ash, a lady of £10,000 fortune, who was under a commission of lunacy, complaint was made thereof to the court, and he was thereupon committed to the Prison of the Fleet, after which the commission of lunacy was superseded and Mr. Packer was discharged. And upon an offer made by him to make a settlement on his wife, an order was made the 19th of March 1702 that Mr. Packer should settle all his estate in Kent and Sussex with the approbation of the Master to the use of himself for life, then to his wife for life, then to the issue of the marriage as usual, with remainder to his own right heirs. And such lands were to be discharged of encumbrances out of the portion and the remainder of the portion was to be at his disposal. And he was to take it from the Master before whom it had been brought during the commission of lunacy.

Mr. Packer never made this settlement; so the portion or the securities for it continued in the hands of the Master, and a great part of it was placed out by him upon government securities. And several subsequent orders were made for the payment of the interest. Mrs. Packer relapsing into her former lunacy, the commission against her was renewed. And Mr. Packer becoming a lunatic also, a commission was taken out against him, and, during such lunacy, he died intestate. And the defendant Isabella took administration, after which Mrs. Packer, who survived her husband, died intestate, and the defendant Windham is her administrator.

The plaintiffs, who are creditors of Mr. Packer by bond and judgments, bring their bill for a satisfaction of their debts out of his assets and insist that the wife's fortune that was in the hands of the Master was liable to the payment of their debts. And, on the other hand, the administrator of the wife insists that the fortune never vested in Mr. Packer, he having never made a settlement according to the order of the 19th of March and, therefore, being under the control of the court and continuing in the Master's hands until Mr. Packer's death, it survived to the wife and is not assets for payment of his debts.

Curia [Lord Cowper] declared the order of the 19th of March was out of the case, that order having not been performed, that, although this court will not help a husband to get his wife's portion without he makes some provision for her, yet, where the husband obtains the legal possession of his wife's portion, this court will not take it from him, that, although a security for a wife's portion be a chose in action and not assignable in law, yet, where the money is paid in on such security in the life of the husband, it becomes his money and, therefore, as to Bacon's mortgage, which was paid in during the coverture, although it was paid into court, yet the same ought in all respects to be looked on as the receipt of P. Packer, the husband, this court, having only according to the common usage of the court laid hold of it in order to see some provision made for the wife and the issue of the marriage, but she being now dead without issue and there being, therefore, no occasion for such provision, His Lordship [Lord Cowper] declared that the money paid in on Bacon's mortgage ought to be looked on as part of Mr. Packer's personal estate and, as such, liable to the payment of his debts.

And, therefore, it was decreed that the money received on that mortgage together with the produce of it should be paid by the Master of the defendant Isabella to be applied in a course of administration. And as to the jewels and goods of the wife, His Lordship was of opinion that such of them as were in her possession or in the possession of any other in trust for her at the time of her marriage or during the coverture are also part of P. Packer's personal estate save as to the jewels. If on the account, it shall appear that Mrs. Packer was entitled to her paraphernalia and, if any of the jewels were in the hands of her committee, the same are to be looked on as in her possession.

And His Lordship [Lord Cowper] declared that, as to all bonds given before the marriage for any part of the wife's fortune, though in the custody of her trustees or of this court, the same did survive to the wife upon the death of the husband and are no part of his personal estate unless the moneys were received or the securities altered during the coverture.

[Related cases: Packer v. Wyndham (Ch. 1715), see below, Case No. 100.]

100

Packer v. Wyndham

(Ch. 1715)

Where a wife dies without issue, her personal property goes to her husband because, where the equities are equal, equity follows the common law, but it is otherwise as to the wife's real property.

Lincoln's Inn MS. Misc. 380, pt. 3, p. 147

Michaelmas term 1715.

Mrs. Anne Ash, who had been a lunatic, married Mr. Packer. And she having a considerable fortune to the value of about £10,000, consisting of two mortgages, a bond, and some jewels, of which the court or the committee by the court's direction had the custody. The court would not let Mr. Packer have her fortune but upon some term of making a reasonable settlement upon her, there being no settlement or articles upon the marriage. Mr. Packer thereupon proposed to settle £500 *per annum*, but his estate being encumbered even to as much as it was worth, no such settlement was ever made. In the meantime, one mortgage of £5500 was without any compulsion fairly paid in, and the Master took the money and, by the direction of the court, put it out again upon government securities. The other mortgage Mr. Packer assigned to creditors. The bond continued as it was, and the jewels were all the time in the custody of the committee. Mr. Packer died, and then the wife died without issue. The question was what should become of the first mortgage money that was so paid in and put out again and of the bond and jewels, the other mortgage being at present, as the Lord Chancellor said, out of the case and not before the court.

It was urged by Mr. *Vernon* that Mr. Packer having in defiance of the court married a lunatic and the court having the custody of her estate and the terms he had offered being unperformed, though the first mortgage money was paid in, yet the court had its hands upon it and it should go to the wife as survivor as a chose in action and not to the husband's executor. And he cited a case of Burdett and [*blank*], in 1700,[1] where a mortgage did in like manner survive to the wife (but it seems that that was a mortgage in fee), though it had been assigned by the husband. He cited also the common case of the Chamber of London where a man that marries an orphan without leave cannot by any act he can do touch her fortune, and sometimes the court will fine the orphan's husband to the value of the fortune.

And *Lechmere* said, as to the jewels that were jewels or other personal estate are not in the wife's possession but in the possession of another, that they are as much choses in action (that the possession of them is not recovered by the husband and wife in the husband's lifetime) as a bond or a mortgage.

The Lord Chancellor [LORD COWPER] said, as to the mortgage which was paid in and the money put out again, it ought to go to the executors of Mr. Packer and not survive to the wife, for the equity in a case ought to follow the law. He said he should look upon the marriage to be a fair marriage and he could lay no penalty upon the husband on that account. And what is the equity the court has over the money no other than this, the court can oblige him that comes for equity to do equity, and, therefore, since Mr. Packer could not come at this money, being in the custody of the court, without the aid of the court, this court, before it will help him to the money, will oblige him to make some reasonable settlement upon his wife and children, so that, when the money is paid into court, it is paid for the use of the husband but subject to that equity. Now, when the wife is dead without issue, that equity ceases as much as if there had been such a settlement made. And where shall it then go? Why the equity shall follow the law, and it shall go to the husband's executors. It seems to me that, since no equity would in such case require a settlement further than upon the wife and her issue and there is no issue, the remaining must of course go to the husband as it would do if a settlement had been made, so, in like manner, where none is made.

As to the bond, the Lord Chancellor [LORD COWPER] said it should survive to the wife and go to her executors etc., for, there being no alteration of the property by calling in the money or otherwise, it is the wife's. And the equity in that case shall follow the law too.

As to the jewels, the Lord Chancellor said that, if they had been in the possession of another by tort and that tort had continued during the coverture, it might indeed have been a question whether they had not been a chose in action as much as a bond and so have survived to the wife. But the possession of the court or committee is the wife's possession and, consequently, the property of them vested in the husband by the marriage and they shall go to his executors.

As to the Case of Burdett, he said, that being a mortgage in fee, the husband could not by any act he could do assign it as he might have done a term for years and, for that reason, the mortgage could not but survive to the wife.

[1] *Burnett v. Kinnaston* (1700), 2 Vernon 401, 23 E.R. 860, Precedents in Chancery 118, 24 E.R. 57, 2 Freeman 239, 22 E.R. 1183, 1 Eq. Cas. Abr. 69, 21 E.R. 882.

[Other reports of this case: Precedents in Chancery 412, 24 E.R. 184, Gilbert Rep. 98, 25 E.R. 68, 2 Eq. Cas. Abr. 138, 583, 22 E.R. 118, 491.]

[Related cases: Buckwell v. Packer (Ch. 1715), see above, Case No. 99.]

101

Bertie v. Lord Falkland

(Ch. 1715)

Where an order of the Court of Chancery is appealed to the House of Lords, the House of Lords enforces its own orders unless the lower court is expressly directed so to do.

British Library MS. Hargrave 81, f. 106

10 November 1715.

This suit was originally for relief against the breach of a condition. Mr. Carie, who was uncle to the plaintiff's wife, having devised his estate at [. . .] to trustees for her during her life in case that, in three years after his death, she married the Lord Guildford, if not, then in trust for the Lord Falkland. The three years passed after the testator's death and she not married to the Lord Guildford and, afterwards, she marries the plaintiff.

The bill, at the hearing in 1698, was dismissed, and, upon an appeal, the Lords decreed the trustees should convey the premises to the use of the appellants for their lives and, after their death, to the Lord Falkland and his heirs.[1] But no such conveyance was ever made, nor was the decree of dismission ever drawn up. Mr. Bertie had several children by his lady, who was then lately dead.

And now the Lord Falkland, by his counsel, moves in this cause that the order of dismission may be entered *nunc pro tunc*, conveyances made, and possession delivered to him together with all deeds and writings belonging to the same. And they urged the cause having been appealed from this court to the Lords and they having relieved the appellants, it was the office of this court to carry the decree of the Lords into execution and that notwithstanding the abatement by the death of Mrs. Bertie.

Of the other side, it was said that, the suit being abated, His Lordship could not move in this cause until it was regularly revived, which was not yet done. Besides, if it were, the court has nothing to do with the matter because the Lords had not left nor ordered anything in it to be done by this court, which had no power to execute the Lord's decree further or otherwise than the Lords gave it power by a particular order.

Curia [Lord Cowper]: This court does not usually direct upon application that orders should be entered *nunc pro tunc* while the parties are living for

[1] *Bertie v. Viscount Falkland* (1697), Colles 10, 1 E.R. 155.

the sake and advancement of justice because, if living, the parties interested may have an opportunity of seeing that the order or decree be fairly drawn up and entered. But, if after so great a length of time as eighteen years, I should do it in this case, the heirs or issue of Mrs. Bertie, who, for aught I can take notice of, may be interested, are not before the court and so I might injure them unheard. But the matter in itself is not before the court. This court is not to execute all the decrees of the Lords or their decrees in every article, but only such and so far as the Lords themselves direct and send down to this court to do or where they cannot do it of themselves, as where, upon an appeal, an account is ordered, this court, in that case, must carry on the account and execute the Lords' decree without any particular directions because the Lords do not take accounts nor have officers nor persons for that purpose. But in other cases, as the Lords have a supreme jurisdiction, so they have a power of executing their own decree and enforcing obedience to them and punishing any breach of their orders by commitment etc.

The application, therefore, must be to them. Besides, here, the Lord's decree is not a bare varying or reversal of the decree below. But it is an original decree of their own. The suit here was for relief against the breach of a condition that they may have the estate notwithstanding Mr. Bertie's marriage to the plaintiff Bertie as if the marriage had been with the Lord Guildford. This court thought they could not be relieved. The Lords, on the appeal, have said they shall have the estate for their lives without taking any notice of the will and then to Lord Falkland, which is quite a new settlement and limitation by this decree, and, as nothing is by it referred to the court, this court has nothing to do in it. And, if the application made here were made to the Lords, it is very likely you would have the same answer that the heir is not before them and ought to be heard. The proper way, therefore, is to apply to the Lords in Parliament setting forth all this matter and praying that the heir may be ordered to show cause, if he can, why the Lord Falkland should not have possession etc.

[Other copies of this report: British Library MS. Hargrave 82, f. 116, pl. 2.]

[Other reports of this case: British Library MS. Hargrave 77, f. 29, British Library MS. Hargrave 303, f. 54, 3 Chancery Cases 129, 22 E.R. 1008, 2 Freeman 220, 22 E.R. 1171, 1 Salkeld 231, 91 E.R. 205, 2 Vernon 333, 23 E.R. 814, 12 Modern 182, 88 E.R. 1248, Holt K.B. 230, 90 E.R. 1026, 1 Eq. Cas. Abr. 110, 21 E.R. 917, Colles 10, 1 E.R. 155, Dickens 25, 21 E.R. 176.]

102

Dagley v. Aubery

(Ch. 1715)

An executor of a will should not pay a legacy to the parent of an infant legatee.

Lincoln's Inn MS. Misc. 380, pt. 3, p. 149

[Upon] an appeal from a judge, the case was [this]. A man, by his will, gives a legacy of £100 to an infant. It appeared by the proofs that, after he had made his will, he said it might be paid to the infant's father, and, accordingly, the executor paid it honestly to the infant's father. Sixteen years after, the infant comes of age, and, becoming a bankrupt, the bill was brought by the assignees.

The Lord Chancellor [Lord Cowper] said eighteen years' acquittance without more would be a presumption of the infant's approbation of the payment.

But it appeared by the proofs that the infant, after he came of age, threatened to sue the executor. The father told him he had honestly paid him £100 and therefore desired him not to trouble the executor and he would keep the £100 and make it £200 for his fortune, whereupon the son acquiesced. But the £200 was never paid, both the father and son becoming bankrupt.

The Lord Chancellor said that showed the acquiescence to be *sub modo*. And, the terms not being performed, he confirmed the judge's decree that the legacy should be paid over again.

Gilbert Rep. 103, 25 E.R. 72

Saturday, 12 November 1715. Dawley v. Ballfrey.

A legacy of £100 was devised to an infant of about ten years of age. The executor paid the legacy to the father and took his receipt. When the infant came of age, the father told him he had such a legacy of his in his hands, but could not pay it immediately, but, however, he would not have him trouble the executor about it, for he would give him £200 for it. Upon this, the son rested satisfied for about fourteen or fifteen years. And he and his father carried on a joint trade together and then became bankrupts. And, upon a commission taken out against the son, this legacy of £100 was assigned, among other things, for the benefit of the creditors. And the plaintiff, the assignee of this commission, brought this bill against the executor to have an account and payment of this legacy.

For the defendant, it was insisted that it would be a hardship on him if he should be obliged to pay it over again, that he had already fairly and honestly paid it to the father whilst he was in good circumstances, and, if application had been made to the defendant sooner, he might have had his recompense over against the father, that the father was the natural guardian of his children and such payments to him have formerly been allowed good, 1 Chan. Ca. 245,[1] though, indeed, the court has thought fit to extend their care for such children farther and disallowed such payment, but, from the circumstance of this case, it was hoped that the defendant would not be answerable for it.

My Lord Chancellor [LORD COWPER]: If the father had not made the son such a promise and the son had required the money in time, the case might have been more doubtful. But this promise of the father drew him in from applying to the defendant sooner, and, since the father had not, nor could not, make good his promise, being a bankrupt likewise, the reason of the son's forbearance was at an end. And he thought the rule of this court in not suffering parents to receive their children's legacies was founded on very good reasons. And, therefore, lest this case might be cited hereafter as a precedent, when the circumstances attending it were forgotten, and to discountenance and deter others from paying such legacies to the parents, though he did not deny the hardship of this particular case, he affirmed the former decree against the executor, this being upon a rehearing.

[Other reports of this case: *sub nom.* Dagley v. Tolferry, 1 Peere Williams 285, 24 E.R. 391, 1 Eq. Cas. Abr. 300, 21 E.R. 1061.]

103

Taylor v. Dixon

(Ch. 1715)

A contract for the sale of land can be set aside on the ground of an inadequate consideration.

Lincoln's Inn MS. Misc. 11, p. 54

15 November 1715.

The bill is brought by the plaintiff, an infant, to be relieved against a fine and deed to lead the uses, the fine being levied by the plaintiff's father and mother and she being an idiot.

The defendant pretends he bought the estate of the plaintiff's father and mother for £50.

Master of the Rolls [TREVOR]: There is no relieving against this deed without setting aside the fine.

Mr. *Cowper*: Why then there is no being relieved where there is a fine in the case.

Master of the Rolls [TREVOR]: No more there is not. It is pretty hard to avoid a fine; however, I think the plaintiff ought to be relieved. And what I go upon is

[1] *Holloway v. Collins* (1675), 1 Chancery Cases 245, 22 E.R. 782, also 1 Eq. Cas. Abr. 300, 21 E.R. 1060.

the smallness of the consideration, which was but £50 and the land is proved to be worth £200. And, by the measure which the Lord Nottingham used to go by in such cases, the plaintiff ought to be relieved.

104

Seal v. Seal

(Ch. 1715)

A court of equity can direct the administration of a decedent's estate according to the terms of his will.

Lincoln's Inn MS. Misc. 11, p. 13

16 November 1715. John Seal, by prochein ami, plaintiff; John Seal, Thomas Seal, and Germain Seal, defendants.

John Seal, the plaintiff's uncle, by will, gives the plaintiff and his heirs his lands in Jersey, and he directs that, in case he should not dispose of his money in the government, that his government securities and other like money should be sold and laid out in lands to the value of £300 or £400 a year. And all the rest of his estate, as well real as personal, after his debts and funeral charges paid, he gave to the plaintiff and his heirs male, remainder to the defendant Thomas and his heirs male, remainder to the defendant Germain and his heirs male. And he made the defendant John Seal executor.

The questions were how much land should be purchased and how settled and whether the residue of the personal estate ought not to be laid out and settled in such a manner as he had entailed such surplus.

Lord Chancellor [Lord Cowper] declared that the testator having distinguished his government securities and moneys of a like nature, which His Lordship took to be Bank or East India [Company] bonds, Exchequer bills, or the like, from his other moneys and his directing £300 or £400 a year to be purchased, which are words of limitation, show that he conceived his government securities and moneys of a like nature to be more than sufficient to purchase £300 a year and might be sufficient to purchase £400 a year. And, in regard the testator's government securities and other moneys of that nature are sufficient to purchase £400 a year, let lands of that value be purchased. And, since the testator has given the residue of his real estate as well as his personal to the plaintiff and his heirs male with remainders over to the defendants successively, let the lands be settled to those uses.

It was insisted on for the defendants that the lands should be settled on the plaintiff for life with remainders to his first and other sons in tail male etc., as is done in cases of marriage articles. But the court would go no farther.

As to the surplus of the personal estate, that was decreed to the plaintiff, for, since there was no direction in the will to invest it in land, My Lord [Lord

COWPER] said he could not say it was the testator's intention it should be so. And, in regard he has taken upon him to entail it in a manner that the law will not allow, it must be paid to the plaintiff when he comes of age. In the meantime, let it be brought before the Master and put out for his benefit.

[Other reports of this case: Precedents in Chancery 421, 24 E.R. 188, 1 Peere Williams 290, 24 E.R. 393, Gilbert Rep. 105, 25 E.R. 73, 2 Eq. Cas. Abr. 38, 346, 716, 22 E.R. 33, 294, 602.]

105

Demainbray v. Metcalf

(Ch. 1715)

Where a pawnee pawns the pawner's goods, even though the original pawner had no notice of the second pawn, the first pawner cannot redeem unless the creditors of the second pawner have been satisfied.

Lincoln's Inn MS. Misc. 11, p. 23, pl. 2

16 November 1715.

The question was if a pawn should be redeemed without paying the pledge not only the money that he had lent on the pawn but whatever else was due to him from the pledgor.

LORD COWPER decreed it should not, for, being only a personal pawn, it is in the nature of an account and not like a mortgage of lands where the mortgagee, after his mortgage, lends more money upon bond, for, by the Statute of Frauds etc.,[1] there can be no charge upon the lands but by a writing.

British Library MS. Hargrave 81, f. 110

If a man pawn jewels or plate to a goldsmith or jeweler for £100 and, before the time for redemption be out, the goldsmith, unknown to the owner, pawns those with others of his own or other people's for a greater sum and, by not mentioning this last pawn, promises payment of the money at a certain time and, afterwards, the goldsmith borrows a further sum of the same person on his note payable on demand and, afterwards, a further sum payable in three months and, in neither of those, takes notice of the pawn and, before the time of the first redemption, he became a bankrupt, the owner of the first jewels shall not redeem them from the last pawn without paying all the several sums, but the goldsmith's own plate shall in the first place be applied to discharge them and as much as that proves deficient, the first pawner must make up and pay to have his goods again.

[1] Stat. 29 Car. II, c. 3 (*SR*, V, 839–842).

Lord Chancellor [Lord Harcourt] cited 1 Car. 97, Sir John Holdford's Case,[1] and said that this was different from a case of lands, that, had the defendant bought those jewels in Knight's shop, that had been buying in a market overt and would have bound the property and barred the petition. It cannot be intended that, having the jewels in his own hands, he would lend any more money without an agreement that they should stand as a security for that also, and he has sworn it, though, indeed, this agreement was not proved.

Goldsborough: There must be four notices unmoved before the other can insist to have cost or object to the parties' being heard for want of having moved according to his notices.

[Other copies of this report: British Library MS. Hargrave 82, f. 122.]

[Other reports of this case: British Library MS. Hargrave 77, f. 30v, pl. 2, British Library MS. Hargrave 303, f. 56v, 2 Vernon 691, 698, 23 E.R. 1048, 1052, Gilbert Rep. 104, 25 E.R. 72, Precedents in Chancery 419, 24 E.R. 188, 1 Eq. Cas. Abr. 324, 21 E.R. 1077.]

106

Waring v. Danvers

(Ch. 1715)

An executor may prefer to pay one creditor of an equal degree before another.

Lincoln's Inn MS. Misc. 11, p. 2

21 November 1715. Wareing v. Danvers, executors of Smith, and several others, creditors of Smith. Master of the Rolls.

The plaintiff, being a creditor of Smith, files an original against the executor. And he serves him a copy of it and demands his debt. Then he takes out a special *capias* against the executor, who having appeared, the plaintiff delivers a declaration and gave rules to plead. And, before the rules were out, the executor confesses judgments to all the other creditors, and then he enters into an agreement with them that the executor, who was also a creditor, should retain his whole debt and that all the rest of the assets should be divided among all the creditors except the plaintiff ratably, share and share alike. And then, the executor pleads these judgments to the plaintiff's action at law, whereupon the plaintiff exhibits his bill to be relieved against these judgments and the agreements as being fraudulent and that he might be paid his debt out of assets.

And it was insisted on for the plaintiff that the executor, after an original was filed, ought not voluntarily to have confessed judgments unless there had been actions really brought against them, much less ought he to have entered into any agreements with the other creditors to exclude the plaintiff. And, therefore,

[1] *St. John v. Holford* (1668), 1 Chancery Cases 97, 22 E.R. 712.

it was prayed that the judgments and agreements might be set aside or, at least, that the plaintiff might come in and have a satisfaction equally with the other creditors.

But, to this, it was answered by Mr. *Vernon* than an executor might prefer one creditor of an equal degree before another. It is true he cannot pay a creditor after an action is brought by another. If he does, such payment will not be allowed. But he may confess a judgment to one creditor after an action brought by another and then pay that judgment, and such payment will be good. And, therefore, the executor's having confessed the judgments in question and since paid them as far as the assets will extend, he has done no more than what, by law, he might, and such payments are good against the plaintiff.

As to the agreements, it was the plaintiffs's own fault he was excluded. He might have come in with the other creditors if he had pleased. But he refused (and so it is proved) and insisted upon his whole debt.

And, for these reasons, the bill was dismissed, but without costs.

Afterwards, upon an appeal to Lord Cowper, the decree was affirmed.

Note Mr. *Vernon* cited Lord Oxford's Case, in Lord Keeper Wright's time, and affirmed in the House of the Lords.[1] The question there was whether an executor might confess a judgment at law to one creditor after a bill brought here by another, and it was held he might, as well as he might confess a judgment to one creditor after an action brought at law by another.

[Other reports of this case: 1 Peere Williams 295, 24 E.R. 396, 2 Eq. Cas. Abr. 257, 460, 22 E.R. 218, 392.]

107

Amery v. Jackson

(Ch. 1715)

Debts entered into by a bankrupt after an adjudication of bankruptcy but before the discharge are not discharged.

Lincoln's Inn MS. Misc. 11, p. 7

25 November 1715. Amery v. Jackson and Gerard.

The plaintiff being a bankrupt and having been discharged by a certificate, he brings his bill to be relieved against a note given by him after the taking out of the commission, on which Jackson sued him at law,[2] suggesting that the note

---

[1] *Darston v. Earl of Orford* (1701), Precedents in Chancery 188, 24 E.R. 91, Colles 229, 1 E.R. 262, 1 Eq. Cas. Abr. 10, 21 E.R. 834, 2 Eq. Cas. Abr. 460, 22 E.R. 391, Lincoln's Inn MS. Misc. 12, p. 180.

[2] *Jackson v. Amery*, Gilbert Cas. 49, 139, 93 E.R. 256, 286.

was given to induce Jackson to sign the certificate and, therefore, was void by the Statute of the 5th of the late queen.[1]

The defendant Jackson insists that he was security for the plaintiff to the defendant Gerrard and, being in danger to be sued, he desired the plaintiff to indemnify and, thereupon, the plaintiff gives him this note, which, though dated after the bankruptcy, he insisted was not discharged by the certificate, it not being for a debt owing at the time of the bankruptcy.

Lord Chancellor [Lord Cowper]: If Jackson has really paid any debts for the plaintiff since the commission of bankruptcy, the certificate will not stand in his way, but he may take his remedy upon the note against the plaintiff, for, as he could not come into the Statute for satisfaction of any debt contracted after the bankruptcy, so neither ought the Statute and certificate be made use of against them.

British Library MS. Hargrave 80, f. 200

Emery v. Jackson.

The defendant had been bound as security for the plaintiff, who, afterwards, became a bankrupt. The defendant had been obliged to pay the debts for which he was surety. And he took a new note from the plaintiff, after which the plaintiff's certificate was allowed and he [was] discharged. The bill was *inter alia* for relief against this note.

Lord Chancellor [Lord Cowper]: The commissioner might equitably have let in the defendant among the creditors so far as to indemnify him, though, at that time, he had not suffered. But the debt from the bankrupt to him arose properly when he was compelled to pay what he was bound as the bankrupt's surety for. And that, being subsequent to the bankruptcy, is not discharged by the allowance for the certificate. No creditors can come in under the statutes[2] but the creditors before the bankruptcy. Those after can have no aid from the Statute, nor are those debts extinguished by it. But they may come upon the bankrupt for satisfaction if ever he be able to make it. He decreed the defendant satisfaction.

[Other copies of this report: Lincoln's Inn MS. Misc. 383, p. 317, Lincoln's Inn MS. Misc. 107, f. 42.]

1 Stat. 4 & 5 Ann., c. 4 (*SR*, VIII, 461–465).

2 Stat. 4 & 5 Ann., c. 4 (*SR*, VIII, 461–465); Stat. 6 Ann., c. 22 (*SR*, VIII, 600–602).

108

Gould v. Lambert

(Ch. c. 1715)

A commission to examine witnesses in a case in the Court of Chancery can be executed in the afternoon.

Lincoln's Inn MS. Misc. 11, p. 52

The plaintiff took out a commission to examine his witnesses, and the commission was not opened until three o'clock in the afternoon of the day on which it was returnable. And then the commissioners examined same witnesses and swore others who were examined the next day. And this was referred to the Master for irregularity.

The Master having reported the depositions of all the witnesses to be irregularly taken and exceptions being taken to the report, the court was of opinion that, as to the witnesses which were examined the next day after the return of the commission, their depositions were irregularly taken though they were sworn the day before. But as to those who were examined upon the day on which the commission was returned, their depositions were regularly taken, for the commissioners might examine witnesses all that day if they pleased and their power did not determine at twelve o'clock of the return day, as was insisted on, for the Court of Chancery is supposed to be always open and to sit in the afternoon as well as the morning. And a commission in this court is not like to a writ at common law which cannot be executed after twelve o'clock of the return day, it being supposed the common law courts rise before that time.

109

Weldon v. Fletcher

(Ch. 1715)

The question in this case was whether the devise in issue lapsed upon the death of the devisee before the time for payment.

British Library MS. Hargrave 81, f. 24, pl. 2

6 December 1715; at the Rolls.

One W., by his will, devises in manner following, *viz.*:

> I give and bequeath my lands in [etc.] unto my nephew William Clark and to the heirs of his body after the decease of C., my wife, conditionally that he pay to my nephew R. Butler £50 to be paid unto him in twelve months after my said wife's decease and, in case the said William Clark shall die without issue and not have paid the said £50, then I give and bequeath the

> said lands unto my nephew, John Clark, and his heirs conditionally that he, the said John Clark, do pay the said £50 unto the said R. Butler.

The testator dies, and the devisee of the £50 assigns it over to the plaintiff and dies. The testator's wife still living, then William Clark, the devisee of the land, sells the reversion to the defendant, who had notice of the devise of the £50.

And, it being a doubt whether that money still continued a charge upon the land or not, he bought the land something the cheaper. The widow dies. And a year after, the plaintiff brings this bill against the defendant, who was the purchaser, to be paid the £50 with interest or to have a sale of so much of the land as should be necessary for the payment of it.

Sir Joseph Jekyll, for the plaintiff, said that this devise was a charge upon the land and was still subsisting notwithstanding the death of the devisee before the time of payment, for it was *debitum in praesenti* though payable *in futuro* and, therefore, the party's dying before the time of payment did not divest the interest that was vested in him by the devise, that notwithstanding the word 'conditionally', this was not a condition but a limitation by construction, and that equity often made such a construction to preserve the intent of the party, that the first devise of the land was to the testator's heir at law, and then it could not be a condition, for a man cannot create a condition by devise to his heir at law and the testator had manifested his intention that this legacy should not determine upon the devisee's dying before the time of payment of devising the land over with the same charge and, if the devisee of the land had died during the life of the testator's wife, the other should not have lost the money nor ought his representative because of the legatee's dying before it was payable.

Sir Robert Raymond, for the defendant, said he admitted that there were such constructions in equity as to decree conditions as expressed in words to be limitations, but that, in this case, it was not material whether a condition or a limitation or whether the money devised be called a legacy, portion, or provision. And he agreed that a man could not devise to his heir at law upon condition, yet, where a condition or limitation is rendered impossible by the act of God, it becomes void and, if it be money to be paid, it sinks into the estate for the benefit of the heir and nothing was more common in the law than this and, if it be so in law, it must be the same in equity, for there will be no color to say that that will be raised in equity which in law was void. So, whether the money be construed a legacy, portion, or provision, it is not to be intended that the testator meant it to be raised or to go to the executor if the party died before it was payable. And he quoted the case of Slayer *et al. versus* Bussey, 17th July 1707; A., seised of lands in fee, devised the same to his wife for life, remainder over, and gives £10 apiece to his daughters, Mary and Sarah, two years after the death of his wife to be paid out of the land; the two daughters survived the wife and died within the two years, and the court decreed this a devise *in futuro* and that no interest vested in the daughters and that the executors were not entitled to either of the legacies.

[Other copies of this report: British Library MS. Hargrave 82, f. 20, pl. 2.]

[Other reports of this case: British Library MS. Hargrave 77, f. 9, pl. 2, British Library MS. Hargrave 303, f. 14, pl. 2.]

110

Brown v. Burton

(Ch. 1715)

Statutory rights, such as mortuaries, are not barred by the general Statute of Limitations.

British Library MS. Hargrave 81, f. 100

7 December.

The plaintiff brought his bill of mortuaries. The defendant [Seaman] Burton pleaded the Statute of Limitations[1] in bar against the plea. It was said that mortuaries were not due by common law but by custom, that the statutes of *Articuli Cleri* and *Circumspecte Agatis*[2] mention them as such as had been accustomed and so the Statute of the 21st Hen. VIII, cap. 6,[3] which ascertains them, and, though those statutes are conceived in negative words, yet they imply an affirmative, as the Statute for Sheriffs,[4] which says they shall not take more than such and such fees, has been adjudged to imply an affirmative that they may take those fees, and, where an action is founded upon a specialty, which every act of Parliament is, such actions are not within the Statute of Limitations. And, therefore, this plea is naught.

Curia [Lord Cowper] overruled the plea.

[Other copies of this report: British Library MS. Hargrave 82, f. 97.]

[Other reports of this case: British Library MS. Hargrave 77, f. 24v, British Library MS. Hargrave 303, f. 47v.]

---

[1] Stat. 21 Jac. I, c. 16 (*SR*, IV, 1222–1223).

[2] Stat. 9 Edw. II, stat. 1 (*SR*, I, 171–174); Stat. 13 Edw. I, *Circumspecte Agatis* (*SR*, I, 101–102).

[3] Stat. 21 Hen. VIII, c. 6 (*SR*, III, 288–289).

[4] Stat. 23 Hen. VI, c. 9 (*SR*, II, 334–336).

111

Goodwin v. Ingoldsby

(Ch. 1715)

Interest is payable after six months on unpaid legacies.

British Library MS. Hargrave 81, f. 27

9 December.

The Lady Napper, to whom the defendant was executor, by her will devised to the plaintiff's wife £200 *per annum* during her life, payable half yearly, and gave several considerable legacies, and made the defendant residuary legatee. The plaintiffs [Goodwin *et ux.*] brought their bill for payment of the arrear of the annuity and to establish the payment of it for the future.

An account of the testatrix's estate was decreed and that the Master should state the value of the residuum. The Master certified the whole to be £12,000 and the residue £6000.

And the plaintiffs now prayed a decree for the annuity with interest and cited the case of the Lady Craven and Lord Craven,[1] where the Lady's annuity was charged upon lands, and, there, interest was decreed her for it.

And so here, the court decreed interest for a month after the first half year.

[Other copies of this report: British Library MS. Hargrave 82, f. 22.]

[Other reports of this case: British Library MS. Hargrave 77, f. 9v, British Library MS. Hargrave 303, f. 15.]

112

Gillet v. Wray

(Ch. 1715)

Where a legacy of a marriage portion is conditioned upon marrying with consent, this condition will be enforced if the legatee has another provision in the will.

1 Peere Williams 284, 24 E.R. 390

A man, by his will, leaves his grand-daughter an annuity of £10 *per annum* for life, and, afterwards, by a codicil to his will, he declares, that, if his grand-daughter shall marry with the good liking of his trustees, then she shall have £150 in lieu of the annuity and her annuity to cease. The grand-daughter, afterwards, marries one worth nothing and without the consent of any of the trustees.

[1] Note *Lord Craven v. Lady Craven* (Ch. 1712), British Library MS. Hargrave 80, f. 75v, Lincoln's Inn MS. Misc. 383, p. 139, pl. 1, Lincoln's Inn MS. Misc. 106, p. 90.

Whereupon it was objected by Serjeant *Hooper* that the restraint of marriage was only *in terrorem* and that the grand-daughter, notwithstanding her having married as above, ought to have the £150 portion.

But the LORD COWPER decreed the contrary, saying here was a provision made either way and, where the provision for the child is in the alternative and there is a condition precedent to the gift of the portion, *viz.* if she marries with consent etc., and that is not performed and the child is still provided for, though not with the greater portion, equity, in that case, does not relieve.

[Other reports of this case: 2 Eq. Cas. Abr. 213, 22 E.R. 181.]

113
Bower v. Oxenham

(Ch. 1715)

A pure bill of discovery must be supported by an affidavit that the plaintiff does not already have the information sought.

British Library MS. Hargrave 81, f. 36

16 December.

The plaintiff exhibited a bill for discovery of a deed of settlement and prayed no relief but did not annex an affidavit to his bill that he had not the deed or that it was lost or mislaid. The defendant therefore demurred.

Mr. *Vernon*, for the demurrer, insisted that the printed rule is general, if a bill etc. and makes no distinction as to the nature of the bill else the plaintiff may be vexatious, which the rule intended to prevent, for, though he had the deed in his own power or custody, it was but leaving out the word 'relief', and yet he might with impunity vex and weary a defendant with a long bill and answering to it and a defendant be without remedy, which was unreasonable.

Mr. *Mead*, for the plaintiff, [said] that he always took the distinction to have been between a bill brought for relief in this court founded on a deed, which the plaintiff had not, and which, if he had, he would not need the aid or assistance of this court, and a bill of discovery only, which everyone was entitled to have. And, therefore, in the latter case, no affidavit was necessary. But, in the former, it was because it was that accident only which gave jurisdiction to the court. And that His Lordship had lately determined accordingly in the case of Lord Harley and Duchess of Newcastle.[1] And he cited a case in the Lord Keeper Bridgeman's time to the same effect.

---

[1] *Holles v. Duchess of Newcastle* (Ch. 1712–1713), British Library MS. Hargrave 80, ff. 90, 128v, 133v, 145v, 147, 151v, 170, Lincoln's Inn MS. Misc. 383, pp. 163, 227, 236,

Lord Chancellor [Lord Cowper]: I do not remember I made that order upon the distinction, for that distinction is wrong, and, instead of preventing vexatious suits in this court, which was intended by the rule, it would encourage and increase them, as has been observed. I remember there was some such case as you mention cited or read in that of the Lord Harley and Duchess of Newcastle, but if the Lord Keeper thought that distinction a good reason for the Lord Keeper, I think it a bad one for the Lord Chancellor. And he allowed the demurrer.

[Other copies of this report: British Library MS. Hargrave 82, f. 31.]

[Other reports of this case: British Library MS. Hargrave 77, f. 10v, British Library MS. Hargrave 303, f. 17v.]

114

Sligh v. Whitton

(Ch. 1715)

The question in this case was when an equity of redemption is forfeited under the Statute of 4 Will. & Mar., c. 16.

British Library MS. Hargrave 81, f. 37

Eodem die [16 December].

The bill was to foreclose and to require the defendant to discover whether he had not made any and what former mortgages or encumbrances prior to the plaintiff. The defendant, by his answer, says she has not made any other but what was assigned or in trust for the plaintiff and demurs to the general question because, by the Statute of the 4th & 5th William & Mary, cap. 16,[1] if any other mortgages had been and not discovered to the subsequent mortgagees, the equity of redemption should be lost and forfeited.

Curia: That forfeiture is only intended where the first mortgagor being paid by the purchaser, the security is not of value to be worth redeeming, and, therefore, for the additional charge and trouble to the mortgagee, he shall forfeit his equity, but not where there is a sufficient [estate] to defray all so that there will be no loss, but, besides, here, the assigning the prior securities to the plaintiff has given the defendant a new equity of redemption not bound by the Statute. He overruled the demurrer.

Query of this case, for, if the equity is never forfeited but where it is not worth redeeming, what signifies the Statute?

[Other copies of this report: British Library MS. Hargrave 82, f. 33.]

260, 262, 268, 291, Lincoln's Inn MS. Misc. 106, pp. 114, 189, 226, 230, 235, Lincoln's Inn MS. Misc. 107, p. 13, pl. 2.

[1] Stat. 4 Will. & Mar., c. 16 (*SR*, VI, 404–405).

[Other reports of this case: British Library MS. Hargrave 77, f. 11, pl. 1, British Library MS. Hargrave 303, f. 18, pl. 1.]

115

Ex parte Spearman

(Ch. 1715)

The owner or lessee of a coal mine, though he mines and sells the coal, is not a coal merchant and is not covered by the Statute of Bankrupts.

British Library MS. Hargrave 81, f. 38, pl. 1

19 December.

Where an owner or renter of a colliery sells the coals he raises of the land, this is not a trading within the Statute[1] to make him a bankrupt. But if he usually buys coals of others to sell them again with his own, that will bring them within the Statute.

Where there is an open account between two, the petition of one of them founded singly on his own computation or guess that the other upon the account is in his debt never was intended by the Statute a sufficient cause to issue a commission. *Per* Lord Chancellor [Lord Cowper].

[Other copies of this report: British Library MS. Hargrave 82, f. 34, pl. 1.]

[Other reports of this case: British Library MS. Hargrave 77, f. 11, pl. 2, British Library MS. Hargrave 303, f. 18, pl. 2.]

116

Smith v. Bromley

(Ch. 1716)

A purchase that was made in bad faith in order to defeat a creditor will be set aside pro tanto.

Lincoln's Inn MS. Misc. 11, p. 14

James Smith and Hannah, his wife, plaintiffs; James Bromley and Amy Latham, Thomas Ellison and Joseph Cope, junior, defendants.

To the Rt. Hon. William, lord Cowper etc. the humble petition of the defendant James Bromley showeth:

[1] Stat. 21 Jac. I, c. 19 (*SR*, IV, 1227–1229); Stat. 10 Ann., c. 25 (*SR*, IX, 685–686).

That the plaintiffs, in January 1707[/08], exhibited their bill against the defendant Cope and others to have satisfaction of the sum of £50 and interest due upon a bond wherein the defendant Cope, as principal, and Joseph Cope, his father and the plaintiff Hannah's grandfather, as surety, were bound to one Honor Dryden, which was paid off by the said Joseph and, by his direction, assigned to trustees for the benefit of the plaintiff;

That the cause being heard 10 June 1710, an issue was directed to try whether the said £50 was the proper debt of the said Joseph Cope, the elder, or of the defendant Cope, his son, and it being found to be the debt of the defendant Cope, the plaintiffs obtained a decree on the 6 December 1710 that the defendant should pay them the said £50 and interest together with their costs to be computed and taxed by a Master;

That the plaintiffs having obtained the Master's report dated 24 February 1710[/11] whereby it was certified that there was due for principal, interest, and costs on the said bond £260, they exhibited their bill against your petitioner and the rest of the defendants to have satisfaction of the said £260 out of some lands purchased by your petitioner of the defendant Cope before the trial of the said issue, to which bill your petitioner put in an answer and thereby showed, as the truth really was, that, by an indenture dated 20 May 34 Car. II [1682] made before the marriage of the defendant Cope with Abigail, his wife, a messuage and lands in Eaton in the County of Chester and a parcel of land called The Oxhope in Sandbach in the same county were so settled that the defendant Cope was only tenant for life with remainders to the issue male of the marriage with a provision for the said Abigail, if she survived her husband, to have £16 a year for her jointure out of the lands in Eaton and with power for the defendant Cope to charge the premises with £200 for debts or younger children's portions;

That the defendant Cope having contracted several debts and Joseph Cope, junior, son of the defendant Cope, being of age, an indenture tripartite dated 20 October 7 Ann. [1708] was made between the defendant Cope and his wife of the first part, Joseph Cope, their son, of the second part, and your petitioner and the defendant Ellison of the third part, reciting the said settlement. It was agreed to the intent the said defendant Cope's debts might be paid that the said lands in Sandbach should be sold and that, out of the purchase money, the defendant Cope's debts mentioned in a schedule, which amounted to £346, should be first paid and that the remainder of such money should be paid to the defendant Ellison and the petitioner to be put out at interest and that such interest should be paid to the defendant Cope during his life and, after his death, £10 a year should be paid thereout to the said Abigail during her life and the remainder to the said Joseph, the son, and after her death, the principal and interest was to be paid to the said son;

That, pursuant to this indenture, the lands in Sandbach were sold by the defendant Cope to one Francis Parrot for £170, which was all paid to the said Cope or his order, but no part thereof was paid to your petitioner;

That, the said £170 not being sufficient to pay all the defendant Cope's said debts, the said Cope and his wife and son did agree to sell the remainder of the said lands and, thereupon, by indenture dated 12 August in the 8th year of the late queen [1709] made between the said defendant and his wife and son of the first part, the said Mr. Parrot of the second part, John Parker and William Watts of the third part, and the defendant Ellison and your petitioner of the fourth part, the said defendant Cope and his wife and son did agree to levy a fine and suffer a recovery of all the premises, which recovery was thereby declared as to the lands purchased by the said Parrot to be to the use of the said Parrot and his heirs, and, as to the remainder of the premises, to the use of the said defendants Cope and Ellison and their heirs;

That the said fine and recovery were accordingly levied and suffered and, upon the 18 May 1710, your petitioner contracted with the defendant Cope and his son for the purchase of the lands in Eaton, which were of the yearly value of £18 or thereabouts, for the sum of £400, which was to be paid by installments and by articles dated 8 June 1710 made between the defendant Cope and his wife of the first part, the said Joseph Cope, the son, of the second part, and the defendant Ellison and your petitioner of the third part, reciting the articles of 20 October 7 Ann. [1708] and the purchase by Parrot and that the purchase money thereby arising had been applied so far as it would extend towards payment of the said schedule debts and reciting the contract for the sale of the remainder of the premises to your petitioner and that the said Joseph Cope, the son, was willing that his said father should have a farther supply for the payment of his just debts out of your petitioner's purchase money; it was agreed that all your petitioner's purchase money, except £200, should be applied in payment of the defendant Cope's debts mentioned in a schedule thereto annexed, which amounted to the sum of £233, and that the remaining £200 should be put out at interest and that such interest should be paid to the said Cope, the son, during the joint lives of his said father and mother and, if she survived, then £10 a year were to be paid to her during her life out of the said interest and, after her death, the said £200 and interest was to be paid to the said Cope, the son, for his own use;

That in pursuance of the last mentioned articles, the defendants Cope and Ellison, by indentures of lease and release dated 10 and 11 July 1710, conveyed the premises in Eaton to the defendant Latham and his heirs, whose name your petitioner made use of as a trustee for your petitioner, and, at the same time, your petitioner entered into a bond to the defendant Ellison for the payment of £400, the consideration of the conveyances at several times therein mentioned;

That the premises purchased by your petitioner being subject to a mortgage made by the defendant Cope to Dr. Jackson for securing £150 and interest, your petitioner paid the sum of £162 11s. 3d. in part of his said purchase money in discharge of the said mortgage being one of the schedule debts discharged in the last articles and your petitioner likewise paid to the defendant Ellison or to his order and towards the farther payment of the said schedule debts and which were accordingly applied for that purpose several sums of money amounting together with the said £162 11s.

3d. to the sum of £310 1s. 10d. besides which the defendant Cope was also indebted to your petitioner by a bond £10 which was one of the schedule debts agreed to be paid out of your petitioner's said purchase so that your petitioner became and was a real purchaser of the last mentioned premises for a full and valuable consideration really paid and secured to be paid in such a manner as is before mentioned;

That the cause was heard 26 July before the Master of the Rolls, who declared your petitioner's purchase ought to be set aside so far as to let the plaintiffs in to receive a satisfaction of what was decreed them in the former cause and decreed that it should be referred to Mr. Browning to take an account what was due for principal and interest on Jackson's mortgage and that your petitioner should account for the £170 raised by the sale of the estate in Sandbach and for what your petitioner had or without his willful default might have received out of the rents and profits of the premises in question, in the taking of which account the Master is to allow your petitioner so much of the said £170 as was applied to discharge the debts of the defendant Cope mentioned in the schedule of the first articles and to make your petitioner all other just allowances and upon the plaintiff's payment of what the said Master should certify to be due for principal and interest on the said Jackson's mortgage discounting the said £170 and what your petitioner had received as aforesaid after such allowances as aforesaid at such time and place as the Master should appoint; it was decreed that the defendants should convey the premises in Eaton to the plaintiffs or whom they should appoint, who should hold the same against the defendant Cope until they should be reimbursed what they should so pay and what was due to them under the former decree together with their costs and the consideration of costs as between the plaintiff and your petitioner was reserved until after the Master's report;

That your petitioner conceives himself aggrieved by the decree:

First, for that your petitioner having really and bona fide paid £310 1s. 10d. and the said £10 in the manner aforesaid in part of his said purchase money and secured the remainder thereof by a bond as aforesaid and which your petitioner is still liable to pay for the benefit of the defendant Cope's wife and son, who being no parties to this suit are not concluded thereby, and your petitioner's purchase being not only contracted for but actually completed even before the issue directed by the first order on hearing this cause was tried, your petitioner humbly conceives that the plaintiff ought not to have been let in to have a satisfaction of their demands out of the estate purchased by your petitioner and rather for that the defendant Cope, by his marriage settlement had only an estate for life therein. However, if it had been thought reasonable to let in the plaintiffs to a satisfaction of their debt out of that estate, yet your petitioner humbly conceives that, before the plaintiffs should receive such satisfaction, they ought not only to pay your petitioner what is due on Dr. Jackson's mortgage, as is decreed, but also what has been really paid out of your petitioner's purchase money towards discharge of the defendant Cope's just debts, for, otherwise, your petitioner must lose that money, the estate not being sufficient to pay all;

Second, for that your petitioner, as he humbly conceives, ought not to have been decreed to account for the £170 paid by Parrot upon his purchase, for, as your petitioner never did receive any part of that money, so neither was there any proof that it ever came to your petitioner's hands nor was your petitioner ever in possession of the lands purchased by Mr. Parrot or had any right so to be;

Third, for that your petitioner humbly conceives that costs ought not to have been reserved as between the plaintiffs and your petitioner, for, since your petitioner, as he humbly apprehends, is now considered by the decree as a mortgagee and to stand in the room of Dr. Jackson, whose mortgage your petitioner paid off, your petitioner, therefore, humbly conceives the plaintiffs ought not to have a redemption of that mortgage out of your petitioner's hands but upon the same terms as mortgagees are usually decreed to be redeemed in this court, *viz.* upon payment not only of principal and interest but also of costs, and your petitioner humbly conceives the plaintiffs ought not to be put in a better condition by your petitioner's paying off that mortgage than they would have been if the mortgage had continued in Dr. Jackson's hands;

For which reasons, your petitioner humbly appeals etc.

Hilary term 1715[/16].

The cause was reheard by Lord Cowper. And it appearing upon proof that the defendant Bromley had made this purchase on purpose to prevent the plaintiff from having a satisfaction of his debt, the purchase was so far set aside as to let in the plaintiff to have satisfaction of his debt.

But in regard that Joseph Cope, senior, was only a tenant for life, it was not reasonable the plaintiff should be put into a better condition by the defendant's purchase than he would have been without, and, therefore, he was decreed to be let into a satisfaction of his debt out of the rents upon paying off Dr. Jackson's mortgage and what the defendant Bromley had paid towards the debts of Joseph Cope, senior, and the plaintiff to hold the estate until he is repaid what he shall pay the defendant.

And, as to his own debt, he is to have a satisfaction of it out of the rents and to hold the premises until paid thereout if Joseph Cope, senior, lives so long.

117

Ex parte Hartop

(Ch. 1716)

Where a bankrupt owes a contingent debt, part of his estate must be set aside to await its accrual or not.

British Library MS. Hargrave 81, f. 38, pl. 2

19 January.

Moss, a freeman of London, on his marriage with Jane, his wife, covenants with Hartop, a trustee, in consideration of Jane's portion that, if she survived him, she should have her election either to take her customary part or £6000 in lieu thereof and, in the meantime, should have and dispose of £500 as her separate estate exclusive of him. And he and his father gave a bond to the trustees in £12,000 penalty to pay the £6000 in case she should make that her election. The marriage took effect. And, afterwards, Sir John Cutler, by his will, give the said Jane a legacy. Moss, the husband, enters the £500 in his book as borrowed from the wife and therein gives her credit for it and for the interest also, and he enters in the same book the legacy in the manner following, *viz*. 'borrowed of my wife, being a legacy left her by Sir John Cutler and paid by Edmund Boulter, who was Sir John's executor'. Moss, the father, dies. Moss, the husband, is his heir and executor. The father leaves a personal estate worth £10,000, which came to the son's hands, who, afterwards, became a bankrupt. And a commission issues. Hartop, the trustee, on behalf of the wife, [prays] to be let in as an immediate creditor for the £500 and interest and for the legacy as the wife's separate estate and a contingent creditor for £6000 and pays contribution for £4000 of it, which the commissioners not admitting, Hartop, the trustee, and Mrs. Moss, the wife, prefer a petition setting forth all these matters and praying that the commissioners may be directed to admit Hartop an immediate creditor for the £500 and interest and for the legacy as the wife's separate estate and to have the contingency settled or secured by the direction of the court.

Mr. *Cooper*, for the petitioners, said that the £6000 is a contingent demand and the wife is a contingent creditor for that sum and, though the contingency may not, yet it may happen and, if it should and, in the meantime, the whole estate is divided amongst the immediate creditors, she must be totally defeated of any satisfaction for her debt, which would be very hard and unreasonable. And he said it was usual in this court in cases of such contingency for the court either to set a value on the contingent interest with the consent of the parties or to order the deposit to answer the contingency where it should happen. And, therefore, he hoped the court would take some such method in this and, if so much of the estate were set apart for that purpose, it might be placed out at interest, which would go to the creditors, and, if the contingency should not happen, the principal too.

Serjeant *Chesshyre*, for the creditors, said this would be a great hardship upon the creditors to be so long kept out of so large a sum of money as £6000, who are like[ly] to be great losers, but they are improper to demand a security before anything is become due. Indeed, in London, a man may arrest another to make him give better security before the debt is payable, but that is supported by the custom only and cannot be done elsewhere. In the case of the Earl of Warrington and Sir James Langham,[1] Sir James gave his daughter £10,000 down and was to give her £10,000 more upon the earl's making a settlement; before the settlement was made, the earl brought his bill in this court to have security for the £10,000, and the cause was heard in 1698 in My Lord Somers's time, and the bill was dismissed, for he was too early to bring his bill, there being nothing then due.

Mr. *Vernon*, *ad idem*, said that it was less reasonable since the last Statute[2] concerning bankrupts to grant what was paid as to the £6000 than before, for, now, when a bankrupt has his certificate confirmed, that will be a discharge against all the debts he owed at the time of his bankruptcy so that the bankrupt, in this case, being a merchant, may after his discharge acquire a new estate, which would be liable to this contingent demand though not so to the present and immediate creditors. And he agreed that, where the contingent demand is certain and fixed, there, it was usual for the court to make such provision as mentioned by Mr. Cooper, but not else. And here, it is wholly uncertain, for the wife, by the articles, has her election to take the £6000 or her widow's part according to the custom and the time of election being not yet come, her present choice, as she is a married woman, cannot conclude her when the contingency happens so that it is entirely uncertain though the contingency should happen whether the £6000 will belong to her or not. And, as to the legacy, it does not yet appear that it is not part of her husband's estate, for, being given after marriage, if it was devised to trustees for her separate use, though it should be devised to her for her separate use, it shall go to the husband. And so it was decreed in Lord Harcourt's time in a case of a gentleman of Lincoln's Inn. And, therefore, that matter should be looked into by the commissioners. And the husband's entering it in his books as borrowed from his wife is no evidence that it was well given to her separate use. And he said that, if His Lordship should think fit to direct any deposit or security for the £6000, he hoped in case the contingency should happen and the wife chose the £6000, that the creditors in such case shall stand in her place as to the widow's part according to the custom of London.

Curia: The £6000 is a contingent debt and so much of it as the proportion of the other debts come to must be set by out of the bankrupt's estate to answer

---

[1] *Earl of Warrington v. Langham* (1698–1699), Precedents in Chancery 89, 24 E.R. 43, Colles 149, 1 E.R. 224, 1 Eq. Cas. Abr. 132, 21 E.R. 936.

[2] Stat. 3 Geo. I, c. 12.

the contingency. And, if that happens and she elects the money, she must make up her contribution for the whole. And the rest of the creditors are to stand in her place as to the widow's part. But, if she chooses her widow's part or that the contingency does not happen, then the money so set apart must be distributed among the other creditors and she must have her contribution money returned. Hartop, as her trustee, is to be admitted an immediate creditor for £538 separate estate and to see whether the legacy be well devised to her separate use; if so, then [he is] to be admitted an immediate creditor for that too.

[Other copies of this report: British Library MS. Hargrave 82, f. 34, pl. 2.]

[Other reports of this case: British Library MS. Hargrave 77, f. 11, pl. 3, British Library MS. Hargrave 303, f. 18v.]

118

Twisleton v. Griffith

(Ch. 1716–1721)

In the case of overreaching by a buyer, the seller will be allowed to redeem his land.

Where a judgment is confessed in connection with a bond, a court of equity will consider the judgment only as a security for the repayment of the money borrowed.

British Library MS. Hargrave 81, f. 241

Hilary [term] 2 Geo. 1715[/16]. This case is reported by Mr. C. Talbott.

The plaintiff's father was tenant for life, remainder to the plaintiff in tail, with remainders over to other persons. The plaintiff being a spendthrift and wanting money to supply his necessities and to buy a commission in the Army, the defendant, an attorney, agreed to purchase the plaintiff's interest in £150 *per annum*, part of the estate, the whole being about £500 *per annum*, and for £1050 really paid to the plaintiff, by fine conveyed that part of the estate to the defendant. The plaintiff's father was about sixty at the time of the purchase and died two years after. The plaintiff had a daughter only living at the time of the purchase, about ten years old. And immediately after the purchase, he bought a commission. But the regiment being afterwards broken and his father dying and the defendant calling upon him to suffer a recovery, the plaintiff brought his bill to be relieved against this absolute conveyance as fraudulent and to be admitted to redeem upon payment of the money really advanced by the defendant and interest.

Lord Chancellor [Lord Cowper]: The good of the state requires that those who take advantage of young heirs and assist them in spending their estates before they have them should be discouraged. It is much more eligible that they should bite upon their necessities before their estates descend to them than after they are gone. This court therefore will incline as far as they can against contracts of this nature. But here, the hazard which the defendant ran is worth money and must be taken into the condition of the purchase. Had the plaintiff died before his father upon failure of issue of the plaintiff, the defendant had lost the estate and his money too. Can you show me any precedent where the court has relieved against conveyances made under these circumstances?

Horsley mentioned one in second Chancery Reports, Nott v. King,[1] as in point.

Vernon, e contra: There, the relief was founded upon the want of a real consideration, none appearing in that case but a paper consideration.

The Lord Chancellor [LORD COWPER] directed precedents to be searched.

On 9 July 1716, the cause came again before him. The precedent of Nott v. King, in the time of Car. II, was produced, but that varied from the present case, for, there, the party to whom the conveyance of the contingent interest was made took at the same time a collateral security for his money, which the court laid hold of to make the whole a redeemable interest.

Another was produced in the time of Car. II, between Muschamp and the Earl of Argliss, Second Chancery Reports 266,[2] which was a stronger case for the plaintiff's relief than the present, and a third between Berny and Pitt of Hampshire,[3] heard before Lord Nottingham 32 Car. II. In that case, Berny, being young and in want of money and entitled to a remainder in tail of a considerable real estate expectant upon his father's death, who was infirm, and having a prospect of a good personal estate from him, borrowed £1000 of Pitt, for which he gave a judgment or recognizance in the penalty of £5000, but defeasanced upon Berney's paying Pitt £2500 upon the death of his father in case he should survive him and interest for £2500 from his marriage if he married in his father's life, and it was declared in the defeasance that, if Berney died before his father, Pitt was to lose the £2500. Pitt, afterwards, advanced a further sum of £1000 upon the same terms. Berney's father died about four years after[wards] in the life[time] of Berney, who then brought his bill to be relieved against these securities. Lord Nottingham declared that he could give no relief but against the penalty upon payment of the £2500 interest and costs, which was paid accordingly under that decree, and the same cause was afterwards relieved by Jeffreys, 2 Jac. II [1686 x 1687], and he relieved Berney upon the head of its being an unreasonable agreement and that bargains for that kind with young heirs who come up here for their education should not be countenanced and ordered a restitution of

---

[1] Perhaps *Nott v. Hill* (1683), 2 Chancery Cases 120, 22 E.R. 875, also 1 Vernon 167, 23 E.R. 391, 1 Eq. Cas. Abr. 275, 21 E.R. 1042.

[2] *Earl of Arglasse v. Muschamp* (1682), 2 Chancery Reports 266, 21 E.R. 675, also 1 Vernon 135, 23 E.R. 369, 1 Eq. Cas. Abr. 133, 21 E.R. 937, note also 1 Vernon 75, 237, 23 E.R. 322, 438.

[3] *Berney v. Pitt* (1686), 2 Chancery Reports 395, 21 E.R. 697, 2 Vernon 14, 23 E.R. 620.

all but the £1000, interest, and cost that had been taxed, and his decree has stood ever since.

[It was] said by *Horsley* that he heard it was affirmed by the House of Peers.

Vernon distinguished the cases, that being of a young heir under the power of his father, this of one that was married and had a child ten years old, that a loan of money, this a purchase of a reversion, that it was never doubted but a man might sell a reversion. If he might not after his father's life, might he after his mother's or after a third person?

Lord Chancellor [Lord Cowper said] that he believed one reason that induced Jeffreys to vary Lord Nottingham's decree was the observation of the public inconveniences that followed the establishing of agreements of that kind, that he could not discern any substantial difference between that case and the present, that, here, the lands now in possession were admitted to be worth £3000, the father's life could hardly be estimated at more than £700 and that, therefore, this bargain agreed with the other as to what was the foundation of the decree in being unreasonable, that the circumstances in which they differed were not material, that, here, the plaintiff by being married young and improvidently was not in a much better capacity to take care of himself than Berney, though a younger man, that there was evidence in favor of Griffiths that he had advised the plaintiff to procure the money of his father or of some other friend and, of the other side, that Griffiths had beat him off from making a more beneficial bargain with his father, that Griffiths was the person upon whom he relied and whom he consulted in everything, and, in the respect, this case is stronger than that of Berney v. Pitt, that he was not without some doubts and vibrations in his own mind, but thought it safer to concur with Lord Jeffreys's decree than by varying to give encouragement to these bargains, that the defendant would be no loser by receiving his principal and interest, that the inconvenience will not be great, if it be known that such bargains are not to be made with heirs, it will only force them when they are straitened to resort to their parents, and, if they are pressed a little before his estate comes to them, it is better than to be so after it is gone, that there is no great inconvenience were it established, that such a contingent reversion is not to be sold but the inconveniences that would follow the allowing such bargains in a court of equity are great and manifest.

The Lord Chancellor [Lord Cowper] decreed a redemption to the plaintiff.

[Other copies of this report: British Library MS. Hargrave 82, f. 240, Lincoln's Inn MS. Misc. 107, f. 121.]

British Library MS. Hargrave 83, p. 17

10 June 1721.

An heir at law, in the lifetime of his father, covenants for a sum of money to convey to the person who advanced the money part of the estate to which he was heir apparent when he should come into possession of it and gives a bond and [a confessed] judgment as a security for the performance of this agreement when it should be in his power to make it good. The father dies. The heir, upon his death, comes into this court to be relieved against his own agreement and the judgment given for performing.

And though there was not the least pretense of any fraud or imposition in the purchaser and though he stood the hazard of the son's dying before his father, Lord Cowper decreed that the judgment should stand only as a security for the money advanced with interest and costs to the defendant.

British Library MS. Hargrave 83, p. 31

The father of the plaintiff Twisleton was tenant for life, remainder to the plaintiff in tail with a remainder over. The plaintiff, being in want of money, applied to the defendant to get him some upon the sale of his remainder. The plaintiff was then no very young man, for he had a daughter fifteen years old or thereabouts as appeared in the cause. It was also proved that the defendant advanced the plaintiff more money than others offered. The defendant gave after the rate of seven years purchase, and the money was actually paid, and a fine was levied by the plaintiff and a covenant to suffer a recovery. After the death of the plaintiff's father, the defendant applied to the plaintiff to perfect the conveyance and suffer a recovery.

Upon his insisting, the plaintiff brought his bill to be relieved upon payment of what was due for principal and interest.

My Lord Cowper took time to consider of the case and was attended by precedents. But the precedent of Nott and Hill, in Mr. Vernon's reports,[1] was not laid before him, for I believe Mr. Vernon only had it and he was of the other side. Lord Cowper, when he made the decree, said that he had some vibration in his mind (that was his expression), but thought it of worse consequence that such contracts should stand than to relieve against them, and he relieved upon payment of what was due for principal, interest, and costs.

[Other reports of this case: 1 Peere Williams 310, 24 E.R. 403, 2 Eq. Cas. Abr. 510, 22 E.R. 431.]

1 *Nott v. Hill* (1683), 1 Vernon 167, 23 E.R. 391, also 2 Chancery Cases 120, 22 E.R. 875, 1 Eq. Cas. Abr. 275, 21 E.R. 1042.

119

Davila v. Davila

(Ch. 1716)

A woman can contract before her marriage to waive her distributive share of her husband's estate if he die intestate.

Lincoln's Inn MS. Misc. 10, p. 256

The plaintiff's husband, by articles before marriage, covenants that his executors, within three months after his death, should pay her £1500, and it is thereby agreed that the £1500 should be in full [satisfaction] of her third and of all claims and demands she might have out of the real and personal estate of her husband, either by virtue of the custom of London 'or otherwise'. The husband dies intestate. The plaintiff permits the defendant, who was next of kin, to take administration, and he pays her part of the £1500. And then she brings her bill for a distributive share of her husband's personal estate, offering to bring into hotchpot what she had received.

The defendant pleads the marriage articles. And it was insisted on for the plaintiff that she was not excluded by this agreement of her distributive share, for, if the husband had made his will and given his wife a legacy, she should have had it, and it is the same thing if he dies intestate and leaves his estate to come to her.

The case of Blandy and Wigmore, at the Rolls,[1] was cited and much insisted on for the plaintiff, which was this. A man, upon his marriage, covenants to leave his wife £500 if she survived him in full [satisfaction] of her dower and thirds. He dies intestate, and she takes administration, and the next of kin bring their bill for a distribution. She insisted she was a creditor for £500 by the marriage agreement and offers, after a deduction of that sum, to distribute the overplus. And, in that case, it was decreed that she should have her election either to take the £500 or to waive that and take her distributive share, but she should not have both. And, therefore, in the present case, it was insisted that the plaintiff might make her election either to claim by the Statute[2] or the articles.

But notwithstanding that case, Lord Cowper allowed the plea, for he was of opinion that the words 'or otherwise' did exclude her of all she could claim under the Statute of Distributions.

[Other reports of this case: 2 Vernon 724, 23 E.R. 1075.]

---

[1] *Blandy v. Widmore* (1716), 2 Vernon 709, 23 E.R. 1066, 1 Peere Williams 324, 24 E.R. 408, 2 Eq. Cas. Abr. 352, 22 E.R. 300.

[2] Stat. 22 & 23 Car. II, c. 10 (*SR*, V, 719–720).

120

Pagett v. Hoskins

(Ch. 1716)

If a man marries an executrix, who makes a devastavit, *the husband is liable to make satisfaction after the death of the wife so far as assets of the testator came to his hands.*

Lincoln's Inn MS. Misc. 11, p. 30

4 February 2 Geo. Thomas Paget, esq., and Mary, his wife, and Elizabeth Whitcomb and others, plaintiffs; Dame Jane Hoskyns, administratrix of her son, Sir Bennet Hoskyns, and others, defendants.

In August 1696, Peter Whitcomb, a freeman of London, being seised and possessed of a very considerable real and personal estate, intermarried with Elizabeth Sherrard with whom he had a portion of £5000. And, in October 1701, she died leaving issue, the plaintiffs Mary and Elizabeth.

By articles of agreement dated 1 September 1702 between the said Peter Whitcombe of the one part and Richard Sherrard of the other part, the said Peter Whitcomb, in consideration of the marriage and portion and of love and affection and for securing a provision for the plaintiffs, his daughters, and in performance of his promise and agreement made before the marriage and for other considerations, covenants with the said Richard Sherrard to pay the plaintiffs, Mary and Elizabeth, £3000 apiece at twenty-one or day of marriage with interest at five percent from his death and, in case of the death of one, the survivor to have £5000 with like interest.

Soon after the executing the said articles, the said Peter Whitcomb intermarried with Mrs. Gertrude Arundel, with whom he had a portion of £6000. And, soon after such his marriage, *viz.* in September 1704, he died having made his will and the said Gertrude, his wife, executrix, who proved the same. And, by virtue thereof, she possessed herself of all or a great part of his personal estate. And Gertrude, being with child of a son born after the death of his father, who was afterwards named Peter and lived about ten months, the said Gertrude, during that time, received the rents and profits of the real estate and cut down and sold timber and wood to the value of £2000.

After the death of Peter, the posthumous son, the said Gertrude obtained letters of administration of his personal estate, and, by virtue thereof, she pretended title to the arrears and rents of his real estate, which she had received, and to the timber and wood sold by her in the lifetime of her said posthumous son.

In Hilary term 1706[/07], the plaintiffs Mary and Elizabeth, by the said Richard Sherrard, their next friend, exhibited their bill against the said Gertrude and others setting forth the said articles and will and that the said Peter Whitcomb, their late father, was a freeman of London and that they were entitled by the custom of London to their orphanage or customary part of the said Peter

Whitcomb's personal estate and that the said Gertrude, their mother-in-law, having possessed herself thereof did convert the same to her own use and delayed coming to an account with the plaintiffs or to pay them their portions and interest settled by the articles or their customary parts of their said father's personal estate, to which bill, the said Gertrude put in her answer. But, before the other defendants had answered or any farther proceedings were had in the cause, she, having raised out of Peter Whitcomb's estate about £6000, married Sir Bennet Hoskins [1675–1711] who received the £6000 with her as a portion, after which she died [in 1709] having first made her will pursuant to a power in her marriage settlement. And [she made] the said Sir Bennet sole executor, who proved the same, and, by virtue thereof, he possessed the personal estate of the said Peter Whitcomb, which had come to the hands of the said Dame Gertrude, his late wife, and the other part unadministered by her.

After the death of Dame Gertrude, the suit was revived and carried on against Sir Bennet Hoskyns. And, on 16 November 1711, the cause was heard before the then Lord Keeper [Lord Harcourt], who referred it to a Master to take an account of the debts that were owing by the said Peter Whitcomb, the father, at his death and of the charge of his funeral and also an account of the said Peter Whitcomb's personal estate which came to the hands of the said Gertrude or Sir Bennet Hoskins or to any other for their use or by their order and to state the same specifically and to make all just allowances and what should appear to be the remaining estate of the plaintiff's said late father subject to the said articles and, in case the plaintiffs' third part of the said estate should not be sufficient, to make good the said portions of £3000 apiece to the plaintiffs with interest. Then, the court reserved the consideration how the same should be satisfied until after the Master had made his report. And the Master was to take an account of the personal estate of the said Peter Whitcomb, the posthumous son, which had come to the hands of the said Gertrude or Sir Bennet Hoskins or to any others by their orders, out of which Sir Bennet was to be allowed for the dower of Dame Gertrude and all other just allowances. And what should appear to be in the hands of Sir Bennet Hoskyns of the plaintiffs' said late brother's personal estate was to be divided into three equal parts, two whereof were to go to the plaintiffs Mary and Elizabeth and the other third part to the defendant Sir Bennet Hoskins in the right of his wife. And all parties were to have their costs.

Before the account was taken by the Master, Sir Bennet died, and, the suit thereby abating, it was revived against Dame Jane Hoskyns [d. 1724] as administratrix of her son, Sir Bennet.

On 19 June 1714, the cause was heard before the Lord Chancellor [Lord Harcourt], who ordered that the former decree should be carried on against the defendant Dame Jane Hoskyns as administratrix of her son, Sir Bennet, and that all parties who had any of Sir Bennet's estate in their hands should account before the Master, but, although the said account is to be carried on according to the said former decree, yet the assets of the said Sir Bennet's estate are not to stand charged with what of the said several personal estates and rents and profits of the real estate that came to the hands of the said Dame Gertrude farther than what of the said Gertrude's personal estate came to the hands of Sir Bennet exclusive of her said portion of £6000.

The plaintiffs, conceiving themselves aggrieved by the last decree, petitioned for a rehearing touching the said £6000, for that the assets of Sir Bennet Hoskyns ought to be charged with at least two-thirds of the said £6000 subject to the plaintiffs' demands and the will of the said Peter Whitcomb as directed by the former decree, the whole sum of £6000 having been received by the said Gertrude as part of the personal estate of the said Peter Whitcomb. And they insisted that there was the greater reason to subject the assets of the said Sir Bennet to the payment of the plaintiffs' proportionable part of the said £6000, for that the said Sir Bennet knew of and was privy to the plaintiffs' demands and, in his marriage settlement he made upon the said Gertrude pursuant to an agreement for that purpose betwixt them, the said Gertrude demanded her dower to Sir Bennet's trustees to make good any deficiency that might happen in the personal estate of the said Peter Whitcomb whereby the said £6000 might be lessened or drawn back from the said Sir Bennet and, in case the administratrix of Sir Bennet Hoskyns should be permitted to carry away the whole £6000, as it seems intended by the said last decree, the plaintiffs would be entirely stripped not only of the provision made for them by their said father by the said articles but also of the customary part of their said father's personal estate.

Lord Chancellor [Lord Cowper]: Sir Bennet having in his marriage settlement taken notice that the account of Peter Whitcomb's personal estate was not stated and having taken security to indemnify him against the account, he takes the portion with full notice the account was unsettled, and, consequently, he must take it subject to the account and as part of the personal estate of Peter Whitcomb in Dame Gertrude's hands unaccounted for. And, therefore, he ordered that the clause in the former decree whereby the £6000 was excepted or excluded should be struck out and the Lady Hoskins should account for the whole assets of Sir Bennet Hoskyns.

Note, in this case, it was said by Mr. *Vernon* that, if a man marries an executrix, who makes a *devastavit*, in law, the husband is not liable to make satisfaction after the death of the wife, but equity goes further and charges the husband after the death of the wife so far as assets of the testator came to his hands.

British Library MS. Hargrave 77, f. 52v, pl. 1

Hilary [term] 1715[/16].

A., having two children, daughters, by a former wife, by some voluntary deed, covenants to raise for them £3000 apiece as portions. And, afterwards, he intermarried with B., with whom A. received a portion of £600. A., being a freeman of London, dies, leaving a personal estate supposed to amount to £18,000, including the said £6000 portion, which was then included and most of it put out in government securities in the name of B. during the marriage, and a real estate of £700 *per annum*. [She], afterwards, intermarries with Sir [*blank*] Hoskins, knight, who, by a deed, recites that B. had represented herself to have £6000 besides her jointure, and, as a consideration of that fortune, he settled on her £300 *per annum*, but he takes notice that the estate of A. was then unliquidated; if it should fall out that her fortune should come short of £6000, she covenants to make good that deficiency out of her jointure. B., afterwards, dies. Sir Hoskins dies, leaving his mother executrix.

And, it, afterward, coming out that A. died entitled to a very considerable personal estate but that the person whom A. employed in his lifetime and was employed after his death as manager and receiver thereof had sunk, embezzled, or otherwise made away with or, by misfortune, lost all except the abovesaid £6000, the daughters of A., after they were in possession of the £700 *per annum* and upon the death of B., exhibited their bill, setting forth several matters. And they prayed that they might have their dividend of the said £6000 according to the custom of London, which counsel for the defendant very strenuously opposed.

And he argued that Sir [*blank*] Hoskins, as a consideration for the said £6000, had made her a jointure and so he was a valuable purchaser, and he said, if any person had actually bought those government securities, though he had not altered the property and they could be traced out, yet that the two daughters, in such case, could have no relief against such a purchaser.

But His Lordship [Lord Cowper] declared that Sir [*blank*] Hoskins having married the widow of a freeman whose estate was then unliquidated and himself even then taken notice that it was so, and that the £6000 and all other moneys that she or Sir [*blank*] had received of the estate of A. should be accounted for, and the plaintiffs receive their dividend according to the custom of London.

[Other copies of this report: British Library MS. Hargrave 303, f. 90.]

[Other reports of this case: Precedents in Chancery 431, 24 E.R. 193, Gilbert Rep. 111, 25 E.R. 78, 2 Eq. Cas. Abr. 684, 22 E.R. 574.]

121

Nunnes v. Hill

(Ch. 1716)

A contract for the sale of shares of stock in a company is covered by the Statute of Frauds.

Lincoln's Inn MS. Misc. 11, p. 21, pl. 1

9 February 1715[/16].

The plaintiff brings his bill to have a specific performance of an agreement for the accepting the transfer of £4000 South Sea stock at 98 percent.

The defendant pleads the Statute of Frauds and Perjuries[1] and says the agreement concerned merchandise and that no agreement was made in writing nor any part of the money which was to be given for this stock was paid down. And he avers the stock is for the carrying on of trade and merchandise.

Curia [Lord Cowper]: The Act intended to divide all property into lands and tenements and goods, wares, and merchandises. Now, if a contract of goods of £10 value is not good unless in writing etc., can it be supposed the Statute should not extend to what is of a higher nature and value?

The word 'goods' in the civil law is very extensive, and I do not see why it should not extend to all personal things. I allow the plea.

122

Cheyney v. Apreece

(Ch. 1716)

Legacies given for charitable uses abate in proportion with other the legacies in the case of a deficiency of assets to pay off the decedent's creditors.

Where land is given to charitable uses by a defective will, the defect is not cured by the Statute of Charitable Uses.

Lincoln's Inn MS. Misc. 10, p. 171

11 February 1715[/16]. Upon Mrs. Rebecca Hussey's will.

In this case, these points were decreed:

First, that legacies given for charitable uses should abate in proportion with other legacies in case of a deficiency and the charity legacies are not to have preference;

Second, that a will not duly executed according to the Statute[2] whereby lands are given to charitable uses could not operate by way of appointments within the

---

1 Stat. 29 Car. II, c. 3 (*SR*, V, 839–842).

2 Stat. 29 Car. II, c. 3, s. 5 (*SR*, V, 840).

Statute of Queen Elizabeth,[1] and so it was decreed and settled by Lord Cowper in the Case of Sidney College,[2] where the will had but two witnesses, though there was a codicil attested by three, for, if lands are to pass by the will as a will and not as an appointment, it must be executed according to the Statute;

Third, that the testator having devised a house, of which she had a lease subject [. . .] to a rack rent, to A.B. for the remainder of her lease, the devisee must take it *cum onere* and the rent shall not be paid out of the personal estate of the testatrix.

123

Musgrave v. Parry

(Ch. 1716)

A will must be construed according to the words used by the testator and not by what the judge may think is fair.

2 Vernon 710, 23 E.R. 1067

25 February.

Sir John Chardine devised the surplus of his estate to his grandchildren living at the time of his decease to be paid to them at twenty-one or marriage (with survivorship and also £100 apiece for mourning to each of such grandchildren. R.L.). There were two grandchildren born, the one within four months, the other within six months after his decease.

For the plaintiffs, the grandchildren born after his decease, it was insisted that a child *in ventre sa mere* is capable of taking, may be vouched, a bill may be brought on its behalf, and an injunction [made] to stay waste. (So Lutterel's Case, cited in Hale v. Hale, Pre. Ch. 50, *et vide* Scatterwood v. Edge, 1 Salk. 229.[3]) The mother may justify the detaining of writings on the behalf of a child *in ventre sa mere*, a limitation *haeredibus de corpore procreatis* shall include issue after born, and so *e converso procreandis* includes issue already born. And the Case of Palmer and Creaghcroft was cited, *quod vide*, and cases cited in a note there, and also the

---

[1] Stat. 43 Eliz. I, c. 4 (*SR*, IV, 968–970).

[2] *Attorney General v. Baines* (Ch. 1707), 3 Chancery Reports 150, 21 E.R. 753, Precedents in Chancery 270, 24 E.R. 131, *sub nom. Attorney General v. Barnes*, 2 Vernon 597, 23 E.R. 990, Gilbert Rep. 5, 25 E.R. 4, 1 Eq. Cas. Abr. 97, 21 E.R. 908, British Library MS. Hargrave 80, f. 13, Lincoln's Inn MS. Coxe 89, vol. 3, pt. 2, p. 30.

[3] *Hale v. Hale* (1692), Precedents in Chancery 50, 24 E.R. 25, also 2 Eq. Cas. Abr. 637, 22 E.R. 534; *Scatterwood v. Edge* (1697), 1 Salkeld 229, 91 E.R. 203, also 12 Modern 278, 88 E.R. 1320, 1 Eq. Cas. Abr. 189, 21 E.R. 980, 2 Eq. Cas. Abr. 337, 22 E.R. 287, King's Inn Dublin MS. 92, p. 1.

cases cited in a note to Weld v. Bradbury, *ante*, p. 705; Darbison v. Beaumont, 1 P. Wms. 229.[1]

Lord Chancellor [Lord Cowper]. The words 'living at the time of his decease' must be restrictive words and can be of no other use, else the devise had been to his grandchildren. A will must be expounded according to what is contained in it, and we must not make or vary the will to provide for children or grandchildren not provided for by the will. And he decreed it for the grandchildren living at the testator's death and excluded the two born after his decease.

Lincoln's Inn MS. Misc. 13, p. 56

29 February 2 Georgii.

Sir John Chardin, by his will dated 20 September 1711, among other legacies gave to all his grandchildren, male and female, which should be living at the time of his decease and to every of them the sum of £100 apiece for mourning and he devises the residuum in the following words, *viz.*:

> As, for, and concerning all the rest, residue, and remainder of my estate whatsoever and wheresoever not before devised, after payment of my debts, funeral expenses, and legacies, I give and bequeath the same and every part thereof unto and amongst all and every my grandchildren, whether male or female, which shall be living at the time of my death to be equally divided between them, share and share alike, and, if any of them die before they attain the age of twenty-one years or be married, then I will that the share of him or her so dying shall go to the survivors or survivor of them.

The testator had nine grandchildren living at his death. And, after his death, two more grandchildren were born, *viz.* the defendant Charles Parry, born about six months after the testator died, and the defendant Mary Musgrave, born about four months after.

The plaintiffs, who were the other nine grandchildren, brought their bill for an account of the personal estate and a distribution according to the will.

Curia [Lord Cowper] declared that the two grandchildren of the testator who were born after his death were not by his will entitled to any share of the said surplus nor to the legacies of £100 apiece given for mourning.

[1] *Palmer v. Cracroft* (1707), 2 Vernon 578, 23 E.R. 976; *Weld v. Bradbury* (1715), 2 Vernon 705, 23 E.R. 1058, also 1 Eq. Cas. Abr. 203, 21 E.R. 990; *Darbison, ex dem. Long v. Beaumont* (1713–1714), 1 Peere Williams 229, 24 E.R. 366, also Fortescue 18, 92 E.R. 743, 1 Eq. Cas. Abr. 214, 21 E.R. 999, Dodd 366, 3 Brown P.C. 60, 1 E.R. 1177, Lincoln's Inn MS. Misc. 10, p. 184, Lords' Journal, vol. 19, p. 696, *sub nom. Lay v. Beamont* (Ex. 1709), Eq. Cases Exch. 604.

Lincoln's Inn MS. Misc. 13, p. 166

Sir John Chardin, by his will, gave to all his grandchildren, male and female, which should be living at the time of his death £100 apiece for mourning. And, after several other legacies, he devised all the residue of his estate whatsoever unto all and every of his grandchildren, whether male or female, which should be living at the time of his death to be equally divided amongst them, share and share alike, and, in case any of them should die before they attained the age of twenty-one or marriage, he directed the shares of them so dying should go to the survivors. He left several grandchildren at his death and had two more born soon after.

It was decreed by Lord Cowper that the posthumous grandchildren were not entitled to a share of the surplus nor to the legacies of £100 apiece given for mourning.

[Other reports of this case: 1 Eq. Cas. Abr. 71, 203, 21 E.R. 884, 990.]

124

Anonymous

(Ch. 1716)

In this case, the testator gave a portion to only one daughter, and he gave legacies to all of his other children.

British Library MS. Hargrave 77, f. 52

25 February, Hilary, 1715[/16].

A., by will, gives all his real estate, being about £470 *per annum*, to B., his eldest son, in tail charged with £200 *per annum* during the life of C., his widow. Afterwards, he gives D., his elder daughter, £1500 for her portion besides several legacies which had been given her by other persons and he had received for her. And, then, he gives to the rest of his younger children the like sum of £1500 to be paid at their age of twenty-two or marriage, but he provides, if any of them die before age or married against the consent of the mother or guardians, then her fortune to go to and amongst the rest. And, then, he wills, if there be any surplusage of his estate which remained undivided, which he declares is uncertain because in government securities, that such surplusage be divided amongst all his children, share and share alike. And, afterwards, he gives B., his eldest son, £100. And, afterwards, the devisor dies leaving B., his eldest son, and D., his daughter, and two more sons and two daughters.

And, if it, afterwards, appears that there is a surplus of £7000, B. brings his bill that he may have a dividend upon that construction of this will.

Which cause being at the Rolls, His Honor [Trevor] declared that the real estate devised to B. was not to be taken as a portion and that the £100 was to be taken as a legacy. Therefore, he decreed that A. was not entitled to any dividend of the surplusage.

From which decree, A. appealed to the Lord Chancellor [Lord Cowper], who asked the question, if that £100 devised to B. had been £1000, then whether it would not have been taken as a portion. And he declared that, upon the construction of the will, the devisor had given a portion to none but D., his eldest daughter, and that £1500 devised to his younger children were to be taken only as legacies and not as portions and, therefore, that B., the plaintiff, was well entitled to an equal share of the said surplusage.

[Other copies of this report: British Library MS. Hargrave 303, f. 89v.]

125

Anonymous

(Ch. 1716)

The separate estate of a wife is not liable to pay the debts of her bankrupt husband.

British Library MS. Hargrave 77, f. 51v, pl. 2

28 February, Hilary vacation 1715[/16]. Lord Cowper.

A., by a bond dated and executed two days before his marriage with B., covenants that he will have nothing to do with the estate, real or personal of B., who was a widow, without her consent and by her direction and that B. should have the entire command and disposal by will of her personal estate and receive the rents of her real estate and dispose thereof in £20,000 penalty. After their marriage, B. and A. join in a deed whereby B. consents that part of her estate may be sold to pay off debts particularly enumerated in two schedules thereto annexed and £1000 and odd moneys therein mentioned to be the debts of A. and £700 and odd moneys, the debts of B. as executor to C. So there remained an overplus of above £200, which was thereby disposed. And, sometime afterward, some differences arising between A. and B., they agreed to separate. And, thereupon, B. covenanted to allow A. a clear annuity of £80 with restrictions from meddling with her estate or receiving the rents under forfeiture of that annuity.

Afterwards, A. became a bankrupt. And the assignees got into their possession a great part of the goods of B., which, upon application to the court, were restored to B. upon B.'s giving security for their value to abide any order to be made upon a bill to be brought by the assignees by the time limited, *viz.* so many goods as B. would make an oath to be her own proper separate goods.

And it being alleged upon the hearing of the cause that, since the coverture, A., by B.'s consent, had taken several mourning hangings, the proper goods of B., which he promised to give in exchange as part to buy new damask and had the remainder of the money from B. but he applied the money and the money arising by the sale of the mourning hangings to his own use and went a trust[1] for the new furniture against B.'s knowledge, His Lordship [Lord Cowper] declared that no part of the estate of B. ought to be applied to satisfy the debts of A. or any goods that were the goods of B. before the marriage or bought with her estate since and that the before mentioned damask belonged to her. And the debt thereby contracted, the debt of the bankrupt, and the £80 *per annum* and arrears was made subject to the bankruptcy, but that B. had not committed any act whereby she could forfeit the command and disposal of her estate.

[Other copies of this report: British Library MS. Hargrave 303, f. 88v, pl. 2.]

126

Frederick v. Wynne

(Ch. 1716)

A court of equity can give relief where a bond has been lost.
Forbearance to sue is a good consideration for a contract.

British Library MS. Add. 35990, f. 142, pl. 3

29 February. At My Lord Chancellor's house.

The bill set forth that the intestate [Crispe] was indebted to the plaintiff by a bond and that, since his death, the defendant, being one of the administrators, promised to pay within such a time upon being forborne to be sued, since which the bond is lost or mislaid, and he prays performance.

The defendant, by his answer, admits the bond and that he promised payment. But he says that it was upon a presumption of assets to come to his hands by the intestate's interest in the Convex Lights, which came to nothing and that he did not promise to pay out of his own estate.

When the cause came on, the only proof was a letter from the defendant to the plaintiff wherein he says:

> I promised to pay you the debt of the late Common Serjeant Crispe but was so unfortunate as not to meet with you. It would be a kindness if you would take the interest and stay for the principal until [etc.]. But, if that does not consist with your convenience, I will come to town and endeavor to pay the whole.

It was objected that this was not a promise to pay out of his own estate, but out of the assets only, and that the words 'endeavor' implied no more, the defendant being a gentleman of a good estate. But, if it might be carried so far, yet this was

[1] Sic in MSS.

not an agreement in writing within the Statute of Frauds,[1] or, if it was, then the plaintiff ought to bring his action at law and not come into equity.

Cowper, Lord Chancellor: I must retain the bill because the bond is lost so the plaintiff is disabled from proving the consideration of the promise at [common] law, and, therefore, it is proper for relief here.

This must be taken to be a promise to pay out of his own estate because he desires time which was complied with and that is forbearance. And such a promise in consideration of forbearance was good at common law. But the Statute of Frauds has provided that it shall not be good for the future unless the agreement or some memorandum or note thereof shall be in writing signed by the party etc. This is not a case within the first part of the division, because the original promise was not in writing, but directly within the express words of the latter, being a memorandum in writing signed by the party that he had made an absolute promise.

The word 'endeavor' does not go to the payment but only to the time in which he would do it; so an inference can be drawn thence that it was to be out of the assets.

I remember a case when I was very young where H. had made a parol promise to pay the debt of another. This not being in writing, the promisee could bring no action at law, but he prefers his bill in this court and in canvassing the plaintiff asks him whether he had not money of the original debtor in his hands at the time he made the promise, the defendant, by his answer, confessed he had and, upon advising with Sir Anthony Keck and the great counsel in the Court of Chancery, they gave their opinion that the court would decree him to perform upon the presumption that he made the promise on the credit and consideration of that money, and, thereupon, he paid the debt.

He decreed for the plaintiff and the defendant to stand in his place to be satisfied out of the assets.

11 Viner, Abr. 428

Hilary term 1715[/16].

An administrator writes a letter to his intestate's creditors, *viz*. 'I promised to pay you what money was due to you before I went out of town, but it will be a kindness to me if you will stay until next winter, but if not, I will endeavor to pay you.'

Per curiam: A promise to pay on a forbearance before the Statute of Frauds was accounted a good consideration to charge the executor or administrator *de bonis propriis*. And, since a writing is sufficient after a parol promise and, by this letter, it appears that the administrator had made a promise and confirmed it by this letter, [it was] so decreed that the administrator should be bound by the

[1] Stat. 29 Car. II, c. 3 (*SR*, V, 839–842).

promise and should answer debts and costs out of his own estate, but have satisfaction out of the assets, if any.

[Other copies of this report: 2 Eq. Cas. Abr. 456, 22 E.R. 388.]

127

Norcliff v. Lee

(Ch. c. 1716)

Where a man knows that his intended wife has settled her property and then proceeds to marry her, he cannot have the settlement set aside fraudulent.

British Library MS. Hargrave 81, f. 74

1 March.

The bill is to set aside a settlement made by the plaintiff's wife during the treaty of marriage as fraudulent.

Mr. *Vernon, pro querente*: She was then a widow and had several leaseholds, houses, and other estate. In expectation of having which in marriage, the plaintiff has married and, by articles, tied himself for a particular provision for his wife of that consideration. We are endeavored to be defrauded by this voluntary settlement. These kinds of settlements or conveyances thus made in breach of that faith and fairness upon which contracts ought to proceed and which are all grounded upon a supposed mutual candor and integrity and which ought in conscience to be a rule to the parties are usually set aside in this court as fraudulent. It is true in Mr. Justice Turton's Case, in Lord Nottingham's time, His Lordship was of opinion that, before marriage, the woman was *sui juris* and, therefore, might well dispose of her estate or make provision for herself in case of accidents or for her children by her first husband unknown to the second, but, upon appeal, the Lords were of a different opinion and reversed his decree. And ever since, the judgment of this court has been accordingly.

Curia [Lord Cowper]: If, pending a treaty of marriage, the woman, being entitled to an estate or fortune, aliens or settles it out of her power without the consent or knowledge of the man and afterwards before this is discovered and, in view and confidence of her having this fortune or estate, the treaty proceeds and a marriage is had, this voluntary settlement or alienation is fraudulent and shall be set aside in equity. But it appearing fully in the proofs in this case that the plaintiff had notice during the courtship that his wife had made the settlement of which he now complains and that, if he would have her, he must take a naked woman and yet that he would marry her, the bill must be dismissed, but without costs.

[Other copies of this report: British Library MS. Hargrave 82, f. 70.]

[Other reports of this case: British Library MS. Hargrave 77, f. 19, pl. 2, British Library MS. Hargrave 303, f. 37v.]

128

Hawkins v. Watts

(Ch. c. 1716)

An agreement to pay interest is for simple interest unless compound interest is expressly contracted for.

British Library MS. Hargrave 81, f. 76

Eodem die [1 March].

The plaintiff, about 1702, had lent the defendant £80, for which he gave the plaintiff a mortgage of lands worth £40 *per annum*. Afterwards, the plaintiff makes up the money £300 and take a further mortgage for £300 principal money and promises to pay one M., an attorney, who claimed a sum of money from the defendant for law charges. The plaintiff neglects to call for his interest or to pay M. the sum he promised but makes up several accounts of the interest. And now the plaintiff, having brought [an action of] ejectment for recovery of the possession, brings his bill also to foreclose or to have his principal and interest according to the last mortgage and costs both at law and in equity. The defendant submitted to redeem on the foot of the first mortgage and to pay what other sums he had since lent him with interest and swears he offered to do so before the [action of] ejectment [was] brought. The plaintiff, at the hearing, insisted to have interest for several sums in which the arrear of interest was from time to time cast up.

Master of the Rolls [Trevor]: There is no precedent at all in this court of such compound interest. It was decreed otherwise by the Commissioners [to Hold the Great Seal], of which I was one. But the cause coming to be heard before My Lord Somers, he asked my opinion and I was against the decree because, there, every time the account was made up, there was more money lent and added to the interest in arrear and so a new principal [was] made. But here, nothing has been added to the interest in arrear, and, therefore, I cannot allow interest for that interest. As to M.'s demand, which was part of the consideration of the last deed, nothing has been paid. If anything had been paid by the plaintiff, he would be allowed it again with interest. But, since nothing has been paid, the executing the last deed of mortgage is not to be taken as an account stated and to bind the defendant. And, therefore, the account must be taken on the foot of the first mortgage and the money really paid is to carry interest and the defendant is to redeem paying all such money and interest and the cost at law in two months after the report, but no costs in this court.

[Other copies of this report: British Library MS. Hargrave 82, f. 72.]

[Other reports of this case: British Library MS. Hargrave 77, f. 20v, pl. 1, British Library MS. Hargrave 303, f. 39.]

129

Adaliza v. Baldwin

(Ch. c. 1716)

Persons who have contingent interests are not necessary parties to suits involving the administration of a decedent's estate.

Any person may bring a bill in an infant's name for the infant's benefit.

British Library MS. Hargrave 81, f. 78

4 March. Francis Herbert Adaliza, per dictum Francis, proxime amicum v. Baldwin, surviving executor of Alice Bernard, defuncti.

Mrs. Bernard, by her will, devised to the plaintiff Adaliza the residuum of her personal estate to be paid her at her age of twenty-one or day of marriage and, if she died before either, then the devise is to one Meyrick, her niece, for her life and, afterwards, to her children, and, if she should die without children, she devises it over to others in like manner. And this bill being brought *inter alia* for a discovery of the testator's estate, it was said for the defendant that they might object for want of proper parties because the persons who were to take in case of a contingency were not made parties; secondly, that the suit was not for the infant's benefit or with her or her parents' desire and would have that examined into in court the[1] father and mother being there.

Curia [Lord Cowper]: The devisees over, being entitled to the residuum only upon a contingency, need not be made parties to the bill, and any person may bring a bill in an infant's name for the infant's benefit. It is an office of humanity and charity to take care of those who are not capable of taking care of themselves. And, if the bill is not in truth for the infant's benefit, the *prochein ami* sues at his own charge. It is he [who] must pay the costs, so it is no prejudice to the infant. Here the *prochein ami* is the infant's uncle and a person of great estate and quality and the parents may not see into the reason and advantage of having such a bill and the accounts taken as is desired. But I, by daily experience, do see it that it is for the infant's advantage to have his accounts taken and settled here.

[Other copies of this report: British Library MS. Hargrave 82, f. 74.]

[Other reports of this case: British Library MS. Hargrave 77, f. 20v, pl. 2, British Library MS. Hargrave 303, f. 39v.]

[1] though *MS.*

130

Bothomly v. Lord Fairfax

(Ch. 1716–1719)

A recognizance is not perfected until it is enrolled; therefore, it does not have priority until the date of enrollment, but it has only the force of a bond before enrollment.

The deposition of a person who afterwards becomes incompetent to testify as a witness can be admitted into evidence.

2 Vernon 750, 23 E.R. 1090

11 March.

The estate of the late Lord Fairfax being by him devised for payment of debts and decreed to be sold and the money arising by sale to be applied for that purpose and first to pay mortgages, judgments, and recognizances that affected the land and then other debts, all creditors were at liberty to come before the Master and prove their debts.

J.S. had a recognizance from the late Lord Fairfax for £500, but the recognizance was not enrolled. And the question was whether J.S. was to be considered as a creditor by recognizance or only as a bond creditor.

It was insisted that a recognizance at common law need not to be enrolled, but it takes its force from being acknowledged and being taken by the proper officer. And, for that purpose, he cited the case of Hall and Winckfeild, in Lord Hobart, fol. 195, 222,[1] and if enrollment was necessary, it might yet be enrolled. A statute staple by the Statute of Acton Burnell[2] is to be enrolled within a limited time, but not so of a recognizance at common law. And, although in the case of Cro. Eliz. 355, Hollingworth *ver.* Ascue, and 2 Roll. Abr. 149,[3] a recognizance not enrolled is adjudged to be a bond, that seems to be a strain, because, although under hand and seal, it is not delivered and delivery is essential to a bond.

Lord Chancellor [Lord Cowper]. The recognizance not being enrolled is imperfect. And, although the court may permit the enrollment of it after the time elapsed, yet it is always done with caution, that it shall not prejudice any intervening purchaser. And the Statute of Frauds and Perjuries[4] provides that judgments shall not, by having relation to the first day of the term, bind purchasers nor affect the land but from the time of signing of them in the margin, but it is silent as to recognizances and pocket securities, which are more dangerous to

---

[1] *Hall v. Wingfield* (1617), Hobart 195, 80 E.R. 342, also Moore K.B. 883, 72 E.R. 973, 1 Brownlow & Goldesborough 69, 123 E.R. 671.

[2] Stat. 11 Edw. I (*SR*, I, 53–54).

[3] *Hollingworth v. Ascue* (1594), Croke Eliz. 355, 78 E.R. 604, 2 Rolle, Abr., *Obligation*, pl. I, 1, p. 149.

[4] Stat. 29 Car. II, c. 3 (*SR*, V, 839–842).

purchasers. And, therefore, it is more reasonable that this recognizance should not bind but from the time of the enrollment. And it may fairly be presumed that the debt was otherwise satisfied or secured when the recognizance was not enrolled. And he decreed J.S. should be considered as a bond creditor only.

Lincoln's Inn MS. Misc. 10, p. 248

11 March 1717[/18].

[It was] adjudged on exceptions to the Master's report that, where a man had devised his lands to be sold for payment of his debts, he had by this put all his debts on an equal foot and that debts on simple contracts should be paid equally with bonds and should carry interest from a year after the testator's death, from which time a legatee is usually allowed interest.

Second, [it was adjudged] that where a judgment was obtained on a bond and the principal and interest was more than the penalty, such overplus interest should be paid, but it should be considered only as a debt on a simple contract.

Lincoln's Inn MS. Misc. 384, p. 98, pl. 1

16 January [1719].

Lord Chancellor [Lord Parker] cited the case of Lady Nolcroft in the Common Pleas, when the judges of that court asked the opinion of the judges of the King's Bench whether, when a person is examined when he is not a party in interest and, afterwards, he comes to be concerned in interest so as he cannot be a good witness, his depositions can be read at a trial at law, they were of the opinion they might be read as evidence, like the case of one that becomes *non compos* [*mentis*] or loses his speech or is beyond the sea or is sick.

Lincoln's Inn MS. Misc. 384, p. 151, pl. 2

9 April 1719.

Lord Chancellor [Lord Parker]: Where a person is examined before he comes to be concerned in interest and after he comes to have an interest whereby he is incapacitated for being a witness, his depositions are evidence at law, for depositions which are once good evidence will ever be so. So, if a witness afterwards becomes dumb or a lunatic or is sick or beyond the sea, here, he is legally dumb. The reason why depositions cannot be read at law as evidence when the witness is living is because the law requires the best evidence, but when the depositions are the best or only evidence that can be had, it is reasonable they should be good evidence. But this court cannot direct they should be good evidence if they are not so at law.

Peere Williams quoted 1 Salk. 286, Tilly's Case,[1] where depositions *in perpetuam rei memoriam* in Chancery were not evidence at law, the witness being alive though, after the depositions were taken, happened to be concerned in interest.

Lord Chancellor [LORD PARKER]: You may distinguish that case from the present, for, there, the depositions were not to be made use of in a cause then depending as here they are.

[Other reports of this case: 1 Peere Williams 334, 24 E.R. 413, Precedents in Chancery 336, 24 E.R. 158, 1 Eq. Cas. Abr. 144, 217, 21 E.R. 945, 1001, British Library MS. Hargrave 80, f. 99v, pl. 1.]

131
Duke of Beaufort v. Lord Dundonald

(Ch. 1716–1717)

Where a testator intends to alter his will but is prevented by accident and fails to do so, the will takes effect at his death as written.

Lincoln's Inn MS. Misc. 12, p. 221

12 March 1715[/16]. The Duke of Beaufort by his next friend, plaintiff; the Lord Dundonald and the Duchess of Beaufort, his wife, *et al.*, defendants.

The late duke of Beaufort,[2] by his will, gave to the defendant, the duchess, his wife, all her jewels, rings, and other garments of her person and all other his jewels whatsoever and the furniture of his houses in London and Middlesex. And he gave the furniture of the house at Bodmington to the plaintiff, his son, to go along with the house.

It was decreed by the Master of the Rolls [TREVOR] that, by the general devise of all other the testator's jewels, his George, Garter sword set with diamonds and other jewels which he wore as a Knight of the Garter did pass by this devise and that a library of books, which was in the house at Bodmington, did pass by the word 'furniture', but that some furniture, which was bought for that house and packed up in boxes in order to be sent down thither, but not sent, could not be deemed or taken to be any part of the furniture of the house at Bodmington.

Lincoln's Inn MS. Hill 29, p. 7

Hilary 3 Geo. I.

---

[1] *Tilley's Case* (1704), 1 Salkeld 286, 91 E.R. 254, also 2 Lord Raymond 1008, 92 E.R. 171.

[2] P. Carter, 'Somerset, Henry, second duke of Beaufort (1684–1714)', *Oxford Dictionary of National Biography*, vol. 51, pp. 592–593.

The late duke [of Beaufort] had devised all his goods and furniture of or belonging to his house at Badminton and Troy in Gloucestershire to his son, the present duke, and he devised to his duchess the residue of all his personal estate and all his household goods and furniture in London and Middlesex.

The duke, sometime before his death, had taken down some of the furniture of the Badmington House and sent it to London to have it cleaned and had bought several goods at London for the Badmington House, all which he had ordered to be packed up in boxes and directed they should be sent by water to Letchlade and from thence by land carriage to Badmington. The boxes were marked with a B and directed as usual. The goods were put into a barge, but the River Thames being at that time very low, the goods could not be brought up so high as Letchlade, and, before the water was high enough to carry them as directed and designed, the duke died. It appeared upon proof that the duke, designing to leave the town and reside chiefly at Badmington, had bought these goods for that house. It appeared also that the duke had made frequent inquiries after the goods in his lifetime and whether they were yet arrived at Badmington.

Query whether the duchess or the present duke shall have the goods?

This cause had had a former hearing before the Master of the Rolls, who was of the opinion that the goods were to be esteemed as part of the residue of the personal estate devised to the duchess, especially since there was no declaration of the duke's intention in writing. And he decreed accordingly.

Upon a petition of appeal to the Lord Chancellor, it came again to be heard this term.

And Mr. *Brown*, counsel for the duchess, cited a case as similar, *viz.* if A. devise all his wearing apparel to B. and he had a new set of clothes at the tailors at the time of his death, they will not pass by the devise.

Mr. *Ward, e contra*, cited a case which was said to be in print, *viz.* A. devises all his goods and chattels in such a house; at the time of the devise's taking effect, there happened to be £400 in coin in the house. This money shall pass by such general words, though, if there be a devise of a sum of money certain by the same will to the same person, it shall be otherwise.

Lord Chancellor [Lord Cowper] in his decree said Mr. Brown's case I take not to be similar to the present case, though it be law. But put it thus, A. buys cloth and puts it to the tailors who brings it home, but is ordered to carry it back in order for further trimming of it and having by his will devised all his wearing apparel at the time of his death to B. and dies, while the clothes remain at the tailors, I take it they will not pass.

So, if a man devise all that is contained in a box marked A at the time of his death to one and all in a box marked B to another, and after[wards] his will has a manifest, evident, and clear design to make a transposition or alteration of what is in the boxes and openly declares the same, yet, if he dies before it is done, though the design was never so manifest, it shall not alter the devise, for whatever at the time of his death was in either box shall pass with it though never so carelessly or humorsomely thrown in. So if a man had two farms and devise the one with all the stock thereon to A. and the other to B. *eodem modo* and afterwards there appears in him a manifest intent to transfer some of the stock from one farm to the other; nay, though orders are actually given to drive off the cattle from one farm to the other, yet, if it is not done before his death, they shall pass respectively as they were on each farm.

I shall, therefore, confirm the decree of the Master of the Rolls but upon a different reason, not because the devisor's intentions were never declared in writing but because the design and intention was not accomplished at the time of the death of the devisor *ergo etc.*

In this cause, it was said at the bar that there was a valuable library at Badmington House, upon which the Lord Chancellor answered that books were furniture and merely furniture to one who was not bookish, but to one who was and understood the use and value of them, they were the best of furniture.

2 Vernon 739, 23 E.R. 1083

26 January [1717].

The duke of Beaufort, by his will made in 1712, devised to his son, the plaintiff, the furniture of his houses in the counties of Gloucester and Monmouth and all his plate. And leaving several other legacies, he made the defendant, his wife, sole executrix and residuary legatee.

The fact fell out to be that the duke lived about two years after the making of the will and had before his death caused several rooms at Badmington in Gloucestershire to be measured, and he bought hangings, pictures, and other furniture, designed to be put up there and had caused the same, with other goods he had here in town, to be packed up and put into cases in order to be sent down to Badmington, and he had agreed with a bargeman for the carriage of them to Letchlade and with carriers and farmers to carry them from Letchlade to Badmington by land carriage. But, before they were removed from London, the duke, in 1714, died at Badmington.

The plaintiff's bill was (amongst other things) to have the goods so packed up and intended to furnish Badmington. And the question was whether they passed by the devise of the furniture of his houses in Gloucestershire and Monmouthshire or belonged to the duchess as executrix and residuary legatee.

The cause was heard at the Rolls, and the duke's bill was dismissed as to that demand. And, coming on now before the Lord Chancellor [Lord Cowper] on an appeal, he affirmed the decree, that the testator's intention to remove the goods to Badmington and to place them there was not sufficient to make them pass by the devise of the furniture of his house at Badmington.

The words of the decree at the Rolls and affirmed as above are as follow:

> Whereupon, etc. His Honor declared that, as to the said goods claimed by the plaintiff and alleged to have been bought by the late duke as the furni-

ture for his house at Badmington and packed up in order to be sent thither, it appeared by the will that the furniture was given to the plaintiff the duke of Beaufort to go along with the house, and His Honor conceived that the said late duke intended those goods for Badmington, and that, by the proofs in the cause, it appeared that they were packed up and designed to be sent thither, but the late duke dying and the goods never having been there and there being no declaration in writing touching those goods, His Honor was of opinion that those goods could not be taken as part of the furniture of or belonging to the house at Badmington, but that they belonged to the defendant the duchess, as claiming the residuum of the late duke's personal estate, and he did therefore order that the plaintiff, the said duke of Beaufort's bill, as to those goods, do stand dismissed.

Reg. Lib. 1716 A, f. 237.

[Other reports of this case: 1 Eq. Cas. Abr. 201, 21 E.R. 989.]

132

Slinger v. Harrison

(Ch. 1716)

One of several co-defendants can except to a report by a Master in Chancery without being joined by his co-defendant.

British Library MS. Hargrave 77, f. 28v

18 March 1715[/16].

Three defendants put in a joint and several answer which is reported insufficient. They join in exceptions to the Master's report. Afterwards, two of them obtain an order to waive their exceptions and submit to put in a further answer. And the exceptions standing for the day, the plaintiff, by his counsel, insisted that the answer being joint and the exceptions joint, the waiver of the exceptions by two must be a waiver of all because there is not now any joint answer subsisting to which the exceptions can relate.

Curia: Though the answer be joint, yet it is several to and may be sufficient as to one though not so as to the rest. Those who have submitted to answer are cautious. The former was insufficient as to what related to them and, therefore, as the one insisting of his answer ought not to affect the waiver of the others, so their waiver ought not to hinder or prevent his insisting on the sufficiency of his answer. So proceed to the exceptions.

[Other copies of this report: British Library MS. Hargrave 82, f. 116, pl. 1, British Library MS. Hargrave 303, f. 53v.]

133
Rushworth v. Rushworth
(Ch. 1716)

In this case, a daughter had an election to receive a legacy or a portion under a marriage settlement.

Language in a will that leases should go along with freehold lands is not a proper devise.

British Library MS. Hargrave 77, f. 52v, pl. 2

2 April 1716. At Westminster.

Sir James, upon his marriage, *inter alia*, creates a term to raise £5000 for a portion for his daughter and, if more than one daughter, to be divided among them, which was to be paid at eighteen or day of marriage. He, afterwards, in his sickness, makes his will and takes notice that he had forgotten the provision he had particularly made for his daughters by settlement and that he would not then look into it, and he devises to his daughter £5000 to be raised out of the lands and to be paid at twenty-one or day of marriage. And he expressly allowed her £60 *per annum* maintenance until ten years old and £80 *per annum* until and then £100 *per annum* until £5000 payable.[1] But he desired that, if she claimed anything by the settlement, that then she should have no benefit by the will. Afterwards, he annexes a codicil, and he declared that, upon a more mature consideration, he gave his daughter £3000 more to be paid her in the like manner with the £5000 devised by will. Sir James, afterwards, dies. And the contingency of his son's death also happens, upon whose death, the daughter was entitled as well to the £5000 as to the estate out of which that £5000 was to be raised in tail.

The question was whether that contingency, the estate being vested in her upon which the term was created and out of which the £5000 was to be raised, her demand of £5000 was not extinguished or whether she could take the £5000 by the settlement and the £5000 and the £3000 by the will and the codicil.

Curia [Lord Cowper]: It is very plain, by the will, she shall not have both £5000 and £3000. But the plaintiff is at an election which to take, for, though, by this contingency, which the testator could not foresee would happen, the estate be vested in her in tail, yet it is not her demand of £5000 by the settlement extinguished, but in regard, by the will, there is a stated maintenance.

Curia [Lord Cowper] was of the opinion that she ought to be paid at all events according to the will notwithstanding the said estate was vested as not immediately depending upon the legacy until she should elect, which she would not yet do, being a minor.

[1] Sic in MSS.

There was another question. Sir James was seised of some freehold and chattel leases, he does not expressly devise over by limitations. But he wills that they should go along with his freehold. The question was, by *Vernon*, whether these words did not amount to a good devise over in equity of those leases or whether they should be deemed part of the personal estate of the son, to whom they were expressly devised, and vested in the plaintiff as administratrix to her brother.

Curia [Lord Cowper]: [It is] not a remainder. This court never carried it so far. And, therefore, he desired a precedent. But none being cited, [he], therefore, decreed it no devise over but part of the personal estate of the son.

[Other copies of this report: British Library MS. Hargrave 303, f. 90v.]

134

Anonymous

(Ch. 1716)

When the wife of a London freeman accepts a jointure, this does not bar her from her customary share of his estate unless it is expressly stated to do so.

British Library MS. Hargrave 77, f. 53

The Court of Aldermen, at Lord Chancellor Cowper's request, certify by the Recorder that, where a jointure is made expressly in bar of customary dower, that, here, it would amount to a bar and a citizen's widow, in such a case, could not support her claim according to the custom of the City. But, if there was a jointure settled and no mention made that it should bar her of her customary right, the Court of Aldermen did not find any precedent in their court where it had been carried so far that, in such a case, she would be barred of her customary right. [This was] certified at Westminster 2 May 1716.

[Other copies of this report: British Library MS. Hargrave 303, f. 91, pl. 1.]

135

Weston v. Fisher

(Ch. 1716)

All parties in interest can be ordered to be joined in a suit so that complete justice can be done in the case.

British Library MS. Hargrave 77, f. 53v

5 May.

Serjeant *Hooper*, for the plaintiff: It is settled in Cook upon Littleton that, where a remainder in fee was limited to the right heirs of the two several persons, they do not take in joint tenancy but as tenants in common because it must vest at different times. This was before insisted on at the arguing of the defendant's plea in bar to the plaintiff's demand. And the plaintiffs were then ordered to amend their bill. And, then, their case appeared to be otherwise than it was stated by the former statings.

Sir E. Brett purchases lands in Kent to one Bruster to about £500 *per annum* for 1000 years term, which term Bruster had purchased of Sir [*blank*]. And he covenants that Sir [*blank*] should convey those lands to Sir E. Brett in fee. But, before that was done, Sir [*blank*] dies, and he leaves his heir, an infant. Sir E. Brett makes his will and takes notice of the term, and he covenants to convey in fee and if Sir [*blank*] death and of his heir being an infant so that the conveyance could not at that time be perfected, then he devises the land to the defendant John Brett Fisher for life and then to his issue in tail, remainder to the defendant Edward Bro. in like manner. And, after some other limitations, he devises it to the heir of A. and B. The plaintiff is the heir of A., deceased, and so he is entitled to a moiety.

And he brings his bill to stay waste and to have a satisfaction for waste committed.

The defendant insisted that the devisor had only a term of 1000 years in him and so the devise to the plaintiff could not take [effect].

Curia: It does not appear whether Sir [*blank*] had the fee in himself or only as a trustee or whether he was to convey as the trustee for Bruster or that Bruster was to make an application and get such a conveyance. Therefore, that they might come to the truth of that matter, the heir of Sir [*blank*] and the heir of Bruster were ordered to be made parties by the plaintiff's amending his bill.

Note the plaintiff filed his first bill, and, to that bill, the defendant put in his plea that he did not believe Sir E. Brett was seised in fee of those lands. Afterwards, in his answer to the plaintiff's amended bill, he makes his case to be as by the will. At the hearing, he insisted that, the defendant's having in his plea said as above, he shall not now be admitted to say Sir E. Brett was not seised in fee, but only of a term. And then, the defendant confessing him to be so seised, the court was to decree as if he was really so seised in fee.

For the defendant, [it was said] that, as the plaintiffs made their case by the original bill, it was indifferent to the defendant whether Sir E. Brett was seised in fee or no. And, therefore, he did not make any great inquiry after it. Though he did say he believed etc., yet he did refer to the will, but now that the plaintiff had made a new case, it became incumbent of the defendant to look into the title.

[Other copies of this report: British Library MS. Hargrave 303, f. 91v.]

136

Cooley v. Cooley

(Ch. 1716)

A testator's intention must be followed as much as it can be and the best way to attain the testator's intention is to view the whole will and make it as consistent as possible.

British Library MS. Hargrave 77, f. 54

9 May 1716.

The testator, Mr. Cooley, upon his marriage settles £200 *per annum* upon his wife and the issue of that marriage. About a year after, he makes his will, and, thereby, he gives her the £200 *per annum* settled upon her for life according to the settlement, and immediately, without taking any express or other notice of his personal estate, he gives the produce of the rest of the estate to his son, but, if his son die before age, then he gave it to his brothers and sisters, equally to be divided, and their heirs forever. And he made his brother, the defendant, trustee for the uses and purposes in the will, and he made him executor. About an hour after, he adds a codicil, and he, thereby, gives his wife all his leasehold goods and her watch and earrings, 'the rest of my estate I leave for the discretion of' the defendant.

At the hearing, the defendant insisted by virtue of the codicil that he was entitled to the testator's personal estate except the specific legacies devised by the codicil to the wife.

And it was then referred to the Master to take an account of the value of the real and personal estate in order to give a better light into the intention of the will, the defendant having suggested the personal estate was but small. And the Master reported the whole real estate included freehold and chattel leases was under £400 and subject to the jointure and the personal estate £4000. This matter came on the day of exceptions.

And *Sir Joseph Jekyll* and Mr. *Peere Williams*, for the defendant, said it was improbable that a father should devise so great a part of his estate from his own son, who was but nine weeks old. And, therefore, it was impossible he could have offended him. The codicil was executed not above an hour after the will, and it was a clearer explanation of his intent in the will. And, though, by the will, he did only mention his lands, yet the word 'the estate' was sufficient in the will to vest the whole, real and personal. And the testator, being a trading man, had made use of the words 'of the produce', which, in this case, did make no alteration, it being a usual way of speaking among traders of personal estates and so did include the personal as well as the real, and the clause in the codicil only served to make his intent more clear and plain, for, whereas by the will, he makes his brother trustee etc., which words are indeed a little dubious and obscure, yet they doubted not it would have been construed upon those words that the testator meant the whole to his son.

But now, to the codicil, he comes and says 'I leave it to the discretion' etc., which was no more than to desire him to take care and manage it for the best advantage of his son. And by 'discretion' could only be intended management. Besides, it was more plain by saying 'I leave' etc. In all wills, where a testator intends a benefit, he says 'I give, devise, or bequeath' and 'uses to me vesting'. Term [?] But 'leave' in a will did not vest. (And I think they cited some cases.) And, here, wherever the testator designed a benefit, he uses the word 'give'; so immediately before in the codicil, and that variation in expression clearly spoke the testator's meaning.

Sir Robert Raymond: Query that persons penned their wills just as it came into their thoughts. 'I give, devise, or leave' sometimes one way, sometimes another, and any of those are sufficient. The testator had amply provided for his son by his real estate, and the plaintiff was his brother, whom he made executor and had not given him one farthing except he would take the benefit of this construction.

Mr. *Vernon, ad idem*: He took it too the codicil was a plainer declaration of the intent of the testator, and he conceived that a testator making his will and taking no notice of his personal estate, which was a great part of the whole, and makes his own brother executor, having amply provided for his children, if it shall not be intended and construed that the personal estate is well devised to the brother as his executor, for he took it that an executor, although a stranger, was well entitled to a personal estate not devised; much more the plaintiff. And it could not be thought, the testator's personal estate being so great, that he would be altogether silent as to the disposition of it but that he intended it for his executor, because he could not forget his personal [estate] and so would dispose of it one way or other, but that the codicil made it past all doubt that he intended it for his executor. And the leaving to his discretion was leaving to his will and pleasure to dispose of it as he thought fit. And he never heard that 'discretion' in a will signified anything else. And he hoped it would be so construed here.

Curia: It is impossible to come at any certainty in such obscure, perplexed wills. But the testator's intention must be followed as much as it may be. Now, in such sort of illiterate wills, the best way to attain the testator's intention is to take a view of the whole will and make it consistent as well as we can.

[Other copies of this report: British Library MS. Hargrave 303, f. 92.]

Lincoln's Inn MS. Misc. 11, p. 32

Henry Cooley of St. Bride's, London, Esq., gives to his wife, Mary, an annuity or settlement of £200 *per annum* to be paid her clear of taxes, the residue of the produce of the estate to be preserved by his brother for the benefit of his infant son, Henry, but, in case of his death before he came of age, he orders and devises that the estate after the decease of his wife and children should go to be equally divided between his brother and sister of the Cooley family forever together with the product to be thereof made. And he makes his brother, Francis Cooley, sole executor and trustee for the purposes in the will.

The same day, he makes a codicil in the words following, *viz.* 'I give all my household goods and furniture to my wife and her watch and earrings, and all the rest of my personal estate I leave to the discretion of my executor signed and dated the day abovesaid.'

The testator left a wife and one child. And, in a few days after the testator's death, the executor proved the will and prevailed on the testator's widow to deliver to him part of the testator's personal estate to the value of nearly £3000, pretending that he would take care of the widow and her child and be a friend to them and afterwards insists that, by the testator's will, after payment of the testator's debts and funerals, that he is entitled in his own right to all the testator's personal estate.

The bill was brought by the mother and child for an account of the personal estate and to be paid the surplus.

[LORD COWPER] decreed the executor was only a trustee for the plaintiffs in the will and codicil.

137

Buckley v. Arnold

(Ch. 1716)

A conveyance of property that has no value is not a fraudulent conveyance.

22 Viner, Abr. 20

Trinity 2 Geo.

B. and C. are two brothers. Lands are conveyed to C. and his heirs in trust for J.S., a stranger, for his life, remainder to B. in tail, remainder to C. in fee. During the life of J.S., the tenant for life, C., in consideration of 5s., conveys the reversion to B. and his heirs in fee. B., supposing he had an absolute fee in him, devises the lands to his executors to be sold for payment of debts and legacies, and he makes his brother C. and another person executors, and he dies without issue. C. bargains and sells the lands to the defendant Arnold, who had notice of all these transactions etc.

The question was if the defendant, being a purchaser for a valuable consideration, shall avoid the conveyance from C. to B. of the reversion in fee, being voluntary, it being, at the time of the conveyance, a dry reversion in fee expectant upon an estate tail and of no consideration in the eye of the law.

COWPER, Chancellor, was of opinion that the conveyance of the reversion in fee from C. to B. cannot be avoided as fraudulent by a subsequent purchaser, because, at the time of the conveyance, it was of no value, being barrable by the tenant in tail by a recovery with consent of the tenant for life, yet he granted a trial at law upon the importunity of counsel.

[Other copies of this report: 2 Eq. Cas. Abr. 752, 22 E.R. 638.]

138

Edmundson v. Cox

(Ch. 1716–1717)

The widow of a London freeman must renounce all benefits of his will in order to take her customary share contrary to the will.

A voluntary bond is a fraudulent conveyance as to a London widow but not as to legatees.

A bond is a valid debt even though it was never delivered to the payee.

7 Viner, Abr. 202

Trinity 2 Geo.

A bill [was exhibited] by a widow of a freeman of London for her customary share of her late husband's estate. The case was the husband made his will and devised to his wife several shares in the New River Water, with a remainder over etc., and he gave her several legacies. The will was sealed up in a sheet of paper, and enclosed in the same paper was a bond found executed by the testator some time before the date of the will, which bond was conditioned to pay the defendant, being his nephew, the sum of £1000 or to transfer to him £1000 stock in the Million Bank, but this bond appeared to be voluntary and not given upon a valuable consideration etc.

The first query was if this voluntary bond shall be taken as a debt due from the testator and, consequently, to be paid out of the testator's personal estate before the widow's customary share.

Secondly, if the widow must renounce and disclaim all benefit and advantage by the will, as well the devise of the shares in the New River for her life, being real estate, as the devise of personal chattels to her.

Trevor, Master of the Rolls, said the plaintiff must disclaim all benefit and advantage by the will if she will have a decree for her customary share, contrary to the will, and this is the constant course of this court.

Secondly, this bond, being in the nature of a voluntary gift, is fraudulent *quoad* the wife's customary share and shall not stand in her way, and such sort of contrivances to evade the custom are always set aside in this court.

He decreed accordingly.

[Other copies of this report: 2 Eq. Cas. Abr. 276, 22 E.R. 233.]

Lincoln's Inn MS. Misc. 380, pt. 3, p. 168, pl. 2

A citizen of London makes a bond whereby he gives £1000 to B. He executes it but keeps it in his own possession and puts it enclosed in his will. He likewise made another bond and will to the same effect and delivers them to a friend to keep as his will.

The [question] was whether this bond should defeat the wife of her customary part.

The Master of the Rolls [JEKYLL] decreed that it should not.

Then, the specific legatees in the will pray that the bond may not have preference to them.

But the Master [JEKYLL] decreed that he thought the testator intended a benefit to the obligee prior to the other legatees by giving him a security, which, in course has preference.

Lincoln's Inn MS. Misc. 10, p. 258

22 November 1717. Lincoln's Inn Hall.

Richard Edmondson, by will, gives specific legacies to the plaintiff, and he makes the defendant, his nephew, executor, who, after the testator's death, found a bond wrapped up in the will executed by the testator wherein he had become bound to the defendant in the penalty of £2000 for the payment of £1000.

The plaintiff brought his bill for an account of the personal estate and to have his legacies.

The defendant insists that there was not sufficient [assets] to pay all of the testator's debts and legacies and that he ought to retain in his hands so much as was sufficient to pay the bond, preferable to the plaintiff's legacy.

The question was if this bond, which was purely voluntary and never in the obligee's hands until he found it in the will after the testator's death should have a preference to the legacies in the will.

The Master of the Rolls [JEKYLL] would hardly allow it to be spoken to, saying it was a debt both in law and equity, and he cited the case of Clavering and Clavering,[1] where it was decreed and afterwards affirmed in the House of Lords that a voluntary disposition by a deed kept always in the custody of the person who made it should take place of a contrary disposition by a will of the same estate.

---

[1] *Clavering v. Clavering* (1704–1705), 2 Vernon 473, 23 E.R. 904, Precedents in Chancery 235, 24 E.R. 114, 7 Brown P.C. 410, 3 E.R. 267, 1 Eq. Cas. Abr. 24, 21 E.R. 845, 2 Eq. Cas. Abr. 351, 22 E.R. 299.

139

Anonymous

(Ch. 1716)

Where a thing agreed for by a contract is devised by a will or is allowed to descend, which the party had a power over or might have disposed of from the heir, it will be considered as done in satisfaction of the contract.

British Library MS. Hargrave 81, f. 49

6 June.

J.S. gave bonds to settle lands of a certain value to the use of himself for life, then to Mary, the intended wife, for her life, then to the heirs of the body of J.S., the intended husband. After the marriage and before any settlement made, J.S. dies, having by will devised to A., who was the eldest son of that marriage and his heir at law, £100 in money and permits a copyhold estate of which he was seised in fee to descend to the said A. The question was whether those lands should be taken as a satisfaction for the agreement by the bond at least *pro tanto* and whether the £100 legacy should be deemed a part of the satisfaction.

Serjeant *Hooper*: The bond is for settling freehold lands, and what is descended is copyhold, so not the thing intended, and it cannot be construed a satisfaction because of less value and of another nature, for, though both are inheritances, yet the copyhold is but a base tenure and subject by custom to several disadvantages and restrictions to which the freehold is not and among others not to cut down trees without license.

Mr. *Vernon*: The legacy cannot be any recompense or satisfaction in this case. And that a legacy shall not be so was lately decreed in the case of Hooper and Pollexton. By the Statute of Distributions,[1] the heir at law shall have his distribution notwithstanding any real estate that descends to him. And there is no question but an heir at law is capable to take a legacy notwithstanding his being heir, though it may be otherwise in the case of younger children where any provision is made for them by any articles or settlement before marriage.

Sir Joseph Jekyll, for the defendants: Where a thing of the same nature or kind as provided by agreement before marriage is devised by will or is suffered to descend, which the party had power over and might dispose of from the heir, it must be taken to be done in recompense or satisfaction of the agreement *pro tanto* at least.

Curia: The copyhold here suffered to descend is so for a satisfaction of the agreement. So let the Master enquire into the value of the copyhold estate. But, as to the £100 legacy, that is not to be reckoned as any part of the satisfaction. Therefore, the plaintiff must have it with interest.

[1] Stat. 22 & 23 Car. II, c. 10 (*SR*, V, 719–720).

[Other copies of this report: British Library MS. Hargrave 82, f. 47.]

[Other reports of this case: British Library MS. Hargrave 77, f. 14, pl. 2, British Library MS. Hargrave 303, f. 25.]

140

Sufton v. Pilkinton

(Ch. 1716)

A creditor of a decedent can require the executor or administrator to disclose the assets of the decedent's estate.

British Library MS. Hargrave 81, f. 50, pl. 1

8 June.

Where a creditor brings a bill against an executor or administrator, though he does administer and annex an account or schedule, yet he shall be examined on interrogatories to discover the assets and that not only from the time he put in the answer, but generally.

[Other copies of this report: British Library MS. Hargrave 82, f. 49, pl. 1.]

[Other reports of this case: British Library MS. Hargrave 77, f. 14v, pl. 1, British Library MS. Hargrave 303, f. 26, pl. 1.]

141

Carter v. Heneage

(Ch. 1716)

In general, interest upon interest, compound interest, is not favored by the law.

In this case, the court refused to allow compound interest.

British Library MS. Hargrave 81, f. 16

8 June 1716.

A bill was filed in 1714 against a mortgagee in possession to account for principal and interest and to convey the estate to the plaintiff, who was heir at law. The defendant by an answer said that the mortgage was now of forty years standing and that, in the year 1695, a person who conceived himself to be heir (for there was then a great contest at law who was) exhibited a bill against the defendant and that, in answer thereto, the defendant had sworn there was £2200 and odd pounds then due to her for interest beside principal etc. And now she says it was true that there was so much interest due at that time and insists to have interest for that sum from the year 1695 as well as for the principal.

At the hearing, it was referred to the Master to compute the interest. And he was directed to make a rest at the year 1695. The Master, in computing the interest, did not make such a rest nor allow interest upon the interest sworn due at that time, upon which the defendant took exceptions to the Master's report because he had not allowed interest upon that interest, which were overruled, because there was no decree for the Master to allow such interest and the exceptions should have been for not making such a rest as the decree directed.

Mr. *Cooper* said the matter was now fully before the court and they were all ready, if His Lordship pleased, to go into it and see if the defendant ought to have interest upon interest in this case.

It was insisted on for the defendant that, if she had her money paid her at the time she had given in that account, she might have made interest of it and, as interest is always allowed upon a stated account, it not being pretended but that the account given in in this case is true in every particular, it amounts to the same as a stated account. The defendant was called upon for it and gave it in upon oath; therefore, he ought to have the same benefit and advantage as a stated account. And it was said the court, upon the hearing, seemed to be of that opinion by directing the Master to make the arrest in computing interest at the year 1695 in order to see if the account then given in were true.

Mr. *Cooper*: There have been an abundance of cases in this court and many artifices and contrivances made use of by mortgagees much stronger than this to get interest upon interest. But yet I never heard in any one case whatsoever that it was ever allowed by this court. And the reason is plain, because the mortgagee has his remedy whenever he pleases; he may enter upon the estate and received the profit. Interest is never looked upon to carry interest in this court until a decree is pronounced, the report made and confirmed, and then, indeed, from the time that payment is ordered to be made, the whole is become a principal debt and will carry interest from the time payment is to be made.

Mr. *Vernon*: Where a mortgagee has only a reversion and assigns over the mortgage, there, indeed, interest has been made principal because, as to the assignee, the interest and principal were one capital sum and there was no remedy for the mortgagee. But, if interest upon interest be allowed in this case, I do not see any case in which it may not. I never yet heard of any case whatsoever in this court, though many and divers have been the attempts to compass it, where interest upon interest has been allowed a mortgagee, who always has his own remedy.

Curia [Lord Cowper]: Many times, it is very just that the mortgagee should have interest upon interest. But the justice of this court never favors such interest. And I do not know any one case where interest has been allowed upon interest sworn due by an answer. I dare say there is none such, and I am very cautious of making new precedents. Show me any one precedent for it, and, then, it may be done here.

But the counsel not being able to show any precedent, it was decreed that interest should not be allowed upon interest in this case.

[Other copies of this report: British Library MS. Hargrave 82, f. 13.]

[Other reports of this case: British Library MS. Hargrave 77, f. 7, British Library MS. Hargrave 303, f. 9v.]

142

Strode v. Strode

(Ch. 1716)

Upon a suit for a breach of contract, the court can order a Master in Chancery to take an account of the plaintiff's damages.

British Library MS. Hargrave 81, f. 51, pl. 2

10 June.

The plaintiff's testator, who was husband to the defendant, on their intermarriage in consideration of a £4000 portion, covenanted to settle a £400 *per annum* jointure. And afterwards, he conveys lands to trustees for her jointure, which he covenants to be and that they shall continue to be of the value of £400 *per annum*.

Mr. Strode makes his will and the plaintiff and defendant, both, his executors, [and he] devises several specific legacies to the defendant and gives the residue of his estate after his debts and legacies to the plaintiff. The defendant, at first, renounced executorship but, afterwards, resumed it and proved the will, as the other had done before. The testator died the 29th day of September about nine o'clock at night.

As the jointure proved deficient, upon which the defendant claimed the half year's rent because the husband died before twelve o'clock at night, so the rent [was] not completely due to him, and to have the deficiency made good, the plaintiff brought his bill to settle her demands and the satisfaction for the deficiency.

And, upon the decree, the Master was directed to inquire how much the deficiency was and that she should be deemed a creditor for so much to her husband's estate. And the Master was to set a value upon her interest for life for the deficiency, which by report was £9 4s. *per annum* and valued at eight years purchase. To this report, the plaintiff excepted because taxes were not deducted or allowed in the deficiency of £9 4s. *per annum* and because eight year's purchase was too much, she being seventy years old.

Mr. *Vernon*, for the plaintiff: The deficiency in the value of the land must be computed according to what the rent would have been if no such deficiency were and, as the defendant would not have had the rent without a deduction of taxes, she ought not to have a compensation for more on account of the deficiency than she would have had clear if the rents had not been deficient. And he cited the case of Ashby and Ashby in Lord Cowper's time, where the party who was to make good the deficiency had an allowance by the decree not only for taxes but for repairs also, which was carrying it further than it had ever been before.

Sir Joseph Jekyll, for the defendant: This is not to be considered now as an annual payment of rent out of lands, but as a debt, and that is not subject to taxes. The court has by the decree directed the deficiency to be computed and the defendant to be a creditor for so much. And, as the Master has not deducted taxes, so neither has he allowed the defendant any interest for the deficiency. And if she should be obliged to allow for taxes and not have interest given her, the plaintiff would take a benefit of his own laches and wrong, which he ought not to do. Had there not been a deficiency, the defendant would have had her rent every year in her pocket and might have put it out at interest. So that, in this respect also, the defendant is damnified by the breach of covenant and ought to have satisfaction. And as to the eight year's purchase, it is not at all too much, for the usual purchase for life is ten years at least and sometimes more, and, though she be near seventy, she is a healthy strong woman and likely to live long.

Curia [Lord Cowper]: The question is how far the defendant is damnified by the breach of the covenant, for, so far, she is to have a satisfaction and no farther. She cannot be damnified in respect of that which, if the rent had been complete, must have been taken or kept from her to pay the taxes and, therefore, cannot have nor is entitled to any compensation for it.

I will take everything most strongly against a person who willfully breaks his covenant and, therefore, allow the valuation of eight years purchase. And, as to the part deficient, let the Master make the same deduction for taxes as he has done for the other part of the £400 *per annum*. And let the defendant have interest for the deficiency from six months after the first year. And, as to the half years rent, that must go to the defendant, for, the husband, dying on the day it was payable, had no right nor could have any action until the day following. And she must have interest also for the said half years rent from six months after it became due.

[Other copies of this report: British Library MS. Hargrave 82, f. 49.]

[Other reports of this case: British Library MS. Hargrave 77, f. 14v, pl. 2, British Library MS. Hargrave 303, f. 26, pl. 2.]

143

Anonymous

(Ch. c. 1716)

The witnesses of a will must sign and seal the will.

Where a plaintiff's case is dismissed yet he had an honest cause and probable ground of suit, the case will be dismissed without costs.

British Library MS. Hargrave 81, f. 19

13 June; Westminster.

The father of the plaintiffs, being seised of a real estate of about £200 *per annum* and having three daughters, devises it to his wife for life and then to trustees to raise a certain sum for his daughters' portions. And then, subject to that charge, he devises the land to his nephew in fee, but he reserved a power of charging it with the sum of £1000 by deed or will signed and sealed in the presence of three credible witnesses. One part of the will was left with the testator's attorney and the other he kept himself. He added a clause with his own hand in a space that was left between the writing and the seal whereby he ordered his nephew to give a certain number of loaves every Sunday to the poor of the parish.

And upon this clause, it is [that] the plaintiffs found their bill as being a re-publication of their father's will and so a good execution of the power reserved in the settlement. And in order to support this, they proved there were three witnesses present when the clause was inserted and that it was written with his own hand. And they proved also that, after all these transactions of the testator, one of the plaintiffs and the defendant being together, the plaintiff said to the testator 'when you are dead, your nephew will not pay your legacies nor live at your house', upon which the testator said, holding up his fist, 'do you hear Jack will not, you pay my legacies' etc., and the defendant replied, upon the word of a gentleman, that he would pay the legacies he should give by his will and give the poor their bread and live at his house when the estate came to his possession. And it was also insisted on for the plaintiffs that, if this clause should not be reckoned to amount to a re-publication, yet the promise ought to bind the defendant since, probably, that might have been a means of preventing the testator's making a stricter and more regular execution of the power reserved by the deed.

Curia [Lord Cowper]: The clause will not amount to a re-publication according to the power reserved in the deed. It was indeed in the presence of three witnesses, but neither signed nor sealed, and, therefore, it cannot amount to a re-publication in this case. And, as to the promise the defendant will answer, there is no will, so that must fall to the ground, though I do not believe the defendant meant it so at the time he made the promise. But the rules of the court must be followed. And this promise is not sufficient to support the plaintiffs' demand. I must, therefore, dismiss their bill. But as they had an honest cause and probable ground of suit, I will dismiss it without costs.

[Other copies of this report: British Library MS. Hargrave 82, f. 15.]

[Other reports of this case: British Library MS. Hargrave 77, f. 7v, British Library MS. Hargrave 303, f. 11.]

144
Cade v. Price

(Ch. 1716)

A grant of land grants by implication what is necessary for the enjoyment of the land, such as a right of way. But, a grant of one parcel, two parcels adjoining each other, without a reservation a way to the unsold parcel is not an implied reservation of a right of way out of the lands which were expressly sold.

British Library MS. Hargrave 81, f. 55

21 June.

The bill was to have a specific execution of an agreement for the purchase of ground, part of which the defendant had before the agreement laid out as a way to other of his grounds, and, therefore, insisted that the way, being necessary to his other grounds, never was intended to pass by the agreement, at least not so as to deprive him of the benefit of it and render the other grounds of no use to him for want of a way to come at them.

But the Master of the Rolls [TREVOR] decreed for the plaintiff, and he took this distinction, that, in equity as at law, if a man grants lands to another, he grants by implication what is necessary for the enjoyment of those lands, *viz.* a way, but, if he grants one close, having two joining to each other and does not reserve to himself a way to the close unsold or express something to that effect, it is his own fault and the law will not by implication reserve him a way out of the lands which he has expressly sold and given away. But, if a man sell all his lands in such a place except a certain close, there, the exception of the close will take in all the necessary requisites for the enjoyment of it.

And he cited the case of the Lord Ellesmere and Sir Robert Kenaston. The Lord Ellesmere had purchased lands from the lord of the manor, who had reserved certain ponds in the grounds to himself; the Lord Ellesmere turned those grounds afterwards into a park. Sir Robert Kenaston insisted that he had a right to a way to those ponds by implication, having expressly excepted them out of the grant. And the case being referred to the judges at Westminster, it was resolved that the ponds being reserved by the grant to the grantor and his heirs, by implication of law, a way to those ponds was reserved also, but that, if the lands had been all sold by their particular denominations and no mention at all made of the ponds, the grantor would have no right [of way] to the ponds through the grounds of the grantee. And he said that the rules of equity as to compelling a specific execution of an agreement is that, if there be circumvention or surprise in obtaining it or that the agreement be improvident, incautious, or overreaching, not to establish it or carry it into execution, but to leave the party to get by law what he can.

[Other copies of this report: British Library MS. Hargrave 82, f. 53.]

[Other reports of this case: British Library MS. Hargrave 77, f. 15, British Library MS. Hargrave 303, f. 27v.]

145
Saring v. Philpot
(Ch. 1716)

Where a testator gives the profits of a lease to his executors until his son comes of age and the son dies under age, the executors get the profits, even though the son could never have had them.

Lincoln's Inn MS. Misc. 11, p. 18, pl. 1

22 June 1716.

A.B., by will, gives to his son a leasehold estate, but, until he comes to twenty-one, he gives the profits to his executors, whom he makes residuary legatees. The son dies before twenty-one, and the plaintiff takes administration.

It was decreed the executors to account for the profits from the death of the son.

So note the administrator was in a better condition than the son would have been if he had lived, for then he could not have had the profits until twenty-one.

It was agreed the administrator should not have had the profits until the time the infant would have come to twenty-one if the profits had been given the executors for the payment of debts or there had been a deficiency of other assets.

146
Stanhope v. Thacker
(Ch. 1716)

A security interest in land cannot be defeated by a common recovery.

Lincoln's Inn MS. Misc. 11, p. 24, pl. 2

Trinity [term] 1716.

Gilbert Thacker, on the marriage of his son, by a settlement dated 9 July 1670, conveys lands to trustees, the uses whereof as to part were to Mr. Thacker for life, then to his wife for life, remainder to Gilbert, the son, for life, with a provision for supporting contingent remainders, remainder to the first and other sons of Gilbert, the son, begotten on Elizabeth, his intended wife, in tail male, remainder to all and every the daughters of Gilbert, the son, on the body of Elizabeth to be begotten and of the heirs of their several bodies until such time as such daughter or daughters should or might out of the rents, issues, and profits of the premises have received £3000 to be equally divided amongst them and, after receipt had of the said sum by such daughters or for want of such daughters, then to the heirs male of the body of Gilbert, the son, then to the second and other sons of old Gilbert, the father, in tail male, remainder to the right heirs of Gilbert, the son.

Gilbert, the son, had issue by Elizabeth, his wife, one child only, *viz.* Jane, the plaintiff's wife. And, after the death of Elizabeth, Gilbert, the son, married a second wife and had other children.

The plaintiff's wife, after the death of her father, levies a fine and suffers a recovery and declares the use thereof to herself in fee, but, before she suffered the recovery, she assigned over the £3000 portion.

The question was if this fine and recovery barred the remainder to the right heirs of Gilbert, the son, and, if it did not, then whether the £3000 should be raised by a sale or mortgage and should carry interest from the death of Gilbert, the son.

Lord Chancellor [Lord Cowper] was of opinion that, though the recovery was good at law, yet it did not bar the remainders, the estate tail created by the settlement for raising the £3000 being in the nature of a mortgage or security for that sum for portions for the daughters and that the turning the estate tail into a fee simple by levying a fine and suffering a recovery was no more than making it a fee simple security instead of a security depending on an estate tail and would not hinder the persons in remainder from redeeming if they thought fit.

As to interest, the court was of opinion the £3000 ought to be raised with interest from the death of Gilbert, the son. And [the court] directed the plaintiffs to account for the rents and what they fell short of satisfying the £3000 with interest, it should be raised by the sale of so much of the premises as the Master should find necessary.

Note in the arguing of this case was cited the Case of Page and Heywood, in the [Court of] King's Bench.[1] [There was a] devise to a niece in tail upon condition that she married J.S. She suffers a recovery and then marries J.N. And the court was of opinion that this being a collateral condition, it was defeated by the recovery.

Note it seemed to be agreed in this case that, if a man pleads himself to be a purchaser for a valuable consideration and the plea is replied to, he ought to prove the consideration as well as the execution of the deed.

There was another question in this cause, which was this. Mr. Wootton, upon his marriage with the defendant Mrs. Thacker, agrees with Mr. Thacker, her father, to release a sum of £2000, which in the agreement was said to be charged upon the estate of Mr. Thacker and payable after his death to the defendant. And it seems that the sum mentioned in the settlement which charged the land was really £2500. And the question now was whether this agreement should extend to release the whole £2500.

Lord Chancellor [Lord Cowper] was of opinion it should not, for it may reasonably be presumed that this £500 was concealed from Mr. Wootton by Mr. Thacker, for it is plain Mr. Wootton knew nothing of it, and it would be hard in a court of equity to say that, when a man has agreed to release £2000, he shall be compelled to release £500 more.

Upon this, another question sprung up which was to whom this £500 did belong since it was not to be released, whether to Mrs. Wootton as a chose in action which never vested in her husband or to his representative in regard Mr. Wootton had made a settlement upon his wife before the marriage and thereby became a purchaser of her fortune and, this £500 being part of her fortune, it ought therefore to go to his representative.

But to this, it was said that, this £500 being concealed from Mr. Wootton, he could make no settlement in consideration of that part of the fortune and, therefore, there is no reason to extend the settlement to what was not then known to the parties nor could be under their consideration when the settlement was made.

And of that opinion the court seemed to be but reserved the consideration thereof until a further time.

[Other reports of this case: Precedents in Chancery 435, 24 E.R. 194.]

---

[1] *Page v. Hayward* (1704), 2 Salkeld 570, 91 E.R. 481, 3 Salkeld 96, 135, 91 E.R. 714, 736, 11 Modern 61, 88 E.R. 886, Holt K.B. 618, 90 E.R. 1242, 2 Eq. Cas. Abr. 362, 22 E.R. 308.

147

Le Pypre v. Farr

(Ch. 1716)

In this case upon an insurance policy, the insured was required to make discovery of what goods were insured, and the insurer was ordered to pay for them.

Lincoln's Inn MS. Misc. 384, p. 132, pl. 1

28 January. Lord Chancellor's house.

Lord Chancellor [Lord Cowper]: Where a policy of insurance is made, interest or no interest, if the insured had no goods on board, it is in the nature of a wager. If he has any on board and there is part saved, the insurer is entitled to what is saved and to a discovery of what is saved and what was put on board but not of the property or value. And, if the whole being worth but £500, part is saved when £700 was insured, the insurers must take what is saved and pay the whole money, for what is insured more than the value of the goods is in the nature of a wager. And where part of the goods is saved, the insureds need only assign their interest in them to the insurers, but they are not to be at the charge of delivering them into the insurers' hands but are entitled to the whole insurance money.

N.B. The insurers are not entitled to a discovery of what was on board at the time of the loss where the policy is interest or no interest.

N.B. Lord Chancellor Cowper decreed that the insurers should only pay the insureds so much as the insurance money exceeded the value of the goods saved whereby the insureds were to be at the trouble of getting in the goods saved, which seems contrary to Lord Parker's opinion; *vide* Salvador and Parrott.

Lincoln's Inn MS. Misc. 11, p. 124

A bill [was exhibited] to be relieved against an action upon a policy of insurance, the words of which policy were that the goods and merchandises loaded or to be loaded on board the ship *Abraham and Isaac* from the loading thereof at London until the said ship with the goods should be arrived at the coast of Africa and there safely landed and to begin the adventure upon such other goods as should be loaded on board the said ship on the coast of Africa from the loading thereof and so to continue until the said ship with the goods should be arrived at Jamaica and thus safely landed, the said goods to be valued at £600 and the assured not liable to make proof of interest.

The plaintiffs, by their bill, insist that the ship arrived safely on the coast of Africa and that the defendant's agents safely landed, bartered, and disposed of the said goods with which the ship was loaded when she set sail from England, that the supercargo neglecting or not having been able to purchase a cargo of Negroes, the bottom of the ship, by lying so long on the coast of Africa, failed, and the ship was declared unnavigable and what goods were left therein were sold.

And, therefore, it was prayed by the bill that the defendants might give an account of the particulars and value of the cargo and how much was sold, landed, bartered, or disposed of in Africa, and they insist that they ought to answer no more than the value of the goods lost in proportion to the money insured. The defendant, by answer, insists he ought not to set out what goods were on board nor to what value when the ship arrived at Africa.

The answer being reported insufficient, exceptions were taken to the Master's report, upon the arguing whereof, Lord Cowper ordered the defendant to set forth the particulars of the goods, but not property nor value.

Note the defendant by his answer disclaimed all right to what was saved and offered, if there were any goods in Africa, to assign them to the plaintiff, and he insisted that the ship was left on the coast of Africa and that, by reason she did not arrive at Jamaica, the plaintiffs became liable to pay the insurance money.

The defendants, by their second answer, set forth the particulars of the goods.

And, on hearing the cause, Lord Chancellor [Lord Cowper] directed the plaintiffs to pay 50 percent of the insurance money and costs at law, and he sent it to a Master to enquire what part of the goods set forth in the second answer were saved. And he reserved the consideration of what average the plaintiffs should have until after the Master's report.

2 Vernon 716, 23 E.R. 1070

7 November [1716].

[There was a suit] on a policy of insurance on goods by agreement valued at £600, and the insured was not to be obliged to prove any interest.

Lord Chancellor [Lord Cowper] ordered the defendant to discover what goods he put on board, for, although the defendant offered to renounce all interest to the insurers, yet he referred it to a Master to examine the value of the goods saved ('or come to the hands of the defendant or any of his agents'. R.L.) and to deduct it out of the value or sum of £600, at which the goods were valued by the agreement.

The plaintiffs, by their bill, stated that they were assured by one Boddington, who applied to them as the agent of the defendant to subscribe the policy, that the ship was a tight and good ship and well fitted for the voyage, and that there were goods on board her of the value of £600 belonging to the defendant. The defendant, by his answer, said that Boddington had no orders from him to say the goods on board were of the value of £600 or any other value. Reg. Lib. 1716, B. fol. 52.

[Other reports of this case: 1 Eq. Cas. Abr. 372, 21 E.R. 1110.]

148
Awbery v. Middleton
(Ch. 1716)

In this case, under the will in issue, the legacies were a charge on the decedent's land, his personal estate not being sufficient to pay them.

Lincoln's Inn MS. Misc. 11, p. 86

24 October 1716.

A. Middleton, by his will, disposed of some lands, and, after several legacies, he gives the rest of his goods, cattles, chattels, and estate to the defendant, whom he makes executor. And he dies seised in fee of other lands besides those which were devised by the will.

The plaintiffs bring their bill for a satisfaction of their legacies. And the executor having applied all the personal assets in satisfaction of debts, the question was if the legacies were a charge on the real estate not devised by the will.

Mr. *Vernon*, for the plaintiffs: If there had been no disposition of anything but personal estate by the will, it might have been a question whether general words of this kind would carry anything more than the surplus of the personal estate. But here are not only lands before devised but likewise annuities for life, which are in their nature a charge upon land. And so it was decreed in Sir Oliver Ashcomb's Case, where his father had made him executor and desired him to see his will performed, by which will, he had given several annuities, but had not expressly charged them on his real estate, but left that to descend on his son and heir, whom he had made his executor. And the court was of opinion the lands were chargeable with these annuities.

And the case of Sherrard and Sherrard, which was affirmed in the House of Lords, was to the same effect, only in that case, the testator, who had made his son and heir executor, had not desired him to see his will performed.

Sir Robert Raymond, e contra: There are no express words in the will which charge the lands with the legacies. And, as to the annuities, he has directed his executor to pay them, which, we apprehend, plainly shows his intent was that they should be paid out of his personal estate.

Then, as to what is insisted on, that the word 'estate' will carry the real estate to the executor, we think not, for, where the word 'estate' is only coupled with personal things, it can carry nothing of a higher nature.

In the Case of Barkham and Twisden, before Lord Harcourt,[1] the words were 'all my estate, chattels, real and personal', and it was decreed lands did not pass.

---

1 *Markham v. Twisden* (Ch. 1713), British Library MS. Hargrave 80, f. 134, pl. 2.

Lord Cowper: Upon the whole will taken together, I think the legacies are a charge upon the lands. At the beginning of the will, the testator takes notice he was about to dispose of all his goods and worldly estate whatsoever. Then, he goes on and gives away some of his lands, and, after that, he devises annuities for life, which, in their nature, are properly to arise out of land. And, after he has given legacies to the plaintiffs, he gives all the rest of his goods, chattels, and estate to his executor, which words, I think, considering what goes before, must be understood to pass the lands, for the residue must be understood to be what remains after payment of the debts and legacies, though those words are not in the will.

This construction is the more reasonable in regard it is not to disinherit the heir, but only to superinduce a charge upon his estate.

149

Hutton v. Simpson

(Ch. 1716)

The question in this case was whether the words of the will were a condition precedent.

There can no account taken of profits before the title is ascertained at common law.

Lincoln's Inn MS. Misc. 11, p. 90

30 October 1716. Hutton and Addison v. Simpson and Addison.

Thomas Addison, by a will dated 14 August 1702, devises his lands after the death of his wife to Dorothy, one of his daughters, and the heirs of her body and, for default of such issue, to Jane, his other daughter, for life and to her first and other sons in tail with a remainder to his own rights heirs. And he made Dorothy his executrix.

Dorothy, after the making of the will, marries and dies in the life of her father, leaving issue, the plaintiff Hutton.

After the death of Dorothy, the daughter, the testator makes a codicil and, thereby, devises a chattel lease, which he had by his will given to his daughter Dorothy, to the plaintiff, her son. And, taking notice he had made a purchase since his will, he gives the new purchased lands to the same persons to whom he had given his other lands by his will upon the same trusts and to the same uses. And he made his wife executrix. After the making of this codicil, he republishes the will and codicil. And he dies.

The question was between the son of Dorothy and Jane, the surviving daughter, to which of them these lands belonged.

Sir Joseph Jekyll, for the plaintiff: It is a settled rule, if a man devises to another and his heirs and the devisee dies in the life of the testator, his heir cannot take, according to Bret and Rigden's Case in Plowden.[1] And it is the same if the

[1] *Brett v. Rigden* (1568), 1 Plowden 340, 75 E.R. 516.

devise is in tail, according to Hartop's Case, [. . .] 243, and Fuller and Fuller, [. . .] 422.[1]

If the devise, then, to Dorothy is void, the next in remainder must take according to the resolution in the Case of Fuller and Fuller, for the devise being void, it is, as is said in that case, as though it had never been mentioned.

As to the codicil, it makes no alteration in the case. Since the Statute of Frauds,[2] the bare making of a codicil is not a republication of a will, and so it was held in Lord Lansdowne's Case.[3] And a republication since the Statute must be as solemn as the first publication of the will ought to be.

Sir Thomas Powys, on the same side: We deny there was any republication in this case. This is not like the Case of My Lord Bath;[4] he had his will and codicil upon a table when he made his codicil. It is true they were not tacked together, but he afterwards put them in a box together and, having sealed them up, wrote thereon 'This is my will.' But there was no determination in that case.

As to the limitation to Dorothy, it is void, she dying in the life of her father. And there is no difference between a devise in fee and in tail, for the heir must derive from his ancestor, and the limitation to the heirs of the body is only a modification of the estate.

Mr. *Vernon, e contra*: The case between a devise in fee and in tail is very different where the devisee dies in the life of the testator. Where it is in fee, the reason given in Brett and Rigden's Case why it is void is that the testator is supposed to have no regard to the heirs general, for those words are added only to denote the quantity of the estate. But, where the devise is in tail, it is plain the testator has it in his view to keep the estate in the family of the devisee and to provide for his issue.

Lord Chancellor Cowper: My present thoughts are that the words 'and for default of issue of Dorothy' are very material and *prima facie* seem to me to be a condition precedent, for to say that Jane shall take whilst there is issue of Dorothy living is to say the express contrary of what the testator has said, for he has said by his will that she should not have the estate until there is a failer of issue of Dorothy.

I will consider of it. If the authorities are against me, I must submit.

Afterwards, Lord Chancellor [Lord Cowper] gave his opinion that the matter in question was a matter of law, and, as there was no obstruction against

---

1 *Hartopp's Case* (1591), Croke Eliz. 243, 78 E.R. 499, also 1 Leonard 253, 74 E.R. 231; *Fuller v. Fuller* (1595), Croke Eliz. 422, 78 E.R. 664, also Moore K.B. 353, 72 E.R. 624, 1 Eq. Cas. Abr. 216, 407, 21 E.R. 1000, 1137.

2 Stat. 29 Car. II, c. 3, s. 6 (*SR*, V, 840).

3 *Penphrase v. Lord Lansdown* (1712), 10 Modern 96, 88 E.R. 642, 1 Comyns 384, 92 E.R. 1122, 2 Eq. Cas. Abr. 769, 22 E.R. 653.

4 *Penphrase v. Lord Lansdown* (1712), *ut supra*.

trying the title at law, he would retain the bill for twelve months that the issue of Dorothy might bring an [action of] ejectment if he thought fit.

As to the account of profits, he would give no direction, it being a settled rule of equity that no account of profits can be taken until the title is ascertained at law.

[Other reports of this case: 2 Vernon 722, 23 E.R. 1074, 1 Eq. Cas. Abr. 7, 196, 216, 407, 21 E.R. 832, 985, 1000, 1137, *sub nom.* Sympson v. Hornsby, Precedents in Chancery 439, 452, 24 E.R. 196, 202, 2 Eq. Cas. Abr. 439, 496, 660, 22 E.R. 374, 420, 554, Gilbert Rep. 115, 120, 25 E.R. 80, 84.]

150

Peter v. Russell

(Ch. 1716)

A mortgagee who knows of the mortgagor's fraud in obtaining a subsequent mortgage on the same security will be postponed to the second mortgagee.

In this case, there was no evidence of the first mortgagee's knowledge of the fraud.

Lincoln's Inn MS. Misc. 10, p. 214

17 November 1716.

A.B. mortgages a lease of some houses at St. James's to the defendant. Sometime afterwards, he desires the defendant to lend him the original lease to show it to some persons, who he pretended were treating with him about improving the premises by building. The defendant, knowing nothing of the mortgagor's real design, lets him have the lease, and then he goes to the plaintiff, shows him the lease, and, upon that, the plaintiff agrees to lend him money upon a mortgage of the premises. The mortgagor, after he had kept the lease about an hour, then returns it to the defendant, and, afterwards, the mortgagor makes a second mortgage to the plaintiff, who brings his bill to be relieved against the first mortgage, suggesting that the defendant was privy to the fraud or, at lease, was aiding and assisting to it.

This cause was heard before the Master of the Rolls [Trevor], who decreed the defendant to redeem the plaintiff's mortgage in six months or be foreclosed.

And now, it came on upon an appeal to the Lord Chancellor [Lord Cowper], who declared, if a man will combine with the mortgagor and assist him in borrowing money upon his estate and conceals his own mortgage, he makes himself a party to the fraud. And, in such case, his mortgage shall be postponed.

I will go a step further. If the first mortgagee is not aiding or assisting to the fraud, but is only passive and does not discover his mortgage to a person who he knows is about lending money on the estate when he has an opportunity, in such a case also, the first mortgage should be postponed.

But neither of these cases comes up to the case in question. The defendant knew nothing of the mortgagor's design nor that the plaintiff was about lending him any money. The pretense the mortgagor made for borrowing the lease was probable enough and the defendant might reasonably lend him to lease for a short time for such a purpose. And, therefore, I cannot come into the reasons upon which this decree is founded, and I am of opinion the bill ought to be dismissed with costs unless the plaintiff will redeem the defendant's mortgage and pay him what the Master shall certify to be due to him for principal, interest, and costs.

Note, in this case, Mr. *Vernon* cited the case of one Gargrave,[1] a Yorkshire attorney, who having a mortgage on an estate of a gentleman in that country, a person who was about lending money to the mortgagor meets <Gregory> Gargrave and asks him if he had any mortgage upon that gentleman's estate but does not tell him the reason of asking him that questions. Gregory, not thinking himself obliged to satisfy everyone that asked him what encumbrance he had upon the mortgagor's estate, did not say that he had any mortgage thereof. This person afterwards take a mortgage of the same estate, and, when he had discovered that <Gregory> Gargrave had a prior mortgage, he brought his bill to set it aside because <Gregory> Gargrave had not disclosed it to him when he enquired if he had any encumbrance upon the estate. And, for that reason, the plaintiff was relieved against the first mortgage. But, afterwards, upon an appeal from the Rolls, where the cause was heard, an issue was directed to try whether <Gregory> Gargrave had any notice that the plaintiff, when he spoke to him, was about lending the mortgagor money and it being found that he had not, the decree was for that reason reversed.

[Other reports of this case: 2 Vernon 726, 23 E.R. 1076, Gilbert Rep. 122, 25 E.R. 85, 1 Eq. Cas. Abr. 321, 21 E.R. 1075.]

151

Freeman v. Freeman

(Ch. 1716)

The intent of a devisor can be inferred from the context of the devise.

Lincoln's Inn MS. Misc. 10, p. 217

20 November 1716.

The bill was to have a legacy of £550 raised out of an estate, which, by the will, was chargeable with the payment of it.

---

[1] *Ibbottson v. Rhodes* (1706), 2 Vernon 554, 23 E.R. 958, 1 Eq. Cas. Abr. 229, 231, 21 E.R. 1010, 1074.

The legacy was only mentioned to be 550, but it is not said in the will whether pounds or what else, but there was no difficulty in understanding it to be meant pounds. But the principal question was if the will was executed so as to charge the land, the witnesses having proved that the testator sealed and published his will in their presence and bid them take notice that was his will, but they did not prove that he signed it.

Lord Chancellor [LORD COWPER]: The Statute[1] says every will for the disposing of lands must be signed as well as sealed by the testator or some person by his direction. I do not say it is necessary that three witnesses should see him sign it, but, here, you do not prove that the testator so signed his will. Let there be an issue [out of Chancery] to try whether the will was duly executed or not.

Note it was said by Serjeant *Hooper* that sealing has been held to be a signing within the Statute.

8 Viner, Abr. 51

A bill [was exhibited] for a legacy. The testator devises 550, omitting pounds, to his daughter Mary, the now plaintiff, and he also devises £550 to his daughter Barbara etc. The defendant insists that the devise of 550 to the plaintiff is void for uncertainty, not saying 550 what.

COWPER, Chancellor: The subsequent devise to the other daughter makes this extremely clear, that the testator meant £550, and it is as certain and good as if the word 'pounds' had been expressed.

[Other copies of this report: 2 Eq. Cas. Abr. 359, 22 E.R. 305.]

152

Lord Pawlet v. Parry

(Ch. 1716)

The question in this case was whether a legacy should be paid out of the decedent's real property where the personal assets of his estate were not sufficient to pay it.

Lincoln's Inn MS. Misc. 10, p. 211

27 November 1716.

A.B. makes his will and begins it in this manner, *viz.*, 'as to the disposal of my estate, I will that it be disposed of as follows', and then he goes on and, in the first place, gives his land to his son Charles in tail, remainder to his son Francis in tail, with remainders to his three other sons in tail successively in like manner. Then, he gives his son Charles his leasehold estate, and he gives his daughter

[1] Stat. 29 Car. II, c. 3, s. 5 (*SR*, V, 840).

£1500 to be paid within three months after marriage by his son Charles, and he makes him executor.

There being a deficiency, as it was apprehended, of personal assets to pay the daughter's legacy, the question was if, by the will, it was charged on the land.

And it was insisted on by *Sir Joseph Jekyll* that, by the first words in the will and by the testator's making the devisee of his real estate executor also of his personal estate, there was a plain charge upon the land and, for this, he cited the case of Cloudsley and Pelham, before Lord Jefferies and affirmed upon an appeal to the Lords,[1] where a man devised his land to his son in tail with several remainders over and, in the close of his will, he gives him his personal estate and makes him executor and desires him to see his will performed. And, in this case, it was decreed that the land was charged with debts notwithstanding the estate devised to the son was only an estate tail.

The case of Sherwood and Sherwood was also cited where a man had devised his real estate to his brother and had given an annuity to his wife for life but had not said out of what it should issue, and it was decreed at the Rolls and affirmed in the House of Lords that it should issue out of the land.

But it was said in answer to that case that the land was the proper fund for an annuity and besides that was a devise in fee and not in tail, as in the present case.

Lord Chancellor [LORD COWPER]: This is a very doubtful case, and I do not know that I have in any case that has come before me charged land with legacies where there is so little foundation for it as there is here.

If the devise to Charles had been a devise in fee, I should make no doubt of charging the land with the legacy. Let the Master see what is the value of the real estate and also of the personal at the time of making the will. Perhaps that may be of some use to form a right judgment of this case.

[Other reports of this case: Precedents in Chancery 449, 24 E.R. 200, Gilbert Rep. 123, 25 E.R. 86, 2 Eq. Cas. Abr. 369, 497, 22 E.R. 313, 421.]

---

[1] *Clowdsley v. Pelham* (1686), 1 Vernon 411, 23 E.R. 552, 1 Eq. Cas. Abr. 197, 21 E.R. 986.

153

Mendez v. Cholwell

(Ch. 1716)

The property of third parties in the hands of a bankrupt factor cannot be seized by the bankrupt's creditors.

Lincoln's Inn MS. Misc. 12, p. 87

19 December 1716. James Mendez *et al.*, agents for foreign creditors of Bartolini, a bankrupt, against Cholwell *et al.*, assignees of the estate of the bankrupt.

Upon a petition, it was ordered by Lord Cowper that the commissioners should examine whether any of the goods or commodities seized by virtue of the same commission or which came to the custody or power of the assignees or either of them belonged to the petitioners' correspondents and by whom consigned to the bankrupt as their factor and were not paid for or satisfaction made in money or otherwise. And, in case there were any such goods remaining in specie in the custody or power of the assignees, he ordered that the assignees should forthwith deliver them to the person or persons to whom they respectively belonged on payment of such charges and disbursements as the bankrupt or the assignees had paid or disbursed at the Custom House or otherwise in case it should not appear that what was so paid or disbursed by the bankrupt was paid out of the money of the petitioners' correspondents in his hands at the time of the payment thereof. And he further ordered that the said commissioners should examine if any such goods had been sold by the bankrupt or the assignees for which the money payable had been paid to the assignees and, in such case, the said assignees were forthwith to pay such money to such person or persons respectively to whom such goods did belong at the time of such sale after deduction of charges paid at the Custom House or otherwise and also after deduction of what was due to the bankrupt for commission.

In case they were not paid by the petitioners' correspondents' own money as before mentioned and in case any of the money for which such goods had been sold by the said bankrupt or the assignees was still unpaid, he ordered that such money should be paid to the person or persons to whom such goods did respectively belong at the time of the sale or to their agents on payment of such charges as before mentioned and that the receipt or discharge of such person or persons who were entitled to such sum or sums of money or their agents should be a good discharge to the person or persons that should so pay the same.

154

Vigars v. Williams

(Ch. c. 1716)

The creditors of a bankrupt cannot receive the corpus of a trust of which the bankrupt is the trustee.

Lincoln's Inn MS. Misc. 12, p. 88

Vigars v. Richard Williams *et al.*, assignees of a commission of bankruptcy awarded against A.B., defendants.

A.B., as factor for the plaintiff, sells goods to C. for eight month's credit. C. gives B. a note for money payable to B. or order for value received payable eight months after date. And B. gives a receipt on the bill of parcels for the money by a note which, when received, was to be in full [satisfaction] of the bill. Before the money became due, B. becomes a bankrupt.

The MASTER OF THE ROLLS was of opinion the money belonged to the plaintiff and not to the creditors, for the bankrupt was only a trustee in the note for the plaintiff. And he said it would have been the same although the bankrupt had given a receipt in full upon taking the note without referring to the note in the receipt.

155

Ostano v. Williams

(Ch. c. 1716)

The creditors of a bankrupt cannot receive the property which the bankrupt holds as a factor and surety.

Lincoln's Inn MS. Misc. 12, p. 89

Ostano v. the same assignees [Richard Williams *et al.*, assignees of a commission of bankruptcy awarded against A.B.]. [decided the same day as Vigars v. Williams.]

In this case, the bankrupt had sold goods as the factor for the plaintiff on six month's credit and had agreed in consideration of a double commission to insure the money for which the goods were sold. And, therefore, it was insisted that the money belonged to the bankrupt's creditors and not to the plaintiff, for the goods were sold at the risk of the bankrupt.

But the MASTER OF THE ROLLS decreed the money to the plaintiff, for, though the factor insures the money to the principal, yet that did not alter the nature of the debt. The money is due to the principal, and he might maintain an action against the buyer though he did not know when he bought the goods but that they belonged to the factor. And the factor in this case is only in the nature of a surety.

156

Anonymous

(Ch. 1716)

The words 'rest of my lands' in a will include remainders as well as lands in possession.

British Library MS. Hargrave 81, f. 48, pl. 1

A devise to J.S. for life 'and all the rest of my messuages, lands, and tenements after the death of J.S. I give to B. and his heirs paying thereout £100 to C.', this is a charge upon all the lands and, by this devise, all the testator's lands pass to B., as well those not devised to J.S. as those that were, some in possession and some in remainder, for the word 'rest' extends as well to quantity as quality and so the lands not before devised passed thereby as well as the remainder of those devised to J.S.

[Other copies of this report: British Library MS. Hargrave 82, f. 45, pl. 1.]

[Other reports of this case: British Library MS. Hargrave 77, f. 13, British Library MS. Hargrave 303, f. 23, pl. 1.]

157

Rosewell v. Boddington

(Ch. 1717)

In this case, the lands in issue passed to trustees and could not pass by a subsequent will.

Lincoln's Inn MS. Hill 29, p. 14

Hilary 3 Geo. I.

The case was this. The plaintiff's great-grandfather was seised of several lands in fee, and the plaintiff's grandfather purchased several copyhold lands, which were not, and surrendered 26 May 1662, at which time the great-grandfather and the grandfather conveyed by bargain and sale the said freehold estate to A.B. in trust for the use of the grandfather and his wife for life, remainder to the heirs of his body, and the grandfather did covenant to surrender the copyhold estate to the same uses. The grandfather married and had issue, three daughters, and one of the daughters was the mother of the plaintiff. The grandfather, in 1712, devised all the said estates and other estates to trustees to be sold and the rents, values, and profits to be divided equally among his grandchildren by the said three daughters, which were several.

And now the plaintiff, who was the only child of one of the daughters of the grandfather, brought his bill in Chancery against the trustees, legatees, etc. to have the legal estate that is one-third part of the entailed estate secured to him and his proportion with the other grandchildren of the trust estate devised as aforesaid.

And these several questions were made: first, whether the bargains and sales conveyed any legal estate or raised any uses, (1) because it was not enrolled, (2) because no lease for a year, nor (3) any livery of seisin; second, whether the copyhold estate so devised to grandchildren otherwise provided for and not surrendered should pass by the will.

It was argued for the plaintiff that the said bargain and sale was at least a good equitable settlement and would carry the estate as a covenant to stand seised. 2 Roll, Abr., 286, 287, and 1 Mod., Scudamore and Crossing, a strong case at common law.[1] And the copyhold would not pass in regard the grandchildren were otherwise provided for. And there was the like case in this court between Townsend and Kettle [*blank*] in Lord Somers' time and, though he decreed the copyhold would pass, yet the House of Lords reversed his decree; Salk. 181.[2]

The Lord Chancellor [Lord Cowper] said there is no doubt but this bargain and sale was a good equitable settlement and, therefore, that the will could not operate but only on such estates as were not comprised in the said deed. And he said had he been in the House of Lords when Townsend's Case was there, the decree had not been reversed, for it was carried by one only and he would have made them even. But now, I decree that the plaintiff and the two other heirs at law shall have all the said estate comprised in the marriage settlement in thirds and also the copyhold estate not surrendered, for I would prevent an appeal. But they cannot have any benefit by the will, and, therefore, the devised estate other than the estate in the said deed shall be distributed among the rest of the legatees according to the intent of the testator. But the said plaintiff is to pay 40s. costs to those who are named defendants for form's sake, but the rest of the costs are to be paid out of the trust estate, and the trustees are to account before the Master and, when that is done, let an application be made to the court to settle any difficulties that may arise.

---

[1] *Crossing v. Scudamore* (1671), 1 Modern 175, 86 E.R. 810, also 1 Ventris 137, 86 E.R. 94, 1 Freeman 368, 89 E.R. 274, 2 Levinz 9, 83 E.R. 428, 2 Keble 754, 784, 84 E.R. 476, 495, Lincoln's Inn MS. Misc. 500, ff. 149, 155.

[2] *Kettle v. Townsend*, 1 Salkeld 187, 91 E.R. 170, also 1 Eq. Cas. Abr. 123, 21 E.R. 929.

158

Bird v. Lockey

(Ch. 1717)

A court of equity can intervene in the execution of a power only when there was a grossly unfair and inequitable execution of it.

No rights pursuant to a power vest before the power has been executed.

Lincoln's Inn MS. Misc. 10, p. 245

10 February 1716[/17].

Hannah Standish, by will, gives £1200 to be distributed between the four children of John Lockey as he should think fit, and she makes him and another executors. And she declares that none of the children shall call for their legacies until a year after her death.

One of the children died in the life of the testatrix, and another died within the year after her death. The father gives one of the surviving children £900, who releases all his right to the legacy. And, afterwards, the father, by his will, gives the plaintiff, who was the other child, £400 and declares it to be in full of her proportion of the £1200.

And now, the plaintiff brings her bill against the representative of the father and of her brother, who had the £900, he being dead, and of her sister, who died after the testatrix, to have the remainder of the £1200 and all the interest which became due for the whole, which exceeded the £400 given her by her father's will.

The representative of the son who received the £900 insisted on a share of the interest, and the representative of the daughter who died after the testatrix insisted on a share of the remaining £300 and of the interest.

Lord Chancellor [Lord Cowper]: The father had only a bare authority and no interest. And, at the end of one year, he ought to have made a distribution of the £1200 amongst the surviving children, and, not having done so, but kept the money, his estate ought to answer for interest. But, in computing interest, let the Master see what interest was due when the £900 was paid and how much of that sum was principal and how much interest, and let the remaining principal sum carry interest from that time.

As to the daughter that died after the testatrix and before the legacy became payable, what interest had she in this legacy? There was no certain interest vested in her; she had indeed an equitable right vested in her. So, as in the case the father had made a very extravagant and unequal distribution, as for instance to have given her 1s. only, she might have come into this court and have been relieved (for the execution of these powers are in some measure under the direction of this court), but she dying before the legacy became payable and having nothing but such an uncertain equity, her representative cannot now claim anything in this money, nor can the representative of the son who received the £900 claim any part of the remainder, he having released.

He decreed the remaining £300 and the interest to the plaintiff.

Note, in this case, it was said by Mr. *Vernon* that, if this had been a joint devise and one of the children had died in the lifetime of the testatrix, the other should have had the whole by survivorship.

And [it was said] by *Sir Thomas Powys* that, if a legacy is given to four equally so that they are tenants in common and one dies in the lifetime of the testator, his share shall not survive, but shall be a lapsed legacy.

So, if lands are given to two and their heirs equally so that they are tenants in common and one dies in the lifetime of the testator, his moiety shall not survive, but it shall descend to the heir at law of the testator. But otherwise it is where the devisees are joint tenants.

[Other reports of this case: 2 Vernon 743, 23 E.R. 1086.]

159

Brown v. Barkham

(Ch. 1717)

Lincoln's Inn MS. Misc. 14, p. 128

11 February 1716[/17]. Brown v. Barkham; Newcomen v. Barkham; Barkham v. Newcomen.

These causes received judgment the 11th February 1716[/17]. The question was between Newcomen and Barkham on the words of the will of Sir Edward Barkham dated the 9th of January 1709[/10], which are as follows, *viz.*:

> My will and meaning is that all my debts shall be justly paid and satisfied, and, to that end and purpose, I give and devise all my manors, lands, tenements, and hereditaments whatsoever and wheresoever which I am seised of or entitled unto in the County of Lincoln or elsewhere in the kingdom of England and also the equity of redemption thereof unto my trusty friend Sir William Massingberd of Gunby in the County of Lincoln, baronet, and Dimock Walpole of Lowth in the said County of Lincoln, gentleman, and to their heirs forever upon the special trust and confidence and to the intent and purpose that they, the said Sir William Massingberd and Dimock Walpole, and the survivor of them and his heirs shall sell the same or such part or parts thereof as they in their discretion shall think fit and, out of the money arising by sale thereof together with the rents and profits of the whole estate until the same be sold, to raise such sum and sums as will pay and discharge all my said debts and all such sum and sums of money as I shall by this my will or by any codicil give away in legacies and, after my debts are paid and the money raised for said legacies according to this my

> will, then I do hereby direct that all the rest and residue of my said manors, lands, tenements, and hereditaments, which shall remain unsold, shall be settled and conveyed by my said trustees upon my cousin Robert Barkham of Wingfleet, esquire, and the heirs male of his body and, for want of such heirs male, then to the heirs male of the body of Sir Robert Barkham, my great-grandfather, and for want of such heirs male, then to my right heirs forever. And I also direct and appoint my said trustees to pay the overplus of the money, if any be, that shall remain in their hands after deducting all their charges and expenses which they shall be at, in, and about the execution of this my will unto my said cousin Robert Barkham or to such heirs male as shall be entitled to the residue of my said manors and lands. *Item*, I give unto my dear sister Newcomen the sum of £2000 of lawful money of Great Britain the same to be raised within one year after my decease, and my will and meaning is that my said trustees and the survivor of them and his heirs do from time to time put the same out at interest in their own names with the approbation and consent of my said sister for her sole and separate use and maintenance during her natural life and with which her husband shall have nothing to do or have any control therewith and that her receipt alone shall be a sufficient discharge to my said trustees as if she was sole and unmarried. And, from and after the decease of my said sister, then my will is that the said £2000 shall go and be paid to the eldest son of my said sister, and, if my said sister shall have no son at the time of her decease, then my will is that £1000 part thereof shall go and be paid to the executors and administrators of my said sister and the other £1000 residue thereof shall go and be paid unto my said cousin Robert Barkham or his heirs male.

And he gave the rest of his personal estate unto his said cousin Robert, and he made him executor. But, if his cousin Robert should not be in England at his decease, then he made Massingberd and Walpole executors in trust for his cousin Robert until he should return. But, in case his said cousin Robert should die before he returned, then he made his heir male executor and gave him all his personal estate.

The testator's sister Newcomen claimed the residue of the said estate as heir to her brother and heir at law to her great-grandfather, Sir Robert Barkham, the devisee Robert Barkham dying in Spain in the lifetime of the testator without issue.

The defendant Edward Barkham claimed as being sufficiently described by the will as the person to take and by the intention of the testator, he being the heir male to his brother, Robert Barkham, the devisee, who died without issue, and also the heir male of the body of Sir Robert Barkham, great-grandfather of the testator, that is the son of Robert Barkham, who was the second son of Sir Robert Barkham, the great-grandfather.

The argument delivered by Lord Cowper in court upon making his decree in the above cause [was as follows]. If this question on these words of the will so clearly signifying the intent of the testator was propounded to the best natural understanding unprejudiced by the learning of the law, the only doubt would be as was observed from the bar how this comes to be a question of any difficulty. And, indeed, it does only become so by the artificial reasoning of the law, as Lord Chief Justice Coke somewhere thinks it as opposite to natural, which I take to be right reason. But I admit that, since neither custom nor statute laws have fixed nor can fix such rules of construction as may be found necessary or at least convenient to be established whenever rules of that kind have obtained for any considerable time in the books of good authority or *a fortiori* in judicial constructions, they ought to be received and submitted to as part of the law and, consequently, to be followed, generally speaking, in courts of equity rather than its professors should not know what to depend upon or how to advise their clients, and this though such rules should happen on a strict inquiry not to have much of natural or inartificial reason to support them.

In order, therefore, to deliver my opinion in this case, I will inquire how far this court is hindered by any such rule or established distinction in law from pursuing it in its decree. The plain and obvious meaning of the testator in these words of the will on which the present question arises, which there can be no doubt, was that the conveyance should be made not to a female being heir general but to a special heir, the heir male of the body of his great-grandfather or to such person as at the time of the conveyance would have held the lands had it been entailed on the great-grandfather and the heirs male of his body.

The first objection insisted on is that it has been often adjudged and is established for law that he who can take by the words 'heir of J.S.' as a purchaser by any kind of conveyance immediately must be at the time of such taking properly the heir of J.S. and that, therefore, if J.S. be then living, none can take by virtue of these words, either as his heir apparent or his heir presumptive, because such person is not properly his heir, it being a known maxim of law *quia non est haeres viventis.*

To this I answer that neither that maxim nor any of the authorities built upon it do at all affect the present case, where the ancestor is dead before the remainder falls into possession or the conveyance is asked. And, therefore, he that claims here as heir male of the body of the great-grandfather is not the less so for the said maxim. And, therefore, Archer's Case, 1 Coke,[1] which has been cited for the plaintiff is avoided, which is only that a man cannot claim as heir by purchase or as heir male in the life of the ancestor.

Secondly, if that maxim had been strictly adhered to in description of a purchaser, which it has not been in the Case of Burchet and Durdent and Long and Beamont,[2] to be mentioned hereafter more at large, yet there is much more rea-

[1] *Baldwin v. Smith* (1597), 1 Coke Rep. 63, 76 E.R. 139, also Croke Eliz. 453, 78 E.R. 692, 2 Anderson 37, 123 E.R. 533.

[2] *Durdant v. Burchett* (H.L. 1690), *James v. Richardson* (H.L. 1685), Pollexfen 457, 86 E.R. 610, also 2 Ventris 311, 86 E.R. 458, T. Raymond 330, 83 E.R. 172, 2 Levinz

son so to have done than in the present to insist that the person claiming as heir male of the body should be also simply the heir since, were the ancestor living, the person claiming as heir is not so. The words are not verified of him in any legal sense but, in this case, all the words taken together are verified in the person claiming by them in a legal and proper sense, as in cases of descent of an estate tail male is allowed on all sides.

And, therefore, there is no argument or authority can be drawn from cases which turn on that maxim to affect this case since that would be to argue from cases where the words are not true concerning the person claiming by purchase in any legal sense and the question is only if they do not sufficiently describe him as a purchaser, as undoubtedly they would do in cases of a descent. What reason or authority there is for that distinction is the main [point] of the present enquiry. And I shall consider it therefore more at large hereafter.

At present, I am only clearing my way to it and laying aside these cases which depend on the rule above mentioned as neither the same nor like to the case in question so that we may also lay by the Case of Chaloner and Boyer, cited for the plaintiff, 2 Leon. 70;[1] a devise in remainder to the heirs of the body of his eldest son then alive when the remainder was to fall into possession none living, the ancestor is not in a legal sense anymore the heir of the body than the heir simply. As also the case Dyer 99a and b,[2] B. makes a feoffment to the use of his wife for life and, after, to the use of his right heirs of the body of himself and his wife; they have issue; then the wife dies, the issue cannot enter because the father is living and so he cannot be the heir of the body of his father during his father's life.

But note, if, in that case, the father had been dead too, it would have been very hard to have said the heir of the two bodies properly become so and, so clearly described, should not have taken the remainder unless he had been also the heir general of his father and also the heir general of his mother so that, if his father or mother had issue male by a former marriage, the heir of their two bodies must have been defeated. But of this more when I come to it in the method I have laid down to myself.

232, 83 E.R. 533, 3 Keble 832, 84 E.R. 1039, T. Jones 99, 84 E.R. 1166, 1 Ventris 334, 86 E.R. 216, 1 Freeman 458, 472, 89 E.R. 343, 353, 1 Eq. Cas. Abr. 214, 21 E.R. 998, Lincoln's Inn MS. Misc. 557, f. 94, pl. 2, Skinner 205, 90 E.R. 95, Comberbach 153, 90 E.R. 400, Carthew 154, 90 E.R. 694, Holt K.B. 223, 224, 90 E.R. 1022, 1023, 1 Eq. Cas. Abr. 214, 21 E.R. 999, Dodd 60; *Darbison, ex dem. Long v. Beaumont* (1713–1714), 1 Peere Williams 229, 24 E.R. 366, Fortescue 18, 92 E.R. 743, 1 Eq. Cas. Abr. 214, 21 E.R. 999, Dodd 366, 3 Brown P.C. 60, 1 E.R. 1177, Lincoln's Inn MS. Misc. 10, p. 184, Lords' Journal, vol. 19, p. 696, *sub nom. Lay v. Beamont* (Ex. 1709), Eq. Cases Exch. 604.

[1] *Challoner v. Bowyer* (1587), 2 Leonard 70, 74 E.R. 366.

[2] *Anonymous* (1553), 1 Dyer 99, 73 E.R. 217.

The second objection is cases have been cited and more may occur in reading on this subject which prove that none can take as a purchaser by the words 'heir male', the ancestor being dead.

The principal case of Cowden, Hobart 30,[1] cited and strongly relied on for the plaintiff, proves no more, the words of devise being 'to the right heirs male and posterity of me and my name forever'. So Ashenhurst's Case, in the end of that report,[2] a devise shall 'remain to my heirs male forever'. So Starling's Case, in Chancery, 8 Will. III,[3] written precedents, a deed of trust to convey 'to the right heirs male of him the said Sir Samuel forever' apply but one of those words truly to himself and this may be admitted and the present case not touched, for, in legal propriety of speech, none can be heir male that is not simply heir, for, if the heir general be a female, the next male relation to the testator can only say he is a male but not the heir male in any legal sense of those words, neither would they carry an estate to him in words of limitation or descent anymore than in words of purchase, except in cases of wills where the words of the testator are in such cases intended and supplied.

But, in the present case, where the words conjointly taken are all in legal propriety of speech true of the person designed and true of none other, whether they do not amount to a sufficient description so as to enable the person described to take by way of purchase is quite a different question.

And, therefore, admitting none can take by purchase as heir, the ancestor being living, nor where the ancestor is dead, as heir or heir male without being the heir, yet I hold one may take by purchase as heir male of the body of a person deceased without being also the heir general of the same person.

To make this good, I shall observe this method. First, I support my opinion with reasons drawn from principles or settled points of law for, as I promised, as to the plain intent of the testator considered by natural reason, there can be no question. And in the next place, I apply myself to answer such authorities as come up to it which are principally assertions or opinions mentioned in some books which set up a distinction that these words are sufficient to describe the person who is to take by descent and not by purchase but without sufficient ground or authority in law for such distinction.

The principle of law I argue from and which I shall show must be overthrown if the said distinction be allowed is this, that a person may take as a purchaser by words of description as well as by names, which are distinguished in law books from other kinds of description. Co. Litt. 3a and b,[4] many cases to prove this. And the law is thereby known to be so.

---

1 *Counden v. Clerke* (1614), Hobart 29, 80 E.R. 180, also Moore K.B. 860, 72 E.R. 955, 1 Eq. Cas. Abr. 213, 22 E.R. 998.

2 *Curtis, ex dem. Beard v. Ashenhurst* (1609), Hobart 34, 80 E.R. 184.

3 *Starling v. Ettrick* (1695), Precedents in Chancery 54, 24 E.R. 27.

4 E. Coke, *First Institute* (1628), f. 3.

The words 'heir', 'heir male', 'heir male of the body', the ancestor being dead and the person claiming as heir general are but descriptions.

Now, if one that may take as a purchaser by words of description, it necessarily follows that that must be a sufficient description for such purposes which has all the requisites to make the most perfect description that can be, for to allow of any description in such case and yet reject the most perfect is to make the law incongruous and indeed absurd. But the description contained in the words which make the present case has all that can be required to make a description perfect and complete, for it is altogether true it is certain and it is expressed in proper words and terms of art.

They are true and no more than are true of Edward Barkham, who is certainly the heir male of the body of Sir Robert, the great-grandfather, or, otherwise, he would not take by descent by virtue of that description, which it is admitted he would do, for words of limitation will not carry an estate by descent to one of whom they are not verified.

Indeed, the books which say they are not good words of purchase in this case, foreseeing the force of the argument I am now using, endeavor to make them appear not true by alleging that the person who can take as purchaser must be the heir as well as the heir male of the body, which relies on this reason, that the word 'heir' is not true of any but the heir general.

I readily admit that the word 'heir', singly and simply considered, is true only of the heir general, but taken together with the words used on purpose to restrain it, which here accompany it, it is true of one who often is not also the heir general. The words of description taken as written and intended they should be taken are true, but, taken separately as not written nor intended, they are not all true. Therefore, they shall not operate unless they are separately true as well as jointly.

This is a most unfair and disingenuous way of construction and not to be endured, nor is it thought of in any parallel instance.

Supposing a man having lands in a manor where is the custom of borough English and he has land at the common law and having two sons, devises the latter to his heir according to the custom of borough English, must the devisee be defeated because he is not also heir at the common law, his elder brother being living, which probably would be the only reason of making any devise, since, if his elder brother had been dead, the land would have descended to the devisee.

So, if a man having gavelkind land devises other lands to his heir in gavelkind, shall they not take because not the heir as well as heirs in gavelkind? In some manors, the eldest is the only heir. Suppose lands devised to my heir according to the custom etc. In short, this construction is to say here are words, proper words, used on purpose to limit the general sense of the word 'heir' and to distinguish the heir special intended from the heir general and adapted by the law for that end, and yet the person distinguished must be also the heir general, the person from whom he is meant to be distinguished, or he cannot take as a purchaser or thus that, though the law allows of the distinction of an heir special and an heir general, yet a man cannot take as the one without being also the other.

The second requisite to a perfect description is that it should be certain, *id est* be competent to the person claiming by them and to no other. That the words are so in the present case to Edward Barkham, the defendant, is clear by the pedigree proved and allowed in this cause, by which it is evident he is in fact the heir male of the body of the great-grandfather and that no other pretends to be so.

The third requisite to complete a description is that it should be in proper words. This is more in my opinion than is necessary in the case of a will. But it happens also to be in the present case. The words 'heir male of the body' are the aptest and most artful words the law knows by which to describe that special heir and to distinguish him from the heir general. It is observable there is not so much here as that redundant epithet often but improperly made use of in such kind of descriptions of special heir, for it better belongs to the heir general, though not necessary or of any use even in that case, so that the art of man cannot more correctly and perfectly describe the heir here intended to take by purchase than is done.

Then, since the law does admit purchasers to take by descriptions, it must of necessary consequence admit of this description, even in the case of a purchase, it being not only true and certain, but even correct and perfect.

The next settled point of law I argue from is that the words 'heir or heirs of J.S.' are admitted to be sufficient to entitle the heir general to take by purchase.

Now, I argue *a pari* that there is full as much, indeed, the same reason that the heirs male of the body of J.S. should be sufficient to enable him who is to take by purchase, though he be not generally and simply the heir, for the first is but a *descriptio personae* and the latter is as has been shown as full and perfect a description as that can be. It is observable the word 'heir' is also in its primary and necessary use a word of descent or limitation of the estate and not of purchase. It became so only accidentally as sufficiently describing the person, after the death of the ancestor, who would in a course of descent inherit the fee if he left any and who is meant to take by purchase. But it is not necessary that the ancestor should leave a fee to descend. His heir can take as heir by purchase without that. Just so are the words in question as certain a description of the person who would take as the heir male of the body if the ancestor had died having had a qualifying fee so limited to him.

These words are, I admit, in their primary and most perfect use words of descent or limitation, but so is the word 'heir' too, as I observed before. And if the one happening to be a sure and perfect description of the person becomes thereby a good word of purchase, why must not the other do so too? This gives me the occasion here to take notice of one of the false colors used to support a difference between these two cases, *viz.* that this case of a purchase is not within the Statute *de Donis.*[1] The proposition that it is not within the Statute is certainly true, for the Statute does not meddle with the subject matter, i.e. what are good words of purchase and what not. But the inference that, therefore, they are not a good *descriptio personae* of a purchaser is plainly wrong, for they might become good words of purchase by a necessary consequence drawn from the Statute, though not directly within the provision or intent of it.

If the common law had not known any of these special inheritances or descents and the said Statute had first created them, which it did not, yet, when these special descents had been once made part of the law why a purchaser might not be described by words of descent, which were at the common law, I do not see nor can any sound difference be assigned, the one being as certain, clear, and, after the Statute, as legal a description as the other.

But that which clears this matter beyond all doubt is that these special heirs described by the words which the question arises upon were at the common law the Statute *de Donis* treats none of these inheritances but only confirms them against alienations, as Littleton is express in his chapter of estates tail and Lord Coke, in his *Commentaries*,[2] fully agrees, and the lands descended to the special heir at the common law according to the limitation though another was the heir general.

This being so, can a reason be assigned why a word of art properly denoting the heir general at the common law, though he has no inheritances descending to him shall be a good description of a person to take by purchase but as artful and proper and full a description of a special heir equally known and allowed by the common law throughout the kingdom shall not. The special heirs at the common law are not the less words of purchase, because his estate, in some measure, confirmed by the Statute *de Donis* and made not alienable in the common form of alienation *post prolem suscitatem* as before it might, the description is not less perfect after the Statute confirming and allows this special heir than it was before. Thus I think it is sufficiently proved that the description of the purchaser in the present case must be good in law or the law be inconsistent with itself and, if so, to understand the law would be a work purely of memory and not at all of judgment. But it must be remembered and enumerated what perfect descriptions of the persons are good to purchase by and what not.

Having before observed that most of the authorities relied on for the plaintiff are not all to the present purpose and why I shall in the next place consider those authorities that are to the purpose of the present case and do assert the contrary opinion, I have already shown that the principal Case of Cowden [in] Hobart is not at all pertinent to this, the devise there being to the right heirs male, which describes a person the law ordinarily knows not in any case, either of descent or purchase, unless he be the heir.

---

[1] Stat. 13 Edw. I, Westminster II, c. 1 (*SR*, I, 71).

[2] T. Littleton, *Tenures*, ss. 13–31; E. Coke, *First Institute* (1628), ff. 18b-27b.

But I admit that Hobart, in proving the point, which is an extremely plain one, says *obiter* and clearly further than necessary to support that judgment that, where a limitation is by way of purchase to the heir male or female of the body, he must be as well the right heir as the heir male or female of the body that shall take, for this is clearly out of the letter and intent of the Statute of Westminster.[1]

To take off the weight of this authority, at least in great measure, I observe, first, that I have before proved that this reason, *viz.* that it is out of the Statute of Westminster, is no good one, because it does not at all want it, being before as perfect a description of an heir special at the common law as the heir was of the heir general and both equally words of descent in their original signification. Second, the words 'heir male of the body' are admitted on all sides to be good words of purchase so that he who takes by them must be the heir male of the body, but it is required when the words taken together do not, that he must be also the heir general. Now, if it was material that the Statute meddles only with descents, and not purchases directly, these words would not be good words of purchase for want of being within the Statute, though he was the heir also.

The Case of John de Mandavill, Co. Litt. 36b,[2] clearly proves the heir of the body of his father is a good name of purchase. They are the very words of Coke. But, if the Statute was material, the heir in tail general considered as a purchaser would want the aid of the Statute as much as the more special heir in tail male.

The question is not if the Statute had created these special inheritances, whether as good words of purchase, they are within the Statute, but, where it would not have been a necessary consequence from the Statute, they should become good words of description and thereby of purchase.

This opinion of Lord Hobart was neither the point in judgment nor necessary to it. I am persuaded, had this been the principal point in view and he had thought closely on that subject, he would not have been satisfied with that opinion or disposed of a valuable property upon a distinction without a difference. And I rather think so, because a little after, in the same case and argument, he said thus. If the principal case had been to the heir male of anyone's body, it might have had some help from the Statute of Westminster so that, in the same report and argument as printed, he says the same case is clearly out of the letter and intent of the Statute and, soon after that, it might have had some help from it.

To make this better consist, I inclined to think he delivered himself in the first place no further than the subject in question required, *viz.* that where the limitation is to the heir male or female, the person taking must be the heir as well as male or female, but, if the principal case had been to the heirs male of anyone's body, then and indeed, it might have had some help from the Statute of

[1] Stat. 13 Edw. I, Westminster II, c. 1 (*SR*, I, 71).

[2] E. Coke, *First Institute* (1628), f. 26b.

Westminster and thus all consist well and properly, so that it is more than suspicious that the words 'of the body' were inserted by some unskillful amanuensis.

But, if otherwise, then it will bear no other reflection than this great man having unnecessarily and with a side view let drop this opinion in the course of this argument he could not proceed much further in it without showing some remorse of judgment in that particular and a questioning in some measure what he had before said.

The principal case of Shelly, Coke 1,[1] is not at all to this case. The limitation indeed is to the heirs male of the body of E.S., but the judgment for the son of the elder son there turns out on this that the grandfather having an estate for life limited to him in the same deed which lead the uses of a recovery, they became words of limitation and not of purchase and so whether good or not as words of purchase never came into question.

Indeed, there, the counsel, which was Coke, for the grandson, the defendant, argues that the second son Edward could not take as a purchaser even before the birth of his client, the grandson, because there was a daughter of the eldest son living, who was the heir at law. But the court takes no manner of notice of this point, and Sir Christopher Wray, Chief Justice, when he enumerates the causes of the judgment, does not make that point to be one nor indeed could he, for holding the words there to be the words of limitation and not of purchase, it could never come in question whether the second son could before the birth of the grandson take by them as words of purchase, so that there is no more than a proposition affirmed by a counsel *arguendo* and that without any authority cited, which comes up to prove it, as I shall next observe, for, here, My Lord Coke transcribes this opinion into his *Commentaries on Littleton* 24b,[2] which has been also much insisted on as an authority for the plaintiff, and, among the authorities noted in the margin to support it, is Shelley's Case, *viz.* solely his own argument there as counsel.

The next is the Case of Farrington, 9 Hen. VI, 23, 24, and the said case argued again 11 Hen. VI, 12.[3] There, the limitation is to the next heir male of J.S. and to the heirs male of his body and also the remainder was to vest in possession before the next male relation, who claimed by those words, was born. In this case, there are two reasons why the next male relation could not take, neither of which are in the present case or in that they are cited to prove. The limitation is to the heirs male of J.S. and not to the heirs male of the body. And next the person claiming was not *in esse* when the contingent remainder should have vested.

---

[1] *Wolfe v. Shelley* (1581), 1 Coke Rep. 88, 76 E.R. 199, also 1 Anderson 69, 123 E.R. 358, Moore K.B. 136, 72 E.R. 490, Jenkins 249, 145 E.R. 176, 3 Dyer 373, 73 E.R. 838.

[2] E. Coke, *First Institute* (1628), f. 24b.

[3] *Farrington v. Darel* (1431–1432), YBB Trin. 9 Hen. VI, f. 23, pl. 19, Mich. 11 Hen. VI, f. 12, pl. 28.

The next is 37 Hen. VIII, Br., tit. 'done',[1] remainder limited to the right heirs of J.S., which J.S. is attainted in the life of the tenant for life and dies, that point adjudged is that, by the attainder, J.S. having no heir, none can take as his heir [is] very far from proving what it is cited to prove.

Another case cited in the margin of C. Litt. 24; Br. tit. [*blank*] 1 and 40, Sir William Hussey's Case.[2] This is rather against the opinion it is cited to warrant. Sir John Hussey enfeoffs to the use of a son a term for life, remainder to the use of heirs male of his body, he is attainted and dies and then his wife dies; by the opinion of Wherewood, Sir William, the eldest son, should take as a purchaser, though he could not be the heir in any legal sense of a person attainted, *sed aliter alii sentierunt*, and then *tamen per aliquos* the opinion *de Wherewood est melior* and in supporting that assertion, this case is *inter alia* put if a gift be with a remainder to the heirs female of his body of a man who has issue, a son and a daughter, the daughter shall have the land although she is not the heir.

The other authority is Dyer 374, which is only an imperfect report of Shelley's Case, before observed on, so that there is not one of the authorities cited which, in the least, support this assertion that he who would take as a purchaser by the name of heir male of the body must be also the heir general. But one of those authorities, such as it is, is in point against it.

From this instance and others which might be given, it appears that whenever one finds, though in books of good authority, opinions laid down which are not judicial opinions and which seem repugnant to natural reason as well as to the reason of the law, i.e. to be inconsistent with other known settled points in law, one ought not too easily to depend on such opinions for law but search them to the bottom and, generally, it will be found they have no foundation but that the law is at least very inconsistent with itself.

But if, after what have been observed, these authorities are yet of some weight, as falling from the pens of so great men, though not in any point in judgment, yet I proceed to show in the next place that the judicial authorities which have been to the contrary greatly overweigh those opinions.

First, in Pollex., 1, 457, the Case of James and Richardson and, afterwards, another case on the same will by the name of Burchett and Durdant, 2 Vent. 311, the first settled in the House of Lords, the second adjudged in [the Court of] Common Bench on the authority of the former, in a devise, a remainder was limited to the heirs male of the body of B., now living. This was adjudged a sufficient description for a devisee to take the remainder by purchase, even in the life of B., the ancestor.

Now, this is by much a stronger case than the present. Here, the person is strictly, all the words of limitation taken together, as was certainly meant they should, require him to be, but only want to put it out of all doubt to be the heir

[1] Brooke, Abr., *Done & remainder*, pl. 42.

[2] *Hussey's Case* (1545 x 1546), Brooke, Abr., *Nosme*, pl. 1, 40.

general; there, the person who takes is neither the heir general nor the heir male of the body, the ancestor being living, besides, in that case, to come at the intent of the party, a known maxim of the law is dispensed with *quod non est haeres viventis*; in this there is no maxim of the law against but only some extra-judicial opinions I have before shown.

The words, 'now living' served in that case only to show that some person then living was intended. But that person living at the time of the devise was no more as heir in the lifetime of the ancestor than if he was not *in esse*.

It is observable that Pollexfen, in arguing that case, takes it as a principle that, if there be a sufficient description or design of the person, the remainder vests.

The next stronger case is that of Long and Beamont, in the House of Lords, on a writ of error on a judgment in the Court of Exchequer, a devise after several terms for years and several estates tail successively 'to the heirs male of my aunt Elizabeth Long lawfully begotten and, for want of such issue, to my own right heirs'. Here, the words 'now living' are wanting and yet the person described took as a purchaser in the life of Mrs. Elizabeth Long, though, in propriety of the law, he was then neither the heir general nor special, but, when she came to die, another might properly and first be the heir male of her body.

Next, in the Case of Long and Beamont, the words 'of the body' are wanting but supplied by implication only from the words 'lawfully begotten and for want of such issue'. But, in the present, the words, as before observed, are neither redundant nor deficient but proper and artful, nor is anything wanting in the person described but something they do not require *ex vi termini*.

The last authority I shall mention is the case of Pibus and Mitford, 1 Ventr. 372, 26 Car. II, Kings Bench,[1] a covenant to stand seised to the use of his heirs male begotten or to be begotten on the body of his second wife; Wilde, Rainsford, and Hale, Chief Justice, support this limitation for the issue male of the second wife, though there was a son by a former wife. This judgment indeed relied on another point, *viz*. that a use for life resulted to the covenantor, i.e. until he might have an heir properly speaking, which could not be until his death and, that being held, the words turned into words of limitation and not of purchase and the lands were adjudged to come to the issue male or the heirs male on the body of the second wife by descent.

But for the better support of this judgment, the said notion of a resulting use for life being very fine spun and plainly labored to support the intent of the parties, even in a deed, Lord Chief Justice Hale argues strongly and, in my opinion, clearly proves that the words 'heirs [of the covenantor] on the body' of his second

[1] *Pibus v. Mitford* (1673–1674), 1 Ventris 372, 86 E.R. 239, also 2 Levinz 75, 83 E.R. 456, 3 Keble 239, 316, 338, 84 E.R. 697, 741, 754, 3 Salkeld 337, 91 E.R. 859, T. Raymond 228, 83 E.R. 119, 1 Modern 98, 121, 159, 86 E.R. 761, 780, 800, 1 Freeman 351, 369, 89 E.R. 262, 275, Lincoln's Inn MS. Misc. 500, ff. 214v, 224, 236.

wife were good as a description to enable the heir of the covenantor of the body of this second wife to take by purchase if it had been a remainder and not an estate vested.

Indeed, he introduces his argument by saying in answer to the objection that he must be the heir general as well as the heir of the body who would in that case take by purchase of this I am not well satisfied but then he proceeds to aver and prove the contrary opinion, *viz.* that the remainder being limited to the heirs of the body of the second wife begotten by the covenantor, such a limitation will make a special heir to serve the turn, i.e. to take by purchase. He gives these reasons, first, because at the common law before the Statute *de Donis*, notice was taken that this was a special heir etc. On the special penning of the deed, it is apparent the covenantor took notice that he had an heir at common law, which, by the way, is also true in this present case on a will. Therefore, it cannot be intended he meant here such an heir as should be the heir general to him. This would be *contradictio in adjecto*. Littleton 352;[1] a feoffment on condition that the feoffee give the land to the feoffor and his wife and the heirs of their two bodies begotten; the feoffor dies leaving his wife; before the estate tail granted to them the feoffee ought to make the estate as near the intent of the condition as may be, *viz.* to let the land to the wife for life without any impeachment of waste, remainder to the heirs of the body of the husband on her begotten, if the husband and wife die before the reconveyance, then the conveyance is to be to the issue and to the heirs of the body of the father and mother begotten. Then he goes on. Suppose this had been to a second wife being the issue by a former, the book 12 Hen. IV[2] says that there it shall be in another manner. Note here the reporter mistook the Chief Justice, for the book does not contradict it but supports his opinion, putting *arguendo* the case being in Littleton and says it shall be performed express etc.

Now, this case put by the Chief Justice Hale is a case in point or a much stronger, for, if a man, having issue by a former wife, takes a second wife and makes a feoffment conditioned that the feoffee give the land to him and his second wife and to the heirs of their two bodies begotten and both die leaving the issue by the former wife, yet the conveyance shall be to the issue or heir of his body by the second wife and the heirs of the body of his father and mother begotten. Then Lord Hale proceeds to cite the case of the issue of Roberge, the wife of Merevil, Fitzherbert, 23, 2 Edw. III, 1 (43, 50),[3] which is the same case in all those books. By all those cases, it appears that no regard his had whether the son be the heir of the husband if he be the heir of the two bodies.

---

[1] T. Littleton, *Tenures*, s. 352.

[2] YB Mich. 2 Hen. IV, f. 5, pl. 20 (1400).

[3] Hil. 17 Edw. II (1324), Fitzherbert, Abr., *Taile*, pl. 23, YB Hil. 2 Edw. III, f. 1, pl. 1 (1328).

Therefore, it seems that the issue by the second wife shall take this by way of a contingent remainder, for the heirs of the body of the second wife is a good name of purchase, i.e. though there be issue who is the heir at law by a former wife.

I have not read any case against this. Hilary 16 or 26 of Eliz.; there was this case. A man taking notice in his will that his brother was dead, had a son, and that himself had three daughters, who were his heirs, he gave them £2000 and then gave the land to his heir male, provided if the daughters troubled his heir, then the devise of £2000 to be void. It was resolved that the devisor taking notice that others were his heirs, the limitation to his brother's son by the name of heirs male was a good name of purchase.

In the present case, the heir general is also, as has been observed, taken notice of by a legacy in money. If it be said that, in the case cited by Hale, that it is plain the heir general could not be meant to take as the heir male where the heir general was tied not to disturb the heir male. I answer, if the plainness of the intent will do, can anything be plainer than that, in this present case, the testator did not mean the heir general should take by the words 'heir male' of the great-grandfather?

Justice Wilde said he was of the same opinion with Hale in this point so that he, it appeared, became convinced by the argument of the Chief Justice. And, since the minute of it is so unanswerable, I wonder it did not convince everyone that heard it at large. If this point had rested here, surely the opinion of these two judges delivered individually and supported by reasons unanswerable and good authorities would have more than counterbalanced the opinion of Coke, arguing as counsel only in Shelley's Case, where, after all he had said, the point was overlooked by the court. And, as to Hobart's opinion, I think it clear from the observations made that nothing is to be fairly collected from what he mentions in Cowden's Case of it but that he doubted of the law in the point in question.

Trinity 8 Will. III, in [the Court of] Common Bench, rot. 1484, 2d *pars*, cited by Sir Robert Raymond, esquire. Barker and Wall, special verdict;[1] a devise, 'I give to Daniel, my eldest son, and his heirs male forever, if a female,[2] my next heir shall pay the said female £12 *per annum* so long as she shall live and have all the rest to him, I mean my next heir to him and his heirs male forever.' The testator died having two sons, Daniel and John. Daniel had issue, Jane, the lessor of the plaintiff, and died, Jane surviving, the heir at law to her father and grandfather, and judgment is given for John Wall, the younger son of the testator, though not his heir at law.

This case is also much stronger than the present, for, here, John, the younger son, as purchaser takes by the description of heir male, which, being not the heir,

---

[1] *Baker v. Wall* (1697), 1 Lord Raymond 185, 91 E.R. 1019, 2 Eq. Cas. Abr. 299, 307, 22 E.R. 252, 259.

[2] feme *MS.*

he is not in any propriety of legal speech, and this only because it is clear from the expressions in the will that the testator did not intend that the being of an heir female should hinder the person he meant by the words 'heirs male' from taking.

Is not the same matter as clear in this will that, when the testator says the heirs male of the body of his great-grandfather shall take, he did not intend that such taker should be hindered by the being of an heir female from whom the words properly, not improperly as in the cited case, this distinguishes the defendant?

The Case of Goodright and Cornish, 4 Mod. 259,[1] is nothing to the present case. It was a devise to John, his eldest son, for fifty years if John so long live and, after, to the heirs male of the body of the said John. John was the heir to the testator, yet it was adjudged that he not being a tenant for life, it was a contingent remainder ex[ecutory], the estate tail not executed in John so as that he could suffer a common recovery. Whether this remainder would vest in an heir male of the body of John, though he should leave an heir female general, is not so much as brought in question.

On the whole, I am of opinion that the words 'heirs male of the body' of the great-grandfather are in law good words of purchase to him who is that their male of the body, though he be not the heir general on these grounds. To recapitulate them very shortly, first, because common sense, natural reason, and the undoubted intent of the testator cry aloud for this justice; second, because the authorities to the contrary considered by themselves strictly are brought to a very little compass and weight; and, third, because such weight as is left in them notwithstanding the observations made is much over-weighed by the authority to the contrary, even in much stronger cases.

There remains but one consideration of little difficulty, *viz.* how is this trust to be executed and in what manner the conveyance is to be directed, as to which it is not material, at least it makes no difficulty, that the remainder is limited to the heirs male etc. in the plural number. It is the doctrine of Shelly's Case and others and most undoubted law that 'heirs of J.S.' are good words of purchase to the heir of J.S. Indeed, more proper and artful than if the singular number had been used, because, when the plural number is made use of, it denotes both the person to take and the estate to be taken, *viz.* the fee to the right heirs of J.S. and his heirs.

So, in the present case to the heirs male of the body of the great-grandfather, they describe the person to take and the estate also, i.e. the conveyance to be made to the person who, at the time of the conveyance, is the heir male of the body of the great-grandfather, *viz.* Edward Barkham, the defendant, and to the

[1] *Goodright v. Cornish* (1694), 4 Modern 255, 87 E.R. 380, also 12 Modern 52, 88 E.R. 1159, Skinner 408, 90 E.R. 181, Holt K.B. 227, 90 E.R. 1024, 1 Salkeld 226, 91 E.R. 200, 1 Lord Raymond 3, 91 E.R. 898, Comberbach 254, 90 E.R. 461, 1 Eq. Cas. Abr. 189, 21 E.R. 980, 2 Eq. Cas. Abr. 337, 22 E.R. 287.

heirs male of the body of his great-grandfather, Sir Robert Barkham, which I decree accordingly.

And in decreeing this, I follow the law in matters executory at the common law when those of performance of conditions are the law, as has been already shown, takes a greater or, at least, the same latitude to execute the intent of the condition as near as may be when a strict pursuing of the letter of it would be ineffectual.

[Other reports of this case: Precedents in Chancery 442, 461, 24 E.R. 197, 207, 1 Strange 35, 93 E.R. 368, Lincoln's Inn MS. Misc. 506, p. 1, Gilbert Rep. 116, 131, 25 E.R. 81, 92, 2 Vernon 729, 23 E.R. 1078, 1 Eq. Cas. Abr. 215, 21 E.R. 999, 2 Eq. Cas. Abr. 717, 22 E.R. 603.]

160

Anonymous v. Foster

(Ch. 1717)

A devise of 'goods, chattels, and estate whatsoever' passes personal and real estate.

Lincoln's Inn MS. Misc. 10, p. 254

22 February 1716[/17]. [blank] v. Lydia Foster.

William Goodman, by will, taking notice that he was entitled to the reversion in fee of a house in London after the death of the plaintiff and his wife, devises all his right and interest in that house to the defendant, his wife, and her heirs, and then he declares his will to be that his wife should sell the said house to pay a debt of £100 which he owed, and he makes no disposition of the surplus of the money which should arise by such sale; then he devises five other houses which were in mortgage for £250 to his wife for life, remainder to his brother and sisters and their heirs. And then comes this clause, *viz.* 'And after payment of my debts, legacies, and funeral expenses, all the rest, residue, and the remainder of my goods, moneys, and estate whatsoever I give to my wife', and he makes her executrix.

The testator died seised in fee of another house besides those particularly devised by his will.

The questions were between the testator's wife and his heir at law:

First, to whom the surplus of the money arising by the sale of the house which was devised to be sold did belong;

Second, whether the house not particularly devised by the will descended to the heirs at law or passed to the wife by the general words in the will.

As to the first, it was decreed for the wife, the houses and all the testator's interest therein being expressly given to her by the will and, besides the surplus of the estate being given to her, the word 'estate' will carry it to her.

As to the second, the Master of the Rolls [Jekyll] was of opinion that the house not mentioned in the will passed to the wife by the words 'all my estate', for though that word is coupled with personal things and, therefore, in such case, generally speaking, must be understood to mean things of the same nature with those with which it is joined, yet, where a man, as in the present case, by his will, gives away part of his personal estate and part of his real estate and then gives all the remainder of his 'goods, chattels, and estate whatsoever', that will pass the remainder of his lands as well as of his personal estate.

161

Earl of Shaftesbury v. Countess of Shaftesbury

(Ch. 1717)

Where goods in a house are devised, no goods pass by that devise but such as are actually there at the time of the testator's death.

A nuncupative will cannot take the place of a written one.

Lincoln's Inn MS. Misc. 10, p. 249

25 February 1716[/17].

There were two questions in this cause, one was upon the late earl's will whereby he had given to the defendant, his wife, all his plate and household goods which should be in his house at Reigate at the time of his death. When the earl made this will, he had a house at Reigate in Surrey, which he held under a lease for years, and, after he made his will, he traveled into Italy and died at Naples. During the earl's absence, Mr. Truelock, his steward, out of good husbandry, agrees with the lessor for a sum of money to accept a surrender of the lease, and, thereupon, he removes all the household goods at Reigate to another house of the earl at Kensington. And then, he acquaints the earl by letter with what he had done, who returns an answer to his steward approving of his conduct in that matter.

The earl, after this, makes a codicil and thereby gives his wife all his plate, pictures, etc. which he had in his house at Naples, but he takes no notice of the goods which had been removed from Reigate. And the question was if the goods at Reigate passed by the will, they not being there [at the] death of the earl.

Lord Chancellor [Lord Cowper]: My notion has always been that nothing will pass by such a devise but what was actually in his house at the death of the testator unless removed tortiously and unlawfully or with a fraudulent intent to defeat the will. But this is not either of those cases, for the goods were lawfully removed by the steward who had a general power to act in the earl's absence and what he did was assented to afterwards by the earl. And, therefore, I am of opinion the countess is not entitled to any part of these goods.

As to the second question, the case was this. The earl, some little time before his death, being then in a declining condition, called three of his servants to him and, in their presence, gives the countess £100, and, after this, he makes two codicils to his will but, in neither of them, takes any notice of this £100. And if the countess should retain it was the question.

Lord Chancellor [Lord Cowper]: As to the gift of this £100, I do not see how I can make it good. It is neither a legacy nor has it been proved as a nuncupative will. And as to what has been insisted on for the countess, that this was a *donatio causa mortis*, there were two codicils made afterwards, so that I think it was absorbed in the subsequent acts.

British Library MS. Hargrave 81, f. 2

25 February 1716/17.

The late earl of Shaftesbury [1671–1713], *inter alia*, devises as follows, *viz.* 'Item, I give to my wife all such goods as shall be at my house at Reigate at the time of my decease'. And, afterwards, the said earl went for his health and resided at Naples, during which time his steward, without any orders from the said earl, removed all or most part of the Reigate furniture to another house, but not by collusion or with intent to defraud, as was admitted of all sides. And, afterwards, he acquainted the earl therewith, who never contradicted what was done or seemed dissatisfied with it. And, afterwards, by a codicil to his said will, he gave his said wife all his goods which at the time of his decease should be at his house at Naples. And he gave her, the day before he died, £100 to bear her expenses into England.

The counsel for the plaintiff insisted that the goods devised by the codicil were in lieu of and ought to be taken as a satisfaction for the goods of the Reigate house. But if not, yet no more could pass by that devise than should happen to be there at the time of the testator's death.

But for the defendant, the Lady Shaftesbury, it was said that the earl not having his will with him might probably have forgot in what manner he devised the Reigate goods or, if he had not, yet that it was not probably that he should know that such removal would defeat that devise and, since he had not declared that he intended one as a satisfaction for the other, the presumption was strong that he intended her the benefit of both. And they insisted strongly that the removal of the goods by the steward without any direction from the earl would not defeat the devise, though the earl did not afterwards contradict it, perhaps through negligence or forgetfulness.

Lord Chancellor [Cowper]: I always was and am still of opinion that, where goods in a house are devised, no goods will pass by that devise but such as are actually there at the time of the testator's death. The words here are in the future tense and no goods can pass that were not there when the testator died, unless such as were fraudulently or tortiously removed, and a consent after the goods were removed is equivalent to a direction to do it.

The next thing that is for judgment before [me] is the bond for £250, which money the defendant, who is the testator's widow, had very commendably and frugally saved out of her fortune before her marriage and, at her marriage, by the earl's consent, was put into her brother's hands for her security and which the earl all along to the time of his death declared he looked upon as his lady's. Here is a series of declarations and actions and very many circumstances which show a permanent intention in the earl. And I must own I cannot help falling in to support it.

As to the declaration of the earl to give the defendant £100 to bear her charges, that cannot be supported here. A nuncupative will cannot take place where there is a written one. It wants the force of the Statute. But the defendant being in court and informing My Lord that the £100 was given her in specie, most of it in pistoles, with a declaration by the testator that it was to bear her charges into England, the court directed the Master to see if the £100 was paid in specie and, if it were, that the defendant should not account for it and that what maiden jewels the defendant wore for ornament should be deemed paraphernalia if there did not appear a deficiency in the testator's estate.

[Other copies of this report: British Library MS. Hargrave 82, f. 1.]

[Other reports of this case: British Library MS. Hargrave 303, f. 1, British Library MS. Hargrave 77, f. 3, 2 Vernon 747, 23 E.R. 1089, 1 Eq. Cas. Abr. 201, 21 E.R. 989.]

162

Longden v. Bealing

(Ch. 1717)

A person cannot act contrarily to his own contract by selling something and then taking it for himself.

British Library MS. Hargrave 81, f. 6

2 March 1716[/17].

The defendant being Gentleman Usher to King William and there being £500 due to him upon the civil list, he obtained a promise of the place in the Custom House in the bill mentioned, but, before he obtained a grant thereof, King William died. And early in the reign of the late queen, the defendant obtained a grant thereof by letters patent during Her Majesty's pleasure and enjoyed the same several years. And, afterwards, wanting money, he contracted with the plaintiff, a very young man, for the sum of £700, to assign the said letters patent to the plaintiff. And by deed poll bearing date the 26th day of November 1712, the defendant, for the consideration aforesaid, assigned the said letters patent to the plaintiff and thereby covenanted to surrender the same unto the plaintiff, his executors, administrators, and assigns and covenanted that, if the plaintiff, at any time during the continuance of the said letters patent in his the defendant's or plaintiff's own name or in any other name that the plaintiff should appoint, that the defendant should assist the plaintiff in obtaining such renewal. And after[wards], by a bond penal reciting the said deed poll, the defendant obliged himself that, if, within the term of three years, the said letters patent should be forfeited, superseded, or any ways made void other than by the defendant's death or the misbehavior of the plaintiff, to repay the plaintiff the sum of £250.

Sir Joseph Jekyll, for the plaintiff: The plaintiff, being but a young man, had not perhaps got the defendant into such express and full covenants as he should have done, but we take it that it was the intent of the parties, and so we have it fully in proof, that it was then intended and understood that the defendant should not again have the benefit of the office, but that, upon all contingencies other than those expressed[1] in the bond, the defendant was to use his interest for the plaintiff's benefit. But now, the defendant pretends that the letters patent being determined by the queen's death, any person was at liberty to obtain a grant of the said employment and, that not being a contingency stipulated for, the defendant might, notwithstanding his agreement, obtain it for himself. And, accordingly, he, in three months after the queen's death, got a grant of it and turned the plaintiff out, which we apprehend to be very unreasonable, for, by that way of reasoning, he might have procured the letters patent to be suspended the very next day after he had assigned them and got a new grant for himself, that being as little provided for as the other.

Mr. *Cox*: After the queen's death, all grants were continued by Act of Parliament[2] for six months and, by proclamation, for three months more, in which time, we have in proof that the plaintiff applied to the defendant to assist the plaintiff to renew the letters patent, which the defendant then refused and got it for himself in three months after the queen's death. And it is proved by the defendant's brother-in-law, who made the writings, that he apprehended the intent of the agreement to be that the plaintiff should enjoy the employment during the defendant's life. And [there was] no talk, as he remembers, of the defendant's ever having it again.

For the defendant, it was insisted on by Mr. *Cooper* and Mr. *Vernon* that the defendant had not done anything contrary to his agreement, for the letters patent being determined by the queen's death and not by any fraud in him, he was by the letter and intention of the agreement, as far as it appears by the writing, as much at liberty to apply for the employment as any other person was and that it would be of a very dangerous consequence to admit witnesses to prove the intent of the parties to be other than what is expressed in the writing.

---

1 excepted *MS*.

2 Stat. 6 Ann., c. 41, s. 8 (*SR*, VIII, 739).

But the court [Lord Cowper] decreed the new grant to the plaintiff and that the defendant should account to the plaintiff for the profits and also pay the plaintiff his costs.

[Other copies of this report: British Library MS. Hargrave 82, f. 5.]

[Other reports of this case: British Library MS. Hargrave 303, f. 2, British Library MS. Hargrave 77, f. 3v.]

163
Ellis v. Dame Lanesborough
(Ch. 1717)

Proof that the last installments of a debt or a rent were paid is good evidence that prior installments had been paid also.

British Library MS. Hargrave 81, f. 8

10 May 1717.

The case was that Ellis, the plaintiff, lent £200 to A. and took a bond for it in the name of one Mr. Smith, with whom he left the bond in order to receive the money. Smith received several sums for interest and in part of principal, for which he endorsed receipts on the bond. And he dies, leaving his wife executrix, who received at two payments the remainder of the principal and interest, for which she also endorses receipts, and dies, leaving the defendant, the Lady Lanesborough, her executrix in trust for charities. The bond was of all hands acknowledged to have been taken in trust for the plaintiff, who now pretends by his bill that the testators received the money to their own use and never paid the same to him.

But it appearing by an account set forth by the defendant that the two last sums endorsed on the bonds were received by the plaintiff and that being also fully proved, the Lord Chancellor [Lord Cowper] said the plaintiff's was an unfair bill in regard it took no notice of the stated account nor of those two payments. And he said there was no occasion to run into the proof of the other payments, for it was like receipts for rent and there was a strong presumption that the former receipts were satisfied upon good proof of the two last sums paid. And the bill was dismissed with costs.

[Other copies of this report: British Library MS. Hargrave 82, f. 7.]

[Other reports of this case: British Library MS. Hargrave 77, f. 4, British Library MS. Hargrave 303, f. 3v.]

164

Batchelor v. Serle

(Ch. 1717)

Even though the executors of a decedent's will are given legacies, they are entitled to take the undisposed of residuum.

Lincoln's Inn MS. Misc. 10, p. 251

William Allen, by will, gives several legacies, and, amongst others, he gives to his brother, John Searle, the elder, and his wife and four sons the sum of £70 to buy them and their two maid servants mourning [clothes], and he gives his horse and furniture to John Serle, son of John, the elder, and he makes him and his brother George, another son of John, the elder, executors.

The plaintiff, being a half-sister of the testator, brings her bill for a distributive share of the surplus of his personal estate, which was indisposed of by the will. And it was much insisted on for the plaintiff that the executors having these bequests given them by the will were excluded from the surplus.

[Lord Cowper] decreed the surplus to the executors notwithstanding.

[Other reports of this case: 2 Vernon 736, 23 E.R. 1081, Gilbert Rep. 125, 25 E.R. 88, 1 Eq. Cas. Abr. 246, 21 E.R. 1022.]

165

Attorney General, ex rel. v. Spalden

(Ch. 1717)

In the administration of a decedent's estate, bond creditors have priority over creditors by simple contract and charitable legatees.

Creditors and legatees of a decedent's estate will be satisfied out of the real assets of the estate where the personal assets are insufficient.

Lincoln's Inn MS. Misc. 10, p. 219, pl. 2

17 May 1717. Attorney General, at the relation of the Governors of the Grammar School of Ashborne v. Dorothy Spalden, widow, Elizabeth Figs, and Thomas Taylor, executors of Anthony Spalden, John Spalden, heir at law of the testator, and the two trustees named in his will.

Anthony Spalden, by a will dated in April 1710, gives £8 a year to the vicar of Ashborne and his successors and the like annuity to the preacher to read prayers at certain stated times in the parish church of Ashborne in Derbyshire. And he gives £340 to trustees to be laid out in lands and settled for the payment of these annuities. He gives his lands in Ireland charged with some annuities to the relators upon trust to sell the same and buy lands in England and on such lands to build almshouses and the persons to be placed there to have 2s. 6d. per week and a new gown once a year. He gives the surplus of his estate as the annuities should determine to the relators upon trust to purchase lands and thereon to build two school houses, one for teaching thirty poor boys and the other for thirty poor girls, and to pay the master and mistress £30 a year apiece. If any surplus should remain, then, with such surplus, the relators should buy lands and thereon build four houses for the maintenance of four clergymen's widows. And, if any surplus should remain after all this, then the relators were to apply it for the benefit of the Town of Ashborne as they should think fit.

He lived three years after making the will and bought a piece of land and built thereon two school houses and put in a master and mistress and allowed them £10 a year each for teaching the children. And, after his death, the lease and release by which that land was conveyed to him was found tied up and a label affixed to the string whereon was written with the testator's own hand these words, *viz.* 'my lease and deed for the charity school in Ashburne'.

The personal estate fell short to answer the debts and charities, and the heir claimed the lands purchased after the will as descended on him.

Curia decreed an account of the testator's estate and, if it appeared that the personal estate was not sufficient to answer the debts and legacies and that the personal estate should be exhausted in the payment of such of the debts as charged the real estate, then so far the debts by simple contract and the charities were to stand in the room of the bond creditors and have a satisfaction out of real assets. But this direction was to extend only to the charities given out of the two first surpluses and not to the last surplus which was given to be applied for charity in general.

He decreed that the label fixed to the deeds of purchase of the lands bought after the will being in the testator's own handwriting was a good appointment of the lands comprised in those deeds to the charity schools mentioned in the testator's will.

166

Godolphin v. Libby

(Ch. 1717)

A mortgagee of land from a decedent's estate takes with notice of and subject to the rights of the devisee.

Lincoln's Inn MS. Misc. 10, p. 222, pl. 1

The same day [17 May 1717].

A man bequeaths by will a leasehold estate to one for life and, afterwards, to other purposes mentioned in his will, and he leaves other assets sufficient to pay all his debts. The administrator *cum testamento annexo* mortgages this estate to the plaintiff, who brings his bill to foreclose the persons interested under the will.

It was decreed the mortgage was not good, for the mortgagee, taking it from the administrator *cum testamento annexo*, must be affected with notice of the will. And the bill was dismissed with costs.

167

Piggott v. Penrice

(Ch. 1717)

The word 'executor' ex vi termini *can concern only personal estate.*

An heir shall not be disinherited but by express words or a necessary implication.

A power can be exercised only according to its terms.

Lincoln's Inn MS. Misc. 11, p. 88

18 May 1717.

Upon an appeal from the Rolls, there were two questions in this cause. The first arose upon the will of Mrs. Neeson whereby she made her niece, the Lady Penrice, executrix of all her goods, lands, and chattels. The testatrix had no leasehold lands, but only an estate in fee of a fourth part of a freehold estate. And her debts were more than her personal estate would suffice to pay.

The question was if these lands passed by the will to the executrix. The will was executed in the presence of three witnesses.

It was insisted on for the defendants that this must amount to a devise of the land, for, otherwise, the word 'lands' in the will must be rejected, which shall never be if any construction can be put upon it.

Lord Chancellor [Lord Cowper]: This is such a case that a judge in his private inclination might wish to determine in favor of the appellants. The words of the will are not sufficient to pass lands. The word 'executor' *ex vi termini* can concern only personal estate.

In the next place, if any land was supposed to pass, it is uncertain what estate passed in the land. The law has guarded inheritances, and an heir shall not be disinherited but by express words or a necessary implication.

The next question arose upon a settlement made by the plaintiff's wife upon her marriage, whereby she settled her estates to the use of herself and the plaintiff for their lives, with a remainder to his right heirs, proviso that Mr. Pigott and his wife or she alone by any deed executed in the presence of three witnesses (but not to be menial servants) might revoke all the uses except the limitation to Mr. Pigott for his life.

Mrs. Pigott, being very ill, writes a letter to Mr. Edwards, who drew the settlement, and acquaints him that she had been prevailed on to make the settlement against her inclination and it had troubled her conscience. And she desired him to prepare a deed of revocation and to settle the estate on her niece, the Lady Penrice, subject to the payment of several charities mentioned therein. And she says she cannot die satisfied if this was not done. But, before any actual revocation was made, she died. And there was some proof that Mr. Edwards had been somewhat dilatory in the matter.

And the question was if this letter should amount to a revocation.

In this case was cited the Duke of Albemarle's Case,[1] where he had made a deed with a power of revocation by a writing executed in the presence of three witnesses, who should be peers of the realm. In that case, there being a question upon the execution of the power that, if the duke had been travelling abroad when he executed his power and could not have had three peers to have been witnesses, they would have supplied that defect.

Lord Chancellor [Lord Cowper]: If all things had been ready for revoking the uses and, by any contrivance of the husband, the execution of it had been prevented, I think I need not say, I should have relieved in such a case. But here was nothing of this nature done. Now, shall I say that, where there is a power of revocation and several circumstances to be observed, that a letter only signifying a desire or interest to revoke shall amount to a revocation? Surely, no.

The decree must be affirmed.

[Other reports of this case: Precedents in Chancery 471, 24 E.R. 211, Gilbert Rep. 137, 25 E.R. 96, 1 Comyns 250, 92 E.R. 1057, 1 Eq. Cas. Abr. 209, 21 E.R. 995, 2 Eq. Cas. Abr. 191, 22 E.R. 164.]

168

Wilson v. Norris

(Ch. 1717)

In this case, a principal debtor was ordered to pay the debt at the suit of the surety against the principal and the creditor.

British Library MS. Hargrave 81, f. 9

21 May 1717.

A., in the country, being indebted to the defendant Norris in the sum of £130 for silks, Norris employed the defendant Rooke as his attorney to get the money. And he employed the plaintiff to arrest A., who accordingly arrested him. And, being in custody, Rooke agreed to take a bond for £100 from the said A. and his brother and, for £20, the bond of the said A. And, A. having a

[1] *Duchess of Albemarle v. Earl of Bath* (1692–1693), 3 Chancery Cases 55, 22 E.R. 963, 2 Chancery Reports 417, 21 E.R. 704, Nelson 196, 21 E.R. 824, 2 Freeman 121, 193, 22 E.R. 1099, 1155, 2 Eq. Cas. Abr. 671, 22 E.R. 564.

mortgage for £100, Rooke proposed that to be a security for the remaining £10 and charges. But, as the mortgaged premises lay too far from him, he desired the plaintiff would give his note for £20 and take an assignment for his security, which the plaintiff first refused, but Rooke assuring him that he should be indemnified against the note and should never be troubled upon it until he had received the value by the mortgage and that he would endorse the note, the plaintiff was prevailed upon to give a note for £20 to the defendant Norris. But Rooke pretended then to be in haste and so could not endorse the note, nor was the mortgage assigned, though it was agreed the plaintiff might at any time have had that, but it proved to be worth nothing. The plaintiff heard nothing of the note for several years after and thought it had been made up another way. At last, Norris arrests the plaintiff, who brings his bill to be relieved against this note. Norris swears he never gave Rooke any orders to make such promise to the plaintiff, as in the bill is mentioned, and Rooke [swears] that he never made any such.

Mr. *Vernon*, for the defendant, said this was a transaction of several years standing and now the plaintiff would fain set aside what appears to be a manifest agreement in writing by a pretended parol agreement proved only by his own followers.

Lord Chancellor [Lord Cowper]: The note is a good note to the defendant Norris. But there appears to me a satisfactory evidence that the plaintiff gave the note upon Rooke's promise to indemnify him, for, besides the evidence that is given of it, I see no other probable inducement for him to do it. Therefore, he decreed Rooke to pay the £20 and interest to Norris and [decreed] the plaintiff his costs.

[Other copies of this report: British Library MS. Hargrave 82, f. 7, pl. 2.]

[British Library MS. Hargrave 77, f. 4v, pl. 1, British Library MS. Hargrave 303, f. 4.]

169

Angier v. Angier

(Ch. 1717–1718)

A divorce a mensa *is a matter for an ecclesiastical court, not a court of equity. However, a contract for separate maintenance is enforceable by a court of equity.*

Lincoln's Inn MS. Hill 29, p. 35

Trinity 4 Geo. I.

Abell, a relation of Anger's wife, sues Anger, the husband, in the ecclesiastical court, to end which suit they both enter into an agreement that Anger should allow his wife £52 *per annum* for separate maintenance and agreed that further articles should be drawn up more at large, which articles he afterwards refused to sign, on which she now brings her bill to enforce a performance of that special agreement.

He answers that he is willing they should live together.

His counsel at the bar objected, first, that she did not sign this agreement and, second, that this affair of separation only belongs to the ecclesiastical court, and for the court to enforce this agreement would be to decree a separation which the Court of Chancery cannot do.

Her counsel proved by affidavits that there was sufficient ground for separation and separate maintenance and said that her bringing her bill proved she consented to the agreement and that this matter is proper for this court because it is only to decree for her a separate maintenance while they are separate and not to decree a separation, that this case of one Cutting, in this court, was like this. He made such an agreement as this with his wife; on her bringing her bill, he pleaded that this matter belonged to the ecclesiastical court, but, afterwards, he consented to come into this court, though, as to the jurisdiction, the plea was overruled, for his covenant could not give the court more authority than it had before. So the Case of Sir James Oxendon in this court.[1] There, the lady had agreed before marriage that her portion should be in trustee's hands to be laid out to the use of Sir James for life, remainder to her for life, and then to her children. Sir James was very barbarous to her, and the money was not laid out. The lady brought her bill against Sir James and the trustees, and, as she desired in her bill, the court decreed the whole interest of her fortune for her separate maintenance.

Lord Parker, Chancellor: The single question is whether this is a matter of this nature in which he can make an agreement. If it be, it is within the jurisdiction of this court of course. Now here, she says that his behavior to her was such that it was impossible for them to live together. He says in answer that her behavior to him was very ill and seems even inclined too that they should live separately. Now, this is a matter proper for the ecclesiastical court, and, if so, consequently, it must be proper for such an agreement as this, when the persons concerned would not have the whole world know of this matter.

The next thing is whether he has made this agreement. And I think he has without any manner of surprise.

As to the objection that she has not signed it. The agreement is with another person, Abell, to end the suit in the ecclesiastical court. And it was very proper to make such an agreement with him, with whom he was litigating in the ecclesiastical court. The agreement then is good. And how must it be enforced? The ecclesiastical court has no jurisdiction to enforce it merely because the original matter of the agreement is of their jurisdiction. And if this court does not, as surely it may, enforce it, this good agreement will again fall to the ground.

---

[1] *Oxenden v. Oxenden* (1705–1706), 2 Vernon 493, 23 E.R. 916, Precedents in Chancery 239, 24 E.R. 116, Gilbert Rep. 1, 25 E.R. 1, 1 Eq. Cas. Abr. 67, 21 E.R. 881.

He decreed that they should go before the Master and he settle proper articles to make this agreement effectual in law, that Anger should allow his wife £50 *per annum*, and the arrears since the agreement was made and that he should be indemnified from all trouble she might bring on him in law, for, though she or any other cannot really hurt him, yet he ought not to be put to any trouble. The husband has, I think, in this case given sentence against himself, for he thinks it proper they should be separate.

Lincoln's Inn MS. Misc. 380, pt. 3, p. 200

26 June 1718. Abell v. Anger.

A husband and wife quarrel. The wife provokes the husband by indecent language and behavior. The husband beats the wife. Afterwards, the wife goes from the husband. Afterwards, there is a meeting between the husband and the wife's friends, and the husband agrees in writing to allow his wife £50 *per annum* to live separate and not be liable to her debts [*blank*].

[Other reports of this case: Precedents in Chancery 496, 24 E.R. 222, Gilbert Rep. 152, 25 E.R. 107, 2 Eq. Cas. Abr. 150, 22 E.R. 129.]

170

Stanley v. Smith

(Ch. 1717)

There is no bringing into hotchpot but between the children themselves.

Lincoln's Inn MS. Misc. 10, p. 218

29 June 1717.

In this case, it was said by Mr. *Vernon* and not denied by anyone that there shall be no bringing into hotchpot but between the children themselves, so that, if a citizen leaves a wife and one child and that child has been advanced in his father's lifetime but not fully, such child, as between him and his mother shall not bring into hotchpot, but he shall have another third of his father's personal estate without regard to what he has received. And so it was decreed in the Lord Delaware's Case.[1]

In like manner, if there are several children and all except one have been fully advanced, the child unadvanced shall have the whole orphanage part of his father's personal estate as well as the other children's share as his own.

[1] *Dean v. Lord Delaware* (1708), 2 Vernon 628, 23 E.R. 1011, 1 Eq. Cas. Abr. 156, 21 E.R. 955.

171

Wheatley v. Wheatley

(Ch. 1717–1718)

Where a London freeman gives legacies to his children, after his death, his estate will be divided into three parts, one-third to the widow, one-third to the children, and one-third will be used to pay his legacies so far as it will extend, and, if it falls short, the legacies will abate in proportion.

Lincoln's Inn MS. Misc. 10, p. 209

5 July 1717.

The plaintiff's father, being a freeman of London, had by his will disposed of his personal estate without taking any notice of the custom of London and had thereby given some specific legacies, as Bank and East India [Company] stock, to some of his children and pecuniary legacies to others. And a bill being brought for an account of the testator's estate and that the plaintiffs might have their legacies and their customary shares also, the court, upon hearing the cause, decreed an account and reserved the consideration of the plaintiff's demands until after the Master's report. And now, it came on upon the equity reserved.

And it was insisted on for the defendants that, the plaintiffs' legacies being more than the orphanage share of each child came to, they ought not to have both, the custom of London being that, if the legacy exceeds the orphanage part, such orphanage part shall be deducted out of the legacy and the remainder only is accounted as a legacy.

Lord Chancellor [Lord Cowper]: Since the legacies given to each child exceed their orphanage shares, it will come to the same thing, whether the orphanage part is deducted out of the legacy and the overplus taken out of the testamentary part or whether the children take their orphanage parts in the first place and then take their legacies out of the testamentary part, for what the children lose one way they get the other. And, therefore, let the estate be divided into three parts, *viz.* one-third to the widow, one-third to the children, and let the remaining third be applied towards satisfaction of the plaintiffs' legacies so far as it will extend, and, if it falls short, the legatees must abate in proportion.

Note the Lord Chancellor seemed to be of opinion that, if a legacy given to a child is less than his orphanage share, he shall not have both, but the orphanage share shall go in satisfaction of his legacy.

Note Mr. *Vernon* insisted that, as to the specific legacies, the children to whom they were given could only have one-third thereof in regards the testator had a power over no more than one-third, and, for this, he cited the case of Web and Web, at the Rolls, which was afterwards confirmed upon an appeal to the Lord Chancellor,[1] where, a freeman having given a leasehold estate to one of his children, [it was] decreed that such child should only have one-third of such lease, for the testator had no power to dispose of more. But the Lord Chancellor did not seem to concur in opinion with that decree and, therefore, in the principal case, decreed that the specific as well as the pecuniary legatees should have their legacies in proportion out of the testamentary part, for he said he saw no reason why a specific legatee should be in a worse condition than a pecuniary one.

Lincoln's Inn MS. Misc. 10, p. 228

The special matter of the Master's report as to the custom of London was reheard before Lord Parker. And the question was whether, if a freeman gives a legacy to a child out of his whole estate taking no notice of the custom of London and such legacy is less than the orphanage part, the child shall have both. And it was strongly insisted that, if the orphanage part is more than the legacy, then the legacy is swallowed up in the orphanage part. But, if the legacy exceeds the orphanage part, then the orphanage part *pro tanto* shall be a satisfaction of the legacy and the overplus only above what the orphanage will satisfy shall be taken out of the testamentary part. And my Lord Chancellor [Lord Parker] seemed to be of this opinion, but he sent it to the Lord Mayor and aldermen to certify the custom. But nothing farther was done, the parties upon enquiry finding the custom to be so.

By the custom of London, if an orphan dies under twenty-one, his share shall survive to the other children and shall not be distributed according to the Statute,[2] by *Vernon*.

Lincoln's Inn MS. Misc. 384, p. 30

21 May. In the Inner Temple Hall.

A freeman had several children. By his will, he gives them several legacies, some whereof amounted to more than their orphanage part and some less.

The query is whether their orphanage share shall go in satisfaction of their legacies *pro tanto*, there not being sufficient [assets] to pay both.

Cowper: This is like the case of a wife who must abide by the will or the custom only and cannot take by both, as in Cox v. Edmundson.

Sir Thomas Powys, contra: This is against reason, for the custom does not meddle with the testamentary part, which is looked upon as an intestate estate. If legacies are given and there happens to be a deficiency of assets, all must abate in proportion. Here, one has a £1500 legacy, another £500, and the orphanage part

[1] *Webb v. Webb* (1710), 1 Peere Williams 132, 24 E.R. 325, 2 Vernon 668, 23 E.R. 1036, 2 Eq. Cas. Abr. 363, 22 E.R. 309.

[2] Stat. 22 & 23 Car. II, c. 10 (*SR*, V, 719–720).

is £800; so one would have £700 more than the orphanage part, but the other would have nothing more.

Lord Chancellor [Lord Parker]: I think this does not so much depend upon the custom as upon reason. Here, the freeman is disposing of his whole estate, and it is different from the case where he disposes only of the testamentary part, for, there, they may take by the custom and the will both. Here, the customary share cannot be had and the legacy both. If the customary share goes in part payment of the legacy, the intent of the father will be better observed, for they will have the whole which was designed them, though some will have more.

But the custom being insisted on, let it go to the Lord Mayor and the Court of Aldermen for their certificate whether, when a larger legacy is given than the orphanage part, that is not a satisfaction by the custom *pro tanto*.

172
Wheatley v. Warner

(Ch. 1717–1718)

An executor of a decedent's estate may pay one bond creditor in preference to another bond creditor, and the unpaid creditor will be subrogated to the rights of the creditor who has been satisfied.

Lincoln's Inn MS. Misc. 380, pt. 3, p. 173

[There was a] settlement on a marriage of a copyholder by a recovery to the husband and wife for their lives, remainder to the heirs of their bodies, remainder to the heirs of the husband. The husband becomes indebted to A. and to B. The husband borrows £100 of C., and the husband and wife surrender the copyhold into the hands of two copyholders and the wife is solely examined to the use of C. by way of a mortgage. And the husband gives a bond to C. for the £100 as a further security. The husband dies before the day of payment, and C. is not admitted. The wife pays the £100 out of the personal estate.

A. and B. bring their bill to charge the copyhold with so much as had been paid out of the personal estate. And the question was whether the wife shall not claim as a purchaser as having charged her own estate to enable the husband to take up the money.

It was agreed, where there are no creditors, she shall have satisfaction where she charges her own estate for the benefit of her husband. And [the question was] whether the court will supply the surrender so as to charge the estate of the wife, the surrender being never presented and no admittance.

Lord Chancellor [Lord Cowper]: The plaintiff having, as it is admitted, a just demand of a debt, he stands a fair creditor in the court. [In the] next place, it is admitted there were assets left sufficient to pay his debts. Another bond creditor has exhausted these assets in satisfaction of his debts; then, the creditor who wants these assets is to stand in the place of him and receive what benefit he was entitled to throughout. And here C. had a lien on the copyhold estate in equity during the wife's life and the remainder limited to the husband in fee. But I question whether the surrender out of court into the hands of the copyholders and the examination by them be good, whether that be an evil custom. The custom of most manors is that the wife shall be examined by the steward. Let the custom be enquired into.

Counsel: Then we desire it may be enquired also whether, by the custom of the manor, whether a surrender by a tenant in tail without a recovery will not bar the issue.

An executor [in] equity prefers one bond creditor by payment or judgment [by confession], and [it is] good against those in equal degree.

173

Anonymous

(Ch. 1717)

Expenses that are contracted for are payable only for the duration of the contract.

Lincoln's Inn MS. Hill 73, p. 1

31 July 1717. Sir Joseph Jekyll; Rolls.

The plaintiff was sent to Bilbao by the defendant as master of a ship to carry it safe to Spain to lade and unlade as he thought fit upon the allowance of £6 *per mensem* for himself and 30s. for his man. The ship was taken by a Spanish privateer and adjudged a good prize at Bilbao, upon which the plaintiff appeals to the superior court of admiralty at Madrid and stays in Spain twenty-four months, for which he demanded reasonable costs, the allowances agreed to by the defendant. But it appearing that he was only master of the ship and not the agent or factor to the part owners (the office of the master being only to convoy, to lade, and unlade, etc.) that he acted without the privity of the owners, the allowance was only made to the time of the capture, otherwise the charge of the plaintiff staying at Spain had been more than the loss of the ship.

174

Anonymous

(Ch. c. 1717)

A contract to pay a proportion of the costs of defending a lawsuit is valid and enforceable.

Lincoln's Inn MS. Hill 73, p. 2

The vicar of Lampeter, being informed that he had a right to receive the small tithes of apples, pears, etc. in kind, demanded them of the parish. They, thinking it an innovation, refuse and enter into articles that whosoever the vicar should make defendant in the cause should represent the whole parish and that the whole parish would acquiesce in the judgment given and bear an equal share of the charge of any suit or suits, action or actions, commenced in any ecclesiastical or other court. The vicar recovered against the defendant, who became plaintiff in this suit, and the whole parish.

But the defendant in this cause and one who died insolvent did according to their articles in writing bear their proportion of the charge. The defendant pretended that he knew of no such articles as obliged to bear any share of the charge in any but the ecclesiastical [court].

The Master [was ordered] to compute his share and costs for the present suit.

175

Anonymous

(Ch. c. 1717)

Unless a will specifies otherwise, interest on general legacies does not accrue until there is a demand for payment.

Lincoln's Inn MS. Hill 73, p. 3, pl. 1

If general legacies are left and the legatees demur and make no demand of them, they shall only have interest from the time of their exhibiting their bill by way of demand. But where it is specified by the will that they shall bear interest from the death of the testator, though the will lie dormant twelve years etc., interest must be allowed for that term.

176

Anonymous

(Ch. c. 1717)

Where an estate tail is devised subject to debts and legacies payable out of the profits and the value of the estate is very small, a court of equity can order the estate to be sold in order to pay the debts and legacies.

Lincoln's Inn MS. Hill 73, p. 3, pl. 2

When an estate tail is left subject to debts and legacies and children's fortunes to be raised out of the rents and profits of the estate so that the estate should not be sold, but yet, if the profits of the estate are so small that it would be many years before the legacies and portions could be satisfied, Baron Price was of opinion the estate ought to be sold to discharge them. Otherwise, how could those portions [be paid] which were to be paid when the children came to the age of twenty-one or marriage when perhaps, by the mesne profits of the estate, they would be raised within treble that time?

177

Anonymous

(Ch. c. 1717)

In this case, a surety was held liable for a bond debt, the principal debtor being insolvent and the debt being unpaid.

Lincoln's Inn MS. Hill 73, p. 4, pl. 1

[Upon a] judgment upon a bond in 1696 [that was] sued execution in 1715, the surety for the bond prayed to be relieved against the plaintiff and to have a perpetual injunction to stay execution upon that judgment for that it charged but could not produce the bond cancelled but, if it had been produced, satisfaction of the judgment ought to be acknowledged upon record.

An injunction was upon the hearing denied, it plainly appearing the debtor was insolvent and the surety had been in the Fleet [Prison] etc. in a very low condition, far from being able to satisfy the judgment until within a very little time before the taking out of execution.

178

Anonymous

(Ch. c. 1717)

A court will not order specific performance of an oral lease.

In a suit involving land, the reversioner in fee as well as the devisee for life must be a party.

Lincoln's Inn MS. Hill 73, p. 4, pl. 2

The plaintiff prayed that the defendant might be compelled to perform the articles of an indenture by [which] a lease for twenty-one years was granted to the plaintiff. The agreement was reduced into writing but never was signed and sealed by either party. By virtue of the parol lease, the plaintiff entered and held the same about the term of seven years during the life of the lessor, upon whose death, the devisee of the lessor, taking the farm etc. in Whitchurch, Oxfordshire, to be underlet, demanded an advancement of the rent to £50 from £43, to which the plaintiff at first agreed, by which it appears he waived his right of twenty-one years to come. It is in direct opposition to the Statute of Frauds and Perjuries,[1] for if this should be allowed because the tenant entered, no parol lease but what might elude the Statute, which was made in order to prevent the very mischief for which the plaintiff deserves to be relieved. [. . .] the bringing of evidence to declare what agreement was made between the parties. The defendant had a verdict at law before.

The plaintiff was ordered by the Master of the Rolls [Jekyll] to deliver possession to the defendant [and] to be allowed for what he had laid out towards next year's crop. The defendant was only a devisee for life, but they should have made the reversioner of the fee party to the suit. If there had been any lasting improvements made, the devisee for life ought not alone to allow for it, but he in reversion.

[1] Stat. 29 Car. II, c. 3 (*SR*, V, 839–842).

179

Basset v. Clapham

(Ch. 1717)

A provision in a marriage settlement for the children of another marriage is voluntary and can be set aside by the parties' creditors.

Lincoln's Inn MS. Misc. 11, p. 18, pl. 2

2 August 1717. Edward Basset and the creditors of Clapham, plaintiffs; Christopher Clapham *et ux.* and trustees, defendants.

Christopher Clapham, before his marriage with his first wife, conveyed his lands to trustees and their heirs to the use of Clapham for life, then to the trustees to support contingent remainders, then to his wife for life, then to the first and every other son of that marriage in tail male, and, for want of such issue, to the first and other sons of any other wife in tail male, and, for want of such issue, to all his daughters in tail, and for want of such issue, to his own right heirs.

Then, Mr. Clapham mortgaged part of the said estate for 500 years and, after the mortgage and after the marriage with his present wife, he levied a fine of all the lands in the first settlement to Sir Robert Marsham, now Lord Romney, and his heirs, as to part of the said lands, to the use of Clapham for life, then to the trustee and his heirs to support contingent remainders, then to his present wife for life, then to the first son etc. and, as to the other part of the said lands, to the use of Sir Robert Marsham and his heirs in trust to be sold and the money arising by such sale to be applied to pay the mortgage and all other debts of Clapham which affect that part of the estate before limited to the use of his present wife.

There being at present no issue, the said creditors prefer their bill against Clapham and the trustee of the first settlement and the trustee of the second settlement to have the lands sold according to the direction of the second settlement. And they allege that the limitations in the first settlement to the first son of Clapham by his second wife is a voluntary limitation and is fraudulent in respect to the plaintiffs, the creditors.

And on hearing the cause by consent before His Honor [JEKYLL], it was decreed the said estate to be sold according to the direction of the second settlement and that the trustee of the first settlement and the trustee of the second settlement should join with Mr. Clapham in conveying the said estate to a purchaser and that the money arising by such sale should be brought before a Master to be applied accordingly.

[Other reports of this case: 1 Peere Williams 358, 24 E.R. 425, 2 Eq. Cas. Abr. 748, 22 E.R. 634.]

180

Ex parte Burslem

(Ch. 1717)

An infant can be declared to be a bankrupt.

Lincoln's Inn MS. Misc. 12, p. 25

9 August 1717.

The creditors of [John] Burslem having applied for a commission of bankruptcy against him, he petitioned Lord Cowper alleging that he was under the age of twenty-one years and that several crafty persons, taking advantage of his infancy and inexperience in matters of trade, had overreached him in dealing in hops, and, therefore, he prayed that, in consideration of his inexperience in matters of trade, no commission might issue out against him but that he might have a reasonable time to get in his effects and pay his debts.

The petition was rejected, and a commission was issued.

181

Burdet v. Holden

(Ch. 1717)

For the purposes of a will, a posthumous child is the testator's child at the time of the testator's death.

Lincoln's Inn MS. Hill 29, p. 33

Michaelmas 4 Geo. I.

The plaintiff's father devised lands *in haec verba*, 'I give to my cousin C. my lands in B. in case I have no son at the time of my death.' The plaintiff was *in ventre sa mere* at the time of the father's death.

Cowper, Chancellor, decreed the plaintiff was within the words of the will; he was a son had or left at the time of his death.

Ex relatione Dr. Abney.

182

Anonymous

(Ch. 1717)

In this case, it was impossible to prove the value of goods sold for the purposes of the salvage of a lost ship.

Lincoln's Inn MS. Misc. 380, pt. 3, p. 153, pl. 2

[There was a] policy of insurance for £1000 at 18 guineas percent on an East India voyage, interest or no interest in the ship. The insured makes a trading voyage and stops at several ports and barters his goods and remits part of his effects to his wife during the voyage. Afterwards, the husband dies on board the ship. And, in performing the ceremony of his funeral by firing the guns, the ship is set on fire and burnt.

The bill was brought by the insurers to have an account of the profits made at the several ports and places of trade as salvage by way of discharge.

[It was] decreed that no salvage shall be accounted for in this case. And the Chancellor [Lord Cowper] said this was not like a law case where, on a voyage insured to Guinea, the effects are landed there, therefore, the goods were sold there, the ship was lost, the salvage shall be accounted for there. But, in the principal case, the goods were bartered at the several ports and the judgment of the merchant and the hazard in bartering was intermixed with the goods and so it is next to impossible to estimate the value at the several ports.

Note it was proved that £1300 was lost in the ship.

183

Amhurst v. Litton

(Ch. 1717)

The words 'to save harmless from all damages' mean that the promisor puts himself in the place of the promisee.

Particular words in an instrument control general words.

Lincoln's Inn MS. Misc. 380, pt. 3, p. 154

Litton, the testator, makes his wife executor, being an infant. The father of the infant and the infant enter into articles with Rob[inson] Litton, the heir at law, that the infant should take out administration and should choose Rob[inson] Litton for her guardian and should assign all the testator's personal estate to him. Rob[inson] Litton covenants that the widow should have her jewels and likewise a legacy given by her husband and covenants to pay certain legacies given to the servants of the family within two years and, afterwards, covenants to pay all the debts and legacies and other moneys due from the testator's estate. And at the end of the covenants is that he will save harmless the infant from all damages etc. for or by reason of the will. Part of the legacies are paid in full, and, afterwards, it appears that the estate is deficient.

Lord Chancellor [Lord Cowper]: It might be the intent of the parties, for aught I know, that R. Litton should pay all the debts and legacies whatsoever and they might have had the honor of the family in view upon such an agreement, and, if the words seem to be reasonable in themselves, the court will not put a construction on them to alter the reasonable and apparent meaning. But the words in the bond of the covenant 'to save harmless from all damages by reason of the will' that the intent was only to put himself in the place of the infant, and, therefore, the particular words at the end shall control the general words in the beginning.

He ordered an account of assets and of the debts and legacies and said, perhaps, some of the debts, being £16,000, may be by specialty, then such debts ought to be taken out of the real estate and, if that proves deficient, then the legatees must refund.

Note this suit was commenced on a dormant debt six years after the articles. It was said at the bar that, at common law, that, if a legatee or creditor request payment and the executor desires the party to stay a little and he shall be paid, the creditor etc. afterwards shall not be put to prove assets, for, by length of time, he may not be able so well to prove assets.

[Later proceedings in this case: Mosely 131, 207, 211, 25 E.R. 312, 353, 355, Fitzgibbons 99, 94 E.R. 671, 1 Barnardiston K.B. 217, 94 E.R. 148, 2 Eq. Cas. Abr. 602, 22 E.R. 506, 5 Brown P.C. 254, 2 E.R. 661.]

184

Lee v. Scawen

(Ch. 1717)

A bona fide *purchaser for value from a bankrupt is not liable to the claims of the bankrupt seller's creditors.*

Lincoln's Inn MS. Misc. 380, pt. 3, p. 155

Farringdon, being greatly indebted to Moreton, makes a bill of sale of all his goods to Moreton to the value of £70,000. Moreton, being indebted to Scawen in three bonds of £5000 each, requests Scawen to advance £20,000 more to him and tells him of the bill of sale from Farringdon to him and offers that as a security for the whole debts, which is accordingly done. But, before this assignment to Scawen, Morton had assigned part of Farringdon's goods to Heathcoat to secure £5000 with a power to Heathcoat to sell the goods in case the money was not paid at a certain day. Heathcoat had no notice that the goods ever belonged to Farringdon. Farringdon becomes bankrupt, and, afterwards, Morton becomes bankrupt. [An action of] trover was directed to be brought for part of the goods, and [there was a] verdict that Farringdon was bankrupt at the time of making the bill of sale and, consequently, Scawen becomes a creditor of Farringdon. Heathcott now insists that he is a fair purchaser having no notice of the bill of sale by Farringdon. And now [an action of] trover was directed to be brought by the assignees of Farrington against Heathcott.

It was said at the bar that the very bill of sale made by Farringdon was an act of bankruptcy. The goods were actually delivered to Scawen, and he, after the time limited, sold the goods to pay himself.

Lord Chancellor [Lord Cowper] said Heathcott appears to be a purchaser for a valuable consideration without notice; therefore, though creditors be concerned, I will not give any directions that shall any ways prejudice a fair purchaser.

185

Crosse v. Crosse

(Ch. 1717)

A devise to 'poor relations' will be construed to be for first cousins or closer relations only.

Lincoln's Inn MS. Misc. 12, p. 131, pl. 1

14 October 4 Geo. [1717].

Thomas Crosse, by a codicil, gave a sum of money to be laid out in the purchase of lands for the benefit of a charity in Clerkenwell parish, and he directed that the minister etc. of the said parish should pay yearly to five of the testator's poorest relations £10 apiece.

It was decreed that the words 'poorest relations' shall not be carried further than first cousins.

186

Sturrane v. Robinson

(Ch. 1717)

A court of equity will not supply the want of a surrender of a copyhold in favor of a natural child against the heir at law.

Lincoln's Inn MS. Misc. 10, pp. 191, 205

27 October 1717. Thomas Sturrane and Mary, his wife, plaintiffs; William Robinson, defendant.

George Stalker, being seised of a customary estate held of the manor of Caldbeck in the County of Cumberland, by the custom of which manor, lands pass by deed and surrender, and having a natural daughter, *viz.* the plaintiff Mary, grants this estate to her and her heirs, and he covenants in the deed for him and his heirs to make further assurance, and he dies without making any surrender.

The defendant recovers by a verdict at law this estate as heir to Stalker, and the plaintiffs bring their bill to be relieved and that the defendant might make a surrender pursuant to the covenant for further assurance.

The cause was heard by the late Master of the Rolls [TREVOR], and the bill was dismissed in regard this court would not supply the want of a surrender in favor of a natural child against the heir at law.

And now, it came on to be heard before the Lord Chancellor [LORD COWPER] upon an appeal.

And it was insisted on by Mr. *Vernon*, on the behalf of the plaintiffs, that the plaintiff Mary ought not to be considered as a volunteer and, though she was a natural child, yet she was such a child as the father by the law of nature was bound to provide for; besides, the covenant for further assurance was a sort of lien upon the estate and went with it to the heir, who was bound by the covenant of his ancestor.

On the other side, it was said by *Sir Thomas Powys* that a natural child was not regarded in the eye of the law nor has this court ever supplied a defective conveyance in favor of such a one against the right heir. In the case of Kettle and Townsend, in Lord Somers' time, which was affirmed in Parliament,[1] the court would not supply the want of a surrender in favor of a grandchild, much less ought it to be done in favor of a natural daughter.

And of that opinion was the Lord Chancellor [LORD COWPER], who said he must leave the plaintiffs to their remedy at law upon the covenants.

Note Mr. *Vernon*, in his argument in the Case of Sturrane and Robinson, *quod vide ante* 191, cited the Case of Taylor and Wheeler,[2] which was this, a man makes a mortgage by a surrender of a copyhold estate and by the custom of the manor of which it was held, which custom among others of the said manor was confirmed by an Act of Parliament, every surrender was to be presented at the next court or else it was void, the mortgagee not knowing the custom of the manor keeps the surrender by him and never presents it. The mortgage continued for about eight years, during which time, the mortgagor had the possession and pays the interest. And then he becomes a bankrupt. The commissioners assign this copyhold estate, and the assignees recover in [an action of] ejectment. And the mortgagee brought his bill and was relieved notwithstanding it might

---

[1] *Kettle v. Townsend*, 1 Salkeld 187, 91 E.R. 170, 1 Eq. Cas. Abr. 123, 21 E.R. 929.

[2] *Taylor v. Wheeler* (1709), 2 Salkeld 449, 91 E.R. 388, 2 Vernon 564, 23 E.R. 968, 1 Eq. Cas. Abr. 122, 312, 21 E.R. 928, 1068.

be presumed that the creditors of the bankrupt had entrusted him with goods or money upon the credit of this estate.

186a

Richmond v. Peere Williams

(Ch. 1717)

The legacy of the wife of a bankrupt that vests after her husband's discharge is not liable to seizure by his creditors.

Lincoln's Inn MS. Misc. 11, p. 33, pl. 2

A legacy was given to a woman payable upon a contingency. She marries, and her husband becomes a bankrupt. After a commission is taken out, he is discharged upon a certificate, and then the contingency happens whereby the legacy becomes payable. And, thereupon, the commissioners assign this legacy.

[Lord Cowper] decreed that the legacy becoming vested in the wife after the certificate could not be assigned by the court.

Lincoln's Inn MS. Misc. 10, pp. 193, 205

[27 October 1717].

Upon an appeal from a decree made by Baron Price in the absence of the Lord Chancellor, the case was that one Wallinger bequeathed to the defendant Williams several mortgages upon trust to pay several legacies and particularly £1000 to the defendant Richmond's wife, then an infant and unmarried, at the age of twenty and, if she died before the legacy became payable, it was to go over. Richmond, by the treachery of a maid servant, draws in the defendant Frances to marry him and shortly afterwards becomes insolvent. And a commission of bankruptcy is thereupon awarded against him. And the commissioners, amongst other effects of the bankrupt, assign this legacy to the plaintiffs before it became due. And the defendant Frances having attained the age of twenty years, the plaintiffs bring their bill to have this legacy paid them by the defendant, Mr. Williams, who, as to that part of the personal estate, out of which this legacy was payable, was appointed executor of the testator's will.

The cause was heard before Baron Price, who decreed the legacy to the plaintiffs. And now, it came on upon an appeal before the Lord Chancellor [Lord Cowper].

And it was insisted on for the plaintiffs that the legacy belonged to them as being part of the bankrupt's estate, for, though it was a chose in action, yet, by the statutes of Queen Elizabeth and King James,[1] it was assignable. The bank-

[1] Stat. 13 Eliz. I, c. 7 (*SR*, IV, 539–541); Stat. 1 Jac. I, c. 15 (*SR*, IV, 1031–1034); Stat. 21 Jac. I, c. 19 (*SR*, IV, 1227–1229).

rupt himself before his bankruptcy might have released this legacy before it became payable and, if the trustee had paid it to him, it had been a good payment.

On the other side, it was said for the wife that the legacy was not become due when it was assigned and thus it did not vest in the plaintiffs; however, if it did, yet that the plaintiffs stood in the place of the bankrupt and, therefore, could be in no better condition than he would have been if he had brought his bill to be paid this legacy, for, if he had done so, the court would not have aided him for the recovery of it but upon the terms of making some settlement out of his own estate upon his wife and the children of the marriage or, if he was not capable of doing that, upon agreeing to do it out of the legacy and, therefore, the plaintiffs ought now to do what would have been expected from the bankrupt in case he had brought his bill.

And of that opinion the Lord Chancellor [Lord Cowper] seemed to be, and he said that the terms which would have been expected from the husband if he could not have made a settlement out of his own estate would have been to have consented to have settled this money for the benefit of himself for life, then for his wife for her life, then for the issue of the marriage and, if no issue, to the survivor of the husband and wife, and, if he would not have come into these terms, this court would have given him no assistance but left him to get his wife's legacy as he could.

But it being admitted on both sides that this was a new case, the Lord Chancellor [Lord Cowper] said he would consider of it.

[Related cases: Jacobson v. Peere Williams (Ch. 1717), see below, Case No. 188.]

187

Stanton v. Platt

(Ch. 1717)

A settlement of land on the only child of a London freeman is not an advancement.

The child of a London freeman can receive a legacy as well as his or her customary part of the estate, where there is no attempt to defeat the will.

The legacies of a London freeman are to be paid out of the testamentary part of his estate only.

If there is a deficiency in a London freeman's estate, all the legacies abate in proportion, but the customary part of his estate is not liable.

The custom of London does not cover estates of inheritance.

Lincoln's Inn MS. Misc. 11, p. 71

8 November 1717.

A citizen of London marries [off] his daughter and makes a settlement of lands on her and her husband and their issue. And, afterwards, he makes his will, and, having a wife and no other child, he gives £1000 to his wife and a leasehold estate to trustees for the separate use of his daughter, who was parted from her husband. And he gives several other legacies but takes no notice of the custom.

The husband brings his bill to have an account of the personal estate and his wife's share by the custom.

It was decreed the settlement of lands was no advancement nor any part of an advancement of the daughter [and] that, notwithstanding such settlement, she should have her share by the custom, secondly, that the daughter should have her legacy as well as her customary part, she not coming here to break through the will and that all the legacies should be paid out of the testamentary part and, if any deficiency, all the legatees to abate in proportion and that the daughter should have her proportional part of the leasehold estate, which should be taken out of the testamentary part and not out of her customary share.

2 Vernon 753, 23 E.R. 1092

Mr. Platt, a freeman of London, having an only daughter, advanced her in marriage by the settling of a real estate, and the husband and wife separated, and the husband went beyond the sea. Mr. Platt died, having by his will devised some houses (leasehold) to a trustee for the separate use of his daughter, for her life and, after her decease, to Thomas Stanton, the plaintiff's son.

First, the advancement by land is no bar to the custom, any more than if devised or descended.

Secondly, if it might go in part, yet it would be the same thing, because there was but one child, and the advancement in part falls in again to the child's part.

Thirdly, that what was devised to the trustee for the daughter cannot go in part of the orphanage nor be any bar to it, but, if the legatory part is not sufficient, the legatees must abate in proportion.

7 Viner, Abr. 210

Michaelmas 4 Geo.

Stanton brings a bill for one-third of his wife's father's personal estate. A settlement by agreement etc. was made on the marriage, and the father gave with his daughter an estate as for her marriage portion etc. By will, the father gave £1000 to his wife and five tenements, which were his on leases, to trustees in trust for the daughter's separate use, and he made the wife executrix. Stanton, being beyond the sea, left the wife and children upon the mother, who maintained them.

By Cowper, Chancellor: First, an advancement of a daughter by a real estate as her portion etc. was not an advancement within the custom; but, if it were in land, the certainty does appear, and the land must be valued and brought into hotchpot; the custom has no relation to an estate of inheritance; if a freeman lays out his money, the custom is defeated, but, if there was any provision made by agreement etc. that, instead of money as a portion etc. the father should diminish his personal estate by making a purchase, it might be a question how far this would be within the custom. But lands descended or purchased are not.

Secondly, that Stanton must have one-third of the clear personal estate, deducting the widow's chamber, paraphernalia, etc.

Thirdly, that the five tenements given to the separate use of the wife should not go in part of this one-third to which the husband was entitled, for that the daughter had no election in this case. She could not choose the one-third, because that was in the power of the husband and to his account, and, as the five tenements are here given to the trustees, it is of a different kind from the husband's one-third; nor is it to the same person; so it cannot go in part of satisfaction within the meaning of the testator. In cases of the custom, the legatee has an election, whether he will renounce his legacy or his one-third part. Here, the father has under all events, *ex abundanti*, made a provision for the separate use of his daughter out of the part which the father had power to dispose of.

Fourthly, if the legacies fall short, everyone must abate in proportion, but, if the daughter's separate provision fall short, which the father intended her, the court ought to lay hold on that which the husband ought to recover when the account is taken, and it ought to be brought before the Master, especially if the husband's going away were without the wife's default.

Fifthly, this specific legacy of the five tenements must be valued, and every one must abate in proportion.

Sixthly, The wife and executors must have her £1000 besides her one-third part.

[Other copies of this report: 2 Eq. Cas. Abr. 266, 22 E.R. 225.]

188

Jacobson v. Peere Williams

(Ch. 1717)

A legacy to a wife that has not vested at the time of the husband's bankruptcy is not liable to his creditors.

Lincoln's Inn MS. Misc. 10, p. 207

9 November 1717. Jacobson v. Peere Williams, Richmond, *et ux.*

Lord Chancellor [Lord Cowper]: The bill, as before me, does not entitled the plaintiffs to what they demand, for, at the time of the commissioner's assignment, the legacy was not payable and, consequently, the plaintiffs had no title when they brought their bill, for there was only a possibility that the legacy might become one, and a possibility is not assignable. The bill must be dismissed, but without costs.

Lincoln's Inn MS. Misc. 380, pt. 3, p. 153, pl. 1

Michaelmas term 4 Geo.

A devise of £1000 [was made] to an infant when she should attain the age of twenty-one after the death of her mother; the infant marries; after[wards], the husband becomes bankrupt, and the legacy is assigned to the creditors as part of the husband's estate. The husband is discharged by a certificate according to the Act of Bankrupts.[1] The creditors bring the bill to have this legacy against the husband and wife after the wife had attained the age of twenty-one and the mother dead.

Lord Chancellor Cowper decreed that the legacy was a possibility only and, therefore, not assignable, for nothing vested in the wife before the age of twenty-one and here was a double contingency before it could vest.

Note that was a devise at twenty-one and not a devise that immediately vested and to be paid at twenty-one. Note the Chancellor said I cannot decree it unless you have a new simple assignment.

[Other reports of this case: 1 Peere Williams 382, 24 E.R. 435, Gilbert Rep. 140, 25 E.R. 98, 1 Eq. Cas. Abr. 54, 21 E.R. 869, 2 Eq. Cas. Abr. 124, 22 E.R. 106.]

[Related cases: Richmond v. Peere Williams (Ch. 1717), see above, Case No. 186a.]

189

Crawford v. Delaney

(Ch. 1717)

A trustee must account to the beneficiary for any interest earned by the trust funds but not for any loss where the investment of the trust fund was reasonable.

Lincoln's Inn MS. Misc. 10, p. 219, pl. 1

12 November 1717.

The plaintiff deposited a sum of money in the defendant's hands, who gave the plaintiff a note acknowledging the receipt of it and promising to keep it as his own or to put it out at interest as occasion should offer.

The plaintiff brought his bill for an account of this money. And the question was if the defendant should answer for interest for this money.

Lord Chancellor [Lord Cowper]: I decree the defendant to account for this money and to answer what interest he has really made of it. And, for that purpose, let him be examined on interrogatories, and, if, in taking the account, it shall appear that any part of the money which has been put out at interest upon security has been lost, the defendant shall not make it good if the money was

[1] Stat. 3 Geo. I, c. 12.

placed out upon a reasonable security and it appeared to be the trust money when it was lent.

190
Wisdome v. Harding
(Ch. 1717)

In this case, there was insufficient evidence to prove the existence of the alleged contract that was sought to be enforced.

Lincoln's Inn MS. Misc. 380, pt. 3, p. 156

Friday, 15 November.

The plaintiff and defendant discoursing about the price of hops, a memorandum is drawn up that agreed that the defendant should deliver a load of hops to the plaintiff within six days after Weyhill fair at the price fixed and mentions that the plaintiff had given a guinea earnest [money]. And an attorney is sent for to draw up articles. But then the plaintiff and defendant differ as to the wording of the articles; part of the articles being written, the attorney goes away. He tells them he would come to them when they had agreed to the matters, but the company broke up without doing anything further. And they leave the memorandum and articles at the place, a public house, where they were. A., the servant of the house, finds the memorandum and articles and delivers them to the master.

Afterwards, the plaintiff brings a special action on the case against the defendant in the [Court of] Common Pleas. And the court not being able to make an order on a third person, *viz.* the master, to produce the memorandum, *ex assensu* of the plaintiff and defendant, the plaintiff, fearing lest his witnesses should differ a little from the memorandum, agreed that the note should be suppressed. And on trial, the plaintiff was nonsuited.

Two years after the nonsuit, the plaintiff brings in this bill, having got a new witness, A., the servant of the public house, who swears he saw the guinea paid by the plaintiff to the defendant. And the bill was to have a discovery of the memorandum and to have a performance of the agreement.

The defendant pleads the Statute of Frauds and Perjuries,[1] and the plaintiff falsifies the plea. And he proves by A., the servant of the house, a witness not produced at the former trial, that the plaintiff paid a guinea as part of the agreement, by another witness that the defendant pulled some money out of his pocket and said 'here is the plaintiff's guinea that he gave me for the bargain of hops'. But, for the defendant, three persons, all that were in the company at that time, swear that they did not see any guinea given to the defendant.

[1] Stat. 29 Car. II, c. 3 (*SR*, V, 839–842).

The Lord Chancellor [Lord Cowper], at first, dismissed the bill without costs. But after the plaintiff's counsel's informing the court that the plaintiff consented to suppress the note at the trial because his witness swore that the agreement was to deliver a load of the best, which varied from the agreement on the note, then the Chancellor said dismiss the bill but without costs, for it appears there was no perfect agreement. Supposing the guinea given on the first memorandum for, before the company broke up, they sent for an attorney to draw up articles in the wording of which they differ and both the note and articles so begun were left on the table when the parties went away and then the memorandum did come to the defendant's possession after the trial at law and he does not now produce it, yet he gives a fair answer to that, that he thought no further use would be made of it when the plaintiff was nonsuited.

191

Elie v. Osborne

(Ch. 1717)

Trustees to preserve contingent remainders can join with the tenant in tail in a fine to bar the entail because they are trustees for the benefit of the tenant in tail.

2 Vernon 754, 23 E.R. 1093

15 November.

James Steer, on his marriage, settled the lands in question on himself for ninety-nine years if he so long lived, remainder to trustees and their heirs to preserve contingent remainders during his life, remainder to his wife for her jointure, remainder to the heirs of his body on the body of Mary, his intended wife, remainder to his own right heirs. The issue were John, James, and Mary. James, the father, and John, his eldest son, with the heir of the surviving trustee, join in a feoffment and fine to Doughty and his heirs. John and James, the sons, died without issue, James, the father, yet living.

The question was whether the purchaser had a good title or that the trustees joining should be a breach of the trust.

The plea was allowed.

Lord Chancellor [Lord Cowper]: It is absurd to say that the trustees may not join with the tenant in tail, for, although the father was living, he was but barely tenant for ninety-nine years if he lived so long and the estate tail vested in the son in equity, but the legal estate in the trustees and their heirs during the life of the father, and they are trustees purely for the tenant in tail and to preserve his estate, and not to stand in opposition to him for the sake of those who are to come after him.

192
Weekes v. Erle
(Ch. 1717)

A lack of a surrender of copyhold lands that have been devised to younger children will be remedied by a court of equity even though the younger children had other provisions.

A person who pays off a debt secured by a mortgage is subrogated to the rights of the creditor-mortgagee.

Lincoln's Inn MS. Misc. 11, p. 4

18 November 1717. Weekes *et al.* v. Mr. Erle and his wife and Mr. Wilcox and his wife *et al.*

The plaintiffs are creditors of Carew Raleigh, son and heir of Sir Charles Raleigh, and they bring their bill to have satisfaction of their debts out of the real and personal assets of Carew.

The defendants Erle and Wilcocks married two of Sir Charles Raleigh's daughters and insist as to some copyhold land, which the plaintiff Thorp claims by virtue of a mortgage made to him by Carew, upon whom it was pretended it descended upon the death of his father, that this was devised by Sir Charles Raleigh to his mother for life and then to his daughters and, though there was no surrender to the use of the will, yet, being a provision for younger children, it ought to be supplied in a court of equity.

On the other side, it was said the daughters had portions given them by the will and, therefore, having other provision made for them, the want of a surrender ought not to be made good in their favor, especially in prejudice of creditors.

Lord Cowper was of opinion that, notwithstanding the additional provision made for the daughters, the want of a surrender ought to be ordered. But as to the plaintiff Thorp, who was a mortgagee without notice of the defendants' title, he decreed he ought to be paid his mortgage money with costs. But then on the other hand, since Carew had taken upon him to mortgage an estate which belonged to his sisters, the defendants were decreed to come in as creditors by simple contract and have a satisfaction out of Carew's assets for so much as they should pay in discharge of the mortgage.

But, upon further consideration, it appearing that the mortgagee had a judgment from Carew as well as a mortgage, he decreed that the defendants should stand in the room of the mortgagee as to the judgment and have a satisfaction out of Carew's assets prior to the bond creditors.

193

Outram v. Round

(Ch. 1717)

In this case, a married woman was not required to specifically perform her contract to convey her land.

Lincoln's Inn MS. Misc. 11, p. 21, pl. 2

20 November 1717.

The plaintiff's wife and the defendant's wife were jointly seised of an estate in fee under the will of one Cotterel. The plaintiff agrees with the defendant to give him £105 for his wife's share of this estate. And, pursuant to this agreement, a lease and release were executed by the defendant and his wife. And therein was a covenant from the defendant that he and his wife would levy a fine in the following terms to the use of the plaintiff and his heirs.

At the time of executing these deeds, the plaintiff paid part of the consideration money to the defendant; another part of it was set off by a debt that the defendant owed the plaintiff,

and, for the remainder, the plaintiff gave the defendant his bond. Pursuant to this covenant, a fine was prepared, and the defendant and his wife went to the Chief Justice's chamber in order to acknowledge it. But, when they came there, the defendant's wife refused to join in the fine. And the plaintiff now brings his bill to have a specific performance of the covenants.

The defendant says he has used his best endeavors to prevail of his wife to join with him in a fine but that she would not, and he offers to pay back what he has received with interest, and she insists that she ought not to sell her inheritance against her will.

Curia: There has been some instances wherein the court has decreed the husband specifically to perform an agreement which he has made for a thing to be done by himself and his wife, and there may be some circumstances which may make it reasonable so to do. But, as this is breaking in upon the privilege which the law gives a married woman of not parting with her estate against her will, I think this power should be executed sparingly. And, in the present case, I see no reason to decree the husband to procure his wife to levy a fine. The defendant must pay back what he has received with interest and costs as also he must pay what he owed the plaintiff at the time of the contract with interest likewise, and, upon the payment of this, the plaintiff must deliver up the conveyances to be cancelled, and the defendant is in like manner to deliver up the bond, which the plaintiff gave him for part of the purchase money.

[Other reports of this case: 2 Eq. Cas. Abr. 145, 22 E.R. 124.]

194

Blackstone v. Clark

(Ch. 1717)

In this case, according to the terms of the will in issue, the share of a deceased daughter went to her children and not to the testator's widower.

Lincoln's Inn MS. Misc. 11, p. 152 [bis]

21 November 4 Geo. Blackstone *et al.* v. Sir Samuel Clark and George Monet, executors of John Blackstone.

The testator, by a lease and release, conveyed an estate in Essex to the defendants and their heirs upon trust to sell the same after his death and apply the money arising by such sale and the rents and profits in the meantime unto such persons and at such times as he should by his will dispose the same and, in case he should die without making any will, then, upon trust to dispose the same unto and amongst all the children of the testator, John Blackstone, and unto John Blackstone, his grandson, in equal shares and proportions and, in case any of the said children should die before such sale leaving issue behind them, then the issue of their respective bodies should have the share of the parent so dying to be paid to sons at twenty-one and to daughters at eighteen or marriage.

Afterwards, the testator makes his will and, taking notice of this conveyance, he appoints the defendants, whom he made executors, and their heirs to pay all the moneys to be raised by the said sale after a deduction of the trustees' charges and £100 which he gave to a charity school and £100 to his daughter-in-law, Elizabeth Blackstone, unto and amongst all his children then living and his grandson, John Blackstone, in equal shares and proportions, and, in case any of his said children should happen then to be dead, his will was that his, her, or their representative child or children should have the part and share of the child so dying, if sons, to be paid at twenty-one, if daughters at eighteen or marriage.

The testator had three sons and a daughter at his death. The daughter was married at her father's death, and she died in a short time after her father and before any sale was made, having left several children by the plaintiff Curwen, her husband, who has taken administration to his wife.

The bill, *inter alia*, is to have a sale of the estate and a distribution of the money according to the will. The question was to whom the share of the testator's daughter belonged, whether to her husband as her administrator or to her children.

Lord Chancellor [LORD COWPER] declared that the words in the will 'then living' are relative to the time of payment and distribution of the money which should be raised by the sale of the estate and that this was the plain meaning expressed, that, if any parent to whom a distributive part thereof is given should die before such distribution made, the child or children of such parent should be entitled to such parent's distributive part, and that, therefore, Mrs. Curwen's children were well entitled to her distributive share and the rather for that there has been no affected delay in the sale of the said estate and making a distribution thereof according to the said will.

And, therefore, he decreed the several trusts and dispositions of the will be executed and performed, and he it referred to a Master to see the same done accordingly and that the estate be sold to the best purchaser and that a distribution be made of the moneys arising by such sale [and] be distributed according to the will as aforesaid, and, if any parent shall die before such distribution made, then the share of the parent so dying do go to his or her child or children.

195

Wainwright v. Bendloes

(Ch. 1717)

Debts are to be paid out of lands devised to be sold for that purpose, and that land is not to be exonerated out of the personal estate.

Lincoln's Inn MS. Misc. 10, p. 213

27 November 1717.

Mr. Bendloes, by his will, devises his lands to be sold for the payment of his debts, and he gives the surplus of the money to the plaintiff Wainwright, his brother-in-law, and to the defendant, his own brother. And he gives some part of his goods to the defendant. And the residue of his personal estate he gives to his sister, the plaintiff's wife, and he makes her executrix.

The question was if the personal estate should be applied to exonerate the real estate in favor of the defendant, a devisee of a moiety of the surplus of the lands devised to be sold.

It was insisted on by Mr. *Vernon* that, where the personal estate is devised away, there, an heir at law or an *haeres factus* shall not have the aid of the personal estate to exonerate the real. But it is otherwise where the executor takes the personal estate *quatenus* executor, as the plaintiff's wife does in this case.

Lord Chancellor [Lord Cowper] decreed the debts to be paid out of the lands devised to be sold for that purpose. There is nothing given to the devisees out of the lands devised to be sold, but the residue only. And what is that but the residue after all the debts are paid. And should the debts be paid out of the personal estate, the bequest of the residue of the personal estate to the testator's sister might be wholly defeated.

[Other reports of this case: 2 Vernon 718, 23 E.R. 1071, Precedents in Chancery 451, 24 E.R. 201, Gilbert Rep. 125, 25 E.R. 87, 1 Eq. Cas. Abr. 271, 21 E.R. 1039.]

196

Anonymous

(Ch. 1717)

A court of equity will compel the buyer of land to pay the purchase price and accept a conveyance.

Lincoln's Inn MS. Misc. 380, pt. 3, p. 157

A bill [was exhibited] to have a specific performance of articles for the purchase of lands. The defendant, in her answer, swears there was no such articles. It appeared that the defendant had a hard bargain and was to give near thirty year's value. The defendant proved by the two witnesses to the articles; one said he verily believe both the plaintiff and defendant signed to the articles; the other that the plaintiff signed the articles, and both say they do not remember the sum but believe it was about £400, and another proof [was] that the defendant had owned she had agreed for the purchase of the plaintiff's land and that the articles were left in the possession of the defendant.

For the defendant, [it was said] this court that is a court of conscience will never assist a hard and an unconscionable bargain as to give thirty years value for land. The defendant absolutely denies any articles, and the plaintiff has no positive proof that the defendant did execute any articles; so there is no agreement. By the Statute of Frauds and Perjuries,[1] here is no positive proof how much this purchase money was. The witnesses say about £400, and the plaintiff has since conveyed it to trustees for payment of his debts.

The Lord Chancellor [Lord Cowper] decreed that the defendant should take a conveyance and should pay costs. She has absolutely denied any articles at all, and it appears plain to me, take the whole evidence together and even by her own confession at other times. One witness says that she said that she could not execute the conveyances because she had put the articles in the hands of a friend, who was gone to Ireland. Therefore, since she conceals the articles, I will take the same [to be] agreed for for a purchase at a medium in what the witnesses swear they believe the sum was.

For the defendant, [it was said] but the plaintiff must procure his trustees to convey and must make the defendant a good title; if not, he must pay costs.

Chancellor [Lord Cowper]: Yes, and, if you have a mind, examine the plaintiff on interrogatories to discover encumbrances.

---

[1] Stat. 29 Car. II, c. 3 (*SR*, V, 839–842).

197

Anonymous

(Ch. 1717)

A court of equity has jurisdiction over cases for escapes where there was a bond given for the security of the sheriff.

Lincoln's Inn MS. Misc. 380, pt. 3, p. 160, pl. 1

A bill [was exhibited] by a sheriff against his under-sheriff to have satisfaction for an escape out of a bond given to the plaintiff as his security. The defendant insisted that suit of a bond ought to be prosecuted at common law and not in this court by the [Statute of] 8 & 9 Will.[1] and the jury have a power to ascertain damages according to the several breaches assigned.

The Lord Chancellor [Lord Cowper]: That Statute does not take away the jurisdiction of this court; this court has concurrent jurisdiction.

198

Mason v. Lake

(Ch. 1717)

Where a lawyer recovers money on behalf of his client, he may retain his fees and expenses out of the recovery before paying the residue to his client or to his client's order.

Lincoln's Inn MS. Misc. 380, pt. 3, p. 160, pl. 2

A. was indebted to the plaintiff £500. A. had a ship taken wrongfully and employed B. Lake, the defendant, his servant, in carrying on a prosecution in the Admiralty court against the captain and had agreed to allow him £100 *per annum* during the management of that affair. A. writes to Mason, the plaintiff, that, when he had recovered in the Admiralty court, he had ordered B. Lake to pay him. B. Lake writes to the plaintiff that, when the money was recovered, he would pay him according to A.'s orders.

The defendant, after a tedious prosecution and money by him expended, recovered in the Admiralty and now insists that he himself ought to be first satisfied out of the money in his hands for his salary and other charges.

The plaintiff insisted that the defendant, by his own letter, had contracted that the plaintiff should be paid when the money was received.

Lord Chancellor [Lord Cowper]: I cannot understand the defendant's letter any other wise than that he would pay him having first satisfied himself. The defendant has been an industrious man and has left no stone unturned in the

[1] Stat. 8 & 9 Will. III, c. 18 (*SR*, VII, 213–215).

management of this affair. I cannot decree that he shall have nothing for his pains and lose money out of his own pocket too.

199

Fane v. Duke of Devonshire

(Ch. 1717)

In this case, the court held that an appointment was invalid because the maker lacked the mental capacity to know what he was doing when he exercised it.

Lincoln's Inn MS. Misc. 380, pt. 3, p. 161

Lord Harry Cavendish, in 1683, made a marriage settlement wherein £12,000 is absolutely settled on an eldest daughter in case there was no son, and, in the same deed, there is a power to raise £10,000 more to be given to such child or children as he should by deed appoint. In 1700, Lord Harry Cavendish, being very ill and given over by the doctors, was desired by his friends to settle his affairs. And the deed was read to him, and he gave direction to draw up a deed pursuant to the power and give the £10,000 to his daughter, his only child. This was two days before his death. Two hours before his death, this deed of appointment is executed, and the deed recites, pursuant to a power given him in his marriage settlement etc. Lord Harry was in his right understanding an hour and a half after the executing.

The Lord Chancellor [Lord Cowper] decreed that he thought it impossible for Lord Harry Cavendish, on a death bed, to be capable of conceiving the import of a settlement which was so long and so tedious that he with his utmost attention to the reading of it could not say that he was master of the contents of it. Therefore, he thought that alone might be sufficient to set aside the deed of appointment.

And, so to the appointment itself, he thought it was not executed according to the intent of the settlement, for he has at all events made a provision for an eldest daughter in case there was no son for that this further provision seems to have been designed for younger daughters only in case there was no son and, in a further provision for a daughter, for whom he had so plentifully provided for.

This decree was confirmed in the House of Lords.

[Other reports of this case: 6 Brown P.C. 137, 2 E.R. 984, 2 Eq. Cas. Abr. 660, 22 E.R. 554.]

200

Rawley v. Wilcocks

(Ch. 1717)

A devisee of specific lands cannot set aside a mortgage of them that was made post mortem *to a* bona fide *mortgagee, but, when the debt is paid off, he or she will receive the lands.*

Lincoln's Inn MS. Misc. 380, pt. 3, p. 162, pl. 1

A. devises that £500 should be raised out of his copyhold estate for R., his daughter's, portion. No surrender is made. After the death of the devisor, B., the son and heir, is admitted into the copyhold. B. mortgages the copyhold to C. and surrenders to him.

R., the daughter, brings her bill against the heir and mortgagee to have her £500 charged upon the copyhold estate.

The Lord Chancellor [Lord Cowper] decreed that he must presume that the mortgagee was a fair purchaser without notice since no notice has been proved. R., the daughter, is in the nature of a debtee by simple contract. Therefore, upon B.'s paying off the mortgage, the copyhold must be surrendered to R. in order to satisfy her demand.

201

Bayles v. Coultson

(Ch. 1717)

A devise to a creditor is a satisfaction of the debt.

Lincoln's Inn MS. Misc. 380, pt. 3, p. 162, pl. 2

A., on his marriage with B., articles to lay out £1400 in lands to be settled on himself for life, then to his wife for life for a jointure, then etc. A. dies before any purchase was made, and he devises land to his wife for life near the value of the income of £1400 that it had been laid out in a purchase and devises to her her jewels, household goods, stock on the ground, etc.

The Lord Chancellor [Lord Cowper] decreed that the devise being near the value of the income of the £1400 shall be taken as satisfaction for it.

Another point in this case was the husband devised a term to his wife for life and after to his son C. for life and after his death to the issue of his body and, after failure of issue, then he devised it to D. for life and, after his death, to the issue of her body and, for failure of issue if his wife were then alive, he devised it to his wife and her executors. The wife dies; then the son dies. And the question was whether the limitation to D. were good after the failure of the issue of the body of C. or whether it should go in the course of administration to C.'s father's brother [and] his mother's sister, they being the next of kin to C.

The Lord Chancellor [Lord Cowper] said he thought it might be a good limitation to D., for it is devised to C. for life only and, it being limited to their heirs of his body and the testator thought all this might happen in the compass of one life, therefore, last of all, he devises to the wife if she were living. But he said he would look into the books that there might not be a clashing of opinions.

In this case, the executor of the mother of C. insisted to have an allowance for so much as the mother, as guardian to her son, had expended beyond the income of the son's estate, that being then in jointure.

The Lord Chancellor ordered the master to enquire if anything and what was necessary to be expended beyond the profits of his estate for his education.

The limitation of the term was in trustees to permit the son to take the profits for life and, after his decrease, to permit his issue to take the profits and, for failure of issue of his body, etc.

202

Green v. Burwell

(Ch. 1717)

A court of equity can settle an account based upon a settlement made for a spendthrift.

Lincoln's Inn MS. Misc. 380, pt. 3, p. 163

A father makes a settlement to trustees in trust that they shall pay £100 *per annum* for the benefit and advantage of B., his younger son, but that it should not be paid him quarterly but in such manner and in such proportion as they in their discretion should think proper so that his son should not be able to demand any money from them or be able to squander that away, which he intended should continue a provision for him all his life. B. marries Burwell's, the defendant's, daughter. The defendant tells B. he had rights to an estate of £800 *per annum* and that he would carry on a suit for him and, after the suit begun, in consideration of money already laid out, B., by articles, covenants that the defendant should have a quarter part of the estate when recovered. The decree in that suit was that B. should have his annuity free from taxes and the taxes heretofore allowed should now be paid for his benefit according to the settlement. As to the rest of the bill, it was dismissed.

Then, the defendant brings in an account of £950 charges, and that account is signed and witnessed. The items in that account are gross sums, one of £600, another of £200, and, after[wards], B. assigns the annuity to the defendant in consideration of the £950. And the deed was endorsed that it was agreed among the parties that the annuity should continue for the benefit of B., his wife, and children.

After the defendant's arrest, B., who is now in prison, brings this bill to open the said account and to have his annuity. The defendant brings a cross-bill to have the assignment of the annuity confirmed to him and to have a maintenance for his daughter, B.'s wife, and against the trustee to make him pay over again so much of the annuity as he had paid to B. after notice of the assignment.

The defendant in his answer offers to bring in his vouchers and now submitted to discharge the plaintiff out of prison.

I shall make this allotment to the infant children. If he had not, I should have opened the account. Strictly, a stated account is to be looked upon only as it was plainly intended as a security to ensure somewhat for the maintenance of the wife and children. Let one moiety be applied accordingly to the original trust for the benefit and advantage of the plaintiff and the other moiety to be paid to the wife for the maintenance of herself and the child, and her receipt is to be a discharge; no costs on either side [are given].

The defendant should have paid costs if he had gone according to the strictness of his case. The trustee has acted a fair part.

203

Creswick v. Ward

(Ch. 1717)

A settled account is a binding and enforceable contract.

Lincoln's Inn MS. Misc. 380, pt. 3, p. 164

The plaintiff and defendant had dealings, one with the other, and, upon an account, the plaintiff appeared indebted to the defendant in the sum of £2300, for which he gave a bond to the defendant, and, at several times within six months afterward he paid £600 or £700. Two years afterwards, an account is stated, and then it was objected by the plaintiff that he ought to be allowed interest or interest ought to be deducted from the time of the several payments. But, at last, the plaintiff signed the account without any such allowance. Afterwards, another account is stated, in which account interest in deducted from the payment of £1000, but the plaintiff [was] under an arrest by the defendant at the time of the second account, on which account £200 was due from the plaintiff to the defendant.

This bill was to have these accounts opened and interest to be deducted from the respective times of payments and then it would appear the plaintiff was not indebted to the defendant.

For the plaintiff, it was said the error appears on the verity of the account, and it is not to be maintained by parol proof. This count always takes care that nothing shall be allowed beyond the legal interest and here the interest was six percent and, though this be a voluntary act, yet it being so does not alter in cases of procuration and continuation.

Lord Chancellor [Lord Cowper]: I do not find the plaintiff was under any arrest at the time of settling the first account. He made that objection and, after all, voluntarily signed the account. The inconvenience that would attend opening such accounts would be much greater than keeping people to their own agreements though it exceed legal interest and would encourage people to sign accounts after such a manner as they know they would easily break through. This sum was due on a balance of an account. The defendant took his money at several payments [and] was forced to bring actions; these are great inconveniences. I cannot relieve. I confirm the decree.

204
Jolliff v. Madgewick
(Ch. 1717)

The question in this case was whether the marriage settlement in issue had been improperly altered.

Lincoln's Inn MS. Misc. 380, pt. 3, p. 166

A father, on his son's marriage, settles his estate in trustees to himself for life, then to his son for life, then to the son's wife in jointure, then to the heirs of the body of the son on his wife begotten. There was but one deed of settlement, which was left with the son, the now plaintiff. The husband, being a seafaring man, gives it to his wife, who delivered it to the defendant, who is the trustee in the settlement.

The suit is against the trustee to have the settlement. On the producing of it in court, it appeared that the release had been erased in the date and dated a day before the lease.

Lord Chancellor [Lord Cowper]: Let the Master examine on oath both the husband and trustee touching the erasure. The husband seems willing to have the deed in his possession to take advantage of the inadvertency of the settlement in settling the estate to the heirs of his body which vests a tail in him, which he may destroy by a fine. Therefore, let the deed be brought before a Master for the benefit of all parties. The father is still alive. Supposing the erasure to be before the execution, then nothing passes by law, and it is only an evidence of an agreement, and this court cannot well carry on that agreement into execution and make a better settlement than what has been made.

205

Eclin v. Barnardiston

(Ch. 1717)

Laches cannot be proved without having been properly pleaded.

Lincoln's Inn MS. Misc. 380, pt. 3, p. 167

Articles [were made] to purchase wherein is a covenant that the lands had been usually let for the eight last years for £126 *per annum*. The articles before execution is endorsed and that it was agreed between the parties that, if the plaintiff, the purchaser, should within one year after the purchase discover that the lands had been let for less within the eight years, then the defendant would refund after the rate of nineteen year's purchase the value given. Two years after, the plaintiff discovered that he had let one part of the land to one A. and had given him £20 and had lent him £30 more to take a lease at such a rent, and, with another tenant, the defendant had agreed to pay his tithes and parochial duties and a receipt in the tenant's name.

This bill was brought to have a performance of the articles and to be repaid according to the agreement endorsed.

For the defendant, it was said by Mr. *Cooper* a court of equity may in several cases well dispense with the circumstance of time. In this case, the defendant had covenanted in the body of the articles that the land had been usually let for that rent for the last eight years. By this count, the defendant, his heirs, and executors would be always liable to an action, to prevent which comes this special agreement and amendment. I will not have this covenant continually to hang over, for, perhaps, my evidence may be lost, but, if you make any discovery within twelve months, which is a reasonable time, that I agree to it.

For the plaintiff, [it was said] the defendant has not insisted on this in his answer. If he had, we could have amended our bill and put that matter in issue. But besides, there is a fraud in this case. The circumstance of time is within common relief of a court of equity.

Lord Chancellor [Lord Cowper]: You do not put that matter in issue in your answer, but you endeavor to prove the land of the value according to the agreement. The circumstance of time is the slightest thing a court of equity has to dispense with and here especially where there is suspicion of fraud. The Master must enquire how much less the land has been let for etc.

206

Thornhill v. Heath

(Ch. 1717)

A guardian can be required to make an account annually.

Lincoln's Inn MS. Misc. 380, pt. 3, p. 168, pl. 1

A bill [was exhibited] against a guardian to have him account annually and that the infant might have a purchase of lands that were very convenient for him and that the defendant might have a liberal maintenance that therewith he might be able to assist his sister and aunt [who were] wholly unprovided for.

Lord Chancellor [Lord Cowper]: Let the defendant account annually; if the defendant be an administ[rator] in trust, yet he has a right to retain. Let the Master enquire if the purchase be convenient. But the making the purchase will be taking away the personal estate, which is in the power of the court, and vesting it in land, which is not in the power of the court, and it will not bind the infant or any creditor.

207

Plume v. Beall

(Ch. 1717)

Where a will has been admitted to probate in an ecclesiastical court, a court of equity will not set the will aside on the ground of fraud.

Lincoln's Inn MS. Misc. 380, pt. 3, p. 168, pl. 3

A. makes his will in writing and devises several legacies, and the residue of the estate he gives to the defendant in trust for charitable uses. This will was written in a kind of paper book, and the particular legacies and dispositions were in distinct pages, and the rest of the page [was] blank. Part was written by his own hand and part by Dr. Thompson's by the testator's directions. This will was proved in the spiritual court.

This bill was brought by the executor to have the direction of the court as to the payment of a legacy to the defendant. It appeared in the will that a legacy of £100 given to the defendant was written in her own hand. Dr. Thompson swore that he had seen the writing of the defendant and verily believed it to be her own handwriting. And it was proved in the cause that, in the testator's last sickness, the defendant came and tended him and that the testator two hours before his death said he had forgotten to give a legacy to the defendant and bade them take notice he then gave to her £2 3s. and a silver cup. And, after the testator's death, the defendant, at her desire, watched the testator's corpse and, in the same room, the will lay in the scrutoire.

The Lord Chancellor [Lord Cowper] decreed the legacy of £100 to be paid to the defendant, for, though here were strong suspicions of fraud that this legacy might be inserted by the defendant herself, yet, as the will was proved in the spiritual court in a proper jurisdiction, the court would not set aside any part of a will regularly proved there.

Mr. *Vernon* said that, in Lady Knapper's Case,[1] the will was regularly proved in the spiritual court, and, after there appeared to be an interpolation fraudulently inserted, on an application to the spiritual court, that part of it was set aside.

[Other reports of this case: 1 Peere Williams 388, 24 E.R. 438, 2 Eq. Cas. Abr. 421, 22 E.R. 358.]

208

Long v. Long

(Ch. 1717)

Where a person devises that his debts and legacies be paid out of rents and profits of land, part of the land can be sold for the immediate payment of the debts and legacies.

Lincoln's Inn MS. Misc. 380, pt. 3, p. 169

A man devises that all his funeral expenses, debts, and legacies should be paid out of the rents and profits of his freehold and leasehold lands and out of all his real and personal estate whatsoever. And then he devises his leasehold and freehold lands to B. for life, remainder to his first and other sons in tail. B., the plaintiff, brings this bill against the trustees to enable him to sell so much of the lands as to discharge the debts. It was objected that this charge ought to proceed from the estate given to the plaintiff and, by a sale, it would affect the estate in tail, which was not intended by the testator.

The Lord Chancellor [Lord Cowper] decreed a sale of the leasehold lands as much as should be sufficient to pay the debts. And he said that he thought the leasehold estate very proper for that purpose.

[1] *Lord Effingham v. Napier* (1724), 5 Brown P.C. 221, 2 E.R. 640.

209

Gibson v. Fellows

(Ch. 1717)

A person cannot be required to answer to matter in a bill of complaint that would be criminal in him, such as compounding a felony.

A court of equity will not hear evidence of a felony.

Lincoln's Inn MS. Misc. 380, pt. 3, p. 170

The defendant served as steward formerly to the plaintiff. And, on an account stated between the plaintiff and defendant, £245 appeared to be due to the defendant, which the plaintiff paid, and mutual releases were given. And then the plaintiff discharged the defendant from being his steward. The plaintiff said the defendant detained from him his court rolls. The plaintiff being told that the defendant kept them [in] such a summer house, the plaintiff and defendant being together in the same house, the plaintiff gets a constable and some other persons and breaks open the door of the summer house, upon which the defendant carries them before a justice [of the peace] and charges them with felony and with the taking away £275, upon which the plaintiff enters into a bond for £275 to the defendant.

The plaintiff brings this bill to be relieved against the bond and to have a discovery of the consideration thereof and sets out this whole matter.

The defendant demurred to the bill because it required him to answer to a matter that would be criminal in him by compounding the felony. And the demurrer was allowed.

Then the plaintiff amends his bill and, in general words, demands what was the consideration of the bond, to which the defendant answers he really lost £275, which he really believes came to his hands or to some other person in company with him and under his management.

The plaintiff proved that the defendant was always reputed a poor man and that, some days before this matter happened, he borrowed £10.

The Lord Chancellor [Lord Cowper] said he would not go into the proof of the felony. The plaintiff best knew whether he was guilty of it or no. If he was not guilty, why did he not stand trial at law? The defendant has positively sworn that he had £275, which he says he verily believes came to the plaintiff's hands.

Serjeant *Hooper* said that, at a trial at Exeter, that the judge admitted them into proof that the consideration of a note [was] *pro turpi causa*, which was a compounding of felony.

210

Williams v. Callow

(Ch. 1717)

In this case of a failed marriage, the court ordered the interest from the wife's marriage portion to be paid to her for her separate maintenance.

2 Vernon 752, 23 E.R. 1091

Williams, a glover, agreed to give his son £1500 and turn over his trade and house to the son, and Mrs. Callow was to give £600 portion with her daughter. But Mrs. Callow insisted she could give but £500 until the son prevailed that, if she would give a bond for £600, he would return £100.

The marriage took effect. The husband proved drunken, rude, and abusive to his wife, and wasting his stock. His father got him to re-assign back his house for an annuity of £60 *per annum* for his life. And, afterwards, he came to an agreement with Mrs. Callow to take a bond for £500 (payable to a trustee), the interest whereof was to be paid to him during the joint lives of himself and wife and, if he survived, the principal to be paid to him. And he gave a release of the portion to Mrs. Callow.

Williams, the husband, brought a bill to set aside the release he had given to Mrs. Callow and to have a legacy of £150 given to his wife by her grandmother and to have the portion made up to £600, although he had delivered up the last bond for £100.

The wife having given a release to the mother before marriage (of the grandmother's legacy) and the treaty being for £600 portion and no mention made of the legacy, the bill was dismissed as to that demand and also as to the £100, which the son promised to remit to his mother and, accordingly, after marriage, gave up the bond.

Mrs. Williams, the wife, brought her cross-bill to have the interest of her portion for her separate maintenance.

And the Chancellor [Lord Cowper] decreed it accordingly, declaring that this was a stronger case than that of Sir James Oxenden;[1] there, [she was] only relieved from the ill behavior and beastliness of Sir James; here cruelty is mixed with it. Sir James Oxenden was of substance to have maintained his wife and lived suitable to his estate; here, the husband has wasted all, and has no fixed habitation, but goes from alehouse to alehouse, and both cases are alike in that the wife's fortune was in trustees, the bond for the £500 being taken in Mr. Callow's, the wife's brother's, name.

---

[1] *Oxenden v. Oxenden* (1705–1706), 2 Vernon 493, 23 E.R. 916, Precedents in Chancery 239, 24 E.R. 116, Gilbert Rep. 1, 25 E.R. 1, 1 Eq. Cas. Abr. 67, 21 E.R. 881.

211

Beavoir v. Hyett

(Ch. 1717–1718)

A purchaser of land takes only what his vendor had.

A person can be ordered to abate a nuisance of blocking ancient lights.

British Library MS. Hargrave 81, f. 10

4 December 1717.

One Mortimer, being seised in fee of four houses on Tower Hill [London], sold two of them to the defendant about the year 1687 and, after[wards], in the year 1702, sold the other two to the plaintiff, who now brings a bill to stop two lights in one of the defendant's houses and also to pull down a closet that jutted out of the third story. The window lights were for the staircase in the first and second stories, and those, as well as the closet, were pretended to be in a party wall and, as such being ruinous, the plaintiff had a right to pull down and build up without lights and oblige the defendant to bear half the charge. And to support his pretensions, the City Surveyor had certified it to be a party wall and fit to be pulled down and that the closet hung over the ground, by which projection, the plaintiff had lost so great a breadth or surface of his ground.

Lord Chancellor [Lord Cowper]: When there was a unity of possession, the owner had liberty to build in what manner he thought fit. And, when he sold two of the houses, the lights etc., not particularly mentioned, passed with them, and the owner, or whoever claims under him, must hold subject to the terms of that sale. It was the business of the last purchaser to see what was conveyed by the first, for he must take subject to it and can be in no better a condition than his vendor. And, therefore, if the lights and closet were there when the defendant purchased, and I think if they were there even before the plaintiff purchased, the plaintiff can have no right to destroy them. And he directed a trial upon that issue.

[Other copies of this report: British Library MS. Hargrave 82, f. 8, British Library MS. Hargrave 77, f. 4v, pl. 2, British Library MS. Hargrave 303, f. 4v.]

Lincoln's Inn MS. Misc. 11, p. 50

22 November 1718.

The bill was brought for an injunction to stay the defendant's building whereby, as it was alleged, he was stopping up the plaintiff's ancient lights. And, upon the hearing of the cause, an issue was directed to try whether the lights were ancient lights or not.

It was found for the plaintiff that they were ancient lights. And, now, it came on for further directions on the equity reserved.

It was decreed by LORD PARKER that the defendant should in three weeks abate so much of his building as stopped up the plaintiff's lights and, if he did not do it within that time, the Master was to appoint commissioners to see it done. The defendant was to pay costs both at law and in this court.

212

Coulthrop v. Codrington

(Ch. 1717)

A devise made in a foreign country charged on foreign land bears interest at the legal rate of interest of that country though the money is to be sent to England.

British Library MS. Hargrave 81, f. 11

4 December 1717.

The devisor, *inter alia*, devises in those words, 'my plantation in Antigua to the defendant burdened with £500 sterling, which I give to my cousin Coulthrop.'

Attorney General [*Northey*]: The plaintiff, by his devise, has a good lien upon the other estate of the testator if the plantations should prove deficient.

The defendant insisted that, the devise being made in Antigua and charged upon plantations there, the £500 ought to be computed as money there and that the plaintiff ought to allow the charges of remittance and that he ought not to have interest.

But the Lord Chancellor [LORD COWPER], being of opinion that the word 'sterling' in the devise showed a plain intention that it should be English money, he decreed the defendant to pay the plaintiff £500 English. But such charges as merchants were usually at in remitting money from Antigua to England, the defendant was to deduct. And he said that the will, being made in Antigua and charged on lands there, was to be taken as a real devise and mortgage and, therefore, the plaintiff was to be allowed the largest legal interest in Antigua for one year after the testator's decease.

[It was] agreed *per omnes*, if it had been a personal devise, the plaintiff might have charged the defendant's person with the payment and need not have gone to Antigua for the money.

[Other copies of this report: British Library MS. Hargrave 82, f. 5.]

[Other reports of this case: British Library MS. Hargrave 77, f. 5v, pl. 1, British Library MS. Hargrave 303, f. 5.]

213
Lyddal v. Bishop of Durham
(Ch. 1717)

Before a bill of review will be allowed, the final decree must be performed and the court costs must be paid.

Upon a bill of review for newly discovered matter, the affidavit thereof must be made by the party himself and not by his lawyer.

4 Viner, Abr. 411

7 December, 4 Geo.

The original bill was brought to settle the boundaries of the plaintiff's manor. And, upon the first hearing, an issue was directed out to be tried at law, and there was a verdict for the plaintiff. Upon the equity reserved, there was a final decree for quieting the plaintiff's possession and that the defendant should pay costs etc.

The defendant moved for leave to file a bill of review upon an affidavit by his solicitor that certain new evidence was discovered since the verdict and decree in favor of the defendant, that this new matter now discovered was a sufficient ground for a bill of review, as well as any error apparent in the decree itself, etc.

The question was if the bishop shall have leave to file the bill of review before he has paid the costs decreed against him.

It was insisted on by the counsel for Sir Henry Lyddall that the party ought not to file a bill of review before he has performed the decree and that this is constantly allowed for good cause of demurrer to a bill of review and that payment of costs is part of the decree, which ought to be performed as well as any other part of it. And an old book of orders and rules of the court printed in 1623[1] was produced, wherein there was a rule *tempore* Bacon, Chancellor, and another in the year 1656[2] to the effect following, *viz.* that no bill of review shall be allowed until after the decree be performed in all parts, unless such performance would extinguish the party's right or title at law, as a conveyance of land, release, etc., and also there must be leave of the court for filing such bill of review, etc., that a bill of review would be a suspension of the payment of the costs decreed, and that Sir Henry Lyddall would be kept out of his costs until the bill of review was determined, and, if the bishop, who is of a great age, should happen to die, Sir Henry would lose them quite, for he cannot revive the suit for costs only, etc.

E contra, it was said for the bishop that the rules produced on the other side were obsolete and had been out of use for several years in many particulars and,

[1] F. Bacon, *Ordinances for the Better and More Regular Administration of Justice in the Chancery* (1623).

[2] *Collection of Such of the Orders Heretofore Used in the Chancery* . . . (1656).

therefore, were not to be taken as standing rules of the court, that, for many years last past, bills of review have been brought without leave of the court upon motion or petition and it was never insisted on as irregular, that, in lieu thereof, a deposit of £50 is left with the Register upon filing the bill of review, so that it is plain these old rules have not been observed of late years, that soon after the restoration, the rules and orders of the court were revised and corrected by Clarendon, Chancellor, and that these last are taken now to be the standing rules and orders of the court, as they are printed and called *Ordines Cancellariae*,[1] and, in that book, there is no such order as they have insisted on the other side, that a bill of review is like a writ of error at law, which suspends the execution of the judgment, the costs decreed is not a duty, but a consequence only of a decree against the party, that, if the decree be reversed, of consequence, the costs are gone and, therefore, ought to wait the event of the bill of review.

Per Cowper, Chancellor: I think the old orders that have been read are reasonable and just and ought to be observed to prevent unconscionable delays by bills of review, which would be brought in all causes of consequence and value if they might be filed without leave of the court and before the decree performed. And I think payment of costs ought to be performed rather than any other part of the decree, especially in this case, where the new matter discovered was in the power of the party and it was his fault and neglect it was not discovered sooner. So let the event of the bill of review be what it will, the other side ought to have costs, as in the like case of a new trial granted upon the like grounds. Where a sum of money is decreed, the money must be paid before a bill of review is filed, though it must be refunded if the decree be reversed upon the bill of review, but, in the present case, if the decree should be reversed, yet the costs ought not to be refunded, which makes it a much stronger case. I think the party himself should make an affidavit that this new matter was discovered since the decree and that the affidavit of a solicitor is not sufficient, for the bishop himself, or some other agent of his, might be informed of this matter before, at least if the bishop, by reason of his age, high station, and quality, may be excused from making an affidavit of the particular matters and facts, yet, at least, he should have an affidavit to corroborate that of his solicitor. But this affidavit of the solicitor alone is not a sufficient ground for a bill of review. And, therefore, the counsel for the bishop must take nothing by their motion.

[Other copies of this report: 2 Eq. Cas. Abr. 176, 22 E.R. 150.]

4 Viner, Abr. 415

Michaelmas 4 Geo. [1717]. Bishop of Durham v. Lyddal.

[1] *Ordines Cancellariae, Being Orders of the High Court of Chancery, from the First Year of King Charles I, to This Present Hillary term, 1697 . . . to Which Is Added the Rules and Orders of the Court of Exchequer* (1698).

A bill of review was brought and demurred to. And, afterwards, the counsel for the plaintiff in the bill of review moved the court to discharge the bill, as not being regularly filed, upon payment of costs out of the £50 deposited in court upon the filing thereof, and the same was granted.

[Other copies of this report: 2 Eq. Cas. Abr. 175, 22 E.R. 150.]

[Other reports of this case: 2 Cooper *tempore* Cottenham 434, 47 E.R. 1236, 2 Brown P.C. 63, 1 E.R. 794.]

214
Meller v. Edisbury

(Ch. 1717)

The priorities of judgments are determined by the date they were signed.

Lincoln's Inn MS. Misc. 10, p. 224

11 December 1717.

The estate of Joshua Edisbury being decreed to be sold for the payment of his debts and the judgments being to be paid according to their priorities, the question upon the Master's report was touching the priority of three judgments, one of which was a judgment at the Grand Sessions in Wales and was signed the 24th March and the other was a judgment in the [Court of] Common Pleas and signed the 8th of April following but was entered up as of the preceding term. And it was much insisted that this last judgment was prior to the judgment in Wales though signed afterwards, for although, by the Statute of Frauds etc.,[1] in the case of purchasers, judgments shall affect lands but from the time of signing, yet this case was not within the Statute, for the dispute is not between a judgment creditor and a purchaser but between one creditor by judgment and another, which has the priority. And, therefore, this case stands upon the common law as it was before the Statute. And, by that, all judgments relate to the term in which they are entered up.

But by the Lord Chancellor [Lord Cowper], it was held that the court in paying creditors out of money arising by the sale of an equity of redemption could have no better rule to go by than what the Statute had directed, which was that judgments should be considered only from the time of their signing and, though this case was not literally within the Statute, for here was no actual purchase, yet he thought a creditor by judgment might be considered to be in the nature of a purchaser, for he is supposed to lend his money upon the security of his judgment and its affecting the land. And, therefore, he decreed that the judgment first signed should be the first paid.

[Other reports of this case: Precedents in Chancery 478, 24 E.R. 215.]

[1] Stat. 29 Car. II, c. 3 (*SR*, V, 839–842).

215

Stafford v. City of London

(Ch. 1718)

A suit will be dismissed for the non-joinder of a co-lessee as a party.

1 Strange 95, 93 E.R. 407

The plaintiff, being a co-lessee with A., brought his bill to have the rent apportioned on a partial eviction. And, because the other lessee was neither plaintiff nor defendant (for, if he refused to be a plaintiff, he might be made a defendant), the bill was dismissed with costs. And instances were cited where bills have been dismissed for want of parties as well as where causes have been put off only.

[Other reports of this case: 1 Peere Williams 428, 24 E.R. 457, 2 Eq. Cas. Abr. 1, 59, 166, 244, 22 E.R. 1, 52, 142, 208, 4 Brown P.C. 635, 2 E.R. 433.]

216

Merrel v. Bennett

(Ch. 1718)

Where a mortgagor-debtor does not pay the interest when it is due, it can be added to the principal debt due and be subject to the payment of interest in the future.

A contract for compound interest is valid and enforceable.

A mortgagee in possession must account to the mortgagor for any profits received from the land.

Lincoln's Inn MS. Misc. 380, pt. 2, p. 1

Chancery. Hilary term 4 Geo.

A mortgagor having paid neither principal nor interest, several accounts from time to time were stated between him and the mortgagee, upon which the interest was made principal and together with the principal was agreed between them to carry interest from the respective times of stating the accounts. Afterward, the mortgagee was put into possession and new accounts were made up between them, in which the interest was in like manner made principal and agreed to carry interest, but no allowance was made in those accounts for the profits of the mortgaged estate that had been received by the mortgagee.

Upon a bill by the mortgagee to redeem or to foreclose the equity of redemption, it was insisted in behalf of the mortgagor that those stated accounts in which the interest was made principal were impositions upon him and that he ought not to be bound thereby, it being contrary to the known equity of the court that interest should carry interest. And for that purpose, the Case of Sir Thomas

Meers[1] was cited, where My Lord Harcourt held and decreed that, where there was a covenant in the mortgaged deed, that, if interest should not be paid from time to time within three months after it became due, such interest should be made principal and from that time carry interest, that such covenant was void and such interest should not carry interest according to that agreement.

Lord Cowper said that it was very reasonable for a mortgagee at the end of the year to insist either on the payment of the interest that was due or that such interest should be made principal and from that time carry interest and that it looks much fairer in this manner to demand the interest, or on non-payment, to have it made principal than to make an addition of some small new sum of money to the interest and then make it altogether principal. This looks like a designed temptation to the mortgagor to come into that which otherwise he might not have been prevailed upon to do.

Therefore, as to those accounts which were made up before the mortgagee came into possession, he decreed that they should stand with liberty only of falsification if any plain mistakes should appear. But as to those accounts which were made up when the mortgagee was in possession, he said that those were manifestly an imposition on the mortgagor, who was thereby to pay interest upon interest without any deduction on account of the profits received. And the mortgagee could do this with no other view but either never to account for those profits at all or at least to hold them without interest.

He said likewise that, where a mortgage is made at first to carry interest of five percent only, that being then the usual value of money, if the value of money afterward rises to six percent, it is not unreasonable for the mortgagee to insist upon having either his money or interest after the rate of six percent after that time and, in case they come to such new agreement for six percent, it shall bind the mortgaged lands not only against the mortgagor himself, but against any new mortgage subsequent to the first though precedent to this new agreement if the first mortgagee had no notice of such new mortgage.

Lincoln's Inn MS. Misc. 380, pt. 3, p. 175, pl. 2

A mortgagor and mortgagee came to an account annually, and then the interest by agreement is turned into principal. And [it was] decreed good by the Chancellor [Lord Cowper].

In this case, Sir Thomas Mears's Case was cited, in the late Chancellor Harcourt's time where, in a mortgage, it was covenanted that the interest due yearly should carry interest. Harcourt decreed the covenant unreasonable and void. Sir

[1] *Meers v. Lord Stourton* (Ch. 1711), British Library MS. Hargrave 80, f. 43v, pl. 2, 2 Eq. Cas. Abr. 246, 22 E.R. 209, on a different point of law, Dickens 21, 21 E.R. 174, 1 Peere Williams 146, 24 E.R. 332, 2 Salkeld 512, 91 E.R. 437, 2 Eq. Cas. Abr. 14, 22 E.R. 11, cited in *Bosanquet v. Dashwood* (1734), Cases *tempore* Talbot 38, 40, 25 E.R. 648, 649.

Thomas Mears told His Lordship he had always inserted such a covenant in his mortgages. Harcourt told him 'Sir Thomas, as often as it comes into this court before me, I will set it aside.' Sir Thomas replied 'I shall do so and perhaps after Your Lordship has left the seat.'

217

Middleton v. Lord Onslow

(Ch. 1718)

A provision in a will that, if a daughter marry without the consent of a parent, she will have only a reduced portion is valid and enforceable.

Lincoln's Inn MS. Misc. 10, p. 238

22 January 1717[/18]. Mary, Constance, Diana, and Anne Middleton, four of the daughters of Mr. Middleton, plaintiffs; Lord Onslow and Elizabeth Middleton, widow, executors of Mr. Middleton, Richard Hockenhull and Elizabeth, his wife, the other daughter of Mr. Middleton, *et al.*, defendants.

Mr. Middleton, by his will, devised his estate to Lord Onslow and the defendant Elizabeth Middleton for 2000 years to raise £16,000 for portions for the plaintiffs and the defendant Elizabeth Hockenhull to be paid at eighteen or marriage provided, if any of the daughters should marry under the age of twenty-one years without the consent of the testator's wife if living in writing under hand and seal or, in case of her death, without the like consent of the trustees therein named or the survivor, then every such daughter so marrying without such consent should have only £1000 and the residue of the portion intended for such daughter should go amongst the other daughters equally and be paid when their original portions become payable.

Elizabeth, one of the daughters, after she was nineteen married the defendant Hockenhull without the consent of her mother.

It was decreed that she should have only £1000 and that the remainder of her share of the £16,000 should go to and be equally divided between the plaintiffs, her sisters.

[Later proceedings in this case: 1 Peere Williams 768, 24 E.R. 605, 2 Eq. Cas. Abr. 254, 259, 22 E.R. 216, 220.]

218
Anonymous
(Ch. 1718)

A plaintiff cannot sue an action in contract without having strictly performed his part of the contract.

In this case, the court did not allow the terms of a contract to be varied by prior mutual variations in its performance.

British Library MS. Hargrave 81, f. 12

February 1717/18.

The plaintiff, being a farmer of alum mines in Yorkshire, entered into a contract with the defendants to deliver to them yearly during the term of seven years 250 tuns of alum by quarterly proportions at a certain price therein agreed upon. And he covenants to deliver the same at some quay at the port of London. The plaintiff, for about four years after[wards], delivers the alum at a quay in Southwark, from whence the defendants constantly fetched it all that time without making the least objection. But, afterwards, the prices of alum falling so as the bargain became prejudicial to them, the defendants neglecting taking the alum as usual, upon which the plaintiff gave notice of its being at the quay and fixed also a notice upon the Exchange, of which the defendants taking no notice, the plaintiff brought his action at law. And at the trial, the defendants insisting that the agreement was to deliver the alum at a quay in London, and not at Southwark, the plaintiff was nonsuited, upon which he brought his bill in this court for relief and performance of the articles, suggesting that, though the courts of law were tied down by the strict letter of the covenant, yet equity had often relieved, that the plaintiff living at Yorkshire and not knowing the exact distinction of London and Southwark and the country people took Southwark and the Strand to be London, as much as Cheapside, that, as long as the bargain was to the defendants' advantage, there was no exception taken to the place, for that was as constant a quay for them as any in London, and the plaintiff could as easily have delivered to them at any quay in London as there, and, as the plaintiff had done everything that was the intention of the agreement, though he had not exactly complied with the letter of it, he hoped the court would compel the defendants to perform their part and not suffer them, after they enjoyed the benefit so long as it was good for them, not to evade it now upon a mere quibble because it turns to their disadvantage.

Upon hearing the plaintiff's counsel only, the Lord Chancellor [Lord Cowper] dismissed the bill with costs.

[Other copies of this report: British Library MS. Hargrave 82, f. 10.]

[Other reports of this case: British Library MS. Hargrave 77, f. 5v, pl. 2, British Library MS. Hargrave 303, f. 5v.]

219

Wingrave v. Palgrave

(Ch. 1718)

A court of law cannot rewrite a private person's contract in order to make it more reasonable.

Lincoln's Inn MS. Misc. 380, pt. 3, p. 175, pl. 1

In Sir [*blank*] Pelgrave's settlement, a term is created to raise portions for such daughter or daughters as should be living at the time of his death. Sir Pelgrave had a daughter, who was married and left a daughter, and died in Sir Pelgrave's lifetime.

The bill was to have the portions raised for the daughters of the daughter.

The Chancellor [Lord Cowper] dismissed the bill, for the contingency never happened on which the term was to arise, and, therefore, the court cannot create a term for that purpose though it be never so reasonable.

Lincoln's Inn MS. Misc. 10, p. 260

4 February 1717[/18]. Winspeare v. Palgrave.

Sir Austin Palgrave, on his marriage, settles lands to the use of himself for life, remainder to the first and other sons of the marriage in tail male, remainder to trustees for 500 years, remainder to his own right heirs. The trusts of the term were that, if there should be no issue male, the trustees should raise the sum of [*blank*] for daughter's portions to be paid them at twenty-one or marriage. Then follows a proviso whereby it is declared that, if there shall be no daughter of the marriage living at the death of Sir Austin and his wife should not be enceinte of any daughter or, there being such daughters, they should die unmarried and under twenty-one, then, in either of those cases, the term should cease and be void.

The plaintiff married a daughter of Sir Austin, who died in the lifetime of her father. And he now brings his bill to have his wife's portion raised by virtue of the trusts of the term.

The bill was dismissed without any difficulty, the court [Lord Cowper] declaring that, if this had even been an unforeseen case when the settlement was made, yet they could not supply such an omission, for this court is to execute the trusts of settlements and not to supply the omissions which may fall out to be in them.

[Other reports of this case: 1 Peere Williams 401, 24 E.R. 444, 2 Eq. Cas. Abr. 655, 22 E.R. 550.]

220

Attorney General v. Burdet

(Ch. 1718)

An appointment by a tenant in tail to a charity binds the reversioner in fee.

2 Vernon 755, 23 E.R. 1093

15 February.

An appointment by a tenant in tail to a charity shall bind the reversioner in fee. And as an authority in point, the case of Christ's Hospital and Hawes was cited. Duke's *Charitable Uses* 84.[1] The Statute of Charitable Uses[2] supplies all defects of assurance where the donor is of capacity to dispose and has such an estate as is in any way disposable by him, whether by fine or common recovery. And the case also of the Attorney General and Hawley[3] was cited, that the appointment by a tenant in tail barred the remainderman.

221

Bury v. Bury

(Ch. 1718)

A supplemental bill lies to bring additional necessary parties into a lawsuit in order to have an account.

Lincoln's Inn MS. Misc. 12, p. 176, pl. 1

19 February 1717[/18].

Upon the hearing of this cause, an account was directed to be taken of a trust estate. But some necessary parties not being brought on to hearing, the court ordered the plaintiff should bring them before the Master to account accordingly.

In order to do which, the plaintiff brought a supplement bill against those persons. And that cause being brought to hearing, they were ordered to account according to the former decree.

---

1 *Christ's Hospital v. Hawes* (1620), Herne & Duke 47.

2 Stat. 43 Eliz. I, c. 4, s. 1 (*SR*, IV, 968–969).

3 *Attorney General v. Hawley* (Ch. 1713), British Library MS. Hargrave 80, f. 139.

222

Mocatta v. Murgatroyd

(Ch. 1718)

Where a person acts negligently so that a third person is thereby enabled to perpetrate a fraud, he will be estopped to assert his own claim against the persons who were defrauded.

Lincoln's Inn MS. Misc. 10, p. 225

22 February 1717[/18]. Moses Mocatta *et al.* v. Murgatroyd, Ford, and Leith Adams, administratrix of Thomas Adams.

The plaintiffs bought several shares of the *Molly Pinck* of the defendant Ford, who had before mortgaged the whole ship to the defendant Murgatroyd for £70. And the defendant, after such mortgage, entrusts Ford with the original bill of sale which had been made to Ford of the ship under pretense (as Murgatroyd swears by his answer) that Ford wanted it to show to a merchant that was about freighting the ship who desired to be satisfied that Ford was the owner of the ship. And, during the time that Ford had this bill of sale in his custody, he sells to the plaintiffs and makes bills of sale of the shares by them respectively bought. And they, knowing nothing of the mortgage to Murgatroyd, caused endorsements to be made of the shares which they had bought upon the original bill of sale that so it might appear what shares had been sold away.

After this, Ford sells all the remaining shares except one-sixteenth to several other persons, who sold to the plaintiffs, but no endorsement or memorandum was made of the sale of these shares.

The plaintiffs, being thus entitled, fit out the ship upon several voyages, and, after they had been in possession some time, the defendant Murgatroyd sets up a title at law under his mortgage, Ford being become insolvent.

And the plaintiffs now bring their bill to be relieved, suggesting a fraud in the defendant Murgatroyd in letting the original bill of sale go out of his hands without endorsing his mortgage, by which means, the plaintiffs were drawn in to become purchasers of part of the ship, which they would not have done if they had known that such mortgage had been made.

Lord Chancellor [Lord Cowper] declared that the defendant Murgatroyd incautiously and negligently trusted the said Ford with the original bill and, after the endorsements had been made thereon of other bills of sale, delivered back the same to the defendant Murgatroyd and he accepted it with those endorsements, which ought to be taken as an agreement in the defendant Murgatroyd to the sale of so many parts of the said ship as are endorsed on the first bill of sale. And, therefore, such bills of sale as are endorsed ought to be preferred before the defendant's mortgage except the bill of sale to Thomas Adams, who was a witness to the mortgage.

Lincoln's Inn MS. Misc. 10, p. 242, pl. 2

22 February 1717[/18].

The plaintiffs bought several shares of the ship *Molly Pinck* of the defendant Ford, who was the owner of that ship, in April, May, and June 1713. In March before, Ford had mortgaged the whole ship to the defendant Murgatroyd and makes him an assignment of the original bill of sale, which is left in Murgatroyd's hands and about two months after, he lets Ford have the original bill of sale under pretense, as Murgatroyd swears in his answer, to show to some merchants, who Ford pretended were about freighting this ship.

Ford, having got the bill of sale into his hands, shows it to the plaintiffs, and, there being no endorsements thereon of the mortgage, the plaintiffs were drawn in to become purchasers of several shares in the ship. And Ford made several bills of sale to the plaintiffs of their respective shares, and a memorandum thereof was made upon the original bill of sale. And then Ford returns the bill of sale to Murgatroyd with these endorsements.

Murgatroyd, after this, leaves the bill of sale with one Haynes, his attorney, in order (as he also swears by his answer) to receive the mortgage money of Ford, and Ford, by some means, gets the bill of sale from Haynes and sells more shares to other persons, who, afterwards, sold to the plaintiffs. And some of these shares were also endorsed on the bill of sale.

Ford absconding and the plaintiffs having bought all the shares of the ship except one-ninth, which Ford kept, they fit her out for a voyage, and, after her return, they refit her for a second voyage. And just as she was ready to sail, Murgatroyd brings [an action of] replevin for the ship. And, thereupon, the plaintiffs exhibit their bill, suggesting that all this was a contrivance between the defendants to cheat the plaintiffs.

Upon the hearing of the case, Lord Cowper declared that Murgatroyd having incautiously or negligently parted with the original bill of sale and after it was returned to him with the endorsements taking no notice thereof to any of the plaintiffs but acquiescing so long as he did under what Ford had done is an evidence of an after consent to the sales which were endorsed on the bill of sale. And he, therefore, decreed that such of the shares as are so endorsed should take place before the defendant Murgatroyd's mortgage. But as to the other shares, which are not endorsed, they must be postponed to the mortgage and redeem Murgatroyd.

[Other reports of this case: 1 Peere Williams 393, 24 E.R. 440, 2 Eq. Cas. Abr. 612, 22 E.R. 514.]

223

Short v. Long

(Ch. 1718)

Where a decedent's estate is not sufficient to pay the debts and legacies, the estates in fee and the leaseholds will be abated proportionably.

Lincoln's Inn MS. Misc. 10, p. 222, pl. 2

24 February 1717[/18]. Long v. Short.

[It was] decreed by Lord Chancellor [Lord Cowper] that, where a man had devised a freehold estate to his son and a leasehold estate to his grandson and there was a deficiency of personal assets to pay the bond creditors, the burden of such deficiency should not fall wholly upon the leasehold estate, but should be borne by both estates in an average, for it was as much as the testator's intention that the specific devise of his leasehold estate should take place as that of the freehold. And, therefore, let the Master put a value upon both estates, and, according to such valuation, let each of the devisees pay in proportion towards such of the bond debts as the personal estate will not extend to pay.

2 Vernon 756, 23 E.R. 1094

24 February.

The testator devised his real estate to his son for life and to his first and other sons in tail, with remainders over. And, by the same will, he devises specifically a leasehold estate to his daughter, and he made his son executor, the assets falling short to pay debts.

The question was whether the deficiency was to be charged upon the real or upon the leasehold estate.

Lord Chancellor [Lord Cowper] decreed the deficiency to be borne equally in proportion to the value of each estate, the fee simple estate devised to the son being liable to debts by specialty by the Statute against Fraudulent Devises.[1] And the leasehold, although specifically devised, is liable to debts. And, both being devised, the intention of the testator stands equally between the devisees. And both estates being liable, each ought to contribute its proportion.

[Other reports of this case: 1 Eq. Cas. Abr. 114, 21 E.R. 921, *sub nom.* Long v. Short, 1 Peere Williams 403, 24 E.R. 445, 2 Eq. Cas. Abr. 223, 22 E.R. 190.]

---

[1] Stat. 3 Will. & Mar., c. 14 (*SR*, VI, 320–321).

224

Pool v. Sandford

(Ch. 1718)

Where a lessee of a glebe has destroyed the boundaries of it, he will be required to identify the extent of the glebe lands.

A dispute over a private right of way should be tried in a common law court, not in a court of equity.

Lincoln's Inn MS. Misc. 380, pt. 3, p. 174, pl. 1

Hilary term 4 Geo. [1718].

A bill [was exhibited] for tithes and to have one-half an acre of the glebe intermixed with the defendant's land to be set out and to have a [right of] way through, which the plaintiff time etc. [of which memory does not run] has used to carry his tithes.

The defendant says the one-half acre is intermixed with eleven acres of his own land and that he does not know what part is the glebe and that he has all along paid 2s. 6d. yearly in satisfaction of the one-half acre, which the plaintiff formerly accepted. As to the way, this is a private right and, therefore, ought to be tried at law, and especially [in] this case where the plaintiff never had a verdict at law. If he had, perhaps a bill for quieting the possession might be proper.

Lord Chancellor [Lord Cowper]: The one-half acre of glebe must be set out and at the defendant's own charge, for it is through his neglect in not preserving the boundaries that the knowledge of it is lost. And, if the commissioners cannot ascertain the one-half acre, let them set out half an acre most convenient for the plaintiff. This is a very common case; people rent the glebe and destroy the boundaries and, for the necessity, the parson is obliged to let them have it at a quarter of the value. This was the Case of the Dean and Chapter of Westminster v. Honsden. The plaintiff's bill must be dismissed as to the way, for it is a private right and [there should be a] trial at the common law.

225

Proby v. Curst

(Ch. 1718)

Where a devisor does not require a devisee to give security to act pursuant to the terms of the will, the court will not require security to be given.

Lincoln's Inn MS. Misc. 380, pt. 3, p. 174, pl. 2

An estate is charged with a portion and several debts and legacies. The owner, being about to make a jointure, recites in the deed that such and such things were paid off and that only £5000 remained unpaid, and, afterwards, he dies. This recital, not being on an account stated and the party interested not being a party to the deed, cannot be an estoppel, especially in this case where the fact is not true.

[There was a] devise of goods and money to A. for life and that A. should give them to B. at his death. B. brings this bill against A. to make him give security that there be no embezzlement.

The defendant answers that he had offered to give his bond.

Lord Chancellor [Lord Cowper]: The testator has entrusted the defendant and not required any security. Therefore, this court will not demand it. The defendant has offered his own bond. Therefore, let the bill be dismissed with costs. The defendant must give an inventory of goods in specie that are durable and of the value of those that are perishable.

226

Note

(Ch. 1718)

A court of equity will enforce a trust for the separate maintenance of a married woman.

Lincoln's Inn MS. Misc. 380, pt. 3, p. 174, pl. 3

On marriage, a separate maintenance is made in trust for the wife. The wife by her *prochein ami* brings her bill for the separate maintenance against the husband and the trustee. And [the court] decreed the maintenance to the wife.

227

Holder v. Holder

(Ch. 1718)

A devise must be made by positive, not negative, words.

Where there is no express trust, if a father purchase land in his son's name, it will be held to be a provision and advancement for such son.

8 Viner, Abr. 269

Hilary term 4 Geo. 1717[/18].

The father, in his will, taking notice that his son J. had much disobliged him, declares thus, 'I do hereby resolve not to give him any more than £20 a year for life to be paid him quarterly.'

N.B. This was a bastard son, to whom the father had by a former will given £80 a year, but, in the second will, he took notice of his ill behavior at the university and devises that estate to his legitimate son.

By the Master of the Rolls [JEKYLL], the bastard son shall take nothing by this will, the words not amounting to a devise.

[Other copies of this report: 2 Eq. Cas. Abr. 359, 22 E.R. 305.]

Lincoln's Inn MS. Misc. 380, pt. 3, p. 206, pl. 2

Trinity after term, 10 July 1718, before the Lord Chancellor [LORD PARKER].

The father has three sons, A., B., and C., and has lands in R., S., and T., and makes a voluntary settlement of R. to B. And afterwards, being displeased with B., he, the father, bargains and sells in consideration of £1000, but not paid, his lands in R. [and] S. to his son C., who recovered the lands. Afterwards, the father settles all the lands on A., his eldest son. And the father and A., the son, bring a bill suggesting that he, the father, was not of a disposing memory, having the gout in his head, when he settled the lands on B. Many letters passed between the father and [B], when he was in favor and possession, wherein the son expresses himself by saying 'our estate' and 'our harvest' etc., which gave a strong suspicion of a trust. The father dies, and A. revives the proceedings in his father's cause.

By the father's bill, it was insisted that the conveyance to B. was obtained by fraud. But now at the hearing, it was insisted to be a trust only for the father and that here was a *suggestio falsi*, for it is in consideration of £1000, which is agreed was never paid, and, though the father may make a voluntary gift to his son, yet, if that conveyance be such where money is necessary to be paid for the perfecting of it, there, the suggestion being false, the conveyance is void. And he cited

Englefield's Case by Chancellor Jeffries.[1] Sir John Englefield, seised for life, remainder to trustees to preserve contingent remainders, [remainder] to his entail, remainder to his brother Edward. Sir John Englefield and the trustees, before any son was born, in consideration of £1000, convey to Edward, the brother. Afterwards, Sir John Englefield has a son, Sir Charles Englefield, who brought his bill against Edward and the trustees and had a decree to have the estate because the suggestion in consideration of money was false. And Sir Charles enjoys the estate to this day.

On the other side, it was insisted, if a father purchase in his son's name, if there be no express trust, the court will intend it [to be] a provision and advancement for such son.

To which the Chancellor [Lord Parker] agreed.

Here, an heir at law or a devisee shall not come and say this was a fraudulent conveyance and a false suggestion; it is a purchaser only [who] has that liberty. And in this settlement, here is a reservation of an annuity of £100 *per annum* to the father and £20 *per annum* to a stranger, which shows it to be no trust.

Claverin v. Claverin,[2] cited, was confirmed in the House of Lords. A voluntary conveyance of lands in R. to A., his son, which the father kept by him in his study. Twenty years after, he makes another voluntary settlement of all his estate, and therein he gave other lands, being a larger estate, to his son A., and the lands before settled on A. he gives to his son B. It was decreed A. shall have both estates by the first and second settlements. And a case before his present honor [Jekyll], Easter term last, Waldred against Guillam;[3] A. makes a voluntary settlement on B. and keeps it locked up in his own possession. B. gets an attested copy of the settlement. Afterwards, A. burns the settlement and makes another voluntary settlement on C. It was decreed by Sir Joseph Jekyll that the first volunteer, who had an attested copy, should have the lands.

This bill is brought suggesting fraud. But now, that is waived, and it is now insisted to be a trust. We have not had an opportunity to make a defense as to that. We, possibly, might have given an answer to these letters had the plaintiff put us upon it by his bill.

Lord Chancellor [Lord Parker]: It seems to me to be impossible to make a decree when you have not so much as mentioned it to be a trust in your bill. The bill must be dismissed with costs.

---

[1] *Englefield v. Englefield* (1686–1691), 1 Vernon 443, 446, 23 E.R. 575, 576, 2 Vernon 236, 23 E.R. 753, 79 Selden Soc. 901, Lincoln's Inn MS. Misc. 557, f. 149, 1 Eq. Cas. Abr. 165, 281, 21 E.R. 961, 1046.

[2] *Clavering v. Clavering* (1704–1705), 2 Vernon 473, 23 E.R. 904, Precedents in Chancery 235, 24 E.R. 114, 7 Brown P.C. 410, 3 E.R. 267, 1 Eq. Cas. Abr. 24, 21 E.R. 845, 2 Eq. Cas. Abr. 351, 22 E.R. 299.

[3] *Naldred v. Gilham* (Ch. 1718–1719), see below, Case No. 237.

In this case, the father had given A., his servant, £20 to be paid him out of the estate when his son W. should recover the estate from his other son J.

Chancellor [Lord Parker]: He cannot be a witness unless he were paid or had released. Perhaps [it would be] otherwise if he had been a legatee generally out of the personal estate.

In this case, part of the consideration of the conveyance besides the £1000 was to enter into a bond to his brother-in-law of £1000 for his sister's portion and that he had actually entered into the bond and had paid the annuity.

228

Middleton v. Duke of Kingston

(Ch. 1718)

The question in this case was whether a fraudulent conveyance to shield property from forfeiture for an anticipated subsequent treason should be set aside for the benefit of the traitor's creditors or the property should be forfeited to the crown.

Lincoln's Inn MS. Misc. 380, pt. 3, p. 175, pl. 3

Middleton v. Duke of Kingston and Attorney General.

The late earl of Mar,[1] on his marriage with the lady Pierpoint, daughter of the duke of Kingston [1665–1726], had a term of years mortgaged to him for £10,000 of which the earl of Mar had a legal estate as to £8000 and the equity of redemption as to the rest, but, being much in debt, he bid his steward tell his creditors he would pay them out of this money when it should be paid to him. Afterwards, the 6th of August 1714, just before he went into Scotland, he executed a conveyance to Dr. Stragham, which was mentioned in the deed to be in consideration of £8000 paid, and the receipt of this money was endorsed on the back of the deed, but no money was actually paid. The earl had before this appointed his steward to state the accounts with his creditors and said what debts he allowed should be paid out of the mortgage. The earl, when he executed this deed, desired Stragham to acquaint the duke with what he had done, for he believed his [. . .] would call him into the country before the duke came to town. And, in a few days after, he went into Scotland. The earl, at the time of executing the deed, left a discharge to be given to the duke for the money. In October, Stragham assigned to the plaintiff a trust for himself and the other of the earl's creditors. The earl was attainted by Act of Parliament 10 January 1714[/15].[2]

[1] C. V. Ehrenstein, 'Erskine, John, bap. 1675, d. 1732', *Oxford Dictionary of National Biography*, vol. 18, pp. 552–558.

[2] Stat. 1 Geo. I, stat. 2, c. 32.

The bill is brought by the plaintiff for himself and the other creditors to have the benefit of the assignment.[1] The Attorney General in his answer insists on the forfeiture to the crown. The duke was ready to convey to whom the court should order.

Master of the Rolls [JEKYLL]: If, in this case, a bill had been brought against Stragham and the earl, putting the treason out of the case, then, if the defendant had admitted this parol declaration of the trust to be for the use of his creditors, I would have decreed it notwithstanding the Statute of Frauds[2] against parol declarations of trusts, for he said the Statute was intended against parol evidence of the declaration of trust, but it was admitted by the parties that the trust was so, and so the mischief intended to be prevented by the Statute was in view. And so it was determined soon after the making of that Statute in this court.[3] But the parties might plead and cover themselves by the Statute. But this case is different. The deed was made when he had intended treason in contemplation and the consideration of the deed was false, no money having been paid and what he said at that time was false that Stragham was to dispose of the money. It was said the forfeiture of the treason could relate but to the time mentioned in the attainder and not [. . .] process at common law, in which case, it relates to the time of the treason committed.

He would not deliver his opinion at present but said it was proper for the Court of Exchequer and that the Attorney General should file a bill of intrusion.

But the Attorney [General, *Northey*] said he should not trouble himself about it, for this was a proper jurisdiction to determine it. He cited the Case of the Marquess of Powys. He, soon after the Revolution, went into France and there made a conveyance of his estate for the benefit of creditors and, soon after, went into Ireland and was in the Rebellion and was tried in the Exchequer and the first verdict was that it was not a fraudulent conveyance to screen his estate from forfeiture, but there was a new trial and [it was] found that it was fraudulent, and [it was] so decreed.

---

1 Stat. 13 Eliz. I, c. 5 (*SR*, IV, 537–538).

2 Stat. 29 Car. II, c. 3 (*SR*, V, 839–842).

3 Perhaps *Potts v. Turvin* (1681), 79 Selden Soc. 856.

229
Starkey v. Brooks
(Ch. 1718)

In this case, the legacy to the executor was ordered to be paid out of the decedent's estate, and not out of the surplus.

Lincoln's Inn MS. Misc. 380, pt. 3, p. 177

Starkey v. Brooks, Lee, and Copper.

A bill [was exhibited] by the plaintiff as co-heir with the defendant Copper to Philip Starkey against Brooks and Lee, who were the executors of Philip Starkey, for an account of the real and the personal estate of Philip Starkey and that no more of the real estate might be sold than is necessary for the payment of the debts and legacies and that the surplus after that be a resulting trust for the heir at law. This was on a will; the words were:

> I give my manor of Statton in Cheshire to my executors hereinafter named and their heirs and assigns forever to be sold for the best price they can get by his executors or the survivor of them or the heirs of the survivor and the money raised by the sale and the clear rents and profits in the meantime to be paid towards the discharge of my own debts and the debts of my brother and the legacies given by my will for so much as my personal estate shall fall short of paying them.

In this will, he gave to the plaintiff, C. Starkey, £40 and gave £10 to the defendant Copper, the other co-heir, and £100 to Brooks, his executor, to be distributed by him among his children. He cited Crompton v. North, Chancery Cases; Gore v. Blake; Dockley v. Dockley. Parol proof was read in this case.[1]

Lord Cowper: It is a part of the trust that the legacy to the executor should be paid out of the estate, and it is not out of the surplus as was insisted. Every case stands on its own circumstance. Therefore, he did not mind the precedents cited. The heir, in this case that is, confessed and avoided though there is not a direct proof of the debt and yet the family had a notion that this sum was owing to this legacy is weakened by the proof of the opinion of the family that so much was due. The £10 legacy to the other co-heir is in the same thread with the like legacy given to his two brothers Coppers. So it is not a simple legacy given to the heir to exclude him from having more. But it is small legacy of the like sum given to the others. The proof [is] that it was offered to him by the drawer of the will to give

[1] *North v. Crompton* (1671), 1 Chancery Cases 196, 22 E.R. 759, also 1 Eq. Cas. Abr. 272, 21 E.R. 1040; *Gore v. Blake* (1668), 1 Chancery Cases 98, 22 E.R. 712, 1 Chancery Reports 263, 21 E.R. 568; *Docksey v. Docksey*, 2 Eq. Cas. Abr. 507, 22 E.R. 429 (Ch. 1708), 3 Brown P.C. 39, 1 E.R. 1163 (H.L. 1710).

the surplus to the executor, but he would not; then the drawer said then they will not take the trust. He still refused to do it though it was in order to make them take the trust. If he was minded to give it them, why did he not? [See] Compton v. North as to parol evidence. He gives his personal estate to be sold for the payment of his debts and legacies and funeral charges and the debts of his brother so far as the same will extend. That is the foundation of the trust. Then, as to the estate, describing it particularly, he gives the same to his executors by their name of office, 'to [his] executors hereinafter named, their heirs, and assigns forever, to be sold and disposed of.' So they were to sell the whole. If they were to take the surplus, he would have said they should sell only what was necessary to be sold. It is to be sold for the best price *bona fide* he could get now, one who is to be absolute owner. It would be sufficient if he executed the trust of sale, and he need not have been bound so strictly. It is not given as a reward for the executing of the trust, for it is given to them jointly and the survivor of them. This giving of it jointly so as the trust survives shows he did not design it to be beneficial for them. He would have taken care of them equally between them. If they were to have the surplus, why are they tied down to act *bona fide* [for] the best price they can get? Men are not in danger of cheating themselves. The money raised by such sale [is] not said so far as would be necessary, but they are to employ the whole money with the rents, issues, and profits to the discharge of the debts and legacies so that the declaration of trust is that they are to sell the whole and dispose of what arises, speaking generally. So they are excluded from taking a benefit if they are to pay the whole. This is different from the cases cited and is a most strong implication of the will for the heir at law. And it is tantamount to saying that they are trustees for the whole of any surplus.

The Master must take account first of the personal estate and so much as is necessary to be sold, and the heir at law [shall] join; if the personal estate will pay off all the debts and legacies, shall the executors have it to their own use. Costs [are to be paid] out of the estate on both sides.

[Other reports of this case: 1 Peere Williams 390, 24 E.R. 439, 2 Eq. Cas. Abr. 496, 22 E.R. 421.]

230
Marchant v. Rootes
(Ch. 1718)

A contract for a small consideration joined with love and affection is binding unless there was fraud and contrivance involved.

Lincoln's Inn MS. Misc. 380, pt. 3, p. 179

1 May 1718, before SIR JOSEPH JEKYLL.

Marchant, the plaintiff, in 1713, made her will and thereby gave several legacies and gave the residue to the defendant and made him executor. And in 1715, she made a bill of sale of all her estate, goods, etc. in consideration of 1s. paid and in consideration of love and gratitude towards the defendant, who heretofore had been serviceable to the plaintiff in lending her money and in managing her affairs etc. and on condition that Rootes should pay the legacies in her will. And it was then agreed that the defendant Rootes should give the plaintiff a bond conditioned to pay £10 *per annum* to the plaintiff during her life, which bond was afterwards executed and delivered to the plaintiff. The plaintiff was upwards of eighty years old at the time of making the bill of sale. Afterwards, both the will and bond came into the possession of the defendant, but, by what means, it did not appear. And the plaintiff in her bill does not pray a discovery how they came to his hands.

The plaintiff brings her bill to be relieved against this voluntary gift. For the plaintiff, it was said, first, the plaintiff was extremely old and therefore easily to be imposed on; secondly, the recompense which was the £10 *per annum* was come into the possession and thereby in her power to defeat it, which is a strong badge of fraud; thirdly, this annuity was not to commence until six months after and the plaintiff had bereft herself of everything and [had] nothing to subsist on in the meantime, and this bond was not given at the time of the bill of sale.

It was answered for the defendant, first, though the plaintiff was old, yet it fully appears that she was of perfect understanding. The deed was read over to her, and she was fully satisfied therewith. And, as the plaintiff has not sought a discovery how the will and bond came into the defendant's possession, therefore, [she] cannot take advantage of that circumstance. And the plaintiff had formerly experienced the kindness of the defendant, so she still depended upon that for her subsistence until the six months.

Master of the Rolls [JEKYLL]: As to the unequal consideration in a deed to the thing granted, we must distinguish where it is a bargain driven; then, if the consideration appear to be grossly unequal, there is color for this court to interpose. And, where the consideration is joined with love and affection, here, unless there be fraud and contrivance, it is always binding. I cannot relieve the plaintiff, for, though she be old, yet it appears she was of perfect understanding. And it plainly appears that she had a great esteem for the defendant, both at the time of making her will, which continued for some years after the making the bill of sale.

231

Corsham v. Dudley

(Ch. 1718)

A settlement can be a satisfaction for a legacy received by the settlor for the benefit of the beneficiary of the settlement.

Lincoln's Inn MS. Misc. 380, pt. 3, p. 180

Easter term 4 Geo. [1718], in Chancery.

A suit [was filed] in the spiritual court for a legacy devised and due thirty-five years since. The plaintiff brings this bill and shows an equitable satisfaction after this manner. The executor paid the legacy to the legatee's father, who indemnified the executor. After[wards], the father, on his son's marriage, settles land on him of greater value than the legacy. At the hearing, the plaintiff produced a receipt given by the legatee on payment on the legacy twenty years since.

The defendant said then the plaintiff ought to have brought this bill for the receipt, and payment had been a proper plea of the spiritual court. Then, the plaintiff waived the receipt and relied on the equitable satisfaction by the father's settlement.

The Master of the Rolls [Jekyll] decreed that a satisfaction for the legacy. The representative of the father ought to have been made a party to the suit.

232

Sparman v. Place

(Ch. 1718)

A secured creditor has priority over the prior creditors of his debtor of whom had no notice when he lent his money but not over those of whom he did have notice.

Lincoln's Inn MS. Misc. 380, pt. 3, p. 181

A., mortgagee, purchases in several after encumbrances without notice of B.'s mesne encumbrance, and, after, he purchased the equity of redemption. At the end of the purchaser's deed, several particular encumbrances are recited, the equity of redemption of all which are granted and of all other his mortgaged estate and after[wards]. A. purchases in afterwards other encumbrances.

The Master [of the Rolls, Jekyll] decreed that A. should be satisfied the encumbrances bought in before the purchase of the equity of redemption, having no notice of B.'s encumbrance. But the encumbrances taken in afterwards shall not have preference to B.'s mortgage, for A., by the purchase deed, had notice of other encumbrances by the words 'and of all other his mortgaged estate'; otherwise, if particular encumbrances had been recited without those general words.

It was objected in this case that, if the encumbrances bought in by A. before his purchase of the equity were bought at an under rate, he ought to be allowed no more than what he actually gave for them, for it is not reasonable that A. should be the gainer and B., an honest creditor who had preference to these after encumbrances, should by A.'s purchasing them be defeated of his whole debt.

And a case in Salkeld was cited by the contrary side, where a difference is taken where a trustee or executor buys in at an under rate and where a man acts in his own right.

233

Wade's Case

(Ch. 1718)

Legacies for portions for younger children who have no other maintenance carry interest from the testator's death.

Lincoln's Inn MS. Misc. 380, pt. 3, p. 182, pl. 1

[Where] portions [are given] to younger children by a legacy, who have no other maintenance, the legacies shall carry interest from the death of the testator.

[Where] administration is granted to the wrong persons, they are administrators in trust for him that has right.

234

Chancey v. Wootton

(Ch. 1718–1720)

A legacy given to a creditor is a satisfaction of the debt.

Lincoln's Inn MS. Misc. 380, pt. 3, p. 182, pl. 2

Before the Master of the Rolls, Sir Joseph Jekyll, Hilary term at Lincoln's Inn Hall after term. Cheny v. Wooton.

Kenrick gives a bond to Wooten, his servant, for £100 in consideration of her faithful service, she having served him several years and had no wages paid her and her wages amounted to £70. After[wards], Kendrick dies, and, by his will, he gives her £500 in consideration of her good services. The executor had a very considerable residue.

The Master [of the Rolls, Jekyll] decreed that the £500 legacy should go in satisfaction of the bond debt.

Barnard, solicitor, in this case: Part of the £70 was but money [. . .] by Wooten.

Lincoln's Inn MS. Misc. 11, p. 5

Hilary term 1719[/20], at Lincoln's Inn Hall.

Mr. Kendrick had a housekeeper, to whom he owed about £100 for wages. He gave her his bond to pay her £100 with interest. Afterwards, he makes his will and gives her £500 for her faithful services, and he makes Mr. Chancey executor.

Mr. Chancey pays the bond debt but refuses to pay the legacy on a pretense that she got some of the assets into her hands and converted them, and, thereupon, he brings his bill for a discovery. And she brings a cross-bill for her legacy.

Upon the hearing, it was insisted by Mr. Chancey's counsel, though not in issue in the cause, it not being mentioned either in his bill or answer, that the legacy was a satisfaction of the debt.

And so it was decreed to be, though not insisted on in the pleadings.

Lincoln's Inn MS. Misc. 384, p. 35

Kendrick, by his will, gave the defendant, his housekeeper, a legacy for her faithful service charged on land, and he was indebted to her by bond in a less sum, which the plaintiff, the executor, had paid and had not in his bill charged it to be a satisfaction.

Yet the Master of the Rolls [Jekyll] was of opinion it was a satisfaction of the bond debt.

10 Modern 399, 88 E.R. 781

A servant maid had lived long in a place without receiving any wages. Her wages were at last by the master computed to amount to £100, and a bond was given for the same. The master, soon after dying, gave her a legacy of £500, which he thus expressed, 'for her faithful services'.

Now, it was said that, this bond being for the money due for her service and this legacy being given her for her faithful services, it was plain that the testator intended this legacy in satisfaction of all that was due to her.

[Other reports of this case: 1 Peere Williams 408, 24 E.R. 448, Select Cases *tempore* King 44, 25 E.R. 213, 2 Eq. Cas. Abr. 354, 22 E.R. 301.]

235

Richardson v. Sprag

(Ch. 1718)

A devise to children and grandchildren will be paid per capita.

Lincoln's Inn MS. Misc. 10, p. 244

Easter 1718. Before Sir Joseph Jekyll, Master of the Rolls.

Elizabeth Sprag, by will, gives freehold and copyhold lands to such of her daughter or daughter's children as should be living at the death of her son James Roberts.

The question was whether the children of the daughters that died in the life of the son should take equally with the surviving daughters.

It was decreed that the grandchildren of the daughters who were dead should take equally with the surviving daughters of the testatrix. *Vide* Peirce and Hunt, Pol. 645.[1]

[Other reports of this case: 1 Peere Williams 434, 24 E.R. 460, 2 Eq. Cas. Abr. 368, 22 E.R. 313.]

236

Anonymous

(Ch. 1718)

Parol evidence is not admissible to vary the words of a will.

Where an executor uses money belonging to a decedent's estate, he must pay interest at the legal rate of interest.

Lincoln's Inn MS. Misc. 380, pt. 3, p. 182, pl. 3

Easter term 4 Geo. [1718], before the Lord Chancellor Parker, in the Inner Temple Hall.

A man makes his will and begins 'as to the disposition of all my worldly estate' and therein devises a legacy of £500 to A. and makes A. his executor. A bill [was exhibited] against A. to account, and he submits to account for the residue. [There was] parol proof that the testator directed the scrivener to give the residue of his estate to his executor and the scrivener told the testator that would go to him of course and would look like ignorance in him to insert such a clause.

[1] *Price v. Hunt* (Ex. 1684), Pollexfen 645, 86 E.R. 674, Dodd 53, 289, also Lincoln's Inn MS. Misc. 557, ff. 46, 68, 81, Georgetown Univ. Law Lib. MS. B88–7, pp. 505, 532, 565.

This was a special report made by the Master on the account taken. But the parol proof was not referred to him.

Mr. *Cowper* cited the case of Littlebury v. Buckley, in the House of Lords,[1] and said that the judgment of the House in that case was founded on this distinction that, at the common law, the residue goes to the executor, and the ancient practice of the Court of Chancery was so too, but, afterwards, forty or fifty decrees were that, if the executor had a specific legacy, he should not have the residuum, and, in that case, the Lord Guernsey said that parol proof ought to be admitted to prove that the testator intended the executor should have the residuum, because this was in support of the common law and, since that, parol proof has always been admitted.

Lord Parker: We cannot now consider this case otherwise than as it was directed to the Master. Therefore, the parol proof cannot now be admitted, and the defendant has submitted away his residue. And I must confess I am strongly biased for the defendant. Therefore, the defendant shall be satisfied both his debt and legacy before he shall account for the residue.

It was decreed that, in regard the executor had money paid to him which he employed in the way of his trade, he should account for the largest interest, *viz.* 6 percent, the course of interest at that time. And it was asserted that this was the constant practice after the parties had compromised matters in court.

The defendant was debtee, legatee, and executor.

I was in court, but could not hear well, but Mr. Bartie reported the case to me.

237

Naldred v. Gilham

(Ch. 1718–1719)

A court of equity will not give a remedy to a donee but will leave the parties to their remedies at common law.

Lincoln's Inn MS. Misc. 384, p. 26, pl. 1

9 May 1718.

A bill [was brought] to have the benefit of a prior voluntary settlement which had been destroyed by Catherine Naldrett, who made it, and of which the plaintiff had a copy.

The Master of the Rolls [Jekyll] decreed that the plaintiff shall hold against the defendant and his heirs. But this [is] not to prejudice the question whether the defendant's wife be entitled to dower, she not being before the court.

---

[1] *Buckley v. Littlebury* (1711), 3 Brown P.C. 43, 1 E.R. 1165, 1 Eq. Cas. Abr. 245, 21 E.R. 1021, also 2 Vernon 677, 23 E.R. 1040, Lincoln's Inn MS. Misc. 10, p. 86.

Ayloffe, for the plaintiff, quoted Clavering and Clavering's case, in the House of Lords, in January 1705, that a prior voluntary conveyance takes the place of a subsequent; the same case [was] between Goodwin and Goodwin, Ch. Rep. 173.[1]

Lincoln's Inn MS. Misc. 11, p. 37

12 December 1718.

The plaintiff's aunt, he being then an infant of about ten years of age, makes a voluntary settlement to the use of herself for life, remainder to the plaintiff in fee without a power of revocation. She keeps both parts of the settlement in her own custody and, about seven years afterwards, cancels them. And she makes a second settlement, which was also voluntary, to the use of herself for life, remainder to the defendant in fee, and she delivers the last settlement to the defendant together with the title deeds. Sometime after this, the defendant being about to marry the daughter of Mr. Toriano, it was proposed by Mr. Toriano to give his daughter £2000 portion in case the defendant could make it appear that he was worth £4000, in order to which he produced the second settlement. And it appearing that the estate of his aunt was settled upon him in reversion after her death, Mr. Toriano was satisfied, and the marriage proceeded.

The aunt being dead, the plaintiff brought his bill to be relieved against the second settlement. And having produced a copy of the first settlement and proved it to be a true copy, the court, upon hearing the cause, conceived that the cancelling the first settlement was fraudulent and decreed the second settlement and all the deeds and writing to be delivered up to the plaintiff.

And now, it came on upon an appeal to Lord Chancellor [Lord Parker].

And it was insisted on for the defendant by Mr. *Vernon* that this court ought not to aid any person who claims under a voluntary settlement, but leave him to [the common] law.

In the case of Stapleton and Stapleton, in Lord North's time, the plaintiff, claiming under a voluntary settlement, brought his bill for a discovery of some matters which he wanted in order to make out his title against the devisee of the tenant in tail under the settlement, who, without suffering a recovery, had disposed of the estate by his will, and the court would not assist the plaintiff in that case.

As to the case of Clavering and Clavering, which was much relied on in the other side and, upon the authority of which case, it was said this decree was made, it was said that Sir John Clavering, who claimed under the voluntary settlement, did not come for the assistance of a court of equity to make good the

[1] *Clavering v. Clavering* (1704–1705), 2 Vernon 473, 23 E.R. 904, Precedents in Chancery 235, 24 E.R. 114, 7 Brown P.C. 410, 3 E.R. 267, 1 Eq. Cas. Abr. 24, 21 E.R. 845, 2 Eq. Cas. Abr. 351, 22 E.R. 299; *Goodwin v. Goodwin* (1658), 1 Chancery Reports 173, 21 E.R. 451, also 1 Eq. Cas. Abr. 23, 21 E.R. 845.

settlement; no, he was a defendant, and it was the devisee under the will who came to be relieved against this settlement, and, therefore, that case was no authority to support the present decree.

And by Mr. *Williams*, who argued on the same side, was cited the Case of Sturvater and Robinson, November 1716,[1] which was thus. A man made a settlement upon a bastard son to take effect after his death, and he covenants for himself and his heirs to make further assurance, and he dies. After his death, it appearing the settlement was not good at law, the bastard son brought his bill against the heir at law for a specific performance of the covenants, but the settlement being purely voluntary, the court would not decree a performance of the covenant but dismissed the bill and left the plaintiff to bring his action at law upon the covenant.

And so, he insisted the plaintiff ought to be left in the principal cause. He ought to try his title at law, for, if the copy of the settlement is evidence in this court, it will be so at law and, if it is not so at law, it ought not to be good evidence here.

And of that opinion, the Lord Chancellor [LORD PARKER] seemed to be, for he did not see there was any equity in the case whereon to ground a decree in favor of the plaintiff, and, if it was tried at law, he believed it would appear the copy of the settlement was not fairly obtained, for it appeared fully upon the proofs that the woman, notwithstanding the first settlement, looked upon it that she had power over the estate and it is pretty strange it should not appear throughout this cause how the plaintiff came to get this copy.

He said he thought the rule mentioned by Mr. Vernon that this court would not assist a volunteer was right. Suppose the plaintiff had brought his bill in the life of his aunt for an injunction to stay waste, suggesting she was committing waste and praying a discovery of the settlement. Would this court have assisted him? Surely no.

Upon the whole, he seemed inclinable to dismiss the plaintiff's bill and leave him to make the best of his case at law. But he said he would be attended with the case of Clavering and Clavering and see how far he was tied up by that precedent. 17 November 1719.

The Lord Chancellor [LORD PARKER] delivered his opinion and dismissed the bill with costs, it appearing that the plaintiff's aunt kept both parts of the first settlement in her own custody and it being very probably that the plaintiff got the copy by some undue means.

Lincoln's Inn MS. Misc. 384, p. 95, pl. 2

12 December; rehearing.

[1] Note *Studevil v. Robinson* (1719), see below, Case No. 418.

Lutwyche, for the plaintiff: At the Rolls, the case of Clavering and Clavering governed this case. The plaintiff, nephew of Katherine Naldrett, brings his bill to have the benefit of a prior voluntary settlement, which had been cancelled, supposed by Katherine Naldrett, who made it, there being no power of revocation and the plaintiff having proved a copy of the deed dated 16th February 1707. The deed under which the defendant claims is dated in October 1713. The first deed [was] Katherine Naldrett in consideration of natural love and affection and 10s. to stand seised to the use of the plaintiff, her nephew, and his heirs.

Cowper: Clavering and Clavering, the same case, [was] affirmed upon an appeal. A voluntary settlement kept secret by the person who made it [is] yet good against a subsequent voluntary settlement.

Ayloffe: Here, the question is between two voluntary settlements, and the first should take place. Goding and Goding, 1 Ch. Rep. 173, 192.[1] The cancelling of the deed does not destroy the title. Ingram and Withers, December 1717.

Raymond, for the plaintiff: This decree is grounded on a supposed fraud, and we are condemned in costs. If there is no fraud, they ought to go to law and not have the assistance of a court of equity. The same evidence to establish the deed here will be good at law. The rule of evidence is the same. Clavering and Clavering differs, for, there, the deed was subsisting, only kept secret.

Vernon: It is a known rule that a court of equity will not assist a voluntary conveyance. [It is] quite different from Clavering and Clavering, where the plaintiff did not come for the aid of this court but only for a discovery as not having the first deed in his hand, and the deed being in the defendant's hands, Lord Keeper Wright only decreed him to produce it at a trial at law. Here Katherine Naldrett, who made the settlement, might have mortgaged or sold it and there had been no fraud. Stapleton and Stapleton, 1673.

Williams: Katherine Naldrett intended to have power over the settlement and, being ignorant of the law, employs an attorney to prepare it, but he does not insert any power of revocation. It is proved, when her will was drawn and she was informed she could not dispose of this estate, she was much surprised and said she then had been imposed upon. She had the power to have settled it on the marriage of her nephew, and his marriage took effect on the confidence of this settlement. A court of equity will not assist a volunteer either to supply livery of seisin or an attornment or a surrender, as, in November 1716, in [*blank*] v. Robinson,[2] where there was a customary estate, which passed the deed and surrender settled on a bastard son by deed, but no surrender and, not being good at law, this court would not help it though there was a covenant for further assurance and only against a remote male heir.

---

1 *Goodwin v. Goodwin* (1658), *ut supra*; *Bingham v. Hussey* (1660–1661), 1 Chancery Reports 192, 21 E.R. 547.

2 Note *Studevil v. Robinson* (Ch. 1719), see below, Case No. 418.

[The] proof [was that] the first deed was cancelled two years before the date of the second and a will intervening. In 1715, the defendant married with the daughter of Torians, who declared his daughter should not marry the defendant unless he made out that he was worth £4000, and his estate under this settlement was valued at £1100 and the lady's fortune £2000.

Lutwyche, in reply: If Katherine Naldrett by law could not destroy this settlement, there being no power of revocation, then she was guilty of a fraud. In Stursaire and Robinson, the settlement was defective in point of law, and the custom [was] not observed. Here was once a good settlement, and it was unlawful to cancel it. It is different from the cases of subsequent purchasers or mortgagees.

Cowper: If there had been a power of revocation and that power not strictly pursued, the second deed had not been good, either at law or in equity. At the time of executing the deed, [there were] no thoughts of the defendant's marriage. Therefore [there was] no consideration.

Lord Chancellor [Lord Parker]: It is very necessary to look into the case of Clavering and Clavering. If it is in point, the Master of the Rolls was bound by it. But there is a great difference between assisting a voluntary settlement and setting one aside. I always understood the rule to be that, where it is merely voluntary, *omne gratuitum*, this court will not interpose unless there had been fraud. Could a bill have been brought against Katherine Naldrett herself for discovery of this deed, or, if it were not with impeachment of waste and she had committed waste, would this court hinder her? This case is not fully before the court. Suppose she had given directions to the attorney who drew the deed to leave it in her power to dispose of the estate otherwise and he had been as wise as the person who drew the will and had told her that she might destroy the deed, it had been a fraud upon her. Here does not appear any ground of equity, for, if the copy of the deed is evidence here, it is the same at law. Nay, sometimes that is evidence to a jury which would not be so here. Anciently, a deed was not looked upon as effectual until delivered to the party. It will appear upon a trial, how the plaintiff came by this copy which will be material if the bill is retained until the copy is established at law. It may be proper to quiet the possession by an injunction of this court. I will look into the case of Clavering and Clavering before I direct a trial.

Afterwards, 17th of November 1719, the Lord Chancellor dismissed the bill.

Lincoln's Inn MS. Misc. 384, p. 198

17 November 1719.

The bill was to have the benefit of a prior voluntary settlement whereby Katherine Naldrett had settled her estate on the plaintiff, her nephew, in fee after her own death without a power of revocation. Afterwards, she cancelled this deed, which was dated 16th of February 1707, and settled her estate on the defendant by a deed dated in October 1713.

J. Cole proves he saw Katherine Naldrett execute the first deed whereby she covenanted to stand seised to the use of herself for life, remainder to the plaintiff and his heirs and that the plaintiff's father, three years after, brought this deed to him and that he made two copies, one of which is proved in the cause.

On the other side, there was a strong presumption that Katherine Naldrett intended to have power over her estate. It is proved that, when her will was made and she was told she could not dispose of this estate, she was much surprised and said she had been imposed upon. And then she cancelled this deed and settled the estate on the defendant.

Lord Chancellor [Lord Parker]: I am convinced in my conscience that Catherine Naldrett thought she had power to dispose of her estate and there not being inserted a power of revocation was an imposition upon her. Here, the two copies were made by the direction of the plaintiff's father, which shows he was afraid she would cancel this deed. And nobody had the confidence to ask her in her lifetime for one of the copies. Both deeds are voluntary, and here is no fraud that equity should interpose. If this bill had been brought against Catherine Naldrett to compel her to bring the deed into court as belonging to the plaintiff's inheritance and she had insisted that she was imposed upon and always intended to have her estate in her own power, would this court decree for the plaintiff? This is not a fit case for equity to interpose.

[I will] dismiss this bill without costs.

[Other reports of this case: 1 Peere Williams 577, 24 E.R. 525, 2 Eq. Cas. Abr. 52, 287, 22 E.R. 45, 241.]

238

Burnett v. Theobalds

(Ch. 1718)

A court of equity can decree the quiet enjoyment of a watercourse.

Lincoln's Inn MS. Misc. 10, p. 227

The plaintiff, being lessee for twenty-one years under a lease for 1000 granted of the manor house of Stockwell and a conduit of water and the pipes and water coming from the conduit to the house and being interrupted by the defendant who had enlarged his wash house and thereby taken in a force cock which was made about twenty years ago for the forcing water down to the house, brought his bill for an injunction to be quieted in that enjoyment of this watercourse.

And the defendant claiming no right to the watercourse but insisting on an agreement by the plaintiff to permit him to make use of the water, which he could not prove, it was decreed that the plaintiff should quietly enjoy this watercourse and should be permitted to go into the defendant's wash house not only to remove the branch of the pipe which the defendant had laid but likewise from time to time at all seasonable times to amend the main pipes and force cock as there should be occasion. The defendant was decreed to pay costs.

The like decrees were made for the quiet enjoyment of watercourses in the case of Lord Guernsey[1] and also in the case of Dr. Sloane for an ancient watercourse at Chelsea.

[Later proceedings in this case: 1 Peere Williams 609, 24 E.R. 538, 2 Eq. Cas. Abr. 280, 22 E.R. 236.]

239

Cotton v. Cotton

(Ch. 1718)

Where a maintenance for a child is to be raised after the commencement of a future term, it cannot be raised presently by a sale of the reversion.

Even in the case of a hardship, a court cannot re-write a person's contract.

Lincoln's Inn MS. Misc. 10, p. 261

10 May 1718. Cotton *et al.*, younger children of Sir Thomas Cotton, plaintiffs; Sir Robert Salisbury Cotton, eldest son of Sir Thomas Cotton, *et al.*, defendants.

Sir Robert Cotton, the plaintiffs' grandfather, settles lands by indentures dated 17 July 1701, the uses whereof as to part were to Sir Thomas, his son, for life, then to his wife for life, remainder to trustees for 500 years, remainder to the defendants in tail male, with remainders over.

The trusts of the term were that, in case Sir Thomas Cotton should die leaving any younger child or children by him begotten on the body of his wife which should be living at his death, then it should be lawful for the trustees, out of the rents of the said estate limited for the said term or by lease thereof for the said 500 years or by the felling of timber or by any other means, as they should think fit and for the advantage of such child or children, to raise such sums of money for the portions of such child or children and pay the same in the manner following, *viz.*, if there should be but one younger child, then £3000 should be raised for such younger child and, if there should be two or more such younger children, then £5000 should be raised and be equally divided between them; if daughters, at eighteen or marriage and, if sons, at twenty-one, and, until such portions should be payable and paid, to raise for such only child £60 a year for his or her maintenance and education, but, if more than one, then to raise and pay them the yearly sum of £50 apiece by equal half-yearly payments at Lady Day

[1] *Lord Guernsey v. Rodbridges* (1708), Gilbert Rep. 3, 25 E.R. 3, 2 Eq. Cas. Abr. 518, 22 E.R. 437.

and Michaelmas, the first payment to be made at the first of the said days which should happen after the commencement of the said term.

Sir Thomas Cotton died leaving his wife and nine younger children, having made his will and some provision for them out of his personal estate after the death of his wife, who is yet living. The plaintiff Philadelphia has attained her age of eighteen, and she and the rest of the younger children bring their bill against the defendant, their elder brother and the trustees of the term. Philadelphia insists that, her portion being become payable, it ought to be raised by the sale of the reversionary term and be paid to her together with the arrears of the £50 a year maintenance from the death of her father. And the rest of the plaintiffs insist upon the like maintenance. And, the better to support the demand of maintenance, it was urged on the behalf of the plaintiffs that they had no other provision in the present but by the settlement and that it could never be the intention of Sir Robert Cotton when he made this provision for the younger children that they should be destitute of a maintenance until their portions should become payable.

Master of the Rolls [Jekyll]: As to the plaintiff Philadelphia's share of the £5000, she having attained eighteen, I am of opinion it ought to be raised out of the reversionary term with interest from the time it became payable though the Lady Cotton is still living. And let the Master see what part of the trust estate is proper to be sold or mortgaged for that purpose.

But, as to the point of maintenance, I am of opinion there is no pretense for it, the settlement being express that the first payment of the maintenance is to be made at the first of the days of payment which should happen next after the commencement of the term, which term by the settlement does not nor can commence until after the death of My Lady Cotton, who is living.

As to the hardship of the case in respect of the plaintiffs, this court cannot take that into consideration but must judge upon settlements as they find them and as the parties have thought fit to make them. It would be to no purpose to make deeds if this court should construe them according to what may be for the convenience or inconvenience of the parties.

Lincoln's Inn MS. Misc. 384, p. 26

10 May.

Where a maintenance for a child is to be raised after the commencement of a future term, it cannot be raised presently by a sale of the reversion. See Graves v. Mattison, 2 Jon.; Corbett v. Maidwell, 201, in Salkeld 159.[1]

---

[1] *Greaves v. Mattison* (1682), T. Jones 201, 84 E.R. 1216, also Skinner 38, 90 E.R. 19, 1 Eq. Cas. Abr. 336, 21 E.R. 1085; *Corbett v. Maidwell* (1709–1710), 1 Salkeld 159, 91 E.R. 147, also 3 Chancery Reports 190, 21 E.R. 764, 2 Vernon 640, 655, 23 E.R. 1019, 1027, 1 Eq. Cas. Abr. 337, 21 E.R. 1086.

240

Marks v. Marks

(Ch. 1718)

An executory devise, a possibility, and a condition in a devisee can pass to the devisee's heirs and personal representatives.

Lincoln's Inn MS. Misc. 384, p. 27, pl. 2

12 May 1718.

William Marks, by his will in 1697, devised the premises to his wife Ann for life and, after her death, to his second son, Daniel, and his heirs provided and upon condition that, if Nathaniel, his third son, should within three months after the death of Ann pay £500 to Daniel, his executors, or administrators, then he gives and devises it to Nathaniel and his heirs. Nathaniel dies in the life of Ann.

The heir of Nathaniel brings his bill within three months after the death of Ann to be admitted to pay the £500.

Powys, for the plaintiff: At law, the heir is entitled to perform the condition and may make the tender when a time is limited. Co. Litt. 206; 1 Ch. Ca. 89.[1]

Mead, for the defendant: This is a condition precedent and is become impossible by the act of God, and a court of equity will never relieve in such a case unless the party who is to take advantage hinders the performance. Bertie v. Lord Faulkland, 3 Ch. Ca. 135.[2] This was but a possibility in Nathaniel, which he cannot convey or devise.

N. argued before the Lord Chancellor 20 May. See *Liber Decretorum* 56.

Master of the Rolls [Jekyll]: I think this is not a condition because the heir cannot enter, but it is an executory devise. Loyd v. Carew, Ca. Parl. 137; Brett v. Rigden, Plow, 341.[3]

Raymond, for the plaintiff: Executory devises came in about Queen Elizabeth's time. The first case was Hainsworth and Pretty, Cr. El. 833, Moor. 644,[4] which was before Pells v. Brown, Cro. Jac. 590.[5] A possibility may descend or

---

[1] E. Coke, *First Institute* (1628), f. 206; *Wallis v. Crimes* (1667), 1 Chancery Cases 89, 22 E.R. 708, also 1 Eq. Cas. Abr. 107, 21 E.R. 916.

[2] *Bertie v. Lord Falkland* (Ch. 1698), 3 Chancery Cases 129, 22 E.R. 1008, note also above, Case No. 101.

[3] *Floyd v. Cary* (1697), Shower P.C. 137, 1 E.R. 93, also 2 Freeman 218, 22 E.R. 1170, Precedents in Chancery 72, 106, 24 E.R. 35, 51, 1 Eq. Cas. Abr. 260, 21 E.R. 1032; *Brett v. Rigden* (1568), 1 Plowden 340, 75 E.R. 516.

[4] *Haynsworth v. Pretty* (1601–1603), Croke Eliz. 833, 919, 78 E.R. 1059, 1140, Moore K.B. 644, 72 E.R. 813.

[5] *Pell v. Brown* (1620), Croke Jac. 590, 79 E.R. 504, also Palmer 131, 81 E.R. 1012, 2 Rolle Rep. 196, 216, 81 E.R. 746, 760, Godbolt 282, 78 E.R. 165, J. Bridgman 1, 123

may be released, though it cannot be assigned. It was said by Lord Cowper that, if a condition precedent will admit of an equivalent, there is no difference between a condition precedent and subsequent. Purefoy v. Rogers, 2 Sand. 380.[1]

Master of the Rolls [JEKYLL]: A man cannot grant or even release an executory devise before it is executed; therefore, it may be distinguished from a possibility. This is not a limitation because the fee passes. Lampet's Case, 10 Co. 50;[2] Earl of Essex's Case. Here, it did not vest in the ancestor, not being executed. How then can it descend or how can the heir take as a purchaser?

The Case of Leister v. Cockroft, in this court, was referred to the judges whether an estate was to arise to the issue after the death of the husband who left a wife *enceinte*. The question was whether it could vest in the infant *in ventre sa mere*. It was adjudged it did.

You may speak to this case before the Lord Chancellor.

Lincoln's Inn MS. Misc. 384, p. 56

20 May 1718.

Sir Thomas Powys, for the plaintiff: The case [is thus]. William Marks, being seised in fee and having issue three sons, Theodore, Daniel, and Nathaniel, by his will the 12th April 1697, devises in these words:

> I give the premises to my wife Ann for her life and, after her death, to my son Daniel and his heirs provided and upon this condition, that, if my son Nathaniel shall within three months after the death of my wife Ann pay or cause to be paid to Daniel, his executors, administrators, or assigns the sum of £500, then I give and devise the premises to Nathaniel and his heirs.

Nathaniel dies in the life of Ann. Daniel, on his marriage, makes a settlement of the premises, under which some of the defendants claim, and also [there is a] mortgage to other defendants. But they having notice of the plaintiff's title can be in no better case than Daniel himself.

The question is whether the plaintiff, who is heir to Nathaniel, can now gain the estate by paying the £500 to Daniel, having brought his bill for that purpose within three months after the death of Ann.

We are opposed by the defendants upon this notion, that [only the] father ought to have paid the money and, he dying before the time of payment, we cannot have the benefit of this devise. But I hope we shall, for, first, this was origi-

---

E.R. 1157.

[1] *Purefoy v. Rogers* (1671), 2 Williams Saunders 380, 85 E.R. 1181, also 2 Levinz 39, 83 E.R. 443, 3 Keble 11, 84 E.R. 566, 1 Eq. Cas. Abr. 189, 21 E.R. 980, Lincoln's Inn MS. Misc. 500, ff. 192, 194b.

[2] *Lampet's Case* (1612), 10 Coke Rep. 46b, 77 E.R. 994, *sub nom. Lampit v. Starkey*, 2 Brownlow & Goldesborough 172, 123 E.R. 880.

nally a good limitation though it is not within the compass of a single life. The first case upon an executory devise was Fulmerston's, quoted in Pells and Brown, Cr. Jac. 590. But Loyd v. Carew, Cas. Parl. 137, proves this a good limitation. That case was upon a deed; this is upon a will, which is much stronger.

[As to] this objection that this was personal to Nathaniel, but it is not, for here is no laches and a time is first. Lit., sec. 334; a feoffment to A. and his heirs upon condition that the feoffor at such time pay such a sum to A., that he may re-enter; though the feoffor may die before the day, yet his heir may tender the money. Therefore, it is not personal. So sec. 336; a feoffment upon condition that the feoffee, at such a day, shall pay; if he alien, the alienee may tender.[1]

This is a devise to Nathaniel and his heirs; consequently, his heir is entitled to the benefit of the condition. Here was an interest vested in the father. Therefore, this is not to make the heir a purchaser. Contingencies or possibilities may descend to an heir. If a man, before the Statute *de Donis*,[2] had made a feoffment to one and the heir of his body, there was a possibility of a reverter in the feoffor, which would descend. There may be an executory devise of a chattel, as M. Maning's Case, 8 Co. 94, to A. for life, remainder to B. was a possibility in B.; Lampet's Case, 10 Co. 50.[3] So, there may be a contingent fee upon a fee, which, being in the ancestor, may descend to the heir. The contingency, indeed, was not fulfilled in the time of the ancestor, but yet the contingency itself was in him. Shelley's Case, 1 Co. 98.[4] And what the heir takes, what might have vested in the ancestor, he shall take by descent, though it originally vested in the heir. So is Wood's Case, there quoted 99a;[5] A. covenanted with B. that, when C. enfeoffed him, he would stand seised to the use of B. and his heirs; B. dies before the feoffment, yet the heir of B. shall be adjudged too late in the course and nature of descent, yet there was neither right, title, use, or action in B., but only a possibility of a use, which could not be released or discharged by B., but, because, if the condition had been performed, it might have vested in the ancestor, therefore, the heir shall claim by descent.

So in Chapman's Case, there quoted 98, Plow. 284;[6] A. covenants with C. to make him a lease for twenty-one years; before the lease was made, C. dies, and the lease was made to the executors so that the term first vested in them, yet it was assets in their hands. If it had vested in C. and the act of God making it im-

---

1 T. Littleton, *Tenures*, ss. 334, 336.

2 Stat. 13 Edw. I, Westminster II, c. 1 (*SR*, I, 71).

3 *Clark v. Manning* (1609), 8 Coke Rep. 94, 77 E.R. 618; *Lampet's Case* (1612), *ut supra*.

4 *Wolfe v. Shelley* (1581), 1 Coke Rep. 88, 76 E.R. 199, also 1 Anderson 69, 123 E.R. 358, Moore K.B. 136, 72 E.R. 490, Jenkins 249, 145 E.R. 176, 3 Dyer 373, 73 E.R. 838.

5 *Wood's Case* (Wards 1560 x 1561), 1 Coke Rep. 99, 76 E.R. 222.

6 *Chapman v. Dalton* (1565), 1 Plowden 284, 75 E.R. 434.

possible to be performed according to the strict words, it was to be done as near as it could be.

In the present case, the land is proved worth but £1000, which must be looked upon as devised to Nathaniel but first to be a security to Daniel for £500, it being plain that the devisor intended his younger sons £500 apiece. So in Wallis v. Crimes, 1 Ch. Ca. 89,[1] where the condition, though precedent, was looked upon but in the nature of a penalty for securing the money and there is no real difference between a condition precedent and subsequent where it will admit of an equivalent. Here the heir of Nathaniel may perform the condition by the intent of the devisor.

Sir John Chesshyre: The question is where this real right did not vest absolutely in Nathaniel subject to a cesser upon his non-payment of £500 to Daniel at the time limited. The intent of the devisor is apparent that it should be to him and his heirs. This is a reasonable contingency and good in its original creation in the devisor. It gives the stakes to Daniel to hold and keep as security to compel Nathaniel to pay him £500. It was not an estate or interest in Nathaniel but a right real which descends and by which the land is bound. As soon as the condition is performed, the estate in Daniel ceases. It is a possibility which is not grantable or transferrable but may be released or extinguished because it binds the land. Supposing a right to descend, the question is whether it is become impossible by the act of God that the condition thereto annexed should be performed. Lit, sec. 334. It may be performed where a time is limited. But, where no time is limited, it is uncertain and personal and cannot be performed by the heir or executor. Spring v. Dame Caesar, 1 Rol. Ab. 439, Winch 103, W. Jones 389, upon a writ of error, where the judges were divided;[2] Vesey v. Parlow, Trinity 4 Ja., Common Pleas, rot. 751, in [an action of] ejectment, R. Hobson, seised in fee, settled to the use of himself for life, then to his daughter Mary and the heirs of her body, provided she paid £300 within seven years after she came into possession to his daughter Sarah, otherwise to Sarah and the heirs of her body. Mary died leaving two daughters; the £300 not being paid within the seven years, Sarah entered. There were two questions, first, whether this was a condition or a limitation; second, whether the heir of Mary could perform it. The court, in Hilary [term] 1690, were of opinion it was not personal but the heir might have performed it had it been within the time but, because the time of payment was elapsed and the money not paid, therefore, it was forfeited though the heirs of Mary were infants.

In the present case, the time of payment not being elapsed, the plaintiff may pay the £500 to Daniel and, from that time, there will be a cesser of the estate in Daniel and the fee will vest in the plaintiff.

---

[1] *Wallis v. Crimes* (1667), *ut supra.*

[2] *Springe v. Caesar* (1636), 1 Rolle, Abr., *Condition*, pl. F, 1, p. 420, also pl. D, 1, p. 469, W. Jones 389, 82 E.R. 204, *sub nom. Cooper v. Edgar* (1624), Winch 103, 124 E.R. 87.

Raymond: The first objection is to the creation of the estate; Scatterwood and Edge, Salk. 229;[1] second, that it is personal to Nathaniel. The first has been fully answered. Third, that the ancestor taking nothing, the heir, who is mentioned by way of limitation, cannot take by purchase. Had the condition been that, if a stranger should pay the £500 to Daniel within the three years, then the land to go to Nathaniel and his heirs, though Nathaniel had died before the three years, yet his heir might have taken, according to Wood's Case in Shelley's [Case], 1 Co. 99, the rule there laid down has been confirmed by many cases since, that a possibility or remainder upon a contingency may descend to the heir. Bro., *Feoffment to Uses*, 53; 3 Co. 20, Boraston's Case; Poll. 55, Weale and Lower.[2]

As to the second question, whether this be personal to Nathaniel, the circumstances in this case are very material. The intent of the devisor seems to be that his two younger sons should be equally provided for. Therefore, this is to be looked upon only as a mortgage, especially being within Littleton's reason that it is no prejudice to the person who receives it. Co. Lit. 219b;[3] a condition of a mortgage that the mortgagor and B. shall pay, yet, if B. dies, the mortgagor alone may tender. Winch, *Entries*, 401.[4]

Pauncefort: This is a possibility coupled with an interest. Wellock v. Hammond, in Boraston's Case, 3 Co. 19; Yelver. 85; Sir Francis Winnington's Case, 2 Co. 59, that payment of money is not personal; Dyer 1; Pibus v. Mitford, 1 Vent. 372; 1 Sand. 150.[5] This ought to be looked upon as a mortgage in Daniel and which is the only provision that the devisor has made for Nathaniel.

---

1 *Scatterwood v. Edge* (1697–1700), 1 Salkeld 229, 91 E.R. 203, also 12 Modern 278, 88 E.R. 1320, 1 Eq. Cas. Abr. 189, 21 E.R. 980, 2 Eq. Cas. Abr. 337, 22 E.R. 287, King's Inn Dublin MS. 92, p. 1.

2 Brooke, Abr., *Feffements al uses*, pl. 59; *Hynde v. Ambrye* (1587), 3 Coke Rep. 16, 76 E.R. 664, 1 Eq. Cas. Abr. 190, 194, 21 E.R. 980, 984; *Weal v. Lower* (1673–1689), Pollexfen 54, 86 E.R. 509, also 2 Freeman 107, 22 E.R. 1089, 1 Eq. Cas. Abr. 266, 21 E.R. 1035.

3 E. Coke, *First Institute* (1628), f. 219b.

4 *Cooper v. Edgar* (1623–1624), H. Winch, *Beau Pledeur*, p. 401, also Winch 103, 115, 124 E.R. 87, 96.

5 *Wellock v. Hammond* (1590), 3 Coke Rep. 20, 76 E.R. 672, also 2 Leonard 114, 74 E.R. 403, Croke Eliz. 204, 78 E.R. 460; *Clark v. Sydenham* (1606), Yelverton 85, 80 E.R. 58, also 1 Brownlow & Goldesborough 136, 123 E.R. 714; *Pilkington v. Winnington* (1598), 2 Coke Rep. 59, 76 E.R. 551, also Jenkins 253, 145 E.R. 180; *Anonymous* (1512), 1 Dyer 1, 73 E.R. 1; *Pibus v. Mitford* (1673–1674), 1 Ventris 372, 86 E.R. 239, also 2 Levinz 75, 83 E.R. 456, 3 Keble 239, 316, 338, 84 E.R. 697, 741, 754, 3 Salkeld 337, 91 E.R. 859, T. Raymond 228, 83 E.R. 119, 1 Modern 98, 121, 159, 86 E.R. 761, 780, 800, 1 Freeman 351, 369, 89 E.R. 262, 275, Lincoln's Inn MS. Misc. 500, ff. 214v, 224, 236; *Wade v. Bache* (1668), 1 Williams Saunders 144, 85 E.R. 152, also 1 Siderfin 360, 82 E.R. 1156, 2 Keble 341, 84 E.R. 213.

Hooper, for the defendant: This is a question purely at law, and the plaintiff has no need to come into this court, for the encumbrance does not hinder his recovering at law. We admit it a good executory devise in its original creation. There is a great difference where it depends on the act of him who is to take a benefit by it and whereon the act of a third person and where no act is to be done. Here, nothing vested in the ancestor; therefore, nothing could descend to the plaintiff. The cases on conditions do not come up to this case because they are annexed to the estate of the party from whom it moved.

Lutwyche: This case is not anywhere adjudged. It is the same here as it would have been at law upon a special verdict in [an action of] ejectment. The words taken strictly are with us. The only question is if the intent be so too. Here the fee vested in Daniel, and, if Nathaniel had paid the money, he would have had an absolute fee. Before the first fee can be defeated, the terms of the will must be fulfilled. It is not said if Nathaniel or his heirs pay, yet it is to be paid to Daniel, his executors, or administrators. Therefore, it was intended to be personal to Nathaniel. The devise is to Nathaniel and his heirs, which are words of limitation not of purchase. Bret v. Rigden, Plowd. 342; Scatterwood and Edge, 1 Salk. 229. The cases which have been quoted do not come up to this case, for here is a condition precedent, which must be performed by the person himself who is to gain the estate. This estate could not descend because it never vested in the ancestor and nothing could vest before an act done, which was not performed in his lifetime. Suppose it had been if Nathaniel shall pay £500 to Daniel in the life of Ann; it is plain the plaintiff could not take. A condition must descend strictly to the heir at law, not to a special heir, and the heir is in of his ancient estate. In the case of Loyd and Carew, the words were strictly performed and the only question was upon the remoteness of the contingency. Spring v. Caesar, W. Jon. 389, is for us, for there was a condition subsequent, which two judges held was personal and could not be performed by the heir. This is not a possibility which may descend, as Manning's Case, 8 Co. 94, of a term for years where it is looked upon as a devise to the second person subject to an estate for life in the first. As to Wood's Case, in Shelly's [Case], 1 Co. 99a, there, the condition was not to be performed by the party himself, but by a third person.

Sawyer: The intent of the testator seems to be that the money should be personally paid by Nathaniel. Poll. 55, Weale v. Lower; it was to A. for life and, if he pay the money, then to him and his heirs; A. died without paying; [it was] adjudged his heir could not pay.

Mead: This is not like the case where the condition is to be performed by the mortgagor, for, there, the heir is privy to the condition and may perform it only in those cases where he is to be restored to the old estate. But here, he is to gain a new one. The heir cannot take as a purchaser, and it is plain nothing vested in the ancestor, for something must be first done, which is not yet performed. Wood's Case is different, for the condition was to be performed by a third person who may make the heir a purchaser though a man cannot make his own heir a purchaser. The calling it a real right in the ancestor is begging the question. Here could be no right to the land, for, this being a condition precedent and become impossible by the act of God, no estate can arise to the plaintiff. If the ancestor had lived, he could not be compelled to perform it but would have his election. Therefore, it is not a security, as Wallis v. Crimes, 1 Ch. Ca. 89. If the ancestor had paid, he had gained an absolute fee, which he might dispose of. So it is not certain that the plaintiff would have had any benefit by this devise. Bertie v. Lord Falkland, 3 Ch. Ca. 135; where a condition precedent becomes impossible by the act of God, a court of equity cannot help. Therefore, the plaintiff cannot perform this condition.

Powys, in reply: First, we had a necessity to come into this court to set aside an encumbrance and to know to whom we must pay the £500.

Second, they lay a great stress upon the words of the will. But those make for us and prove that Daniel was not to have the land in fee, for the money might be paid to his executors or administrators.

Third, they say this is a remote contingency. But we have cited much stronger cases. Nathaniel surviving the devisor, it was an interest vested in him.

Fourth, it is said to be a contingency which must happen precedent to the vesting of the estate. But it is no more than happens in all executory devises.

Fifth, that we have not a right to perform this condition though we come within the three months after the death of Ann, but here is no real difference between this case and Lit., sec. 334, there being a time limited, though it is otherwise where no time is limited, for then it must be performed in the life of the parties.

Chesshyre: This is manifest that Daniel's personal estate was to have money in exchange for land, but Nathaniel was to have land in exchange for money. The cases of conditions and limitations are within the same reason. Limitations were invented to prevent the fraud of heirs, who, perhaps, would not enter. Therefore, all acts may be done by those who take upon limitations as might have been done by heirs in case of conditions.

Lord Chancellor [Lord Parker]: I will consider of this case. You must attend the Master of the Rolls and me with a copy of the will.

Vide Liber Decretorum; [it was] decreed for the plaintiff.

Lincoln's Inn MS. Misc. 11, p. 125

21 May 1718.

William Marks, having three sons, by will, devises lands to his wife for life and, after her death, to his second son, Daniel, and his heirs, but subject to this condition, *viz*. that, if Nathaniel, his youngest son, should within three months after the death of his mother, pay £500 to Daniel, his executors, administrators, or assigns, then the testator devised the lands to Nathaniel and his heirs. Nathaniel died in the lifetime of his mother. And the plaintiff, who is his heir, within three months after her death, brings his bill to be admitted to perform the condition and that, upon payment of the £500, he may have the lands.

It was insisted on for the plaintiff that this was an executory devise, the contingency was to happen within three months after the death of one life. In all executory devises, the contingency must happen within a life or lives in being or within a short time after; otherwise, it may run into a perpetuity. In the Case of Loyd and Cary, Cases in Parl. 137, it was carried to a year, which was thought a reasonable time.

As to the objection that no estate ever vested in Nathaniel and, therefore, nothing could vest in his heir and, consequently, he could not perform the condition, it is true no estate is vested in the heir, but there is a right that is descended upon him, a right to have the estate upon performing the condition. And when the condition is performed, the estate vests.

If there is a contingent fee in the ancestor, it will descend on the heir and be contingent in him. And when he has performed the condition, he will be in by descent. There are many cases to this point in the third point in Shelley's Case.

We are in the case of a will. The land is proved to be of the value of £1000, and it is plain the testator intended one son should have the land and the other £500 so as to make an equal division between them. And the land, in the meantime was to be in the nature of a security.

Serjeant *Hooper*, for the defendant: It is insisted that this is an executory devise. I shall not much object against that, since the Case of Loyd and Cary. But there is a difference between an executory devise which is to take effect where no act is to be done and where there is some act to be done before it can take place.

Now here is an act to be done, but by whom, not by the heir, but by the ancestor. But has he done it? No. Why then, nothing vested in him and, consequently, nothing can vest in his heir.

Mr. *Mead*, on the same side: The cases which have been cited on the other side are where the estate has been in the ancestor, as where a man enfeoffs another and his heirs upon condition that, if the feoffor pay a sum of money, the estate is to be void. Now, in that case, the heir may perform the condition and revest the old estate in him. But, in our case, there was never any estate in the ancestor.

Now, I believe there can be no case where a condition which was to be performed by the ancestor may be performed by the heir so as to give him a new estate, which never was in the ancestor.

In the Case of Bertie and Lord Falkland, in Lord Somers's time, it was laid down for a rule that a court of equity will never interpose to aid the non-performance of a condition precedent. But in the case of a condition subsequent, it may be otherwise, for that is in the nature of a penalty or forfeiture, and, if it is not performed, the court may make satisfaction some other way to the party who has suffered by the non-performance of the condition.

Adjournatur.

Lincoln's Inn MS. Hill 73, p. 10

The testator made to Daniel and his heir provided always nevertheless subject to the payment of £500 [. . .] his brother Nathaniel at his age of twenty-one. Nathaniel dies before he attained the age of twenty-one.

[Where] an estate [is] made to a man and his heirs, if the feoffee dies without heirs, it reverts to the donor. (N.B. Tom Latham's Case.)

An executory devise that depends upon the performances of some act in the father, nothing can descend to the son without the father's performing that act. (N.B. [. . .] Case.)

A devise to Ann, his wife, for life, remainder to Daniel Marks and his heirs subject to this condition that, if Nathaniel pay the sum of £500 [. . .] three months after the death of Ann to Daniel, his executors, and administrators if the estate should remain to Nathaniel, his heirs, and assigns forever. This is a condition precedent to be performed by the devisee, Daniel, himself and the estate to arise from the performance of such acts, and, nothing being vested in the father, nothing can descend to the heir at law.

Lincoln's Inn MS. Misc. 380, pt. 3, p. 209

Easter term 4 Geo.

William Marks had five sons, Theodore, William, Ezekell, Daniel, and Nathaniel, and, being seised of lands in Northampton and also of lands in question, by a settlement, 10 April 1680, granted those in Northampton to trustees to sell after his decease and the money to be paid according to his will, the overplus to Theodore, provided if Theodore, his heirs, or assigns should within one month after his decease pay £500 as he should appoint by his will, then, the trust should determine and the lands go to Theodore and his heirs. Afterwards, in the year [*blank*], he makes his will and, reciting that trust, appoints the payment of the £500, *viz.* £400 to his son William and £100 to Ezekell, and devises the lands in question to Ann, his wife, for life, remainder to Daniel upon this condition, 'if my son Nathaniel do and shall within three months of the decease of my wife pay or cause to be paid to Daniel, his executors, or administrators the sum of £500, then I give the said land to my son Nathaniel and his heirs'. Soon afterwards, the devisor died, and Ann entered and, in conjunction with Daniel, made a settlement of these lands upon his marriage. And several other encumbrances were made by Daniel. Then, Nathaniel died, leaving William Marks, the now plaintiff, his son and heir. Afterwards, in May 1715, Ann died.

And, in July following, within three months, William Marks comes into this court to know to whom among the several encumbrances to pay the £500 appointed by the will of the grandfather, the chief questions being whether the heir Nathaniel could pay the £500 and perform the condition.

That point was urged by itself at the bar last Easter term, and the Lord Chancellor desired the assistance of the Master of the Rolls. And now, they both delivered their opinions.

Master of the Rolls [JEKYLL]: The equity which brings this matter into this court is that the defendant Daniel had so conveyed and encumbered this estate that so it became difficult for the plaintiff to know to whom to pay the money. Now, before this can be settled, the court must determine a question in law, whether the heir of Nathaniel, upon payment or tender of the money, might enter. And I am of an opinion that this is not personal to Nathaniel, but goes to his heir. If this was a condition at common law, there is no doubt but the heir might enter, Litt., § 334, and, in a case of a condition for the payment of money at a certain time by the feoffor of an estate, if the feoffor, before the day, re-enfeoff another, this second feoffee may pay the money. Litt., § 336. But I admit the present case is not of a condition, but an executory devise. Wherein then does the difference consist? All the difference can amount to is only this. In the case of a condition, the heir has a right antecedent to the condition to enter, for the heir does not gain a new estate but only invests himself of the old one. But, in our case, the heir is to gain perfectly a new estate which the ancestor never had.

In answer to this, it is to be considered that this is a condition to create an estate, which the law will construe liberally. 1 Inst. 219, C. It is said a condition that is to create an estate is to be performed as near to the intent and meaning of the condition as may be if the letter and word of the condition cannot be performed.

But besides, this is the case of a will in which great latitude is allowed by the law to come at the meaning of the devisor. Now, in our case, his meaning seems to be this upon a view of the whole will. He is distributing his estate among his children; to some money; to others land. In the proviso for Theodore's payment of £500 recited in the will, it is worded 'if Theodore, his heirs, or assigns shall pay' etc. Now, no one can imagine that, by the difference of words in this proviso and that in question, the testator's intention was different. In both cases, the devisor seems to be aiming at a method of charging those several lands with £500 apiece.

Let us now consider whether, by this will, Nathaniel himself had anything in the lands in question. I conceive he had a future interest or a possibility which might descend to the heir though the right never vested in the ancestor. That such a future interest in a term will go to the executor or administrator is known law. Welden's Case, Pl. Com. 519, is full to that point.[1] It may also be released, as in Lampet's Case, 10 Co. 48b. Now why such a future possibility should in a term go to the executor or administrator and, in a freehold, not go to the heir, the proper representative, I cannot imagine.

[1] *Welcden v. Elkington* (1578), 2 Plowden 516, 75 E.R. 763.

At common law, such a possibility arising by an act executed will come to the heir as before the Statute *de Donis*. The reversion upon an estate tail was only a possibility, and yet it should go to the heir, and even a possibility may go to the heir, which could not possibly vest in the ancestors. 1 Inst. 338b. So the same possibility will go to the heir where the limitation is by a use. 1 Co. 98, Shelley's Case, and Wood's Case, there cited, is very strong. And though it is there said that a future interest or a possibility cannot be released, that was before Lampett's Case, where it is determined such a possibility may be released. And I believe it would be so now. In 1 Roll. Ab. 420,[1] there is a case of a fine by A. and B. to the use of A., in fee if B. does not pay 10s. at Michaelmas after and, if he does then pay it, it shall be to the use of A. for life and afterwards to B. in fee; B. dies before Michaelmas, and Rolle says it seems the heir of B. may pay the 10s., for this is not more personal, being the payment of money, than in the case of Litt., p. 334, upon a mortgage between Spring and Julius Caesar, the same case is reported in Winch 303, 304, etc., and, though, in Jones 309, it is said the court were divided, yet Coke and Jones were of opinion the performance of the condition was not personal, and they did not see the difference between this case and that quoted out of Littleton. And since this reason was not contradicted by any of the other judges and reported by Rolle as law, I must take it for law.

Now, since these several possibilities are judged to go to the heir, I do not see why such possibility created by a will, since executory devises are allowed, should not go to the heir also. The Case of Brett v. Rigden, cited, in Plo. Com., for the defendants is nothing to the purpose because there was indeed no devise to the ancestor, he being dead before the devisor. But, in the present case, here is a complete devise and such as the ancestor might here have taken.

But it was insisted for the defendants that the plaintiff's father had an election to pay or not to pay the money and, therefore, it must be personal in him. I admit it, but then such an election is always given in favor of him who is to pay, the receiver having no estate at all and in Littleton's case, p. 334, the mortgagor had equally an election and yet it is not personal in him. Lord Coke, in his comment upon that section gives four reasons for Littleton's opinion, which all concur in the present case. The first is a day is appointed. It is so in the present case. As to the second, if the heir in our case takes by virtue of this executory devise, as has already been shown, he does [it] in the nature and course of a descent. It is the same thing as where, in Coke's second reason, the condition is descended to the heir. The two remaining [. . .] are plainly the same in our case. So Littleton is indeed an authority in point. It is not to be made a question whether this future interest or possibility being to arise beyond a life is good by way of executory devises at this time since the resolution of Floyd and Cary's Case in the House of Lords, which allows a twelve month more than a single life.

---

1 *Springe v. Caesar* (1637), 1 Rolle, Abr., *Condition*, pl. F, 1, p. 420, also pl. D, 1, p. 469.

Upon the whole then, I am for the plaintiff as to the point of the law. Indeed, it was insisted on further for the plaintiff that, if the law were against him, yet, in equity, he would have a good title upon payment of the £500, the estate in Daniel being to be looked upon as a security for £500. And for this, the case of Wells and Crimes, in 1 Chan. Cas. 89, was quoted. But now, lest anyone should go away with this dangerous opinion that another construction in this case ought to be made in a court of equity than would be in a court of law [*blank*].

Lord Chancellor [Lord Parker]: The Master has set this matter in a very clear light. I am of the same opinion. And, if we look upon this case on every side, it appears the right is clearly for the plaintiff. The will shows the intendment that, though the word 'heirs' be left out, in the case of Nathaniel, yet he should be in the same condition with Theodore. The question here is indeed a question at law, whether, Nathaniel dying before the time of payment, his heir, paying the money, shall be entitled. The method in which I have endeavored to satisfy myself in this case has been by considering this proviso, first, as upon a feoffment and, then, as upon a will and, lastly, as it would stand in equity as a provision for the payment of money.

First, at common law, if William Marks had made a feoffment to B. for life, remainder to Daniel and his heirs, provided, if Nathaniel, within three months after the death of B. pay to Daniel £500, then it shall go to Nathaniel and his heirs, Nathaniel could take no benefit of this condition because [it is] contrary to the maxim in law that a condition cannot limit over an estate to another, but can only be taken advantage of by the maker, but, in the case of a feoffment by A. to B. and his heirs upon condition that, if A. pays £500 to B. within three months, then A. shall have his estate back again, if A. dies before the three months are expired, his heir, though not mentioned, may pay the money and enter. Litt., p. 334.

But now consider it upon the Statute of Wills,[1] and it is the same upon the Statute of Uses[2] since executory devises and springing uses have been allowed of. At first, they began when merely future and sprang out of the estate of the devisor. Afterwards, they were extended beyond a life, as if an estate was devised to A. for life, remainder to B. and his heirs upon condition that, if C. pay a sum of money to B. within a certain time after the death of A., then the remainder shall go to C. and his heirs. This has been allowed of, and it is no more than granting the advantage of a condition to another person which, by a common law conveyance, could go only to the maker himself. Now, this advantage is in its own nature descendible because it is nothing against that very right, which, if it had gone to the devisor himself, would have descended to his heirs. Take this as a possibility or a future interest, and the cases mentioned by the Master of the Rolls show plainly that this is a right descendible to the proper representative,

1 Stat. 32 Hen. VIII, c. 1 (*SR*, III, 744–746).

2 Stat. 27 Hen. VIII, c. 10 (*SR*, III, 539–542).

whether of a term or an inheritance, the former to the executor or administrator, the latter to the heir. But, if we consider it, as I have done, as a condition, the case is yet stronger because this benefit of a condition is what is taken notice of before by the common law to be descendible and, since, by the Statute of Wills and Uses, the benefit of a condition is allowed to go over to a stranger, that stranger ought to have it as fully and completely as the feoffor himself would have at common law, that is it shall go equally to the heirs of the one and the other.

If we consider this matter as it stands in a court of equity, I agree entirely, were the law against the plaintiff, as if he had paid the money at the day, this court could not have intermeddled. But if the law upon payment at the day be with him, it will be another consideration whether this court would not relieve him against the next time of payment. This is the case of a mortgage; equity looks upon the mortgagee's estate, which is become absolute by the passing of the day, as only a security for the money and, therefore, will defeat it upon payment though after the day.

Now, in our case, Daniel's interest is merely personal. By the express words of the will, the money is to be paid to him or the executors. The estate of inheritance is given to Nathaniel and his heirs, subject only to this encumbrance. And though this court has not relieved against an heir at law upon a condition precedent to raise an estate out of the heir's estate, yet, when it is to be raised only out of the estate of the devisee, it may very well do it. Nathaniel, therefore, would have the equity of redemption, and, this estate of Daniel being only his security for the money, if this, therefore, had been the case, I think this court, therefore, would relieve. But the present case does not warrant that assistance.

To return then to the question in law, which is now whether the death of Nathaniel has not destroyed the benefit of the condition as to his heir. And this contains a question, first, whether this condition be such as may be performed after Nathaniel's death, *scil.* whether the estate must not first vest in the ancestor before the heir can take. As to the first, I think it is clearly not personal in Nathaniel, but performable by his heir. The payment of 12d. or 10s. or such small sum that bears no proportion to the estate may be considered perhaps only as a ceremony by which to declare the mind of the person. And, therefore, if, in the case of Spring and Julius Caesar, the two judges continued in their opinions, it must be, as I conceive, because the sum was so small and they looked upon it as a mere ceremony. But where the sum is £500, it must be looked upon as a certain, valuable, and considerable thing. And since Englefield's Case, in the second Report,[1] the payment of money is a thing of all things the least personal, it not being material who pays it.

---

[1] *Regina v. Englefield* (1591), 7 Coke Rep. 11, 77 E.R. 428, also Moore K.B. 303, 72 E.R. 595, 4 Leonard 135, 169, 74 E.R. 779, 800, Popham 18, 79 E.R. 1139, 1 Anderson 293, 123 E.R. 480.

If, therefore, the heir in one case pays the £500, all the purposes in the will are answered as much as if Nathaniel himself had paid it. And this exactly answers the case of Litt., p. 334, and agrees to all the reasons given by Lord Coke, which reasons are not adapted to the institution of the common law only, but to the nature of the thing. The case of Littleton and ours are exactly the same to the present purpose; the benefit of the condition by the common law goes to the feoffor and, in our case, to the devisee. And this benefit being equally by the Statute of Wills vested in the devisee, his heir shall equally come in. Otherwise, the benefit would not go equally.

As to the second, Wood's Case, 1 Co. 99a, proves evidently that an heir may take by descent by virtue only of a possibility of right which was in the ancestor.

It has been objected that this has been a condition precedent, but I take it to be a condition subsequent. It would indeed have been precedent if it had been to raise an estate out of the heir's estate, but now it is only to defeat Daniel's estate, and Nathaniel himself comes into the place of the heir at law. But, indeed, this is a mere verbal dispute. No matter whether it be precedent or subsequent, if the performance by the heir be looked upon as the performance of Nathaniel, it shall have the same effect as if Nathaniel himself had paid the money. I think, therefore, at law, the plaintiff would have good title on payment at the day.

But yet he came very properly into this court because of the hazard he ran in paying the £500 to Daniel. There must be a decree in the nature of a redemption, that is, he must pay the principal and interest from the day of payment and have the estate conveyed over to him. The money must be brought before the Master, who must see what demands are upon it and adjust the proportions of the several claimants.

Lincoln's Inn MS. Misc. 384, p. 82

17 November 1718.

Master of the Rolls [Jekyll]: William Marks, seised in fee, conveys to trustees to the uses of his will in 1697. By his will, reciting the settlements, he gives the premises to his wife for life with this proviso 'If my son Nathaniel within three months after the death of my wife pay to Daniel £500, then I give it to Nathaniel and his heirs.' Daniel mortgages to the defendants. The wife dies in 1715, and, within three months after her death, the plaintiff, the heir of Nathaniel, brings the bill against Daniel and the mortgagees and makes his equity that he knew not to whom to pay the £500. The question is whether the plaintiff as heir of Nathaniel, on payment or tender, might enter. I am opinion he might. If it were to pay money on a mortgage, he might. Lit., sec. 334, 336; C. Litt. 219.

The stranger may pay. This is not a condition but an executory devise. To distinguish the cases, it is said the heir has a right to perform the condition and does not gain a new estate. But here the ancestor having nothing, the heir must gain a new estate. A condition must be performed as well as it can. This is upon a will, which is to be construed favorably. The intent was that some should have land and others money. In the case of payment to Daniel, it is if he, his executors, administrators, or assigns shall be paid. But it is by Nathaniel. Nathaniel had a possibility or a future interest, which might go to the heir. It is so in a term. Lampet's Case. There is no difference. The second reason in Lampet's Case, 48, extends to both. Lit., sec. 643. A possibility at common law descends to the heir as before the Statute *de Donis*. 2 Inst. 335.[1] The heir is in by descent though it could not vest in the ancestor, C.L. 378; Hob. 130,[2] as by law, so by limitation of a use. Shelley's Case, 38. Wood's Case; there it is said it cannot be released, but the law is otherwise since Lampet's Case. Spring and Caesar, Jon. 383. There is greater latitude in wills than deeds. Brett and Rigden, Plow., is not in point.

Here is a complete devise, which the ancestor might have taken. [It was] objected the plaintiff's ancestor had an election, but that is of him that is to pay, not of him who is to receive. Lit., sec. 334; C.L. The first reason is a time was limited; second, the condition descends; third, there is no prejudice; fourth, a consequence [is] the intent performed. [There is] an authority in point. The possibility [is] to arise after a life [is] no objection since Loyd and Carew, Cas. in Parl., which gives twelve months.

Therefore, as to the point of law, I am of opinion with the plaintiff, Wallis and Crimes, 1 Ch. C. 89, that, if the law were against him, yet equity should help him. But it is a dangerous notion that equity should alter the law, and that case is but a trust. Wellock and Hamond in Boraston's [Case], C. Rep. 20; a limitation is not a condition. If the law were against the plaintiff, I should think he ought not to be relieved, but, it being for him if he had entered, equity follows the law. The plaintiff is proper here. If he had paid Daniel after notice of the encumbrance, he had paid it in his own wrong. The court may declare that the defendants are affected with notice of the will. Daniel's covenanting that he was seised in fee does not alter the case.

Lord Chancellor [Lord Parker]: The Master of the Rolls has stated the matter very clearly. I am of the same opinion that the right is with the plaintiff. The will shows plainly the intent. In the deed, it is, if Theodore, the eldest son, his heirs, etc. should pay, but, in the will, if Nathaniel should pay. And it must mean the same thing though the word 'heirs' is omitted. The question is a question of law. The method I satisfied myself was, first, to consider it as a feoffment, if A. conveys to B., provided, if he pay before such a day, then he may enter and, if he die before, his heir may tender; he may release it though not assign it to a stranger. Lit. 347. No remainder could be a limitation over on Daniel's estate. The construction on the Statute of Wills is the same as the Statute of Uses. An estate may be given upon a condition, which, if not too remote, may be for the benefit of the grantor or a third person though lawyers, to save the maxim that

1 E. Coke, *Second Institute* (1642), p. 335.

2 E. Coke, *First Institute* (1628), f. 378; *Oates v. Frith* (1614), Hobart 130, 80 E.R. 280.

a right cannot be assigned, have invented other terms (Weal v. Lower, Pol. 55) called a possibility or executory devise. Taking it either way, it vested in Nathaniel and descends to his heir.

Consider it as a condition; it is stronger. When assigned to a third person, it is as it was in the grantor. If it had not been paid at the day, equity would not help in this case unless it were prevented by some accident. It is otherwise in a mortgage, which is but a security for money. Here, Daniel has an estate in fee redeemable on payment at a day. The inheritance is given to Nathaniel only subject to this encumbrance though this court will not help against a condition precedent. Yet, where it is not against the heir but a devisee, it will, being in the nature of a mortgage. The devisee has the same advantage, the devisor had. This is different from a condition precedent whereon an estate is to arise to defeat the heir at law. The point is whether the condition is defeated by the death of Nathaniel or may be performed by the plaintiff, the heir.

I think it is not a personal act of Nathaniel. The payment of a small sum which bears no proportion to the value of the land is to be looked upon only as a ceremony, which was the reason, I suppose, the judges went upon in Spring v. Caesar. Payment of money is the least personal of anything, as in Ingledon's Case, C. 7 Rep.; Lit., sec. 334.[1] And the reasons are agreeable not only to the law but also to the nature of the thing. Wood's Case, in Shelly's Case. The right did descend. The condition well vested in the plaintiff as representative of his ancestor. The case is exactly the same with Lit., sec. 334.

The great point is whether the devisee has the same advantage [as] was intended him, which here he has. The difference made is that Littleton is a condition subsequent and this is a condition precedent. But there is no great difference where money is to be paid. He who is to perform a condition must do so if he will take advantage of it. If it is performed, there is no difference between a condition precedent and subsequent. This advantage vested in Nathaniel. He not releasing or extinguishing, it descends to the plaintiff. It was necessary for him to come into this court.

Here must be a decree for the plaintiff in the nature of a redemption. The Master must see what demands there are to this money. What remains must be laid out in land and settled according to Daniel's marriage articles until the purchase. The interest of the money is to be paid to the same uses.

British Library MS. Add. 36651, f. 91, pl. 2

Michaelmas [term] 5 Geo., 1718. William Merks, plaintiff; Daniel Merks *et al.*, defendants.

The case was that William Merks, in 1697, made his will, having three sons, *viz.* Theodore, Nathaniel, and Daniel. And he devised lands valued £40 *per an-*

[1] *Regina v. Englefield* (1591), *ut supra*; T. Littleton, *Tenures*, s. 334.

num to Ann, his wife, for her life and, after her decease, then to Daniel and his heirs forever 'provided nevertheless that, if Nathaniel shall within three months after the decease of my said wife pay or cause to be paid unto the said Daniel, his executors, administrators, or assigns, the sum of £500, then I do devise my said close and premises to the said Nathaniel Merks, his heirs and assigns forever'.

The testator died, and Ann, his wife, entered and made a lease for years of the said lands to Daniel, by virtue of which Daniel was in possession. And he and Ann joined in a conveyance of part to certain trustees upon the marriage of one of the daughters of Daniel, who are all defendants before the court, and made a mortgage of the rest to other of the defendants. But all the defendants had notice of the proviso and limitation in the will.

Nathaniel died in the lifetime of Ann, the wife, and he left issue, the plaintiff, William Merks, his son and heir. Then Ann, the wife, died.

And the plaintiff brought this bill within three months after her decease and, thereby, makes tender of the £500 and prays for the direction of the court to which of the defendants he ought to pay it, and he prays to be let into possession according to the limitation of the will.

There are two points: first, whether this was a good executory devise to Nathaniel in its original creation in respect that it is not limited to take effect in the compass of lives in being, the proviso allowing three months after the decease of the wife; second, supposing it to be a good executory devise to Nathaniel, whether it is not to commence upon such a condition precedent as is personal to Nathaniel so that his heir, not being named in the proviso, cannot perform it or whether it is a condition coupled with an interest in the lands so as to descend to the heir and the heirs, upon the performance thereof, to be entitled.

Sir Thomas Powys, for the plaintiff said it was a good executory devise in its original creation according to Pell and Brown's Case, Cr. Ja. 590. He owned that the general doctrine of executory devises is that they must be limited to take effect in the compass of lives in being at the time of the creation lest they should tend to perpetuities, but, though this be a general rule, yet, where they are limited to take effect upon the payment of money, the law will allow a reasonable time for raising the money and three months, considering the largeness of the sum, is a reasonable time in this case. And, in the Case of Floyd and Carew, B. Shower's Parl. Cases 137, twelve months was allowed and held good by the House of Lords.

Second, he said that this is a condition coupled with an interest in the land and that it would descend and was not personal to Nathaniel though the proviso be that if Nathaniel pay, leaving out the word 'heirs'. He said that here being a time fixed for the performance of the condition, the heir, though not named, may perform it according to Lit., sec. 334, which is that, if a mortgage be made upon a condition to be void if the mortgagor pay such a sum at such a day, if the mortgagor die, his heir may perform the condition at the day. And, in the case at bar, the limitation is to Nathaniel and his heirs, so that the heir has an interest therein as well as in the case above.

He said it was objected that nothing vested in Nathaniel; therefore, nothing could descend to his heir.

He responded that a vesting in Nathaniel in point of estate in land was not necessary, for it is the same as a reversion which, before the Statute of *Donis*, remained in the donor, which, though it was a mere possibility and no estate in the land, yet it did descend to the heir of the donor. And so it is in the case of limitations of chattels. Where a lease for years is limited to a man for life with a remainder over, the executors of him in remainder shall take, as in Matthew Manning's Case, 8 Rep. 95. And Wood's Case, cited in Shelly's Case, 1 Co. 99a, is stronger than the case at bar, *viz.* A., seised of the manor of S., covenanted with B. that, when J.S. should enfeoff him of D., that then he would stand seised of the manor of S. to the use of the covenantee and his heirs; the covenantee dies, his heirs within age; J.S. enfeoffed the covenantor of the manor of D., and it was adjudged that the heir of the covenantee did take the manor of S. in the course and nature of a decent and yet there was neither right, title, use, nor action in the ancestor, but only a possibility of a use, which could not be released or discharged. But, inasmuch as it might possibly have vested in the ancestor, the heir shall be in by descent.

He said that this being upon a will, the intent of the testator must be regarded and it seems to be intended only in the nature of a mortgage for the payment of this sum.

Serjeant *Chesshyre* said it should be construed a limitation and that the estate given to Daniel should cease upon the payment of the £500 at the time limited. But he seemed to agree that, if it was not paid at the time, infancy or want of notice etc. would be no excuse.

He said that a possibility and also a right to have the estate upon the performance of the condition did vest in Nathaniel and did descend to his heir and Nathaniel might have released or extinguished it though he could not have granted it over.

That the heir might perform the condition in this case, he cited Lit., sec. 334, 337; 1 Roll Ab. 420, Winch 103, 105, 115; and the Case of Dacy [?] and Barlow, in the Common Pleas, Trin. 4 Jac. II, rot. 751 or 707, upon a special verdict; 1 Roll Ab. 496; Jones 139.[1]

Sir Robert Raymond, to the second objection, said that that ground was overruled by the authority of Floyd and Carew's Case, before cited.

[1] T. Littleton, *Tenures*, ss. 334, 337; *Springe v. Caesar, sub nom. Cooper v. Edgar* (1637), *ut supra*.

To the first, he said that the rule in Shelly's Case and Wood's Case, there cited, is very strong in favor of the heir's taking by descent; so are Bro., tit. *Feoffment to Uses*, 59, and Lord Hale's opinion in Pollexphin 55.[1]

Mr. *Panceford* said it was not to be construed only a condition, but a limitation, according to the Case of Willock and Hammond, 3 Co. 20b; he cited also Yelv. 85; 1 Saund. 150.[2]

For the defendant, Serjeant *Hooper* insisted first that the condition was personal to Nathaniel and the heir, not being named in the proviso, could not perform it. He said that it never vested in Nathaniel and, therefore, could not descend. And there is a diversity between a possibility which is to vest upon an act to be done and where it is to vest without any act to be done by the party that is to take, and, in this case, it was to vest upon an act to be done by Nathaniel, and, until Nathaniel did the act, it cannot vest and, consequently, it could not descend.

As to what was urged from the case of reversions upon gifts in tail before the Statute of *Donis*, that they did descend to the heir of the donor, he said that that was by reason that, before the Statute of *Quia Emptores Terrarum*,[3] which was made very near the time of the Statute of *Donis*, if a man made a feoffment in fee, the feoffee held of the feoffor and, if the feoffee died without heirs, the feoffor had the land again by a condition implied. Therefore, if the cases mentioned in Co. Lit. were before the Statute of *Quia Emptores Terrarum*, nothing can be argued from them.

Lutwyche said that, in all times, judges have been jealous of executory devises as tending to perpetuities and, therefore, have never extended them further than lives in being. And they ought to be held strictly to the conditions upon which they are to arise. And he cited the Case of Scattergood and Edge, Salkeld's Rep. 229.

Mead said this case was very different from that of Lit., sec. 334, and the other cases cited in relation to the heir's being let in to perform the condition, for, in all those cases, the ancestor had once the estate in him, but this is a possibility of a new estate which was never in the ancestor, but it is to arise to the ancestor upon his performance of the condition. And it is admitted that the heir must take by descent or not at all, for he cannot take it as a purchaser. He said the defendants are purchasers though with notice and they are to be favored in a court of equity, which will not assist in the performance of a condition precedent to create a new estate to their prejudice, as is held in 2 Ch. Rep. 89,[4] though, in

---

[1] Brooke, Abr., *Feffements al uses*, pl. 59; *Weal v. Lower* (1673–1689), *ut supra*.

[2] *Wellock v. Hammond* (1590), *ut supra*; *Clark v. Sydenham* (1606), *ut supra*; *Wade v. Bache* (1668) *ut supra*.

[3] Stat. 18 Edw. I, c. 1 (*SR*, I, 106).

[4] *Wallis v. Crimes* (1667), *ut supra*.

the case of a condition subsequent, the court often gives relief, as in the case of a forfeiture or the like.

The arguments above were made last term. And now, the Master of the Rolls [Jekyll] delivered his opinion. He said it was a mere question at law. But Daniel Merks having made several encumbrances upon the estate, it was necessary for the plaintiff to bring this bill for the direction of the court to whom the £500 should be paid.

He said that the general query is whether the plaintiff William, as heir at law to Nathaniel, upon payment or tender of the £500 at the day, may enter.

He said that, in the case of a condition of re-entry reserved to the feoffor on payment at a certain day, if the feoffor die before the day, his heir may pay the money at the day and enter though he was not named in the condition. So is Lit., sec. 334. So it is in the case of a condition that the feoffee pay etc. Lit., sec. 336. But the case at bar is not to be construed a condition but an executory devise. And all devises are chiefly governed by the intent. The plaintiff's father had a possibility or interest to have this land on the payment of £500 at the time limited by the proviso. And this was such an interest as will descend. There are many instances of possibilities of terms for years going to executors or administrators of those persons to whom they were limited, as in Welden's Case, Plow. Com. 519; Lampett's Case, 10 Rep. 48; and several other cases. And, before the Statute of *Donis*, the donor upon a gift in tail had but a possibility which did descend to his heir. 2 Inst. 335. And, in many cases, the heir shall be in by descent of a remainder that could not possibly ever vest in the ancestor, as in the case in Co. Lit. 378b; Hob. 130.[1] And, as the heir shall take advantage of such conditions created by conveyances operating by the common law, the same also holds in conveyances operating by way of a use, as in Shelly's Case and Wood's Case, before cited.

He said that the Case of Brett and Rigden, Plow. Com., did not come up to this case, for, there, the death of the devisee before the devisor prevented the devise from ever taking effect and made it as no devise at all; so nothing could descend.

As to the other query, that this is not limited to take effect in the compass of lives in being, he said that the Case of Floyd and Carew, adjudged in the House of Lords, overruled this point, for, there, the time was twelve months, and, in this case, there are only three months after the death of the wife.

Lord Parker, Chancellor, was of the same opinion. He said that, if it was to be considered merely as a condition created by a common law conveyance, it could not be limited to a stranger so as to enable him to defeat the estate limited to Daniel or to raise a new estate to himself. And, therefore, it must be construed as a limitation or executory devise. And, by that construction, Nathaniel might

[1] E. Coke, *First Institute* (1628), f. 378; *Oates v. Frith* (1614), *ut supra*.

take the benefit of it by performing the condition. But, if this be considered merely as a condition that the feoffor, upon payment of such a sum at a certain day, may enter, his heir may take advantage of it though not named in the condition, whether the conveyance operated by the common law or by way of a use or by the Statute of Wills.

He said he took this to be in the nature of a mortgage, and, if a mortgage in fee be made for securing a sum of money and the mortgagee die and the money is not paid at the day, but afterwards the money is paid to the heir, in this case, the heir is in equity but a trustee for the executor though, in law, the estate was absolute in the heir on the failure of the payment at the day, which shows that the intent and design of the parties is to be considered, *viz.* that it was only intended as a security for money. And so it was in this case.

This case is not like the cases where a small sum, as a penny or the like, is by a proviso or condition appointed to be paid before the party shall be enabled to revoke, defeat, or take by force of a proviso or condition, as in the Case of Spring and Sir Julius Caesar, for such provisoes or conditions cannot be taken as a security for such small sums, but such a payment is to be understood only as a ceremony enjoined to be performed in order to make the act of revocation etc. more notorious. And, therefore, after the day of payment is past, the court will not aid or relieve in such cases. But, in the case at bar, the sum to be paid is half the value of the land and the land is a security for it.

He said that, though the land did not vest in Nathaniel, yet a right to have it upon the performance of the condition did vest in him and does descend to the heir. And, in that respect, the case is the same as in Lit., sec. 334.

As to the other point, he said he agreed with the Master of the Rolls that it was overruled by the authority of the Case of Floyd and Carew.

He decreed for the plaintiff.

Lincoln's Inn MS. Hill 73, p. 104

J.S. devises to A. and his heirs proviso, if B., within three months after his death, pay £500 to A, his heir, administrator, or assigns to the use of C., the tenant for life, then B. to have the estate. B. dies during the life of C. Query if the heir of B. shall pay the money and direct the estate of A. B. survived the divisor but died in the life of the jointress, tenant for life; upon the death of the jointress, the heir of B. offered to pay the £500 within the three months.

The Master of the Rolls [Jekyll] [gave] his opinion for a trial at law to determine whether the right of entry, upon the offering the payment by the heir, would entitle him at law. C.L., sect. 334; C.L., fol. 219b.[1]

This is no condition but an executory devise. In the case of a condition, the heir has a right antecedent, and [it] only re-vests the old estate, whereas, by the

[1] E. Coke, *First Institute* (1628), ff. 206, 219.

executory devise, the heir is to create an estate. The father had such a future interest, as though not vested in the father, shall descend to the heir. Welden's Case, Plowden. The future interest of a term shall go to the executors and [there is] no reason why the future interest of an inheritance shall not go to the heir. Littleton, sec. 643; Lampet's Case.

By the Statute *de Donis*, the donor had only a possibility of reverter, but that should revert to the heir, and he should be in by descent though nothing could vest in his ancestor. C.L. 378b; Hob. 130.[1] Lampet's Case settles the doctrine of releasing future interests, which he conceived a standard. Roll's Ab., 420, 469.[2] The answer to the defendant's objection, C.L., sect. 334, that the plaintiff's father had an election. But the election is always construed in favor of the payor. Floyd and Carew allowed twelve months [to be] a reasonable time for the payment of money upon a future devise, and so the objection that it would tend to a perpetuity, it being limited to be paid three months after the death of the tenant for life and so no end; it might be more etc. 1 Chan. Rep. 89.[3]

Lord Chancellor [Lord Parker]: [In] consideration of the proviso at common law, C.L., sect. 347, when the condition of payment of money vests in the ancestor immediately and descends to his heir, but [it is] not assignable by the ancestor to a third person.

Upon the Statute of Wills and Uses, executory devises and uses have always been allowed of. A man may give an estate to a man and his heirs upon a condition if it is not too remote. It is the right of the condition and [is] descendible to his heir, being such as, had the devisor not assigned to the third persons, it had from him descended to his heir so that the [. . .] that the advantage of a condition could be assigned is and has been for a long time destroyed.

The heir of a mortgagee is only a trustee for the executors.

This case seems exactly in the nature of a mortgage, and the redemption is given to the [. . .].

Whether the benefit of the advantage of the condition was lost by B. dying before he could pay the money and, therefore, not vesting in the ancestor, could not descend to his heirs, [he was] of opinion that it was not personal to the ancestor and consequently may be performed by his heir and that heir, who stands in the place of the ancestor to take the estate if the ancestor had paid, shall stand in his place to pay the money in order to take it.

A decree for the plaintiff is in the nature of a redemption to pay the £500 and to be put in possession.

---

1 E. Coke, *First Institute* (1628), f. 378; *Oates v. Frith* (1614), *ut supra*.

2 *Springe v. Caesar* (1637), *ut supra*.

3 *Wallis v. Crimes* (1667), *ut supra*.

[Other reports of this case: Precedents in Chancery 486, 24 E.R. 218, 10 Modern 419, 88 E.R. 789, 1 Strange 129, 93 E.R. 429, 1 Eq. Cas. Abr. 107, 21 E.R. 915, 2 Eq. Cas. Abr. 335, 364, 22 E.R. 285, 309.]

241

Bradburn v. Woodcock

(Ch. 1718–1719)

In this case, a suspicious gift was enforced but a suspicious debt was not.

Lincoln's Inn MS. Misc. 384, p. 28, pl. 2

The plaintiff brought his bill against the defendant to be repaid £300 left in his hands as a deposit to secure and indemnify him for having married the plaintiff at an uncanonical hour.

The defendant by answer said that the plaintiff courted the daughter of Is. Hawkins [who had] a considerable fortune and that he was very instrumental in the match, that the plaintiff owned his obligation, and that he could never sufficiently requite them, that, the night before the marriage, the plaintiff brought the defendant a bag of money, which the defendant did not then count, but after found it about £200, that, the next morning, the plaintiff brought the defendant another £100 and presented him with it freely and voluntarily. And he admitted that the plaintiff had given him a note for £500, which he said was to indemnify him, which he submitted to deliver up.

It appeared by proof that the defendant was the Curate of Ruston upon Trent and had a power of granting licenses from the chancellor of the diocese, that he would not grant a license to the plaintiff before he had brought him to such unreasonable terms, which was urged by Mr. M. as a very great breach of trust, which he ought not to have advantage of, that he had instilled jealousies into the plaintiff that the lady might be removed and that the parson, Mr. Brown, whose curate the defendant was and whom the defendant durst not disoblige and who had married the other daughter of I. Hawkins, was averse to the plaintiff, that, therefore, all possible expedition and secrecy was to be used, that, on the plaintiff's telling the defendant he had not sufficient ready money, the defendant told the plaintiff a friend of his, Mr. Browne, would advance the money, which the plaintiff borrowed accordingly upon his and the lady's bond, that the plaintiff had before presented the defendant with 10 guineas on his contract the plaintiff with the lady, that the plaintiff having presented him with £200 overnight did not satisfy the defendant, but, the next morning, the defendant refused to marry the plaintiff until he brought the other £100 into the church.

This appearing to be the case, the great doubt was whether the court had ever gone so far as to compel the refunding of money in such cases, which the Master of the Rolls [Jekyll] conceived it had not.

Mr. *Mead* quoted a case which was mentioned by Mr. Robins, which he said he found amongst Mr. Poley's papers, but he did not remember the names, in Lord Keeper Wright's time, where money which the maidservant had obtained for assisting the plaintiff was decreed to be refunded with costs.

Lord Chancellor: You must let me see the precedent because this differs from the other cases.

The bill was dismissed.

Street v. Allen, before Lord Cowper, the first time, by W. Cowper; a bond was given to the lady's father for payment of £100 if he should survive his daughter and the marriage took effect. The plaintiff paid some interest on the bond. That bond was decreed to be delivered up and the interest to be refunded.

Goldsmith v. Bruning, at the Rolls, 2 December 1700, and reheard before Lord Keeper Wright and affirmed; see 150.[1]

Lincoln's Inn MS. Misc. 384, p. 187, pl. 1

1719.

Lord Chancellor [Lord Parker]: I cannot see how the plaintiff can be relieved. A man courts a woman and desires a clergyman to marry them. He tells them he would [not] without acquainting the relations unless they would give him a sum of money, *viz.* £300, which was paid accordingly. This is not like marriage brokage contracts. No fraud is charged in the bill, only that it was deposited to indemnify him. But of that there is no proof. The plaintiff was eager to get a fortune and that he could not over pay the parson, and, therefore, he gave him the £300. There is no proof that the parson demanded it, and the defendant positively denies it and swears it was a voluntary gift to him. But I think he has not behaved himself very fairly, for the plaintiff says he gave the defendant a bond for his indemnity, which the defendant denied at first but afterward owned it was not a bond but a note for £500, which must be delivered up. But as to the £300, the bill must be dismissed.

Lincoln's Inn MS. Hill 73, p. 15

The bill was to be relieved against a promissory note given by the plaintiff to the defendant and likewise to have the sum of £300 restored to the said plaintiff, to which end it set forth that the plaintiff did make his address to one Mary Hawkins, a young lady (but of age), who had £260 *per annum* in land and £1100 in money in her own hands and, being favored by the young lady, he desired Mr. Woodcock, the defendant, the curate of the parish, to marry them the same night the father of the said Mary was buried, which indecency he scrupled at. He desired them to defer it for a short time, but, at the desire of the plaintiff, went to the said Mary, who had a great confidence in him and advised her seriously not

[1] *Goldsmith v. Bruning* (1700), 1 Eq. Cas. Abr. 89, 21 E.R. 901.

to deceive and break her promise with the plaintiff, but however the parties being very pressing to have the ceremony over, the defendant absolutely refused to perform it unless the plaintiff would indemnify him from any costs or charges he may be put to for doing the same in the ecclesiastical courts etc. as he pretended, upon which the plaintiff gave him a note of £500 for value received payable upon demand. But, at last, he refused to marry them without (as the plaintiff declared, but denied by the defendant) the sum of £300 paid down to him, which he procured the plaintiff from one Mr. Brome in the town, but Mr. Brome not having above £200 said to the defendant 'there is a debt owing by you to me, if you will pay me that, I will endeavor to furnish you with the other £100 the next morning', which accordingly the defendant did. And the plaintiff did give the said sums of £200 and £100 to the said defendant. And to have that restored as unjustly detained was the end of the bill, it being only a deposit, as the plaintiff set forth, in the defendant's hands.

The defendant, by his answer, said he was ready to deliver up the promissory note of £500 but that, as for the £300, it was an absolute gift of the said plaintiff for the service he had done in forwarding the said match.

It did not appear there was any contract or agreement or that the said defendant made the said match but, having a great influence over the lady, it was for his assistance, My Lord deferred giving judgment.

Mr. *Mead* cited an anonymous case from Mr. Pooly's reports, where a man that was courting a woman in the Strand gave the maid £50 and a note for £100 more and, after the marriage, brought his bill and recovered both with costs.

After being attended with precedents, he decreed a perpetual injunction against the note but no relief for the money paid, as told by Bridger, the solicitor in the cause.

[Other reports of this case: Gilbert Rep. 147, 25 E.R. 103.]

242

Anonymous

(Ch. 1718)

A court of equity will not grant relief against a final judgment at common law unless new facts are alleged so as to make out a new case.

An executor can retain assets to satisfy debts owed to him by the decedent's estate.

Lincoln's Inn MS. Hill 73, p. 6

17 May 1718. Lord Parker, Chancellor.

A bill was dismissed for that, after having gone through the whole course of law, the plaintiff comes into Chancery for relief in the same thing that he had recovered at law without setting forth any new matter in his bill in equity. The case was a mother raises £400 for the advancement of her son, [*blank*] O'Hara, but takes a bond from him to secure to her the interest of the said sum during her life at the rate of £24 *per annum*. The son buys a commission and, being very much straitened in his circumstances through great misfortunes, was supplied with necessaries by an uncle and aunt, his mother refusing to do anything for him, and with several sums of money to a very large account. The son, being sensible of the kindness his uncle had done him, was very uneasy until he was secured his money. And, being in a condition not like to live long, he frequently desired his uncle to sell his said commission and satisfy his just debt. And he made a will and left his aunt some acknowledgment for her care and tenderness to him and made his uncle executor. The uncle, before the death of the son, sold the commission. And the question was whether the said money, there never having been any account stated between them, should be reckoned as a payment of the debt of the uncle or whether it should be assets in his hands and liable to other debts.

My Lord [Parker] decreed it should be reckoned a fair payment and not assets. And he said further that, if the son had recovered and after he had empowered his uncle to sell the commission to pay himself and the commission, by virtue of such power, had been sold and he had repented of it and would not agree to such payment, the uncle would have been very proper for relief in equity.

But as to what was said in relation to the mother's debt, her not having called upon her son for the interest during his life, that, therefore, it should be esteemed a gift, My Lord was quite of another opinion, for she was entitled to call for it when she would, either of her son or any representative of him. And though it might be so far intentionally a gift in the mother as only to keep her son by such bond hanging over him in a due obedience, yet it not appearing so by any words of the mother or any other plain circumstances, it was decreed to be a debt remaining upon the estate of the son and to be satisfied out of the assets.

There was an objection made that the uncle had paid himself out of the money he received some debts after the death of the said son as the apothecary's bill etc., which he ought to be upon the foot with other creditors.

But My Lord said that those debts were raised upon the credit of the uncle and he stood bound for them and that, therefore, he ought to pay himself those as well as any other debts.

243

Pave v. Fisher

(Ch. c. 1718)

A devise over of a testator's personal estate after a devise for life is good.

Lincoln's Inn MS. Hill 73, p. 12

Charles Pave etc., plaintiffs; John Fisher etc., defendants.

The bill was brought to have a trust performed and to have an account, to which end it set forth that [*blank*] did borrow £400 and £200 of Mr. Freeman and [*blank*] of Bristol, for the securing of which several sums with interest, the testator did by indenture subject his real estate and, by his last will, did confirm and ratify the said deed. And he devised his lands to two persons in trust that they should sell the same and, after the two debts above mentioned and other just debts were satisfied, they should pay the remainder to his wife. And such of his personal [estate] (all which he before gave his wife for life and made her sole executrix) that his wife should leave behind her at the time of her death, he did devise over to [*blank*].

My Lord Chancellor said that, in that case, if money had been out upon security and the wife had changed the security, yet he thought the devisee of the husband would be entitled to it after the death of the wife.

He decreed an account to be taken of the rents and profits of the estate received by the trustees and that the same should be sold and the two debts specially mentioned and other the just debts of the testator should be satisfied. And he gave leave for any creditor to go before the Master to make out his just debt and the remainder to be paid to the wife, the trustees to have their costs out of the trust estate and to have all just allowances.

244

Mayor and Town of Arundel v. Wilde

(Ch. c. 1718)

A court of equity will take jurisdiction of a case in order to prevent a multiplicity of litigation.

Lincoln's Inn MS. Hill 73, p. 14

The bill was exhibited to have an account, and it set forth that the said Town of Arundel was entitled to a toll of 2d. for every load of plank and likewise 2d. for every load of timber that was brought through the River Arundel or the sea and landed at the said Town of Arundel and that the defendants had brought 600 or a very great number of loads within a short time and that they might set forth what number of loads they had brought. And to have an account stated for the same was the bill.

The defendant expressly denied by his answer that he had brought above twenty-seven loads.

My Lord decreed that there was no foundation of equity in the bill, that they had never been at law, where their remedy lay to try the right of this corporation to such toll, and that he would not order any account for such a sum as 40s. 2d. And so he dismissed the bill with costs.

My Lord said, indeed, if the Mayor and Town had had several suits at law and recovered and still others refused to pay the said toll and combined together to defraud the said Town of such toll, to have the said toll settled in Chancery and to avoid multiplicity of suits, there might be some equity.

Sir Robert Raymond desired that the bill might be retained (as he said it often had been done) for a year upon condition that the plaintiffs try the cause at law within that time.

245

Hewett v. Ireland

(Ch. 1718)

A gift to a child to be born includes a child already in being.

Lincoln's Inn MS. Misc. 384, p. 27, pl. 1

19 May.

A trust was created by a deed for the benefit of such daughter or daughters as shall be begotten by A. on the body of B. A. had at the time of the making of the deed a daughter born, who married the defendant.

The query was whether this daughter could take.

Lord Chancellor [Lord Parker]: Yes, certainly, for it would be absurd to suppose a man should make a provision for a child not *in esse* and neglect a child already born. So '*procreatis*' often extends to those born after and '*procreandis*' to such as are born before [so] that the intent of the parties may be fulfilled.

246

Fremoult v. Dedire

(Ch. 1718)

Where a man contracts before marriage to give his wife a sum of money and later dies insolvent, his widow takes proportionately with his bond creditors.

Lincoln's Inn MS. Misc. 384, p. 29

21 May. Crayford v. Didier.

The plaintiff is the widow of Abraham Didier. There was a marriage contract between them in Holland, which he afterwards confirmed in England, whereby she was to have the benefit of her own estate which should come to her by donation or otherwise in the case she survived her husband and also to have £60 *per annum* for life out of his clearest estate and £30 in Romney Marsh for her dower.

The query is how this agreement shall be executed here, for the husband left bond creditors and but £5 *per annum*, which was liable to this agreement.

Mead, for the plaintiff: In Holland, this contract would take place of all other creditors, though the husband had become a bankrupt, and it should be construed here accordingly, as in the Case of Foubert v. Tusk;[1] a contract in France was executed here according to their law.

But query if that was not of a personalty.

Lutwyche: The plaintiff can only come in *pari passu* with the creditors by specialty. The husband was a native of England, but the plaintiff was a Dutchwoman. Didier, also by will, charged his real estate with the payment of his debts, which is not within the Statute of Fraudulent Devises.[2]

Lord Chancellor [Lord Parker]: The real estate over which Didier had a power must be sold for the payment of his debts. As to the wife's demands, I think she is entitled to the benefit of the contract as far as may be. As to the £60 *per annum*, that was no specific lien on any lands in certain. And, there not being sufficient [assets] to answer that, she must come in for a satisfaction out of the personal estate in equal degree with the other creditors by specialties and a value must be put upon her estate for life, as in Berisford v. Powele's Case.[3]

Lincoln's Inn MS. Misc. 12, p. 304, pl. 1

21 May 1718. Crayford v. Dedier.

---

[1] *Foubert v. Turst* (1703), Precedents in Chancery 207, 24 E.R. 101, 2 Eq. Cas. Abr. 475, 22 E.R. 404, 1 Brown P.C. 129, 1 E.R. 464.

[2] Stat. 3 Will. & Mar., c. 14 (*SR*, VI, 320–321).

[3] Note *Powell v. Beresford* (Del. 1707), 2 Lord Raymond 1282, 92 E.R. 341, 2 Eq. Cas. Abr. 761, 22 E.R. 646.

The plaintiff, a Dutchwoman, was the widow of Abraham Didier. On her marriage, he entered into a contract with her in Holland whereby he agreed that she should have the benefit of her own estate, which should come to her by donation or otherwise, if she survived him, and that she should have £60 *per annum* for life out of his clearest estate.

The husband died, leaving bond creditors.

For the plaintiff, it was insisted that, in Holland, this contract would take place of all other creditors, even though the husband had become a bankrupt, and that, in the case of Foubert v. Tust, in the House of Lords, a contract made in France was executed here according to their laws.

Lord Chancellor [Lord Parker] declared the plaintiff was entitled to the benefit of this contract accordingly as to the wife's estate. But, as to the £60 *per annum*, there not being sufficient assets, the plaintiff was to come in as a creditor by specialty.

[Other reports of this case: 1 Peere Williams 429, 24 E.R. 458, 2 Eq. Cas. Abr. 37, 257, 22 E.R. 31, 218.]

247

Rawlings v. Powell

(Ch. 1718)

The question in this case was whether a pecuniary legacy to the testator's creditor of a greater sum is a satisfaction of an unliquidated debt that is less than the legacy.

Lincoln's Inn MS. Misc. 384, p. 35

23 May 1718; upon exceptions.

Parker, Lord Chancellor: The question is whether a legacy of a greater sum shall be a satisfaction of a debt which is less, though not liquidated, but depending upon a running amount.

Cowper, for the plaintiff: In the common cases, a larger legacy is a satisfaction unless the intent of the testator appears otherwise. It was referred to the Master to state the nature of the debt and of the personal estate. And it appears that, if the debt is not satisfied by this legacy, the will must be defeated, for he gives £1300 in legacies and the whole personal estate amounts to but £1200. It might have been stronger for the defendant had there been a surplus.

Mead: The reason of the rule is taken from the civil law. *Debitor non praesumitur donare.*[1] In the Case of Chancy v. Kendrick, lately at the Rolls,[2] Kendrick, by his will, gave the defendant, his housekeeper, a legacy for her faithful service

---

1 *Black's Law Dictionary* (rev. 4th ed. 1968), p. 490.

2 *Chancey v. Wootton* (Ch. 1718–1720), see above, Case No. 234.

charged on land and was indebted to her by bond in a less sum, which the plaintiff, the executor, had paid and had not in his bill charged it to be a satisfaction. Yet the Master of the Rolls was of opinion it was a satisfaction of the bond debt.

Sir Thomas Powys, for the defendant, quoted Cuthbert and Peacock, Salk. 155;[1] a man may be both just and kind. Suppose a man owes his particular friend £499 and, by his will, gives him a legacy of £500, it would be absurd to say it is a satisfaction.

Peere Williams, for the defendant: If a man, in his will, says he gives, it ought not to be construed the same as to pay. The least proof of the testator's intent will bring it out of the common rule.

N.B. There was another point, whether the plaintiff as executor was entitled to the surplus though he had a specific legacy. But the defendant, by his answer, did not claim it.

Lord Chancellor [Lord Parker]: This does not come properly before me now upon the special matter of the Master's report. But you should have excepted to the report or rehear the cause. If the defendant has concluded himself from claiming the surplus, you must take it upon the terms in the answer, which are that he demands both his debt and legacy. I will consider of this case.

British Library MS. Hargrave 81, f. 28

10 December.

Powell, a drugster in London, had some dealings with the defendant, who was also a drugster in London. The account was then open, and, being well acquainted and they happening to be together at Epsom in Powell's last sickness, he makes his will and, without taking any notice of the dealings or that he was indebted to him, devises £500 to the defendant and makes him sole executor. And he makes no disposition of the residue. And the plaintiff, as next of kin, brings his bill for the residue. The cause was heard and came on to be reheard upon the defendant's petition.

Mr. *Vernon*, for the plaintiff: Where portions of provisions have been made by wills, for children or relations, if the testator was by covenant to pay or his land stood charged to pay or that he was otherwise debtor to such children and relations and took no notice of the debt or charge in his will, this, though in case of a portion or provision, which the testator as a parent was obliged to make, has constantly been held to be a satisfaction for the debt, charge, or covenant. In the case of Jesson and Jesson,[2] where the father's estate was charged or he was debtor to his children £5000, he, by his will, makes as large provisions for his children as the debt or charge, this was decreed a satisfaction, though, in the case of a child, there being no mention of the debt or charge, but the devise general, much more

[1] *Cuthbert v. Peacock* (1707), 1 Salkeld 155, 91 E.R. 143, also 2 Vernon 593, 23 E.R. 986, 1 Eq. Cas. Abr. 205, 232, 21 E.R. 992, 1012.

[2] *Jesson v. Jesson* (1691), 2 Vernon 255, 23 E.R. 766.

shall it be so when the devise is to a stranger, as here, the defendant and he had dealings. No account was stated or settled between them in the testator's lifetime, but upon account so set out in the defendant's answer, the defendant makes the balance to be £300 due to him so that a legacy of £500 was much more than his debt and, therefore, to be taken as a devise in satisfaction of that debt and he having the overplus, which is a beneficial devise to him, he ought to be excluded of the residue, and that should be distributed.

Mr. *Mead*, of the same side, said that, where the devise exceeded the value of the debt or demand, it was constantly deemed by the justice of this court a satisfaction or compensation for the debt etc. But, where the thing devised was short in value, there, it has been allowed a satisfaction *pro tanto.*

Mr. Serjeant *Hooper*: The case of Forster and Mount,[1] at the arguing of which I was present, was the first breach in this point upon the common law, which makes every testator's personal estate not particularly devised and which remains after debts, legacies, and funeral expenses discharged, be such remainder more or less, a gift to the executor of his care and trouble in executing that office, and it is, therefore, a gift in law to him. And the resolutions of the Lords since in the cases of the Lady Granville and Duchess of Beaufort and of Buckley and Littlebury[2] *et alii* have gone against that judgment and according to common law.

Mr. *Williams*: Since these cases mentioned by Mr. Serjeant, the Lord Chancellor Harcourt decreed accordingly in the case of Ball and Smith,[3] where Mr. Smith devised to his wife £500 and made her executrix and did not dispose of the remainder, it was, notwithstanding the legacy, decreed to her as executrix. It is objected that the defendant has put his case and defense upon a wrong point, which is against him, that it is not his act but the act of his counsel, which ought not to prejudice the defendant, especially where the mistake proceeds from the variety of judgment in such cases. And, the cause being now [upon a] rehearing, the whole matter is open to all the parties, and the court, it is hoped, will judge upon the whole according to the reality of the case and its circumstances.

Curia [Lord Parker]: The case cited of legacies to children or relations who have a charge upon the testator's estate do not come up to nor are precedents ex-

[1] *Foster v. Munt* (1689), 1 Vernon 473, 23 E.R. 598, 1 Eq. Cas. Abr. 243, 21 E.R. 1020, 2 Eq. Cas. Abr. 433, 443, 22 E.R. 368, 378, Dodd 78, Lincoln's Inn MS. Misc. 498, p. 27, Lincoln's Inn MS. Misc. 503, p. 93, Lincoln's Inn MS. Misc. 504, p. 88.

[2] *Lady Granville v. Duchess of Beaufort* (1709), 2 Vernon 648, 23 E.R. 1023, 1 Peere Williams 114, 24 E.R. 317, 1 Eq. Cas. Abr. 245, 21 E.R. 1021, 2 Eq. Cas. Abr. 415, 22 E.R. 352; *Buckley v. Littlebury* (1711), 3 Brown P.C. 43, 1 E.R. 1165, 1 Eq. Cas. Abr. 245, 21 E.R. 1021, also 2 Vernon 677, 23 E.R. 1040, Lincoln's Inn MS. Misc. 10, p. 86.

[3] *Ball v. Smith* (1698–1711), 2 Vernon 633, 675, 23 E.R. 1014, 1039, 2 Freeman 230, 22 E.R. 1178, 1 Eq. Cas. Abr. 245, 21 E.R. 1022, 2 Eq. Cas. Abr. 133, 434, 22 E.R. 114, 369.

actly for this case. In cases of precedents, we must go to the right reason of them and of the judgment, for, by following the precedents implicitly, we make another upon that and then another upon this and so on until we [shall have] run a great distance from the truth of the reason of the judgment or groundwork. Here, the nature of the debt will make a considerable difference in the reason of the judgment to be given. It is well observed by Mr. Mead, if the fact be so, that the nature of the debt is money to be paid the defendant upon the balance of account. The thing devised to him is money, *viz.* £500. So both are of the same nature and kind and, therefore, proper and natural to be taken as a satisfaction. But, if the fact be otherwise, the consequence may be so too, for, if a man has a running and open account with another and it is uncertain whether he owes that person anything or not or, if anything, how much, and he, without taking any notice of this dealing or account, devises to the other a certain sum or thing, I cannot think he intended this as a satisfaction of what he did not know nor could be apprised of nor has taken notice of, but must take it for an independent debt. The case of Foster and Mount was founded upon particular circumstances and upon the fraud that appeared. The resolutions since in the House of Lords have left the matter so fluctuating and uncertain one knows not how to judge. In cases of rehearings as well as appeal, the whole matter is open at least to the party who does not petition, the nature of the debt here not being ascertained.

He gave no judgment, but referred it to the Master to state the nature of the debt. *Vide* the following case.

[Other copies of this report: British Library MS. Hargrave 82, f. 23.]

[Other reports of this case: British Library MS. Hargrave 77, f. 10, British Library MS. Hargrave 303, f. 15v, *sub nom.* Rawlins v. Powel, 1 Peere Williams 297, 24 E.R. 397, 2 Eq. Cas. Abr. 438, 491, 22 E.R. 373, 417.]

248

Target v. Gaunt

(Ch. 1718)

In this case, the words in the will in issue, 'died without issue', meant having no issue living at the time of death.

Lincoln's Inn MS. Misc. 10, p. 259

24 May 1718.

William Targett, by a will dated 9 April 1692, devised a leasehold estate to his son Henry for life if the term should so long continue and no longer and, after his decease, to such issue of Henry as he should give it to. And, in case Henry died without issue, then, the testator bequeathed the premises to his brother for the remainder of the term. Henry died without issue after the testator. And the question was if the limitation over to the testator's brother, being of a term was good.

Lord Parker: The dying without issue in this case must not be taken in a legal sense, for that, in the case of an inheritance, would be whenever there should be a failer of issue. But it must be understood in a vulgar sense, that is in case there shall be no issue of Henry living at the time of his death, for then it was that his issue, if they took at all, were to take, for it is given to him for life and, after his death, to such of his issue as he should give it to so that, if he had issue and gave it to such issue, then they were to take, but, if he should die without issue, that is if there should be no issue of his body living at the time of his death, then the estate was to go over.

He decreed it to the testator's brother.

Lincoln's Inn MS. Misc. 384, p. 32

24 May.

S., being possessed of a term in gross, devises it to his son H. during his minority and, if he attain twenty-one, then for life and no longer and, after his death, then to such of his issue as he should give the same by will and, after his death without issue, then to Albinus, under whom the plaintiff claims.

And the query is whether this be not a limitation after an estate tail and, consequently, void and, if it be, then the next of kin to the tenant in tail will be entitled to the term.

Raymond, for the defendant: There can be no limitation of a term in gross after an estate tail. This is not if he shall die without issue living at the time of his death. If a real estate be devised to A. for life and if he dies without issue, then over, it carries an estate tail to A. by implication.

Hooper, for the plaintiff: No estate can pass by implication which destroys the estate expressly given, as in Popham v. Ramfields, 1 Salk. 236; a devise to P. for life and, after his death, to his sons in tail male and, if he dies without issue, then over to B.; the query before Lord Trevor and the other judges was whether P. had an estate tail and could suffer a recovery; it was adjudged he could not.

Mead: The intent of the testator is to take effect if it may be by the rules of law. The words import no more than an estate for life to H. with a power for him to give the residue of the term to his issue, provided, if he did not execute that power, then to go over, for, if H. had had issue and had not executed that power, the issue could not have taken it but Albinus who had the devise over. The case of Peacock v. Spooner was to the wife and her issue and, if she died without issue, then over. It was a good devise over, but, then, the wife would have given away the term to a stranger from the relations of her husband, whose the term was. And, therefore, it might be the more favored.

Lord Chancellor [Lord Parker]: The plaintiff may redeem. The will devises the term to H. for his life and no longer. At law, if a devise of land be to A. and, if he dies without issue, then to B., this gives the issue of A. an estate tail by implication but, in [case] of a term, it will not descend to the issue. Here, it may be construed if he dies without issue living at the time of his death. Here, the act of the devisee must determine whether his issue shall take or not. Lodington v. Kime, 3 Lev. 431. Here can be no estate tail, and it must be taken if he die without issue living at the time of his death. Therefore, I think this estate vested in Albinus, and, consequently, the plaintiffs are entitled.

[Other reports of this case: 1 Peere Williams 432, 24 E.R. 459, 10 Modern 402, 88 E.R. 782, Gilbert Rep. 149, 25 E.R. 104, 1 Eq. Cas. Abr. 193, 21 E.R. 983, 2 Eq. Cas. Abr. 343, 22 E.R. 292.]

249

Trafford v. Ashton

(Ch. 1718)

In this case, the portions were to be raised by the sale or mortgage of the lands and not out of the issues and profits of the land.

Lincoln's Inn MS. Misc. 11, p. 27

26 May 1718. Trafford *et ux.*, Lister *et ux.*, and Curzon *et ux.*, plaintiffs; Sir Ralph Asheton *et al.*, defendants.

Sir Ralph Asheton, the defendant's uncle, upon his marriage by settlements dated 19 May 1680 conveys lands to the use of himself for life, remainder to trustees for 99 years, remainder to the first and other sons of the marriage in tail male, remainder to Richard Asheton, brother of old Sir Ralph, for life, remainder to his first and other sons in tail male, remainder to the right heirs of old Sir Ralph. The trusts of the term of 99 years were that the trustees, out of the rents and profits of the premises, should pay to Mary, the intended wife, for life and, after Sir Ralph's death, to raise such maintenance for the eldest son as therein is mentioned and upon further trust that, in case Sir Ralph Asheton should happen to die without issue male begotten on the body of Mary, his intended wife, and should leave one or more daughters begotten between them and that, for want of issue male of the said marriage, the premises, by virtue of the said settlement, should descend or come to the said Richard Asheton or any of his issue male or their heirs male, that then the said trustees should, out of the rents, issues, and profits of the premises raise, levy, and pay to all and every the daughters of the said Sir Ralph and Mary, his intended wife, the several sums following, *viz.* if there should be no son and but one daughter, then such daughter should have £5000 for her portion and, if there should be two or more daughters, then such daughters should have out of the issues and profits of the premises the sum of £8000 to be equally divided between them.

Sir Ralph and his wife are dead without issue male and have left three daughters, who are married to the plaintiffs, Trafford, Lister, and Curzon, two of which daughters married since Sir Ralph's death.

The plaintiffs bring their bill against the defendant, Sir Ralph Asheton, who is the son of Richard, the remainderman, and against the trustees of the term to have the portions raised by sale or mortgage of the term together with interest from the death of old Sir Ralph, who survived his wife.

The question was if the portions should be raised by sale or mortgage in regard the settlement had prescribed no other way for raising the portions than by the rents and profits and whether the plaintiffs should have interest.

It was objected for the defendant that here was no certain time limited by the settlement for paying the portions, to which it was answered that the trusts of the term were to raise the £8000 so soon as conveniently might be, which must be understood presently, for so it is in the judgment of law.

Lord Chancellor [Lord Cowper]: There is a clause in the settlement that, if there is issue male, that then the trustees may by the rents and profits raise £1000 apiece for daughters' portions to be paid at twenty-one or marriage. Now, it is admitted that, if there had been issue male, the term might have been sold for raising the portions in that case in regard there was a limited time in the settlement for paying them. But can it be supposed that Sir Ralph Asheton, when he made this settlement, had a greater regard to the remainderman than to his eldest son and that he could intend the term should be sold in prejudice of an elder son if there had been one and yet in favor to the remainderman? It should not be sold if there was no issue male of the marriage.

I decree the £8000 to be raised by sale or mortgage of the term, and, as to interest, that is a consequence of the other, for, if the portions are to be raised by a sale, that sale might have been made immediately after the death of Sir Ralph and, therefore, from that time, interest ought to be computed.

See the preceding case, which was cited in this case; see also 1 Ch. Reports, Lady Backhouse v. Middleton, fo. 173; Hughes and Collis, fo. 179, and 2 Ch. Rep., Lingon v. Foley, 205.[1]

[Other reports of this case: 2 Vernon 660, 23 E.R. 1029, 1 Peere Williams 415, 24 E.R. 451, 1 Eq. Cas. Abr. 213, 21 E.R. 998, 2 Eq. Cas. Abr. 641, 22 E.R. 537.]

---

[1] *Stanhope v. Thacker* (Ch. 1716), see above, Case No. 146; *Backhouse v. Middleton* (1670), 1 Chancery Cases 173, 208, 22 E.R. 748, 765, also 3 Chancery Reports 39, 21 E.R. 722, 2 Freeman 132, 22 E.R. 1108; *Hughes v. Collis* (1641), 1 Chancery Cases 179, 22 E.R. 751, *Lingon v. Foley* (1674), 2 Chancery Cases 205, 22 E.R. 912.

250

Atwood v. Atwood

(Ch. 1718)

A writ of homine replegiando *does not lie against a husband for confining his wife.*

Lincoln's Inn MS. Misc. 10, p. 266

Last day of Easter term 1718.

The defendant [the husband of the plaintiff] came to show cause against granting a writ of *homine replegiando* for the plaintiff, his wife, which had been granted unless cause [be shown] upon a suggestion that the defendant confined his wife.

And it was now insisted on for the defendant that this was new and without precedents and that never any such writ had been granted for the wife against her husband, for, if she is ill used by him, she may bring her [writ of] habeas corpus [?] or may exhibit articles.

For the wife, it was said that it appeared by affidavits that the wife's estate was settled for her separate use and that her husband had used her very ill and confined her because she refused to settle her estate upon him.

Lord Chancellor [Lord Parker]: This writ ought not to be granted in this case. The husband, by law, has a right to confine his wife to prevent her doing any harm, but he is not to imprison her. If he uses her cruelly, the proper method is to libel in the spiritual court *propter saevitiam*. However, this court will interpose if the husband goes about to compel his wife to undo the contracts which he has made with her or her trustees.

And, therefore, he ordered that she should be quieted in her estate and that there should be an injunction to stay waste until an answer and farther order.

Lincoln's Inn MS. Misc. 384, p. 36, pl. 1

26 May.

Upon a motion for a [writ of] *homine replegiando* for the plaintiff, who is the wife of the defendant and, by her bill, sets forth the articles before marriage whereby she was to have power over her own estate and that the defendant used her hardly and confined her in order to make her deliver up her articles, the Lord Chancellor [Lord Parker] ordered her to be set at liberty and be put into possession as before until answer and further order.

Gilbert Rep. 149, 25 E.R. 105

Monday, 26 May 1718.

In this case, it was held by the court that a wife cannot, either by herself or *prochein ami*, bring a [writ of] *homine replegiando* against her husband, for he has by law a right to the custody of her, and he may, if he thinks fit, confine her, but must not imprison her; if he does, it will be good cause for her to apply to the spiritual court for a divorce *propter saevitiam*. But the nature and proceedings in a writ *de homine replegiando* are such as cannot be maintained by a wife against her husband.

[Other copies of this report: Precedents in Chancery 492, 24 E.R. 220, 2 Eq. Cas. Abr. 778, 22 E.R. 661.]

251

Anonymous

(Ch. 1718)

A person who receives money to invest for the payor must account to the person who paid the money.

Lincoln's Inn MS. Hill 73, p. 20, pl. 2

Trinity term, June 14.

The plaintiff's bill [was] to call the defendant to an account for monies put into his hands by the plaintiff and which he was to allow the plaintiff at the rate of £4 per cent. The defendant pleads that he had remitted £167 to the plaintiff's brother and that the money he had in his hands was for a security to indemnify him in his dealings with his brother. The defendant had £800 or more money of the plaintiff in his hands but then refused to trust the brother anymore when he had so much money in his hands, which, had he thought the plaintiff's money was a security for any such debt, he would not have stopped.

The defendant was ordered to be examined upon interrogatories upon bringing the sum of £167, the sum in question, into court. Costs were reserved until after the examination.

252

Spence v. Allen

(Ch. 1718)

A witness can be re-examined after the publication of the depositions where the interrogatories are objected to as leading but the error of the leading questions was de minimis.

Lincoln's Inn MS. Misc. 10, p. 265

19 June 1718.

A motion was made for a new examination of witnesses after publication had passed, the interrogatories having been reported leading and an order made for suppressing the depositions. And it was alleged that, unless the plaintiff might examine his witnesses over again, it would be a very great hardship upon him in regard he would be forced to go to the hearing without any evidence. And, therefore, it was prayed that he might examine the same witnesses upon new interrogatories to be settled by a Master. And the Case of Bawdes and Amherst[1] was cited where the like order was made by Lord Cowper in the like case.

This was much opposed by the other side as a thing of dangerous consequence.

But notwithstanding, Lord Chancellor [Lord Parker] upon perusing the interrogatories, being of opinion that they were not so leading but that a counsel might easily fall into the mistake of drawing them in the manner they were, he thought it would be hard that the plaintiff should be deprived of the benefit of his evidence through such a mistake as this. And, therefore, he granted the motion.

Lincoln's Inn MS. Misc. 384, p. 39, pl. 1

19 June.

[There was a] motion that, interrogatories being reported [to be] leading, the plaintiff may exhibit new ones after publication and so not lose material evidence.

Raymond, for the plaintiff, produced a precedent of Lord Cowper, Bawd v. Amhurst.

There were produced for the defendant Harding v. Coxeter [and] Dolbon v. Allison.

The Lord Chancellor [Lord Parker], after hearing the interrogatories and himself reading the depositions, declared that the interrogatories were not plainly leading nor drawn with that intent ad that it would be hard the plaintiff should lose the benefit of such material depositions barely for the mistake of his counsel.

Therefore, he gave the plaintiff leave to examine *de novo* paying all the costs.

Lincoln's Inn MS. Hill 73, p. 23

[The question was] whether the witness might be re-examined after publication passed. Harding and Coxeter [was] against it.

My Lord [Parker] ordered that the plaintiff should re-examine his witness as to those points in the interrogatories which were called leading and that he should not lose the benefit of examining them for the small blunder in his counsel.

Precedents in Chancery 493, 24 E.R. 221

In this case, interrogatories and the depositions of witnesses taken on them had been suppressed, for that the interrogatories were leading. And then publication passed. And now the court was moved that a new set of interrogatories might be

[1] *Bawdes v. Amhurst* (Ch. 1714–1715), see above, Case No. 47.

drawn and settled by a Master for the examination of this witness, whose evidence was very material and yet must be wholly lost if the court would not indulge them this way. And, though the practice has been always against it and it was insisted to be of dangerous consequence, yet one precedent being produced to this purpose and the interrogatories which had been suppressed were such as might have been drawn by many other counsel without any apprehension of their being leading, the court, to let in the party to the benefit of this witness's testimony, ordered interrogatories to be put in and settled by a Master for his examination over again.

[Other reports of this case: Gilbert Rep. 150, 25 E.R. 105, 1 Eq. Cas. Abr. 232, 21 E.R. 1012.]

253

Brown v. Brown

(Ch. 1718)

The question in this case was whether the executors of a will, having been declared by the testator to be trustees, should take the undisposed residuum of the estate.

Lincoln's Inn MS. Misc. 10, p. 252

14 June 1718.

Edmund Brown, by will, after several legacies, gives all the rest of his estate after debts and legacies paid to his executors, who were his nephews and niece, in trust to hold to them and the survivor and the executors of the survivor in trust that they should with all convenient speed put out the surplus upon security and, with the yearly income, should pay an annual sum to as many of his nearest relations and kindred as they or the survivor should find necessitous or see convenient. And, for their care and pains to be taken therein, he gave to each of his executors (having in the former part of his will given them legacies) the farther sum of £20 to be allowed them out of his estate. And he willed that, in case any of his next of kin or nearest relations, *viz.* his brothers and sisters and their children, should want necessaries and that his executors should find them in want, then he bequeathed to such relation £10 a year for life, anything in his will to the contrary notwithstanding, but he made no disposition of the surplus in any other manner. And the question was to whom it belonged.

Mr. *Vernon* insisted for the plaintiff that there were not only particular legacies given to the executors, but they are expressly declared in the will to be executors in trust and, besides, the £20 legacies given to the executors are given them for their labor and pains, which alone is sufficient to exclude them from the surplus.

As to the case of Buckley and Littlebury, *quod vide ante*,[1] there was a proof that the testator intended that the surplus should go to the executors and that proof was admitted to be read and, since that case, the court has admitted the like proof to be made of the testator's intention where the next of kin come to take away the surplus by reason of particular legacies given to the executor.

Lord Chancellor [LORD PARKER]: Every executor is an executor in trust.

The Master of the Rolls [JEKYLL], being present in court, said that, in the Case of the Duchess of Beaufort,[2] the plate was given to the duchess for life and that, after her death, it should go as an heirloom and what the Lords went upon in that case was that there was a good reason for inserting the plate in the will because it was to go after her death as an heirloom and, therefore, they would not suppose that the duke intended thereby to exclude the duchess from the surplus.

As to Foster and Munt's Case,[3] the executors were strangers and had only £5 apiece given them for their labor and pains.

As to Buckley and Littlebury's Case, proofs were admitted because the executors had the law on their side and such proofs were for supporting the law.

In Lord Harcourt's time, there were two cases that seemed to contradict the Case of Foster and Monck, so that, as the resolutions now stand, it is difficult for practisers, this point being so fluctuating, to advise their clients. I am sure I found it so.

In the principal case, the court took time to consider of it.

Lincoln's Inn MS. Misc. 380, pt. 3, p. 186

Trinity term 4 Geo. [1718].

Edward Brown, the testator, had five brothers and seven sisters, some of which died in the testator's lifetime leaving children. Edward Brown makes his will as follows, in the beginning it is 'I make, constitute, and appoint A., B., and C. my executors in trust', being both nephews and nieces to the testator, desiring them to take on them 'the trust and execution of this my will'. After several legacies, he devises to A., his executor, £50 'for his care and pains herein' and devises £100 to B. and £40 to C., and he devises particular legacies to all his brothers and sisters and all their children and that, upon payment of their several legacies, they shall give releases of all accounts, bequests, legacies, and demands whatsoever or else the legacies to be void. Then follows:

all the rest and residue of my estate after my debts and legacies [are] paid I devise to my executors etc. in trust as aforesaid on the condition that they shall

[1] *Buckley v. Littlebury* (1711), 3 Brown P.C. 43, 1 E.R. 1165, 1 Eq. Cas. Abr. 245, 21 E.R. 1021, 2 Vernon 677, 23 E.R. 1040, Lincoln's Inn MS. Misc. 10, p. 86.

[2] *Duke of Beaufort v. Lord Dundonald* (Ch. 1716–1717), see above, Case No. 131.

[3] *Foster v. Munt* (1689), 1 Vernon 473, 23 E.R. 598, 1 Eq. Cas. Abr. 243, 21 E.R. 1020, 2 Eq. Cas. Abr. 433, 443, 22 E.R. 368, 378, Dodd 78, Lincoln's Inn MS. Misc. 498, p. 27, Lincoln's Inn MS. Misc. 503, p. 93, Lincoln's Inn MS. Misc. 504, p. 88.

put out the surplus to interest or continue it on their own securities and, out of the income, shall pay annually to such of his nearest relations as shall be necessitous or as they shall see convenient, and I give to my executors £20 apiece for their care and pains and of any of my nearest relations I mean brothers and sisters and their children [who] shall complain to my executors that they want necessaries, then my executors shall pay to such person any sum not exceeding £10.

This bill is brought to have a distribution of the residue.

First, whether the executors shall have the residuum, they being legatees and executors in trust, or it shall go in distribution;

Second, what interest the nearest relations have in the residuum (if it had been real estate, no time being mentioned, they take for life) but this being personal, whether the nearest relations shall not take the whole not in a course of distribution, but all of them equally, the child as well as the parent;

Third, whether the release directed to be given on payment of their particular legacies shall not bar such legatees, being the nearest kindred, of the residuum.

For the defendants, it was said, though the executors are said to be in trust, yet that trust is for a particular purpose only, *viz.* the payment of those annuities, and, when that is satisfied, it comes within the common case where an executor is likewise a legatee. And the late practice has been that a legacy shall not bar an executor of the residuum; it only shows the intent of the testator that the executor shall have something at all events and shall be as certain as the other legatees. One of the executors, in her answer, says she believes the testator did not intend that they should have the residuum, but, however, if the court should be of opinion that the executors have a right to the residuum, she claims her part.

Have you examined the defendants as to that? If not, I cannot take notice of it. This distribution of the income among the nearest relation as the executors shall see convenient this court is not to intermeddle until executors abuse this trust, and then this court is to interpose and control the discretion of the executors. But the parties desiring the direction of this court, let them propose a scheme to the Master.

Master of the Rolls [Jekyll]: I do not think the case of Littlebury and Buckley to be in the least contrary or to shake the authority of Foster and Munt, where a legacy of £5 apiece was given to the executors for their care and pains, adjudged this bars the executor of the residuum. But the Case of Littlebury etc. admitted of parol proof only that the testator intended the executor should have the residuum in support of the common law and not that he should have the residuum without proof. The Case of the Duchess of Beauford, who was made executrix and the use of the plate given her for her life and that, after her death, the plate should go as an heirloom to the family, it was determined that the duchess should have the residuum, and the reason [was] because it was not a particular legacy but that she should have the plate for her life only and that it should go as heirloom.

But, in My Lord Chancellor Harcourt's time, there were two cases determined directly that a legacy should bar the executors of the residuum. The first was Smith v. Bawes; the other [*blank*]. In the first case, the Chancellor desired to be attended with precedents, and I was a counsel in that case and know that he was attended very slightly with precedents and, after the Case of Foster and Munt, there was a great run of precedents that the executor being legatee should not have the residuum.

Lord Chancellor [Lord Parker]: This is a very intricate and [. . .] will. Let me be attended with a copy of the will and precedents. It seems to be pretty strong against the executor.

The Master of the Rolls [Jekyll] seemed inclined that the release would be a bar.

254

Warner v. Jenkins

(Ch. 1718)

A defendant can be required to make discovery of his own gross negligence.

A banker who receives stolen negotiable instruments through his own gross negligence must return them to the rightful owner.

Lincoln's Inn MS. Misc. 380, pt. 3, p. 188

Lottery orders and tickets are endorsed by the owner to blank to be disposed of by the plaintiffs [Warner and Snow, goldsmiths]. Snow having the orders etc. to the value of £700 in a bag and being at the Bank of England, the bag is taken from him, that this was the 28th of April 1715. Snow, the same day, gets advertisements dispatched to all the goldsmiths and bankers by the beadles of Goldsmiths' Hall and publishes advertisements in the *Daily Courant* and *Gazette* until the 8th of July. One Samuel Snow, who had got one of these orders of £50 and twenty-six lottery tickets of £10 each, goes to the defendants [Jenkins and King], bankers in Lombard Street, and takes up money on them. This Samuel Snow was a broker on the Exchange and formerly had dealings with the defendants and had cheated them by imposing a blank ticket of £10 for a benefit of £50 and had been guilty of several other miscarriages in his way of business, which the defendants confess they have heard a general report of.

The dealings between Samuel Snow and the defendants was after this matter. One Player deposited £550 in the defendants' hands, for which he had the defendant's note payable on demand and for which Player was to have no interest from the defendants, but Samuel Snow gave a note to the defendants to pay him interest for the £550. Weekly, Samuel Snow brings tickets and other securities to the defendants, for which they advanced him money not exceeding the £550, and their securities were deposited and taken back again on payment on the money two or three times a day, and these securities were bundled up together with a paper about them in which was written Snow's securities for so much money, but no entry of these transactions were made in their book. This the defendant proved by some witnesses, goldsmiths, was the method and practice of bankers. The money advanced by Player was to answer interest to the defendants and to save the trouble of computing interest from time to time with Snow.

This bill was brought to know how the defendants came to these tickets and what consideration they gave for them and whether they had not notice these tickets had been lost.

The defendants disclose the matter before recited and that they had examined their servants, who say they did not know of such notice left at their shop so as to apply it to the tickets and orders when they came to their hands and that they frequented Baker's Coffee House, the place where the reward was to be paid, and that they read over the advertisements with a general view and not as to anything that concerned them, that they do not remember when the tickets and orders came to their hands, but that, the 6th of August, Player took up his money and then the orders and tickets came to be distinguished in their books.

The plaintiff proved by the beadle of the Goldsmith's Company, who, in his examination, says he assuredly believed he left one of those advertisements at the defendants' shop, which was in his division.

The plaintiff likewise proved that the defendants turned the tickets into an order, that they employed for this purpose an officer in the office, who being befriended, entered at a time that was not an office hour, and that this person was usually employed by the defendants but only this time for the defendant [. . .], that, if such a way of advertising shall be taken as notice to a purchaser, no man can be secure in the purchase of any government securities, this is not proper for this court, for, if the plaintiff has a title and the defendant have notice, then [an action of] trover lies at common law.

Lord Chancellor [Lord Parker]: I do not take this to be a matter of such great consequence as it is represented. I am sure the contrary would be only an encouragement to thieves and rogues. It is proper to have a discovery in this court. I do not know whether they can maintain [an action of] trover because the plaintiffs had the possession only and no actual assignment. As for the evidence of the beadle, he says as much as any honest man can say without their happened any particular circumstance to make him remember. The defendants will not discover when the tickets came to their hands. And this method of taking securities without making entries in their books, though the defendants have not proved direct fraud, yet it is such a gross negligence as will at any time cover fraud. The defendants say they are not bound to take notice of advertisements or that they forgot it. I think it is not necessary to determine how far such public notice shall be binding on purchasers, but, here, the defendants not owning when the tickets came to their hands, for aught I know, the defendants might had had the advertisements in their hand when the tickets were brought. Therefore, here being such gross negligence, I think the defendants ought to make the plaintiffs satisfaction. These tickets were had of a person who formerly had imposed on them. Here is no proof that seems to affect the defendants' credit, but here is such a gross negligence as can hardly be distinguished from fraud. When a man does all that in him lies to give them notice and notice actually [was] left with the defendants, common justice required him to look into it. The defendants have not made it part of their case that the tickets came to him a long time after the notice. That possibly might have altered the case.

The defendants applied to the court and desired His Lordship would make a declaration that they had not been guilty of any fraud and that His Lordship would not give costs against them because that would look like a punishment and that they acquiesced in His Lordship's decree.

Chancellor [Lord Parker]: I reserve costs until the defendants have made satisfaction.

One circumstance in this case was the defendants, after the 6th August, sold one ticket to A., who offered to sell it to B. No, says B., it is one of the tickets that has been so often advertised, on which A. carries the ticket to the defendant who re-paid his money, and B. informed the plaintiff concerning the tickets.

Lincoln's Inn MS. Hill 73, p. 21

16 June.

The plaintiff had lost some Exchequer orders, and he immediately sends to all the goldsmiths in London, among the rest, to the defendant, as he truly believed, which was as much as any honest man in such a case could swear unless some accident which at that time happened might fix it in his memory. And he put it into the News and ordered a reward to any that should bring it again to be paid at Barker's Coffee House, which the defendant confessed by his answer, was the house he most used. These orders came to the defendant's hands etc.

My Lord [Parker] ordered the orders to be assigned to the plaintiff, the defendant to be accountable for the interest which had been made upon them and to be examined upon interrogatories as to that point.

255

Aulston v. Greenway

(Ch. 1718)

The jury are the judges of the credibility of a witness.

Lincoln's Inn MS. Hill 73, p. 113

18 June 1718; exceptions. Sir <Robert> Oliver Aulston v. Greenway.

First exception, which [was] brought to enquire into the consideration to a mortgage, which was since a decree made in this cause, [was] to the Master's second report, for that the Master has allowed £400 which was to be paid to one Colonel Russell for a gratuity to him for getting him, Robert [Aulston], made a baronet in 1696, a man very weak and in poor circumstances and there does no time appear that the money was paid or, if it was, was a very unreasonable gratuity, but it does not by any proof appear when it was paid. Foulks, a defendant, confesses that £160 was paid for fees of making Sir Oliver a baronet in 1696. Foulks had a mortgage from Sir Oliver for £1500. It is very possible that might be given as a security for the sum of £400 if ever it was paid.

Colonel Russell, upon his examination, says that he did receive £400 of the defendant Foulks agreed to be paid to him for procuring a warrant for creating the complainant a baronet from King William and that Greenway was no ways privy to the said agreement.

Foulks, in his examination, swore he paid among other things £40 to one Wells, who positively denies any such payment.

Foulks, it appears by Sir Richard Hoare's books, did receive £800 and that he did pay part of it over, but it does not appear that it was for the use of the plaintiff or by his order or to any person the plaintiff dealt with.

N.B. If a man examines a witness which he might except to as interested, he, by that, allows him a witness, but, if, by anything afterwards, the witness appears to have sworn anything that is false, he, by that means, may be disallowed afterwards.

The jury are to try the credit of a witness for, until then, a man's oath is evidence and not a man's saying he will not believe him etc.

Foulks charges the plaintiff with £9 paid to Aubrey for wood and coals, and Awbrey, upon examination, swears he never received but £2 19s. 00d. A trial was ordered at law whether the several sums so sworn to be paid by Foulks were so paid to the plaintiff or to his use by an issue between the plaintiff and the defendant to be settled by the Master, costs reserved.

Second exception, for that the Master has charged the plaintiff with the sums of £70 and £100 demanded by Gimbert, a broker in Long Lane, for [*blank*] and interest for the same, whereas they were only debts of a simple contract, but, by the decree, the mortgage of Gimbert is ordered to be a security for such debt. [It was] overruled as an exception to the decree.

Third exception, for that the Master has allowed the sums of £300 and £350, whereas there was only proof of part of the same sums paid. Heather and Southern, examined, [were] proof [of] the plaintiff's due execution of the endorsement of a sum of £350 as money lent by Greenway and Gimbert. The deposit of £5 [is] to remain until after the trial of this issue at the sittings after term.

256

Cornwall v. Pitts

(Ch. 1718)

The term 'poor relations' in a will is an expression of endearment only.

Lincoln's Inn MS. Misc. 380, pt. 3, p. 193, pl. 1

21 June.

Sir J. Kingsmill devises several legacies to several relations and an annuity chargeable on his fee simple estate to the daughter of his cousin Wyndham and, afterward, devises an estate to Wyndham in tail, remainder to his cousin Pory in tail, etc. And, afterwards, he devises that the residue of his personal estate should be divided among his poor relations as hereinbefore named in such proportion as his executors should think proper.

The late Master [TREVOR] decreed that the words 'poor relations' did not signify the circumstances of his relations that were to take, but was an expression of endearment.

Second, none were entitled to the distribution but such as were both relations and legatees and that such relations as were mentioned only to describe another person as the children and so were not entitled to anything.

Third, the devisees of land were not entitled to any part of the residue of the personal estate.

Fourth, the annuity charged on the real estate is likewise not entitled to a part of the residue.

The two first points were affirmed by LORD COWPER.

And now [there was an] appeal by the annuitant.

Lord Chancellor [LORD PARKER]: I think the annuitants are likewise the objects of his favor. I do not know [how] to distinguish between legacies and devisees.[1] They are entitled to a part.

[Other reports of this case: 1 Peere Williams 327, 24 E.R. 410.]

[1] Sic in MS. for legatees and devisees.

257

Wright v. Pilling

(Ch. 1718)

In a bill to redeem, an unsecured bond debt cannot be tacked to a mortgage, but a judgment debt can be.

New matter is admissible in evidence upon a rehearing.

Lincoln's Inn MS. Misc. 380, pt. 3, p. 191

22 June. Appeal.

Cockroft mortgages the land in question to A. in 1699. Pilling, the plaintiff, obtains a judgment Hilary [term] 1704[/05]. Cockroff, March the 10th, 1704[/05], mortgages the same land to Wright, the defendant, and, March the 12th, sells him the equity of redemption. March the 23rd, the sheriff executes the [writ of] *fieri facias* on the judgment and sells the term to R. in trust for the defendant. After[ward], the defendant, having the mortgage [of] 1699, brings his bill in Easter [term] 1705 to redeem the mortgage, upon which followed an agreement and the mortgage was assigned to the defendant. The mortgaged estate was only an estate for the life of Cockroft and his wife. In 1716, Wright brings his bill to redeem the defendant on paying his mortgage only without the judgment. And [it was] so decreed by the Master.

For Pilling, it was insisted that he ought to be satisfied his judgment as well as mortgage, for a judgment debt, though it be only a general encumbrance on all the party's lands he has at that time, yet this is [as] much to be favored in a court of equity as a paid mortgagee who takes a first mortgage.

Lord Chancellor [Lord Parker]: A bond debt cannot be tacked to a mortgage. Whether it shall against the heir of the mortgagor is another case.

Counsel: The Case of Barron against Eubank[1] was cited. Charlton Whitlock mortgages his manor of A. to the bishop of Ely, then grants estates for lives to R., S., and T. Afterwards, R. obtains a judgment against C. Whitlock and afterwards purchases in the bishop of Ely's mortgage. It was decreed that R. should be satisfied his judgment as well as the mortgage before the others should be let in. This was before the Master of the Rolls [Trevor].

At law, he will be paid his honest debt unless equity takes it from him. He has a security affecting the equity of redemption as much as a paid mortgagee, who has equity and a legal title. Wright cannot be in a better condition than Cockroft himself. Then if he had come to redeem, he must pay both judgment and mortgage. We are a fair purchaser without notice. For Wright, a judgment or statute is a general lien, which is reduced to charge a particular estate as the law assigns it to him. But in a mortgage, he is a purchaser of particular lands *pro*

[1] *Bacon v. Eubank* (Ch. 1715), see above, Case No. 69.

tanto. And it is like a dower and a jointress in dower. She is content to take such an estate as arises to her by law.

As to C. Whitlock's case, it differs from this, for there Eubank, who had the judgment, was likewise the purchaser of an estate for life and the judgment was allowed because he was a purchaser for life.

The Lord Chancellor [Lord Parker] seemed to be of an opinion that the judgment should be likewise satisfied.

But Wright agreed to take what was due to him and convey. Nosworthy and Sir J. Maynard was cited where the judgment debt was to be satisfied before redemption.

In this case, Cockroft was the only witness that proved the deeds of conveyance to Wright two days before the execution. The Chancellor [Lord Parker] declared that his evidence cannot be admitted, for there is a strong presumption of management to shelter himself from the judgment.

Before the Master, a week's time was given to Pilling to try the validity of Wright's purchase, which he did not think fit to do.

The Lord Chancellor [Lord Parker]: Though he declined then, yet, on appeal from the Master, the whole matter lies open before me, and the invalidity of Cockroft's evidence did not appear to the counsel, but, otherwise, in the House of Lords, nothing can be read there but what was actually produced in this court. This appeal is to be enrolled as my decree. It is an application to the Keeper himself to hear the cause before he makes it his decree.

Chancellor [Lord Parker]: Wright supposing this estate for life but a slender security has not thought fit to stir in the matter until twelve years after and now sets up his title; therefore, I would not have made the defendant to account for the profits during his possession.

Lincoln's Inn MS. Misc. 384, p. 33

21 July 1718. Appeal from the Rolls.

The plaintiff purchases the equity of redemption of the defendant. Cockroft, afterwards finding a prior mortgage, would have taken that in, but the defendant Pilling, who had a judgment subsequent, gets the mortgage and would tack the judgment to it.

Vernon, for the plaintiff: A judgment creditor cannot by buying in a prior judgment or other encumbrance give himself a preference, but the encumbrances must take place according to their priority. But a purchaser or mortgagee who has a specific lien on the land may. This is a term for years, and the defendant's judgment was signed prior to the plaintiff's purchase, but execution was not taken out until after.

Lutwyche, for the defendant: The defendant's judgment is a specific lien, and we have the law with us.

Cowper: The plaintiff is not a fair purchaser nor is a creditor by a judgment and had the term in execution and a bill of sale from the sheriff.

Curia [Lord Parker]: The question is whether this judgment ever affected the land, for, otherwise, the bill of sale by the sheriff under the execution was void.

Williams, for the defendant: If there be two mortgages and a judgment creditor subsequently purchases in the first mortgage, he shall hold all against the second mortgagee.

Vernon, in reply: They cannot controvert our purchase upon an appeal or rehearing. There is a difference between a purchaser or mortgagee who has a specific lien and a judgment creditor or other encumbrancer, for, in the first case, if he can protect himself at law, equity will not hinder him. But a judgment cannot be tacked to a prior judgment and so gain a preference. There is the same difference between a jointress, who has a lien on specific lands, and a doweress, who has only a general lien. In Sir William Bassett's Case,[1] where there were several judgments in one hand, yet they could not be tacked together. So a mortgage cannot be tacked to a statute. So a grantee of an annuity takes in a satisfied statute, but he could not protect it, as in Serjeant Maynard's Case upon Noseworthy's statute. Here the term is not bound until execution is taken out by the Statute of Frauds.[2] And it may be distinguished from all the cases that can be cited.

Curia [Lord Parker]: All is open, and new matter may be admitted upon a rehearing. The plaintiff should ask to try the validity of his purchase deed, which is proved but by one who cannot be a witness, for otherwise here will be a decree upon a deed which is neither admitted nor proved. If it was without valuable consideration, then the sale by the sheriff to the defendant will take place. Let it be tried whether the plaintiff's deeds were executed and when and upon what consideration.

The defendant's counsel offering to pay the plaintiff what he paid for the purchase with interest and costs, he accepted it. And so ended the cause.

[Other reports of this case: Gilbert Rep. 150, 25 E.R. 105, Precedents in Chancery 494, 24 E.R. 221, 2 Eq. Cas. Abr. 613, 22 E.R. 514.]

[1] *Simons v. Simons* (1704), 2 Freeman 274, 22 E.R. 1206, *sub nom. Earl of Bristol v. Hungerford* (1705), 2 Vernon 524, 23 E.R. 938, 1 Eq. Cas. Abr. 44, 142, 21 E.R. 862, 944.

[2] Stat. 29 Car. II, c. 3 (*SR*, V, 839–842).

258

Sparks v. Palgrave

(Ch. 1718)

When a plaintiff-donee agrees to forebear to sue, he then becomes a purchaser.

If a person pays the consideration money for the benefit of another, that other person is a purchaser for a valuable consideration.

Where a verdict to recover lands is general and the lands cannot be found, a commission to set out the lands or lands of the like value will be granted by a court of equity.

Lincoln's Inn MS. Misc. 380, pt. 3, p. 193, pl. 2

23 June.

In 1686, Sir Ant[hony] Palgrave is indebted £100 by bond to C. Sparks, father of the plaintiff. In 1692, Sir A. Palgrave surrendered all his copyhold lands in such a manor to Ch. Sparks on condition to be void on payment of £300. The surrender was made without the privity of Sparks and with intent to borrow £200 more of him. But, when Sparks was acquainted, he refused to advance more money. It was proved, before the surrender, Sparks had sued Sir Anthony Palgrave for payment of the £100. In 1694, Chr. Sparks is admitted [to] such and such copyhold lands, which afterwards proved not to be copyhold but freehold.

Sir R. Palgrave, the defendant, sets out a settlement by his grandfather, Sir J. Palgrave on his son, Sir A.'s marriage, which in consideration that his wife had settled her lands and for continuing his estate in his blood, name, and family to A. Palgrave for life, then to his wife for life, then to the first son of the marriage in tail etc., remainder to his first son in tail by any other wife. Sir A. Palgrave had no son by his first wife, but Sir R. Palgrave, the defendant, was the only son by a second wife. That settlement mentioned several copyhold lands to be intermixed with the freehold lands before settled. Then follows a covenant to surrender those copyhold lands to the same uses.

The plaintiff brought [an action of] ejectment and recovered those copyhold lands generally as are mentioned in the surrender but takes possession of the wrong parcels. This bill is to foreclose and to have a discovery where the copyhold lands lie or to have other lands set out for him.

The defendant claims as a purchaser by the settlement [of] 1652. For this was cited 1 Lev. 150, Jenkins v. Keymis, Hardres 398, same case.[1] The consideration of a marriage portion will extend to the issue of a second marriage and to all the limitations throughout the deed. If A. pays money, it is, in consideration of which a conveyance is made to B., this is a good consideration. A covenant

[1] *Jenkins v. Keymish* (Ex. 1664–1666), 1 Levinz 150, 83 E.R. 343, Hardres 395, 145 E.R. 515, also Lincoln's Inn MS. Misc. 499, p. 209, British Library MS. Lansdowne 1109, f. 181v, Exch. Repts. *temp.* Car. II, 26.

for a valuable consideration is sufficient to raise a trust in this court. We have an equal equity with them, and [one] that [is] prior in time. And though the plaintiff has a legal title, let him make use of it at law. But he ought not to be assisted by this court. They must find out the lands as well as they can. The surrender of the copyholds to the plaintiff was merely voluntary and without the plaintiff's knowledge.

For the plaintiff, [it was said] the settlement in 1652 is merely voluntary as to the defendant. The same settlement may be good in part and be on good consideration and yet may be voluntary or fraudulent as to the residue. In case we had not consented to the surrender, we had been only a trustee. If a man is pressing for his debt and the debtor give him real security for it, it is the same as if the money had been lent at that time. We are a fair purchaser without notice. Therefore, we beg the assistance of this court either that we may have the specific or other lands of equal quantity or that we may have a commission for that purpose.

Lord Chancellor [Lord Parker]: The admission must pursue the surrender. And, therefore, if that be general of all his copyhold lands belonging to such a manor and you take a particular admission, it is at their peril, and the admission is void. In the settlement of 1652, it is such copyhold lands as were used with the farms therein settled so that the defendant must make out that the copyhold lands are used etc. and where those copyhold lands are. Though the plaintiff's admission be void, yet the heir is entitled to be admitted, even at this day, for the surrender has bound the estate in law and, if it be not made perfect to the father, it shall be made good to the son and heir without the assistance of the defendant or this court.

Here are different considerations that suit the different limitations in the deed. Money paid by one to convey to another, [there is] no question that this is a good consideration. The condition of the portion to the first marriage and the continuing the estate in his own name and blood to the other limitations, these latter uses cannot be said to be fraudulent, but are honestly made and, therefore, cannot be set aside by the Statute of Fraudulent Conveyances.[1] But yet such a voluntary conveyance cannot come into this court to enforce such a settlement against a purchaser without notice. It is not *meritorium*; it is *omnium gratuitum*, as they call it, and a court of equity will never enforce it. The plaintiff was not a purchaser at first, but when he agrees to it and forebears his suit and takes it for his security, he is now become a purchaser. The verdict is general to recover the copyhold lands, and, if the copyhold cannot be found, then a commission to set out other lands of the like value [will be granted].

---

[1] Stat. 3 Will. & Mar., c. 14 (*SR*, VI, 320–321).

Lincoln's Inn MS. Hill 73, p. 25, pl. 2

Upon a marriage portion, deeds [were] drawn to provide for the issue of that marriage with a further provision for any children by a second wife in case of failure of issue of the first and, though the money given was a consideration for the first issue not for the second, but it is a sufficient consideration to raise a use to persons of the name and family.

Lord Chancellor [Lord Parker]: If one man pay the consideration money for the benefit of another, that other person is a purchaser for a valuable consideration.

259

Sloan v. Cheny

(Ch. c. 1718)

Only parties and their privies can file bills of revivor, but others may bring original bills in the nature of a bill of revivor.

Lincoln's Inn MS. Hill 73, p. 27, pl. 2

This [was] confirmed in a case before Lord King at his house 16 November 1725 upon a demurrer.[1] A devisee of part of the real estate was executor; so, as to the arrears, he was privy but not to the estate. He was obliged to alter the bill in the nature of a bill of revivor as devisee.

And Serjeant *Glyde* cited a case of an executor, who was likewise a mortgagee, and, by the opinion of Mr. *Vernon*, they were forced to revive as executors and have a bill in the nature of revivor as mortgagee.

260

Nuce v. Nugent

(Ch. 1718)

Only parties and their privies can file bills of revivor, but others may bring original bills in the nature of a bill of revivor.

Lincoln's Inn MS. Misc. 380, pt. 3, p. 195

23 June.

Above twenty years since, the plaintiff brought a bill to redeem or foreclose. And now, the plaintiff, with other co-plaintiffs, who are the parties interested, brings the bill of revivor.

---

[1] *Huet v. Lord Say and Seal* (Ch. 1725), see below, Case No. 718.

The Master declared the whole proceedings void for want of an order to revive the proceedings in the former cause. None are entitled to revive but parties and privies, as heirs and executors. But others may bring a bill in the nature of a bill of revivor and so have an order, as Sir Hans Sloan, who purchased of Lord Cheney, who commenced a suit against the duchess of Beaufort[1] for a watercourse and had gone on to examine witnesses, and [he was] ordered to stand in the place of him from whom he purchased.

A bill [lies] to foreclose the mortgagor, trustee, heir, and executor and, likewise, the mortgagor, heir, or executor or administrator in a mortgage in fee.

If the heir disturb the executor to whom it belongs, the court will punish him.

Lincoln's Inn MS. Hill 73, p. 27, pl. 1

A devisee or purchaser cannot revive [a suit] but privies only, as heirs, executors, and administrators.

261

Parslow v. Weedon

(Ch. 1718)

The Statute against Fraudulent Devises does not apply to inter vivos *gifts.*

Lincoln's Inn MS. Misc. 384, p. 37, pl. 1

27 June. Inner Temple Hall.

The question was whether a voluntary conveyance of lands could be affected by a subsequent bond creditor.

Vernon: It has always been taken to be fraudulent as against a bond creditor.

Lord Chancellor [Lord Parker]: Where the donee is likewise the heir, it may be a question whether the descent is broken by the conveyance. Before the Statute of Fraudulent Devises, the lands were not liable in the hands of the devisee. The Statute has only provided for the case of the devise, but not of a gift in the parties' lifetime. If there had been any secret trust for the donor, it might be fraudulent as in a gift of goods with a secret trust for the donor. But a man may *in extremis* give away either his lands or goods, and they will not be liable to his creditors.

Vide Finch 99; st. 127 El., c. 4; 13 Eliz., c. 5.[2]

---

[1] Perhaps *Sloan v. Cheny* (Ch. c. 1718), see above, Case No. 259.

[2] H. Finch, *Law*, p. 99; Stat. 27 Eliz. I, c. 4 (*SR*, IV, 709–711); Stat. 13 Eliz. I, c. 5 (*SR*, IV, 537–538).

Query of this case, for the counsel were not well satisfied.[1]

Lincoln's Inn MS. Misc. 11, p. 141

Trinity 1718.

It was decreed by LORD PARKER in this case that, if a man conveys away his estate, whether upon consideration or not, it is good against creditors.

Mr. *Vernon* cited this case to the LORD PARKER, who said that, before this case, he took it to be otherwise according to former precedents but that now it was so settled.

1 Eq. Cas. Abr. 149, 21 E.R. 950

Trinity 1718.

Though, by the Statute against Fraudulent Devises,[2] a man is prevented from defeating his creditors by his will, yet any settlement or disposition he shall make in his lifetime of his lands, whether voluntary or not, will be good against bond creditors, for that was not provided against by the Statute, which only took care to secure such creditors against any imposition which might be supposed in a man's last sickness, but, if he gave away his estate in his lifetime, this prevented the descent of so much to the heir and consequently took away their remedy against him, who was only liable in respect of the lands descended. And as a bond is no lien whatsoever on lands in the hands of the obligor, much less can it be so when they are given away to a stranger.

262

Anonymous

(Ch. c. 1718)

A legacy to a wife that is not vested at the time of her husband's bankruptcy is not liable to his creditors.

Lincoln's Inn MS. Hill 73, p. 22

The plaintiff was wife to one who, soon after the marriage, became bankrupt. She had a legacy left her to be paid at the age of twenty and, if she died before, then to etc. She brought her bill to be relieved against her husband and the assignees of the estate of the bankrupt, who demanded it. The husband broke and the certificate from the commissioners was signed before she was the age of twenty so that there was no right vested in her and so consequently [it was] not liable to the assignees.

---

1 E.g. *Jones v. Marsh* (1735), Cases *tempore* Talbot 64, 25 E.R. 664; *Brunsden v. Stratton* (Ch. 1719), see below, Case No. 420.

2 Stat. 3 Will. & Mar., c. 14 (*SR*, VI, 320–321).

263

Anonymous

(Ch. c. 1718)

A judgment creditor who has several judgments can execute only one of them on the debtor's land, but a mortgagee who has a judgment against his mortgagor can be satisfied for both out of his debtor's lands.

Lincoln's Inn MS. Hill 73, p. 24, pl. 1

Lord Chancellor: A man cannot tack three judgments together so as to hold the land until he is satisfied the whole because his legal estate is gone as soon as one judgment is satisfied. But a mortgagee that has a judgment shall protect his judgment by his mortgage and be satisfied both before he relinquishes the land.

264

Anonymous

(Ch. c. 1718)

The question in this case was whether a debtor can redeem a mortgage without also satisfying a judgment debt to the mortgagor.

Lincoln's Inn MS. Hill 73, p. 24, pl. 2

[Upon] a judgment upon a term of years, the term was sold before a [writ of] *fieri facias* was sued out upon the judgment. A bill to redeem the first mortgage [was filed] without satisfying the judgment which the first mortgagee had got into his hands.

265

Anonymous

(Ch. c. 1718)

A person who has an interest in the outcome of the lawsuit cannot testify as a witness.

Lincoln's Inn MS. Hill 73, p. 24, pl. 3

In an execution sued and goods taken, if any[one] comes and lays a title to them and produces a bargain and sale, the man against whom execution sued shall not be allowed as a witness to prove it for a valuable consideration and protect his own goods.

266

Anonymous

(Ch. c. 1718)

Jointures and dower rights are encumbrances on land.
Jointresses and doweresses are purchasers.

Lincoln's Inn MS. Hill 73, p. 24, pl. 4

In an appeal to the Lord Chancellor is only that he would not make a decree as his own which he has not heard.
Jointress and doweress [are] the same as an encumbrancer and a purchaser.
A general encumbrancer, as a woman in dower, must stand to receive such lands as by law they are entitled to s[. . .] a purchaser and jointress etc.

267

Proctor v. Johnson

(Ch. c. 1718)

An account can be ordered to be taken of a decedent's estate.

Lincoln's Inn MS. Hill 73, p. 36, pl. 1

Upon a devise of £100 to her daughter to be paid at twenty-one or the day of marriage, but, if she die before that age, £50 of it to the plaintiff, the Lord Chancellor decreed an account to be taken of the assets of Jane Hanfield.

268

Anonymous

(Ch. c. 1718)

The payment of a decedent's debts will be marshalled so that all of the debts will be paid.

Lincoln's Inn MS. Hill 73, p. 36, pl. 2

A bill was brought to charge the real estate of the testator with debts of simple contracts, there being a large personal estate.

[It was] decreed that, where there are debts that will charge the lands, as all specialties and others that will fall only on the personal estate, that the real estate shall repay back to the personal estate so much of that money as the personal estate has paid in discharge of those debts which would affect the real estate [so] that all the testator's debts might be paid.

269

Anonymous

(Ch. c. 1718)

Where a lessee makes repairs, they are considered to have been made for his own benefit and not for the benefit of the lessor.

Lincoln's Inn MS. Hill 73, p. 37

A lessee for years has a mortgage of the inheritances and lays out £700 in repairs before his term is expired; it shall be construed the repairs of the lessee for [. . .] and not of the mortgagee in possession, and he shall be redeemed without any allowance made for such repairs.

270

Willis v. Lucas

(Ch. 1718)

In this case, a person was held to have a devise of an estate by necessary implication.
Parol evidence cannot be used to explain a will concerning land.

Lincoln's Inn MS. Misc. 384, p. 38

1 July.

John Lucas, by his will, devises the premises to his second son, Samuel, him and his heirs paying legacies to his other children and, after the death of Samuel and his wife, then to the sons of Samuel. The question is whether the wife of Samuel has an estate for life by implication or whether, during her life, it descends to the plaintiffs, the heirs at law of the devisor.

Mead, for the plaintiff: In the Case of Gardiner v. Sheldon, Vaughan 262, it is a rule which has never been shaken that the heir at law shall never be excluded by a constructive, but only by a necessary, implication. Spirt v. Bence, 1 Cr. Ca. 368.[1]

Raymond, for the defendant: I do admit that distinction where the devise is to the heir and where to a stranger. Here, the defendant is to pay £10 *per annum* to the heir at law out of the rents and profits, which is a strong implication that he is excluded, because he cannot have both the land and £10 *per annum*. Here, it happens that part of the lands are gavelkind and so the devise is to one of the

[1] *Gardner v. Sheldon* (1671), Vaughan 259, 124 E.R. 1064, also 1 Freeman 11, 89 E.R. 9, 2 Keble 781, 84 E.R. 494, 1 Eq. Cas. Abr. 197, 21 E.R. 986; *Spirt v. Bence* (1634), 1 Croke Car. 368, 79 E.R. 921.

coheirs and, if the sons of Samuel are heirs of the devisor, the implication is necessary that the wife shall have it.

Peere Williams: In gavelkind, they are but one heir. It cannot descend to the rest. Reading v. Royston, Salk. 242, in the King's Bench,[1] there was a devise to one daughter. The question was whether she should take a moiety or the whole by purchase. It was adjudged she took the whole because it could not descend in part.

Yorke: A necessary implication is not where it is impossible for any other to take but where the intent of the devisor is apparent upon the words of the will. A descent must be entire.

Chesly's reply: If the wife of Samuel is to take, she will have the land clear when the heir of Samuel will be liable to pay the £10 a year, for Samuel and his heirs are to pay it.

Vernon: This is not like the case of a devise to him who is completely the heir.

Lord Chancellor [Lord Parker]: You cannot read parol evidence to explain a will concerning land, as in Lord Falkland's Case.[2] This is a very unskillful will. The intent must govern. There is no difference between the construction here and at law; therefore, it is proper at law. The intent was that the annuities should be paid, and the implication is strong that the wife should have it for life. The plaintiff must bring his [action of] ejectment or, to save expense, may make a case for the opinion of the judges.

Lincoln's Inn MS. Hill 73, p. 28

John Lucas had three sons, John, [*blank*], and Samuel. The testator devises his lands to his youngest son, Samuel, and subjects it to the annuities and after the death of the said Samuel and his then wife, then to the heirs of James, they likewise paying the annuities. The wife of Samuel insists she is entitled to an estate for life by implication upon the words of the will after her husband's death, his being now dead.

2 Cr. 75; Gardner v. Shelden;[3] the bill [was] brought by the four daughters and co-heirs of John, the son and heir of John, the testator, to call the defendant,

---

[1] *Reading v. Royston* (1703), 1 Salkeld 242, 423, 91 E.R. 214, 368, also 1 Comyns 123, 92 E.R. 994, 2 Lord Raymond 829, 92 E.R. 54, Precedents in Chancery 222, 24 E.R. 108, 2 Eq. Cas. Abr. 333, 22 E.R. 284.

[2] *Bertie v. Viscount Falkland* (Ch. 1697), 2 Vernon 333, 23 E.R. 814, 1 Salkeld 231, 91 E.R. 205, 3 Chancery Cases 129, 22 E.R. 1008, 2 Freeman 220, 22 E.R. 1171, 12 Modern 182, 88 E.R. 1248, Holt K.B. 230, 90 E.R. 1026, Colles 10, 1 E.R. 155, Dickens 25, 21 E.R. 176, 1 Eq. Cas. Abr. 110, 21 E.R. 917, British Library MS. Hargrave 81, f. 106, British Library MS. Hargrave 82, f. 116, pl. 2, note also above *Bertie v. Lord Falkland* (Ch. 1715), Case No. 101.

[3] *Horton v. Horton* (1605), Croke Jac. 74, 79 E.R. 63; *Gardner v. Sheldon* (1671), *ut supra*.

the wife of Samuel, to account for the rents and profits of the said estate, being not entitled to any estate by implication.

Chesshyre: The difference between an estate given to one for life and to remain to another after the death of [*blank*], who would be entitled to take by descent and when to one, who is a stranger and not as heir at law, there is no necessary implication that the stranger should take. It must be a necessary implication that includes the heir at law.

The heir at law by the express words of the will is not to take during the life of the wife; therefore, it seems a necessary implication that the wife should have it until the heirs can take and not that it should descend to the heirs at law, who are expressly excluded until after the death of the wife.

Williams: The eldest son, the heir is by the will to have an annuity of £10, which implies he is not to have the lands but only that £10 *per annum*, and, therefore, if it is given [*blank*].

Reading v. Royston, Salkeld, vol. 1, 242; a man had two daughters, seised in fee, devised his [land] to one of his daughters and her heirs; the question was whether she was in by descent in one moiety and by purchase in the other. It was held that she was in by descent in no part because they both made but one heir and consequently what descends must descend to both.

Whitcomb v. Whitcomb;[1] a man [had] two daughters by his first [wife] and a son by his second wife; he makes his will but says nothing of his lands, by which the son inherited and was seised and died soon after.

N.B. There was a devise of an annuity of £10 *per annum* to John, the heir for life.

Vernon: The annuities are charged to be paid by Samuel and his heirs only, and, therefore, if the implication should take place, the annuity would not be secured to the devisees.

Lord Chancellor [Lord Parker]: If the plaintiff has a right, setting [?] aside the mortgage, which was satisfied [. . .] that was set up by the defendant by which he was prevented from pursuing his right at law, that ought not to be procured [?] that the title upon the construction of the will might be tried, a matter of law, it being by the words 'the heirs of Samuel' are obliged to pay the annuities even whether he has the estate or no by the £10 *per annum* for life to John, the heir, exclude the heir in point of time. There are no exclusive words of the heir in the cases mentioned.

The case referred to before, Cr. 2, 75, Horton v. Horton, in [an action of] replevin upon a demurrer, the case [was] A. made a lease for years of the lands in question upon condition that he should not alien to any besides his children, the lessee devises part of the term to [*blank*], his son, after the death of his wife and made two strangers his executors; the lessor entered for a breach of the condition.

---

[1] *Whitcombe v. Whitcombe* (1709), Precedents in Chancery 280, 24 E.R. 135.

But, upon arguing, [it was] found for the defendant.

Query if the lessee ought not to have made his sons his executors to have performed the condition.

10 Modern 416, 88 E.R. 788

J.S. had three sons, A., B., C., and daughters. And, being seised in fee of land, part whereof was gavelkind, he devised it by his will to C., his youngest son, he or his heirs paying £10 a year to A., £10 a year to B., so much a year to the daughters, etc. for the term of his life, and, after the death of C. and his wife, then it was to go to the sons and daughters of C. according as he should have one or other, equally to be divided between them.

C. dies, living his wife; his wife enters, as conceiving it a devise by implication to her for her life. The heir at law, supposing the land not at all disposed of by the will, during the intervening time between the death of C. and the death of his wife, and that it ought, therefore, in the interim, to descend to him, brought his [action of] ejectment at common law. But the wife, protecting her estate by a mortgage, nonsuited him.

He, therefore, now brought his bill to discover these encumbrances and whether they were not satisfied.

The wife, in her answer insists, in the first place, that this is a devise to her by implication for life and, secondly, that, though, by the rigorous rules of law, this should not be so, yet that this estate being her chief dependence and her father-in-law having often told her before the making of his will that he would give it her for life and having, likewise, after the making the will declared that he had done so, she hopes the plaintiff shall not have the aid of a court of equity to get that from her which her father-in-law so plainly designed to give her.

For the plaintiff: The difference taken in the Yearbook 13 Hen. VII and 2 Cro. 75,[1] as to estates by implication, *viz.* that, where the estate is devised after the death of the wife to the heir at law, there the wife shall take by implication, but not where the devise is over to a stranger, was insisted strongly upon in favor of the plaintiff as also the rule laid down in the case of Gardiner v. Sheldon, that an estate should never be raised by implication, unless where it was a necessary and unavoidable one.

It was urged in favor of the wife that, by a necessary implication in the meaning of the law was not to be understood a natural necessity that the estate could go nowhere else, but a necessity arising from the plain intention of the testator in his will. It was also urged, that the heir at law, by having £10 a year given him, when by law he was entitled to the whole, was evidently by the intention of the testator as much excluded from having the land descend to him in

[1] *Stoner's Case* (1497), YB Mich. 13 Hen. VII, ff. 4, 11, also YB Trin. 12 Hen. VII, f. 19, pl. 1, Keilwey 32, 72 E.R. 189, 64 Selden Soc. 161, 115 Selden Soc. 363; *Horton v. Horton* (1605), *ut supra*.

the meantime as if the devise had been to him after the death of C. and his wife, that, if the land should descend to the heir at law, it would not in him be subject to the payment of the annuities, which would be plainly contrary to the intention of the testator. It was also insisted upon that part of these lands being in Kent must be taken to be in the nature of gavelkind, and then all the sons and their representatives make but one heir, in which case, the descent must be entire. But this cannot be because, as to a third of the land, the representative of C. being heir at law and the person to whom the devise is made, it will be a devise of that by implication to the wife, according even to the rule insisted upon by the other side. Then there remains two-thirds to descend, which will be a descent neither by custom nor by the common law; not by the custom, for that is already broken in upon by the estate by implication raised by the will; not by the common law, for these two-thirds must go to the two sons or their representatives and the representatives of C. And here again, the wife must have by virtue of their own rule an estate by implication in the third part of the two-thirds, because the devise is to the representative of C., heir at law, according to this way of taking it, of a third part of the two-thirds.

PARKER, Lord Chancellor, was of opinion that the wife ought to have an estate for life by implication, the heir at law being excluded by the annuity.

But this being matter triable at law, he directed an issue accordingly, where the wife was ordered to waive her encumbrances and insist only on her title at law.

Parol evidence was offered to prove the intention of the testator to give it his wife, but the Chancellor refused to receive it.

[Other reports of this case: 1 Peere Williams 472, 24 E.R. 478, 2 Eq. Cas. Abr. 343, 363, 22 E.R. 293, 309.]

271

Geen's Case

(Ch. 1718)

In this case, the devisor created a trust, not a legacy.

Lincoln's Inn MS. Misc. 380, pt. 3, p. 205, pl. 2

Trinity term 1718, in which the former case [Kingsman v. Kingsman (1706)[1]] was cited.

A. devises all her estate as her mother should think fit and declared that she had not given any legacies. [There was] parol proof that the daughter, the devi-

---

[1] *Kingsman v. Kingsman* (Ch. 1706), 2 Vernon 559, 23 E.R. 962, Lincoln's Inn MS. Misc. 380, pt. 3, p. 205, pl. 1.

sor, had often told the mother that she might give £180 to Anne, her half-sister, if she thought fit.

[There was a] bill to discover if there was no secret trust.

[The] answer [was] she might or might not give £180, and she was to judge of Anne's behavior.

Lord Chancellor [Lord Parker]: If you take it as a legatee, I think it will overthrow the Statute of Frauds.[1] But it [is] on her answer, and the parol proof ought not to be admitted to dispose as she should think fit. She submits it to the discretion of the mother. [Upon] a trust to dispose money among her children, if she gives all to one, the court will interpose unless there be strong causes to the contrary. She, by her answer, admitted she would give it to her if she behaved herself well. I think she ought to have shown some misbehavior. This must be taken as a trust to be given in case the party does not misbehave herself. I think this is not a case to be decreed [of] course. I do not know as to the time whether she has not use [?] for this payment of it. Let her pay the £180 but no interest.

272

Berney v. Holbert

(Ch. c. 1718)

A court of equity will not order specific performance of a contract where to do so would prejudice a third person.

A tenant for life of land subject to a mortgage must either pay the interest on the debt or pay off one-third of the remaining debt.

Lincoln's Inn MS. Misc. 380, pt. 3, p. 206, pl. 1

[Upon a] trust by a devise of lands for the payment of debts and legacies, it was said by counsel, where all the debts are chargeable in conscience, that they are all to come in an equal degree, this being not legal assets, without any preference. *Cuius est dare eius est disponere.* He might have made the legacies payable first if he would.

Query the contracts by articles for the purchase of these lands with the heir.

Lord Chancellor [Lord Parker]: The court cannot decree a performance, for the contract will not bind the other parties. But the plaintiff may oblige the heir to make good to him the damage he receives. He, at last, became the purchaser himself for £10,000 and sold to the plaintiff for £8000. The court can never decree a specific performance of articles that will prejudice a third person, though it be with a trustee that has the legal estate. It has lately been determined that, if one contract for a purchase with the trustee, the purchaser may pursue the legal title but cannot expect any assistance from this court. But, if they come

[1] Stat. 29 Car. II, c. 3 (*SR*, V, 839–842).

here, the court will order a sale for the best purchaser. The trustees and legatees etc., as well as the heir who contracted ought to be parties. In this case, the tenant for life receives the rents and profits and does not keep down the interest; his personal estate [in] the executor's hands shall make it good. He may either keep down the interest or pay off the one-third part of the principal.

273

Crookshanks v. Beard and Wise

(Ch. 1718)

A surety has no subrogation rights against the principal debtor's obligor where the obligor's transaction is separate from the debt that the surety agreed to pay; thus a surety cannot garnish his principal debtor's debtor.

Lincoln's Inn MS. Misc. 380, pt. 3, p. 197

Friday, 11 July 1718, before the Lord Chancellor.

The end of the plaintiff's bill is to have satisfaction against Wise for the payment of the customs of certain goods which were the defendant Wise's and of which Wise had the benefit. The case was this as it appeared on the opening of the bill. Wise was a merchant in London trading into Caceo[1] and, having a considerable quantity of tobacco in the Thames, applied to Beard, his father-in-law, and prevailed with him to enter his tobacco in his own name and as his own proper goods and to give security for the payment of the customs. According[ly], he applies to the plaintiff and one Brown to become surety with him for the payment of the customs. After this, Wise disposes of the tobacco, and Beard becomes insolvent, and Brown [becomes] a bankrupt, so that the whole charge was now to lie on the plaintiff.

It was insisted for the plaintiff that, as Beard would now in equity be entitled to have satisfaction from Wise, though there was no counter-bond or security to indemnify him, so the plaintiff should now stand in Beard's place and that, as Wise had received an advantage from the payment of the customs of his goods, it was fit he should pay for it.

The Lord Chancellor [LORD PARKER] said that the credit given by the plaintiff was given to Beard and was entirely personal that he knew nothing at all of Wise and, therefore, he should not follow the goods in Wise's hands nor have any satisfaction for the advantage Wise received by the credit he gave to Beard, especially in this case where Wise was not guilty of any fraud. If there had been any fraud in the case, as if he had hired the plaintiff to become surety or any way contributed to that end, Wise should have paid for it. So if I have a mortgage of £500 on my estate and, being on a treaty of marriage, desire J.S. to give security to the

[1] I.e. Caicos.

mortgagee for the mortgage money so that the mortgage deeds may be delivered up, if J.S. prevail with A. and B. to join in a bond with him to the mortgagee so that the mortgage deeds are delivered up and, afterwards, J.S. becomes insolvent, A. and B. shall never resort to the land or to me to be indemnified; so that, if I agree with a man to build me a house and he employs other persons in building of it, the credit they give to him is personal, and, if he becomes insolvent, they shall never resort to me, so that the plaintiff's bill was dismissed with costs.

274

Brown v. Thomas and Wilson

(Ch. 1718)

In a suit against a trustee for the specific performance of a contract, the beneficiaries of the trust are necessary parties.

Lincoln's Inn MS. Misc. 380, pt. 3, p. 198, pl. 1

11 July 1718.

[There was a] trust to sell to raise money to be paid to B. Thomas. The trustee is informed that the estate would sell better if the whole were leased to one tenant, and, accordingly, articles to make a lease to Brown, the plaintiff, [were executed]. The bill was to have a specific performance.

It was objected that the *cestui que trust* ought to have been a party, for the defendants have in their answer set forth this trust so that the plaintiff might have made them parties.

Lord Chancellor [Lord Parker]: Suppose this court should decree a performance. The *cestui que trust* might come and set aside this decree as prejudicial to him. Though the trustee does absolutely agree, yet this court will not decree the performance, but the plaintiff may recover elsewhere against the trustee. I do not know whether he can recover in this case because, at the time of the agreement, the trustee said he did not know whether he could do it; so the plaintiff would be a purchaser with notice.

The bill was dismissed.

275

Anonymous

(Ch. 1718)

A court of equity will prohibit a lord of a manor from oppressing his tenants by holding unnecessary courts.

Lincoln's Inn MS. Misc. 380, pt. 3, p. 198, pl. 2

There was a bill of peace to ascertain the customs and fines and to make the lord [of a manor] hold court and not oblige the tenants to [attend] special courts, for which they pay 40s.

On complaint, the lord tells them he will hold courts every three weeks and oblige them to attend.

The Lord Chancellor [LORD PARKER] directed several issues and said, if the lord will hold courts every three weeks when there is no business either for the lord or the tenants, this is oppression and proper for this court. This keeping of courts is likewise in the nature of a trust. Let the lord hold a court once every year at Michaelmas.

276

Powell v. Bowman

(Ch. 1718)

The question in this case was whether trust moneys could be traced to a purchase of lands.

A parol declaration of the settlor cannot create a trust.

Lincoln's Inn MS. Misc. 380, pt. 3, p. 198, pl. 3

There was a devise for an estate to be sold for the payment of debts, the residue to be laid out in a purchase of other land to be settled, *viz.* for paying such an annuity, then to A. for life, remainder to the plaintiff's heirs. The estate is sold, and the money is put out on a bond to B. The money to be laid out was £1300. A., afterwards, purchases an estate of the value of £1100 to her and her heirs. A. dies. The plaintiff brings this bill claiming the lands purchased by A. to him and his heirs as being purchased with the trust. And [there was] proof that A. was indigent and could not have made such a purchase but with the trust money. But there was no proof of either side what became of the money laid out and, secured by the bond, whether it was paid in to A.

Lord Chancellor [LORD PARKER]: No parol declaration of the party can be admitted of a trust since the Statute of Frauds.[1]

1 Stat. 29 Car. II, c. 3 (*SR*, V, 839–842).

Vernon: Only in the case [of one] who paid the consideration money [can] parol proof [be] admitted in such a case. And it shall be a resulting trust. But it has never been carried further than this. Hammond v. Webb and Cranmer; a purchase with the very rents and profits, the party that received them carried them to the party who made the purchase. Money can have no earmark. The Case of Chatley v. [*blank*];[1] the executor in trust finds a bag of money of £1300 hidden behind the hangings in his house at Uxbridge and, with this money, he buys an estate to him and his heirs, and the executor was not worth 1s., and he died seised. The court decreed, money having no earmark, they could not decree the estate to be a trust estate.

Lord Chancellor [Lord Parker]: This is a blind case because it does not appear what became of the £1300. Here are some indications that it was the trust money and proof likewise on the other side. If the person that has covenanted to lay out such a sum in lands, now secured by a bond, and afterwards receives this money and lays it out in land to him and his heirs, this might be a trust. But this has not been made to appear here. Indeed, it is very hard to trace money by an earmark. Let the Master enquire how the £1800 was paid. And, if it was paid to her, it will differ from the cases cited.

277

Harris v. Duke of Kent

(Ch. 1718)

A tenant who holds over has the right to harvest his crops.

Where a lease of a coppice is ended by the landlord before the tenant could have a benefit by cutting it, the tenant should have an allowance for it.

Lincoln's Inn MS. Misc. 10, p. 229

16 July 1718.

The plaintiff was a lessee of a farm under the defendant's father, and, after the expiration of the lease, he held over. Part of this farm consisted of a coppice, which was usually cut every seven years. And the defendant, being minded to unite this farm with another and to let them both together, gave the plaintiff warning at Lady Day [25 March] to quit the farm at Michaelmas [29 September] following. But, afterwards, there was some treaty between the plaintiff and the defendant's steward about the plaintiff's taking both farms, but, that breaking off, the plaintiff sows some part of the land before Michaelmas with wheat and refuses to quit the farm. And, afterwards, he begins to cut down the coppice, which was then between five and six years growth.

[1] *Kendar v. Milward* (1702), 2 Vernon 440, 23 E.R. 882, Precedents in Chancery 171, 24 E.R. 83, 2 Eq. Cas. Abr. 365, 744, 22 E.R. 430, 631.

Upon this, the defendant brings an [action of] ejectment and likewise an action of trespass against the plaintiff, who thereupon brings his bill for an injunction and that he may be permitted to reap his crops which he had sown and to cut the coppice.

The plaintiff obtained an injunction as to his continuing in the farm until he had reaped his crop, but he was enjoined from cutting the copse. And, accordingly, he reaped his crop at the usual season, and, at Michaelmas following, he delivered up possession of the farm so that, when the cause came to be heard, the principal question was whether the plaintiff should have an allowance for the value of the copse.

Lord Chancellor [Lord Parker] seemed to be of opinion, where a man was tenant at will, it was not necessary to give warning, but either party might determine the tenancy at will without giving warning. But query.

But, as to the copse, His Lordship was of opinion and so decreed that the plaintiff ought to have an allowance for it according to the value it was of when he left the farm, for, having paid six years rent for it without reaping any profit, it was but reasonable he should have an allowance made him by his landlord if he thought fit to determine the will and thereby prevent him from cutting his copse.

278

Bagnall v. Henton

(Ch. 1718)

A devise to several persons to share and share alike creates a tenancy in common.

Lincoln's Inn MS. Misc. 384, p. 40

17 July.

A. has three children and gives them by his will £200 apiece and, if either of them died before twenty-one or marriage, then to the survivors. One dies in the testator's lifetime.

Lord Chancellor [Lord Parker]: The testator's intent was that, if one died, the others should have it. And it is the same though one died before the testator, the surplus being devised to them, share and share alike, makes them tenants in common and the share of the person dying in the testator's lifetime remains not disposed of. If one was incapable to take the whole, [it] would vest in the others. I would see precedents.

Vernon: In Billingsly and Shower's Case, there was a devise to two executors and one died; his share was adjudged to his representative, but the decree was afterwards reversed.

Lincoln's Inn MS. Hill 73, p. 33

Bagwell v. Heaton.

A devise [was given] to the grandchildren of the testator by two daughters, five by one of his daughters and two by another, of £200 apiece to be paid to the grandsons at the age of twenty-one, and the granddaughters at twenty-one or day of marriage, and, if any of them died before he or they attained such age as is limited, that share was to survive to the rest of them, share and share alike. One of them died in the life of the testator. Godolphin, *Legacies*, 3, 100 sect.; 2 Roll's Abr. 301.[1] And the residue of his estate he bequeathed to his four daughters, their heirs, executors, administrators, etc. equally to be divided between them, share and share alike, which makes them tenants in common.

The defendants Edens, the grandchildren of Ely, ask the £200, which was given to one of the grandchildren and [who] died.

A case was mentioned by *Sir Robert Raymond* as in Lord Cowper's time; a devise of £500 apiece to his children equally to be divided and that it should survive.

The Lord Chancellor [Lord Parker] decreed that the legacy which was given to the granddaughter who died in the life of the testator and which was to survive was to be paid to the surviving children as agreeable to the testator's intention in the same manner as if the granddaughter had died after the death of the testator. As to the residue devised to the said daughters, he desired to be attended with precedents [and] adjourned.

Mr. *Vernon*: Billingsby v. Shower; a devise of the residue of the estate [was made] to two executors; one of them dies before any division was made. It was adjudged that is was a joint devise and should survive to the other executor. But, afterward, it was reversed. And several cases have followed in confirmation of the last judgment that the executor of the executor shall have it.

Lord Chancellor [Lord Parker]: As to the residue devised to the four daughters, three-fourths [was] ordered to be paid immediately to those who were entitled. As to the other part, jud[gment was] adjourned, all parties to have costs out of the estate.

[1] J. Godolphin, *Orphan's Legacy*.

279

Lord Thomond v. Earl of Suffolk

(Ch. 1718)

In this case, the payment or release of a debt that was bequeathed was not an ademption of the bequest.

A husband is liable for his wife's debts while she is living, but not after her death.

Lincoln's Inn MS. Misc. 11, p. 134

18 July 1718.

The plaintiff being indebted by bond for the payment of £2000 to the countess dowager of Thomond, his grandmother, and the Lady Henrietta Thomond being also indebted to her by a bond in £2000 more, she makes her will dated 26 April 1716, whereby reciting those two bonds, she bequeaths the moneys due thereon to her granddaughter, the Lady Mary O'Brien, the plaintiff's sister, and all securities given for the same. And she declares that, if all or any part of the two sums of £2000 should be paid in to her before her death, then she gave to her said granddaughter the sum of £4000 or so much money as the said principal so paid in should amount unto, as the case should fall out. But the surplus of her personal estate she directs to be laid out for the benefit of her grandchildren in the manner therein mentioned.

After making this will, the testatrix voluntarily without any consideration executes a general release to the plaintiff, but she never delivers up his bond.

The Lady Mary O'Brien survived the testatrix and, afterwards, died, and the plaintiff took administration to her. And he, thereby, is become entitled to the legacy given to her.

The Lady Henrietta Thomond married the defendant, her second husband, and is since dead. And he refusing to take administration to his wife, the plaintiff took out administration. And now, he brings his bill against the defendant, the Lord Suffolk, for a discovery of what he possessed of his wife's estate and that, out of her assets, he may pay the £2000 and interest due on her bond and, against the executors and residuary legatees of the testatrix, to be paid the £2000 and interest secured by the plaintiff's bond, for, though that debt was not actually paid in to the testatrix, yet she having released it, it was the same thing according to the intention of the will as though it had been actually paid.

The defendant, the Lord Suffolk, confessed by answer that his wife had a jointure of £1500 a year in Ireland and that he and his wife agreed with the plaintiff to surrender her jointure to the plaintiff in consideration of £1000 a year in money to be paid by the plaintiff in England, that the jointure was accordingly surrendered and, thereupon, the plaintiff covenanted with the defendant and his countess to pay the £1000 and that the £1000 a year was accordingly paid. But the greatest part was received by the countess and that, since her death, he had received £500 for the last half year, which became due in her lifetime. He also confessed that he and his wife had sold a small estate in Ireland, which she was entitled to and that part of the money had been applied to his use.

Lord Chancellor [LORD PARKER]: If the countess of Suffolk had been an executrix and the assets of her testator had come to the defendant's hands, no doubt, but, even after her death, he would be liable so far as assets had come to his hands to pay the testator's debts. But to call the husband to an account after his wife's death for what he has received out of her estate in order to have a satisfaction of her debts seems to me very extraordinary.

The husband is responsible in his wife's lifetime for her debts though he did not receive one penny portion with her. But, I think, after her death, let him have received what he will with her, he shall not be affected with her debts. This seems to be an undoubted rule of equity as well as law.

As to the £500 received by the earl of Suffolk after her death, if it had been a debt due to her before marriage and he had received it after her death, it would have been assets for the payment of her debts, for he would have received it as executor *de son tort*. But this was a debt owing to him; the plaintiffs' covenant for paying the annuity being made with the earl and his countess. The bill must be dismissed as to this demand.

As to the other £2000, I do not see by anything that appears in the case that there was any intention in the testatrix to change her mind. She could not at the making of her will have any view of the case which afterwards fell out. And I am of the opinion that the releasing the debt is the same as though it had been actually paid, and it is no more than if she had received it with one hand and given it back to the plaintiff with the other.

The plaintiff must be paid this £2000 out of her assets.

Lincoln's Inn MS. Misc. 506, p. 8

21 July 1718.

The countess of Thomond, April 26, 1715, made her will, and, in it, devised to her granddaughter, the Lady Mary Obrian, the sum of £1000 and then there follows this clause:

> And whereas my grandson, the Lord Thomond, does owe unto me the sum of £2000 on bond and my daughter, the Lady Henrietta Thomond, does owe to me £2000 more on bond, I do hereby further bequeath unto my said granddaughter, the Lady Obrian, the said several sums of £2000 and £2000 owed to me by said grandson, the Lord Thomond, and my said daughter, the Lady Henrietta Thomond, and the bonds and the securities for them with all the interest due at my death and, in case all or any part of these sums be paid in, then I give the said Lady Mary Obrian the sum of £4000 or so much as the sum paid in shall amount to according as the case shall fall out.

The countess of Thomond, on September 29, 1715, releases to Lord Thomond the £2000 owing to her by him and afterwards dies. Lady Henrietta Thomond afterwards marries the earl of Suffolk, and she dies. Lady Mary Obrian, the legatee, dies, and Lord Thomond takes out administration to her and now brings a bill against the earl of Suffolk and the executors and the residuary legatees of the countess of Thomond for satisfaction of the legacies. The questions were whether the release to Lord Thomond was an ademption of the legacy of £2000 to Lady Mary Obrian and whether the earl of Suffolk is to pay the bond entered into by his countess, when *sole*, after her death.

Mr. *Vernon, Mead*, and *Melmoth* were counsel for Lord Thomond. And they insisted that this release to Lord Thomond was the same as receiving the money and paying it back again to him and, if it had been so, then it had come within the words of the will and, if the bond had been assigned over on a consideration, the subsequent legacy of £4000 or so much as should have been received would have risen.

There was cited the Case of Pollet, Raym. 335.[1] In the case of Orme v. Smith,[2] solemnly determined by Lord Harcourt, February 1711, the plaintiff was indebted to the testator Smith by bond in the sum of £370 and gave a warrant of attorney to confess judgment. Smith makes his will, in which was this clause: 'I give and bequeath unto my only uncle [*blank*] Orme £500, *viz.* the bond and judgment which he gave me for about £400 he owes to me and £100 in money.' The plaintiff and testator, before his death, stated accounts and the plaintiff paid him all that was due but £80, and the bond and warrant of attorney were delivered up and the testator gave a warrant of attorney to enter up satisfaction, and the plaintiff gave the testator a new bond for £80, and it was decreed he should be paid the whole £500, the bond of £80 being taken for part.

As to the other question, whether the earl of Suffolk was liable to pay this bond after the death of the countess, they first endeavored to show that assets were come to his hands which was thus. The countess had a considerable jointure in Ireland, which was agreed to be exchanged with Lord Thomond for £1000 *per annum* during the life of the countess, in pursuance of which agreement, articles were executed by which the earl did consent with Lord Thomond that the countess should resign her jointure and that he should be in possession of it until it was resigned. The matter stood on this covenant, and it was not resigned, but the £1000 *per annum* was constantly paid and at the time of the countess's death there was £500 in arrears which was paid to the earl after her death and this was insisted on to be assets. There was also some part of the jointure sold during the coverture for £500. The jewels which she had before the marriage were reckoned of the value of the £500. It was argued that these things coming to the earl not

---

1 *Pawlet's Case* (1679), T. Raymond 335, 83 E.R. 174.

2 *Orm v. Smith* (1711), 2 Vernon 681, 23 E.R. 1042, Gilbert Rep. 82, 25 E.R. 58, 1 Eq. Cas. Abr. 302, 21 E.R. 1061, British Library MS. Hargrave 80, f. 78, pl. 3.

by purchase or valuable consideration but by marriage, he ought to be charged on account of them, for where a debt is owing by a woman when *sole*, if she dies after marriage, the husband at law, indeed the husband, will not be obliged to pay it, yet, in equity, the court will follow the assets wherever they are. So, if a wife, being executrix, die the debts being unpaid, the assets are liable as far as they go. If a woman be a trustee by virtue of which trust great sums of money come to her hand, if she dies, they shall be liable to the trust. Freeman and Goodale, Chan. Rep. 295.[1] A woman bought goods when *sole*, she marries and dies. A bill was brought against the husband to which he demurred. The demurrer was overruled.

On the other side, Mr. *Lutwyche*, Mr. *Cowper*, Serjeant *Whitaker*, Mr. *Williams*, and Mr. *Talbot*, of counsel for the earl and the residuary legatees, urged that the bonds were given specifically and what remains is to be given to them. As to the £2000 owed by the Lord Thomond himself and afterwards released to him, it was a revocation of the legacy, it was an alteration of her intention by giving it to one when she before intended to give it to another. If a man leave the legacy of an horse and gives it away to another before he dies, the legacy is gone. The same if a testator gives away a particular debt, if the debtor voluntarily pay in the debt, the legacy shall stand, but if the testator call it in, it is an ademption or revocation of the legacy. Swinburne.[2] So here the release is the voluntary act of the testator. As to the latter clause of the legacy, if the £4000 be paid in or any part thereof, that is on a condition precedent if it be paid in, but it was not paid in and the condition did not happen so the words are against them and the intention was so, *viz.* if the personal estate was increased by it, but the £2000 released does not augment her personal estate as payment of it in would have done. It is sunk in that branch of the family intended to be provided for by the legacy, for it is taken away from the granddaughter and given to the grandson.

As to the latter question, whether the earl ought to be charged, it was insisted that, as to the £500, the half year's annuity paid after the countess's death, he ought to be admitted as a purchaser because Lord Thomond could not be admitted into possession of the estate without his consent, that he was entitled to it at law without the interposition of this court. If he were not, they would be proper to charge him, that he had notice of this bond before marriage, and it is not to be resembled to the case of an executrix or administratrix because they give in an inventory whereby the husband may know how much they are indebted.

Lord Chancellor Parker: As to the bond of £2000 from the plaintiff himself and which was released, I think, since there appears nothing from which I can infer the testatrix changed her mind as to what she intended her granddaughter, that it is no revocation of the legacy. I take this release to be a payment and a return of the money. If it had been a receipt, nobody would have doubted of

[1] *Freeman v. Goodham* (1676), 1 Chancery Cases 295, 22 E.R. 808, also 1 Eq. Cas. Abr. 60, 21 E.R. 874.

[2] H. Swinburne, *Brief Treatise of Testaments and Last Wills.*

it. It is said she has changed her mind and given it to her grandson. True, she has so, but she has not changed her mind with respect to her granddaughter so as to take it from her and give it to her grandson. When she says 'if the bonds are paid,' the meaning of that is if they are discharged; the bonds are only securities. If they continue, she is to have them specifically; if not, she is to have them out of the personal estate. And this seems reasonable from the circumstances of the family. If there might be a reasonable intention to take it in that strict sense that nothing but payment should discharge, you say right. But does anyone think that, when the testatrix speaks only of payment and afterwards releases it, she had that in view? This does not bear any proportion to her other legacies which she gives to her other grandchildren. The surplus is given among nine, and this lady had nobody to take care of her, no other parent. And thus she gives her £4000. And does it then look reasonable that this granddaughter should bear the whole deduction than that it should be shared among the nine? That would be exceeding hard. And when she gives the residue of her estate to her grandchildren, that must depend upon what she gives away in her life. I think a release, in this case, amounts to the payment of the money and a giving it back again. There are many such cases in law. A lease and a release is looked on as a feoffment, and setting money off from a debt is a receipt and paying it back again. So this answers the intent of the parties as well as the receipt of the money from her grandson and giving it him back again. The releasing of it is doing it in that way which was least trouble. And I think the plaintiff's being a person to whom it was released makes no difference, for he recovers it as in her place and it is she who recovers it. The plaintiff, thus, must have a decree as to that £2000.

As to the other £2000, the question is how far the earl of Suffolk is bound to make it good. He is neither administrator nor executor nor in any way the representative of his wife. I doubt not but, if the wife had been executrix, the husband had been responsible because the assets had been liable and the demand had been *in rem* and he receives it subject to the trust and, if the husband disposes of the estate, it is a *devastavit*. He is to pay the debts because he has those very things which were to pay them and, if the creditor had got a judgment *de bonis testatoris*, he might have gone and taken the goods and it is the same where the wife is a trustee, for the parties have a right to follow the trust estate though there had been a conveyance, unless it were without notice and on a valuable consideration. But if you come to demand a debt due from the wife and to call the husband to an account for it after her death, I do not know any reason for it. The law says the marriage makes a gift of all the wife's goods to the husband. In the cases I have mentioned, as the husband is responsible for the goods of the testator and the trust estate, so he is answerable no farther than the assets go and the trust estate reaches. But in respect of the wife's debts, he is liable not only as far as her estate goes, but to the whole. And, if you had sued this bond in her lifetime, the husband must have been charged with the whole, though he had not a penny with her. And as, in her lifetime, he is responsible for her beyond what he receives, so, after her death, he is not responsible at all, not even as far as what he had with her. As the law on the one hand exposes the husband to a great hazard, so, on the other hand, it gives entirely to him all that the wife has. He must take it as it happens. If the law were altered and the husband liable no farther than what he receives, what the plaintiff contends for might be reasonable. But as it now stands, I cannot think so. But then, as to the particulars as to the £500 for which part of the jointure was sold, the money which he received for her jointure during the coverture was his; he could give it away and dispose of it as he would. As to the £500 annuity received after her death, if it was a debt to her and not to him, he ought to be accountable for it, for then he is executor *de son tort*. The question then is whether this be a rent or anything due to her. I take it, if it were so, that the plaintiff comes with an ill grace, for that is to say that he has broken his covenant and would profit by the breach of it, for, if it had been paid on the day which it ought to have been paid on, he could not have come and proposed it as assets. But I do not see that it is a part of her estate. The earl of Suffolk has covenanted that she shall surrender, and this is a price paid to him for that agreement. And the effect of this could be no other than to bind him and thus the countess of Suffolk might after his death come in and say she had not agreed to it. She thus not having surrendered and the earl not being discharged from his covenant, I look on it as a price paid to him and thus he receives it as his own estate. I think thus there is no ground to order the earl to an account, nor do I find that he has received any part of her personal estate since her death.

Lincoln's Inn MS. Misc. 384, p. 46, pl. 2

21 July.

The countess dowager of Thomond devises in these words, 'Whereas Lady Henrietta owes me £2000, now I do hereby bequeath the sum of £2000 to my granddaughter Lady Mary O'Brien', who is married to the plaintiff. Lady Henrietta afterwards pays in the £2000 to the testator. The first question is whether this extinguished the legacy to Lady Mary O'Brien; the second question is whether the defendant's late wife having committed a *devastavit* as executrix, the defendant was accountable for it here, though not at law.

Vernon, for the plaintiff: If a man devises to A. £500, which is due to him upon a bond, if he after[wards] release to the obligor, the legacy is extinct. But it is otherwise if the money be paid in.

Second, if a *feme sole* is indebted, marries, and dies before it is recovered, at law, the husband is not liable, but he is here. So, if a man marries a trustee, the husband is liable here so far as he has possessed the estate of his wife, of which he is not a purchaser. So, if a wife be an executrix or is possessed of a term and is indebted on a bond, the term is chargeable in the hands of the survivor.

N.B. By Lord Cowper, if a tenant for life commit waste and die, this court will make the executors answer for it out of the personal assets so far as they are increased by the waste, though there is no remedy at law.

Mead: By the civil law, ademption of a legacy is not to be presumed any more than a revocation of a will. Raymond 335. As to the second point, see Freeman v. Goodham, 1 Ch. Ca. 295. In the case of Orme and Smith, before Lord Harcourt, February 1711[/12], the plaintiff was indebted to the testator, J.S., by a bond and a [confessed] judgment of £500 which he paid off except £80; the testator, by his will, gave the plaintiff the sum of £500, 'which he owes me by bond and judgment'. The plaintiff brought his bill for the £500, he having paid off the debt after the making of the will, and it was decreed to him as a legacy of so much money.

Lord Chancellor [Lord Parker] decreed the first point for the plaintiff on the authority of this case. But as to the second point, he would not make the defendant liable for his wife's debts here further than he was [liable] at law.

British Library MS. Hargrave 81, f. 14

22 July 1718.

The countess of Suffolk, the defendant's grandmother, by will, gave the plaintiff's wife £4000, *viz.* £2000 due from the plaintiff by bond and £2000 due from the defendant, the earl of Suffolk's wife. And, if any part of the said several sums should happen to be paid in her lifetime, then she willed that so much should be paid out of her personal estate. And, afterwards, the testatrix gave the plaintiff a general release, which vacated the bond, and died. The plaintiff, afterwards, married the said legatee, and the defendant, who was executor, married the other obligee. And the plaintiff exhibited his bill against the defendant for the said several sums of £2000 each. As to the £2000 due to the plaintiff, it was argued by his counsel that the release, though it extinguished his debt, yet it no ways altered the devise to his lady. And they cited the Case of Orme v. Smith, where the obligee devises £150 due to him by bond to the obligor and, afterwards, the obligor pays the testator £100 of the money, takes up the old bond, and gives a fresh bond for the residue. The question was whether such payment and alteration of the debt was not a revocation of the legacy, since it manifestly altered the intention of the testator. But it was then looked upon that the money was voluntarily paid, without being called for by the testator; the devise was good.

And as to the other £2000, it was insisted that the defendant, having married the obligee, was liable to pay her bond, for that, where a man married a woman, although without a contract, and possesses the estate etc., in that case, he stands in her place and is liable to any demand against the wife as far as her estate will go in the same manner as an executor and, therefore, if a man marries a woman possessed of a term for years, who dies, that term is afterwards liable to her debts and so all her other estate that can be found. Otherwise, it would be very hard, for, suppose a man should marry a woman who was a trader and worth £5000 but indebted as much to several persons, the creditors might by that means be stripped of their debts without a remedy and the husband run away with all.

Lord Chancellor [LORD PARKER]: By the general release, the bond is undoubtedly vacated. But it does not appear by that the testatrix had altered her intention, for, suppose the money had been actually paid, it is evident that would not have altered her intention as to the sum devised, for, there, it is expressly provided to be paid out of her personal estate and the release is no more than if she had received it with one hand and given it back with the other. It only saved the trouble of telling it over. And there is the less reason to take it as an alteration of her intention, as the devisee was her daughter. And it does not alter the case at all that the now plaintiff, who after[wards] married the daughter, was the person to whom the release was made. He now seeks a satisfaction for this legacy out of the testatrix's estate in right of his wife and what right she had is now vested in him.

And, as to the other £2000, that the defendant, the Lord Suffolk, as representative to his wife, was liable as far as assets should be found to pay such debts as she owed before her marriage. And that a husband in equity stood as an executor is a new doctrine. An executor or administrator is liable so far as assets. And, if they waste any part of the assets, they are liable to answer for it; so is a trustee for his trust. But the case of a husband is quite otherwise. The marriage is a conveyance or gift to the husband of all his wife's personal estate, whether he makes any settlement or not, and it is the same in equity. And the husband is liable not only as far as her fortune goes, but, if he receive nothing, he is nevertheless bound to pay all the debts of the wife, be they never so many. But, if the husband die before judgment, he is not liable. They then become the proper debts of the wife again so that, as the law exposed the man to a manifest disadvantage in that respect, it gave him the wife's fortune as a recompense. And marriage was never looked upon as a fraud. A term of the wife's is indeed liable to her debts after death, and the reason is because the husband cannot entitle himself to the term but by administration and, *quoad* administrator, he should be so far liable.

[Other copies of this report: British Library MS. Hargrave 82, f. 11.]

[Other reports of this case: British Library MS. Hargrave 77, f. 5v, pl. 2; British Library MS. Hargrave 303, f. 7, 1 Peere Williams 461, 24 E.R. 474, 2 Eq. Cas. Abr. 134, 567, 22 E.R. 114, 478.]

280

Drake v. Robinson

(Ch. 1718)

The question in this case was whether copyhold lands will pass by general words in a will or by a devise of the residue of the real estate where there is any freehold land to answer those general words.

Lincoln's Inn MS. Misc. 10, p. 231

18 July 1718.

A.B., by will, devised all his estate not settled upon his eldest son for the payment of his debts. And he died seised both of freehold and copyhold land not settled, but the copyhold was not surrendered to the use of the will.

The question was if the court should supply the defect of a surrender, it being objected that, where there is no surrender to the use of the will, copyhold lands will not pass by general words in a will nor by a devise of the residue of the real estate where there is any freehold land to answer those general words.

The court reserved the consideration of this matter until after the Master had taken the account.

It was said by Mr. *Vernon* and so agreed that, if freehold and copyhold lands are particularly devised for the payment of debts and there is no surrender to the use of the will, the copyhold shall bear a proportion of the debts with the freehold.

[Other reports of this case: 1 Peere Williams 443, 24 E.R. 464, 2 Eq. Cas. Abr. 232, 22 E.R. 197.]

281

Winder v. Hiccock

(Ch. 1718)

If a creditor is in possession of lands under a statute and gives up possession, not being evicted, what is afterwards received shall be taken to be received in discharge of the debt.

Lincoln's Inn MS. Misc. 10, p. 232

Horatio Moor, in 1701, acknowledges a statute to the defendant Burgh for £1000 and, in May 1703, confesses judgment to one Goff, under whom the plaintiffs claim, for £2000. After this, Burgh assigns his statute to the defendant Hiccock for £537, and Hiccock extends his statute and was in possession for about two years of the extended lands. And then, he and Moor state an account touching what was due on the statute, upon the balance of which account there appeared to be due to Hiccock about 40s., who, thereupon, delivers up the possession of the lands to Moor.

Hiccock, in 1702, before Goff's judgment, lent Moor several sums on bonds and notes, and Moor promises to give him a mortgage, but, failing to do it, Hiccock puts the bonds and notes in suit and recovers judgments thereon about three months after Goff's judgment. And, after Hiccock had delivered up the possession of the extended lands, he and Moor settle another account of what was due on the judgment recovered by Hiccock. And upon the balance thereof, there appearing to be due £1500, Moor agrees to make Hiccock a mortgage for securing that sum, and Hiccock agrees to vacate the statute. And, accordingly, 6 December 1705, Moor makes a mortgage to Hiccock for securing £1500 with interest. And, in that mortgage, it is recited that Hiccock had agreed to acknowledge satisfaction on the statute. Hiccock, before he took this mortgage, had notice of Goff's judgment. Moor dying shortly afterwards, Hiccock never vacated the statute.

Moor's estate not being sufficient to satisfy all the encumbrances, the question was upon the Master's report after a decree which had stated this matter whether the statute was still a subsisting encumbrance and whether, by virtue of that, Hiccock might not protect his mortgage so as to have a satisfaction of the £1500 prior to Goff's judgment, which the plaintiffs claimed.

Lord Chancellor [Lord Parker] seemed to think that the statute was discharged at law, for, if a man is in possession of lands under a statute and quits the possession, not being evicted, whether to the cognisor or any other, what is afterwards received shall be looked upon to be received in discharge of the statute, and it appears that, when Hiccock quitted possession, he had received about £620 and, the estate being upwards of £200 a year, the statute must have been satisfied long ago. However, if it was not, yet, as this case is, he could not come in for a satisfaction prior to the plaintiffs for more than is really due of the £1000, for which the statute was given, for, he having taken a new security after he had notice of Goff's judgment and at the same time agreed to vacate the statute, though such new security proves to be deficient, by reason of Goff's judgment, which is prior, yet he shall not by virtue of his statute come in for a satisfaction of his mortgage before Goff's judgment of which he had notice when he took that mortgage, for his agreement was to vacate his statute and take a mortgage subject to Goff's judgment.

It was insisted on for the defendant that the mortgage ought to have a relation to the time when Hiccock first lent his money, which was when the bonds and notes were given, in regard that Moor then promised to make Hiccock a mortgage. And, as to this, the Case of Kildare and Kent was cited, *quod vide ante*, f. 24.[1]

---

[1] *Earl of Kildare v. Kent* (1702), 2 Freeman 253, 22 E.R. 1192, *sub nom. Shepherd v. Kent*, Precedents in Chancery 190, 24 E.R. 92, 2 Vernon 435, 23 E.R. 879, 1 Eq. Cas.

But it was said this was not like to that case, for, there was a note in writing promising to make a mortgage and that [was] relied on as the security, which was a sort of lien on the estate. But here were notes and bonds given for security and the agreement for a mortgage [was] only parol.

Curia [Lord Parker]: Let the Master take an account whether the statute is satisfied by the rents received since the defendant quitted possession, and, if anything remains due, let the defendant, as to so much, come in for a satisfaction prior to the plaintiffs.

Note it was said by Mr. *Vernon* to be lately decreed that, though if a second mortgagee gets in an encumbrance which is prior to the first mortgage, he shall protect himself against the first mortgage of which he had no notice, yet it is otherwise where a judgment creditor gets in a prior encumbrance.[1]

282

Butler v. Duncomb

(Ch. 1718–1719)

In this case, the marriage portion in issue was not payable according to the terms of the settlement until a later date even though the woman had married and reached the age of twenty-one.

Lincoln's Inn MS. Misc. 384, p. 43, pl. 2

21 July.

The question is whether a term for fifty years being created by a marriage settlement after a limitation to the husband for life, then to the wife for life for her jointure, then to the first and other sons in tail male and for default of such issue to trustees for 500 years to raise £3000 after the commencement of the term for daughters' portions out of the rents and profits or by sale or mortgage to be paid at their age of twenty-one or day of marriage, the tenant for life being dead without issue male leaving a daughter, who is married to the plaintiff, the £3000 can be raised presently by a sale or mortgage of the term in the life[time] of the jointress.

Sir Thomas Powys, for the plaintiff: All of the difficulty arises upon the words 'after the commencement of the term', for, otherwise, it might be sold presently. These words are not in the articles before the marriage, but are slipped into the settlement after pursuant thereto for, in those articles, the term is to commence after the death of the tenant for life without issue male and the portions are to be paid at twenty-one or marriage, which ought not to be defeated by the other words, as in 2 Jones 201, Greaves v. Mattison; Corbet v. Maidwell, Salk.

Abr. 142, 21 E.R. 944, Colles 253, 1 E.R. 273, Lincoln's Inn MS. Misc. 10, p. 24.

[1] Perhaps *Wright v. Pilling* (Ch. 1718), see above, Case No. 257.

159; Gerrard v. Gerrard, 2 An. R., Ch. Rep. 190;[1] if Sir Charles Gerrard die leaving one daughter, then, for raising her portion at twenty-one or marriage, which should first happen after the death of himself and Honora, his wife, who is living, though here seemed to be a condition annexed to the time of payment, which is not in our case, yet the age of twenty-one or marriage being the proper time for it to take effect, it was decreed to be raised at that time.

Cowper: The settlement cannot control the original articles, and, when a portion is payable at twenty-one or marriage, it ought not to be deferred longer, for, perhaps, the portion then may be of no service.

Vernon: We are now upon a trust and a provision for a younger child, which this court always construes favorably. In Hilliard and Jones,[2] there was a term for raising portions at twenty-one or marriage after the death of the father and mother, yet there was a sale of the term in the life[time] of the father. So in Staniforth v. Staniforth,[3] the mesne intent of the parties is to be observed. This is now a certain interest which cannot be defeated, there being a failure of issue male. And here is no maintenance provided besides this portion.

Mead: The trust of this term was contingent in the creation, for, had there been issue male, the term might never have commenced. But now, it is become certain that it must commence.

Lutwyche, for the defendant: The question arises upon the words 'after the commencement of the term'. In point of time, it is not yet commenced. [There is] no difference between the term and the trust of the term. If the reversion is to be sold, it will scarcely raise the money. In Staniforth v. Staniforth, before the Master of the Rolls, if the husband and wife died without issue male and left daughters at the time of their death, then for the daughters' portions at twenty-one or marriage, it was raised in the life[time] of the mother.

Raymond: Here are particular words which carry it further than any cases which have been cited. There was the case of Cotton v. Cotton, see [no.] 112, 10 May last, before the Master of the Rolls;[4] the trustees of a term were by the felling of timber and profits to raise a maintenance and £5000 to be paid at twenty-one, the first payment to be 'after the commencement of the term'; the Master of the Rolls would not allow any maintenance during the life of the mother, who possessed the land. There is no difference between maintenance and portions.

---

1 *Greaves v. Mattison* (1682), T. Jones 201, 84 E.R. 1216, also Skinner 38, 90 E.R. 19, 1 Eq. Cas. Abr. 336, 21 E.R. 1085; *Corbett v. Maidwell* (1709–1710), 1 Salkeld 159, 91 E.R. 147, also 3 Chancery Reports 190, 21 E.R. 764, 2 Vernon 640, 655, 23 E.R. 1019, 1027, 1 Eq. Cas. Abr. 337, 21 E.R. 1086; *Gerrard v. Gerrard* (1704), 2 Vernon 458, 23 E.R. 894, 2 Freeman 271, 22 E.R. 1204, 1 Eq. Cas. Abr. 337, 21 E.R. 1086.

2 *Hellier v. Jones* (1689), 1 Eq. Cas. Abr. 337, 21 E.R. 1085.

3 *Staniforth v. Staniforth* (1703–1719), 2 Vernon 460, 23 E.R. 895, 1 Eq. Cas. Abr. 337, 21 E.R. 1086, see also below, Case No. 362.

4 *Cotton v. Cotton* (1718), see above, Case No. 239.

Lord Chancellor [LORD PARKER]: This case goes further than the other cases. A man may limit it so that it shall not be raised during the precedent estates. Here, the interest is running on, but the trustees are not to do it until 'after the commencement of the term'. I would not go further than the precedents, which I would see and consider of.

18 February 1718/19.

Upon the plaintiff's petition, it was ordered that he have liberty, with the trustee, to sell the moiety of his wife's fortune for their present subsistence, the plaintiff covenanting that the other moiety should be settled on the wife when it should be raised.

N.B. This was before any judgment was given whether the whole should be raised before the commencement of the term.

British Library MS. Hargrave 77, f. 5v, pl. 1

22 July 1718.

In consideration of a £4000 portion paid to the father, he settles upon the son £400 *per annum* for life, remainder to the wife for life, remainder to the first and every other son in tail male, and, if the husband and wife should die without issue male, remainder to trustees for 500 years and after the commencement of the term to raise £3000 by mortgage, demise, or otherwise for daughters' portions, remainder to the right heirs of the father.

The son dies and leaves issue of the marriage only one daughter, who was married to the plaintiff at fourteen years of age by ill practice. The plaintiff now exhibits a bill to enable the trustees to raise the £3000. And the mother being living, many cases and many inconveniences were cited on both sides. A certain provision [was] made. The children [were] disobedient and threw themselves away against the parents' inclinations. No provision or maintenance is provided. [It is] very hard to subsist by a mother's benevolence and compassion, unnatural many times etc.

Settlements must be taken as made. After commencement can mean nothing but the beginning of the term. Consider the inconveniences on both sides, nature, prevalent, unequal. Suppose the settlement had been to sons in tail, remainder, as before, to the daughter and they had had sons, for 100 years and no recovery suffered, the daughters had procured to advance on the contingency which had afterwards happened, these would be the gross sum and 100 years interest, which would devour the estate. And it would be the same in this case.

[Lord Chancellor PARKER:] A stranger to many cases in this court, but I acquiesce with the noble [judges] whom I succeed that, if the matters *res integra* were now before me, that I should not go so far as some cases already cited. But if [it is] so settled by this court, it is all one and then becomes a law which everyone when he makes a settlement considers and casts about how far it will operate and settles accordingly, but there appears such a manifest disadvantage and it is a matter of such importance that I would gladly consider the cases of this nature, which I will follow, but not go one step farther than they have gone.

[Other copies of this report: British Library MS. Hargrave 303, f. 6.]

2 Vernon 760, 23 E.R. 1096

22 July.

[There was a] settlement to the husband for life, to the wife for life, and to first and other sons in tail, in default of such issue, to trustees for 500 years, remainder to the defendant Duncombe, the grandfather, who made the settlement, and his heirs.

The trust of the term is declared to be in trust that, after the commencement of the term, the trustees shall by and out of the lands, tenements, and hereditaments raise for the portions of such younger children as George, the son, should have by Anne, his wife, the sum of £4000 to be raised and paid out of the rents and profits (as to the effect of such a trust, in respect of the words 'rents and profits') or by demising, selling, or mortgaging the premises to be paid to the child or children at twenty-one or marriage, which shall first happen. The husband died and left only a daughter, who, when of the age of fifteen, married the plaintiff in the lifetime of the mother.

The question was whether the portion should become payable in the lifetime of the mother.

The objection relied on was that it was not to be raised until after the commencement of the term and the term does not properly commence until it comes in possession, but it was a vested remainder on the making of the settlement and was no contingent remainder. And he cited the case of Cotton and Cotton, where a maintenance was to arise and be paid at the first feast that should happen after the commencement of the term, heard at the Rolls and decreed it did not commence until after the death of the wife.

For the plaintiff were cited the cases of Hellier and Jones, where a term was sold in the lifetime of the father to raise portions at twenty-one or marriage; Greaves and Mattison, T. Jones 201; if he die without issue male of his then wife.

Curia advisare vult.

The cause coming on afterwards (Easter Term 1719) to be further heard, the court declared the portion was not payable until after the decease of the jointress, nor would it carry interest in the meantime. But Mr. Butler being a considerable tradesman in Guildford, the court thought it not reasonable that the whole money, when payable, should be secured or laid out for the benefit of the wife and children. But he decreed, the wife being present in court and consenting, that Mr. Butler might sell or dispose of a moiety of it as he thought fit.

Lincoln's Inn MS. Misc. 11, p. 122

9 May 1719.

A term of 500 years was limited by the marriage settlement of the plaintiff's father and mother, after the death of the father and mother, upon trust, after the commencement of the term to raise portions for the daughters. The father being dead, the plaintiffs, in the life of the mother, bring their bill to have the portion raised upon the reversionary trust.

Lord Chancellor [Lord Parker]: The question is when is the portion to be raised. I answer, in the words of the settlement, after the commencement of the term. Though the trusts of the term are in the affirmative, yet they imply a negative, as, when it is said a portion is to be paid at twenty-one, it implies it is not to be paid sooner. So, where it is said, as here, to be raised after the commencement of the term, it implies it is not to be raised before. But when does the term commence? Why, after the death of the wife.

But then, it has been insisted on that the portion is payable at twenty-one and the plaintiff's wife is of age and, therefore, the portion ought now to be raised. I think not. The meaning is the portion shall be raised after the commencement of the term if the daughter is of age or married, but, if not, then, though the term is commenced, yet she shall wait until the portion becomes payable.

I admit a right to the portion vests at twenty-one but not a right to have the portion raised immediately unless the term is commenced.

I am persuaded the intention of the parties was that the portions should not be raised in the life of the father or mother. And, for that reason, the words 'after the commencement of the term' were added. There is no case where the words have been express to raise the portion after the commencement of the term that the portion has been decreed to be raised sooner.

However, I will not dismiss the plaintiffs' bill, for the right to the portion vested in the plaintiff's wife, though not to have the portion raised until the commencement of the term and then it must be raised, but not with interest but from the time the term commences. I will, therefore, retain the bill, that, if the plaintiffs' occasions require it, they may raise money upon the credit of this decree.

Lincoln's Inn MS. Misc. 384, p. 174

11 May.

Lord Chancellor [Lord Parker]: I have not seen any precedents to my satisfaction. The case arises upon a deed of settlement of the plaintiff's wife's father. There is a limitation of a term of 500 years after the mother's death upon a trust that, after the commencement of the term, the trustees should raise £3000 for the daughters' portions to be paid at twenty-one or marriage out of the rents and profits or by mortgage or sale. She, being twenty-one, has married the plaintiff in the life[time] of her mother, who brings his bill to have her portion raised. So the question is when the portion shall be raised. I answer in the words of the deed, after the commencement of the term, which implies a negative, not before. Then, the question is when the term commences? Not until after the death of the mother, who is still alive. But does it not arise in equity sooner than at law? No.

But it is said this portion is payable at twenty-one and, therefore, should be raised at that time. But the intent was that she should not have it before twenty-one though the term should commence sooner and also not before the commencement of the term. If money is to be raised at twenty-one but the deed which appoints it is not sealed until after, it is void, but the money is due presently. Here, it is to be raised after the commencement of the term and cannot be paid before it is raised. When words are used only to obviate one accident and that accident happens, to construe it otherwise is not to construe but expunge. But does this not clash with former authorities? No, for there is one case where portions to be raised after the commencement of the term have been raised before. Corbet and Maidwell, Salk. 159. If this were *res integra*, this court would not go so far, but it should not go further. If the money were to be raised presently, it would be very hard on the reversioner. If it were mortgaged, the reversioner might be foreclosed before the term commenced. [There are] no precedents for setting aside express words. The right to the portion is vested in the plaintiff, but it is not to be raised until the commencement of the term.

[I will] retain the bill that the plaintiff may raise money on this portion if he has occasion though the portion itself cannot be raised until the term commences. The plaintiff, the husband, may dispose of a moiety of his wife's portion for his advantage in trade. No interest is due until there is a default of payment, which cannot be until the portion is payable.

Lincoln's Inn MS. Hill 73, p. 38

21 July. Lord Chancellor.

Vernon: Case [. . .] Stanniford v. Stanniford; Lady Garrard v. Garrard. A term vested in trustees for raising portions expectant upon an estate for life may be sold during the life of the tenant for life, being to be paid the children at the age of twenty-one or marriage after they have attained such age.

N.B. Lord Chancellor [Lord Parker]: All remainders vest immediately that do not depend upon a contingency.

The marriage settlements [are] to the husband and wife and the issue male and, in failure of issue male, to trustees to raise fortunes for daughters.

Mead: Though the term is a vested remainder, yet the trust of the wife is contingent because, if there was issue male, there had been no use made of it.

Lutwyche, for the defendant: The term does not commence until the death of the father and mother. The words of the settlement [. . .] after the commencement of the term to be sold, mortgaged, etc. for the fortunes of younger daughters.

Stanniford v. Stanniford; an estate [was] limited to the husband for life and after to the wife for life and, in case the husband and wife died without issue male and left a daughter, then a term vested for raising such fortunes for daughters. It was decreed that the reversion should be sold in the life of the jointress.

Cotton v. Cotton; an estate was limited to the lady for a jointure and then a term to raise fortunes for the younger children which were eight (the words next after the commencement of the term the first payment to be made at such a feast); the court could not assist them against such words though there was no provision for their maintenance. Hellier v. Jones.

Sir Robert Raymond: The term is undoubtedly vested in the trustees immediately, but the execution of the trust is not to be enforced until after the commencement of the term (which words can have no other construction but commencement in possession or computation of time). Corbet v. Maidwell, Salkeld.

Williams: A daughter though first born was decreed to be a younger child and only in opposition to a son.

Lord Chancellor [Lord Parker]: There being no maintenance for the issue during the life of the father and mother is upon the natural supposition of the father and mother providing for their issue.

The reversioner, who was by the settlement to pay £3000 if the trustees can raise this fortune during the life of the jointress and interest charged for such sum may be forced to pay or at least been charged with even more than the testator could bear, which depends upon the length of the particular estate precedent lasting.

He was of opinion that, without the words 'from and after the commencement of the term', it might have been raised before the term commenced but by these words 'from and after' is express limitation that it shall not vest until that commencement, and very natural it is to suppose the words were put in to prevent the inconveniences that would have attended the want of them, which was (as is before mentioned) the overcharging the inheritance beyond what it could possibly bear.

Adjourned [and] attend with precedents.

My Lord observed in the cases cited that there were no express terms limited that the term should commence from.

Lincoln's Inn MS. Misc. 11, p. 132

The trusts of the term were that the trustees or the survivor should after the commencement of the term by and out of the lands limited to them for the 500 years or by sale or mortgage thereof raise £3000 for the daughter of the marriage to be paid at twenty-one or marriage, which should first happen.

In this case, Mr. *Vernon* cited the Case of Stanyport and Stanyport, which was that, in a marriage settlement, a term of years was limited and the trusts thereof declared to be that, if the father and mother died without issue male and there should be daughters of the marriage, the trustees should raise portions for such daughters to be paid at twenty-one or marriage. The father died without issue male leaving a daughter, and, though the mother was living, yet there being a failer of issue male and it being the intention of the parties that, when there was a failer of such issue, the portions should be raised. It was decreed that the portion should be raised by the reversionary term.

[Other reports of this case: 1 Peere Williams 448, 24 E.R. 466, 10 Modern 433, 88 E.R. 797, 1 Eq. Cas. Abr. 339, 21 E.R. 1088, 2 Eq. Cas. Abr. 674, 22 E.R. 566.]

283

Carter v. Barnardiston

(Ch. 1718–1719)

The question in this case was whether a devisee of a life estate can suffer a common recovery and destroy contingent remainders so that the person in reversion has a right of entry.

An estate will be in abeyance in order to preserve estates, not to destroy them.

A tenant in tail after debts are paid may suffer a recovery before the debts are paid.

Lincoln's Inn MS. Misc. 384, p. 53

21 July 1718; at the Rolls.

Sir Thomas Powys, for the plaintiff: Sir Michael Armine devises the premises in question to Evers Armine for life with several contingent remainders in fee. Evers Armine suffers a recovery whereby all the contingent remainders are destroyed. The question is whether the heir of the devisor had a reversion and consequently a right of entry.

This is the same case with Purefoy v. Rogers, 2 Sand. 380.[1] It is upon a devise and not by transmutation of possession. If there is an estate for life given by will and the next limitation is upon a contingency, it vests in the heir of the devisor until the contingency happens. It is not the same with a devise to the heirs of J.S., who is living, for here the testator does not intend it shall go from his heir presently. If a man devises to A. for life, remainder to a monk, the remainder is void and the reversion continues in the devisor and his heirs.

Sir Edward Northey: If a man limits by his will an estate for life with remainders on a contingency, the fee remains in the devisor until the contingency happens, for it is absurd that a tenant for life should gain an indefeasible fee when he commits a forfeiture. [See] the opinion of Gascoign, Co. 135, and Chudley's Case, Popham 83; Salkeld 234.[2]

---

[1] *Purefoy v. Rogers* (1671), 2 Williams Saunders 380, 85 E.R. 1181, also 2 Levinz 39, 83 E.R. 443, 3 Keble 11, 84 E.R. 566, 1 Eq. Cas. Abr. 189, 21 E.R. 980, Lincoln's Inn MS. Misc. 500, ff. 192, 194b.

[2] *Dillon v. Freine* (1589–1595), 1 Coke Rep. 113, 135, 76 E.R. 261, 305, Popham 70, 79 E.R. 1184, also 1 Anderson 309, 123 E.R. 489; *Cole v. Rawlinson* (1703), 1 Salkeld 234, 91 E.R. 207, also 2 Lord Raymond 831, 92 E.R. 55, Holt K.B. 744, 90 E.R. 1309, 3 Brown P.C. 7, 1 E.R. 141, 2 Eq. Cas. Abr. 300, 22 E.R. 252.

Chesshyre: If a tenant for life with a remainder over limits a forfeiture, he in remainder is not obliged to enter until five years after the death of the tenant for life. 2 Sand. 380. There is indeed a devise to the heir of the devisor, but that being void because the heir cannot take by devise but is in by descent, therefore, it is the same with our case. It has been a doubt whether a remainder was good to one *in ventre sa mere*. Hob. 338, Ratcliff's Case.[1] A fee is not in abeyance, but when there is a necessity for it, as in the case of a parson. 1 Syd. 353; Salk. 229.[2] Until the contingency happens, the reversion descends.

Cowper: This is a new case which is nowhere determined. By the words and intent of the will, it is manifest the devisor designed Evers Armine should have but an estate for life and that he should not take any more unless he had issue. By law, if a tenant for life endeavors to gain a tortious fee, he forfeits the estate and a right of entry is given to the next in remainder in reversion. Here, the fee remains in the heir of the devisor undisposed of until the contingency happens. It is absurd that a tenant for life should have it in his power to defeat the whole will of his testator to whose bounty he owes his own estate for life. The weight of reason is very strong on our side, and the other side only depends upon a chicanery of law.

Vernon: We apprehend the authorities make for us, but, if they are laid out of the case, the reason of the thing is certainly with us, for whatever the testator has not disposed of must remain in him and descend to his heirs.

Acherly: Wherever a devise or use is limited to the heir of the devisor, it operates nothing but is in him by descent. Leonard Lovey's Case, 10 Co. 78.[3]

Gilby: Abeyance is a fiction of law, which is never favored and is to be set up only to support a right. Plowd. 554, Walsmith's Case.[4] An estate does not pass out of the grantor but when it vests in the grantee. If the fee was in abeyance before the recovery, yet it could not be so after but vested in the heir of the devisor.

Lutwyche, for the defendant: There is no difference between a will and a deed as to the effect of the recovery. Wherever there is an estate for life, all the subsequent estates are remainders, and, if they are contingent and the particular tenant commits a forfeiture, they are all destroyed. The fee passed immediately out

[1] *Lord Sheffield v. Ratcliffe* (1625), Hobart 334, 80 E.R. 475, also W. Jones 69, 82 E.R. 36, 2 Rolle Rep. 501, 81 E.R. 943, Godbolt 300, 78 E.R. 176.

[2] *Snow v. Tucker* (1663–1667), 1 Siderfin 153, 82 E.R. 1027, also *sub nom. Snow v. Cutler*, T. Raymond 162, 83 E.R. 86, 1 Levinz 135, 83 E.R. 335, 1 Keble 567, 752, 800, 851, 83 E.R. 1115, 1224, 1251, 1280, 2 Keble 11, 145, 296, 84 E.R. 7, 91, 185, 1 Eq. Cas. Abr. 188, 21 E.R. 979; *Scatterwood v. Edge* (1697), 1 Salkeld 229, 91 E.R. 203, also 12 Modern 278, 88 E.R. 1320, 1 Eq. Cas. Abr. 189, 21 E.R. 980, 2 Eq. Cas. Abr. 337, 22 E.R. 287, King's Inn Dublin MS. 92, p. 1.

[3] *Prowt v. Worthen* (1613), 10 Coke Rep. 78, 77 E.R. 1043, also 2 Brownlow & Goldesborough 103, 123 E.R. 839.

[4] *Attorney General v. Walsingham* (1573), 2 Plowden 547, 75 E.R. 805.

of the devisor. Co. Lit. 442b. When there is a freehold vested and the remainders are contingent, the fee is in abeyance until it is seen whether the remainders will vest or not. If the fee was once out of the devisor, when did it come back to him again? The wrong is done to the remaindermen but none to the heir of the devisor. Had it been upon a grant, it would be so, and this is the same case. It is nowhere adjudged that the heir of the devisor has a right of entry.

Selby: All the arguments against tenants for life's gaining a tortious fee turn as strongly against his power to suffer the recovery; here is a fee gained. The question is whether anybody can defeat that fee. It is admitted the remaindermen to whom the wrong was done cannot because their estates are destroyed, neither can the heir of the devisor to whom no wrong was done because he had no reversion.

Raymond: We hope the principles laid down in our law books will hold good. As he who has a fee can have no more, so, where he grants a fee, he can have nothing remaining in him. C. L. 378.[1] The inheritance passes immediately out of the grantor. Where there is an estate for life, remainder to the heirs of J.S., no remainder can be limited over. And, where no remainder can be limited, there can be no reversion. Leonard Lovy's Case. There can be no limitation after a contingent fee. The law books say the fee is in abeyance. C. L. 342; Hob. 338.[2] There is no difference between a will and a deed where the party intends to dispose of the whole fee. And here, the whole fee is given away from his heir. Shall the will have a different effect upon an accident which could not be foreseen? This is a tort only to the remaindermen, but the heir of the devisor is not wronged. Poph. 83.[3] The opinion of Gascoigne does not affect this case and, besides, is not law. It is if a tenant for life, remainder to the heirs of J.S. make a feoffment, it is a forfeiture though the heir of J.S. cannot enter. But it is not said the heir of the donor may. As to the case in Saunders, it is not determined what estate was given to S., for, if he had but an estate for life, it is nothing to the purpose.

Peere Williams: If the tenant for life had committed waste, the heir of the devisor could not bring an action of waste, which proves he had no reversion. The contingent remainders may be destroyed though no forfeiture is committed, as in a feoffment by a tenant in tail. There are no authorities against us. Saunders quoted Noy 102; Beck's Case, Lit. Rep. 32.[4]

Powys, in reply: If a man devises to A. for life, remainder to the right heirs of J.S. and the tenant for life dies before J.S., the heir of the devisor shall have it again. It is the same thing if the tenant for life makes it impossible that the heir of J.S. should take, for, if J.S. dies without an heir, the testator did not intend the remaindermen should have it until after the contingency happened. This is exact-

---

[1] E. Coke, *First Institute* (1628), f. 378.

[2] E. Coke, *First Institute* (1628), f. 342; *Lord Sheffield v. Ratcliffe* (1625), *ut supra.*

[3] *Dillon v. Freine* (1589–1595), *ut supra.*

[4] *Palmer's Case* (1611), Noy 102, 74 E.R. 1068; *Beck's Case* (1629–1630), Littleton 253, 285, 315, 344, 124 E.R. 233, 249, 264, 277.

ly the same case with Purefoy and Rogers, Sand. It is absurd that a wrong should be done by a tenant for life and no one be able to punish him for it.

Northey: If persons are *in esse* and capable, they will take. But where they are not *in esse*, it is the same as if they were not capable. Boreton and Nicholls, Cr. Ca. 363,[1] quoted by Hale in Purefoy and Rogers.

Chesshyre: They admit it is a forfeiture but say it is a wrong to nobody, which is absurd. There is a right remainder in the devisor when the contingency becomes impossible, either by the act of God or any accident, and the whole fee was not out of the devisor until the contingency happened. 2 Rol. Ab. 418; 6 Co. 17, Cleer's Case.[2]

Master of the Rolls [JEKYLL]: The intent of the testator appears to pass the whole fee out of him, though not immediately. But the remainders must expect until the contingency happens; like a devise to an infant *in ventre sa mere*, it does not vest presently but, in the meantime, descends to the heir. Now, it was the intent of the devisor that the freehold should pass, which it would have done if the tenant for life had permitted it. When the tenant for life has done this act, if the heir of the devisor has any right remaining in him, he may enter. Purefoy and Rogers is the same with this case.

A case must be made for the opinion of the judges of the [Court of] Common Pleas.

Lincoln's Inn MS. Misc. 384, p. 98, pl. 3

16 January [1719]; at the Rolls.

Sir John Chesshyre: Sir Michael Armine, seised in fee, 28 March 1688, makes his will and devises, after his debts [be] paid, to Evers Armine for life and, if he leave issue male, to such issue male and his heirs and, if no such issue, to Styles and his heirs. *Vide* the printed case.[3] Evers Armine received the profits for his life. In Hilary [term] 1675, Evers Armine suffered a recovery. In June 1680, Evers Armine died. In 1717, Lady Torrington, the heir of Sir Michael Armine, the devisor, conveys to the plaintiff.

The several points [are]: first, tenant for life, remainder in contingency, where the fee is until the contingency happens; second, the effect of the recovery, whether a bar to the heir; third, the effect of the fine of Hilary 1697, whether a bar to the heir of the devisor, first, whether anything passed by the fine, second, if a bar, only to a moiety, one party being under age; third, as to the other moiety, whether the fine could bar, debts not being paid; fourth, whether the heir of the devisor was bound to enter for the forfeiture; fifth, no bar against contribution

---

[1] *Boreton v. Nicholls* (1634), Croke Car. 363, 79 E.R. 917.

[2] 2 Rolle, Abr., *Remainder*, p. 418; *Parker v. Clere* (1599), 6 Coke Rep. 17, 77 E.R. 279, also Moore K.B. 567, 72 E.R. 763, Croke Eliz. 877, 78 E.R. 1102, Croke Jac. 31, 79 E.R. 24.

[3] *Carter v. Barnardiston* (1718), 1 Peere Williams 505, 24 E.R. 492.

for Pickworth against Willowby; sixth, whether it is proper to be determined in equity.

As to the first, there are no cases in the law that the fee is in abeyance, which is only for necessity, not where a person is capable to take, but a fiction of law. *Vide* Hob. 338, in Sheffield and Ratcliff's Case. It is only to prevent a vacuum. [First,] the consideration is at law; second, by way of use; third, by devise. In all, where the person is certain, there is no abeyance though the use is contingent, as a tenant for life, remainder to J.S. to have a fee on condition, the estate rests in the feoffor. Lit. Rep., Beck's Case, 255; Plowd. 323.[1] Nothing is given to the tenant for life but an estate for life, and, if he dies, the grantor shall enter, which proves nothing. More 11; Hob. fo. 12.[2] A devise to A. for life, remainder to B., passes in fee and B. dies without an heir, it reverts in the life of A. A right of entry is in the heir of the devisor for the forfeiture. Poph. 83; Rep. 135, Chudley's Case.[3]

Objection: The devisor did not design to keep anything in him.

It is true when in prejudice of the devisees, not when for their benefit. The reversion descends until the contingency happens.

Second, on the Statute of Uses,[4] though the estate is in the feoffee, the use undisposed of remains in him. 6 Rep. 17; Lit. Rep. 255; 10 Rep. 85, Leonard Lovei's Case.[5]

Third, it is stronger on a devise, as to one *in ventre sa mere*, which formerly was looked upon as void. Dyer 304b; 1 Syd. 153, Snow and Cutler; Purefoy and Rogers, 2 Sand. 380; Lord Hale's opinion was the foundation of that resolution; 3 Lev., Godbolt and Freestone.[6]

As to the force of the recovery by the tenant for life, it was void as to the heir of the devisor. 1 Rep., Pelham's Case. By the Statute 14 Eliz., it is declared void. Though it is a forfeiture, it is like a feoffment. Co. L. 362a.[7]

---

[1] *Beck's Case* (1629–1630), *ut supra*; *Regina v. Earl of Northumberland* (1567), 1 Plowden 310, 75 E.R. 472.

[2] *Anonymous* (1551), Moore K.B. 11, 72 E.R. 405; *Holder v. Taylor*, Hobart 12, 80 E.R. 163, also 1 Brownlow & Goldesborough 23, 123 E.R. 641 (1613).

[3] *Dillon v. Freine* (1589–1595), *ut supra*.

[4] Stat. 27 Hen. VIII, c. 10 (*SR*, III, 539–542).

[5] *Parker v. Clere* (1599), 6 Coke Rep. 17, 77 E.R. 279, also Moore K.B. 567, 72 E.R. 763, Croke Eliz. 877, 78 E.R. 1102, Croke Jac. 31, 79 E.R. 24; *Beck's Case* (1629–1630), *ut supra*; *Prowt v. Worthen* (1613), *ut supra*.

[6] *Anonymous* (1571), 3 Dyer 303, 73 E.R. 682; *Snow v. Tucker* (1663–1667), *ut supra*; *Purefoy v. Rogers* (1671), *ut supra*; *Godbold v. Freestone* (1694), 3 Levinz 406, 83 E.R. 753.

[7] *Page, ex dem. Bowes v. Griffin* (1588–1590), 1 Coke Rep. 3, 76 E.R. 8, also 2 Leonard 60, 74 E.R. 358, 4 Leonard 123, 74 E.R. 772, Moore K.B. 271, 72 E.R. 574, 1 Anderson 227, 123 E.R. 444; Stat. 14 Eliz. I, c. 8 (*SR*, IV, 600); E. Coke, *First Institute* (1628), f. 362.

As to the force of the fine in Hilary 1697 by Barnardiston and Armine Bullingham, it was an innocent act. It did not turn the estate into a right. Sir T.B. had no interest or possession. Therefore, he could pass none. [By] 24 January 1697, the bargain and sale, which is the grant only of Ar. Bab. and the confirmation of Barnardiston, all passed from A.B. The fine four days after could work only by confirmation or release; it does not displace any estate and, therefore, can be no bar. 10 Rep. 96, Seymor's Case; 9 Rep. 96.[1] Whether the deed and fine are one conveyance as to a purchaser, 2 Rep., Lord Cromwell's Case,[2] not where he is a wrongdoer. The force of it is taken off notwithstanding the non-claim, for they could not enter and were not bound to enter. The devise is to the trustees to receive the profits until the debts were paid. If the heir had brought an [action of] ejectment, he could not have recovered until the debts were paid, nor could he know when the debts were paid. Therefore, his not entering cannot bar him. The trust is not until the debts might be paid, 4 Rep. 81, Sir Andrew Corbet's Case,[3] but until the debts are paid. Where the heir is the cause of the debts not being paid, he shall not take advantage of it, so, in tenants by *elegit*, and the time elapsed shall not be taken as part of the time. Blackburn's Case, 3 Cr. 800, Noy 53 or 73.[4] If the heir is the wrongdoer, his assignee is affected with it. Carter 77.[5]

Here, Evers Armine, the tenant for life ought to have entered and paid the debts. Salk. 153.[6] The possession of the trustee is the possession of all that have right. If my trustee levies a fine, I am in possession. If a tenant for years hold over, he is not a possessor but a tenant at sufferance.

Lastly, though we might enter, we were not bound to enter. If my tenant for years or life levies a fine, I am not bound to enter until the estate is determined. Hard. 400.[7] There is a difference between the owner of the estate and a stranger. There is no period of time when the debts are to be paid. Fines are favorably construed to quiet purchasers. 25 Assiz., pl. 11; 1 Rol. Ab. 661, 6; F., tit. *Disseizin*; Blunden and Row, Cr. Ca. 303; 2 Cr. 660; Lit., sec. 588, 589.[8] The person to

---

[1] *Heywood v. Smith* (1612), 10 Coke Rep. 95, 77 E.R. 1070, also 1 Bulstrode 162, 80 E.R. 853; *Reynel's Case* (1612), 9 Coke Rep. 95, 77 E.R. 871.

[2] *Lord Cromwell v. Andrews* (1601), 2 Coke Rep. 69, 76 E.R. 574, also 2 Anderson 69, 123 E.R. 550, Jenkins 252, 145 E.R. 178, Croke Eliz. 15, 78 E.R. 281, Moore K.B. 471, 72 E.R. 703, Gouldsborough 116, 75 E.R. 1034, Yelverton 3, 7, 80 E.R. 3, 5, Savile 115, 123 E.R. 1044, 1 Anderson 230, 123 E.R. 445, 3 Dyer 354, 73 E.R. 796.

[3] *Corbet's Case* (1599), 4 Coke Rep. 81, 76 E.R. 1058.

[4] *Blackburn v. Lassels* (1600), Croke Eliz. 800, 78 E.R. 1029, Noy 33, 74 E.R. 1003.

[5] *Thomasin v. Mackworth* (1662), Carter 75, 124 E.R. 833, also O. Bridgman 502, 124 E.R. 713.

[6] *Anonymous* (1689), 1 Salkeld 153, 91 E.R. 141.

[7] *Focus v. Salisbury* (Ex. 1665), Hardres 400, 145 E.R. 517.

[8] YB 25 Edw. III, Lib. Ass., f. 117, pl. 11 (1351); YB 26 Edw. III, Lib. Ass., f. 127, pl. 39 (1352), 1 Rolle, Abr., *Disseisin*, pl. G, 6, p. 661; Fitzherbert, Abr., *Disseisin*; *Blunden v. Baugh* (1633), Croke Car. 302, 79 E.R. 864, also W. Jones 315, 82 E.R. 166;

whom the wrong is done has his election whether he will admit himself disseised of a rent. But it is not at the election of the wrongdoer.

In equity, though a trustee does a wrong which would prevail at law, yet it may be set aside. If the plaintiff is entitled to Pickworth, it must be exonerated by Willowby by Lord Cowper's decree, which is not reversed as to that point.

Lutwyche, for the defendant Mortimer, the heir at law of Evers Armine: The House of Lords have determined that Evers Armine was a tenant for life and, by his recovery, the contingent remainders are destroyed. Now, the plaintiff's title is only under the countess of Torrington, who is the heir at law of the devisor. This case has not been anywhere directly determined. Co. Lit. 380; a lessee for years may make a feoffment, and the fee shall pass, and it is a disseisin of the freehold. Where there cannot be an entry and the estate could not be defeated but by an entry, the estate is indefeasible.

There is no difference between contingent remainders created by a deed or a will. No entry was proved, and the recovery passed after a fee simple forty years ago. No case was cited to overthrow this rule of law except Purefoy and Rogers, where it was a question whether it were an executory devise. It was determined that, wherever there is a freehold to support the remainders, it is a contingent remainder and the fee is in abeyance. And there is no difference between a deed and a will. Lit., sec. 647.[1] The case of an infant *in ventre sa mere* is different, for, there, it is an executory devise. See Harwood and Edge, Salk. 229,[2] which may be good after a reasonable number of years. But, if there be an estate for life precedent, it is a contingent remainder. As to the case of having a fee on a condition, it is not the same, for the estate remains in the feoffor until the condition is performed. This is founded on the maxims of law. The heir of the devisor has no wrong done him. Therefore, he ought not to enter against the devise of his ancestor.

As to the forfeiture, could he have brought an action of waste, there may be forfeitures of which no advantage can be taken, as where there is a tenant for life, remainder for life. If the uncertain chattel interest for the payment of debts is still continuing, yet that does not hinder the freeholder from making a feoffment. There cannot be two fees simple, neither could a remainder have been limited after the contingent remainders.

Serjeant *Pengelly*, for the defendant Barnardiston: The bill is not proper, but the title is at law, and they may take their remedy by [an action of] ejectment. And they ought to have affirmed their title at law before they come hither to redeem.

Powsely v. Blackman (1620), Croke Jac. 659, 79 E.R. 569, also Benloe 103, 73 E.R. 973, Palmer 201, 81 E.R. 1042, 2 Rolle Rep. 241, 284, 81 E.R. 774, 803; T. Littleton, *Tenures*, §§ 588, 589.

[1] T. Littleton, *Tenures*, § 647.

[2] *Scatterwood v. Edge* (1697), *ut supra*.

Curia [JEKYLL]: As to the objection that it is not proper here, I take it Lord Cowper decreed that he was proper. And the question in the House of Lords was not that he was not proper, but that he was not proper with that title.

Serjeant Chesshyre: We are proper here to have the debts paid.

Curia [JEKYLL]: If it is taken that there has been sufficient profits received to pay the debts and the interest of the trustees determined, then they were proper at law, but that is not so.

Pengelly: The plaintiff has no title, either in equity or law, by the recovery suffered by Evers Armine. The whole fee was gained, and there was no reversion in the devisor. The devisor made a disposition of the whole fee and so that one of the limitations must necessarily take effect. The first limitation, being a freehold, was a proper support of a contingent remainder. If it took effect, the whole fee was gone from the heir of the devisor. One of the contingencies must take effect upon the determining of the particular estate. If either of the remaindermen died in the life of Evers Armine, it would vest in their heirs and they would take by descent. 1 Ins. 378b; to two joint tenants and to the heirs of him who die first. 1 Rep. 98, 99.[1] It is said, though it is so in the case of a conveyance at common law, yet it is otherwise in a will. But it is the same, for a will is a conveyance by act of Parliament. Gardner and Sheldon, Vaug. 269.[2] Where a devisor disposes of the whole fee, nothing remains in him. The devisor could not make any further limitation over; the reason is because he had nothing in him. Taylor v. Biddulph, 2 Mod. 292.[3] The difference is between an executory devise and a contingent remainder, in the first case, the estate descends to the heir, not in the other. [It is] not proved by one case that the reversion descends, but that the fee is in abeyance. 1 Co. 130b, 135b; 2 Rol. Ab. 418, pl. 4; 5 Co. 20; Ins. 378a.[4] The reason is that the whole fee passes out of the grantor. 1 Co. 135b.[5] It is not said that the heir has a right of entry where it is said that the feoffment of L. destroys contingent remainders. 11 Hen. VI, fo. 12.[6] It is only the saying of the counsel, [it was] not said that the donor shall be in of his reversion.

---

1 *Wolfe v. Shelley* (1581), 1 Coke Rep. 88, 76 E.R. 199, also 1 Anderson 69, 123 E.R. 358, Moore K.B. 136, 72 E.R. 490, Jenkins 249, 145 E.R. 176, 3 Dyer 373, 73 E.R. 838.

2 *Gardner v. Sheldon* (1671), Vaughan 259, 124 E.R. 1064, also 2 Keble 781, 84 E.R. 494, 1 Freeman 11, 89 E.R. 9, 1 Eq. Cas. Abr. 197, 21 E.R. 986, Lincoln's Inn MS. Misc. 500, f. 160.

3 *Taylor, ex dem. Smith v. Biddall* (1678), 2 Modern 289, 86 E.R. 1078, also 1 Freeman 243, 89 E.R. 173, Carter 182, 124 E.R. 904, 1 Eq. Cas. Abr. 188, 21 E.R. 979.

4 *Dillon v. Freine* (1589–1595), *ut supra*; 2 Rolle, Abr., *Remainder*, p. 418, pl. H, 4; *Main v. Scot* (1596), 5 Coke Rep. 20, 77 E.R. 80, also Moore K.B. 452, 72 E.R. 689, Croke Eliz. 449, 479, 78 E.R. 689, 731, Popham 109, 79 E.R. 1217, 2 Anderson 18, 123 E.R. 523, Jenkins 26, 145 E.R. 182; E. Coke, *First Institute* (1628), f. 378.

5 *Dillon v. Freine* (1589–1595), *ut supra*.

6 YB Mich. 11 Hen. VI, f. 12, pl. 28 (1432).

As to Purefoy and Rogers, Hale said it was clear the reversion was in the devisor, but that he had not disposed of the whole fee, but left a provision for the heir. The question there is made whether it was an estate for life or a fee. And it is taken as an estate for life. Plunket v. Holmes, 1 Lev. 11, Raymd. 28.[1]

As to the second point, whether the recovery were void, that there was no reversion in the devisor, 2 Leon. 219, Humfreston's Case. Therefore, the recovery was not void by the Statute 14 Eliz. or Hen. VIII.[2]

In all the case quoted, there was a reversion. The Statute of Uses does not execute an estate in abeyance. In. 251, 330; Lit., sec. 415, 416, 611.[3]

As to Beck's Case, though there is a possibility of reverter, if it be displaced, it is destroyed. Lit. Rep. 157;[4] that the fee is in abeyance though the contingent remainder is not executed. Where lands are given to an abbot and his successors, which is [dissolved], the donor shall have it again, but not if the abbot had made a feoffment.

As to the fine 2 March 1688, whether it is a bar to Lady Torrington and the reversion was turned to a right, no distinction that the bargain and sale and fine shall be taken as one consequence to a purchaser but not to a wrongdoer. 2 Lev. 52, 55; Hard. 401; 2 Rol. Ab. 394, pl. 1.[5] If the plaintiff has a right of entry, it is as heir of the devisor and no other. If a tenant for life or years levies a fine, the lessor has five years after the estate determined. But where a stranger levies a fine, he must enter within five years after the fine was levied. 9 Co. 105; Dyer 354, pl. 35; 1 Ven. 241; 2 Ven. 334; Plow. 374.[6] The uncertain chattel interest for the payment of debts is not different from a certain chattel interest estate.

---

1 *Plunket v. Holmes* (1661), 1 Levinz 11, 83 E.R. 271, T. Raymond 28, 83 E.R. 15, also 1 Siderfin 47, 82 E.R. 961, 1 Keble 29, 119, 83 E.R. 792, 848.

2 *Humphreston's Case* (1574), 2 Leonard 216, 74 E.R. 490; Stat. 14 Eliz. I, c. 8 (*SR*, IV, 600); Stat. 32 Hen. VIII, c. 31 (*SR*, III, 787).

3 E. Coke, *First Institute* (1628), ff. 251, 330; T. Littleton, *Tenures*, §§ 415, 416, 611.

4 *Mannington's Case* (1628), Littleton 156, 124 E.R. 184.

5 *Whaley v. Tankard* (1672), 2 Levinz 52, 83 E.R. 445, also 1 Ventris 241, 86 E.R. 162, T. Raymond 219, 83 E.R. 114, 3 Keble 30, 37, 110, 84 E.R. 577, 581, 622; *Focus v. Salisbury* (1665), *ut supra*; *Barton's Case* (1615), 2 Rolle, Abr., *Recoverie common*, p. 394, pl. B, 1.

6 *Bicknell v. Tucker* (1612), 9 Coke Rep. 104, 77 E.R. 883, also 1 Brownlow & Goldesborough 181, 123 E.R. 741, 2 Brownlow & Goldesborough 134, 153, 123 E.R. 857, 869; *Lord Cromwell v. Andrews* (1577–1601), 3 Dyer 354, 73 E.R. 796, also 110 Selden Soc. 370, 2 Coke Rep. 69, 76 E.R. 574, Jenkins 252, 145 E.R. 178, Moore K.B. 471, 72 E.R. 703, 1 Anderson 230, 123 E.R. 445, 2 Anderson 69, 123 E.R. 550, Yelverton 3, 80 E.R. 3, Savile 115, 123 E.R. 1044, *sub nom. Andrews v. Blunt*, Moore K.B. 105, 72 E.R. 470, 3 Dyer 311, 73 E.R. 704, 1 Anderson 17, 123 E.R. 300, Benloe 201, 123 E.R. 141, *sub nom. Andrews v. Lord Cromwell*, Croke Eliz. 891, 78 E.R. 1115, Noy 44, 74 E.R. 1013; *Whaley v. Tankard* (1672), *ut supra*; *Dighton v. Greenvil* (1687–1698), 2 Ventris 321, 86 E.R. 464, also Comberbach 50, 77, 90 E.R. 337, 354, 1 Shower K.B. 36,

Supposing the law against the plaintiff, he has no right of contribution for Pickworth out of Willowby, but it is barred by the fine. Hard. 512.[1] An equitable interest is barred by a fine. Sir W. Jones 211, 416; 1 Co. 67; Dy. 374, pl. 16; 5 Co. 124.[2] A court of equity will not help against a fine and non-claim. The plaintiff has no reversion; if he had, it is barred.

Peere Williams, for the defendant Coppin, [was] stopped by the Master of the Rolls.

Curia [JEKYLL]: Serjeant Pengelly's objection is of consequence, that it is a title at law. What decree does the plaintiff pray?

Chesshyre: The debts are not yet paid. [It is] within Sir Andrew Corbet's Case. We pray that the uncertain interest may be set aside.

Curia [JEKYLL]: If it is within the reason of Sir Andrew Corbet's Case, then the court will put a reasonable construction on the devise for the payment of debts. The plaintiff says he is kept out by him that claims under Evers Armine, but the plaintiff's estate comes in after the estate in the trustees and after Evers Armine's life. If there has been a sufficiency for the payment of debts, the question is whether that estate is standing out.

[The case was] put off until Saturday seven night.

24 January.

Peere Williams, for the defendant Coppin: The defendant Coppin is a purchaser of a rent charge created in 1697 on Willowby for £3500 from A. Bullingham. 1 February 1709, he agreed to accept of £7000 for it. 5 May 1710, [there was a] decree Coppin [was] to be paid first and the estate sold. The plaintiff has purchased the title of the heir of Sir Michael Armine, the devisor. The plaintiff's claim is very stale, for Sir Michael Armine died in 1668. The plaintiff's title accrued in 1679 when Evers Armine died.

He answered to Serjeant Chesshyre's argument: (1) whether, on the will of Sir Michael Armine, the fee was in abeyance; (2) if, on the recovery of Evers Armine, the heir of Sir Michael might enter; (3) where the uncertain interest in the trustees is determined; (4) the operation of the fine in 1697, whether it bars the contribution of Willowby to Pickworth and whether it bars the heir of the devisor; (5) whether the plaintiff's title is not a legal [one] without impediment and against a purchaser and, therefore, should be left to the law.

89 E.R. 432, 4 Modern 247, 87 E.R. 375, 1 Skinner 260, 90 E.R. 118, Colles 64, 1 E.R. 182; *Stowel v. Lord Zouch* (1569), 1 Plowden 353, 75 E.R. 536.

[1] *Wolstan v. Aston* (Ex. 1669), Hardres 511, 145 E.R. 573.

[2] *Sawle v. Clearke* (1629), W. Jones 208, 211, 82 E.R. 111, 112, also Latch 64, 72, 82 E.R. 276, 280, Benloe 174, 73 E.R. 1035; *Thynne v. Cary* (1639), W. Jones 416, 82 E.R. 218; *Baldwin v. Smith* (1597), 1 Coke Rep. 63, 76 E.R. 139, also Croke Eliz. 453, 78 E.R. 692, 2 Anderson 37, 123 E.R. 533; *Gerrarde, qui tam v. Worseley* (1580), 3 Dyer 374, 73 E.R. 839, also 1 Anderson 75, 123 E.R. 361; *Saffyn v. Adams* (1605), 5 Coke Rep. 123, 77 E.R. 248, also Croke Jac. 60, 79 E.R. 50.

First, the fee is in abeyance. [It was] determined by the House of Lords that the remainders were contingent, therefore, in abeyance, C.L. 342a, and in no person, consequently, not in the heir of the devisor by descent. There is no reason for the distinction where a remainder in fee is limited to some person on a condition precedent and where to the heirs of J.S., as if to A. for life and, if B. does such an act, then to B. in fee. This is a contingent remainder though to a person certain. So it is the same with a remainder to the heirs of a person in being.

Consider it, first, on a feoffment, second, on a grant without livery, third, on a will.

First, it is admitted that the fee is in abeyance on a feoffment. Lit. Rep. 322, Beck's Case. A. makes a lease to B. for the life of C.; B. dies before C.; the grantor cannot be the occupant against his own grant. C.L. 342b, 343a. [It is] in abeyance, as the fee of a parson of a church, only one is temporal, the other perpetual. If a lease for years is to A., remainder to the heirs of B., the remainder is void because the freehold is in abeyance.

Second, on a grant, which passes only what may lawfully pass, if I grant a reversion with attornment to A. for life, remainder to the heirs of B., it is in abeyance.

Third, on a will, it is said whatever estate is not disposed of remains in the devisor. But here, the fee is disposed of, here being a freehold to support it, the remainder is contingent. [It is] the same rule with grants. By proper words, a will may put the fee in abeyance. Hob. 74, Barn's Case.[1] A. covenants to stand seised to the use of A. for life, remainder to the use of the heirs of B.; the doubt there is whether the fee in abeyance is transferred by the Statute of Uses.

In a covenant to stand seised, it may remain in the covenantor, which it cannot in a will, 1 Co. 101b; 1 Lev. 200,[2] as if I covenant to stand seised to the use of A. for life, remainder to B. in fee and A. refuses, B. shall not take presently as he shall in a devise. And so if to the use of a monk for life, remainder to B. in fee. Perkins, sec. 507.[3] It may descend to the heir in a case of necessity, as if to A. for years, remainder to the heirs of B. in fee. Noy 23, Cr. El. 878.[4]

But here is a freehold good to an infant *in ventre as mere* as an executory devise. But, if to A. for life, remainder to an infant *in ventre sa mere* and A. suffered a recovery, it would destroy the remainder. If to A. for life, remainder to the heirs of the body of B., there is a reversion. But here, it is in fee, and nothing is left, and, if A. should commit waste, it destroys the particular estate, and no action of waste could be brought.

---

1 *Barnes's Case*, Hobart 74, 80 E.R. 224.

2 *Wolfe v. Shelley* (1581), *ut supra*; *Palmer v. Lawson* (1667), 1 Levinz 200, 83 E.R. 367, also 1 Siderfin 332, 82 E.R. 1139, 2 Keble 110, 130, 150, 156, 217, 84 E.R. 70, 82, 98, 135.

3 J. Perkins, *A Profitable Book.*

4 *Payne v. Ferrall* (1602), Noy 43, 74 E.R. 1012, Croke Eliz. 878, 78 E.R. 1103.

Second, the heir of the devisor could not enter for the forfeiture by the recovery of Evers Armine in 1675, which is forty-three years ago, for the heir of Sir Michael Armine, the devisor, had no reversion. The reason is that the wrong is done to the reversion, and, where there is no reversion, there is no wrong done, and, therefore, there is no forfeiture. In a grant to A. for life, remainder to the heirs of B., if A. dies before B., the grantor may enter because the particular estate is determined, which is a possibility when not interrupted. 2 Rol. Ab. 418, C.J., n. 81b, 12b; C.L. 251a.[1] It is for necessity because nobody else can take but the grantor. There can be no occupant of a fee simple if the gift were to A. for life, remainder to the heirs of B. during the life of C.; the occupant would have it. Lit. Rep. 343.[2] The lord cannot have it by escheat.

If a man seised of a rent grants it to A. for life, remainder to the heirs of B. [and] A. dies before B., it shall not revert to the donor but shall be extinguished, and more reason that the feoffee of a tenant for life should have it if to A. in tail, remainder to the heirs of B., the donor has a possibility. If the donee dies without issue in the life of B., it reverts. But, if the donee makes a feoffment, the feoffee shall have it. Lit. Rep. 290.[3] This possibility [is] like a gift to a mayor and commonalty where it shall revert if they be dissolved but not if a feoffment had been made.

He answered to the cases.

Poph. 83; the opinion of Gascoign is denied to be law. It is to A. for life, remainder to the heirs or heirs of the body of B. 10 Co. 78, 85, Leonard Lovey's Case; 6 Rep. 176, Sir Edward Cleer's Case; 1 Leo. 11; 1 Syd. 47; Ray. 28, Plunket v. Holmes; Purefoy and Rogers, 2 Sand. 380; 2 Lev. 39; 3 Keb. 11. As it is reported in Levinz and Keble, [it is] different from this case. Sampson Shelton, seised in fee, devises to his wife for life and, if she should have a son and christen him Sampson Shelton, then to him in fee, remainder to his own right heirs. It is admitted in the end of the case to be a contingent remainder; so there is no devise until a son be born and so christened. Therefore, until then, the fee must descend, it being a condition precedent. Salk. 224, Lodington and Kime.[4] It is said there is gained a tortious fee, which is good against all but the heirs of the devisor. This is not mentioned in Levinz and, therefore, not said by the court. But Salkeld's opinion is if a tenant for life suffer a recovery, it is void as against the remainder or reversion. But, if there is no remainder or reversion, it is not void. 2 Leon. 219, Humfreston's Case; Beck's Case, Lit. Rep. 159, 253, 285, 315, 344;

[1] E. Coke, *First Institute* (1628), f. 251.

[2] *Beck's Case* (1629–1630), *ut supra*.

[3] *Beck's Case* (1629–1630), *ut supra*.

[4] *Loddington v. Kime* (1695), 1 Salkeld 224, 91 E.R. 198, also 3 Levinz 431, 83 E.R. 766, 1 Lord Raymond 203, 91 E.R. 1031, 1 Eq. Cas. Abr. 182, 21 E.R. 974, 2 Eq. Cas. Abr. 331, 22 E.R. 282.

Cr. Ca. 363, 401, Boreton and Nicholls, affirmed in error. If it is law, the plaintiff has no title to will.

Objection: That it was not the intent of the devisor that the tenant for life should gain the whole fee, but it was the devisor's own fault not to make trustees to preserve the contingent remainders. As waste by a tenant for life or years was not punishable before the Statute of Gloucester[1] because it was the party's own fault that he did not provide against it by a covenant, here, the plaintiff is not hurt, for the fee is given away from him, and he could not have it if no recovery had been.

Third, where the uncertain interest in the executors for payment of the debts is not determined but it was determined when sufficient [assets] might have been raised, but the law is settled that, if I devise the rents and profits until the debts shall be paid, it is the same as might be paid.

4 Co. 81b, Sir Andrew Corbet's Case; these debts might have been paid in seven years. Evers Armine was one of the executors as well as the devisee for life. Therefore, his entry was lawful as executor, though but one of the executors, for he might release a debt. But he ought to have applied the profits towards payment of the debts, yet he must hold over, Moor 556, 754, Ross's Case,[2] as if he had suffered the remainderman to enter. And the words 'until the executors shall have raised' is the same as 'might have raised'; the difference is where the entry of the heirs is wrongful that they shall hold over, but not where the entry is lawful. Who must hold over? The executor of Sir Michael Armine. But he is the person who did the wrong. And, because he did the wrong, must he hold over? It is absurd and only in favor of a mortgagee who has a good security for his debt.

Fourth, as to the operation of the fine in 1697 by Sir Thomas Barnardiston and Armine Bullingham, it is a bar to the uncertain interest and to the heirs of the devisor. 10 Rep., Seymour's Case; 4 Rep. 70, Hind's Case.[3] The fine and the bargain and sale made but one conveyance.

There is no difference whether it is to a purchaser or whether to a wrongdoer. 2 Lev. 52, Whaley v. Tankard, where the feoffment and fine made but one conveyance, though a disseisin and at six months distance. Then the chattel interest is barred and so is the equitable interest, for trusts now are the same as uses were. 1 Jon. 416, Thyn and Townsend.[4] A fine and non-claim is a bar to an equitable interest. Hard. 512.[5]

---

1 Stat. 6 Edw. I, c. 5 (*SR*, I, 48).

2 *Rosse's Case*, Moore K.B. 556, 72 E.R. 755.

3 *Heywood v. Smith* (1612), 10 Coke Rep. 95, 77 E.R. 1070, also 1 Bulstrode 162, 80 E.R. 853; *Libb v. Hynde* (1591), 4 Coke Rep. 68, 76 E.R. 1037, also 1 Anderson 285, 123 E.R. 475.

4 *Thynne v. Cary* (1639), *ut supra*.

5 *Wolstan v. Aston* (Ex. 1669), *ut supra*.

It is no objection that it is a matter of account, the same as a mortgage, The legal title of Sir Michael Armine, the devisor, is likewise barred by the fine. 9 Rep. 95, pl. 373.[1] If a lessee for years levies a fine, the lessor has five years after his estate determines, but not where a stranger, for, there, he has but five years after the fine was levied.

Fifth, whether the plaintiff's title as heir to Sir Michael Armine, the devisor, is a legal title and [there is] no impediment, we will be bound not to give the uncertain chattel interest in evidence. So that is out of the case. But there is equity for the plaintiff's having a contribution out of Willowby, but the plaintiff claims all the manors. And, if that claim is dismissed, he may establish his title at law. The plaintiff's interest cost but £500; therefore, it is not to be favored.

(1) The fee is in abeyance. (2) The recovery bars the heir of the devisor. (3) The chattel interest is barred by the fine. (4) The equitable interest is likewise barred. (5) The plaintiff's is a mere legal title and against a purchaser.

Master of the Rolls [JEKYLL]: How does the bill put the case?

Vernon: It only states the case and prays relief generally.

Curia [JEKYLL]: He does not pray contribution if the title at law is with him, but, if that is against him, he prays contribution.

Sir John Chesshyre's reply: First, as heir at law of the devisor, we claim the equity of redemption of Pickworth. The great point is whether the fee is in abeyance. We admit that, in a grant to A. for life, remainder to the heirs of B., the fee is in abeyance. There has been no answer to the cases on a devise whether the person is certain though the use is uncertain. There is no case whether, in a devise, the fee is in abeyance. In A. and B.'s case, it was the first time it was made a question, for the court was reproved for it.

Objection: That, as to the manor of Willowby, it is a title at law.

But where the principal point is a matter of equity and there happens to be incident a point of law, it is properly to be determined in equity. There is no case where an uncertain interest can be said to be determined where the heir at law does not insist upon it. Blackburn, 3 Cr. The heir may say it is determined, but not the person who did the wrong, not paying the debts.

If the term is standing out, we cannot recover at law. It is proper here to know what debts are paid and to have the rest satisfied and, as to Pickworth, to have contribution against Willowby and to have it assigned to us and to redeem Pickworth.

Objection: But the mortgagees are not before the court, for the executor has brought it in. Plunket and Holmes, 1 Lev. 11, is in point with us. Lewis Bowles's Case, 11 Rep.; 1 R. Archer's Case, 66; Rol. 204; 2 Mod. 292.[2]

---

[1] *Reynel's Case* (1612), *ut supra*.

[2] *Bowles v. Bury* (1615), 11 Coke Rep. 79, 77 E.R. 1253, also 1 Rolle Rep. 177, 81 E.R. 413; *Baldwin v. Smith* (1597), *ut supra*; *Taylor, ex dem. Smith v. Biddall* (1678), *ut supra*.

As to the recovery, it is admitted, if the heir has a reversion, the recovery is void. Humfreston's Case.

As to the fine, the fee was out of the parties to the fine before it was levied. Therefore, *partes finis nihil habuerunt.* 24 January 1697 [was the] deed; 28 January the fine. So the estate was gone before, and the fine does not turn it to a right or bar any person.

If a lessee for years disseises the lessor and makes a feoffment, he may enter presently or stay until the lease is ended. A court of equity will relieve against a fraud though there were a fine and non-claim, as Darby's Case and Lord Warrington and Booth on another Statute.[1] Query Hard. 512.

The staleness of the demand was no objection before Lord Cowper or the House of Lords. Barnard's Case, Hob. 74;[2] there was no resolution. The intent of the devisor must follow the rules of law. But here, no rule is broken.

One executor may dispose of the whole interest and may release it. Where a trustee has done a wrong for which he is not punishable at [common] law, yet he may be punishable here.

Curia [Jekyll]: This case has been fully argued. At first, it was not objected that the bill was not proper here.

Mr. Vernon said the plaintiff is proper to have the chattel interest removed without which he cannot recover at law. But, in the arguing his case, it has been considered whether this is a continuing estate or not. As to the manor of Willowby, here, one of the executors entered and took the profits. It is said the law will construe him to enter as of his rightful estate and not tortiously. Now, if he has entered and nothing hindered him from taking the profits, it is not like Sir Andrew Corbet's Case, where the heir kept the trustee out. A creditor might have come upon Evers Armine's estate for life; so may the heir at law. He who claims under Evers Armine, who should have applied the profits, cannot object to the heir at law. As to Pickworth, the plaintiff has not the mortgagee before the court; therefore, he cannot redeem.

If the plaintiff cannot in this court be considered as heir at law, perhaps, he may as a creditor to have contribution, both as mortgagee and heir at law. The chief question that is to be considered by me is how you have need to come into this court.

---

1 *Murray, ex dem. Earl of Derby v. Eaton* (Ex. 1679–1680), T. Jones 237, 84 E.R. 1234, T. Raymond 260, 286, 319, 388, 83 E.R. 134, 147, 165, 176, Pollexfex 491, 86 E.R. 622, 2 Shower K.B. 104, 89 E.R. 823, Skinner 95, 90 E.R. 45, Lincoln's Inn MS. Misc. 556, ff. 42, 48, 56, 55, 73, Georgetown Univ. Law Lib. MS. B88–7, pp. 108, 121, 138, 170, Lincoln's Inn MS. Maynard 25, f. 16; *Earl of Warrington v. Booth* (H.L. 1714), 4 Brown P.C. 163, 2 E.R. 111, British Library MS. Hargrave 80, f. 175; Stat. 21 Jac. I, c. 16 (*SR*, IV, 1222–1223).

2 *Barnes's Case*, Hobart 74, 80 E.R. 224.

Sir Thomas Powys, for the plaintiff: If we are barred of Willowby by the fine, we are entitled to contribution out of it. As to the uncertain interest, a court of law will not take an account. If I extend land upon a [writ of] *elegit*, I may come here for an account.

Vernon, for the plaintiff: This objection that we are not proper here comes very late, for that was before Lord Harcourt and Lord Cowper, who ordered the heirs of Sir Michael Armine and Evers Armine before the Master to be bound by the account. And the House of Lords have reversed the decree, but without prejudice to the heirs of Sir Michael or Evers Armine. We cannot try our right without the assistance of this court. And in many cases where the parties have joined issue, the court will determine any point of [common] law which is incident to the chief question.

We are likewise proper for the judgment of the court as to the right of redemption of Pickworth. Here is not a matter of fact proper for a jury, but only a question of law proper for the judgment of the court. If any trustee conveys away the trust estate by a fine or any other conveyance, it will not prejudice the trust. Bovey and Smith, Michaelmas 1682;[1] the defendant, a trustee, conveyed away the estate to a purchaser without notice, but, afterwards, he purchased the estate himself after there had been a fine and non-claim. Lord North decreed the estate was subject to the trust and although it had been freed in the hands of a purchaser without notice.

Curia [Jekyll]: If the plaintiff has taken in the mortgage of Pickworth, has not he a right to bring into this court the heir of Evers Armine, who claims the equity of redemption if it is necessary in order to have contribution against Willowby? But it has been insisted by the plaintiff that he has not only a right to contribution but that he has a right to the whole manor of Willowby. How does that come to be determined here, supposing the estate of the trustees is ended?

Sir Thomas Powys: If Evers Armine had been living, we might have come against him for an account of what he had received as a trustee not only for payment of the debts but for him who was entitled after. So have we if he has paid the profits over into other persons with notice.

Curia [Jekyll]: If another executor had entered and received the profits, could not Evers Armine have come for an account? Yes, if the court is satisfied with the plaintiff's title. Has not the plaintiff a right for an account against a trustee who has held over? And, if he has a right to the equity of redemption of Pickworth, it is proper to be determined here. Lord Harcourt, Cowper, and the House of Lords thought it proper in this court.

I would have the assistance of the judges if it were usual for the Master of the Rolls. But it is not. Therefore, I must determine it myself. Let it stand over. 10 March.

---

[1] *Bovey v. Smith* (1682), 1 Vernon 60, 84, 144, 23 E.R. 310, 328, 377, 2 Chancery Cases 124, 22 E.R. 877, 1 Eq. Cas. Abr. 256, 384, 21 E.R. 1029, 1120.

Master of the Rolls [JEKYLL]: The plaintiff is not entitled to the aid of the court against Mr. Mortimer. It is proper to have that title determined as to Pickworth upon Mr. Mortimer's bill.

As to Willowby, the plaintiff is not entitled because the uncertain interest in the executors is determined by sufficient of profits received to pay the debts. The land has borne its burden. Sir Andrew Corbet's Case, 4 Co. 81. The next estate was Evers Armine's. The plaintiff is not entitled to an account against his representative.

As to contribution, the plaintiff cannot have it as he makes his case. The plaintiff claims title to both manors. The fine and non-claim by Sir Robert Barnardiston is a bar only to a moiety of the manor of Willowby.

As to the nature of the estate demised by Sir Michael Armine, they say the fine is not a bar to Lady Torrington because *partes finis nihil habuerunt*. But the deed though precedent and the fine are but one conveyance. There is no distinction between a rightful and a wrongful estate and the same rule [applies] as to their conveyances. Armine Bullingham joined with Sir Thomas Barnardiston in the fine. Armine Bullington was no disseisor.

On the Statute of Limitations,[1] the title accruing to Sir Michael Armine's heir was in 1680 on the death of Evers Armine. The heir was not then an infant, but it does not appear whether she was under coverture at that time.

But query whether the plaintiff is not entitled to the aid of this court though not to that particular relief which I have mentioned. The plaintiff has the [common] law with him. He has a right to the assistance of this court to discover whether he has been disinherited and how. I cannot help the plaintiff to the discovery of the deeds in order to bring his [action of] ejectment.

The question has never been determined and is very difficult.

First, query whether a man by a will can put an estate in abeyance.

Second, whether Sir Michael Armine has so done by this will.

Third, whether a possibility remained in the heir of the devisor.

Fourth, whether the recovery by Evers Armine has destroyed it, first, on a common law conveyance; second, by way of a use; third by a devise. 1 Ins. 342b, Gascoign's opinion [is] contrary to law.

First, it is plain an estate may be put in abeyance by a feoffment with livery and nothing remains but a possibility of reverter. Pollex. 70, Carpenter and Smith, admirably well argued by Lord Pollexfen.[2]

Second, by way of a use, a man may put an estate in abeyance. Lit. 159, 253; Beck's Case is very loosely reported; 1 Co. 120, Chudley's Case does not say that a use cannot be in abeyance, but only, if it be, it is not executed by the Statute. Barn's Case, Hob. 74; Co. 17, Sir E. Cleer's Case; 10 C. 78, Leonard Lovey's

[1] Stat. 21 Jac. I, c. 16 (*SR*, IV, 1222–1223).

[2] *Carpenter v. Smith* (1672–1673), Pollexfen 70, 86 E.R. 515, also 3 Keble 18, 93, 122, 176, 84 E.R. 570, 613, 629, 661.

Case; Pollexf. 65, Lower and Weale, Hale's opinion that the use may be in abeyance. Lit. Rep. 254; whatever may be by a common law conveyance may be by a use. In no case [is there] less power over a use than over a common law conveyance.

Third, whether a man may put an estate in abeyance by a devise, the words of the Statute of Wills are a man may give and dispose of his estate as he thinks fit. The same rule is in the case of a will as of a use. He may do the same and more than by a common law conveyance. There are no other limits but the rules of law, as Couden and Clark, Hob. 29,[1] a man may by will put the estate in abeyance, as Archer's Case, 1 Co. 6b; Cr. El. 878, Plunket and Holmes, 1 Leo. 11; Raym. 28; 2 Mod. 292, Taylor and Biddulph.

The second question is whether this will has put the estate in abeyance. I take it this is stronger than a devise to A., remainder to the heirs of B., who is living, for, here, the heir of the devisor was intended to be disinherited in all events. 11 Hen. VI, 12; there was a reversion left in the heir of the devisor. Plunket and Holmes, 1 Lev. 11; Raymd. 28; 1 Syd. 47. In Levinz, it is neither wrongly reported nor grounded upon a mistake because, there, it is taken the heirs were purchasers, which is contrary to law. Fentwick v. Milford; Godbolt and Freestone, 3 Lev. 406; Moor 437, may be distinguished from this case, there being a reversion by descent and the devise void. Purefoy and Rogers, 2 Sand. 380; here was a reversion subject to a contingency. Where there is a reversion, it descends immediately but will open again to let in the remainder. In all three cases, nothing could bar this reversion but the contingency happening. Hob. 338, Sheffield and Ratcliff. Abeyance is only for necessity, which is where the heir could never have it, as in this case. The case of a feoffment or uses or a will is the same where a man grants all out of him and whatever is not out of him remains in him.

First, I think a man may put an estate in abeyance by a will; second, the estate is put in abeyance by this will; but, third, there may be a possibility, though in abeyance.

Here is a possibility of reverter from the estate in contingency being capable of being destroyed, as it was in this case. There is no reason why this possibility should not take place, as it would in the limitation to A. for life, remainder to the heirs of B., and A. dies before B. It is true the tenant for life, Evers Armine, gained a fee by the recovery. But query whether it was not a base fee determinable on the entry of the heir of the devisor. 1 Ins. 344; Lit. Rep. 317.

I may dispose of my own possibility, but not of a third person's. In the case of a donor and donee before the Statute *de Donis*,[2] the possibility of reverter could not be barred by the donee before the issue was born, 1 In. 19a, on an execu-

[1] *Counden v. Clerke* (1614), Hobart 29, 80 E.R. 180, also Moore K.B. 860, 72 E.R. 955, 1 Eq. Cas. Abr. 213, 22 E.R. 998.

[2] Stat. 13 Edw. I, Westminster II, c. 1 (*SR*, I, 71).

tory devise. Pell and Brown, Cr. Ja. 590.[1] A common recovery does not bar. It is strong in favor of the present case. If a tenant in tail makes a feoffment, it is a fee, but a bare one. Li., sec. 690, is obscure. Machill and Clark, 2 Salk. 619.[2]

How did this recovery operate? Not as a forfeiture, it being no prejudice, but an advantage, to the heir. 1 Ins. 251. Yet the estate for life is determined. All the contingent remainders are destroyed, there being no freehold to support them. But this does not touch the possibility in the heir of the devisor. By the Statute 14 Eli., a recovery by a tenant for life is void against him to whom a reversion shall or may appertain and which it may in this case.

If a tenant for life destroys the intent of the will by which he himself claims, it gives a right of the heir to revenge it. And if, while he is endeavoring to defeat the remaindermen, he destroys his own estate, it is very just. And judges should be as like to construe it so. Therefore, I am of opinion that the possibility is not destroyed. 1 Salk. 225, Lodington and Kime, a manuscript of it which I have seen says that the fee is good against all but the heir of the devisor. I would propose that deeds proved here may be read at [common] law. It is agreed the estate in the executors is determined, there being sufficient estate received to pay the debts.

I will retain the bill for twelve months that the plaintiff may try his title at law by bringing an [action of] ejectment.

28 October 1719; an appeal from the Rolls.

Lord Chancellor [Lord Parker]: I think the point in abeyance is not material, for, if a feoffment be made to A. for life, remainder to the right heirs of B., in which case the fee is in abeyance, is it in the power of the tenant for life to gain a fee? If the particular estate determines before the death of B., it reverts; so if a tenant for life determines his estate by his own act.

Reeves, for the plaintiff: As to the fine and non-claim, it will bar only a moiety. It is no bar to the contribution from Willowby.

As to the abeyance, [it is] not saved. Where a man devises on a contingency, it vests in the heir of the devisor until the contingency falls. 49 Edw. III, 16; 10 Rep. 50, Grant's Case, cited in 1 Cr. 435, 1 Co. 95.[3] Where a remainder is limited on a condition precedent, there is no necessity that the estate should be in abeyance. To A. for life, remainder to the heirs of B. is immediate, and [there are] no future words. But, if there are conditional words, as, if the heirs of B. should

[1] *Pell v. Brown* (1620), Croke Jac. 590, 79 E.R. 504, also Palmer 131, 81 E.R. 1012, 2 Rolle Rep. 196, 216, 81 E.R. 746, 760, Godbolt 282, 78 E.R. 165, J. Bridgman 1, 123 E.R. 1157.

[2] *Machil v. Clerk* (1702), 2 Salkeld 619, 91 E.R. 524, also 7 Modern 18, 87 E.R. 1068, 11 Modern 19, 88 E.R. 856, 2 Lord Raymond 778, 92 E.R. 19, 1 Comyns 119, 92 E.R. 992, Holt K.B. 615, 90 E.R. 1240.

[3] YB Pas. 49 Edw. III, f. 16, pl. 10 (1375); *Grant's Case* (1587), 10 Coke Rep. 50, 77 E.R. 1001, Croke Car. 435, 79 E.R. 978, 3 Coke Rep. 90b, 76 E.R. 842.

pay such a sum, then to them, the fee would not be in abeyance. There is no intention in the devisor to disinherit his heirs at law unless Evers Armine should die without issue. 1 Salk. 229, Scatterwood and Edge; 2 Sand. 380, Purefoy and Rogers; and Plunket and Holmes, 1 Lev. 11, are authorities in point. Ke. 190.

Acherly, for the plaintiff; *Yorke*, for the plaintiff: [As to the] Statute of Wills, the intention of the devisor is to be pursued. The construing the reversion in fee to be in the heir of the devisor is according to the intent of the devisor that Evers Armine should have but an estate for life. 1 Syd. 153; Cr. Eliz. 2. Though the fee were in abeyance, yet here is a possibility of reverter, as before the Statute *de Donis*. 1 Salk. 231; 1 Ins. 252a. The reason why a recovery by a tenant for life is a forfeiture is not because it displaces the reversion, but because there is a condition in law broken by the recovery. This notion of a possibility is that it might take effect upon the removal of some impediment. Statute 19 Eliz., c. 6.[1] Recoveries suffered by particular tenants are void against such persons to whom a reversion or a remainder shall or may appertain, which it may in this case. Here is no rule of law broken [and] no perpetuity.

The second question is whether it is proper in this court. First, the bill is a bill of foreclosure; therefore, it is originally proper here [and there is] no fact to be tried. Second, it is proper for a contribution. And the question of [common] law arises incidentally.

Chesshyre, for the plaintiff: The first question is whether the fee is in abeyance. Co. Lit. 19a; 1 Co. 135; Poph. 83; 1 Lev. 11, Plunket and Holmes; 2 Mod. 292, Taylor v. Biddulph, the opinion of North. To A. for life, remainder to the heirs of B.; A. dies before B.; there is no descent to the heir of the donor to support the contingent remainder. 2 Sand. 380, Purefoy and Rogers.

The first difference is that it was to the heir of the devisor, but it was in the heir by descent, not by devise.

Second, it did not vest, there being no son; *ergo*, it descended. 1 Salk. 153, Lodington and Kime. This case is good against all but the heir of the devisor. Query whether the heir of the devisor is barred by the common recovery. It is but a common assurance. By the Statute 14 Eliz., it is void for the tenant for life.

Third, [as to] the force of the fine in Hilary 1697, *partes finis nihil habuerunt*.

Fourth, the heir of the devisor could not enter for the forfeiture, the debts not being paid.

Fifth, though the heir might have entered, yet he was not bound to enter. 2 Ch. C. 124.

Sixth, it is proper to be determined in equity. If points of law are incident to the chief question, it is usual to have the assistance of the judges. The [Court of] King's Bench cannot hold a plea in *quare impedit*, but, if it comes on a writ of error or upon a plea in abatement, they will determine it.

[1] Stat. 14 Eliz. I, c. 8 (*SR*, IV, 600).

Lutwyche, for the defendant Mortimer: The plaintiff's title is forty years old and is not to be favored. As to Willowby, [on] an ejectment bill, the defendants [are] purchasers and entitled to all legal advantages.

Lord Chancellor [Lord Parker]: If any points should appear to me doubtful, I can order a case to be sent to the judges. We are upon a will, and Plunket and Holmes and Purefoy and Rogers are in point upon a single contingency. Co. Lit. 342, 367; Lit., sec. 613. If you would speak to the point, you should show that, though the fee is not in abeyance upon a single contingency, yet it is upon a double one, you must say either that these cases are not law or not to the purpose. There is no case in the books which was the consequence of the estate being in abeyance nor how it ended. The judges only considered it in expectancy. You shall have all advantages, as the benefit of the statutes of Limitations and Descents,[1] if a case is made.

Serjeant *Pengelly*, for the defendant Barnardiston: The first question is whether it is proper to determine the points of law in this court. The Master of the Rolls's direction is very proper that the plaintiff should bring his [action of] ejectment. If the title at law is against the plaintiff, he has no equity. The plaintiff ought either to give up that part of the bill which prays possession or else establish his title at law first. The question whether the debts are paid or whether, sufficient [assets] being raised to pay the debts, the interest in the trustees is determined is a question at law and no impediment. It is said to be necessary for the heir to discover whether the debts are paid. But, when the plaintiff has that discovery, he is not entitled to anything more. Though the right of contribution or foreclosure may be proper here, yet they are but subsequent and depend upon the first point whether the plaintiff has the law with him.

Whether the fee was in abeyance at law, the plaintiff will have the benefit of the same arguments as here; so as to the fines. I agree, if there is any interest undisposed of, it will remain in the heirs of the devisor. But here, the whole fee is given from the heir so that he has no injury done to him. 2 Leon. 219, Humfreston's Case. There is the same constructions of wills as of a conveyance at common law.

As to the effect of the recovery, Lit., sec. 415, 674; 1 Ins. 161, 356a, the reversion is discontinued by the recovery. Lit. Rep. 259, Beck's Case; 2 Roll, Ab., 418. It is not warranted by the yearbook.

Lord Chancellor [Lord Parker]: As to the fine, as to one moiety, the plaintiff does not insist but that five years are past if it be a bar [for] length of time. The plaintiff's title cost but £500. If the recovery was void, it gave the heir of the devisor an immediate right of entry. If there had been a descent to the son of Evers Armine, it had taken away the right of entry. The entry of Sir Thomas Barnardiston was wrong. Then he makes a mortgage in fee as having a title in

[1] Stat. 21 Jac. I, c. 16 (*SR*, IV, 1222–1223); Stat. 22 & 23 Car. II, c. 10 (*SR*, V, 791–720).

opposition to all others, not in privity to the trust. Consequently, there was no fraud in his levying the fine. [For the] effects of the fine, [see] 5 Co. 124, Saffin's Case; 1 Co. 67; [it is] a bar even to an uncertain interest. Archer's Case; a man is barred though he could not enter. 9 Co. 105. As to contribution, [see] Hard. 512. If the fine is a bar at law, it is so here. It is within the Statute of Fines,[1] it being an interest.

As to Plunket and Holmes, 1 Lev. 11, Raymd. 30, it is only an estate tail in Thomas.

(*Curia*: But it is a fee in the next taker.)

As to Purefoy and Rogers, 2 Sand. 380, the devisor reserved the reversion and did not give it from his heir. The plaintiff is proper at law, and there is no equity.

The Lord Chancellor [LORD PARKER] put it off until a further day, this day sennight 4 November. I would have you show me authorities contrary to Purefoy and Rogers and Plunket and Holmes, which I think are very strong for the plaintiff. This is not two contingencies but one which works two ways. I think the question is whether the fee is given from the heir in all events. See if there is any distinction in the books upon double contingencies and whether the fine operates any otherwise than against the feoffors or that the heir cannot enter.

4 November.

Raymond, for the defendant, answered to Plunket and Holmes, Lev. The resolution that the reversion descended was unnecessary, and the only point then in question was whether the contingent remainders were destroyed.

He answered to Purefoy and Rogers, 2 Sand. 380, first, the devise was to the heirs of the devisor if the contingency did not happen. Second, it was not determined what estate was devised upon the contingency. If it was only an estate for life, it is not to the purpose. If the fee was not in abeyance, yet it is barred by the recovery.

As to the fine, a fine by a moiety will not bar, but that is because of the privity. Here, it is between strangers; *ergo*, a bar. The decree is right that it is properly triable at law. As to Willoughby, it is merely a legal title, and he only prays possession. Indeed, where matters of law are intermixed with equity, it is proper for this court. But here is no equity. This court will not decree possession. The question whether the interest in the trustees is determined is triable at law.

Peere Williams, for the defendant Coppin: First, nothing descended to the heir of the devisor; second, the operation of the fine; third, the Statute of Limitations; fourth, the interest in the trustees determined; fifth, the plaintiffs are not proper in equity.

First, if a lease be to A. for life, remainder to the heirs of B., it is said the fee simple is in abeyance. Co. Lit. 242b, 243. The law is the same on a devise as on a

[1] Stat. 14 Eliz. I, c. 8 (*SR*, IV, 600)

grant. The Statute of Wills enables a man to dispose of his lands as he shall think fit. 2 Mod. 291, Taylor and Biddulph, North's opinion; Hob. 74; 1 Co. 101a, 154; 1 Leo. 210; cases when, on a covenant to stand seised, the old use remains in the covenantor, but [it is] otherwise on a devise.

As to Plunket and Holmes, 1 Lev. 11, 1 Syd. 47, Raymd. 28, the only question before the court was whether the contingent remainders were destroyed. The opinion that the reversion descended was extrajudicial, and there might be a devise to the eldest son.

As to Purefoy and Rogers, 2 Lev. 39, 3 Keeb. 11, 2 Sand. 380, it is different from this case. A devise is to the heir of the devisor. If the contingency should not happen, there is no contingency or possibility of its coming to the heir of Sir Michael Armine. Whether Evers Armine has issue or not, it is given away from the heir. The plaintiff's title is at law. [There is] no impediment. This court cannot give possession; it will only remove impediments. What decree would the plaintiff pray? [There is] no equity. In [an action of] ejectment, the defendant may have many advantages which he ought not to be deprived of.

Talbot, for the defendant Barnardiston, whose title has held for above forty years, [said] the plaintiff is a volunteer; the defendant is a purchaser. The plaintiff does not know what decree to pray unless it is to alter the possession, which has been good for above forty years.

In all the cases which have been cited, the devisor intended his heir should have it. If the contingency did not happen, here, he intended to give it away from his heir in all events.

Chesshyre, in reply: We are proper in this court to have a redemption of Pickworth and, in order to that, to have our title determined, which will have an influence as to Willoughby. Both depend on the same question. It is proper to have a distribution from Willoughby.

The defendants' arguments are matter of favor, as their being purchasers etc. But they had notice of the will. The fee is not in abeyance. It is admitted there is no case in point for the defendants. Common sense is against the defendant. No distinction is attempted between a determination of a particular estate by the act of God and the act of the party. 11 Hen. VI, 12; 1 Rep. 135; Pop. 83. Law and reason are both with the plaintiff.

As to the fine in 1697, the party who levied it was but a tenant at will; ergo, partes finis nihil habuerunt. Everybody may say so who might be barred with it. If the fine be void, there needs no claim. It only extends to a moiety of Willoughby. The estate in the trustees is not yet determined, for the debts are not yet paid. If the reversion descended, the recovery by the tenant for life is void by the Statute 14 Eliz.; ergo, it is out of the case.

As to the Statute of Limitations, no descents are cast to toll the plaintiff's entry.

Reeves, in reply: Plunket and Holmes and Purefoy and Rogers have been attempted to be distinguished from this case because here is a double contingency. But there is no difference in law between a single and a double contingency.

The Statute of Limitations is not a bar because, at the death of Evers Armine, both the co-heirs were married, though they were unmarried at the time of the recovery. But they were not bound then to enter. 1 Jon. 208; Hunt and Born, Hilary 1 Ann., Salk. 244.[1] The Statute of Fines bars the right; the Statute of Limitations only bars the remedy. *Ergo*, if a new right accrues, it voids the Statute of Limitations.

As to the moiety of Willoughby, Torrington was unmarried in 1698 and might have entered, but she married again. The plaintiff may say *partes finis nihil habuerunt*. Where a tenant for years or at will buys a fine, not having altered the estate, it is void. Farmer's Case, 3 Co. 77; 9 Co. 141, 191a, Beaumont's Case.[2] There was but one descent to toll our entry in 1701, but the heir was a married woman. Saffin's Case, 5 [. . .].

Acherly [and] *Yorke*: The last case in Hardres[3] is that an equitable interest is barred by a fine. Yet it is admitted that a fine by a mortgagee will not bar the right of redemption. *Ergo*, it is repugnant. As to the descent, both co-heirs were under coverture at the time of the disseisin and descent.

Lord Chancellor [Lord Parker]: I will not determine this myself but will have the opinion of the judges. As to Pickworth, it is merely in equity. This case will not be determined if I should send them to law, for the plaintiffs may be entitled to a decree for part though the jury should find for the defendant for the other part on the fine etc. Here are no controverted facts to be tried. I should do the parties service by determining it here and save them the expense of a special verdict.

The first point, as to the equity of redemption of Pickworth, that will depend upon the effect of the recovery by Evers Armine. The devise upon a contingency to the issue of Evers Armine and to Styles is void and consequently undevised. It is not then in the heir at law. There is no reason why it should be in abeyance but that it should be in the power of B.A. to destroy the will. At common law, abeyance was invented only to preserve estates, not to destroy them.

Beck's Case is a most extraordinary one. There is no color to say here was nothing in the heir of the devisor. Plunket and Holmes [and] Purefoy and Rogers are in point. But it is said that there was a devise to the heir. But had the devisor nothing in him, he could give nothing to his heir. The double contingency does

[1] *Saul v. Clarke* (1626–1629), *ut supra*; *Hunt v. Burn* (1703), 1 Salkeld 244, 91 E.R. 216, also Holt K.B. 255, 90 E.R. 1039.

[2] *Fermor v. Smith* (1602), 3 Coke Rep. 77, 76 E.R. 800, also 2 Anderson 176, 123 E.R. 607, Jenkins 253, 145 E.R. 180; *Beaumont's Case* (1612), 9 Coke Rep. 138, 77 E.R. 928.

[3] *Wolstan v. Aston* (Ex. 1669), *ut supra*.

not alter the case. It is said that, in all events, the fee was given from the heir in this case. But here was a possibility of a tort being a forfeiture. This right must be given over, as in the case of trustees to preserve contingent remainders. He might have limited a fee over to take place if Evers Armine should determine his estate before his natural death. *Ergo*, such a right descended to his heir. So the question is whether, upon Evers Armine's suffering the recovery, the fee did not vest in the heir of the devisor.

The second point is whether, supposing the right of entry descended, it is not barred by the fine and non-claim or the Statute of Limitations. Here, the heir of the devisor could have no right of entry on the death of Evers Armine, but the recovery suffered only gave him a right of entry. As to the fine, the fee of Evers Armine is tortious only as against the heir of the devisor, but rightful against all others.

Armine Bullingham and Sir Thomas Barnardiston joined in the fine. They have a good fee against all but the heirs of the devisor. They had a right of entail and a right of entry. *Ergo*, it cannot be said *partes finis nihil habuerunt*. I do not see but this fine will be a bar as to one moiety of Willoughby.

The third point is what right there is of contribution. It arises upon the will of Sir Michael Armine. But it was for the benefit of Stiles and Barnardiston, not for the heir at law, for, if he is barred of the land itself, he is barred of having contribution.

If the trustee receives sufficient [assets] to pay the debts, the land is discharged and the trustee is accountable and the estate in the trustee ceases.

I think the points are very clear. But, if it is desired, I will send them to the judges of the [Court of] Common Pleas.

The two first points were accordingly sent for the judges' opinions.

N.B. In this case of Carter and Barnardiston, it was determined in the House of Lords that a tenant in tail after debts paid may suffer a recovery before the debts are paid. And so it was determined by Lord King in Sterwood and Cooper upon the will of Sir William Whitlock. *Vide* Keen and Fenn.[1]

[Other reports of this case: 1 Peere Williams 505, 24 E.R. 492, 2 Eq. Cas. Abr. 224, 375, 430, 475, 692, 703, 22 E.R. 190, 319, 366, 404, 582, 591, 3 Brown P.C. 64, 1 E.R. 1179, *sub nom.* Loddington v. Kime, 1 Salkeld 224, 91 E.R. 198, 3 Levinz 431, 83 E.R. 766, 1 Lord Raymond 203, 91 E.R. 1031, 1 Eq. Cas. Abr. 182, 21 E.R. 974, 2 Eq. Cas. Abr. 331, 22 E.R. 282.]

[1] *Keen v. Fenn* (1736), Lincoln's Inn MS. Misc. 384, p. 120.

284
North v. Mawd

(Ch. 1718)

Where a will requires security to be given for the future payment of a legacy, the legacy vests as of the date of the death of the testator.

Lincoln's Inn MS. Misc. 384, p. 41, pl. 2

4 July 1719.

A legacy is given to A. to be paid or secured within seven years after the death of the testator. A. dies before the seven years expires.

Query whether the time of payment was annexed to the substance of the devise.

The Master of the Rolls [JEKYLL], at first, thought it a lapsed legacy, but, afterwards, he was of the opinion that the wife, who was residuary legatee, must give security presently and, therefore, that it was vested.

A legacy was given to four daughters at twenty-one and, if one die, then the other three daughters shall have the whole. It happens that two die before twenty-one.

Curia: It will not survive after the death of the second daughter.

Lincoln's Inn MS. Misc. 10, p. 240

Eodem die [1 August 1718].

A man devises several specific legacies to his wife, she paying £50 to his son seven years after the testator's death, and he directs that she should give security to his trustees named in the will to pay this £50 to the son according to the will. The son died before the seven years were expired. And the question was if this was a lapsed legacy.

It was decreed it was not. Had it stood simply without the last clause, which directs the giving security, it would have been lapsed. But the testator having directed his wife to give security for this £50, that makes it in the nature of a debt, and it shall go to the executor or administrator of the son.

285

Note

(Ch. c. 1718)

The bankruptcy of a plaintiff does not cause an abatement of a lawsuit.

Lincoln's Inn MS. Hill 73, p. 20, pl. 1

A bill is not abated by the death of one of the executors nor by the plaintiff's becoming bankrupt, for the assignees may make use of the bankrupt's name and recover.

286

Anonymous

(Ch. 1718)

The wife of a deceased London freeman is by the custom entitled to her widow's chamber out of the whole personal estate and to a whole third part of what remains as her widow's part.

British Library MS. Add. 36651, f. 88v, pl. 1

Trinity [term] 4 Geo. I, 1718.

A freeman of London having a wife and two children died intestate leaving a personal estate. The wife having married a second husband, the children brought their bill to have an account of their father's personal estate and to have their shares according to the custom of London etc.

Lord Parker, Chancellor, said that, in this case, the estate is to be divided into three equal parts, that, in the first place, the wife is by the custom entitled to her widow's chamber out of the whole and to a whole third part of what remains as her widow's part. Then, the children are to have another third part, which is called the orphanage part. The other third part, called the dead man's part, must be divided between the wife and the children according to the Statute of Distributions,[1] *viz.* one-third to the wife and the other two-thirds to the children so that the wife in this case is entitled to four-ninths and the children five-ninths. And he decreed accordingly.

---

1 Stat. 22 & 23 Car. II, c. 10 (*SR*, V, 719–720).

287

Davis v. Davis

(Ch. 1718)

Where an executor has voluntarily paid legacies and the assets afterwards prove deficient to pay the decedent's debts, the legatees will be ordered to refund.

8 Viner, Abr. 423

A bill [was exhibited] by an executor against a legatee to refund a legacy voluntarily paid him by the executor, the assets falling short to satisfy the testator's debts.

[It was] decreed that the defendant should refund to the plaintiff and that an executor may bring a bill against a legatee to refund a legacy voluntarily paid, as well as a creditor, for the executor, paying a debt of the testator out of his own pocket, stands in the place of the creditor and has the same equity against the legatee to compel him to refund, contrary to the opinion in 2 Vent. 358, Noell v. Robinson, and 2 Vent. 360, Hodges v. Waddington,[1] by Sir Joseph Jekyll, Master of the Rolls.

[Other copies of this report: 2 Eq. Cas. Abr. 554, 22 E.R. 466.]

Dickens 32, 21 E.R. 178

3 May 1718.

An executor having voluntarily paid legacies and the assets afterwards proving deficient, the legatee was decreed to refund.

[1] *Noel v. Robinson* (1682), 2 Ventris 358, 86 E.R. 484, also 1 Vernon 90, 543, 460, 469, 23 E.R. 334, 580, 585, 594, 2 Chancery Reports 248, 21 E.R. 670, 2 Chancery Cases 145, 22 E.R. 887, 1 Eq. Cas. Abr. 299, 21 E.R. 1059; *Hodges v. Waddington* (1683), 2 Ventris 360, 86 E.R. 485, also 2 Chancery Cases 9, 22 E.R. 821, 1 Eq. Cas. Abr. 236, 21 E.R. 1015.

288

Lawson v. Lawson

(Ch. 1718)

A married woman cannot take a gift from her husband, but she can take from him a gift causa mortis.

Lincoln's Inn MS. Misc. 384, p. 41, pl. 1

17 July.

The husband, a little before his death, delivers a purse of gold and a Bank note for £100 to his wife for her use. The query was whether it were a good donatio causa mortis. There was quoted Lady Shaftesbury's Case, by Lord Cowper, where Lord Shaftesbury presented my lady with £100 in money and bills to bear her charges from Italy, where he died soon after. And it was decreed a good gift, for, though the husband and wife are but one person in law, yet, in equity, they are considered as different persons to many purposes. So, in the Case of Nantwell, quoted by Mead. But there, the wife had a separate maintenance; so in Lady Herne's Case. In the present case, [there] were notes signifying gifts to the wife and so it could not be proved in the nature of testamentary codicils.

The Master of the Rolls [Jekyll] took time to consider of it and would be attended with precedents.

1 August.

It stands for judgment. It was ordered to be reported specially by the Master. I do not care to favor such gifts further than the law allows. Vide Drury v. Smith, 45.

19 March 1718/19.

The Master of the Rolls [Jekyll] decreed both the purse of gold and the Bank note to be a good gift causa mortis.

Lincoln's Inn MS. Misc. 10, p. 241

Eodem die [1 August 1718].

The defendant's husband, being wounded at Preston by the rebels and, finding he could not live, gives his wife 100 broad pieces. And, soon afterwards, he dies, having sometime before made his will and his wife and another executors.

Upon a bill brought against her by her children for an account of the personal estate, she insists to retain these broad pieces as being given her by her husband.

Curia was of opinion it was a *donatio causa mortis.*

Lincoln's Inn MS. Misc. 11, p. 92

1 August 1718.

Captain Lawson having been wounded at Preston and likely to die and having sometime before made his will and about seventeen days before he died, he drew a bill upon a man at York, who was one of the executors in his will, for £100 payable to the plaintiff, his wife. And at the bottom of it, he writes that it was for the use of his wife to buy her mourning [clothes] and subsist her until her life rent shall come in. And a few days after, *viz.* the 21st of July, he delivers to her a purse of gold containing about £100 and bids her made use of it to buy her necessaries for her own use and no other. And he died about twelve days after worth about £8000.

The question was if the wife was entitled to these two sums. And the Master of the Rolls [JEKYLL], having taken time to consider of it, this day, delivered his opinion and decreed them to the wife.

He said the gold was properly a *donatio causa mortis*. It must operate as a legacy after his death, for his wife could not take it during his life.

As to the £100, for which the bill was drawn, I take it to be an appointment that she should have that sum out of his estate. If she had received the money before her husband died, it would have been an appointment how that money should have been applied.

Things of this kind are not much to be favored. And had the money been considerable, it might have admitted of another consideration, but, the sums being small with respect to the whole estate, he was of opinion the wife ought to have them both.

[Other reports of this case: 1 Peere Williams 441, 24 E.R. 463, 2 Eq. Cas. Abr. 575, 22 E.R. 484.]

289

East India Company v. Atkins

(Ch. 1718)

A defendant can be required to make discovery of his own fraud.

Lincoln's Inn MS. Misc. 384, p. 45

26 July 1718.

A bill [was brought] for the discovery of the defendant's trading contrary to his agreement. The defendant demurred and pleaded the Act of 9 Will. III and 6 Ann.[1] enacting severe penalties, which the defendant by his discovery would subject himself to. The plaintiffs' bill set out a covenant of the defendant to make a true discovery and not to plead or demur to any bill in equity. And the plaintiffs waived their share of the forfeitures. The question was how far this covenant bound the defendant to make a true discovery.

[1] Stat. 9 Will. III, c. 44, s. 71 (*SR*, VII, 444–445); Stat. 6 Ann., c. 71 (*SR*, VIII, 824–829).

Chesshyre, for the defendant: By all laws, no man is bound to betray himself. A covenant not to take a benefit of the law is void at law, much more in equity. They may take what benefit they can of the covenant at law.

Cowper: The plaintiffs cannot waive the penalties which the crown is entitled to. A covenant or bond not to exercise a trade is void.

Raymond: In the Exchequer, in cases of the Crown, excise men and others are bound to discover, but not to a common informer, though he offer to waive the penalties.

Vernon: An usurious bond is not binding. One insisted, when he made such a contract, [they] forced the parties to make affidavits that they would not seek relief either at law or in equity, yet they were relieved.

Mead: When the East India Company made the sailors enter into bonds not to demand wages, they were set aside. In the Case of Nandeach, there was an affidavit that he would not seek relief in equity, yet he was relieved here. Fenwick, Co. Lit. 53; C. 345b; 2 Vernon 365, Stiles [. . .].

Sir Thomas Powys, for the plaintiff: We may have an account of waste or tithes if we waive the penalties.

Talbot: The defendant might have discovered without this covenant, and the court could have decreed upon it that force is not unlawful. *Quilibet potest renuntiare juri per se introducto.*

Lord Chancellor [Lord Parker] was of the opinion that, so far as the plaintiffs had it in their power to waive the penalties, the defendant ought to discover. But he said he would consider how far the defendant might by the covenant subject themselves even to undergo a penalty, having acted contrary to a penal law.

Lincoln's Inn MS. Misc. 384, p. 77

7 November 1718.

Vernon, for the defendant: The plaintiff's bill is for discovery of the defendant's trading, offering to waive the penalties. And it insists on the defendant's covenant to discover.

First, as to waiving the penalties, [it is] not in the plaintiff's power. The discovery they seek is of goods put on board the *Tuskan Pink* and, at Maderas, put on board the *Stringer Galley*, belonging to the plaintiffs, and carried to the Indies. And the goods were sent to Holland and there sold for the defendant's use. This discovery will subject the defendant to the penalties of the Statute 9 & 10 Will. III and 6 Ann. Pursuant to 10 Will. III, three-fourths are given to the plaintiff and one-fourth to the informer. The plaintiffs, being the informers, may upon that Statute waive the whole penalty. But pursuant to 6 Ann., the whole value of the goods are forfeit, one-half to the Crown and one-half to the informer. Therefore, the plaintiffs cannot waive the one-half.

Objection: The Act extends only to private traders. But they cannot be in a better case than the Company traders. We are in the common case that a court of equity will not compel a man to subject himself to any penalties therefor.

Second, they insist on the covenant which is a new one. It is that the defendant shall discover and not plead or demur to any bill brought by the Company, and they waive all penalties. First, we are not plaintiffs to be relieved against the covenant but are defendants, and the plaintiffs would have a specific performance as to the manner of gaining it. It was when we were just going abroad they sometimes gain such covenants from seamen to defraud them of their wages, which the court always sets aside. The plaintiffs' undertaking to waive penalties, which induced the defendant to enter into the covenant, is void. The difference [is] between setting aside a covenant and performing it in specie. A man may waive his privilege but not in all cases. If a man covenants not to redeem or confirm it with an oath, as Stisted's Case, yet it is void. If a man borrows on a mortgage and covenants that, if he will not pay the money, the interest shall yearly carry interest, the court always sets it aside. A court of equity cannot be bound by a private covenant. This is that a man shall not use part of his defense. If you can bar him of part, you may of the whole. If it were that a man shall not defend a cause but the bill be taken pro confesso, it is void. A court of justice should withstand all attempts of this kind. The covenant is that the defendant shall not plead. But, if he does, are the hands of justice tied up? What weight this covenant is of in a court of equity, if the covenant is executory as for a purchase, it may be carried into execution. But this is not so. This court is to relieve against the rigor of the law and against penalties, not to assist them. The rule is founded upon reason and justice and was never shaken until this attempt which does not come to set aside the covenant. But we only insist on our common right of defending ourselves against it. We hope we shall not be obliged to make this discovery.

Sir Thomas Powys, for the plaintiffs: We hope the plea shall be overruled. The Statute directs that the party shall take an oath not to carry on a private trade. The plea goes to the whole bill. 9 Will. extends only to private traders. So, as to the outward voyage, the defendant is not liable to any penalties, and the forfeiture belongs to the Company, no information being brought by any other person. Therefore, they can waive it. If a man sues for tithes or waste and waives the penalties, he is entitled to a discovery and to have the single value. 6 Ann. extends to the homeward voyage, and one-half is given to the crown and one-half to the informer. A man may covenant not to commit fraud. In cases of a mortgage, the covenants are inconsistent with the nature of a mortgage. This covenant was on very valuable consideration, which was a great profit to the defendant. It goes along with a trust, and it is not like interest upon interest, nor like the taking away of seamen's wages. A man may renounce a privilege. If a man promises to give judgment by default, this court will compel him. *Conventio vincit legem; volenti non fit injuria*. This covenant is only inconvenient for the defendant who might gain a great deal honestly but would gain more fraudulently. The question is which shall suffer, the Company or the person guilty of the fraud. The taking away the means takes away the satisfaction due to the Company. They say they made 200 percent for the company and have made the same for themselves. They covenant to have it determined here and not at law where we cannot have a discovery. They had all this in view and knew the consequence when they made the covenant. [There was] no accident since to alter the case. It is a matter of great consequence and will set aside the Statute and ruin the Company. It concerns the public.

Lord Chancellor [Lord Parker]: I think, where the plaintiffs' waiver of penalties is to free the defendant from them, it must appear plainly that he can waive them, which, here, it does not. But the plea goes too far as to the main point. This covenant is to be considered that it lies within the only knowledge of the defendant if he has been guilty of a fraud. They gave him the opportunity by his being entrusted, however reasonable, yet, if against law, it is void. I think it is not to disable the court to do justice but enables them so to do as to hindering him from his defense. It is not a defense of justice, but of fraud. [This is] not like the case of a mortgage, which is only a security for a debt, and the court cannot be hindered from doing justice. This is only insisting that the plaintiff is not entitled to know the truth from him. It is only a matter of privilege not to discover, not a matter of natural right. If the plaintiff had no right before to have a discovery, the covenant gives him a right. The defendant will be subject to penalties, but the court will not make this covenant void, which cannot be of force until a man is a knave, who is not to be protected. The law of England does not hinder a man from giving a right to examine him on oath for discovering a fraud. If you go to law, there can be no discovery, without which they cannot recover. Therefore, this plea must be overruled, and the defendant must answer.

[Other reports of this case: 1 Strange 168, 93 E.R. 452, 1 Comyns 346, 92 E.R. 1105.]

290

Smith v. Bridges

(Ch. 1718)

In this case, the legacy in issue was held to be a contingent legacy.

Lincoln's Inn MS. Misc. 13, p. 45, pl. 1

27 July 1718.

Deborah Bradford, by will, gave to the plaintiff Deborah Smith half her plate and linen and £1000 when she should attain the age of twenty-one or be married and the surplus of her estate to her executors upon several trusts.

[The Master of the Rolls, Jekyll] decreed the legacy to the plaintiff Deborah was a contingent legacy and did not arise until the plaintiff's age or marriage.

291
Vincent v. Farnandez
(Ch. 1718)

A Jewish father has a duty to support his Protestant children, and this duty includes making provisions for them by a will and, if he fails to do so, the court will order provisions to be made for them out of his estate.

Lincoln's Inn MS. Hill 73, p. 42

1 August 1718.

Upon the death of a Jew father, a daughter, who, in the lifetime of the father, turned Protestant, sued to have a maintenance allotted to her by the Chancellor according to the Statute of Anne, c. 30,[1] which enacts that, if any Jewish parent, to compel such child to change his religion, refuse such child fitting maintenance, the Lord Chancellor etc. may make such order for the maintenance of the child as he etc. think fit.

The father had made a will and left his estate, which was computed at £40,000 to the Portuguese Jews at Amsterdam in charity and, by his will, ordered the money to be paid within three months after his death. The executors alleged that they had paid it away as the will ordered. The testator died in June 1718.

My Lord [Lord Parker] was of an opinion that that was no sufficient authority to remit the estate immediately for fear of debts and that, if upon this Act, she is entitled to a maintenance, he declared he took it to be a debt upon the estate, that the words of the Act were very large and ought to be construed for the benefit of the child.

He advised the executors to come to some composition.

Judgment was adjourned.

Lincoln's Inn MS. Misc. 384, p. 46, pl. 1

1 August.

Upon a petition of the child of a Jew who was turned a Protestant Christian and, therefore, disinherited by her father and his personal estate given to the Jewish synagogue of Amsterdam, the question was upon the Act of 1 Ann. whether the child was entitled to a maintenance after the death of the father. The executors pretended they had paid away all the estate according to the will.

Lord Chancellor [Lord Parker]: This is not like the case of a justice of the peace who can only compel a father to maintain his child during his life, but the Lord Chancellor, by this Act, may compel the deposit of a sum of money and this

[1] Stat. 1 Ann., c. 24 (*SR*, VIII, 74).

is to be extended as far as possible. I will consider of it but recommend it to the legatees to make a reasonable allowance. It is in the nature of a debt.

Lincoln's Inn MS. Misc. 11, p. 40

The plaintiff was the daughter of a Jew, and, having been brought up in the Christian religion under her mother, who had been a Jew but was converted to the Christian religion, she presented her petition to the Lord Chancellor, praying that she might have a maintenance out of the estate of her father, who was dead and by his will had given away all his estate from her. And this was grounded upon the Statute of the year first of Queen Anne, ca. 30, sess. 1. And if the court could make any order for the plaintiff's maintenance out of her father's estate, he being dead and having given it away, was the question.

Lord Chancellor [Lord Parker] was of opinion this case was within the intent of the Statute and there was nothing in the letter of the Act to the contrary, for the Act empowers the court to make such order for the maintenance of the Protestant children of Jewish parents if such parents refuse to maintain them, as the court shall think fit, and the Act does not say the court shall order the parent to allow a reasonable maintenance for such Protestant child, but shall make such order for the maintenance of such child as they shall think fit, which must be out of the estate of the parent. And this may be done as well after the death of the parent as in his lifetime.

As to that part of the Act which says this is to be done when the parent refuses to allow his Protestant child a maintenance in order to compel him to change his religion, His Lordship was of opinion that it was not necessary for the child to prove that the father declared he would not maintain him unless he changed his religion, for, if so, the Act would be of little effect, but he thought the proof lay on the other side and that, if the parent did not make it out that he had some other goods sufficient cause for withdrawing a maintenance from the child, it should be presumed he did it for the reason mentioned in the Act.

[Other reports of this case: 1 Peere Williams 524, 24 E.R. 499, 2 Eq. Cas. Abr. 513, 22 E.R. 433.]

292

Bampfield v. Chenhale

(Ch. 1718)

A devise of shares of stock in a company does not include any unpaid dividends that had accrued at the time of the death of the testator.

Lincoln's Inn MS. Misc. 10, p. 239

1 August 1718.

It was decreed that a devise of 'all my stock in the South Sea Company and all my right and interest therein' did not carry a devise of the dividends which were due for this stock at the death of the testator, though Mr. *Vernon* insisted upon the contrary and said, if a man bequeaths a bond, he gives all the interest due upon it as well as the principal.

The Master of the Rolls [Jekyll] compared this to a devise of a leasehold estate as where a man devises a leasehold estate and all his interest therein, that will not carry the arrears of rent, and the words 'all his interest' etc. do not enlarge the preceding words, for a devise of the stock is a devise of all his interest in that stock.

293

Hughes v. Sayer

(Ch. 1718)

The words in a will 'died without children' mean children living at the death of the testator.

A devise over of a personal estate upon the devisee's dying 'without children' is good.

Lincoln's Inn MS. Misc. 11, p. 93

Eodem die [1 August 1718].

John Hughes, by will, directs his personal estate to be divided into ten parts. And he gives four parts to his sister Mary and, after her decease, to her children. And he declares that, if either of them died without children, his will was that the survivors or survivor should have the share of the deceased.

One of the children died leaving no issue. And the question was if the share of that child should go to the surviving children or belonged to the administrator of the child that died.

Upon the hearing of this cause, the Master of the Rolls [Jekyll] took time to consider of this question. And now, he delivered his opinion. It is said the word 'children' has been taken to be synonymous to the word 'issue'. Wild's Case, in the Reports; Pollex. 112; and in Vent., King and Melling.[1] However, in this case, he was of opinion it must be understood to be children living at the death of the person dying and not to be a dying without issue generally, for a dying without issue generally extends to future issue and a person is said to be dead without issue not only if he leaves no issue at his death but whenever there is a failer of issue. And, if the words in the present case, *viz.* if either died without children, were to be taken in that sense, the limitation over, being of a chattel, would undoubtedly be void. But he said he was of opinion that dying without children must be restrained to the death of the party, for, then, it is that there must be a survivorship. And, therefore, he decreed the limitation over to be good and that the surviving children ought to have the share of the child that died.

2 Vent. 349, *contra.*[2]

1 Peere Williams 534, 24 E.R. 504

John Hughes, after several legacies, by his will, directed that the surplus of his personal estate should be divided by his executors into ten shares, three shares whereof should be paid to his nephew and niece, Paul and Anne Hughes, children of a deceased brother, and, upon either of their dying without children, then to the survivor, and, if both should die without children, then to the children of the testator's other brothers and sisters.

The question was whether this devise over of a personal estate upon the devisee's dying without children was good or not.

And His Honor [Jekyll], having taken time to consider it, gave judgment that the word 'children' when unborn had been, in the case of a will, construed to be synonymous with issue and, therefore, would in a will create an estate tail (6 Co. 17, Wild's Case[3]); and, if the word 'children' was understood to be the same with issue in the present case, then, the devise over of the personal estate upon a death without issue would be void, but that, here, the words 'dying without children' must be taken to be children living at the death of the party, for that it

[1] *Wild's Case* (1599), 6 Coke Rep. 16, 77 E.R. 277, also 1 Eq. Cas. Abr. 181, 21 E.R. 973, Gouldsborough 139, 75 E.R. 1050, *sub nom. Richardson v. Yardley*, Moore K.B. 397, 72 E.R. 652; *Warman v. Seaman* (1675), Pollexfen 112, 86 E.R. 530, also 2 Chancery Cases 209, 22 E.R. 914, 1 Freeman 306, 22 E.R. 1227, Reports *tempore* Finch 279, 23 E.R. 153, 3 Keble 544, 84 E.R. 870, 73 Selden Soc. 197, 217, 248; *King v. Melling* (1672), 1 Ventris 214, 225, 86 E.R. 144, 151, also Pollexfen 101, 86 E.R. 526, 2 Levinz 58, 83 E.R. 448, 3 Keble 42, 52, 95, 84 E.R. 584, 589, 614, 3 Salkeld 296, 91 E.R. 835, 1 Eq. Cas. Abr. 181, 21 E.R. 973.

[2] *Broadhurst v. Richardson* (1681), 2 Ventris 349, 86 E.R. 479, also 2 Chancery Reports 153, 21 E.R. 644.

[3] *Wild's Case* (1599), 6 Coke Rep. 16, 77 E.R. 277, also 1 Eq. Cas. Abr. 181, 21 E.R. 973, Gouldsborough 139, 75 E.R. 1050, *sub nom. Richardson v. Yardley*, Moore K.B. 397, 72 E.R. 652.

could not be taken in the other sense, that is whenever there should be a failure of issue, because the immediate limitation over was to the surviving devisee and it was not probable that, if either of the devisees should die leaving issue, the survivor should live so long as to see a failure of issue, which in the notion of the law was such a limitation as might endure forever.

And, therefore, by reason of the limitation over in case of either of the devisees' dying without children, then to the survivor, the testator must be intended to mean a dying without children living at the death of the parent. Consequently, the devise over is good.

[Other reports of this case: 2 Eq. Cas. Abr. 291, 22 E.R. 244.]

294

Hudson v. Harrison

(Ch. 1718)

An arbitral award that has been made an order of the court is subject to the correction of the court upon exceptions.

Lincoln's Inn MS. Misc. 10, p. 242, pl. 1

6 August 1718. Lord Chancellor.

Exceptions were taken to an award by arbitrators pursuant to a submission of the parties which had been made an order of court. And the question was if exceptions would lie in this case.

And after the court had taken time to consider of it, [Lord Parker] was of opinion the exceptions would lie, and one of them was allowed. And the award was confirmed as to the rest.

295

Anonymous

(Ch. 1718)

The first process of contempt against a menial servant of a peer is a sequestration nisi.

1 Peere Williams 535, 24 E.R. 505

Mr. *Hale* moved for a sequestration *nisi* for want of an answer against a menial servant of a peer of the realm as the first process for contempt in the same manner as in the case of the peer himself.

And, though the motion was granted by the Master of the Rolls [Jekyll], yet the Register refused to draw it up, as thinking it against the course of the court.

Upon which Mr. *Hale* moved it again before the Lord Chancellor [Lord Parker], who, upon reading the Statute,[1] granted the motion likewise, it appearing to be both within the meaning and words of the Statute, and, if it were not so, as it was plain no attachment would lie against their persons, consequently, there would be no remedy against them and they would have a greater privilege than their lord if the process against such menial servants were to be a subpoena.

296

Cope v. Cope

(Ch. 1718)

An administrator of a decedent's estate should make an account to the heir and the decedent's creditors and not to the executor of an after discovered will.

Where a bond given to a decedent cannot be found after his death, there is a presumption that the debt was paid or forgiven.

A bill for an attachment lies to garnish money that is owed to the plaintiff and that is in the hands of a third party.

Administration of a decedent's estate can be granted pendente lite *where the will is in dispute.*

A recital in one record of another record is not proof of the record.

Lincoln's Inn MS. Misc. 384, p. 72

16 October; Inner Temple Hall.

Seymour, an administrator, *pendente lite*, receives £3781 and, after[wards], a will being found, pretends he paid it to the executor, Samuel Cope, who gave him a general release. The question is whether this release is a discharge. The executor being insolvent and a bill brought by a creditor and the heir to have an account and for the personal estate to ease the real estate in favor of the heir, the Master does not state whether any money was paid to the executor but that £2400 was paid for debts and that he accounted with the executor for the rest.

Sir Thomas Powys: The release was obtained from the executor when in prison and after two bills brought against him.

Acherly: In equity, the assets may be followed in any person's hands. First, the bill is brought by the widow, Rachel Cope, to have her article made good, and so [she] is a creditor in equity. The second [is brought] by the heir to have the personal estate come in aid of the real. Winch, *Entries*, tit. 'Debt'.[2] The administrator is chargeable at law *durante minore aetate*.

---

[1] Stat. 12 & 13 Will. III, c. 3, ss. 1, 2 (*SR*, VII, 638).

[2] *Chandler v. Thompson* (1622), H. Winch, *Beau Pledeur*, p. 353, also Hobart 265, 80 E.R. 411.

Lutwyche, for the administrator: We paid the money to the executor without fraud knowing him to be insolvent. At law, we are discharged and ought not to pay twice.

Cowper: We could not refuse to pay to the executor.

Raymond: At law, the executor only could demand an account from the administrator *pendente lite*. And the bill cannot prevent it without an order of court. In the House of Lords, Lord Orford's Case,[1] a voluntary payment by an executor after a bill brought to a creditor in equal degree [was] allowed.

Powys in reply: The administrator paid after he had put in his answer and submitted to the account. Lord Orford's Case is different, for the court would not grant an injunction for one creditor against another.

Mead: The heir's is an attachment bill. The payment is not to a creditor; so [it is] not like Lord Orford's Case. But if it had been to a creditor of an inferior nature, he must have paid it again. Decree that the creditors be satisfied out of the testator's personal estate in the course of administration [and] the executor and all other persons who possessed the personal estate to account and to have all just allowances.

Lord Chancellor [Lord Parker]: Seymour has not accounted but insisted he ought not. He must account. If this payment had been after the decree, it had not been good. At law, the question is whether this money was not attached in his hands, he being the proper person to pay it. The administration *pendente lite* is as good and of the same nature with *durante minore* aetate, it being to secure the estate until another is capable. He, after a suit is commenced by a creditor, pays it to the executor; it is not a good bar. If the executor had demanded it, he was not bound to pay him. The decree has not determined it. At present, I think he could not pay it to the executor. If he could and any undue advantage made by him, it ought not to prejudice other creditors. The Master must proceed to make him account notwithstanding this bar he has insisted on.

Lincoln's Inn MS. Misc. 11, p. 1

16 October 1718.

The case upon the Master's report was this. There was a contest in the spiritual court touching the will of A.B., and, during that contest, administration *pendente lite* was granted to the defendant, Seymor, who possesses the testator's assets. And, thereupon, a creditor of the testator, while the administration was in force, exhibits her bill against the administrator for a satisfaction of her debt out of the assets in his hands. Seymor puts in his answer, sets out an account of the assets he had received, and offers to come to an account. After the will is proved, another person, who had a demand out of the testator's personal estate

[1] *Earl of Orford v. Daston* (1702), Colles 229, 1 E.R. 262, Precedents in Chancery 188, 24 E.R. 91, 1 Eq. Cas. Abr. 10, 21 E.R. 834, 2 Eq. Cas. Abr. 460, 22 E.R. 391, Lincoln's Inn MS. Misc. 12, p. 180.

brings a bill against the executor and Mr. Seymor in the nature of an attachment bill, praying that the assets in Mr. Seymor's hands might remain there and not be paid away.

The causes were heard, and Mr. Seymor is decreed to account for what he had received, having all just allowances. And when he came before the Master, he insisted that he had accounted with the executor and had paid over to him what was remaining in his hands, who was the proper person to receive it and that the executor had given him a release and, therefore, he ought not to account over again to the plaintiffs. And, if the payment by Mr. Seymor, who was a temporary administrator after his administration determined to the executor pending a suit in this court wherein both were made defendants was a good payment was the question.

Lord Chancellor [Lord Parker] was pretty clear it was not, the plaintiff's bill being in the nature of an attaching of the money in his hands and he ought not to have parted with it without applying first to the court. But, however, he said the matter was not ripe for the judgment of the court until the Master had taken the account and it appeared whether Mr. Seymor had really paid any money to the executor or not (for that had not been proved). If he had and the payment was a good payment, it ought to be allowed him under just allowances, which the Master is directed to make him. But, if he was not, it ought not to be allowed. But that question will come most properly before the court upon exceptions to the Master's report.

In this case was cited Lord Oxford's Case, in the House of Lords, and the last case in Winch's *Entries*, tit. Debt.[1]

British Library MS. Hargrave 81, f. 79

Five causes.

These suits were concerning the estate of Joseph Cope, out of which the plaintiff and defendants had several demands, either as creditors or legatees, and the defendant, Rachel Cope, his widow, was both a creditor by bond before marriage for £500 and demands the residuum as executor.

One H. was heir at law to the testator, and he brought his bill to have the testator's personal estate applied to exonerate the real [estate]. And one Tordin Hastings, who was a relation of the testator, was another defendant. He was indebted to the testator by two bottomry bonds, one of £10 and the other for £60, but neither of them could be found after the testator's death. Hastings, by his answer, owned[2] the bonds and that neither of them had been paid, but he insisted that the testator had never made any demands for them and intended, as he be-

---

[1] *Earl of Orford v. Daston* (1702), *ut supra*; *Chandler v. Thompson* (1622), *ut supra*.

[2] I.e. admitted.

lieved, to forgive them and had, therefore, as he believed, cancelled them. The answer was replied to, but no proof was made of any demand.

Sir Joseph Jekyll, pro querente: Though it be necessary at law to produce the bond in question in order to recover because of the *profert hic in curia*, yet, in equity, it is not if it plainly appeared the bond was executed and that the obligor has not paid it. And this court will in such cases supply that want. Here, the bonds are admitted by the defendant to have been executed and not satisfied. He, therefore, prayed a decree for the payment of that money.

[*blank*] for the defendant: It was said that, where a bond cannot be produced to charge the party with it, it shall be intended to have been satisfied or intended as a gift to the obligee and, therefore, cancelled by him. And the presumption is stronger in this case because no demand has been proved and that the defendant was a near relation and in low circumstances when the bonds were given.

And the court decreed accordingly that the bill as to those bonds should be dismissed, but without costs as to exonerating the inheritance.

It was said and agreed to by counsel on both sides that such exoneration can only be out of the surplus, for the will of the party must be first performed. Therefore, the exoneration must be postponed until the legacies as well as debts and funeral expenses are discharged and this court will compel an application of all the assets accordingly and so it has been frequently adjudged and decreed in this court.

And [it was] decreed here accordingly.

[Other copies of this report: British Library MS. Hargrave 82, f. 75, British Library MS. Hargrave 77, f. 21, British Library MS. Hargrave 303, f. 40.]

Lincoln's Inn MS. Hill 73, p. 44

16 October 1718. Temple Hall.

N.B. An attachment bill is only proper when money is in a person's hand who cannot himself pay the demand but must pay it to another, as an executor perhaps, who ought to pay that debt. Then, it is very proper by a bill to attach the money in that person's hands that the money may lie in his hands and that it may be applied in satisfaction of his demand.

N.B. Administration is granted often by the ecclesiastical court *pendente lite* where a will is in dispute as well as *durante minore aetate*, for, in the first case, there is no one that can take upon him the executorship until the dispute is settled, and, in the last, no one of sufficient discretion to understand it.

N.B. A recital in one record of another is no proof of the record, for a record ought to be made up of itself.

297

Anonymous

(Ch. 1718)

Where a defendant pleads and then answers, the answer supersedes the plea.

Lincoln's Inn MS. Hill 73, p. 109, pl. 1

18 October 1718. Serjeants' Inn Hall. Lord Chancellor. Demurrers and Pleas.

N.B. Where a man first pleads and after, in the end, answers the bill, his answer overrules the plea.

298

Browse v. Welman

(Ch. 1718)

A mistake in a decree should be corrected on a petition to rehear, and not by an original bill.

Lincoln's Inn MS. Hill 73, p. 65

19 October.

The bill [was] to have the will of Thomas Barton performed. The plaintiff had a legacy of 20s. per week. The defendants answer that they had paid debts due on specialties, mortgages, etc. to £170 12s. more than the testator's personal estate amounted to. The plaintiff desired that those debts which would affect the real estate should be paid out of it so that the intent of the testator might be fulfilled and the legacy paid out of the personal [estate] or that the plaintiff might be decreed to be paid out of the real estate.

The plaintiff had had a hearing of this cause before and an account of the personal estate only directed to be taken. And now, he says he is informed that the real estate ought to be affected and, therefore, brings this bill, an original bill, in aid of the former decree, saying that the decree was wrong, whereas they should have petitioned by a petition signed by two counsel to have had it reheard, which is the only method to have any mistake in a decree settled. And, therefore, the Lord Chancellor [Lord Parker] dismissed this second original bill and left the plaintiff to pursue the common method of rehearing.

N.B. No bill or action can be brought without joining all the executors though some have renounced.

A motion [was] made to tax [the] attorneys at law's bill, the plaintiff being ready to pay what should be reported due.

299

Bacon v. Clark

(Ch. 1718–1719)

When a portion is devised to be raised by rents and profits, it may be raised by a sale.

Lincoln's Inn MS. Misc. 11, p. 33, pl. 1

25 October 1718. Nicholas Bacon and Elizabeth, ux., daughter of Abraham Clark, deceased, plaintiffs; Abraham Clark, defendant.

Abraham Clark, seised in fee of houses and land in London and Middlesex in possession and of lands in Witchingham in Norfolk in reversion after the death of Horace Herne, by will dated 25 February 1711[/12], devised to his wife for life his estate in London and Middlesex and, after her death, to the defendant, his only son, and his heirs, and, after the death of the said Horace Herne, he devised the estate in Witchingham to the defendant and his heirs upon condition that he paid to the plaintiff Elizabeth, his sister, £1000 within twelve months after the death of one Elizabeth Herne and, if the defendant or his heirs should neglect paying the said £1000, it should be lawful for the plaintiff Elizabeth to enter upon the said estates in London, Middlesex, and Witchingham and take the rents until she should be paid the £1000.

Soon after making the will, the testator died. And Elizabeth Herne died in September 1713, but Horace Herne and the testator's wife are still living. And the plaintiffs now bring their bill that the defendant may pay the £1000 with interest or that the reversion may be sold for raising it.

The defendant insists the £1000 is not become payable and that he is the heir at law and has no other provision from his father.

The Master of the Rolls [Jekyll] declared that the portion became payable within twelve months after the death of Elizabeth Herne,[1] and he decreed the reversion to be sold for raising it with interest from the time it became due.

Lincoln's Inn MS. Misc. 384, p. 75

27 October; Master of the Rolls.

Clark devises a London estate to his wife for life, remainder to the defendant in fee and a N. estate, after the death of Horace Hern, the tenant for life, to the defendant in fee on condition that the defendant pay the plaintiff £1000 within twelve months after Elizabeth Hern's death, proviso, if not paid, the plaintiff to enter and take the profits. The wife and Horace Hern are both alive, but Elizabeth Hern died September 1713.

The plaintiff's bill is to raise the £1000 presently by a sale of the reversion.

[1] Horace *MS.*

Objection: The testator intended the money should not be raised until the estate came into possession by directing, if it were not paid, the plaintiff to enter and take the profits. There was quoted Butler v. Duncombe, now under the consideration of the Lord Chancellor, and Corbet v. Maidwell, in Salk. 159; Boreston's Case, 3 Co. 19.[1]

Master of the Rolls [JEKYLL]: Had this been a devise in possession, it has not been an equitable charge, but the devise would enure by way of limitation, not condition, because the devise is to the heir at law and the plaintiff would have a remedy at law and might have entered. The proviso that, if it were not paid, then the plaintiff might enter must be construed in case the estate came in possession.

The £1000 carried interest immediately. The money must be raised with interest from twelve months after the death of Elizabeth Hern. A sale must be of so much of the reversion as shall be necessary.

Lincoln's Inn MS. Misc. 384, p. 185, pl. 2

9 June 1719.

Abraham Clark, by his will, devises his lands etc. in Middlesex to his wife for life and then to the defendant, his heir at law, he paying £1000 to the plaintiff, the testator's daughter, within twelve months after the death of Elizabeth Hern and, in case the money be not paid, then the plaintiff to enter and receive the rents and profits.

The plaintiff brings her bill to have the money raised, Elizabeth Hern being dead, which the Master of the Rolls [JEKYLL] decreed to be raised by sale.

Vernon, for the plaintiff: The defendant now appeals and insists that the plaintiff is not entitled to have her portion raised until she could enter for non-payment, which must be after the death of the testator's wife, but that provision for the payment does not exclude the raising it by sale etc. He gives after the death of Horace Hern an estate in Norfolk to the defendant on the same condition.

Northey, for the defendant: The defendant is the testator's eldest son. And, if the plaintiff's portion is to be now raised, he will be in a worse condition than the younger children, which could not be the intent of the testator. The will does not say that the portion shall be raised out of the lands.

Raymond: The giving an entry for non-payment shows the intent at what time it should be paid and that he did not design a sale. The estate is but £130 *per annum*, which is all leasehold except £19 *per annum*, and the mother is alive. The mention of the death of Elizabeth Hern shows the intent that it should not be raised until the estate came into possession.

---

[1] *Butler v. Duncomb* (Ch. 1718–1719), see above, Case No. 282; *Corbett v. Maidwell* (1709–1710), 1 Salkeld 159, 91 E.R. 147, also 3 Chancery Reports 190, 21 E.R. 764, 2 Vernon 640, 655, 23 E.R. 1019, 1027, 1 Eq. Cas. Abr. 337, 21 E.R. 1086; *Hynde v. Ambrye* (1587), 3 Coke Rep. 16, 76 E.R. 664, also 1 Eq. Cas. Abr. 190, 194, 21 E.R. 980, 984.

Lord Chancellor [Lord Parker]: When a portion is to be raised by rents and profits, it may be a sale, which is taking all the profits at once. This case is stronger, for, here, the entry is given only in default of payment in twelve months after the death of Elizabeth Hern and it was impossible to raise it within that time by receiving rents and profits. The giving an entry will not put the plaintiff in a worse condition than if there had been no such clause. If it were not to be sold until it comes into possession, it would not benefit the defendant, for it carries interest.

I think the decree is right.

[Other reports of this case: 1 Peere Williams 478, 24 E.R. 480, Precedents in Chancery 500, 24 E.R. 224, 2 Eq. Cas. Abr. 208, 641, 22 E.R. 177, 538.]

300

Shales v. Barrington

(Ch. 1718)

Parol evidence is not sufficient to settle or convey any estate nor to destroy an estate fairly settled by deeds and conveyed.

Even where a devise is made of an estate for the payment of debts, the decedent's personal estate should be first used to pay his debts.

A devise of a personal estate means such estate as the devisor shall die possessed of.

Lincoln's Inn MS. Hill 73, p. 45

28 October.

A bill was brought by Shales, who had married a sister of Sir Charles Barrington, to establish some deeds executed by Sir Charles during his life as also his last will. And John Barrington brings a cross-bill to set aside those deeds and the last will as obtained by surprise, circumvention, etc. and that the estate ought to go as by a former settlement upon the heirs male, which was Sir John Barrington. But by those deeds and by the will, Sir Charles gives his estate to his sister, Mrs. Shales, during her life and to her male heirs taking upon them the name of Barrington. There was by Charles' will a trust of a term raised to pay the debts and legacies, and the residuum of his personal estate he gave to Sir John Barrington, the plaintiff in the cross-bill.

But, upon the most clear and undeniable proof, the deeds and will were established.

N.B. The evidence for the defendant in the original bill was only parol evidence as to what they had heard Sir Charles say and, therefore, as by the Statute of Frauds and Perjuries,[1] no parol evidence is sufficient to settle or convey any

[1] Stat. 29 Car. II, c. 3 (*SR*, V, 839–842).

estate; so no parol evidence ought to be held sufficient to destroy an estate fairly settled by deeds and conveyed.

The counsel for Sir John Barrington insisted then that the term that was raised for the payment of debts and legacies should be so applied and that the personal estate, the residue of which was given to Sir John Barrington, should come in aid of the deficiency of the said term; otherwise, that it was a void devise.

But it was held by the Lord Chancellor [Lord Parker] that, where a devise is made of an estate for the payment of debts, that the constant construction has been that the personal estate ought, for, unless it would be to the damage of creditors by simple contract or to specific legatees, where the intent of the testator is plain and direct, but never to make a residuum only of the personal estate, that such a one might take who had no specific legacy. Sir Charles might have paid most of those debts before he died, perhaps, had he lived sometime longer and, though a devise of land can only extend to such land as the devisor was possessed of at the time of the devise, a devise of a personal estate has a future view and shall mean such estate as the devisor dies possessed of and so, by that means, there might possibly have been a residuum.

Mr. *Vernon* mentioned Lady Gainsborough's Case,[1] where the real estate was made subject to debts and those debts particularly named and even the funeral charges mentioned as such a debt as he designed should fall upon the real estate and the lady was made executrix. But the proof of the intention of the testator was what guided this cause which was Mr. Webb, who said that it was the intent of the testator that all the personal estate should be at My Lady's disposal and that he said by making her executrix and charging his real estate with his wife's [?] debts without giving a particular devise of it would be sufficient.

The counsel for Mr. Shales insisted to have their costs considering the very unnecessary charges they had been put to in the plaintiff's cross-bill examination etc.

But the Lord Chancellor [Lord Parker] would not give costs, for, though he was not heir at law, he was in the place of an heir at law disinherited and, though he thought they had carried it on a little too far considering the weakness, he thought it would be a little too hard to decree him to pay costs. And he said it was absolutely necessary to bring the cross-bill, for Sir John had a specific legacy and [. . .] his children and though the plaintiff in the original bill did in the same bill confess the said legacies, yet that was no security to the legatee for supposing the plaintiff in the original bill had got his bill dismissed which he might have done upon paying the defendant's costs.

An account was ordered of the personal estate and the term to assist if there should be a deficiency in the personal estate.

[1] *Countess of Gainsborough v. Earl of Gainsborough* (1692), 2 Vernon 252, 23 E.R. 764, 2 Freeman 188, 22 E.R. 1152, 1 Eq. Cas. Abr. 230, 21 E.R. 1010.

[Other reports of this case: 1 Peere Williams 481, 24 E.R. 481, 2 Eq. Cas. Abr. 237, 22 E.R. 202.]

301
Bransby v. Kerrick
(Ch. 1718)

The question in this case was whether an executor and legatee who had defrauded the testator into making a will in his favor should be declared a constructive trustee for the benefit of the heir at law.

Lincoln's Inn MS. Misc. 384, p. 73

The plaintiff's son, having made several wills whereby he gave his estate to the plaintiff, his father, was at last prevailed upon by the defendant, who was no relation, through false insinuations, particularly that the plaintiff would not assist his son with money to supply his occasions etc., to make a new will whereby he directs the defendant to pay his debts and makes the defendant executor. But he does not give anything to the plaintiff father. One witness proved that the will was read to the testator as cont[aining] a devise to the father.

Lord Chancellor MACCLESFIELD decreed that the defendant should take no benefit by the will but be deemed a trustee for the plaintiff and should account for the real and person estate of the testator and should convey the freehold and surrender the copyhold to the plaintiff and pay costs.

N.B. There was an appeal to the House of Lords.[1]

29 October 1718.

Vernon, for the plaintiff: Equity may set aside a will made by the plaintiff's son. Thynn and Egham's Case,[2] where the heir was executor, but intending to make his wife executrix the executor promised she should have the same benefit, was decreed. The plaintiff is the testator's father, and the former wills were made in his favor. The defendant was an entire stranger. A witness says the will was read as a devise to the plaintiff, the father, and the design of this will was only to pay the debts, but not to be for the benefit of the defendant. It is like the case of a deed read in another manner to an illiterate man, which is not his deed. Lachford's Case[3] on Oldham's will, who intending to provide for a relation at Cam-

---

1 *Kerrich v. Bransby* (1727), 7 Brown P.C. 437, 3 E.R. 284.

2 *Thynn v. Thynn* (1684), 1 Vernon 296, 23 E.R. 479, 1 Eq. Cas. Abr. 380, 21 E.R. 1116.

3 *Oldham v. Litchford* (1705), 2 Freeman 284, 22 E.R. 1214, 2 Vernon 506, 23 E.R. 923, 1 Eq. Cas. Abr. 231, 21 E.R. 1011, 2 Eq. Cas. Abr. 44, 22 E.R. 39.

bridge, had charged his real estate but did not execute the will according to the Statute;[1] the heir undertaking to make good the will, it was decreed.

Raymond, for the defendant: A will cannot be set aside here, but it must be tried at law. [In] Masters v. Button,[2] it was sent to law though [there were] circumstances of fraud between the wife and the servant, whom she promised to marry after her husband's death; yet it could not be set aside here. The court cannot decree gratitude. The testator intended to give his estate to another, a stranger.

The Lord Chancellor [Lord Parker] took time to consider in what manner the plaintiff should be relieved.

14 November.

The Lord Chancellor decreed that the defendant should take no benefit by the will but should account for the real and personal estate of the testator, but be allowed for the debts paid by him and have all other just allowances. The defendant is to pay costs and to convey the freehold and surrender the copyhold to the plaintiff.

[This was] reversed in the House of Lords.

See Masters v. Button, L.B. 92, *contra*, Bodville v. Roberts in Bath and Mountage, 3 Ch. Ca. 103.[3]

Lincoln's Inn MS. Misc. 12, p. 234

14 November 5 Geo. [1718].

The son lying sick at Leicester, his father took Kerridge with him and went to visit him and gave him money but not sufficient to pay all his debts. When the father returned, he left Kerridge behind, who persuaded the son to make his will for the payment of his debts, and he gave his estate from his father to himself.

The court decreed Kerridge to be a trustee for the father and that the father should be empowered by actions in the name of Kerridge to get in and recover the personal estate of the son.

It is a rule in equity that persons circumvented and imposed upon by a will ought to be relieved.

2 Lee 563, 161 E.R. 441

Herridge v. Bransby.

This case in Chancery was mentioned by Mr. Lutwyche in the cause of Powis v. Andrews, 1 Lee 251.[4]

---

1 Stat. 29 Car. II, c. 3, s. 5 (*SR*, V, 840).

2 *Masters v. Button* (1715), see above, Case No. 55.

3 *Roberts v. Wynn* (1664), 1 Chancery Reports 236, 21 E.R. 560; *Earl of Bath v. Earl of Mountague* (1693), 3 Chancery Cases 55, 103, 22 E.R. 963, 992.

4 *Andrews v. Powis* (1728), 1 Lee 242, 251, 161 E.R. 90, 93.

Lord Chancellor Macclesfield, on pretense that a will had been obtained by fraud and imposition, decreed it to be void as to real estate therein devised, and he declared that Herridge, the executor of the will, should, as to personal estate, be a trustee only to the use of the deceased's father.

Herridge appealed to the House of Lords,[1] who were of opinion that the Chancellor had no power to appoint the executor to be as a trustee and that it was a novel invention without any color or foundation. And they reversed the decree in every part of it, by which the will stood and the executor was re-established as sued.

[Other reports of this case: 1 Eq. Cas. Abr. 133, 406, 21 E.R. 937, 1136, 2 Eq. Cas. Abr. 421, 508, 767, 22 E.R. 358, 430, 652, 7 Brown P.C. 437, 3 E.R. 284]

302

Calmady v. Calmady

(Ch. 1718)

If a testator gives a younger son more than the others, the distribution of the surplus of the estate must be equal without respect to the inequality of the will, and there will be no hotchpot.

An advantage given in the lifetime of a father is not within the Statute of Distributions.

A legacy to younger children is construed to include posthumous children.

In this case, a necklace was ordered to be taken apart so that some of the specific jewels could pass by a specific bequest separately from the others.

Lincoln's Inn MS. Hill 73, p. 51

31 October 1718.

The plaintiff, administrator *cum testamento annexo* to his father, his older brother, Josias, dying, brought his bill against the widow [. . .] Kelmady to have an account of the personal estate of her husband. And the widow's cross-bill was to have her jointure established, which the defendant to the cross-bill said was of assart lands.

One question was whether some money that the wife had saved during the coverture out of the allowance of her husband should be liable to distribution. She had £50 *per annum* by a deed for separate use and the profit of the dairy etc. which then was spent in the family.

The second question was, in the will a diamond croisade, was desired to go to the heir male of the estate as an heirloom but, afterwards, before the death of the testator, he turned it into a diamond necklace and presented it to the plaintiff,

[1] *Kerrich v. Bransby* (1727), 7 Brown P.C. 437, 3 E.R. 284.

his then wife, and whether this shall go to the wife or by the devise though it was altered and given to her by the heir male.

N.B. The diamond cost a great deal more than the croisade sold for. It was given originally with the design that the son should, it being a jewel that had continued in the family some time, give it to his wife whenever he married, the testator being then a widower but the testator marrying his now widow thought fit to present it to his own wife.

If a jointure estate be evicted from a widow, she is empowered by the Statute 27 Hen. VIII[1] to enter upon any estate in fee or in tail her husband was possessed of and is not to take a recompense out of the personal estate.

That Statute of Distributions of Intestate's Estates[2] does not extend to this case where legacies are specifically devised to some of the children by will and the distribution has always been equal [?] without regard to such legacy, for that Statute only says what has been given by the father in his lifetime for the advancement of any child or children shall be brought and put into hotchpot so as to make all the younger children equal. But I suppose they are not obliged to do it unless it be to their advantage. If a man has married a lady whose father gave her a considerable fortune, he is not obliged at the death of the father to bring that fortune in order to provide for the younger children. It would be a little hard in the present case where there are several children and one had a portion of £3500 given with her in marriage in her father's life[time] if she should be obliged, being expressly within the words of the Statute of an advancement in the life of the father to put that into hotchpot and the rest of her sisters carry off each £1500 apiece by virtue of a specific legacy which would not be liable to such hotchpot. It prevents the intention of the Act, which was to make the younger children's fortune equal [if]

devised to him as an heirloom.

Lincoln's Inn MS. Misc. 380, pt. 3, p. 234

Mr. *Vernon*: If a man gives a younger son more than the rest by the disposition of his will, the distribution of the surplus must be equal without respect to the inequality of his will, and there must be no hotchpot, it not being an advantage in the life of the father and so not within the Statute of Distributions. A legacy to younger children is always interpreted advantageously so as to take in posthumous children.

Lincoln's Inn MS. Misc. 384, p. 75, pl. 1

31 October.

---

1 Stat. 27 Hen. VIII, c. 10, s. 5 (*SR*, III, 541).

2 Stat. 22 & 23 Car. II, c. 10 (*SR*, V, 719–720).

Vernon: If a man give one younger child more than another by his will, the distribution of the surplus must be equal without regard to the inequality of the legacies, and there must not be any hotchpot, it not being an advancement in the heir's lifetime and, therefore, not within the Statute of Distributions.

A legacy to younger children is always construed beneficially so as to take in posthumous children.

11 Viner, Abr. 181

Michaelmas, 5 Geo.

Mr. Calmady having a crocheat of diamonds, which was his first wife's, in 1695, makes his will and, amongst other things, devises this crocheat to his eldest son and that it should go in succession to the heir of his family as an heirloom. Afterwards, in 1699, he marries a second wife, the now defendant, and turns this crocheat into a necklace and adds several new diamonds to it of the value of £200, which was more than the value of the crocheat. The plaintiff, as heir to Mr. Calmady, though not the eldest son, to whom it was specifically devised, demands this crocheat of the defendant, the widow of Mr. Calmady.

Counsel for the defendant insisted that the defendant was entitled to it as part of her paraphernalia, which the husband cannot give away from his wife by will, though he may dispose of it in his lifetime, and the wife shall retain it against the devisee or executor of her husband unless in the case of creditors, who cannot otherwise have a satisfaction of their debts.

Counsel for the plaintiff said that, though, formerly, it was a doubt whether the husband could devise any part of the paraphernalia of the wife, yet, of late, it has been held that the husband may devise specifically jewels of his own which he permitted his wife to wear, though they shall not go to his executor or to a general residuary legatee and that, in this case, there being no direct proof of an express gift to the wife, only a permission to wear them, they are well devised to the heir as an heirloom and that the altering and turning the crocheat into a necklace and permitting his wife to wear them was no revocation of the devise.

Parker, Chancellor, seemed to doubt at first that turning the crocheat into a necklace, adding new diamonds to it, and permitting his wife to wear it was a revocation of the devise. But, at last, he ordered the Master to examine and separate the old diamonds from the new, and he decreed the diamonds of the crocheat to the plaintiff as heir at law and specifically devised to him as an heirloom.

[Other copies of this report: 2 Eq. Cas. Abr. 628, 22 E.R. 528.]

303

Castleman v. Pitts

(Ch. 1718)

In the pleading of a deed, a mistake in the date is not material.

In this case, the conditions of a contract were performed, and an account and payment were ordered by the court.

A voluntary bond creditor has priority over simple contract creditors in the administration of a decedent's estate.

Lincoln's Inn MS. Misc. 384, p. 75, pl. 2

3 November.

A bill [was exhibited] to have satisfaction of a bond of £1500 out of the assets. The condition of the bond recites a deed of settlement on the defendant and that, if the defendant enjoy the estate accordingly, then the money is to be paid the plaintiff. The date of the deed is mistaken, and the bond is voluntary.

Mead, for the plaintiff: If the condition of the bond is void, then the bond is single and good against the executor of Palmer, the obligor, though voluntary there being assets to pay the other creditors. If this bond is not a specific lien on the trust estate, yet it ought to be satisfied out of the assets.

The condition recites two deeds, one of real and the other of personal estate, if P. enjoy according to the trusts, then to stand good; the quantum of the personal estate is also mistaken.

The bond was given on this occasion. Ford, the grandfather of Palmer, the obligor, on J.'s [?] marriage, promised to give him £10,000 and directed counsel to make a settlement on him to that value and to recite that it was in consideration of that promise. There were two deeds to convey the real and personal estate to P. after the death of Ford, these settlements being made by the intervention of Ford's wife. P. enters into the bond of £1500 to her trustees with the condition above mentioned.

Cowper, for the defendant: We have not the full benefit of the condition of the bond, part of the estate being limited to A. And, if he has issue, we may be defeated.

Vernon, in reply: We are proper here for discovery of the assets and for satisfaction. The court never directs an action [at law] when it can decree without. They have the full benefit of the condition, both of the real and personal estate according to the trusts of the deeds.

Objection: We are volunteers and the defendants are purchasers, that Ford promised to leave P. the best part of £10,000. But it appears Ford would not be bound to it and P. died before Ford. So the will had been void; then the wife obtains this settlement which the defendant enjoyed. Therefore, it is a good consideration for the bond.

Suppose it voluntary, it had bound the assets against other creditors had it not been with the intent to protect the estate against creditors.

Lord Chancellor [Lord Parker]: How far this is proper, here, the plaintiffs cannot go to law, the bond being to a trustee. There could be no defense against it; though, at law, the mistake of this date is not material, at law, the deeds must be set out, and, if the date is not the same, the defendant could not show that he did not enjoy according to the deed.

As to the merits, there is no occasion for consideration against executors where the party himself was liable, there being no secret trust. But here was a consideration, for, otherwise, Ford would not have made the settlement and the defendant was bound in gratitude to give this bond to his grandmother.

The condition is well performed, he being to pay within six months after Ford's death if he should enjoy according to the trusts of the deeds. The condition had not been performed if the estate were defeated by a prior settlement or if there had been an estate tail precedent. The terms are fulfilled according to the expectation of the obligor. There must be an account and satisfaction out of the personal estate first and then out of the real with interest from six months and costs.

Lincoln's Inn MS. Misc. 12, p. 12

3 November 1718. Mary Castleman v. Meniconi, Pitt, *et al.*

A voluntary bond for the payment of £1500 to the plaintiff entered into by Thomas Palmer, to whom the defendant Meniconi was executor, was decreed to be good against the creditors and to be paid prior to the simple contract creditors with interest and costs.

Lincoln's Inn MS. Misc. 13, p. 322, pl. 1

3 November 1718.

It was decreed that, if the debts of Thomas Palmer and the legacies devised by his will should not be paid out of his personal estate, then the creditors by simple contract and the legatees were to stand in the place of the plaintiff, a creditor by bond, for a satisfaction of their debts and legacies out of the real estate of the said Thomas Palmer so far as his personal estate should be exhausted in satisfaction of what should appear due on the plaintiff's bond with interest and costs.

304

Pinder v. African Company

(Ch. 1718)

A surety is discharged when the original principal debtor becomes later joined by other joint debtors.

Lincoln's Inn MS. Misc. 384, p. 47

4 November.

The plaintiff was a surety to the [African] Company for one Bullard in a bond for the performance of covenants in an indenture which recited that Bullard and T. were their factors at Barbados, and it contained covenants for their daily accounting for such time as they or either of them should be continued by the Company. T. dies, and Bullard acts solely for some time afterwards. The Company elects Bates and Steward to act jointly with Bullard. The question is whether the plaintiff is bound for Bullard after Bates and Steward are joined with him.

The Master of the Rolls [JEKYLL] was of opinion that it was a bare authority in Bullard and to be construed strictly and the adding of Bates and Steward to him determined that authority and, therefore, that the plaintiff was not liable afterwards. And he relied upon Lord Arlington v. Merrick, 2 Sand. 403; Knight v. Cole, 3 Lev. 273.[1]

305

Gonawra v. Toot

(Ch. 1718)

Where a defendant has committed a fraud on the plaintiff in regard to an oral contract to make a lease, a court of equity will order the lease to be made.

Lincoln's Inn MS. Misc. 384, p. 94

6 November.

Vernon, for the plaintiff: Where the Statute of Frauds[2] has been used to cover a fraud, the court has always relieved. The first case was in Lord Nottingham's

---

[1] *Lord Arlington v. Merricke* (1672), 2 Williams Saunders 403, 85 E.R. 1215, also 3 Keble 45, 59, 84 E.R. 586, 593; *Knight v. Cole* (1690), 3 Levinz 269, 273, 83 E.R. 684, 686, also 1 Shower K.B. 150, 89 E.R. 505, Carthew 118, 90 E.R. 673, 1 Eq. Cas. Abr. 170, 21 E.R. 965, *sub nom. Cole v. Knight*, 3 Modern 277, 87 E.R. 183, Holt K.B. 620, 90 E.R. 1243, *sub nom. Knight v. Low*, Dodd 121.

[2] Stat. 29 Car. II, c. 3 (*SR*, V, 839–842).

time,[1] where there was an absolute conveyance and a defeasance which the defendant would not execute but insisted on the Statute overruled; the next case, in Lord Jeffreys's time, Goucher and Goucher, where putting the party into possession was such an executing of the agreement in part as was good against a subsequent purchaser; Foxcroft and Lister, in the House of Lords,[2] where there was a building lease contracted for and the contractors [had] begun to build, Lord Keeper Wright dismissed the bill, [but it was] reversed by the House of Lords. Taylor and Pike, where standing by and seeing the party lay out his money in building on the defendant's ground bound him; so Raw and Port,[3] where the second son being privy to the marriage settlement of his elder brother and not discovering that the estate was entailed upon him.

Raymond, for the defendant: The bill is to have a lease according to the defendant's promise, the plaintiff having laid out money on the premises. The defendant insists on the Statute of Frauds, not having signed any agreement nor agreed upon certain terms. He says what the plaintiff has laid out was not for lasting improvements. The defendant admits he saw the plaintiff build a stable which cost about £10. It is proved that the defendant told the plaintiff his word was as good as his bond and promised the plaintiff a lease when he should have renewed his own from Hudson, his landlord.

Lord Chancellor [Lord Parker]: This is stronger than most of the other cases. Here, the defendant is guilty of a fraud and ought to be punished for it. The best way of punishing him is by making a lease to the plaintiff. Though the terms were uncertain, it is in the plaintiff's election for what time he will hold it. And he does elect to have it for the defendant's term. The defendant must make the plaintiff a lease for his term at the old rent and pay him costs.

306

Anonymous

(Ch. 1718)

Exceptions cannot be taken to the credibility of witnesses until after publication is passed.

Lincoln's Inn MS. Hill 73, p. 58, pl. 1

6 November 1718.

Lord Chancellor [Lord Parker]: Exceptions cannot properly be taken to the credit of witnesses until after publication is passed, for, though the witnesses

[1] Perhaps *Potts v. Turvin* (1681), 79 Selden Soc. 856.

[2] *Lester v. Foxcroft* (1700), Colles 108, 1 E.R. 205.

[3] *Raw v. Pote* (1691), 2 Vernon 239, 23 E.R. 755, Precedents in Chancery 35, 24 E.R. 19, 1 Eq. Cas. Abr. 169, 355, 21 E.R. 964, 1098.

are known to the parties to be [. . .] of very ill reputation, he does not know until he sees the depositions whether their evidence relates materially to him or no.

307

Boswell v. Perry and Parsons

(Ch. 1718)

A person interested in the outcome of a lawsuit is not competent to testify as a witness. However, in this case, the witnesses that were objected to were not interested.

Where a person takes someone else's property, such as building materials, he must pay for them.

Lincoln's Inn MS. Hill 73, p. 58, pl. 2

The plaintiff made a contract with the trustees enabled by the [*blank*] of Queen Anne, for the stopping of Dagenham Breach,[1] which was that he should have £16,000 paid at several times, which was £6000 when the breach was stopped for a month and the water did not overrun the works and the rest when the walls were completed and a certificate made of it by the trustees. But the plaintiff failing in his project, he received nothing from the trustees, but he brings his bill to be allowed for his materials etc. and wood, which [was used by] the defendant Perry, who was employed by the trustees to carry on this work.

The bill against Parsons was to make him stand to his agreement, which he had made with the plaintiff to stand to a quarter part of the profit and loss.

An objection was raised by the defendants' counsel against reading one [blank] for a witness, he being, as they alleged, one concerned in interest (and therefore, indeed, ought to have been a party to the bill) and that he was to swear to his own benefit and in order to throw a greater load upon the defendant Parsons, for that person and some others who were to be read as witnesses had a sort of a parol promise that they should go such a share and Parsons was to go a third part if they quitted their pretensions to any share, otherwise Parsons was to go but a sixth share. So they thought it not right for those gentlemen to be witnesses that they might throw off their shares and by that means lay a third share upon Parsons.

But My Lord [Parker] was of opinion as that, as such a parol promise was not sufficient to have entitled those gentlemen to have come in for a share in the profit if such project had succeeded, they could not by such be loaded with the damage and that they were not concerned in interest and, therefore, the account might go on without them. And he ordered their depositions to be read.

[1] Stat. 13 Ann., c. 20 (*SR*, IX, 968–971).

He ordered an account between the plaintiff and Perry for what materials he had and made use of of the plaintiff, and Parsons [was ordered] to stand the share of the charge according to his agreement with Boswell.

308

Anonymous

(Ch. 1718)

Firebote does not extend to lead mines or iron works.

Lincoln's Inn MS. Hill 73, p. 61

Lord Chancellor [Lord Parker]: Firebote only extends to such a fire as is necessary for the house, such as it was at the time of the lease. And [he said] that, if a man lease ground and lead mines or iron works and grants to the tenant firebote, it shall not extend to the working of the mines, or, if a man enlarges his house with abundance of rooms and fires, it shall not extend to such enlargement.

309

Kitson v. Robins

(Ch. 1718)

The customary share of a London freeman's widow is her proportion of his estate and not any specific property.

Lincoln's Inn MS. Misc. 384, p. 81, pl. 1

15 November.

Vernon: A specific legatee shall not contribute to the debts until the other personal estate is applied in the first place, but he shall be preferred to the other legatees.

A freeman of London devised a leasehold in five house to the plaintiff and real estate to his wife for life, remainder to B., and other personal estate to her for life. Upon a bill against the widow, she elects to take by the custom [of London] and waives all benefit of the will as to the personal estate. [It should be] decreed that the personal estate devised to her shall go and be paid to the other persons entitled as legatees of the residue.

Raymond, for the defendant, who represents the widow: We are entitled to one-half of the personal estate in specie.

Vernon, in reply: It has not been determined that, by the custom, the widow is entitled to half of the personal estate specifically. But it is generally otherwise. The plaintiff is a specific devisee of the houses. The widow's claim is in the nature of an encumbrance. The specific legatee is to have a preference, and the encumbrance is to fall on the other legatees, who are only entitled to the residue.

Lord Chancellor [LORD PARKER]: I take it to be clear that the plaintiff shall enjoy the houses. The widow shall not be a tenant in common of the personal estate by the custom, but the freeman may dispose of which moiety he pleases, but he shall leave her the value of the other moiety. It would be inconvenient if she should have a moiety in specie. If there is a deficiency, the legacies must abate in proportion, but the plaintiff, the specific legatee, must enjoy these houses, there being a sufficiency of assets to pay all except the residuary legatees.

Lincoln's Inn MS. Misc. 380, pt. 3, p. 231, pl. 1

15 November 1718. Kitson and Roberts, executors of Kitson.

Kitson, a freeman of London, devises his freehold to his wife for life and also his leasehold estate, consisting of five houses, for life, remainder to B., and he devises the rest of his estate to C. and D. The wife makes it her elections to adhere to her customary part.

It was said by counsel, not contradicted, that specific legatees shall be satisfied and the last disturbed, for legatees at large or pecuniary legatees shall first be obliged to pay debts and encumbrances before the specific legacies shall be charged.

Lord Chancellor [LORD PARKER]: I take it to be the custom of the City that a wife is to have a third or a moiety of the whole estate her husband leaves behind him and not a moiety of a third of every particular of which the estate consists so that this custom will be satisfied though he should at pleasure by his will specifically dispose of any part of his estate, provided he leave enough for her customary share.

8 Viner, Abr. 423

Trinity, 5 Geo.

If a freeman of London dies without issue, his wife is entitled by the custom to the moiety of her husband's personal estate in value, but not in specie. If a freeman of London makes his will and disposes of his whole estate without any notice of the custom and gives several specific legacies and several pecuniary legacies and devises the residuum to A. and the widow waives her legacy and claims a moiety of his personal estate by the custom, if the residuum be sufficient to answer her moiety or share, it shall be taken out of the residuum, but, if that fall short, then the pecuniary legatees shall abate in proportion, and, if the residuum and pecuniary legacies be sufficient to answer her moiety, the specific legatees shall not be brought in to contribute, but enjoy their legacies entire.

British Library MS. Add. 36651, f. 91, pl. 1

Michaelmas [term] 5 Geo. I, 1718.

A freeman of London made his will and devised all his estate to his wife for her life and, after her decease, he devised five houses, being leasehold, to J.S. and the residue of his estate, after the death of his wife, to J.D. and he devised some pecuniary legacies to other persons.

The legatees preferred a bill in this court, and the wife came into court and made an election to take a moiety of her husband's estate, being all personal and [there being] no children and waived the devise to her by the will. She, afterwards, dying, the suit was revived against her executor.

She had entered into the five houses devised, as above, and was in possession of them at the time of her death, insisting to have a moiety of them by the custom in specie. And her executor now insisted on the same.

Sir Robert Raymond said that it seems *prima facie* that, by the custom, the wife might insist upon a moiety of the personal estate in specie and could not be compelled to take the value thereof though he never knew any case adjudged the one way or the other.

But Lord Chancellor PARKER said he did not take the custom to be so, for that it would be impossible that she should have a moiety of each spoon or utensil or the like small items and that a tenancy in common should be created of every individual part and, in the case of a house, it would create great confusion, for, if it were so, she must have a moiety of each house or a third part if there were children and hold that in common. Therefore, he said he took the custom to be that she shall have a moiety of the value of the personal estate.

Therefore, he decreed that her executor should be paid a moiety of the value out of the residue if sufficient. If not sufficient, then it is to be made up out of the pecuniary legacies but the specific legacy, *viz.* the houses, were not to be touched unless there be a deficiency in the former.

Lincoln's Inn MS. Misc. 11, p. 65

15 November 1718. Upon an appeal from a decree at the Rolls.

A freeman of London devised to his wife five leasehold houses and a copyhold estate for life, and, after her death, he devised it over. He gave the house he lived in and all other his personal estate to his wife for life with a power to dispose of £500 at her death. And, after her death, he gives all except the £500 to some of his relations. And he made his wife and the defendant Robins executors.

The widow brought her bill for a moiety by the custom and to have the other moiety by the will for her life with a power to dispose of £500 and also for the real estate for her life.

Upon the hearing of this cause, the Master of the Rolls declared the widow could not claim by the custom and the will too. However, if she insisted on her customary share, that would not bar her of claiming the real estate by the will, and, therefore, that was decreed to her for life. But, as to the personal estate, she having at the hearing made her election to take her customary share, it was decreed to her, and the other moiety was decreed to be paid to such persons to whom the whole was given by the will after her death.

Upon hearing the appeal, LORD PARKER declared the decree was right only it wanted to be explained a little, and, therefore, he decreed that the widow was to have her moiety in the first place, then the legacies were to be paid, and, after that, the residuary legatees were to have what was left, but, if the personal estate over and above what was specifically bequeathed was not sufficient to answer the widow's moiety, then a sufficient part of the specific legacies were to be sold to make good the deficiency.

In this case, the Lord Chancellor [LORD PARKER] declared that a freeman, having a wife and no child, might give away what part of his estate he pleased, provided he left a moiety in value for his wife, for the custom must be understood not that the widow shall have one half of every individual thing but only that she shall have a moiety of the value of the personal estate.

[Other copies of this report: 2 Eq. Cas. Abr. 277, 555, 22 E.R. 234, 466.]

[Other reports of this case: *sub nom.* Kitson v. Kitson, Precedents in Chancery 351, 24 E.R. 164, Gilbert Rep. 28, 25 E.R. 20, 2 Eq. Cas. Abr. 275, 22 E.R. 232, British Library MS. Hargrave 80, f. 131.]

310

Miles v. King

(Ch. 1718)

A written contract will be enforced as written, even though one party lied to the other during the negotiations therefor.

Lincoln's Inn MS. Misc. 11, p. 70

15 November 1718. Richard Miles, plaintiff; John King and William King, executors of Richard Graw, defendants.

The defendant having taken a lease from Stamper of a farm in Essex for twenty-one years and a half at £40 *per annum*, he stocks the farm, and, about two years after, he comes to an agreement with the plaintiff to let him an underlease and to sell him his stock for £450. Accordingly, he makes an underlease to the plaintiff at £50 a year. The plaintiff pays this rent to the testator for about three years and, after his death, pays some rent to his executors. And now, the plaintiff brings his bill to be relieved against a fraud which he suggests had been imposed on him by the testator, for that he agreed to make him a lease at the same rent as he paid Stamper, which was only £40 a year, whereas he had made a lease at £50 a year. And it was fully proved in the cause that Stamper was paid no more than £40 a year.

On 28 October 1718, the cause was heard before the Master of the Rolls [JEKYLL], who declared that the rent of £50 *per annum* was inserted in the lease in question by fraud and imposition on the plaintiff and that the agreement for the purchase of the stock and goods for £450 and for the lease at the rent which the testator paid Stamper was an entire agreement and the testator having executed in part by paying the £450 and by entering on the estate was entitled to be relieved against the reservation of the rent and to have a performance of the agreement. And, therefore, he decreed an account to be taken of what was due for rent at £40 a year and, upon payment of what should appear due, the counterpart of the lease was to be delivered up and the defendants, the executors, were to assign over the original lease to the plaintiff for the remainder of the term and to pay costs.

The defendant appealed to the Lord Chancellor for these reasons:

First, for that the counterpart of the said lease under the plaintiff's hand and seal and proved to be drawn and engrossed by the plaintiff's own attorney was better evidence to prove what the agreement was than the parol evidence produced by the plaintiff and the said underlease could not have been so drawn if the plaintiff's attorney had not had the original lease by him;

Second, parol evidence to vary the agreement from the written lease ought not to be allowed to overthrow the lease in writing, for, if so, every written agreement must subsist by parol evidence and deeds in writing which vary from the parol evidence would be invalid and the Statute of Frauds[1] become useless;

Third, the defendants, having found the counterpart of the lease under the plaintiff's hand and seal, made a fair defense and, therefore, ought not to have been condemned in costs.

Lord Chancellor [LORD PARKER]: The agreement was not that the plaintiff should pay the same rent as the testator paid, but he agreed for the land at £50 a year and, to draw the plaintiff in to pay that rent, he told him a lie, *viz.* that he paid £50 a year himself. Why now is there any reason the plaintiff should be relieved for this reason because he told him a bare, simple lie, which for aught appears has done him no hurt, for there is no proof the land is not worth £50 a year? And, for aught I know, it may be worth £60 a year.

Now, there is a difference between an agreement which has reference to another matter to reduce it to a certainty and an agreement which is made certain by the parties themselves. Suppose a man is treating about settling lands on the marriage of his son and he proposes to settle all the lands he purchased of J.S. and a settlement is made and, after, it appears that some of the purchased lands are left out of the settlement. Perhaps the court may relieve in such a case.

But suppose a man proposes to settle all the lands he purchased of J.S. and then gives in a particular of those lands and that is agreed to by the parties. Shall

[1] Stat. 29 Car. II, c. 3 (*SR*, V, 839–842).

a man, after these lands are settled, come into this court and say the lands contained in that particular were not all the lands purchased of J.S.?

It is a dangerous thing to allow or parol proof in these cases. The bill must be dismissed, but without costs.

311

Anonymous

(Ch. 1718)

A legatee can sue for his legacy without joining the other legatees as parties.

If there were initially sufficient assets in a decedent's estate to pay all debts and legacies and one legatee was paid his legacy, the subsequent insolvency of the executor will not require that legatee to refund any part of his legacy.

Lincoln's Inn MS. Hill 73, p. 62

15 November 1718.

Two infants were residuary legatees of the testator's personal estate, which was given to the executor in trust for them. One sues in the proper court, the spiritual one, to have an account of the estate and that she might have her moiety of the residue. The spiritual court ordered the executor to give in an account of the testator's estate upon pain of excommunication, which is all the penalty they can inflict. The executor brought in the accounts, the moiety of which amounted to the sum in question, which was declared by the spiritual court to belong to the plaintiff before them.

But before they gave a sentence, the executor brought a bill in Chancery to stay proceedings in that court and that he might have his account taken there and be discharged of his trust.

The injunction was granted upon the executor's bringing in that money, which was by the spiritual court declared to belong to the petitioner, before the master, which was done. And now, the petitioner desired that it might be paid out to her, which was opposed by the other infant because the executor was insolvent, but was for having that money which was declared to belong to the other to go as the residue of the estate and to be divided between them and so both to bear a proportion of the loss by the executor's being insolvent.

But the Master of the Rolls [Jekyll] was of opinion that the money which the petitioner was suing for in a legal manner and the sum ascertained that belonged to her in the spiritual court and the injunction confirming that sum to her, it must be paid her and that the injunction can never be taken to be in aid of the laches of the other infant, who was not a party to the proceedings in the spiritual court, and, that one single legatee may sue there or in this court without making the other legatees parties and that any legatee may sue for this legacy though there are infants that are legatees and is not obliged to be put off until they are at age and, if there are sufficient assets acknowledged by the executor and the legatee is paid such legacy, the after insolvency of the executor shall not oblige him to refund assets [that] were at the time of the suit in the spiritual court allowed by the executor.

N.B. At that rate, a man [would] be put off forever of his legacy if there are infants legatees very young perhaps and they die near their age and leave infants [. . .] estates personal to infants.

312

Lady Pierpoint v. Lord Cheney

(Ch. 1718)

The question in this case was whether a maintenance for a child should be raised by a sale of the assets of the estate during the lifetime of her father.

Lincoln's Inn MS. Misc. 11, p. 72

18 November 1718.

Upon the marriage of Lord Kingston with Mrs. Baynton, an Act of Parliament[1] was obtained for settling lands of the now duke of Kingston, father of the lord Kingston. And, as to part of the lands, which was of the yearly value of £947 a year, the limitations were to the use of the duke for life, then to lord Kingston for life, then to trustees for 1000 years upon trust that, if there should be one or more daughters of the marriage, the trustees, by the rents and profits of the term or by sale or mortgage of the term, should raise £20,000 for the portions of such daughters to be paid them at twenty-one or marriage and, in the meantime, to pay them the following maintenances, *viz.* £300 a year to the daughters until they attained twelve years of age and afterwards £400 *per annum* and such maintenance to be paid quarterly at the feasts etc., the first payment to be paid at the first of the said feast days as should happen next after the death of the Lord Kingston.

Lord Kingston is dead, having left the defendant, his only son, and the plaintiff, his only daughter, who brings her bill by her next friend to have her maintenance raised during the life of the duke of Kingston by a sale of the reversionary term. And if such maintenance should be raised during the life of the duke was the question.

Mr. *Vernon*, for the plaintiff, cited the Case of Gerrard v. Gerrard.[2] In that case, the portions were to be paid at eighteen or day of marriage, which should first happen after the death of the father and mother. In favor of the daughter,

[1] Private Act of 4 & 5 Ann. (*SR*, VIII, 483).

[2] *Gerrard v. Gerrard* (1704), 2 Vernon 458, 23 E.R. 894, 2 Freeman 271, 22 E.R. 1204, 1 Eq. Cas. Abr. 337, 21 E.R. 1086.

the court decreed the portions to be raised in the life of the mother, the father being dead.

It was insisted for the defendant that there had been no case where a reversionary term had been sold or mortgaged for raising a maintenance only, for, if so, there must be an annual mortgage made, by which means, if the duke of Kingston[1] should live for some years, the estate may be swallowed up or, at least, there may not be sufficient [assets] to raise near the portion when it becomes payable, for the estate is but £947 a year and, therefore, as this court are guardians of infants and their estates, it was hoped in this cause the court would not direct the term to be sold or mortgaged, for that might rather turn to the prejudice of the infant.

Lord Chancellor [Lord Parker]: All persons declare against raising portions on reversionary terms by inserting clauses in marriage settlements that the portions shall not be raised in the life of the father. I think my predecessor [Lord Cowper] much in the right in declaring in the Case of Corbett v. Maidwell[2] that this matter had gone a great way.

Can it be imagined that the parties, when they made this settlement, intended that there should be an annual mortgage made for twenty years together as it may happen to be the case, by which means it may fall out to swallow up the estate? But, however, I must now take it as it stands upon the Act of Parliament, and I cannot say but this is no other than what has been done in former cases, but, still, I think the court may consider how far it is for the interest of the plaintiff to have the whole maintenance raised. And, therefore, it is proper the court should know what is the real value of the estate. And, to that end, let the Master look into the value and report it and what is fit to be allowed for maintenance, and I reserve the further consideration until after the report.

If it comes out that it will turn to the infant's prejudice to sell or mortgage the term for raising her maintenance, I should think it would be best for the infant that no more should be raised than what is absolutely necessary for her maintenance and let the estate stand debtor to her for the remainder.

[Other reports of this case: Precedents in Chancery 503, 24 E.R. 226, 1 Peere Williams 488, 24 E.R. 485, 2 Eq. Cas. Abr. 642, 22 E.R. 538.]

---

1 Kent *MS.*

2 *Corbett v. Maidwell* (1709–1710), 1 Salkeld 159, 91 E.R. 147, also 3 Chancery Reports 190, 21 E.R. 764, 2 Vernon 640, 655, 23 E.R. 1019, 1027, 1 Eq. Cas. Abr. 337, 21 E.R. 1086.

313

Thorold v. Thorold

(Ch. 1718)

In this case, in the will in issue, it was the intent of the testator that the required release by the devisees referred only to the confirmation of his will and not to any debts he owed them otherwise.

Lincoln's Inn MS. Misc. 11, p. 104

18 November 1718.

Sir John Thorold, by a voluntary settlement in 1685, charged some lands with £1000 apiece to his three sisters payable at marriage and £60 a year maintenance in the meantime.

And having married [off] two of his sisters and paid their portions, he makes his will and gives his two married sisters £500 apiece and to the plaintiff £100 a year for her life upon condition that all his said sisters should execute such a release, confirmation, and assurance to the defendant, who was a remote relation and to whom he had devised his real estate, of all right, title, and interest to all his lands, tenements, and estate as the defendant or his counsel should reasonably desire.

The defendant refusing to pay the annuity given by the will unless the plaintiff would execute a release in the words of the will whereby she would have released the £1000 secured by the settlement and payable at her marriage, she brought her bill for her annuity.

Lord Chancellor [Lord Parker]: It seems to be plainly the intent of the testator that his sisters should confirm his will and not release any debt that he should owe them. And, therefore, I decree the plaintiff to execute a confirmation of the lands to the defendant, the devisee, according to the will with an exception or saving not to prejudice the security she has for her £1000.

Note there was a covenant in the settlement from Sir John Thorold to pay the portions and maintenance.

Lincoln's Inn MS. Misc. 384, p. 85, pl. 2

18 November.

Sir J. Thorold, in 1685, covenants to give his three sisters £1000 apiece on their marriage and £50 *per annum* in the meantime. Two of them marry, and their portions are paid. In 1712, Sir J., by his will, gives a legacy of £500 apiece to his two married sisters and £100 *per annum* for life to the plaintiff, his unmarried sister, provided, 'if my three sisters shall not execute such releases, confirmations, etc. of my real estate as counsel shall reasonably advise', then the legacies to be void. Then he gives his personal estate to his executors to pay his debts and the legacies on the before mentioned condition. And also, he gives the plaintiffs a reversion in fee.

The query is what release the plaintiffs must execute having these demands on the real estate under the settlement and the will.

Lord Chancellor [Lord Parker]: It is objected, if she does not release these demands, she releases nothing. But it is as good as the release of the other sisters, who are paid. If she releases her demands to the land, she may resort to the personal estate. The query is upon the testator's intent and whether the release required by the defendant, the heir, is reasonable. The defendant offers to except the reversion in fee out of the release because it is given the plaintiff by the same will, but it is also directed by the same will that his debts should be paid. Therefore, it is reasonable that they should be excepted. And the plaintiff's demands out of the real estate are certainly debts. The intent must be construed that the sisters should not give the heir any trouble but should confirm the will. Therefore, the plaintiff is to be relieved upon joining in a release only for the confirmation of the will, but it shall not prejudice her demands out of the real estate.

314

Lemon v. Lemon

(Ch. 1718–1719)

A devise of land to the testator's wife which is not expressly stated to be in lieu of her dower rights does not exclude her from claiming dower in his other land.

Lincoln's Inn MS. Misc. 11, p. 34, pl. 1

Michaelmas term 1718.

[It was] decreed that a devise of lands to the testator's wife for her life, it not being said to be in full or satisfaction of dower, did not exclude her from claiming her dower in other lands, which were devised to the heir at law.

In this case was cited the case of Lawrence and Lawrence,[1] which was said to be the very same with the present case, where it was first decreed by Lord Somers that the wife was barred of her dower but, upon a rehearing before Lord Keeper Wright, that decree was reversed. Afterwards, it came on before Lord Cowper, who would do nothing in it, but he advised the parties to appeal. Accordingly, they did so, and Lord Keeper Wright's decree was affirmed.

---

[1] *Lawrence v. Lawrence* (1699), 2 Vernon 365, 23 E.R. 829, 2 Freeman 234, 22 E.R. 1180, 3 Brown P.C. 483, 1 E.R. 1448, 1 Eq. Cas. Abr. 218, 21 E.R. 1002, 2 Eq. Cas. Abr. 386, 388, 22 E.R. 330, 331, *sub nom. Lawrence v. Dodwell*, 1 Lord Raymond 438, 91 E.R. 1190, 3 Lord Raymond 151, 92 E.R. 615, 1 Lutwyche 734, 125 E.R. 384.

Lincoln's Inn MS. Misc. 384, p. 80, pl. 3

14 November.

The defendant had £40 *per annum* for life devised to her by her husband, and the rest of his real estate was devised to the plaintiff. The defendant brings a writ of dower. The query is whether she is barred by this devise or can have both. Lawrence and Lawrence, by Lord Somers, [held] that she would not take both; [it was] reversed by Lord Keeper Wright, whose decree was affirmed in the House of Lords.

Lord Chancellor [Lord Parker]: This point is determined by the House of Lords. The bill must be dismissed with costs.

8 Viner, Abr. 366

Trinity 5 Geo.

J. Lemon devised lands to his wife for her life, and he devised other lands to the plaintiff, his brother, and his heirs. The defendant, the wife of the testator, entered into the lands devised to her, which were of more value than her dower, but not devised to her expressly in lieu and satisfaction of dower. And, afterwards, she brought [an action of] dower against the devisee of the other lands, and she recovered dower against him with costs, who, thereupon, brings his bill in this court to be relieved against the judgment, the lands devised to her by her husband being of greater value and she in possession of them.

The Case of Lawrence and Lawrence, in the House of Lords, was cited for the defendant, as a case in point that the wife shall have dower notwithstanding a devise to her for life of lands by her husband, unless declared to be in lieu and satisfaction of dower.

Lord Parker said this point is determined already by the House of Lords that there is no relief in this case in equity; therefore, the bill must be dismissed.

[Other copies of this report: 2 Eq. Cas. Abr. 353, 22 E.R. 300.]

315

Chaplin v. Horner

(Ch. 1718)

Where money was contracted to be laid out in a purchase of land and settled in fee and the obligor dies not having received the money and made the purchase, the heir of the obligor and not his executor shall have the money, but if the obligor received any of this money, this is a good payment, and it shall not be repaid.

Lincoln's Inn MS. Misc. 384, p. 49, pl. 1

18 November.

James Chaplin, on his marriage, covenants to lay out £2000 in land to be settled on himself in tail, remainder to his right heirs; £1300, part of it, was paid by the trustees to him. But before the rest was laid out, he dies. And the plaintiff is his heir. The query is whether the rest shall be taken as land or money. 1 Ch. Rep. 30.[1]

The Master of the Rolls [Jekyll]: The plaintiff, the heir, is entitled to have the rest laid out in land though it was in the ancestor's power to have it remain in money. Therefore, the payment to him by the trustees was good. But he has determined the rest should be turned into land for the benefit of his heir. It is a covenant indeed which he might have controlled, but he has not so done.

Vernon quoted Kettleby v. Atwood, where it was determined several ways, but the query being between the heir and administrator, it was at last decreed for the heir. Cann and Cann, in Lord Jefferys' time, and Legate v. Shewell, where a man covenanted to purchase and settle on himself in tail, yet the court would not compel him to lay the money out because he might presently suffer a recovery and turn the land into money again.[2]

N.B. The tenant in tail did happen to die before any recovery was suffered and the remainderman Shadwell still enjoys the estate under the decree. But in Dr. Shadwell's Case, *alias* Colwell and Colwell, Lord Cowper said precedents had gone too far on a will because the person who would be entitled under the settlement should have the chance that the tenant in tail might die before the recovery was suffered and should not be deprived of that contingency. Parker v. Stanley, 9 May 1715, same case, but the difference was where the dispute is with the party himself and when between his heir and executor, for, here, money covenanted to be laid out is looked upon as land and belongs to the heir.

Lincoln's Inn MS. Misc. 384, p. 64, pl. 2

18 November 1718.

By a marriage settlement, A. covenanted to lay out £2000, his wife's portion, in land with all convenient speed to be conveyed to him and his heirs. A. died intestate. The £2000 was not paid down, but, after, £1350 was paid to A. and £650 remained unpaid at his death. He left issue only a daughter, who brought a bill against the widow, who was administratrix.

His Honor [Jekyll] decreed what remained unpaid to be laid out in a purchase and settled accordingly but not the £1300, which had been paid in to the father.

---

1 *Ferrers v. Ferrers* (1628 x 1629), 1 Chancery Reports 30, 21 E.R. 498.

2 *Kettleby v. Atwood* (Ch. 1685–1687), 1 Vernon 298, 471, 23 E.R. 481, 596, 2 Chancery Reports 404, 21 E.R. 700, 1 Eq. Cas. Abr. 273, 21 E.R. 1041; *Cann v. Cann* (Ch. 1687), 1 Vernon 480, 23 E.R. 605; *Legat v. Shewell* (1706), 1 Peere Williams 87, 24 E.R. 306, 2 Vernon 551, 23 E.R. 957, Gilbert Rep. 141, 25 E.R. 99, 1 Eq. Cas. Abr. 394, 21 E.R. 1127, 2 Eq. Cas. Abr. 530, 22 E.R. 447.

[Other reports of this case: 1 Peere Williams 483, 24 E.R. 483, 2 Eq. Cas. Abr. 721, 22 E.R. 607.]

316

Bromfield v. Witherly

(Ch. 1718)

Where a solvent trustee invests the trust funds in stocks, the beneficiary does not receive any capital gains, but, if the trustee is insolvent, the beneficiary does because, if there were capital losses, the insolvent trustee could not reimburse the beneficiary.

Lincoln's Inn MS. Misc. 380, pt. 3, p. 231, pl. 2

19 November 1718.

A trustee puts out £1000 trust money in stock. The stock happens to rise to the value of £1100, and then he sells out.

It was decreed that the *cestui que trust* should have the improvement if it appears that the trustee is insolvent.

This I suppose must be understood where the trustee leaves enough to answer the trust and the improvement is not enough to satisfy all his creditors that, there, what is left in the first place be appropriated to the discharge of the trust and the improvement made by the trusted money, for, here, the trustee runs the risk of stock jobbing with other people's money and, therefore, the *cestui que trust* who stands to the peril ought to have the advantage, for though I suppose a case wherein there is enough left to answer the trust and not enough to pay debts, yet it may happen otherwise and there may not even enough be left to satisfy the trust. But where a trustee is able and rich, there is as much as the *cestui que trust* runs no hazard. If the stock sinks in value, the trustee must make satisfaction, the trustee shall also have the improvements where the stock rises. Where an executor or trustee puts out money to interest upon security, there the interest shall go to the *cestui que trust*. The reason is that in placing out money to interest, if a trustee takes due care about security, he runs little or no hazard. But in buying or selling stock, which is a sort of a gaming, it is otherwise.

Lincoln's Inn MS. Misc. 384, p. 85, pl. 1

19 November.

Mead, for the defendant, quoted Weedon v. Parslow, before the present Lord Chancellor, 27 June,[1] where a voluntary settlement was decreed to be not fraudulent against a subsequent bond creditor.

Vernon, for the plaintiff: It has formerly been held, if a trustee or executor had put out money at interest, if a loss had happened, he must have borne it; so

[1] *Parslow v. Weedon* (1718), see above, Case No. 261.

he should have the gain. But that has been since exploded, and the trustee must answer for what advantage he makes.

The Lord Chancellor [Lord Parker] sent it to a master to see what trust money came to the defendant's hands and to state any matter specially. If a trustee puts it out at interest, if he takes care of the security, he runs no hazard. But putting it into stocks is like gaming. Therefore, the plaintiff is entitled to the whole advantage. The trustee must only answer for the common interest, but, if he is insolvent, the stocks themselves are liable.

Precedents in Chancery 505, 24 E.R. 227

In this case, a difference was taken by My Lord Chancellor [Lord Parker], that, if an executor or trustee of money places it out in the funds or on other security, whereby he gains considerably, that he shall have the whole benefit thereof to himself in respect of the hazard he run of being a considerable loser thereby, which he must have borne, but, if such trustee or executor were an insolvent person at the time of placing out such trust money, there the *cestui que trust* shall have the whole benefit gained thereby, as he only could have borne the loss thereof if any had happened, the trustee or executor, by reason of his insolvency, being incapable thereof and, consequently, running no hazard at all.

[Other reports of this case: 1 Eq. Cas. Abr. 239, 398, 21 E.R. 1017, 1130.]

317

Wilson v. Fielding

(Ch. 1718)

Where a decedent's personal estate is insufficient to pay his creditors, the heir must refund any inheritance he received.

The personal assets of a decedent's estate, though only to be come at in equity, shall be applied as legal assets ought to be with respect to the debts as they stood at the death of the testator.

A court of equity will not to assist an executor to give a preference to one creditor of the decedent before another.

Lincoln's Inn MS. Misc. 384, p. 86, pl. 2

21 November 1718.

The plaintiff, being a simple contract creditor having got a judgment at law but the executors pleading want of assets, brings a bill to have a satisfaction of his whole debt out of equitable assets. The defendants, the executors, offer to pay him proportionally with the other creditors.

Vernon, for the defendants: All creditors are equal in conscience and, where there are only equitable assets, all must be paid equally. As equity will not take away the benefit of the law from a creditor, so it will never aid one creditor to defeat another. A creditor by specialty may take his satisfaction out of the personal assets at his election and shall not be hindered by this court. And in that case, a creditor on a simple contract shall stand in his place to affect the real assets. But this court has never gone farther.

Sir Thomas Powys, for the plaintiff: Where creditors have no lien upon the land and a man creates a trust for payment of debts, all must be paid equally. But it is otherwise where I have a lien by a judgment precedent; he who gets judgment has, both in law and equity, a preference of inferior creditors on all assets. Here, the executor has paid away all the personal assets to the simple contract creditors, to whom he confessed judgments. The defendants, the mortgagees, coming into a sale, the surplus is paid to the heir and so is equitable assets. The mortgagees having a bond, the executors confess judgment on that bond and pay off half the mortgage in favor of the heir out of the personal assets.

Vernon: There is no precedent where there are only equitable assets that any preference has been given to one creditor against another. The court would even go out of the way to do equal justice.

Lord Chancellor [Lord Parker]: I think that this is not within the common rule. I am not satisfied with the rule that all equitable assets shall go equally. It is so where anything of bounty is given, but not where there is an equal right, for, where equitable assets or a trust is in the executors, it is to go in the course of administration, it being personal assets. Though they cannot be come at by law, executors may confess judgment to whom they will. If, in the life of the testator, there had been one creditor superior to another, he shall have the preference by law. (It should not be put in the power of the executor by the aid of equity to pay which creditor he pleases and to defeat the rest, but all should be equal.)

If, in this case, the heir at law is to refund to the executor, the creditors shall be paid proportionally. If a man devises his real estate for payment of his debts as to those who have a lien on the land, it shall go according to law. But, as to the other creditors, it must go equally.

N.B. The Lord Chancellor seems to make a difference in equitable assets, *viz.* between such as are merely equitable and such as would be assets at law but cannot be come at without the assistance of a court of equity.

Lincoln's Inn MS. Hill 73, p. 67

21 November 1718.

Equitable assets [are] not to go equally to the creditors. Where indeed lands are given to pay debts, all debts are then equal. If there were assets in trust for the testator, they are personal assets (as if a man has an Exchequer note taken in trust) and liable to the creditors, and it is not the testator's putting them in trust that shall defeat their having a satisfaction of their debts.

The plaintiff in this case was a creditor of an equal degree at the time of the testator's death but had got judgment against the executor.

But the Lord Chancellor [Lord Parker] said that, if this judgment was to have the preference, it is really decreeing that the executor (and so in all cases) may pay which creditor he pleases, which consequence would be very fatal.

It is a constant rule in equity that, where debts that bind the real estate are paid out of the personal estate, the heir is obliged to refund so much as those debts have exhausted out of the personal or so much as is wanting to satisfy the debts of a lower nature. But where the heir at law is decreed to refund, My Lord [Parker] said it was certainly right in equity to have it distributed among the several creditors and not to have any creditor run away with the whole assets. And so he decreed that an account should be taken of the debts of the several creditors and the money to be distributed among them.

Lincoln's Inn MS. Misc. 380, pt. 3, p. 232

The testator mortgaged his land for such a sum of money and gave a bond for the performance of covenants comprised in the mortgage deed and dies indebted to several persons by simple contract. The mortgagee gets a judgment upon this bond, and the executor pays a great part of this judgment out of the personal estate, by which means the assets proved insufficient to discharge the debts by simple contract.

A bill was, therefore, brought by the creditors against the heir to oblige him to refund out of what he had been eased in respect to the land descended to him by a discharge of the great part of the mortgage debt out of the personal estate as far as was necessary for the discharge of debts.

And it was decreed that he should refund.

After the death of the testator, one of the creditors by simple contract had by a suit at [common] law against the executor turned his simple contract debt into a judgment debt. And the question was whether this money so decreed to be refunded for the benefit of all the creditors equally or for the advantage in the first place of him that had turned his debt into a judgment debt. The executor and the rest of the creditors had offered this judgment creditor to be paid in equal proportion with the rest. But he refused it, insisting upon his judgment.

In behalf of the rest of the creditors, it was urged that debts by simple contract are in justice and conscience as much debts as debts by bond or judgment. Therefore, according to the rules of equity, if he that will have equity must do equity, if a judgment creditor stands in need of the assistance of this court to make the assets which at law would be no assets, the court will never give him this assistance unless he will consent to come in equally with the rest of the creditors who in conscience and equity have as just demands as himself. Thus, if a man subjects his land by will to the payment of debts, the Court of Chancery always decrees without distinguishing what the nature of the debts are, whether simple contract, bond, or judgment debts, shall be paid in equal proportion out of his land thus subjected by will to the payment of debts.

It was insisted by the counsel of the other side that nothing was more common than for bills to be brought by creditors for the discovery of assets, that, if it should happen in this case that bonds taken in trust for the testator should be discovered, it was never yet heard of that a creditor should be told in this court these bonds are assets in equity and now shall not have the assistance of this court to make them assets at law unless you will quit the advantage the law gives you, leave the superiority of your debt, and be content to stand upon the level with the rest of the creditors.

Lord Chancellor PARKER: The doctrine that seems to be laid down by the counsel for the creditors that there is this standing difference between assets in law and assets in equity, that though the former shall go according to the course of administration prescribed by the law, that yet the latter shall without any regard to this go among all the creditors equally however different the nature of their debts are is a doctrine without any reason or foundation and would establish a rule in equity directly contrary to the known rules of law as to the order in which debts are to be paid.

Indeed, as to the case put of lands devised by the testator to be sold for the payment of debts, it is so, and this court does always direct the profit arising from the sale equally among all the creditors. But then this land may be considered as a gift of the testator among all his creditors. As to the testator, the donor has not thought fit to make any distinction between his creditors; so this court, which is in the nature of a trustee for the testator, will make none either.

But, generally, there is no difference [between] assets in law and assets in equity, but both must be distributed by the executor in a course of administration. Had, therefore, this judgment creditor been in possession of his judgment at the time of the death of the testator, I would not have taken the benefit of his judgment from him, but would have decreed the refunding for his benefit in the first place. But this is not the case. This judgment is obtained against the executor and whether voluntarily does not appear. And it will be impossible for me to distinguish; it is enough that it may be a voluntary [judgment] confessed by the executor, who has it, by this means, in his power to give a preference to a simple contract creditor at any time to a bond creditor and so, in reality, overturn the course of administration. And though this, at law, may be done, and, had payment, therefore, been made to this judgment creditor, there had been no remedy. Yet a court of equity shall never be assisting to the enabling of an executor to the doing of it.

The money was, therefore, decreed to be refunded for the equal benefit of all the creditors.

Lincoln's Inn MS. Misc. 11, p. 73

21 November 1718.

Wilson, being a creditor by simple contract of the defendant's husband, brings an action against the defendant for his debt. There were several other creditors by simple contract and likewise a creditor by a mortgage. The assets being insufficient, all the creditors by simple contract except the plaintiff agree to take the assets in average. The mortgagee brings his action against the defendant on the bond for performance of the covenants and recovers judgment thereon, and then the defendant pleads this judgment to the plaintiff's action and that she had not assets *ultra*. Upon that, the plaintiff takes a judgment *quando* assets *acciderint*.

The defendant pays over all the assets to the mortgagee in satisfaction of his bond. Afterwards, the estate is sold, and the plaintiff now brings his bill that he may stand in the room of the mortgagee and be paid out of the money for which the real estate had been sold and which was now remaining in the hands of the heir.

The heir admits that the estate was sold and that he has the money in his hands. And he submits to pay so much as the mortgagee received out of the personal assets in satisfaction of the mortgage.

The other creditors also bring a bill that, pursuant to the agreement, the assets may be distributed equally.

It was insisted on for the defendant, the executor, and the plaintiffs, the creditors in the other cause, that this money was only equitable assets and under the disposition of the court and, if so, the most equitable way of disposing them is to dispose them equally among all the creditors.

The plaintiff has no remedy at law. His judgment is only *quando* assets *acciderint*, which must be understood legal assets.

Sir Thomas Powys, for the plaintiff in the first cause: We are no party to the creditors' bill. We come singly against the executor and the mortgagee and, having a judgment at law, are proper to have a satisfaction out of assets, though equitable only. The plaintiff, having a judgment, though for a simple contract debt, has by that means a preference before other creditors who have not judgments, and, therefore, he has a right to be paid out of everything that belonged to the testator, whether legal or equitable.

Lord Chancellor [Lord Parker]: As to the rule that equitable assets shall be applied to pay all debts equally, I am not satisfied in that. Suppose a man has an Exchequer annuity in another person's name or anything of that nature. Shall the creditors say that this ought to be applied equally? No, surely. Whatever is personal assets, though only to be come at in equity, shall be applied as legal assets ought to be with respect to the debts as they stood at the death of the testator. But, if a creditor, after the death of the testator gets a judgment against the executor, whether by the consent of the executor or otherwise, it matters not, for the court cannot distinguish. And such a judgment creditor comes here for a satisfaction out of assets which are only made assets by a rule of equity. This court ought not to be assisting to the executor to give a preference to one creditor before another but ought to divide these assets equally between the plaintiff and the other simple contract creditors who have brought their bill for that purpose.

And, though the plaintiff is no party to the creditors' bill and so that bill is not properly a cross-bill, yet that bill coming on to be heard at the same time, one entire decree may be made in both causes.

And, therefore, he decreed the money in the hands of the heir to be divided equally between the plaintiff and the other creditors.

2 Vernon 763, 23 E.R. 1098

The executrix applies part of the personal assets in paying off a mortgage. The plaintiff Wilson, who was a creditor by simple contract, brings his action against the executrix, who pleaded *plene administravit*, and he takes a judgment against the executrix to be satisfied out of assets *quando acciderint*. And now he brought his bill against the heir to compel him to refund so much of the personal assets as had been applied to pay off the mortgage.

And *Hillersden* and others [said] the plaintiffs in the other cause, being likewise creditors by simple contract, brought their bill to compel the heir to refund and to be paid their debts.

And the question was whether Wilson, by virtue of his judgment, was to be preferred to the other creditors in point of payment.

[It was] adjudged that the plaintiff Wilson being only relievable in equity, all the creditors should be paid in proportion, for the judgment could not avail him at law, no assets coming afterwards to the hands of the executors. But, if there had been personal assets, as a lease for years, a bond, or the grant of an annuity in a trustee's name, then, although a creditor could not come at it without the aid of a court of equity, yet the assets should be applied in a due course of administration. But, in this case, the compelling the heir to refund is a matter purely in equity and a raising of assets where there were none at law.

[Other reports of this case: 10 Modern 426, 88 E.R. 792, 1 Eq. Cas. Abr. 143, 21 E.R. 944.]

318

Anonymous

(Ch. 1718)

Where a surety agrees to be liable for a lesser sum than the principal debtor's debt, he is liable to pay what remains unpaid up to that agreed sum.

Lincoln's Inn MS. Hill 73, p. 69, pl. 1

Lord Chancellor [LORD PARKER]: Where a man gives a bond for payment of £100, part of a sum of money secured by another security, the meaning of that bond must be not that, if the parties who are bound by the first security do not pay £100, that then the second security will pay £100, but that, if the first security does not pay the whole, that then the second security will pay the rest so far as £100 will go.

319

Note

(Ch. 1718)

A devise or gift of household goods includes plate regularly used in the family.

Lincoln's Inn MS. Hill 73, p. 69, pl. 2

N.B. Plate that is used constantly in the family will pass by the name of household goods.

320

East India Company v. Winder

(Ch. 1718)

Where a plea is too broad, it must be totally overruled.

An infant must make discovery of other person's actions, though not his own so as to subject himself to penalties.

An infant's contracts that are for his benefit are valid; where he has received a consideration, his contracts are only voidable.

Lincoln's Inn MS. Misc. 384, p. 89

21 November 1718; at Serjeants' Inn Hall.

[There was a] bill and plea the same with East India Company against Atkins,[1] but the defendant, in his answer, says he is ready to prove that, at the time of his signing the covenant to discover and at the putting in of his plea, he was an infant. He was a bookkeeper and had a salary. [It was] insisted, first, the matter of infancy should have been set out in the plea, second, notwithstanding infancy, the defendant is bound to discover.

Vernon, for the defendant: First, the plea is put in by a guardian and it is proper to insist on infancy by answer rather than by plea, as it is proper to deny notice by answer.

Objection: The plea covers too much; therefore, it must be overruled.

Answer: Not so. It may be good for part and overruled for the rest, as if a plea insists he is a purchaser of Black Acre and White Acre and, as to Black Acre, denies notice, it is good, but, as to White Acre, does not deny notice, it is bad, though a demurrer must be vicious throughout and cannot be good for part.

---

[1] *East India Co. v. Atkins* (1718), see above, Case No. 289.

Curia [Lord Parker]: Pleading to screen what would overthrow the plea if discovered is too large. Where a plea is too large, it must be totally overruled. It is stronger than a demurrer, for a plea is one, a demurrer is several in its nature. An infant must discover other men's actions though not his own so as to subject himself to penalties. The laws of nature give a man a right to know what concerns his own interest. And where it tends to justice and no positive law interposes, a man's voluntary covenant gives another a right over him. An infant's covenants for his benefit are good; where he has a *quid pro quo*, they are only voidable. By the rules of common honesty, a capable infant may answer mismanagement.

He overruled the plea but so as the defendant may not answer what will subject him to penalties.

Vernon: If a bill be brought against a person not concerned in interest, he may demur for that the plaintiff might examine him as a witness and that his answer is not evidence.

321

Worsley v. Merrick

(Ch. 1718)

In this case, the beneficiary of a trust of land had satisfied the condition of the gift so as to be the beneficial owner of the land held in trust for him.

Lincoln's Inn MS. Misc. 11, p. 75

22 November 1718.

Sir William Merrick, the defendant's grandfather, by will, gives to the defendant £5000 to be paid at twenty-one, and he directs his trustees, out of the interest, to allow him such maintenance as they think fit. The trustees not acting, the defendant's father, who was executor, took on him the management of the testator's estate and educated his son at Eton School. And, when he was grown up, he bought chambers in the New Square in Lincoln's Inn for him and took the lease in the son's name.

The son continued some time in the chambers, but, having a mind to go into the Army, the son and father came to an agreement to lay out part of the £5000 in buying a commission, which was done. After this, the father contracts to sell the chambers to the defendant Dodson for £600. And it was agreed between them that a new lease should be taken in the son's name for the life of the defendant Dodson and another person to be nominated by Dodson. And the father agreed the son should assign the lease to Dodson. The lease was accordingly executed by the proprietors of the ground to the defendant Merrick, and his father sent to him to execute an assignment to Dodson. But, before such assignment was made, the father died, having made his will and disinherited the defendant, who was his only son and given all the surplus of his personal estate to his daughter, who is since married to the plaintiff, and he made her executrix.

The question was whether the money to be paid for the chambers belonged to the executrix of the father or should be paid to the son.

On 22 February 1717[/18], the cause was heard at the Rolls. [It was] declared the chambers appear to have been purchased by the father in his son's name and to have been declared by him to be for the use and benefit of the son, whereby they became the property of the son, and that he is entitled thereto in law and equity.

From this decree, the plaintiff appealed. And, as to the chambers, it was insisted on for the plaintiff that they were bought with the father's own money whereby there did by operation of law arise or result to him a trust of what was purchased in the name of the defendant and there was no declaration, grant, or assignment in writing by the father in his lifetime or by his will of any trust in the chambers for the benefit of the son, as by the Statute of Frauds[1] is required. Nor did it appear by any evidence that the father intended the son should have any benefit of the chambers but in case he applied himself to the study of the law. But it appears by proofs that the defendant rejected his father's design and, afterwards, agreed to assign the chambers as his father should desire.

Lord Chancellor [Lord Parker]: When the father purchased the chambers, it must be supposed that his intention was that his son should study the law. Now, if the son immediately after this refuses to study the law, it would be too hard to say that he shall have the property in the chambers, as in the case which Mr. *Vernon* put, that, if a man intends to send his son beyond the sea and buys a cargo of goods and puts them on shipboard in the son's name and the son refuses to go to sea; surely, the son shall not have the goods in this case.

But now, in the case before us, the son had been for some time in the possession of the chambers and had studied the law. But, when he was twenty-four, he had a mind to leave the profession of the law and go into the Army. I think he had so far performed the condition precedent upon which the chambers were given him as to give him a property in the chambers. And, therefore, as to them, the decree must be confirmed.

---

[1] Stat. 29 Car. II, c. 3 (*SR*, V, 839–842).

322

Truelock v. Truelock

(Ch. 1718)

A London orphan can be estopped by his own acts to claim his orphanage share of his father's estate.

Lincoln's Inn MS. Misc. 11, p. 34, pl. 2

24 November 1718.

The plaintiff's father, being a freeman of London, makes his will and gives part of his real estate to the plaintiff and the other part to the defendants, his younger sons, after the death of his wife. And he gives £300 apiece to his two daughters to be paid at marriage and £200 apiece more if his executors thought fit. And he gives the profits of his trade to his executors to pay his debts or raise portions. And he gives the surplus to the defendants, and he makes his wife and the plaintiff, his eldest son, executors, and they prove the will.

Two years after the testator's death, the two daughters marry. And, previous to such marriages, articles are entered into, reciting the will and that the portions were £500. And, thereby, it is agreed that part of the portions should be paid down and the residue at a certain time afterwards and that, upon payment thereof, the daughters and their husbands shall execute releases to the plaintiff and his mother of all claims to the testator's personal estate, either by virtue of his will or the custom of London or otherwise.

The portions are afterwards paid, and releases are executed accordingly.

The plaintiff and his mother frequently declare their acquiescence under the will and press and importune the younger children so to do. And, during all the mother's lifetime, it was understood by them all that the custom should be waived and the estate distributed according to the will.

The mother and all the children lived together in the testator's house for several years after his death, and the trade, for four years, was carried on in the mother's name by the two younger sons, who were apprentices to the father. And, at the end of the four years, the mother, in consideration of £1000, delivers up the trade to the two younger sons, and, when one of the younger sons married, she and the plaintiff quitted the house and left him and the other brother in possession thereof and of the stock in trade. And the plaintiff, who was privy to the agreement for delivering up the house by the mother, never contradicted it, nor did he during all the mother's life, who lived nine years after her husband's death; [he] never claimed any right to the trade or to any share of the personal estate by the custom.

The mother, before her death, made her will and, thereby, distributed her plate and household goods amongst her children pursuant to a power given her so to do by the testator's will. But she made no disposition of the surplus of her estate nor named any executor. And, after death, the plaintiff took administration *cum testamento annexo* and, two years after her death, brings his bill for an orphanage share of his father's personal estate and for his mother's customary share thereof, as he was her representative, or, if he had done any act to exclude him from claiming by the custom, that he might have an account of the ten years profits of the trade after the death of the testator.

Master of the Rolls [JEKYLL]: A bare acquiescence under the will or some declarations of a child after his father's death that he will not insist on the custom where nothing is given him by the will I do not think is sufficient to bar him of his customary share. But, in the present case, there are words accompanied with facts and facts that are inconsistent with claiming by virtue of the custom. The plaintiff has not only declared all along that he would acquiesce under the will, but he has joined in the probate of that will and carried it on to an execution. And, therefore, I think he is not entitled to claim anything by the custom.

As to the profits, I am of opinion that the devise of the profits for ten years to pay debts or raise portions was not an absolute bequest of the profits of the trade for ten years but only until sufficient [money] was raised thereout to pay the debts and the daughters' portions, though the devise was to the executors, and that, after the debts and portions be paid, the trade would belong to the younger sons as residuary legatees. And, for this, he cited the Case of Sir John Packington and Austen,[1] where a devise was of an annuity of £200 a year to the wife towards payment of the testator's debts, it was decreed that, after payment of the debts, the annuity should cease though the devise was to the wife.

And, as to any account of the profits of the trade in respect of the debts and portions, it being proved that the plaintiff was privy to the mother's giving up the trade to her younger sons and acquiescing under it, the plaintiff's bill was dismissed as to both his demands.

[1] *Packington v. Wyche* (1707–1712), Eq. Cases Exch. 619, order of 9 December 1707: Public Record Office, E.126/18, f. 681; order of 30 May 1709: Public Record Office, E.126/19, f. 153, 3 Brown P.C. 44, 1 E.R. 1166, 2 Eq. Cas. Abr. 507, 744, 22 E.R. 429, 632, Lords' Journal, vol. 19, p. 448, Lincoln's Inn MS. Misc. 503, p. 281.

323
Sorrell v. Clark

(Ch. 1718)

Where a creditor of an inferior nature by fraud gains an undue preference from an executor, the court will relieve against it.

Lincoln's Inn MS. Misc. 384, p. 90

24 November; at the Rolls.

[There was a] bill by a judgment creditor against the defendant Clark, as executrix of her husband, and Nichols, a bond creditor, to compel him to refund, suggesting a fraud to defeat the plaintiff and that Nichols had notice of the plaintiff's judgment and the executrix is insolvent.

Vernon, for the defendant: As against the executrix, they are proper for an account but not against Nichols, the creditor. If a simple contract creditor recovers or is voluntarily paid his debt by an executor, though he had notice of superior debts, he was never compelled to refund either in law or equity, but it is otherwise in the case of legatees. Ven. 358, 360.[1]

Master of the Rolls [Jekyll]: Nothing wants more the help of the legislature than the case of executors, the law being very hard upon them in some cases and, in others, giving them too great power in the administration of assets. If a creditor of an inferior nature by fraud gains an undue preference from the executor, I should relieve against it. [It is] like the case of Johnston of Cow Lane, who, having a lease, placed it over into the hands of an insolvent person. Here was relief, though none at law. I think a voluntary payment by an executor is different from being compelled by the creditor's recovering. Why may not a creditor be compelled to refund as well as one legatee to another to make an equality? It is on the same reason. Here, the defendant Nichols, the bond creditor, knew the state of the assets. [There was] no proof that he had notice of the plaintiff's judgment. If there were such proof, I would relieve the plaintiff.

Vernon: This was never attempted to make a creditor refund in this court. Here is no proof of fraud. There is no difference whether a creditor is voluntarily paid or recovers his debt. If a judgment by confession is good payment to avoid that charge, it is good likewise as to the creditor though the executor is liable to a *devastavit*.

1 *Noel v. Robinson* (1682), 2 Ventris 358, 86 E.R. 484, also 1 Vernon 90, 543, 460, 469, 23 E.R. 334, 580, 585, 594, 2 Chancery Reports 248, 21 E.R. 670, 2 Chancery Cases 145, 22 E.R. 887, 1 Eq. Cas. Abr. 299, 21 E.R. 1059; *Hodges v. Waddington* (1683), 2 Ventris 360, 86 E.R. 485, also 2 Chancery Cases 9, 22 E.R. 821, 1 Eq. Cas. Abr. 236, 21 E.R. 1015.

Master of the Rolls [Jekyll]: I would relieve the plaintiff if I could. If there were proof of notice of the plaintiff's judgment, the defendant's knowing likewise the quantum of the assets, I would decree for the plaintiff. The bill must be dismissed but without costs.

324

Rex v. Hare

(Ch. 1718)

A minor error in a sheriff's return of a writ will not result in an abatement.

Lincoln's Inn MS. Misc. 384, p. 91, pl. 1

25 November.

Bootle, on a demurrer to a plea in abatement to a *scire facias*, recites letters patent supposed to be void. The writ is returned *in comitatu ubicumque fuerit in Anglia* omitted. It is the constant form of the Register [for] *scire facias*es and *certioraris* from Edward III to this time; [there are] but two or three instances of the contrary. Register, 150, 69, 208; 8 Rep., the Prince's Case; Plowden, Sand.[1] are *ubicumque fuerit* without an 'etc.' though Queen and Bude, Hilary 9 Ann., on a *scire facias* returned *ubicumque fuerit in Magna Britannia*, the writ [was] quashed. The execution was that it ought to be *ubicumque fuerit in Anglia*. Some writs returned *in Anglia* [are] not sufficient to alter the course of the court. So in Liverpool [and] Bendley, the same with this returned.

Curia [Lord Parker] overruled the plea.

[Other reports of this case: 1 Strange 146, 266, 93 E.R. 439, 513.]

325

Cart v. Rees

(Ch. 1718)

A husband is entitled to the administration of his deceased wife's estate.

Lincoln's Inn MS. Misc. 384, p. 91, pl. 2

27 November.

The defendant is executor of his brother, J. Rees, whose wife was executrix and residuary legatee of A. The husband dies without taking out an administration to his wife. The plaintiff, as mother and next of kin to the wife, takes out

[1] *Registrum Brevium*; *The Prince's Case* (1606), 8 Coke Rep. 1, 77 E.R. 481; *Regina v. Earl of Northumberland* (1568), 1 Plowden 310, 75 E.R. 472.

administration to her and brings a bill against the representative of the husband for an account of the wife's estate.

Vernon, for the defendant: If there were choses in action of the wife and they are recovered by her representative, it is in trust for the husband.

Mead: This is a trustee's calling the *cestui que trust* to account.

Chancellor [LORD PARKER]: By the Statute of Distributions,[1] the husband is entitled though he does not take out administration to the wife, and whoever takes out administration is but a trustee for him.

The bill was dismissed.

326

Turton v. Benson

(Ch. 1718–1719)

Marriage brokage bonds are unenforceable.

Assignees of a bond take it subject to all of the personal defenses against the assignor.

A fraudulent bond is not enforceable.

Lincoln's Inn MS. Misc. 384, p. 50

1 December 1718.

A bill is [exhibited] to be relieved against a bond for the payment of £1000 to Benson in seven years after the plaintiff's marriage with Benson's daughter. Before the marriage, there was a settlement made by the plaintiff of £300 *per annum* in consideration of £3000 mentioned to be the lady's fortune. To enable the plaintiff to make this settlement, the plaintiff's mother surrenders her jointure and swears she would not have so done had she known the lady's fortune was not so much. Benson dies, and the defendant is the administrator. His creditors have this bond assigned to them amongst the rest of his effects, there not being assets. And they bring a cross-bill against Turton to have a satisfaction of this bond.

The questions are two, first, whether the plaintiff, being a party to the fraud, can be relieved; second, whether the bond's being assigned to the creditors will alter the case.

As to the first point, that these bonds obtained when the young person's affections are engaged and the marriage was ready to be consummated are always set aside as fraudulent were quoted Kemp v. Coleman, 1 Salk. 156; Duke of Hamilton v. Lord Mohun, 158, when Lord Cowper compared it to marriage brokage bonds.[2]

---

[1] Stat. 22 & 23 Car. II, c. 10 (*SR*, V, 791–720).

[2] *Kemp v. Coleman* (1707), 1 Salkeld 156, 91 E.R. 144, also 1 Eq. Cas. Abr. 88, 21 E.R. 900; *Duke of Hamilton v. Lord Mohun* (1710), 1 Salkeld 158, 91 E.R. 147, also 1

Vernon, for the plaintiff: Bonds and covenants to re-convey or to pay back part of the consideration money have always been set aside in this court.

Master of the Rolls [JEKYLL]: The only difference here is that the party himself to the fraud comes to be relieved against it. And this is principally a fraud upon the mother. If a man makes a fraudulent conveyance, it is good against himself and his heirs.

2 December.

If the assignment of this bond to the creditors, though without the plaintiff's privity, carried the legal interest, a court of equity would not take the law from them, but it carries only an equitable interest.

Powys, for the defendant: The first case on marriage brokage bonds was Sir J. Keen, *alias* Hale and Potter, in Show. Ca. Parl. 76.[1] The next was Sir Nicholas Butler and Chaney, but there was a fraud upon the father, who made the settlement, and he came to be relieved and not the party to the fraud.

Vernon, in reply: We have had much stronger cases in this court. Bacon v. Bladwell, in May 1684, before Lord Jeffreys,[2] where the plaintiff covenanted to re-demise lands at £120 *per annum*, which were agreed by the marriage articles to be £200, yet the defendant was decreed to account at £200. Redman v. Redman, December 1685,[3] the husband being in debt, the wife's father would not agree to the match until he was clear; the wife herself proposed to the husband's brother to pay off the debts to the husband to give him a counter-bond, which was set aside. Gale v. Ludlow, 28 November 1687,[4] where the wife borrowed money to appear [to have] a greater fortune; the person who lent the money lost it as a party to the fraud. Lamby v. Hamond, Michaelmas 1704, reheard 24 May 1705,[5] where the husband having a leasehold estate and his mother, on his marriage, surrendering her jointure, he privately assigns this leasehold estate to her and gives her a bond as a consideration for the surrender, yet it being a fraud against the wife and her relations, they were both set aside. This is within the same reason as marriage brokage bonds. And the party only who is aggrieved can come to set it aside.

As to the second point, the assignment of the bond to creditors cannot alter the case, though it might if the plaintiff had agreed to the assignment. They have not parted with anything to purchase this bond [so] that they stand in the

---

Peere Williams 118, 24 E.R. 319, 2 Vernon 652, 23 E.R. 1025, 1 Eq. Cas. Abr. 90, 21 E.R. 901, 2 Eq. Cas. Abr. 386, 22 E.R. 330.

1 *Hall v. Potter* (1695), Shower P.C. 76, 1 E.R. 52, also 1 Eq. Cas. Abr. 89, 21 E.R. 900.

2 *Peyton v. Bladwell* (1684), 1 Vernon 240, 23 E.R. 440.

3 *Redman v. Redman* (1685), 1 Vernon 348, 23 E.R. 514.

4 *Gale v. Lindo* (1687), 1 Vernon 475, 23 E.R. 601, also 1 Eq. Cas. Abr. 88, 21 E.R. 900.

5 *Lamlee v. Hanman* (1704–1705), 2 Vernon 466, 499, 23 E.R. 900, 920.

same place with the party himself. That was the case of Hanakenius v. Richmond and Bosviler v. Brandon,[1] where assignees could not be in a better case than the bankrupt.

Mead quoted Goldsmith v. Bruning,[2] by the late Master of the Rolls, where the defendant having married a servant who had been serviceable in promoting the plaintiff's match, the plaintiff gave her a note for £100 and after[wards] voluntarily paid her £50 in part; yet the defendant was decreed to refund, though he swore in his answer he should not have married his wife but upon the credit of this note.

The Master of the Rolls [Jekyll]: As to the second point, I am of opinion that the assignment of this bond to Benson's creditors does not make any difference in this case. So the only question is whether the plaintiff ought to be relieved against the representative of the person guilty of the fraud. This bond was first assigned with the rest of Benson's effects to Sir Theodore Janson,[3] who was his principal creditor, for the equal benefit of all the creditors. He has now assigned it over to Mrs. Richardson, the plaintiff in the cross-cause.

Curia. If Sir Theodore Jansen could have any benefit by this bond, his assignee would stand in his place. But he took this security only as it could be assigned to him and had but an equitable interest, the legal interest of a bond not being assignable. A man cannot have the money when it is not payable in equity. If a bond be satisfied by a collateral security and another has it assigned to him, it cannot be set up again. It imports the assignee of a bond to enquire of the obligor whether it is satisfied or not, which if he neglects to do, he is guilty of a laches. Here, the plaintiff in the cross-cause can be in no better case than Sir Theodore Janson unless the plaintiff Turton has authenticated the assignment. If it were not part of Benson's assets when the benefit of it was not nor could be assigned to his creditors, that which makes the only difficulty is the deposition[4] of Dor[othy] Jones, who says that the plaintiff offered, if the creditors would abate £400, he would pay off the bond, but they would not agree to this proposal. And the Lord Cowper used to say, if the parties will not accept of the terms of peace when offered, they shall never take advantage of the other's good nature because it was made upon the condition of being then accepted. But it is proved the plaintiff promised Mrs. Richardson that, if the bond was assigned to her, he would not endeavor to avoid it. Now here, the assignment was not proposed to be for Richardson's benefit only, but of all the creditors equally. And the plaintiff's promise

---

1 *Bosvil v. Brander* (1718), 1 Peere Williams 458, 24 E.R. 470, 2 Eq. Cas. Abr. 113, 146, 22 E.R. 96, 125.

2 *Goldsmith v. Bruning* (1700), 1 Eq. Cas. Abr. 89, 21 E.R. 901, *sub nom. Smith v. Bruning*, 2 Vernon 392, 23 E.R. 852.

3 E. Veale, 'Janssen, Sir Theodore, first baronet (c. 1658–1748)', *Oxford Dictionary of National Biography*, vol. 29, pp. 785–786.

4 disposition *MS.*

must be understood to be personal to her alone. This is a *nudum pactum* and is voluntary. And a man cannot talk away his debts in equity any more than he can at law. She should have then bound the plaintiff by some solemn act, which she has not done. It is proved that the plaintiff intended to bring a bill against Benson himself and gave instructions to counsel to prepare it. But that proceeding was prevented by his death.

Therefore, I must consider it upon the first cause only, which is against the proper representative of the person guilty of the fraud. I am very glad so many cases have been cited to warrant my opinion, for I did not remember my case where there had been relief for the party himself who was privy to the fraud. And those cases are very strong, for it was not the parties who settled that were relieved in those cases, though they may certainly be relieved when any such case happens because the terms proposed are the conditions of the settlement. The reason why the parents have not come hither is because the parties themselves may have relief here. The great objection is that the plaintiff is a party to the fraud. But here it is upon the level with the other party, for he was not in a state of freedom, his affections being engaged and settled irrevocably and the marriage almost consummated. A guardian or other person concerned in the marriage may not take advantage of brokage contracts.

As to the evidence of the fraud, it is plain. The mother had a right to know the terms and she swears she would not have parted with her jointure if the fortune were not £3000 and the deed produced to her to execute recites it so to be, which is a *suggestio falsi*, though the very consideration of her enabling her son to make this settlement and Mulsoe, who drew the deed, took it to be so. The plaintiff must be looked upon as an innocent and not the master of himself and must be relieved and the bond be delivered up, and the creditors' bill must be dismissed.

Lincoln's Inn MS. Misc. 11, p. 77

Hilary 1718[/19]. Turton v. Katherine Benson, widow and administratrix of John Benson; and the creditors of John Benson v. Mr. Turton and Katherine Benson.

The case was that the plaintiff married the daughter of John Benson and enters into articles dated 29 June 1710 made before the marriage whereby, in consideration of a £3000 portion, which he thereby acknowledges to have received, he agrees to settle £300 a year for the jointure of the wife and afterwards for the issue male of the marriage. And, by a bond bearing date with the articles, Turton becomes bound to John Benson to pay him £1000 without interest in seven years.

John Benson dies in January 1714[/15], having about a year before entered into a bond to Sir Theodore Jansen for the payment of £1000 with interest, in which bond John Benson's son was also bound. And, for the better securing of this £2000,[1] John Benson, by an assignment bearing even date with the bond to Sir Theodore Jansen, assigns over the plaintiff Turton's bond to him.

John Benson died insolvent and, in March following, the creditors enter into articles with Mrs. Benson, the administratrix, that her husband's place of Secondary of the Wood Street Counter should be sold and that £3000 of the money arising by such sale and the effects mentioned in a schedule, of which Turton's bond was a part, should be distributed equally.

It was insisted on for the plaintiff that the mother was a party to the articles, that she was made to believe that her son was to have £3000, and, upon that inducement, it was that she must be presumed to come into an agreement to release her jointure.

On the other hand, it was insisted for the creditors that this agreement was made with Turton himself, who was of age and a barrister at law, that if it was a fraud upon the mother, it was a fraud put on her by the son and not Mr. Benson. However, if this is such a case wherein Mr. Turton could have been relieved against Mr. Benson if he had been living, yet the case is different in respect of the creditors, who now stand in the room of Sir Theodore Jansen, for this bond having been assigned to him as a collateral security for securing a debt owing him on a bond from John Benson, and Sir Theodore having been paid his whole debt out of the assets of John Benson, they now stand in his place and are entitled to the same equity as he would have had against the plaintiff Turton, who it was insisted could not have been relieved against Sir Theodore Jansen.

Mr. *Vernon*, for the plaintiff, cited the following cases.

Peyton and Gladwell, in Jeffreys's time;[2] Bradwell agreed to settle lands for a jointure on the plaintiff and to settle other lands on the plaintiff's husband and his heirs. The husband agreed to re-demise part of the jointure and to release the covenant. The jointure was, in pursuance of this agreement, actually re-demised and the covenant released. And, after the husband's death, Gladwell was decreed to account with the widow and administratrix of the husband for the profits of the jointure lands received in the life of the husband and to a make a settlement according to his covenant.

Gale v. Lindo, in 1687; a woman, being about to marry, borrows £170 of her brother in order to make her fortune appear more considerable than it was, and she gives a bond for it. And, after the death of her husband, she herself came to be relieved against this bond, and she was relieved accordingly.

Lamlee v. Haman, Michaelmas 1704; a woman was prevailed on to part with her jointure to her son to enable him to make a settlement on his marriage, and, in consideration of that, he agrees to assign to her a leasehold estate which he was possessed of. And, it being apprehended by the relations of the wife, who treated the match, that the mother agreed to release her jointure without any

[1] Sic in MS.

[2] *Peyton v. Bladwell* (1684), 1 Vernon 240, 23 E.R. 440.

consideration in order to enable her son to make a jointure, there was a relief against this agreement.

Goldsmith and Brunning, before the late Master of the Rolls [Trevor]; the defendant's father having been aiding to the plaintiff's marriage, the plaintiff in consideration thereof gave her a sum of money and also a note to pay her a further sum. And, afterwards, the plaintiff brought his bill to be relieved against the note and to be repaid the money he had paid the defendant's wife. And it was decreed that the defendant should not only deliver up the note but pay back the money which his wife had received and this notwithstanding the defendant insisted that he married upon the inducement of the note and the money and looking on it as his wife's portion.

Master of the Rolls [Jekyll]: I am of the opinion the creditors are not in a better case than the administratrix of Benson. The creditors perhaps would be entitled to claim in the room of Sir Theodore Jansen. But that will not make the case better, for I think Sir Theodore Jansen would not have been in a better condition than Mr. Benson himself would have been. It is to be considered Sir Theodore Jansen had not a legal title to this bond, but only an equitable assignment. And, therefore, having a security which was not good in equity, he could be in no better condition than Benson himself, and, consequently, the creditors can be in no better condition than Sir Theobald Jansen.

Suppose a man assigns a satisfied bond as a security for a just debt. Shall such an assignee set up this bond now in equity? Will the bond which was satisfied before be made better by assigning it? No, surely.

It is incumbent on a person who takes an assignment of a bond to go to the obligor and be sure that the bond is a good bond. If he does not, it is his own fault, and he shall not take advantage of his own laches.

As to what is proved of some offer made by Turton to pay part of the bond, I think that ought not to be of any prejudice to him, for offers made and not accepted signify nothing. I have often heard Lord Cowper say a man should not be bound by any offers made during a treaty which afterwards broke off or upon terms which were not accepted.

This court always relieved in cases of this nature. And I am of the opinion even the parent himself would be relieved in such cases, as suppose a parent settles lands on the marriage of his son and the son agrees to pay back part of the fortune, I think in that case the parent would be relieved and the settlement set aside.

Upon the whole, here having been an underhand agreement made with the plaintiff without the privity of his mother and after the plaintiff's affections were settled, I am of the opinion the plaintiff ought to be relieved and the bond delivered up.

Lincoln's Inn MS. Misc. 11, p. 189

Turton v. Benson and Richardson.

Upon an appeal to Lord Chancellor [Lord Parker] from the Master of the Rolls's [Jekyll] decree, *quod vide ante*, fo. 77, Lord Chancellor [LORD PARKER] said agreements of this kind have been always discountenanced and relief given in this court, even to the parties who were privy to the fraud.

The taking the bond in question in a private manner was fraudulent and Mr. Benson has by a deed under his hand and seal declared that the marriage portion was £3000, which was false in fact. Why then consider whether the creditors are in a better condition than Mr. Benson himself, if living, would have been?

I think no assignment of this bond by Mr. Benson could mend the case, for, if it would, it would be in the power of the party who has committed the fraud to prevent this court from relieving against such practices. Besides, the creditors have no assignment of this bond, nor have they parted with anything for it. They have only agreed that the assets shall be got in by the administratrix and applied to pay the debts ratably. And now, they come here to demand this bond as part of the assets of Benson, but, if Benson could not have recovered this money, neither can his creditors.

The decree must be affirmed.

Note, in this case, Mr. *Vernon* cited the case of Bovey and Smith.[1] The trustee of an estate sold to one who had no notice of the trust, and a fine was levied by the trustee and five years non-claim passed. Afterwards, the trustee re-purchases this estate. Though the fraud was purged when the estate was in the hands of the purchaser without notice and it could not be taken from him, yet when it came back again to the person who committed the fraud, the court laid hold of it.

Lincoln's Inn MS. Misc. 384, p. 195

14 November [1719]. Rehearing.

The original bill is to be relieved against a bond of £1000 given by the plaintiff to Benson to refund part of the portion of £3000 which he was to give his daughter on her marriage with the plaintiff. Benson being dead and the bond assigned to Richardson and others of Benson's creditors, they bring a cross-bill to have satisfaction of this bond.

Lutwyche, for the plaintiff: The bond is dated in June 1710 conditioned to pay £1000 in seven years without interest. The portion agreed to be paid by Benson was £3000, in consideration of which the plaintiff's mother agreed to surrender part of her jointure to enable the plaintiff to make an equivalent settlement. Kemp v. Coleman, 1 Salk. 156; Duke of Hamilton v. Lord Mohun, Salk. 158. The bill is against the administrator of Benson. The plaintiff was not privy to the assignment of the creditors. The bond was first assigned as a collateral security by Benson to Sir Theodore Jansen, and, afterwards, it was agreed it should be

[1] *Bovey v. Smith* (1682), 1 Vernon 60, 84, 144, 23 E.R. 310, 328, 377, 2 Chancery Cases 124, 22 E.R. 877, 1 Eq. Cas. Abr. 256, 384, 21 E.R. 1029, 1120.

assigned for the benefit of the other creditors, Sir Theodore being paid off. This may be compared to a marriage brokage contract and is of as dangerous a consequence.

Sir Robert Raymond: This is within the cases that have been mentioned. There have been cases where the party himself was relieved. Redman v. Redman, 1665, where, the husband being in debt, the brother was to give a bond to the creditors of the husband and the husband gave a counter-bond to the brother, yet the husband was relieved against the counter-bond. Gale v. Ludlow, where the lady's brother gave her a bond that she might appear [to have] a better fortune and she promised to deliver it up, yet the brother was not relieved, but the bond remained in force. Goldsmith v. Bonning; a note was given to the lady's maid and the money paid on the note was recovered back again; the defendant married the maid on the credit of the note.

Vernon: Relief was never denied in such cases as this. Lamly v. Hamond, Michaelmas 1704; the mother, on her son's marriage, was to surrender her jointure, and he privately agreed to assign a leasehold estate; yet that agreement was set aside as fraudulent. Bacon v. Bladwell, 9 March 1684; the defendant agreed to settle on his nephew who married the plaintiff, an estate in possession of £200 *per annum* and £100 *per annum* more at his death, but the defendant made the plaintiff's husband agree to re-demise the estate at £150 *per annum*; yet it was decreed for the defendant to account for £200 *per annum*. Sloan v. Fowler, where the son of the defendant married the plaintiff's daughter and the defendant not being willing to settle his estate unless the lady's fortune were greater, his son proposed to give the defendant a bond to make up the fortune, yet the lady's father was relieved and [the court] set aside this bond.

Chesshyre, for the defendant: The creditors of Benson, who will not have above 11s. in the pound and on the credit of the plaintiff's bond paid off Sir Theodore Jansen's debt, and it is proved that the plaintiff offered to pay Sir Theodore Jansen £600 if he would abate the rest. 1 Syd. 133.[1] If a feoffment be made by fraud and the feoffee conveys over in good conscience, the fraud is purged. 2 Cro. 5, Ellis v. Ward; Sarret v. Fielding, on a usurious bond, by Lord Somers.[2] The plaintiff drew a bill on A. payable to Mrs. Dod or order; the bill came into the defendant's hands, who was a creditor of Mrs. Dod; though the plaintiff had good equity against her, she not having paid any consideration for the bill, yet the court would not relieve against the defendant, who had got better security.

Cowper, for the defendant: This case is different from all the cases cited. It is proved that the plaintiff promised Mrs. Richardson that he would not dispute

---

[1] *Prodgers v. Langham* (1663), 1 Siderfin 133, 82 E.R. 1014, also 1 Keble 486, 83 E.R. 1068.

[2] *Ellis v. Warnes* (1604), Croke Jac. 33, 79 E.R. 26, also Moore K.B. 752, 72 E.R. 883, Yelverton 47, 80 E.R. 34, 1 Brownlow & Goldesborough 85, 123 E.R. 681; note *Fielding v. Serrat* (K.B. 1696), Holt K.B. 27, 90 E.R. 912, Comberbach 375, 90 E.R. 537.

the validity of this bond. If the plaintiff had been privy to the assignment to the creditors, he could not be relieved against it.

Talbot: Where the party has been relieved, it was where he was manifestly imposed upon. Here, the plaintiff was not imposed upon, though his mother was. And she is not a party to this suit. The case is different with respect to the creditors and with respect to the administrator of Benson. Though, by the assignment of a bond, only an equitable interest passes, yet, in many cases, an assignee is in a better case than the assignor, as where a purchaser with notice of a prior equitable title conveys over to another without notice.

Lutwyche, for the plaintiff, in reply: It is proved the plaintiff intended to bring a bill against Benson in his lifetime to be relieved against this bond and took advice of counsel. But before the bill could be filed, Benson died.

As to the objection the plaintiff was privy to the fraud, that would hold against all the cases. [There is] no difference by the bond's being assigned to creditors.

As to the cases of purchasers, they have the law with them. Here, the creditors have parted with nothing to get this bond into their hands. Sarah Jones's deposition is that the plaintiff told Mrs. Richardson, if this bond were in Benson's hands, he would dispute the validity of it, but he would not if it were assigned for her benefit. It was only an act of generosity. And, in truth, it is not assigned for her benefit only, but of all the other creditors.

Raymond: If this should be determined otherwise, it would overturn all the cases cited. It is different from the cases of purchasers, for, here, the creditors paid no consideration for the assignment of the bond. Turton, in his answer to the creditors' bill, swears directly contrary to Jones's deposition.

Vernon: Whoever takes an assignment of a bond cannot be in a better condition than the obligee himself. The creditors are not purchasers of this bond; they have not parted with anything to gain it. The creditors' agreement to share the assets was not made by the inducement of this bond. All the right the creditors have is to the estate of the debtor. In the case of a bankrupt, the assignees are in no better case than the bankrupt. Taylor v. Wheeler, Salk. 449,[1] where a bankrupt made a surrender to the plaintiff, which was not presented, the plaintiff was relieved, though the creditors had the [common] law with them. Ferrers v. Cherry; Bovey v. Smith.[2] Here, the mother was principally imposed upon, and she swears she would not have parted with her jointure had she known the lady's fortune was not so much.

---

[1] *Taylor v. Wheeler* (1709), 2 Salkeld 449, 91 E.R. 388, also 2 Vernon 564, 23 E.R. 968, 1 Eq. Cas. Abr. 122, 312, 21 E.R. 928, 1068.

[2] *Ferrars v. Cherry* (1700), 2 Vernon 383, 23 E.R. 845, 1 Eq. Cas. Abr. 3, 331, 21 E.R. 830, 1081, British Library MS. Hargrave 80, f. 89; *Bovey v. Smith* (1682), 1 Vernon 60, 84, 144, 23 E.R. 310, 328, 377, 2 Chancery Cases 124, 22 E.R. 877, 1 Eq. Cas. Abr. 256, 384, 21 E.R. 1029, 1120.

Lord Chancellor [Lord Parker]: These agreements have always been discouraged in this court. And one of the parties to the agreement has generally been relieved. The agreement is under Benson's hand and seal that Turton was to have a £3000 portion with his wife. And Turton's mother is a party to the deed and is imposed upon. If Benson had disclosed the truth, she would not have agreed to the settlement. This fraud proceeded originally from Benson. This is as gross an instance as ever came before the court.

Secondly, consider whether the creditors are in a better case; if it were in Benson's power to alter the case, the power of this court would be eluded. The bond or penalty cannot be assigned, but only what is justly due on the bond. If the party to the fraud were only to be relieved, it might alter the case. So if he had given a new bond to the creditors. Here, the creditors have no color for their bill, for here is not any proper assignment of the bond, but only an agreement that the administratrix of Benson shall recover this bond debt. The creditors have not parted with anything to purchase this bond. The agreement between the creditors is just one, but it is not founded upon the credit of this bond. That the plaintiff's office of Secondary of the Counter should be sold is very advantageous to the creditors and what they could hardly have compelled him to do.

The chief end of the agreement was to prevent the administratrix from making an undue preference of any one creditor and to prevent suits. As to what passed between the plaintiff and Mrs. Richardson, it was only a compliment and the time does not certainly appear when the discourse was. She did not make any agreement with him about it. It is equitable that this debt should be got in. Creditors are only to be favored with respect to the debtor's estate. And this bond is not to be looked upon as part of it. I affirm the Master of the Rolls's decree.

Lincoln's Inn MS. Misc. 506, p. 15

Michaelmas 6 Geo.

The plaintiff Turton was married to Katherine, one of the daughters of Mr. Benson, who is since dead, and his wife, the defendant, has taken out administration to him. Before the marriage, it was agreed that the portion should be £3000. The settlement was to be £300 *per annum* besides other lands to be settled on the children of that marriage and to enable him to make that settlement, the mother agreed to surrender part of her jointure. After the plaintiff's affections were engaged, then Benson pretended he could give no more than £2000, and then he insisted on a bond for the repayment of £1000 to be paid within seven years, which was accordingly given. Benson died insolvent. And, within the seven years, Turton, the plaintiff, brings this bill against the administratrix of Benson to be relieved against this bond. The creditors of Benson bring a cross-bill against the plaintiff and defendant in the original bill to contest this bond.

Mr. *Lutwyche* insisted for the plaintiff that there were many cases express for giving relief. Salk. 150, Duke of Hamilton and Lord Mohun;[1] where the question was not of returning a portion, but it was compared to that; it was insisted on as part of the marriage agreement that there should be a release of accounts, and it was said in that case that, if there were no compulsion, yet it ought to be set aside for that it was of the same nature with marriage brokage bonds.

There have been stronger cases where the party himself has been relieved, as these cases which I had from Mr. Vernon, Rodmayne v. Rodmayne, 1685;[2] upon a treaty of marriage, the man being in indifferent circumstances, it was insisted that he should first pay all his debts. There was one which he was not able to pay and thus applied to his brother, who gave his bond to the creditor and took a counter-bond from his brother, upon which the marriage took effect. The wife was privy to all of this transaction. The husband dies, and the wife takes administration. The brother, who had paid the money to the creditor, brings a bill against the administratrix to be reimbursed, but the court refused it as being fraudulent. Gale and Lindo; a lady desirous the marriage should take effect, but not having a competent fortune, she prevailed on her brother to give her a bond for a large sum of money and promised, when the marriage should take effect, she would give it him up. The marriage took effect, and the husband died, and she took administration, and the brother's bond was accounted by this court as assets, and he was obliged to pay it. Goldsmith and Bruning; a note was given to a servant who was instrumental in procuring the marriage. This servant was married to the defendant Bruning; a bill was brought to set aside the note, and, though it was insisted on by the husband that he was a purchaser and that he married her on the credit of the note, yet the note was set aside and ordered to be delivered up. This case was before Sir John Trevor, then Master of the Rolls. As to our case, I think it is not altered by the assignment of the bond, for though the money had been paid for that bond, yet the party that comes under it cannot be in a better case than he under whom he claims. But here was no money given. It was only a security for a debt and a collateral one too. No declaration that no advantage should be taken of it against creditors, though it had been more solemn than is pretended, would have availed because it is *nudum pactum*.

Mr. *Vernon*: The £3000 is the consideration mentioned in the deed, which is under hand and seal. There are cases much stronger than this, and I do not know one that has come before the court which has been decreed relief. Lumley and Hammond, Michaelmas 1704; the mother, for the advancement of her son, agreed to part with her jointure, and the son, by a private agreement between him and his mother, assigned a leasehold estate to her in lieu thereof, but, in regard there was no mention made of this in the marriage treaty and the son was in possession of the leasehold estate, the wife, who was the representative of the

[1] *Duke of Hamilton v. Lord Mohun* (1710), *ut supra.*

[2] *Redman v. Redman* (1685), *ut supra.*

son, did by a decree of this court recover the leasehold estate from the mother. Innumerable are the cases that might be mentioned on this head. Butler and Chaney; Slone and Fowler. As to our equity against the creditors, it is only an assignment by way of a collateral security. But had it been an original security, yet, if a man will take an assignment of a chose in action, which is assignable only in equity, he must take it subject to such relief as a court of equity will give.

Serjeant *Chesshyre*, *contra*: I must agree it is now settled as a principle in this court that any underhanded dealings to the prejudice of the settlement are not allowed, but then the case must be very plain against the parties themselves or their representatives, but such ill things are not easily to be presumed. Benson lived until November 1714, and no discontent showed in his lifetime. The bond was assigned in his lifetime to Sir Theodore Janson, and, though it be not proved that he knew of it at the time of the assignment, yet it is proved that he knew of it afterwards. These other creditors come in on good consideration and without notice. Serrat and Fielding,[1] in Lord Somers's time; Serrat was a cheesemonger in Cheshire; Dodd was a grocer who had occasion to return money and applied to Serrat to give him a bill and he would pay him the money. Serrat, at first, refused to give a bill or send advice unless he had the money before the post went out (11 in the forenoon); but Dodd being busy in the shop and not at leisure to pay the money, did at last get a bill of Serrat upon a promise to pay the money and sent it away by the post. The money was never paid to Serrat. The person in town accepts the bill, which was afterwards assigned without a consideration to Fielding, who was a creditor of Dodd. Serrat brings a bill to have up this bill of exchange against Dodd and Fielding as being without a consideration. It was urged that Fielding had not advanced one groat and so would stand in as good a case as he did before. But Lord Somers was of opinion that Fielding having an advantage by it, *viz*. the setting off his debt, Serrat could not be relieved.

Mr. *Cowper* and Mr. *Talbot* were of the same side.

Lord Chancellor [Lord Parker]: These private agreements have always been discouraged, and all the cases have been of parties that have had the benefit of the settlement. As to what is said of Turton's imposing upon Benson, suppose it be so, that does not at all excuse Benson, that he did not give the account to Mulso, who treated on the behalf of Turton and his mother and with whom he agreed to give £3000. And when this agreement comes to be put into writing, it is under his hand and seal. I am convinced in this case that the matter began from Mr. Benson. Indeed, if Turton had proposed to his mother and Mr. Mulso, his uncle, £2000 and, upon their disagreeing, it had been brought up to £3000, that had looked as if it had proceeded from him. But £3000 is the only sum proposed. There was no other, and the mother thought it too little. I think this is as gross an instance as ever came before the court, but then the question

[1] Note *Fielding v. Serrat* (K.B. 1696), Holt K.B. 27, 90 E.R. 912, Comberbach 375, 90 E.R. 537.

will be whether the creditors are in a better condition than Mr. Benson. I think no assignment of Mr. Benson can mend it, for that would be putting it out of the power of the court to intermeddle. I think the person to whom it is assigned must stand in the place of him that made the assignment. And, therefore, if a man assigned a bond a great deal whereof is paid, shall he to whom it is assigned have more than is due? Surely not. But though the party himself who is guilty of the fraud cannot make it better, yet it is another question whether the injured person may not. But I do not think here is any new contract which can make it better. Sir Theodore Janson is paid off and thus out of the case. Mr. Turton was not privy to the assignment to him.

Then, let us see how it stands with respect to the creditors. There is no assignment to them at all. They parted with nothing in consideration of the bond. And it is so far from being an assignment that there is a covenant that the administratrix shall get in all the estate. And so the contest is to be between the administratrix and the several debtors. So the effect of the agreement is no more than this, they have endeavored to prevent any undue preference and agreed that all the money shall be equally divided among them. It is true they have let in the simple contract creditors, but that might be to prevent the administratrix letting them get judgments and so might prefer them before the bond creditors. It seems to me very reasonable they should consent to this agreement without any preference. If this bond were reckoned part of the estate and, thereupon, they had released all the rest, that might have been a different case. But they are to have the whole estate divided among them as the administratrix gets it in.

The creditors' bill was dismissed, and Mr. Turton had a perpetual injunction as to the bond.

2 Vernon 764, 23 E.R. 1099

The plaintiff Turton, on the marriage of Benson's daughter, was to have £3000 portion, and, in consideration thereof, his mother agreed to surrender part of her jointure to enable her son to make the settlement. There were no articles in writing, but, in the settlement made by Mr. Turton, it is mentioned to be in consideration of £3000 portion. But Mr. Benson, who was secondary of one of the Counters in London, prevailed on Turton to agree between themselves, unknown to his mother, and those who treated for the marriage on his behalf, to give a bond to repay £1000, part of the £3000, at the end of seven years, but without interest.

Benson being dead, the bill was brought against his widow and administratrix to have the bond delivered up as unduly gained and imposed upon him by Benson a little before the marriage without the consent or privity of his mother or friends that treated on his behalf.

Richardson and others, as creditors of Benson, brought their bill to have the benefit of the bond, charging a collusion between Turton and Mrs. Benson and that she made but a faint defence of their prejudice and charging that Turton, since the death of Benson, had promised to pay the money, and, in confidence that it would be paid, it was assigned over to the creditors.

The bond was decreed to be delivered up as obtained in fraud of the marriage agreement. The assignment to the creditors did not alter the case; a bond, which is assignable only in equity, is still liable to and attended with the same equity as if remaining with the obligee.

And as to any promise made by Turton that he would pay it, that was but *nudum pactum* and not binding.

The decree, in Michaelmas 1719, was affirmed upon an appeal to the Lord Chancellor.

Lincoln's Inn MS. Misc. 380, pt. 3, p. 229

Michaelmas term 1719.

Mrs. Turton, a widow and possessed of an estate in land as her jointure to the value of £400 *per annum* and having a son of the age of twenty-two and a barrister at a law, entered into a treaty of marriage for her son with Mr. Benson. The agreement was that Mr. Benson should give with his daughter a portion of £3000 and, in consideration of this fortune, Mrs. Turton agreed to settle immediately the £400 *per annum* which she had an interest in for her life as her jointure upon her son and £300 *per annum* of this very land was to be settled upon Mr. Benson's daughter as a jointure proportional to her fortune, which was £3000. When all things were thus agreed upon and the affections of the young people were engaged, Benson, the father of the young lady, takes Turton, the son, aside and tells him that his circumstances would not allow him to give £3000 with his daughter but that, however, he would do his utmost, *viz.* give him £2000 and let him have the other £1000 for seven years without interest, but that he must give a bond for the repayment of the £1000 at the end of the seven years, without which the match should not go on. Turton, rather than the match should be broken off, gives the bond.

Afterwards, marriage articles, to which Mrs. Turton, the mother, was one of the parties, were prepared and executed in pursuance of the agreement, *viz.* £3000, the portion, and £300, the jointure, and Mrs. Turton actually quitted to her son the interest she had for her life, knowing nothing of this bond. The marriage took effect.

Mr. Benson owed Sir Theodore Johnson a considerable sum, for which debt he and his son were both bound. And Sir Theodore, not satisfied with this, procured from Mr. Benson an assignment of this bond thus obtained from Turton, his son-in-law, as a collateral security for his debt.

Benson, the father, four years after the marriage, dies very considerably indebted to Sir Theodore, Mr. Richardson, and others, both by bond and simple contract. The assets left were sufficient to pay the bond debts but not the debts by simple contracts.

The question was whether Turton, the seven years being expired, should be obliged to pay the £1000, for which this bond was given, to the creditors of Mr. Benson.

Lord Chancellor PARKER: All agreements of this nature are odious and have ever found relief in this court as often as they have come in before it, even in favor of those very persons that were parties to the agreement. In this case, here are plainly two agreements, the one open and above board and the other secret and private and derogatory of the former. By the first, the fortune is £3000; by the latter, it is reduced to £2000. And it is plainly to the deceit of the mother, a party to the settlement and who, upon the consideration of this fortune, quitted her jointure in order to make this settlement. And, it the bond be naught *quoad* Benson, no assignment of his can make it good; to hold that would be in effect to give up the power and jurisdiction of this court over frauds, for, no matter how fraudulent and vicious the agreement was, make but an assignment and that will cure all. When bonds are assigned, the meaning is, there, the assignee is to have all equitable advantages that the assignor could have had. Suppose a bond is assigned, upon which both principal and interest is discharged. Shall the assignee recover the penalty which the assignor had no right to? I do not say that this bond is so void as that no subsequent agreement upon good consideration could make it good, but nothing like this is in this case.

As for Sir Theodore and the assignment to him, his debt being paid, he is entirely out of the case. As for the deed of composition, as they call it, between the administratrix and the creditors, there is nothing in it to influence this case, nor can there, from the nature of the agreement, be found so much as one single reason drawn from this bond to [induce] them to enter into it. It is only an agreement made between the creditors for preventing the wasting of the assets in law, expenses, and restraining the administratrix from giving that preference to debts that by law she might.

As for Turton's promise to Mrs. Richardson, if true, for it was positively denied by Turton how far in honor it may bind him, is nothing to me. It was a promise made upon a supposition of an assignment to be made to her, but nothing of that nature was done, or can she be supposed to become a party to this agreement upon account of this promise. The making of the profits arising from the time of the sale of the office are assets. The preference the administratrix might have given to other debts had she refused are plain and good reasons for her to come into it.

The creditors are entitled to favor, yet this is only with respect to the estate of the debtor.

[Other reports of this case: 10 Modern 445, 88 E.R. 803, 1 Peere Williams 496, 24 E.R. 488, 1 Strange 240, 93 E.R. 498, Precedents in Chancery 522, 24 E.R. 234, 1 Eq. Cas. Abr. 45, 88, 21 E.R. 862, 900, 2 Eq. Cas. Abr. 87, 22 E.R. 75.]

327

Burdet v. Hopegood

(Ch. 1718–1721)

A posthumous child is the child of his father for the purposes of a will even though born after the will takes effect.

Lincoln's Inn MS. Misc. 384, p. 91, pl. 3

5 December; Serjeants' Inn Hall on the Master's report.

Sir Robert Burnet, the plaintiff's father, devises, in case he shall leave no son, then all his personal estate to the defendant, his executor, and his real estate to the defendant upon trust by mortgage or sale etc. to pay his debts and legacies. And he leaves the plaintiff, a son, *in ventre sa mere*.

Lord Cowper was of the opinion that there being a son left, the condition precedent was not fulfilled as to the personal estate. But he sent it to the Master to state the value of the real estate and the debts.

Now the question is whether the trust does arise and, if not, whether the debts and legacies are payable.

Vernon, for the plaintiff: The personal estate is subject to the debts. If he devises his real estate for payment of all his debts, it is but as a supplement and the personal estate is to be applied in the first place, unless there be negative words to exempt it. The cases are very numerous. Lord Meath and Moor, in the House of Lords;[1] Lord Meath had vested his English estate in trustees for payment of his debts and devises all his personal estate to his Lady yet it was subject to reimburse the real estate. But in Lady Gainesborough's [Case],[2] which is the only case to the contrary, Mr. Milman, who drew the will, was directed by the testator to give his Lady his personal estate exempt from the debts. Milman told him she would have it as executrix without other words, the real estate being subject to debts. [It was] decreed below the personal estate to Lady Gainesborough. It was affirmed in the House of Lords, and parol evidence was admitted.

Raymond, for the defendant: The question upon the personal estate is properly to be determined here. And we hope it is not in this case subject to the debts and legacies, for it differs from the other cases and is not given [to the] defendant as executor but all his other personal estate is given the defendant for his trouble and as a token of his affection and kindness etc.

Lord Chancellor [Lord Parker]: If the point of the real estate which is proper for the determination of a court of law is given in favor of the defendant,

---

1 *Coote v. Moore* (1691–1692), cited in *Roper v. Radcliffe* (1712), 9 Modern 181, 189, 88 E.R. 387, 391.

2 *Countess of Gainsborough v. Earl of Gainsborough* (1692), 2 Vernon 252, 23 E.R. 764, 2 Freeman 188, 22 E.R. 1152, 1 Eq. Cas. Abr. 230, 21 E.R. 1010.

the point of the personal estate will not be material because the debts must be paid by the defendant. But the testator only considered his having no son and his daughters being well provided for, he gives all his estate to the defendant. But he, having left a son, did not design he should be unprovided for. Let a case be stated for the opinion of the judges of the King's Bench.

N.B. The question is whether the devise of the real estate is a substantive independent clause and not subject to the conditions precedent of the devisor's not leaving a son at the time of his death and, if not, whether the plaintiff being in *ventre sa mere*, the devisor left a son at the time of his death.

1 Peere Williams 486, 24 E.R. 484

Sir Robert Burdet *versus* Hopegood.

Robert Burdet, Esq., in the lifetime of Sir Robert Burdet, the plaintiff's grandfather, being seised in fee of the manor and priory of Modney in the County of Norfolk, by his will dated 17th December 1711, devised the premises in case he should leave no son at the time of his death to his cousin Francis Hopegood and his heirs, and, as a reward for the trouble which the testator had given him and for the many obligations he had to him, he gave him all his personal estate and made him sole executor and died, leaving his wife *privement ensient*, which child afterwards proved to be a son, the now plaintiff.

And one of the questions was whether Hopegood, the devisee, was entitled to these lands in regard, as was objected, the testator died without leaving a son at the time of his death.

Hereupon, Lord Chancellor Parker referred it to the judges of the King's Bench, who were unanimously of opinion that the plaintiff, Sir Robert, though not born, had yet an existence in the eye of the law as *in ventre sa mere*, which, in many respects, was regarded as if a woman takes poison to kill her child then in her womb and the child is born alive and, afterwards, dies of that poison, the woman is guilty of murder. *Vide* Beale v. Beale, *ante*, 244.[1] Also, a child *in ventre sa mere* may be vouched and may be a devisee. And it would be hard to disinherit such an only child, nor could it be imagined the testator ever intended so to do.

The certificate of the judges was as follows:

> We are of opinion that the devise of the said manor and priory of Modney etc. to Francis Hopegood and his heirs was not an absolute devise but subject to the contingency of the testator's leaving no son at the time of his death so that, such contingency not happening, the devise to the said Francis Hopegood and his heirs cannot take place, the testator, as we humbly conceive, having expressed no intention in the will of disinheriting his only

---

[1] *Beale v. Beale* (1713), 1 Peere Williams 244, 24 E.R. 373, also Gilbert Rep. 93, 25 E.R. 64, 2 Eq. Cas. Abr. 639, 22 E.R. 536.

son, the consequence of which is that Mr. Hopegood is not entitled to the premises. /s/ *John Pratt, Robert Eyre, Littleton Powys, John Fortescue Aland.*

With which His Lordship agreed, and, accordingly, on the 5th of October 1721, he decreed the defendant Hopegood to deliver up possession of the premises and account for the rents and profits which he had received.

Lincoln's Inn MS. Misc. 11, p. 53

Burdett v. Francis Hopegood, executor of Francis Burdett, father of the plaintiff.

The plaintiff's father makes his will and charges his lands with the payment of his debts, and, taking notice that his daughters were sufficiently provided for by his marriage settlement, he declares that, in case he should have no son at the time of his death, that then he gives to the defendant all his lands etc.

The testator died, leaving his wife *enceinte* with the plaintiff. And the question was whether the defendant was entitled to these lands.

Lord Cowper declared he was not, for the contingency upon which the lands were given to the defendant had never happened, for the words 'leaving no son' must be understood leaving no son born or *in ventre sa mere.*

Note, in this case, when it came on upon the equity reserved as to another point, Mr. *Vernon* cited the Lady Gainsborough's Case to be this. Lord Gainsborough sent to Mr. Milbourn to make his will, and, having thereby charged his Rutlandshire estate with the payment of his debts, he makes the Lady Gainsborough, his wife, executrix. And he directs Mr. Milbourn to add that he gave his wife all his personal estate exempt from the payment of his debts. But Mr. Milbourn told him there was no manner of need of inserting those words in the will, for the making his wife executrix was sufficient of itself to give her the personal estate, and, thereupon, the Lord Gainsborough being overruled by Mr. Milbourn, the words were left out of the will. And, upon a bill brought by Lady Gainsborough to have the personal estate exempt from the debts, it was fully proved that Lord Gainsborough would have inserted those words in his will if he had not been overruled in it by Mr. Milbourn. And, when the cause came to be heard, the question was if this parol proof should be read. And the court was of opinion it should. And upon the reading of it, it decreed the personal estate to the plaintiff and that she should have it exempt from the debts. And this decree was affirmed in the House of Lords.

[Other reports of this case: 2 Eq. Cas. Abr. 292, 22 E.R. 245.]

328
Simpson v. Watson

(Ch. 1718)

A demand for a legacy can be barred by the legatee's laches.

Lincoln's Inn MS. Misc. 384, p. 93, pl. 1

5 December.

A bill [was filed] for a legacy of £100 given by the will of J. Miller to J. Dennis in 1676.

Vernon, for the defendant: This legacy was given forty-two years ago, and [there is] no excuse for not demanding it sooner only that the legatee was a seafaring man. Though the Statute of Limitations[1] does not bar a legacy or a bond debt, yet the length of time is a presumption of satisfaction. As to the evidence of an acknowledgment of the husband of the executrix that it was not paid and his offering the plaintiff 20s. for a release, it is very slight and of little weight and does not prove this to be the same legacy but a release to another legacy. [There was] no promise of payment nor any demand though assets were left and the legatee [was] in necessitous circumstances. The plaintiff and the others brought a bill in 1715 for other demands on the testator's estate, and [there was] no notice of this legacy, which bill was dismissed for want of prosecution.

Mead, for the plaintiff: [There is] no entry of payment in the books of the executrix, who was sued by another legatee who recovered. The defendant admits assets. We submit what interest shall be paid.

Lord Chancellor [Lord Parker]: In 1715, a bill is filed for the plaintiff and others for the other legacies, and [there is] no mention of this legacy. [There is] no demand for above thirty years after the testator's death. And twenty-seven years after the legatee's death [is] stronger than a case of a bond which may be lost. But it is said this is supported by the confession, which plainly relates to the other legacy. The bill must be dismissed without costs.

---

1 Stat. 21 Jac. I, c. 16 (*SR*, IV, 1222–1223).

329

Dann v. Chandler and Kesling

(Ch. 1718)

A contract for wages cannot be assigned before the wages are due and payable.

Lincoln's Inn MS. Misc. 384, p. 93, pl. 2

5 December; Serjeants' Inn.

E. Plunker, having a ticket for her late husband's wages, in 1714, assigns it to the plaintiff to secure £35 and delivered it to the plaintiff. The defendant Kesling had a bill of sale of this ticket in 1713 from D. Plunker himself, which was before the money was earned or the wages due. The defendant gets it unfairly into his custody. Brewster v. Edes, before Lord Keeper Wright, same case, decreed it could not be sold or assigned before the wages were due, [was] quoted by *Horsely*.

Master of the Rolls [JEKYLL]: The ticket must be delivered up to the plaintiff to remain as a security or pledge for what is due, and the defendant may redeem. The overplus must be paid to the defendant Chandler, the executor of Plunker. The ticket could not be assigned or pass the wages before they were due. In Thompson v. Lord Haversham, before the Lord Cowper,[1] an advowson could not be sold in the life of the defendant Haversham.

N.B. That case is different because the court there went only upon the inconvenience of an heir apparent parting with his estate in the life of his ancestor, especially without a valuable consideration.

N.B. The plaintiff being a purchaser for a valuable consideration without notice of the defendant's title and the defendant having got possession of this ticket unfairly, for that reason, the decree seems to be just.

330

Morgan v. Saunders

(Ch. 1718)

The question in this case was whether a suit in equity lies to discover a deed of entail whereby the devisor had no power to give his estate to the defendant by will.

Lincoln's Inn MS. Misc. 384, p. 95, pl. 1

10 December.

Vernon, for the defendant, quoted Stapleton and Stapleton, by Lord North, where a tenant in tail devised his estate to A., and the issue in tail, in order to maintain a [writ of] formedon, brought a bill against the devisee to discover who

---

[1] *Thompson v. Lord Haversham* (Ch. 1715), see above, Case No. 96.

was the tenant to the *praecipe* when the recovery was suffered. The defendant demurred, and [it was] allowed because a man cannot impeach a settlement or title in equity when the party had the power to make the settlement. Therefore, the plaintiff must by his bill offer to confirm the estate of a jointress or tenant for life before he is entitled to a discovery. But it is otherwise where the party who makes a settlement or will has no power, as where he is but a tenant for life.

This bill is to discover a deed of entail whereby the devisor had no power to give his estate to the defendant by will.

Justice Tracy: Here is very strong evidence of an entail, for the devisor had prepared a deed to lead the uses of a recovery but died before the recovery was suffered. So this differs from Stapleton and Stapleton, for, there was a recovery suffered and that bill was to discover whether the recovery was good. Here, the debts being charged by the will on the real estate, they are not to be defeated.

He sent [it] to the Master to see the value of the estate and the debts. He reserved consideration whether a trial shall be to try if the devisor was seised in fee.

331

Countess Dowager of Montacute v. Maxwell

(Ch. 1718–1720)

The Statute of Frauds cannot be pleaded in order to support and to further a fraud.

Lincoln's Inn MS. Misc. 12, p. 236

1718. Mountague v. Sir George Maxfield.

The will was proved in the ecclesiastical court. The bill was to set aside the will as to the real estate. The issue directed was whether *compos* [*mentis*] or not. It was found non *compos* [*mentis*], yet the court would not meddle with the personal estate for want of jurisdiction.

Lincoln's Inn MS. Misc. 384, p. 232

Lady Montague v. Sir George Maxwell.

The bill was to have the benefit of an agreement on a marriage whereby the plaintiff was to have power over her own fortune, but, before the agreement could be reduced into writing, the plaintiff and defendant married.

The defendant pleads the Statute of Frauds,[1] there being no writing signed by him, and he also pleads the enrollment of a former plea.

Vernon, for the plaintiff: The enrollment of any interlocutory order cannot prevent its being reheard. Here is such new matter charged in this amended bill as will bring it out of the Statute of Frauds. The agreement appears by a note pre-

[1] Stat. 29 Car. II, c. 3 (*SR*, V, 839–842).

pared but not signed by the defendant. There are letters by the defendant promising to perform his agreement and that the writings were preparing by his counsel. And as an assurance that he would perform it, he took the Sacrament. If the reducing the agrement into writing is prevented by fraud, it is out of the Statute. The first case on the Statute was in Lord Nottingham's time.[1] There was an absolute conveyance, and the other party would not execute a defeasance; [it was] out of the Statute. In Moor v. Hart,[2] a letter that Hart would give his daughter £1500 bound him. Foxcroft v. Lister;[3] there was a parol lease, and the lessor suffered the lessee to build. If a writing be drawn contrary to the intent of the parties or read contrary, it is out of the Statute.

Talbot, for the plaintiff: The note mentioned in the bill was drawn by the plaintiff and not delivered to the defendant until after the marriage, and then the defendant refused to sign it. The plea does not go in bar of a discovery of the fraud, but to that we have answered.

Lord Chancellor [Lord Parker]: You plead the allowance of the former plea, not only to the former bill, but to that part which is amended. The defendant does not deny the several letters set forth in the bill. If the plaintiff did write to the defendant requesting him to settle her estate on her and the defendant, before marriage, answers her letters promising to perform her desire, and, on that condition, the marriage takes effect, does this not bring it out of the Statute? This case is extremely gross. If there is a parol agreement before marriage and the reducing of it into writing is hindered by fraud, it is proper for this court to relieve. So, in the case of a building lease by parol and the lessor suffers the lessee to build, it is out of the Statute because the Statute, which was to prevent fraud, shall not be eluded by fraud. Here, it is charged the defendant has studied to avoid his own agreement by pretending Mr. Molony, his counsel, was out of town so that the writings could not be finished. This case is extremely varied by these new charges in the bill. And I think it is not barred by the Statute of Frauds. Let the plea stand for an answer with liberty to except.

British Library MS. Add. 36651, f. 96

Michaelmas 6 Geo., 1719.

The bill was to have a discovery and execution of an agreement made between the plaintiff and the defendant before their intermarriage whereby the defendant did agree that the plaintiff, who was entitled to a very great fortune should have the disposal thereof as she should think fit notwithstanding the coverture. And the bill charges that the said agreement was reduced to writing and read over to and agreed to by the defendant.

[1] Perhaps *Potts v. Turvin* (1681), 79 Selden Soc. 856.

[2] *Moore v. Hart* (1682–1684), 2 Chancery Reports 284, 21 E.R. 680, 1 Vernon 110, 201, 23 E.R. 352, 412, 1 Eq. Cas. Abr. 22, 21 E.R. 844.

[3] *Lester v. Foxcroft* (1700), Colles 108, 1 E.R. 205.

The defendant pleaded that the plaintiff did before, *viz*. in [*blank*] term 1717, bring a bill in this court for the same matters, to which the defendant pleaded that Statute of Frauds, for that the said pretended agreement nor any note thereof was put in writing or signed by the defendant or any other by him authorized. And, in support of the said plea, he did answer that neither the defendant nor any other person authorized by him did ever sign the said pretended agreement or any note thereof or any other note or agreement whatsoever etc. And he avers that the said plea was argued before the Lord Chancellor Cowper and allowed by him and the said allowance was enrolled. And, therefore, he now pleads the said allowance and enrollment in bar of this amended bill etc.

Upon arguing this plea before Lord Parker, Mr. *Vernon*, for the plaintiff, said there were several cases within the letter of the Statute of Frauds which were out of the intent and for which relief has been given by this court. And so are all cases of fraud where the party, by fraud and contrivance, seeks to evade the Statute, as in this case, where the defendant, by fraud, evaded the signing of the agreement. And, if that fraud is apparent and notorious, appearing to the court by facts (as in this case it does), the court will give relief.

His letters under his hand make it clear that here was such an agreement. And he says he had given directions to his counsel to draw the writings pursuant to the agreement. And, upon this fraudulent pretense of drawing the writings, he evaded signing the agreement until the marriage was solemnized; so that these letters are not only evidence of the agreement but also of his fraud and contrivance to evade the signing of it.

This is like the case adjudged in the court where a man was to lend money upon a mortgage and he ordered the conveyance to be by a deed of feoffment and a separate deed of defeasance. After the feoffment and livery of seisin were executed, the mortgagee refused to sign the deed of defeasance and claimed an absolute estate. And, upon a bill brought to redeem, he pleaded the Statute of Frauds. But the court overruled the plea because it was out of the Statute, for the intent of the Statute was not to support, but to prevent, such frauds as this was. So, in the case of a mortgage, the deed was absolute without any defeasance, yet it appearing that the mortgagee received interest for the purchase money from the mortgagor, it was held to be out of the Statute because it appeared to the court by evidence of fact that it was only a mortgage and yet the words of the Statute are as strong in that case as in this.

So where there was a parol agreement for a building lease and the lessee entered and the lessor stood by and saw the lessee lay out money in building upon the leased premises and said nothing to hinder it, the court looked on that as a fraud and obliged him to execute a lease according to the parol agreement.

In the case at bar, the agreement was made in the most solemn manner and that the defendant might prevail with the plaintiff to put off the signing it until after the marriage, he promised to receive the Sacrament to bind his promise of performing it and, at the time of the marriage, he actually did receive the Sacrament. And, after the marriage, he agreed that she should draw up a case to be put to the doctors of the Sorbonne whether he was bound in conscience to perform it.

He also cited the Case of Moor v. Hart, that a letter written by the father promising to give £1500 with his daughter was held a promise in writing within the Statute. And, in the case at bar, the defendant's letters make it evidence that there was an agreement, and they are a promise in writing to perform that agreement. One of his letters is that his affairs called him into Scotland but that he would first come to town to perform his agreement and then he should go with a good conscience. And, in another letter to her, he says that he had given directions to his lawyer to draw the writings, by which it is apparent that he, by fraud and contrivance, evaded the signing of the agreement.

Panceford said there was no provision or settlement made for her by Sir George Maxwell, nor does this agreement relate at all to his estate, but only to secure her own fortune to herself. And, therefore, it seems to be out of the intent of the Statute, and the rather for that, in many cases, a court of equity will take care to provide for a wife out of her own estate.

Lutwyche, contra, said, if they would bring this case out of the Statute as being an agreement executed in part by the marriage, then it would follow that no agreement in consideration of marriage could be within the Statute if a marriage did ensue.

He agreed that, in case of notorious fraud, the court has relieved. But this is not such, but, at most, it is only a breach of a promise or oath. And, if she was content to take his promise or oath, she may thank herself for it. The defendant, by his answer, denies that the agreement was put in writing before the marriage, but he confesses that, after the marriage, the plaintiff drew it up in writing, but the defendant refused to sign it.

This bill is the same in substance with the former, save only that they have added some few circumstances. Therefore, the allowance of the plea to the former bill is a good bar to this.

Mr. *Talbot*, for the defendant: Every breach of promise is in some measure a fraud. But the cases adjudged to be out of the Statute are of plain, notorious frauds.

Lord Parker: This is an amended bill, and the defendant has pleaded the allowance of a plea to the original bill, which is a very strange plea.

It appears by his letters that there was an agreement, and it is not disputed but that it was to the effect in the bill. And he says in one of his letters that he was coming to London to perform his agreement, which is a promise or agreement under his hand to perform that agreement.

If there is a parol agreement between the intended husband and wife before marriage and it is not put into writing until after the marriage but it is then put in writing and signed by the husband, this is good within the Statute of Frauds although an agreement between a man and his wife is void.

If it appears that there was an agreement in writing, as is charged by the bill, but that the defendant evaded signing it by fraud and that fraud appears by the facts, it will be out of the Statute.

The plea was overruled, but it was ordered to stand for an answer with liberty to except.

Lincoln's Inn MS. Misc. 11, p. 167

March 1719[/20]. Viscountess Mountague v. Maxwell.

The plaintiff brought her bill to have a specific performance of a parol contract made by the defendant before the marriage with the plaintiff to make her a settlement. He pleaded the Statute of Frauds and Perjuries, and the plea was allowed.

The plaintiff amended her bill and set out several circumstances which were not in the former bill. And to this the defendant pleaded the original bill and the allowance of the plea which was put in thereunto and that the proceedings were signed and enrolled. And then he pleads again the Statute of Frauds and Perjuries.

Note there was a memorandum drawn up but not signed and a charge in the bill of many solemn promises and assurances to make a settlement.

Mr. *Vernon*, for the plaintiff, cited the Case of Mr. Moor of the new playhouse v. Dr. Hart, which was thus. Dr. Hart wrote a letter to Mr. Moor, who was in a treaty for a marriage with the Doctor's daughter, telling him he would give £1500 with his daughter if the marriage took effect. The treaty continued some time and, at last, the marriage was had. And, in this case, it was decreed that the letter was an agreement in writing within the Statute, and this decree was afterwards affirmed in the House of Lords.

He also cited the Case of Foxcroft and Lister, where a parol agreement was to take a lease and the party put into possession was decreed to be out of the Statute. And this decree was also affirmed in the House of Lords.

He said the first case upon this Statute was before Lord Nottingham,[1] where a man had made a mortgage, which was by an absolute conveyance, and a defeasance was to have been executed at the same time, but, after the mortgagor had executed the conveyance, the mortgagee refused to seal the defeasance. This was plainly a fraud and, though within the letter of the Statute, yet it was plainly within the intent and meaning of it, for the Statute was made to prevent frauds and not to protect against frauds.

Lord Chancellor [Lord Parker]: If a parol agreement is made before a marriage and a settlement is after the marriage made in pursuance of such agreement, though this promise would not bind, yet, when it is performed, it is a good consideration so as to make this settlement not voluntary. The reason why the

---

[1] *Potts v. Turvin* (1681), 79 Selden Soc. 856.

court has carried parol agreements into an execution where part is performed, as where, upon an agreement for a building lease, the party enters and goes to building and then the lessor takes advantage and will not perform the agreement is because there is fraud in the case, for it is a very unfair thing for the lessor to stand by and see the party lay out his money and then refuse to make him a lease. And the court has gone so far as to carry these agreements into execution though the decree that must be made in such cases is founded upon the deposition of witnesses. But the reason of this must be because the fraud of the parties in such cases is greater than the fraud intended to be prevented by the Statute.

Let the first part of the plea be overruled and the other part stand for an answer.

Lincoln's Inn MS. Misc. 380, pt. 3, p. 183

Sir George Maxwell, in his courtship of his present lady, promises that she shall have the disposal of her own estate, and the lady gives Sir George a paper containing her demands, which she desired Sir George to carry to counsel to be drawn up into form. Sir George carries it to counsel. The lady enquires from time to time whether the settlement was finished. At length, the wedding day was come. The lady again asks for the settlement; Sir George tells her the counsel had not finished it, but, upon his word and honor, everything should be done according to her desire. After the marriage, the lady sends Sir George a letter wherein she insists on her settlement; Sir George sends her an answer wherein he says it was highly reasonable she should have her own estate in her own disposal etc.

Now the bill is brought to have a specific performance.

The defendant pleads the Statute of Frauds and Perjuries.

For the plaintiff, it was insisted that this was an agreement carried into execution in part by the marriage.

Lord Parker: This differs from the common case of an agreement to make a lease for years and the intended lessee enters and lays out money; this is an agreement in part carried into execution; therefore, it is proper for the court. But, in our case, it is directly contrary to the Statute of Frauds, for, if there be a marriage, then all such agreements are to be carried into execution, then this Statute signifies nothing. This is no fraud but a bare breach of promise. She has waived the settlement and relied on his promise only. There may be an instance of fraud proper for this court, as, if the husband brings another like that he is to execute and signs that, this is a fraud.

He dismissed the bill.

[Other reports of this case: Precedents in Chancery 526, 24 E.R. 235, 1 Eq. Cas. Abr. 20, 21 E.R. 842, 2 Eq. Cas. Abr. 592, 22 E.R. 497, 1 Peere Williams 618, 24 E.R. 541, 1 Strange 236, 93 E.R. 494.]

332
Davison v. Milton
(Ch. 1718)

A contract in consideration of marriage is enforceable even though it was made after the marriage took place if the general negotiations took place before the marriage.

Lincoln's Inn MS. Hill 73, p. 109, pl. 2

The defendant demurred to the plaintiff's demand, which was to compel the defendant to execute articles which were minuted and signed on one part, which was to allow 50s. per week to the plaintiff and his wife during their living together. But this agreement was subsequent to the marriage and, therefore, was objected as no consideration, which, had it been before, would have been an undoubted one. The defendant had drawn in the plaintiff to marry his daughter, who was represented by the defendant himself, who was father to the plaintiff's wife, as [having] great a fortune, but, at least soon after the marriage, the father talked of giving £2500 to the plaintiff as a fortune but, after alleging it would be an inconvenience to pay down so much money out of trade, agreed to pay 50s. per week, which agreement was so far executed as that he paid it for a long time.

This agreement was not within the Statute of Frauds and Perjuries,[1] for that Act says only where the party that is to be charged has set his hand. Here, the defendant has signed the minutes and the objection that the other side was not obliged by the agreement by not having signed it that is by the plaintiff's suing to have them put in execution. The consideration of this agreement, though subsequent to the marriage in point of time, [was] a very sufficient consideration. And, therefore, the demurrer was overruled and the articles ordered to be carried into execution.

333
Anonymous
(Ch. 1718)

A trustee's wife does not have dower rights in the corpus of the trust.

Lincoln's Inn MS. Misc. 380, pt. 3, p. 184, pl. 1

A. makes a voluntary settlement to B., but he keeps it in his own possession. Afterward, C., who was heir to A., by fraud, procures A. to burn the deed. The question was whether C.'s wife should be endowed of this land, which her husband had obtained by fraud.

---

1 Stat. 29 Car. II, c. 3 (*SR*, V, 839–842).

Master of the Rolls [Jekyll]: A trustee's wife shall not be endowed. C., having obtained these lands by fraud, is a trustee for him that has the right. Therefore, his wife shall not be endowed.

334

King v. Cotton

(Ch. 1718)

A court of equity cannot rewrite a settlement on the ground of compassion in order to give a maintenance not provided for by the settlor.

Lincoln's Inn MS. Misc. 380, pt. 3, p. 184, pl. 2

Sir Thomas Cotton [d. 1715], the father, upon his marriage, settles to the use of himself for life, then to trustees for 500 years to raise £2000 if but one younger child and £5000 if more to be paid at the age of eighteen or marriage and a maintenance of £50 *per annum*, the first payment to be made the first quarter day after the death of the wife. Sir Thomas Cotton died leaving nine children.

A bill [was exhibited] against Sir Robert Salisbury Cotton [1694–1748], the defendant etc., to have maintenances in the lifetime of the mother.

It was insisted for the children that this was a compassionate case of younger children wholly unprovided for, that the court ought to exert the jurisdiction in cases of this nature, that Sir Robert, the defendant, has an estate of £5000 *per annum* descended to him.

Master [of the Rolls, Jekyll]: I cannot decree a maintenance when it is expressly agreed by the parties that the maintenance is to be paid the first quarter after the death of the father and mother. This court has no discretionary power in consideration of compassion. The rules and proceedings of this court are as much known and as certain as the courts at common law. The mother is amply provided for and must maintain them. One of the younger children has attained the age of eighteen [and] therefore entitled to her portion and, though the term be reversionary after the death of the father and mother, yet it vests and is saleable at the respective ages of eighteen or marriage. Though the mother be living, so much of the term of £500 years as is necessary for her portion [will] be disposed of by sale or mortgage as is most advantageous for the estate with interest from eighteen. Though the portion be payable at eighteen, yet this court will take care of the infant and order the money to be put out to interest. But if she be married, it must be immediately paid to her.

335
Tichburn v. Johnson
(Ch. 1718)

Fraud must be pleaded with particularity.

Lincoln's Inn MS. Misc. 380, pt. 3, p. 185

[Where] general fraud is suggested in a bill, they cannot give evidence of a particular fraud, for this would be a hardship on the defendant, who would not know how to defend himself.

[Where a] trustee refuses to act, though it be not necessary to bring him before the court, yet, if a sale be necessary, he must come in before the Master and join in the sale.

336
Perryman v. Perryman
(Ch. 1718)

The Statute of Limitations applies to suits in equity.

Lincoln's Inn MS. Hill 73, p. 107

The defendant pleads the Statute of Limitations.[1] The case was upon an agreement made by the defendant's testator with the plaintiff, who married his daughter, which was that the plaintiff should have £500 upon the marriage, and a usual settlement [was] made and £100 more at the birth of the first child, but, if she died within a year without issue, he was to pay back £100 out of the £500, upon which two bonds were mutually given, one that the plaintiff to pay £100 if the wife died within a year without issue, the other that the defendant was to pay £100 more upon the birth of the first child. The wife died within two months after the marriage and no settlement [was] made. The agreement with the defendant's testator was never sealed. It was no specialty though signed, not being under hand and seal.

The agreement was made 1701, and the defendant lived until 1704, and no action was brought until after his death, 1716.

Mr. *Williams*, for the plaintiff, said the Statute of Limitations is no plea because the cause of action is not yet accrued and, therefore, not within the Statute, for, though the promise was made 1701, it was upon the execution of the settlement, which, as yet, is not executed and, consequently, (Lord Warrington v.

[1] Stat. 21 Jac. I, c. 16, s. 3 (*SR*, IV, 1222–1223).

Booth, House of Lords[1]) no cause of action accrued, but the plaintiff was always ready to execute such agreement and that the agreement was prepared by Mr. Reeve, counsel, and engrossed and was delivered to the father of the plaintiff's wife during the life of the wife, who, being ill at that time, the father delayed the execution until to avoid. (Lord Hollis's Case, Ventris.[2])

Chesshyre, in answer to Mead, [said] that, though the bill was proper to a discovery, it being against an executor to discover assets (that if they had any demand at law, they might know whether there was sufficient assets in the executors to satisfy the demands), yet the court will not likewise grant a relief so as to make the bills convertible a bill for relief and for discovery.

The Statute of Limitations is no plea against a fraud.

Lord Chancellor [Lord Parker]: The plaintiff could not have executed the settlement, the wife dying so soon after. The Statute is as good a plea to a bill in equity as to a suit in law of things of the same nature. He allowed the plea.

N.B. [It is a] very good covenant in a deed where two persons are executors or trustees each to be bound only for his own acts or receipts etc.

337

Anonymous

(Ch. 1718)

A bill can be dismissed for want of prosecution after a replication has been filed.

Lincoln's Inn MS. Hill 73, p. 98, pl. 1

[On the] second seal [day] after Michaelmas term 1718, a bill was dismissed for want of prosecution after a replication had been filed, but [the court] discontinued any proceedings for above those terms after upon an affidavit of notice.

The Master of the Rolls [Jekyll] said he thought it very proper a time should be fixed. And he said it was very proper.

And Mr. Register said it was often granted.

---

1 *Earl of Warrington v. Booth* (1714), 4 Brown P.C. 163, 2 E.R. 111, British Library MS. Hargrave 80, f. 175.

2 *Lord Hollis's Case* (1680), 2 Ventris 345, 86 E.R. 477.

338
Coke v. Wilcocks
(Ch. 1718)

A defendant can deny by the means of a plea notice of claims to property purchased.

Lincoln's Inn MS. Misc. 13, p. 35, pl. 2

18 December 1718.

The defendant pleaded that he was a purchaser for a valuable consideration, and he denied notice by his plea. And it was objected that he ought to have denied notice by his answer, for, otherwise, if the plea is allowed, the plaintiff cannot take exceptions to the answer as to the notice. And for this was cited 1 Vern. 185.[1]

But this objection was overruled by Lord Chancellor [LORD PARKER], saying, if a man could not deny notice by his plea, he could never plead without answering too.

[Other reports of this case: Mosely 74, 25 E.R. 279.]

339
Anonymous
(Ch. 1718)

The parties to a mortgage have six months to redeem or to accept a redemption. A special receiver must put up an indemnity bond.

Lincoln's Inn MS. Hill 73, p. 98, pl. 2

18 December 1718. Master of the Rolls, last seal.

A mortgagee cannot be obliged at an hour's warning to take his money, but [he] has six months allowed to accept it as the mortgagor has to pay it. Upon a motion, this was to oblige the mortgagee to accept immediately, which was denied because it would not have been granted even upon the hearing and, therefore, they could not ask more upon a motion as they could get by a decree.

The Master of the Rolls [JEKYLL] said that the court never appointed a receiver of an infant's estate without a security taken from them to answer the rents.

But Mr. *Vernon* said that he believed that the court had appointed sometimes a receiver not by the power of the court but at the request of the executors, as in this case, which was upon Mr. Bromley's estate of Cambridge, which was in Barbados. There were executors appointed by Mr. Bromley, who, during his

[1] *Price v. Price* (1683), 1 Vernon 185, 23 E.R. 404.

life, had put his estate of Barbados under four trustees, who the executors desired might be empowered by the court to act under the same trusts, it being absolutely necessary that the estate should be put into somebody's hands in January, and this motion was [made] 18 of December; otherwise, it would be to the prodigious damage of the infant's estate.

340

Cullum v. Cullum

(Ch. 1718)

For the purposes of the contract in issue, the words 'younger children' did not refer to daughters where there was no son.

Lincoln's Inn MS. Misc. 12, p. 330

22 December 1718.

By articles on the marriage of Thomas Cullum with the plaintiff Savilla, his wife, he agreed to settle lands for her jointure and that part of her portion should be laid out in long Exchange annuities. And he assigned to trustees on trust out of the profits to pay £60 a year to the plaintiff's mother for her life and the remainder of the profits to Mr. Cullum for his life and the whole to him for life after the death of the mother and upon trust after the death of Mr. Cullum to sell the annuities for or towards the maintenance and education and preferment of the younger children of the said Thomas Cullum on the body of the said Savilla begotten in such proportions as they should during their joint lives by any writing attested by two witnesses appoint. And, until the annuities should be purchased, the mother was to receive the £60 a year and Mr. Cullum the remainder of the produce. But there is no direction what is to be done with the annuities in the case of no appointment or that there should be no younger children.

Mr. Cullum, in pursuance of these articles, settles lands to the use of himself for life, to his wife for her jointure, remainder to the first and other sons of the marriage, remainder to his own right heirs. And it is therein declared that, in case he should have an eldest son and one or more younger children, sons or daughters, by him begotten on the body of his wife, that it should be lawful for him by any deed or writing to charge the jointure lands after his wife's death with any sum not exceeding £1000 for or towards portions for such younger children.

Mr. Cullum having no son and but two daughters only by his wife, he, by will, devises the reversion of the jointure lands to trustees to sell to pay such debts as his personal estate would not extend to pay and then to raise so much money as should be sufficient to make his two daughters portions £2000 apiece to be paid within six months after the death of his wife, and the residue he directs to be applied for other purposes.

The plaintiff brought her bill, amongst other things, that the trustees, in whose hands the remainder of her portion which was made a provision for younger children was, might pay it to her as executrix of her late husband.

The cause was heard by the Master of the Rolls [Jekyll] in Lincoln's Inn Hall, who declared that, as to the £2000, the residue of the plaintiff's portion, which, by the articles, was to be for the maintenance and preferment of the younger children by the plaintiff, the persons who could be entitled thereto ought to have been younger children of the testator at the time of his death, which the defendants Savilla and Katherine were not. And, therefore, he declared they were not entitled to the £2000 but that the said £2000 ought to be taken as part of the said testator's personal estate. But His Honor [Jekyll] declared that the said defendants were entitled to £2000 apiece under the will of the said testator to be raised out of the lands subjected thereto.

Lincoln's Inn MS. Misc. 11, p. 56, pl. 2

22 December 1718.

By articles made on the plaintiff's marriage with Mr. Thomas Cullum, deceased, £2000 was appropriated for younger children's portions. Mr. Cullum died leaving two daughters only by the plaintiff.

The Master of the Rolls [Jekyll] declared that daughters, if there was no son, were not to be taken to be 'younger children'.

341

Babington v. Greenwood

(Ch. 1718–1720)

Where a widow's claiming by the custom does not disturb the will, she shall have what is given her both by the will and by the custom.

Lincoln's Inn MS. Misc. 12, p. 202

The plaintiff's father, being a freeman of London and having no real estate but only a personal estate, does by articles in 1694 on his marriage with Frances, his wife, now the wife of the defendant, in consideration of a £1500 portion to be paid to the trustees, covenant within two years after their marriage to pay £1500 to the trustees. And his wife's father covenants likewise to pay them at the same time £1500 for his daughter's portion, which two sums are thereby directed to be laid out in the purchase of lands to be settled on the husband for life, remainder to the wife for life for her jointure and in bar of dower, remainder to the issue of that marriage. The marriage takes effect. The two plaintiffs are the only issue of that marriage.

The husband, by his will in 1703, devises £3000 apiece to the plaintiffs to be paid at twenty-one. And, taking notice of his marriage articles and that a purchase and settlement had been made pursuant thereto, he confirms that settlement and devises the same lands to his wife according to the settlement for life and, after her death, to his children, the plaintiffs. And he gives the residue of his personal estate to the plaintiffs for their lives and, in case of their deaths, to his wife, the defendant, whom he makes executrix. And he dies.

The wife proved his will and gave security to the Chamberlain of London for £5645 9s. 7½d., being the surplus of his personal estate.

And now, the plaintiffs, having attained their full age, brought this bill against the defendant and his wife, who was the widow and executrix of the plaintiff's father, for an account of his personal estate and to have their several legacies paid them.

The defendant, the wife, by her answer, insisted that her late husband, the plaintiffs' father being a freeman of London, she was entitled to a third part as his widow by the custom. And whether she should be allowed it or not in regard of the marriage articles aforesaid was the principal point in question.

In Michaelmas term 1718, the cause was heard before the Lord Chancellor [Lord Parker], who declared that, from the time of the articles, the money was a debt, which the husband was obliged to pay, that it was no part of his personal estate from that time, but it must be looked upon as land, and then it could be no bar of her customary share of the personal estate, that the custom did not operate at all until the parties' death and, then, whatever personal estate was left was to go according to it. And he decreed accordingly.

Lincoln's Inn MS. Misc. 11, p. 76

18 March 1719[/20].

A freeman, on his marriage, articles to add £1500 to his wife's fortune and that both shall be laid out in lands and settled on the husband for life, then to the wife for life in bar of her dower and thirds at the common law, and then to the issue of the marriage.

[Lord Parker] decreed that this settlement did not exclude the wife from coming in for her share by the custom, notwithstanding the lands were to be bought with money coming out of the personal estate, for, though the land was not bought, yet it must now be considered as land.

Lincoln's Inn MS. Misc. 11, p. 166

19 March 1719[/20].

A citizen makes his will without taking any notice of the custom of London. And he gives legacies to his wife and children, and the surplus, except his plate, which he gives to his wife, he directs should be put out for the benefit of his children. The wife refuses to abide by the will and claims her share by the custom.

Upon hearing the cause, the consideration how the testamentary part should be disposed of was reserved. And now it came on upon the Master's report. And the question was if the widow should have the plate in regard she would not acquiesce under the will, but claimed her customary share. And it was said she could not claim by both.

And the Case of Bedell v. Bedell was cited by *Peere Williams*, for the widow, where it was decreed by Lord Parker that a woman may take by the custom and the will too if what she takes by the will is not inconsistent with the custom or breaks into the customary part.

Mr. *Mead*, *e contra*: It is a settled rule that, if a woman goes about to defeat the will and insists upon the custom so as that the will cannot take place throughout, she can take nothing by the will. Now, by her insisting on the plate, she has lessened the legacies given to the children.

Lord Chancellor [Lord Parker]: If the wife's claiming by the custom does no ways disturb the will, there is no reason why she should not have what is given her by the will. But, indeed, if her claiming by the custom defeats the will, she shall not then have the benefit of both.

Now, in the present case, her claiming the plate does not defeat the will, for the children will have the legacies given them by the will and they will likewise have all the surplus except the plate, which was not given to them, but to the wife.

Note the testator, on his marriage, had by articles agreed to lay out a sum of money in land to be settled for the jointure of the wife. The money was not laid out. And the question at the hearing was if this did not bar the wife of her customary share.

It was decreed it did not, for though it went out of the personal estate, yet it should be considered as land.

Lincoln's Inn MS. Misc. 384, p. 150

18 March.

The defendant is the widow of William Babington, a freeman of London. He, by articles before marriage, covenants to lay out £1500 added to her portion of £1500 in the purchase of lands to be settled on the defendant for her jointure and in bar of dower out of his lands, tenements, and hereditaments. The query is whether she is barred of her customary share of his personal estate.

Mead, for the plaintiff: The defendant is compounded with and should be barred because the personal estate is lessened by this purchase, like Hancock and Hancock, where the settlement of a leasehold was a bar, by Lord Cowper. It is not like Atkyns and Waterson, where lands were settled. But here, the husband had no lands.

Vernon, for the defendant: The Common Serjeant was of the opinion that any provision for the wife, even out of the husband's real estate, would be a bar, but that was exploded in Atkyns and Waterson. In Staunton v. Platt, Michaelmas 1717, where the plaintiff, on her marriage, was advanced by a settlement on her father's land, yet there was no bar of her orphanage part of his personal estate.

In Hancock's Case, there were words to bar her. It might as well be a bar to her share of the personal estate by the Statute of Distributions. Articles to settle is in this court the same as a settlement made. He might have barred her by laying out his whole estate in land.

Lord Chancellor [Lord Cowper]: Here, the settlement is only to be in bar of dower out of his lands etc., which is as strong as if there were negative words that it should not bar her of her customary share. This cannot be looked upon as his personal estate, for whatever is contracted for is a debt. This must be taken as land and may be entailed.

Mead, for the plaintiff. The defendant has a legacy of £50 in plate or money, which she must relinquish if she claims her customary share. Cox and Edmonson. She must entirely abide by the will or the custom. Langston and Langston, where she could not take a devise even of lands and her customary share both.

Lord Chancellor [Lord Cowper]: Where the will is defeated by her claim of her customary share, she cannot take both. But she may where it is not inconsistent with the will. I do not see any reason why a devise of land should hinder her from having her customary share too, because the personal estate is not lessened by the devise. Where it is mentioned to be in bar of her customary share, she has her election, which she will abide by.

On 19 March 1719, on a petition, it was ordered the plaintiff to have her legacy and customary share.

[Other reports of this case: Precedents in Chancery 505, 24 E.R. 227, 1 Peere Williams 530, 24 E.R. 503, 2 Eq. Cas. Abr. 276, 721, 22 E.R. 233, 607.]

342

Morris v. Nixon

(Ch. 1719)

An agreement that was the result of fraud can be rescinded.

1 Strange 144, 93 E.R. 438

On a treaty of marriage, the attorney for the lady told the intended husband that his client desired a remainder might be limited to him. The husband consented; and, when the settlement was read before execution, the lady objected to this remainder, whereupon the gentleman acquainted her that it was done at her request, which she denied. But, however, it being a remote remainder and they unwilling to defer the matter, the writings were executed.

And a bill was brought into this court, where the remainder was set aside as a fraud and imposition.

343
Tremain's Case
(Ch. 1719)

A court of equity can by its officer remove an infant from one place to another and keep him at the latter place.

1 Strange 167, 93 E.R. 452

[Tremain] being an infant, he went to Oxford [University], contrary to the orders of his guardian, who would have him go to Cambridge [University].

And the court sent a messenger to carry him from Oxford to Cambridge. And, upon his returning to Oxford, there went another, *tam* to carry him to Cambridge, *quam* to keep him there.

344
Scotton v. Scotton
(Ch. 1719)

A child's legacy can be satisfied by a provision made subsequent to the will.

1 Strange 235, 93 E.R. 494

A daughter having married without her father's consent, he gave her no portion, but he made his will and, thereby, gave her £50 to be lent out for her, and she to have the use of it. Her husband, being informed of this legacy, applies to the father for the money presently, who gave it him and took a receipt for it in lieu of her portion and of the legacy given by his will. The father died without altering his will, upon which his daughter and her husband sue the administrator in the spiritual court for the legacy, and the administrator brings his bill in this court.

Vernon, for the plaintiff, quoted Birkenhead v. Birkenhead, in Lord Egerton's time, where the father having by will given £1500 apiece to his three daughters, afterwards, married one of them and gave £1500 portion, and died without altering his will, and it was adjudged the portion was a satisfaction of the legacy.

Master of the Rolls [Jekyll]: Whether this be a case relievable in the spiritual court I am not certain. I rather think this receipt is not pleadable there, being a release of a legacy before it is due. But, in this court, it amounts to an agreement of the son-in-law to discharge the legacy. Besides, the precedents here run all this way, that a child's legacy is satisfied by a provision subsequent to the will. Let the proceedings in the spiritual court be stayed.

345

Hagshaw v. Yates

(Ch. 1719)

A person whose title to property is both at common law and in equity will prevail over a person who has only an equitable title.

1 Strange 240, 93 E.R. 497

By PARKER, Lord Chancellor: Where a legal estate and equity meet in the same person, they shall destroy a prior title which is only equitable. And, where the inheritance of land mortgaged for a term is conveyed by a defeasible but equitable title and, afterwards, conveyed to another by a legal and equitable title, the latter shall have the benefit of the equity of redemption.

346

Webb v. Whittington

(Ch. 1719)

Where a plaintiff makes a default at a hearing, he can have a rehearing upon the payment of court costs for the default.

Lincoln's Inn MS. Misc. 384, p. 98, pl. 2

20 January.

The plaintiff made default at the hearing and got an order for a rehearing on paying the defendant 5s. costs of the day and depositing 10s. with the Register. The defendant moves that he may have his costs taxed, as where the defendant makes default.

Lord Chancellor [LORD PARKER]: This is not like where the court makes a decree for the defendant and, on a rehearing, reverses it. There, it is the mistake of the court. This is the same with the defendant's making default or rather stronger.

Let it be the standing rule that the plaintiff must pay the defendant his costs to be taxed, but he need not make a deposit of 10s. with the Register.

Vernon quoted Price v. Higgins, where the same order was made.

Lincoln's Inn MS. Misc. 13, p. 133, pl. 1

7 February 1719. Webb v. Whittingham.

The plaintiff, as heir at law to his uncle Whittingham, brought his bill to discover the defendant's title, who claimed by a settlement made by [. . .] Whittingham with a power of revocation, who, after the execution thereof, had interlined and erased the deed in several material parts. And, therefore, it was insisted that such interlineations and erasures amounted to a revocation or that it made void the deed. And he cited the case of Pigot v. Pigot, that a bond interlined or erased after the execution shall be void, but it is otherwise as to a deed; it will not make void the estate, and Cro. Ca. 399, and 2 Levinz, f. 35, were cited.[1]

The matter [was held] triable at law, and the bill was dismissed with costs.

347

Weeden v. Norwich

(Ch. 1719)

A deed is only evidence of a title, and a party can prove the claim or title by other evidence if the title deed be lost.

Lincoln's Inn MS. Misc. 384, p. 125, pl. 2

26 January 1718/19.

A bill [was exhibited] that the defendants may redeem or be foreclosed and for the aid of the court, the plaintiff having lost the assignment of the mortgage deed.

Curia: The plaintiff's assignment is plainly proved by Serjeant Hanbury's notes taken out of the mortgage deed and here is the original mortgage of two assignments 20 May 1687. This deed is lost, but there is the draft [?] with Mr. Dod's notes and the receipt for £700. The first mortgage in 1687 was made by Sir Roger Norwich to Edward Barwell 7 May 1708. The defendant Sir Er. Norwich's endorsement that the lands should stand a security for £1200 then due for principal and interest [was] proved by Serjeant Hanbury. The plaintiff is to be assisted here against the defendants who claim under a subsequent settlement. The loss of a deed is not a loss of the title. It is only the evidence of a title. The defendant, the Lady Norwich, had notice that there were some encumbrances on the estate; so, she cannot be looked upon as a purchaser without notice, for she ought to have enquired into them. The defendant, Sir Er., must pay off the mortgage or, if the defendants are foreclosed, he must make Lady Norwich compensation of her marriage articles. He has made an ill defense and denies that he knew of the plaintiff's mortgage, which is satisfied. Therefore, he must pay the costs.

Vernon, for the plaintiff, [cited] Sir J. Bank's Case, that he, being a purchaser, might protect himself at law by a deed, which he had stolen out of Serjeant Ellis's study. He insisted that there was no equity for one purchaser against another

[1] *Winchcombe v. Pigot* (1614), 11 Coke Rep. 26, 77 E.R. 1177, also 2 Bulstrode 246, 80 E.R. 1096; *Miller v. Manwaring* (1635), Croke Car. 397, 399, 79 E.R. 947, 948, also W. Jones 354, 82 E.R. 186; *Zouch v. Claye* (1672), 2 Levinz 35, 83 E.R. 441, also 1 Ventris 185, 86 E.R. 126, 2 Keble 872, 881, 84 E.R. 551, 558.

and that law and equity will prevail against equity only, as in Serjeant Maynard and Nosworthy, L.D. 124.

348

Winnington v. Foley

(Ch. 1719)

An infant trustee to preserve contingent remainders can be compelled to join in a common recovery to defeat remainders.

Lincoln's Inn MS. Misc. 384, p. 127, pl. 1

27 January. *Ex parte* Winnington.

[A petition was exhibited] that an infant heir of a trustee might convey to the petitioner to enable him to suffer a recovery. Winnington was the tenant for ninety-nine years if he should so long live, remainder to a trustee to preserve contingent remainders, remainder to the first and other sons of Winnington in tail. Winnington has a son of twenty-one years of age, who prefers this petition.

Master of the Rolls [Jekyll]: This is a new case. The best way is to get an act of Parliament. If I should direct the trustee to convey, the petitioner cannot make a safe title by suffering a recovery because this infant trustee is not within the Act of Parliament, 7 Ann.[1]

N.B. The Lord Chancellor [Lord Parker] decreed the trustee to convey.

[Other reports of this case: 1 Peere Williams 536, 24 E.R. 505, 2 Eq. Cas. Abr. 695, 749, 22 E.R. 584, 635.]

349

Watkins v. Pacy

(Ch. 1719)

Where trustees lose the corpus of the trust, they are not liable if they acted prudently and reasonably, but they are liable if they acted with fraud or gross negligence.

An answer under oath has the weight of evidence, and a single witness cannot prevail against it.

Lincoln's Inn MS. Misc. 384, p. 126

27 January.

The plaintiffs, infants, bring their bill against the defendant, the trustee, who had put out the trust money on a bad security to compel him to make good

[1] Stat. 7 Ann., c. 19 (*SR*, IX, 89).

the trust money, suggesting that the defendant did or might have known it not to be good security and that he did not act with that fairness a trustee should in that part of the money lent on the security was his own but that he would now turn the loss upon the plaintiffs.

Sir Thomas Powys, for the defendant: Formerly, trustees had all the benefit of the trust money and, then, they were liable to make good any loss that might happen. But now, they have no benefit of the trust and, therefore, are not answerable if they use the caution a prudent man should. And no fraud or neglect is proved upon them.

Vernon: They ask that the trustee should answer for £490 and interest lent on a mortgage out of his own pocket when the principal was but £290 and the rest the improvements made by the defendant. The furthest that it has been carried is that the trustees should take the security. But the trustee, not having anything for his pains, is never so punished unless guilty of plain fraud or neglect. In Lord Nottingham's time, the trustee was liable to make good the security. But in Lord Cowper's time, no trustee was bound to warrant a security unless he acted fraudulently. Where trustees or executors have been moneyed men, the court has sometimes held them very straightly because of the fraud of taking the good securities themselves and turning the bad ones on the trust. The defendant's answer is falsified but by one witness, which it is not sufficient. They pretend we had notice that the title was bad, but that must be plainly proved. In one Gargrave's Case,[1] it was sent to law to try whether he had notice or not; Gargrave, the trustee, was the attorney in the cause of Moncktown and Shipley; the defendant pleads a stated account 8 November 1711 between the defendant and W.W., the plaintiff's husband. The benefit was saved to the hearing. At that time, the plaintiffs did not insist that the defendant should make good the security.

Curia [LORD PARKER]: There not having been proved any fraud or gross neglect in the defendant, the trustee, he dismissed the bill without costs.

Lincoln's Inn MS. Misc. 380, pt. 3, p. 201

Tuesday, 27 January, before Lord Chancellor PARKER.

A. makes his will and makes the plaintiff, his own daughter, his executor and appoints the defendant supervisor of his will. The defendant takes out administration *durante minore* aetate and places out the trust money at interest. £250 was placed out in a defective mortgage. The plaintiff Watkins, after his intermarriage with the infant, states an account of his wife's estate with the defendant and receives the securities and money and gives a release. And now he brings his bill to make the defendant to account to him £492, being the principal and interest due on the defective security. And he suggests that the defendant,

[1] Note *Ibbottson v. Rhodes* (1706), 2 Vernon 554, 23 E.R. 958, 1 Eq. Cas. Abr. 229, 231, 21 E.R. 1010, 1074.

being an attorney, lent the money knowing it to be a defective security and that he had received a gratuity for so doing or, at least, had paid himself with the infant's [money] a bad debt due to himself from R., the mortgagee.

The plaintiff proved that the defendant and R., the mortgagee, lived both in the same town and were acquainted, that R., in 1703, had mortgaged the same lands to S., and that the defendant was a witness to that mortgage and, in 1704, took an assignment of that mortgage from S. and then advanced £110 paid to S. and R. and mentioned to be the defendant's money. In 1705, the defendant had a bill of sale from R. of all his goods.

The defendant, in his answer, says that he thought it a good security even at the time when the account was made up with the plaintiff and that, at the time of the mortgage taken, he advised with counsel, who told him that a recovery was necessary, which was accordingly had and that he had no gratuity or reward whatsoever.

The plaintiff proved that, before the mortgage, that the defendant and one Clarkson, after[wards] the attorney of the same town, were traveling to Lincoln to the assizes and that Clarkson told the defendant that he heard that he had or was about to lend money on R.'s lands and cautioned him and said that the estate was settled by R.'s father. But there was no proof that the defendant made any answer to him. The plaintiff proved there had been dealings between the defendant and R. on his own account, but this was much about the same time as the mortgage, that the defendant had taken a bill of all R.'s goods and had sold them so that he then knew him to be an indigent person, that there was an account stated between the defendant and R., and that £105 was due to the defendant and an £105 was an additional sum lent on the same security.

For the plaintiff, it was said, though we cannot give any direct proof of any advantage to the defendant but only from the whole circumstances collected together, yet here is gross negligence, *scil.* the defendant did not enquire after any title deed. He says he advised with counsel, who told him a recovery was necessary. How could the counsel have advised a recovery unless he saw the settlement? And here is express notice by Clarkson.

The defendant proved by the witnesses to the release that, on the delivery over of the securities, no objection was made and that the plaintiff seemed fully satisfied. For the defendant, it was said, formerly, it was the practice of the court that, if a trustee lent the money, it was at his hazard, but then the advantage and interest made was his own, but, now, the course is altered, as a trustee has not now the advantage of the interest, so he is not chargeable with the principal in the case of a bad security. We took a prudent care in the putting out of this money. We took an assignment of a mortgage. The mortgagor was in possession and his father before him. As to the notice by Clarkson, that will never be accounted notice in this court. The Case of Munton v. Shipley, where one meets another in the market and asks him if he has any encumbrances on such lands, the other answers no; this was no notice but an idle question. But, if he had told him he was about lending money on such an estate and then asked if he had any encumbrances on it, this would be notice. So in our case, it was only travelling discourse, and it may be not attended to by the defendant. He made no answer. A trustee shall not be saddled with the payment of money for neglect only. It was never carried so far in this court. He has a hard part; as it is, he is allowed nothing for his labor and pains unless there be a special provision for it in the deed. They have not the least pretense we have made any advantage by this mortgage and so must suppose we did mischief for mischief's sake.

A trustee is not bound to come into a court of equity to have the direction of the court in placing out the money. But he must act prudently[1] and reasonably.

It was said, where a trustee has £1000 and puts it out on two securities [and] one proves defective, the *cestui que* trust may either insist on all the principal, *viz.* £1000, but then shall have no interest gained by the £500 or else must be contented with the £500 and interest. So, if there were several other good securities, he shall lose the interest of all of them if he insist on the principal cost.

The security in this case was defective. Thus, R.'s father made a settlement after marriage to himself and his wife for their lives, remainder to the heirs of the body of the wife begotten by the husband, remainder over. The father dies. The wife makes a lease for years to the son and, so being in possession, makes this mortgage, and he dies before the mother. He suffered a recovery which was not good because [there was] no good tenant to the *praecipe*, the freehold being in the mother.

Lord Chancellor [Lord Parker]: This bill is not brought to rectify the account; this cannot be set aside but for fraud. Suppose the executor had been guilty of a gross neglect and after[wards] the infant comes of age and having time and leisure to look into the securities and afterwards executes a release. Shall a court of equity set aside this release because I was negligent to enable me to take an advantage of another's negligence? This is what I never heard of. I did not look about me, and there was a fraud put upon me trusting your honesty and not my own understanding. And here, though the husband was transacting for an infant, his wife, that will not alter the case, for the husband is immediately entitled to this estate; therefore, if he give a discharge, whether he received the money or not, the wife is forever bound. Here was the appearance of a security. It was not land the party had nothing to do with. I believe he might know of the settlement. He says in his answer that he did not know it to be a defective title. Clarkson might tell the defendant this story, but that does not seem to be material, for he made no answer. I cannot account for the recovery if they had not known something of this settlement. I take it to be a mistake in Pacy concerning the title, and [he was] led into it by his counsel, who told him it would be a good security if there was a recovery. And the plaintiff himself is led into the same mistake, for

1 prudentionably *MS.*

he writes the defendant that his counsel told him he had a good title and shall make this mistake to be so penal in the defendant, which the plaintiff himself is led into. He never called on the defendant to make him satisfaction until after a decree against him in this court. He was computing, if I take the interest, I shall lose the principal on the bad security; if I insist on the principal, I shall lose the interest. It is plain he had hopes of prevailing in his suit. What temptation had the defendant to throw away an infant's money? He swears he had no premium at all. In other respects, he seems to have acted much to the defendant's advantage. The ace of the recovery was to trustees to sell to pay the infant's money first. This was to save the expense of a decree of foreclosure, the security being scanty. He has charged himself with £450 interest. If there had been any reason to think the security insufficient and he had lent the infant's money to pay himself, there he had been chargeable. But that is not the case. I take it to be clear if a trustee call in money and afterwards puts it out on a bad security; yet, in this instance, the trustee making no profit to himself, therefore, shall not answer for the loss of it. Let the bill be dismissed but without costs.

It was said in this case, if an executor [on] trust is not answerable for gross negligence, it will give great encouragement and opportunity to cheat and squander away trust money.

The Lord Chancellor [Lord Parker] said Clarkson's deposition cannot prevail against the answer of the defendant, for it is an oath against an oath.

It was said, where a trustee lends out his own money beside the trust money and does not declare at the time of the money lent that it is the trust money, he shall not turn the bad security on the trust.

350

Savage v. Collins

(Ch. 1719)

Where a testator has a power of revocation, his or her will is not an execution of the power where the will does not refer to it and does not devise inconsistently to it.

Lincoln's Inn MS. Misc. 384, p. 134

31 January. At the Lord Chancellor's House.

The question is whether the will of the defendant's wife is an execution of a power of revocation, the power not being referred to by the will.

Sir Thomas Powys, for the defendant: In the case of an inheritance, it is so, as Scroop's Case.[1] She devises £500 to A. in case she leave no child and all the residue of her personal estate to the defendant, her husband, whom she makes

[1] *Scrope's Case* (1612), 10 Coke Rep. 143, 77 E.R. 1143.

executor. Where that is a power and a will [is] inconsistent, it is an execution of the power.

Vernon: If there is a power of revocation and the circumstances are observed in a will, it is an execution of the power though it is not referred to. If the will is not a revocation, it is void. She disposes of her estate as being absolute owner of it.

Kettleby: The power in the deed is that she may revoke by any deed or will executed in the presence of three witnesses. The devise of the residue does not depend upon the same contingency as the devise of £500 to A., which is in case she leave no child. She made the will seven weeks before she had a child born.

Cowper, for the plaintiff: Where there is a direct contradiction between the deed and the will, they cannot both subsist. Here is no revocation, no more than if she had made her husband executor only. The devising to him the residue does not alter the case. Here, the intent was only that her husband should have the residue in case she left no child, but she did not design to give it away from her child. There is no inconsistency between the deed and the will.

Mead: The deed gives the estate to her executors, administrators, and assigns if she should have no child or it should die before twenty-one subject to a power of revocation.

Lord Chancellor [Lord Parker]: Here is no express revocation. The only question is whether that is a necessary implication or inconsistency. If there had been no power of revocation, how had this will been? The deed gives it to her, her executors, administrators, and assigns in case she should have no child or it should die before twenty-one. She had £150 to her own separate use, out of which the present legacies may take effect. She gives the residue of her personal estate to her husband. Her personal estate was what was to her separate use and what belonged to her upon the contingency of the child's dying. So it would stand that if there were no power of revocation. And it remains so if the deed is not altered and if she does not make use of her power, which I think she has not done. There not being any inconsistency or necessary implication that it is revoked, it would be hard to leave it in the husband's power not to give the child one farthing.

Lincoln's Inn MS. Misc. 11, p. 42

31 January 1718[/19].

Before the marriage of the defendant with his wife, a deed of trust was made whereby the defendant's wife assigned to trustees several securities and other personal things amounting to £3500 upon trust that they should pay the interest thereof to the wife for her separate use during the coverture between her and the defendant, her husband, and, if he survived her, then he was to have the interest for his life unless he married again and then it was to go to the issue of the marriage if there were any, but, if there was none, he was then to have it for his life notwithstanding his marriage, and, after the death of the survivor of the defendant and his wife, the trust estate was to go to their issue, but, if they left none, then to go to the executors or administrators of the wife, in which deed was a power for the wife by any deed or by her will under hand and seal attested by two witnesses to alter or revoke the trusts and appoint new ones.

The wife, about a year after her marriage, being then with child, makes her will and, without taking any notice of the deed of trust or the power which she had to revoke it, directs £80 to be laid out in a monument for her father, gives £5 to the poor of the parish where she lived, and £10 to a friend, and some specific legacies, and, in case she should die without issue, she gives £500 to her sister, and all the residue of her personal estate she gives to the defendant, her husband, and makes him executor. And, in a short time afterwards, she dies leaving one child only.

And the question was whether this will was a revocation of the deed of trust.

Sir Thomas Powys and Mr. *Vernon*, for the defendant, insisted the will was a revocation. They are inconsistent one with the other. The devise to the husband is an immediate devise and unless the deed is revoked by the will, the will is a mere nullity.

If the will can work upon nothing else, it must operate upon the trust estate, and that it can operate upon nothing else is plain, for the wife lived but a year after the marriage, and, instead of laying up anything out of the interest, the husband spent more in her maintenance and for her funeral and sickness than what the interest amounted to.

As for the objection that the power is not taken notice of in the will, that is not necessary according to Scroop's Case.

On the other side, it was insisted that the deed and will are very consistent, for the devise of the residue to the husband must be understood to be an appointment how the residue should go in case she should have no children, for, by the deed of trust, the trust estate was to go to her executors if there was no issue.

Lord Chancellor [Lord Parker]: The only question is how far the will is inconsistent with the deed, for, if it is so, it must amount to a revocation of the deed. There is no express revocation, and, therefore, it must be a revocation by implication if at all.

Suppose there had been no power of revocation. How would it have stood then? Why, the wife had a power to dispose of her estate if there was no issue. Now, is not this a very proper will to dispose of the estate in case she should have no issue? It is true she has given away legacies to the amount of £15 and directed £80 to be laid out in a monument for her father. Now, to answer this, there was a year's interest of £3500, which is a great deal more than what the legacies came to.

Indeed, the defendant, by his answer, says his wife left nothing, but then he deducts for her funeral and physic, which is pretty extraordinary, for must not a man bury his wife if she has a separate estate or must she, in such case, pay for her board? So that I do not see but that part of the will is very consistent with the deed.

Then, as to the residue given to the husband, why may not that be expounded to be what she had the power to give away in case she had no issue? I think it ought to be so construed since there is no actual revocation.

He decreed the will to be no revocation of the deed.

Lincoln's Inn MS. Misc. 13, p. 133, pl. 2

31 January 1719. Dr. Savage and Collins, an infant v. Collins.

Frances, late wife of the defendant Collins, before her marriage, assigned over her personal estate to Dr. Savage in trust for herself for life, to the defendant, her husband, for life, if children and he marry again, the child or children to have the profits, if no child or the child dies before twenty-one, then to her executors or administrators, [with] a power for the wife, by deed or will with three witnesses, to revoke.

Frances makes a will and thereby devised £80 for a monument, £500 to her sister if she died without a child, and she gives the rest and residue of her estate to her husband, whom she made executor; she leaves one child.

The question was if this will was a revocation of the deed.

It was agreed, if the will was altogether inconsistent with the deed, it would be a revocation, as in Scroop's Case. But here, it was held not to be inconsistent, the words are 'her estate' and the 'residue of her estate', which do not carry or import a necessary implication that she intended to revoke the deed.

And, therefore, [it was] decreed the defendant to account.

351

Shilston v. Tate

(Ch. 1719)

A court of equity will intervene in a contract case where an unforeseen accident occurred.

Lincoln's Inn MS. Misc. 384, p. 135

31 January.

The question was how a contract for Negroes who were sold for sugar at Montserrat should be performed, whether for the value of sugar at the time of the contract or of the delivery of the sugar. At the time of the contract, sugar was worth about 12s. per hundred, but the French having destroyed the island, sugars were treble that value at the time the sugar was agreed to be delivered, which was the next harvest, so that the Negroes, who were sold at £30 a head, which was the highest price, would be then sold at £100. The Negroes were sold about July 1699, and the contract was that so many hundredweight of sugar should be paid for each Negro.

Lord Chancellor [Lord Parker] considered the sugar as money and this being an unforeseen accident, the value should be taken as at the time of the contract, for had this accident been foreseen, it is not to be imagined the parties would have contracted for the delivery of so much sugar in specie, which would have been above treble the value of the Negroes.

But query whether, if this accident had not happened and the sugars had risen or fallen in their value before the time of delivery, the value of the sugar must not have been taken as at the time of the delivery, the contract being that so many hundredweight of sugar should be paid for each Negro at the next harvest, and whether it would not have been so if the value of money had altered and the contract had been for money.

352

Goodman v. St. John

(Ch. 1719)

The doctrine of lis pendens *is for the benefit of plaintiffs not defendants.*

Lincoln's Inn MS. Misc. 384, p. 136

6 February; at the house of the Lord Chancellor.

Vernon, for the defendant: A *lis pendens* is only for the benefit of the plaintiff that he may not be defeated by any conveyance or act of the defendant, and, therefore, if a man purchases from a defendant *pendente lite*, he is in the same case with the defendant. But a defendant can have no benefit by a *lis pendens*. The doctrine of *lis pendens* is sometimes very hard, and it were to be wished that a public register were kept of all bills and what lands are demanded by them that resort might easily be had to them.

Raymond: A plaintiff may be said to attach his right by filing his bill, but it is a new attempt for a defendant to claim a benefit by a *lis pendens*.

Vernon: If a man surceases three terms, he cannot have the benefit of a *lis pendens*, for, then, his bill may be dismissed for want of prosecution. But there must be a recent prosecution.

Lord Chancellor [Lord Parker]: The notion of a *lis pendens* is not from the notoriety of it, for, if so, a judgment at law or a trial at *nisi prius* would have the same effect. But the reason of it is because, without it, the court cannot do justice if it should be in the power of the defendant to delay or prevent a plaintiff of his remedy by conveying to other hands though without notice.

The Lord Chancellor [Lord Parker] asked Mr. Vernon: If there be a decree that lands are liable to one trust and, afterwards, [there is] a second decree that the same lands are liable to another trust, which decree shall take place, whether it be like two judgments whereof the prior takes place?

Vernon: The rule *Qui prior est tempore potior* [*est in*] *jure* holds good in this case unless the *cestui que trust* under the second decree gets the law on his side, as in Christ's Hospital v. Stewkly.353

353

Lawley v. Lawley

(Ch. 1719)

In this case, a power to make leases was properly exercised.

Lincoln's Inn MS. Misc. 384, p. 137, pl. 3

9 February.

[Upon] a power for trustees to join with Sir Francis Lawley, Dame Ann, or Sir Thomas, who were tenants for life, to make leases for twenty-one years or any number of years determinable on three lives so as the rents be not less than the rents then reserved, the plaintiff Sir Thomas was to have the fines.

Sir Robert Raymond, for the plaintiff: The plaintiff admits that the power is not strictly pursued at law, the rents not being reserved to the trustees nor they joining and some part not being then in lease, which concerns the second power for Sir Thomas Lawley to renew or let after the death of Sir Francis. Such parts were in lease at Sir Francis's death so as the rent be reserved to the trustees and the ancient and accustomed rent or such rents as now are or the most that can be gotten for the same.

Knott: The intent of the power is observed, which was the full rent then in being should be reserved. If there has been a forfeiture, there may be a compensation made to Lady Lawly. Therefore, it is good in equity.

Mead, for the plaintiff: The intention of the parties at the making of the settlement by Sir Francis on the marriage of Lady Lawley was the rents were to be for the benefit of Lady Lawley, but the plaintiff Sir Thomas was to have the fines. If no part could be leased or renewed by the plaintiff, Sir Thomas, but what was then leased by Sir Francis, it would be in Sir Francis's power to defeat him from making any leases and consequently from having any fines. So, if he must reserve the rack rent, there is no prejudice to Lady Lawley by the plaintiff's making the leases in question, the ancient rents being reserved.

Cowper, for the defendant, Lady Lawley's representative, she being now dead: In 1681, Lady Lawley joined with her son, Sir Thomas Lawley, in making the second settlement, she having then a jointure on the premises. The leases should have been made according to the power and the rents be reserved to her trustees, whereas Sir Thomas reserves the rents of My Lady's jointure to himself without consulting with the trustees. As to one lease to B., that was a lease in being at £30 *per annum*, and Sir Thomas renews it at £20. The intent must appear from the settlement itself. They may lease what was in lease at the death of Sir Francis. Therefore, they cannot lease what was not then in lease, reserving the ancient rent, or what was in being seven years before the settlement or the best rent. The last refers to what was not in lease at Sir Francis's death or at the time of the settlement.

Vernon: As to how, for the plaintiffs are proper, there is no equity. They say the trustees lived at a distance, but there is no proof of any request to them. Sir Thomas has willfully not pursued the power. Where purchasers under the power are to have the benefit of the execution of the power, equity may interpose, but not for the person himself to take advantage of his own neglect. Suppose he had not executed the power. It is the same if he had not pursued it. Here are incurable defects. It is of such lands as should be in lease at the death of Sir Francis at the time of making the settlement. It should have been considered whether it were proper or convenient. But, when the settlement is made, it cannot be altered. There was a second power to lease if there was no lease then in being. Here was a lease in being to B. If it were surrendered to the plaintiff, it would not do, for it should be to the trustees. The old rent was £20 *per annum* reserved during the life of R.B. and after at £30. The rent the plaintiff has reserved is but £20; therefore, it is not the old rent.

Sir Thomas Powys, in reply: It is said that equity will assist him who purchases under the execution of a power but not him who executes the power, for the settlement was made in consideration of £6000, which was the fortune of the plaintiff's lady. A parol lease is as good as one in writing. Here, part was let on a parol lease. If the tenant had held it twelve years, it had been an accustomed rent.

Raymond: The defendant is no sufferer, but he has had the benefit of the settlement, for the rents of her jointure have been paid her. They are trustees for her as to the rent. But, for us, as to the fines, Sir Francis would not make leases of part which should not turn to our prejudice.

Lord Chancellor [Lord Parker]: Upon the construction of the deed, two things are to be considered, what interest My Lady had before and what she was to have after the settlement. It seems here is an estate to Sir Francis and his lady, then to trustees upon trust, which is not strictly a power to join in leasing. As to the rents, they are trustees for My Lady and, as to all the other profits, for him in remainder. And they could be compelled by Sir Thomas to join. But they could not of themselves make any lease good. They might make two sorts of leases, first, to bind My Lady or the person who joined, the other to bind the remaindermen. As to the first, the person joining was bound though the power was not pursued. But, as to the second, the remaindermen could not be bound unless the power were pursued. Here, the intent was only that My Lady should be secure of the ancient rents. The rest was to be for the benefit of Sir Thomas, who might have demanded of the trustees to make a lease, even to himself. And, if he paid the ancient rents, he would have the benefit of the rest. Therefore, the plaintiff had a right to compel the trustees to join in any lease. If B.'s lease had fallen in My Lady's lifetime, it might have been a question whether £20 or £30 *per annum* should be reserved, but, now, it is out of the case. As to the other lease, it is good as to the plaintiff, and My Lady is to be answered only the rent reserved by Sir Francis at the time of the settlement. And the leases are good as against the plaintiff.

[Other reports of this case: 9 Modern 32, 88 E.R. 296, 2 Eq. Cas. Abr. 71, 578, 22 E.R. 62, 486.]

354

Bishop of London v. Webb

(Ch. 1719)

A lease without impeachment of waste does not permit the lessee to alter permanently the leased premises.

Lincoln's Inn MS. Misc. 11, p. 45

10 February 1718[/19].

The plaintiff obtained an injunction to stay the defendants from digging brick earth in a field lying in the manor of Ealing, which belonged to the Bishop [of London] in the right of his bishopric upon an affidavit that the defendant, who was only a lessee, was digging of brick earth to the prejudice of the inheritance.

The defendant put in his answer and set forth that he was an under lessee under a lease for 200 years granted in Edward VI's time and that the lease was made without impeachment of waste and that, therefore, he ought not to be restrained from digging for brick earth and the rather for that there was twenty-nine years to come of the lease and he had only taken for fifteen years and was bound to dig but one acre in a year and to level every acre before he began to dig another.

Upon the plaintiff's coming to show cause why the injunction should not be dissolved upon the coming in of the defendant's answer, it was insisted on that, though the lease was without impeachment of waste, yet that would not justify him in what he was doing, for he was digging at least nine feet deep, as appeared by the affidavits, which was in effect to destroy the inheritance and take away the very thing granted. And, therefore, it was prayed that the injunction might be continued as was done in the case of Vane v. Lord Bernard,[1] where My Lord Bernard was tenant for life without impeachment of waste, and, upon a quarrel with the plaintiff, his son, who was the next remainderman in the settlement, he pulls down a great part of the mansion house and sells the materials. And, in that case, an injunction was granted, for he was in effect taking away part of what was granted by the marriage settlement.

Lord Chancellor [Lord Parker]: I have for a long time thought that these words 'without impeachment of waste' had been carried too far. After the Statute of Gloucester,[2] which gave treble damages and the place wasted, these words were inserted in deeds to prevent people's being liable to actions upon that Statute. But I believe they never were intended to give a man a property[3] in anything that he severed from the inheritance. However, as the law now stands, a tenant for life without impeachment of waste may cut down timber and sell it, but

---

[1] *Vane v. Lord Barnard* (1715), see above, Case No. 58.

[2] Stat. 6 Edw. I, c. 5 (*SR*, I, 48).

[3] in properly *MS*.

though this is so, yet I think a man, by virtue of those words, cannot take away the very thing which is granted to him, as the defendant, if he is suffered to go on in his digging, would do, for, though he is obliged to level as he digs, yet that does not oblige him to fill up, so that, when he has done digging, the ground will be a perfect pit and there will be no way to carry off the water.

Let the injunction be continued, but not to extend to stay the making into bricks the clay which is dug upon the one acre which is begun to be dug.

Lincoln's Inn MS. Misc. 384, p. 141, pl. 2

19 February.

There was a motion to show cause for an injunction to stay waste. The defendant claims under a lease without impeachment of waste made by Bishop Bonner.[1] The defendant digs to make bricks, which the plaintiff insists is to destroy the inheritance and the land will be overflowed with water and so the evidences altered.

Mead, for the defendant: A tenant without impeachment of waste may open new mines. This is not like the Case of Lord Barnard, who pulled down Raby Castle, which was settled on the issue of the marriage, nor like cutting down trees, which are the ornament of the seat.

Vernon, for the plaintiff: Lord Cowper decreed Lord Barnard's Case upon former precedents. If a house is settled and the tenant for life is without impeachment of waste, he cannot pull down the house. In Lord Barnard's Case, though the castle was in great part pulled down before the injunction was granted, yet he was decreed to put it again into repair and to pay costs.

Wilkinson: This is not like trees or mines, which are part of the profit.

Lord Chancellor [Lord Parker]: At common law, [a writ of] prohibition to commit waste lay. There, the Statute[2] gives treble damages. Now, the clause 'without impeachment of waste' was at first designed to exempt them from the penalty. If a tenant for life cuts down trees, the property of them is in him who has the inheritance. If this clause could signify nothing unless it gave a liberty to make bricks, I could not hinder it. But, at the time of making this lease, there could not be any expectation that it would be used for making bricks. I am afraid the digging nine feet deep may be of ill consequence to the inheritance because it cannot be made level again. I would not have the injunction to hinder him from making the earth already dug into bricks, but he must not dig any more until the hearing of the cause. The writ of estrepement at common law is like an injunction.

[Other reports of this case: 1 Peere Williams 527, 24 E.R. 501, 2 Eq. Cas. Abr. 758, 22 E.R. 643.]

---

[1] K. Carleton, 'Bonner, Edmund (d. 1569)', *Oxford Dictionary of National Biography*, vol. 6, pp. 552–556.

[2] Stat. 6 Edw. I, c. 5 (*SR*, I, 48).

355

Ekins v. East India Company

(Ch. 1719)

Where both parties to a lawsuit are members of a corporation, they may inspect the books of the corporation, but not where one only is a member.

The medium of interest means the medium during the time of the transaction and also the medium of what might be gotten under those circumstances.

Lincoln's Inn MS. Misc. 11, p. 187

The plaintiff, under a license from the defendant, sent his ship in 1699 upon a voyage to the East Indies. And, putting in at Batavia, one of the defendant's agents, who wanted a ship for their service, by undue means, possessed the plaintiff's ship and cargo and sailed away with her to Pulo Condore in June 1702. And the plaintiff brought his bill for a satisfaction of the loss he had sustained.

On 11 November 1715, the cause was heard before Lord Cowper, who declared that the defendants ought to answer for the ship stores and cargo as came to the hands of the defendants or their agents according to the value they were of at the time when it came to their hands, but not to answer for what the plaintiff might have lost by the voyage. And it was sent to a Master to compute the value, and interest and costs was reserved. The Master reported the value at £3700, but, the defendants taking exceptions, an issue at law was directed to try the value. And the verdict found it £3400.

On 24 January 1716[/17], the cause was heard on the equity reserved, and it was decreed the plaintiff should have interest from the 9th June 1702 and that such interest should be Indian interest. And, in regard Indian interest did not bear a certain rate, the Master was to make his computation of interest at a medium rate of interest and the plaintiff was to allow what it would have cost to have insured the remittance of so much money from India to England.

The defendants, after this, appealed to the House of Lords, and the appeal was dismissed with £100 costs.[1]

The Master certified the medium rate of interest to be £8 percent and, at that rate, computed the interest.

The plaintiff excepts to the report because the Master had not computed interest at £12 percent or at least not less than £10 percent.

On 17 February 1718[/19], upon arguing this exception, the report was confirmed.

[1] *East India Company v. Ekines* (1718), 2 Brown P.C. 382, 1 E.R. 1011.

Note, on arguing the exception, a case was cited between Harvey and the East India Company,[1] [who] were decreed to pay 15 percent for £30,000, and another cause between Brown and Captain Litton,[2] where the defendant submitted to pay 10 percent for a sum of money of the plaintiff's husband, which the defendant took into his hands in the East Indies and common interest from the time he arrived in England.

Lincoln's Inn MS. Misc. 384, p. 140, pl. 3

12 February.

Upon a motion by the plaintiff that the Company might produce their books before the Master that the plaintiff might the better discover the value of India interest in the year 1702, which the defendants were decreed to pay for a ship of the plaintiff, which they had seized on at Batavia. The Master had examined witnesses and settled the interest at £8 percent.

For the defendant, it was insisted that this was a new attempt for a man to arm his adversary against himself, that a man must produce his books of accounts, which concern dealings between the parties themselves, not what concerns the dealings with others, as in Lane and Nichols, where Turkish interest was decreed, both being partners in Turkey.

Lord Chancellor [Lord Parker]: In the common law courts, where both parties are members of a corporation, they may have liberty to inspect the books of the corporation, but not where one only is a member. This is a new attempt and may be of ill consequence. And the Master does not certify that he wants more light.

He denied the motion.

Lincoln's Inn MS. Misc. 384, p. 187, pl. 2

15 October 1719.

The plaintiff had a decree for Indian interest, which the Master was to settle at a moderate medium. The Master allowed £8 percent. The plaintiff excepts for that it ought to be £12.

Chesshyre, for the defendant: The transaction arose at Batavia, which is a Dutch settlement, where interest at the highest is but 6 percent, and, at Fort St. George, it is but 9, but, at Bengal, it is £15 percent. The Master did right in having regard to the place where the transaction arose, rather than where interest is at the highest.

---

[1] Note *Harvey v. East India Company* (1700), 2 Vernon 395, 23 E.R. 856, Precedents in Chancery 128, 24 E.R. 62, 2 Eq. Cas. Abr. 281, 22 E.R. 237.

[2] *Brown v. Litton* (1711), 1 Peere Williams 140, 24 E.R. 329, 10 Modern 20, 88 E.R. 606, 2 Eq. Cas. Abr. 5, 452, 722, 740, 22 E.R. 4, 385, 608, 628, British Library MS. Hargrave 80, f. 21v.

Cowper, for the plaintiff: The plaintiff has been kept out of his money seventeen years so that the 8 percent from that time will not be more than 4½ if it had been constantly paid.

Lord Chancellor [LORD PARKER]: That is if you compute interest upon interest. But here, you are allowed simple interest.

Cowper: As to Batavia, that belongs to the Dutch, and, where the question is between Englishmen, interest ought to be rated according to what it bears in our own colonies. In Harvey v. East India Company, £15 percent was allowed.

Curia [LORD PARKER]: The medium of interest must mean the medium during the time of the transaction and also the medium of what might be gotten under those circumstances. The security of money or the badness of the security is the true measure, not the difference of places. I think the Master has done right.

[Other reports of this case: 1 Peere Williams 395, 24 E.R. 441, 2 Eq. Cas. Abr. 238, 533, 534, 722, 22 E.R. 202, 449, 450, 608, 2 Brown P.C. 382, 1 E.R. 1011.]

356

Bailey v. Scott

(Ch. 1719)

Where an executor uses the decedent's estate to buy land, the unpaid legatees cannot get payment out of the land.

Lincoln's Inn MS. Misc. 11, p. 41

17 February 1718[/19]. Master of the Rolls.

The plaintiffs bring their bill against the defendant, who was the executor of an executor for a satisfaction of legacies given them by the will of the first testator out of lands purchased by his executor, suggesting that he had laid out the assets of the first testator in purchasing these lands and that there were no other assets left to pay these legacies. And there was proof that the executor had declared that the lands were purchased with the assets of the first testator. But notwithstanding that, the plaintiffs' bill was dismissed though there was no purchaser in the case. And for this was cited the Case of Keck v. Web, in Lord Somers's time, where trustees of lands had employed one Hamond to receive the rents and he lays out the money he received out of the trust estate in a purchase of lands and takes the conveyance in the trustees' names and, they afterwards dying insolvent, the *cestui que trust* brings a bill to follow the money and to have a satisfaction out of the lands. And the bill was dismissed by Lord Somers for the trustees were debtors for the money, which their receiver had received. And, upon an appeal to the Lords, the decree was affirmed.

Mr. *Vernon* cited the case of a mealman of Uxbridge,[1] who was left executor and found a considerable sum of money hidden in a wall in his testator's house, which he immediately laid out in a purchase, and the residuary legatee brought a bill to follow the assets, it appearing that the executor was worth nothing at the testator's death and that the purchase could be made with no other money but that which he found in the wall. And the late Master of the Rolls [Trevor] decreed for the plaintiff, but that decree was afterwards reversed.

It was said that My Lord Chancellor [Lord Parker] declared in the Duke of Kingston's Case, last term,[2] that, if a trustee of a sum of money purchases land and does not leave assets sufficient to answer the trust money, a court of equity will presume he made the purchase with the trust money and in pursuance of the trust though there is no declaration of trust to that purpose.

357

Anonymous v. Maxwell

(Ch. 1719)

A defendant in a court of equity who is beyond the jurisdiction of the court must put in his answer by a commission.

Lincoln's Inn MS. Hill 73, p. 70, pl. 1

19 February 1718[/19].

A man, prisoner at Tunis, to which place no English ships go directly but by the way of Leghorn or Genoa, by the affidavits proved, had brought his action for seaman's wages and recovered, upon which a bill in equity was preferred for a discovery. And an injunction [was] craved for want of Maxwell, who was the defendant in equity, having put in his answer from Tunis, notwithstanding the difficulty of getting a commission returned from Tunis.

His Honor [Jekyll] could not break the rules of the court though he thought it a very hard case, for the defendant was in slavery and the wages [were] the only means of his redemption, and he put one to get Maxwell's answer.

[Other reports of this case: 1 Peere Williams 523, 24 E.R. 499.]

[1] *Kendar v. Milward* (1702), 2 Vernon 440, 23 E.R. 882, Precedents in Chancery 171, 24 E.R. 83, 2 Eq. Cas. Abr. 365, 744, 22 E.R. 430, 631.

[2] *Middleton v. Duke of Kingston* (Ch. 1718), see above, Case No. 228.

358
Note
(Ch. 1719)

An executor of a will, after probate of the will, can recover the testator's debts.

Lincoln's Inn MS. Hill 73, p. 70, pl. 2

N.B. Probate only empowers an executor to recover debts, for he is liable to all debts before.

359
Wycherley v. Shrimpton
(Ch. 1719–1720)

A marriage is a sufficient consideration for a marriage settlement.

A will or a contract cannot be set aside on the ground of fraud where the fraud was committed by a third person.

Lincoln's Inn MS. Misc. 11, p. 94

21 February 1718[/19]. Shrimpton v. Wycherley.

In this case was cited by Mr. *Vernon* the Case of Cheeke and Lord Lisle,[1] which was this. The plaintiff married the defendant's daughter, and, before the marriage, there were articles entered into between the plaintiff and the defendant whereby it was agreed that the plaintiff should make a settlement upon his wife, for which time was given by the articles, and the defendant agreed that, upon the plaintiff's making such settlement, to pay the plaintiff a sum of [blank] as a portion with the defendant's daughter. The wife died before the settlement was made, and, she being dead without issue and so no occasion for making any settlement, the plaintiff brought his bill to be paid the portion.

And though it did not appear that the plaintiff had been guilty of any laches or that he had been so much as called upon to make the settlement, yet the agreement being mutual and the portion being to be paid upon making the settlement and that being now not to be made, the Lord Keeper [Lord Parker] assisted by Judge Rainsford decreed the portion not payable.

Lincoln's Inn MS. Misc. 506, p. 21, pl. 2

Hilary 6 Geo.

---

1 *Cheek v. Lord Lisle* (1673), 1 Freeman 302, 303, 22 E.R. 1224, 1225, 89 E.R. 219, 221, Reports *tempore* Finch 98, 23 E.R. 53, 2 Keble 794, 84 E.R. 502, 73 Selden Soc. 23, 52.

Wycherley, being very old and near his death, was prevailed upon by fraudulent persuasions and importunities to marry the now defendant's wife against his own inclinations, he declaring that a physician was more proper for him than a wife, and to make her a jointure, within two or three days after which he died. And his widow married Mr. Shrimpton. The bill was brought by the heir to set aside this marriage settlement, being obtained by fraud and made on a person who brought no fortune.

The court was unanimous that it could not be set aside because, the marriage taking effect, that was a valuable consideration of itself and there was no proof to charge the wife as being *particeps fraudis*, that the persons guilty of the fraud were such as had no benefit themselves by the settlement, that, if the wife had been proved to have been concerned in the fraud, they would have discountenanced such proceedings and have striven hard to have set it aside.

Lincoln's Inn MS. Misc. 384, p. 127, pl. 2

Shrimpton *et ux.* [v.] Wycherly and Lister. 28 January. Lord Chancellor [Lord Parker], Chief Justice King, Chief Justice Pratt, Tracy.

Mead, for the plaintiff: A bill [was exhibited] that the plaintiffs may redeem a mortgage made by Wycherly to Lyster and that the plaintiff Elizabeth may be let into a jointure settled by W. Wycherly, her former husband. [In] 1696, Daniel Wycherly mortgaged to Lyster for £1000. Interest was paid by D. and W. Wycherly, his son. A deed of 10 September 1696 gives a power for W. Wycherly to make a jointure. [On] 20 December 1715, W. Wycherly marries the plaintiff and [on] 18 December executes that power. And he dies on 31 December, thirteen days after, having made his will and the defendant executor in trust for the plaintiff Elizabeth.

Acherly, for the defendant Wycherly: The defendant is the nephew and heir of W. Wycherly. He says that Daniel Wycherly, being tenant for life, had no power to enable W. Wycherly to make a jointure and the power was not well executed, W. being imposed upon.

Clive, for the defendant Lister: He submits to the redemption by him who has the right.

Acherly: The defendant, who has brought a cross-bill to set aside the plaintiff's jointure as obtained by fraud and contrivance of the defendant Shrimpton when W. Wycherly was on his death bed, that the defendant proposed Elizabeth Jackson to Wycherly for his wife intending to marry her himself after Wycherly's death.

Hungerford opens the answer of the defendant Shrimpton *et ux.* He says that the plaintiff[1] Wycherly had provoked his uncle, W. Wycherly, who thereupon

1 Sic in MS.

declared he would marry to be revenged on him, that the defendant Elizabeth had a fortune of £1100. And they deny any imposition.

Sir Thomas Powys, for the plaintiff Shrimpton *et ux.*: [In] 1696, Daniel Wycherly settles on himself for life, remainder to his son W. Wycherly for life with a power for W., the son, to make a jointure.

Chesshyre: All the evidence is proper at law. We do not come into this court to have any defect in the deed supplied.

Mead: We only desire to have the mortgage or other impediments set out of the way, that we may try our title at law. We have proved the deed was well executed and prepared by Mr. Webb and approved by Wycherly himself, and we have proved the marriage.

Proofs: Harris, who married the plaintiffs, says he asked Wycherly whether he had considered of what he was about to do; Wycherly answered yes and that it was a young lady to whom he had great obligations and she would accept of him for a husband and that Wycherly was of perfect understanding.

Lutwyche, for the defendant Wycherly: We have proved Shrimpton had contrived this imposition on Wycherly several months before and had him kept very poor on purpose to effect this match, which he told Wycherly was the only expedient to get money, that Wycherly then told Shrimpton he had more need of physicians than a wife, that he incensed Wycherly against the defendant, his nephew, by false suggestions. If Wycherly was so far in his senses as we cannot plead at law *non est factum*, yet we are proper in this court to set aside this deed for notorious fraud and imposition. It is proved that Wycherly had extreme unction and received the Sacrament according to the Church of Rome before he married the plaintiff so that then he was in a dying condition.

Cowper: We are proper to be relieved against the execution of a power obtained by fraud when Wycherly was in a dying condition. The lady was only the instrument of Shrimpton to bring about his designs, and before a wife was mentioned to Wycherly, Shrimpton had declared he would live at Wycherly's estate. Perhaps no case exactly like this can be cited. But fraud may be relieved against in any shape.

Vernon: It is said they would meet us at law, but fraud is proper in this court. Here are all the circumstances of fraud that can be. The marriage is so far from sanctifying the fraud that it aggravates it. We do not insist that he was *non compos* [*mentis*] or not adequate but that here was a whole train of circumstances and suppression of the truth when Wycherly was easy to be imposed upon. Shrimpton was the agent throughout and incensed Wycherly against his nephew by suggesting what was false, that he would not lend Wycherly any money to pay his debts and that the best way of being revenged was by executing this power. If the plaintiff Elizabeth had married an innocent man, it might have been hard to have punished him, but here she has married him who was party to the fraud.

The Master of the Rolls [JEKYLL]: What decree does Mr. Wycherly pray?

Lutwyche: That this jointure deed may be set aside and that Mr. Shrimpton and his wife may levy a fine of the estate to Mr. Wycherly.

[The case was] put off until another day.

3 February.

Sir Thomas Powys, for the plaintiff: It is a very considerable question whether, when a marriage is not avoided or avoidable, a court of equity can set aside the incidents or consequences of the marriage by reason of false suggestions. It has been frequent that a man *in extremis* has married on purpose to entitle his wife to her dower or free bench. [It is] nothing to affect Mrs. Shrimpton, who is innocent. If Mr. Wycherly had lived many years and she had been entitled to any estate, he would have had the benefit of it. We have proved frequent declarations of Wycherly that he would execute his power to make a jointure that he might be revenged on his nephew for refusing to join in a sale to pay his debts, that Wycherly applied to one Mrs. Lee to help him to a wife, that he had perfect understanding; in his will, which is proved, he calls her his loving wife.

Hungerford: Suppose there was a fraud in representing the lady [had] a great fortune when she had no fortune and, in consideration thereof, a jointure is made; it could never be set aside. There is no statute of limitations against a marriage. After the mortgages are paid off, the jointress will not have above £100 *per annum*. The witnesses say the deed was obtained by force and fraud, which was plainly put into their mouths.

Chesshyre, for the plaintiff: We do not come here to have a defect in the deed supplied, but only on a common equity to remove an impediment [so] that we may come at our legal remedy. Consider it as at the time of the marriage, as at the time of Wycherly's death, as if the plaintiff Elizabeth had married a stranger. And as she has married the plaintiff Shrimpton, the marriage could not have been dissolved or the consequence of it prevented. C.L. 28a; Bacon's *Essay on Marriage*. An idiot may contract marriage. 1 Ro. Abr. 348, 355; Stanford, *Pleas of the Crown*, 35; Co. Lit. 40.[1]

If Wycherly had an estate of inheritance, the plaintiff had been dowable and equity could not deprive her of it. A jointure comes by Statute[2] in lieu of dower. The accident of the husband's dying cannot alter the case. Secondly, if the plaintiff had lived [as] a widow, the defendant could not have set aside the deed. Third, if she had married a stranger, it is admitted the deed would be good. Fourth, as she has married the plaintiff Shrimpton, it was by the advice of her mother. It is denied by the answer that there was any contract between the plaintiffs in Wycherly's lifetime; therefore, it is not to be presumed. Swinburn, *De Sponsalis*, 139. There is not sufficient evidence that the plaintiffs exasperated Wycherly against his nephew, [there] being but one witness against the ancestor. If there

[1] E. Coke, *First Institute* (1628), ff. 28, 40; 1 Rolle, Abr., *Baron & Feme*, p. 348, pl. X, 2, 3.

[2] Stat. 27 Hen. VIII, c. 10, s. 4 (*SR*, III, 540–541).

is any doubt in this cause, it is proper to be tried at law. The will of Jones of the Savoy appeared here with very ill grace, but being sent to law, it appeared there [to be] clear of any fraud. Bodwill and Roberts in Bath and Montague, 3 Ch. Ca. 61, 94;[1] where a will obtained on false suggestions could not be set aside by this court.

Mead, for the plaintiff: The plaintiffs only come against the mortgagee on the common equity to remove impediments. The court will not direct the trying of a fraud. But here, the marriage and the deed are one transaction. And the matter is doubtful and deserves a further examination. [There is] nothing to charge Mrs. Shrimpton with being privy to any force or fraud. Therefore, she ought not to lose her jointure no more than if she had married a stranger. The subsequent marriage cannot affect what was antecedent, for she may survive her husband. And if any accession of fortune had come to her in Wycherly's lifetime, he would have had it. [There is] no pretense of insanity. No circumstance of force is proved. But it was a deliberate act. [There is] no proof that she represented herself [to have] a greater fortune. [There was] no suppression of truth in the plaintiffs' telling the tenants he would come and live among them. [It is] not sufficient to set aside the deed. [There was] no precedent quoted. Packer v. Wyndham;[2] the estate of a lunatic under the custody of the court was decreed to the husband after her death though he married the lunatic in contempt of the court.

Curia: Let it stand until tomorrow morning.

Lutwyche, for the defendant: The case of dower or free bench is not like this, for that is a necessary consequence of the marriage, but this is not. A will may be set aside in equity though it be good at law, as Bransby and Kerrick.[3] So a marriage settlement may be set aside, as Miller and Nixon. Though the marriage of an idiot may be good, yet his settlement is void. We have proved misrepresentation, exasperating Wycherly against his nephew, using force, and threatening. Mrs. Shrimpton is not innocent, but suffered herself to be Shrimpton's instrument.

Cowper: Shrimpton declared he had contrived this fraud in such a manner that no court of equity could set it aside. This case is without precedent, but fraud may be relieved against in any form. Wycherly was in want and depended on Shrimpton to supply him, but he pretended there were no rents in the tenants' hands [in order] to marry the plaintiff after Wycherly's death, for she told Shrimpton that they should live bravely and keep their coach. How long was Wycherly to live when the marriage was only with a view of an after marriage with Shrimpton?

---

[1] *Roberts v. Wynn* (1664), 1 Chancery Reports 236, 21 E.R. 560; *Earl of Bath v. Earl of Mountague* (1693), 3 Chancery Cases 55, 103, 22 E.R. 963, 992.

[2] *Packer v. Wyndham* (1715), Precedents in Chancery 412, 24 E.R. 184, Gilbert Rep. 98, 25 E.R. 68, 2 Eq. Cas. Abr. 138, 583, 22 E.R. 118, 491.

[3] *Bransby v. Kerrick* (1718), see above, Case No. 301.

Vernon: The jointure may be set aside. In Cheek and Lord Lisle,[1] where it was provided that the portion should be paid when the settlement was made, the lady died before the settlement was made; so the plaintiff was not entitled to the portion. Baskervile v. Baskervile;[2] where the money was not paid, no settlement was made; the contract must be entirely performed. Lady Clifford and Lord Burlington;[3] Lord Clifford was a tenant for life with a power to make a jointure; the court helped the execution of the power in one part, but not in the other, there being fraud in suggesting the estate to be £1000 *per annum*, which was but £600.

All agreements must be clear of fraud which can have any aid from a court of equity. Here, all manner of frauds have been practiced. Shrimpton managed the settlement and gave Mr. Webb 16 guineas for making it sure. Wycherly's will was made but the day before he died, which made Shrimpton executrix. Bodwin and Roberts [was] that a will cannot be set aside here, but, by the civil law, it may be set aside if gained by excessive flattery or solicitation, for the will should be perfectly free. Here, Wycherly married only for the sake of money, but he did not gain one farthing.

Acherly: The defendant referred our bill for scandal in charging a precontract between the plaintiffs, but Lord Cowper was of opinion that nothing could be scandalous but what was impertinent. A jury cannot try a fraud, but it is proper for this court. Soliribblehill and Brett;[4] the court set aside the defendant's lease given for procuring the marriage of Mr. Thynn of Egham; by Lord Keeper Wright, it was sent to law, where there were two verdicts for the deed, but on appeal to the House of Lords, there was relief, it not being proper to send it to law. The same case with Hale and Potter.[5]

[The case is] to stand for judgment.

3 March 1719[/20]. At the Lord Chancellor's House. Lord Chancellor [LORD PARKER], Chief Justice PRATT, Master of the Rolls [JEKYLL], KING, TRACY.

The judges are all of opinion that there is not sufficient evidence to affect Mrs. Shrimpton so as to set aside the deed, consequently, that she must be admitted to redeem the mortgage. The plaintiff Shrimpton has undertaken to pay

---

1 *Cheek v. Lord Lisle* (1673), 1 Freeman 302, 303, 22 E.R. 1224, 1225, 89 E.R. 219, 221, Reports *tempore* Finch 98, 23 E.R. 53, 2 Keble 794, 84 E.R. 502, 73 Selden Soc. 23, 52.

2 *Baskervile v. Baskervile* (1703), 2 Vernon 448, 23 E.R. 886, Precedents in Chancery 186, 24 E.R. 90.

3 *Lady Clifford v. Earl of Burlington* (1700), 2 Vernon 379, 23 E.R. 841, 1 Eq. Cas. Abr. 346, 21 E.R. 1092.

4 *Scribblehill v. Brett* (1701–1703), 2 Vernon 446, 23 E.R. 885, Precedents in Chancery 165, 24 E.R. 79, 4 Brown P.C. 144, 2 E.R. 97, 2 Eq. Cas. Abr. 585, 22 E.R. 492.

5 *Hall v. Potter* (1695), Shower P.C. 76, 1 E.R. 52, also 1 Eq. Cas. Abr. 89, 21 E.R. 900, 3 Levinz 411, 83 E.R. 756.

all of Wycherly's debts not secured by a mortgage and must keep down the interest of the mortgage. The plaintiff must have possession and an account of the profits.

2 Eq. Cas. Abr. 391, 22 E.R. 334

Wicherly v. Wicherly.

The remainderman brings a bill to be relieved against a jointure made by the tenant for life even upon his deathbed in consideration of and previous to his marriage by virtue of a power reserved to him.

But LORD PARKER, assisted by PRATT, Chief Justice, and the Master of the Rolls [JEKYLL], denied relief.

360

Tompkins v. Cullen

(Ch. 1719)

A court of equity will aid defective executions of powers in favor of younger children or creditors, but it never will aid the non-execution of powers.

Lincoln's Inn MS. Misc. 11, p. 48

3 March 1718[/19]. Daniel Tompkins and Alice, his wife, daughter of Edwin Sandys, plaintiffs; Sir Rushout Cullen [1661–1730] and others, defendants.

On the marriage of the said Edwin Sandys with Alice Rushout, daughter of Sir James Rushout [1644–1698], a settlement was made by Samuel Sandys, father of Edwin, of lands in Worcestershire and Oxfordshire by lease and release dated 11 and 12 October 1694, and, as to part of the lands, *viz.* a farm called Piddington in Oxfordshire, the same was limited to the use of Edwin Sandys for life, then to trustees for 400 years, remainder to the first and other sons of the marriage in tail male, remainder to the first and other sons of Edwin by any other wife, remainder to the defendant Martin Sandys, brother of Edwin, for life and to his first and other sons in tail male, remainder to Samuel Sandys and his heirs.

As to the 400 years term, it was declared to be upon trust that, in the case of issue male of the marriage and one or more younger son or sons, daughter or daughters, then the trustees should out of the rents of the premises or by mortgage or sale thereof raise all and every such sum and sums of money not exceeding £5000 in the whole as the said Edwin and Alicia, his intended wife, or the survivor of them should from time to time by any deed or writing or by his or her last will in writing attested by two or more witnesses should direct, limit, or appoint.

The marriage was had, and, afterwards, Edwin Sandys died, leaving the said Alicia, his wife, *enceinte* with a son and two more children by her, *viz.* the plaintiff Alice, who has since married the plaintiff, Mr. Tompkins, and the defendant, Samuel Sandys.

Mr. Edwin Sandys, before his death, when he was ill of the sickness where of he died, made his will. And, without taking any notice of the settlement, he gives all that his manor of Wickamfort, which, by the settlement, was settled on the issue male of the marriage, with a remainder for a term of 500 years to raise £6000 for daughters' portions in the case of no sons, and his farm at Piddington to his wife and brother, Martin Sandys, and their heirs upon trust that they should raise £6000 to be disposed of as follows, *viz.* £2000 to the child his wife should be *enceinte* with at his death, provided such child should prove to be a son, to be paid at his age of twenty-one years, but, if a daughter, £2500 to be paid at twenty-one or marriage and the residue of the £6000 to be paid to the plaintiff Alice at twenty-one or marriage. And he made his wife, Martin Sandys, and son, Samuel, executors. And he gave the residue of his estate to his son, Samuel.

The child of which the wife was *enceinte* proved to be a son. The wife died after her husband, and the plaintiffs, having married, brought their bill to have the plaintiff Alice's share of the £6000 raised or at least so much of the £5000 as the Piddington estate was charged with by the settlement as was proportionable to the plaintiff's share of the £6000 given by the will.

And, if the power given to the husband and wife and the survivor of them to appoint how much of the £5000 should be raised for daughters and younger sons portions upon the 400 years term [was well pursued], the wife having never by any writing confirmed her husband's will nor made any appointment whatsoever, was the question.

The Master of the Rolls [Jekyll], having taken time to consider of this case, upon the 19th March 1718[/19], delivered his opinion that, supposing the power of appointing had been solely vested in Edwin Sandys, this court would have said it had been well executed though he has taken no notice of his power and though, instead of appointing the portions to be raised out of the lands chargeable therewith, he has devised the lands themselves and coupled other lands with them.

But he was of opinion that Mr. Sandys, in the life of his wife, could not execute this power by himself without his wife and that, therefore, the power was never executed.

This court will aid defective executions of powers in favor of younger children or creditors, but it never will aid the non-execution of powers. And that I take to be the difference that this court has always gone upon. This is a case much to be favored, but I cannot alter men's deeds. The bill must be dismissed.

Lincoln's Inn MS. Misc. 384, p. 146

9 March. Tomkins v. Sands.

The question was whether a power to charge £5000 for daughters' portions is well executed. A term of 400 years of Piddington is limited to trustees to raise £5000 for daughters in case there should be issue male in such a manner as Edwin Sands and Alice, his wife, or the survivor should limit or appoint. Edwin, in the life of Alice, makes his will and devises Piddington and another estate, over which he had no power, on trust to raise £6000, £2000 to the child his wife was enceinte with and the residue to the plaintiff, his daughter. The trust was of the 400 years term.

N.B. in case there be issue male and also one or more younger sons or daughters, then to raise such sums not exceeding £5000 as the said Edwin and Alice or the survivor of them should by deed or by his or her will appoint.

Master of the Rolls [Jekyll]: It must be executed by both in the lifetime or by the survivor.

Mead, for the plaintiff: Alice's surviving has confirmed this execution by not making any contrary disposition. Parker and Parker, before Lord Harcourt;[1] there was a power to appoint for younger children by a will to be executed before three witnesses £7000. He, by a will not so executed, charges £8000; it was a good execution of the power. Smith and Ashton, 1 Ch. Ca. 268, Thwaytes and Day; there was a power to limit particular lands.[2] He appointed a rent charge; it was good. Melmouth's [Case], where an infant on marriage covenanted to execute a power, [the court] decreed the heir to execute it; Hollingshed and Hollingshed; Dr. Garth's Case.[3]

Sir Thomas Powys, for the plaintiff: If a husband and wife levy a fine of the wife's land and the husband declares the uses, it is good. But if they declare contrary uses, it is void. If she does not, it is an agreement to the husband's declaration of the uses.

Vernon, for the defendant: The power was not well pursued. In Dr. Garth's Case, there was a covenant to execute the power, and, it [not] being executed by the party, the court did. Here is only a sum not exceeding £5000 to be raised; so there is no certainty. They might have raised but £1000. The will does not take notice of the power, but directs £6000 to be raised for younger children out of Piddington and etc.

Master of the Rolls [Jekyll]: This is a case of great compassion. Let it stand over that the parties may agree to an accommodation.

Afterward, 19 March, the parties not agreeing, it came on to be heard again before the Master of the Rolls [Jekyll], and he dismissed the bill.

---

[1] *Parker v. Parker* (1714), Gilbert Rep. 168, 25 E.R. 118.

[2] *Smith v. Ashton* (1675), 1 Chancery Cases 263, 22 E.R. 792, also 1 Freeman 308, 22 E.R. 1229, 89 E.R. 226, Reports *tempore* Finch 273, 23 E.R. 150, 3 Keble 551, 84 E.R. 874, 1 Eq. Cas. Abr. 345, 21 E.R. 1091, 73 Selden Soc. 191, 221; *Thwaits v. Dye* (1689), 2 Vernon 80, 23 E.R. 661, 1 Eq. Cas. Abr. 343, 21 E.R. 1090, Brasenose Coll. Oxford MS. 59, p. 81, Dodd 80, *Lords' Journal*, vol. 14, p. 474, note *Thwaites v. Deye* (1701), Colles 179, 1 E.R. 238, and *Lords' Journal*, vol. 17, pp. 64–65.

[3] *Hollingshead v. Hollingshead* (1708), Gilbert Rep. 167, 25 E.R. 117; *Garth v. Lady Blanfrey* (1695), Gilbert Rep. 166, 25 E.R. 117, 2 Eq. Cas. Abr. 659, 22 E.R. 554.

361

Marsingill v. Flyerden

(Ch. 1719)

Where a defendant pleads a good bar to a claim for an account, he need not set forth the account in his pleading.

Lincoln's Inn MS. Misc. 11, p. 55, pl. 1

7 March 1718[/19].

The bill was for an account of dealings between the plaintiff and the defendant since the year 1710.

The defendant answered and admitted the dealings, but he said that, in November 1717, he and the plaintiff stated accounts together and the plaintiff, upon the balance, was indebted £900, for which the plaintiff gave a note payable on demand with interest and the vouchers on each side were delivered up. And he insists on the account and that he ought not to set forth any other account, but he says nothing as to any subsequent dealings.

The Master reported the answer insufficient, and the defendant took exceptions.

And the Master of the Rolls [JEKYLL] was of opinion that the defendant having set forth a good bar in his answer, he was not obliged to set forth any account previous to the stated account. But he was ordered to answer as to subsequent dealings.

362

Staniforth v. Staniforth

(Ch. 1719)

A bill of revivor lies to revive a bill of review.

If a deposit was made upon a former bill of review, there was no need of a new deposit upon a bill of revivor thereto.

Lincoln's Inn MS. Misc. 384, p. 144, pl. 3

9 March. Staniforth v. Williamson.

There was a plea and demurrer to an original bill in the nature of a bill of review. A former decree is not to be altered but by a bill of review for error apparent in the body of the decree or for new matter. No process is prayed *ad revivendum* or *ad revidendum*. The plaintiff is the devisee of Jonathan Staniforth. The decree was against him that a term should be sold for raising £1500 for the defendant's wife. The limitation was, if John and Christian Staniforth die and leave no issue male of their two bodies and shall leave one or more daughters at their death, then the term of 500 years from their death for raising £1500 for the daughters' portions. In 1714, there was a decree that the term should be sold after the death of the father without issue male in the life of the mother, who lived until 1717.

Vernon: A devisee cannot revive or bring a bill of review but may bring a bill in the nature of a bill of revivor or review. The plaintiff is wrong in form. Jonathan Staniforth must have deposited £50 and have performed the decree unless it was dispensed with. His devisee cannot be in a better case.

As to the new matter, there was no affidavit. The bill suggests that, since the decree, the defendant has received satisfaction out of her father's personal estate by the custom of York, not since some orders of the court; since, the defendant married and had a settlement in consideration of her fortune of £1500. And a term was purchased under the decree.

Serjeant *Chesshyre*, for the plaintiff: The term was contingent and not vested, it not being certain that there would be a daughter living at the death of the mother. Yelv. 85;[1] a term was limited to two joint tenants and the executors of the survivor, and both sold the term. It was adjudged void, it being only a possibility. A bill of review is like a writ of error. It must be brought by those in privity. But this is in the nature of such a bill; therefore, it is good.

Lutwyche: This is like pleading an outlawry to a writ of error to reverse it, which is not a good plea. We hope we shall not be stopped from going into the merits. £50 was deposited by J.S.; the purchase money is not yet paid.

Curia [Lord Parker]: The report of a best purchaser was confirmed against Jonathan Staniforth, and he never complained. You who claim under him should not.

Raymond, for the plaintiff: If a sale is decreed and there is any fraud in it, it may be come at by an original bill. The mother died in 1717.

Mead: The first cause of the demurrer is that there is no error; no proper process is prayed; second, that the plaintiff as devisee is not entitled to revive or review, which proves the process is proper; third, there is no affidavit when the new matter was discovered, [it is] not necessary, being plainly subsequent to the decree; fourth, they affirm no error in the decree. We join issue that there is.

N.B. there was a special verdict found upon this case before Mr. Justice Montagu at the York Assizes. Therefore, this is not a clear case like the case before Mr. Justice Tracy. And it was determined a contingent term and not vested.

Curia [Lord Parker]: As to the new matter relating to the purchase, it is an original bill to set aside a purchaser, a purchaser confirmed against the party under whom the plaintiff claims. It is a good plea to so much.

Second, as to the bill of review, the plaintiff claims as executor as well as devisee of J.S., who deposited £50. The decree could not be performed before the bill was brought.

---

1 *Clark v. Sydenham* (1606), Yelverton 85, 80 E.R. 58, also 1 Brownlow & Goldesborough 136, 123 E.R. 714.

Third, it is pleaded that the limitation is to the father and mother for life etc. and refers to the deed. If it is to A. from the death of B., who has a precedent estate, it is a vested interest. Shall the daughter if she marries in the life of the mother have no provision? But if this is not a good term at law, how can this court help it?

I will not preclude the plaintiff from being heard on this point, though I think it strong against him, but I will allow the plea to the purchaser. Here, the defendant is not excluded by express words. There are two cases, first, if they die leaving no issue male, second, and shall have one or more daughters. The copulative does not relate to the time of their death, but it is sufficient if daughters be born at any time. Lord Powlett's Case is contrary to Lord Rivers's Case.[1] A portion was payable at eighteen or marriage; she died before, yet it was raised. In Lord Darby's Case, there was no time of payment; the child died in minority, yet the portion was raised by the trustees.

Lincoln's Inn MS. Misc. 11, p. 58

9 March 1718[/19].

Old Jonathan Stanniforth <the plaintiff's father> makes a settlement to the use of himself for life, then to his wife for life, remainder to the heirs male of his body begotten on the wife. And then, the words of the settlement are 'and, in case the said J.S. and his wife shall die without issue male and shall have issue one of more daughters, then to trustees for 500 years from the decease of the survivor to raise of £1500 for daughters' portions'. And no time was appointed for payments.

He dies leaving his wife and one daughter but no son. The daughter, in the lifetime of her mother, having attained twenty-one, brings her bill against the heir at law to have her portion raised, and she had a decree for that purpose.

The defendant, after the decree was signed and enrolled, brings a bill of review and assigns for error that the portions ought not to have been raised during the mother's lifetime, for, unless the plaintiff had survived her mother, she was not entitled.

Before any further proceedings were had upon the bill of review, the plaintiff in that bill died, having devised the estate to the now plaintiff, who brings a new bill, partly in the nature of a bill of revivor to revive the bill of review and partly

---

[1] *Lady Pawlett v. Lord Pawlett* (Ch. 1685), 1 Vernon 204, 321, 23 E.R. 415, 496, 2 Freeman 93, 22 E.R. 1079, 2 Ventris 366, 86 E.R. 489, 2 Chancery Reports 286, 21 E.R. 680, 1 Eq. Cas. Abr. 267, 21 E.R. 1036, Lincoln's Inn MS. Misc. 498, p. 14, Lincoln's Inn MS. Misc. 503, p. 83, pl. 2, Lincoln's Inn MS. Misc. 504, p. 80, *Lords Journal*, vol. 14, p. 87; *Earl of Rivers v. Earl of Derby* (Ch. 1688), 2 Vernon 72, 23 E.R. 656, 1 Eq. Cas. Abr. 268, 21 E.R. 1037, Lincoln's Inn MS. Misc. 498, pp. 16, 89, Lincoln's Inn MS. Misc. 503, pp. 85, 113, Lincoln's Inn MS. Misc. 504, pp. 81, 103, *Lords' Journal*, vol. 14, p. 195.

original. And he has alleged new matter discovered since the decree, *viz.* that part of the personal estate of old Jonathan Staniforth, by the custom of the province of York, came to his daughter and ought to go in satisfaction of her portion.

The defendant pleads the former decree and also demurs for not making the usual deposit of £50 nor making an affidavit of the new matter.

Mr. *Vernon*: The plaintiff, being a devisee, is not entitled to bring a bill of revivor or a bill of review, there being no privity between him and the defendant in the original cause.

I must admit that the court, rather than there should be a failer of justice, does allow a devisee to bring a bill in the nature of a bill of review or a bill of revivor. But here, the plaintiff is wrong in form, for he does not pray for process *ad revidendum et revivendum* but prays for process generally to appear and answer. And, besides, he has not made the usual deposit.

To this it was answered that there was £50 deposited upon the former bill of review and, therefore, no need of a new deposit, that being still in the Register's hands.

And, as to praying for process, it was said that the process could be prayed for in no other manner, for, he being entitled, as was said by Mr. Vernon, only to bring a bill in the nature of a bill of review and revivor, he could not pray for process *ad revidendum et revivendum*.

As to the merits of the former decree, it was said by Serjeant *Chesshyre* that, by the words of the settlement, the term was to arise upon a contingency, *viz.* if there should be a daughter at the death of the survivor of J.S. and his wife, and, therefore, the portion ought not to have been raised during the lifetime of the mother, for, though the father was dead and it was certain that there could be no issue male, yet it was not certain whether the daughter would survive her mother and, unless she did so, the term could never arise. And, therefore, this differed from the Case of Corbet and Maidwell, in Salkeld's reports, and the Case of Sir Thomas Greives, in Sir Thomas Jones's reports,[1] for, in those cases, the terms were vested and there was nothing contingent but the death of the father, which was uncertain only as to the time.

Lord Chancellor [Lord Parker]: If the deposit was made upon the former bill of review, there was no need of a new deposit, but, indeed, I do not see this is proper to be objected upon a plea or a demurrer, for, if a deposit is necessary and it is not made, there should have been an application made to the court by a motion, for, until the deposit is made, the defendant is not obliged to answer the bill.

As to the merits, there does not seem to be any great reason to vary the decree, for I think it would be hard if, after the death of the father without is-

1 *Corbett v. Maidwell* (1709–1710), 1 Salkeld 159, 91 E.R. 147, also 3 Chancery Reports 190, 21 E.R. 764, 2 Vernon 640, 655, 23 E.R. 1019, 1027, 1 Eq. Cas. Abr. 337, 21 E.R. 1086; *Greaves v. Mattison* (1682), T. Jones 201, 84 E.R. 1216, also Skinner 38, 90 E.R. 19, 1 Eq. Cas. Abr. 336, 21 E.R. 1085.

sue male, the daughters' portions should not be raised during the lifetime of the mother. And I think the contingency upon which the term was to vest did happen upon the death of the father without issue male. However, it may not be improper to have this matter reconsidered.

The plea and demurrer must be overruled.

[Other copies of this report: 2 Cooper *tempore* Cottenham 432, 47 E.R. 1234.]

[Other reports of this case: 2 Vernon 460, 23 E.R. 895, 1 Eq. Cas. Abr. 337, 21 E.R. 1086.]

363

Peeres v. Barwick

(Ch. 1719)

A court of equity will enforce a foreign judgment.

Lincoln's Inn MS. Misc. 384, p. 147

11 March; Lord Chancellor's house.

The first question was whether this court [of Chancery] can execute a decree made in Barbados and confirmed here by the King in Council.

The second [question was] whether a decree there can be varied by this court.

Raymond: Though the common law courts cannot take notice of what is determined in any other court, yet this court is so far in the nature of the civil law courts, which constantly execute one another's sentence, as the Court of Admiralty will execute a sentence in the civil law courts beyond the sea, that, when the person is here, it may compel performance of a decree in the plantations, as it may decree an account of lands in Ireland when the trustee is here.

This bill is to have an account of a plantation in Barbados.

Second, the defendant pleads a decree in Barbados and confirmed here by the King in Council to so much of the bill as seeks an account precedent to and settled by the decree.

Curia [Lord Parker]: [I will] allow the plea because the decree may not be impeached.

Vernon: All courts of equity have an equal jurisdiction. Therefore, a decree made in Barbados was never impeached here by way of appeal or by original bill.

N.B. the other question was not determined but reserved until the hearing.

N.B. there is a record in the [Court of] Common Pleas where notice is taken that the defendant was fled into Holland and there is a letter missive by the justices of the Common Pleas to the States of Holland to request them to execute the judgment of the Common Pleas, which is the only instance of this nature, according to *Mead*.

364
Hawkes v. Hawkes

(Ch. 1719)

An heir at law is entitled to discovery of title deeds.

Lincoln's Inn MS. Misc. 11, p. 55, pl. 2

11 March 1718[/19].

The plaintiff makes a title to lands as heir to his father, and he charges that the defendant has gotten into possession of the lands and has also possessed the title deeds and other writings relating to them. And he prays a discovery thereof and that they may be delivered to him.

The defendant pleads a voluntary settlement in bar to any relief as also to the discovery of deeds and writing.

And the plea was overruled, for an heir at law is entitled to come into this court to have a discovery of deeds and writings though he claims as heir at law generally and not under any settlement.

365
Nixon v. Muscall

(Ch. 1719)

A plea of auter action pendant *does not lie where the first suit is for a different relief.*

Lincoln's Inn MS. Misc. 11, p. 56, pl. 1

Eodem die [11 March 1719].

The defendant pleaded a former suit depending in the Court of Chancery of Durham for the same matters for which the plaintiff seeks relief by his now bill.

Upon arguing the plea, it appeared that one of the matters for which the suit was commenced in Durham arose at Newcastle and, consequently, out of the jurisdiction of that court and was, therefore, a matter for which the plaintiff could have no relief there.

And the plea, being insisted on, was overruled.

Lincoln's Inn MS. Misc. 384, p. 148

11 March.

Sir T. Powys, for the defendant: The bill [was exhibited] against the defendant, an attorney, for an account and to have his bill taxed. The defendant pleads to the jurisdiction, that there is a bill now depending in the County Palatine of Durham before the Chancellor there for the same matter and both parties live within the County Palatine. Sir Humphrey Mackworth's Case, where there was a cause depending in the Grand Sessions of Wales; he brought a bill here; the defendant pleaded the matter, and the plea was allowed, though it was suggested that some witnesses lived out of the jurisdiction.

Mead, for the plaintiff: We allege in our bill that the matters arise out of the jurisdiction and that our witnesses are likewise out of the jurisdiction. Here, the defendant pleads to all matters not answered to, whereby it cannot appear to the court how much the plea covers.

Curia: He avers by his plea that all matters not answered to are contained within the bill depending in the County Palatine and he swears no witnesses live out of the jurisdiction. It is generally true that, if a bill suggests fraud, the plea must deny the fraud, but that it is proper in another place which has jurisdiction. If I can show any part of the bill not answered to which the plea should not cover, the plea must be overruled. Here, part of the bill is for matter which the Chancery of Durham could not relieve in. Therefore, as to such matter, the plea is not good.

366

Bretland v. Earl of Oxford

(Ch. 1719)

Upon a bill of review for new matter discovered after the decree, the petitioner must allege the time and manner of the discovery with particularity.

Lincoln's Inn MS. Misc. 11, p. 56, pl. 3

11 March 1718[/19].

The plaintiff exhibited a bill of review upon new matter discovered after the account was taken. The defendant demurs, first, because the plaintiff had no leave of the court, second, because he had not performed the decree before he brought his bill by paying the money reported due from him, which was upwards of £7000, third, he has not made a proper affidavit as to the discovery of the new matter.

As to the two first causes of the demurrer, it was said to be determined in the Case of the Bishop of Durham and Sir Harry Liddall[1] that no bill of review ought to be brought without leave of court and that the court never grants leave for a bill of review unless the party first performs the decree, provided such performance does not extinguish the things in demand.

To this, it was said by the plaintiff's counsel that, as to the objection that the plaintiff had no leave of the court for bringing this bill, it was too late to object that now. The defendant might have applied to the court before he had pleaded or

[1] *Lyddal v. Bishop of Durham* (1717), see above, Case No. 213.

demurred for an order to stay the proceedings on this bill, but he could not take advantage of it on a demurrer.

As to the not performing of the decree, it was said that the plaintiff had formerly submitted to an order for appointing a receiver to receive the rents of £500 a year of the plaintiff's estate towards satisfaction of the defendant's debt and the receiver was actually in possession, which, in effect, was a performance of the decree.

But notwithstanding, the court allowed the demurrer. But the new matter not being so particularly charged in the bill as to the time and manner of its discovery as it ought to have been, the court gave the plaintiff leave to amend his bill and affidavit.

And, as to the payment of what was reported due to the defendant, the plaintiff consenting to convey the £500 a year to the two senior Six Clerks as a security for what should be found due on the account, the court dispensed with the plaintiff's performing the decree.

Lincoln's Inn MS. Misc. 384, p. 149

11 March.

Mead, for the defendant: Upon a plea and demurrer to a bill of review to reverse a decree in 1709 and set aside several orders to account and to have the account taken *de novo*, the plea [was that] the decree was signed and enrolled. The bill suggests new matter that the plaintiff has since the decree found several accounts whereby it appears that Serjeant [Reginald] Bretland's estate was not indebted to the plaintiff in that cause, who was the Earl Rivers. The defendant pleads and demurs. He sets out all the former proceedings in the usual manner and that the plaintiff had no leave to bring this bill and he has not performed the decree.

Vernon, for the defendant: If this were permitted that, on such a discovery of new matter, a decree might be reviewed, accounts would the endless. In 1705, on the first bill, the accounts were chiefly taken out of Serjeant Bretland's own book, and he appeared indebted £7656 to Earl Rivers.

[As to the] 1709 decree, first, they are wrong in form. There was no leave to exhibit this bill. Second, the decree was not performed; not only a principal sum but also costs must be first paid. Third, there is no error in the body of the decree. Fourth, there is not sufficient new matter. These accounts are mentioned in the report in the former cause, and the affidavit of this new discovery is very loose.

Sir H. Liddell and the Bishop of Durham; first, it was settled that, until costs be paid by the defendant, the court would not give leave to bring a bill of review. Second, it was discretionary whether the court would give leave. Third, no bill of review could be brought without such leave.

Chesshyre, for the plaintiff: If we can open this decree, there will appear £3000 due to us. First, they say we are wrong in form, not having leave, but that is not matter of a demurrer but should be by a motion. Second, we have deposited

£50. Third, they say we have not performed the decree. But a receiver is appointed of the trust estate. Fourth, our affidavit is that all or most of the rentals and vouchers necessary to make out the account are discovered since the last report.

Curia: The decree is not complained of, which is only to account. But the grievance is the last report, which is confirmed. The affidavit should have been positive that all the papers and accounts have been found since the last report, whereas the affidavit is positive only to twelve rentals of Serjeant Bretland's own handwriting, which is not material. There being no proof that they are true, no vouchers found since, here was an account stated by Serjeant Bretland in his answer. Shall this new discovery set it aside where there is no account given of how they came to be found since the report and not before? If this had been in other person's hands, it might have made some difference. But these accounts were in your own hands. I allow the demurrer.

Hanakenius v. Jacobson, in the House of Lords,[1] where letters found since the decree, though in the party's own custody, was sufficient ground for a bill of review, though it was not allowed by Lord Chancellor Cowper.

[Other copies of this report: 2 Cooper *tempore* Cottenham 444, 47 E.R. 1240.]

367

Cliff v. East India Company

(Ch. 1719)

An officer of a corporation can be compelled to answer an interrogatory as to what is found in the company's books so long as that information is not secret.

Lincoln's Inn MS. Misc. 506, p. 19

Easter 5 Geo.

The plaintiff's testator had given the Company information of a clandestine trade carried on by A. on which the Company prosecuted A. on the Statute,[2] which gives part to the informer, but did not put in the testator, but Woolley, their own Secretary. Afterwards, the Company dropped the prosecution having compounded the matter with A., but gave no allowance to the plaintiff's testator, who was the real informer. To prove of this, interrogatories were exhibited to Woolley, the Secretary of the Company whether any composition was made between the Company and A. and what sum of money was given by A. and what minutes, notes, and memorandums are entered in the Company's books relating

---

[1] *Jacobsen v. Hennekenius* (1714), 5 Brown P.C. 482, 2 E.R. 811, *Hennekenius v. Jacobsen* (Ch. 1712–1713), British Library MS. Hargrave 80, ff. 97, 146v, Lincoln's Inn MS. Misc. 383, pp. 174, 261, Lincoln's Inn MS. Misc. 106, pp. 29, 228.

[2] Stat. 5 Geo. I, c. 21, s. 4.

to this matter. To this last interrogatory, he demurred because, being a servant to the Company, he was not obliged to discover what was in their books without their particular leave.

But the demurrer was overruled because the interrogatory did not require the discovery of any secret transaction, but only the entry book.

368

Lloyd v. Symmonds

(Ch. 1719)

A defendant need not give an answer in pleadings that might subject him to criminal penalties.

Lincoln's Inn MS. Misc. 506, p. 20, pl. 1

Easter 5 Geo.

The plaintiff had bought of the defendant, who was a parchment maker in the country, several skins of parchment which were sent up to town without being stamped according to 9 & 10 Ann.[1] The plaintiff was prosecuted for having these in his custody to his damage of £50. He brings his bill here against the defendant for a discovery whether he had paid the duties on these parchments or not. To this bill the defendant demurs.

Lord Chancellor [LORD PARKER] held the demurrer good because to answer in this case might subject him to the penalties of divers acts of Parliament.

369

Eubank v. Noyes

(Ch. 1719)

Interest on unpaid legacies is payable after one year after the testator's death.

Lincoln's Inn MS. Misc. 384, p. 165, pl. 2

18 April.

William Wogan, by his will in 1710 gives a legacy of £1000 to Richard Noyes, senior, and £1000 to Richard Noyes, junior, the last to be paid within six months after the testator's death, directs his real estate to be sold for the payment of his debts and legacies, and makes J. Symonds residuary legatee and devisee. The question is whether the Noyeses are entitled to have interest for their legacies raised out of the real estate and from what time.

---

[1] Stat. 10 Ann., c. 18, ss. 116, 117 (*SR*, IX, 617–618).

Vernon, for the defendant Symonds: Both the real and personal estate are made subject to the debts and legacies by sale or mortgage. We admit that such debts as in their own nature carry interest should be paid with interest. But the personal estate being exhausted by the debts, the real ought not to be subject[1] to interest against the residuary devisee.

Cowper, for the defendant Noyes: Where a legacy is given out of the personal estate only and no mention is made of interest but the surplus is devised over, yet the legacy will carry interest against the residuary legatee whether a time be limited for the payment of the legacy or not. This case is stronger, the real estate being likewise subject. When no time is limited, it generally carries interest from a year after the testator's death.

Mead: The real estate is devised to Noyes to be sold or mortgaged for the payment of the debts and legacies. Therefore, the legatee is in the nature of a mortgagee.

Curia: The question would have been considerable had the personal estate been large, for Noyes being the trustee as well as a legatee, as soon as he received sufficient of the profits to pay his own legacy, interest would cease and would go for the benefit of the residuary legatee. Noyes might have mortgaged privately and paid the legatees. The other legatees must have interest at 5 percent being charged on land from a year after the death of the testator. As to Noyes' and his son's legacies, he reserved the consideration of interest until after the account was taken. And it is [to be] seen whether Noyes has received sufficient to pay his and his son's legacies.

N.B. Where legacies are charged on land, they carry 5 percent; where only on the personal estate, they carry 6 percent.

Curia: Let the Master compute interest at 5 percent for Noyes senior's legacy from a year after the testator's death and for Noyes junior's legacy from six months if he do not find that Noyes received sufficient to pay the legacies.

Lincoln's Inn MS. Hill 73, p. 71

Easter term 1719.

[The question as to] legacies [was] whether they should have interest upon a rehearing. They were charged upon the real and personal estate by the will to mortgage or sell and, in one [of the] legacies the time when it should be paid.

It did not appear from the will but if the testator thought there might be a residuum of his personal estate, for, by the words of the will, the residuum of the real estate after payment of debts and legacies was to be conveyed to [*blank*] Symonds and likewise the personal estate.

Interest was allowed to the legatees where no time was fixed for the payment [. . .] from a year after the death of the testator to the other legatees.

---

[1] sufficient *MS.*

370

Dewer v. Chaworth

(Ch. 1719)

Where a married woman is an executrix, her husband is only a nominal party to a suit involving the decedent's estate.

A writ of ne exeat *can be discharged upon the giving of a bond as security to pay any future judgment.*

Lincoln's Inn MS. Misc. 384, p. 165, pl. 1

18 April 1719.

Upon a motion by the defendant to discharge a [writ of] *ne exeat regno*, [the case was thus]. The plaintiff is the defendant's son by a former husband, and he brings his bill for an account of his father's personal estate against the defendant, his executrix, who has married the defendant Chaworth. She, having put in her answer and being entitled to one-third of a plantation at Antigua for her dower, was going over thither, but, the plaintiff having stopped her by a [writ of] *ne exeat*, she moves to discharge it, suggesting she had occasion to go and take care of her affairs at Antigua and it would be much to her prejudice to detain her here.

The plaintiff insisted he should have occasion to examine her upon interrogatories and that her husband ought to give security to answer the event of the account, which he refused to do, and quoted Hole and Dubois and Moore and Munell.[1]

But, there, they were going abroad on purpose to defeat the plaintiffs.

Curia: The argument is because the husband is here and you may sue him, therefore, the wife should be discharged. But suppose he should die and the wife be gone beyond the sea; there would be a failure of justice. Here the husband is only a nominal party. [I will] discharge the [writ of] *ne exeat regno* on the defendants' giving security in £600 to abide by the order on the hearing, and the plaintiff is likewise to give £200 security.

---

1 *Dubois v. Hole* (1708), 2 Vernon 613, 23 E.R. 1002, 1 Eq. Cas. Abr. 65, 21 E.R. 879; *Moor v. Meynell* (Ch. 1719), see below, Case No. 386.

371

Woodward v. Harcourt

(Ch. 1719)

The question in this case was whether a court of equity will order specific performance of a land related contract where third persons have frustrated the expectations of the parties thereto.

Lincoln's Inn MS. Misc. 384, p. 166

20 April.

The defendant, being Clerk of the Crown in the [Court of] King's Bench, proposed to the plaintiff to build a proper house in Gray's Inn to keep the King's Bench Office in. The plaintiff accordingly, covenants to build such a house, and the defendant covenants to take a lease for twenty-one years at £35 *per annum* and also covenants to remove the Crown Office thither. But, upon the defendant's application, the Court of King's Bench refuse to give leave.

The plaintiff brings his bill for a specific performance. The defendant insists that the condition is become impossible by the act of the Court of King's Bench and, therefore, that the plaintiff might bring his action [at common law] for damages but is not entitled to a specific performance. And he offers to take the lease for twenty-one years. The plaintiff is damnified by being obliged to pay a ground rent to the benchers of Gray's Inn for forty-one years, whereas, [if] the Crown Office had been removed thither, the benchers would not have insisted on any ground rent and, therefore, would have the defendant pay the said ground rent during the forty-one years and not only for twenty-one years.

Curia: Let the Master look into the agreement of the benchers of Gray's Inn with the plaintiff and what damage the plaintiff has sustained and the benchers be made parties, and then I will endeavor to quiet this matter.

372

Bedle v. Browne

(Ch. 1719)

In this case, the court of equity refused to order specific performance of a lease where third persons frustrated the intentions of the parties thereto.

Lincoln's Inn MS. Misc. 384, p. 167, pl. 1

20 April.

The plaintiff, being possessed of a house, the defendant, in November 1717, applied to him to let the defendant a lease. The plaintiff had then let a lease to Cross, but he being willing to waive it and having lodgers in the house, the plaintiff and defendant came to an agreement that the defendant should have a lease for seven years at £16 *per annum* as soon as the plaintiff should be capable of making such lease. And the plaintiff, being a scrivener, drew up a memorandum in his pocket book, which was signed by the defendant but not by the plaintiff. The defendant was then in lodgings, which he was to quit Christmas following.

The plaintiff brought his bill to compel the defendant to accept of the said lease. The defendant, by answer, insisted that the inducement to him to come into the said agreement was that possession should be delivered to him before Christmas Day, that he went to the tenants to know when they would quit, that they said that they had a year to come and would not quit, that, on application to the plaintiff, he said he could not tell when possession would be delivered but that he would make the defendant stand to his bargain though possession were not delivered in twenty years, that the defendant, being turned out of his lodgings and thus disappointed of the house, was forced to take other lodgings, and, therefore, he hoped the court would not compel him to take the said lease, the terms being unequal and the plaintiff, not having signed, could not be compelled to deliver possession.

The court dismissed the bill with costs.

373

Gould v. Rutland

(Ch. 1719)

If a married woman make a warrant of attorney, it is void as a deed, but, if she has a separate power, a court of equity will enforce it.

The reason that the law gives a married woman's estate to her husband is because he is liable to her debts.

Lincoln's Inn MS. Misc. 384, p. 167, pl. 2

22 April.

The plaintiff, after his marriage with his late wife, agrees that part of her estate should remain in trustees' hands and that they should pay the profits during her life in such manner as she, by deed executed in the presence of two witnesses, should appoint. The trustees pay all the profits to her. The question is whether she had a power to make a *donatio causa mortis* of this separate estate.

Vernon, for the plaintiff: The power, being after marriage, is voluntary and the donations also are voluntary and are derogatory of the rights of the marriage. Therefore, they are to be construed strictly and not to be aided.

Lord Chancellor [Lord Parker]: I think it is not material how she came by this power, but the argument would only be a matter of favor. The point is what the power is. The objection is that this disposition is not by a writing etc. A wife's will is void not because of want of power but for want of the husband's consent.

And, where she has a separate estate, it passes by her will. This is the same as the case of lands before the Statute of Wills[1] where a gift in the lifetime was good though to take effect after the death, which was good.

It is absurd that she had power to dispose of it absolutely and not upon condition. If a married woman make a warrant of attorney, it is void as a deed, but, if she had a separate power, a court of equity would make it good. If there was a demand from the trustees, there must be such a deed as is directed. But if they pay it into her hands, she may pay it over either in satisfaction of a debt or as she pleases. It is admitted she might have given 100 guineas with her own hands. But she has given some East India bonds to R.; if R. had paid it over, it had discharged the trust and had been good.

It is said her act is not complete, but it is, for, if she had given 100 guineas, reserving the interest during her life, it had been good. And here, the husband is not to control such a disposition. As to her lottery tickets, if she had delivered them over to a person who sold them, it had been a good sale. The clause is that the husband shall not meddle contrary to her direction. Here, he would meddle contrary to her direction. Here, she may dispose as if she had been unmarried.

So the only question is whether, in such case, this disposition had been good against her administrator. The reason of the law of England giving the wife's estate to the husband is because he is liable to her debts, which is not by any other law. I take it that the husband here intended she should have the same power as if unmarried. The direction were only to be observed by the trustees, but when they had delivered them over to the wife, she had an absolute power to dispose of it as she pleased. Here, the person to whom the lottery tickets were delivered for the benefit of the defendants, having delivered them to the plaintiff, is guilty of a breach of trust; so of the East India bonds. And the defendant has a right to demand them of the plaintiff. The question whether all these are part of the separate estate is proper to be enquired before the Master.

Lincoln's Inn MS. Hill 73, p. 72, pl. 1

22 April.

A bill was brought by the plaintiff as administrator to his wife for some East India bonds amounting to £700, which was put out by the wife during her life into one [. . .], a defendant's hand in trust for Rutland and her niece. It was alleged by them that this money was part of her separate maintenance, which was but £100 *per annum*.

It was decreed for the niece against Sir [*blank*] Gould.

[1] Stat. 32 Hen. VIII, c. 1 (*SR*, III, 744–746); note also Stat. 34 & 35 Hen. VIII, c. 5, s. 7 (*SR*, III, 903).

374

Awbrey v. Awbrey

(Ch. 1719)

A bill of discovery lies to discover waste.

Lincoln's Inn MS. Misc. 506, p. 20, pl. 2

Easter 5 Geo.

A bill [was exhibited] to have a discovery of what trees were cut down by the defendant. The defendant, who was the plaintiff's father, and Mary, his wife, were seised in her right for her life without impeachment of waste, remainder to the plaintiff. Mary dies. In her lifetime, the defendant had cut down a great number of trees. To have a discovery was the end of the bill.

The defendant demurs because the waste was committed in the lifetime of his wife and that he was seised only in her right and thus not obliged to answer any waste done in her lifetime.

The demurrer was overruled.

Lincoln's Inn MS. Hill 29, p. 44

Easter 5 Geo. I.

A bill [was exhibited] to discover what trees were cut down by the defendant etc. The case was that the plaintiff's father and Dame Mary, his wife, were seised in her right for 99 years without impeachment of waste, remainder to the plaintiff.

The defendant demurs because that this waste was committed in the lifetime of the said Mary, that he, the defendant, was seised only in her right, and that he is not obliged now she is dead to answer to any waste committed in her life.

The counsel for the defendant said that this being in the right of the wife and she being dead, an action of waste lies at common law.

Lord Chancellor [LORD PARKER] said an action of waste does not lie against him for this. *Vide* Foliamb's Case, in Co. 5 Rep. 115.[1]

The demurrer was overruled.

---

[1] *Foliamb v. Bowes* (1601), 5 Coke Rep. 115, 77 E.R. 235.

375

Davison's Case

(Ch. 1719)

Where a solicitor commits malpractice, he will not be charged for the expense resulting therefrom, nor can he charge his client for it.

Lincoln's Inn MS. Hill 73, p. 72, pl. 2

[As to] Davison, a solicitor, a motion [was] made that he might pay the charges of an irregularity in practice, which was so reported by the master, and costs taxed.

But My Lord [PARKER] ordered that the solicitor should not pay the charges of it but should not be allowed anything for his own trouble, as attendance etc.

376

Lord Coningsby v. Higgins

(Ch. 1719)

A defendant cannot be required to make a discovery of his own criminal maintenance of an action and thus incriminate himself.

Lincoln's Inn MS. Hill 73, p. 96

24 April 1719.

A bill was brought by Lord Coningsby[1] against the defendants to discover the right and title of the plaintiff to heriots and likewise to [. . .] what fraudulent conveyances have been made to deceive the lord of the manor. [. . .] refused to pay a heriot to the plaintiff. Lord Coningsby's agent seized an ox as a heriot, for which the defendant Rod, an attorney, brought his action in the Exchequer,[2] towards the carrying on of which suit the defendant advanced several sums of money and subscribed for more by the instigation of the defendant Rod, the attorney.

The defendants demurred as to this part which requires a discovery of what combination [and] contrivance the defendant Rod and the rest made in order to carry on the suit because it was criminal and would particularly be against Rod, the attorney, maintenance.

No one can demur upon his answer. A demurrer must be certain and specific what it is the defendants demur to. The defendants answer part of the bill

---

[1] A. E. Stokes, 'Coningsby, Thomas, first earl of Coningsby (1657–1729), *Oxford Dictionary of National Biography*, vol. 12, pp. 949–954.

[2] Note *Rodd v. Lord Coningsby* (Ex. 1723), Exch. Cases *tempore* Geo. I, p. 583.

and generally, at last, say, as to all that they have not answered, they did demur, which general demurrer Mr. *Vernon* said was never allowed, that, when a man has, as to part of the bill, given a very evasive answer, he should demur to the rest so that it cannot be referred as insufficient because that is a direct bar, *viz.* the demurrer, to the rest so that the plaintiff can have no discovery until after the demurrer be overruled.

The defendants to this bill did not appear to be tenants of the manor who might lawfully so far unite against the lord as to try the title of My Lord to heriots. Some of the defendants were not concerned in right but were charged to have got money subscriptions etc. in order to support those suits, which would be criminal and direct maintenance.

Upon assigning a cause of demurrer, a man may assign another cause at the arguing of the demurrer than is particularly mentioned in it, but will pay costs; indeed, if the cause assigned in the demurrer is not allowed, as Mr. *Mead* said and Mr. *Talbot*, but the Lord Chancellor [Lord Parker] [held] contra. The demurrer was overruled.

The Lord Chancellor said it would have been proper to have made a plea. The defendants may plead that, if they been charged as strangers, having no interest, had united etc., they could not be obliged to set it forth because that would be a direct maintenance and so a good bar to a discovery from them.

377

Beckley v. Newland

(Ch. 1719)

In this case, the defendants were proper parties, being the distributees of the decedent's estate that was in issue.

Lincoln's Inn MS. Hill 73, p. 93

Articles were made between Sir George Newland and Beckley, who had married two nieces of one Sturges, that whatever legacies etc. should be given by will or codicil to either of them should be equally divided.

Mr. Sturges, by Sir George's influence, gave his estate among the children of Sir George but the rents and profits of them to Sir George, his executors, administrators, and assigns during the minority of Sir George [. . .] towards the maintenance and education of them. The estate was about £1000 *per annum*.

A bill [was exhibited] to discover what had been laid out for their education and how much had been laid out in the repairing and beautifying any part of the estate. (The defendants were the sons of Sir George, and his wife [was] another defendant.)

A demurrer [was filed] for that the plaintiff had nothing to do with asking the defendants any of these questions, that they are not concerned in interest and, therefore, only proper to be examined as witnesses.

But that was answered, for Sir George Newland's dying intestate, his estate was come to the defendant's hands according to the Statute of Distributions[1] so that, if the surplus of this estate (the profits of which was devised to Sir George during the infancy of his youngest son) is taken as a beneficial devise or legacy, it will take so much out of the hands of the several defendants who have [been] distributed the estate of Sir George, who died intestate, and which will be assets to charge them and so diminish the personal estate of Sir George.

The demurrer was overruled, and they were ordered to answer.

[Other reports of this case: 2 Peere Williams 182, 24 E.R. 691, 2 Eq. Cas. Abr. 22, 22 E.R. 18.]

378

Rex v. Town of Morpeth

(Ch. 1719)

The question in this case was whether a writ of mandamus *lies to reinstate a schoolmaster at a school founded by a royal grant.*

Lincoln's Inn MS. Hill 73, p. 118

Rex v. Bailiff and Burgesses of Morpeth, Northumberland.

Lutwyche: A [writ of] *mandamus* [went] to restore the under schoolmaster of Morpeth. The bailiff and burgesses had turned him out. In the return of the writ to show cause, they have shown no cause. It is an improper return.

First objection: It ought to have shown the very cause why they turned [him] out.

Answer: By the Act of Parliament 1 Geo., for taking the oaths,[2] the office is *ipso facto* void and that declares the cause.

Second objection: It does not appear he was schoolmastering from the publishing of the Act of Parliament and the first of Michaelmas term.

Answer: It appears he [*blank*].

All writs of *mandamus* lie for offices of a public nature that respect public justice.

1 Stat. 22 & 23 Car. II, c. 10 (*SR*, V, 719–720).

2 Stat. 1 Geo. I, stat. 1, c. 3.

Michaelmas 2d of the queen [1703], Vaughan, the prover of guns. A [writ of] *mandamus* [was] given for the restoring the Register of the ecclesiastical court against the opinion of Chief Justice Holt. 1 Siderfin 169.[1]

If he has a freehold in the school, he has an assize or an action of the case. 1 Siderfin 40.[2]

A school founded by Edward VI and the head schoolmaster by the letters patent as [. . .] and not the [. . .] servant but is of a very public nature.

They ought to say he did not take the oaths appointed to be taken in England or in that case and not only the oaths appointed to be taken by the Act of Parliament because the oaths to be taken by Scotchmen are appointed by the same Act.

A peremptory *mandamus* was not granted in Siderfin, not granted to an usher, but it was of a grammar school erected not by letters patent of the king and a free school.

379

Burnett v. Thornicroft

(Ch. 1719)

After a caveat *is entered and a decree is brought to be signed in order to be enrolled, the Secretary of the Decrees immediately sends notice thereof to the party who has entered the* caveat. *If he does not do so, the enrollment will be set aside.*

Lincoln's Inn MS. Misc. 11, p. 47

It was moved to set aside the enrollment of the decree in this cause because the defendant had entered a *caveat* with My Lord Chancellor's Secretary and had no notice afterwards that the decree was brought to be signed, it being alleged that, although the decree was not signed until twenty-eight days after the *caveat* was entered, yet that was not sufficient unless there had been twenty-eight days notice given to the defendant's solicitor that the decree was brought to be signed, for it was said to be the constant course of the court and so it was certified upon further consideration of this matter by forty-five clerks of the office that, if, after a *caveat* is entered, a decree is brought to be signed in order to its enrollment, the Secretary of the Decrees immediately sends notice thereof to the party who has entered the *caveat*. And if he does not lodge a petition for a rehearing in twenty-eight days after such notice, then the Chancellor signs the decree and not before.

---

[1] *Vaughan v. Company of Gun Makers* (1703), 6 Modern 82, 87 E.R. 839, 2 Lord Raymond 989, 92 E.R. 159; perhaps *Anonymous* (1694), Comberbach 264, 90 E.R. 468; *Rex v. Middleton* (1663), 1 Siderfin 169, 82 E.R. 1037, also 1 Keble 625, 629, 83 E.R. 1149, 1152.

[2] *Stamp's Case* (1661), 1 Siderfin 40, 82 E.R. 957.

And there having been no notice in this case by reason of the sickness of the Secretary, the enrollment was set aside.

Lincoln's Inn MS. Misc. 384, p. 142, pl. 1

19 February.

The query was whether a decree may be enrolled a month after a *caveat* was entered or a month after notice that it is presented to be signed by the Lord Chancellor. The Master had reported that, by the practice of the court, there must be twenty-eight days after notice.

Vernon: A *caveat* expires in a month. The only intent of a *caveat* is to delay the enrollment for a month. If no *caveat* is entered, the party may enroll the decree the next day.

Lord Chancellor [Lord Parker] and the Master of the Rolls [Jekyll] inclined that a decree may be enrolled a month after a *caveat* is entered and that there need not be twenty-eight days after notice. But they put it off until the next seal day.

380

Micklethwaite v. Booth

(Ch. 1719)

Where partners conduct a business and then end the partnership and divide the partnership assets, there can be no further account ordered between them.

Lincoln's Inn MS. Misc. 11, p. 108

24 April 1719. Micklethwaite *et ux.*, executrix of Richard Booth, plaintiffs; William Booth, surviving executor of William Booth, his father, defendant.

William Booth, the father, being a grazier in Lincolnshire, makes his will and gives part of his real estate to John, his eldest son, and the residue of his real and personal estate which should remain after payment of his debts and legacies, he gives to Richard and the defendant William, his younger sons. And he makes them executors. And, by a codicil, he declares his executors should receive the rents devised to John for six years towards the payment of his debts and legacies. And he died in January 1702[/03].

His personal estate, which consisted chiefly of stock upon his farms, amounted by the inventory to £5162 0s. 0d. The executors, having proved the will, agreed to carry on the grazing trade with their father's stock in partnership. But no articles were made in writing. Accordingly, they carried on such trade for two years and mutually bought and sold and received and paid, but neither of them kept any account in writing. And, in 1704, which was two years after the father's death, they made a division of the farms and stock between them.

Richard, one of the brothers, being dead, the plaintiff, as his executrix, brings her bill to call the surviving brother to an account. The question was whether he should account.

[It was] adjudged no account should be taken of anything prior to the division in 1704, the two brothers having occupied the farms together without keeping any account of what was bought or sold or what was paid to the landlord for rent or for the debts and legacies of their father.

381

Blunden v. Barker

(Ch. 1719–1720)

The questions in this case were whether a freeman of the City of London can be a purchaser of his wife's customary share of his estate and whether his children can release their orphanage shares.

Lincoln's Inn MS. Misc. 11, p. 127

27 April 1719. Blundell *et ux*. v. Barker *et al.*, at the Rolls

Mr. Hebert, an upholsterer, upon the marriage of one of his daughters with Mr. Barker gives her £4000 for her portion and settles a freehold and a leasehold estate upon her, and, in the settlement, it is declared to be in satisfaction and bar of her orphanage share of her father's personal estate. And, in consideration of the portion and settlement, she covenants to release all her right to her father's personal estate by the custom of London or otherwise.

Afterwards, Mr. Hebert marries a second wife and, before marriage, she gives a bond of £3000 penalty with a condition that, if she survived Mr. Hebert and his[1] executors paid her £400, she would release all her share to his personal estate by the custom.

The plaintiff having married the other daughter of Mr. Hebert and having never received any fortune with her and Mr. Hebert being dead, the plaintiff and his wife bring their bill for her customary share of the personal estate of her father.

[It was] decreed the bond entered into by Mr. Hebert's second wife did amount to an agreement to release and that she was barred thereby to claim her widow's share, though she offered to forfeit the bond, and that the penalty should be deducted out of what should be coming to her.

Secondly, the settling a leasehold estate on a child did not in itself bar that child of his customary share nor should he be looked on as fully advanced thereby, and, though the certain value thereof did not appear by a writing under the father's hand, yet the value might be ascertained and, therefore, such child

[1] her *MS.*

should notwithstanding come in for his customary share, bringing the lease into hotchpot.

But, however, as to the defendant, Mrs. Barker, the settlement being made in satisfaction of her customary share and she having agreed to release, taking the whole together, she was barred.

But, then, a question arose how the widow's share and Mrs. Barker's share should be divided, they being both barred, and there being no other child except the plaintiff's wife. And, as to this, it was sent to the City to certify the custom.

Lincoln's Inn MS. Misc. 384, p. 152

27 April.

A bill [was exhibited] to have the orphanage part of J. Hibbert's personal estate. The plaintiff's wife Hester was one of the daughters of J. Hibbert, a freeman of London. J. Hibbert settled on his wife in bar of her customary share and advanced the defendant Barker, his other daughter, in marriage. 6 March 1715, J. Hibbert made his will, and 29 July 1717 a codicil, and gives the plaintiff's wife a legacy, which the plaintiffs renounce and claim a customary share. The testator, by will, disposes of two-thirds parts of his personal estate to the defendants and releases several debts to the defendants. The defendant Barker, the daughter of J. Hibbert by a former wife, insisted that J. Hibbert, settling on his second wife in bar of her customary share, was a purchaser of his wife's one third, and, therefore, he had the power to dispose of two-thirds and the defendant's advancement appears under her father's hand, which was £4000 in money and an estate in land and the defendant released her father of all demands which was intended of her own real estate descended to her from her uncle, but could not be of her customary share.

Cowper, for the plaintiff: The first question is whether the defendant Mrs. Hibbert, the widow, is barred of her customary share. In 1684, [there was a] settlement of lands before the marriage and J. Hibbert took a bond of £3000 penalty reciting the marriage articles and that, if he left her £400 by his will, then she should release her right to the custom [of London] etc. Afterwards, she and her husband sold the lands. Therefore, she insists she is not barred of her customary share.

The second question is, if she is barred, then a moiety is the testamentary part and the other moiety is to be divided between the children. But the defendant Barker was advanced by her father in marriage. Lord Delaware's Case.[1] Where the certainty of the advancement does not appear under the freeman's hand, the child's advancement is barred. 19 June 1706, the defendant Barker, before her marriage, covenanted to release her father of all demands in respect

[1] *Dean v. Lord Delaware* (1708), 2 Vernon 628, 23 E.R. 1011, 1 Eq. Cas. Abr. 156, 21 E.R. 955.

of the custom or otherwise except what he should voluntarily leave her. If she is thereby barred of her orphanage part, then the whole orphanage part belongs to the plaintiff.

Vernon: First, the plaintiffs are entitled to a moiety of the testator's personal estate as to the widow. Davila and Davila.[1] A man covenants to leave his wife £1500 in bar of her customary share or otherwise, which, by Lord Cowper, barred her of her distributory share, he dying intestate.

Second, the testator having barred his wife, a moiety is the orphanage part, as if all the children are advanced; the same as if dead. Clare and Acmooty.[2] The custom certified [is] the husband [is] not looked upon as a purchaser of his wife's part, but the same as if she were dead. Handcock and Handcock; Rawlinson and Rawlinson.[3]

Third, the defendant Barker [was] fully advanced. [It is] not in a freeman's power to alter the custom by declaring the child fully or not fully advanced. But the certainty must appear under the father's hand and not depend upon an account. Here, the certainty of the advancement only appears by the settlement to be £4000 in money and land of considerable value, but that is never to be allowed. Here the whole legatory part is given to the defendant Barker. 16 February 1684, [in] articles before the testator's marriage with the defendant, he covenants within six months to settle lands of £90 *per annum* on the defendant in lieu of dower and to leave her £400; [on the] same date was a bond of £3000 from the defendant to the testator on receipt of the £400 to release her customary share.

Master of the Rolls [Jekyll]: She is compounded with.

Mead, for the plaintiff: In Hancock and Hancock, it was reheard and settled that the estate went in moieties; the same in Rawlinson and Rawlinson. In Clare and Acmooty, which was where the child was advanced and there was a certificate; the reason [was] the same where the wife is barred.

Clive, for the defendant: The widow is willing to forfeit the penalty of the bond so [long] as she may be let into her customary share.

Master of the Rolls [Jekyll]: In this court, a bond is looked upon as an agreement, but this to bar her of the custom. This is but a possibility, as in Thompson and Lord Haversham, where a possibility of an advowson was granted, but it was held void. Here, as well as at law, it should be certified whether this bond is a compounding with her by the custom. There was a case where a vendor gave a bond to convey to the vendee; the court considered not only the penalty, but took it as a trust and as an agreement and would not leave it to the election of the obligor to forfeit the penalty.

---

1 *Davila v. Davila* (1716), 2 Vernon 724, 23 E.R. 1075.

2 *Clare v. Almuty* (1708), 2 Eq. Cas. Abr. 420, 22 E.R. 358, Lincoln's Inn MS. Misc. 12, p. 199, pl. 1.

3 *Hancock v. Hancock* (1707), 2 Vernon 605, 665, 23 E.R. 995, 1033, 1 Eq. Cas. Abr. 153, 21 E.R. 952; *Rawlinson v. Rawlinson* (Ch. 1714), see above, Case No. 3.

Sir Edward Northey [and] *Lutwyche*, for the defendant Barker: It is our intent that the widow should be barred. Here is a provision for her both out of the real and personal estate. And the articles and bond are but one settlement.

Raymond, for the defendant Barker, the administratrix *cum testamento annexo.* A widow may bar herself of her customary share by her contract without any relation to the custom as she may bar herself of dower, which is stronger because the husband cannot bar her dower as he may of her customary share by laying his personal estate out in land.

Master of the Rolls [Jekyll]: First, where the widow is barred of her customary share, she may bar herself before her right accrues. This court always carries marriage agreements into execution. I conceive she is barred if this bond is to be looked upon as an agreement. I think this is such an agreement which is only executed by her. And the articles which contain the other part of the agreement were executed only by the husband and the wife's trustees. Whether this agreement be within the custom or not, yet she is barred by her contract.

The second point I think is considerable and worth being satisfied. There is a difference between the case of the wife and the children, for she may be barred before her right commences, but the children cannot.

Let it go to the City to certify whether, the wife being barred of her customary share, the orphanage part goes in moieties or thirds.

Sir Edward Northey: First, as to the defendant Barker's release of her right to her customary share, it is void as a release of a future right and also as a fraud upon the custom.

Second, where she is barred by her advancement and where the certainty does not sufficiently appear, the settlement mentions £4000 to be paid by her father in part of her portion and the residue to be in lands of considerable value. But the value of the lands does not appear. A child cannot be barred by any agreement wit the father, being under his power, through a wife may.

Master of the Rolls [Jekyll]: In Dean and Lord Delaware's Case, there were some entries in the father's books made by himself of his daughter's advancement and other entries made by the bookkeeper by his order, and there the certainty sufficiently appeared.

Cowper in reply: Here, it was the intent of the father that the certainty of his daughter's advancement should not appear, for the deed mentions lands settled of a considerable value and the release mentions the same and the defendant's husband is a witness. So the certainty does not appear.

Vernon: The reason of the custom is that no witnesses should be admitted to prove the value of the advancement. A child as well as a wife may be advanced by lands as well as money. Here, the quantum of the portion cannot appear without taking an account, for part of the lands were given as the residue of her portion and part in recompense of a debt.

Master of the Rolls [Jekyll]: First, as to the £4000 part of the portion, I incline to think that that sum is sufficiently certain under the hand of the father.

Second, as to the land called the residue of the portion, I think *certum est quod certum reddi potest* and that is the reason why land may be a composition for the personal estate. But the case does not rest there, for there is a leasehold estate afterwards conveyed and the daughter releases her claim of her customary share. So the question is whether this is not a good agreement between the father and the daughter to bar her. Sir Owen Buckingham's Case, in the House of Lords,[1] where it was adjudged that lands purchased afterwards will not pass by a will; yet, in equity, they will if contracted for before making the will. Here the daughter agrees to what the father might have done without her agreement. Therefore, I think that she is fully advanced.

An account was directed. The plaintiff is entitled either to a moiety or a third of the personal estate accordingly as the City shall certify the custom to be, *viz.* whether, when the wife is compounded with, the freeman has the power to dispose of a moiety or two-thirds.

21 November 1719. Reheard by the Lord Chancellor [Lord Parker].

The defendant appeals for His Honor's [Jekyll's] decree, first, because the certainty of the defendant's portion does sufficiently appear or may be reduced to a certainty; second, that the defendant's release to her father on her marriage ought not to bar her of her orphanage part; third, the plaintiff's father had the power to dispose of two-thirds.

Cowper, for the plaintiff: Clare and Acmooty; where the children were advanced, the widow had one moiety and the other was accounted testamentary. Hancock and Hancock; where the wife was compounded with, the estate went in moieties as if the wife were dead. Rawlinson and Rawlinson, same point.

Vernon, for the plaintiff: The release is a good bar. The defendant was of full age and, on having a marriage portion, released. A future right on possibility may be released on a valuable consideration, as where a wife is compounded with. Davila and Davila, by Lord Cowper, where a woman released what she might claim by the custom or otherwise; in consideration of £1500, she was barred of her distributive share, the husband dying intestate.

[It was] objected that a release given by a child shall be intended [to be] by coercion; but, when it is on good consideration, [there is] no room for such intendment. Fowke and Lewyn;[2] where a portion is given in marriage with a child, it is a bar unless the certainty appears under the father's hand. Here, the certainty cannot appear until an account is taken, for several lands of inheritance and leasehold are settled on the defendant besides £4000 in money. If an account were to be admitted, all cases of advancement would be out of the custom.

Yorke: Though the defendant's release were void in law, being of a future right, yet it is good in equity as an agreement upon a valuable consideration. 14

---

1 *Buckingham's Case* (K.B. 1707), Dodd 211.

2 *Fouke v. Lewin* (1682), 1 Vernon 88, 23 E.R. 331, 1 Eq. Cas. Abr. 69, 154, 156, 21 E.R. 882, 953, 955.

June 1706, the defendant, in consideration of her portion, releases to her father all actions etc. or what may be due to her by the custom or otherwise except what her father should give her voluntarily. [By the] decree of the Master of the Rolls, first, the defendant Hester Hibbert, the widow, is compounded with; second, the defendant Barker's advancement does not appear and, she having released, she is barred; third, whether the testamentary part is a moiety or two-thirds was sent to be certified. 17 and 18 June 1706, the defendant's father conveys several freehold and leasehold estates to the defendant as part of her portion, the freehold after his own death and the leasehold in like manner. 6 March 1715, J. Hibbert's will, reciting that his wife was barred of her customary share, gives her several legacies, gives the plaintiff a leasehold estate and £5000, makes the defendant Barker the residuary legatee.

Sir Edward Northey, for the defendant: First, as to the advancement of the defendant Barker, Dean v. Lord Delaware, entries in the testator's books were sufficient to ascertain the child's advancement though the entries were made by the bookkeeper. 2 Ch. Ca. 185, Annand and Honywood.[1] The reason of the custom is only that the advancement may be brought into hotchpot. Stranger's Case,[2] by the Master of the Rolls, where the children were admitted to prove a further advancement. By the custom, a wife may be compounded with because she is at her own disposal, but a child cannot be barred by any agreement. Co. Lit. 176.[3] The custom is mistaken. The widow is not to have the benefit of hotchpot, but only the unadvanced children. The father cannot give a child a certain sum in satisfaction of the orphanage share. It ought to be certified whether a father can agree with his child to bar the orphanage share.

Lord Chancellor [Lord Parker]: As to the point of the defendant's advancement, the objections are two: first, the uncertainty of the value of the land; second, the uncertainty of how much is to go in advancement and how much in discharge of the debt due to the defendant from her father.

Lutwyche, for the defendant: Upon the Statute of Distributions,[4] land is to be taken as part of a child's advancement, but, by the custom of London, land is not to be taken as part.

Raymond, for the defendant: The certainty of the estate appears though not the certainty of the value, but that is easily ascertained. Suppose a mortgage or bond were assigned as part of the portion, they might be brought into hotchpot

---

1 *Annand v. Honywood* (1680–1682), 2 Chancery Reports 179, 21 E.R. 651, also 1 Vernon 345, 23 E.R. 511, 2 Chancery Cases 117, 129, 22 E.R. 874, 880, 2 Freeman 56, 22 E.R. 1056, 1 Eq. Cas. Abr. 152, 21 E.R. 952, 79 Selden Soc. 824, 879.

2 *Northey v. Strange* (1716), 1 Peere Williams 340, 24 E.R. 416, 2 Eq. Cas. Abr. 264, 291, 439, 22 E.R. 223, 244, 374.

3 E. Coke, *First Institute* (1628), ff. 171–172.

4 Stat. 22 & 23 Car. II, c. 10 (*SR*, V, 719–720).

though it should not appear how much interest is due. [There is] no precedent where a child has been compounded with; therefore, it is proper to be certified.

Peere Williams: If a lease for years or money be settled as a jointure, it is no bar of dower at law; yet, in equity, it will bind her. If this release is to be considered as an agreement, why may not all releases be so?

Talbot: If the defendant's release is void in law and not supported by the custom, there is no room for equity to assist it. It is no inconvenience that a wife may be compounded with, she having no right antecedent to the marriage, but a child has by its birth. By the custom, the certainty of the advancement is to appear. If the thing is subsisting, it may be brought into hotchpot. Though the certainty of the value does not appear, paraphernalia are subject to debts. If the husband devise lands for payment of his debts, he is a purchaser of the paraphernalia and may dispose of them by his will. [This is] the same reason that the husband by compounding with his wife is a purchaser of her share of his personal estate.

Cowper, in reply: If the parties had intended the certainty of the advancement should appear, the value of the lands would have been ascertained. But they are only mentioned to be of considerable value. Therefore, the parties intended that the certainty should not appear. The witnesses differ as to the value of the lands. In all cases, the advancement may be reduced to a certainty and the custom would be precluded.

Vernon: If lands descend on are settled on a child, it is not a bar of the customary share. So where lands are settled on a wife and it is not mentioned to be in bar of the custom, as in Atkyns and Waterson[1] it was certified to be so, it is the party's agreement that is the reason of the law. So, if the child agrees to accept of land on marriage and releases her right to the orphanage part, it is as good as where a wife does. It was never sent to the City to certify whether an agreement were a bar, but only where there were no express words to bar her. Here is a mutual agreement. If it were a devise, the defendant could not take both, but would have her election. Here is no imposition or advantage taken of the child. The father might have invested the personal estate in land or have given away his personal estate in his lifetime. Second, whether the wife be barred, she offering to pay the penalty of the bond. But an agreement is not less binding for the addition of a penalty. It is at least as strong as if there were none. In Clare and Acmooty, all the children were advanced and the wife had a moiety. Dean and Lord Delaware carried a great way; Dean married the widow of Freeman, and a difficulty arose about the certainty of the daughter's advancement, who married Lord Delaware; there the entries in the testator's books were admitted to ascertain it. No case ever went so far.

Lord Chancellor [Lord Parker]: As to that part which is sent to be certified, if there has been a former certificate of that point, it is improper to send it

[1] *Atkyns v. Waterson* (1715–1716), see above, Case No. 83.

thither again. Therefore, I would see precedents. Here is something very special in this case. If it should be certified that, when the wife is barred, the wife is looked upon as dead, it would not give me entire satisfaction for it is not clear that the wife is entirely barred by her bond, for, take it strictly, the bond is forfeited by her claim. I would give an absolute opinion now.

The bond is that the widow shall release her customary share to the executors on their paying her £400. Suppose they should not pay her the £400, then she might claim the customary share. If she releases to the executor, it is not for the benefit of the children but for such uses as the husband shall direct by his will. It is proper to be certified whether a child can release its orphanage share. As a release, it is void because there is no inchoate right in the child, for the father may lay out his personal estate in land. A right to a distributive share by the Statute cannot be released by a child, for it is supposed the father dies intestate and then who must have it? Considered as an agreement, this release is good. It is in consideration of her fortune.

Now the question is not between the father and the daughter, but between her and another daughter, who has a particular provision by his will and the residue to the defendant, his other daughter. The plaintiff will not accept of that provision. The defendant's agreement may be construed not to claim any further part of her customary share than what her father would give her, and he has given her all he can. Therefore, the father seems to have released her from this agreement by devising to her the customary and testamentary share. The question is whether here is a sufficient certainty of the advancement. Nothing can be more certain than land and the thing in specie when it appears. And all the purposes of the custom are answered though it is certain what was given the defendant. Yet it is said not to be certain how much was in satisfaction of the debt. But if her father owed her £40, it would not alter the nature of the case. Here, the freehold lands may be construed to be given in satisfaction of the debt because, by the custom, it is not reckoned as part of the portion. But here, the defendant offers to quit the debt, which puts an end to that question.

The defendant may bring her advancement into hotchpot if it is not barred by her release. The plaintiff is entitled only to one half of one third. If the custom has not been already certified, it must go to the City upon both points: first, whether the husband is a purchaser of his wife's one third; second, whether the child can release its orphanage share.

N.B. This case was afterwards ended by agreement.

Lincoln's Inn MS. Misc. 506, p. 21, pl. 3

Trinity 6 Geo.

Hibbot, a freeman of London, had two wives. By the first, he had a daughter, the defendant Barker. By the second, he had a daughter married to the plaintiff, Blondell. But, on his marriage with the second, he settled a jointure and, by articles, agreed to leave her £500 besides jewels and she, on the receipt of the

£500, was to release her customary share. Hibbot dies and leaves to his daughter by the first wife above three-fourths of his personal estate. The question was whether he could by will dispose of two-thirds, first, one-third as a testamentary part and the other third as belonging to his widow, which he had given her a satisfaction for and she had released, or whether it should be considered as if he had left no widow and so one moiety would be affected by the custom and only a moiety [would be] testamentary. There was cited the case of Hall and Lomly, 4 February 1635, where there was a certificate that, in case of a composition with a wife, one-third ought to come to the children by the custom, not a moiety, but what is very odd it is sent back to know what is fit to be done according to the custom and not what is the custom and then they certify that it is fit the children should have half.

Travin and Pocock, 33 Car. II, is express that, the wife having released according to an agreement prior to the marriage, the orphanage part should be one-third and the other two-thirds legatory.

Hancock and Hancock; it was declared without any certificate that, the wife being fully advanced upon marriage by a settlement and agreement and so barred of her customary part, her share should go to increase the personal estate and the orphanage part should be a moiety. Rawlinson and Rawlinson, upon the like circumstances, divides it into moieties. Chase and Fox; Hall and Plant, 1675; Atkinson and Waterson.[1] In the principal case, it was suggested that the consideration should be whether the advancement of the wife was out of the real or personal estate, that, if it was out of the real, then her customary part should go to increase the testamentary, but, if out of the personal, then it should go indistinctly into the personal estate and be distributed as if there had been no wife because the advancement of the wife had lessened the personal estate.

But the Lord Chancellor [Lord Parker] seemed inclined to make a distinction between where the agreement is in satisfaction of the custom and where it is an agreement to release; where it is extinguished or satisfied, then it should be divided into moieties because then it is as if there were no widow, but, where it is not extinguished, then her part should go to the executors or legatees. It was not said here that the thirds were satisfied, but that she should release to the executors. He doubted whether that would be an extinguishment. He thought it ought to be taken according to the intent of the testator who had it in his power to do as he would. As to the certainty of a child's advancement, he said he had looked into a copy of judge law in Edw. VI and, by that, the custom appeared to be that the father should express the certainty of the goods, which is different

[1] *Chase v. Box* (1700), 1 Lord Raymond 484, 91 E.R. 1223, 1 Eq. Cas. Abr. 154, 21 E.R. 953, Dodd 189, Lincoln's Inn MS. Misc. 10, p. 170, Brasenose Coll. Oxford MS. 59, p. 22, Yale Univ. Taussig MS. 311, vol. 1, pp. 441, 444; *Hall v. Plant* (1676), 73 Selden Soc. 300, *sub nom. Hill v. Blankett*, Reports *tempore* Finch 248, 23 E.R. 136; *Atkyns v. Waterson* (1715–1716), see above, Case No. 83.

from the certainty of the value, for that may appear otherwise. Besides, it would be absurd to ascertain the value of money.

This affair was afterwards compromised.

Lincoln's Inn MS. Misc. 380, pt. 3, p. 216

Michaelmas 1719.

This bill was brought by Mr. Blunden in the right of his wife, the daughter of Ibot, the testator, and by the widow against Mrs. Barker, the other daughter of Ibot, the administratrix *cum testamento annexo* to have a discovery of the estate of the deceased, Mr. Ibot, and to have the will set aside as far as it was prejudicial to the right of his wife, as a daughter of a citizen of London, or to the right of the widow, as wife of a citizen.

Upon the pleadings, the case came out thus. Ibot, the testator, had by his first wife issue, Anne Barker, the defendant, and, by his second, his present widow, one of the defendants, Esther Blunden, married to the plaintiff against the consent of the father. Upon the marriage of Mr. Ibot, the testator, with his second wife, now widow, there were articles of agreement precedent to the marriage entered into by Mr. Ibot and the present widow, the substance of which articles were that Mr. Ibot should leave her at his death an estate in land for her life of £85 *per annum*, £400 in money, and all her jewels and that she should enter into a bond of £8000 penalty to some in trust for Mr. Ibot, the condition of which bond was that, if these terms were made good to her, she would within two months after the death of Mr. Ibot release to his executors all right and title that she might have to any part of his estate, real or personal, by dower or custom of London or otherwise, the bond was entered into accordingly, and, in 1684, the match took effect.

In the year 1706, Mr. Ibot married his oldest daughter, Mrs. Barker, and gave her for her portion, as appears by the marriage settlement, £4000 in money and lands [and] tenements with a reversionary interest of a lease to a considerable value. To this settlement, among others, Mr. Ibot, the father, was a party and the certainty of Mrs. Barker's advancement appeared not otherwise than by the father's being a party to that settlement wherein no value was put upon either the freehold or the reversionary interest of a lease settled upon her. In truth, the value of them amounted to about £9000. But, precedent to the marriage, the father thought fit that Mrs. Barker, his daughter, should before the marriage execute to him a release to which the lawyer that drew the settlement and Mr. Barker, the intended husband, should be parties, wherein his daughter should in consideration of her present advancement release to her father, his heirs, executors, and administrators all interest, right, title, etc. that she had or should have to any part of his estate, real or personal, by the custom of the City [of London], Statute of

Distributions,[1] or otherwise, save what her father should be pleased to give her by his last will. This release was accordingly executed. Mrs. Barker had before this had some small matter in land and money left her by some other ancestors, the interest and profits of which were received by the father, but no account was ever made up between them.

Sometime after this, Mr. Blunden, the plaintiff, marries the other daughter of the testator, Ibot, without his consent. Afterwards, Mr. Ibot makes his will, which, as far as is material to the present dispute, was to this purpose. He gives to his wife during her life the interest of so much Bank and East India stock as amounted to £1200 *per annum*; he gives his second grandchildren by Mrs. Barker £5000 apiece; then he gives a leasehold in trust for Mr. Blunden during the life of his wife and, after her decease, in trust for the children of Mrs. Blunden and, in default of such, in trust for his own right heirs; he gives all his real estate to Mrs. Barker and likewise makes her residuary legatee of all his personal estate. Ibot dies, leaving a very considerable, both real and personal, estate.

The questions in this cause are three:

First, whether Mrs. Ibot be barred by the articles of agreement and the bond from claiming her customary share;

Second, if she be barred, what is to be done with her customary share, *viz.* whether, in this case, the husband is to be considered as dying without a wife and so the estate to be divided into moieties to the testamentary part of the testator or whether the agreement by which the wife is barred; being founded upon the consideration of a settlement upon her out of a real estate, Mr. Ibot should not be considered as a purchaser of his wife's third and so have a right to dispose of all the thirds of his estate by his will;

Third, whether Mrs. Barker is in this case barred from claiming her customary part, either upon account, first, of the release executed to her father or, secondly, for want of a sufficient certainty of her advancement appearing under the hand of the father.

In case the widow be barred and the husband is to be considered as dying without a wife and Mrs. Barker is barred, then Mr. Blunden, in the right of his wife, has a clear title to a moiety of the personal estate of the testator. In case the wife is barred and the husband to be considered as a purchaser and Mr. Barker barred, Mr. Blunden, in the right of this wife, will be entitled to a third. But, in case the wife is barred, Mrs. Barker not barred, and there Mr. Ibot is to be considered as a purchaser, then Mr. Blunden will in the right of his wife be entitled only to a moiety of a third part of the testator's estate.

Upon the hearing of the cause before Sir Joseph Jekyll, Master of the Rolls, he was pleased to decree, first, that the wife was barred, but what the con-

[1] Stat. 22 & 23 Car. II, c. 10 (*SR*, V, 719–720); Stat. 1 Jac. II, c. 17, s. 7 (*SR*, VI, 19).

sequence of that was whether the husband is to be considered as a purchaser he sent to the City to be certified what the custom was.

Secondly, he decreed Mrs. Barker barred both by the release as a subsisting agreement in equity and also because there was not such a certainty appearing under the hand of the father as the custom of the City requires to let her in to claim her share.

Mrs. Barker, not acquiescing under the determination of the Master of the Rolls, brought it before the Lord Chancellor Parker.

The substance of the arguments in support of the decree of the Master and in favor of Mr. Blunden [were as follows]. The cases of Clare and Acmudy, Hancock and Hancock, and Rawlinson and Rawlinson were urged to prove that the wife may by an agreement before marriage bar herself of her customary share and that, when this is done, the husband is always considered as dying without a wife and no difference is made when the estate by which the wife is compoundable is real and when (and in the case of Hancock and Hancock) the wife was barred by a jointure of land and yet [it was] held expressly that the estate should be divided into moieties. In the case of Rawlinson and Rawlinson, the wife was compounded off out of real estate and yet [it was] held that the husband should have but a moiety for his testamentary share. In the case of Clare and Acmudy, the children were all advanced in full, and it was held that, in that case, the father was to be considered as dying without children and the estate was to be divided into moieties: the one moiety to go to the wife, the other to be the testamentary share of the father and [it was] not at all considered what the nature of the estate was, whether real or personal, out of which the children were advanced. Though, in law, the bond can bind no farther than the penalty, yet, in equity, the bond and articles make but one agreement, and therefore, [it is] not in the liberty of the wife, by incurring the penalty of the bond, to free herself from the agreement.

As to the release of Mr. Barker, it was owned that, at law, as a release, it would be void. But it was urged that it would subsist as a good agreement in a court of equity.

It was argued that, if a jointure made precedent to marriage could bar a woman of her dower, that if a woman might by an agreement precedent to marriage bar herself of her customary share, in neither or which cases, the woman has not any right at the time of the bar, *a fortiori* may a daughter release that right which was a right is by her birth already vested in her, though not to take effect in possession until the death of the father.

As to the objection, if a father be allowed to take a release from his children, it will leave room for the father to impose on is children by that authority that a father has naturally over his children, *responsum*, first, that it is not the case here. The advancement was a very handsome, considerable one, and the intended husband and the lawyer that drew the settlement were witnesses to the release. Secondly, if fathers cannot take releases from their children or, some way or other, bar them from the customary share, it will be a discouragement to fathers from the advancing of their children in their lifetime. Thirdly, the father by the advancing of his children never so inconsiderably may according to the custom cut off his children, provided he will be but silent and not let it appear under his hand what that advancement was. [It was] settled in the case of Fowk and Edwin that an advancement in marriage will cut a child off his customary part if the certainty of that advancement does not appear under the hand of the father.

As to the certainty, it was urged that the decree of the Master was right, first, because the father being indebted to the daughter for interest of money and profits of lands by him received at the time of this release and, this account having been never adjusted, it was now utterly impossible to do it and, consequently, impossible to know the certainty of the advancement, which was the remainder after this debt deducted.

Another reason of the uncertainty of the advancement was because no value was put upon the reversionary interest of the lease, not of the freehold lands in the settlement. It had been easy for the father to have put a value upon these things, but it seems to have been omitted on purpose to corroborate the release that upon a supposition that the release should not prove effectual, for the cutting her off the uncertainty of the advancement in this settlement might.

If it had been said that *id certum est quod certum reddi potest* and that this advancement, however uncertain upon the settlement, is yet capable of being reduced to a certainty, it may be answered that it is true it may, *viz.* by the chargeable and dilatory way of either a trial at law before a jury or by an account before a master. But that is not such a certainty as the custom requires which, on purpose to avoid these ill conveniences, has fixed and prescribed the way by which this certainty is to appear, *viz.* the hand of the father. If this were not so, the custom as to the certainty would signify but nothing, for there is nothing but may some such way be reduced to a legal certainty.

It may be objected that the custom not extending to land, the uncertainty of the freehold estate is not material. *Responsum* yet it is material, for, though the custom does not extend to land, yet the real estate as well as the personal making part of the consideration the woman shall quit her dower, yet equity will interpose and hold her to her election and not let her have both.

The Case of Atkins and Waterson, who was a citizen of London, [as to] jointures [of] his wife before marriage with land to which the custom did not extend, sent to the City to certify whether this jointure did not bar her of her customary part but that, had it been made in bar, it would.

Of the arguments over and above what follows in the decree, take [?] as follows.

If a man has a personal estate not sufficient for the payment of his debts and subjects his land to pay them, he will be considered in this court as a purchaser of the paraphernalia of his wife and may dispose of them by his will because, had he not charged his land, they must have gone to pay his debts. *Pari rationi*, the wife when compounded with out of real estate, the husband is to be considered as a purchaser of his wife's thirds.

This release [is] acknowledged to be void at common law, but [it is] said that it will stand good as a release for equity. *Responsum*, according to this way of reasoning, the courts of law and equity directly contradict one another. The law says that some releases are void, others good. Equity says all releases are good, for every release imports an agreement that is not to be endured; the law [is] not to be overthrown but where some equitable circumstance interposes. But here is nothing at all but what is essential to the nature of a release, *viz.* that it imports an agreement.

Lord Chancellor [Lord Parker]: When once the court is possessed in a parallel case of what the custom of the City is by a proper certificate, it is to no purpose to send it again to the City to be certified again. However, since it is now before the City for their certificate of their custom whether, in case a woman be compounded with out of a real estate, the husband will not be considered as a purchaser; it may likewise be sent to the City to know whether the custom allows of such releases between parents and their children, for, though they are void in law, yet, as agreements in equity, they may be supported if the custom of the City does not interpose, for, as to the inconveniences that it is said will attend these releases drawn from the power and authority of parents over their children, [they] are not much because the present case stands free of them and whenever a case shall arise attended with such circumstances as the objection supposes, it will then be a case proper for the relief of this court.

Were not the other point now depending before the City, I would not send this because I very much doubt whether Mr. Blunden will be the better whatever answer be returned upon the certificate of the City, for, as to the first question whether the husband etc., I am of an opinion that admitting the custom of the City in general to be that the husband does not become a purchaser of his wife's third when, before marriage, she agrees to accept of a settlement out of land in bar of her customary share anymore than he would in case the settlement had been of personal estate that notwithstanding as this particular is circumstanced the husband must be considered as a purchaser and consequently will have seconds and thirds of his estate for his testamentary share.

Suppose that, without any precedent agreement, the wife had after the death of her husband released to the executors of her husband all her right to her third by the custom, I demand if the executors of the husband must not have had the benefit of this release? No doubt, they must. If so, what difference in reason is there when that same though it is done in pursuance of a precedent agreement and when without?

The notion that, in this case, the husband is to be considered as dying without a wife does necessarily suppose the wife's third so totally destroyed as to have no more subsistence either in law or the consideration of the parties than if the testator had never married. But here, it is very plain that the wife's right to her customary share does still subsist both in law and the consideration and intention of the parties as a collateral security to the wife that the husband performs his part of the agreement, because, had he failed, she might have claimed her thirds.

As to the release, when the meaning of the parties, the person applying to this court to make the release bind and the will comes to be considered, I much doubt whether Mr. Blunden can reap any advantage from any certificate the City shall make. Mrs. Barker, for the consideration of her marriage advancement, does release to her father all right etc., that she shall have to any part of his estate, either by the Statute of Distributions, custom of London, or otherwise save what he shall be pleased to give her by his last will.

Now, what is to be understood by this clause 'save' etc.? It cannot be save what he should give her out of his own testamentary share, for then it signifies just nothing, for the release did not extend to that or could the parties think it did. It must then have relation to some part of the estate which it was thought by the parties the release did cut her off from, and then the meaning must be this, and very natural meaning it is, [it is] that, in consideration of so handsome a settlement I think fit now to make, you shall promise me to be content with such part of your customary share I shall think fit to give you by my will. And consequently, it was the meaning of the agreement that the father was to be considered as a purchaser of his daughter Barker's customary share and then the meaning of the agreement, which in a court of equity will be equally prejudicial to Mr. Blunden's right as if it were left to its fate at law, where doubtless it would be void.

It is not the father to whom the release was executed that comes in this court to have the benefit of it, but it is a daughter married against the consent of the father that comes into this court in order to support a release void at law as an agreement in equity in order to break in, in a great measure, upon the will of her father to whom the release was executed.

It seems to me a very harsh doctrine, and what it may be was never done for a third person to come into a court of equity to enforce an agreement void in law in direct opposition to the meaning of the parties to the agreement. The father had during his life an absolute power over this release and might, if he had pleased, discharged his daughter from being bound by it.

The question is whether he has not done that which is equivalent. So it seems to me that a will whereby he has given her all her customary share is virtually and in equity a plain declaration that it was never his intention that she should be cut off from this share by this release.

If, therefore, for these reasons, the release will not stand in her way, the next thing to be considered [is] whether the certainty of her advancement does appear under her father's hand as the custom required, for, if it does not , then this advancement will cut her off from coming in. And here, the question is no more than this, whether the certainty of the advancement does sufficiently appear as in the marriage settlement, for the father being a party to it, whatever appears there does appear under the hand of the father.

As for the uncertainty of the freehold estate, that is nothing to the purpose, for the custom extends only to personalty. The personal estate in this advancement is £4000 in money, said in the settlement to be in part of her fortune, and the reversionary interest of a lease, and no value [was] put upon it.

The first objection against this being a sufficient certainty is the uncertainty of the value of this reversionary interest of the lease.

In answer to this, it is to be observed that the custom of the City is not that the certainty of the value of the advancements or the certainty of the sum, but the certainty of the advancement must appear under the hand of the father. It seems to me that there cannot be a greater certainty or less possibility of fraud or collusion than when the thing given to the child appears under the hand of the father. If a father should say he had given a child such a diamond necklace, describing it, is not this better than if he should put a value upon it? It may be more; it may be less than the true worth. Besides, had this reversionary lease remained part of the testator's estate *tempore mortis*, it must have been valued and may, therefore, as well now.

The second objection against the certainty is that Mrs. Barker had both money and land left her by another ancestor and that her father receives in her right the interest of the one and the profits of the other and was at the time of the marriage a debtor to his daughter upon this account and that, therefore, it is impossible now to know the certainty of that advancement, which is the remainder after the debt is deducted.

The reason why the custom of the City requires the certainty of the advancement to appear under the hand of the father is certainly in favor of the unadvanced children that the whole of the advancement may be thrown into hotchpot. If, therefore, it does plainly appear that a child has not been advanced quite so much, but it is only uncertain how much short of that sum the advancement was by reason of a trifling debt to be deducted that cannot be reduced to a certainty. Without doubt, such an uncertainty may be cured by the advanced child's quitting entirely this debt and bringing the whole £4000, for the unadvanced children cannot be prejudiced by bringing in more than the advancement was.

Not to admit this for an answer were to reduce the custom of the City to this absurdity, that, when a man has a right to so much and more, he shall lose that to which he has a certain right because he cannot tell how much more he is entitled to. If, therefore, Mrs. Barker quit her debt, this objection is at an end. But it is capable of another answer if this was insufficient.

Mrs. Barker's marriage portion consisted both in real and personal estate. And now, the freehold estate, to which the custom does not extend, be esteemed to go in satisfaction of the debt; then, the uncertainty of the debt will not create any uncertainty in her advancement as far as the custom of the City is concerned in it. And that seems to be agreeable to the justice of this court in other cases, as where a man indebted in specialties and simple contracts dies leaving both a personal and real estate, this court will not suffer the debts by specialty to be flung upon the personal estate and that being exhausted leaves the debts by simple contracts unsatisfied, the land not being liable to them, but it will decree the debts by specialties to be satisfied out of the land and the debts by simple contract out of the personal estate.

If, in this case, the real estate had not been settled upon Mrs. Barker upon her marriage, but left her by will, Mr. Blunden would have thought it very hard that this debt should have been discharged out of the personal estate and so lessen his wife's share when her sister had so considerable an estate in land left her, out of which the debt might have been deducted.

As to the demand of the widow, Mrs. Ibot, that she should not be bound further than the penalty, there is very little in that, for I esteem the bond and articles of agreement before marriage to make but one entire agreement and the penalty of £3000 as circumstances. Then, it was thought more than a sufficient penalty for the enforcement of it. And though this happens to prove otherwise by an unexpected increase of the testator's estate, yet certainly a court of equity will hold her to her agreement.

Upon the whole, it seems clear to me that Mr. Blunden is in the right of his wife entitled only to one-half of a third of the personal estate of the testator.

British Library MS. Add. 36651, f. 97v

Michaelmas, 6 Geo., 1719. J. Blunden and Hester, his wife, plaintiffs v. Frances Barker, widow, and A. Hibbert, widow, defendants.

John Hibbert, a freeman of London, had two daughters by two wives. By the first wife, he had the defendant Frances, who was married to [*blank*] Barker, deceased. By his second wife, *viz.* the defendant Hibbert, he had the plaintiff Hester, who married Blunden. John Hibbert, upon and before his marriage with his second wife, made a settlement upon her of lands for her jointure and in lieu of her dower and customary part, and she, being then of full age, gave a bond in £3000 penalty to perform the agreements in the said settlement and also that she, upon paying her £400 by the executors of the husband, would execute a release to his executors of all her right to her customary part of his personal estate.

The said John Hibbert, upon the marriage of his elder daughter with Barker, as a portion with her, made a settlement of a freehold estate in land and also of a reversionary interest of a leasehold estate, and he also gave her £4000 in money, and he declared her to be fully advanced. And at the same time, she, being of full age, executed a general release of all demands which she had for or in respect of any legacy left to her by any of her ancestors or for or on account of any claims she then had or might have to any part of his personal estate by virtue of the custom of London or the Statute of Distributions or otherwise.

Hester, the second daughter, married the plaintiff Blunden without the consent of her father. And afterwards, the father died, having first made his will, whereby he devised several legacies to his wife and others. And he made his elder daughter, Frances Barker, his sole executrix and residuary legatee.

Blunden and his wife bring this bill for an account and child's share of the personal estate according to the custom. And, upon a hearing before Sir Joseph Jekyll, the Master of the Rolls, he was of opinion that Frances Barker was barred of her share of the orphanage part, first, because of the release, secondly, because the certainty of her advancement did not appear under the hand of the father.

Upon a rehearing before Lord Parker, the Chancellor, the case was argued again. The points were, first, whether the widow's share of the personal estate, she having released all right to it before marriage, shall enure to increase the testamentary part only or shall go in moieties, *viz.* one moiety to increase the testamentary part and the other moiety to increase the orphanage part. The second point was whether, by the custom of London, the child of a freeman can by her release extinguish or bar her right to her child's part.

Mr. *Vernon*, for the plaintiff, said it was agreed on all sides that a woman, before marriage, may bar herself of her customary part, for so has the custom often been certified. Therefore, that being out of dispute in this case, the first point is how that part shall go, whether the husband who made the settlement upon her before marriage is to be accounted as a purchaser of it and consequently to have the power of devising it by will or whether it ought not rather to sink into the whole personal estate.

He cited the Case of Hancock v. Hancock, where the widow had compounded, as in this case, before marriage and it was decreed that the children should take a moiety of the whole, as in the case she was dead. And he cited the case of Clare and Ackmooty to the same purpose and the case of Davilla v. Davilla, where there was an agreement by the wife, before marriage, to take £1500 in lieu of what she might claim by the custom of London or otherwise, it was decreed that she should be barred of any share of the personal estate though the husband died intestate and her share to increase the whole personal estate.

To the second point, he said the release given by the eldest daughter will bind her. It is not doubted in the case of the wife before marriage though that be only a possibility, *viz.* in case she should survive the husband, and the case of a child is the same. The release given by the defendant was upon a very good consideration, no less than £14,000 fortune in land and money. And it is witnessed by her then intended husband, and she was of full age. At least, it may operate as an agreement, and an agreement by a child of full age in consideration of a settlement made by the father to quit or release her right to her orphanage share is good, though a settlement of itself without such agreement would not bar her. So, if a freemen make a jointure of lands of inheritance to his wife before marriage, it will not bar her of her customary share unless it is so agreed and provided by the settlement.

But, putting the release out of the case, the defendant cannot come in for any further share, because she is an advanced child and the certainty or quantum of her advancement does not appear under the hand of the father as the custom of

London requires, the reason of which is because she cannot throw it into hotchpot as she must do if she will rather take a moiety of the orphanage part than stand to the advancement she, before, has had from her father. It appears by the settlement that part was in land of inheritance and part reversionary leasehold and only £4000 in money. And part of this was left her by a relation and was in her father's keeping so that the value of the fortune received from her father is uncertain. At least, it does not appear under his hand. And so, the custom, as it has been certified, requires before she be admitted to put it in hotchpot.

Serjeant *Chesshyre*, for the plaintiff, said that, where the wife of a freeman is compounded with before marriage or when a child is advanced, it shall fall in to and enure to increase the whole estate and not to increase the testamentary part only.

To the second point, he said there is no right, future or contingent, but what may be released or barred by proper words. And he cited Cook [*blank*]. And this release by the daughter is good if any can be by the custom, as it stands clear of all fraud and contrivance.

But, though the release be void, yet the defendant cannot claim any further share of the father's personal estate because the certainty or quantum of her advancement does not appear under the hand of the father, as the custom requires. It is said that it may be reduced to a certainty. But, if that is to be admitted, there can be no uncertain advancement in any case, for everything may be ascertained by an account. The settlement mentions three things, *viz.* £4000 in money, second, a leasehold, and third, lands of inheritance. And it appears her father was indebted to her for several sums left her by other relations. But it does not appear what part of this was in consideration of the debts owing to her by her father and what was the advancement from her father so that it is altogether uncertain. And, if that be so, the release is out of the case.

Cowper, for the plaintiff: It appears to have been the intent of all the parties that the release should bar the defendant. The husband is a witness to it, and, by leaving the quantum uncertain, when it might easily have been ascertained by the deed, makes it more evident.

Mr. *Yorke*, for the plaintiff, said the first query is whether, in this case, the orphanage part is a third or a moiety. And to that, he said there might be a difference, for, where the father advances a child by making a settlement upon her of lands of inheritance, there might in that case be some color to say that he should become a purchaser of such child's orphanage share, for, there, the land, which was out of the custom, goes to increase the personal estate. But where the advancement was out of the personal estate, that reason will not hold. But, even in the first case, he shall not be accounted a purchaser, for, if a freeman sells his lands, the purchase money falls into his personal estate and it cannot be said that he is a purchaser of the money so as to prevent its being subject to the custom.

Sir Edward Northey, for the defendant, agreed that the certainty of the advancement ought to appear before the advanced child can be admitted to throw into hotchpot. But, though the custom does require that it appear certainly what the advancement was, yet it is not necessary that the precise sum appear, and it is sufficient within the words of the custom if the thing in specie be brought in and the value may be made out by proof. And, in this case, the whole advancement appears under the father's hand to be the land of inheritance, the reversionary, and leasehold, and the £4000. The first is out of the custom, and the last is certain of itself, and the leasehold may easily be ascertained by proof.

As to the release of a bare possibility which cannot by law be released no more than an heir can release his right to the estate of his ancestor in the life of the ancestor, and, therefore, it is void in this case unless it is allowed and supported by the custom.

By the custom, a wife may be compounded with before marriage but not after. But the custom does not hold as to children, at least it has never yet been so certified.

If a father gives a child £100 and declares it to be in full satisfaction of [his] child's part, it is not pretended that that will bar her, though, in law, an acceptance in satisfaction is as strong as a release, but such child may bring it into hotchpot, not with the whole estate but with the orphanage part. 1 Inst. 176; 12 Rep. 113.[1]

Mr. *Lutwyche*, for the defendant, said that the defendant was not bound by the advancement she had received, first, because the certainty of that advancement did sufficiently appear, second, for that this release, being only of a possibility, was void.

What the advancement was appears fully by the settlement signed by the father, *viz.* £4000 in money, a leasehold, and an estate of inheritance. Of these, only what is personal, *viz.* the money and the leasehold, are within the custom, for, if he had vested his whole personal estate in lands of freehold or inheritance, it would have defeated the custom, for the custom differs from the Statute of Distributions, which does account land, unless in the case of an heir at law, to be part of an advancement and to be brought into hotchpot. But a settlement of land by a freeman upon a child is not considered any advancement within the custom. The only query, therefore, as to certainty is in respect of the reversionary leasehold. And that may be ascertained and valued as well as any other part of the personal estate, and, by the proofs, it appears to be worth £1400. And it may be presumed that the freehold was settled as a recompense for what was owing to her by her father.

As to the release, he said a release must be of something that the party has a right to at the time of the release. Otherwise, it is void. Lit., sec. [*blank*]. Here was no right at the time of the release, and it was uncertain whether she should ever have any, for his estate might be lost or laid out in land or he might be dis-

---

[1] E. Coke, *First Institute* (1628), f. 176; Note on the Custom of London, 12 Coke Rep. 113, 77 E.R. 1388.

franchised. So, the release of the heir of the disseisee to the disseisor is void. Lit., sec. [*blank*]. In the case of a wife before marriage, it has been allowed because the custom warrants it, though, at common law, a release of dower before marriage or acceptance of anything in satisfaction did not bar the wife. Vernon's Case, 4 Rep.[1] But it has never yet been certified to be the custom of London that a child may release.

Sir Robert Raymond, for the defendant: As to the certainty of the advancement, he said it appeared by the deed of settlement, which is under the father's hand. The freehold is out of the case, for, if a freeman give land to a child, it is no part of an advancement within the custom. He said it was adjudged in the Case of Lord Delaware that the certainty of a child's advancement appearing by a book kept by the father's bookkeeper where he and the bookkeeper made entries promiscuously was sufficient.

As to the release, it is void as a release because the party had no right at the time of executing it, nor can it be supported as an agreement, there being no words in it sufficient to construe it such.

It is different from the bond given by the wife which is supported by the custom as it has been certified. And there is good reason why it should allow the one and not the other, for a wife, before her marriage, was no way dependant but entirely *sui juris* and might accept or refuse. But the child is dependent, and the influence of the father over it is great and may be made use of to ill purposes.

Peere Williams, for the defendant, said they were willing to have the custom certified how it stands in relation to the father's compounding with a child. As to the wife, we admit it having already been certified and is better supported by reason. And it is consonant to the rules of equity, for, though a settlement of money or a lease for years or the like made upon a wife before marriage is no bar of her dower within the Statute of Hen. VIII, of jointures,[2] yet her agreement to accept them before marriage will bind her in equity.

This release given by the defendant will not amount to an agreement, for all agreements, at their creation are executory in their nature. But this is executed.

As to the certainty of the advancement, it is sufficient if the thing given appear though the value do not. If more were necessary, the custom might easily be evaded.

From the reason of the thing, the father should be taken as a purchaser of the widow's part, for the condition of the bond is in the nature of an agreement to assign over her third part as the husband should direct, and a condition of a bond may in many cases be considered as an agreement.

---

[1] *Vernon v. Vernon* (1572), 4 Coke Rep. 1, 76 E.R. 845, also 3 Dyer 317, 73 E.R. 718, Benloe 210, 123 E.R. 147, 3 Leonard 28, 74 E.R. 519.

[2] Stat. 27 Hen. VIII, c. 10, ss. 4–7 (*SR*, III, 540–541).

Mr. *Talbot*, for the defendant, said that the release given by the defendant is void as a release and it is not to be supported as an agreement, for, if a void lease be to be supported in equity as an agreement, it would overturn the law.

The certainty does sufficiently appear in the case under the father's hand, for the custom as certified is that the certainty of the advancement should appear, and it does not require that the certain sum or valuation should appear.

As to the husband's being a purchaser of the widow's part, he said it was like the case of paraphernalia, which belong to the wife in case the personal estate be sufficient to pay the debt. But where the husband charged his land with the payment of his debts for which his personal estate was not sufficient, he became a purchaser of the paraphernalia.

Mr. *Clive*, for Mrs. Hibberd, the widow, said she ought to be admitted to her third in case she would submit to the £3000 penalty of the bond.

Chesshyre and *Vernon*, *contra*: An agreement contained in a writing with a penalty is as strong as if there was no penalty, and, by her answer, she has submitted to it.

Lord Parker, Chancellor: Suppose the wife, after the death of the husband, without any previous agreement, had executed a release to the husband's executors of her share or customary part of his personal estate. That would not go to increase the children's part. Then taking it for granted that the bond binds the wife as an absolute agreement, which is that she, upon being paid £400 by her husband's executors, shall execute such a release to his executors and that, after the death of the husband, a release is executed accordingly, that will not vary the case. And it seems to be the intent that she should not immediately be barred of her third part but that her right should subsist as a security for the £400 to be paid by the executors and, upon payment thereof, she should release it to the executors to answer the will of the testator.

He said he took the release of the defendant Barker as such to be void because she had no right at the time of the release nor could she force her father to keep his personal estate, which he might lay out in land or otherwise dispose of. But, as an agreement, it may be good if the custom admits it. And, if it is an agreement, [it is] no matter for the value or certainty of the time.

It is to be considered who it is that would enforce this agreement. It is not the father that would have it established, but the other daughter, who is no party to it and would make it effectual to the father whether he would or not, whose intent appears fully that the plaintiff should have nothing that he could give from her. One of the parties to an agreement may release and discharge the other from it.

By the custom, as it has been certified, an advanced child cannot throw its advancement in hotchpot unless the certainty of the advancement appears under the hand of the father. Here, it does appear, for nothing can be so certain as the thing in specie, which is more certain than when the value is expressed. The leasehold or the price of it if sold may be brought in and especially if she quit her demands as a creditor and agrees to take it all as an advancement. It makes it all certain.

As to the lands of inheritance, they are not within the custom. So they may be applied as a satisfaction for the debts.

He said he would have the custom certified, if it was desired, whether a father can compound with a child and how far the custom would warrant such a release. But, as to the other matters wherein the custom has already been certified, he would not have them certified again. But they might search for precedents.

Lincoln's Inn MS. Misc. 12, p. 201

In the case of Blundell and his wife, plaintiffs, and Frances Barker, widow and administratrix *cum testamento annexo* of John Hibert, and others, defendants, it was decreed by the Master of the Rolls [JEKYLL] that the defendant Barker should account for the personal estate of John Hibert, the testator. And he declared that the settlement made on the defendant Esther Hibert, the widow of the testator, and the bond executed by her before her marriage was to be taken as an agreement on her part for compounding for her customary part and that she was barred from claiming any part of her husband's personal estate by virtue of the custom of London. And he decreed the same accordingly.

And, as to the claim of the defendant Barker to a share of the orphanage part of the personal estate, as being one of the children of the said John Hibert, His Honor [JEKYLL] declared she was barred.

The defendant Barker appealed from this decree.

On 25 November 1719, the cause was heard before the Lord Chancellor [LORD PARKER], who declared that he took it to be an absolute agreement that the defendant Esther should perform the condition of the bond, which was that, after her husband's death, she should release to his executors and that the agreement was not that her said part should be extinguished for the benefit of her children but should go to his executors for the benefit of his will.

And, as touching the claim of the defendant Barker, the custom of the City was ordered to be certified, which, not being material to the present question, is here omitted.

[Other reports of this case: 1 Peere Williams 634, 24 E.R. 548, 10 Modern 451, 88 E.R. 806, 2 Eq. Cas. Abr. 258, 268, 22 E.R. 219, 226.]

382

Hawkins v. Turnor

(Ch. 1719)

A court of equity will not give a remedy to a person who comes into court with unclean hands.

Lincoln's Inn MS. Misc. 384, p. 169, pl. 2

4 May.

A bill [was exhibited] to be relieved against a bond of resignation.

Raymond, for the plaintiff: Though such bonds are good at law, yet, if any ill use is made of them by the patron, they are always set aside.

Vernon: The reason of allowing these bonds was to compel residence. In Sands of Gloucester's dispute[1] between the patron and the incumbent touching tithes, the patron put the bond in suit; the incumbent was relieved. The plaintiff is the incumbent of Water Newton in the County of Huntingdon and has laid out £300 on the parsonage house.

Mead: The defendant gives two reasons for putting the bond in suit: first, for a fraud appearing in a cause in this court by the plaintiff; second, for defrauding the defendant in the management of the defendant's estate. But the defendant did not then take advantage of the bond and did not put it in suit until lately. Wood and Lumley, by Blencowe, in the absence of the Lord Chancellor, where a defendant had used the bond to compel the plaintiff to lease the tithes at an under rate, the plaintiff was relieved and an injunction [was] granted though that bond was for resigning to the defendant's own son.

The defendant's proof made the plaintiff a very ill man, who had been guilty of very great fraud and ingratitude to the defendant; therefore, the bill was dismissed with costs.

[Other reports of this case: Precedents in Chancery 513, 24 E.R. 230.]

[1] *Durston v. Sands* (1686), 2 Chancery Cases 186, 22 E.R. 904, 1 Vernon 411, 23 E.R. 552, 2 Chancery Reports 398, 21 E.R. 698, 1 Eq. Cas. Abr. 86, 21 E.R. 897.

383

Savile v. Savile

(Ch. 1719–1721)

The question in this case was whether lands should be sold to pay marriage portions or whether the portions have been satisfied by lands descended.

A will can be revoked by an inter vivos *deed.*

Lincoln's Inn MS. Misc. 384, p. 170

5 May. Lord Chancellor [Lord Parker], Chief Justice Pratt, Master of the Rolls [Jekyll], Chief Justice King, Tracy.

Chesshyre, for the plaintiffs [Lady Dorothy and Mary Savile]: On 20 February 1694[/95], a term of 500 years is limited to trustees for raising £25,000 for the three daughters of Lord Eland, two of whom are the plaintiffs, who are also the representatives of Lady Essex, their sister, deceased. The plaintiffs pray that the defendants Lord Aylesford and Lord Cheney may execute the trust.

Cowper, for the defendants: The question arises upon the marriage settlement of Lord Eland, the plaintiffs' father on 20 February 1694[/95], wherein notice is taken of a former settlement in 1687, whereby premises are limited to Marquess George, the plaintiffs' grandfather, for ninety-nine years if he lived so long, then to his lady for ninety-nine years if she lived so long, then to the first and other sons in tail, then the term of 500 years in question to raise, if one daughter, £20,000, if more, £25,000, provided, if any daughter attain sixteen or be married before the term of 500 years commence, then the portion to be paid six months after the term commenced. Query when the term of 500 years commenced. It could not until the ninety-nine years term which was limited to the wife of Marquess George for her life was determined, which was but a year ago, when the lady died. The condition of the estate [is] not to be considered as it was at the time of the death of Marquess George but as it was at the commencement of the term when the encumbrances were paid off. The great question will arise upon the proviso, which estates descended to the plaintiffs will be a satisfaction of their portions within the intent of the proviso. The intent in general was that the plaintiffs should be secure of £25,000, but should have no more, provided if there be no daughter or such daughter should die before the portions be payable or if the portions be secured by the reversioner or the daughters advanced by Lord Eland or lands or tenements of inheritance descend from Lord Eland of as great value to be sold as their portions amount to, then the term of 500 years to cease. And if the reversioner shall make up such lands as shall be suffered to descend or come to the daughters from Lord Eland the full value of their portions, then the term is to cease. A descent of an estate of inheritance may be of an estate tail as well as of a fee simple, and it may be sold, and in reversion as well as in possession. And we insist that sufficient lands are descended to the plaintiffs to make satisfaction for their portions.

Vernon, for the defendants: The general view of the family was to keep the bulk of the estate in the heirs male and to ascertain what should be the portions of the daughters, which is fixed at £25,000, in money or lands. If the lands are equivalent to the portions, then the term is to cease, if not, it is then to be made up by the reversioner. The lands descended are fee tail or fee simple, which are both an inheritance, part is descended in tail in possession on the plaintiffs.

[It was] objected the plaintiffs, being infants, could not sell to raise their portions whereas the portions were payable at sixteen or marriage. But if there had been an encumbrance on the estate, yet the portions might be raised, though not so conveniently. The lands in Yorkshire of £900 *per annum* are sufficient to descend and the reversion of the jointure of the marchioness of Halifax, who is living, is £1400 *per annum*. As to the method of raising what is remaining of the plaintiffs' portions, it is directed by rents and profits or sale or mortgage, and the reversioner ought to have his election to have it raised by sale or mortgage and not be kept out of the profits during his life.

Mead: The intent of the parties was not that the lands suffered to descend to the parties should be sold, but only that an estimate should be put upon them to make up their portions and £5000. The plaintiffs' infancy, which hinders a sale, ought not to be of weight because an estimate may be put upon the lands.

Talbot: The defendant Sir George Savile is the heir male of the family. It was not the intent of the parties that the plaintiffs should have both the £25,000 and lands of as great value. As to the lands in remainder in tail which descended to the plaintiffs, they are within the meaning of the proviso and a value may be set upon them though it be not so great as if in possession, as in Kemis v. Thomas and Copley v. Copley by Lord Harcourt.[1]

Chesshyre, for the plaintiffs: Portions are always favored. Therefore, this court will aid the want of a surrender of a copyhold in favor of a daughter unprovided for. So where portions are payable at a certain day out of a future term, the court will order an immediate sale of the term. An estate tail is not assets as a fee simple is, as if a man binds himself and his heirs in a bond or lineal warranty; an estate tail is not assets, as Co. Lit. 274b; 6 Jan. 167, 2 Mod. 223, Dr. Vosius's Case; Salk. 236, Countess of Bridgewater; Collier's Case, 6 Co. 16.[2] No estates in fee

---

1 *Thomas v. Kemeys* (1696), 2 Vernon 348, 23 E.R. 821, 2 Freeman 207, 22 E.R. 1163, Colles 112, 1 E.R. 206, 1 Eq. Cas. Abr. 269, 21 E.R. 1037; *Copley v. Copley* (1711) 1 Peere Williams 147, 24 E.R. 333, 2 Eq. Cas. Abr. 639, 22 E.R. 536.

2 E. Coke, *First Institute* (1628), f. 374b; *Paget v. Vossius* (1677), 2 Modern 223, 86 E.R. 1039, also Lincoln's Inn MS. Misc. 500, f. 296, 2 Levinz 191, 83 E.R. 513, 1 Ventris 325, 86 E.R. 210, T. Jones 73, 84 E.R. 1153, 3 Keble 638, 749, 779, 842, 84 E.R. 925, 989, 1007, 1044, 1 Eq. Cas. Abr. 195, 21 E.R. 985; *Countess of Bridgwater v. Duke of Bolton* (1704), 1 Salkeld 236, 91 E.R. 209, also 6 Modern 106, 87 E.R. 866, Holt K.B.

simple are descended to the plaintiffs, but an estate in fee subject to great encumbrances is not to be looked upon as an equivalent. King and Melling, 1 Ven. 232.[1] 6 May.

Cowper, for the defendant: The portions are favorably taken, yet they, any more than creditors, ought not to have a double satisfaction if any estate of inheritance descend which is worth any sum to be sold, that is may have an estimate put upon it. Contingencies may be valued. Sir George Rook and Sir James Banks in 1706.[2] Portions were directed to be raised by rents and profits or a fine at eighteen or marriage. Lord Rosebury's Case, cited, in the House of Lords,[3] decreed that, a time being appointed and the means then mentioned being no more than the trustees might have done without any directions, that the portions might be raised by sale or mortgage. Here, it is stronger for the words 'sale or mortgage' are inserted.

Vernon, for the defendant: We have the letter of the deed with us and equity too. An estate tail in possession or reversion is as much an inheritance as a fee simple. If it be after an old life or a short term of years, surely a value may be set upon it, though it is difficult to fix how much an estate tail after a life is worth. But a ship at sea or a chance in a lottery may be valued and sold. It might be hard if we would force the plaintiffs to take an uncertainty instead of a certain portion. But we desire the contingencies may be sold and the plaintiffs be paid their whole portion of £25,000 by the defendant on the head of satisfaction. In Lord Egerton's time, Birkenhead's Case; Duffield and Smith,[4] where the sister's portion was charged on land which the brother devised away and gave his sister his personal estate; it was held here that the personal estate was a satisfaction, but on appeal, it was reversed being a different fund and no mention of satisfaction. Jesson v. Jesson; Blois and Blois.[5]

[It was] objected that the lands descended could not be sold, the plaintiffs' being infants, no more could a fee simple in possession be sold when the portions were payable, which is sixteen. If there be a second life in a lease, it is of some value. Here is a remainder in tail of £1400 *per annum* after the life of Lady

---

281, 90 E.R. 1054, 1 Eq. Cas. Abr. 177, 21 E.R. 970, 2 Eq. Cas. Abr. 299, 22 E.R. 252; *Collier v. Walker* (1595), 6 Coke Rep. 16, 77 E.R. 276, also Croke Eliz. 379, 78 E.R. 625.

1 *King v. Melling* (1672), 1 Ventris 214, 225, 86 E.R. 144, 151, also 2 Levinz 58, 83 E.R. 448, 3 Keble 42, 52, 95, 84 E.R. 584, 589, 614, Pollexfen 101, 86 E.R. 526, 3 Salkeld 296, 91 E.R. 835, 1 Eq. Cas. Abr. 181, 21 E.R. 973.

2 *Mills v. Banks* (1723–1724), see below, Case No. 620.

3 *Viscount Roseberry v. Taylor* (1702), 6 Brown P.C. 43, 2 E.R. 921, 2 Eq. Cas. Abr. 643, 22 E.R. 539.

4 *Duffield v. Smith* (1692), 2 Vernon 258, 23 E.R. 767, 2 Freeman 185, 22 E.R. 1150, 1 Eq. Cas. Abr. 204, 21 E.R. 991, *Smith v. Duffield* (1690), 2 Vernon 177, 23 E.R. 717.

5 *Jesson v. Jesson* (1691), 2 Vernon 255, 23 E.R. 766; *Blois v. Blois* (1680), 2 Chancery Reports 162, 21 E.R. 646, 2 Ventris 347, 86 E.R. 478.

Dowager Halifax, who is ninety years old. In the beginning of the proviso, the lands are to descend, which may seem to exclude a devise or purchase, but, in the end, are to descend or come. If a man covenants to settle and suffers land to descend, it has been adjudged a satisfaction. If an estate for life is devised to A. for life, remainder to B., subject to an encumbrance, A. is only to keep down the interest during his life. And the defendant Sir George Savile has done so and paid all the maintenance.

The court took time to consider.

Lincoln's Inn MS. Misc. 506, p. 60, pl. 2

Eodem die [15 July 1721].

It was declared by the Lord Chancellor [Lord Parker] that a will may be revoked two ways, either by express terms or by some deed inconsistent with it. An express revocation must be signed by three witnesses, else it is not according to the Statute.[1] But a virtual repeal by a deed inconsistent with the will may be by two witnesses notwithstanding the Statute because the Statute does not hinder it from being a good deed and then, by operation of law, it will be a revocation. This was Lord Lincoln's Case[2] and it was affirmed in the House of Lords, but this ought to be taken as strictly as possible. A mortgage in fee would not be a revocation because, though it be a divesting of the estate, yet it argues no change in mind because it was done only for a security for money; the trust remains the same as before. Therefore, it shall pass. Duffield and Smith, 1692; Wilcox and Wilcox, Trinity 1706.[3] Burton and Abbot[4] was a conveyance to the use of his will of lands *ex parte materna*. He makes no will. It was determined it should go to the heirs of the part of the mother because it did not go out of the party and made no change of the estate.

[Other reports of this case: 2 Atkyns 458, 26 E.R. 677, 11 Modern 327, 88 E.R. 1069, Select Cases *tempore* King 32, 25 E.R. 206, 2 Eq. Cas. Abr. 646, 679, 704, 22 E.R. 542, 570, 591, 1 Peere Williams 745, 24 E.R. 596, Fortescue 351, 92 E.R. 886, Philadelphia Free Library MS. LC 14.81, f. 96.]

[1] Stat. 29 Car. II, c. 3, s. 5 (*SR*, V, 840).

[2] *Earl of Lincoln v. Roll* (1696), Shower P.C. 154, 1 E.R. 105, 2 Freeman 202, 22 E.R. 1160, 1 Eq. Cas. Abr. 411, 21 E.R. 1140.

[3] *Duffield v. Smith* (1692), *ut supra*; *Wilcocks v. Wilcocks* (1706), 2 Vernon 558. 23 E.R. 961, 1 Eq. Cas. Abr. 26, 156, 160, 21 E.R. 847, 955, 958.

[4] *Abbot v. Burton* (1708), 11 Modern 181, 88 E.R. 976, 2 Salkeld 590, 91 E.R. 494, 1 Comyns 160, 92 E.R. 1014.

384
Anonymous
(Ch. 1719)

A contract to settle lands is performed by allowing lands to descend.

Lincoln's Inn MS. Hill 73, p. 73, pl. 1

7 May.

Mr. *Vernon*: If a man covenants to settle lands and suffers lands of equal value to descend, it has been allowed in equity [to be] a performance of the covenant.

385
Anonymous
(Ch. 1719)

The next friend of an infant pauper plaintiff is liable for the court costs of a groundless suit.

Lincoln's Inn MS. Hill 73, p. 73, pl. 2

8 May.

An infant pauper sued by his *prochein ami*, and, at the hearing of the cause, the *prochein ami* was ordered to pay costs, there being no ground for the suit.

386
Moore v. Meynell
(Ch. 1719)

A decree pro confesso *will not be made unless the process of contempt goes to a writ of sequestration.*

A married woman's real estate is not subject to her husband's debts.

Lincoln's Inn MS. Misc. 384, p. 173

8 May.

[It was said] by *Goldesborough*, the Register, where the defendant stands in contempt and will not appear, the plaintiff must go through the whole process of contempt to a [writ of] sequestration, which must be produced under seal and the record of the bill read before the bill can be taken *pro confesso*.

Mead quoted Dubois and Hole,[1] where the defendant, being a married woman, would not appear and process issued against the husband and a [writ of] sequestration [was] produced under seal before the bill was taken *pro confesso*.

Vernon, for the plaintiff: The bill is to have satisfaction of a bond debt and out of the personal estate of the defendant's former husband, Laurence Crabb, to whom she is administratrix. The defendant insists that the intestate had a plantation in Antigua, which is settled on her and that the stock accrues to her, but it has been settled that, if a tenant for life of a plantation buys Negroes and stocks it, he may by his will or otherwise dispose of them provided he leaves as many as he found, much more are they liable to his debts.

Raymond, for the defendant: We hope the plantation itself is not liable to our husband's debts. It was originally the defendant's own, but, in 1692, when she was under age, she joined in a deed and fine which was not registered there within six months and, therefore, is void by the laws of that island. If a fine is levied here, it will bind in Barbados or Jamaica if it be transmitted thither, but not in Antigua.

Vernon, for the plaintiff: The settlement of the stock is void as against creditors because a man cannot secure his personal estate from creditors.

Curia: As to the plantation itself, which was the wife's real estate, it is not subject to the husband's debts, and the deed of the wife whereby she gives her husband power over it is void by an act of the Island, which makes all conveyances etc. void unless registered within six months, which this deed was not. As to the stocks and personal estate, if he had not an estate for life but only during the coverture and bought Negroes, they were his personal estate. It is said the money wherewith he bought them was raised by sale of an estate of hers in Barbados, but, if the money was his, so are the Negroes, as much as if he bought horses.

The plaintiff must have satisfaction out of the personal assets. If there is any difficulty, the Master is to state it specially.

Dickens 30, 21 E.R. 178

By an order (the order is not entered) dated the 11th of April 1719, on an application for the wife to go to her husband, who was in Antigua, it appeared that the plaintiff had had dealings with the late husband of the defendant Ann Meynell, who was his administratrix, and had possessed what effects she could, that she had intermarried with the defendant, John Meynell, that she had come to England upon business and meant to return, that a writ of *ne exeat regno* had issued against her until answer and further order, that, having given bail, she put in her answer, she had applied to have the writ discharged, which the court had ordered

---

[1] *Dubois v. Hole* (1708), 2 Vernon 613, 23 E.R. 1002, 1 Eq. Cas. Abr. 65, 21 E.R. 879.

upon giving security to abide the event of the suit, and that she had given security accordingly.

N.B. The court, upon this application, put terms upon the plaintiff to speed the cause.

387
Leighton v. Leighton
(Ch. 1719–1720)

A purchaser of land has a right to have a discovery of the title deeds to his land.

Once a court of equity has taken jurisdiction to grant an equitable remedy, it will retain the case and grant common law relief in order to give a complete remedy.

Lincoln's Inn MS. Misc. 384, p. 175

11 May.

The plaintiff purchased from the defendants' father, who, as the defendants insisted, was tenant in tail. There were four verdicts for the defendants, but, on Baron Price's certificate after the last trial, this court retained the bill until after a trial at the bar in the [Court of] Exchequer, where a verdict was found for the plaintiff, who prays now a perpetual injunction and an account of the profits. The defendants pray a new trial, having four verdicts against one.

Vernon, for the defendant: The plaintiff is not entitled to an injunction. The plaintiff is a purchaser, yet the defendant claiming under an entail, there is no equity, but the matter is purely at law. Lord Bath and Sherwin, where the court would not grant an injunction, though the House of Lords did.[1] An inheritance is seldom bound by one verdict. A perpetual injunction is never granted unless the plaintiff has equity.

Curia: The question is whether this court ought to interpose and not to leave the matter as it is at law. This was not an issue directed. If the defendant should bring a new [action of] ejectment against the plaintiff, I will not hinder him. If the defendant had no verdict for him, I would not hinder him from trying it again, much less when he has had four verdicts to the plaintiff's one. I do not grant a new trial but only do not interpose to hinder it.

By consent, let there be a trial at the bar of the [Court of] King's Bench next Michaelmas term.

N.B. Afterwards, there being a verdict for the plaintiff, he had a perpetual injunction, which was affirmed in the House of Lords.[2]

---

[1] *Earl of Bath v. Sherwin* (1706–1710), 10 Modern 1, 88 E.R. 596, Precedents in Chancery 261, 24 E.R. 126, Gilbert Rep. 2, 25 E.R. 2, 2 Eq. Cas. Abr. 171, 243, 522, 22 E.R. 147, 206, 440, 4 Brown P.C. 373, 2 E.R. 253.

[2] 4 Brown P.C. 378, 2 E.R. 256.

Lincoln's Inn MS. Misc. 384, p. 211, pl. 2

12 November. William Leighton v. Sir Edward Leighton.

A perpetual injunction was granted to the plaintiff, who was a purchaser from the defendant's ancestor. The defendant claimed under an entail 200 years old and had obtained several verdicts in his favor in the County of Salop, where the lands lie. The plaintiff thereupon came into equity to have a discovery of the title deeds and to have a trial in an indifferent county which might be decisive.

The court thereupon ordered a trial at the bar, which coming out in the plaintiff's favor, the Lord Chancellor [Lord Parker] granted a perpetual injunction to quiet the plaintiff in the possession and that there might be an end of suits and it being in favor of a purchaser.

Lincoln's Inn MS. Misc. 11, p. 181

12 November 1720.

Upon hearing this cause, the court directed the plaintiff should try his title at [common] law and retained the bill for that purpose, the defendant having before the bill [was] brought recovered three verdicts in ejectment under an old deed of entail, which was made 200 years ago. And now it came on upon the equity reserved. And the plaintiff prayed a perpetual injunction. And the Case of Sherwin and Sherwin, which was the Case of the Earl of Bath and the Duke of Mountague, where Lord Cowper,[1] after five verdicts at law, refused to grant a perpetual injunction, but, upon an appeal to the Lords, it was granted.

Lord Chancellor [Lord Parker]: The defendant has set up a hard demand and is entitled to no favor in this court.

The court did not direct an issue at law but left the parties to try their title at law in a proper manner and [ordered] that they should then come back to the court. What did the court mean by this? Did they intend to do nothing when it came back but dismiss the bill? It was as ripe for a dismission at the hearing as now.

I think the cause ought to be at rest. The plaintiff had a right to come here, being a purchaser, for a discovery of deeds and writings and, being now here and the court having cognisance of the cause and the right having been tried and found with the plaintiff, I think there ought to be a perpetual injunction, but no costs, the defendant having had three verdicts in his favor.

[Other reports of this case: 1 Peere Williams 671, 24 E.R. 563, 1 Strange 404, 93 E.R. 596, 4 Brown P.C. 378, 2 E.R. 256, 2 Eq. Cas. Abr. 523, 22 E.R. 441.]

---

[1] *Earl of Bath v. Sherwin* (1706–1710), *ut supra*.

388

Jellard v. Jellard

(Ch. 1719)

A contract to make a marriage settlement can be performed by making a devise in a will.

Lincoln's Inn MS. Misc. 11, p. 113, pl. 2

Philip Jellard, executor of Thomas Jellard, plaintiff; Elizabeth Jellard, relict of Thomas Jellard, defendant.

Thomas Jellard, on his marriage with the defendant, entered into a bond to the defendant's mother with a condition that, if Thomas Jellard should put the defendant's life into a tenement in Stokenham, then in his possession, and should purchase some other estate for her life so as the whole together with the tenement should be of the yearly value of £20 and should convey the said estates to the obligee for the life of the defendant for her life for her jointure or if his executors should within six months after his death pay the defendant £250, the bond was to be void.

Sometime after the marriage, the said Thomas Jellard took a new lease of the tenement for ninety-nine years if the defendant and two others therein mentioned should live so long, but he made no assignment thereof for her benefit nor settled any other lands. But, by his will dated October 1713, he devised two closes called Buddles for her life with remainders over, and he gave her the use of his household goods in his house at Stokenham, which he takes notice was part of her jointure, and he makes the plaintiff executor. And, soon after, he dies.

The defendant, being ancient, insists upon being paid the £250 and to have the closes devised to her for her life besides. And the plaintiff insisting that she ought only to have the tenement, which he was willing to assign to her, and the two closes made up £20 a year, she brought her action and got a judgment. And the plaintiff came to be relieved against the action.

On 28 May 1718, upon hearing this cause before the Master of the Rolls [Jekyll], His Honor declared that the testator having not made a settlement according to the condition of the bond and the defendant having since his death elected to take the £250, the plaintiff ought not to be relieved further than against the penalty. And, therefore, he referred it to a Master to compute interest for the £250 and to tax the defendant her costs. And, upon payment of principal, interest, and costs, he decreed the bond to be delivered up and satisfaction acknowledged on the judgment.

On 6 June 1719, upon an appeal to Lord Chancellor [Lord Parker], he declared the defendant had no power of electing whether she would have the £20 a year or £250 in money, it being the primary intention of the parties that the testator should settle lands of £20 a year on the defendant, but there was no time limited for the doing it, and the testator having in his lifetime put the defendant's life into the lease of the tenement and having by his will taken notice that the said tenement was part of his wife's jointure, the agreement of the parties was in part executed. And he was of opinion that the two closes devised by the will as well as the said tenement ought to go in part of the £20 a year.

And he referred it to the Master to see what was the yearly value of the tenement and the two closes and then to come back for further directions.

Lincoln's Inn MS. Misc. 384, p. 37, pl. 2

28 May.

Jellard, upon his marriage with the plaintiff, enters into a bond to settle on her a certain estate or to leave her £200, but he dies without doing either. The query is whether his executors have their election of which to do.

Master of the Rolls [Jekyll]. The husband himself having made default of settling, the executors have no election, but they must perform according to the desire of the plaintiff.

389

Duke of Bolton v. Deane

(Ch. 1719)

Where a lessee holds over, the lessor is not entitled to the profits until he makes an entry unless his entry is prevented by fraud or accident.

Lincoln's Inn MS. Misc. 384, p. 176, pl. 1

30 May 1719.

Lord Chancellor [Lord Parker]: Where a lessee holds over, by the law, the lessor is not entitled to the profits until his entry, neither is he entitled in equity to an account of the profits unless his entry is prevented by fraud or accident. If, at law, the lessor might have an action of trespass, he may bring his bill here for an account of the profits.

Here, the plaintiff had made a lease for the lives of the lessee's three daughters. The lessee had two daughters of the same name, Elizabeth. The lease determined by the death of the first Elizabeth; so the plaintiff, by this accident, was prevented from entering and, therefore, is entitled to an account of the profits from the time the lease determined.

Lincoln's Inn MS. Misc. 13, p. 132, pl. 2

30 May 1719.

The plaintiff's grandfather, the ninth of Charles II [1657], demised to one Dean, a close of land for 99 years if Anne, Jane, and Elizabeth, his daughters, should so long live, Dean having then a daughter named Elizabeth by his first wife. He, afterwards, married a second wife, by whom he had a daughter, and he baptized her by the name of Elizabeth. The farm, amongst which this close lay, was settled on the defendant for her jointure.

It fell out that the three lives in the lease were dead, but Elizabeth, the daughter by the second wife, being supposed to be the daughter Elizabeth named in the lease, the defendant had held over for several years. And the duke, having discovered that the Elizabeth now living was born nine years after the making of the lease, recovered in [an action of] ejectment. And now, he brought his bill to have an account of the rents and profits for the time the defendant had held over.

Lord Chancellor [Lord Parker]. The plaintiff ought to have made an entry to entitle him to the rents and profits. And he must not come into equity to excuse or supply his own neglect or default. But, in this case, there being a sort of fraud in the lessee's naming two daughters of the same name and the landlord thereby deceived and made to believe the life was living, the Lord Chancellor [Lord Parker] decreed the defendant to account.

[Other reports of this case: Precedents in Chancery 516, 24 E.R. 231, 2 Eq. Cas. Abr. 588, 22 E.R. 495.]

390

Morrell v. Lawson

(Ch. 1719)

Where a bill is brought to establish a charity, the Attorney General must be named as a plaintiff, but this is not necessary where there is a devise to trustees for a charitable use.

A court has jurisdiction over a defendant who has not been served with process where a cross-bill has been filed in his name, he thereby consenting to the court's jurisdiction.

Lincoln's Inn MS. Misc. 384, p. 176, pl. 2

1 June 1719.

Lord Chancellor [Lord Parker]: Where a bill is brought to establish a charity, the Attorney General must be named a plaintiff. But where a devise is to trustees for a charitable use and a bill is brought against them, there is no necessity that the Attorney General may call the matter in question again, so he may if there be collusion to defraud the charity though he be named a defendant.

The objection that, there being three trustees, two only were parties, the other being beyond the sea, was overruled.

Vernon quoted Wilkinson and Parry, where one of the parties was beyond the sea, who, when he returned, might bring the matter over again, not be brought to hearing, yet the cause proceeded that there might not be a failure of justice. This case is stronger, the absent trustee not having acted and being named a plaintiff in the defendants' cross-bill. Therefore, the defendants are estopped from making that objection.

Lincoln's Inn MS. Misc. 11, p. 133

1 June 1719.

The plaintiffs brought their bill claiming an estate, which the defendants insisted upon a title to under a will whereby the same was devised to trustees upon several trusts and, amongst others, for some charities.

And upon the hearing, it was objected that the Attorney General ought to have been a party in respect of the charities.

But, to this, it was said by Mr. *Vernon* that there was no need of making the Attorney General a party where there are trustees for a charity and they are before the court.

But then it was objected that one of the trustees was not brought to the hearing, to which it was answered by Mr. *Vernon* that it appeared by the defendant's answer that he was beyond the sea. And he said it was settled by Lord Cowper in the Case of Wilkinson and Parry upon a view of several precedents that, it appearing by affidavits that a necessary defendant was beyond the sea and not amenable by the process of the court, the cause should go on notwithstanding, for, otherwise, there would be a failer of justice.

391

Griffith v. Levet

(Ch. 1719)

The question in this case was whether the wife should have both the settlement in issue and also the sum payable in default of the settlement, where the settlement was but partially made.

Lincoln's Inn MS. Misc. 384, p. 183

3 June.

Sir Richard Levet, on his marriage with the defendant, in consideration of a £3000 portion, covenants to lay out £4800 within two years in the purchase of lands of inheritance to be settled on himself for life, then to the defendant for life in bar of dower and customary share, then to the issue male and female etc., in default of such settlement, then, she to have £4000 to her own use. Sir Richard did not make such a settlement, but he purchases a copyhold of £150 *per annum*, which he settles on the defendant. And the question is whether this shall be a satisfaction *pro tanto* and bar her claiming the £4000, especially the defendant having a large accession of fortune after her marriage.

Vernon: If Sir Richard is a purchaser of his wife's third, it will be a question whether it will augment his own share or go for the benefit of his children, as in Blunden and Barker,[1] which is sent to the City.

Mead quoted Hook v. Grove.[2]

Master of the Rolls [JEKYLL]: At present, I conceive the defendant, Lady Levet, cannot have both the £4000 and the lands settled on her because it seems to be provided she should have the £4000 only in case Sir Richard had died within the two years. But it will be proper to consider the circumstances of the case, which the Master must state.

392

Trevor v. Trevor

(Ch. 1719)

A court of equity will order specific performance of a marriage contract to settle lands.

Lincoln's Inn MS. Misc. 384, p. 176, pl. 3

5 June. Edward Trevor, eldest son of Sir John Trevor v. John Trevor *et al.*, the other sons etc. of Sir John Trevor.

The bill is to have the performance of articles on the marriage of Sir John Trevor[3] with the widow of Roger Puleston, Esq. [By] 23 October 1669 marriage articles, Sir John Trevor covenants within two years after the marriage to settle for the use of himself for life without impeachment of waste, then to his wife Jane for life, then to the use of the heirs male of his body on the body of his said wife and the heirs male of such heirs male, remainder to the heirs of Sir John Trevor. Sir John afterwards purchased lands in fee, which he has suffered to descend on the plaintiff, but he has settled the premises contained in the marriage articles on the defendant John Trevor etc.

On 20 May 1717, Sir John Trevor died intestate, leaving four sons and two daughters.

Mead opens the defendant Trevor's answer. The premises in Denbigh and Salop [are worth] £230 *per annum*. The intent of Sir John Trevor was to have power over the estate limited to his issue male. There is a covenant that the premises should be to my lady free from encumbrances and, if no settlement was made within two years, then to stand seised of the premises to the same uses until a further assurance should be made.

---

[1] *Blunden v. Barker* (Ch. 1719), see above, Case No. 381.

[2] *Hooke v. Grove* (1713), 2 Eq. Cas. Abr. 218, 389, 22 E.R. 186, 332, 4 Brown P.C. 593, 2 E.R. 404.

[3] K. Ellis, 'Trevor, Sir John (c. 1637–1717)', *Oxford Dictionary of National Biography*, vol. 55, pp. 362–363. Trevor was the Master of the Rolls from 1685 to 1717.

In Trinity [term] 1692, Sir John Trevor and his lady levied a fine of the premises. April 1698, September and October 1699.[1] No uses were declared of the fine until the eldest son's marrying unfortunately, to Sir John for life, then to John, the second son, in tail, proviso, if any of Sir John's sons should marry without his consent, he should have the power to vary the uses. The defendant John is in possession of the premises. The plaintiff is in possession of the Irish estate, which is permitted to descend, £743 *per annum* and the English estate £300 *per annum* and £9000 personal estate, which ought to be a satisfaction of the marriage articles.

Talbot opens the defendant Arthur Trevor's answer, the third son.

Trevor [opens] Tudor Trevor's answer, the fourth son.

Ewer [opens] Lord and Lady Middleton's answer, the daughter.

Gindol, [opens for] Prudentia Trevor, the second daughter.

Chesshyre, for the plaintiff: The bill is to have the benefit of our mother's marriage articles. It is against all our brothers and sisters and the heirs of the surviving trustee. The articles are only executory and only heads of an agreement and are to be carried into strict settlement and trustees are to be appointed to preserve contingent remainders. The first words 'heirs male' are words of purchase. Archer's Case.[2] And the other words are words of limitation. This case was upon a will. The construction of articles is the same. Where it is upon a fine or a feoffment, it may amount to a covenant to stand seised. But here, it would destroy the intent of the first part of the articles if it is not taken strictly. As to the satisfaction, first, the Irish estate we claim under a settlement as issue in tail. If a man covenants to purchase and settle without any mention of particular lands and suffers an estate to descend of equal value, it may be a satisfaction, but not if particular lands are covenanted to be settled. Sir John dying intestate whereby a share of the personal estate came to the plaintiff ought not to be a satisfaction, being a different fund, 23 October 1669 Sir John's marriage articles.

Carter, for the plaintiff: The defendants insist, first, that Sir John was a tenant in tail, second, that the articles were a sufficient settlement. The covenant is that, if no settlement is made within two years, then that Sir John would stand seised to the same uses until such a settlement was made according to his agreement aforesaid. Wherever settlements are to be made in this court, they are to be made strictly and the first taker to be but a tenant for life, as in Lord Stamford and Sir J. Hobart, upon a will.[3] So in Pim and Pim, [?] by Lord Keeper Wright, upon a bond to settle marriage articles. [They] are construed more strictly. The

---

1 Sic in MS.

2 *Baldwin v. Smith* (1597), 1 Coke Rep. 63, 76 E.R. 139, Croke Eliz. 453, 78 E.R. 692, 2 Anderson 37, 123 E.R. 533.

3 *Hobart v. Countess of Suffolk* (1709), 2 Vernon 644, 23 E.R. 1020, 1 Eq. Cas. Abr. 272, 21 E.R. 1040, *sub nom. Earl of Stamford v. Hobart* (1710), 3 Brown P.C. 31, 1 E.R. 1157, note also *In re Maynard's Will* (1691), Dodd 101.

covenant is that the settlement should be as counsel should advise, which certainly would have been in the strictest manner. That Sir John was to be tenant for life without impeachment of waste shows he was not intended to be tenant in tail, for then those words had been useless. The lands settled on John, the second son, are £900 *per annum*. There was no intendment to bar the heir at law unless it is absolutely necessary. Reading and Reading.

Vernon, for the plaintiff: There are two questions: first, how the case stands on the articles; second, whether we have satisfaction. The plaintiff is entitled to the most favorable construction. The cases are much stronger here where the intent has been observed and the first taker made but tenant for life. If it was intended Sir John should have an estate tail, the words 'without impeachment of waste' had been useless. The difference is between a devise and articles, which are upon a contract, which must be strictly taken. Coleman and Bale,[1] where, upon a will that money should be laid out in lands and settled on A. and the heirs male of his body, yet, being executory, A. was directed by Lord Cowper to be made but a tenant for life, but, afterwards, it was reversed by Lord Harcourt, being upon a will. But he declared it would have been otherwise on marriage articles, which cannot be called a settlement executed. Here, the trustees were to take care of the future settlement, and, if they had come here to have the settlement made, it could not have been said that it was already made and Sir John would have been made but tenant for life. Articles will transfer the property in equity as much as if it had been carried into execution. It differs very much from a general covenant to settle lands of such a value, where an equivalent may be looked upon as a satisfaction. But, here, the heir has a specific lien on the ancient estate of the family and cannot be obliged to accept of an equivalent satisfaction.

Second, the personal estate, which came to the plaintiff by the accident of the father's dying intestate, will not be satisfaction, neither would a devise without express words. If the father was indebted to one child and had died intestate, the distributive share would not be a satisfaction. Duffield and Smith.[2] A different fund cannot be a satisfaction. We have a subsistence right to these specific lands.

Northey, for the defendant: Courts of equity have of late taken great liberty in the construction of articles and of wills so as sometimes to make almost new wills. His late Honor [Trevor] always took it that he had a power over this estate. The plaintiffs came for a specific execution of these articles. There was no covenant but for the wife's estate for life. By the words, he had a power over the estate tail. The construction of old articles is the same as when they were first made.

[1] *Baile v. Coleman* (Ch. 1711), 2 Peere Williams 142, 24 E.R. 330, 2 Vernon 670, 23 E.R. 1036, 2 Eq. Cas. Abr. 309, 472, 717, 22 E.R. 261, 402, 603, British Library MS. Hargrave 80, f. 26v, pl. 2.

[2] *Duffield v. Smith* (1692), 2 Vernon 258, 23 E.R. 767, 2 Freeman 185, 22 E.R. 1150, 1 Eq. Cas. Abr. 204, 21 E.R. 991, *sub nom. Smith v. Duffield*, 2 Vernon 177, 23 E.R. 717.

But we insist that, by the covenant in the end of the deed to stand seised to uses, this was a settlement, and there is no room for a court of equity to carry it into execution. If the covenant to stand seised takes place, then, by Shelly's Case, 93 Co. 1 Rep.,[1] Sir John was a tenant in tail. The covenant is to stand seised until a further assurance should be made, which must have been only a confirmation of the same uses. But it will not bring it into the power of a court of equity to model it as a prudent man should have settled. As to the satisfaction, where there is a covenant to settle lands generally, if any lands are suffered to descend, it will be a satisfaction. The reason is the same where particular lands are covenanted to be settled. And there is no case to establish any distinction to the contrary. The court is not bound to execute articles, as for stockjobbing or where the agreement is hard. Here, the plaintiff has ten times the value. There was a fine levied in October 1699 and a deed leading the uses of this estate to the second son etc.

Lutwyche, for the defendant: The settlement in pursuance of the articles was to be made within two years and at the request of the trustees and should be such as should be agreed upon by Sir John Trevor and his trustees. Therefore, there might be a variation of the uses. Therefore, Sir John's not being called upon by the trustees to make any such conveyance implies an intended variation.

Cowper, for the defendant John Trevor: In a court of equity, articles are not always to be carried into execution. Where bills are brought for that purpose, if it is not according to conscience, they are dismissed. Every case stands upon its own circumstances. The question is whether the settlement in 1699 shall be rescinded by the articles in 1669. Where articles are carried into strict settlement, it is where there is no reason to the contrary. The intent of the articles is that the jointure should be free from encumbrances, not that the estate tail should be so, but be left to the consideration of the parties. The settlement to be made was to be to the uses in the articles and should, which imports a new agreement, be limited and agreed upon by Sir John Trevor and the trustees. Now, if the trustees had agreed to settle it on the second son, it had been good. The trustees all died before any settlement was made. Therefore, the whole power vested in Sir John Trevor. If he had a legal power and it is not against conscience, equity will not hinder him where there is in this case any equity.

Lord Chancellor [Lord Parker]: You had best read [depositions] to establish the facts recited in the settlement of 1699 for setting aside the eldest son.

Evan Loyd [was] read. It proves his father's declarations of the undutifullness of the plaintiff etc.

Cowper: As to the point of satisfaction, [see] Slaney and Slaney,[2] by his late honor [Trevor]. There was a devise for life, and a reversion in fee descended was

---

1 *Wolfe v. Shelley* (1579–1581), 1 Coke Rep. 88, 76 E.R. 199, also Moore K.B. 136, 72 E.R. 490, 1 Anderson 69, 123 E.R. 358, Jenkins 249, 145 E.R. 176, 3 Dyer 373, 73 E.R. 838.

2 *Slaney v. Slaney* (1714), 5 Brown P.C. 113, 2 E.R. 568.

adjudged a satisfaction of articles to settle. It was reversed in the House of Lords because it was only a reversion. Mr. Vernon admitted that, where the covenant is only to settle lands of a particular value, lands permitted to descend are a satisfaction, and there is no difference between a particular value and particular lands. The lands purchased after 1699 are equivalent. If there is evidence of an intention of satisfaction, it is much stronger than the common cases where there is no intention proved, but only implied. His Honor [Trevor] had the power to make a will and dispose of the whole Irish estate from the plaintiff. It is in the power of the court either to carry articles into execution or not. We hope, on all the circumstances, these are not fit to be carried into execution.

Raymond, for the defendant: If His Honor [Trevor] had either a legal or equitable power to bar the plaintiff, he has done it by the fines and recovery. His reasons for doing it are mentioned in the deed of 1699. These acts were done with great deliberation upon the notion of carrying the articles into strict execution, which is of much later date than those articles of 1669. The first case was Lord Stamford's in the House of Lords. The construction was before that time the same here as at law. It was reasonable that he should have power over his children. After the two years, it was an estate executed. A covenant to stand seised was good until a further assurance should be made, which was made by the deed in 1699. The covenant is plainly an estate tail, as it would have been in a conveyance at common law. Shelly's Case is in point. If the articles are only executory, the plaintiff has had a satisfaction like a tenant in tail conveying and leaving assets to descend. The leaving to descend is the same as giving.

Peere Williams: It might be hoped that the plaintiff would have acquiesced under the great provision left him by his father and not have endeavored to defeat his father's settlements. Here was an estate tail actually vested in Sir John Trevor. Equity will not interpose where the estate is vested. If the estate had been executed in the words of the articles, equity would not alter it. At law, wherever there is a limitation for life and afterward to the heirs male of the body, the estate tail vests in the first taker. [On] the authority of His Honor's opinion, who has sold part on the same title, the plaintiff is not disentitled but amply provided for. If the younger son had no other provision but this estate, the court would not take this estate from him.

Norris [cited] Popham and Bamfield, in the House of Lords.[1]

Vernon: That case makes against him.

Mead: This attempt is to defeat His Honor's settlements where here is sufficient to take away the provision made for a younger son. If his father had any

[1] *Bampfield v. Popham* (1701–1703), 2 Vernon 427, 449, 23 E.R. 873, 888, 2 Freeman 266, 22 E.R. 1201, 1 Peere Williams 54, 24 E.R. 290, Holt K.B. 233, 90 E.R. 1028, 1 Eq. Cas. Abr. 183, 21 E.R. 975, *sub nom. Popham v. Bamfield*, 1 Vernon 79, 167, 344, 23 E.R. 325, 391, 510, 1 Salkeld 236, 91 E.R. 209, 2 Freeman 269, 22 E.R. 1203, 1 Eq. Cas. Abr. 108, 21 E.R. 916, 2 Eq. Cas. Abr. 308, 22 E.R. 260.

legal advantage which he made use of for the benefit of a younger son, it is hard to set it aside when the heir at law has sufficient assets to make good any breach of covenant.

Objection one: The plaintiff has a specific lien. But the reason is the same as when he covenants generally to settle lands, for, in that case, it is equally a breach of covenant. It was adjudged, when a man leaves his wife more by dying intestate than his bond to settle money upon her amounted to, it is a satisfaction. In Blandy and Wigmore, Hilary 1715, by his late Honor [Trevor], affirmed by Lord Cowper.[1]

Talbot: In the articles, there is no mention of the lady's portion executed before marriage. Where a settlement is after the marriage but in pursuance of articles before, it may be rectified by those articles, but not where the settlement is before marriage. Lestrange v. Baldwin, Common Pleas, Trinity 5 Ann.,[2] money to be laid out and settled, G. legatee will[3] to William for life, then to the heirs male of his body and the heirs male of the body of such heirs male, upon a will certified by three judges of [the Court of] Common Pleas, Trevor, Blencowe, and Dormer, that William had an estate tail, the same with Shelly's Case; the bill was by William to have the money paid to him as being tenant in tail and so he would have a power over the land when purchased.

As to the point of satisfaction, the plaintiff, having more than an equivalent, has no injury done him; therefore, [there is] no equity. Wilcocks and Wilcocks, by Lord Cowper;[4] articles to settle lands of £2000 value, W. left lands of £100 *per annum* to descend [was] decreed to be taken as a satisfaction against a bond creditor. Wilks v. Wilks, 1713;[5] a bond to invest £800 in lands to be settled to the use of the husband for life, then to the wife for life, remainder to the heirs of the body of the husband, a copyhold descended in fee, but of less value; it was decreed by Lord Harcourt to be a satisfaction *pro tanto*.

Lord Chancellor [Lord Parker]: To consider this case clearly, let us suppose the bill was brought within the two years. What settlement should then have been made? If the limitation had been barely to the father for life, then to the heirs male of his body, the court would make him tenant for life only. The addition 'and to the heirs male of such heirs male' makes it far more plain and shows his affection to his heirs male.

---

[1] *Blandy v. Widmore* (1716), 2 Vernon 709, 23 E.R. 1066, 1 Peere Williams 324, 24 E.R. 408, 2 Eq. Cas. Abr. 352, 22 E.R. 300.

[2] Perhaps *Langley v. Baldwin* (1707), 1 Eq. Cas. Abr. 185, 21 E.R. 976, 8 Modern 258, 88 E.R. 183, British Library MS. Hargrave 80, f. 12, pl. 2.

[3] Sic in MS.

[4] *Wilcocks v. Wilcocks* (1706), 2 Vernon 558, 23 E.R. 961, 1 Eq. Cas. Abr. 26, 156, 159, 21 E.R. 847, 955, 957.

[5] *Wilkes v. Wilkes* (Ch. 1713), 2 Eq. Cas. Abr. 35, 218, 22 E.R. 30, 185, Lincoln's Inn MS. Misc. 384, p. 4, pl. 2, British Library MS. Hargrave 80, f. 144v.

As to Shelly's Case, it is a question whether it is truly reported. Anderson says it is not. If taken as a *descriptio personae*, it would be confined to the eldest son only. Lestrange and Baldwin is directly Archer's Case. It is in effect a limitation to each heir male successively. An heir male in common acceptation is a son, but in a legal [sense] signifies a person to take by descent. If the limitation had been to Sir John Trevor for life, remainder to his first son, without trustees to preserve contingent remainders, and he had levied a fine before a son was born, would not the court relieve? A covenant which leaves it in the power of the father is vain. The court would oblige the trustees to agree to these uses.

As to the covenant to stand seised until further assurance, nobody can say until a final settlement. It is merely provisional until a settlement is made to the uses and intent of the articles.

What has since altered it? If the son had been undutiful, I do not know how far equity could interpose, and I should be sorry to see a precedent of this court's judging what behavior would be a forfeiture of a man's estate. I believe Sir John Trevor was of the same opinion. Is it to be conceived if he that had the power to bar the plaintiff that he would have recorded the misfortunes of his family? It was with a view of supporting this point when brought in question. It is strange to suppose that the plaintiff's marriage after the fine would be the reason to guide the uses of the fine.

As to the satisfaction, I cannot see it possible that a right to [alter] the estate is satisfied by not settling another. It has been taken as if the plaintiff came here for a breach of covenant. But that is not so, for the plaintiff comes here on the fact of the trust. If the trustee conveys to another with notice, it is no breach, for the party may come here against the assignee for the land. The plaintiff does not come here for satisfaction for the breach of covenant, but to have the trust performed by conveying the estate in law to him. This differs from the case to settle generally. And, where the demand is against the executor and an estate descends, there it is not strictly as strictly a satisfaction for the breach of covenant, but, by permitting it to descend, it is put in the son's power to perform it specifically by conveying it to the use of himself and the heirs of his body etc. And nothing is wanting but his own act to make it complete.

In Blandy and Wigmore, the covenant was literally performed. It is said, if the younger son had no other provision etc. But suppose the elder had no other, would it not be harder? But this would only be a matter of favor, and compassion is a bad ingredient in a judgment.

I think this was a trust for the first and other sons in tail male etc. And I decree a conveyance accordingly.

5 February 1719[/20], affirmed in the House of Lords; *contra* Harcourt and Trevor.

Lincoln's Inn MS. Misc. 11, p. 129

5 June 1719. Edward Trevor, eldest son and heir of Sir John Trevor, late Master of the Rolls, plaintiff; John Trevor, Arthur Trevor, Tudor Trevor, Prudentia Trevor, younger children of Sir John Trevor, *et al.*, defendants.

Sir John Trevor, upon his marriage with Mrs. Puleston, enters into articles dated 20 October 1669, and he, thereby, covenants with the trustees within two years to settle lands in Denbigh and Salop in such manner as the trustees and their heirs by them or their counsel should direct or appoint to the use of himself for life without impeachment of waste, then to Mrs. Puleston for life, then to the use of the heirs male of Sir John on the body of Mrs. Puleston begotten and the heirs male of such heirs male lawfully issuing, and, for want of such issue, to the right heirs of Sir John Trevor. And, in the articles, there is a covenant from Sir John with the trustees that, if he did not make a settlement within two years, that he and his heirs would stand seised of the premises until such time as a further assurance should be made to such uses, intents, and purposes as are therein before declared.

Sir John, having taken a displeasure against the plaintiff, never made any settlement pursuant to the articles, but he and his lady levied fines of these lands. And, by a deed dated 29 September 1699, they declared the uses of the fines to be to himself and his lady for their lives, remainder to the defendant John Trevor and his heirs male, remainder to the defendants Arthur and Tudor successively in tail male, remainder to such uses as Sir John should appoint, and, for want thereof, to his daughter in fee.

Lady Trevor died in the life of her husband, and, he being also dead intestate, the plaintiff brings his bill to have a specific performance of the marriage articles.

Serjeant *Chesshyre* and Mr. *Vernon*: It was insisted for the plaintiff that he was in the nature of a purchaser and that, therefore, the articles ought to have the most favorable construction, that, according to the constant course of the court, the settlement ought to have been in the strictest manner, *viz.* to the first and other sons in tail male and, if it had been so made, it had not been in the power of Sir John to have barred the plaintiff. And it is plain the intention of the parties was that the lands should be so settled by making Sir John tenant for life without impeachment of waste, which would have been absurd if it was intended he should have been a tenant in tail.

This court has made a difference between a will and marriage articles. In the Case of Coleman and Vale,[1] money, by a will, was directed to be laid out in the purchase of lands and settled to the use of one for life to the heirs of his body and, upon a bill brought to have this money laid out, Lord Cowper directed the lands should be settled on the first and other sons in tail after the death of the

[1] *Baile v. Coleman* (Ch. 1711), *ut supra*.

tenant for life, but, upon a rehearing before Lord Harcourt, this was reversed and for this reason only, because it was upon a will, but, had it been upon marriage articles, he said he should have been of the opinion the lands ought to have been settled in the strictest manner.

The last clause in the articles will make no alteration in the case. It must not be considered as a distinct independent clause, but be relative to and operate with the precedent limitations.

As to what was insisted by the defendants in their answer, that lands of £1100 a year were descended on the plaintiff and that they ought to be taken as a satisfaction of the articles, it was admitted by the plaintiff's counsel that, if the covenant had been to settle lands generally of such a particular value and lands of that or a greater value are suffered to descend, they shall be taken to be a satisfaction. And so it was decreed by Lord Cowper. But, where there are particular lands agreed to be settled, the party has a specific right to those lands, and other lands cannot be a satisfaction.

Sir Edward Northey, for the defendants, admitted, where articles were executory, this court had taken a great liberty and, if this case stood only on the first part of the articles, according to the present course of the court, Sir John would not have been a tenant in tail. But we say the articles are executed by the last clause and, thereby, there was an estate tail executed in Sir John, according to Shelley's Case. And, having levied a fine and barred that entail, the plaintiff can have no title.

I do not know that, in any case where the estate is executed, this court has meddled or altered it. And they cite none of the other side where this court has gone so far. All the cases they cite are only where the matter is executory. And I agree, there, the court has done what the parties themselves perhaps in prudence ought to have done.

But suppose, in our case, the articles were executory, yet a court of equity is not bound to carry an agreement into execution. If the agreement is hard or unreasonable or upon the circumstances of it not fit to be performed, this court will not interpose, but leave the party to his remedy at law.

Now, in the present case, the plaintiff has lands of £1100 a year descended upon him, as is proved in the cause, and, besides, has received upwards of £9000 on account of his share of his father's personal estate. And since he is so well provided, it would be hard to take away the lands in the articles, which are but £239 a year, from the defendant John Trevor and give them to the plaintiff.

Lord Chancellor [LORD PARKER] without any great difficulty decreed the lands to the plaintiff.

1 Comyns 416, 92 E.R. 1137

5 June 1719, in Chancery, and afterwards affirmed in the House of Peers, February 1719.

By articles in 1669, made by Sir John Trevor, late Master of the Rolls, upon his marriage, it was covenanted to make a settlement of lands to the value of £250 *per annum* within two years to the use of himself for his life without impeachment of waste and, afterwards, to the use of his wife for her life and, then, to the use of his first, second, and other sons by such wife in tail etc. and, in case no settlement was made in two years after the marriage, the persons seised should stand seised to the same uses. After the two years, he suffered a recovery and disposed of the estate by will. But all was set aside, and the construction made was that the articles should have been executed so as not to have enabled the Master of the Rolls to defeat the children of the marriage, and, although it was insisted that, by the covenant to stand seised, the estate was now executed to the limitations as expressed in the articles, it was held that ought to make no alteration.

[Other reports of this case: 1 Peere Williams 622, 24 E.R. 543, 9 Modern 161, 88 E.R. 377, 10 Modern 436, 88 E.R. 798, 1 Eq. Cas. Abr. 387, 21 E.R. 1122, 2 Eq. Cas. Abr. 475, 505, 22 E.R. 404, 427, 5 Brown P.C. 122, 2 E.R. 574.]

[Related cases: Hopson v. Trevor (Ch. 1722), see below, Case No. 544.]

393

Manaton v. Manaton

(Ch. 1719)

A rent charge is not payable without a legal demand made for it upon the land.

Lincoln's Inn MS. Misc. 11, p. 111

8 June 1719. Manaton and Kendall, executors of Rachel Manaton, plaintiffs; Richard Manaton, executor of Henry Manaton, executor of Ambrose Manaton, defendant.

The plaintiffs brought their bill to be paid the arrears of a rent charge of £300, which was settled by Ambrose Manaton on his marriage with Rachel, the plaintiffs' testatrix, for her jointure. And, in the settlement, there was a grant of £5 per month *nomine poenae* for every month the rent charge should be unpaid after it was lawfully demanded and a covenant for him and his heirs to pay this rent charge clear of taxes. The rent charge was payable generally. And the question was if any interest should be paid for the arrears and in what manner it should be computed.

It was insisted that, here being a *nomine poenae*, the defendant, who had brought a cross-bill, could not be relieved against that but upon paying the interest and costs.

But the Master of the Rolls [Jekyll] was of opinion the plaintiffs could not be entitled to interest by reason of the *nomine poenae* in regard that did not become payable but upon default of payment of the rent charge after it was lawfully demanded, which must be a legal demand, a demand upon the land, which there had not been in this case. However, there being a covenant for payment of this annuity, he was of opinion the arrears ought to be paid with interest. And, in regard the rent charge was payable quarterly, such interest ought to be computed from the end of three months after each quarter became due.

And so it was decreed by Lord Cowper, as it was said, where an annuity was payable half yearly, the interest was directed to be computed from the end of six months after every half yearly payment.

[Related cases: Manaton v. Manaton (Ch. 1724), 2 Peere Williams 234, 24 E.R. 711, 2 Eq. Cas. Abr. 252, 22 E.R. 214.]

394

Attorney General, ex rel. v. Earl of Arran

(Ch. 1719)

Parol evidence is admissible to explain the identity of a legatee.

Lincoln's Inn MS. Misc. 11, p. 112

9 June 1719. Attorney General, at the relation of the Minister and churchwardens and overseers of the poor of Kew, plaintiffs; Earl of Arran and others, defendants.

The countess of Derby, by her will, gave her house at Kew to the defendant and other trustees to be sold and, with the money arising by the sale, to pay off a mortgage and apply and distribute the money for the benefit of the poor of Kew and Brentford equally at the discretion of the trustees.

The question was between Old and New Brentford to which of the poor in those two places one moiety of the surplus should be applied.

It was proved on the behalf of Old Brentford that the countess for several years before her death gave away yearly a great deal of money to the poor of Old Brentford and distributed coals, clothes, and other necessaries among them.

And, on the other hand, it was proved that the countess contributed towards the support of the charity school at New Brentford and put in some boys into that school and that once she gave money to a poor woman in New Brentford.

Lord Chancellor [Lord Parker], it being very clear upon these proofs that the countess intended this benefaction for the benefit of the poor of Old Brentford, which proofs were read without any difficulty, decreed the surplus money to be laid out in a purchase of lands and that the rents of the lands should be applied for the relief of such poor housekeepers not receiving alms of the parish as the trustees should think fit.

395

Bush v. Earl of Tankerville

(Ch. 1719)

A contract for compound interest is valid and enforceable.

Lincoln's Inn MS. Misc. 384, p. 160, pl. 2

9 June.

Vernon, for the plaintiff, quoted Lady Bromhill's Case, where her mother, the countess of Arglas, being her guardian, came to an account with Sir J. Every, who had a mortgage on the estate and was about to recover the possession, to prevent which the guardian stated an account in behalf of the infant and agreed that the interest should be made principal. And [it was] allowed by Lord Somers, it being for the advantage of the infant. But, regularly, a guardian has not such power.

N.B. A tenant for life of an estate subject to a mortgage is only to keep down the interest during his life. If there be a redemption, he is to pay one-third.

The Master of the Rolls [JEKYLL] cited Sir J. Conway and Morton, in the House of Lords, where an agreement of a tenant for life that the interest due on a mortgage should be made principal was established.

396

Cook v. Gough

(Ch. 1719)

A defendant, whether served with process of not, cannot be examined as a witness without a court order.

Lincoln's Inn MS. Misc. 384, p. 160, pl. 3

12 June. At the Lord Chancellor's House.

The plaintiff had named one Hannah Gregory a defendant but did not serve her with process but examined her as a witness without an order. The Master reported the examination irregular. The plaintiff excepts and insists on a difference where a defendant is served and has appeared and answered, that, there, an order is requisite but not where a defendant is served, that it is an order of course, and it would be hard to deprive plaintiffs of a material deposition. And he, therefore, prayed that the plaintiff might examine her *de novo* paying the costs of the irregularity, as in Spence and Allen,[1] where the interrogatories were leading.

[1] *Spence v. Allen* (Ch. 1718), see above, Case No. 252.

Lord Chancellor [Lord Parker]: It is admitted, where a defendant is served and has answered, that then an order is absolutely necessary. The reason holds stronger in the present case, for, here, the defendant is more under the influence of the plaintiff, who can put the defendant to the expense of answering if he should not swear as a witness to the plaintiff's purpose. Therefore, I overrule the exception. If you can show me a precedent like this case, I will give you leave to examine *de novo*. But Spence and Allen was not like this case, for, there, the interrogatories were not designed to be leading but only happened through the inadvertency of the counsel.

397
Farrington v. Knightly
(Ch. 1719–1721)

Where the executors of a will are bequeathed a legacy, the residuary surplus not bequeathed goes to the testator's next of kin.

An executor of a will is a trustee and not a residuary legatee.

Lincoln's Inn MS. Misc. 384, p. 161

16 June 1719.

The question is upon Mr. Upton's will, whether his executors, the defendants, having legacies of £50 apiece are excluded from taking the surplus.

Vernon, for the plaintiff, quoted Foster and Munt [and] the Duchess of Beaufort's Case.[1]

Raymond, for the defendants, the executors: The law is with us, and so have been the latter resolutions. The presumption that, if the testator intended the executor the surplus, he would not have given him a legacy because it would be included in the surplus may be answered that the testator intended some benefit to the executor though there should be a deficiency of assets; whereas, if he was only to take the surplus, he would have nothing. Foster and Munt was grounded on a fraud. Ball and Smith, by Lord Harcourt,[2] where the wife was executrix and had

---

1 *Foster v. Munt* (1689), 1 Vernon 473, 23 E.R. 598, 1 Eq. Cas. Abr. 243, 21 E.R. 1020, 2 Eq. Cas. Abr. 433, 443, 22 E.R. 368, 378, Dodd 78, Lincoln's Inn MS. Misc. 498, p. 27, Lincoln's Inn MS. Misc. 503, p. 93, Lincoln's Inn MS. Misc. 504, p. 88; *Duke of Beaufort v. Lord Dundonald* (Ch. 1716–1717), see above, Case No. 131.

2 *Ball v. Smith* (1698–1711), 2 Vernon 633, 675, 23 E.R. 1014, 1039, 2 Freeman 230, 22 E.R. 1179, 1 Eq. Cas. Abr. 245, 21 E.R. 1022, 2 Eq. Cas. Abr. 133, 434, 22 E.R. 114, 369.

a legacy and the surplus both. In Littlebury and Buckley, in the House of Lords,[1] parol evidence was admitted, and the executor had the surplus besides his legacy.

Mead: A man cannot be said to die intestate when he has made a will and executors. Here, the executors are relations, and the next of kin have particular legacies. There may be a difference where the executor is a mere stranger. But here, one executor is the testator's sister, the other a sister's son, who would have been entitled to a distributive share. Coatesworth and Brangwine, by Lord Harcourt, who were executors and Coatesworth only a legatee, Lord Harcourt was of opinion that both should take the surplus equally; so in Wingfield and Atkinson, where both executors had legacies, heard and reheard by the late Master of the Rolls [Trevor]; Rawling and Powell;[2] this is a gift in law to the executors, and they are entitled to the surplus.

N.B. The surplus is about £1200.

1 June 1718, Mr. Upton's will makes the defendants, Knightly, his sister, and Captain Upton, his nephew, executors, and he gives them £50 apiece.

Vernon, in reply: In Foster and Munt, there was no proof of fraud and a will, which concerns only personal estate and has been proved in the spiritual court, cannot be set aside for fraud, as in Goss and Tracy,[3] where it was manifest imposition. There have been decrees in our favor and which have been settled in the House of Peers. It is not so material what the law is, provided it be certainly known.

Lord Chancellor [Lord Parker]: If a will cannot be set aside in this court, I have done wrong in Branely and Kerrick.[4] But I considered the executor as a trustee in that case. If a man makes a will but no executor, the court will prohibit the ecclesiastical court. Before the Statute of Distributions,[5] the reason why the executor took the surplus was not that the testator intended it for him but because nobody else could claim it. In Foster and Munt, it was looked upon that, after the Statute of Distributions, the legacy given to the executor was a reward for his trouble in the executorship. If the surplus had been small, I believe the resolution of that case would have been otherwise, but, the surplus being great, it appeared very gross. There have been many cases determined on the authority of Foster

---

[1] *Buckley v. Littlebury* (1711), 3 Brown P.C. 43, 1 E.R. 1165, 1 Eq. Cas. Abr. 245, 21 E.R. 1021, also 2 Vernon 677, 23 E.R. 1040, Lincoln's Inn MS. Misc. 10, p. 86.

[2] *Colesworth v. Brangwin* (Ch. 1712), Precedents in Chancery 323, 24 E.R. 153, Gilbert Rep. 79, 25 E.R. 56, 2 Eq. Cas. Abr. 438, 22 E.R. 373, British Library MS. Hargrave 80, f. 77v; *Wingfield v. Atkinson* (1711), 2 Vernon 673, 23 E.R. 1038; *Rawlings v. Powell* (Ch. 1718), see above, Case No. 247.

[3] *Goss v. Tracy* (1715), 1 Peere Williams 287, 24 E.R. 392, 2 Vernon 699, 23 E.R. 1053, 1 Eq. Cas. Abr. 406, 21 E.R. 1136, 2 Eq. Cas. Abr. 396, 491, 767, 22 E.R. 338, 416, 651.

[4] *Bransby v. Kerrick* (Ch. 1718), see above, Case No. 301.

[5] Stat. 22 & 23 Car. II, c. 10 (*SR*, V, 719–720).

and Munt. As to Ball and Smith, it was very just because the wife was executrix, who is the nearest relation. In Littlebury and Buckley, the reason of the evidence being admitted was because the law gave it to the executor.

This will does not seem to be complete. If there had been some lines obliterated so as they could not be read, it would be hard that the executors should have the whole benefit of it. The testator, in the beginning of the will, speaks doubtfully whether he should leave any personal estate, for he gives such legacies out of his personal estate if he left any.

I would see precedents that I may settle this point if possible.

By a judgment 10 June 1721, the Lord Chancellor [Lord Parker] decreed the surplus to the next of kin.

Lincoln's Inn MS. Hill 29, p. 63

Michaelmas 8 Geo. I.

A. begins his will, by which he bequeaths various legacies and particularly gives £50 to B., whom he makes executor. The whole was written with A.'s own hand, who died before the perfecting and signing it. The question was whether the surplus of A's personal estate should go to B. as executor or according to the Statute of Distributions.

N.B. The will mentioned no reason or on what account A. gave the said legacy to his executor.

Lord Chancellor [Lord Macclesfield] said he looked upon an executor but as a trustee, and, therefore, he decreed the surplus to go according to the Statute of Distributions.

Lincoln's Inn MS. Misc. 12, p. 284

9 June 1721.

Upon the will of Anthony Upton, where the executor had a legacy given him and there was no devise of the surplus, Lord Chancellor [Lord Parker], after taking time to consider of it, decreed the surplus to be distributed amongst the next of kin.

He said the mistake that some cases had gone upon was that the bare making a man executor was a devise of the surplus to him. The word executor does not import that he shall have the estate. He is only in the nature of a manager and trustee.

If a man is made executor and the surplus is not given to him and he dies intestate, his administrator shall not take administration *cum testamento annexo*, but the next of kin of the testator.

He said he had talked with Mr. Vernon, who said he looked upon the point so fully settled, *viz.* that where an executor has a legacy and there is no disposition of the surplus, he is excluded, he had left off making any more cases upon that question.

Note Lord Chancellor [LORD PARKER], in giving his judgment, took notice of the following cases:

Coatesworth and Brandwyn, first heard by Lord Cowper and afterwards by Lord Harcourt; one executor had a legacy and the other none and the surplus was not disposed of; Lord Harcourt divided the surplus equally between them.

In the case of Foster and Mont, the next of kin had legacies as well as the executors.

Bailey and Coell, in 1698, Elizabeth Bird gave all the next of kin legacies and gave small legacies to the executors and made no disposition of the surplus. Lord Somers decreed the surplus to the next of kin.

Ward and Land;[1] a man made his will and gave small legacies to his wife and some others and made A.B. executor, but he did not dispose of the surplus. He lived twenty years afterwards and increased his estate considerably. And he died without altering of his will. The surplus was decreed to be distributed according to the Statute of Distributions.

Westcourt and Jones;[2] A. devises a leasehold estate to his wife for life, and, after her death, he gives the remainder of the term to others upon a contingency, which never happened, but he made no disposition of it in case the contingency did not happen. [It was] decreed the wife [to have] a distributive share of the reversion notwithstanding she had the whole for her life, for the devise to the wife for life was only in the nature of an exception out of the general devise of the term.

And the resolution of the Duchess of Beaufort's Case was grounded on the like reason.

[Other reports of this case: 1 Peere Williams 544, 24 E.R. 509, Precedents in Chancery 566, 24 E.R. 254, 10 Modern 442, 88 E.R. 801, 2 Eq. Cas. Abr. 245, 421, 424, 440, 22 E.R. 208, 358, 360, 375.]

---

1 *Ward v. Lane* (1701), 1 Eq. Cas. Abr. 244, 21 E.R. 1021.

2 *Jones v. Westcome* (1711), Precedents in Chancery 316, 24 E.R. 149, 1 Eq. Cas. Abr. 245, 21 E.R. 1022, Gilbert Rep. 74, 25 E.R. 52, British Library MS. Hargrave 80, f. 54, pl. 2.

398

Jenison v. Lord Lexington

(Ch. 1719)

A contract for the payment of money to a third party, such as the executor of the obligee, is valid and enforceable.

Lincoln's Inn MS. Misc. 384, p. 163, pl. 1

25 June. Seals *post* Trinity Term. Sir Matthew Jenison v. Lord Lexington and Rastall.

Samuel Ellis, being seised for three lives, in 1701, by lease and release, assigns to the defendant, Lord Lexington, for the whole term reserving £9 *per annum* to himself, his executors, and assigns. The plaintiff claims under the heir of the assignor and insists that the reservation of the rent to the executors is void because a rent cannot be reserved to a stranger.

The defendant, the Lord Lexington insists that, as the executor cannot claim because he is a stranger, so neither can the heir because he has no reversion to which the rent might be incident by implication of law, as in Sacheveral and Frogat, 1 Ven. 161, 2 Lev. 13,[1] and, therefore, that it is extinct in point of law and determined by the death of the lessor, as in Co. Litt. 47a.[2]

The defendant Rastall, who is the administrator of Ellis, insists that, though possibly it may not be good as a rent, yet that it is good by way of contract for the payment of a sum in gross, which may be to a stranger. And there is a clause in the deed that, if it be not paid to the executor or administrator, the heir of the assignor may enter, which is a good condition by way of a penalty to enforce the payment of it, as in Co Lit. 213a.[3]

And of this opinion was the Master of the Rolls [JEKYLL] in the absence of the Lord Chancellor. And he dismissed the plaintiff's bill with costs and the rather because he had been before nonsuited at [common] law upon full evidence.

But the [action of] ejectment was for recovery of the land itself, not of the rent.

[Other reports of this case: 1 Peere Williams 555, 24 E.R. 515, 2 Eq. Cas. Abr. 431, 22 E.R. 366.]

1 *Sacheverell v. Frogate* (1671), 1 Ventris 148, 161, 86 E.R. 101, 109, 2 Levinz 13, 83 E.R. 430, also 2 Williams Saunders 361, 85 E.R. 1150, T. Raymond 213, 83 E.R. 112, 2 Keble 798, 819, 833, 839, 84 E.R. 504, 517, 527, 531, Hetley 105, 124 E.R. 378, Lincoln's Inn MS. Misc. 500, ff. 158v, 178v.

2 E. Coke, *First Institute* (1628), f. 47.

3 E. Coke, *First Institute* (1628), f. 213.

399

Wilks v. Fisher

(Ch. 1719)

A bond creditor cannot follow lands which descend and are alienated by the heir because the heir is only personally liable for the debts of his ancestor.

Lincoln's Inn MS. Misc. 384, p. 184, pl. 2

26 June. Seals after term.

Mead quoted Kiddulph and Langhorn, where a bond creditor brought his bill against the executor and heir, who admitted assets by descent. But there being some difficulty in taking the account of the personal assets, the creditor prayed to be satisfied out of the real assets, being equally liable, and not to stay until the account could be settled. [It was] refused here because the personal assets ought to be first applied, but it was reversed in the House of Lords in favor of the creditor, and [it was] ordered that the heir should be reimbursed out of the personal assets.

The Lord Chancellor [Lord Parker] declared that a bond creditor cannot follow lands which descend and are aliened by the heir here further than at law and that, by the Statute of Fraudulent Devises,[1] the heir is only personally liable and not the land any more than before that Statute.

400

Wheddon v. Oxenham

(Ch. 1719)

Where a widow was given a legacy conditioned upon releasing her dower rights and she dies before exercising her election, her legacy lapses.

Lincoln's Inn MS. Misc. 14, p. 95

9 July 1719. Mary Wheddon and William Oxenham *et al.*

William Long, by will, devised to his wife £3000 to be paid to her within six months after his death, provided she should within that time at the request, costs, and charges of his executors by such deed or instrument in writing, as they or their counsel should advise, release and discharge all right of dower and thirds and all other claims and demands whatsoever which she might have, challenge, or demand to have of [and] to any lands or other estate whatsoever, whether real or personal, whereof he should die seised or possessed, except the said £3000. And he charged his real as well as personal estate with the payment thereof. He

[1] Stat. 3 Will. & Mar., c. 14 (*SR*, VI, 320–321).

made the defendant Palmer and Sir Hugh Ackland, since deceased, executors, who proved the will.

Soon after the testator's death, the defendant Palmer spoke to the widow about the legacy and the release mentioned in the will, who said she was not in a condition to talk of business or to consider what to do, and, she being in an ill state of health, he did not press her any further at that time. And, at her desire, the affair was deferred until he and the other executor returned from the Sessions, whither they were going. But before their return, *viz.* ten weeks after her husband's death, she died intestate.

The plaintiff, as administratrix, brought her bill to be paid the said £3000 with interest.

The defendant Oxenham and his wife, who was the testator's daughter and heiress and had proved his will when she came of age, by their answer, insisted that, the legacy being charged on the real and personal estate and the said Elizabeth dying before it was payable and the personal estate not being sufficient to pay the legacy without the real estate or so much thereof as the personal estate would not satisfy, the legacy sank and was extinguished in the lands for the benefit of the daughter and the rather for that the legacy appears to have been given and designed for the wife's support in lieu of her dower if she released her dower, which she did not do, and, she being dead, there was no occasion to raise the money for that purpose.

The bill was dismissed as to the £3000.

[Other reports of this case: 2 Eq. Cas. Abr. 546, 22 E.R. 460.]

401

Anonymous

(Ch. 1719)

The king may be a plaintiff in actions sued by original writs but not in criminal actions.

Where an action is brought against a man and his alleged wife, if the man dies, the action continues against the woman.

Lincoln's Inn MS. Hill 73, p. 117

10 July.

A motion [was made] to make a rule of *nisi prius* a rule of this court fifteen days between the *teste* of the first *scire facias* to the return of the second inclusive one and the other exclusive.

Mr. *Symonds*: If there be one, there must be fifteen days, if [. . .], it must be sworn and eight days notice for trial inclusive is not sufficient.

Chesshyre: 1 Sid. 210; 2 Keble 168;[1] following the words of the writ is a sufficient answer; where the suggestion in the *mandamus* is *debito modo electus*, the return ought to be *non fuit electus*.

Chesshyre: A *mandamus* to proceed to the chief clerk of a town in Warwick [?]; 1 Inst. 325;[2] the king may be plaintiff in actions sued by original [writs] but not in criminal actions; therefore, the Statute of 3 Hen. VIII, c. 30, which extends only to cases where there are plaintiff and defendant, the king shall come within the design.

Pengelly: Where the action is brought against a man and wife [and] the woman says she is not married, if the man dies, the action continues against the woman. The plea is in abatement of the writ against the wife; otherwise, if the man should confess, the woman would be without a remedy.

402

Pellet v. Bainbrigg

(Ch. 1719)

Where an eldest son has died, the next eldest son cannot share in a bequest to 'younger children'.

Lincoln's Inn MS. Misc. 11, p. 115

July 1719. Thomas Pellet and Jane, his wife, one of the daughters of William Bainbrigg by Martha, his wife, and others, daughters of the said William and Martha, as also the said Martha Bainbrigg, plaintiffs; Edward Brett Bainbrigg, son and heir of the said William Bainbrigg and others, defendants.

After the marriage of William Bainbrigg with the said Martha, his wife, Edward Brett, her father, surrendered copyhold lands to the use of William Bainbrigg for life, then to his wife for her life, remainder to Serjeant [William] Leake [d. 1687] and the defendant Wilmot for 500 years, remainder to the first and other sons of William Bainbrigg by Martha, his wife, in tail male, remainder to William in fee. As to the term of 500 years, it was declared to be upon trust that the trustees, by the rents and profits of the premises or by sale or mortgage, might raise for the portions of the younger children of William and Martha such sum not exceeding £1000 to be paid to him, her, or them at such times and in such proportions as the said trustees or the survivor of them or his executors should appoint and, in default of such appointment, to be equally divided between them at their respective ages of twenty-one years.

---

[1] *Hereford's Case* (1664), 1 Siderfin 209, 82 E.R. 1061; *Rex v. Patrick* (1667), 1 Keble 610, 83 E.R. 1141, 2 Keble 65, 164, 84 E.R. 42, 103.

[2] E. Coke, *First Institute* (1628), f. 325.

By another settlement dated in September 1688, the said William Bainbrigg settled other lands to the use of himself for life, then to pay a rent charge to his wife for life, remainder to trustees for 500 years, remainder to the first and other sons of William by Martha in tail male, remainder to William in fee. The trusts of that term were that, if William should have a son and one or more younger children, the trustees, by the rents and profits by sale or mortgage, should raise towards the portions of such younger children such sum and to be paid at such days and in such manner as the said defendant Robert Wilmot, his executors, or administrators should by any writing under hand direct.

By a deed poll dated 21 March 1689[/90], the defendant Wilmot, with the consent of Mr. Bainbrigg and his wife, executed the power in the last settlement and directed, if there should be but one younger child, the sum of £2000 should be raised and paid to him, if a son, at twenty-one, if a daughter, at eighteen or marriage, but, if two or more younger children, then £3000 should be raised and equally divided between them and paid to sons at twenty-one and to daughters at eighteen or marriage.

On 14 August 1706, William Bainbrigg died intestate and left six children, *viz.* William, his eldest son, who, afterwards, died under twenty-one, Martha, his eldest daughter, who, afterwards, died intestate, having first attained twenty-one, and the plaintiff, Martha, his mother, has taken administration to her, the plaintiffs Dorothy, Jane, and Barbara, and the defendant William Brett Bainbrigg.

Serjeant Leake died in the lifetime of Mr. Bainbrigg and neither he and the said defendant Wilmot, in the serjeant's lifetime, nor the said defendant, since his death, ever executed the power touching the portions to be raised by virtue of the 500 years term limited by the first settlement.

The plaintiffs now bring their bill to have the shares of the plaintiffs Jane, Dorothy, and Barbara as also of Martha, the deceased daughter, of the £3000 appointed by the deed poll raised as also the £1000 to be raised by virtue of the first 500 years term.

The defendant Edward Brett Bainbrigg insisted that, the defendant Wilmot having not executed the power touching the £1000, that sum ought not to be raised until the power is executed, for Mr. Wilmot, if he thinks fit, may appoint a lesser sum to be raised; however, if it is to be raised, yet Martha's share ought not to be raised, there having been no appointment made and, consequently, no share of that ever vested in her.

And, as to the £3000, if that was to be raised, he ought to have an equal share with his sisters in that money, he being a younger child at the death of his father.

The defendant Wilmot confessed by answer he had never executed the power touching the £1000, and he said that, by reason of the infancy of the defendant Edward, he was unwilling to make any appointment and he hoped he should be discharged of the trust. And he submitted to the court whether he ought or ought not to make an appointment.

The Master of the Rolls [Jekyll]: Mr. Wilmot having never executed the power and being desirous to be discharged of the trust, it ought to be considered as though he was actually dead. And I am of the opinion the whole £1000 ought to be raised and such of the children whose shares are become payable must be paid them with interest from the time they became due.

But, as to the share of Martha, the daughter, who died after she came of age, I am of the opinion nothing vested in her, the power having never been executed, and, therefore, her share cannot be raised for her administratrix, but it must fall in for the benefit of the rest of the younger children.

As to the £3000, that must be also raised and paid to such of the children whose shares are due with interest, and Martha's share of that sum must be paid to her mother, who is her administratrix. The plaintiff Barbara's share, who is an infant, must be put at interest by the Master.

As to the claim which the defendant, the son, makes to a share of the £3000, as he was a younger son at the death of his father, I am of the opinion that he is not entitled, for, being now become the eldest or only son, he ought not to have any part of what was intended to be a provision for younger children.

Note, in this case, Mr. *Vernon*, for the plaintiffs, cited the Case of Dolman and Chadwick,[1] which was thus. Sir Thomas Dolman, pursuant to a power given him by a settlement to appoint £4000 for his younger children, appoints £2600 to be raised for his second son. Afterwards, the eldest son died, and the estate came to the second son, who insisted that the £2600 ought to be raised for his benefit. But, notwithstanding, the portion was actually vested, yet Lord Cowper without any difficulty decreed the £2600 to the other younger children.

403

Marlow v. Smith

(Ch. 1719–1723)

An infant who borrows money to pay for necessaries is liable to pay that debt after he comes of age.

Lincoln's Inn MS. Misc. 11, p. 119

July 1719.

Upon the equity reserved after a decree, the case upon the Master's report appeared to be that A.B. having married during his infancy without his father's consent and thereby incurred his father's displeasure so that his father would

[1] *Chadwick v. Dolman* (1705), 2 Vernon 528, 23 E.R. 941, 1 Eq. Cas. Abr. 344, 21 E.R. 1091.

make no settlement upon him and being forced to contract debts for necessaries and having likewise borrowed several sums of money to the amount of £130 when he was within half of a year of being of age, after he came of age, he made his will. And he thereby devised an estate to trustees to be sold for the payment of his debts generally without taking any particular notice of the debts contracted during his minority. And he died before he had paid those debts.

The question was if those debts should be paid out of the trust estate.

As to those which were contracted for necessaries, the Master of the Rolls [JEKYLL] made no difficulty of ordering them to be paid. But he doubted as to those which were for monies borrowed. And after he had taken time to consider of it, he ordered those to be paid likewise, first, because they were not considerable, secondly, because [they were] contracted when he was near of age and, perhaps, the persons, who lent the money did not know but he might be of age.

Lincoln's Inn MS. Misc. 12, p. 26

Michaelmas 1723.

Sir Charles Pitfield, by a settlement dated 15 April 1680, conveys lands to trustees to the use of himself for life, remainder to trustees to preserve contingent remainders, remainder to Alexander, his son, for ninety-nine years if he lived so long, remainder to trustees to preserve contingent remainders, then to Jane, the intended wife of Alexander, for life, remainder to their first and other sons in tail male, with other remainders over, with a remainder in fee to Sir Charles Pitfield. Sir Charles dies, and the eldest son of Alexander, during the life of his father, suffers a recovery, his mother being dead. And the heir at law of the surviving trustee for preserving contingent remainders joins with him in making a tenant to the *praecipe*. The uses of the recovery were limited to the son in fee. Charles Pitfield, who suffered the recovery, devised the estate to be sold for payment of his debts. And there was a decree for that purpose.

Serjeant [Nathaniel] Mead [d. 1760], who had been reported the best purchaser of this estate, in the name of one Swinfen, objected to the title because there was not a good tenant to the *praecipe*, for it appeared that Francis Moor, the surviving trustee for preserving contingent remainders, made his will and, after several devises of particular lands, gives the rest of his estate to his wife and her heirs.

And it was insisted on the behalf of the purchaser that the lands of which the testator was seised as surviving trustee passed by the general words of the will and did not descend to the heir at law, who had joined in making a tenant to the *praecipe*.

And, upon the Master's report, who was ordered to state the title, the question was if the trust estate was in the heir or the devisee of the surviving trustee.

It was insisted on for the plaintiffs, the creditors, that the testator intended to devise nothing but his own proper estate, that in the beginning of his will, after the usual preamble, are these words, *viz.* 'as to such estate as the Lord has bestowed on me, I give, devise, and bestow as follows', and then he gives particular lands, and, when he comes to dispose of the residue, he calls it 'the rest of my estate', that is to say the rest of that estate mentioned in the beginning of his will, which the Lord had bestowed upon him, which, properly speaking, was what he had in his own right and not in trust for another. And the Case of Dorrell v. Collins, Cro. Eliz. 6, and Cole and Knight, 3 Mod. 277, were cited.[1]

But notwithstanding, the Master of the Rolls [JEKYLL] was of the opinion that the trust estate passed by the will and that the recovery was not good and, therefore, the purchaser was discharged.

Lincoln's Inn MS. Misc. 12, p. 292

Sir Charles Pitfield, in 1680, on the marriage of Alexander, his son, settled lands to the use of Alexander for ninety-nine years if he lived so long, remainder to A. and B. and their heirs during the life of Alexander to preserve the contingent estates, remainder to the wife for life, remainder to the first and other sons of the marriage in tail, with other remainders over.

Some years after the marriage, the wife being dead, Charles Pitfield, the eldest son of Alexander, in the lifetime of his father together with the heir of the surviving trustee for preserving contingent remainders join in suffering a common recovery to the use of Charles Pitfield and his heirs. And he, having afterwards mortgaged the estate and contracted other debts, made his will and devised the premises to be sold for the payment of his debts, And he died leaving issue, an infant son.

Upon a bill brought by the creditors, the estate was decreed to be sold before a Master, and Mr. Swinfen was reported the best purchaser. But having afterwards a mind to get off from his purchase and objecting to the title, it was referred to the Master to see if a good title could be made to the purchaser. And the Master reported the title to be as is before set forth. But he said that the surviving trustee for preserving contingent remainders, before his death, made his will, and, after a devise of several particular lands, he devised 'all the rest of [his] estate whatsoever' to his wife and that it was insisted that, by this general devise, not only his own estate but also what he had in trust passed to the wife and that she ought to have joined in making a tenant to the praecipe. And the Master submitted it to the court whether a good title could be made to the purchaser.

And now, it came on before the Master of the Rolls [JEKYLL] in the absence of Lord Macclesfield for the judgment of the court upon the special matter of the Master's report. And the single question was whether the freehold of the premises upon the death of a surviving trustee vested in his heir at law or in his wife

1 *Dorrell v. Collins* (1582), Croke Eliz. 6, 78 E.R. 273; *Cole v. Knight* (1690), 3 Modern 277, 87 E.R. 183, also Holt K.B. 620, 90 E.R. 1243, *sub nom. Knight v. Cole*, 3 Levinz 269, 273, 83 E.R. 684, 686, 1 Shower K.B. 150, 89 E.R. 505, Carthew 118, 90 E.R. 673, 1 Eq. Cas. Abr. 170, 21 E.R. 965, *sub nom. Knight v. Low*, Dodd 121.

by virtue of the general devise in the will and, consequently, whether the recovery was well suffered.

For the plaintiffs, the creditors, it was insisted that the lands whereof the testator was seised as surviving trustee for preserving contingent remainders did not pass by the will, for, by the words 'all [his] estate whatsoever,' nothing could pass but what was properly his own estate and in his own power to dispose of. And it was plain he intended to devise nothing else, for, in the preamble of his will, he beings 'as to such estate as the Lord has bestowed on me,' and, then, he goes on and devises particular lands which he was seised of in his own right, and, then, comes the general words, 'all the rest of [his] estate', which are relative words and must mean all the rest of the estate which the Lord had bestowed on him.

And the cases of Dorrell and Collins, Cr. Eliz. 6, and Cole and Knight, 3 Mod. 277 [were cited]. If an executor or administrator grants *omnia bona sua*, the goods of the testator or intestate do not pass, for they are not *bona sua*.

But, notwithstanding what was insisted on, the Master of the Rolls [JEKYLL] was of opinion that the trust lands did pass by the will and the purchaser was discharged.

[Other reports of this case: 2 Peere Williams 198, 24 E.R. 698, 2 Eq. Cas. Abr. 328, 22 E.R. 279.]

404

Pinbury v. Elkin

(Ch. 1719)

A person is said to die without issue not only if he dies leaving no issue at his death, but also, if he leaves issue and there is afterwards a failer of issue, though never so long.

An executor of a will may dispose of the testator's assets notwithstanding a legacy is given upon a contingency so long as he keeps sufficient assets in his hands to pay the legacy if it becomes payable.

A person may make himself a debtor on any contingency whatsoever though never so remote.

Lincoln's Inn MS. Misc. 384, p. 39, pl. 2

11 July. Inner Temple Hall.

Giles Davis devises by his will all his lands etc. to his wife Esther, then came these words 'provided that, if the said Esther Davis, my wife, should die without issue by me, Giles Davis, that fourscore pounds should remain to my brother, John Davis, after her decease.' John Davis, the legatee, survives the testator but dies before the wife. The question is whether it is a vested interest in John Davis and will go to his executor though it is not assignable.

Peere Williams quoted Nicholls v. Hooper, before Lord Harcourt; 2 Vern. 347; where there was a devise of lands to A. and, after his death without issue, then £500 to B.; there being issue left, it could not arise; Powel v. Loyd; a trust to raise money on the death of A. without issue; there was a child left *in ventre sa mere*; query, *vide* Target v. Gaunt, 121, where it was construed leaving issue at the time of his death.[1]

Vernon, for the defendant: We admit, where there is a contingent devise to A., it will vest, but the objection is the remoteness of it. Personalties could not formerly be limited to one for life with a remainder over. Here, the words are not 'without issue at the time of her death'. Indeed, terms for years may be limited further than other personalties.

Lord Chancellor [Lord Parker]: I think, if it were, 'if my wife die without issue generally, then I give £80 to A.', it would not be good. But, here, the chief question is whether they be not special words. If the words had been transposed, it would have passed, for it is given to be paid after the wife's death, provided she die without issue. If I give to my wife such goods to be by her possessed and enjoyed, provided, if she die without issue by me, then £80 to remain to A., it is good. Here, the testator's intent being that if it should be paid at the death of the wife in case there was no issue, it is good and must be paid with interest.

16 July.

Lord Chancellor [Lord Parker] said that, by the civil law, if the time of payment is uncertain, whether it will happen or not, if the legatee die before, it is lapsed. Swinburn, l. 4, sec. 17.[2] And so he doubted upon the contingency, the legatee dying before the wife.

Lincoln's Inn MS. Misc. 11, p. 120

22 July 1719.

Davis, by a will, declares that, if his wife died without issue, a legacy of £80 should remain to his brother. After the death of the testator and during the wife's life, the brother died. And, then, the wife died without issue. The plaintiff, as executor of the brother, brings a bill for the legacy.

The questions were two: first, whether a legacy can arise, being given after a dying without issue; if it can, then, secondly, whether, the legatee dying before the contingency happened, did it not become lapsed or if it shall be paid to the administrator of the legatee.

Lord Chancellor [Lord Parker], having taken time to consider of this case, this day delivered his opinion, *viz.*, first, that the legacy did become payable

---

[1] *Nichols v. Hooper* (Ch. 1712), 2 Vernon 686, 23 E.R. 1045, 1 Peere Williams 198, 24 E.R. 353, 1 Eq. Cas. Abr. 202, 21 E.R. 990, 2 Eq. Cas. Abr. 559, 22 E.R. 471, British Library MS. Hargrave 80, f. 94v; *Anonymous* (1679), 2 Ventris 347, 86 E.R. 478; *Target v. Gaunt* (1718), see above, Case No. 248.

[2] H. Swinburne, *Brief Treatise of Testaments and Last Wills.*

upon the death of the testator's wife without issue. According to the legal sense of the words, a man is said to die without issue not only if he dies leaving no issue at his death, but, if he leaves issue and there is afterwards a failer of issue, though never so long. But, in this case, the words ought to be taken in the vulgar sense, that is, if the wife died without leaving issue at her death, though, if the case had fallen out to have been that the wife had left issue at her death and such issue had afterwards died without issue, I will not say the legacy would not have been payable, for there is a great difference between giving a sum of money after a dying without issue and limiting a remainder of a term after a dying without issue. In the latter case, such remainders are clogs upon property, for, if they were good, such remainders could not be barred. But the other case is not attended with any such inconvenience, for an executor may dispose of the rest of his assets notwithstanding a legacy is given upon the contingency of a person's dying without issue. He need only keep sufficient [assets] in his hands to answer the legacy if it becomes payable.

Suppose a man covenants that his executors shall pay A. £100 if B. dies without issue. Will not that covenant be good? And, if a man may bind his executors by a covenant to pay a sum of money after a person's dying without issue, why may he not do it by his will? But, as to this, I give no opinion though I do not know that, in any case, it has been decreed that such a bequest is not good.

As to the second point, I am of the opinion the plaintiff is entitled to the legacy though the legatee died before the contingency happened, according to 2 Vent. 347.[1]

Lincoln's Inn MS. Misc. 384, p. 186, pl. 2

23 July 1719.

Giles Davis gives by his will his lands and goods to his wife Esther, provided that, 'if Esther Davis, my wife, should die without issue by me, Giles David, that fourscore pounds should remain to my brother John Davis after her decease'. John Davis died in the life of Esther, and the plaintiff is his executor. [The issues were] that it is void in the creation as too remote [and] the words 'without issue' are of various significations, as in the cases of Moor 127; 1 Leo. 285; 1 Ven. 231, another sense; Goodyear and Clark, Syd. 102, 1 Keb. 462, 248, as if it were died without ever having issue.[2] A third sense is without leaving issue at the time of the death, which is called the vulgar sense.

This case is to be taken in the last sense. Otherwise, it would defeat the intent of the testator if it had been generally 'if my wife die without issue by me'.

---

1 *Anonymous* (1679), 2 Ventris 347, 86 E.R. 478.

2 *Newton v. Bernardine* (1583), Moore K.B. 127, 72 E.R. 484; *Lee v. Vincent* (1584), 1 Leonard 285, 74 E.R. 260, also 3 Leonard 106, 74 E.R. 570, Croke Eliz. 26, 78 E.R. 291; *Goodiar v. Clarke* (1663), 1 Siderfin 102, 82 E.R. 996, 1 Keble 73, 78, 169, 246, 462, 83 E.R. 819, 822, 880, 926, 1054.

It might be more remote. But here, it is to be paid after the wife's death if it thus circumstanced that she died without issue, which is agreeable to common sense. It would be absurd if it were to be paid after her death if she leave issue, which might die twenty years afterwards; remainders of terms and goods might be great clogs upon property. But a future gift of money is not so. There is no case where a covenant to pay a sum of money on the death of A. without issue is void. A man may make himself a debtor on any contingency whatsoever though never so remote.

As to the second objection, [see] Swinburn 308, 309; 1 Vent. 347. I doubted whether the legacy was lapsed, the legatee dying before the wife. But now I think on reading those cases that the money must be paid to the plaintiff with interest from the death of the wife, it being a vested legacy.

[Other reports of this case: 2 Vernon 758, 766, 23 E.R. 1095, 1099, Precedents in Chancery 483, 24 E.R. 217, 1 Peere Williams 563, 24 E.R. 518.]

405

Anonymous

(Ch. 1719)

The inhabitancy of paupers determines their settlement for the purposes of the poor laws.

Lincoln's Inn MS. Hill 73, p. 115, pl. 1

A motion [was made] to quash an order of the Sessions which ordered that several persons, seafaring men, living constantly on shipboard in the Thames but in the daytime in the parish of St. Mary Colechurch did serve [. . .]. The Statute[1] is not only binding, but [also] inhabitancy. Service of forty days is a good settlement. These persons served three months.

The judgment [in] eyre [was] that inhabitancy makes the settlement.

[1] Stat. 3 Will. & Mar., c. 11 (*SR*, VI, 314–315).

406
Notes

(Ch. 1719)

A judgment debtor may re-enter upon his land where the debt has been satisfied under a writ of elegit, *but not under a writ of extent.*

Lincoln's Inn MS. Hill 73, p. 115, pl. 2

A *reddidendum* is a writ upon the bail piece when the parties hand over to the court at the return day.

Signing an interlocutory judgment, a plea is entered under the first letter of the plaintiff's name instead of the defendant's, upon which the plaintiff signs the judgment for want of a plea regularly entered.

The defendant may enter upon a [writ of] elegit when the debt is satisfied (though it be otherwise in [writs of] extent).

407
De la Rose v. Hodges

(Ch. 1719)

Property held by a bankrupt as a trustee cannot be reached by the creditors of the bankrupt trustee.

Lincoln's Inn MS. Misc. 384, p. 164, pl. 1

14 July.

1717, December 23, the defendant, Sir Joseph Hodges, gave the plaintiff a note promising to transfer £1500 South Sea [Company] stock to the plaintiff on demand and to account for the dividends for value received. And, the 30th January, he transferred £3000 stock to Sir Lambert Blackwell, who transferred to the defendant Mack in trust as to £1500 for the plaintiff. 31 January, Sir Joseph becomes bankrupt, and the assignees claim the £1500 as part of the bankrupt's estate.

Mead, for the plaintiff, quoted a case before Lord Cowper, *Ex parte* Sesiman, where a merchant abroad consigned effects to a factor here, who sold part to the East India Company on credit and afterwards [became] bankrupt; it was decreed that neither the money in the East India Company's hands nor the effects in the factor's hands were liable to the factor's bankruptcy.

It was proved that the plaintiff transferred the £1500 to Sir Joseph the 23rd December without consideration and that Sir Joseph declared it was in trust for the plaintiff.

Master of the Rolls [JEKYLL]: In regard Sir Joseph, at the time of giving the note, had more than the £1500 stock in the South Sea Company, he was of opinion that the stock was bound from that time and Sir Joseph was but a trustee for the plaintiff and, therefore, it was [not][1] liable to Sir Joseph's bankruptcy.

408

Finch v. Earl of Winchelsea

(Ch. 1719)

A life tenant is not required to pay interest on encumbrances on his life estate if this would render it of no value to him.

Lincoln's Inn MS. Misc. 384, p. 188

17 October.

Cowper, for the defendant, quoted the Case of Boteler and Allington, by Lord Harcourt.[2] The rule that a tenant for life must keep down the interest of an encumbrance is subject to this exception, unless the profits are not sufficient for that purpose and also for a reasonable maintenance for the tenant for life because the tenant for life is not to be starved for the benefit of the remaindermen. An estate of £1700 *per annum* was limited to Mr. Boteler for life, remainder to his first and other sons in tail, subject to an encumbrance of £24,000, and there was a direction to sell timber, which produced £10,000, and the profits of the estate would barely keep down the interest, yet the court allowed Mr. Boteler £400 *per annum* and the possession of Woodhall House and Park.

The Master was to allow Lord Winchelsea a reasonable allowance, which he settled at £600 *per annum*. The plaintiff excepts.

Curia [LORD PARKER]: In these cases, the allowance of maintenance is discretionary, that is it is sometimes allowed by the course of the court and sometimes disallowed. The discretion of the court is not merely voluntary, but to be guided by the nature and circumstances of the case according to equity and justice. How it is according to equity and justice that Lord Winchelsea should have an allowance suitable to his honor and dignity and not be starved for the sake of a remainderman? The Master has allowed £600 *per annum*, which is but a reasonable allowance though there are great encumbrances. The decree has provided that the creditors shall not be prejudiced. And, as to Mr. Finch, the remainderman, he will have as much or more when he comes into possession.

He overruled the exception.

---

[1] The word 'not' is supplied by the editor.

[2] *Butler v. Allington* (Ch. 1714), Lincoln's Inn MS. Misc. 384, p. 14, pl. 1, British Library MS. Hargrave 81, f. 69, British Library MS. Hargrave 82, f. 66, British Library MS. Hargrave 77, f. 19, pl. 18; British Library MS. Hargrave 303, f. 36.

[Other reports of this case: 1 Peere Williams 277, 24 E.R. 387, 1 Eq. Cas. Abr. 2, 21 E.R. 828, 2 Eq. Cas. Abr. 257, 460, 683, 22 E.R. 218, 392, 574, British Library MS. Hargrave 80, f. 149.]

409

Wind v. Jekyll

(Ch. 1719)

In this case, the devise of the term in gross in issue was a declaration of a trust, and the devisee was given the residue of the term.

Lincoln's Inn MS. Misc. 384, p. 189

19 October.

J. Seed, possessed of a term in gross, devises to his wife for so many years as she should live, remainder to J. Clark. J. Clark, in the life of the wife, devises to A., to whom the plaintiff is executor. The defendant is executor of J. Clark, and he insists it was not in the power of J. Clark to devise it, it being only a possibility. The question is whether this possibility is devisable.

Peere Williams, for the plaintiff: A devise is but an equitable appointment. Moor 806.[1] It is hard that a man should have a property which he cannot dispose of. Fulwood's Case, 4 Co. 64; Lampet's, 10 Co. 46;[2] that a man cannot grant a possibility, it being a chose in action, yet there is no case that he cannot devise it. 1 Ch. Ca. 8, Goring and Bickerstaff.[3] It may be disposed of by will by proper words. Woods and Sanders, Pol. 35; it is to the son if he survived A. and B.; Pinbury and Elkin, *ante*.[4]

Lutwyche, for the executor: There is a great difference between a property and a possibility. It is admitted that the possibility cannot be granted nor assigned. The reason is as strong that it cannot be given by will.

Curia [Lord Parker]: If he had made an executor in trust, it would vest; so if the executor be made the residuary legatee.

Lutwyche: A possibility is looked upon as not vested; therefore, it cannot be transferred.

---

1 *Cole v. Moore* (1607), Moore K.B. 806, 72 E.R. 917.

2 *Cartwright v. Roberts* (1591), 4 Coke Rep. 64, 76 E.R. 1031; *Lampet's Case* (1612), 10 Coke Rep. 46b, 77 E.R. 994, *sub nom. Lampit v. Starkey*, 2 Brownlow & Goldesborough 172, 123 E.R. 880.

3 *Goring v. Bickerstaff* (1662), 1 Chancery Cases 4, 22 E.R. 665, also 2 Freeman 163, 22 E.R. 1132, Pollexfen 31, 86 E.R. 502.

4 *Wood v. Saunders* (1669), Pollexfen 35, 86 E.R. 503, also 1 Chancery Cases 131, 22 E.R. 728; *Pinbury v. Elkin* (Ch. 1719), see above, Case No. 404.

Lord Chancellor [Lord Parker]: The rule laid down, that it is hard that a man cannot dispose of his own, is too large, and we cannot now consider the reason of the law, but what the law is. By the law, a man cannot assign what he has not. But cannot he by a will? As to land, he cannot, but, as to personal things, he may. The reason is because, as to land, the heir would have it if not disposed of. But, before the Statute of Distributions,[1] there was no person to take personalties; therefore, the executor must have taken or nobody.

Land purchased after will not pass by a will, but personal estate will. Suppose a man has made an executor in trust *quoad* this term. Should he take this for his own benefit? No. He is subject to the trusts of the will. Here, a man makes his wife executrix as to all the rest except this term, and, as to that, she is a trustee for the devisee. If it had been a bond, it had been the same. I think it very reasonable to construe this a declaration of a trust and that the devisee ought to have the residue of this term.

[Other reports of this case: 1 Peere Williams 572, 24 E.R. 522, 2 Eq. Cas. Abr. 296, 421, 22 E.R. 249, 358.]

410

Cud v. Rutter

(Ch. 1719–1720)

Specific performance of a contract will not be ordered where money damages would be a complete and adequate remedy.

Where a defendant cannot specifically perform a contract, a court of equity will not order it.

Lincoln's Inn MS. Misc. 12, p. 295

27 October 1719.

The plaintiff bought £1000 South Sea [Company] stock of the defendant the 14th October 1718 to be delivered the 20th of November following at £104 10s. percent. And he paid the defendant 2 guineas in part of the payment. And, thereupon, the defendant gave the plaintiff the following note, *viz.* 'Received of Mr. John Cud the sum of £2 2s. 0d. in part of payment of £1000 South Sea stock, which I promise to deliver on the 20th November 1718 at 104 & ½ percent. London 14th October 1718.'

The stock rising, the defendant did not transfer the £1000 South Sea [Company] stock according to his agreement. And, thereupon, the plaintiff brought his bill for a specific performance.

[1] Stat. 22 & 23 Car. II, c. 10 (*SR*, V, 719–720).

The defendant, by answer, insisted he ought only to pay the difference and that such was the intention of the parties when the agreement was made and that the plaintiff did not on the 20th of November call upon the defendant to transfer the stock.

It was proved by one witness that a day or two before the 20th of November, the plaintiff and the defendant were together and then the plaintiff desired the defendant to be ready to transfer the stock, upon which the defendant grew angry and said he would have nothing to do with the plaintiff and had ordered one Gough to transfer the stock to the plaintiff and that the plaintiff, afterwards, went to Gough, who said he had no order about it.

And another witness said that, twice or thrice after the 20th of November, at the plaintiff's desire, he asked the defendant to transfer the stock, who said he had been tricked into the agreement and would not transfer the stock.

The Master of the Rolls [Jekyll] decreed the defendant should transfer £1000 South Sea [Company] stock to the plaintiff, he paying £1042 18s. 0d., the residue of the purchase money with interest from the 20th of November 1718, but thereout the plaintiff was to be allowed what had been received for dividends since the time of the contract together with his costs to be taxed by a master.

The defendant appealed from this decree to Lord Chancellor Macclesfield. And the reasons alleged were:

First, for that the agreement was not mutual or equitable, the defendant being under a promise to deliver the stock on the 20th November, but the plaintiff was not obliged then to accept it, and it was proved that South Sea stock was £106 10s. per cent at the time of the contract and, therefore, the agreement was not a reasonable and fair agreement;

Secondly, the plaintiff has not proved he demanded the stock on the 20th of November or that he then offered to pay the purchase money, which, if the agreement was reciprocal, it was incumbent on him to have done, as well as for the defendant to have tendered the stock, and without such demand and tender of the money at the day, the plaintiff seems not to be entitled to a decree for a specific performance, especially in the cases of delivery of stock, which is always fluctuating;

Thirdly, the decree seems to be grounded on the plaintiff's intention only, which appeared to be to have the stock transferred to him and not to take the difference, whereas the defendant's intention was just the contrary, and, by the proofs, it appears that either party was to pay the difference as it should happen by the fall or rise and, at the time of the contract, the defendant declared he had not the stock;

Fourthly, the plaintiff, before the bill was filed, tendered the difference as it was on the 20th of November with the 2 guineas and the interest and the charge of transfer and the plaintiff, if he had gone to [common] law, where was his proper remedy, could have had no more and, though nothing is mentioned in the note about paying the difference, yet that must have been the rule in assessing the damages, for he could be damnified no more than that came to, and, though the plaintiff should pretend damages in having sold stock upon the credit of the agreement, yet that ought not to avail him, for he might have got any other person to have transferred stock to him at the market price.

This cause came on upon the appeal 2 July 1720.

It was insisted for the defendant that it was a discretionary act of the court whether to decree a specific performance of a contract or not. If there was anything unfair or hard in the contract, the court would not decree it.

In the Case of the Marquess of Normanby and Lord Berkeley, it was said by Lord Somers that all contracts which are good in law are to be carried into execution in this court. But then, he said that an agreement which is to be carried on here must be reasonable in itself and must be in writing, and the court has a discretionary power to judge of the whole circumstances of the case.

The present contract appears to be a very hard and unreasonable contract. If it is a legal contract, the plaintiff has his remedy at [common] law. And there is no reason he should have any assistance from this court or have any decree for a specific performance, especially when it has fallen out by the extraordinary rise upon the stock that, if the defendant s decreed to perform this contract, it must be his ruin.

For the plaintiff, it was insisted that the agreement was fair and reasonable in itself. Both parties run a hazard. One thought the stock would rise, and the other that it would fall.

As to the hardship of the case, it is to be considered how the contract was at the time of the making. There was nothing then hard or unreasonable in it. And it is owing to the obstinacy of the defendant that it is now become a hard bargain. Had he performed the contract when he should have done it or at the time when the bill was bought, it would have been no great matter, but that which occasions the hardship is the extraordinary rise upon the stock, which was accidental and could not be foreseen.

Lord Chancellor [Lord Parker]: This is the first agreement of this kind that has been brought into this court to be carried into execution.

If the defendant was not ready to transfer the £1000 stock according to his contract, the plaintiff might have bought £1000 stock more of some other person, and then the damage would have been settled. But would no stock do but the defendants? Did ever anyone come into this court to have a specific performance of a contract for the sale of a quantity of malt, for instance? No, surely. If the party does not deliver it at the day agreed on, he may buy it of some other person, and he may bring his action for the damage he sustains by the breach of the contract.

It must be understood by the parties in all contracts for stock that the specific stock is not to be delivered but the difference is to be paid. Indeed, if the same quantity of stock is not to be got, it might alter the case. And, therefore, this court carries an agreement for the sale of land into execution because, if the party has not the land, he cannot have the same thing another way.

It is no objection to say you are in possession of a decree. No, it is no decree until it is signed by me, for all decrees, though made at the Rolls, are mine when signed by me.

Let there be an inquiry by the Master whether the plaintiff did really buy any stock to make good any contract that he had made, and, if he did, the defendant must pay the difference with interest. But no costs [are to be given] on either side.

Lincoln's Inn MS. Misc. 384, p. 190, pl. 3

27 October.

The bill was to have a specific performance of an agreement whereby the defendant was to transfer £1000 South Sea [Company] stock to the plaintiff at 105½ percent on the 20th of November 1718.

Vernon, for the defendant, insisted that this was a stock jobbing bargain and not to be countenanced in a court of equity, but that the plaintiff ought to take his remedy at law upon the note and recover damages, there being no precedent where such an agreement has been carried into execution, that, in Attorney General and Wills, the defendant was decreed to transfer stock deposited in his hands as a pledge, that, where the agreement is only to pay the difference on such a day, it is in the nature of a wager, that here was only two guineas paid down to bind the bargain.

Master of the Rolls [Jekyll] was of opinion that this was a fair transaction and decreed the defendant to transfer £1000 stock in specie to the plaintiff at this time and to account for the dividends from the 20th of November 1718, and to pay costs.

[This was] reversed by the Lord Chancellor [Lord Parker] and left to [the common] law 2 July 1720.

5 Viner, Abr. 538

Trinity 6 Geo. [1720].

A bill [was exhibited] for a specific performance of an agreement to transfer stock. The case was thus. The defendant agreed with the plaintiff to transfer to him £1000 South Sea stock upon the 20th of November then next following at the rate of £104 percent and gave him a promissory note under his hand for so doing, and he received two guineas of the plaintiff in part of the consideration money. But the defendant, in drawing the note, had put in the usual words 'or pay the difference', which the plaintiff struck out and would not agree to. And then, the defendant signed the note. After the bargain was made and before the time of delivering the stock, the South Sea stock did rise considerably in value, and the defendant did not deliver the stock at the day. But, a few days after, he offered to pay the difference, and he submits so to do by his answer. But the plaintiff insists to have the stock actually transferred to him and refuses to take the difference etc.

Sir Robert Raymond and Mr. *Vernon*, for the defendant, insisted that buying the stock in this manner to be delivered at a future time at a certain price was in the nature of a wager upon the rise and fall of a stock, and, therefore, paying the difference is a sufficient performance of the contract, that a contract for the sale of stock differs from other contracts for the sale of a house, lands, etc., for, in such things, there may be a particular convenience or benefit to the buyer in this individual house etc., but it is not so in stock, for one £1000 is as good as another £1000 stock and it is to be purchased daily in Exchange Alley, that the plaintiff has his remedy at law for the damages, *viz.* the difference, and that is the justice of the case between the parties, that it is discretionary in the court to decree a specific performance of an agreement, and that, in many cases, the court will leave the party to his remedy at law for the breach of a contract etc.

Sir Joseph Jekyll, the Master of the Rolls, said, that this is a fair and reasonable agreement, and he saw no reason why the court should not in this case as well as others decree a specific performance of the contract, especially since it was insisted upon by the plaintiff at the making the agreement that he should not be obliged to take the difference but would have the stock actually be delivered to him. And it is more for the advantage of the buyer to have the stock than the difference, and it saves him the trouble of buying it of another and paying brokerage. And he decreed that the defendant do transfer the stock and pay the dividends since the 20th of November, the plaintiff to pay interest of the money to that time, and he ordered costs to the plaintiff.

On an appeal from this decree, Parker, Chancellor, upon opening the cause, asked if the plaintiff was at the South Sea House upon the day appointed for transferring the stock to demand it and tender the money. And he seemed strongly against the plaintiff and urged the law in the case of a bargain for corn to be delivered upon a day certain at such a market at such a price and the corn is not delivered according to the contract, the buyer shall not by a bill in equity compel the seller to a specific performance of this agreement, but the buyer is left to his remedy at law for breach of the agreement to recover damages, *id est* the difference between the price agreed on by the parties and the price of corn upon the market day.

It was said it was the common justice of this court to compel the party to a specific performance of his agreement if the same was just and reasonable and fairly obtained, that this was a just, reasonable, and fair agreement in all the circumstances, it was the current price of the stock at that time, and there was no imposition upon the defendant, that the subsequent rise could not alter the case, for it was an equal hazard that it might fall, and the parties, in such contracts executory, must take their chance. They compared it to the case of a contract for so many bales of silk or any other merchandise to be delivered at a future day at a certain price; if the value of the silk or other goods does rise before the day, that is no excuse for non-performance of the contract. So, in the case of a contract for lands, if the lands rise in value, yet the party ought to execute his agreement. They said that, from the time of the contract to the time appointed for the delivery, the stock did not rise above £12 percent, that it was not more at the time of filing the bill, which was in January 1718; nay, it was not more at the time of the decree pronounced by the Master of the Rolls in Michaelmas Term last, and, though the stock has risen since to a vast price, between £900 and £1000 percent, if the plaintiff suffers by that, it is his own fault in not performing his contact sooner, when he was demanded so to do, and, in not obeying the decree, as he ought to have done, that whatever has happened since cannot alter the case, that the contract was reasonable at the time it was made, and so it was when the bill was filed and the decreed pronounced.

It was said for the defendant that the rule was laid down too generally for compelling the execution of agreements between the parties, that this court would not compel the party to perform a hard agreement, though it was fair at the time it was made, but leave the other party to his remedy at law, that it was very unreasonable now to compel the defendant to transfer £1000 South Sea stock to the plaintiff at £104 10s. percent when it was worth £1000 percent, that paying the difference at the day was a good performance of this contact, that the plaintiff knew that the defendant had no stock when he made the bargain with him and, therefore, could not expect to have the stock delivered to him, but to have the difference if the stock should happen to rise before the time, and he had no more intention to take the stock than the other had to deliver it, and this appears by his non-attendance at the South Sea House upon the day to accept and pay for the stock. They cited the case of Marquess of Normandy and Lord Berkeley, *tempore* Lord Somers, Chancellor,[1] who said in that case that the court would not carry agreements into execution unless the contract was reasonable and fair in every particular, because they cannot mitigate damages upon the circumstances of the case, as a jury may do, but must decree the whole contract to be performed.

It was replied that the plaintiff, some days before the stock was to be delivered, told the defendant that he expected to have the stock delivered to him, but the defendant said that he had not the stock, and, therefore, he would not deliver it, and, afterwards, the defendant kept out of the way for some days, and the plaintiff could not find him, and that was the reason he did not attend at the South Sea House to accept the stock, that this being occasioned by the defendant's own unfair dealing, the plaintiff ought not to suffer by it, and, upon the account, the plaintiff ought to be relieved in equity, because he is remediless at law for want of a legal demand and tender upon the day.

---

1 *Marquess of Normanby v. Duke of Devonshire* (1697), 2 Freeman 216, 22 E.R. 1169.

PARKER, Chancellor: There is no reason to bring this bill for a specific performance of this agreement, because there is no difference between this £1000 South Sea stock and another £1000 stock, which the plaintiff might have bought of any other person upon the very day, and the plaintiff does not suffer at all by the non-performance of the agreement specifically if the defendant pays him the difference. These sorts of contracts are commonly understood to mean no more than to transfer the stock or pay the difference. And this fully answers the intention of the parties, and the party has thereby the entire benefit of his contract as fully as if the stock were actually delivered, for he may buy of any other person and be no more money out of pocket than if the stock were delivered to him according to the agreement. This differs very much from the case of a contract for lands, some lands being more valuable than others, at least more convenient than others to the purchaser. But there is no difference in stock; one man's stock is of equal benefit and convenience as another's.

Secondly, it appears that the defendant had not the stock when the contract was made, and this court will not decree a specific performance of a contract when the party has not the thing to deliver. Suppose a contract for the sale of land and the party has not the land at the time he contracted for the sale of it, this court would not decree a specific performance of the agreement. If there be a contract for the sale of malt or any other commodity and the seller has not the malt or other things agreed to be delivered, this court will not compel the party to perform his agreement but leave the buyer to recover his damages at law for non-performance of the agreement.

Thirdly, in contracts for stock, being subject to sudden rise and fall, the day is the most material part of the contract, and, therefore, it is not proper for a court of equity to carry [them] into execution. The decree might be beneficial to the plaintiff one day and to his prejudice the next. I shall always discourage bills of this kind, but, since the defendant did shuffle with the plaintiff and not offer to pay him the difference until two months after the day, I will not dismiss the bill, but let the Master enquire what the difference was at the day, and the defendant to pay it to the plaintiff with interest, but no costs.

The decree was reversed by PARKER, Chancellor.

[Other copies of this report: 2 Eq. Cas. Abr. 160, 22 E.R. 136.]

[Other reports of this case: 1 Peere Williams 570, 24 E.R. 521, 2 Eq. Cas. Abr. 18, 22 E.R. 15.]

411
Buckley v. Stanlake
(Ch. 1719)

In this case, the legacy in issue vested in the devisee and then passed to his administrator.

Lincoln's Inn MS. Misc. 11, p. 173

4 November 1719.

John Thompson, by will, gives the rectory of Furnex Pelham in Hertfordshire, which he held by a lease for lives, to his wife Katherine for life and, after her death, to his daughter Katherine and her heirs, but, in case his daughter should die before she should be married, then he devised the rectory to his wife and her heirs subject to and chargeable with the payment of several legacies and, among others, of £100 apiece to Robert and John Fletcher. And he made his wife executrix. Robert Fletcher died soon after the testator, and then Katherine, the daughter, died under age and unmarried.

Katherine, the mother, who survived her daughter, by her will, gave the premises to the defendant upon trust to sell the same and discharge the legacies charged thereon by her husband's will and then to pay her own debts and legacies.

The question upon the exceptions to the Master's report after the hearing was whether, in regard the legacies were given upon a contingency and Robert Fletcher dying before such contingency happened, his legacy did not become lapsed or whether it was not a vested legacy and should go to his administrator.

Lord Chancellor [Lord Parker] was of opinion the legacy vested and should go to the administrator of Robert.

See the Case of Pinbury and Elkin, *ante* 120, and 2 Vent. 347; see the Case of Smell and Dee, Salkeld 415.[1]

Lincoln's Inn MS. Misc. 11, p. 232

4 November 1719. Edward Buckley *et al.* v. George Stanlake *et al.*

John Thompson, seised of a rectory in Hertfordshire under a lease for lives, by his will, devised the premises to his wife for life and then to his daughter and her heirs. And he declared that, if his daughter should die unmarried, then he gave the premises to his wife and her heirs subject to and chargeable with the payments of several legacies, and, among others, he gave to Robert and John Fletcher, sons of his uncle, Thomas Fletcher, deceased, £100 apiece.

Katherine, the daughter, died an infant and unmarried after her father's death and during the life of her mother.

---

[1] *Pinbury v. Elkin* (Ch. 1719), see above, Case No. 404; *Smell v. Dee* (1707), 2 Salkeld 415, 91 E.R. 360, also 1 Eq. Cas. Abr. 295, 21 E.R. 1056.

The mother, after her daughter's death, devised the premises to the defendant upon trust to pay the legacies charged thereon by her husband's will and then for other purposes.

The cause was heard and a sale was decreed. And the Master was to take an account of the debts and legacies remaining unpaid.

It appearing by the Master's report that Robert Fletcher, who survived the testator, died in the lifetime of Katherine, the daughter, a question was made whether the legacies given to them shall now be paid to their representatives. It being insisted on that the legacies being given upon a contingency, *viz.* the daughter's dying unmarried, and the legatees' being dead before the contingency happened, they never vested in the legatees and consequently could not be payable to their representatives, but became lapsed.

But LORD PARKER was of opinion the legacies were not lapsed, for there was an interest vested in the legatees though it was contingent. And, therefore, he ordered the legacies of £100 each to be paid to Robert and John Fletcher, the administrators of the said Robert Fletcher.

Lincoln's Inn MS. Misc. 384, p. 191, pl. 2

4 November.

John Thompson, by his will, gives £100 apiece to his nephews, John and Robert Fletcher. Then, he devises his lands etc. to his wife Katherine for life and, after her death, to his daughter Katherine and her heirs, but, if she die unmarried, then to his wife Katherine and her heirs, subject to the raising of the several legacies to John and Robert. John and Robert died before the daughter Katherine, who likewise died unmarried. The query is whether the legacies vested in John and Robert so as to go to the plaintiffs, who are their executors.

Lord Chancellor [LORD PARKER] was of opinion that the legacies vested in John and Robert, though the raising of it depended on a contingency, *viz.* the daughter's dying unmarried. *Vide* Pinbury v. Elkin, *ante.*

412

Warley v. Wimbush

(Ch. c. 1719)

A judgment creditor of a decedent's estate has priority over a creditor by a decree.

Lincoln's Inn MS. Misc. 11, p. 233

The plaintiff's wife being administrator of John Ebrall, her first husband, and his personal estate not being sufficient to pay all his bond debts, she paid the remainder out of her own money. And then she brought her bill against the heir at law, praying that she might stand in the room of such bond creditors as she had so paid and have a satisfaction out of the real assets. And, upon the hearing of the cause, it was so decreed.

After this decree was obtained and the account was taken of what was due to the plaintiff and an order was made upon the hearing of the Master's report that the estate should stand charged with the sum reported due and that the plaintiff should be at liberty to apply for a sale, the defendant Wimbush put a bond in suit against the heir at law, wherein the testator was bound as a surety for his brother, who was dead insolvent, and obtained a judgment.

And now, the plaintiffs brought their bill to stay the proceedings at law upon the judgment and praying that the money decreed the administratrix might be paid out of the real estate before the defendant's judgment.

The Master of the Rolls [JEKYLL] decreed against the plaintiffs and said he never knew any case where a judgment creditor in respect of real assets was postponed to a creditor by a decree.

413

Como v. Vincetti

(Ch. 1719)

A court of equity does not have jurisdiction over reprisals for a foreign debt until after a final judgment in a court of admiralty.

Lincoln's Inn MS. Misc. 384, p. 192

6 November. Como and Corticelli v. Vincetti *et al.*

Northey, for the plaintiffs: In 1693, one Justiniani at Genoa was indebted to the plaintiffs £3000. The plaintiffs, not obtaining justice there, obtained letters from Lord Sunderland to Sir J. Norris to seize by way of reprisals. Afterwards, the Lord Forbes, under Sir J. Norris, took three Genoese ships, but he seized them upon suspicion they had contraband goods and got them condemned in the [Court of] Admiralty as prize. The effects are sold, and the money came to the defendant's hands.

And the bill is to have a satisfaction out of that money of what is due to the plaintiffs. Reg. 129; Molloy [*De Jure Maritimo*].

Vernon, for the plaintiffs: The defendants insist that they are only trustees for Marquis Sauli and the other proprietors of the ships, but, if they are trustees for him, they are liable to any demands against him. Otherwise, there would be a failure of justice, process not running into foreign parts. The defendants insist by answer that these ships were not taken by way of reprisals, but for carrying contraband goods, but we have proved the contrary. The ships and effects were sold for £18,000, which was left in the defendants' hands for the benefit of all entitled.

Lord Chancellor [Lord Parker]: You should have applied to the Admiralty and have proceeded against the effects and money in the defendants' hands and might have a remedy there. There is no color for coming here. If Sir J. Norris did not give orders to Lord Forbes to seize as reprisals, Lord Forbes could not seize, and he says himself he took the ships for contraband goods. This court cannot interpose until there is a sentence in the [Court of] Admiralty that they are reprisals.

Cowper, for the defendants: [By the] Statute 4 Hen. V,[1] letters of marque must be under the great seal; query, here was only a letter from Lord Sunderland to Sir J. Norris.

It was put off until Monday next.

N.B. In July 1710, articles [were made] between Lord Oxford and the proprietors of the ships whereby they lend to the Crown £18,000, and, thereupon, the ships were discharged, and the defendants, who are trustees for the proprietors, had this money transferred into the South Sea Company.

9 November.

Dr. *Henchman*, for the plaintiff: First, as to the effects of the reprisals, Grotius, lib. 3, c. 2, p. 4,[2] the property is altered by the capture for the benefit of the parties for whom the capture is made, *ad lumeram* [?] *debiti*. It is *bellum privatum et species violente executionis*. The sentence in the [Court of] Admiralty does not vest a right, but only declares it.

Second, the reason why the plaintiffs did not prosecute their right in the Admiralty [is] the ships were delivered at Port Mahon by the order of the Crown, and the money is vested in trustees; therefore, it is proper here and not in the Admiralty.

Third, the release of the ship is not a release of the debt in equity.

Sir Nathaniel Lloyd, for the defendant: First, whether the plaintiff has a property in the ships by the capture; second, whether the defendants are trustees for the plaintiffs. The plaintiffs did claim regularly in the proper court and ought to proceed there. There is no proof that Sir J. Norris sent orders to Lord Forbes to seize these ships as reprisals. I admit reprisals are an execution, but Lord Forbes swears he seized them on suspicion of having contraband goods, not by way of reprisals, and these ships were not condemned as reprisals. If the plaintiffs were wronged by that sentence, they might have appealed. In the Admiralty, the cause before the condemnation is in the queen's name, though, afterwards, in the name of the captors. Therefore, she had a power to discharge them.

Cowper, for the defendant: First, whether the plaintiffs are proper in this court, the defendants are innocent. It is hard they should suffer for the injury of another. The great question is whether these ships were taken by way of reprisals. Where reprisals are made, the property vests in the parties to whom the letters

[1] Stat. 4 Hen. V, stat. 2, c. 7 (*SR*, II, 198–199).

[2] H. Grotius, *De Jure Belli et Pacis*, book 3, chap. 2, ss. 4, 5.

are granted, and the Crown has no interest. The difference is between letters of marque under the great seal and a private letter to the Admiral to make them a seizure. In the first case, the Crown cannot release, as it may in the other. Here, the ships were seized for contraband goods, but retained by way of reprisals.

Hale, for the defendant: The retaining of the ships by way of reprisals will not cure the original defect in the seizure, and the whole bill is founded on the seizure as reprisals. Grotius, lib. 3, cap. 2, sec. 4, 5. Reprisals are to be granted only where *jus denegatur*, not where the debtor is insolvent, as in this case. The defendants are purchasers of their exemption by their loan to the Crown, and the Crown was fully satisfied.

Lord Chancellor [Lord Parker]: It is not clear whether the plaintiffs have gone through the whole process at Genoa. But I think the plaintiffs are entitled to letters of marque if they are not yet satisfied. Letters of marque are only authorities to the parties to seize and then it is *privatum bellum*, consequently what the party takes is his own until he is satisfied. And it is gained at his expense. And it is no wonder Grotius says that property vests. But it is otherwise where the prince gains it at his own expense. There, it is a public war, and the prince may make peace when and upon what terms he pleases.

Second, it is clear the ships were not seized by way of reprisal by Lord Forbes's deposition and the proceeding in the [Court of] Admiralty. If they were taken for reprisals, they must be condemned as such in Admiralty, even upon letters of marque, and the plaintiffs could not come into this court to make a demand upon them until after sentence there. Two seizures are inconsistent. The retaining is not a seizure.

Third, there is no excuse for not proceeding in the Admiralty.

Fourth, if the seizure had been rightly made, yet I think the Crown might discharge even after the seizure.

There is no equity for the plaintiffs from the articles.

He dismissed the bill without costs.

414

Abington v. Clement

(Ch. 1719)

Where a tenant in tail has the power to destroy contingent remainders, a court can order land that was devised in order to pay the decedent's debts to be sold for that purpose.

Lincoln's Inn MS. Misc. 384, p. 228

9 November 1719.

J. Compton devises his real estate to his executors for payment of his debts out of the rents and profits. And he directs that, after his debts are paid, they shall stand seised to the use of the plaintiff, Isabella Abington, for life, remainder to the next heir male of her body, remainder to the heirs female of her body, remainder to the defendant in fee.

The creditors join with Isabella and bring a bill for a sale. The first question was whether the debts should be paid out of the rents and profits or by sale. The second was whether the plaintiff Isabella had an estate tail or only an estate for life.

Vernon, for the plaintiff: In Dormer (Justice) v. Sheldon,[1] it was settled that not only debts but portions also may be raised by sale where it is directed to be by rents and profits. In Trevor v. Luck, a bond creditor had a decree for a sale. Secondly, the plaintiff Isabella has an estate tail. In Bale v. Coleman,[2] there was a difference taken between articles executory and a will. In the first case, it would be carried into strict settlement; in the other, it would be construed an estate tail.

Cowper, for the defendant: The debts ought to be paid out of the rents and profits for the benefit of the defendant, the remainderman, the plaintiff not having any issue. The defendant ought to have a chance for the estate. C. 147.[3] In Dr. Shadwell's Case,[4] where an infant was within three months of age and land was covenanted to be purchased and settled on him accordingly, which he would not have directed had the plaintiff been of age because he might immediately have suffered a recovery and defeated the remainders, but the Lord Chancellor said he would give the remainderman a chance for the estate, for it was possible the infant might die before a recovery could be suffered, which happened accordingly.

Master of the Rolls [Jekyll]: In Penlia v. Hollis, it was adjudged where there was a tenant for life to destroy those remainders. But, where there is a tenant in tail, in equity, he may defeat any remainder.

He decreed a sale.

---

1 *Sheldon v. Dormer* (1693), 2 Vernon 310, 23 E.R. 802.

2 *Baile v. Coleman* (Ch. 1711), 2 Peere Williams 142, 24 E.R. 330, 2 Vernon 670, 23 E.R. 1036, 2 Eq. Cas. Abr. 309, 472, 717, 22 E.R. 261, 402, 603, British Library MS. Hargrave 80, f. 26v, pl. 2.

3 *Throckmerton v. Tracy* (1555), 1 Plowden 145, 75 E.R. 222, 2 Dyer 124, 73 E.R. 272, 124 Selden Soc. 93.

4 *Colwell v. Colwell* (*tempore* Cowper).

415

Clark v. Acton

(Ch. 1719)

In this case, the legacies in issue were charged on the decedent's land.

Lincoln's Inn MS. Misc. 384, p. 229

10 November. Westminster.

J. Green, by his will in 1679, devises his real estate to his wife for life, provided she suffer A. to enjoy a lease, remainder to Ed. Green and the heirs male of his body, remainder to the right heirs of Robert Green. Then he appoints some charities and gives several legacies to the plaintiffs, which he directs to be paid by him who should have the land within one year after possession. Then he gives other legacies, which he directs should be paid by his wife, whom he makes executrix. The wife is dead; so is Ed. without issue male. Robert is living so that the remainder to his heirs is void.

The defendants claim as heirs at law. And the bill is to have the plaintiff's legacy raised out of the land.

The first question is whether the personal estate is exempted. The second question is whether the defendants are chargeable, not claiming under the will, or whether the wife ought not to have paid the legacy after one year's possession.

First, that the personal estate is to be applied in the first place unless expressly [declared otherwise]. Christ's Hospital v. Garraway.[1]

Master of the Rolls [Jekyll]: First, the personal estate is exempted, the testator directing only some particular legacies to be paid by his executrix, and *expressio unius est exclusio alterius.*

Secondly, I think the defendants are chargeable, for the testator does not say that the legatee shall be paid by such person as shall have the possession by virtue of the will, but, generally, such as shall have the possession.

Thirdly, I think it was the testator's intent that the wife should not be charged because he annexed a proviso to her to enjoy the land and does not mention her paying the legacy charged on the land but only the legacy paid out of the personal estate, and, if he had meant otherwise, he would have directed the legacy to be paid within a year after his death and not a year after possession. And though it is to be paid by him who should be in possession and the heirs at law are females, yet, since the testator intended to disinherit his heirs on a contingency, *a fortiori*, he intended to charge them with these legacies.

The plaintiff must have a satisfaction of their legacies from the defendants with interest from a year after the defendants came into possession. As to the

---

[1] *Christ's Hospital v. Gallway* (Ch. c. 1714), see above, Case No. 5.

contingent remainder to the heirs of Robert Green, I hardly know how the law is since Long v. Beamont, in the House of Lords.[1]

Lincoln's Inn MS. Misc. 11, p. 236

10 November 1719.

A.B., by will, gives legacies to the plaintiffs, and he devises his real estate to his wife for life, remainder to B. in tail, remainder to C. in tail, remainder to the right heirs of J.S. And he directs that the legacies shall be paid by him who shall be in possession of the premises within one year after such possession.

All the remaindermen in tail died without issue, and, the wife being dead and the contingent remainder having never vested, J.S. being living, the plaintiffs bring their bill against the heir at law for a satisfaction of their legacies.

The heir insisted he did not claim under the will, but as heir at law of the testator and that the lands were not charged by the will with the legacies.

The Master of the Rolls [JEKYLL] was of opinion that the lands were charged with the legacies, for, the direction being that the legacies should be paid by the person in possession generally and not restrained to the devisees of the land, the defendant who claimed as heir was liable to pay the legacies within one year after he came into possession.

Secondly, although the words of the will were that the legacies should be paid by 'him' in possession in the masculine gender, yet that word took in both male and female in this case and would extend to the wife.

Note the testator, after making his will, had sold away part of the lands, and, therefore, it was insisted on by the defendant that the legatees ought to abate in proportion to the value of the lands which had been so sold.

But His Honor [JEKYLL] was of opinion there ought to be no abatement, for, though the sale of part of the lands was a revocation of the devise of so much of the land as was sold, yet it was no revocation of any part of the legacies and the rest of the lands would remain charged.

---

1 *Darbison, ex dem. Long v. Beaumont* (1713–1714), 1 Peere Williams 229, 24 E.R. 366, Fortescue 18, 92 E.R. 743, 1 Eq. Cas. Abr. 214, 21 E.R. 999, Dodd 366, 3 Brown P.C. 60, 1 E.R. 1177, Lincoln's Inn MS. Misc. 10, p. 184, Lords' Journal, vol. 19, p. 696, *sub nom. Lay v. Beamont* (Ex. 1709), Equity Cases Exch. 604.

416
Bowers v. Littlewood
(Ch. 1719)

In the administration of a decedent's estate, there is no representation among collateral kin after brothers' and sisters' children, therefore, the decedent's uncle takes the estate and not the cousins.

Lincoln's Inn MS. Misc. 384, p. 194

13 November.

Upon the Statute of Distributions of Intestate Estates,[1] the question is whether the words that there shall be no representation among collaterals after brothers' and sisters' children, Pett v. Pett, Salk. 250,[2] do relate to the brothers' and sisters' children of the intestate or of the collaterals.

Vernon, for the defendant: The defendant is the uncle; the plaintiffs are the children of the aunt of the intestate. It was adjudged so by Lord Somers, and it is the constant course of the spiritual court.

Peere Williams, for the plaintiff: Words relate to the next antecedent, which here is 'collaterals'. In Pett v. Pett, the question was between a brother's child and another brother's grandchild.

Lord Chancellor [LORD PARKER]: I think that case is stronger because a grandchild may be called a child. It relates only to the brother's children of the intestate. If an uncle leaves two children and the aunt leaves three, they shall take *per capita* equally.

Lincoln's Inn MS. Misc. 11, p. 174

John Bowers and Mary, his wife, and Elizabeth Todd, plaintiffs; Thomas Littlewood, defendant.

John Church and Katherine, his wife, had issue Thomas, who survived his father and, afterwards, died intestate. The plaintiffs Mary and Elizabeth are the daughters of George Amyas by Elizabeth, his wife, who was the sister of the defendant and also the sister of Katherine Church.

The defendant, the uncle of Thomas, took administration to him. And the plaintiffs, who are the nieces of the defendant and cousins german of Thomas, the intestate, bring their bill for their distributive shares.

---

[1] Stat. 22 & 23 Car. II, c. 10, s. 4 (*SR*, V, 720).

[2] *Pett v. Pett* (1700), 1 Salkeld 250, 91 E.R. 220, also 3 Salkeld 138, 91 E.R. 738, 12 Modern 409, 88 E.R. 1415, Holt K.B. 259, 90 E.R. 1041, 1 Lord Raymond 571, 91 E.R. 1281, 1 Comyns 87, 92 E.R. 973, 1 Peere Williams 25, 24 E.R. 280, 2 Eq. Cas. Abr. 435, 22 E.R. 370.

The defendant demurs for that it appears of the plaintiffs' own showing that the defendant was the uncle of Thomas, the intestate, and next of kin and that the plaintiffs Mary and Elizabeth are only cousins german of the intestate and not related to him in equal degree with the defendant. And the question was upon the words of the Statute,[1] which says there shall be no representatives amongst collaterals after brothers' and sisters' children, whether brothers' and sisters' children must be understood the brothers and sisters of the intestate or of the collaterals.

Lutwyche: This has been settled in the Case of Pett and Pett, Salk. 250, that it must be the brothers and sisters of the intestate.

And so Mr. *Vernon* said it had been settled by Lord Somers.

Williams, e contra: 'Collaterals' are the next antecedent.

Lord Chancellor [Lord Parker] allowed the demurrer without any difficulty.

The pedigree stood thus.

```
          Thomas Littlewood
                  |
__________________|____________________________
|                      |                      |
Thomas                 Katherine              Elizabeth
(defendant)            m. John Church         m. George Amyas
                       |                      _____|_______
                       |                      |           |
                       Thomas                 Mary        Elizabeth
                       (intestate)            (plaintiff) (plaintiff)
```

So that the defendant was the uncle to the intestate and the plaintiffs Mary and Elizabeth, children of Elizabeth, aunt to the intestate.

[Other reports of this case: 1 Peere Williams 594, 24 E.R. 531, 2 Eq. Cas. Abr. 439, 22 E.R. 374.]

[1] Stat. 22 & 23 Car. II, c. 10, s. 4 (*SR*, V, 720).

417
Forth v. Chapman
(Ch. 1719–1720)

In this case, the devise over in issue was a valid executory devise.

Lincoln's Inn MS. Misc. 384, p. 230, pl. 3

17 November [1719]; at the Rolls.

Walter Gower, possessed of a term in two houses, by his will, devises to Chapman in trust for William and Walter Gower, and he gives all the residue of his estate to William and Walter Gower, his nephews, and, if either of his said two nephews shall depart this life and leave no issue, then over to the daughter of his brother, under whom the defendant claims. Walter dies without issue; William survives and conveys to the plaintiff the equity of redemption, there being a mortgage on the premises. The question is between the plaintiff, who claims under William, and the devisee over, William being dead without issue.

I think the devise over is not good by way of an executory devise but is void. If the words were if they die without issue, it should be clearly void. There is no distinction between the same words in the limitation of a freehold and a term. That the same words should not express the same intent is absurd. To construe it without issue at the time of his death is to put new words into the will. 1 Syd. 450;[1] leaving no issue and dying without issue is the same thing. There is no difference between dying without issue and departing this life and leave no issue. D. Norfolk's Case; 1 Leo. 285;[2] a devise to the son and if he die, not having issue, is the same as if he die without issue. [This is] stronger than the present case, for these words might seem to refer to the time of his death.

The precedents left with me do not come up to this case. Trinity 1709, Wicks v. Wicks; to C. for life and if he die before the expiration of the lease and leave no issue then living must refer to the time of his death; *ergo*, it is good. 17 December 1718, Hughes v. Sayer,[3] which was before me; the residue was devised to the three plaintiffs and, if any of them die without children, then to the survivor was good because the survivorship takes place at the time of their death.

---

[1] *Love v. Windham* (1670), 1 Siderfin 450, 82 E.R. 1211, also 2 Chancery Reports 14, 21 E.R. 602, 1 Levinz 290, 83 E.R. 412, 2 Keble 637, 84 E.R. 401, 1 Ventris 79, 86 E.R. 55, 1 Modern 50, 86 E.R. 724, 1 Eq. Cas. Abr. 191, 21 E.R. 982.

[2] *Howard v. Duke of Norfolk* (1681), 1 Vernon 163, 23 E.R. 388, 3 Chancery Cases 1, 22 E.R. 931, 2 Swanston 454, 36 E.R. 690, Pollexfen 223, 86 E.R. 568, 2 Chancery Reports 229, 21 E.R. 665, 2 Freeman 72, 80, 22 E.R. 1066, 1070, 79 Selden Soc. 904, 922, 999, Dodd 42, Oxford Bodleian Library MS. Rawlinson C.347; *Lee v. Vincent* (1584), 1 Leonard 285, 74 E.R. 260, also 3 Leonard 106, 74 E.R. 570, Croke Eliz. 26, 78 E.R. 291, Moore K.B. 147, 72 E.R. 497.

[3] *Hughes v. Sayer* (1718), see above, Case No. 293.

He [Jekyll] decreed for the plaintiff. On 25 June 1720, he was reversed. 25 June 1720; reheard by the Lord Chancellor.

Solicitor General *Yorke*, for the plaintiff: [There was a] devise of the remainder of the estate to the defendant in trust as aftermentioned. Then he devises 'to William Gower and, if either of my two nephew, William and Walter Gower, shall depart this life and leave no issue, then' over to the defendant. The question is whether these words are the same as dying without issue or tie it up to the parties' death. If the same words are used in the limitation of terms as of inheritance, they will signify the same thing, dying without issue, an estate tail. D. Norfolk's Case.

Lord Chancellor [Lord Parker]: If there is any case where a devise to a man and if he die without issue without giving it to the issue, I do not remember. Leo. 285; a lessee devises to his son and if he depart this world not having issue. Syd. 420, Love v. Windham.[1]

Serjeant *Chesshyre* [cited] Hopkins v. Williams, 1708, by Lord Trevor; a devise of a freehold to Edward Body and if he happen to die and depart this life not having issue [creates] an estate tail.

Lincoln's Inn MS. Misc. 11, p. 140

Samuel Forth, plaintiff; Francis Chapman *et al.*, defendants.

Walter Gore, possessed of several houses which he held under a lease from the dean and chapter of Bangor, makes his will, and, after several legacies, he gives the residue of his estate, both real and personal, to the defendant John Chapman in trust only the lease of the School of Bangor for the use of his nephews, William Gore and Walter Gore, during the lease as hereafter mentioned. And then he gives several other legacies. And then he goes on and says, as for the remainder of his estate as well as his house in Shaw's Court with all the rest of his goods whatsoever, he gave to his nephew, William Gore, and, if either of his two nephews should depart this life and leave no issue of their respective bodies, then to the daughter of his brother, William Gore, and the children of his sister Sibley Price. And he made his nephew, William Gore, and John Chapman executors, who proved the will.

Walter Gore died without issue, and William survived him and is also dead without issue, having made his will and [made] his wife executrix, who sold the leasehold premises to the plaintiff.

The question was whether the devise over was good by way of an executory devise or was a void limitation. And the Master of the Rolls [Jekyll] having taken time to consider of this matter, he now gave his opinion that the devise over was a void limitation.

[1] *Love v. Windham* (1670), *ut supra*.

He said, if the words had been that, if my nephews shall die without issue, it shall then go over, there is no doubt but such a limitation over had been void. And he said he thought there was no difference between those words and the words in the present case.

In the case of an inheritance, they would be of the same import. And he saw no reason why they should not be so in the case of a leasehold estate. He cited the case of Love and Windham, 1 Sid. 450, which he said was a case which had been often cited and was good law, and the Case of Lee, 1 Leo. 285, upon which he principally relied.

He took notice of the Case of Weeks and Weeks, in Lord Cowper's time, where the words were that, if the devisee died before the expiration of the term without issue then living, then to go over. This was adjudged to be good by way of an executory devise, and no doubt but it was right, for the word 'then' confined the dying without issue to the death of the devisee. But this case differs very much from the present case.

This decree was afterwards reversed upon an appeal to Lord Parker. *Vide post* 210.

Lincoln's Inn MS. Misc. 11, p. 210

Upon an appeal to Lord Parker from the Master of the Rolls' decree, *quod vide ante* 140, the decree at the Rolls was reversed.

Lord Chancellor [Lord Parker] said the plain meaning of the words in the will are that, if the nephews left no issue at their deaths, then the estate should go over. The words 'dying without issue' are not in all cases to be taken in a legal sense, *viz.* whenever there is a failer of issue.

The only difficulty in the present case is in respect to the objection that has been made, that the devise of the leasehold is coupled with a devise of freehold land and that, therefore, the construction of the words 'leaving no issue' must be the same when applied to the leasehold, as where it is applied to the freehold and, had it been a limitation of a freehold, it would have been an estate tail.

But I do not know whether there is any absurdity in applying the words in a different sense in respect to the leasehold and the freehold. However, if the same construction must be put upon the words with respect to both estates, why should not the freehold give way to the leasehold as well as the leasehold give way to the freehold?

The bill was dismissed.

Note, in this case was cited by Mr. *Williams* the Case of Target and Gaunt,[1] before Lord Parker, where a man devised a term to one for life and, after, to such of his issue as he should appoint and, if he died without issue, then he devised it over. It was decreed the limitation over to be good.

---

[1] *Target v. Gaunt* (1718), see above, Case No. 248.

[Other reports of this case: 1 Peere Williams 663, 24 E.R. 559, 2 Eq. Cas. Abr. 292, 359, 22 E.R. 245, 306.]

418

Studevil v. Robinson

(Ch. 1719)

A devise or descent is a satisfaction of an obligation to the devisee or heir.

Lincoln's Inn MS. Misc. 384, p. 199

18 November.

Vernon, for the plaintiff: The plaintiff Ann, the widow of Bridgman, married Studevil, who confessed a judgment to perform an agreement to purchase and settle £60 *per annum* within seven years, the £60 *per annum* to be settled on the eldest son living at his death and his heirs. He had a son, Thomas, who gave him a release of the marriage articles. Studevil, the father, by his will, gave Thomas an equivalent estate. But Thomas died in the life of his father, whereby the devise was void and the estate descended on George, the next son. The question is whether this descent is a satisfaction of the marriage articles. Wilcocks and Wilcocks, Trinity 1706, by Lord Cowper;[1] a freemen of London covenanted to purchase and settle £200 *per annum* but died without purchasing and suffered an equivalent estate to descend. The plaintiff brought his bill to have the purchase made, but it was dismissed. There are many cases where it has been construed that an equivalent is a satisfaction, though not expressed. Kemys and Thomas,[2] where a portion of £5000 was charged on particular lands with a maintenance until twenty-one and, afterwards, another portion of £5000 was charged on other lands with a different maintenance without mention of the first portion, which was provided by the marriage settlement. The plaintiff brought her bill for both portions. It was adjudged she should have but one portion.

Cowper, for the defendant George Studevil, the infant: The first question is on the release of Thomas; the second, as to the satisfaction. If the settlement had been made within seven years according to the articles, Thomas had been but tenant for life and the remainder had been to the defendant George. It is provided by the articles that, if no settlement should be made, then £1000 should be left to the eldest son.

Lord Chancellor [Lord Parker]: The release is of no avail. But is not the devise of an equivalent to the eldest son an actual settlement according to the ar-

[1] *Wilcocks v. Wilcocks* (1706), 2 Vernon 558, 23 E.R. 961, 1 Eq. Cas. Abr. 26, 156, 21 E.R. 847, 955.

[2] *Thomas v. Kemeys* (1696), 2 Vernon 348, 23 E.R. 821, 2 Freeman 207, 22 E.R. 1163, 1 Eq. Cas. Abr. 269, 21 E.R. 1037, Colles 112, 1 E.R. 206.

ticles? Thomas, the eldest son, being dead, it descends on the defendant George, as it would have done if the settlement had been made. He is by the articles within seven years to settle £60 *per annum* on the eldest son or leave him by his will £1000. If he had settled after the seven years, it had been good in equity, for the design of the articles is performed; it is to be settled on the eldest son living at the time of his death. As to the second son, George, who was the eldest at the time of his death, it was the design that the devise should be in satisfaction of the marriage articles, though the first son died in the life of the father after having released. The estate descends on George. Can he say that he will have a performance of the articles and have this estate too, which is expressly given in satisfaction?

This is stronger than any cases cited, for, had there been a settlement made, the less land would have descended and George ought not to have satisfaction out of the personal estate.

Let the Master see if the land descended is an equivalent; if not, it is a satisfaction *pro tanto.*

The testator gave a bond to Croply for £300 conditioned to purchase an annuity and settle on his daughters. By his will, he gives £300 to his executors to purchase an annuity and settle it accordingly. It is a fulfilling of the bond.

Cowper quoted Slaney and Slaney,[1] where the House of Lords adjudged that a reversion of equal value descending was not a satisfaction.

Lord Chancellor [Lord Parker]: There, it was not expressed to be in satisfaction, as it is here.

Lincoln's Inn MS. Misc. 11, p. 160, pl. 2

18 November 1719. Ann Stutteville, executrix of Thomas Stutteville, plaintiff; George Stutteville, son and heir of Thomas Stutteville by his first wife, and others, defendants.

Thomas Stutteville intermarried with Anne, the daughter of Sir George Stearne, with whom he had no portion, but, sometime after the marriage, Stearne paid and secured to be paid to Thomas Stutteville £300 as a marriage portion, in consideration whereof Thomas Stutteville executed an indenture wherein it is recited that Thomas Stutteville had not then an estate of £60 *per annum* to settle on the said Anne, his wife, but he did by the said indenture covenant to convey within seven years lands of the value of £60 *per annum* over and above reprises and free from encumbrances to the use of the said Thomas and Anne Stutteville during their lives and the life of the longer liver of them and, after their decease, to the use of the heirs of the body of the said Anne by the said Thomas begotten or to be begotten, with a remainder to the said Thomas Stutteville in fee, and also that, if the said Thomas Stutteville should die within the said seven

[1] *Slaney v. Slaney* (1714), 5 Brown P.C. 113, 2 E.R. 568.

years and before such assurance, that then he should by will give and assure the said Anne £1000, which she should dispose of after her death to her children by the said Thomas begotten, *viz.* £800 part thereof to her eldest son and £200 residue thereof to her next born child, and, for want of such issue, that then the said Anne should quietly enjoy the said £1000 without interruption, and, if Anne should die before such assurance and should have issue of her body at her death, that then the said Thomas Stutteville should settle upon the eldest of the sons of the body of the said Anne living at the time of the death of the said Thomas lands of £60 *per annum* and, for default of such issue, to the daughter or daughters of the said Anne, and, for default of such settlement, should by will give to the eldest son of the body of the said Anne living at his death £1000 and, in default of such issue, should give to the daughter or daughters the said £1000.

Thomas Stutteville confessed a judgment of £1000, which was defeasanced for the performance of the covenants in the said indenture.

Thomas Stutteville had issue by the said Anne, two sons and three daughters, *viz.* Thomas, who is dead without issue, George, Anne, married to Thomas Fauran [?], Diana, Susannah, married to James Robinson. Thomas Stutteville, the father, prevailed with his son to release the said covenant in the said indenture of 1689.

Thomas Stutteville, the father made his will and devised to his son Thomas his manor of Woodham Ferris and all the lands and hereditaments thereto belonging to hold to him and his heirs upon condition that he should pay within a year after the death of Roger Stutteville and Abigail, his wife, the testator's father and mother, £600 as follows, *viz.* £500 part thereof to the testator's daughter Diana and £100 to his son George with a power to enter for non-payment and upon a further condition that Thomas Stutteville, the son, and his heirs should accept the same premises in full [satisfaction] of all claims and demands by virtue of the indenture of February 1689 and, if he refuse so to do or should insist upon the express terms of the said settlement, then he should have no benefit by his will and, in such case, he gave the said premises to his wife and her heirs, she paying the said two legacies. He gave to his son George his estate at Wood [*blank*], Cheavely Dillingham, and Burrough Green to hold to him and his heirs; to his daughter Diana £500, and he gave other legacies to his other children, [and he] made his wife executrix and residuary legatee.

The plaintiff brought her bill to have the directions of the court touching the execution of her testator's will.

The defendant George Stutteville insisted by his answer that, his brother Thomas dying in his father's lifetime, the devise to him of the lands in Woodham Ferris was void and that the same were descended on him the defendant as heir at law of the testator discharged of all payments and conditions and that the £500 given to Diana and charged on those lands was become void, or, if it was subsisting, it ought to be paid out of the personal estate.

[It was] insisted likewise that the testator having by an express covenant obliged himself, if he survived his wife, to settle lands of £60 a year upon his eldest son which should be living at his death and also to give such son £1000 in case he neglected to make such a settlement and the testator dying without making such a settlement or making such a devise, the defendant is entitled to be paid the said £1000 out of his father's personal estate.

Lord Chancellor [Lord Parker]: The first thing the father was obliged to do was to make a settlement. And, therefore, it would have been a good performance of the covenant, though he had made the settlement after the expiration of the seven years and after the death of his wife.

As to the devise to Thomas, the eldest son, though the devise is fallen, yet the charge of the £500 and £100 is still subsisting. It is plain the father's intent was that the son should have Woodham Ferris in full [satisfaction] of the articles or that his wife should have it to make good the articles, and, therefore, the defendant George ought not to take the lands but in performance of his father's covenants in those articles if the lands are equal in value to £60 a year. And, therefore, let that be enquired by the Master. And, if they are not of the value of £60 a year, let so much land be purchased out of the personal estate as will make up the £60 a year.

In this case was cited the Case of Wilcox v. Wilcox. A man agreed on his marriage to settle lands generally, and he leaves lands to descend on his son. It was decreed to be a satisfaction of his marriage agreement.

In the principal case, there was another question, and, as to that, the case was this. One Thomas Cropley, in kindness to the defendant Susanna Robinson, who had married without the consent of Thomas Stutteville, her father, pays £300 into Stutteville's hands, and, thereupon, Stutteville gives a bond to Cropley to pay him £18 a year for his life and, after his death, to lay out the £300 in purchasing an annuity for the life of Susanna to be settled in such manner as that her husband should not receive it but that the same should be divided into twelve equal parts and one part thereof constantly paid her on the first day of every month into her own hands or into the hands of such person as she should appoint by a writing, and, until the said annuity should be purchased, he should pay the interest of the £300 to Susanna or as she should appoint.

Cropley died in the lifetime of Thomas Stutteville. And Stutteville, by his will without taking any notice of this bond, gives his executrix £300 to be laid out in purchasing an annuity for the life of his daughter Susanna to be settled in such manner as her husband could not receive it, but that the same should be divided into twelve equal parts and one part thereof be constantly paid on the first day of every month into her own hands or into the hands of any person she should alone by a writing appoint to receive the same and, until the said annuity should be purchased, the interest of the £300 at five percent should in like manner be paid by his executrix to Susanna as before directed, and, if she died before such annuity was purchased leaving issue, then he directed the £300 to be paid to such children at twenty-one.

The question was if Susanna should have two annuities purchased for her.

Lord Chancellor [Lord Parker] declared the annuity given by the will was in performance and discharge of the bond, and he ordered the £300 to be brought before a Master and laid out in the purchase of an annuity for the defendant Susanna according to the will.

419

Heaton v. Hassell

(Ch. 1719)

What the law gives the husband by the marriage is a good consideration for his making a settlement, but the husband's making a settlement does not vest in the husband the choses in action of the wife, unless it be expressly so agreed between the parties and it appears to be part of the consideration of the settlement.

Lincoln's Inn MS. Misc. 384, p. 201, pl. 1

18 November.

The defendant is the widow of T. Hassell and had a bond of £500 given to her whilst unmarried. Her husband, by his will, directs his debts to be paid out of this bond. The question is whether the husband is a purchaser of this chose in action or whether it survives to the defendant. This bond is not specified in the marriage settlement, but £160 is settled on her in consideration of her fortune generally.

Lord Chancellor [Lord Parker]: Here the defendant is made executrix. Suppose another person had been executor or residuary legatee. Could he have had it? And the creditors cannot be in a better case.

Cowper, for the plaintiff: If the settlement was made expressly in consideration of this bond, he would have been a purchaser of it.

Lord Chancellor [Lord Parker]: The settlement is made in consideration of her fortune, that is only what the law gives him in her right by virtue of the marriage. You may as well say that he is a purchaser of the inheritance of his wife's land as of her choses in action when she survives.

British Library MS. Add. 36651, f. 95

Michaelmas 6 Geo., 1719

The bill was against the defendant, as executrix of her late husband, to have a discovery of assets and a satisfaction of a debt of £150 in which the testator was indebted to the plaintiff by a bond.

The defendant, by her answer, said that only £100 came to her hands, which she has administered.

The case upon the pleadings was that the defendant, before her marriage with the testator, was seised of a real estate in Lincolnshire and had also £500 owing to her by a bond. And, before the marriage, the husband, 'in consideration of a considerable fortune' (so are the words of the deed), settled a leasehold estate on the wife by way of a jointure and also, by another deed, settled a freehold estate likewise in jointure and upon the issue of the marriage (but this deed was not produced at the hearing), both which made her jointure to be £160 *per annum*. The husband, by his will, devised all his estate, real and personal, for the payment of his debts. And he requests of his wife, whom he made executrix, that she would sell her estate in Lincolnshire for that purpose if his own proved deficient.

The defendant, by her answer, insisted on the settlements made on the marriage etc. and on her title to the Lincolnshire estate and, as to the bond debt of £500, that the security, having never been altered by her husband in his lifetime and it being a chose in action, did survive to her and could not be devised by the will nor was assets in her hands to answer the plaintiff's demands so that the whole estate was covered.

Mr. *Cowper*, for the plaintiff, said the plaintiff had no hopes but from the £500 due on the bond. And the settlement made by the husband being in consideration of her portion, of which the £500 due to her on the bond was part, the husband is a purchaser of it in the eye of a court of equity. Therefore, it is assets in equity. She had no other portion but that £500 and the estate in Lincolnshire, which she has since sold for £700, as appears by the deposition of one of her trustees.

Lord Chancellor PARKER was of opinion that it survived to the wife and was not assets liable to the plaintiff's debt. And he said they might as well make the Lincolnshire estate liable as the £500 due to the wife on the bond, for that that as well as the bond debt was a part of the portion and it was the husband's folly that he did not alter the security in his lifetime. But he said that, if the £500 was expressed in the deed of settlement of the freehold estate as part of the consideration, that might alter the case and the defendant having confessed that some assets came to her hands, let them go before a Master to see what did come to her hands and how administered and the defendant to produce the deeds and writings and, if the £500 be mentioned as part of the consideration, then to report that or anything specially.

2 Eq. Cas. Abr. 467, 22 E.R. 398

Michaelmas, 6 Geo. I.

The defendant had lands to the value of £700 and also £500 due to her upon a bond, which remained in the defendant's hands. Her husband, before marriage, makes a marriage settlement, and, in consideration of a considerable fortune and portion with his intended wife, he does grant etc., but the particulars wherein her portion did consist did not appear by the deed. And the question was, if this bond to the defendant for £500, part of her portion (being a chose in action and not called in by the husband), should be assets in equity to satisfy a debt of the husband, the wife having enjoyed the benefit of the settlement made to her out of her husband's estate, which would have been liable to the debts.

PARKER, Chancellor, decreed an account to be taken of the husband's assets, but not of this £500 bond. His Lordship said the case was so very clear that the defendant's counsel need not to argue it. Creditors, in this case, cannot be in a better condition than the executor of the debtor. And can it be imagined that, if another person had been made executor to the husband and such executor had brought a bill against the wife to compel her to assign this bond, that the court would have decreed for the executor? What the law gives the husband by the intermarriage is a good consideration for making a settlement, but the husband's making a settlement does not vest in the husband the chose in action of the wife, unless it be expressly so agreed between the parties and that appears to be part of the consideration of the settlement, for, then, the husband is a purchaser and well entitled to them in a court of equity.

420

Brunsden v. Stratton

(Ch. 1719)

The Statute for Preventing Fraudulent Devises does not prevent a person from making a voluntary settlement and breaking the descent to his heir.

A testamentary trust to pay all of the testator's debts does not distinguish one debt from another in their payment.

Lincoln's Inn MS. Misc. 11, p. 137

18 November 1719. Brunsdon *et al.*, creditors of William Stratton, plaintiffs; Mary Stratton *et al.*, executors of William Stratton, and several others, defendants.

Upon the marriage of William Stratton with the defendant Mary, Charles Raymond, her father, enters into a bond to Stratton, who was then an infant and not capable of making any settlement, with a condition to pay him £1000 so soon as he should attain twenty-one and make a suitable jointure settlement to the defendant Mary, his intended wife, for it and, in the meantime, to pay interest for the £1000 and also to pay him £500 at the death of Raymond, he the said Stratton augmenting the jointure settlement to Mary, his intended wife, proportionably to it.

Stratton, after the marriage, becomes greatly indebted, and Raymond pays the £1000 towards Stratton's debts. And he dies. After his death, J. Raymond, his son and executor, pays the £500, and, thereupon, he makes a settlement to the use of himself for life, then to his wife for life, then to trustees for 5000 years upon trust to raise £2400 for the issue of the marriage to be paid at such times and in such manner as he should by his will or any writing appoint, and, for want thereof, amongst all his children equally.

Afterwards, he makes his will and, thereby, confirms the settlement, and he gives all his lands in possession and reversion to his wife and the defendants Raymond and Itchener and their heirs. And he also gave them his personal estate upon trust that they should sell the same or any part thereof or mortgage the whole or any part and, with the moneys arising by the premises, pay and discharge all his debts. And he gives further directions touching the surplus that should remain, and he makes his wife and the two trustees executors.

The plaintiffs bring their bill to have their debts paid out of the real and personal estate and the trusts of the will executed.

The first question was if the settlement made by the testator was voluntary as to the children and void against the creditors in regard the marriage agreement seemed to extend no farther than to the making of a settlement for the jointure of the wife.

The Master of the Rolls [JEKYLL] was of the opinion it was not voluntary as to the children, it being made in consideration of the wife's portion, and that the words in the bond, 'jointure settlement', imported a settlement on the issue of the marriage as well as on the wife.

And, by Mr. *Vernon*, it was insisted and agreed to by the court that, if the settlement had been voluntary, it would have been good against the creditors according to the opinion of the Lord Chancellor in the Temple Hall, 1718, in the Case of Parslow and Weedon[1] and some subsequent cases, for Lord Parker, in that case, was of the opinion, a man, by a voluntary settlement, might break the descent and prevent his estate from coming to his heir and the Statute for Preventing Fraudulent Devises[2] has not restrained it.

Mr. *Vernon* said before this court, according to former precedents, he took it to be otherwise, but, now, it is so settled.

A second question was whether the bond and simple contract creditors should be paid *pari passu* in regard the estate is devised to the executors. And, therefore, it was said that, when the estate is sold, the money will be legal assets in their hands and ought to be applied in a course of administration.

But the Master of the Rolls [JEKYLL] was of opinion that, though the trustees are also executors, yet here is a plain trust declared in the will and it is not like where a man devises that his executors shall sell his lands to pay his debts, for, in that case, the money, when the estate is sold, is legal assets and must be applied as other assets are by law to be applied. But, in the principal case, the trust being to pay all the debts, the court, in executing that trust, makes no distinction between one debt and another. Nay, this court has gone so far as to let

---

1 *Parslow v. Weedon* (Ch. 1718), see above, Case No. 261.

2 Stat. 3 Will. & Mar., c. 14 (*SR*, VI, 320–321).

legatees, where the trust has been to pay debts and legacies, come in to be paid equally with creditors.

But, upon asking Mr. *Vernon* if it was not the course of the court to do so, he said it had been so formerly, but it was otherwise now.

[Other reports of this case: Precedents in Chancery 520, 24 E.R. 233, 2 Eq. Cas. Abr. 52, 260, 22 E.R. 46, 220.]

421

Turner v. Smith

(Ch. 1719)

In this case, the contract in issue was not so far carried into execution as not to be within the Statute of Frauds.

Lincoln's Inn MS. Misc. 384, p. 233

23 November.

The bill is to compel the defendant, a lessee, to execute a counterpart of a lease. The defendant entered by a parol lease but, afterwards, it was agreed by parol that a lease should be in writing for eleven years at £160 *per annum* and the plaintiff was to put the tenements into repair, which he has not done. It is proved that the defendant approved of the draft of the lease and has paid the rent ever since he has been in possession. The question is whether this is an agreement so far carried into execution as not to be within the Statute of Frauds.[1]

Lutwyche, for the plaintiff, cited Foxcroft v. Lister; *antea*, Gomesera v. Foot.[2]

Vernon, for the defendant: In those cases, the lessee built at the connivance of the lessor. But a bare entry is not sufficient to bring it out of the Statute.

Master of the Rolls [Jekyll]: This is an agreement touching lands, which, by the Statute is to be in writing signed by the party. There have been cases out of the Statute though within the words, as where a defendant admits an agreement by an answer; so, where a man is put into possession and lays out money but that is grounded upon a fraud in the lessor. And, in those cases, the lessee would lose his money. Butcher v. Butcher,[3] the first case after the Statute; where a man builds upon another's ground, the landlord standing by and permitting it, is bound. Here, the plaintiff must show that he performed all on his part of the agreement before he can come into this court. But here, he has not put the tenements into repair according to his agreement by parol and the lease contains only

[1] Stat. 29 Car. II, c. 3 (*SR*, V, 839–842).

[2] *Lester v. Foxcroft* (1700), Colles 108, 1 E.R. 205; *Gonawra v. Toot* (Ch. 1718), see above, Case No. 305.

[3] *Butcher v. Stapely* (1686), 1 Vernon 363, 23 E.R. 524, 1 Eq. Cas. Abr. 21, 21 E.R. 843.

part of the plaintiff's agreement, and nothing is mentioned in the lease about these repairs, but the defendant was forced to repair at his own expense.

I am of opinion that, if the plaintiff had performed his whole agreement, it would not have brought this case out of the Statute of Frauds, for all the cases cited were of the tenant's laying out money upon another's estate. But here, the plaintiff would only have repaired his own. The entry of the tenant does not bring it out of the Statute, for, by his entry, he is subject to pay the rent.

He dismissed the bill with costs.

422

Atwood v. Lamprey

(Ch. 1719)

An annuity charged on land is liable to pay land taxes.

Lincoln's Inn MS. Misc. 384, p. 234, pl. 1

24 November.

The question is whether an annuity is subject to taxes. A. mortgages land to the plaintiff for 1000 years to be void if he paid B. £12 *per annum* for life.

Lutwyche, for the defendant: It is not by way of a demise and re-demise or by way of a reservation, nor is it issuing out of the land.

Vernon, for the plaintiff, quoted Sir Thomas Seliard's Case,[1] where portions were charged on land and a maintenance which should not exceed the interest of the portions, it was adjudged the maintenance was subject to taxes.

Master of the Rolls [JEKYLL]: In the mortgage, there is a covenant to pay the £12 *per annum*. By the words of the Act,[2] a deduction is to be made where any charges are upon land whereby the owners of the land do not receive the full yearly value. I think it is so where there are equitable charges. The question here is whether the mortgagor is the true owner. He is in equity though the legal interest is in the mortgagee. When the annuity was granted, there were no land taxes. But those are by act of Parliament, and all annual payments are subject unless expressly excepted. And this is granted in lieu of dower, which is subject. *Ergo*, this is subject to taxes.

---

[1] Perhaps *Jellard v. Jellard* (Ch. 1719), see above, Case No. 388.

[2] Stat. 6 Geo. I, c. 1.

423

Livings v. Higham

(Ch. 1719)

A legacy to support Quaker preachers is valid, not being for a superstitious use.

Lincoln's Inn MS. Misc. 384, p. 234, pl. 2

15 December. At the Rolls.

Upon a Quaker's will, His Honor [JEKYLL] doubted whether a legacy given to his executors for the maintenance of their public Friends, i.e. preachers, was good or whether it was not a superstitious use. And now, he was of opinion it was good, and he relied upon the authority of John v. Gale, by Lord Cowper, 11 November 1707.[1]

N.B. *Gregson*, solicitor for the defendant, [said] where, by a deed, £15 *per annum* was settled for the benefit of an Anabaptist congregation, the court doubted whether it were not void for uncertainty and referred it to the Attorney General to state; he certified that there was not sufficient certainty.[2] The court was of opinion as to the other question, whether it was not a superstitious use, that it was not but was in the Toleration Act.[3] It was reheard Michaelmas 1712 before Lord Harcourt, who sent it to be tried at law, and it was found a legal use.

Lincoln's Inn MS. Misc. 11, p. 147, pl. 2

Livings *et ux*. v. Anthony Neat *et al*., executors of Richard Richardson.

The testator, by his will after several legacies and, amongst others, a legacy of £10 each to his executors, gives the surplus of his estate to his executors for them to dispose of as they shall see meet. And, by a codicil, he directs that any such surplus shall be disposed of by his executors to some honest public fund that wants a settlement; if not, to some honest Friend and at such terms as that he may entertain such traveling ministers of the Gospel as the testator used to do. And he further directs part of the profits to be disposed of to such faithful Friends, men or women, that should travel to preach the Gospel towards helping them towards their charge that leave their families and travel in that service. And, if his executors should see meet, they might give that or other parts of his estate to such of his relations as they might judge deserving.

The testator was a Quaker, and the plaintiff's wife was his only child. And he having made little provision for her by his will, it was insisted on for the plain-

1 *Johns v. Gale* (Ch. 1712), British Library MS. Hargrave 80, f. 121.

2 *Johns v. Gale* (Ch. 1712), *ut supra*.

3 Stat. 1 Will. & Mar., c. 18 (*SR*, VI, 74–76).

tiffs that the directions in the codicil touching the surplus were void and that the surplus ought to go according to the Statute of Distributions.[1]

The Master of the Rolls [JEKYLL] declared the executors were only trustees as to the surplus and were bound to settle and distribute the whole. But, in regard the power of distribution thereof was by the will vested in them, His Honor ordered they should attend the Master and propose how and to whom and in what manner they would have the said surplus settled and distributed and the court on the Master's report would give further directions, His Honor declaring that the trust for the traveling ministers, as they are called in the codicil, is not an unlawful trust. But he was of the opinion the executors could not appoint the whole residue of the estate but only part thereof for that purpose.

424

Pitfield v. Waller

(Ch. 1720)

Where a devise does not create an estate tail, a limitation over is valid.

Lincoln's Inn MS. Misc. 384, p. 235, pl. 1

26 January 1719[/20].

Anthony Tytler, by will, in 1668, recites that he was possessed of a long term of years in three houses. He devises them to trustees upon trust to permit his daughter Elizabeth Phipps to receive the rents and profits during her life and, from and after her decease, to permit and suffer such person and persons as shall be heir of heirs of her body and, for want of such issue, to his daughter Moor. The question is whether the limitation over is good.

Raymond, for the defendant: The word 'heir' is properly a word of limitation, not a *descriptio personae*. If a term is limited to A. for life and then to the heir or heirs of the body of A. with a limitation over, it is void. The words 'to such person as shall be his heir' make no difference.

Mead: Here are no words which tie it up to the time of Elizabeth's death. Forth v. Chapman, *ante quod vide*; James v. Richardson, Poll. 466.[2]

---

[1] Stat. 22 & 23 Car. II, c. 10 (*SR*, V, 719–720).

[2] *Forth v. Chapman* (Ch. 1719–1720), see above, Case No. 417; *James v. Richardson* (H.L. 1685), *Durdant v. Burchett* (H.L. 1690), Pollexfen 457, 86 E.R. 610, also 2 Ventris 311, 86 E.R. 458, T. Raymond 330, 83 E.R. 172, 2 Levinz 232, 83 E.R. 533, 3 Keble 832, 84 E.R. 1039, T. Jones 99, 84 E.R. 1166, 1 Ventris 334, 86 E.R. 216, 1 Freeman 458, 472, 89 E.R. 343, 353, 1 Eq. Cas. Abr. 214, 21 E.R. 998, Lincoln's Inn MS. Misc. 557, f. 94, pl. 2, Skinner 205, 90 E.R. 95, Comberbach 153, 90 E.R. 400, Carthew 154, 90 E.R. 694, Holt K.B. 223, 224, 90 E.R. 1022, 1023, 1 Eq. Cas. Abr. 214, 21 E.R. 999, Dodd 60.

Master of the Rolls [JEKYLL]: This is a plain case. The limitation over is good. The query is whether the words are to denote the quantity of the estate or are only a description of the person. I think they are only a description of the person. Peacock v. Spooner, in the House of Lords; Daffron v. Goodman, by Lord Somers; Webb v. Webb, by Lord Harcourt, contra, do not influence this case; Loyd v. Carew, Ca. Parl. 137; Cotton v. Heath, Poll. 26.[1]

Lincoln's Inn MS. Misc. 11, p. 149

Charles Pitfield v. Anne Waller *et al.*

Anthony Titler, possessed of three leasehold houses, by his will dated 7 January 1668[/69], devised them to trustees upon trust to permit Elizabeth, his wife, to receive the rents during her life and, after her decease, to permit Mary Moor, his daughter, to receive the rents of the two front houses during her life and, after her death, such person or persons as should be heir or heirs of the body of his said daughter to receive the rents during the remainder of the term.

The plaintiff is the heir of the body of Mary Moor, *viz.* son and heir of Alexander Pitfield by Elizabeth, his wife, who was the daughter and heiress of Mary Moor, and, as such, the plaintiff claims the leasehold premises devised to his grandmother. And he brings his bill to have the lease assigned to him.

The defendant claims the premises under the will of the said Mary Moor. And whether they belong to the plaintiff or the defendant was the question.

The Master of the Rolls [JEKYLL] was of the opinion that the words 'to such person as should be heir of the body of Mary Moor' did not enlarge the estate devised to her for her life, but they describe the person who was to take after her death and that the plaintiff was the person who was described by the will to take after the death of Mary Moor.

Note, in this case, the Master of the Rolls [JEKYLL] said that, in the case of a contingent limitation of a term, it was not necessary that the contingency must happen within the compass of one life. And, for this, he cited the Case of Loyd v. Cary, in Lord Somers's time, where the contingency happened in six months after the death of the tenant for life, and, therefore, having not fallen out within the compass of a life, it was for that reason decreed not to be a good limitation. But that decree was afterwards reversed by the House of Lords.

---

[1] *Peacock v. Spooner* (1688–1690), 2 Vernon 43, 195, 23 E.R. 638, 727, 2 Freeman 114, 22 E.R. 1094, 1 Eq. Cas. Abr. 362, 21 E.R. 1104; *Dafforne v. Goodman and Bolt* (1699), 2 Vernon 362, 23 E.R. 828, Precedents in Chancery 96, 24 E.R. 46, 2 Freeman 228, 231, 22 E.R. 1176, 1179; *Webb v. Webb* (1710), 1 Peere Williams 132, 24 E.R. 325, 2 Vernon 668, 23 E.R. 1036, 2 Eq. Cas. Abr. 363, 22 E.R. 309; *Floyd v. Cary* (1697), Shower P.C. 137, 1 E.R. 93, also 2 Freeman 218, 22 E.R. 1170, Precedents in Chancery 72, 106, 24 E.R. 35, 51, 1 Eq. Cas. Abr. 260, 21 E.R. 1032; *Cotton v. Heath* (1638), Pollexfen 26, 86 E.R. 500, 1 Eq. Cas. Abr. 191, 21 E.R. 981.

[Related cases: Marlow v. Smith (1719–1723), see above, Case No. 403, 2 Peere Williams 198, 24 E.R. 698, 2 Eq. Cas. Abr. 328, 22 E.R. 279; Marlow v. Pitfield (1719), 1 Peere Williams 558, 24 E.R. 516, 2 Eq. Cas. Abr. 316, 22 E.R. 435; Pitfield's Case (1728), 2 Peere Williams 513, 24 E.R. 841.]

425

Selby v. Robinson

(Ch. 1720)

An obligation to act when requested is a good consideration for a promise even though no request has been yet made.

Lincoln's Inn MS. Misc. 506, p. 21, pl. 1

Hilary 6 Geo.

A trust of 100 *per annum* was granted to one *pro concilio impendendo.* It was decreed to be performed for that, though he had not given advice, yet it was a good consideration that, when he should be asked, he was obliged to give it and, if it were not, yet a trust may be granted without consideration when it is raised, though it cannot be raised without one.

426

Tuck v. Gifford

(Ch. 1720)

Words in a will that direct that debts and legacies are to be paid charge the testator's land with the payment thereof.

Lincoln's Inn MS. Misc. 11, p. 146

1 February 1719[/20]. Master of the Rolls.

The words of the will were 'as to such estate wherewith it has pleased God to bless me, I dispose thereof as follows, in the first place, I direct all my debts and legacies shall be paid.' And then, the testator goes on and disposes of his real and personal estate.

[Jekyll] decreed that, by the words, 'in the first place, I direct all my debts and legacies shall be paid', the lands were charged with the debts.

427

Fletcher v. Dalbois

(Ch. 1720)

In a will, the words 'if she attain her age' and 'when she attains her age' are synonymous. In this case, the time of payment was annexed to the substance of the devise.

Lincoln's Inn MS. Misc. 384, p. 204, pl. 2

15 February.

Margaret Eleridge, by her will, gives the residue of her personal estate to trustees for the sole use and benefit of her daughter Mary at her age of twenty-one. Mary dies before. The question is whether it vested.

Master of the Rolls [Jekyll]: I think it is not vested. In this case, the trustees are also executors, so the naming of the trustees does not vary the case. If it were to other trustees, it would not have vested at her age. 'If she attain her age' or 'when she attains her age' are synonymous. Here, they are not trustees for her benefit until she arrives at twenty-one. The construction of trusts must be according to the rules of law. Here, the time of payment is annexed to the substance of the devise. The question seems more difficult, who are entitled to it, whether the trustees or the next of kin to the testatrix. I am of opinion that the trustees cannot have it, for they are barely trustees and nothing is intended for their benefit, but it remains part of the testatrix's estate undisposed of.

Maynard: Where there was a devise to trustees in fee to particular uses but no use is limited of the fee, Lord Cowper decreed they were trustees for the heir at law.

428

Spinke v. Storr

(Ch. 1720)

Where two persons join in lending a sum of money on a mortgage and take the security in both their names, there is no survivorship.

Lincoln's Inn MS. Misc. 11, p. 147, pl. 1

17 February 1719[/20].

[It was] decreed that, where two persons join in lending a sum of money on a mortgage and take the security in both their names, there shall be no survivorship though it does not appear how much was lent by the one or how much by the other. But, otherwise, it is in the case of a joint purchase though the purchase money is paid equally or in different proportions by the purchasers, for, in the first case, the debt is distinct and the taking a joint security does not alter the nature of the debt. And, therefore, if one of the parties dies, the survivor shall be a trustee for the executor of the party dying *quoad* his debt.

It was said by the Master of the Rolls [JEKYLL] it had been decreed there should be no survivorship of an equitable joint estate.

Mr. *Vernon* mentioned the Case of Garraway and Christ's Hospital,[1] where it was decreed that a man having lent money and taken the security in the name of himself and his wife and died, the wife should have it by survivorship and the money should not be assets of the husband.

429

Pepper v. Fryar

(Ch. 1720)

Evidence is admissible to explain facts in reference to a will but not to explain the meaning of the words of a will.

Lincoln's Inn MS. Misc. 384, p. 201, pl. 3

Hilary, 6 Geo., 11 February.

20 February 1717[/18], Christian Fryar's will gives the plaintiff's wife, Ann, her eldest daughter, £1000 payable at twenty-one or marriage. Afterwards, 15 May 1718, she gives a note for £500 to the plaintiff Pepper payable in November following as an augmentation of her daughter's portion. There was besides the mother's legacy of £1000 a portion of £2000 provided by a settlement of the father.

The first question is whether this note is a satisfaction of the legacy *pro tanto*; second, whether parol evidence can be admitted where a resulting trust belonged to the heir, whether the surplus belonged to the executor, who had a specific legacy. Calmady v. Calmady, a legacy is a satisfaction of a debt; Docksey v. Docksey, parol evidence was admitted; Littlebury v. Buckley.[2]

Mead, for the defendant: It is proved that Mrs. Fryar declared she intended the note of £500 to be in part of the legacy of £1000 and designed to have altered her will, but was prevented by death.

Vernon, for the plaintiff: It is of great consequence to admit parol evidence contrary to the will. It may indeed be admitted where it is consistent with the construction of law or to explain who was meant where two persons are of the

---

[1] *Christ's Hospital v. Gallway* (Ch. c. 1714), see above, Case No. 5.

[2] *Calmady v. Calmady* (Ch. 1718), see above, Case No. 302; *Docksey v. Docksey*, 2 Eq. Cas. Abr. 507, 22 E.R. 429 (Ch. 1708), 3 Brown P.C. 39, 1 E.R. 1163 (H.L. 1710); *Buckley v. Littlebury* (1711), 3 Brown P.C. 43, 1 E.R. 1165, 1 Eq. Cas. Abr. 245, 21 E.R. 1021, 2 Vernon 677, 23 E.R. 1040, Lincoln's Inn MS. Misc. 10, p. 86.

same name. Lytton v. Lytton,[1] where it was to explain what was meant by the lands out of the settlement; it was admitted here, but rejected by the House of Lords, and there is no case where it was admitted since, by Lord Cowper assisted with judges. If a legacy be given to a creditor of a greater sum, it is a satisfaction, not where the debt is subsequent to the will or the legacy less than the debt.

Lord Chancellor [Lord Parker]: Examinations are allowed to ascertain facts, but not to expound the words of the will. As to the declarations of the party, there is a distinction. Where the words are doubtful, it is no evidence to explain them, but only where the words are clear and some circumstance intervenes, which creates an ambiguity, you may read [depositions], it not being to control the will, but to explain a fact, where it was intended the note should be in augmentation of the portion provided by the settlement or that given by her will.

Let the Master look into the value of the estate. I reserve further directions.

Lincoln's Inn MS. Misc. 12, p. 328

18 February 1719[/20]. Pepper *et ux.* v. Fryar and Wenyeve, executors of Christian Fryar.

Christian Fryer, by her will, devised to the plaintiff Anne, her eldest daughter, £1000, to her second daughter £800, and to her youngest £500 at twenty-one or marriage. And she made her three brothers executors.

After making her will, the testatrix married her eldest daughter to the plaintiff Pepper and gave him a note for £500, and she sickened on that day and died in five days after. But, in her sickness, she declared she intended her daughters but £1000 and would have altered her will for that purpose, but she was prevented by sudden death.

The question was whether parol evidence should be admitted. The case of the Dovey and Dovey, cited, and Littlebury and Buck were read; Litton v. Litton, *contra.*

Lord Chancellor [Lord Parker]: Proof is always to be admitted to prove the circumstances of the family and the condition of the estate as if there are two persons of the same name. If a devise is to J.S. after the death of the wife, it may be proved that J.S. is the heir at law and, consequently, a devise to the wife by implication. And the circumstances that the estate is not sufficient to pay all the legacies if the £500 note is not to be taken to be a satisfaction of so much of the legacy is proper to be proved. But you shall never be admitted to prove the meaning of the words in a will or what was the testator's intention by any devise in his will.

---

[1] *Viscountess Falkland v. Lytton* (1709), 3 Brown P.C. 24, 1 E.R. 1152, 3 Chancery Reports 169, 21 E.R. 758, 2 Vernon 621, 23 E.R. 1008, 1 Eq. Cas. Abr. 210, 21 E.R. 996, British Library MS. Hargrave 80, f. 13v.

But, here, the question is whether the testatrix has not in her lifetime paid down £500, part of the £1000 she intended her daughter should have after her death.

And, therefore, he ordered the proofs to be read, and, then, he directed an account to be taken to see whether the estate would hold out. And he reserved the further determination until after the Master's report.

[Other reports of this case: 2 Eq. Cas. Abr. 353, 772, 22 E.R. 300, 657.]

430

Woodroffe v. Wood

(Ch. 1720)

An heir who destroys a will that devised land to another will be ordered by a court of equity to convey the land to the devisee.

Lincoln's Inn MS. Misc. 384, p. 202

24 February; at the Lord Chancellor's house.

A bill [was exhibited] that the defendant may convey an estate at Walton to the plaintiff which was given to the plaintiff by the will of J. Storer, which was burned with the defendant's privity. The plaintiffs were Anthony and J. Woodroff, executors.

Vernon, for the plaintiff: This court has often decreed possession without sending it to law where a deed or will has been suppressed. Haines v. Haines, Michaelmas 1702;[1] the younger son destroyed his father's will at the funeral, by which his eldest brother was disinherited. [It was] decreed the devisee to hold and enjoy though the eldest son was not privy to the fraud. Here, he is privy. Santom v. Romsey; where articles were destroyed by the defendant, he was committed until he admitted by his answer that the articles were of the purport as set out in the bill. Lord Dacres' Case, Hob.; where an estate was forfeited by Lord Dacres, [it was] decreed the Crown was to enjoy until the title deeds were produced, which were vehemently suspected to be destroyed, though the title was merely at law.

Mead: Everything is to be presumed against a person guilty of such a fraud. Hamden v. Hamden, heard at the Rolls, affirmed by Lord Cowper, affirmed in the House of Lords,[2] where a will was suppressed; [it was] decreed to be taken as in the bill though it was insisted it was proper at law. J. Woodroff proves that

---

[1] *Haines v. Haines* (1702), 2 Vernon 441, 23 E.R. 883, 1 Eq. Cas. Abr. 402, 21 E.R. 1133.

[2] *Hampden v. Hampden* (1708–1709), Dickens 26, 21 E.R. 176, 1 Peere Williams 733, 24 E.R. 590, 3 Brown P.C. 550, 1 E.R. 1492.

Cooper, an Anabaptist preacher, read Storer's will. A deponent heard part, the devise to the plaintiff and his heirs, he paying £12 *per annum* for life to the testator's daughter if unmarried, but, if she married, then only £8 *per annum*, and that it revoked all former wills and writings.

Hannah Monk [testified] that Elizabeth Wood, the defendant's wife, said that the maker of the will being dead, that she had made the will safe and had delivered it to William Glover and had given him a hive of bees and a guinea and that they had burned the will and deeds.

Chamberlain proved the draft of J. Storer's will in 1713 and that the remainder in fee was given to the plaintiff.

N.B. Part of the draft is wanting; so it does not appear how the estate is limited over, whether it is to the plaintiff or not.

Cowper, for the defendant: Where this court has decreed possession upon the suppression of a will, it has been where there was a sufficient certainty of the limitation of the estate. Here is not sufficient certainty, *ergo*, it should be sent to law, the defendant being the heir at law.

Lord Chancellor [Lord Parker]: It is plain by this draft that the defendant Elizabeth Wood, the testator's daughter, was not to have the estate, but only £12 or £8 *per annum* for life. The engrosser of the will swears that the remainder in fee was given to the plaintiff. The proof is very full. The person who destroyed the will ought not to go to a jury who may favor him. The defendant Wood must convey to the plaintiff and pay costs and account for the personal estate.

Dickens 32, 21 E.R. 179

24 February 1719[/20].

The heir at law destroys the will, whereby the estate was, as it was alleged, devised to the plaintiff. The heir at law was decreed to convey the estate to the plaintiff and his heirs. A trial was denied whether there was such a will as set out in the bill.

431
Hinton v. Bolton
(Ch. 1720)

A defendant, in his pleadings, can waive the benefit of the Statute of Frauds.

A court of equity does not carry trusts created by wills into strict settlement, as it does marriage articles.

A devise to a man 'and his issue' creates an estate tail.

Lincoln's Inn MS. Misc. 384, p. 204, pl. 1

24 February.

The plaintiff is the natural daughter of Robert Hodson, and she brought her bill to have a surrender of a copyhold, which was made by the defendant to her for life and then to her issue, rectified and limited to her and the heirs of her body. Hodson had surrendered it to the use of his will and, by his will, devised it to the defendant Bolton and Sanderson and their heirs but under a secret trust for the plaintiff. Sanderson, in his lifetime, surrendered a moiety to the plaintiff for life, remainder to her issue, and, after his death, the defendant surrendered the other moiety to the same uses but, for default of issue, to such uses as the defendant should declare by will.

The bill suggested that it was not the intent of Hodson that the defendant, who was but a trustee, should have any benefit, but that the plaintiff ought to have a power over it.

The defendant, by answer, said that he was a stranger to the trust; only that Sanderson, before his death, told him that it was intended by Hodson as a provision for the plaintiff and the issue or heirs of her body and he hoped he had done right in surrendering his moiety to the same uses as Sanderson had done.

Lord Chancellor [Lord Parker] was of opinion that, if the defendant had not admitted the trust by his answer, it had been within the Statute of Frauds.[1] But as he had admitted it, it was plainly an estate tail, for that this court does not carry trusts created by wills into strict settlement, as it does marriage articles, as in Bail v. Coleman's Case,[2] that, as this surrender is made, the issue of the plaintiff would all take jointly and only an estate for life because, in surrenders, the word 'heirs' is as necessary to create an estate of inheritance as in conveyances, whereas, in wills, to a man 'and his issue' carries an estate tail.

Therefore, he decreed the defendant to surrender the premises to the plaintiff and the heirs of her body.

---

1 Stat. 29 Car. II, c. 3 (*SR*, V, 839–842).

2 *Baile v. Coleman* (Ch. 1711), 2 Peere Williams 142, 24 E.R. 330, 2 Vernon 670, 23 E.R. 1036, 2 Eq. Cas. Abr. 309, 472, 717, 22 E.R. 261, 402, 603, British Library MS. Hargrave 80, f. 26v, pl. 2.

432

Hern v. Wood

(Ch. 1720)

An assignee of a lease who assigns over to a third person is not liable to the covenants of the original lease.

Lincoln's Inn MS. Misc. 384, p. 206, pl. 1

2 March 1719[/20]. Hern v. Wood and Lennard.

The question was how far an assignee of a lease who assigns over to a third person is liable to the covenants of the original lease.

Vernon: There have been but two cases, one where an assignee to avoid repairs assigned over to an almsman; the other where he assigned over to a prisoner, but this being a plain fraud, the lessor was relieved.

Lord Chancellor [Lord Parker]: The lease is made on the credit of the lessee, and, therefore, he is liable at law. But the assignee is entirely a stranger after he has assigned over, though, while he is in possession, he is subject to the action of the lessor. If the assignee assigns back again to the first lessee, who proves insolvent, the lessor is not damnified.

14 January 1710[/11], the plaintiff makes a lease to the defendant Wood for seven years with a covenant to uphold. Wood assigned the lease to the defendant Margaret Lennard, his mother. January 1714[/15], the house happened to be burned. The bill is against the defendant Lennard for a specific performance of the covenant to uphold, the defendant Wood being insolvent. The defendant Lennard insists she never accepted of or executed any assignment of the lease but only continued in possession to look after Wood's affairs, he having absconded, that she paid the rent, but it was Wood's money. Hill proves a draft of an assignment to Lennard and that she was present, but it was executed only by Wood.

The bill was dismissed.

Lord Chancellor [Lord Parker]: The reason why an assignee of a lease is not liable at law after he has assigned over is because there is no privity of contract between him and the lessor and the law gives him a power of assigning over. But when the assignee is liable at law in respect of repairs etc. and then assigns over to an insolvent person, this being a plain fraud, perhaps a court of equity may relieve. But this court cannot relieve where the assignee at the time of his assignment over was not liable at law.

Lincoln's Inn MS. Misc. 13, p. 133, pl. 3

2 March 1719[/20]. Herne v. Wood and Lennard.

A bill [was filed] to discover whether the defendant Wood, who was insolvent, had assigned over his lease to the defendant Lennard and to have the house rebuilt, being burnt down in the fire in Thames Street.

It was insisted on behalf of the defendant that the plaintiff, having had a discovery, he ought to have no further relief. A jury would in that case consider the circumstances and mitigate the damages.

Lord Chancellor [Lord Parker]: This is the hardest case imaginable, for the lessee remains liable to the covenants and that was the security which the lessor took for his rent and covenants, and, in an assignment, it is, therefore, proper for the lessee to take a covenant from the assignee to perform the covenants in the lease.

Where the assignee is not intended to be liable, he may take a derivative term. And, if the assignee assigns over, I see no reason for equity to relieve. He may assign back again to his lessee. As the law makes him liable as assignee, so the same law does discharge him when he ceases to be an assignee and has assigned over.

433

Spindlar v. Wilford

(Ch. 1720)

A mortgagee of copyhold lands has constructive notice of any charges on the land that appear in the court roll.

Lincoln's Inn MS. Misc. 384, p. 206, pl. 2

4 March; rehearing; Spindler v. Willfull and Ryder.

The bill is for arrears of an annuity of £5 *per annum*. In 1614, Mary Thorn, seised of two copyhold tenements in Holywell Street in the parish of Stepney, granted this annuity in fee. In 1687, the plaintiff purchased the annuity. And the tenements are descended upon the defendant Wilford, who, in 1707, mortgaged to Ryder without notice.

N.B. In 1686, there was a decree for this annuity.[1]

Master of the Rolls [Jekyll] decreed the tenements to be chargeable with the arrears and the defendant Wilford's person while in possession. But, as to Ryder, not being affected with notice, the plaintiff was to redeem here.

The plaintiff appeals. First, the plaintiff's charge is prior to Ryder. Second, Ryder came in with an implied notice, for she purchased under the copy of court roll and this charge appears on the rolls and it is incumbent on a purchaser to look into his title.

Vernon, for the plaintiff: We do not insist that the defendant Ryder had actual notice nor do we desire that it should be presumed she had. But we say she had constructive notice, as if the agent has notice or the party claims under a will. It is the same here where she claims under copy of court roll.

[1] *Spindlar v. Wilford* (1686–1687), 2 Vernon 16, 23 E.R. 621.

Lord Chancellor [LORD PARKER]: This is a case where the plaintiff is entitled to all the favor that can be. There was a former decree in 1686 for this annuity. The original grant is by surrender to A. and his heirs upon condition to pay £5 *per annum* to B. and his heirs and, on default of payment, the land to be to B. and his heirs. I do not remember that it has been determined upon a copyhold what shall be the effect of such a condition, for the grantee cannot enter as at law, but must apply to the lord,[1] who may grant it to the annuitant. It is not barely an equitable interest, but it carries with it a right to apply to the lord for an actual admittance. If the lord should admit the annuitant, this court would interpose. If the tenant of the land would pay the arrears here, the defendant has not a legal title. She has only a surrender from one who held the land upon condition. Here, both parties have only an equitable interest. The defendant would be freed by the assistance of this mortgage from a former decree and the constant payment of this annuity. But she must know this charge if she knew her own legal title. The plaintiff has a right to have this £5 *per annum*. The former decree should have been for a surrender to a third person to secure this annuity to the plaintiff. The plaintiff must have a satisfaction of the arrears from those who have been in possession. The Master must settle a conveyance to secure the £5 *per annum* to the plaintiff for the future and then to secure the mortgage made to the defendant Ryder. The plaintiff is to have his costs.

434

Syred v. Syred

(Ch. 1720)

An incomplete devise to pay debts and portions for younger children can be cured by the making the heir at law a trustee to execute the devise.

British Library MS. Hargrave 81, f. 216

Friday, 11 March 6 Geo., at the Rolls.

James Syred, by will, 20th September 1717, devised part of his estate to be sold by his executor for the payment of his debts and portions for his younger children but did not devise the same to any person for that purpose so that, upon his death, the same descended to his eldest son and heir at law, who was an infant under the age of twenty-one years.

Yet, by a bill brought by the younger children to have the estate sold and their portions raised, the Master of the Rolls [JEKYLL] was of opinion that the infant heir at law was but a trustee within the Act of 7 Ann.,[2] for enabling infant trustees to execute conveyances of their trust estates, and he directed him to

[1] land *MS.*

[2] Stat. 7 Ann., c. 19 (*SR*, IX, 89).

join in a conveyance accordingly to the purchasers and the Master to settle the conveyance.

[Other copies of this report: British Library MS. Hargrave 82, f. 218, pl. 1; Lincoln's Inn MS. Misc. 107, f. 100.]

435

Woodward v. Woodward

(Ch. 1720)

Pending an appeal, no new matter can be introduced to vary the case.

A decree made at the Rolls is not a decree until it is signed by the Chancellor, and then it becomes the decree of the Chancellor.

Pending an appeal to the Lord Chancellor from a decree by the Master of the Rolls, the plaintiff can add parties in order to execute the decree.

A demurrer that is good in part and bad in part will be overruled in toto.

Lincoln's Inn MS. Misc. 384, p. 236, pl. 4

11 March 1719[/20]. At the Lord Chancellor's house.

W., the plaintiff's grandfather, devised to the defendant, his eldest son, for 99 years if he should live so long, remainder to the heirs of his body, remainder to the plaintiff's father for 99 years if he should live so long, remainder to the heirs of his body, remainder to A. and the heirs of his body. The defendant, not having a son, committed waste. And the bill was for an injunction and an account of what waste had been done.

Master of the Rolls [JEKYLL] decreed accordingly. The defendant appealed. Pending this appeal, the plaintiff discovered that, in point of law, he had not a good title and, therefore, purchased in A.'s title, who had an estate tail vested. And he brings a supplemental bill to establish this title whereby it will appear that the decree at the Rolls is right.

The defendant demurs for that, pending an appeal, no new matter can be introduced to vary the case.

Lord Chancellor [LORD PARKER]: Before Beaumont v. Long, in the House of Lords,[1] the law was taken that this remainder was void, there being no freehold to support it. If it be considered as a present devise, it is so, but, if as a future executory devise, it may be good. Scatterwood v. Edge, Salk.[2]

---

[1] *Darbison, ex dem. Long v. Beaumont* (1713–1714), 1 Peere Williams 229, 24 E.R. 366, Fortescue 18, 92 E.R. 743, 1 Eq. Cas. Abr. 214, 21 E.R. 999, Dodd 366, 3 Brown P.C. 60, 1 E.R. 1177, Lincoln's Inn MS. Misc. 10, p. 184, Lords' Journal, vol. 19, p. 696, *sub nom. Lay v. Beamont* (Ex. 1709), Eq. Cases Exch. 604.

[2] *Scatterwood v. Edge* (1697), 1 Salkeld 229, 91 E.R. 203, also 12 Modern 278, 88 E.R. 1320, 1 Eq. Cas. Abr. 189, 21 E.R. 980, 2 Eq. Cas. Abr. 337, 22 E.R. 287, King's

As to the supplemental bill, generally, no new matter may be introduced pending an appeal, but the cause ought to be reheard upon the same evidence. The decree at the Rolls is no decree until signed by me, and then it is my decree. But the demurrer is not good because it goes not only to so much of the supplemental bill as prays the benefit of the decree at the Rolls; if it went no farther, it would be good. But it goes to so much of the bill likewise as seeks an account of waste. A plaintiff's being entitled to such account, the demurrer must be overruled.

Dickens 33, 21 E.R. 179

The defendant appealed from a decree pronounced by the Master of the Rolls in the original cause. Before it was brought on, the plaintiff filed a supplemental bill to carry the decree into execution, apprehending he had not proper parties to the decree when pronounced. The defendant demurred, *inter alia* for that the appeal was not determined.

The demurrer was overruled.

436

Ashton v. Curzon

(Ch. 1720)

In this case, the defendant's plea was held to be insufficient to bar the plaintiff's claim.

Lincoln's Inn MS. Misc. 11, p. 150

11 March 1719[/20].

The defendant pleaded a settlement made by his wife before marriage of the rectory of Whaley in Lancashire held by a lease for lives under the archbishop of Canterbury, whereby the rectory was conveyed to the defendant and his heirs in consideration of a settlement made by him at the same time upon his wife. And he averred he had no notice at or before the making of the settlement of the plaintiff's title.

It was objected that he had not carried his denial of notice for enough, for he might have notice of the plaintiff's title after the settlement and before the marriage, and, if so, he would be affected with it.

Lord Chancellor [Lord Parker]: It is said in the plea that, shortly after the making the settlement, the marriage was had. But it is not said how soon afterwards. I think it must be very clear and full notice that must affect a man after a settlement and before the marriage. But, if that were so, the defendant ought to plead it and set forth that he had no notice until after the settlement and set it

Inns Dublin MS. 92, p. 1.

out what manner of notice he had and that it was just before his marriage, when he could not retreat. And I think that would be sufficient.

As to the present case, the denial of notice is not sufficient, it not appearing how soon the marriage was had.

It was then insisted on for the defendant that the defendant might put in an answer and set forth whether he had any notice before his marriage and so it had been done in cases of the like nature. And upon this, the plea was ordered to stand over and, in the meantime, the Lord Chancellor would be attended with precedents.

In this case, it was said by counsel and agreed to by the court that, if this plea was overruled for the informality of denying notice, the defendant might turn it into an answer and insist upon the same matters as he had done by his plea and he would have the benefit of it as to the discovery that is covered thereby.

437

Plomer v. Johnson

(Ch. 1720)

An executor of a will cannot bring a lawsuit before the probate of the will.

Lincoln's Inn MS. Misc. 11, p. 152, pl. 1

Eodem die [11 March 1720].

The plaintiff as executor brought a bill to revive, and he had not set forth that he had proved the will. The defendant demurred, and the demurrer was allowed good, for an executor is not entitled to bring any suit until he proves the will, though it is not necessary for him in his bill to offer to produce the probate under seal.

438

Green v. Smith

(Ch. 1720)

The Statute of Frauds does not cover contracts for the sale of shares of stock in a company.

Lincoln's Inn MS. Misc. 11, p. 152, pl. 2

Eodem die [11 March 1720].

The plaintiff brought a bill to be paid money due upon a contract for stock.

The defendant pleaded the Statute for empowering the Mayor and Court of Alderman to appoint brokers[1] and that, in pursuance of that Act, he was ap-

[1] Stat. 8 & 9 Will. III, c. 32 (*SR*, VII, 285–287).

pointed a broker and had entered into a bond of £500 penalty to the Mayor of London conditioned, among other things, not to buy or sell stock for himself and that he had taken an oath faithfully to discharge the office of a broker. And he insisted that the discovery prayed by the bill, if the things therein charged were true, might subject him to the penalty of the bond. And, as to so much of the bill as sought the discovery of any parol agreement, he pleaded the Statute of Frauds and Perjuries.[1]

The Master of the Rolls [JEKYLL], upon opening, disallowed the plea as very frivolous. As to the Statute of Frauds, he said it did not extend to South Sea [Company] stock, there being no such thing in being at the time of the Statute.

But query, for I have been told by Mr. Mead that Lord Cowper adjudged *contra* upon a plea of the Statute of Frauds etc.,[2] for he was of opinion that a contract for stock was within the Statute though there was no such stock in being at the time of the Statute as well as a contract for any new invented commodity.

Note it was said by the Master of the Rolls [Jekyll] in another cause that, if a man confesses a parol agreement, it shall bind him notwithstanding the Statute of Frauds. And so, he said, it was adjudged soon after the making of that Statute.

The Master of the Rolls [JEKYLL] seemed to doubt very much whether a settlement made after marriage in pursuance of a parol agreement before marriage was not voluntary in regard it was made in pursuance of an agreement that was not binding to the party.

But Mr. *Vernon* seemed to differ in opinion, and he said the man, in that case, had done nothing but what, in justice, he ought to do and, therefore, the settlement was not voluntary.

Query.

439

Loyd v. Read

(Ch. 1720)

Where an annuity is purchased and held and the interest is received by the purchaser, he or she is the owner of it even though it is in the name of a third person.

Lincoln's Inn MS. Misc. 384, p. 237

15 March 1719[/20].

The question was whether an Exchequer annuity of £14 *per annum* purchased by Mrs. Stevenson, the defendant's grandmother, in the name of the defendant was an absolute gift to the defendant or the defendant was only a trustee.

---

[1] Stat. 29 Car. II, c. 3, s. 5 (*SR*, V, 840).

[2] Perhaps *Nunnes v. Hill* (Ch. 1716), see above, Case No. 121.

Mrs. Stevenson received the interest during her life and, by her will, has given [it] to the plaintiff.

Lutwyche, for the defendant: This is stronger than the common cases where a purchase in the name of a child or grandchild is construed to be a gift and an advancement. But here, the defendant is in some measure a purchaser, for his father, in order to induce Mrs. Stevenson to purchase this annuity entered into a bond of the same date with the annuity to pay her the money or allow her £7 *per annum* for life in case the annuity should not be duly paid her.

Vernon, for the defendant: In the case of an advancement, it is the same as a voluntary conveyance, and the party cannot revoke it.

Mead, for the plaintiff: In the case of a purchase by the father, it is not presumed an advancement if the father declares his intention otherwise. Here, the grandmother had the interest during her life and the same reason for her having power to dispose of it.

Lord Chancellor [Lord Parker]: It has been taken that a purchase of land in the name of a child has been a provision for him. Here, it is the grandmother, and she receives the interest during her life so as it could not be a provision during the life of the grandmother.

As to the father's bond, there is no mention of any advantage to the granddaughter, but he only hoped that, the granddaughter's use [?] being in the grandmother, she would not give the annuity from her. So the bond does not vary the case. The grandmother always thought that she had power over this annuity. It is plainly a trust for the grandmother. The plaintiff, who claims under the grandmother's will is entitled to the annuity, and the defendant must deliver up the tally and order and pay costs.

[Other reports of this case: 1 Peere Williams 607, 24 E.R. 537.]

440

Edgley v. Blackburne

(Ch. 1720)

In this case, the devise in issue did not create an estate tail by implication.

Lincoln's Inn MS. Misc. 11, p. 188, pl. 2

22 March 1719[/20].

Lands were devised to Ewer Edgley for life without impeachment of waste, then to trustees to preserve contingent remainders, then to the first and other sons in tail male of Ewer Edgley, a remainder to his daughters in tail. Then follows these words, 'and if he shall die without leaving issue or that such issue shall die without issue', then he devises it over.

It was argued by Mr. *Williams* that these last words created an estate tail in Ewer Edgley. And he cited a case, which was this. Lands were limited to one for life, remainder to his first, second, third, fourth, fifth sons in tail male and goes no farther as to the sons, and then follows, 'and if he shall die without issue male', then the lands are limited over. This, he said, was adjudged an estate tail by implication.

Lord Chancellor [Lord Parker] said the reason why it was so adjudged was for that, otherwise, if there was a sixth son, which there might be, he could not take. He said, in the present case, the words must be understood to mean the issue mentioned before, that is to say, if he should die without sons and daughters or, leaving such, they should die without issue. And, therefore, he thought there was no estate tail by implication in Ewer Edgley.

[Other reports of this case: 1 Peere Williams 600, 24 E.R. 534, 2 Eq. Cas. Abr. 62, 182, 313, 324, 660, 702, 22 E.R. 55, 156, 265, 276, 277, 554, 590.]

441

Wall v. Theedam

(Ch. 1720)

The party that first brings the case to a hearing has the right to open the case and proceed with his evidence first.

A bill of complaint cannot be scandalous unless it is also impertinent.

The Court of Chancery cannot set aside a will.

British Library MS. Hargrave 83, p. 7, pl. 1

In the cause of Wall and Theedom, there were cross-bills. Theedom's bill had been filed some years before Wall's, but Wall had set down the cause for hearing. It was disputed whose bill ought to be opened first.

My Lord [Lord Parker] consulted the Register and ordered his bill to be opened first who had set down the cause for hearing.

Lincoln's Inn MS. Misc. 384, p. 152

22 April.

The defendant excepted to the Master's report that the plaintiff's bill was not scandalous. The bill charged that the testator's will was altered etc. by the defendant, who wrote it and made himself the residuary devisee.

Vernon, for the plaintiff: A bill cannot be scandalous unless it be impertinent. It is necessary to be charged and put in issue; otherwise, it cannot be proved. If a bill prays a discovery from a defendant of what is criminal, the defendant may demur because no man ought to be compelled to accuse himself. But yet it is necessary to be charged [so] that it may be proved, as in Wycherly and

Shrimpton,[1] where Lord Cowper was of opinion that, although the suggestions in the bill were of a very heinous nature, yet they were not scandalous because relevant. So in Sacheverel and Sacheverel.[2] If the will was only concerning personal estate, it being proved in the spiritual court, it could not be shaken here. And then those charges could not be relevant. But here the testator was seised of a real estate, which is disposed of by the will, and we are proper here to discover whether there were any forgery or imposition in obtaining this will.

The defendant having excepted that the bill was scandalous and impertinent, the Lord Chancellor [Lord Parker] overruled the exception.

Lincoln's Inn MS. Misc. 384, p. 210, pl. 3

8 November.

The bill was to set aside a forged devise of the surplus to the executors. The forgery appears plainly upon the will itself.

Lord Chancellor [Lord Parker]: This court cannot set aside the will. The proper remedy is in the spiritual court where you may have relief though it is proved in common form. It is not like Bransby v. Kerrick,[3] where it was the man's will though obtained by false suggestions; therefore, I decreed the executor [to be] but a trustee. Here, this was not the testator's will, but [it was] plainly inserted without his knowledge. [I will] retain the bill until it is determined in the ecclesiastical court.

Lincoln's Inn MS. Misc. 11, p. 180

8 November 1720. Wall v. Theedham.

A bill [was exhibited] to set aside a will which had been proved in the spiritual court on the account of fraud, it being charged that the words in the will which gave the surplus to the executors were inserted without the testator's privity or, at least, added after his death, and that it was so appeared pretty plainly by the will, for, before the devise of the surplus, the testator had given the executors £10 apiece and a suit of mourning.

Lord Chancellor [Lord Parker]: It does seem to me as if there had been some unfair practice. But what can I do with it here? This matter is proper for the spiritual court. And, if it is as you say, that court would set aside that part of the will which has been foisted in. The will has been only proved in common form, and, therefore, it is still open to be contested in the spiritual court. And I will give the plaintiff an opportunity of doing it and retain the bill for that purpose.

Note in this case was cited the Case of Bransby and Kerridge, before Lord Parker,[4] where a will was set aside, which had been proved in the spiritual court,

---

1 *Wycherley v. Shrimpton* (1719–1720), see above, Case No. 359.

2 *Sacheverell v. Sacheverell* (1717), 1 Strange 35, 93 E.R. 368.

3 *Bransby v. Kerrick* (1718), see above, Case No. 301.

4 *Bransby v. Kerrick* (1718), see above, Case No. 301.

but that was upon the head of fraud, for it really was the testator's will, but he had been drawn in to make it by several false suggestions and fraudulent transactions. But this differed from the present case, for the will in question is supposed not to be the testator's will as to what concerned the disposition of the surplus, which is a matter properly and only cognizable in the spiritual court and, if it is proved there, that the devise of the surplus was foisted in without the testator's privity, that court will grant a probate only of the rest of the will.

[Related cases: Wall v. Theedam (Ex. 1711), Dodd 227, Equity Cases Exch. 664.]

442

Seagood v. Neale

(Ch. 1720–1721)

An oral contract to sell land is unenforceable pursuant to the Statute of Frauds.

Lincoln's Inn MS. Misc. 11, p. 209

1 May 1720.

A bill [was exhibited] to have a specific performance of an agreement for the sale of lands. The plaintiff agreed to sell the defendant some lands for the sum of £246, and the defendant paid the plaintiff a guinea in part [performance], and, at the same time, he wrote a letter to Mr. Leonard, an attorney, in the words following, *viz.* 'Sir, be pleased to show the bearer the writings and let him have them, I having agreed for the disposal of them. Your humble servant, /s/ *R. Neale.*'

The defendant first demurred, and the demurrer was overruled. Then he answered and submitted the agreement and the payment, but he said it was by parol only, and he insisted on the Statute[1] and offered to pay back the guinea.

Note Leonard had a mortgage on the estate, and he is made a defendant. And the bill, as to him, is to have a redemption.

Lord Chancellor [Lord Parker]: The letter is nothing. The intent of the Statute is to prevent perjury in witnesses who might swear the purchase money was more or less or that there were more or less land included in the agreement. Now, this letter does not prevent that mischief, for here is nothing certain in this letter. It does not appear what houses were here agreed for or to whom of for what.

In the Case of Moore and Hart,[2] there was a parol agreement for giving a portion, the marriage was had, and a letter from the father, whereby it appeared

---

[1] Stat. 29 Car. II, c. 3 (*SR*, V, 839–842).

[2] *Moore v. Hart* (1682–1684), 2 Chancery Reports 284, 21 E.R. 680, 1 Vernon 110, 201, 23 E.R. 352, 412, 1 Eq. Cas. Abr. 22, 21 E.R. 844.

he had proposed to give a £1500 portion with his daughter, was decreed to bring the case out of the Statute. But the reason why the court has gone so far is because the marriage cannot be undone. And so, where an agreement has been executed on one side, the court has carried it into execution on the other, as, where an agreement has been by parol for a lease and the party has been put into possession and has laid out money, the court has carried this into execution, for, otherwise, the party who refuses to stand to the agreement shall have the benefit of the money laid out and so take advantage of his own wrong.

The bill must be dismissed with costs.

1 Strange 426, 93 E.R. 613

S. agreed to sell an estate in land to O. and wrote to his agent to deliver the title deeds to O., he having agreed to dispose of it to him. Afterwards, S. sold this estate to D., who had notice of this transaction. O. brought a bill against S. and D., insisting that the letter brought the case out of the Statute of Frauds and Perjuries.

But Lord Chancellor [Lord Parker] held it did not because the agreement does not appear in it.

Lincoln's Inn MS. Misc. 384, p. 241, pl. 1

1 May. At Westminster. Seagood v. Neal and Lennard.

A guinea paid in part [performance] of a contract for land does not bring it out of the Statute of Frauds. Where cases within the words are construed not to be within the intent of the Statute, they are either expounded upon a fraud, as when a mortgagee has an absolute conveyance and refuses to execute a counterpart or where the agreement is carried into execution as by putting into possession etc. or where it is grounded upon a letter or other writing. The whole terms of the agreement must appear in such writing.

[Other reports of this case: Precedents in Chancery 560, 24 E.R. 251, 2 Eq. Cas. Abr. 49, 22 E.R. 43.]

443

Appleyard v. Wood

(Ch. 1720)

A devise of a trust of copyhold lands is within the Statute of Frauds.

A person who is a beneficiary of a will is not competent to be a witness to its execution, but this rule does not apply to someone who afterwards acquires an interest.

Lincoln's Inn MS. Misc. 11, p. 208, pl. 1

12 May 1720.

The question was whether a copyhold estate surrendered to the use of a will would pass, though the will was not executed according to the Statute of Frauds,[1] it being insisted that the land passes by the surrender so that the will was only in the nature of an appointment and that copyhold land is not within the words of the Statute, which extends only to lands[2] devisable, which copyhold was not before the Statute.

Lord Chancellor [Lord Parker]: The copyhold passes by surrender. But, in this case, the surrender was to A. and B. and their heirs to the uses in his will so that nothing passes by the will but a trust. Now, if a trust of lands is devised, must not the will be executed according to the Statute? I shall not determine the question whether the will must be executed according to the Statute or no. It is certain it is within the mischief and, if it is not within the Statute, I do not know but a parol will may be sufficient where there is no surrender to the will.

Upon the whole, Lord Chancellor [Lord Parker] seemed to be of opinion that the will must be executed according to the Statute.

Note it was agreed in this case that, if a will executed in the presence of three witnesses who were at the execution of it competent etc. good witnesses and might have been examined to prove the will etc. afterwards one of the witnesses happens to be a party interested in the estate by something that fell out after the execution of the will, as by taking a lease of some of the land or being heir to one of the devisees or the like, yet, if the will is proved by the other witnesses to be executed in the presence of three witnesses, it is well enough, for the Statute does not say the will must be proved by all three witnesses. But otherwise it is if one of the witnesses is a devisee or legatee in the will.

---

1 Stat. 29 Car. II, c. 3 (*SR*, V, 839–842).

2 wills *MS.*

8 Viner, Abr. 1289

A., seised in fee of copyhold lands, makes a surrender to the use of B. and C. and their heirs to the use of his will, and he devises the lands to D. Query if a devise of copyhold lands is good in this case without the circumstances required by the Statute 29 Car. II of Frauds in devises of lands be duly observed.

Parker, Chancellor, was of opinion that the circumstances required by the Statute of Frauds in devises of lands, ought to be observed in this case, for, by this surrender, the fee of the copyhold was in the surrenderees and only a trust devised by the will, which cannot pass by the devise without the circumstances required by the Statute of Frauds in relation to devises of lands to be duly observed.

But the counsel insisting that a devise of copyhold is not within the Statute of Frauds, Lord Chancellor [Lord Parker] said that, if the surrender had been only to the use of the will, that might have been a question in this case, but now it is not. However, he inclined to think it necessary in that case, but would not determine that point now, that not being the case before him.

[Other reports of this case: Select Cases *tempore* King 42, 25 E.R. 212, 2 Eq. Cas. Abr. 232, 764, 22 E.R. 197, 648.]

444

Cater v. Web

(Ch. 1720)

A remainderman is not entitled to possession of title deeds held by the life tenant, but a reversioner is.

Lincoln's Inns MS. Misc. 11, p. 208, pl. 2

16 May 1720.

The defendant's husband, by will, devised the land in question to the defendant, his wife, and, after her death, to the plaintiff in fee. The plaintiff brings his bill for the deeds and writings offering to confirm the estate of the tenant for life.

[It was] decreed the writings to be brought before a Master, for the plaintiff claiming a remainder only and not as a reversioner, he was not entitled to the deeds and writings, for, he being a stranger and not the heir at law, he could not confirm the defendant's title in regard that, notwithstanding such confirmation, the heir at law might dispute the title. But otherwise it is where the reversioner comes for the writings, for, upon his confirming the estate of the tenant for life, the writings shall be delivered to him.

445

Bale v. Wivell

(Ch. 1720)

A court of equity will grant relief against fraud and order a bond to be re-delivered.

Lincoln's Inn MS. Misc. 384, p. 208, pl. 1

16 May.

A bill [was exhibited] to be relieved against a bond to repay £350 to the defendant on the death of the plaintiff's wife without issue, it being gained when the plaintiff's affections were engaged to the defendant's daughter and no part of the marriage contract. Turton v. Benson.[1] The bond was dated 9 May 1715; the settlement the 11th; the marriage the 19th.

Lord Chancellor [Lord Parker]: This is a fraud. It was first proposed to the plaintiff's father, and he rejected it with indignation, and, then, the defendant drew in the plaintiff. An agreement may be reasonable to refund part in case the wife die within a limited time, as a year or two, because the husband's expense would be lessened. But here, if the wife had lived forty years and then died without issue, it was to be repaid. The bond must be delivered up to the plaintiff.

446

Hobart v. Burridge

(Ch. 1720)

This case concerned the administration of a decedent's estate.

Lincoln's Inn MS. Misc. 11, p. 155

23 May 1720. Mary Hobart, only daughter of Francis Hobart, an infant, plaintiff; John Burridge and others, defendants. At the Rolls.

Upon the marriage of the plaintiff's father with Mary Burridge, articles were entered into whereby Francis Hobart, senior, the plaintiff's grandfather, covenanted to surrender some copyhold lands to the use of the plaintiff's father for life, then to Mary, his intended wife, for life, then to the use of the eldest or only son of the marriage and his heirs charged with the payment of £1400 unto and amongst all other the children or child of that marriage in such proportions and at such times as the plaintiff's father by a will or writing should appoint and, for want of such appointment as the wife, if she survived, should appoint and, for want of her appointment, then to and amongst such said child and children in equal proportions at twenty-one or marriage. Francis, the grandfather

[1] *Turton v. Benson* (Ch. 1718–1719), see above, Case No. 326.

surrendered the lands pursuant to the articles. Mary, the wife, dies, leaving issue, the defendant Francis, her son, and the plaintiff and Hannah, her two daughters.

The plaintiff's father, after his wife's death, by a deed poll reciting the articles and surrender, limits and appoints the trustees to whom the surrender was made to surrender the premises after his death to the use of his son and his heirs charged with and subject to the payment of £1400 to trustees [and] their executors at the end of one month next after his death in trust for the plaintiff and her sister, Hannah, in equal proportions and to be paid them at their respective ages of twenty-one or marriage and, after the end of the said month and until they should attain the age of sixteen, there should be unto or for their use in lieu of interest £20 apiece for their maintenance and, from sixteen until twenty-one or marriage, £25 apiece.

Shortly afterwards, the father died and, after his death, Jane, his youngest daughter, died, an infant of tender years. And the defendant Burridge has taken administration to her during the minority and for the benefit of the plaintiff and her brother.

447

Howard v. Rooke

(Ch. 1720)

Where a person makes a contract to convey real estate and dies before executing the conveyance, his heir will be ordered to make the conveyance and the purchase money will be ordered to be paid to the executor.

Lincoln's Inn MS. Misc. 11, p. 156

23 May 1720. William Howard, plaintiff; Elizabeth Rooke, executrix of Edward Rooke, and Edward and Elizabeth, son and daughter of Edward, deceased, defendants. At the Rolls.

The plaintiff contracts with Edward Rooke, the defendant Elizabeth's testator, for the purchase of ground rents in Drury Lane for £1260, and he paid him a guinea in part. And, thereupon, Rooke gives a receipt in these words:

> Received July 8th, 1719, of Mr. William Howard the sum of £1 1s. 0d. as earnest of my estate in Drury Lane, being eight houses of the value of £70 *per annum* and £12 improved rents *per annum*, which on making a good title and conveyance of the same to his order, I am to receive the sum of £1260 of lawful money. Witness my hand. /s/ *Edward Rooke.*

Shortly after and before any conveyance executed or prepared, Rooke died, having made his will dated 11 July 1719 and his wife executrix. And he leaves the estate to descend upon the defendant, his son.

The bill is for a specific performance of the agreement.

[JEKYLL] decreed a performance of the articles and that the money should be paid to the executor, the estate upon the foot of the articles being to be considered in equity as turned into money, and the heir was decreed to convey when he comes of age, and, in the meantime, the plaintiff is to hold and enjoy.

448

Payne v. Stratton

(Ch. 1720–1725)

Witnesses may be examined to prove the application of the words in a will but never to prove the meaning of the words in a will or the testator's intention.

If a chattel real is devised to one for life and, if he dies without issue, to another, the devise over is void and the whole term is in the first devisee.

Lincoln's Inn MS. Misc. 11, p. 188, pl. 1

29 May 1720.

In this case, it was said by Lord Chancellor [LORD PARKER] that you may examine witnesses to prove the application of words in a will, as where the testator devises to his son John and he has two sons of that name, but you shall never examine to prove the sense or meaning of the words in a will or what was the testator's intention.

Lincoln's Inn MS. Misc. 12, p. 137

16 January 1724/25.

The case upon the special matter of the Master's report after the hearing was that William Pain, by will, gives one moiety of his real and personal estate to his sister, Anne Paine, and to the heirs of her body lawfully begotten or to be begotten, and, for want of such issue or heirs of her body, he gives the said moiety after the decease of his said sister Anne to the children of his sister, Mary Stratton, equally among them.

The testator died seised and possessed of a considerable real and personal estate, and the greatest part of the personal estate consisted of South Sea [Company] stock.

Anne Paine, the testator's sister, brought her bill against the executor and the children of her sister Stratton, praying that the South Sea stock might be transferred to her, she claiming an absolute interest in the personal estate by the devise to her and the heirs of her body.

And the question was whether the devise over to the children was void as to the personal estate.

And the Commissioners [to Hold the Great Seal] JEKYLL and GILBERT seemed to be clear of opinion that the plaintiff had an absolute interest in the personal estate and might dispose thereof as she thought fit and that the devise over was void.

But Commissioner Raymond being absent, they said they would consult with him and then give judgment.

Commissioner JEKYLL said the judges have made the same construction on devises of chattels real as of freehold lands so that, if a chattel real is devised to one for life and, if he dies without issue, to another, the devise over is void and the whole term is in the first devisee and that it is the same as a devise to one and the heirs of his body of a chattel real, remainder to another; the remainder over is void. And this, he said, was the Case of Love and Windham.[1] And yet, he said, it was against the common acceptation and the grammatical construction of the words that a man who leaves issue and such issue afterwards dies without issue, that this man is said to have died without issue. But this cannot now be shaken.

Note, in the principal case, were cited the cases of Pinbury and Elkin, C, 120, and Forth and Chapman, *liber* C, 140, 210.[2]

[Other reports of this case: 3 Brown P.C. 99, 1 E.R. 1203, 2 Eq. Cas. Abr. 325, 348, 22 E.R. 277, 296.]

449

Palmer v. Palmer

(Ch. 1720)

Where the funds are different, the sums are different, and the times of payment are different, all gifts to the same recipients by settlements and devises by wills and codicils are payable.

Lincoln's Inn MS. Misc. 384, p. 238, pl. 2

23 June 1720. At the Rolls: affirmed by the Lord Chancellor.

The question is whether the plaintiffs, the granddaughters of Sir Anthony Craven, are entitled both to the portion provided by a settlement and also to the portions given to them by his will and codicil. In 1708. Sir Anthony made a voluntary settlement upon trust to raise £2000 to be paid the plaintiffs at twenty-one or marriage. But he always kept the deed in his own custody. In 1712, by will, he gives the plaintiffs £500 apiece and, by a codicil, he gives the plaintiffs £500 apiece more if his son Samuel, who was an alien, should be naturalized and enjoy the premises, which happened accordingly.

---

[1] *Love v. Windham* (1670), 1 Siderfin 450, 82 E.R. 1211, 2 Chancery Reports 14, 21 E.R. 602, 1 Levinz 290, 83 E.R. 412, 2 Keble 637, 84 E.R. 401, 1 Ventris 79, 86 E.R. 55, 1 Modern 50, 86 E.R. 724, 1 Eq. Cas. Abr. 191, 21 E.R. 982.

[2] *Pinbury v. Elkin* (Ch. 1719), see above, Case No. 404; *Forth v. Chapman* (Ch. 1719–1720), see above, Case No. 417.

Master of the Rolls [JEKYLL]: Sir Anthony's having the deed in his own custody did not give him a power of destroying it like the case of Clavering v. Clavering, 1704, in the House of Lords.[1]

Second, if Sir Anthony had forgot his former provisions or was under a false persuasion in a collateral matter, it would not avoid the legacies. The funds are different, the sums are different, and the times of payment are different.

Third, satisfaction is not to be presumed in a case of bounty, but only in a case of a debt; *ratis debitor non praesumitur donare.* Savile v. Savile; Duffield v. Smith, in the House of Lords, December 1692.[2] There was no satisfaction because the funds are different.

Fourth, the cases where portions were not twice raised were when both are charged on real estate. Jesson v. Jesson; Kemys v. Thomas; Copley v. Copley, 6 July, 10 Ann. [1711].[3]

Here, the plaintiffs are entitled to £1000 apiece by the deed and to £500 apiece under the will and to £500 apiece by the codicil.

Lincoln's Inn MS. Misc. 13, p. 72, pl. 3

23 June 6 *Georgii.* Theodosia Palmer, plaintiff; Samuel Palmer and others, defendants.

Sir Anthony Craven, by indenture 28 April 1708, conveyed the manor of Sparsholt in Berkshire to trustees to the use of himself for 99 years if he lived so long, after the determination of that term, then the premises should stand charged with £1000 apiece to the plaintiff and Anne Palmer, her sister, his two granddaughters, to be paid at twenty-one or marriage and to be raised by the rents of the premises or by mortgage and £40 a year apiece in the meantime.

Afterwards, Sir Anthony Craven makes his will and thereby gives to the plaintiff and her sister Anne and the defendant Elizabeth Pountney, another granddaughter, £500 apiece subject to the provisos thereinafter mentioned and declared that, if the will of William Craven, his son, should be adjudged a good will as to such legacy as was given to the defendant Elizabeth Pountney, then he gave the £500 which he had given to her to the plaintiff and her sister. And, if either of his three grandchildren died before their legacies became payable, the

---

[1] *Clavering v. Clavering* (1704–1705), 2 Vernon 473, 23 E.R. 904, Precedents in Chancery 235, 24 E.R. 114, 7 Brown P.C. 410, 3 E.R. 267, 1 Eq. Cas. Abr. 24, 21 E.R. 845, 2 Eq. Cas. Abr. 351, 22 E.R. 299.

[2] *Savile v. Savile* (Ch. 1719–1721), see above, Case No. 383; *Duffield v. Smith* (1692), 2 Vernon 258, 23 E.R. 767, 2 Freeman 185, 22 E.R. 1150, 1 Eq. Cas. Abr. 204, 21 E.R. 991, *sub nom. Smith v. Duffield*, 2 Vernon 177, 23 E.R. 717.

[3] *Jesson v. Jesson* (1691), 2 Vernon 255, 23 E.R. 766; *Thomas v. Kemeys* (1696), 2 Vernon 348, 23 E.R. 821, 2 Freeman 207, 22 E.R. 1163, 1 Eq. Cas. Abr. 269, 21 E.R. 1037, Colles 112, 1 E.R. 206; *Copley v. Copley* (Ch. 1711), 1 Peere Williams 147, 24 E.R. 333, 2 Eq. Cas. Abr. 639, 22 E.R. 536, British Library MS. Hargrave 80, f. 48.

legacy of her or them so dying to go to the survivor. If either of them married in his lifetime without his consent, then he revoked her legacy and gave her 1s. only and gave her legacy to the unmarried equally or such as should be married with his consent. And, afterwards, by a codicil [he] thereby directed that, if the defendant Palmer should, either by his will or by any other deed enjoy the said manor, then he gave to his said granddaughters the further sum of £500 apiece and to be paid out of his personal estate subject to such provisos and contingencies of death and marriage as were mentioned in his will.

The plaintiff brings her bill to be paid the portion provided by the settlement and the legacies given her by the will and codicil. And the question was if the legacies were not a satisfaction of the portions by the settlement or whether the plaintiff should have both.

The Master of the Rolls [Jekyll] declared that the plaintiff was entitled to the sum of £1000 given her by the said deed and the two sums of £500 each given her by the testator's will and codicil, there being no power of revocation in the settlement and the said £1000 being thereby charged on the said testator's real estate only and the two sums of £500 being charged on the testator's personal estate and being given upon contingencies could not be taken to be in lieu or satisfaction of the said £1000 given by the deed. And, therefore, he decreed both to the plaintiff.

450
Savile v. Blacket

(Ch. 1720–1722)

A person who prevents another from making a will will be considered as a trustee to carry out the intentions of the decedent who would have made a will but for the prevention.

Lincoln's Inn MS. Misc. 12, p. 235

6 July 1720.

Sir William Blackett left two sons, William and John, and two daughters. He might have more, but two were all named in the case. Sir William Blackett made his will, and he made his son John executor and residuary legatee. He, afterwards, married one of his daughters to Savile and agreed to leave her worth £500 more than he had already given her by his will. The son, upon notice of this, promised he would pay the £500. And he was decreed so to do. And, although the son denied he made such a promise and the proof did not come up to an express promise, yet the said Chancellor [Lord Parker] declared he would take it as all one, whether the son made an actual promise to pay the money or used such words as made the father believe he would do it.

British Library MS. Hargrave 83, p. 3

Blackett v. Blackett.

Thynn and Thynn,[1] a case cited by *Sir John Chesshyre* in the case of Blackett and Blackett. Thynn had made his son executor and residuary legatee, but, afterwards, he altered his mind and determined to make his wife executrix and residuary legatee and would have made a new will for that purpose. But his son said 'Sir, you are weak and in pain; do not give yourself the trouble of making a new will. I faithfully promise it shall be as you intend and your wife shall have the residue of your personal estate as duly as if she had been declared in the will the residuary legatee.' The court decreed the son to be only a trustee of the residuum for the wife.

Oldham and A.,[2] cited also by *Sir John Chesshyre* in the same case. The uncle of Oldham had by his will devised to him £40 *per annum* out of certain lands. There were but two witnesses to the will. The uncle, being apprised that this devise was not valid for want of such a number of witnesses as the Statute of Frauds[3] requires, wrote to A. to let him know that he intended for this reason to make a new will; A. wrote back to him and promised by his letter that the devise should be punctually complied with and, therefore, he need not be at the trouble of making a new will. The uncle dies without altering his will; A. refuses to pay the annuity; Oldham brings his bill; A. pleads the Statute. [The plea was] overruled, and [he was] decreed to pay the annuity to Oldham.

Lincoln's Inn MS. Misc. 12, p. 29

25 January 1721[/22].

Sir William Blacket, by a settlement, was tenant for ninety-nine years if he lived so long, remainder to trustees for preserving contingent remainders, with a remainder to his first and other sons in tail, with other remainders over. And, in the settlement, there was a power for Sir William to charge the estate with £1000 for daughters' portions to take effect after his death. The trustees for preserving etc. having surrendered to the eldest son, a recovery was suffered, in which Sir William joined, and a new settlement was made. And, afterwards, Sir William, by his will executes his power.

And the question [was] if Sir William had not extinguished his power, it being insisted on that this was a power annexed to his estate and, therefore, having parted with his estate, he had extinguished his power.

It was agreed to be otherwise if the power was not annexed to the estate.

---

1 *Thynn v. Thynn* (1684), 1 Vernon 296, 23 E.R. 479, 1 Eq. Cas. Abr. 380, 21 E.R. 1116.

2 *Oldham v. Litchford* (1705), 2 Freeman 284, 22 E.R. 1214, 2 Vernon 506, 23 E.R. 923, 1 Eq. Cas. Abr. 231, 21 E.R. 1011, 2 Eq. Cas. Abr. 44, 22 E.R. 39.

3 Stat. 29 Car. II, c. 3, s. 5 (*SR*, V, 840).

Lord Chancellor [Lord Macclesfield]: The suffering of the recovery of itself is not an extinguishment of the power, for the charge was not to take place until after his death. And, therefore, being only a tenant for ninety-nine years if he lived so long, the power was not annexed to his estate. But then his joining in a new settlement will amount to an extinguishment of the power, for there is no doubt but a man may release a power or declare it shall be extinguished, and, though Sir William Blacket has not declared so in the new settlement, yet he has done what amounts to such a declaration.

[Other reports of this case: 1 Peere Williams 777, 24 E.R. 610, 2 Eq. Cas. Abr. 568, 672, 22 E.R. 479, 564.]

451

Collington v. Bromfield

(Ch. 1720)

An arbitral award that was entered as an order of the court by the consent of the parties can be attacked only by a bill of review.

British Library MS. Hargrave 83, p. 1, pl. 1

13 July 1720. First seal after Trinity term.

An award was made by the order of the court and the consent of the parties is in the nature of a decree. And, if a party to the award brings a bill in the cause after the award is finished but before he has complied with the terms of it, his proceeding is wrong and he has no right to an answer, for such a bill is a bill of review and is to be governed by the printed rule concerning a bill of review.

This bill was for a discovery of matters in the manner of obtaining the award in order to set it aside. His Honor [Jekyll] said the bill could not now be brought without special license of the court though, perhaps, before the award be confirmed, such a bill of discovery might not be improper and yet he knew no instance of such a bill being brought upon an award.

452

Anonymous

(Ch. 1720)

The question in this case was whether a contract to buy land should be set aside due to major fluctuations in the general economy.

British Library MS. Hargrave 83, p. 1, pl. 2

Eodem die [13 July 1720].

The South Sea [Company] stock then rising, the effects of that began now to appear in court by attempts to lay open purchases again to new biddings notwithstanding persons had been confirmed the best purchasers.

The court seemed to hold that, if there had been a deposit, if one party was compellable to stand to the bargain, the other should also be bound.

Some of the suggestions for laying these purchasers open again were that, by the rise of land and the advanced price which might now be had, all the creditors might be fully satisfied, whereas, if the terms of the former biddings stood, half of them would not be satisfied, that, by the death of some of the parties, the suit was abated, that some of the principal creditors had not notice of the bidding. And several other allegations and contrivances were brought before the court in order to have the advantage of a new bidding.

The court determined none of these motions, but referred them to a master to state the circumstances of the sale[1] of purchase.

453

Anonymous

(Ch. 1720)

The question in this case was the proper investment of assets paid into court.

British Library MS. Hargrave 83, p. 2

Eodem die [13 July 1720].

There were also several motions that the master might be at liberty to subscribe lottery annuities into the South Sea Company. The court said they could not order it, the terms which the South Sea Company would give not being then known. My Lord [Lord Parker] said he could not give leave to fling a merryman with the infants' money; besides, the Act of Parliament[2] gave no authority for subscribing these annuities belonging to infants as it did for the long

---

[1] Sic in MS.

[2] Stat. 5 Geo. I, c. 19.

annuities. But he made this order that the master might sell or dispose of the annuities for the advantage of the infants. And this was the farthest he would go, except in one case where the annuities were devised to the son and, after him, to the father. In this case, at the instance and request of the father, he gave leave that the annuities should be subscribed.

454
Attorney General v. Acton

(Ch. 1720)

A devise must be certain in order to be a proper testamentary disposition.

Lincoln's Inn MS. Misc. 11, p. 177

14 July 1720.

A.B., by his will, gives £100, or £50 perhaps, to be distributed in books for the poor of Stanton. And he gives other legacies in the like uncertain manner as to the poor of Stanton 50s. or £5 [and] to Cousin C., £50, £30, or £20.

Upon a bill brought for the legacies given to the poor against the executors, who admitted assets, it was insisted on for the defendants that the word 'perhaps' is an adverb and governed by the verb 'give' and it makes the bequest wholly uncertain.

Now, in money legacies, the least is to be taken even where the bequest is to a charitable purpose. And so is the civil law.

The last words in a will are to be regarded as being supposed [to be] the last intention of the testator. Godolphin, 429.[1]

Master of the Rolls [Jekyll]: The will, though it is proved to be a will and must now be so taken, seems to me to be no more than the heads[2] of a will. The uncertainty is not relative to the £50 only, but it goes to the whole devise and tears it up by the roots. And, therefore, I am of opinion the whole devise is void for uncertainty. But, in regard the defendants have submitted to pay £50, I may decree it upon that foot.

---

[1] J. Godolphin, *Orphan's Legacy.*

[2] I.e. outline.

455

Atwell v. Marriot

(Ch. 1720)

If a defendant pleads a matter which, if true, is a flat bar to the plaintiff's title and that plea is overruled for not being well pleaded, he may by an answer insist upon the same matter again in bar of the discovery.

Lincoln's Inn MS. Misc. 11, p. 165

30 July 1720.

The defendant pleaded herself a purchaser under her marriage settlement, and she denied notice at the time of the settlement, but she had not denied notice before the marriage. And for this cause, the plea was overruled.

The defendant put in an answer and amended the denial of notice. And she insisted upon the same matters as she did by her plea in bar of any relief or other discovery than what she had made by her answer. And the question was if she could do this.

Note the bill was for a discovery of a settlement made by the plaintiff's great-grandfather prior to the defendant's marriage settlement.

Lord Chancellor [Lord Parker]: There is no difference between a plea and an answer but this, that the plea is to cover something that may tend to the defendant's prejudice. Now, if a defendant pleads a matter which, if true, is a flat bar to the plaintiff's title and that plea is overruled for not being well pleaded, he may by an answer insist upon the same matter again in bar of the discovery. But, if the plea is not a flat bar in itself to the plaintiff's title, as in the principal case, for the plaintiff's title under the first settlement may be good notwithstanding the defendant's settlement, in that case, the defendant cannot turn her plea into an answer and insist on the same matters in bar of the discovery.

456

Loyd v. Griffith

(Ch. 1720)

A Roman Catholic heir can sell land to a Protestant.

Until a sale or conformity by a Roman Catholic heir, the Protestant heir may enter and take the profits, having such an interest that he may maintain an action of ejectment.

Lincoln's Inn MS. Misc. 11, p. 157, pl. 1

2 August 1720.

Upon arguing the defendant's plea, these things were laid down by the Master of the Rolls [JEKYLL]:

First, that the Statute of 11 & 12 King William,[1] which gives the profits of lands etc., where the Papist does not conform, to the Protestant heir, does not hinder the descent to the Papist heir, but, notwithstanding the Statute, the legal estate descends to the Popish heir and he may sell to a Protestant;

Secondly, until such sale or conformity, the Protestant heir may enter and take the profits and he has such an interest that he may maintain an [action of] ejectment as a tenant by elegit or statute staple may do and, until he has entered and recovered in [an action of] ejectment, he cannot bring a bill in equity for an account of the profits.

457

Clavering v. Johnson

(Ch. 1720)

Where trustees have approved the accounts of their agent, a suit for an account by the beneficiary of the trust should be against the trustees only and not against their agent.

Lincoln's Inn MS. Misc. 11, p. 157, pl. 2

The plaintiff brought his bill against the defendants, who were trustees for him under the will of his mother, for an account of the profits of his estate received during his minority and also against the defendant Johnson, who had acted as a bailiff under the defendants, the trustees.

The defendant pleaded several accounts stated with the trustees and the balance paid and vouchers delivered.

It was objected that the trustees could not state any account whereby to conclude the plaintiff, they being only trustees and accountable to him.

---

[1] Stat. 11 Will. III, c. 4, s. 4 (*SR*, VII, 587).

But, notwithstanding, the plea was allowed by the Lord Chancellor [Lord Parker], who said the defendant Johnson was only a servant under the trustees and they were the proper persons to settle his accounts and, although, as between Johnson and the plaintiff, those accounts could not be [look]ed into, yet, as between the plaintiff and the trustees, all accounts would be still open and they would be answerable for all the money which came to the hands of the defendant Johnson.

[Other reports of this case: Precedents in Chancery 535, 24 E.R. 240, *sub nom.* Clavering v. Westley, 3 Peere Williams 402, 24 E.R. 1120, 2 Eq. Cas. Abr. 9, 225, 22 E.R. 8, 191.]

458

Duke of Dorset v. Girdler

(Ch. 1720)

Where a person is in possession of land and another person sets up a title to that land but does not disturb the plaintiff's possession, but only announces he will do so in the future, a bill to perpetuate testimony is proper.

Lincoln's Inn MS. Misc. 11, p. 178

3 August 1720.

The plaintiff's bill is to examine witnesses who are aged and infirm *in perpetuam rei memoriam* for established his title to the sole fishery in the River A. And the bill charges that the defendant [Serjeant Joseph Girdler (d. 1724)] threatens to set up a right to a separate fishery in that river after the witnesses are dead. But he does not charge that the defendant had given the plaintiff any interruption in the enjoyment of his fishery.

As to so much of the bill as sought to examine witnesses *in perpetuam etc.*, the defendant demurred for that the plaintiff had not established his title at a trial at law and for that he is under no incapacity of bringing his action.

And for support of this demurrer was cited the Case of Winne and Harris, before Lord Keeper Wright, where there was the same demurrer to a bill brought for the examination of witnesses *in perpetuam etc.* touching a right of common and, upon great debate, the demurrer was allowed.

But, in answer to this case, it was said that the plaintiff had there suggested that the defendants had entered on the common and committed trespasses and he might have brought his action and, therefore, it was improper to bring a bill to establish the testimony of his witnesses until his right has been settled by a trial at law. But, in the present case, the plaintiff does not say by his bill that the defendant has interrupted him in the enjoyment of his fishery, but only threatens to do so when his witnesses are dead, and, therefore, the plaintiff cannot bring any action at law.

Lord Chancellor [LORD PARKER]: It is most certain that, if a man will bring a bill to examine witnesses *in perpetuam etc.*, pretending title to an estate of which the defendant is in possession, such a bill may be demurred to. But, if the plaintiff is in possession and another only sets up a title but does not disturb the plaintiff by entering on that estate, but only gives out he will do so, such a bill is very proper, for, otherwise, the plaintiff is without a remedy, for he cannot bring an action.

Indeed, if the plaintiff does not show by his bill that the defendant has disturbed him and, in fact, he has done so, the defendant may then plead his title and that he has interrupted the plaintiff and insist that the plaintiff ought to bring his action. And until he has done so and established his title at law, he ought not to examine his witnesses *in perpetuam rei memoriam*. But, if no such interruption or disturbance appears by the bill, a demurrer is improper.

The demurrer, for these reasons, was overruled.

Lincoln's Inn MS. Misc. 384, p. 239, pl. 2

The bill was to examine witnesses *in perpetuam rei memoriam* on a suggestion that, when the plaintiff's witnesses were dead, the defendant threatened to controvert a right of a fishery. The defendant demurred, for that the plaintiff had not established his title at law. It was overruled

Lord Chancellor [LORD PARKER]: The difference is, where a person is in possession, he cannot bring an action against a man for pretending a right without an actual disturbance. His only means to prevent a disturbance is by perpetuating the testimony to maintain his possession. But, where a man is out of possession, he shall not be admitted to bring a bill to perpetuate testimony before he has established his title at law.

[Other reports of this case: Precedents in Chancery 531, 24 E.R. 238, 2 Eq. Cas. Abr. 181, 22 E.R. 155.]

459

Anonymous

(Ch. 1720)

If a plaintiff has taken no action in a lawsuit for a year, he cannot proceed without giving the defendant notice by a subpoena.

British Library MS. Hargrave 83, p. 4, pl. 1

5 August 1720. The last seal after Trinity term.

If a plaintiff has rested a year without any process carried on, he cannot move the court for any order without first taking out a subpoena for the defendant to make an attorney. And if the defendant becomes in the nature of a plaintiff, as in account, and proceedings have rested above a year, he must take out such a subpoena against the plaintiff before he can move for any order, which was the present case.

460

Anonymous

(Ch. 1720)

Where a defendant is in default, having made no defense, a court of equity will grant an injunction to stay proceedings that are properly in another court.

British Library MS. Hargrave 83, p. 4, pl. 2

Upon a motion for an injunction to stay proceedings at law for debts and to stay a suit in the ecclesiastical court for some legacies, it was suggested that the executor had brought a bill in order to adjust an account of the assets for the due and proportional payment of the debts and legacies of the testator.

The Master of the Rolls [Jekyll] said he could not do it, for the legatees were proceeding in a court that had the proper jurisdiction. But the motion being made upon notice and there being no defense, he granted it.

461

Pool v. Sacheverel

(Ch. 1720)

A public advertisement for witnesses to come forward in a case is an invitation to perjury and is punishable as an attempted subornation of perjury.

British Library MS. Hargrave 83, p. 5

The marriage of one Mrs. Sacheverell had been long controverted. And, at length, upon an appeal to the [Court of] Delegates, [it was] held good by them unanimously. A daughter of this marriage claimed a parcener's share of Sacheverell's estate and had been long kept out of it by the dispute about her mother's marriage. Poole [a solicitor], by the advice of an eminent practiser, who desired his name might be concealed, published an advertisement in the *Gazette* offering a reward to any person that would come in to prove that the persons' names who were entered in the register book of the Fleet and were insisted upon to be the feigned names of Mrs. Sacheverell and her husband did belong to other persons and that the entry there was not upon their marriage.

It was urged by *Sir Robert Raymond* that this was a most scandalous attempt to suborn evidence. My Lord Chancellor [Lord Parker] had ordered precedents to be searched. And he insisted upon one where Mr. Justice Tracy had committed a person for endeavoring to suborn.

He [LORD PARKER] spoke of Mr. Poole as one whom he knew to be a very honest man and whom he believed incapable of a design to suborn evidence and which he would not do to gain the estate in question. But he thought to divest himself of all prejudices in doing justice and must not be swayed by the private opinion he had of a man. This was a matter wherein the justice and credit of the nation was concerned. The *Gazette* went abroad, and if such a *si quis* to all rogues to come in, give evidence, and earn money went abroad in a paper published by authority, foreigners must have a strange opinion of our proceedings. He ordered, therefore, Poole to be committed and an advertisement to be published in the *Gazette* that the person who had published the former advertisement in the *Gazette* was committed by order of the Court of Chancery. He spared Poole's name and said he would not have that inserted because it might hurt his reputation, which he would favor as much as he could being persuaded that he did not intend to suborn any evidence. But his private judgment of him was not a reason for dispensing with the punishment of a proceeding which evidently had a direct tendency to invite men to swear for reward and if it was not discouraged and punished in the first instance, it might become a common practice and would be the safest and surest way of tempting men to perjury.

[Other reports of this case: 1 Peere Williams 675, 24 E.R. 565, 2 Eq. Cas. Abr. 222, 22 E.R. 189.]

462

Knipp v. Wall

(Ch. 1720)

The question in this case was how the share of a child of a citizen of London should be treated after the death of the father, the child having died under age in the lifetime of the father.

One defendant can have an account taken by a Master in Chancery against a co-defendant.

British Library MS. Hargrave 83, p. 6

Michaelmas, 25 August 1720. The case of Sir Randal Knipe *et al.*

A. dies, being a citizen of London. He leaves three children and a wife. One of the children dies under age. It was questioned by the Master of the Rolls [JEKYLL] how the orphanage part should go.

Mr. *Mead* said it had been settled in two cases in this court that it should survive to the other orphans by the custom of the City and should not go according to the Statute of Distributions.[1] One was the case of Rawlinson and Rawlinson in Lord Harcourt's time;[2] the other was the case of Ambrose and Ambrose in Lord Cowper's time.

N.B. In this case, the Master of the Rolls [Jekyll] upon consulting the Register said that one defendant might have an account against another defendant as well as against the plaintiff where the cause was sent to a master.

Lincoln's Inn MS. Misc. 11, p. 158

25 October 1720. Knipe v. Wale *et al.*

A freeman of London dies, and he leaves a wife and three children, *viz.* two sons by his first wife and a daughter by his second wife, the youngest son having attained twenty-one dies; then the daughter dies, being about seven years of age, and the elder brother takes administration to her.

The question was if the daughter's orphanage part did belong to the surviving brother by the custom of London.

It was agreed on all hands her share survived by the custom, she dying under age, and was not subject to the Statute of Distributions.

But the Master of the Rolls [Jekyll] seemed to make some doubt whether it did not survive to the mother as well as the brother.

But this was much exploded at the bar. And Mr. *Mead* said it had been decreed in the Case of Ambrose and Ambrose and Rawlinson and Rawlinson that the orphanage share of a child dying under age, by the custom, went to the surviving children, upon which the Master of the Rolls [Jekyll] desired to see that precedent.

Lincoln's Inn MS. Misc. 384, p. 208, pl. 2

25 October.

Burgess Draper, a freeman of London, leaves three children. One dies under age. Query whether the orphanage share goes to the surviving children exclusive of the mother.

Mead quoted Ambrose v. Ambrose, by Lord Cowper, [and] Rawlinson v. Rawlinson, by Lord Harcourt, that the mother is excluded.

Precedents in Chancery 537, 24 E.R. 241

In this case were cited a case of Ambrose v. Ambrose and another of Rawlinson *cont.* Rawlinson, where it had been certified to be the custom of London, and it was accordingly decreed by the Lord Chancellors Harcourt and Cowper, successively, that, if a City orphan dies before twenty-one, his orphanage part survives to the other orphans and that he can make no disposition by will to con-

---

[1] Stat. 22 & 23 Car. II, c. 10 (*SR*, V, 719–720).

[2] *Rawlinson v. Rawlinson* (Ch. 1714), see above, Case No. 3.

tradict it, but, if he dies after twenty-one, at which time he might have by will disposed of it, there, though he die intestate, it shall go, according to the Statute of Distributions, between his mother and surviving brothers and sisters and that, in the other case, the survivorship holds only as to the orphanage part belonging to himself, for that, if he had by survivorship the part of any other of his brothers or sisters, that should go according to the Statute of Distributions.

And it was also said that, if a man married an orphan, yet, until twenty-one, his right was not so vested as to prevent his wife's share from surviving in case she died before twenty-one, though, whether the marriage was before or after twenty-one, the husband was fineable and might be committed if he had not the license of the Court of Orphans.

[Other reports of this case: 2 Eq. Cas. Abr. 267, 22 E.R. 226.]

463

Ramsden v. Oldfield

(Ch. 1720)

Marriage is a good and valuable consideration to support a contract.
An objection to the lack of proper parties can be waived.

British Library MS. Hargrave 83, p. 7, pl. 2

26 August 1720.

Upon a treaty of marriage between the plaintiff and her husband, since deceased, the estate to be settled upon her was given in at £1000 *per annum*. But it appearing that there was an encumbrance of a £100 *per annum* annuity payable to the defendant Oldfield, it was insisted on the behalf of the plaintiff that the estate should be cleared of this encumbrance. And one Appleyard, who was concerned in making the match, promised that it should or that he would be bound to make the jointure good to the plaintiff to the value of £1000 *per annum*. Thus far, as I take it, the proof was parol. *Sed quaere*. But there was a letter under Appleyard's hand, in which he expressed himself thus, 'I will oblige myself to clear the jointure lands of the annuity.'

The plaintiff now brought her bill against the defendant as being consenting to this promise and against the heir and executors of Appleyard to make it good.

Query whether the executors and heir of Appleyard were not decreed to pay the plaintiff an equivalent for the annuity issuing out of the jointure lands.

Lincoln's Inn MS. Misc. 384, p. 209

27 October.

On the marriage of the plaintiff with her late husband, his father settled lands which were subject to a charge of £100 *per annum* to Oldfield and agreed to give the plaintiff a bond to indemnify against that charge and desired one Appleyard to join in that bond. Appleyard writes a letter promising that he would so do and that he thereby obliged himself to do it. Ramsden, the father, dying insolvent, the bill was against the heir and executor of Appleyard, having devised his estate for the payment of debts.

The Lord Chancellor [Lord Parker] looked upon Appleyard's letter as a bond executed and decreed the plaintiff's jointure to be disencumbered out of Appleyard's estate.

Lincoln's Inn MS. Hill 29, p. 51

Michaelmas 7 Geo. I.

On the hearing of the cause this day, it appeared to be this. John Ramsden, senior, in 1690, charges his estate with an annuity of £100 *per annum* payable to Oldfield for life, and, about 1709 on a treaty of marriage between his son and the plaintiff, the plaintiff's counsel insist that security be given to indemnify the estate proposed to be settled as a jointure on the plaintiff from this annuity, on which Ramsden, senior, writes to Mr. Appleyard, acquainting him therewith and desiring him to be a security. Appleyard, in return, writes to him 'You may assure yourself I am very ready to join with you in signing a bond for the performance of the covenant you mention for the taking the payment of the annuity on yourself, and I do hereby oblige myself thereto.'

On showing this letter to the plaintiff's counsel, they were satisfied. The writings were signed, and Ramsden, junior, and the plaintiff were married, Ramsden, senior, executing the bond alone without Appleyard's joining in the same. Ramsden, senior, then Appleyard, then Ramsden, junior, die.

The plaintiff, the widow of Ramsden, junior, now brings her bill to have the jointure estate relieved of this annuity against Oldfield, suggesting the annuity was obtained by fraud without consideration etc. and against the executor and the devisee of Appleyard and the administrator *de bonis non* of Ramsden, senior, who denies assets.

Lord Chancellor [Lord Parker] made the following decree.

First, as to the annuity granted to Oldfield being so long duly paid and acquiesced under as since the year 1690, it can scarcely be contested. There is no color to pretend a fraud in it, and, though there was no consideration, being without fraud, it is well. Therefore, as to Oldfield, the bill is dismissed with costs.

Second, as to relief of the plaintiff against Appleyard, the objections are (1) that it is a voluntary undertaking of Appleyard without consideration, (2) that it is for the benefit of a person other than him to whom the undertaking was made and the letter written, (3) that it has been slept on now these eleven or twelve years and been paid by Ramsden, junior. In answer to these, it is plain Appleyard wrote this for the encouragement of the match, that the lady's counsel insisted on a security, and that this letter was in answer to one Ramsden sent him and was showed to the plaintiff's counsel for their satisfaction. As a private letter, it is a present engagement, for he says 'and I do hereby oblige myself'. These words answered their design, and the counsel did very well in resting on this satisfaction, and, as they would not allow it without, it was not voluntary, for, however voluntary it was with respect to him who made it, yet it is part of the consideration of marriage. And, though the lady acknowledges in her answer to the cross-bill that it was no consideration with her to the marriage, yet, as it is a consideration of and a part of the settlement, it is a part of the terms of marriage and so a consideration sufficient, for it is not necessary to the consideration of a contract that the party making it should profit by it; it is sufficient if another loses by it.

As to the letters being written to Ramsden, senior, it alters not the case since it was written for the satisfaction of the plaintiff's counsel as such. As to its being slept on and not demanded of Appleyard, he never agreed to enter into a sole bond without Ramsden, senior.

And as to the acquiescence with regard to the father and not suing Ramsden, senior, it would have been hard for a lady at the time of living with her husband's father to commence a suit against him and to disturb the peace of the family at a time too when it was very probable in a course of nature Ramsden would outlive Oldfield.

Wherefore I think an account must be taken, and, if the executor of Appleyard has sufficient assets, the plaintiff must be indemnified out of the personal estate. If not, the devisee of Appleyard's real estate must pay the annuity, and a part of the real estate should be set aside for that purpose as a security for the payment of the annuity while due.

The plaintiff must have her costs.

Lincoln's Inn MS. Misc. 12, p. 286

A marriage being treated on and the estate which was agreed to be settled being subject to an annuity, a relation of the father of the intended husband writes a letter wherein he promises to become bound with the father to indemnify the estate from this annuity.

The marriage took effect, and the wife, after the death of her husband, brings a bill for a specific performance of the agreement in the letter and that the defendant might indemnify her jointure from the annuity.

It was decreed the defendant, pursuant to his promise in his letter, though it was a *nudum pactum* and collateral to the marriage agreement, should indemnify the estate from the annuity.

4 Viner, Abr. 453

Michaelmas, 7 Geo.

A bill [was exhibited] to be relieved and indemnified against an annuity of £100 *per annum* charged upon the plaintiff's jointure and payable to the defendant Oldfield for his life etc. upon this case. Mr. Ramsden, the plaintiff's late husband, treating with the plaintiff's friends and relations about a marriage with the plaintiff, did propose to settle certain lands in jointure upon her. The proposals being laid before counsel in order to draw a settlement, it was objected upon looking into the title that the lands proposed to be settled in jointure were subject to this rent charge of £100 *per annum* to the defendant Oldfield for life. And the plaintiff's counsel did insist that Mr. Ramsden ought to give security to indemnify the plaintiff's jointure from this charge, and, thereupon, Mr. Ramsden did give a bond to indemnify. But that not being thought a sufficient security, he offered to get the defendant Appleyard, a man of a considerate estate, to be bound with him for a security. And, upon his application to Mr. Appleyard, who was his friend and kinsman, Mr. Appleyard, by letter directed to Mr. Ramsden, writes thus, *viz.* that he is willing to be bound with him, *viz.* Mr. Ramsden, to indemnify the lady's jointure from the said annuity and does by this his letter oblige himself so to do. This letter being produced to the plaintiff's counsel, he was satisfied with it, and, thereupon, the settlement was made, and the marriage took effect, and there was a bond drawn pursuant to this agreement, which was executed by Mr. Ramsden, but never executed by Mr. Appleyard. Mr. Ramsden died insolvent in 1717. And Mr. Oldfield's annuity being secured by demise and re-demise of part of the jointure lands, he brought an [action of] ejectment against the plaintiff to recover his rent charge.

And, thereupon, the plaintiff brings her bill in this court against the executors of her husband and against the executors of Mr. Appleyard and also against his heir at law, to whom he devised all his real estate subject to the payment of his debts. The principal point in this case was if the heir at law and devisee subject to the payment of debts of Mr. Appleyard should be liable to indemnify the plaintiff's jointure from this rent charge by force and virtue of this letter to Mr. Ramsden without having executed the bond to indemnify Mr. Ramsden, the plaintiff's husband dying insolvent and the executors of Mr. Appleyard having no assets.

The defendant's counsel insisted that the heir at law of Mr. Ramsden, as well as his executors, ought to have been made a party to his suit, for, if he had assets by descent, he would be liable to satisfy the whole; Mr. Appleyard, being only a surety, supposing his heir to be bound by this letter, ought not to be charged. Secondly, [he argued] that Mr. Appleyard had no consideration for indemnifying the plaintiff's jointure from encumbrances, and, therefore, it was a *nudum pactum* and not binding; thirdly, that this promise of Mr. Appleyard was in its nature barely executory and parties concerned in interest ought to have come into this court for a specific performance of this agreement in his lifetime and during Mr. Ramsden's lifetime and then Mr. Appleyard might have made himself safe by taking a collateral security; fourthly, that this letter cannot bind his heir at law and devisee.

Parker, Chancellor: It is not so much as suggested in all the pleading in this cause that Mr. Ramsden left assets real or personal to save the defendant harmless from this rent charge. And the exception of want of proper parties ought to have been made before the cause was at hearing if the defendants would take advantage of it. And, therefore, he overruled the exception. Secondly, [he held] that there was a sufficient consideration for this promise or undertaking of Mr. Appleyard, *viz.* the marriage, and such a consideration is good at law, for, though no profit accrues to the promisor, yet the other party, without this promise, would be subject and liable to a loss or damage, and that is a sufficient consideration to support an [action of] *assumpsit* at common law. Thirdly, [he held] that this promise of Mr. Appleyard is direct and positive in the present tense, *viz.* 'and I do by this my letter oblige myself so to do', and, though this letter was directed and sent to Mr. Ramsden, yet it was written with an intent to be shown to the plaintiff's counsel to satisfy him that the lady's jointure should be indemnified from the rent charge. And it seems it did so, for, immediately thereupon, the jointure was accepted and the match was made, which very likely would not have gone on without it. Fourthly, though this letter of Mr. Appleyard's would not bind his heir at law, it not being in the nature of a debt by specialty, but by simple contract only and the heir not named in it, yet it will bind him as devisee of the real estate subject to the payments of debts, for, thereby, the lands are liable to the payment of all debts whatsoever.

And he decreed an account to be taken of what is due to the defendant Oldfield for the arrears of his annuity to be paid by a day to be appointed by the Master, otherwise, the injunction in this cause to be dissolved, that the plaintiff be reimbursed what she shall so pay by the defendant, the devisee of Mr. Appleyard, who is to give such security as the Master shall approve to indemnify the plaintiff from all future payments.

[Other copies of this report: 2 Eq. Cas. Abr. 390, 22 E.R. 333.]

464

Emblyn v. Freeman

(Ch. 1720)

When lands are settled or devised upon trust to be sold and any part of the money is undisposed of, it shall go to the heir.

Lincoln's Inn MS. Misc. 11, p. 175

Michaelmas term 1720.

Joshua Aylworth conveys his estate to trustees to be sold after his death and, out of the moneys arising thereby, to pay his debts and several specific sums of money thereby appointed to be paid. And, after the payment thereof, he directed that the overplus of the money should be divided amongst the plaintiffs and the defendants Mary Emblyn etc., share and share alike, a sum of £200, which, if the remainder amounted to so much less, should be liable to a note under the hand of him the said Joshua Aylworth and payable to the persons therein named, being first taken thereout, and he directed the trustees to pay the £200 according to the note.

There being no note found or produced after Aylworth's death, the Master of the Rolls [JEKYLL], upon a bill brought for the sale of the estate, decreed that Aylworth having made no appointment as to the £200, it belonged to his heirs at law. And he ordered the same to be paid accordingly out of the surplus moneys arising by the sale of the estate.

The persons entitled to the surplus appealed to the Lord Chancellor from this decree.

Lord Chancellor [LORD PARKER]: The only question is whether the £200 is to be considered as real or personal estate. I think nothing is more certain than that, when lands are settled or devised upon trust to be sold and any part of the money is undisposed of, it shall go to the heir. Suppose there had been no disposition of the surplus at all, it must have gone to the heir according to Ratcliff and Roper's Case.[1]

Then it was insisted by Mr. *Cowper* that Mr. Aylworth, in this case, had disposed of the whole surplus but subjected it to the payment of £200 as he should appoint by the note and, he having made no such appointment, the £200 must sink into the surplus.

Lord Chancellor [LORD PARKER]: Mr. Aylworth does not direct that the surplus shall be liable to the £200 note, but he says the £200 shall in the first place be taken out of the surplus and applied to discharge this note so that the £200 must be first taken out before the surplus can be divided, and, when it is taken out and there is no such note, it will belong to the heir.

The decree must be affirmed.

Lincoln's Inn MS. Misc. 384, p. 215, pl. 1

19 November.

Joseph Aylworth, 21 April 1715, conveys his land to trustees to sell to pay debts, the surplus to be divided among four after a sum of £200 taken thereout, which is to be subject to a note or disposition of Joseph Aylworth. Joseph Aylworth dies without making any disposition. Query whether it is part of his personal estate or shall go to his heir.

Lord Chancellor [LORD PARKER]: In Roper v. Ratcliff, in the House of Lords, it was adjudged that, where land is to be sold for a particular purpose, the surplus is to be looked upon as part of the land undisposed of. It is the same

---

1 *Roper v. Radcliffe* (1712–1714), 9 Modern 167, 181, 88 E.R. 380, 387, 10 Modern 89, 230, 88 E.R. 639, 706, 5 Brown P.C. 360, 2 E.R. 731, 2 Eq. Cas. Abr. 508, 620, 621, 622, 625, 771, 22 E.R. 430, 520, 521, 525, 655, British Library MS. Add. 36651, f. 101, Chancery Cases *tempore* Harcourt, 242, 430.

in this case, the land not being turned into money in the lifetime of Joseph Aylworth. The Master of the Rolls' decree was affirmed.

465
Galley v. Selby
(Ch. 1720)

The mortgagor of an advowson, not the mortgagee in possession, has the right to present his nominee to the church.

Lincoln's Inn MS. Hill 29, p. 55

Michaelmas 7 Geo. I.

A bill was brought against the defendant, who had presented his own clerk to a living fallen vacant, to have the plaintiff's clerk instituted and inducted, the plaintiff being grantee of the next avoidance from Charles Stafford, who had before mortgaged the estate and advowson to the defendant.

It was allowed by all that, at law, a mortgagee only has a right to present, but, in equity, he being looked on only as a trustee of the estate, the mortgagor must present.

And Serjeant *Comyns* [said] and [it was] allowed *per curiam* [Lord Parker] that, where the mortgagor does but bring his bill to redeem, by the court of Chancery, he will be allowed to present. And so it was decreed in case of Sir John Philips v. Harcourt.

Lord Chancellor [Lord Parker], in the decree, said this was a common case. A person having made a mortgage in which is included the advowson and the church becomes vacant, he has a right to come into this court and demand the presentation, for, as the mortgagee is looked on only as a trustee of the whole estate for the money lent, though the presentation be not worth money, yet the advowson is and may be sold. And, therefore, he decreed the presentation by the defendant was void, and, in case Serjeant Selby does not present the plaintiff's clerk in fourteen days, the plaintiff's clerk must be instituted and inducted without.

1 Strange 403, 93 E.R. 595

It is a rule in equity that, though, in the case of a mortgage in fee, the legal right of presentation is vested in the mortgagee, yet they will interrupt that presentation and compel the ordinary to institute the clerk of the mortgagor anytime before foreclosure, it not being any part of the profits of the estate. 2 Vern. 401.[1]

[1] *Amhurst v. Dawling* (1700), 2 Vernon 401, 23 E.R. 859, also 1 Eq. Cas. Abr. 329, 21 E.R. 1081.

Lincoln's Inn MS. Misc. 380, pt. 2, p. 2

Michaelmas term 7 Geo.

Serjeant Selby had a mortgage of certain lands together with an advowson from one Charles Stafford, who, after the making of the mortgage, in the year 1706, made a grant of the next avoidance to the plaintiff. When the next avoidance fell, the serjeant was in possession of the mortgaged lands and both he and the plaintiff presented their respective clerks to the bishop. The bishop refused to admit either of their clerks, upon which the plaintiff brings his bill against the serjeant and the bishop in order to have his clerk admitted.

Lord Chancellor Parker decreed for the plaintiff with costs against the serjeant. He said the mortgagee is no more in a court of equity than a trustee for the mortgagor as to the estate in the land, but, as to himself, he had no other right than to have his own money and for that purpose to receive the profits in order to repay himself out of them. But as to anything else belonging to the land out of which no profits arise, he is still a trustee only for the mortgagor. This is the case of the advowson, which though included in the mortgage because it is of some value to be sold and so increases the security, yet no immediate advantage or profits can be received from it. And, therefore, the mortgagor has a right to present whom he pleases or to oblige the mortgagee to present him, as any other *cestui que trust* has to oblige his trustee to execute those acts for him relating to the estate which he himself could do if the legal estate was in him.

[Other reports of this case: 1 Comyns 343, 92 E.R. 1103.]

466

Anonymous

(Ch. 1720)

In this case, the actions of a testator were a revocation of a devise.

1 Strange 407, 93 E.R. 600

A. makes his will and devises £300 to his daughter, provided she married with the consent of her mother, otherwise, only £200. After this, in his own life, he marries her and gave £200 with her. And this was held a revocation of the devise, so as to deprive her of the other £100.

467

Taylor v. Nevill

(Ch. 1720)

An installment sales contract will be enforced by an order for specific performance in order to prevent a multiplicity of lawsuits.

In this contract of sale, the agreement as to price was sufficiently definite to be enforceable.

Lincoln's Inn MS. Misc. 384, p. 208, pl. 3

29 October. Decree by Baron Price reheard by the Lord Chancellor.

A bill [was exhibited] to have performance of an agreement whereby the defendant was to deliver 800 tons of bar iron in ten years at eighty tons *per annum*, the price to be regulated as R. Taylor and Wallis sold their iron to ready money customers. R. Taylor dies. The question is whether the agreement is determined.

Lutwyche, for the plaintiff: The general intent is to be sold at the market price. R. Taylor was the plaintiff's father; *ergo*, the defendant was not likely to be prejudiced, but the plaintiff. If R. Taylor and Wallis had sold for different rates or had no ready money customers or had left off trade, it is hard to say the agreement was determined when, for ten years, [it was] certain.

Attorney General [*Raymond*], for the defendant: The articles are rendered impracticable by R. Taylor's death. Carrying articles into execution is discretionary [and] not done where there is a remedy at law. This is proper at law.

Objection: The first clause is an absolute agreement; the settling of the price is a distinct subsequent article.

Answer: The whole is but one agreement. This is an essential part.

Lord Chancellor [Lord Parker]: Suppose R. Taylor and Wallis had left off trade. Was the iron to be sold at no price? If they had sold at different prices at different times just before the delivery, how far this contract is proper to be carried into execution. Where it is hard or the ends of justice are not answered, it is not proper, for time past should be left to the law. [For an] agreement for delivery of iron sold for ten years, at law, he must every year call for and demand his iron and, if not delivered, to bring his action.

This bill is to prevent multiplicity of suits, which might ruin both parties. [As to] the nature of the thing, iron is sometimes very scarce and cannot be had everywhere, so the plaintiff's customers might be disappointed and be ruined. It is not like South Sea stock, which may be had every day. Cuddee v. Rutter, ante.[1]

It is said the articles are void by the death of R. Taylor. But, if he was the person relied on, why was Wallis nominated? It is said it was a trust which cannot be transferred. There is no trust but that he should sell his own iron for the best

[1] *Cud v. Rutter* (Ch. 1719–1720), see above, Case No. 410.

price. Articles cannot be construed literally. If both sold at different prices, [it is] but as generally sold at. If it were a contract for the sale of wood and no price was set, the contract would not be void, but [the court] must supply the price according to the market. If Wallis does not sell, you may supply his place.

He affirmed the decree whereby Wallis was to set the price, and the plaintiff was left to recover damages at law for what was past, but to have a specific performance for the time to come.

468

Duncombe v. Evance

(Ch. 1720)

A bill of foreclosure lies only against someone who has an equity of redemption, but not against a prior mortgagee.

A party cannot prove what was not pleaded.

Lincoln's Inn MS. Misc. 11, p. 159

The plaintiff was a mortgagee of the estate of one Thomas Lewis, and the defendant had a prior mortgage upon the same estate. And by virtue of an old term, which was kept on foot having gotten possession by an [action of] ejectment at law, he brought his bill to foreclose the defendant Evance[1] and the heirs at law of the mortgagor.

The Master of the Rolls [Jekyll]: The bill is very improper. No one can be foreclosed but he that has the equity of redemption. The defendant has not the equity of redemption, but a prior mortgage, which he insists ought not to be postponed, and, therefore, as against him, you can pray no foreclosure. But your bill must be dismissed with costs.

Then it was said for the plaintiff that he had an assignment of a term, which had been kept on foot and which was prior to the defendant's mortgage. But that not being set out in the bill nor put an issue in the cause, though proved, it could not be read.

And, therefore, the Master of the Rolls [Jekyll] seemed inclinable to let the plaintiff amend his bill and the cause to stand over.

Then there was a proposal made by the defendant Evance, which the plaintiff came into, that the estate might be sold and both plaintiff and defendant paid.

But the Master of the Rolls [Jekyll] said that could not be done unless the heirs at law would consent. And one of them being an infant and near of age, the cause was ordered to stand over to the next term that the infant, who would then be of age, might signify his consent to a sale.

---

[1] H. Lancaster, 'Evance, Sir Stephen (1654/5–1712)', *Oxford Dictionary of National Biography*, vol. 18, p. 660.

469
Tipping v. Tipping
(Ch. 1720)

No one has a right to a widow's paraphernalia but the creditors of her deceased husband where there is a deficiency of other assets in his estate.

Lincoln's Inn MS. Misc. 11, p. 206

31 October 1720.

The plaintiff's bill was to have a sum of money laid out in a purchase of lands and settled for her jointure pursuant to articles made before her marriage whereby her husband had covenanted for himself, his heirs, executors, etc. And, in regard the personal assets were not sufficient to make good this covenant, the plaintiff was seeking her satisfaction out of the real assets.

And the question was if the paraphernalia should be considered as personal assets and applied towards the satisfaction of the plaintiff's demands in favor of the heir and in ease of his estate.

Lord Chancellor [Lord Parker]: I believe there is such a case in Rolle,[1] as has been cited, that the husband cannot by his will devise the paraphernalia of his wife. But I think there have been some cases in this court where the husband has been allowed to be a purchaser of his wife's paraphernalia.

It is certain the wife shall retain her paraphernalia against the executors or administrators of the husband; and so she shall against legatees. And no one has a right to the wife's paraphernalia but creditors where there is a defect of other assets.

The right which the wife has to her paraphernalia is prior to the right which a legatee has to his legacy, and, if so, it is prior to the right which the heir has to have the personal estate applied in ease of the real estate.

If the creditors who have a lien on the real estate are paid out of the personal assets and there is not sufficient assets to pay the legacies, the legatees shall stand in the room of the creditors and be paid out of the real assets. But they shall never come upon the paraphernalia. And, if they cannot, it would be strange in such a case that the heir should have a right to say that the paraphernalia shall go to pay these legacies.

He decreed the paraphernalia to the plaintiff.

[Other reports of this case: 1 Peere Williams 729, 24 E.R. 589, 2 Eq. Cas. Abr. 499, 573, 627, 22 E.R. 423, 483, 526, 527.]

[Connected cases: Tipping v. Tipping (1721), see below, Case No. 528.]

[1] *Lord Hastings v. Dowglas* (1632), 1 Rolle, Abr., *Executors*, pl. 9, p. 911.

470

Bull v. Bull

(Ch. 1720)

When London orphans claim their orphanage shares, they must bring any advancements into hotchpot.

Lincoln's Inn MS. Misc. 11, p. 182, pl. 1

7 November 1720.

Upon a bill brought for a distribution of a freeman's personal estate according to the custom of London, an account was decreed, and the Master was directed to enquire whether it did appear by any writing under the father's hand what was the quantum of the portions given to such of the children as were advanced in his lifetime. If it did, they were to be let in for their orphanage shares upon bringing into hotchpot what they had received; if not, they were to be looked upon as fully advanced.

Finney v. Finney;[1] in this case, as was said by Mr. *Williams*, Lord Cowper seemed to be of an opinion that an eldest son, upon the Statute of Distributions,[2] as well as the other children, ought to bring into hotchpot what he had received by way of advancement from his father out of the personal estate, for he thought the Statute was very doubtfully penned and that the exception of the eldest son as to bringing into hotchpot only extended to the real estate.

471

Heath v. Percival

(Ch. 1720)

A debtor cannot avoid his obligation by contracting with a third part for the third party to pay it.

Where a bill of discovery lies, the court of equity can grant a common law remedy in order to avoid a multiplicity of actions.

Lincoln's Inn MS. Misc. 11, p. 182, pl. 2

Thomas and William Heath, executors of William Heath, plaintiffs; Whitfield, Hayter, Samuel Percival, residuary legatee of Peter Percival, Ebenezer Sadler, surviving executor of Peter Percival, defendants.

---

[1] *Phiney v. Phiney* (1708), 2 Vernon 638, 23 E.R. 1018, 1 Eq. Cas. Abr. 249, 21 E.R. 1025, Lincoln's Inn MS. Misc. 384, p. 210, pl. 2.

[2] Stat. 22 & 23 Car. II, c. 10, s. 3 (*SR*, V, 720).

Upon a bill for discovery of assets of Peter Percival and to be paid a bond wherein he and Sir Stephen Evance[1] and the defendant Hayter became bound to the plaintiffs' testator for the payment of £1000 with interest, the case was thus. On 8 June 1682, Sir Stephan Evance and Peter Percival being partners and goldsmiths, they, together with the defendant Hayter, entered into the bond in question to the plaintiffs' testator. In February 1692[/93], the partnership was dissolved, and, by an agreement between Sir Stephen and Percival, Sir Stephen took upon him to pay all the partnership debts and covenanted to indemnify Percival. And Percival, in consideration of a sum of money, released all his right in the partnership effects to Sir Stephen. Notice was thereupon given to all the bond creditors to come in and take their money. Some did, and others continued their debts upon their old securities, and, among others that did so, the plaintiffs' testator was one.

But, in 1696, the plaintiffs' testator called in his money. But upon Sir Stephen's agreeing in advance the interest to £6 percent and making an endorsement thereof on the bond, the money was continued. Interest was accordingly paid until the year 1710 by Sir Stephen Evance. And, in February 1711[/12], he failed, and a commission of bankruptcy was awarded against him. And the plaintiffs, as creditors, came in under the commission.

The defendants insisted upon all these transactions and the long acquiescence, it being above twenty-seven years since the bond was given, and that Sir Stephen was in full credit until he failed so that the plaintiffs might have received their money if they had pleased.

And the question was if the plaintiffs and their testator had not so far accepted of Sir Stephen Evance to be their paymaster as to have discharged Percival and the defendant Hayter in a court of equity.

Lord Chancellor [Lord Parker]: The three persons are bound in a bond; whether partners or no is not material. Then they agree among themselves that one shall pay the debt. Will this agreement alter the nature of the original contract? Well, but you say, there was notice of this agreement given to the obligee. What then? Will notice of an agreement that he was not concerned in any ways affect him?

As to Heath's going to Sir Stephen Evance and receiving his interest, you say, by this, he took Sir Stephen as his paymaster. Why, everyone that was bound in the bond was his paymaster.

And, as to the plaintiff's coming in under the commission, that was for your benefit and what has been received under the commission must be allowed. And I see no reason to discharge the estate of Percival from the payment of the debt.

And, therefore, the plaintiffs' being entitled to come here for a discovery of assets and, being here, the court will not send them to [common] law to recover

[1] H. Lancaster, 'Evance, Sir Stephen (1654/5–1712)', *Oxford Dictionary of National Biography*, vol. 18, p. 660.

their debt, but, for avoiding circuity of actions, will decree them debts if there are assets. And, therefore, assets being admitted, let the Master see what is due on the bond, and the defendant, the executor of Percival, must pay it.

Lincoln's Inn MS. Misc. 384, p. 211, pl. 1

8 November.

In 1692, Sir Stephen Evance and the defendants, his partners, entered into a bond to the plaintiff for £1000. Afterwards, Sir Stephen and the defendants agree to determine the partnership and Sir Stephen to take upon himself the payment of all the partnership debts. The plaintiff then applied to him for satisfaction of his bond, but, upon Sir Stephen's proposing to give him £6 percent interest, the plaintiff was content to stay sometime longer. Afterwards, Sir Stephen became bankrupt, and the plaintiff, under the commission, received 7s. in the pound. Query whether the defendants are discharged, especially since the plaintiff might have been paid whilst Sir Stephen was in full credit.

Lord Chancellor [Lord Parker]: The defendants are chargeable by the original contract, which has not been discharged by anything subsequent. And he decreed the plaintiff a satisfaction against the defendants.

[Other reports of this case: 1 Peere Williams 682, 24 E.R. 570, 1 Strange 403, 93 E.R. 595, 2 Eq. Cas. Abr. 167, 630, 22 E.R. 143, 529.]

472

Marsh v. Evans

(Ch. 1720)

Whether the losses of a testator's estate occur before or after his death does not affect the course of administration of his estate.

Lincoln's Inn MS. Misc. 11, p. 160, pl. 1

10 November 1720.

Upon hearing the special matter of the Master's report, a question arose upon the words of a will whereby a man gave legacies to all his children and declared that, if his personal estate should fall short and not pay all his debts and legacies, his daughter should be paid her legacy and the rest of his children should abate of their legacies in proportion. The testator's estate was sufficient to pay all the testator's debts and legacies. But the wife, who was executrix, wasted the assets so that there was now a deficiency to pay all the legacies. The question was if the daughter should now be paid her full legacy.

Lord Chancellor [Lord Parker] was of the opinion she ought, for it was nothing to her by what means the deficiency happened, whether by losses in the testator's lifetime or by losses after his death. The testator could never intend to confine the deficiency to the time of his own death.

[Other reports of this case: 1 Peere Williams 668, 24 E.R. 561, 2 Eq. Cas. Abr. 556, 22 E.R. 468.]

473

Anonymous v. Potts

(Ch. 1720)

A company can be ordered to re-transfer shares of its stock to the assignees of a bankrupt shareholder where the shareholder is beyond the jurisdiction of the court.

Service of process can be made on the agents of a defendant who is beyond the jurisdiction of the court.

British Library MS. Hargrave 83, p. 8

Thursday, 10 November 1720.

[It was] moved that an injunction might be granted to prevent the transfer of South Sea and East India stock which had been accepted by the agents of Mr. Potts, a Dutch merchant resident in Holland, until his answer came in and that service of the subpoena upon his agents might be [held to] good service.

The case was stated to be thus by the bill. Sir Justus Beck had great dealings with a house in Holland, which, by the run of the South Sea times, he apprehended to be in great danger of failing. He writes to Mr. Potts and desires him to stand by the house and support them. Mr. Potts sends him word that he would not venture to do it unless Sir Justus would give him security for what he should advance, which, if he would do, Mr. Potts undertook to assist the house with a very considerable sum of money. Sir Justus gave the security desired in South Sea and East India stock. Mr. Potts sent a procuration to his agents to accept it. The house in Holland broke. Sir Justus Beck failed and assigned to his creditors all his estate and effects for the payment of his debts. They, upon an enquiry, found that Mr. Potts had advanced no money towards the support of the house in Holland upon which the creditors, the assignees of Sir Justus bring their bill and pray that the stock transferred to Mr. Potts and accepted by his agents may be re-transferred to them. And, now, upon an affidavit verifying the facts stated by the bill, this motion was made.

The East India Company opposed the stopping of their transfer by the injunction of the court, Mr. *Hungerford*, their counsel, alleging that the stopping of their transfer might be a prejudice to their stock and bring a discredit upon it among foreigners.

The South Sea Company submitted to the direction of the court.

It was argued against Mr. Hungerford's objection that, if a free transfer were permitted and Mr. Potts should dispose of the stock, the creditors could have no remedy against him, he living out of the jurisdiction of the court.

As to the other part of the motion concerning the service of the subpoena, it was insisted that they who had accepted the stock were only agents of Mr. Potts barely for that purpose and that nothing vested in them, that they were not so much as trustees, had no disposal of the stock, that acceptance was merely a matter of form and might be done by any person, and that a parol order was sufficient to empower anyone to accept.

For the plaintiffs, it was argued as to this point that they who accepted the stock had a procuration from Mr. Potts and that they were the only agents of Mr. Potts that the defendants knew of. And they cited the case of one Coggell, who, having proved a will as executor, went soon after into the Indies, and, a bill being brought against him, the court ordered that service upon his proctor in the [Doctors'] Commons should be good service.

Lord Chancellor Parker granted both parts of the motion in this case.

474

Anonymous

(Ch. 1720)

The Court of Chancery will give relief against fraud and duress even though the amount in issue be very small.

British Library MS. Hargrave 83, p. 15, pl. 2

14 November 1720.

A bill was brought to have a note for £9 19s. that was obtained by fraud and duress delivered up. The suggestions of the bill were fully proved.

My Lord Chancellor Parker said it should not escape the court by being contrived to be under the dignity of it. He decreed the note to be delivered up and the defendant to pay costs.

Query the name of the case. It will be easily found for there was a great run among the causes about this time, the court being often up by nine in the morning and thirteen causes often struck out in one day. The practicers said there was no money stirring to carry on the causes, people being in suspense about their South Sea engagements and contracts.[1]

[1] I.e. the burst of the South Sea bubble in 1720.

475

Phipps v. Earl of Anglesey

(Ch. 1720)

Rent must be tendered on the land leased.

To marry an infant ward of the Court of Chancery without leave of court is a contempt of court.

Lincoln's Inn MS. Misc. 384, p. 211, pl. 3

16 November.

A bill was [exhibited] to have a portion of £12,000, which was provided by a settlement, and £3000, given by a will to the plaintiff's lady by her father, the late earl of Anglesey. The £12,000 was charged on lands in Ireland, which are descended upon the defendant, at her age of eighteen or marriage.

The first question is whether it is to be paid in English money or whether an allowance ought to be for the course of exchange.

Lord Chancellor [LORD PARKER]: If it had been a rent charged on lands in Ireland, it had been payable in Irish money because rent is to be tendered upon the land. But this being a sum in gross and to be paid her at eighteen or marriage and the deed being executed and the parties living here, it must be understood in English money; so if a mortgage be made here of lands in Ireland, and the judges in Ireland have so determined.

The second question is how the fortune should be settled in regard the plaintiff married her when under the care of the court and not being able to make an adequate settlement.

Lord Chancellor [LORD PARKER] ordered it to be settled to her separate use and so as the plaintiff might have the least benefit that was possible. And as to the censure of the court for so great a contempt, both by the plaintiff and Sir Constantine [Phipps][1] and the other persons who were concerned in making the match, the court ordered precedents to be provided. And he declared it should be punished with the utmost severity and the plaintiff to pay costs.

[Other reports of this case: 1 Peere Williams 696, 24 E.R. 576, 2 Eq. Cas. Abr. 220, 754, 22 E.R. 188, 640.]

[1] D. W. Hayton, 'Phipps, Sir Constantine (bap. 1656, d. 1723)', *Oxford Dictionary of National Biography*, vol. 44, pp. 174–178.

476

Windsor v. Tongue

(Ch. 1720)

Void proceedings cannot be cured by a bill of revivor.

British Library MS. Hargrave 83, p. 10

In the case of Windsor and Tongue, My Lord Chancellor [Lord Parker] said that a bill of revivor only renewed the former proceedings and replaced them in the state and condition they were in at the time of the abatement upon which it was brought. But it did not give any sanction or add any validity to the former proceedings. Those that were void or voidable before would remain so after the revivor if they were void for any other cause than merely the abatement upon which the revivor was brought.

N.B. Tongue showed cause against the revivor, and the cause he showed was that there had been several proceedings in the former cause after the abatement before the plaintiff owned her marriage, which was now the cause of the revivor.

477

Saunderson v. Clagget

(Ch. 1720)

A motion for a writ of prohibition to an ecclesiastical court must be grounded on matter appearing on the face of the pleading in the ecclesiastical court.

British Library MS. Hargrave 83, p. 11, pl. 1

Upon a motion for a [writ of] prohibition to the court of the Archdeacon of Sudbury, the Master of the Rolls [Jekyll] declared that, if a prohibition was granted to an ecclesiastical court out of Chancery, it must be upon something appearing on the face of the libel and not upon anything outside it, for there was no way here of bringing matter outside to a trial and no such thing as a declaration in prohibition that ever he remembered in Chancery. And upon consulting the Register, he confirmed his opinion that there could be no declaration in prohibition in this court and that no suggestions outside the libel had ever been admitted here.

[Related cases: 1 Peere Williams 657, 24 E.R. 557, 1 Strange 421, 93 E.R. 609.]

478

Anonymous

(Ch. 1720)

In this case, a writ of ne exeat regno *was continued in force even though the party could not have been held to bail at common law.*

British Library MS. Hargrave 83, p. 11, pl. 2

It was moved that a [writ of] *ne exeat regno* might be discharged, the case being such that the party against whom it issued could not have been held to bail at common law if an action had been brought against him. And he having made an affidavit that he did not intend to go out of the kingdom, the Master of the Rolls [JEKYLL] refused to discharge it.

479

Clifton v. Burt

(Ch. 1720)

In the administration of a decedent's estate, the debts and legacies are to be paid out of the decedent's personal estate.

Creditor are preferred to heirs; heirs are preferred to executors; specific legatees are preferred to pecuniary legatees.

If there are specific and pecuniary legacies and there is a deficiency of assets, the pecuniary legacies abate proportionably, but not the specific legacies.

If the personal assets are used to pay the bond creditors and there are real assets by descent, the legatees may stand in the place of the creditors to affect the real assets.

A void surrender of a copyhold will not to be aided in equity in favor of a legatee.

Real assets have preference over personal assets; specific legatees have preference over general legatees; devisees are preferred over heirs.

Devisees of lands are considered as specific legatees and have preference to heirs.

Devisees of land are preferred to specific legatees of personalty.

Specific legatees are preferred to pecuniary legatees.

Lincoln's Inn MS. Misc. 384, p. 213

19 November. Rehearing.

John Bignold's will gives the plaintiff £500 after the death of his son without issue before twenty-one. He directs his debts and legacies to be paid; then, he devises his freehold and copyhold to his son, John Bignold, in tail and, if he die before twenty-one, then, to the defendant. (John Bignold dies before twenty-one.) He takes notice he had surrendered the copyhold to the use of his will and directs the copyhold to be sold for the payment of his debts and legacies on a deficiency of personal estate. The executors pay away the personal assets in satisfaction of debts.

In 1712, Lord Harcourt decreed the plaintiff to stand in the place of the creditors and to have a satisfaction out of the freehold.

Peere Williams, for the defendant: A specific devisee of a term shall not contribute to a pecuniary legatee. A devisee of a freehold is stronger. A copyhold expressly devised for that purpose excludes the freehold.

N.B. The copyhold was surrendered to two persons who were not tenants of the manor. So it was void in law and not to be supposed for a legatee.

Attorney General [*Raymond*], for the defendant: There is no case where there being a devise of a freehold and also of a legacy that assets have been marshaled to defeat the devisee.

Peere Williams [cited] Hern v. Merrick, by Lord Harcourt,[1] where the heir was a devisee and executor and, to favor his own devise, paid the bond creditors out of the personal assets; the legatees, being the younger children, were not decreed to stand in the place of the creditors.

Lord Chancellor [Lord Parker]: That case determines this.

John Bignold directs that his debts and petty legacies should be first paid; then, he devises to his son in tail and, if he dies before twenty-one without issue, then to the defendant, then he gives the plaintiff £500 to be paid if his son die under twenty-one without issue. Now, he intended that the freehold should not be affected until [there is] a deficiency of the personal estate and the copyhold. As to the copyhold, he is disappointed, the surrender not being good. But it will be supplied in favor of the creditors, not in favor of the legatee. Why should a legatee have a preference of a devisee of land? Suppose it had been but a term for years; so if a personal chattel. Here is a specific devisee of land. It is very harsh to take it wholly away from him to give it to a legatee. The farthest this court has gone is to make them abate in proportion, even in the case of a money legacy only.

I would see Hern v. Merrick, though I am very strong of opinion the same way. 13 December 1720.

Lord Chancellor [Lord Parker]: This case turns upon the rule of marshaling assets.

First, the proper fund for payment of debts and legacies is the personal estate.

Second, an executor does not claim in his own right, but *in jure testatoris*. A specialty creditor may come upon which estate he will, but, if it is against the heir, he may come against the executor to have the real estate exonerated. If the personal estate is not sufficient to pay the whole debt, a creditor on a specialty may call the heir into this court to apply his subsidiary fund where the primary fund falls short. As a creditor is preferred to the heir, so is the heir to the executor; so is a specific to a pecuniary legatee.

---

[1] *Herne v. Meyrick* (1712), 2 Salkeld 416, 91 E.R. 362, 1 Peere Williams 201, 24 E.R. 355, 1 Eq. Cas. Abr. 143, 21 E.R. 944, Chancery Cases *tempore* Harcourt, 279.

Third, if there are specific and also pecuniary legatees and there happens a deficiency of assets, the pecuniary legatees shall abate in proportion, not the specific.

Fourth, the testator may narrow the fund provided for the pecuniary legatees but so as not to prejudice creditors, as by giving specific legacies. A specific legacy is supposed to be severed by the testator from the rest of his personal estate.

Fifth, if the personal assets are swept away by the creditors on a specialty and there are real assets by descent, the legatees may stand in the place of the creditors to affect the real assets.

Sixth, this case goes farther. A. devises lands specifically, and there are not assets to pay the debts and also the legacies. As a specific legatee of a personalty shall not contribute to a pecuniary legatee, so neither shall a specific devisee of lands. Here, the testator has marshaled his own assets and has exempted this specific devise from being subject to money legacies.

Seventh, the testator has provided another fund for the legatees, *viz.* the copyhold, which he has devised to be sold to pay them.

Eighth, the surrender of the copyhold happens to be void in law and is not to be supplied in equity in favor of a legatee; so the fund provided by the testator for the legatees fails. There is no equity to come against the freehold in the hands of the devisee.

The case of Hern v. Merrick governs this, founded on the difference between an heir and a devisee. The heir is liable to make good the assets; so is not a devisee.

First, real assets always have a preference of personal.

Second, specific legatees have preference of general legatees.

Third, a devisee is preferred to an heir.

The decree was reversed whereby the freehold was directed to be sold to pay the plaintiff's legacy.

Lincoln's Inn MS. Misc. 11, p. 234

John Bignold being tenant for life of a freehold farm of £25 *per annum* and of a copyhold farm of £50 *per annum*, remainder of both to his son John Bignold in tail to him and the heirs of his body, reversion in fee to John, the father, he, the said John, the father, by his will in 1706, devised the freehold farm to Joseph Burt and his heirs. He devised the copyhold farm to the said Joseph Burt, James Burt, and Elizabeth Horsnell and their heirs upon trust to sell the same and, with the moneys, to pay his debts and legacies.

He gave a legacy of £500 to the plaintiff James Clifton to be paid three months after the death of his said son John Bignold without issue. He made the defendant and three others executors. The testator, at his death, was indebted £800, *viz.* in £600 by bond and £200 by simple contract. And his personal estate fell short about £50 to pay the debts. John Bignold, the son, died an infant about fourteen months after his father, the testator, without issue.

It happened that the testator had not surrendered the copyhold farm to the uses of his will, and the heir at law evicted the trustees and recovered that farm, whereby the fund that was intended to pay the legacies failed. The defendant Burt, being one of the executors, administered the whole personal estate in the payment of the debts by bond and simple contract and made good the deficiency of £50 out of his own pocket.

Clifton, the legatee of £500, brought his bill against Burt, the executor, who was also the devisee of the freehold farm, to have the personal estate so marshalled that the bond debts might be laid on the freehold farm or to the intent that the personal estate might be spared and sufficient assets left to pay the £500 legacy.

On 4 July 1712, on hearing the cause, the Lord Keeper Harcourt decreed the freehold lands to be sold for the payment of so much of the debts and legacies as the personal estate fell short of paying and the legatees should stand in the place of the bond creditors and have a satisfaction out of the real estate.

On 13 December 1720, on a rehearing of the cause before the Lord Chancellor PARKER, His Lordship was pleased to reverse the decree and to state his argument or reasons after this manner, *viz.* to consider how the matter of equity would stand in this case, first, between the heir at law and the creditors by simple contract, second, between the heir and the money legatees, third, between the legatees themselves, *viz.* devisees of lands, specific legatees, and money legatees.

The personal estate is the primary fund for the payment of debts and legacies, and the real estate is the secondary or subsidiary fund to pay only debts. And it is made so only by a special agreement in cases where the heirs are bound by specialty. And that was the reason which gives the heir a right in equity to compel the executor, who claims not in his own right but is in the nature of a trustee, to administer and apply the personal estate in payment of the debts in exoneration of the real estate, by which it appears that equity prefers the heir to the executor.

First, a creditor by simple contract had a right in equity to have the benefit of the primary fund, to wit to have a satisfaction out of the personal estate and to place the debts by specialty on the secondary or subsidiary fund, to wit the real estate in the hands of the heir.

Second, money legatees had a right in equity to have aid against the heir to place upon him the debts by specialty to the intent they may have a satisfaction out of the personal estate. But the reason was because the law itself had bound the heir to pay the debts by specialty and the same ancestor who had bound the heir to pay those debts had given the money legacies.[1]

And, therefore, it was no wrong in a court of equity to place upon the heir those debts which the law itself had obliged him to pay.

[1] legatees *MS.*

But where money legacies are given out of a particular or special fund and if that fund fails, either for want of title or default of value, such legatees should have no aid in a court of equity against the heir because they were not originally placed on the primary or general fund, to wit the personal estate. But such money legatees ought to resort to the surplus of the personal estate, if any be.

Third, as to the legatees themselves, a specific legacy, to wit a horse, a bed, a jewel, a term for years etc., showed the mind and intent of the testator, that he had severed that species from the rest of his personal estate and that the executors should not apply that species of his estate for the payment of his debts and that, if such a specific legacy should be taken in execution by a creditor, the legatee should be aided in equity to compel the executor to reimburse him the value. Therefore, money legatees should never have aid in equity to compel or have a contribution or abatement against a specific legatee.

Devisees of lands ought to be considered as having specific legacies and are preferred to the heir because the testator himself does in these cases of specific legacies marshal the payment of his legacies and show his mind and intent that those parts of his estate shall not be applied for the payment of debts or legacies. And, therefore, for equity to give aid to a money legatee against a devisee of lands would be to contradict the testator's own marshaling of his estate and would make one part of his will contradict the other.

In general, His Lordship [Lord Parker] concluded that, in equity, a devisee of the real estate should be preferred to a specific legatee of the personal [estate] and that a specific legatee should be preferred to a money legatee.

In the case in question, the testator's intent was apparent, for he had appointed the copyhold farm to be the particular and special fund to pay this £500 legacy, which fund having failed for want of title, there could be no more reason to relieve the legatee of the £500 against the devisee of the freehold than there could be to aid the devisee of the copyhold, whose title in law failed, against the devisee of the freehold, whose title proved good.

And, therefore, His Lordship reversed the decree and dismissed the plaintiff's bill.

[Other reports of this case: 1 Peere Williams 678, 24 E.R. 566, Precedents in Chancery 540, 24 E.R. 242, 2 Eq. Cas. Abr. 556, 22 E.R. 467.]

480

Arne v. Waple

(Ch. 1720)

A party to a contract has the defense of illegal consideration in a common law court and, therefore, has no need of an equitable remedy to assert this defense.

Lincoln's Inn MS. Misc. 384, p. 215, pl. 2

24 November. Arne v. Waple and Emes.

The plaintiff made a contract with the defendant Waple for three shares of the Welsh Copper [Company] to be transferred to the plaintiff at a future day. And the plaintiff gave Waple a negotiable note for value received payable in two months. About two days before the note was payable, the Lords Justices caused to be advertised that a *scire facias* was ordered against the Welsh Copper [Company]. At the day agreed upon, Waple transferred the shares in the books, but the plaintiff did not attend to accept them. Waple, being indebted to Emes, endorsed over this note, which was for £250, to him, but no new money was then advanced. Emes, the endorsee brought an action upon the note against the plaintiff.

And the bill is to be relieved against the note upon this equity, that it was given to Waple upon an illegal consideration and the endorsement to Emes was without consideration, and that the plaintiff Arne could not at [common] law show that it was upon an illegal consideration, the note being for value received.

Lord Chancellor [Lord Parker] was of opinion that, though the plaintiff at law need not prove the consideration of the note, yet, if the defendant should prove that it was upon an illegal consideration, the plaintiff could not recover.

He denied the injunction.

481

Codrington v. Trinity College

(Ch. 1721)

A will speaks as of the testator's death and not as of the making of the will.

British Library MS. Hargrave 81, f. 4

Hilary term 1720/21.

Colonel Codrington,[1] having by his will, which was dated several years before his death, devised unto Mr. Codrington, his relation, part of his estate of the value of £450 *per annum* upon condition that he should pay unto Trinity Col-

[1] S. Mandelbrote, 'Codrington, Christopher (1668–1710)', *Oxford Dictionary of National Biography*, vol. 12, pp. 383–384.

lege in Oxford the sum of £10,000 at several payments therein mentioned. And having also devised to the said College a library in these words, *viz*. 'My library now in the house of Mr. Ives' and the said Mr. Codrington being made executor and having after the testator's death entered upon the lands devised upon condition as aforesaid and paid £7,000, part of the £10,000, the Fellows and Scholars of the said College brought their bill against the executor and Mr. Ives, in whose house the library stood and who refused to deliver the books until he was paid an arrear of rent for their standing of about £200, for the residue of the £10,000 and the said library.

And the executor, Mr. Codrington, brought a cross-bill against the College for such part of the said library as was purchased after the date of the will, there being a great part thereof purchased after, because of these words in the devise, 'now in the possession of Mr. Ives', and also that they should be compelled to pay Mr. Ives for the standing of the books.

And, upon full hearing of both the causes in Westminster before SIR JOSEPH JEKYLL, Master of the Rolls, it was decreed that Mr. Codrington, the executor, having entered upon the estate and paid part of the money, accepted the condition and should therefore pay the residue of the £10,000 and interest for the same from the several times stated by the will for payment thereof. And, for that purpose, the parties were directed to account before the Master. And, as to the after-purchased books, they were decreed to pass by the will notwithstanding the words 'now in the possession of Mr. Ives', for they were adjudged to be in this case words of designation only and not of restriction. And so he said a devise of all my sheep now in such a pasture has been adjudged to pass all such sheep as should be there at the time of the testator's death and so, in all cases where the devise is of things of a fluctuating and chargeable nature.

And the executor was also decreed to pay all the arrear of rent for the standing of the books, as well what became due after the testator's death as before, for what was due in the testator's lifetime was his proper debt and, consequently, to be paid by the executor and what was due after became so by the executor's default, for the College demanded the books of Mr. Ives but he would not deliver them until he had his rent paid and the consent of the executor, neither of which the executor would do. Therefore, he was ordered to pay costs in the original bill, and the cross-bill was dismissed with costs.

[Other copies of this report: British Library MS. Hargrave 82, f. 3.]

482

Jones v. Fulham

(Ch. 1721)

In the settlement of a decedent's estate, bond creditors and legatees have priority over heirs, and heirs have priority over executors.

The intent of a testator is not to be varied by anything that happens after his death.

Lincoln's Inn MS. Misc. 384, p. 216

17 January.

3 June 1697, by marriage articles, trustees were to stand possessed of £4000 to be laid out in lands and settled on Dr. G. Fulham for life, then to Katherine, the wife, for life, then to the heirs of their bodies, remainder to the right heirs of G. Fulham, [with a] power for G. Fulham to charge £3000 for younger children. In the meantime, the money is to be put out at interest and paid to the parties in like manner.

Katherine died in 1699, leaving one son. 21 November 1702, G. Fulham, by will, devises to his son all his estate, real and personal. He appoints his debts to be paid out of his personal estate; if his son should die before twenty-one, he directs his executors to sell his leasehold estate and divide it amongst three persons. And he gives the residue of his personal estate to the widows of clergymen. The son died an infant, and the £4000 is not yet laid out in land. The question is whether the £4000 is to be looked upon as real or personal estate as between the creditors and the heir of Dr. G. Fulham.

Mead, for the plaintiffs, the creditors: Dr. Fulham might make his election whether he would take it as real or personal. He might have devised the reversion in fee. Where money is to be laid out in land and settled on A. in tail, A. may claim the money. At the death of the testator, it was a personal estate.

Talbot: Who are the parties? If it is between the heir and the executor, the heir is preferred; if between the issue of the marriage and the creditors at large, the issue is preferred. But where between creditors and volunteers, the creditors are preferred in all cases. This is neither a legal, real, or personal estate, but merely a trust. The heir has another estate descended on him, so he will not be totally disinherited. If the £4000 had been paid to the Doctor by the trustees and there had been no issue, it has been a good payment. But being paid in the life of the issue, it was decreed a wrong payment. Now, the issue being dead, it is out of the case.

Cowper, for the defendant, the heir: If the question had been between the heir and the executor, it is admitted that the heir would be preferred. The rule is the same against creditors as executors. The money is considered as actually settled. Articles are looked upon specifically executed. Dr. Shadwell's Case.[1] If land had been purchased, there had been no question.

Attorney General [*Raymond*], in reply, cited Chaplain and Horner, 18 November 1718,[2] where money was to be laid out and settled after some precedent limitations, which were determined, to the right heirs of the plaintiff, the plaintiff brought his bill for the money, and it was decreed to him.

Lord Chancellor [Lord Parker]: There are three distinct questions.

First, as to the creditors, the bond creditors' £1000, supposing this real estate, it must be applied so far. If there had been no son and the father had called in part, it had been good. The heir stands in the place. There is no color but that the creditors should be paid out of this money.

Secondly, with respect to the legatees, this court always gives preference to the heir, but so as it is consistent with right and justice. Money being considered as land does not make it really land. How far a man must take notice of the rules of this court, if his intent cannot be answered without another construction, his intent must be pursued rather than the rules of this court, though, generally, the heir has preference of the executor, yet not against the intent of the testator.

Third, as to the gift of the residue to charities, they can only take in the same manner as the executor, who, in this case, is not entitled. *Regula*: the intent of the testator is not to be varied by anything that happens after his death.

[Other reports of this case: *sub nom.* Fulham v. Jones, 2 Eq. Cas. Abr. 250, 296, 22 E.R. 212, 249.]

483

Scudamore v. Scudamore

(Ch. 1721)

Where a bequest to purchase land is not executed, the money goes to the heir.

In the settlement of a decedent's estate, heirs have priority over executors.

Lincoln's Inn MS. Misc. 384, p. 217

3 February.

On 28 August 1699, Lady Jane Scudamore, by will, devises all the rest and residue of her ready money, goods, and chattels, lands, tenements, and hereditaments to her daughter, Mary Prince, her heirs, executors, etc., upon trust and to the intent that she, so soon as a convenient purchase could be had, should lay out the same for the purchasing of a freehold and inheritance of lands etc., which, when purchased, should be conveyed to M. Prince and her heirs to the use of her

[1] *Colwell v. Colwell* (*tempore* Cowper).

[2] *Chaplin v. Horner* (1718), see above, Case No. 315.

for life and, after her death, to her grandson, J. Scudamore, and his heirs, and, if M. Prince should die before such purchase and settlement made, then she gives her ready money and all and singular her goods, chattels, lands, etc. so as aforesaid devised to M. Prince unto her grandson J. Scudamore, [his] heirs, executors, etc., and, if he should die before M. Prince and before such purchase, then she gives her ready money, goods, chattels, lands, etc. to Lord Scudamore, his heirs, executors, etc.

J. Scudamore and Lord Scudamore both died before M. Prince, and no purchase is yet made. The question is whether this is a real or a personal estate. The plaintiff is the executor of Lord Scudamore; the defendant is his heir.

Lord Chancellor [Lord Parker]: This case differs from all the cases that have been determined. First, the person who is to have the inheritance of the land when purchased may claim the money. Second, where the question is between the heir and the executor, the heir is preferred. Third, consider the nature of the thing, here is no express declaration of Lord Scudamore to determine it. Lady Jane Scudamore devises the residue of her personal estate to M. Prince upon trust and to the intent that she should lay it out in land as soon as a convenient purchase could be had. If M. Prince should die before any purchase, there was no direction that it should be then laid out. The words carry it to Lord Scudamore's executors. It is very clear that, if Lord Scudamore had survived M. Prince, this had been a personal estate at his election. But Lord Scudamore did not survive. We must consider it at the time of Lord Scudamore's will and what he understood by his personal estate. M. Prince should have laid it out and settled to herself for life, remainder to the heirs of Lord Scudamore. If his heir had come here to compel her to settle accordingly, she could not have said that it was a personal estate.

N.B. J. Scudamore brought a bill against M. Prince and had a decree that land should be purchased and settled on him, but, he dying before M. Prince, that decree is at an end.

M. Prince is directed to lay out as soon as a purchase could be had. And there is a decree that it should be laid out accordingly. It is inconvenient that M. Prince should have the power to make it a real or a personal [estate] at her pleasure.

Here is an infant under the care of the court. If M. Prince had performed the trust, the infant had been entitled. This vested a right in Lord Scudamore's heir to have it laid out, which does not cease by the death of M. Prince. *Ergo*, the heir is entitled.

[Other reports of this case: Precedents in Chancery 543, 24 E.R. 244, 2 Eq. Cas. Abr. 375, 376, 22 E.R. 320.]

484
Dansie v. Adams
(Ch. 1721)

A note received for a valuable consideration and without notice of the maker's personal defenses thereto is valid and enforceable.

Lincoln's Inn MS. Misc. 11, p. 190

6 February 1720[/21]. Dansie v. Adams, Jones, and Shrimpton. At the Rolls.

The plaintiff agrees to buy five shares of the Lutestring stock of the defendant Jones at £85 per share. And the transfer books being then shut, the plaintiff gives Jones a note for the money payable to him or order in two months for value received, and Jones gives the plaintiff a note to transfer the shares to him on demand at the opening of the books. Immediately after this agreement, comes out the order in the *Gazette* for the issuing of a *scire facias* against the Lutestring patent and other patents.

The defendant Jones gives the plaintiff's note to his broker, the defendant Shrimpton, in order to get it discounted, and the defendant Adams, upon Shrimpton's endorsing it, discounts it at 20 percent. And the note not being paid, he brings his action against the plaintiff upon the note and recovers a judgment. And thereupon, the plaintiff brings his bill to be relieved in regard the shares never were and, as things now stand, ever would be transferred to him, for the Lutestring stock was one of the bubbles which was within the late Act of Parliament for settling the South Sea stock[1] and there was now a *scire facias* depending for repealing the patent of the Lutestring Company, and it was believed their transfer books would never be opened.

The defendant Adams denied by answer that he had any notice upon what account the plaintiff's note was given. And, therefore, it was agreed on all hands that he must have his money and that the plaintiff was entitled to no relief against him, for, if it had been determined that, if a man takes a note which was given for a gaming debt, which is void by the Statute[2] against the person who takes it, and the note is made for value received, in which case, upon a trial at law, the party is not bound to prove the consideration, and he pays a valuable consideration for it without notice upon what account it was given, he shall recover against the party who gave the note.

---

1 Stat. 6 Geo. I, c. 18, ss. 18–22.

2 Stat. 9 Ann., c. 19 (*SR*, IX, 476–477).

485

Earl of Strafford v. Lady Wentworth

(Ch. 1721)

Where a lessor who is a life tenant dies on the day that the rent is payable, where the lessee has the right to hold over after the lessor's death, the rent goes to the remainderman or to the reversioner, but if the lease ends by the death of the lessor, the rent is payable into the lessor's estate.

Where a creditor has a mortgage and, consequently, a right to receive the rents and there being money likewise due to him from the mortgagor upon a note and the mortgagor agrees that the mortgagee shall receive the rents of the mortgaged estate until he is satisfied the note as well as the mortgage, that note will be a charge upon the equity of redemption, and the mortgagor shall not redeem without paying off both.

Lincoln's Inn MS. Misc. 13, p. 152

2 February 1720[/21].

Sir Harry Johnson, being a tenant for life under his marriage settlement, makes leases and reserves the rents half yearly, *viz.* at Lady Day and Michaelmas. And he died at one o'clock on Michaelmas Day. And the question was to whom the last half year's rents belonged, whether to the plaintiff as representative of Sir Harry Johnson or to the reversioner.

Attorney General [*Raymond*], for the plaintiff: The leases became void on the death of Sir Harry Johnson. The books are express that, if a tenant for life makes a lease, upon his death, the lease is void and not voidable. The acceptance of the rent by the reversioner would not make it good. I agree the books say the rent is due the last moment of the day. But this must not be understood twelve o'clock at night, for the time when the rent is to be demanded is sunset. Now, it would be pretty strange to say that, if the tenant does not pay his rent at sunset, when it is demanded, his lease may be avoided, and yet that the rent is not due until six hours after.

Solicitor General [*Yorke*], of the same side: There shall be no fraction of a day. 1 Salk. 44. And, therefore, Sir Harry Johnson having lived until Michaelmas Day, the rent remained due to him. If he had received the rent in the morning before he died, it had been a good payment. Clun's Case, in the 10th Rept.

Lord Chancellor [Lord Parker]: The case is no more than this. The tenant for life makes a lease for years and reserves the rent, payable at Lady Day and Michaelmas and the tenant for life dies on Michaelmas Day in the morning.

It is a question at law whether the executor of the tenant for life shall have this rent. But it is such a question that I shall no more send to law than I would send to the judges for their opinion whether the eldest son shall inherit his father's lands or not, for I think it is as plain a case as ever I knew.

Indeed, if the leases made by Sir Harry Johnson had been made in pursuance of a power which was not well executed and the lessee was entitled to have such defect made good in this court, so that the lease was not determined in equity, it might be a matter of a different consideration.

Note in this case was cited the Case of Cole and Bellasis, a Durham cause, which was referred to Mr. Justice Tracy. Lady Cole, tenant for life, made a lease for years, reserving the rent at Lady Day and Michaelmas, and she died at nine at night of Michaelmas Day, and the judge signified his opinion under his hand that the executors of the lady were entitled to the rent, and the rather because she lived until the rent was to be demanded of the tenant or tendered by him.

Lincoln's Inn MS. Misc. 384, p. 219, pl. 1

8 February.

Lord Chancellor [Lord Parker]: Where a tenant for life, pursuant to a power, makes a lease reserving rent during the term and dies between one and two o'clock in the afternoon of the day on which the rent is payable, the rent shall go to the reversioner. But if the lease be not pursuant to a power, the rent shall go to the executors of the tenant for life. *Ratio*: In the first case, the term continues; in the second, it is determined.

British Library MS. Hargrave 83, p. 11, pl. 3

Thursday, 9 February 1720/21. Lord Strafford v. Lady Johnson.

Upon a motion, the case was [thus]. The father of Lady Strafford, the late husband of the defendant Lady Johnson, being tenant for life of the estates settled upon his marriage with a remainder to the defendant Lady Johnson, his wife, etc., made several leases for years of the estates in settlement, as he had a power to do, some of the leases were by deed and some by parol. He dies about one of the clock in the afternoon of the day upon which the rent reserved

upon the leases was payable. The defendant, the Lady Johnson, after his death, received the rent. Lord Strafford, in the right of his wife, takes out letters of administration to her father and brings his bill against Lady Johnson and the tenants who had paid the rent to her for an account of the rents and profits due at the time of the lessor's death.

The counsel for the plaintiffs argued that the law made no fractions in a day, that the rent becoming due upon any day was due every part of that day and demandable and a payment in the morning would be good and satisfactory, though there were cases which seemed to determine that the tenant was not obliged to pay the rent until the last hour or minute of the day, which was to be understood that it was not due until that time so as to bring an action for it or that non-payment should not induce a forfeiture or give a re-entry until the extremity of the day.

But, however, the law might be inequitable and against conscience that the rent which came in lieu of the profits which were all of them received before the rent day should be lost by the act of God after such time as it was due and legally payable though not absolutely necessary to be paid, for, otherwise, the rent must be lost unless the administrator of the lessor was to receive it, for the leases being determined by the lessor's death, My Lady had no title to the rent by virtue of her remainder.

The counsel for the defendant argued that the rent was not due until the extremity of the artificial day, until twelve at night, as had been determined in the case of Baskerville and Mayowe in Saunders,[1] that it was entirely in the tenant's election whether he would pay it before that time or not, at least it was in his election until sunset, and, if he did not pay it before that time, the lessor's representative would have no title or interest in it nor he himself if the lease happened to determine before the extremity of the time that the rent was payable. And for this, they cited Clun's Case, 10th Report 127.[2] But they insisted that the lessor had a power by the marriage settlement to make leases but that, after his death, the possession of the lessor would be the possession of My Lady, who had the remainder and their rent due to her.

My Lord Chancellor Parker said, if the leases are such that the tenant has a right to hold over after the death of the lessor, the rent will then (as this case is) belong to the person in reverter or remainder. The rent ought to go to his administrator. And he took this distinction. The rent being payable at a certain day during the term ought, if the lessor lives until the pay day, to be payable while the term continues; otherwise, the words will not be satisfied. Therefore, if the lessor lives until the rent day and dies on that day and the term expires with him, the rent by the very words that are usual in leases was due before his death. Otherwise, it would not be payable during the term. But, if the lease has a continuance after the death of the lessor, then the rent may be payable after his death and yet the words may be satisfied. He added that, in case the leases were determined by the lessor's death, he would not leave this matter to [the common] law for the opinion of the judges whether the rent was payable to the administrator or should be lost.

He ordered the deed of settlement to be produced before a master and appointed him to state the case and report what power Sir Henry Johnson had to lease and whether he had executed that power either in law or equity that it might appear to the court whether the terms of the lessees had a continuance after his death.

---

[1] *Duppa v. Mayo* (1670), 1 Williams Saunders 275, 85 E.R. 336, also 2 Keble 576, 84 E.R. 362, Lincoln's Inn MS. Misc. 500, f. 45v.

[2] *Clun v. Archer* (1613), 10 Coke Rep. 127, 77 E.R. 1117, also Croke Jac. 309, 79 E.R. 265, 4 Leonard 247, 74 E.R. 850.

N.B. The case of Lady Cole[1] was cited. It came on at the Durham assizes before Mr. Justice Tracy, who determined it after great deliberation and having advised with the other judges.

Lincoln's Inn MS. Misc. 384, p. 254

23 June.

The plaintiff, as administrator to Sir Henry Johnson, brought a bill against the defendant for an account of the Michaelmas rents, which were received by the defendant as reversioner. Sir Henry Johnson, the defendant's late husband was tenant for life and had made leases reserving rents payable at Michaelmas. He happened to die on Michaelmas Day at two in the afternoon. Query whether the rent belongs to the reversioner or to the administrator of the tenant for life.

Attorney General [*Raymond*], for the plaintiff: [In] Southern v. Bellasis,[2] Lady Cole died at nine at night; the rent belonged to her administrator. By the death of the tenant for life, the lease was determined and the tenant having enjoyed the benefit of the lease, the rent belongs to the administrator of the lessor. The lease has not a continuance because it was not made pursuant to the power, the ancient rent not being reserved. Powers are to be taken strictly. [There is] no help in equity if it is not pursued.

Solicitor General [*Yorke*], for the plaintiff: Nothing can give the defendant, the reversioner, a title to the rent but the continuance of the lease.

Lutwyche, for the defendant: Southern v. Bellasis is not like this case. Query when this rent became due. If it is not due the first moment of the day, it is not due at noon. If Sir Henry himself could not have demanded it, neither can his administrator. 1 Sand. 287, Duppa v. Mayow. The rent is not due at sunset nor until midnight. Lady Cole died at nine at night. The judge was of opinion that the rent was due, she having lived until after the legal time of payment, i.e. sunset. As to a tenant at will, if a lessor determine his will an hour before it is due, the rent is gone; so if he die. A fraction of a day [is] necessary.

The plaintiff is not proper here unless [there is] some equity. If the law has given the defendant this rent, [he is] without equity. If the law has not, he may bring his action [at common law]. If it is a wrong payment, the tenants are prejudiced, not the plaintiff. It is hard against the defendant, the settlement being of her own estate, here being a power for the husband to make leases. If he does not strictly pursue the power, equity will not suffer it to prejudice a jointress. Though

[1] *Southern v. Bellasis* (1701), 1 Peere Williams 180, note 1, 24 E.R. 346.
[2] *Southern v. Bellasis* (1701), 1 Peere Williams 180, note 1, 24 E.R. 346.

it does not appear that the ancient rent was reserved, yet if more is reserved, why it is not as good? Sir James Oxenden[1] died at two o'clock; 1 Inst. 351.[2]

Lord Chancellor [Lord Parker]: I told you my opinion upon that case that, where the leases are subsisting, the rent clearly belongs to the reversioner. But if the leases determine by the lessor's death, how can the reversioner be entitled?

Cowper: If the plaintiff has no right, it is not material whether the defendant has it or the tenants.

Hungerford: The plaintiff must recover by his own strength [or there is] no occasion to come into this court. Barwick v. Forster, 2 Cr. 228.[3] Sir Henry had no right of action at the time of his death; therefore, his administrator is not entitled.

Mead: The question is the same as if between the plaintiff and the tenants. If the plaintiff be not prejudiced, [there is] no right against the defendant. If he be prejudiced, [there is a] remedy at law. [There is] no apportionment[4] of rent in equity. A parson made a lease of tithes reserving a rent at Michaelmas; he died two days before though the tithes were all received by the tenant, yet equity would not compel the tenants to account for any rent to the executors of the parson, [as held] by Lord Cowper.

The Attorney General [*Raymond*] replies: The question is now not with the tenants. The bill is for an account of the rent paid by the tenants, who admit it was due. The tenant might have paid Sir Henry in the morning. Sir James Oxenden's Case must be either a lease pursuant to a power or contrary to law.

Lord Chancellor [Lord Parker]: The first question is properly this, whether the rents belong to the defendant; secondly, if not, whether they belong to the plaintiff; thirdly, and whether any equity arises to the plaintiff by the tenants' having submitted to pay; whether leases made pursuant to a power or by a tenant in fee and the lessor dies before the last hour that the rent is due, it belongs to the reversioner and he may demand it or distrain for it.

Second, the report is imperfect; it does not appear whether more than the ancient rent was reserved or that the leases were not pursuant to the power. Therefore, I will presume that Sir Henry did right and that the leases were pursuant to the power, especially the tenants not complaining. As to those, I dismiss the bill.

If Sir Henry had not made leases pursuant to his power, this court would have compelled him. If upon valuable consideration, this court would supply a

---

[1] *Lord Rockingham v. Oxenden* (1705–1711), 2 Salkeld 578, 91 E.R. 487, Precedents in Chancery 239, 24 E.R. 116, *sub nom. Lord Rockingham v. Penrice*, 1 Peere Williams 177, 24 E.R. 345.

[2] E. Coke, *First Institute* (1628), f. 351.

[3] *Barwick v. Foster* (1609), Croke Jac. 227, 233, 79 E.R. 197, 201, also Yelverton 167, 80 E.R. 111, 1 Bulstrode 1, 80 E.R. 707, 1 Brownlow & Goldesborough 105, 123 E.R. 695, 2 Brownlow & Goldesborough 220, 123 E.R. 908.

[4] appointment *MS.*

defective execution of the power. As to the other leases which appeared by the report were not made pursuant to the power, the defendant cannot be entitled. If she is not, is the plaintiff? I think he is, for payment in the morning had been good though the law allows the tenant to the last hour of the day for payment of the rent. But I will not now determine that point. If the rent is not due to the plaintiff by law, yet he is a proper [party] here, for it is a hard law. And if a man does not through honesty [do that] which he is not compellable to by law, he does well and according to natural justice, and equity may hinder his recalling it, though he may by law. And the person who received the rents is but a trustee for the person entitled.

As to the leases which appear by the report to be determined by Sir Henry's death, the defendant must account to the plaintiff for the rent.

Lincoln's Inn MS. Misc. 11, p. 197

Among other questions in this cause, one was whether a debt by a note should be tacked to a mortgage. And, as to that, the case was this.

Sir William Wentworth, in the year 1691, mortgages some tithes to Dr. Spencer for securing £100 and interest, and, about the same time, he borrow £50 more on a bond and another £50 on a note under his hand. After the death of Sir William Wentworth, Dr. Spencer draws out an account of these securities and, at the bottom are written the following words, which were signed by the plaintiff, who was the son and heir of his father, *viz.* 'Sir, I do empower you to receive the rent of the tithes of Hooton Parnell yearly for the discharge of the interest of the debts above mentioned and for the interest of £50 for which you are bound to Mauliverer and of the principal so far as the rents will extend. Witness my hand 26 February 1693.'

The question was if, by this authority to receive the tithes, the mortgage was charged with the £50 note and that the plaintiff should not redeem one without paying off the other.

Lord Chancellor [Lord Parker]: If a man owes money on a note and gives the party to whom the note is given authority to receive the rents of such a farm until he is paid the debt, that will not amount to a charge upon the farm, for, being an authority only, it may be revoked. But, where a man has a mortgage and, consequently, a right to receive the rents and there being money likewise due to him from the mortgagor upon a note, the mortgagor agrees by a writing under his hand that the mortgagee shall receive the rents of the mortgaged estate until he is satisfied the note as well as the mortgage, that will be a charge upon the equity of redemption and the mortgagor shall not redeem without paying off both.

[Other reports of this case: Precedents in Chancery 555, 24 E.R. 249, 9 Modern 21, 88 E.R. 289.]

486

Anonymous

(Ch. 1721)

Notice must be given to all parties of a motion to strike out a plaintiff who was made a party without his consent.

British Library MS. Hargrave 83, p. 15, pl. 1

Eodem die [9 February 1720/21].

If you move to strike a plaintiff's name out of a bill upon an affidavit the person was made a plaintiff without his consent, you must give notice to the other plaintiffs and defendants. But the court granted the motion this day without notice [. . .] etc.

487

Lord Kingsale v. Miles

(Ch. 1721)

A defendant should be sued by the name by which he or she is commonly known.

Where a person is alleged to be married to someone where the marriage is disputed, the plaintiff must specifically identify the parties to the alleged marriage.

British Library MS. Hargrave 83, p. 15, pl. 3

9 February 1720[/21].

The defendant had demurred to the plaintiff's bill because she was thereby styled Anne Miles, whereas the style ought to have been Anne, commonly called Lady Kingsale, because she was the widow of the late Lord Kingsale. And the plaintiff now brought his bill against her suggesting that she was married to one John Miles and that John Miles was living at the time of her intermarriage with the late Lord Kingsale. And upon this demurrer, the plaintiff was ordered to amend his bill.

Now, the defendant's counsel moved that she might have further time to plead, answer, or demur until the plaintiff gave her a note under his hand who that John Miles was to whom he charged in his bill that the defendant was married and where that John Miles lived, which motion My Lord [Lord Parker] granted, for he said she ought to know what Miles was meant in a case of such obscurity, for, though it had been urged that she might deny generally that she was married to any John Miles, yet if a trial should be directed upon that issue and she comes prepared to prove that she was not married to that John Miles who is thought to be the man meant by the plaintiff or that he was married to another person at the time he pretended to marry her, the plaintiff might then set up another or say that this is not the Miles I meant so that there ought to be a certainty in the person before there can be a certainty in the issue. My Lord added that he had known it said in a like case 'this is not the man I meant to whom the party was married.'

488

Caruthers v. Perry

(Ch. 1721)

The administrator of a decedent's estate is entitled to reimbursement for any expenses of the estate that he paid.

Lincoln's Inn MS. Misc. 12, p. 30

10 February 1720[/21]. Caruthers v. Perry, Hanson, and Lucy, his wife, and Banks.

One Wilson gave the defendant Hanson's wife a legacy to be paid her at twenty-one. The executors lived at Virginia, and they remitted over the £50 to the defendant Perry, who paid it to the defendant Lucy's mother upon her giving him a bond to pay it to her daughter when she came of age. And the plaintiff was bound as surety in this bond. The mother dies intestate, and the defendant Banks takes administration.

Perry assigns over the bond to the defendant Hanson, who had married Lucy. And he puts the bond in suit against the plaintiff, who, thereupon, brings his bill for an injunction and for an account of the assets of the mother and praying that the bond might be satisfied out of her assets.

Lord Chancellor [Lord Parker] decreed the administrator to account and, in that account, to be allowed what he, after the mother's death, had paid for the maintenance of the defendant Lucy during her infancy and for putting her out and what had been so paid was to go in discharge of the legacy, for, though the mother had no right to receive the legacy but for the use of her daughter, yet, in regard the daughter was not entitled to her legacy until she came to twenty-one, if any part of the assets has been applied for her benefit, it ought to go towards the discharge of the legacy though it should break into the principal.

489

May v. Lewen

(Ch. 1721)

Where legacies are given to executors, the executors are only trustees for the next of kin for the residuum of the decedent's estate.

Lincoln's Inn MS. Coxe 89, vol. 3, pt. 2, p. 1

20 February 1720[/21].

There were two executors appointed and £5 apiece given them by the will with these words subjoined, *viz.* 'for their care and trouble'. And it was decreed the surplus of the estate should go to the next of kin.

Lincoln's Inn MS. Misc. 11, p. 192, pl. 3

The same point the next day [25 February 1721] came in question before Lord Chancellor [Lord Parker], where the executors had £50 given them for their care and pains.

He decreed against the executors without difficulty. And Lord Chancellor [Lord Parker] said he had some precedents from Mr. Vernon, who told him he had taken no notes of late years as to this point, he looking upon it as settled that, where the executors had legacies given them and there was no disposition of the surplus, they could not be entitled to it.

2 Peere Williams 159, note, 24 E.R. 683,
9 Modern 11, note, 88 E.R. 282

Lord Chancellor Parker had decreed in favor of the next of kin purely on account of the legacies' being given to the executors for their trouble in the execution of the will.

The case of May v. Lewin was this. Beatrice Miller, by her will of 2nd December 1717, after payment of her debts, legacies, and funerals, devised all her lands and tenements and the rents and profits thereof and the produce of all her money and other personal estate to the plaintiff and the defendant Lewin and their heirs on trust to sell the said real and personal estate and pay the interest of the money arising by such sale to her mother for life. And the testatrix then gave some small legacies to be paid after the death of the mother. And she appointed the plaintiff and the defendant Lewin executors of her will, and she gave them £50 apiece for their trouble therein. But she made no disposition of the residue.

The court declared the executors to be trustees of the residue for the next of kin. Reg. Lib. B. 1720, fol. 196.

Lincoln's Inn MS. Misc. 384, p. 310

Lord Macclesfield: The executor, having a legacy, cannot claim the surplus. Lord King, 28 January 1725[/26], Newel con. Gardiner; the executor shall not have the residue because he had a legacy. Weaver v. Fowler, 26 November 1723; the defendant, a goldsmith, subscribed the plaintiff's annuity into the South Sea [Company] without the plaintiff's privity.[1] The bill for satisfaction was dismissed.

490

Holloway v. Curry

(Ch. 1721)

A settlement made by a debtor in favor of his wife and children in consideration of love and affection is void as against the settlor's creditors.

Lincoln's Inn MS. Misc. 11, p. 192, pl. 1

23 February. At the Rolls.

The plaintiff, being a creditor by subcontract of one Johnson, to whom the defendant Curry was executor, brings his bill for a discovery of assets and a satisfaction of his debts.

The defendants set up a settlement made by the testator after his marriage of a leasehold estate in consideration of love and affection to his wife, which was in trust for his wife and children after his death, which settlement was made after the testator became indebted to the plaintiff.

[The Master of the Rolls, Jekyll] decreed the settlement to be fraudulent as against the plaintiff.

491

Liron v. Liron

(Ch. 1721)

Where executors receive legacies, they cannot take the residuum of the estate.

Lincoln's Inn MS. Misc. 11, p. 192, pl. 2

24 February 1720[/21]. At the Rolls.

The plaintiff's brother, by his will gave several annuities to the plaintiff and to the defendant, her son, and he gave amongst other pecuniary legacies £5 apiece to his executors. But he makes no disposition of the surplus.

---

[1] *Weaver v. Fowler and Nicholls* (Ch. 1723), see below, Case No. 572.

[The Master of the Rolls, JEKYLL] decreed that the executors, having legacies given them by the will, could not be entitled to the surplus.

492

Holditch v. Mist

(Ch. 1721)

In this case, the court refused to grant relief to a director of the South Sea Company against his creditor even though his assets had been seized by an act of Parliament.

1 Peere Williams 695, 24 E.R. 575

The plaintiff having been one of the late directors of the South Sea Company, was sued at law for £800, he having taken that sum of the defendant for £400 South Sea stock, which he had (as he affirmed) put into the subscription books in the name of one Mrs. Peck, whereas, upon search in all the books, it did not appear that there was any sum whatsoever set down in the name of Peck, upon which the defendant Mist brought an action against the plaintiffs, as for so much money received for the defendant's use, and obtained a verdict.

The defendant at law now brought his bill and moved for an injunction, urging that in regard the late act[1] had vested all his estate in the trustees for the South Sea Company and made a provision for the payment of his debts (being late a director) out of his estate, the defendant Mist ought to repair to the trustees, that it would be extremely hard to permit the plaintiff at law to take out execution against the body of his debtor when the legislature had disabled him from paying any of his debts and provided another method for that purpose, and that it was like the case of a bankrupt, where the court had not only granted an injunction, but also released the bankrupt, who, after having given up all his estate and submitted to be examined, had yet been arrested by a peevish creditor.

But the Lord Chancellor [LORD PARKER] refused to grant an injunction, saying there was nothing of this Act of Parliament disclosed in the pleadings or, if there was, yet that the Act was not made in favor of the late directors.

However, afterwards, by consent, the present trustees of the South Sea Company paid the debt in question out of the allowance made by the Act to the plaintiff Holditch.

[Other reports of this case: 2 Eq. Cas. Abr. 724, 22 E.R. 609.]

---

[1] Stat. 7 Geo. I, stat. 1, c. 28.

493

Cann v. Cann

(Ch. 1721)

A release made by a person who was aware of his rights will not be set aside unless there was fraud or surprise.

Lincoln's Inn MS. Misc. 384, p. 143

25 February.

The bill is to set aside a former will by proving a subsequent will in 1681, which is not extant, but is proved to be burned by the daughter of the testator Sir Robert Cann with the direction of her mother. The testator died in 1685. The question is whether the court will at this distance of time direct a trial whether there were such a subsequent will.

Peere Williams: The original bill was filed in 1694. The estate was £1200 *per annum*. In the Statute of Frauds,[1] that will which revokes a former must be signed by the testator in the presence of three witnesses, but other wills are to be attested by three witnesses in the testator's presence but need not be signed by the testator in their presence.

Yorke, for the defendant: The former bill was to establish the second will and was dismissed. This bill charges new discoveries. Lord Somers ordered the defendants to answer the new matter, but the plaintiff not to proceed without leave of the court. Lord Cowper ordered that the plaintiff should proceed as he should be advised. To re-examine matters in issue in a former cause is very dangerous and introductive of perjury.

Vernon, for the plaintiff: In the common case, where a bill is to prove a will *per testes*, though the will is well proved, yet the court never denies the heir a trial at law if he desires it. Jacobson and Hanakennis;[2] where a new discovery of letters which were in his own house was admitted in the House of Lords, though publication had passed, the person entitled to another part of the estate may examine over again what was in issue in this suit about the other part. So a wife may examine matters *de novo* which were in issue in a cause brought by the husband. Here, a bill of review will not lie, as in Jacobson and Hanakennis.

Mead quoted Goss and Tracy,[3] where a bill was brought to establish a cancelled will. The defendant got the testator to make a new will as a corroboration

[1] Stat. 29 Car. II, c. 3, s. 5 (*SR*, V, 840).

[2] *Jacobsen v. Hennekenius* (1712–1714), British Library MS. Hargrave 80, ff. 97, 146v, 5 Brown P.C. 482, 2 E.R. 811, Chancery Cases *tempore* Harcourt, 232, 367.

[3] *Goss v. Tracy* (1715), 1 Peere Williams 287, 24 E.R. 392, 2 Vernon 699, 23 E.R. 1053, 1 Eq. Cas. Abr. 406, 21 E.R. 1136, 2 Eq. Cas. Abr. 396, 491, 767, 22 E.R. 338, 416, 651.

of his former will; the court directed an issue whether the testator designed to cancel his former will by the second; it was found that the first will was not designed to be cancelled by the second.

Lord Chancellor [LORD PARKER]: If this matter were fresh, I should think it very strong for the plaintiffs. By the civil law, if a parent gives his son a legacy and that son should draw his sword upon him, as in this case, it would make the will void. And the eldest son here had done nothing to disoblige his father. Here, two witnesses swear they were witnesses to the second will which had the testator's seal to it and that a great part of the estate was given to the plaintiff's father. A judge should not say he has only an inclination to do justice. The objection that the matter cannot be re-examined is strong one way; on the other, that the witnesses who are secreted by fraud should not afterwards be examined is very hard. If my predecessors had determined either way, I should have gladly acquiesced. I should be glad to see when publication has passed that the matter has been re-examined. In the case of a husband and wife, they are different persons. I should be inclined to send it to law if the inconvenience shall not appear to me insuperable. But if I cannot, I hope it will be sent to law by another court.

British Library MS. Hargrave 83, p. 18

22 August 1721. At the Lord Chancellor's house.

Sir William Can had two sons by two wives, Sir Thomas, the elder, by a former wife, Sir William, the younger, by a wife that was living at the time of his decease. Sir William, the father, was a humorsome man; he had made several wills and had written them all with his own hand. In 1680, he made a will all written with his own hand. And by this will, he left his estate to his younger son charged with an annuity or £6000 to his elder son which he should accept after the death of Sir William, the father. This will was duly proved. And Sir Thomas, the son, accepted the £6000 and acquiesced under the will for ten years. But after that length of time, Sir Thomas brought a bill against the Lady Can, the relict of Sir Thomas's father, and against his brother Sir William. And in his bill, he charged that there was a will made by his father subsequent to that of 1681 or some other writing by which he revoked that writing, and he charged that this will or writing had been suppressed or destroyed by the defendants. They both by their answer denied such subsequent will but gave no answer to the charge as to the writing. Sir William also upon the exhibiting of this bill preferred a cross-bill against Sir Thomas to be quieted in possession. And upon the hearing of these causes, Sir William's prevailed and Sir Thomas's bill was dismissed and he was foreclosed having accepted of the £6000 devised to him. Then Lady Can dies and makes Sir William, her son, executor. And, after her death, Sir William and Sir Thomas came to an agreement by which reciting the will of 1681 to have been duly proved and taking notice of all the matters and controversies between them, Sir William makes over the manor of Brene to Sir Thomas upon condition that Sir Thomas should give him a general release of all demands, which

Sir Thomas accordingly did. Afterwards, in a cause that sprang up between Sir William and other parties, some new light sprang up as to a will made by Sir William, the father, subsequent to that of 1681. Upon this, Sir Thomas brought another bill in which he charged new matter lately come to his knowledge as to a subsequent will that it had been conveyed away, that Lady Can had burnt it, and that, as soon as Sir William, the son, heard it was burnt, he expressed great joy and said then he was safe. To this new bill, Sir William pleaded in bar the dismission of the former bill and the release given by Sir Thomas. This plea was argued in 1695 before Lord Somers, and Sir William was ordered to answer, but there were to be no further proceedings without leave of the court. Sir William put in his answer and absolutely denied all the charge in Sir Thomas's bill. After this, Sir Thomas took a fortnight's time to consider whether he would proceed any farther and then said, 'Well there was another will. I am sure. I saw it myself, but however Sir William, I wish you joy.' Sir Thomas afterwards made his will and thereby he again releases to Sir William upon condition that he paid £1600 which terms Sir William not thinking fit to comply with, the plaintiff, who was son of Sir Thomas and an infant at the time of his death, now brought his bill of revivor having attained his full age.

My Lord Chancellor [Lord Parker] said to set aside such a release would be of the utmost ill consequence, for it is not pretended to have been obtained by any surprise and, at the same time that they endeavor this, they insist upon their own advantage, which they have by the agreement in pursuance whereof this release was given and make no offer of restoring the manor of Brene. Besides, the release itself presumes some right in the releasor to be released and Sir Thomas said he knew there was another will, he himself had seen it. This release, therefore, cannot be supposed to have been given by one ignorant of his right, which makes the principal equity in the case.

My Lord then balanced the evidence on both sides as to the subsequent will and concluded it to be his opinion that no such will was ever executed by Sir Thomas, his father, but he perhaps being a humorsome, unaccountable man, might have prepared a draught of some such will to lay in the way of his elder son to amuse him and, if he did so (as he did many things as odd), that would reconcile all or most that had been said by the evidence on both sides. But supposing there had been a will duly executed and afterwards destroyed by Lady Can, he saw no foundation for setting aside a release made by a man cognizant of his own right and which is not pretended to have been obtained by any fraud or surprise.

[Other reports of this case: 1 Vernon 480, 23 E.R. 605, 1 Peere Williams 567, 723, 24 E.R. 520, 586, 2 Eq. Cas. Abr. 417, 22 E.R. 354.]

494

Dunn v. Smith

(Ch. 1721)

He who seeks equity must do equity.

Where a debtor sues to redeem a mortgage, he or she must pay the creditor the entire debt that is owed even though only part of it was secured by the mortgage.

Partial performance of a contract takes it out of the Statute of Frauds.

Lincoln's Inn MS. Misc. 506, p. 23

Hilary 7 Geo., 1 March 1720[/21].

An estate in land was given to Richard Farro's wife in trust for her for her sole and separate use during the joint lives of her and her husband, the husband not to be permitted to receive any part of the profits, that, in case the wife died before the husband, then it should be in such manner as she should appoint by writing under her hand and seal, subscribed in the presence of two witnesses and, in default of such appointment, to her heirs and assigns forever, but, in case she outlived her husband, then to her during her life, and afterwards, as she should appoint etc. The trustees and the wife, by a fine, conveyed the land to one Reavely, a widow, in fee by way of a mortgage for £350. Afterwards, the husband writes a letter to this Reavely desiring her to lend them £50 upon the same security, telling her that they were in great necessity for the money etc., which letter ran throughout in the plural number, meaning himself and his wife. But it was signed by the husband only. The wife carried the letter to Reavely desiring the effect of it. Afterwards, there was an application made to one Barnton, who had procured the former £350 of Reavely, that he would go to her and persuade her to lend Farro and his wife £50 more, and, accordingly, he did. But, afterwards, Reavely brings the money and takes a bond only of Richard Farro, the husband, for the money. The like was done afterwards for another £50. There were several receipts for the interest of the £350, one by Reavely in her lifetime and the other by the defendant Smith, her administrator, taking no notice of the two £50s. There appeared also a letter from Reavely wherein she inquired where is Parson Farro, that I may get my money of him. Reavely dies. And Smith takes out administration.

The bill is brought by the trustees of the wife against the defendant Smith to redeem the mortgage and to have reconveyances of the land upon the payment of the £350 with interest, the husband it seems being worth nothing. And the defendant insists upon the having the other two £50s to be paid, so that the question was whether the wife's land was chargeable with the two £50s. It was insisted on by the plaintiff that it was not, for that relating to an inheritance in lands, it ought to have been in writing, signed by the party according to the Statute of Frauds and Perjuries,[1] that this was the case of a married woman, who was under the power of her husband and, in that, different from other cases of this nature, that, as this could not have charged the estate at first, so neither could it surcharge it, that it appears from Reavely's receipts, which were only for the £350, that she did not imagine that she had any other security than Farro's bond for the two £50s, which were secured by a quite different way from the £350, *viz.* by the husband's single bond and no covenant from the trustees, not so much as to pay the interest, the £350 by the mortgage in which both the husband and wife were bound.

On the other hand, it was urged that this was the case of an honest creditor, who was likely to lose a just debt if that security should fail and is, therefore, entitled to all the favor the court could show, that, though the wife did not sign the letter, yet she knew the contents of it and carried and delivered it herself, when the letter ran in both their names, that this being to her separate use, she is in the nature of a *feme sole*, that the money was paid to them both, that it was out of the Statute of Frauds because it was not to bind lands originally, but only to stop the equity of redemption. A case was cited in Lord Cowper's time, which was of a personal thing, the plaintiff had pawned a jewel to a goldsmith, one White, who afterwards pawned it to one Metcalfe for more than the plaintiff had pawned it to him.[2] Afterwards, Metcalfe, at the request of White, lent him several more sums of money, at which time there was no mention made of the jewel's being a security for the money, but yet Lord Cowper decreed that the plaintiff should not be admitted to redeem but upon paying all the money that Metcalfe had lent White, while the jewel was pledged to him because, says he, it is to be presumed that he who has a security in his hands does not lend but with a view to that security. He relied much on the case in 1 Ch. 97.[3] There was another case cited of Watts v. Creswell,[4] where the father was a tenant for life, remainder to the son, who was an infant. The son solicited for money to be lent to the father upon the security of the estate; the money was lent to the father, who made a mortgage of the estate in fee, to which the son was a witness, but yet it was decreed that the estate was bound after the father's death in the hands of the son.

(Lord Chancellor [LORD PARKER] said that was a case of fraud and an infant may be guilty of a fraud as well as another person.)

Another case of Kent and Lord Kildare,[5] where, on a promise to give land as security for money lent, it was decreed that such a promise was a lien on the land.

---

[1] Stat. 29 Car. II, c. 3 (*SR*, V, 839–842).

[2] *Demainbray v. Metcalf* (1715), see above, Case No. 105.

[3] *St. John v. Holford* (1668), 1 Chancery Cases 97, 22 E.R. 712, also 1 Eq. Cas. Abr. 324, 21 E.R. 1077.

[4] *Watts v. Creswell* (1714), see above, Case No. 18.

[5] *Earl of Kildare v. Kent* (1702), 2 Freeman 253, 22 E.R. 1192, *sub nom. Shepherd v. Kent*, Precedents in Chancery 190, 24 E.R. 92, 2 Vernon 435, 23 E.R. 879, 1 Eq. Cas.

Ramsdel v. Oldfield;[1] where the party had promised in a letter that he would give land as security for money to be paid on marriage, the marriage took effect before the money was paid or the security given, and yet it was decreed that this should bind the real assets. Note there was a devise of lands for payment of debts.

The Lord Chancellor [LORD PARKER] thought that, on the circumstances of the case, the wife's land ought to be bound for the whole because she was privy to the transaction and solicited for the money and, though the rents of the estate were payable to her and not to her husband, yet, if she had ordered the trustees to pay it to him, that would have been a good payment to her use. This money may be looked on as advanced for her as much as her husband, being for furnishing an house, which was come to him with a small rectory; she could not have disposed of her money better, it being for necessaries. As to Reavely's taking the bond, it is not to be supposed that, when it was offered, she should refuse it, though not thinking to quit any other security and, indeed, it is improbable she should quit land security for the bond of a beggar, for such it appears the husband was and is. As to the Statute of Frauds, lands may be bound without a writing where there is no fraud; had this been only performed on one part, the court would have compelled the other party to perform his part of that agreement. But, where it is performed on both parts, the money is lent, and the creditor has a legal security for his debt, shall this court defeat him of that security? The creditor does not come here to be paid or to have a security, but is in possession of the lands, and it is the debtor who comes here for the equity of redemption. The money was not paid at the day; the estate thus in law is absolute and the wife or her trustees can only come on a foot of equity and must thus do equity by making the party an adequate compensation. As to the receipts, that is nothing, for it is in the power of the person paying to declare what use the money shall be to and not of the receiver. And thus, when money is offered, shall she refuse taking it because it is not the whole or shall she refuse to give a receipt according to the truth of the case, *viz.* that it was the interest of the £350? Besides, there is but one receipt in her lifetime; the others are from the administrator, who knew nothing of the matter.

It was decreed that the plaintiff should be let into possession paying the £350 and the two £50s with the interest due thereon; otherwise, the bill is to be dismissed with costs.

Lincoln's Inn MS. Misc. 384, p. 219, pl. 2

1 March 1720[/21].

Upon the marriage of Richard Farresly with his wife, her estate was vested in trustees to her separate use, but she was to have the power of charging it by a deed attested by two witnesses. Accordingly, in 1706, she mortgaged it to

Abr. 142, 21 E.R. 944, Colles 253, 1 E.R. 273.

[1] *Ramsden v. Oldfield* (Ch. 1720), see above, Case No. 463.

one Mrs. Reively for £350. Afterwards, her husband wanting £100 wrote to the mortgagee in his own and his wife's name to advance the £100 upon the same security and the wife carried the letter but did not sign it. And by her importunity and the advice of one Bernard, who had persuaded the lending of the first mortgage money, Mrs. Reively was prevailed upon to advance this £100, for which Mr. Farresly gave two bonds of £50 each. He is since become insolvent and gone out of England.

The bill is by Mrs. Farresly and her trustees to be admitted to redeem this mortgage. The question is whether the mortgage shall be redeemed without paying off the bonds.

Mead, for the defendant, cited Demainbry v. Metcalf and White, where the plaintiff had pledged a jewel to Metcalf, who assigned it to White, and, afterwards, the plaintiff borrowed more money of White upon his note and, though there was no agreement that the jewel should be a security for that money, yet Lord Cowper decreed that the plaintiff should pay off the notes before he should be admitted to redeem the jewel and relieved upon the case of St. John v. Holford, 1 Ch. Ca. 97, that he [who] will have equity must do equity. Watts v. Creswell.

Lord Chancellor [Lord Parker]: If this had been the estate of the husband, there could have been no question but that he must have paid off the bonds. It is hard for a court of equity to take the estate from the defendant without being paid the bonds, especially when she lent the money on the credit of the mortgage, and Barnard, who prevailed on the defendant to lend the money swears he would not have procured 6d. to be advanced on the husband's bond, who was worth nothing. Besides, the wife had the benefit of this money to buy her necessaries. And this cannot be within the Statute of Frauds etc., being in part carried into execution.

The mortgagee is in possession. If the mortgagor will have equity, she must do equity and must pay off the bonds.

495

Roby v. Daniels

(Ch. 1721)

A London orphan cannot take his orphanage share and also a legacy under his father's will where the will disposes of the entire personal estate.

Lincoln's Inn MS. Misc. 11, p. 193, pl. 1

2 March 1720[/21].

In this case, it was said by the Master of the Rolls [Jekyll] and agreed to by Mr. *Cooper* and Mr. *Lutwyche* that, if a freeman takes upon him by his will to dispose of his whole personal estate without any regard to the custom and gives legacies to his children, who refuse to acquiesce under the will and insist on their orphanage parts, that they shall not have their legacies and their orphanage shares too.

But this was opposed by Mr. *Mead*, who said the later resolutions had been otherwise. And he cited the Case of Wheatley and Wheatley, *quod vide*, 228, and Babington and Greenwood, *ante* 166.[1]

496

Robinson v. Farsyde

(Ch. 1721)

If a person enters upon an infant's estate, he is a trustee for the infant.

If a trustee purchases in encumbrances for less than is due on them, it is for the infant's benefit and the trustee cannot charge the infant's estate with more than he paid.

Where a widow does not claim her dower, it is presumed that she released it to her heir.

Lincoln's Inn MS. Misc. 506, p. 26

2 March 1720[/21].

The plaintiff, an infant, is heir at law to John Robinson, the son of Henry Robinson, who was seised in fee of the lands in Bucton. The defendant married a daughter of Henry, the grandfather, sister to John, the father of the plaintiff, and entered into the lands of Bucton and was several years in possession of the lands. The bill was to be let into possession of the lands and to have an account of the profits. The defendant insisted that he had compounded several judgment debts of the grandfather, in whose lifetime the father died, whose heir the plaintiff is, and that he ought to be allowed the whole of those debts and for the dower of his wife's mother, the plaintiff's grandmother. The plaintiff's father went into the East Indies, and, there, he married and had issue, the plaintiff, and died, living the grandfather. And then, the grandfather died leaving several debts on judgment securities to one Sir William Rearsby and to Doctor Humphrey Robinson, brother to the said grandfather, which debts the defendant compounded for less than half and, upon that account, entered into the lands. Most of the debts were compounded after the defendant was in possession, and one not above half a year before.

---

[1] *Wheatley v. Warner* (Ch. 1717–1718), see above, Case No. 172; *Babington v. Greenwood* (Ch. 1718–1720), see above, Case No. 341.

Henry Robinson — Humphrey Robinson

Henry Robinson:

John Robinson — _____ Robinson m. Mr. Farsyde (defendant)

John Robinson:

Mr. Robinson (plaintiff)

The Master of the Rolls [JEKYLL] had decreed that the plaintiff should be let into possession and have an account of the profits upon paying the defendant what he had compounded the debts for, without allowing anything for dower.

And, on a rehearing, the decree was confirmed. The Lord Chancellor [LORD PARKER] declared that, had the defendant entered in the right of his wife, he should have varied the decree and he should have allowed the defendant the whole money, for, at that rate, a man may be undone if he must account for the profits of an estate which he believed to be his own and, perhaps, has lived answerable to it. In such a case, he would have been as a stranger, and, where a stranger compounds debts that affect the land, he will stand in the place of the creditor and be entitled to the whole sum and the party shall never be let into possession but upon paying the whole. But, where a trustee or a guardian or an executor compound, he shall be allowed only what he paid for them on the presumption that he had money of the parties in his hand or is in expectation of having it. And this rule extends to all those whom this court looks on as trustees. Now, as this case is, the defendant could not be supposed to have entered in his own right or in the right of his wife, for he had notice of John Robinson's being married in the Indies and being dead, leaving issue, and, by virtue of these judgments, he could not enter, for there was no [writ of] *elegit* sued out nor possession delivered, and, if he had sued out an *elegit*, yet that would have affected but a moiety of the lands and, of that moiety, there must have been a valuation so that he could not enter but in the right of the plaintiff, who was an infant, for else he must be a disseisor. But the court will suppose every man an honest man and, when he has but one right to enter by, will suppose that he entered in that right rather than make him a wrong-doer. And anybody may enter for the benefit of an infant where it is by consent and without opposition. And, if he entered for the benefit of the infant, he is looked on by the court as a trustee and is within the common rule of having no allowance for more than what he actually paid.

As to the matter of dower, [there is] no doubt but, if the widow had taken possession of the whole and a bill had been brought against her, she would have had an allowance for her dower, though she had not sued out any writ of dower.

And it would have been the same if she did agree that her daughter's husband should have it, especially if it were by way of a marriage portion. But there is nothing of that in this case. There is no agreement proved that she quitted for the benefit of her daughter or the daughter's husband, and since she waived it and never sued out any writ, nor did she come to any agreement that any other person should have the benefit of it, it is most reasonable to presume that she waived it for the benefit of the heir, who was her grandson, that so, when he came home from the Indies, he might have his estate clear of all encumbrances so that there ought to be no allowance for dower neither.

Lincoln's Inn MS. Misc. 384, p. 220, pl. 1

2 March; rehearing.

Lord Chancellor [Lord Parker]: If a stranger enters upon an infant's estate, he is a trustee for the infant. And if he purchases in encumbrances for less than is due on them, it is for the infant's benefit and the trustee cannot charge the infant's estate with more than he paid.

The Master of the Rolls' decree was affirmed.

497

Gore v. Gore

(Ch. 1721)

A devise in praesenti *to a person who is neither in esse nor expectant is an executory devise that is subject to the same restrictions as a contingent remainder.*

Lincoln's Inn MS. Misc. 506, p. 28

March 1720[/21].

This is a bill brought by the younger son, who is the devisee under his father's will, against a disinherited eldest son, to perpetuate the testimony of the witnesses to the will and to have an execution of the trusts. But there was a question how the trust should be directed on one clause in the will whereby the father devises the lands to trustees for 500 years upon several trusts there mentioned and, afterwards, to the first son of the defendant, his eldest son, and his heirs male and, for want of such issue to the second son, etc. The father takes notice of his eldest son's being unmarried, for he directs that he should marry and pay his wife's portion to his trustees, that he should have the power to settle a jointure. He takes notice of his oldest son's being extravagant and, for that cause, had made no provision for him. The father dies, and the eldest son having no issue, the question was whether the devise to the first son of the eldest son, a person not *in esse*, be a good devise after a trust of 500 years. It was insisted on by the one side that it was void, for that it could not be a devise *in praesenti* because [it was] to a person not *in esse* nor by way of a contingent remainder because there is no freehold to support it nor by executory devise because it is not within a reasonable time. It was compared to the case of Scatterwood and Edge,[1] that the effect of that would be that the estate in the meantime would descend to the defendant Thomas Gore as heir at law, whom the testator intended should have nothing.

Lord Chancellor [LORD PARKER] said that the case of Scatterwood v. Edge was no more than this, 'to one for ten years' and then goes on to make a fresh devise *in praesenti* without saying from after the expiration of the term nor was there anything in the will by which it appeared that the testator intended to wait any while for the commencement of the second devise. It being thus a devise *in praesenti* to a person not *in esse* nor expectant, it was said that you should not wait any number of years nor one day after the testator's death, though he said he did not know how far that may be altered by the late resolution of the House of Lords,[2] that one may wait nine months after the death of the father for a posthumous child. However, it cannot be reckoned by years.

On the other side, it was insisted that it was an executory devise and plainly so intended by the testator, that when once a contingency happens within the time limited by law, then all the remainder estates vest immediately, that, if the trust estate should do more than satisfy the trusts, the surplus ought to go to the heir by way of a resulting trust, being part of the estate not disposed of that the testator intended it as a future devise because he takes notice of his son's not being married and gives it to his first son to be begotten. There was a case in the House of Lord, Bowton and Long,[3] where 'to the sons begotten' was construed a devise *in praesenti*, but 'to the persons to be begotten' a devise *in futuro*.

The LORD CHANCELLOR said that an executory devise is a future disposition of the freehold, but, where the freehold is disposed of *in praesenti* and then there is a future disposition on a contingency, that is a contingent remainder and can never be an executory devise. That is the distinction laid down in Purefoy and Rogers and Pell and Brown.[4] In an executory devise, you may have the same contingencies as on a contingent remainder. This case can be good only by way

---

[1] *Scattergood v. Edge* (1699), 12 Modern 278, 88 E.R. 1320, 1 Salkeld 229, 91 E.R. 203, 1 Eq. Cas. Abr. 189, 21 E.R. 980, 2 Eq. Cas. Abr. 337, 22 E.R. 287, King's Inns Dublin MS. 92, p. 1.

[2] Perhaps *Thornby v. Fleetwood* (1721), 5 Brown P.C. 374, 378, 2 E.R. 740, 742.

[3] *Lay v. Beaumont* (Ex. 1709), Eq. Cases Exch. 604, *Darbison, ex dem. Long v. Beaumont* (Ex. 1713), 1 Peere Williams 229, 24 E.R. 366, Fortescue 18, 92 E.R. 743, 1 Eq. Cas. Abr. 214, 21 E.R. 999, Dodd 366, *Darbison v. Beaumont* (H.L. 1714), Lords' Journal, vol. 19, p. 696, 3 Brown P.C. 60, 1 E.R. 1177.

[4] *Purefoy v. Rogers* (1671), 2 Williams Saunders 380, 85 E.R. 1181, 2 Levinz 39, 83 E.R. 443, 3 Keble 11, 84 E.R. 566, 1 Eq. Cas. Abr. 189, 21 E.R. 980, Lincoln's Inn MS. Misc. 500, pp. 192, 194; *Pell v. Brown* (1620), Croke Jac. 590, 79 E.R. 504, Palmer 131, 81 E.R. 1012, 2 Rolle Rep. 196, 216, 81 E.R. 746, 760, Godbolt 282, 78 E.R. 165, J. Bridgman 1, 123 E.R. 1157.

of executory devise so that the question will be whether this be not too remote, not falling out in the life[time] of his father nor within the due course of nature after his death, that he thought it would be hard to say it was after the resolution of the House of Lords and the Act of Parliament. However, it was purely a matter of law.

And, therefore, he ordered it to be made a case of for the judges of the King's Bench, that the heir at law would be entitled to the surplus if there be any of the trust lands where there is maintenance, that must be allowed; where there is none, it will carry interest.

[Other reports of this case: 2 Peere Williams 28, 24 E.R. 629, W. Kelynge 254, 25 E.R. 599, 9 Modern 4, 88 E.R. 278, 10 Modern 501, 88 E.R. 826, 2 Strange 958, 93 E.R. 967, 2 Barnardiston K.B. 209, 229, 355, 94 E.R. 453, 467, 550, 2 Eq. Cas. Abr. 339, 22 E.R. 289.]

498

Kemp v. Kelsey

(Ch. 1721)

A child of a London citizen can release his or her customary share; such a release is not necessarily void.

A release of the customary share of a London citizen's estate by a husband and wife after the marriage is valid.

Where a bill of complaint is brought to be relieved against a release, the defendant cannot plead the same release in bar.

Lincoln's Inn MS. Misc. 12, p. 74

10 March 1720[/21]. John Wymp and Rebecca, his wife, one of the daughters of John Kelsey, plaintiffs; Kelsey, the widow and executrix of John Kelsey, and Bull and his wife, the other daughter, defendants.

The plaintiffs [exhibited a] bill for an account of the personal estate of John Kelsey, who was a freeman of London, and to have the plaintiff Rebecca's orphanage share thereof by the custom.

The defendant, the widow, pleaded that the plaintiffs, after their marriage agreed to release all their right to the testator's estate and that, accordingly, in consideration of £100, they released to the testator all their right to his real and personal estate by the custom of London or otherwise.

And in the release there was a covenant that the plaintiffs after the testator's death would release to the executors all right by the custom.

And it was insisted for the plaintiffs that the release was no bar to their demand, for that a man cannot release a future or contingent right of his wife, and, at the time of the release in question, there was nothing vested in the plaintiff's wife.

Lord Chancellor [LORD PARKER]: This is not properly a release because it is of a future right. But it amounts to an agreement that the plaintiffs would be barred, and, if a freeman's child will accept of a sum of money and agree to take it in full satisfaction of the orphanage part, such agreement will be binding and such child shall not afterwards claim a share by the custom.

But, in the present case, the agreement was after the marriage, and that may make some difference. And, perhaps, the custom of London may be concerned in this question, whether, after marriage, such a release will bind.

Let the plea stand for an answer with liberty to except that it may be seen what is the quantum of the personal estate and save the benefit of the plea until the hearing.

And now, the cause came on to a hearing. It appeared by the account as set forth by the executrix in a schedule to her answer that the plaintiff's orphanage part would have amounted to £400.

For the defendants, it was insisted that the plaintiffs were not surprised. They understood what they did, and they thought fit to take £100 in the present in satisfaction of what they might afterwards be entitled to by the custom. And that was merely contingent, for the testator might have left nothing at his death. Besides, the plaintiff John has covenanted to release to the testator's executor. And it is pretty extraordinary for him to come into a court of equity to set aside his own agreement.

Lord Chancellor [LORD PARKER]: The customs of London are the remains of the common law, which was that the wife should have one-third of her husband's estate and the children another third. Bracton takes notice of the unreasonableness of this law and that the wife might by an agreement before marriage preclude herself of this right though she could not of her dower.

Now, there has been no law to alter this, but the unreasonableness of it has been so manifest that, by a general consent, it has been abrogated, except in the City of London and the province of York, where it is still kept up. And the reason why it has been kept up in London is owing to the Court of Aldermen's taking orphans' estates into their hands.

As to the present case, the plaintiffs have had £100, and they might have had nothing, for the testator might have died insolvent or turned all his personal estate into land. It will be very strange if a citizen should not be able to make an agreement with his children during his lifetime to discharge himself of the custom and to have it in his power to dispose of his estate as he pleases. Shall this be called a fraud?

I think all cases of this nature ought to be encouraged that men may not marry citizen's daughters without their father's consent upon an expectation of coming in for a share of his estate by the custom when he dies, and, if a citizen's daughter should marry without his consent, it would be very strange that, after the marriage, he may not agree to give the husband a sum of money in satisfaction of what he and his wife in her right may claim by the custom, especially when it is in his power to defeat them of any share by the custom by turning his personal estate into land.

Upon the whole, he declared there was no color for the plaintiffs' demand, and the bill was dismissed with costs.

Lincoln's Inn MS. Misc. 506, p. 30

March 1720[/21].

The defendant is the widow and executrix of Thomas Kelsy, a freeman of London, who left two daughters, the one married to the plaintiff. The bill is to have an account of the father's estate and a moiety of the orphanage part. The defendant pleads that, upon the marriage of the plaintiff with his now wife, the plaintiff executed a release to her father, which recites the receipt of £100 in full [satisfaction] for the customary part and all other demands on the father's estate and covenanted that he would after the death of the said Thomas Kelsy execute any other release or releases to his executrix or administrator as they should from time to time appoint. It was insisted on for the plaintiff that not a farthing was really advanced on the marriage and that one end of the bill was to be relieved against that very release as gained by surprise and misinformation, that it was not proper to plead a release in bar to a bill for relief against that very release. It was said that there had lately been a case so ruled and that it had been held that a release of a future right, especially in the right of the wife, is no bar and that it was taken for granted in Blondel and Barker,[1] for there was not a release before marriage.

On the other side, it was insisted that, if a release may not be pleaded to a bill which seeks relief against the release, then it would always be in the power of the plaintiff to prevent the defendant from having the benefit of his release, for it is but alleging matter of circumvention and praying relief against it, that the release will be of no use. As to the other matter, whether it be releasable, that will depend on the custom, whether, by custom, it may not be releasable. Besides, here is a covenant to execute further releases.

Lord Chancellor [Lord Parker] said that he did not look upon a release from a child of a customary part to be void, that it was not taken for granted in Blondel and Barker, that, indeed, it was not properly a release, but it would be good by way of agreement though it would not be binding so as to oblige a release of what should be left by the father's will. That would be very hard indeed. If it had been a proper release, it would have been so and the person that is afterwards in right would come in. The agreement can be effectual only except the father relinquish it. There is a difference where the release is after a marriage, for though the husband release; yet, possibly, that future right may fall after the husband's death. This matter will turn very much on the custom of London. This advance-

[1] *Blunden v. Barker* (1719–1720), see above, Case No. 381.

ment after marriage will be an advancement as far as it goes. As to the pleading of a release, that is not a proper plea to that part of the bill which seeks relief against the release, but it is a good plea to the rest of the bill.

Let the plea stand for an answer.

Lincoln's Inn MS. Misc. 384, p. 220, pl. 2

10 March.

The plaintiff's wife is the daughter of Thomas Kelsey, a freeman of London. And the bill is for the customary share of his personal estate. The defendant pleads a release by the husband and wife to the testator and claims under his will all the personal estate.

Lord Chancellor [LORD PARKER]: There may be an agreement by a child with the father which may bar the child of its customary share. But here, the release is by a husband and wife after a marriage. How far this shall be a bar cannot be determined now so well as at the hearing. He saved the benefit of the plea until the hearing. Where a bill is to be relieved against a release, the defendant cannot plead the same release in bar.

[Other reports of this case: Precedents in Chancery 544, 24 E.R. 245, 2 Eq. Cas. Eq. 262, 267, 22 E.R. 222, 226.]

499

Mead v. Fotherby

(Ch. 1721)

Where a criminal act has been pardoned, a defendant must answer interrogatories in a bill of complaint in relation to it, since no penalties can result from the answer.

Lincoln's Inn MS. Misc. 506, p. 31, pl. 1

March 1720[/21].

The plaintiffs, the assignees of the commissioners of Thomas Barker, a bankrupt, bring a bill against the defendant, who had several notes of hand from Barker, to discover what interest he took for the money lent, charging it to be an usurious contract and that the interest was 10 percent. The defendant pleaded the Statutes of 12 Car. II and 12 Ann.[1] and that he ought not to answer to such matters as would subject him to the penalties of the Act. On the plaintiff's side, it was said that these things were transacted before the Act of Grace[2] and so [there is] no danger from penalties, that one part of the case is the discounting of a bill at 12 percent, which is a purchase and not a loan, and that, notwithstanding the

1 Stat. 12 Car. II, c. 13 (*SR*, V, 236–237); Stat. 13 Ann., c. 15 (*SR*, IX, 928).

2 Stat. 7 Geo. I, stat. 1, c. 29.

Act, that the 12 percent for the continuance of the forbearance will not make the first contract void; only what is above the legal interest will go in payment of the principal.

Lord Chancellor [Lord Parker] said that the original contract being before the Act of Grace and the continuance being not penal by the statutes against usury, the plea was bad and thus overruled it.

500

Hoover v. Lee

(Ch. 1721)

A court of equity can stop waste though there be no common law action for it.

Lincoln's Inn MS. Misc. 506, p. 31, pl. 2

March 1720[/21].

Lord Chancellor [Lord Parker] said that, where there is an estate for life, remainder for life, remainder in fee, though there cannot be an action for waste, yet there was equity to grant an injunction to stay waste.

501

Nichols v. Nichols

(Ch. 1721)

The Court of Chancery has the power to supervise trustees, including executors of wills.

The Court of Chancery can order an executor to pay an infant's money into the Chancery for safe keeping while proceedings are ongoing in another court.

The doctrine of priority of suit does not apply where different things are sued for in the different courts.

Lincoln's Inn MS. Misc. 506, p. 31, pl. 3

March 1720[/21].

An executor libeled against in the spiritual court for two legacies, £500 each left to two infants, brings a bill that he may be admitted to pay them into this court and may have an injunction to stay the proceedings of the spiritual court. The defendant pleads priority of suit in the spiritual court, that the legacies were payable out of the personal estate and so properly cognizable there, that there is no danger of the monies being lost by being paid to the father, the method of the spiritual court, for they always took security. It was insisted on by the civilians that an injunction ought not to be granted for that here had been a citation, that citation returned, a libel given, an appearance entered without any protest, and so that the Court of Arches was fully possessed of the cause, that that court had a proper jurisdiction in legacies out of the personal estate, at least a concurrent one with the temporal courts, and, in the civil law, where two courts have concurrent jurisdictions, that court which is first possessed of the cause should retain it until it was finally determined, which is called prevention of jurisdiction and, after that, the cause shall not be removed upon any pretense whatever, though the party should be out of the jurisdiction of the court, e.g. where a cause of marriage is instituted in the Consistorial Court of London and, afterwards, the parties remove out of the Diocese of London, the party shall not come and say he is before a wrong judge and so remove it into another court. Lib. 3, Cod., tit. 13, l. 4, *De jurisdictione omnium judicium.*[1] This rule is universally observed in Germany where there are two courts which have a concurrent jurisdiction, the Aulic Council and the Concilium Spirense; when the cause is once lodged in either of those courts, the other shall not draw it to itself. It would be an hardship upon the party that, when he has been at expense until issue joined, he should be drawn to another court, that the rule of prevention is observed between this court and the Exchequer. And priority of suit in the Exchequer is an usual plea to a bill brought here for tithes. As to the safety of the executor, the father is appointed guardian by the election of the infants and might have been appointed to sue for the legacies, though the infants had been under the age of election, a guardian who may sue might certainly give a discharge, that as to the infant's safety, the court always took security, which is reported to the court and the party has liberty to except to it, which is not only to indemnify against the legacies, but against all suits, that there had been a case of Orbin and Fryer, the churchwardens of Kensington, one Pelham left £50 to the poor of the parish; there was a suit in the spiritual court for the money, the executrix pleaded no assets, but offered pro rata, which was refused, it being for a charity; upon a bill brought by the other legatees, an injunction was denied notwithstanding the spiritual court seemed to favor that legacy more than the laws of England. Where there are two jurisdictions, the plaintiff may choose which he will and the defendant must follow. Where a bishop makes a visitation, though that suspends all inferior jurisdictions, yet when once an inferior court is possessed of a cause, though it be inhibited during the bishop's stay, it cannot be drawn away, but must afterwards be finally determined there.

On the other side, it was argued that, if the jurisdiction was denied, this court would be ousted of its prerogative in having the care of infants, that payment to a guardian is no legal discharge, that their security is only personal, which this court looks on as none at all, that the spiritual court cannot put it out to interest as this court can, that in the Case of Gardiner,[2] last seal, there was an injunction granted and, upon cause shown, continued; £1500 was left to the wife; the husband sues in the spiritual court for the legacy; the executor, who was the

1 *Codex*, 3, 13, 4.

2 *Gardiner v. Walters* (1722), 11 Modern 361, 88 E.R. 1089.

brother to the wife, brings a bill that he may be admitted to pay the money into the hands of a Master of this court and to have an injunction to stay proceedings in the spiritual court; the court granted an injunction to the spiritual court and would not let the husband have the money until he had made a provision for the wife. A recognizance with two sureties is the lowest security this court allows, and that affects the land.

Lord Chancellor [Lord Parker] said that there was no dispute of the spiritual court's jurisdiction in personal legacies, but then they have not the only jurisdiction. They have the power to inquire whether one be a trustee, *viz.* an executor, but when once he appears to be a trustee, then this court has a power over an executor, as over all trustees. As to priority of suit, that is certainly right in all cases where there is no subordination for, in subordinate inferior courts, it is very common to remove the cause to a superior court, but there is no subordination from the spiritual court to this. It is every day's practice between the Exchequer and this court; so counties palatine; they are not subordinate courts to this purpose. But then all this is so where the thing asked is the same in both courts. Thus, if the money had been brought here, it had been proper to bring a bill to secure etc., for the suit in the spiritual court is no hindrance to the bringing money here. It is common where suits are at common law. It was questioned whether they should not have stopped after the citation when the bill was filed here, but there is no color for that, for the plaintiff in this court may dismiss his own bill whenever he pleases. We allow the father to sue as prochein ami, but we never order the money to be paid into the father's hands because the son cannot call for it again when he will. He cannot sue his father without obvious inconveniences. If the legacy had been brought into court and the costs in the spiritual court had been paid, it might be proper to continue the injunction, for the end of the suit in the spiritual court would be answered.

It was ordered that the injunction should be dissolved unless the costs of the spiritual court be paid and the money with interest from the end of the first twelvemonth be brought before the Master.

It was said by the counsel that a twelvemonth was usually allowed an executor for collecting the testator's debts.

Lincoln's Inn MS. Misc. 384, p. 221, pl. 1

A bill [was exhibited] by an executor to stay proceedings in the Court of Arches and to have an account taken in this court. The defendants are legatees, and, being infants, they, by their guardian, sue in the spiritual court for two legacies of £500. The defendants plead priority of suit in the spiritual court.

Dr. *Straughan* and *Sayer*, for the defendants, insisted that they have a concurrent jurisdiction and, having priority of suit, the cause ought not to be taken out of that court, that they have the power to appoint a guardian who can give a discharge and that they always take personal security of the person to whom the infant's money is paid.

Mead, for the plaintiff: The spiritual courts have no jurisdiction over infants and cannot order the infant's money to be put out at interest and can only order personal security, which is not allowed here. And this court never permits an infant's money to be paid into the hands of the father. They have no power to appoint a guardian.

Lord Chancellor [Lord Parker]: The ecclesiastical courts have a jurisdiction, but not the only one. They can compel an executor who is a trustee to prove and perform the will, but this court has jurisdiction over all trusts. Second, the court which has priority of suit shall retain the cause as between the executor and this court. But this is not a cause of that kind, which is where the same thing is demanded in both courts. If the money had been paid to the party, there had been an end of the suit in the spiritual court. So, if he had paid the money into court, until the money is paid into this court and all the costs in that court are paid, if their court takes security, it takes off the great objection. But the security is only for the principal money and not to answer for any interest.

I will continue the injunction upon the plaintiff's bringing the money into court within a month. I allow the plea in the meantime.

[Other reports of this case: Precedents in Chancery 546, 24 E.R. 246, 2 Eq. Cas. Abr. 242, 573, 22 E.R. 206, 483.]

502

Richmond v. Tayleur

(Ch. 1721)

An original bill of complaint lies to assert fraud in a former final decree in equity.

Lincoln's Inn MS. Misc. 12, p. 300

11 March 1720[/21].

Mr. Tayleur, on his marriage, enters into articles to lay out a sum of money in the purchase of lands to be settled on the wife and the issue male of the marriage. And a term was to be limited for raising daughters' portions.

The wife dying and leaving issue, only the plaintiff's wife, Mr. Tayleur brought his bill against his daughter, then an infant and unmarried, and against the trustees to have this money laid out.

The cause was heard by consent at the Rolls, and the money was decreed to be laid out in a purchase. And, in pursuance of this decree, a purchase and settlement was made.

Mr. Tayleur being dead, the plaintiffs brought their bill for an execution of the articles and therein take notice of the decree and charge that it was obtained by collusion and that the plaintiff's wife was then an infant and that, by the settlement, which has been made in pursuance of the decree, there is not so great a provision made for the plaintiff's wife as she was entitled to by the articles.

The defendants pleaded the decree signed and enrolled and the settlement made in pursuance of it. And it was strongly insisted that, the decree being signed and enrolled, it could not be impeached by an original bill.

But Lord Chancellor [LORD PARKER] overruled the plea and said the bill was very proper, for the decree was only by consent. And it was in the nature of an agreement among the parties and, unless the articles are fully set out in the original bill, a bill of review will signify nothing in regard to what is now insisted on, *viz*. that the plaintiff's wife is entitled by the articles to more than is provided for her by the decree, will not appear upon the face of the decree and, therefore, it cannot be assigned for error so that an original bill is the only proper remedy.

British Library MS. Hargrave 83, p. 33

There was an absolute decree against an infant in the case of a personal estate. The infant, when he came of age, brought an original bill suggesting fraud in obtaining the decree. The decree was pleaded in bar.

LORD MACCLESFIELD overruled the plea and the court declared that, in case fraud was suggested in obtaining the decree, this was a proper method of showing cause to avoid the decree and that, even in the case of a personal estate, an infant should have time to show cause and might avoid the decree either by a bill of review, original bill, rehearing, or putting in a new answer or any other method by which he may come at the justice of his case.

[Other reports of this case: 1 Peere Williams 734, 24 E.R. 591, Dickens 38, 21 E.R. 181, 2 Eq. Cas. Abr. 516, 22 E.R. 436.]

503

Ex parte Jephson

(Ch. 1721)

Writs of process for bringing a party into the Court of Chancery at the beginning of a lawsuit are to be executed by the Serjeant at Arms, not by the Warden of the Fleet.

Originally, writs of sequestration were only of the thing in issue, but, afterwards, it was extended to all other things.

Lincoln's Inn MS. Misc. 506, p. 34

18 March 1720[/21].

Upon a petition to the Lord Chancellor by the Serjeant at Arms complaining of an irregularity in the issuing the process of the court, the question was whether any commitment ought immediately to be to the Warden of the Fleet.

For the petitioner, it was insisted on that all such process should be directed first to the Serjeant at Arms and that then the prisoner should be turned over to the Fleet [Prison]. It was admitted that, where the commitment is by way of execution, as for contemptuous words spoken of the court or resistance of an officer executing the process of the court, the warrant has been immediately to the Warden of the Fleet to take the party into custody, but that, where the commitment is by way of process, as for not coming in on former process or in order to further proceedings, the warrant was always directed to the Serjeant at Arms, though after an appearance entered with the Register, for that on a return of *non est inventus* by the Warden of the Fleet, no [writ of] sequestration can issue, that there was a case to that purpose, which hung a long while in this court, Frederick and David, who married one Moresco, and his wife,[1] where, after a decree, the party not appearing nor complying with the decree, there issued an attachment to the Sheriff, who took up the defendant, but discharged him on taking a bond for his appearance. The Sheriff returned a *cepi*, and the next process was to send a messenger to bring him into court, but if he should return *non est inventus*, as he must, for there was an affidavit that he was seen in Holland, the question was how the court should come at a sequestration for that, on a return of *non est inventus* by the messenger, no sequestration could go and the amercing the Sheriff would be of no service to the plaintiff, who had been at great expense in obtaining a decree. Upon great debate, it was ordered by the court that the warrant should be directed to the Serjeant at Arms and then, on his returning *non est inventus*, there might go a sequestration. There was another case in Lord Cowper's time, 1716, where one who had been committed to the Fleet had escaped and it was ordered that, when retaken by the Warden of the Fleet, he should for his new contempt be taken into the custody of the Serjeant at Arms. It was urged in this case that the contrary practice was but of late date within ten or twelve years and Goldsborough, the Register, certified the court that this practice was grown in his time, that the entering of an appearance with the Register was in the time of the Lords Commissioners since the Revolution, that all the effect of that was the shortening the process and admitting all to be regular whereas, otherwise, there must be a [writ of] attachment, a proclamation, a commission of rebellion, and then the serjeant at arms, etc., that, if the party was taken upon any of those processes, he was turned over to the Fleet and, if after bringing him up thrice on [a writ of] *habeas corpus*, he did not put in his answer, the matter of the bill was taken *pro confesso* and a decree [was made] accordingly, and, if he did not comply with it, a sequestration issued.

Lord Chancellor [LORD PARKER] inclined in favor of the Serjeant at Arms and said that it did not seem so proper that, where there are two officers, one to go abroad and fetch in the party and another to attend upon the court and receive

[1] *Frederick v. David* (1685), 1 Vernon 344, 23 E.R. 510, 1 Eq. Cas. Abr. 352, 21 E.R. 1096.

and keep him in custody, the warrant for taking the party should be directed to him who is supposed to be either attending the court and receiving his directions there or else at his prison looking after his prisoners, that it was absurd that an officer who is always supposed to take the party along with him out of court should return *a non est inventus* and so the orders are that the party should stand committed, so that the question is whether, since no sequestration can go until the party be first committed or else the court satisfied that he cannot be found in order to be committed, that so the court might try that method of compelling him to comply, the court can be satisfied that he is not to be found but by the return of the Serjeant at Arms.

So the Lord Chancellor ordered that he should be attended with precedents, that if the Serjeant at Arms was entitled to have the fees of that process, the court could not deprive him of them, that nothing but a new law could take them from him, and, though the court by the voluntary appearance of the party could shorten the process, yet they could not divert it into another channel, that, indeed, the Serjeant was entitled to no fees for the attachment, proclamation, etc. because the party appearing, those processes were never executed, but where the process must be executed by somebody, as in the case here supposed, then the Serjeant was entitled to that execution of that process and his fees upon it.

Huggins, the Warden of the Fleet, insisted that, by an appearance, everything precedent was admitted and, in that, was included the serjeant at arms.

The Lord Chancellor said it could not include that the Serjeant at Arms had returned a *non est inventus*.

It was said by a gentleman at the bar that he had heard Serjeant Pemberton give an account of the original of sequestrations, that it was about the latter end of the reign of King James, in the case of Sir Robert Reeve,[1] who, having been committed to the Fleet for non-performance of a decree, said he would not comply, for he lived very well there and had iron chests full of money which he kept in his chamber there; the court ordered certain persons to break open those chests and to take out so much money as would pay the plaintiff.

Goldsborough said that sequestrations had been much more ancient.

The Lord Chancellor said that, originally, sequestrations were only of the thing in question, but, afterwards, it was extended to all other things.

[Other reports of this case: Precedents in Chancery 549, 24 E.R. 247, 2 Eq. Cas. Abr. 710, 22 E.R. 597.]

---

1 *Russel v. Read* (1635 × 1636), Tothill 102, 21 E.R. 136; Eq. Cases Exch. 264; cited in *Hide v. Pettit* (1667), 1 Chancery Cases 91, 92, 22 E.R. 709, 710; T. E. Tomlins, *Law Dictionary*, vol. 2, *sub tit.* 'sequestration'; R. North, *Lives of . . . Baron Guildford* (1826), vol. 1, p. 420.

504
Countess of Shaftsbury's Case

(Ch. 1721)

Where a receiver deposits money belonging to another person with a banker who later becomes bankrupt, the loss falls on the owner of the money and not on the receiver.

Lincoln's Inn MS. Misc. 506, p. 37

Eodem die [18 March 1721].

Upon the petition of the countess of Shaftsbury, there arose a question upon this case. The earl of Shaftsbury being a minor and his estate under the direction of the Court of Chancery in the hands of a receiver, who, by order of the court, was, out of the profits, to pay to the countess, his mother, by quarterly payments £800 *per annum*, which was her jointure, and £600 *per annum* for the maintenance of the young earl, the receiver asked the countess into what banker's hands he should pay her money for her, that, for his part, he deposited all his with Sir Robert Child. She answered that she would have her money as it became due paid into Northcote's shop, that all the family had used to lodge their money there, and she would not change her banker. Accordingly, the sum of £200 which was due to the countess on Michaelmas Day was, sometime before Michaelmas, lodged by the receiver at Northcote's shop, who happened to become a bankrupt and was almost entirely insolvent on Michaelmas Day. The question was whether that loss should fall on the countess.

The Lord Chancellor [Lord Parker] ordered it should not, for that, until Michaelmas Day, the money was not hers nor could she demand it, that what she desired was that the receiver should pay it into Northcote's shop *as it became due* so that, until it was due, Northcote was his banker, not the countess's, that, if Northcote broke on Michaelmas Day, he broke the night before because, Michaelmas Day being an holy day, no goldsmiths pay on that day. But he would not determine whether this loss should fall on the receiver or on the estate, that not being now before him, but that he thought, if the receiver did his duty and was guilty of no neglect, but put out the money according to the best of his judgment, this being a banker that the family used, he ought to be no sufferer by it, but it would be much the same as if he had been robbed of it and, in effect, this was a robbery.

[Other reports of this case: Precedents in Chancery 558, 24 E.R. 250, 2 Eq. Cas. Abr. 691, 22 E.R. 581.]

505

Wentworth v. Underwood

(Ch. 1721)

Where the personal assets of a decedent's estate are insufficient to pay all of the decedent's debts, the unsecured creditors are subrogated to the rights of the bond creditors to go against the decedent's land.

Lincoln's Inn MS. Misc. 14, p. 82

22 March 1720[/21].

The plaintiff, as a creditor by bond of John Underwood, brought his bill on the behalf of himself and other creditors against the widow and administratrix of the said Underwood and against Robert Underwood, an infant, his son and heir, to be paid his debt out of the personal assets and, if they were not sufficient, then out of the real assets.

[The Master of the Rolls, JEKYLL] decreed an account of the personal estate and of the debts owing by the intestate and what should be found in the hands of the administratrix to be applied to pay the debts in a course of administration. And so far as the personal estate should be exhausted in the payment of the bond debts, the creditors by simple contract were to stand in the place of the bond creditors to receive satisfaction out of the real estate. And, after the defendant, the heir, should attain his age of twenty-one, the rents of the real estate should be subject to the payment of the debts by bond. And the infant was to be bound by the decree unless he showed cause against it when he came of age.

506

Savile v. Savile

(Ch. 1721)

The question in this case was whether a purchaser of land can back out of his contract before accepting a conveyance upon forfeiting the money deposited.

Lincoln's Inn MS. Misc. 11, p. 193, pl. 2

25 March 1721. Savile v. Lord Nottingham.

Mr. Frederick, in June last, was reported the best purchaser of a house in St. James's Square for £10,500 and had deposited £1000. And now, upon the plaintiff's petition, it was prayed he might proceed in his purchase.

Note in the Case of Archbishop Tenison, who was reported the best purchaser of an estate in Wales of about £900 a year at £32,000, and of Mr. King, who was reported the best purchase of Mr. Bennet's estate at Rotherhithe of about £950 a year and had deposited £10,000 and had signed and enrolled the decree and the report and orders for confirming it, the Lord Chancellor discharged them from going on with their purchases, but ordered they should forfeit their deposits.

Lord Chancellor [Lord Parker]: I do not see that this case of Mr. Frederick differs from the other cases which have been lately before me. In those cases, indeed, it was said that the parties [were owners of] of South Sea [Company] stock at the time of their biddings and, by reason of the fall of stock, were not able to go on with their purchases. And I do not find that is said in the present case. It is admitted Mr. Frederick is very well able to proceed in his purchase, but he declares he will not and is willing to forfeit his deposit. The rule must be the same between the rich and the poor.

What I went upon in the other cases was the general and universal calamity that has happened and that universal mistake people were under which made them give everything a greater value than it really had. But I declared then that what I did was not to be a rule in future times, for I do not say that there cannot be a case where a man shall not be held to his bidding before a Master where he is willing to forfeit his deposit, though, at present, I do not see any.

As to what is said that, if this was a contract between two private persons upon articles, this court would carry it into execution, I believe no one will say that, if a man came into this court to have a specific performance of a contract for the sale of lands when estates had this imaginary value, that this court would decree an execution of such a contract, but only leave the party to his remedy at law.

[Other reports of this case: 1 Peere Williams 745, 24 E.R. 596, 2 Eq. Cas. Abr. 679, 22 E.R. 570.]

507

Perry v. Bennett

(Ch. 1721)

A court of equity will grant relief against a forfeiture of a lease.

Lincoln's Inn MS. Misc. 12, p. 38, pl. 2

10 May 1721.

The plaintiff's bill was to be relieved against a forfeiture of a lease, the condition whereof was to indemnify the defendant, who was the vicar of the parish of A., against all parish rates and taxes.

The question was if this court will relieve against a forfeiture of this nature.

Lord Chancellor [Lord Parker]: Suppose it had been a mortgage to indemnify a man against a bond and the mortgagor does not indemnify him, shall not the mortgagor be relieved against this forfeiture?

There is nothing more settled than that forfeitures of this nature shall be relieved against.

He decreed that the defendant shall make the plaintiff a new lease upon the same terms as the former lease was made and the plaintiff must pay the defendant the costs he has been put to at [common] law in getting possession. But, as to the costs in this court, the defendant having insisted upon several things which were unreasonable and upon an agreement which he has not proved, in strictness, he ought to pay costs. However, let there be no costs on either side.

508

Stephens v. Tristram

(Ch. 1721)

Where a person signs on behalf of another person a contract that must be in writing, the authority to sign must also be in writing.

British Library MS. Add. 36651, f. 103v

Easter [term] 7 Geo. I, 1721; before Sir Joseph Jekyll, Master of the Rolls.

The bill was to have an execution of an agreement in writing concerning the redemption of a mortgage. The case was that one Cook, *anno* 1684, mortgaged the premises to T. Tristram, the defendant's father, for £38 and, about seven years after, made a second mortgage of the same lands to the plaintiff. *Anno* 1702, Cook and Tristram, the father, came to an account, and then an endorsement is made on the mortgage deed that, upon stating accounts, there appeared to be due for principal and interest £52. But [it was] not there said to be agreed that the lands should stand charged with that as a principal sum to carry interest.

Afterwards, the plaintiff brought his bill against Tristram, the father, to be admitted to pay him off, and, after some proceedings therein, the plaintiff and the now defendant, son to Tristram, the first mortgagee, and who acted for the father, came to an agreement, which was reduced into writing and signed by the plaintiff and now defendant whereby it was agreed that the plaintiff should first pay the defendant's father £5 for the costs of that suit and that, afterwards, he should be admitted to a redemption etc. or to that effect.

The defendant's father is since dead. And now the plaintiff brings this bill against the now defendant as heir and executor to his father thirteen years after the said agreement to have an execution of it.

Note it appeared that the £5 was paid to the son for the father's use soon after the agreement.

There were two points: first, whether this was a good agreement in writing within the Statute of Frauds,[1] being signed only by the son upon an authority from his father by parol.

And it was held by the Master of the Rolls [JEKYLL] that it was not good, for there ought to have been an authority in writing from the father, for, though it is not required by the Statute in express words, yet, being within the same mischief, it is within the meaning of the Statute.

The second point was, in case a redemption was decreed, whether interest should be allowed for the £52 agreed to be due at the time of the endorsement taking it to be as a principal sum from that time or that interest should be only allowed for the original sum of £38.

To this the Master [JEKYLL] cited the case of the Lord Delaware v. Cutler, adjudged by Lord Somers assisted by Chief Justice Holt *et al.*, where it was said by Chief Justice Holt that, upon an action of *insimul computasset* at law, the jury always give judgment for the sum stated in damages and, thereupon, interest was allowed in that case, though it appeared that the accounts had been stated every year as the interest became due. And so, in this case, interest ought to be allowed for the £52 as a principal sum, for this court ought not to take away this advantage to which the defendant is entitled by law.

Note it was insisted by the plaintiff's counsel that the payment of the £5 in pursuance of the agreement was an execution in part and, therefore, makes it valid and out of the Statute.

But the Master of the Rolls [JEKYLL] held otherwise because that related only to the suit then depending, being for the costs and did not concern the mortgage.

509

Burnett v. Chetwood

(Ch. 1721)

A translation is not an infringement of an author's copyright.

The Court of Chancery has the power of censorship over improper religious books.

Lincoln's Inn MS. Misc. 506, p. 50

Easter 7 Geo.

A bill was brought by the plaintiff, as executor of Burnet, the author of *Archaeologia Sacra*, against the defendant for an injunction to stay the printing and publishing of a translation of the said book, suggesting it to be an injury to the executor in whom the property of the book was vested by 8 Ann., c. [*blank*].[2]

[1] Stat. 29 Car. II, c. 3 (*SR*, V, 839–842).

[2] Stat. 8 Ann., c. 21 (*SR*, IX, 256–258).

It was insisted on for the defendant that a translation of a book was not within the intent of the Act, which, being intended to encourage learning by giving the advantage of the book to the author, could be intended only to restrain the mechanical art of printing and that others should not pirate the copy and gain an advantage to themselves by reprinting it, but not to hinder a translation of the book into another language, which, in some respects, may be called a different book and the translator may be said to be the author inasmuch as some skill in languages is requisite thereto and not barely a mechanic art, as in the case of reprinting in the same language, that the translator dresses it up and clothes the sense in his own style and expressions and, at least, puts it into a different form from the original and *forma dat esse rei* and, therefore, should rather seem to be within the encouragement than the prohibition of the Act.

Lord Chancellor [LORD PARKER] said that, though a translation might not be the same with the reprinting the original on account that the translator has bestowed his care and pains upon it and so not within the prohibition of the Act, yet this being a book which, to his knowledge, having read it in his study, contained strange notions intended by the author to be concealed from the vulgar in the Latin language, in which language it could not do much hurt, the learned being better able to judge of it, he thought it proper to grant an injunction to the printing and publishing it in English, that he looked upon it that this court had a superintendency over all books and might in a summary way restrain the printing or publishing of any that contained reflections on religion or morality.

An injunction was granted.

[Other copies of this report: 2 Merivale 441, 35 E.R. 1008.]

510

Comber v. Smith

(Ch. 1721)

An executor of a will can commence a lawsuit before probate.

Lincoln's Inn MS. Misc. 506, p. 51, pl. 1

Easter 7 Geo.

A *subpoena scire facias* was sued out by an executor to revive a decree for things which lay in Middlesex. The defendant pleads that the executor had proved the will in the Court of the Archdeacon of Surrey and not in the Prerogative Court of Canterbury, though there were *bona notabilia* both in London and Chichester. And he insisted that this probate was a nullity and would not entitle him to a decree for things in Middlesex.

The Lord Chancellor [LORD PARKER] said that he thought it not necessary that the will should be proved at all before the hearing of the cause, that, if a proper probate were produced, then it would be time enough, that an executor may bring a bill or an action before probate, for he may release before probate. He may sue out a writ before probate, and it is sufficient if, in the declaration, he plead it with a profert, which is not to entitle him to his action, but only to show that he has a probable cause of action, and that is the true old meaning of *inde producit sectam*, *viz.* produces some probable cause of action, whether by the oath of some person or otherwise, but not that it is for that reason or cause that he brings his action, for the profert is not the title to the action. It is not necessary to allege that the probate was granted by the ordinary of the place nor cannot be put in issue, as it might if that was the title to the action. Nay, though the probate were a forgery, that cannot be pleaded. Otherwise it is in a case of an administrator, for, before administration is granted, he is not entitled to an action.

The plea was overruled, and the decree was revived, but no proceedings are to be upon it until a proper probate be produced.

[Other reports of this case: 1 Peere Williams 766, 24 E.R. 605.]

511

Smith v. Withers

(Ch. 1721)

Where a London orphan is given a legacy in lieu of his customary share, he can take the legacy and waive an accounting of the customary share or vice versa, *but he cannot have an account and then make an election.*

Lincoln's Inn MS. Misc. 506, p. 51, pl. 2

Easter 7 Geo.

The bill was brought by the plaintiff, who was the daughter of the defendant's testator, who was an alderman and freeman of London, to have an account of the estate and to have a distribution of the orphanage part.

The defendant pleads that the testator gave a legacy to the plaintiff in bar of her customary part and all other demands and that the plaintiff, being of full age, did accept the said legacy being money in the Chamber of London, which was assigned to her, and that, by the will, she was directed on receipt of the legacy [that] she should release her customary part, though she refused to do it when she received the legacy. It was insisted on by the defendant that the acceptance of the legacy barred the plaintiff of her orphanage part and so she was not entitled to an account.

On the other side, it was insisted on that the plaintiff had taken the legacy, yet it was only *de bene esse* until she had an account of the personal estate so she might judge what the orphanage part would amount to, until when she was not obliged to make her election according to the Case of Hoskins and Styles, where, upon the death of an intestate who left a considerable estate, there was a sum of money given to a person for his share of the distribution by another person entitled to a share likewise. There was a release actually given but set aside in this court because the true value of the estate was not known to the party who released. It was urged that, having an election, she was not obliged to determine it until the whole estate was disclosed, and, for that purpose, a case was cited of [*blank*] and Thorpe.

Lord Chancellor [Lord Parker] said it was not the intent of the will that she should have an account of the estate and then make her option. But on the contrary, this legacy was left to prevent the trouble of an account, and, therefore, she is confined to a month's time, and, if she does not accept the legacy in satisfaction, the intent of the will was that she should run the hazard whether the same should prove more or less and not that she should have an account first. And, therefore, it is not like the case where an option is left. I look upon it that the acceptance of this legacy in satisfaction would be a bar without any release, though a release be required by the will, but this acceptance is not in satisfaction because, at the time of the acceptance, she refused to release her customary part. The plea must be overruled, but, if she proceeds to take an account, she cannot afterwards choose the legacy.

7 Viner, Abr. 211

Michaelmas vacation 1721.

Sir W.W., in 1718, made his will, giving to his daughter £7000 and to his son and executor all the rest of his estate. He declared that this legacy to the daughter was in satisfaction of all she could claim etc. under the custom and she was to declare within one month after his death whether she would abide by that or not, and she was to release etc. The testator lived two years after this will, and, after his death, the daughter marrying within a fortnight, they were both made acquainted with the will. And the executor and son came one morning and made a delivery of some plate etc. specifically devised and also assigned an annuity in the Exchequer, which was given to the daughter, etc. And, being asked to execute a release, some time was desired for consideration etc.

In Michaelmas vacation, the question was, on a plea to the discovery and account prayed by a bill, whether what the daughter and her husband had done did amount to such an acceptance as did determine their election and to exclude them from a share by the custom.

And by Lord Chancellor [Lord Parker], the plea was allowed because they had not made any election by the bill to waive the will, but with a saving to any farther claim or right they might make, i.e. by amending their bill and running the hazard of the account of the personal estate, for, whether it be more or less, they must abide by the event of it. He declared that it was the testator's intention that, if she accepted of the legacy, she was to take that in satisfaction of the whole under the custom and that he never intended she should have an account of the personal estate to see whether it was her best way to abide by the one or the other; she was to have no such liberty. And, therefore, he confined her to a month's time to declare herself so that all objections made from her, being under any surprise or having anything misrepresented unto her, is out of the case. It is likely Sir W.W. thought the custom very hard, and he had a mind to tie her down. But yet this must be a complete acceptance by her of all that he had imposed. But, in this case, it does not appear that all was finished and completed; some things she did accept of. But the executing of the release was put off and other matters for farther consideration, so that this was not a full and entire acceptance, though he thought that, if all had been done and accepted of without the release, that was not so necessary to be done within the month, but might be executed at any time. [Other copies of this report: 2 Eq. Cas. Abr. 268, 22 E.R. 227.]

512
Frederick v. Frederick
(Ch. 1721)

Where a person contracts to become a London freeman and fails to do so, his estate, after his death, will be distributed according to the custom of London.

Lincoln's Inn MS. Misc. 384, p. 221, pl. 2

19 May 1721.

In 1674, license was granted by the Court of Aldermen for the late Mr. Frederick to marry his wife, who was an orphan, provided Mr. Common Serjeant do approve of the settlement made, and it is mentioned that Sir John Frederick, the father, and Mr. Frederick had engaged and promised to take up his freedom within a year. The marriage immediately took effect, but Mr. Frederick, though called upon by the Court of Aldermen about two years after, never took up his freedom. The lady's fortune was £25,000, and the settlement was not adequate. Mr. Frederick by a will gives his eldest son only £1000 and the like to his daughters and the rest of his personal estate, about £400,000, to his second son.

The bill is by the widow and the eldest son and the daughters to have such part of their father's estate as they should have been entitled to if he had taken up his freedom.

Talbot, for the plaintiff: [There are] instances in this court where a husband was ordered to take up his freedom. Willis, who married Sir Edward Hans' daughter.[1]

1. The marriage took effect before the credit of the license and took effect immediately.

[1] *Hannes v. Waugh* (1713), 2 Eq. Cas. Abr. 754, 22 E.R. 639.

2. The husband's agreement with the Court of Alderman was not waived before the marriage and could not be after.

3. A year was given to take up his freedom; therefore, it could not be waived before the year expired. Acts of the court subsequent to the marriage show it was not waived.

4. The Court of Aldermen could not waive it; neither could the parties after the marriage.

5. [There is] no implied waiver. Nobody could compel Mr. Frederick in his lifetime to perform his agreement without disobliging him, and he could have defeated it by laying the personal estate in land. But that is no reason to excuse the performance of an agreement because it is contingent.

6. Where it is proper in a court of equity for a specific performance, it is only to consider that as done which is agreed and ought to have been done, as in the case where money is covenanted to be laid out in land. [It is] the same in reason as if he had covenanted to leave one third to his wife and another to his children.

Attorney General [*Raymond*], for the plaintiff:

1. This agreement not being under hand and seal is no objection. Here is a contract made with a competent court. If it had been within this court upon the marriage of a ward of the court, the court would have carried it into execution.

2. This was part of the terms required by the Court of Alderman, without which they would not have granted their license.

3. [There is] nothing to distinguish this from the common case's unalterable rule, where a man upon a valuable consideration covenants to do an act, this court looks upon it as done.

[It was] objected that the custom only operates upon the estate of a freeman and [there is] no such thing as an equitable freeman, but we consider him as to this purpose as an actual freeman.

4. The settlement was not adequate. If it were, it would not avoid the other part of the contract.

5. [There are] frequent instances where the husband was compelled to take up his freedom. Were it otherwise, it is where the husband is no trader. This was a just and reasonable agreement, not by compulsion.

6. Who could have compelled Mr. Frederick to take up his freedom? He would have cut off everybody.

7. [It was] objected he might have defeated the plaintiffs by laying out his personal estate in land. That contingency was where a man was to be a tenant, yet the money was not paid to the tenant in tail but was ordered to be laid out [so] that the remainderman might have a chance for the land.

8. [It was] objected [that there is] no precedent like this. Every new case must be without a precedent.

9. [It was] objected the disappointment of legatees. That is very frequent.

10. The plaintiffs are purchasers under this marriage contract.

Solicitor General [*Yorke*], for the plaintiff:

1. Neither the resolutions of the courts of common law nor the decrees of this court are grounded merely on precedents, but on the general rules and reasons upon which former cases were founded. Therefore, the want of precedents is no objection.

2. This order was not made for the advantage or grandeur of the City, but the performing of the duty of a guardian.

3. This agreement is in part carried into execution by the court's granting the license.

4. If the bill had been against Mr. Frederick in his lifetime, he would have been decreed to have performed it.

5. [There is] no alteration by his death as to the effects. [It was] objected that, where an heir or executor are decreed to do an act which the ancestor ought to have done, it is where they can perform the very act. [This is] not a true rule because the court will consider the act as done by the ancestor.

6. [There was] no restraint upon Mr. Frederick from purchasing land. But that not being done, the personal estate is all subject to this agreement and to the custom [of London] and the plaintiffs are entitled to the benefit of this accident.

7. This is an *inofficiosum testamentum* by the civil law. And if the plaintiffs prevail, there will be an equal provision for this family.

Cowper for the plaintiff:

1. The settlement is only in bar of dower, not of the customary share.

2. In the settlements, [there is] no provision for younger children if there were an elder son. But they were taken care of by this agreement with the Court of Alderman.

Lord Chancellor [Lord Parker]: There are two points: first, whether this were part of the marriage agreement; second, whether it ought to be carried into execution. I will consider of it.

Lincoln's Inn MS. Misc. 506, p. 53

Easter 7 Geo.

The plaintiff was the widow of Sir John Frederick, the son of Sir John Frederick, an alderman of London, and she brought a bill against his representatives for an account of the personal estate and to have a third according to the custom of London. Young Mr. Frederick, afterwards upon his father's death Sir John Frederick, makes his addresses to the plaintiff, who was then a City orphan and her fortune [was] in the Chamber of London and he gained her consent to marriage. And all things were agreed on between the friends on both sides, and a settlement answerable to her fortune was actually prepared and executed so that there wanted nothing but a license from the Court of Orphans. Accordingly, application was made to the court for a license, who, thereupon, made an order that he should have a license provided the Common Serjeant should approve of the settlement that was made and, if it was not satisfactory, he should make it up to the satisfaction of the Common Serjeant. But at the same time, they required

Mr. Frederick to promise that he would take up his freedom of the City. Accordingly, he did promise and the said Sir John, the father, did engage that he should take up his freedom of the City within a twelvemonth. The marriage was had. Sir John, the father, dies. Afterwards, the son dies having never taken up his freedom and leaves a great personal estate, but nothing to his wife, from whom he had for many years lived separate and had greatly abused her. This was the occasion of the bill in which there were two points: first, whether this was any part of the marriage agreements, to take up the freedom; second, whether the plaintiff can have any advantage of it if it were after the death of her husband.

It was insisted on for the defendant that this was no part of the marriage agreement, for that had been all settled between the parties before it came before the Court of Aldermen. The agreement was completed and the writings actually executed; all that the application to the Court of Aldermen was for was only a license to marry, for the words of the order are that 'they should have license to marry provided Mr. Common Serjeant should approve the settlement made and, if he should not, Mr. Frederick should make it up to the satisfaction of Mr. Common Serjeant and the said Mr. Frederick, being thereunto required, did promise, and the said Sir John, on his behalf, did engage that Mr. Frederick should take up his freedom of the City within a twelvemonth', that the last clause was independent [of] the marriage and only put in to take advantage of gaining Mr. Frederick to be a freeman of the City, that this was warranted by the subsequent entry in the City books, which is 'it is agreed that, for the future, if any person not free of this City shall address for license to marry a City orphan, he shall first be required to take up his freedom', which shows that their view was with regard to the benefit of the City by increasing the number of citizens.

In 1676, it is taken notice of that Mr. Frederick had not taken up his freedom of the City according to his engagement, and he was, therefore, summoned. What was then done does not appear. In 1680, it is again taken notice of that he had not taken up his freedom and ordered the Common Serjeant to look into the marriage agreement. But the court never urged the taking up his freedom for the benefit of his wife or children, which shows that they did not look upon it as a part of the marriage agreement. If it had been so, they would not have allowed a twelvemonth for doing it when the marriage was to be had immediately so that, if he had died within the twelvemonth, it could not be said that he had broken his agreement though he had not taken up his freedom. It cannot be said that this was founded on any custom, for the subsequent entries show the contrary. They did indeed use to require it where the person that applied for a license was to gain his living by exercising a trade in the City because, otherwise, by the laws of the City, he could not carry on his trade. It must be admitted that, in other respects, he was not to be considered as a freeman. It will not be pretended that he could be chosen sheriff or fined for not serving. Besides, what effect can there be of this order now he is dead? Nor, indeed, if he had been living, would any action have lain against him upon the foot of this order? Nor could any bill have been brought to have compelled him to take up his freedom, for, if it be any agreement, it is an agreement with the Court of Aldermen, which is mentioned as a court of record and this court would have supposed that they had the power to enforce their own orders. But, if the court had decreed it and he would not perform it, he could only have been in contempt and his estate in sequestration during his life. Lenyon and Williams;[1] a tenant in tail mortgaged lands and covenanted to suffer a recovery; a bill was brought by the mortgagee to have a performance of that covenant, and there was a decree against the tenant in tail. He refused to suffer a recovery and, for non-performance of the decree, he was committed to the Fleet [Prison] and died in contempt, and so the mortgagee lost his mortgage money.

If the Court of Aldermen acted as a political parent in this affair and neglected to compel him to do it, that is their fault and cannot be helped when it is neglected so long until the thing is impossible to be done. But it looks as if they thought they could not compel the doing of it, when, after taking notice several times that it had not been done, they only ordered that the Common Serjeant should look into the settlement, which was all, as they thought, they could do. This is not like the case of carrying articles into execution, where a court of equity looks upon that which is agreed to be done as done, for, where a person covenants to settle an estate to the use of himself in tail and afterwards to another in fee, the remainderman cannot compel an execution of the covenant, for it is a standing maxim in this court that articles or a trust for the remainder or reversion in fee shall not be carried into execution when it is after an estate in tail because, as soon as it is done, it is liable to be destroyed. Dr. Shadwell's Case[2] was the case of an infant. This case is not like the case of an heir or an executor that may do the same thing which the ancestor or testator ought to have done. But this is a personal thing which can be done by nobody but Mr. Frederick and, he being dead, cannot be done at all. And though the thing cannot be done, yet they are contending to have the consequence of it as if it had been done. This bill is not for a specific performance, but for consequential damages, which is further than a court of equity ever went. They come to have the benefit of this against the trustees for younger children, for, if this prevails, the legacies to the younger children must be defeated, for they are specific legacies of Bank annuities etc. This case differs from others in that the land remains or the money remains which is to make good the agreement in those cases. But, in this case, there is nothing remaining. It is a personal act and dies with the person, which being gone, there can be no execution of the agreement, *viz.* Mr. Frederick cannot now take up his freedom. What is now prayed is more than ever was known, that the court should first declare the order to amount to a covenant or an agreement and then decree the consequences of such an agreement [as] if it had been

[1] *Weal v. Lower* (1673–1689), Pollexfen 54, 86 E.R. 509, 2 Freeman 107, 22 E.R. 1089, 1 Eq. Cas. Abr. 266, 21 E.R. 1035.

[2] *Colwell v. Colwell* (*tempore* Cowper).

performed. There are cases where there might be as much need of relief and yet this court confessedly cannot relieve, as in the case of a forfeiture of a copyhold; nay, not against a penalty where the damages cannot be ascertained. Tall v. Ryland, 1 Ch. 183.[1] There would be as little reason to have decreed Mr. Frederick to have performed this agreement as there would be in the case of an agreement to settle on oneself in tail, remainder in fee, for, as in that case, the remainderman might be barred by a common recovery. So, in this, if Mr. Frederick had taken up his freedom, yet he might have barred his wife of her third by giving it away or laying it out in lands. Nay, had he been disenfranchised afterwards, which is a contingency that might have happened, the custom could never have operated. If he be a freeman, he must be a freeman throughout, and then the Court of Aldermen would have a right to the management of his estate and his children would be orphans of the City and could not marry without the consent of the Court of Orphans, all which is not so much as pretended here. Indeed, if a man entering into marriage articles should declare that he was a freeman and, in regard that his estate would be subject to the custom there, needed no provision further and it should afterwards appear that he was no freeman, this would be a fraud, and the court would go as far as they could to make compensation. And yet, in the case of [*blank*] v. Brockman, the court under very strong circumstances denied relief though it appeared that he was an ill husband and left his estate not to his grandchildren as here, but to a stranger, a woman whom he had lived with in an unbecoming manner. But here is no fraud except every neglect of performing what is agreed be a fraud. Besides, this might have been a great disadvantage for younger children. Mr. Frederick at the time of the marriage was worth but £5000 besides the settled estate. If the wife, besides her jointure, were to have a third and the eldest son, who was amply provided under the settlement, a share of another third, what would be left for the younger children? And yet it is pretended on the other side that the intent of the obliging him to take up his freedom was to make provision for younger children, but surely this would be but an odd way of providing for them.

On the other hand, it was insisted on that this was an agreement and that it was a part of the marriage settlement that there would have been no doubt if this had been a covenant with the plaintiff's father and a bill had been brought in his lifetime but that agreement must have been carried into execution. Now, here was a contract with the Court of Orphans, which is a political parent and has the superintendency over the orphan as a parent would have had. And a contract with the court is the same as if it had been with a natural parent, that here was an express agreement that he should take up his freedom without which he could never have legally married her or taken her fortune out of the Chamber of London. It must be a strange construction and farfetched imagination to take

[1] *Tall v. Ryland* (1670), 1 Cases in Chancery 183, 22 E.R. 753, also 1 Eq. Cas. Abr. 91, 21 E.R. 902.

this not to be part of the settlement. And though it be objected that the court did not know what was in the settlement and, therefore, had no reason to apprehend that there was not sufficient provision made by that, yet there is no proof that the court did not know what was in the settlement. And, unless we are to intend a court negligent of its duty, we must take it that they did look into the settlement.

It is the constant practice of a court of equity that, when a man covenants for a valuable consideration to do an act at a certain time, to consider that act as done at the time, the plaintiff does not come for consequential damages. But looking upon Mr. Frederick as a freeman, to claim the benefit of the custom, it has been objected that the custom affects only actual freeman. As to this purpose, he is an equitable freeman, and, as to this purpose, it will be the same as an actual freeman whatever he be as to other matters, such as serving offices, etc. As to the objection that the settlement alone was answerable to the fortune, if the guardian has got the plaintiff a better provision than usual, fairly and by agreement, she is equally entitled to the benefit of it as in any other case.

Post, 61.

Lincoln's Inn MS. Misc. 506, p. 61

Trinity 7 Geo.

This cause being heard last term, the Lord Chancellor [LORD PARKER] now pronounced a decree in favor of the plaintiffs, the widow and children.

The question is whether the widow and the children shall be entitled to a distribution of Mr. Frederick's estate in the same manner as if he had actually taken up his freedom. The rule they rely upon is that, where there is an agreement to do an act, though that act be not done, yet, in equity, they ought to have the same benefit as if it had. This is, therefore, a contest with Mr. Frederick, that is with his representatives, whether they shall distribute his personal estate in the manner he had agreed on. An agreement between parties by deed will certainly conclude them if of full age, but none others will be bound thereby. Therefore, the settlement in this case before the marriage agreed on with the mother is no more than proposals and will not conclude the Court of Aldermen, who were not parties, yet were the proper guardian. They knew nothing of the transactions of this settlement so that the Court of Aldermen were at liberty when this settlement came before them to have refused it or altered it or added to it or they might have agreed with Mr. Frederick by parol (for it was before the Statute of Frauds[1]) to make a further provision. And now, it appears that they were not content with the settlement, but did insist on something further, *viz.* that he should take up his freedom. The proof is strong, for it is on record in a court that has a proper jurisdiction, as strong a proof as need be of a fine, for this is in the nature of a fine.

[1] Stat. 29 Car. II, c. 3 (*SR*, V, 839–842).

It is a concord and agreement to have a marriage properly done; it is the proper business of the Court of Aldermen.

It is said that they intended it for the benefit of the City and not of the marriage, but surely it shall never be supposed that an agreement which may be honestly intended for the benefit of the orphan shall be expounded for a knavish design without any proof at all. If any of the aldermen had said so, I should have no regard to it, but have thought that man a knave and the others honest. But it is said the license is absolute only let Mr. Common Serjeant approve the settlement, which it is presumed he approved since the money was accordingly paid out of the Chamber of London. But probably the reference to the Common Serjeant was only for the validity of the settlement, not the quantum, for the aldermen would now be as good judges of that as he. But suppose the whole was referred to the Common Serjeant, yet the taking up his freedom was part of the settlement and the settlement could never be considered by the Common Serjeant abstractedly from the freedom since that was directed in the very order of reference.

As to the objections that he had a twelvemonth's time to take up his freedom in and he might have died within that time, that is so small a time that there could be no apprehension of any ill consequence within that time, for there could not be many younger children within that time, nor is it to be supposed that, within one year's time, a man should be so displeased with his wife as to leave all from her and, if he dies intestate, she would have a share of the distribution.

As to the general order which follows that everyone who should marry a City orphan should be obliged to take up his freedom, it appears that that was intended for the benefit of the City orphan and not the City, for there is a power left of compounding it and to make an equivalent, which may be done with respect to the orphan, but there can be no equivalent with regard to the City. But it is said the length of time which passed without compelling him to take up his freedom shows it was waived. It appears by the summons that it was intended for the benefit of the orphan and that it was not waived before the marriage. And, if so, who could waive it? The Court of Aldermen could not release it, for they were but trustees.

And as to the length of time, that can be no objection to the wife or children, for there could be no laches in them. But it is said it is a matter which turns upon the custom and, if not within the custom, it cannot be brought within it by a court of equity. Why not? Should not contracts relating to customs be enforced as well as others? It has been done where there has been a fraudulent assignment of a citizen's estate. It is said the City could not make him sheriff. I agree they cannot, but that only proves that he was not an actual freeman.

It is said the City shall not have the guardianship of his children. I agree it, for that is not a claim against Mr. Frederick and there can be no valuable consideration for that and it is not to be expected that this court would decree away a guardianship from itself to the Court of Orphans.

But it is said it is now too late since he is dead and there can be no specific performance. It is true the man that is dead can perform nothing specifically. But with respect to the wife and children, the taking the freedom was only to entitle them to their several shares of the personal estate. Therefore, all that the court can do is to take care that the effect of the agreement be answered. Suppose a man, after he had sold his estate, should article to settle that very estate on a third person who had no notice of the sale; in that case, there could be no specific performance, but yet this court would decree the settlement of other lands. The business of this court is to see that the parties should have the benefit of an agreement not executed the same as if it had been executed.

It is said he might have laid it out in lands and then the wife and children would be entitled to nothing. It is true he might. And who hindered him? But is that a reason why the wife and children should not be entitled to what he has not laid out so? It is a stronger case, which sometimes happens in this court, of an agreement to lay out money in lands to be settled in tail; in that case, the issue or remainderman may come and compel an execution of the agreement after the death of the tenant in tail, and yet, in that case, he might have docked the entail, but he could not the money. The argument is no more than this, had you given notice or had I been aware of your design to insist upon this contract, I would have found out a way of eluding it. You did not deal kindly with me not to give me warning, for, if you had, I could have cheated you. This is a fair experiment of knowing what he would choose to do with his money, and it would have been unjust to have bought lands on purpose to elude his agreement though a court of equity could not reach him. The case that has been put of a tenant in tail who has sold his lands and covenanted to make further assurances but yet refused to levy a fine or suffer a recovery is not like this case, for there the issue in tail or remainderman does not claim under the tenant in tail so that they cannot be bound by any covenant of his. But here is nobody before the court but Mr. Frederick or those who represent him and claim under him. This is, therefore, rather like the case of a man who sells land by bargain and sale and dies before enrollment; this court will oblige the heir to enroll it.

I think clearly that Mr. Frederick was bound by the agreement, and his executors and devisees claiming under him.

[It was] decreed that the executors come to an account for the personal estate. The £6500 and the money which came out of the Chamber of London should be laid out in lands according to the marriage settlement, but what money came since is not to be laid out that way. The trustees must account for the interest of it until Mr. Frederick's death and all the personal estate is to be divided according to the custom [of London] and the third part, which is not subject to the custom, is to be distributed according to the will as near as may be and the children who have legacies by the will but insist upon the custom must quit their legacies and the widow must have her chamber and paraphernalia.

[Other reports of this case: 1 Peere Williams 710, 24 E.R. 582, 1 Strange 455, 93 E.R. 632, 1 Brown P.C. 253, 1 E.R. 549.]

513

Manningham v. Anonymous

(Ch. 1721)

A court of equity will grant relief against a bond to pay for worthless shares of stock in a sham corporation.

British Library MS. Hargrave 83, p. 16

Friday, 9 June 1721.

Manningham bought ten shares of Welsh Copper at £40 per share and gave a note of £400 under his hand for value received. And the person with whom he contracted gave Manningham a note under hand promising to transfer the ten shares to him. He soon after offered Manningham a transfer which Manningham declined accepting and said it was time enough, after which, the *scire facias* being ordered against the Welsh Copper Company, the value of the shares sunk to nothing. Upon that Manningham brought his bill to be relieved against his note for £400. The defendant, by his answer, admitted that the shares cost him but 20s. per share.

And though the defendant had not begun any suit upon the note, the Master of the Rolls [Jekyll] granted an injunction to stay proceedings upon the note.

It was said upon this motion that His Honor in a like case had ordered a master to state the facts that His Honor might judge whether the Welsh Copper was within the Act made against this kind of dealing, for, if it was, then every contractor had an equity to be relieved against a contract which was made for a thing which could not be contracted for lawfully.

And upon this case, Mr. Hale, afterwards Chief Baron of Ireland and then Baron of the Exchequer here, told me that he moved in the Exchequer upon a South Sea contract that the injunction might extend to stay an arrest upon the contract, his client being a merchant, and it was granted.

514

Moreton v. Kent

(Ch. 1721)

Where a married executrix dies, the residuum of the testator's estate goes to the testator's heirs at law and not to the husband of the deceased executrix.

Lincoln's Inn MS. Misc. 11, p. 205

12 June 1721.

Joseph Emes, by will, devised to trustees his real estate upon trust to sell the same and to discharge his debts with the money arising thereby, and, after payment of his debts, he directed the residue of the money arising by the sale of his said estate to be paid to his sister, the defendant Kent's wife, and, after some legacies, he gave the residue of his personal estate to his said sister. And he made her executrix, who proved the will and, afterwards, died, leaving issue by her said husband, three daughters.

The defendant Kent took administration to his wife and administration *de bonis non cum testamento annexo* of the said testator.

The plaintiffs are creditors, and they bring their bill to be paid their debts out of the personal estate and, if that was not sufficient, to have the real estate sold for that purpose.

Upon the hearing of this cause, a question arose, to whom the surplus of the real estate, after the payment of the debts, did belong, whether to the defendant Kent as administrator to his wife or to his children as heirs at law to the testator.

[Lord Parker] decreed it to the heirs at law.

515

Peachy v. Duke of Somerset

(Ch. 1721)

A copyholder who violates the land use customs of the manor forfeits his copyhold both at common law and in equity.

Yale Univ. Taussig MS. 311, vol. 1, p. 53

Trinity term 1721.

Sir Henry [Peachy] exhibited his bill in Chancery to be relieved against several forfeitures of a copyhold estate held by the said Sir Henry of the duke, of which forfeitures the duke had taken advantage by entry and brought an [action of] ejectment thereupon. The causes of forfeiture were four: first making leases without license; second, lopping and topping trees; third, digging stones in a quarry, part of which quarry extended into the duke's copyhold though the first digging was within Sir Henry Peachy's freehold; fourth, removing hedges which originally separated and were between the copyhold of the duke and Sir Henry's freehold.

Sir Henry Peachy, upon the birth of his son, before which some of these forfeitures were committed, made a surrender to the use of himself for life, remainder in tail to the use of his son. There was no admittance upon this surrender, but rent was afterwards accepted for several years.

The points were, first, whether all the causes of forfeiture being such wherein the duke might receive a full pecuniary satisfaction and his inheritance was not worse, a court of equity, upon tender of full satisfaction, would not relieve against such forfeitures; second, whether, upon the aforesaid state of the case, these forfeitures could be extended any further than to the estate for life of Sir Henry.

Mr. *Talbot*, for the plaintiff, urged that, though, in law, Sir Henry might not strictly speaking be tenant for life because there was no admittance upon this surrender and so it might be said that the old fee simple continued notwithstanding the surrender, yet, in equity, it was otherwise.

(*Sed quaere per me* [Philip Ward], for, if the forfeitures were previous to the surrender, perhaps the reason why the duke did not accept the surrender was because he would not waive the forfeitures. *Sed quaere* as to the subsequent acceptance of rent, whether this would not be a waiver.)

Secondly, as to the forfeitures, they are always discountenanced in Chancery. They were at first contrived only for the sake of something else and not for their own sake and, therefore, being only originally designed for the security of the party to whom given, the reason of inventing them is fully satisfied in conscience where such use is made of them as will answer that end and secure the party or fully make him whole again by other satisfaction for any damage sustained by the breach of the condition, which is what Sir Henry tenders by this bill.

In a freehold at common law, the forfeiture of a tenant for life gives advantage to him in the next immediate remainder. It is otherwise in cases of copyhold, for, there, the lord is only to take the particular estate forfeited, which is to rest in him only while it continues.

Lincoln's Inn MS. Misc. 506, p. 58

Trinity 7 Geo.

A bill was brought by the plaintiff, who was a copyholder, against the defendant, the lord of the manor, to be relieved against a forfeiture which he had incurred by cutting down some trees which grew upon the copyhold estate. It was insisted on for the lord of the manor that this was not relievable, that the ground of relief was where the court can make an adequate satisfaction, as in the case of a mortgage, which is intended only for security of money, that there is a great deal of difference between conditions in law, which are intended for the prevention of the doing an act, and the conditions of the party, in which it appears to be the intent of the party to secure something else and then there may be relief because the court can make compensation, but no compensation can be made in this case so that there is no handle for a court of equity to lay hold on, that, should the court relieve in such cases as these, it would be so far from answering the intent of the party that it would entirely defeat it and be an encouragement to copyholders to break their customs, that the court would not relieve on a *nomine poenae* for breaking up meadows because it is not supposed that that was inserted for securing the value of the thing, but that the intention of the party was to prevent the doing of it, which intention would never be answered if, after it was done, there might be relief in this court, that it differs not from a tenant for life's making a feoffment in fee or suffering a common recovery or where an action of waste is brought against a particular tenant, in such cases, the court never relieves, for the law, by such acts, makes one man's estate become another's and, to relieve in those cases, would be to alter the law. There was a case [*blank*] where the lord of a manor brought an [action of] ejectment against his copyholder as having forfeited his copyhold by making leases and committing willful waste; the copyholder brought a bill to be relieved against the forfeiture; it appeared that he had made repeated leases and encouraged the other tenants to shake off their obedience to their lord and not comply with the customs of the manor, which he called badges of slavery, but the bill was dismissed inasmuch as copyholders are only tenants at will and, though the law has confirmed an inheritance to them, yet that is only an inheritance according to the custom and while they perform and observe the customs of the manor, but, when they refuse to comply with the customs, the law will not give them any relief, but consider them only as tenants at will, for the customs are the qualifications of a copyholder's estate, which, if he does not perform, he, thereby, determines his estate. In the case of Thomas and Porter, 1 Ch. 92,[1] it was laid down for a rule that a copyholder shall not be relieved for voluntary waste. The case of Cox and Hickford[2] was permissive waste, but, he being obstinate, the court considered it as voluntary. [In] the case of Cox and Brown, 1 Ch. Rep.,[3] there were particular circumstances and creditors were concerned.

The bill was dismissed, it being a voluntary waste.

Lincoln's Inn MS. Misc. 384, p. 224

14 June 1721.

A bill [was exhibited] to be relieved against a forfeiture of a copyhold which the plaintiff held of the defendant, as lord of the manor of Petworth. The defendant insisted on the advantage the law gave him and on three causes of forfeiture,

---

[1] *Thomas v. Porter* (1668), 1 Chancery Cases 95, 22 E.R. 711, also 1 Eq. Cas. Abr. 121, 21 E.R. 927.

[2] *Cox v. Higford* (1710), 2 Vernon 664, 23 E.R. 1032, 1 Eq. Cas. Abr. 121, 21 E.R. 927.

[3] *Cox v. Brown* (1656), 1 Chancery Reports 170, 21 E.R. 540.

making leases without license, topping of trees, and digging in a quarry of stone. The plaintiff offers by the bill any satisfaction and says he had no intent to act contrary to the custom and that the leases are delivered up to the defendant, that the plaintiff, by a marriage settlement, is but a tenant for life [and it is] hard that his issue should forfeit the leases being determined that they were made soon after the plaintiff came of age and by Dee, who was the deputy to the defendant's steward and the plaintiff was ignorant of the custom.

Serjeant *Chesshyre*, for the plaintiff, [cited] Tothill 107; 1 Ch. Rep. 170, Cox v. Brown; Wheeler v. Honor, Syd. 58, Ray. 51; 2 Ch. Rep. 134.[1]

Cowper [cited] Shelly v. Mason, by lord Coventry; 1 Ch. Ca. 95; Whistler v. Cage; Cox v. Higford, by lord Harcourt; Lord Darby v. Morley;[2] Cudmore v. Raven, first, that the plaintiff was ignorant; the forfeiture was not willful; second, that the lord is compellable to grant a license to let; third, equity will relieve where satisfaction may be made. Rolle's Abr. 509.[3]

Serjeant *Pengelly*, for the defendant: First, the plaintiff may forfeit the inheritance; second, the reason why leases are a forfeiture is because a copyholder takes upon himself to be an owner. A disseisor to the lord would alter the tenure. To cut trees is assuming a right to the inheritance. Voluntary waste is always a forfeiture. A lease to commence *in futuro* is a forfeiture though [there was] no entry. Owen 63; Moore 305.[4] The plaintiff must take notice of the custom. Ro. Abr. 807; Cro. El. 498.[5] A condition in law is stronger than in a deed. Infants are bound. There was a confederacy between the plaintiff and Dee. Altering bound the forfeiture. Lib. 268. No precedents are in point.

Attorney General [*Raymond*]: First, a copyholder is bound to take notice of a custom.

Second, [there is] no relief against a voluntary act or condition in law.

Third, [there is] relief only when fraud, accident, or trust. [There is] no relief where a tenant for life makes a feoffment or levies a fine. [There is] no equity to take away the law.

---

1 *Western v. Tolpitt* (1595), Tothill 108, 21 E.R. 138, 117 Selden Soc. 203, 249; *Cox v. Brown* (1656), 1 Chancery Reports 170, 21 E.R. 540; *Wheeler v. Honour* (1661), 1 Siderfin 58, 82 E.R. 968, T. Raymond 41, 83 E.R. 23, also 1 Keble 154, 166, 83 E.R. 870, 878; *Morgan v. Scudamore* (1678), 2 Chancery Reports 134, 21 E.R. 638, also Reports *tempore* Finch 464, 23 E.R. 251, 79 Selden Soc. 562.

2 *Thomas v. Porter* (1668), 1 Chancery Cases 95, 22 E.R. 711, also 1 Eq. Cas. Abr. 121, 21 E.R. 927; *Cox v. Higford* (1710), 2 Vernon 664, 23 E.R. 1032, 1 Eq. Cas. Abr. 121, 21 E.R. 927; *Nash v. Earl of Derby* (1705), 2 Vernon 537, 23 E.R. 948, 1 Eq. Cas. Abr. 121, 126, 21 E.R. 927, 932.

3 1 Rolle, Abr., *Copihold*, p. 509.

4 *Penn v. Merivall* (1597), Owen 63, 74 E.R. 902; *Tresham's Case* (1582), Moore K.B. 172, 72 E.R. 511.

5 *East v. Harding* (1596), 1 Rolle, Abr., *Copihold*, pl. D, 7, p. 507, Croke Eliz. 292, 498, 78 E.R. 546, 749, also Moore K.B. 392, 72 E.R. 648, Owen 63, 74 E.R. 901.

Fourth, the cases on non-payment of fines admit a satisfaction. Cox v. Higford, in favor of the defendant; [there can be] no relief because of obstinance, which is equal to willful waste. Cases turn on circumstances. [There is] no relief on a proviso not to assign without license. [There is a] *nomine poenae* not to turn meadow into pasture. Lord Aylesford would not relieve [against] Lord Somers's rule in Bertie v. Lord Falkland. Cage v. Russell, Vent. 372; Cro. Ja. 368; 4 Co. 21b.[1]

Solicitor General [*Yorke*]: First, this forfeiture does not arise from any particular custom of this manor, but the general custom of all copyholds.

Second, relief here would encourage the mischief which the law would prevent.

Third, a lord is not bound to grant a license.

Fourth, [there is] no relief against a breach of a condition in law nor in cases of a willful forfeiture. Equity may relieve where the forfeiture is for non-payment of money or not doing that of which the value only was considered at the time of the agreement, but not where the intent is to prevent a mischief and of which the value was not considered and does not admit of a compensation. Otherwise, it would defeat the end of the forfeiture and alter the law.

Acherly cited 2 Cro. 403, 3 Bulstr.; Yelv. 144; Br. 84.[2]

Serjeant *Chesshyre* replies, first, if the steward had granted a license, in equity, the lord would be bound. So, if the lord or his steward is a witness to a lease. 1 Ro. Abr. 854.[3]

Second, [it is] a feoffment by a tenant for life *et ux.* to A. and his heirs to the use of the wife for life. Owen 64; 1 Leo. 174.[4]

Third, if a tenant for life levies a fine *sur cognizance de droit* and by deed declares such uses as the tenant for life may, equity would relieve against the forfeiture.

Fourth, it is proved that licenses were granted in this manner at 4d. per pound in the annual rent which brings it within the reason of a compensation.

---

[1] *Viscount Falkland v. Bertie* (1696), 2 Vernon 333, 23 E.R. 814, also 1 Salkeld 231, 91 E.R. 205, 3 Chancery Cases 129, 22 E.R. 1008, 2 Freeman 220, 22 E.R. 1171, 12 Modern 182, 88 E.R. 1248, Holt K.B. 230, 90 E.R. 1026, Colles 10, 1 E.R. 155, Dickens 25, 21 E.R. 176, 1 Eq. Cas. Abr. 110, 21 E.R. 917; *Cage v. Russel* (1681), 2 Ventris 352, 86 E.R. 481, also 1 Eq. Cas. Abr. 108, 21 E.R. 916; *Ford v. Hoskins* (1615), Croke Jac. 368, 79 E.R. 315, also 1 Rolle Rep. 125, 195, 81 E.R. 376, 427, Moore K.B. 842, 72 E.R. 941, 2 Bulstrode 336, 80 E.R. 1168; *Brown's Case* (1581), 4 Coke Rep. 21, 76 E.R. 911, also Moore K.B. 125, 72 E.R. 483.

[2] *Frosel v. Welsh* (1616), Croke Jac. 403, 79 E.R. 344, 3 Bulstrode 214, 81 E.R. 181, also J. Bridgman 49, 123 E.R. 1192, Godbolt 268, 78 E.R. 157, 1 Rolle Rep. 415, 81 E.R. 575; *Wilson v. Weddell* (1608), Yelverton 144, 80 E.R. 97.

[3] 1 Rolle, Abr., *Estate*, p. 854.

[4] *Hone* [*How*] *v. Clerk* (1588 x 1589), Owen 64, 74 E.R. 903; *Dove v. Williot* (1589), 1 Leonard 174, 74 E.R. 160, also Croke Eliz. 160, 78 E.R. 418.

Fifth, [there is a] distinction between a forfeiture at law and in equity. Thomas v. Porter, 1 Ch. Ca. 95.[1] [For a] *nomine poenae* not to plow up meadow, [there is] no relief because [it is] stated damages. Ayre v. Hutt, in the Duchy, by lord Aylesford.

Sixth, [it was] objected [that] relief in such cases would be an encouragement to tenants to commit forfeitures. But, if this court decrees the plaintiff to pay a cons[iderable] fine and costs, it would be a sufficient discouragement.

Hungerford: If there is no relief in this court, the plaintiff insists of a trial at law whether these acts are a forfeiture.

N.B. The waste was committed in 1693.

Talbot: First, the case of the plaintiff and his son are different. The plaintiff is only a tenant for life by a marriage settlement and a surrender made and accepted to those uses, and though there was no admittance, yet [there was] a trust for the son, and this court would compel the lord to admit.

Second, the son is a proper [party] in this court to preserve his equitable interest.

Third, forfeitures are neither under [the jurisdictional headings of] fraud, accident, or trust, yet [they are] proper for relief in equity.

Fourth, [it was] objected [that there is] no relief against breaches of conditions in law; [this is] false, for non-payment of fines [for] permissive waste is relieved. Cox v. Higford; nine years after the lord's entry.

Fifth, both the leases determined in 1707. [There was] no entry for a breach.

Lord Chancellor [Lord Parker]: These forfeitures arise from the imbecility of the tenure. At first, he was but a tenant at will, now, he is a tenant according to the custom of the manor, i.e. as long as he observes the custom. But when he takes upon himself a greater power than the custom allows, it is a forfeiture as much as where a tenant for life makes a feoffment. This forfeiture does not arise from any damage for which a compensation may be had. This is the law. It determines his estate without a ground of relief in equity. If it be a hard law, this court cannot repeal it. It is not unconscionable to take advantage of the [common] law any more than an act of Parliament. The common law was at first acts of Parliament, though the records are lost. [There is] no handle for a court of equity to lay hold of so as to restore the party. Where money is to be paid at a day, if the party has interest from that day, it is according to the original intent of the parties.

But these forfeitures arise from the nature of the tenant's estate. Indeed, forfeitures for non-payment of fines or rent only consist in a payment of money. Copyholders have now a great advantage by the law [so] that [there is] no reason to extend them further. In the case of permissive waste, compensation may be made. If a house is repaired before an action is brought, it is a good excuse at law, without circumstances of equity in this case.

---

[1] *Thomas v. Porter* (1668), 1 Chancery Cases 95, 22 E.R. 711, also 1 Eq. Cas. Abr. 121, 21 E.R. 927.

If the lord had encouraged the leases, this court would hinder his taking advantage of the forfeiture. The plaintiff's [. . .] in the steward is an aggravation [and] no objection against the lord. The steward does not take advantage of the forfeiture.

If equity relieves in this case, it must in all. If leasing without license be continued, it will be an evidence in time against the lord. The plaintiff's discourses in the copyhold court are aggravations. Topping a timber tree makes it a pollard, and it becomes the property of the tenant; therefore, it is equivalent to cutting it down. In some manors, the property of timber trees is not in the lord, but here it is. Even when it is not, yet the tenant's cutting is a forfeiture.

[There are] no equitable circumstances in this case proper here for a discovery without a forfeiture the defendant insisted on. It is not proper now to determine the case of a plaintiff's son. A lord may take advantage of a forfeiture by a trustee. If the son commits treason, the estate cannot be forfeited. If trustees of a freehold commit a felony, the lord by escheat is not liable to the trust [for the] admission of a tenant. [Where a] lord admits a remainder[man], there is not a fine until after the admittance. [There is] nothing in this case for this court to relieve on. The judgment in ejectment being given is not to prejudice the plaintiff. The plaintiff must bring a new [action of] ejectment.

Lincoln's Inn MS. Misc. 12, p. 59

14 June 1721.

The plaintiff was a copyholder of the defendant's manor of Petworth in Suffolk, in which there is a custom that, if a tenant makes a lease of his copyhold for more than a year and a day without the license of the lord, for which license 4d. in the pound is to be paid to the lord for a fine, it is a forfeiture of his copyhold.

The plaintiff having made a lease of some copyhold land held of the defendant's manor for eleven years at £13 a year without license, the defendant brought an [action of] ejectment. And the plaintiff's bill was to be relieved against this forfeiture.

The defendant insisted that the plaintiff had not only forfeited his copyhold by making the said lease but likewise by lopping timber trees, digging in a quarry, and destroying the boundaries.

The plaintiff, by his bill, offers to procure the lease to be delivered up and to pay his fine for the license, which he should have taken.

Serjeant *Chesshyre*, for the plaintiff: This court has frequently relieved incases of forfeitures of freehold, as where there is a clause of re-entry in case of alienation. It has been settled that, where there is a controverted point between the tenant and the lord and the tenant disputes it and it is found against him, yet it shall not be a forfeiture, even at law. And he cited 1 Canc., Cox and Brown, and 1 Sid., Wheeler and Honour.

Mr. *Cowper*, of the same side: I apprehend the precedents are that, in all cases, where there has been a forfeiture for cutting timber or not taking up a copyhold, this court has relieved.

Shelly and Mason, 5 Car. I, in Lord Coventry's time; a copyholder made a lease without license, and the lord entered, and, upon a bill to be relieved, the tenant was decreed to be restored and the lord to account for the profits. 1 Canc. 95;[1] a copyholder had not taken up his copyhold; the lord entered, and the copyholder was relieved.

Cox v. Higford, in Lord Harcourt's time; [upon a] bill to be relieved against a forfeiture for waste committed, the defendant insisted the waste was voluntary. It was proved that the lord for three years together called upon his tenants to repair and he was obstinate and would not, and, for this obstinacy of his, the court would not relieve but dismissed the bill.

Lord Chancellor [Lord Parker]: The Case of Cox and Higford was permissive waste. But can you show any case where the waste was voluntary that this court has relieved?

Mr. *Hungerford*, of the same side: I take it that the rule has been that, where the party who claims by reason of a forfeiture can be put into the same condition by this court as he was in before the forfeiture was committed, the court will relieve.

Attorney General [*Raymond*], for the defendant: I do not know any case where this court has relieved against a voluntary forfeiture. Fraud, accident, or trust are the three things in which this court relieves, but not against a man's voluntary act. Did this court ever relieve in case a tenant for life levies a fine or makes a feoffment? There was an attempt in the Duchy Court [of Lancaster] to be relieved against a *nomine poenae*, but it was denied. Equity is tender in breaking in upon fundamentals upon privileges annexed to estates by law.

Solicitor General [*Yorke*], same side: As to the forfeitures insisted on by the defendant, they are forfeitures at law. The bill to be relieved against them implies as much. If the court, in some general cases and upon circumstances, has relieved, yet there are no such circumstances in the present case. But, on the contrary, there are circumstances which ought to induce the court to deny relief, for the plaintiff has been endeavoring to alter the tenure and to stir up the tenants to deliver themselves from the customs of the manor and to prejudice the interest of the lord.

Mr. *Lutwyche*: A copyholder is only a tenant at will according to the custom of the manor. Now, if he takes upon him to make a lease, it is a determination of his will and a setting up for another sort of estate than what the law allows him.

If the plaintiff is entitled to relief, what compensation can be made to the lord? The court can give him his costs, they cannot assess damages.

---

1 *Thomas v. Porter* (1668), *ut supra*.

The case that comes the nearest to the present case is that of a tenant for life's making a feoffment or levying a fine. Now, might not the same be said in that case as in the present? Might not a tenant for life come into this court and say let me be relieved for I might have made a lease for ninety-nine years and avoided the forfeiture? So here, they say the plaintiff might have had a license from the lord and have saved his forfeiture.

Serjeant *Pengelly*, same side: As to the forfeitures, we say they were all voluntary and willful. And the reason why the law makes these things forfeitures is not because the lord is deprived of his fine but because the tenant takes upon himself to act as though his estate was a freehold, which may in time tend to defeat the lord of his right. If a tenant at will takes upon himself to make a lease for years, it is a disseisin, and he thereby gains an inheritance in the reversion.

The case is the same as to copyhold. Where a man takes upon himself to make a lease of it, he acts as though he had a freehold, and it is a determination of his estate. East and Harding [*blank*] adjudged that a lease of a copyhold to commence *in futuro* was a forfeiture.

The plaintiff has made several leases, one in 1693, another in 1694, and the last in 1714 so that his forfeitures have been repeated. And, in time, these leases may be made use of to show that the estate is not copyhold.

The plaintiff cannot pretend ignorance, for these forfeitures are annexed to the estate and are conditions in law which go along with it. And conditions in law bind more strongly than conditions in fact. They will bind infants.

As to what is insisted, that the deputy steward made the last lease and was a witness to it, we say he was not a steward at that time. However, supposing him to be so, we insist the laches or neglect of the steward shall not turn to the prejudice of the lord or excuse the forfeiture.

As to the cutting down the hedges and fences, some of these lay between the freehold and the copyhold, others between copyhold and copyhold. Now, the grubbing up these hedges may be of ill consequence to the lord, for, in time, he may not know where to find his land. Litt. rep. 268;[1] destroying boundaries was adjudged to be a forfeiture.

As to the cutting the trees in The Grove, our proof is there was no occasion to cut several of those trees. If the act itself is illegal, it is no excuse to say that he party intended well. If what a man does is an injury to another, let his intention be what it will, it will not excuse him.

As to the Case of Shelly and Mason, cited by Mr. Cowper, it is a very extraordinary one. A lord was decreed to account for the profits of an estate on which he has entered for a forfeiture.

A lord, in the case of a forfeiture, may make a grant without an entry.

---

1 *Watts v. Maydwell* (1629), Littleton 268, 279, 124 E.R. 240, 246, also Hutton 104, 123 E.R. 1132.

Mr. *Mead*, same side: Cage and Russell, 2 Vent. 352; a rule was laid down, the most general that I know of. By that case, it must be admitted it does appear that this court will relieve in cases of penalties. But there are cases of forfeitures where this court will not relieve, as for breach of a condition precedent.

In the Case of Bertie and Lord Falkland, it was laid down by Lord Somers that this court will not relieve in the case of the breach of a condition precedent unless there were any underhand practice to hinder the performance of the condition. But, in the case of a condition subsequent, it is otherwise, for that goes only by way of defeasance. Where the law annexes a condition to an estate, if the court relieves, it would be to make a new law.

In the case of Hamond and Ange, before the present Chancellor, where a lord prevailed on the plaintiff to come to the court and be admitted to an estate which the lord said was copyhold and it afterwards appeared to be freehold, the plaintiff was relieved, but that was upon the head of fraud.

In the cases of relief, where the lord insists on a forfeiture, it is grounded upon this, that the lord makes an undue use of the power which the law gives him.

I believe, in all cases where the court has relieved, it has been only against one single act. And no case can be produced where the court has relieved against continued and repeated forfeitures, as in the present case.

As to the Case of Cudmore and Raven, cited on the other side, the plaintiff, being a Quaker, was called upon by the lord to take the oath of fealty, and, he refusing and the lord insisting on this as a forfeiture, the Quaker brought his bill and was relieved. But here was a case of hardship and oppression. Perhaps the lord did not insist upon any of his other tenants swearing fealty but singles out a Quaker, who he knows scrupled to take an oath. In such a case as that, it was highly reasonable the court should relieve, for it is well known that it is frequent in copies to respite fealty.

Lord Chancellor [Lord Parker]: This is a case of very great consequence, and it is very strange to me that there has been no precedent for these 100 years past that comes up to this case.

A copyholder is considered in most cases as a tenant at will. It is true he is a tenant at will according to the custom of the manor, and the lord cannot determine the will but where the custom allows it. But if the custom allows it, what hinders, but the lord may determine it.

It is very right what has been observed, that a copyholder shall not make a lease but according to the custom is a condition in law annexed to his estate. And, therefore, if the tenant takes upon him to make a lease contrary to the custom, it is usurping upon the lord, and, by law, it is a determination of his estate. And, if the law says a copyholder's estate is determined in such a case, shall this court say it shall not be determined?

It is agreed that there shall be no relief in equity in a case of waste. Can there be any difference between a freeholder and a copyholder as to waste? Shall a freeholder who commits waste have no relief though the party has a treble satisfaction and recovers the place wasted besides? And shall a copyholder be in a better condition when there is not that compensation to be made?

As to what is said that the action of waste is grounded upon an Act of Parliament and there can be no relief against an act of Parliament, why, the forfeiture of a copyhold for waste committed is given by law, and the reason will hold as strong in the one case as the other.

As to forfeitures for the non-payment of a fine or rent, the intention of the law in making them forfeitures is for the security of the lord. And the reason why the court relieves in those cases is because, if the party has a satisfaction by being allowed interest, it is the same thing whether the fine or rent is paid at one time or another.

Now, what circumstances are there for relief in this case which might not be shown in any of the case where the court has denied relief?

Upon the whole matter, the Lord Chancellor [Lord Parker] seemed to be of opinion that the plaintiff was not entitled to be relieved. But no decree was pronounced, there being some matters sent to be tried at law, which I do not particularly remember.

Note there was another case cited and the decree was read in court, which was the Case of Nash and Lord Derby, 21 February 1705[/06], before Lord Cowper, which was this. The plaintiff was a copyholder and had a right to cut timber for repairs by an assignment of the lord. And he cut timber without an assignment, but he applied it for repairs, whereupon the lord brought his [action of] ejectment, which was tried. And he had a verdict for the forfeiture. All the trees which were cut were not above the value of £3, and the copyhold was worth £300. The plaintiff brought his bill and was relieved upon paying the value of the timber and full costs at law and in this court. And it was referred to a master to settle the value of the timber. And, upon payment thereof with costs, it was decreed that the defendant should re-admit the plaintiff, paying the usual fees, but without any fine.

British Library MS. Add. 36651, f. 104v

The original bill was to be relieved against a forfeiture of some copyholds belonging to the plaintiff which he held of the duke's manor of Petworth in the County of Sussex and to have an injunction to stay execution upon four judgments in [actions of] ejectment by default, which the defendant had obtained upon the said pretended forfeitures. There was also a supplemental bill wherein the son of Sir Henry Peachy joins to discover the several matters insisted on by the defendants as forfeitures of the said copyholds and insisting that Sir Henry Peachy by his marriage settlement was only tenant for life of the said copyholds, a surrender having been made on his marriage and the uses limited by the settlement to him for life with a remainder to his first and other sons so that Sir Henry could not by any forfeiture prejudice the inheritance.

The duke, by his answer, insisted on four several causes of forfeiture:

First, in making leases of part of the said copyhold lands for eleven years without license of the lord;

Second, for lopping and heading timber trees;

Third, for grubbing up and leveling the fences within the copyhold etc. and also such as divided the copyhold from his own freehold lands.

Fourth, for opening and digging stone quarries within the copyhold lands.

As to the first, of making leases without license, the custom of the manor was proved both by an old decree in 36 Eliz. and by witnesses that copyholders could not lease for a longer time than a year and a day. They produced two leases made by the plaintiff *anno* 1694 for eleven years each and a third dated *anno* 1714 for eleven years to which one Bernard, the defendant's steward, was a witness.

As to the second and third, *viz.* lopping and heading the timber trees and grubbing up the fences, it appeared on the proofs that the said trees were in a close called The Grove, containing five acres, four of which were copyhold and formerly divided into three several closes by quick hedges in which some trees grew and were also in like manner divided from that acre that is freehold, that Sir Henry Peachey, thirty years ago, planted the said timber trees in rows as avenues to his house and grubbed up the hedges and laid the ground level for the ornament to his house so as now there is no boundary between the freehold and copyhold to distinguish the same, that the trees in the copyhold within The Grove were all headed but the rest not, which was done after the great wind *anno* 1703 to make them uniform as was pretended.

As to the fourth, of digging stones, it appeared that the quarry was first opened in Sir Henry's freehold and so carried on into the copyhold lands, but it did not appear when it was first opened or whether it was carried into the copyhold since Sir Henry became tenant or not.

Serjeant *Chesshyre*, Mr. *Cowper*, Mr. *Hungerford*, and Mr. *Talbot*, for the plaintiff, urged that relief against forfeitures was the proper business of a court of equity and never denied but upon particular reasons, especially where an adequate compensation could be made, so are all redemptions upon mortgages and penalties for non-payment of rents or fines of copyholders. Therefore, if the plaintiff can put the defendant in the same circumstances as before or make an adequate compensation for the damage, he must be relieved.

Copyholds are not forfeited but by the willful act of the copyholder. Moor 622.[1] And, in the case of a forfeiture for non-payment of a rent or fine, the lord must first demand them of the person of the tenant before he can take advantage of the forfeiture. Hob. 135.[2] So, in the case of permissive waste and such like involuntary forfeitures, there must be personal notice before the lord can enter.

---

[1] *Dalton v. Hamond* (1600), Moore K.B. 622, 72 E.R. 799, also Croke Eliz. 779, 78 E.R. 1010, *sub nom. Hobart v. Hammond*, 4 Coke Rep. 27, 76 E.R. 942.

[2] *Denny v. Lemman*, Hobart 135, 80 E.R. 285.

Mr. *Talbot* particularly insisted that, Sir Henry Peachy being only a tenant for life, the forfeitures could only affect his estate for life and not the remainder in tail vested in his son by virtue of the marriage articles. He said it was objected that, though there was a surrender and presentment in pursuance of those articles, yet there has been no admittance or fine paid according to such surrender, to which he answered that, in a court of equity, it will be considered as done, especially being in pursuance of marriage articles.

As to the cause of forfeiture in making leases without a license, he said the reason why that is a forfeiture is because the lord thereby loses his fine for a license; so it is the same as the case of a lease with a clause of re-entry for non-payment of the rent, in which case, this court has always relieved.

To the second cause of forfeiture in heading and lopping the timber trees, he said the difference is objected between voluntary and involuntary acts and, though this is a voluntary act, yet it appears not to have been done with an intent to commit waste but for the sake of beauty and ornament to the house, and the same may be said as to the third cause of forfeiture in grubbing the hedges the trees that grew in the hedges being of little or no value.

As to the fourth, *viz.* digging the quarry, he said it was an open quarry at the time of Sir Henry Peachy's admittance as appeared by the evidence and not shown when it was first carried into the copyhold land.

Serjeant *Pengelly*, *contra*: The inheritance in law remaining in Sir Henry Peachy for want of an admittance, his acts of forfeiture will affect it. All these acts are voluntary and are all such as would be evidence of a freehold and, therefore, not relievable in equity. But, even in case of a forfeiture by permitting the house to be out of repair for thirty years after notice to repair it though only permissive waste, yet this court denied relief, as in the Case of Fox v. Hickford, 1 Chanc. Cases 95. And, for these cases of forfeitures, the estate is in the lord before actual entry.

Sir Robert Raymond, Attorney General, said it was a general rule that this court relieved in three cases, *viz.* of fraud, accident, and trust but never against a voluntary act unless it had in it some circumstance which brought it within that general rule. If a tenant for life of a freehold make a feoffment, there is no relief in this court against the forfeiture though a recompense was offered, for this court cannot alter a limitation or condition annexed by the law to an estate, so a devise to A. for life, remainder to the heirs of his body is an estate tail executed though the intent of the testator is express that A. should have only an estate for life.

This court will often relieve in case of circumstances as of time and allow a thing to be done or performed *nunc pro tunc* as in the case of mortgages and entries for non-payment of rents and also of a *nomine poenae* for non-payment of rent, but, upon a penalty for plowing meadow or pasture contrary to an agreement, no relief was ever granted. And it was denied in the Case of Eyre v. Hutton, in the Duchy Court, in which the judges assisted.

As to the objection that Sir Henry Peachy is only a tenant for life and, therefore, these acts of forfeiture cannot affect his son, I respond, if they do not, then the son has no cause to pray for relief now because, if there be no forfeiture of the inheritance, he may defend himself at [common] law when he come to take in remainder.

As to Sir Henry Peachy, it is said in excuse that he was a stranger to the customs of the manor. I respond these are forfeitures by the common law, not by a particular custom and, if otherwise, yet every copyholder is bound to take notice of the customs of the manor at his peril.

Objection: The leases are attested by the lord's steward.

Response: His act cannot prejudice the lord, and the steward told the plaintiff a license was necessary.

The Case of Thomas and Porter, cited on the other side, is an authority for the defendant, for, in that case, it was said by Lord Bridgman that, in the case of a voluntary forfeiture, he would not relieve, so an issue was directed to try whether the waste was willful or not and it was found it was not. And, in the Case of Cox and Hickford, the copyholder continuing obstinate after notice to appear, it was looked upon as equal to a voluntary waste and, therefore, relief was denied. All the other cases wherein relief has been decreed were upon acts of omission, as non-payment of fines upon admittance etc. and where a recompense can be made.

There is also a difference between conditions in a deed, as by contract or agreement etc., and conditions in law. In the first, the court can consider the intent of the parties, as in the case of a mortgage which is only intended as a security for money. But the intent of the parties cannot be considered in the case of conditions in law. And, therefore, against such, there is no relief, as if a tenant for life levy a fine or make a feoffment unless he that was to take advantage of the forfeiture had been guilty of some fraud or concealment of deeds or the like. So, in actions of waste to recover the places wasted, no relief was ever in this court. And conditions in law are so strong that they will bind infants, and to relieve against them would be to alter the law.

The Case of Cox and Brown, in 1 Chanc. Rep. 170, is cited where relief was given in the case of a voluntary forfeiture, but that depended on particular circumstances, the plaintiff being an executor and there were creditors concerned. So, in 2 Ch. Rep. 234,[1] the court relieved in a case where the lord insisted on an extravagant fine. And perhaps in cases of dispute between a lord and a copyholder, every act or refusal will not be a forfeiture, as if a custom was doubtful and insisted on, that might be an excuse. But, in this case, the customs were certain and settled by an ancient decree to this purpose.

---

1 *Morgan v. Scudamore* (1678), *ut supra.*

Mr. *Atcherly* cited the Case of Nash v. the Earl of Darby, where a copyholder demanded wood to be set out by the woodward, and, upon his refusal, she got two tenants to set it out for repairs, which there was no custom to warrant; the lord brought an [action of] ejectment and had judgment, but relief was decreed in this court on paying the full value of the timber.

Lord Chancellor [Lord Parker] cited a case in Tothill where a copyholder cut timber and employed it in repairs without license, and he had relief in this court because there was only a circumstance wanting and, there, the custom was disputed.

Note they cited the Case of Eyre v. Hutton, in the Duchy Court; a bill [was exhibited] to be relieved against a *nomine poenae* for so much per acre for plowing meadow or pasture ground, and Lord Bridgman would not relieve because he said it was stated damages by the agreement of the parties.

Chesshyre, in reply, insisted that, as to these two parcels of copyhold forfeited by the two leases made above twenty years ago, the lord was barred to take advantage of it by the Statute of Limitations.

Mr. *Talbot* [said] that, as to the inheritance, Sir Henry Peachy is to be looked upon only as a trustee for his son. Two of the leases were made over thirty years ago, and it would be hard to insist on forfeitures after such a length of time.

Lord Parker, Chancellor: It is a case of great consequence. A copyholder is only a tenant at will, and the copyhold is part of the demesnes of the manor, but *consuetudo manerii* has established his estate which, at first, the lord might have determined at pleasure.

To relieve against forfeitures arising upon conditions in law would be to revoke and alter the law. So, if it arises upon an act of Parliament, as in the case of waste, where the Statute gives the place wasted and treble damages, must this court say the Parliament have made an unreasonable law and that the forfeiture is unconscionable.

Recompense is a handle which this court takes hold of to give relief in some cases. But, in this case, there can be no recompense. That is the foundation of relief on mortgages, failure at the day being recompensed by giving interest from that time.

The law has annexed these conditions to the copyholder's estate. He must be content to enjoy it upon these terms. But, in the case of non-payment of rent or a fine, this court will relieve because compensation may be made and nothing but the circumstance of time is wanting.

Cases in equity turn upon particular circumstances. If the lord had been present when the leases were made and had driven the bargain for the leases, that might have been proper for relief, but the steward's being a witness is rather an aggravation, for he told the plaintiff he ought to have had a license. And, if relief was to be had in this case, all copyholders might make leases without license.

As to the trees, to lop a timber tree is as prejudicial to the lord as to fell it and take it away, for then it is no longer timber but a pollard and the property is in the tenant. Though neither lord nor tenant, without the consent of each other, can cut timber, yet if the tenant cut a tree, the lord may take it away, or, if the tenant take it, the lord may bring [an action of] trover, for then it became his when severed from the land.

The son is not now properly before the court. But, for argument's sake, suppose the father is a trustee for him as to the inheritance, acts of forfeiture by the father will affect and be a forfeiture of the son's inheritance. So if the father commit treason and the lord that is in by the forfeiture or escheat is not subject to the trust.

If Sir Henry Peachy had been admitted upon the surrender, then his act could not have affected the son because the admittance is a grant to the son as well as to the father. The lord cannot compel an admittance, nor is a fine due until the admittance. So, by not being admitted, the lord is injured.

As to that part of the estate comprised in the lease made *anno* 1714, he said he was clear that that was a forfeiture and not relievable; so the defendant might take out a *scire facias* upon the judgment in the [action of] ejectment for that part (note the judgment was above a year ago) if he thinks it better for him to do so than to bring a new [action of] ejectment.

As to the other parts to which the other acts of forfeiture related, he directed new [actions of] ejectment to be brought, there not being a full proof of those causes of forfeiture. And he would dismiss the bill as to relief, but he retained it until after the trial in order to give costs as the case should come out.

The dismission as to the son is to be without prejudice if he shall afterwards think fit to bring his bill in this court.

[Other reports of this case: 1 Strange 447, 93 E.R. 626, Precedents in Chancery 568, 24 E.R. 255, 2 Eq. Cas. Abr. 227, 22 E.R. 193, 6 Viner, Abr., *Copyhold*, p. 113.]

516

Ewer v. Earl of Shaftesbury

(Ch. 1721)

Where a power to raise a sum of money out of land is exercised in favor of a third party, that donee is not liable for any waste committed by the person who exercised the power.

Lincoln's Inn MS. Misc. 384, p. 242

30 June.

A bill [was exhibited] to have £2000 raised, which was given the plaintiff by Mr. Miclelthwayte pursuant to a power. Sir J. Cropley, by will, devised his estate to Mr. Miclelthwayte for life with a power for him by a deed or will to limit £2000 to be raised by mortgage or sale to be paid to such person after his death as he should appoint. Pursuant to this power, Miclethwayte, by deed, appoints this £2000 to be paid to the plaintiff.

The defendant, to whom the next estate for life was devised, insisted that Mr. Miclethwayte committed waste and raised a considerable sum of money in his lifetime by the sale of timber and, therefore, that the value thereof ought to be deducted out of the £2000.

N.B. The inheritance is given to Greenwich Hospital.

Master of the Rolls [JEKYLL], first, considered whether there was any remedy, either in law or equity, for him who had the inheritance against the representative of Miclethwayte for the waste committed in his lifetime and was of opinion there was not;

Second, whether equity could deduct the value of the waste out of this £2000, it is to be raised by mortgage. Suppose the mortgagee had committed waste, he must have accounted for it. Miclethwayte had an absolute power over the £2000. He might assign it for a valuable consideration; it was subject to debts. Lassells v. Lord Cornwallis.[1] He ordered a deduction to be made of the value of the timber.

14 July.

Master of the Rolls [JEKYLL]: First, my opinion was founded upon a supposition that Mr. Miclethwayte had a property in the £2000. If he had and had come against the person who had the inheritance, it might have been objected by way of rebutter that he had received part by cutting down the timber. But the defendant, the earl of Shaftesbury, being only tenant for life, cannot have any property in the timber. Duke of Newcastle's Case,[2] where it was blown down.

Second, the plaintiff does not claim under or as representative of Miclethwayte, but under an execution of a power.

Third, Miclethwayte might have appointed it to his executors or administrators and then it had been assets. But he had a power to do otherwise and he to give it to a stranger, which he has done.

Fourth, Miclethwayte might have released or extinguished his power, but it is a great strain to say that, in equity, he had so done by committing a tort when he was liable to be punished by law.

Fifth, here is a damage done to the inheritance, but the remedy is gone by the party's death. No property was in Miclethwayte.

[1] *Lasselles v. Lord Cornwallis* (1704), Precedents in Chancery 232, 24 E.R. 113, 2 Vernon 456, 23 E.R. 898, also 2 Freeman 279, 22 E.R. 1210, 1 Eq. Cas. Abr. 242, 21 E.R. 1019, 2 Eq. Cas. Abr. 467, 22 E.R. 397.

[2] *Duke of Newcastle v. Vane*, cited at 2 Peere Williams 240, 241, 24 E.R. 714.

517

Baker v. Norton

(Ch. 1721)

The question in this case was whether a court of equity can order a faulty settlement to be corrected according to the terms and intent of the contract to make the settlement.

Lincoln's Inn MS. Misc. 11, p. 194

30 June 1721.

John Norton, upon the marriage of Alice, his daughter, with the plaintiff's father, makes a settlement by a lease and release dated 16 and 17 January 1717[/18]. And, thereby, in consideration of the then intended marriage and for making a provision for Alice, the daughter, for her life and for a provision for the issue of the body of the plaintiff's father on the body of Alice and for the advancement of the issue of the body of the plaintiff's father on the body of Alice to be begotten, John Norton settles a house to the use of himself for life, then for the separate use of Alice for life, and after the decease of John Norton and Alice, his daughter, to the use of the heirs of the body of Thomas Baker, the plaintiff's father, on the body of Alice to be begotten, and, for default of such issue, to the use of the heirs of Thomas Baker.

John Norton and his daughter are both dead, but Thomas Baker is living, and the plaintiff is the only son of Thomas Baker by Alice, his wife. And, in regard the limitations over after the death of John Norton and Alice are, as it was apprehended, contingent and consequently void by the determination of the particular estates on which they depended during the [life] of Thomas Baker, the plaintiff brings his bill against the heir at law of John Norton, upon whom the legal estate was descended, to supply the defect of this settlement, for, as the settlement was penned, the issue of the marriage is entirely defeated, which is contrary to the agreement of the parties, which was to make a provision for the issue, and so it is recited in the settlement, and, if Norton himself had been alive, this court would have decreed him to make the settlement according to the marriage agreement; so his heir at law, who stands in his place, ought to do the like, the settlement being made upon a valuable consideration.

Mr. *Mead, e contra*: The difference has always been where the marriage agreement is executory only and where it is carried into an execution. In the latter case, this court has not relieved. And he cited the Case of Taylor and Taylor, before the late Master of the Rolls [Trevor], where a man, upon the marriage of his son, settled lands to the use of himself for life, then to the intended wife for life, then to the first and other sons of the marriage, but there was no limitation to the son of the father, who made the settlement for his life as usual, and he brought his bill to supply this defect, it being plainly an omission in the settlement, and what made it more evident to be so, there was a power given to the son in the settlement to make leases, which plainly showed it was intended he should have had an estate for life, but, notwithstanding, the court would not help him and dismissed his bill. And, upon an appeal to Lord Harcourt, he affirmed the decree.

The Master of the Rolls [JEKYLL] made a doubt whether the limitation to the heirs of the body was contingent. And he seemed to think the eldest son might take in the lifetime of his father. And, therefore, he sent it to the judges of the [Court of] Common Pleas to certify their opinion upon a case to be drawn up. But he said, if the [common] law was against the plaintiff, equity ought to relieve, for, had the marriage agreement appeared by a separate deed and the settlement had been contrary to the agreement, the court would have directed the settlement to have been made according to the agreement, and, therefore, he did not think it would alter the case, because the agreement appeared in the settlement itself.

What created the doubt in the Master of the Rolls as to the matter in law was the Case of Beaumond and Long, in the House of Lords,[1] which was contrary to what the law was taken to be before that case.

Lincoln's Inn MS. Misc. 384, p. 241, pl. 2

30 June 1721.

The bill was to have the unskillfulness of a marriage settlement rectified. The deed recited that the estate was to be settled for a jointure for the wife and a provision for the issue of the marriage. The limitation was to the wife for life and, after her decease and of J. Norton, the grandfather, then to the use of the heirs of the body of the husband and wife . The wife died and J. Norton, but the husband is alive, no estate being limited to him. The query is whether the contingent remainder to the heirs of his body is not void in law, and, if it is, whether equity will relieve.

The Master of the Rolls [JEKYLL] was very doubtful whether the limitation was not good in law since the case of Long v. Beamont, in the House of Lords, where Mr. Speccot, by will, devised to the heirs male of his aunt Long lawfully begotten, and the Lord's adjudged it good though Mrs. Long was living. Upon this point, they sent it to the judges of the Common Pleas, but they said that, if the law were against the plaintiff, yet equity would rectify the settlement, it being intended to be a provision for the issue of the marriage, who were in the nature of purchasers.

[1] *Lay v. Beaumont* (Ex. 1709), Eq. Cases Exch. 604, *sub nom. Darbison, ex dem. Long v. Beaumont* (Ex. 1713), 1 Peere Williams 229, 24 E.R. 366, Fortescue 18, 92 E.R. 743, 1 Eq. Cas. Abr. 214, 21 E.R. 999, Dodd 366, *sub nom. Darbison v. Beaumont* (H.L. 1714), Lords' Journal, vol. 19, p. 696, 3 Brown P.C. 60, 1 E.R. 1177.

Mead, for the defendant: That case was upon a will. This is upon a deed. There is no case where the deed was altered unless by articles precedent to the Statute of Frauds.[1]

He cited Taylor v. Taylor, by the Master of the Rolls [Trevor], affirmed by Lord Harcourt, where the limitation in a deed was to the father for life, then to the first and other sons of the son in tail with a power to the son to make leases, but no estate was given to the son, though it was insisted that the implication was very strong that the son was intended to have an estate for life, yet, because it was a settlement executed and not articles executory, this court would not relieve.

518

Low v. Low

(Ch. 1721)

Where daughters' portions are to be raised by a settlement and also by a will, the donee must elect one or the other even where they are to be raised out of different lands.

Lincoln's Inn MS. Misc. 11, p. 198

A settlement was made by the plaintiff's father for raising portions and maintenances for the plaintiffs, his daughters. And a term was created for that purpose. The portions were payable at eighteen or marriage. And, afterwards, the plaintiff's father, by his will, taking no notice of the settlement, gives the plaintiffs, his daughters, larger portions payable at twenty-one or marriage, and he gives them larger maintenances in the meantime than what they were entitled to by the settlement. And he devises lands to other trustees for raising these portions, amongst which lands were part of the lands comprised in the settlement.

The plaintiffs bring their bill to have their portions raised. And they insist they are entitled to the portions both under the will and the settlement in regard they are different sums, different trustees, different lands are charged, and the portions are payable at different times. And if they should have both was the question.

The Master of the Rolls [Jekyll] said it was a very clear case, and he decreed the plaintiffs should only have one of the portions provided for them by the settlement and the will. And, in regard they were under age and could not now make their election, he reserved a liberty for them to apply to the court when they came of age, and, in the meantime, he directed the maintenance provided by the will should be paid, for that being the largest maintenance and apparently for the plaintiffs' benefit, the court might so far elect for them.

---

[1] Stat. 29 Car. II, c. 3 (*SR*, V, 839–842).

As to what was insisted on, that the portions were different and payable at different times and charged on different lands, it made no alteration in the case, as was determined in the Case of Keymish and Thomas, quod vide B, 30.[1]

519
Ex parte Chion
(Ch. 1721)

Shares of stock held in the name of the agent of the purchaser are held in trust for the purchaser.

Assets held in trust by a bankrupt cannot be seized to satisfy the creditors of the trustee-bankrupt.

Lincoln's Inn MS. Misc. 384, p. 243, pl. 1

4 July.

The plaintiff, living in Holland, wrote to Sir Justus Beck to purchase in his own name £1000 Bank stock, which he accordingly did. And, the same day, bills were drawn for the money. And it was immediately paid, and it was entered in Sir Justus's books that the petitioner was a creditor for £1000 Bank stock. Afterwards, Sir Justus became bankrupt, the stock remaining in his name. The question was whether it was liable to his debts.

Talbot objected that Sir Justus had absolute power over it, and it was the same as money, and, on the credit of this, he was trusted.

Lord Chancellor [Lord Parker] was of opinion that Sir Justus was only a trustee and this was no part of his estate, that, he being a great remitter, nobody could think that all the stock in his name was his own. He said it would ruin all the commerce if what was transacted only by commission should be liable to the debts of the trustee.

2 Eq. Cas. Abr. 114, 22 E.R. 97

Trinity [term] 1721.

A trader in London, having money of J.S., who resided in Holland, in his hands, bought South Sea [Company] Stock as factor for J.S. and took the stock in his own name, but he entered it in his account book as bought for J.S., after which the trader became bankrupt. It was determined that the trust stock was not liable to the bankruptcy by Lord Parker, who said it would lessen the credit of the nation to make such a construction.

[1] *Thomas v. Kemeys* (1696), 2 Vernon 348, 23 E.R. 821, 2 Freeman 207, 22 E.R. 1163, Colles 112, 1 E.R. 206, 1 Eq. Cas. Abr. 269, 21 E.R. 1037.

520

Mudge v. Mudge

(Ch. 1721)

In this case, the conveyance in issue did not create a covenant to stand seised in the heir.

Lincoln's Inn MS. Misc. 506, p. 60, pl. 1

15 July 1721.

A man conveys lands to his wife for her use for life and, after her death, to her son and the heirs of his body and, if he die without heirs of his body, then to another and then follows a covenant for him and his heirs with her and her son William for further assurances. The defendant is heir at law to the covenantor and son to William. The question was whether this should work as a covenant to stand seised. It was made a case and sent to the judges of the Common Bench, who gave their opinion that it was a good covenant in the creation, but void by descending to the heir.[1]

Upon a bill brought for an account of the rents and profits against the defendant, the Lord Chancellor [Lord Parker] dismissed the bill, saying, if he did not make good the conveyance, he would not decree against it unless it were on behalf of a purchaser for a valuable consideration without notice.

In this case was cited the case of Gozaker and Robinson,[2] where the father had made a defective conveyance to a natural son and a covenant for further assurances. A bill was brought for further assurances against the heir, and the Master of the Rolls, Trevor, dismissed the bill because it was a voluntary conveyance. And that dismission was affirmed by Lord Cowper.

521

Beech v. Crull

(Ch. 1721–1722)

The question in this case was whether one can make a binding contract for the future delivery of an object not presently owned.

Upon the argument of a demurrer, all of the alleged facts of the bill of complaint are taken as true and cannot be disputed.

Lincoln's Inn MS. Misc. 384, p. 243, pl. 2

22 July 1721.

---

[1] *Mudge v. Mudge* (1719), 1 Comyns 332, 92 E.R. 1098.

[2] *Fursaker v. Robinson* (1717), Precedents in Chancery 475, 24 E.R. 213, Gilbert Rep. 139, 25 E.R. 97, 1 Eq. Cas. Abr. 123, 21 E.R. 929.

A bill [was exhibited] to compel the defendant to repay £1500, which the plaintiff had paid the defendant for the third subscription in the South Sea Company. The defendant demurs that the plaintiff's remedy was at law, the plaintiff, in the bill, charging that the defendant had given him a bond to deliver to the plaintiff the subscription as soon as the receipts should be delivered out for the same. The plaintiff charges that he can have no remedy at law because no receipts are given out and that the defendant voted at a general court against deliver[ing] out receipts, so he has been instrumental in hindering the plaintiff from a recovery at law and that the contract between the defendant and the Company being void, consequently, the private contracts are void and that the defendant at the time of this contract really had no subscription.

Solicitor General [*Yorke*], for the defendant: It has been adjudged that, although a person has not the stock at the time of the contract, yet, if he has it at the time of the delivery, it is sufficient. The receipts are not yet given out, yet they may hereafter [. . .][1] equity. The meaning of the contract is only that the buyer should stand in the place of the seller.

Talbot, for the defendant: All the circumstances are as much before the court on a demurrer as at the hearing, the bill being taken for true. The having no remedy at law is not a sufficient ground for equity to help.

Master of the Rolls [Jekyll]: This is a question of great consequence. Upon a demurrer, the court is to judge whether there is any probability of the plaintiff's being relieved. It is not necessary to determine that the court will certainly relieve at the hearing. It is sufficient if there be a probability. On a demurrer, all allegations of the bill are admitted and are not to be considered.

My opinion of these contracts is as bad as possible. The plaintiff comes here to avoid this contract. Though these contracts are of bad consequence, yet, if they have the sanction of law, this court will not take it away because there must be but two rules of property.

First, I think the defendant's voting in the general court will not make this contract void.

Second, the bill charges that the defendant had not at the time of the contract subscribed £500 nor was possessed of it, whereas the bond implies that he had so done. A right was transferred to the plaintiff at the time of the contract. It is not like the sale of stock itself to be transferred at a future day. If a man affirms he has subscribed £500 and sells what he affirms he has so subscribed, this is a *suggestio falsi*, and the buyer depended on that affirmation and is thereby deceived. Nobody can say that equity will not release, for he never had it in his power to perform his contract as he would if he had been possessed of such subscription.

[1] wt *MS.*

This case is not fit to be stifled by a demurrer, but it is proper to come before the court in judgment.

Precedents in Chancery 588, 24 E.R. 264

29 April [1722].

The plaintiff bought £500 third subscription of the defendant at 205 percent premium, for which he paid in ready money £1525, and the defendant, at the same time, gave the plaintiff a bond to deliver him £400 in the said third subscription when the receipts should be delivered out of the same by the company.

And no receipts being delivered out, this bill was brought to have the money refunded, the plaintiff by his bill offering to deliver up the bond. The defendant demurred to the plaintiff's bill for want of equity, and, by way of answer, offered to transfer to him the stock given by the company for the £500 paid in upon the subscription.

And the demurrer was allowed.

My Lord Chancellor [Lord Parker] said the plaintiff's equity was that he was now to pay but 209 percent for this subscription, and he complains that he had not the receipt delivered out, which would have obliged him to pay £1000 percent, and he said there was no color in the world to demand back this money, but he must take back the stock given by the company in lieu of it, as he agreed to stand in the seller's place, and would have been glad to do so if it had proved an advantageous bargain; so must he too now that it comes out to be otherwise. But he said that the plaintiff might proceed at law if he thought fit upon his bond and make the best of it there.

522

Gardiner v. Walters

(Ch. 1721–1722)

Where a husband comes into a court of equity in order to get his wife's portion, the court will require the husband to make a suitable settlement on his wife.

An executor of a decedent's estate is a trustee for the payment of the debts and legacies.

Courts of equity have a concurrent jurisdiction with the ecclesiastical courts to see that trusts are duly executed.

Lincoln's Inn MS. Misc. 11, p. 212

29 July 1721. William Gardner, executor of William Gardner, his father, plaintiff; Walker and Jane, his wife, daughter of William Gardner, the testator, defendants.

The defendant Walker having married the defendant Jane, his wife, who was entitled to a portion of £1500 by the will of her father, they libeled in the spiritual court against the plaintiff to be paid this legacy. And, thereupon, the plaintiff exhibited his bill in this court to stay the proceedings in the spiritual court and to pray the directions of this court touching the payment of the portion in regard the defendant had made no settlement upon his wife.

At the hearing of the cause, it was insisted on for the defendants that this court had never interposed where the husband had a remedy to come at his wife's portion without the assistance of this court. Indeed, where the husband and wife are plaintiffs and come here for the aid of the court to get at the wife's portion, the court will see that the husband makes a suitable settlement on the wife, and, if he cannot do that out of his own estate, they will settle the fortune. But, otherwise it is where they are brought in here and do not stand in need of the assistance of the court.

Lord Chancellor [LORD PARKER]: The executor is a trustee for the payment of the debts and legacies, and this court has a concurrent jurisdiction with the spiritual court to see that trust duly executed.

Can it be reasonable for this court to interpose when the husband is a plaintiff and comes here to be paid a legacy given to his wife and yet not to do it when the executor, who is but in the nature of a trustee, is the plaintiff and comes here for the direction of this court? If it were so, no suit would be brought here for a legacy given to a woman who had married improvidently.

Let the husband go before the Master and make proposals, and I reserve the consideration touching the payment of the £1500 portion until after the Master has made his report.

1 Strange 503, 93 E.R. 662

An executor brought his bill for the direction of the court touching the payment of a considerable legacy left by his testator to the defendant's wife, who was his daughter. And he insisted to have the same put out for the benefit of the wife and her issue and, likewise, for an injunction against the defendant's proceeding in the spiritual court in a suit there instituted for the legacy.

On the hearing, the defendant insisted that he, having commenced his suit in a proper court, ought not to be enjoined, or, if he ought, yet there could be no reason to direct the money to be put out as insisted on by the bill, it having been never done but in cases where the husband has brought the bill to compel the executor to pay the money. And no precedent was produced where such directions had been given upon a bill brought by the trustee.

And by MACCLESFIELD, Lord Chancellor: Then, it is time to make one. Can the difference who is plaintiff in equity alter the reason of the thing? If it should, it will but be for the husband, instead of coming here, to go into the spiritual court, as to be sure he will, and so get the whole into his power. There must be the usual direction, that the money may be disposed of for the benefit of the wife.

[Other reports of this case: 11 Modern 361, 88 E.R. 1089.]

523

Deane v. Norcliff

(Ch. 1721)

The whole interest on a debt is fully payable even where it exceeds the penalty for non-payment of the principal.

Lincoln's Inn MS. Misc. 11, p. 199, pl. 2

1 August 1721.

The plaintiffs are creditors by bond of John Harris, and they bring their bill to have satisfaction of their debts out of an estate which he had settled on trustees for the payment of his debts and the raising of portions for his younger children.

The interest due on the plaintiff Deane's bond has exceeded the penalty, and the cause having been heard and the estate decreed to be sold and the plaintiffs to be paid what the Master should find due for principal and interest, the plaintiff Deane petitioned that the Master might compute the whole interest due for the principal sum notwithstanding it exceeded the penalty, which was ordered accordingly, it being a debt to be paid out of a trust estate.

524

Attorney General v. Grantham

(Ch. 1721)

Where a person is accused of contempt of court for not preforming a decree, he can object to any irregularity of the procedure of the accusation without performing the decree.

Lincoln's Inn MS. Misc. 11, p. 199, pl. 1

7 August 1721.

In this case, it was laid down as a rule by Lord Chancellor [Lord Parker], if a man is brought into contempt for the not performing of a decree, he may be admitted to move to refer the irregularity of bringing him into contempt to a Master though he has not performed the decree, but, where there are two things decreed to be done at different times and he is in contempt for not performing the decree in both instances and, as to one of them, he is brought into contempt regularly, but not so as to the other, he shall not be admitted to move to refer the irregularity of the proceedings in the latter case nor be heard as to any other matter whatsoever until he has performed that part of the decree touching which he has been regularly brought into contempt.

525
Periam v. Monson
(Ch. 1721)

A contingent interest in a trust of money is devisable.

Lincoln's Inn MS. Misc. 11, p. 204

8 August 1721.

Israel Mayo, by his will, gives £3000 to trustees upon trust for his son George during his life and, after his death, in trust for such wife and children as he should have in such manner as therein is mentioned, and, in case he should have no children at his death or, there being such, all of them should die under twenty-one, then he gives this £3000 to all his daughters equally. One of the daughters of the testator died in the lifetime of George, her brother, and, by her will, she gives her contingent share of this £3000 to A.B., and, after her death, George, her brother, died without issue.

The question was if this contingent interest was devisable.

Lord Chancellor [Lord Parker] without any difficulty held the devise good. And he said it was exactly the Case of Pinbury and Elkin, *quod vide ante* 120.[1]

Lincoln's Inn MS. Misc. 12, p. 52, pl. 1

8 August 1721.

Israel Mayo, by will, gives £3000 to trustees upon trust for his son George to receive the interest during his life and, after his death, in trust for such wife and children as he should have in such manner as therein is mentioned and, in case he should have no children living at his death or, there being such, they should all die under the age of twenty-one years, then he gives the £3000 to all his, the testator's, daughters equally. One of the testator's daughters died in the lifetime of George, the son. And, by her will, she devised her contingent share to the plaintiff.

The question was if the daughter had such an interest as she could devise in this money.

Lord Chancellor [Lord Parker], without any difficulty, was of the opinion she could, and he said this was exactly the Case of Pinbury and Elkin, *quod vide Liber* C, fo. [*blank*].

---

1 *Pinbury v. Elkin* (Ch. 1719), see above, Case No. 404.

526

Wallis v. Wallis

(Ch. 1721)

Where a testator gives legacies to his wife and children under a condition that they not dispute his will or disturb the administration of his estate, they may nevertheless claim their statutory shares of any undisposed of surplus.

Lincoln's Inn MS. Misc. 12, p. 52, pl. 2

8 August 1721,

Peter Wallis, the plaintiff's grandfather, having, before his marriage, settled an annuity on the defendant, his wife, for life, makes his will. And, thereby, he gives his wife another annuity of £60 a year for her life, and he also devises to her some lands for her life and the use of his household goods and plate for her life. And he subjects the lands to the payment of an annuity of £45 a year to the defendant Judith, his daughter, for her life. And he declares that what he gave his wife was upon condition that, if she claimed dower in any part of his real estate or any share of his real or personal estate, either at common law or by the custom of London or otherwise howsoever other than what she might claim by his will, then what was given her to be void. Then, he directs his trustees to put out £400 upon securities and to pay the interest to the plaintiff Sarah, his daughter-in-law, for life and then to pay the £400 to the other plaintiffs, her children, equally. He confirms an annuity of £45 a year formerly settled on the plaintiff Sarah for life, and he gives the lands charged with that annuity to the defendant Simon, his son, for life. And he declares that, if his daughter Judith or son Simon claimed any greater or other share of his estate, either real or personal, other than what was devised to them by his will, either by the custom of London or otherwise howsoever, then the devises to them should be void. He gives some lands to the plaintiff Peter and his heirs. He releases to his son Simon all debts he owed him upon the express condition that he should release to his executrix within six months after his death all claims or demands which he should or ought to have in or to any part of his, the testator's, personal estate by the custom of London or otherwise except what he might claim by the will. He discharges the defendant Judith from all expenses he had been put to in her maintenance upon the condition she should not sue or molest his executrix for any arrears of her annuity, which was never designed her, but at his discretion, until after his death. And he declares his meaning to be in this and such like clauses in his will to induce his family to be content with such share and proportion of his estate as he had thereby allotted them and that they should enjoy the same in peace and quietness without strife and contention as it was his earnest desire they should. Then, he gives his wife two cows, two horses, and some implements of husbandry and

£20 for mourning [clothes] and some other legacies to some other persons. And he makes his wife executrix.

But he makes no disposition of the surplus. And the question was to whom it did belong, whether to the plaintiffs' grandchildren in regard the testator's wife and children are excluded by the will of any further part of his estate except what he had thereby given them or whether the wife and children, though excluded by the will, might not yet claim the surplus, that is to say whether it does not belong to her as executrix or to her and the children by the Statute of Distributions.[1]

Those who argued for the grandchildren said that the widow and children being expressly excluded by the will of any share of the testator's estate except what was thereby given them, they could not claim the surplus by the Statute, for that was inconsistent with the will and contrary to the plain intent and meaning of the testator. And they insisted much on the words 'or otherwise' in the condition annexed to the bequests to the wife.

And they cited the case of Perira and Perira, in Lord Cowper's time, which was thus. A woman, by articles before her marriage, agrees to accept of what was thereby agreed to be settled upon her in full satisfaction of what she might claim by the custom of London or otherwise. Note, by the articles, she was to have £1500 paid her if she survived her husband. The husband died intestate. And the plaintiff brought her bill against the defendant, who had taken administration, to have her £1500 paid her and her distributive share of the personal estate by the Statute. As to the plaintiff's demands of her distributive share, the defendant pleaded the articles in bar. And, upon arguing the plea before Lord Cowper, the plea was allowed.

Mr. *Mead*, likewise, cited the Case of Vachel and Vachel, *quod vide Liber* C, fo. [blank],[2] which was thus. A man gives his son 1s. by his will and declares he should have no other advantage out of his estate but what he had given him by the will. And he having made no disposition of the surplus of his personal estate, the son brought his bill for his distributive share thereof. And it was decreed to him by the late Master of the Rolls. But, upon an appeal to the House of Lords, that decree was reversed.

But, as to this case, Lord Chancellor [Lord Parker] said it was plain the father there intended to disinherit his son.

On the other side, it was argued on the behalf of the wife and children, and, as to the wife, it was said she ought to have the surplus as executrix and, if she claims it as executrix, she does not claim inconsistently with the will or any dispositions thereby made.

---

[1] Stat. 22 & 23 Car. II, c. 10 (*SR*, V, 719–720).

[2] *Vachel v. Vachel* (1669), 1 Chancery Cases 129, 22 E.R. 727, 1 Eq. Cas. Abr. 361, 21 E.R. 1103.

And, as to the words 'or otherwise', the testator must be understood to mean that she should not disturb his will by any claim of dower or by the custom of London or in any other way whatsoever.

As to the Case of Perira and Perira, that was upon marriage articles, and, therefore, it differs very much from the present case, which arises upon a will. When a man is entering into marriage articles, he may have it in his view that he may die intestate. But can that be said when a man is making his will? Can it be supposed, when a man is making his will and disposing of his estate, that he has it in his view to die intestate *quoad* a particular part of it?

Lord Chancellor [LORD PARKER] said he thought the distinction was very right between a deed and a will. When a marriage agreement is made, it may be very proper to provide against everything that may happen and to say that this is all the wife shall have out of the husband's estate. But, when a man is making his will, he cannot be supposed to be making a provision for excluding his wife and children from the surplus of his personal estate when, if that was his intention, he might very easily exclude them from the surplus by giving it away from them.

The testator, by his will could not intend to dispose of his whole estate but only that he has pretermitted the surplus. The testator has by his will given his wife the use of his goods for her life and directed that she should not waste them so that it is plain she cannot have the surplus as executrix.

He decreed the surplus to be distributed according to the Statute.

527

Hales v. Andrews

(Ch. 1721)

A devise made in a foreign country of an annuity to be paid in sterling where the devisee lives in England is to be paid in English money in the foreign country and the cost of sending the money to the devisee in England is to be paid by the administrator of the decedent's estate.

Lincoln's Inn MS. Misc. 12, p. 167

21 August 1721.

A.B., having an estate both in England and Barbados, makes his will in Barbados, and he gives an annuity of £50 a year sterling to one who was living in England.

And the question was if this annuity should be paid at Barbados or in England and whether in Barbados money or English money.

It was decreed the annuity was to be paid at Barbados in sterling money and the plaintiff was to allow for the charges of returning it to England.

528

Tipping v. Tipping

(Ch. 1721)

Where a widow learns her husband's trade secret after his death, she must give it to his executors as part of his estate.

11 Viner, Abr. 244

Michaelmas 8 Geo. [1721].

On a question in Chancery, whether the widow was to account to executors for the receipt of Tipping's Water, Lord Parker declared that, if the secret was imparted to her by her husband, then it became a matter of her own knowledge, part of her understanding, which could not be taken from her. But, if she learned the art by finding the receipt after her husband's death or had the knowledge communicated to her by any servant etc., then the executors were to have the benefit of this receipt.

[Other copies of this report: 2 Eq. Cas. Abr. 467, 22 E.R. 398.]

[Connected cases: Tipping v. Tipping (1720), see above, Case No. 469.]

529

Trott v. Dawson

(Ch. 1721)

A trustee is entitled to be reimbursed his expenses in administering the trust.

Lincoln's Inn MS. Misc. 12, p. 31

7 November 1721.

Philip Ludwell[1] and Lady Frances Berkeley,[2] his wife, in 1684, conveyed an eighth proprietorship in Carolina to Thomas Amy and his heirs. Amy was a trustee in this conveyance for four other persons, and, for several years, he had acted as a proprietor and was at some trouble and expense in that matter.

The plaintiff's wife was one of the co-heirs of Amy and claimed as such a moiety of the proprietorship in their own right. And they brought their bill for an account of the profits against the defendants, who had purchased under the *ces-*

[1] P. H. Wood, 'Ludwell, Philip (b. c. 1637, d. after 1710)', *Oxford Dictionary of National Biography*, vol. 34, pp. 723–724.

[2] T. L. Snyder, 'Berkeley, Frances Culpeper Stephens (bap. 27 May 1643 – ca. 1695)', *Dictionary of Virginia Biography*, vol. 2, pp. 450–451.

tuis que trust, and against the other co-heir of Amy. And the defendants brought their bill against the co-heirs of Amy to have the legal estate conveyed to them.

The trust was fully proved; so the only question was whether the legal estate should be taken from the heirs at law without making them satisfaction for the trouble and expense which Amy had been put to in acting in the trust as a proprietor.

And, notwithstanding it appeared that he had never acted after the *cestuis que trust* had conveyed, yet the court decreed that the plaintiffs in the original cause should be allowed not only what Amy had expended in acting in the trust but likewise for his trouble therein, for the defendants could not be in a better condition than the *cestuis que trust*, under whom he claimed. And, if they had brought their bill, they must have made that allowance.

This decree was reversed upon an appeal to the Lords, 1729; see the case.[1]

1 Peere Williams 780, 24 E.R. 612

The plaintiff was a trustee for one Archdale, as to an eighth of the proprietorship of the province of Carolina, and he was put to great trouble and charge in relation to the affairs of the province. This business, charge, and trouble was all undergone during such time as Archdale was the *cestui que trust*. And, afterwards, Archdale assigned his interest to the defendant, who, being sued by the plaintiff Trott for the money expended by him in relation to the premises, brought his cross-bill against the plaintiff, the trustee, in order to compel him to convey over the trust estate to the defendant, who, as was insisted, ought not to allow for any of this charge and trouble, which was all upon the credit of Archdale.

Lord Chancellor [Lord Parker]: Dawson, the assignee of Archdale, cannot be in a better case than Archdale, under whom he claims, wherefore, as Archdale would not have had the assistance of a court of equity without paying for the charge and trouble which Trott had been at in relation to this trust, so, by a parity of reason, the defendant Dawson, as claiming under Archdale, must do the same thing, which it was incumbent upon Archdale to have done.

[Other reports of this case: 2 Eq. Cas. Abr. 740, 22 E.R. 628, 7 Brown P.C. 266, 3 E.R. 173.]

1 *Danson v. Trott* (1729), 7 Brown P.C. 266, 3 E.R. 173.

530
Anonymous
(Ch. c. 1721)

Tradesmen who fit out a ship for a voyage do not have a lien on the ship or on the freight.

Lincoln's Inn MS. Misc. 12, p. 32

It was decreed that the tradesmen who had fitted out a ship for a voyage had no lien, either on the ship or the freight, and that neither the ship nor the freight was liable to make good the debts which the captain had contracted for the fitting out of the ship.

531
Leyliard v. Humphreys
(Ch. c. 1721)

Where a landowner contracts to sell land and, before the conveyance is made, he or she contracts to sell the same land to another person, the second contract is unenforceable on account of the fraud.

Lincoln's Inn MS. Misc. 12, p. 33

Lady Leyliard v. Sir William Humphreys and *e contra*.

The defendant, 20 August 1720, enters into articles with the plaintiff to purchase an estate of her at thirty-five years purchase, and he pays her £1000 in part, and no time was limited for conveying the estate to the defendant.

Before this, she had articled with Mr. Jacob to sell him the estate. And, after the articles with the defendant, *viz.* on the third of November, she gives Mr. Jacob £100, and, in consideration thereof, he delivers up his articles. But, before those articles were delivered up, she writes a letter to the defendant telling him that she was willing and able to make him a good title and was ready to convey to him free from encumbrances.

The plaintiff's bill was for a specific performance of the articles, and the cross-bill was to have the articles delivered up and the £1000 repaid.

And it was insisted on by Sir William Humphreys that it was a fraud and imposition on him by the plaintiff to take upon her to sell the estate when she had before articled to sell it to another and the writing the letter to him before Jacob had delivered up his articles was a continuation of the fraud, and, besides, Sir William bought this estate with a design to sell his South Sea stock and pay for it and, the plaintiff's not being able to make good her contract had prevented him disposing of his stock to a good advantage.

It was decreed the £1000 to be paid back with interest and the articles to be delivered up and chiefly for this reason, because the plaintiff had been guilty of a fraud in articling with the defendant to sell him the estate when she had before entered into articles to sell it to another and keeping both articles for some time on foot.

532

Deg v. Deg

(Ch. c. 1721)

Where there is a devise of land to trustees, the money arising by the sale of such lands is equitable assets.

Lincoln's Inn MS. Misc. 12, p. 34

Mr. Deg, by will, devised lands to trustees and their heirs upon trust and to the intent to sell the same for payment of his debts and, afterwards, to pay several legacies, and he makes the trustees executors.

The question was if the money arising by the sale of these lands are equitable or legal assets, the trustees being made executors.

Mr. *Williams*: This being a devise to executors, it shall be legal assets. It is true, if it had been a devise to trustees only, it would have been equitable assets and, being such, this court will distribute them equally among all the creditors. And he cited 1 Leo. 224 and [. . .] 920.[1]

The Master of the Rolls [JEKYLL]: I agree that, if the testator had directed his executors to sell to pay debts, the money arising by sale would undoubtedly have been legal assets in their hands. Nay, if it had been a devise to the executors to sell, it would have been a devise in fee, and the money would have been legal assets.

But the devise in the present case is to trustees and their heirs upon trust etc., which makes nothing but a trust. And, therefore, the money arising by the sale of these lands must be equitable assets.

[Later proceedings in this case: 2 Peere Williams 412, 24 E.R. 791, 2 Eq. Cas. Abr. 500, 674, 22 E.R. 424, 566.]

1 *Alexander v. Gresham* (1590), 1 Leonard 224, 74 E.R. 205; *Anonymous* (1619), 1 Rolle, Abr., *Executors*, pl. G, 6, p. 920.

533

Pickering v. Sherrard

(Ch. 1721)

The creditors of a decedent's estate cannot reach the widow's paraphernalia unless the personal estate is insufficient to pay them.

As between a doweress and the heir at law or devisees of the decedent's real estate, a court of equity will order encumbrances on the dower land to be paid off by the estate.

Lincoln's Inn MS. Misc. 11, p. 207

13 November 1721.

Sherrard Pickering, the plaintiff's husband, gave a bond to leave his wife £700, and, by will, he gives his personal estate to the defendants, his executors, upon trust to pay his debts, and, if any surplus, he gives it to his wife. But, if the personal estate was not sufficient, he directs his executors, to whom he devised his real estate, to sell and mortgage a sufficient part thereof to make good the deficiency of his personal estate.

The plaintiff brings her bill to have her £700 paid her and to have her dower out of the real estate, and she insists upon her paraphernalia.

The personal estate was not sufficient to pay all the debts, and, therefore, it was insisted by the executors that the paraphernalia ought to go towards the payment of the debts, for this differed from the case where the dispute lies only between the widow and the heir, for, here, the testator has by his will subjected his real estate to the payment of his debts whereby he is become in the nature of a purchaser of his wife's paraphernalia.

Lord Chancellor [Lord Parker] decreed the plaintiff her paraphernalia unless, upon the account, it should appear that the personal estate was not sufficient to pay such of the testator's debts as did not affect his real estate and, if so, then the paraphernalia was to be applied towards the satisfaction of such debts.

As to the plaintiff's dower, there being a mortgage for years on the real estate, it was insisted on by the defendants that the plaintiff was not entitled to her dower and that the court ought not to assist her in removing that term out of the way.

But, as to that, it was decreed that the plaintiff should have her dower notwithstanding the term and that the Master should set out the dower and that the plaintiff should have an allowance for it from the death of her husband, for, as between the doweress and the heir at law or devisee of the real estate, this court has always removed terms of years out of the way.

As to the Case of Radnor v. Vandebenbe,[1] which has been cited, Lord Chancellor [Lord Parker] said there was a purchaser in that case and an assignment of an old term to protect the purchase, which being a common method that had prevailed in Westminster Hall, the House of Lords, for that reason, would not assist the doweress against a purchaser.

534

Babington v. Babington

(Ch. 1721)

Where a surrender of a copyhold estate is made to the use of a will, it is not necessary that the will be executed according to the requirements of the Statute of Frauds.

Lincoln's Inn MS. Misc. 11, p. 211, pl. 1

Michaelmas term 1721.

It was decreed by the Master of the Rolls [Jekyll] after he had taken time to consider of it that, where a surrender of a copyhold estate was made to the use of a will, it was not necessary the will should be executed according to the Statute of Frauds etc.[2]

535

Downam v. Mathews

(Ch. 1722)

Tradesmen, in the usual course of their dealings, can set one debt off against another debt of the same nature.

Lincoln's Inn MS. Misc. 384, p. 256

25 January 1721[/22].

N. Biss, deceased, being a dyer, the plaintiffs dealt with him in the way of his trade by sending woolen cloths etc. for which Biss used to pay by dying other cloths, and there were mutual accounts between them. Biss, at his death, was indebted to the plaintiffs for cloths sold etc., and the plaintiffs were indebted to

---

[1] *Countess of Radnor v. Vandebendy* (1683–1697), Shower P.C. 69, 1 E.R. 48, *sub nom. Lady Bodmin v. Vandenbendy*, 1 Vernon 179, 356, 23 E.R. 399, 520, 2 Chancery Cases 172, 22 E.R. 899, *sub nom. Lady Radnor v. Rotheram*, 2 Freeman 211, 22 E.R. 1165, Precedents in Chancery 65, 24 E.R. 32, 1 Eq. Cas. Abr. 219, 21 E.R. 1002, 2 Eq. Cas. Abr. 383, 22 E.R. 326.

[2] Stat. 29 Car. II, c. 3 (*SR*, V, 839–842).

him for dying. The question is whether the plaintiffs can set off a debt against a debt as against the defendants who are creditors of Biss of a superior nature.

It was proved that this was their usual manner of dealing, and the plaintiffs offer to pay what was due from them upon the balance.

Solicitor General [*Yorke*], for the defendant, insisted that this would alter the law that the plaintiffs, who are creditors of an inferior nature, should retain a satisfaction for their whole debts and the defendants, who are creditors of a superior nature, must abate, that stoppage is no payment, that, before the Statute of Bankruptcy,[1] if there were mutual accounts, they could not be set off, and that Statute was introductive of a new law.

Lord Chancellor [Lord Macclesfield]: Though stoppage is no payment, yet it is reasonable in this case to set a debt against a debt, being between tradesmen and the usual way of dealing and the reason why they dealt with each other; even at [common] law it would be so. It is not like debts of a different nature, as rents or specialties.

He decreed the plaintiffs only to pay the balance.

Lincoln's Inn MS. Misc. 12, p. 28

25 January 1721[/22].

The plaintiff, being a clothier, sells clothes to the defendant's intestate, who was a dyer. And he, on the other hand, dyes cloth for the plaintiff, and he dies. The defendant takes administration, and he insists that the plaintiff ought to pay what he owed the intestate for dying and come in as a creditor and be paid as in a course of administration for what the intestate owed him for cloth.

It was proved that the plaintiff and the intestate, in the course of their dealings, upon settling accounts, had set off one debt against another.

Lord Chancellor [Lord Macclesfield]: I believe it is always understood among traders, when they deal together, that their dealings shall be set one against the other. And it seems to be highly reasonable it should be so; otherwise, the late Act of Parliament empowering commissioners of bankrupts etc. must be supposed to have enacted what is unreasonable in itself.

Indeed, where the debts are of a different nature, as where there is a bond on one side and a debt on a simple contract on the other, it may be of another cons[equence] and yet, even in that case, if there was the least proof of any agreement of the parties to set one against the other, this court would so decree it.

He decreed an account to be taken and that the plaintiff should pay only what upon the account he should be found to owe to the intestate more than what the intestate owed him.

[Other reports of this case: Precedents in Chancery 580, 24 E.R. 260, 2 Eq. Cas. Abr. 9, 22 E.R. 8.]

---

[1] Stat. 5 Geo. I, c. 24.

536

Sandys v. Sandys

(Ch. 1722)

In this case, according to the settlement in issue, a daughter's marriage portion was ordered to be paid though her father was still living.

Lincoln's Inn MS. Misc. 12, p. 35

26 January 1721[/22]. Sandys and his wife v. Sir Richard Sandys.

By a settlement made by the defendant on his marriage, lands were settled to the use of the defendant for his life with a provision for supporting contingent remainders, then to his intended wife for her life, remainder to the first and other sons in tail male, then to trustees for 500 years, remainder to the defendant and his heirs. The trusts of the term were that, in case there was no issue male and there should be one or more daughters, then the trustees by sale or mortgage of the term and by the rents and profits of the lands comprised therein, over and above what should be expended in the maintenance of such daughters, should raise portions for the said daughters, *viz.*, if but one, £5000 and, if two or more, then £6000, to be paid at twenty-one or marriage. Then there is a direction that, until the portions became payable, the trustees should out of the rents raise maintenances for the daughters at the rate of four percent.

There was a clause that, if the defendant gave any of his daughters in his lifetime portions equal to what they should be entitled to by the settlement, then the portions of such daughters were not to be raised. There was likewise a power reserved by the settlement for the defendant to limit a jointure to a second wife.

The defendant's wife died and left no son but four daughters. And the plaintiff having married one of them, he and his wife brought their bill against Sir Richard Sands and her father and the trustees to have her portion raised and paid by sale or mortgage of the reversionary term.

Upon hearing this cause, it was sent to the Master to state the value of the estate. And it now came on upon the Master's report, which had certified the estate to be £587 a year.

Lord Chancellor [Lord Macclesfield]: If there had been a son and daughters, neither the one nor the other would have anything during the father's lifetime. Now what reason is there that, when there are only daughters, they should be in a better condition than an eldest or only son?

I am tied up by former resolutions, yet, if this case differs from these resolutions, I shall think myself at liberty to vary my determination. I think the raising of portions for daughters in the lifetime of their father is an encouragement to them to marry without their father's consent.

It is admitted the maintenance cannot be raised during the life of the father, it being to be raised by the rents and profits. One would think there was as much reason to raise maintenances as portions, as much reason the daughters should have bread as be married.

However, at length, the Lord Chancellor [Lord Macclesfield] said he did not see that this case differed from the former cases, and he was not willing to change the course of the court. That was more proper to be done in another place.

And, therefore, he decreed that a fourth part of the estate be sold for raising the plaintiff's wife's portion. As to interest, he thought there ought to be none raised, the estate being a reversion only, which yielded no profits.

[Other reports of this case: 1 Peere Williams 707, 24 E.R. 580, 2 Eq. Cas. Abr. 643, 22 E.R. 539.]

537

Hanger v. Eyles

(Ch. 1722)

A court of equity will not specifically enforce a contract where the plaintiff cannot fully perform the bargain.

Lincoln's Inn MS. Misc. 11, p. 211, pl. 2

January 1721[/22].

The plaintiff [Sir George Hanger] brought his bill to compel the defendant to perform [articles] by him entered into for the purchase of the plaintiff's estate at Farmingham in Kent of about £350, for which the defendant had agreed to pay £15,500, bring about forty years purchase.

The defendant among other things insisted that the manor as well as the lands in Farmingham were agreed to be conveyed to him and that, upon looking into the title, it appeared that the plaintiff had no title to the manor.

Note, in the articles, the manor is not particularly mentioned, but there are general words, *viz.* all his manors, messuages, etc.

The plaintiff insisted that there was no value put upon the manor in the particular of the estate, that, upon discourse with the defendant, he told him he had a title to the manor, that he had a receipt for the consideration money, and that he maintained the pound and had lopped the trees and had been in possession about thirty years.

But the plaintiff having no other title to the manor and having said during the treaty that he had a title, for this cause only, the bill was dismissed, though it was proved there was no value put upon it in the purchase.

Lincoln's Inn MS. Misc. 384, p. 257, pl. 1

26 January 1721[/22].

The bill was for specific performance of articles at forty-six year's purchase. On 23 July 1720, by articles, the plaintiff covenants, before Michaelmas, to convey to the defendant the capital messuage and manor etc. at Farningham in Kent, in consideration whereof, the defendant covenants to pay £15,500.

N.B. The estate was £330 *per annum*. N.B. the particular mentions the manor whereas the plaintiff had none. The proof [was] that no value was put upon the manor, and no stress was laid upon it.

Lord Chancellor [Lord Macclesfield]: I will dismiss the bill.

21 Viner, Abr. 540

Hilary term 8 Geo. I.

A bill [was brought] for a specific performance of articles for the purchase of lands etc. in Kent. The case was the plaintiff agreed to sell the manor and lands in A. in Kent to the defendant by a particular, wherein the manor and royalties are mentioned, but no value [was] set upon them therein. It happened that the plaintiff had no title to the manor, but he had been in possession of the royalties several years.

The defendant objected against going on with the purchase that this was a contract at a South Sea price, *viz.* forty-six years purchase and, secondly, that, though no value was set upon the manor and royalties by the particular, yet they are valuable in themselves, and it was a great inducement to him to purchase the estate. And, therefore, since the plaintiff cannot strictly perform his part of the agreement by conveying the manor, he ought not to have the aid of a court of equity to compel the defendant to pay the money, since he cannot have the full benefit of the agreement.

And for this last reason, the bill was dismissed, but without costs if the plaintiff would deliver up the articles.

[Other copies of this report: 2 Eq. Cas. Abr. 20, 689, 22 E.R. 17, 579.]

538

Amphlet v. Soley

(Ch. 1722–1723)

In paying the debts of a decedent's estate, the freehold and copyhold estates subjected to the debts will be sold and the money arising by sale of the freehold be first applied where the copyhold was not surrendered to the use of the will and then the moneys arising by sale of the copyhold and then the personal estate specifically devised for that purpose and then the freehold lands devised to children.

Where an executor is also a trustee for all the creditors, it is a breach of trust in him to pay off debts of the estate for his own personal benefit at the expense of the other creditors.

Lincoln's Inn MS. Misc. 11, p. 229

12 February 1721[/22]. Master of the Rolls [Jekyll].

John Soley, by will, devised freehold and copyhold lands to be sold for the payment of his debts. He devised other freehold lands to some of his children and gave them also specific legacies out of his personal estate.

Upon a bill brought by the creditors for a satisfaction of their debts, it was decreed that an account should be taken of the personal estate and the rents and profits of the real estate and that the freehold and copyhold estates subjected to his debts be sold to pay the debts and the money arising by sale of the freehold be first applied, the copyhold having not been surrendered to the use of the will, and, in the case of a deficiency, then the moneys arising by sale of the copyhold to be applied to pay the debts and, if that should fall short, then the personal estate specifically devised to be applied for that purpose and, if there should still remain any deficiency, then the freehold lands devised to the children were decreed to be sold to pay the debts which should remain unpaid.

Lincoln's Inn MS. Misc. 12, p. 19

6 December 1723.

This cause, *quod vide Liber* C, 229, came on again upon the Master's report. And the question was whether John Soley should be allowed some mortgages paid out of the personal estate, which were an encumbrance upon an estate, which had been settled on him on his marriage and the father had covenanted in the settlement with the trustees to pay off these mortgages but had left one unpaid and had likewise covenanted the estate was free from encumbrances except the mortgages which were covenanted to be paid off. And there appeared to be other mortgages which are not mentioned in the settlement. And the defendant had paid off these mortgages out of the personal assets after this suit commenced. And it appeared by the Master's report that the real and personal assets were not sufficient to pay all the debts.

Master of the Rolls [Jekyll]: The defendant was a trustee as well as an executor. And, as he was a trustee for all the creditors, it was a breach of trust in him to pay these mortgages in ease of his own estate after a bill was brought. And he ought not to have an allowance for what he has so paid, but he can only come in as a creditor by virtue of the covenant in his marriage settlement made with the trustees.

If the defendant could be entitled to this allowance, which he insists on, it would come around again upon him, for the creditors in such case would be entitled to stand in his place and have a satisfaction out of the mortgaged estate for so much as the personal estate has been exchanged in payment of the mortgages.

The defendant had likewise paid some bonds since the suit was commenced, out of the personal estate. And the question was if he should have an allowance of these debts in regard there would not be sufficient [assets] to pay all the creditors.

And it was said that this differed from the payment of the mortgages, for these debts were not paid in ease of the executor, but were debts he was bound to pay and might have been sued for at law, and an executor had a right by law to prefer one creditor before another in equal degree. And, though it was after the bill was brought, yet that would not alter the case, for, before a final decree, an executor might pay another creditor according to the Case of Mason and Williams, in 2 Salk., and Lord Orford's Case, *quod vide, liber* C, 3.[1]

The Master of the Rolls [JEKYLL] said, in the Case of Lord Orford, there were some particular circumstances. And he thought the law in this court as to this point was not fully settled. And it not appearing by the Master's report when these debts were paid, whether before or after the answer was put in and whether, if after the answer was put in, before or after the decree, it was sent back to the Master to state the times when the debts were paid.

Note, upon reading the decree, it appeared there was a mistake in the directions there given, for there was no distinction made touching the payment of the debts out of the estate subjected by the will to the debts and that which was devised to the younger son.

As to the first, all the creditors as well those by simple contract as those due by specialties were to be paid ratably, share and share alike. But, as to the other estate, the creditors by specialties only are affected, that by virtue of the Statute of Fraudulent Devises,[2] and, therefore, the creditors by simple contract were not to come in ratably with the bond creditors and be paid out of that estate.

And of that opinion was the Master of the Rolls [JEKYLL].

539

Backwell v. Eaton

(Ch. 1722)

In this case, the legacy in issue lapsed and did not survive to the other legatees.

Lincoln's Inn MS. Misc. 11, p. 230, pl. 1

A.B. devised the residue of his real and personal estate to his four children equally to be divided between them, and he dies. One of the children dying in his lifetime, the question was whether his part should go to the three surviving children or be a lapsed legacy.

---

[1] *Mason v. Williams*, 2 Salkeld 507, 91 E.R. 433; *Earl of Orford v. Daston* (1702), Precedents in Chancery 188, 24 E.R. 91, Colles 229, 1 E.R. 262, 1 Eq. Cas. Abr. 10, 21 E.R. 834, 2 Eq. Cas. Abr. 460, 22 E.R. 391, Lincoln's Inn MS. Misc. 12, p. 180.

[2] Stat. 3 Will. & Mar., c. 14 (*SR*, VI, 320–321).

Lord Chancellor [LORD MACCLESFIELD], after taking time to consider of it, was of opinion it was lapsed and should not go to the surviving children. But he went pretty much upon some expressions in the will.

This was reported to me by Mr. Martin who was counsel in the cause.

540

O'Neil v. Mead

(Ch. 1722)

A specific legacy will not be abated in exoneration of the real estate in the hands of the heir.

Where real estate is devised as well as the personal estate, the legatee takes the real estate burdened with any mortgages.

Where there are debts by bond, which are a lien on the real estate, and both real and personal estate is devised, those debts shall be paid out of the specific legacies if the rest of the personal estate is not sufficient and not out of the real estate.

Lincoln's Inn MS. Misc. 11, p. 213

6 March 1721[/22].

Thomas Coppin, having mortgaged his real estate, devises it to trustees and their heirs for the benefit of his two sons charged with £500 for the plaintiff's wife, who was his daughter. He gives a leasehold estate and his plate and household goods to his wife. And he dies leaving debts by bond, which, by an instrument under his hand and seal, were charged upon the mortgage, and some debts by simple contract.

The plaintiffs brought their bill to be paid the £500 given the daughter against the executors, the widow, and the testator's son, the other son being dead. And the cause being heard and an account directed, it came back upon the Master's report for farther directions.

The question was between the son and his mother whether the debts on the mortgage and the bonds, which were charged on the real estate by the testator in his lifetime, should be paid out of the real estate or out of the specific parts of the personal estate given to the wife, there being but very little personal estate besides.

Master of the Rolls [JEKYLL]: It is a settled rule in this court that a specific legacy shall not be applied in exoneration of the real estate in the hands of the heir. And, in this case, the real estate is devised as well as the personal estate, and, therefore, the son must take the real estate *cum onere*. If, indeed, there were debts by bond, which are a lien on the real estate, as it is assets at [common] law and both real and personal estate is devised, those debts shall be paid out of the specific legacies if the rest of the personal estate is not sufficient and not out of the real estate.

[Other reports of this case: 1 Peere Williams 693, 24 E.R. 574, 2 Eq. Cas., Abr. 556, 22 E.R. 468.]

541

Decaster v. Halley

(Ch. 1722)

The question in this case was whether a contract for the sale of shares of stock is within the Statute of Frauds.

Lincoln's Inn MS. Misc. 11, p. 214

7 March 1721[/22].

A bill [was exhibited] for a specific performance of a contract for the sale of South Sea [Company] stock. The defendant pleaded the Statute of Frauds and Perjuries[1] and averred that no money was paid in part of the purchase.

In this case, it was said by *Sir John Chesshyre* that the like plea was pleaded in the [Court of] Common Pleas to an action on the case upon a contract for South Sea stock, and, the court being divided in opinion whether stock was within the words 'goods and merchandises' mentioned in the Statute, they ordered a case to be made in order to be considered by all the judges in Serjeants' Inn, which was done. And six of the judges were of opinion for the defendant and six for the plaintiff. And, thereupon, the Chief Justice of the Common Pleas [King] ordered that the action should be tried to the intent a special verdict might be found and a writ of error afterwards brought. But, upon the trial, the plaintiff proved he paid £100 in part of the purchase money, and, thereupon, he obtained a verdict; so the matter in law was never determined.

Lord Chancellor [Lord Macclesfield] was not willing to allow the plea, it going only as to one matter and the defendant has not by demurrer taken advantage of the great price of the stock, which was sold at £840 percent, and he insisted that this court ought not to decree a specific performance of a contract for South Sea stock at so great a price, and, therefore, with the defendant's consent, the benefit of the plea was saved to the hearing that he might then take advantage of that matter so that, in case of an appeal, he might insist both upon the Statute and the greatness of the price, which, if the plea was allowed, he could not do.

1 Stat. 29 Car. II, c. 3 (*SR*, V, 839–842).

542

Pauling v. Dennis

(Ch. 1722)

Where a plea of the Statute of Limitations is overruled because it was improperly pleaded, it cannot be re-argued at the hearing on the merits of the case.

Lincoln's Inn MS. Misc. 11, p. 215, pl. 1

Same day [7 March 1722].

The defendant pleaded the Statute of Limitations[1] but had not averred that he made no promise within six years, but only said 'not having made any promise' etc. And for this cause, the plea was overruled.

It was insisted on by Mr. *Mead* that the benefit of the plea might be saved until the hearing.

But the Master of the Rolls [JEKYLL] said the benefit of a plea of the Statute of Limitations was never saved. And upon asking Mr. *Goldsbrough*, he said it was done in the Case of Lawley and Lawley[2] lately, but he never knew it done before. Mr. *Mead* insisted it had been done several times.

The Master of the Rolls [JEKYLL] said, the plea being ill pleaded, there was no reason to save the benefit of it to the hearing, and, besides, it was a plea not much favored either at [common] law or in equity.

543

Ivy v. Gilbert

(Ch. 1722)

Where it is the intention of the settlor of a trust that the beneficiary is to receive money out of the income from land, the land cannot be sold to raise the money.

Lincoln's Inn MS. Misc. 12, p. 91

13 April 1722.

Roger Pomroy being seised in fee of lands in Devonshire does pursuant to articles before marriage by indenture 29 May 1651 settle the premises to the use of himself and his wife for their lives, remainder to their first and other sons in tail, remainder to four trustees for 120 years to raise daughter's portions, *viz.* in trust that the trustees out of the rents, issues, and profits of the premises as well by leasing and demising the premises for one, two, or three lives or any number of years determinable upon one, two, or three lives or for twenty-one years abso-

[1] Stat. 21 Jac. I, c. 16 (*SR*, IV, 1222–1223).

[2] See *Lawley v. Lawley* (Ch. 1719), see above, Case No. 353.

lute, reserving the ancient rents, raise daughters' portions, *viz.* £1500 if but one daughter, if more, £1500 among them equally, without mentioning any time of payment. And he limits the reversions to himself in fee.

Roger Pomroy has issue, only one daughter, Joan, married to the defendant's father, Humphry Gilbert.

On 29 and 30 March 1706, Roger Pomroy, who made this settlement, by indentures of lease and release, settled the reversion in fee expectant upon his own and his wife's death [without] issue male and on failure of issue male of his own body and subject to the 120 years to the use of trustees for ten years, remainder to his kinsman Hugh Pomroy for life, remainder to his first and other sons in tail male, remainder to the defendant John Gilbert, son of his daughter Joan, for life, remainder to his first and other sons etc. in tail etc. The trust of the ten years was that, in case his son-in-law Gilbert and his wife would release the £1500 portions secured by the 120 year's term, the trustees of the ten years should raise £1900, *viz.* £1500 of it to be laid out in a purchase of land for the benefit of his son-in-law and daughter Joan and the £400 residue of the £1900 to be paid to the son-in-law himself.

Roger Pomroy, who made this settlement, dies, having issue only his said daughter Joan. And the surviving trustee of the said 120 years dying, administration is granted to Joan. And Joan, the daughter, and her husband, Humphry Gilbert, by the direction of Hugh Pomroy, who had the immediate remainder for life, join in the assigning this term in mortgage to the plaintiff for £1500, which is paid to Humphry in satisfaction of the portion secured by the term of 120 years. And Hugh Pomroy covenants to pay the money.

Hugh Pomroy is dead without issue. And Humphry Gilbert, the son-in-law, and Joan, his wife, are dead, leaving issue, the defendant John Gilbert, who has issue, John Gilbert, another defendant.

And now, the plaintiff, the mortgagee, brings a bill against the several defendants to foreclose them and also against the executors of Hugh Pomroy to discover assets to satisfy Hugh Pomroy's covenant. And the question is whether, by the words of this trust, this portion could be raised by mortgage or any other way than by annual profits or leasing and whether there having been sufficient [money] raised by the profits to pay the portion, the land has borne its burden and [is] to be no longer charged with the portion or mortgage.

Objection: The plaintiff is an honest mortgagee and the term of 120 years is a subsisting term at law and the defendant's claim under a voluntary settlement and the power to raise the portions being by rents, issues, and profits, the word 'profits' when not said 'annual profits' has been frequently understood any profit that the land would yield, either by leasing, selling, or mortgage and the words 'as well by leasing and' are only additional and not restrictive. To say that all the profits during Hugh Pomroy's life, who was the remainderman for life, should be applied towards raising the portions would be a great and undesigned hardship upon Hugh Pomroy and might defeat the whole profit of his estate for life, which would be to starve the tenant for life and to starve him who was of the name and blood of him that made the settlement and to starve him for the benefit of a remoter remainderman, which is not to take effect until after his the said Hugh's death without issue male.

This is a construction against all the rules of equity as well as against the intention of the party himself.

If I devise lands, part for the payment of debts and, afterwards, to A. for life, remainder to B. in fee, yet, though A's estate is only after debts paid, yet A. shall not bear the whole burden of the debts, for that would entirely defeat the devise as to him, which is to destroy part of the will. But, especially, it would be harder in the case considering the chief regard in the case, which Roger Pomroy seems to have for his kinsman Hugh Pomroy, who was both of his name and blood and whom the donor Roger Pomroy, as he named him first in the will, so it was with an intention of preferring him to the persons to whom the subsequent limitations were made. And as it would be a hardship to the tenants for life to pay it out of the profits, so it would be a prejudice for the daughter to pay her portion by driblets, which ought to be paid at once at the marriage as the most beneficial manner for her advancement.

Also, it was observed that a portion was favored in equity, even as much almost as a creditor, it being a debt of nature from a parent to a child. And, in the case, the daughter is as a purchaser of her portion, it being in consideration of the mother's marriage and the mother's portion. And, if the words would any way bear it, the court would assist it with the most favorable construction. And, therefore, as the word 'profits' would extend to a mortgage, it should be taken in the sense, especially where the next limitation in the settlement to the term securing the portion was a remainder in fee to the heirs at law of Roger Pomroy that made the settlement. And, if, on the death of Roger Pomroy that made the settlement, the heir at law had entered and taken the profits, these profits taken by the heir at law should never have gone in discharge of the portions. And, as the heir at law could never have said this against the daughter, to whom the portion was due, and, as the heir at law could not have said so, so cannot the persons under the second settlement in regard they claim under the limitation to the heirs at law and stand in the place of the heir.

Also, it was said the same was imperfect, *viz.* the trust of the term of 120 years was to raise the portions out of the rents, issues, and profits, as well by leasing the premises for one, two, or three lives or twenty-one years absolutely, reserving the ancient rent, so that there is no word to answer those words 'as well'. The words might be understood to raise the portions by rents and profits as well as by leasing, it being in case of a western estate, where fines are usually raised by leasing, might be *in majorem cautelam* to empower the trustees to make leases though the general word before, *viz.* 'profits', included the same. And it is usual to say in a marriage settlement in trust to raise the portions by rent, issues, and profits or by sale, lease, or mortgage, though all this is implied by the word 'profits'. And that was very hard in a court of equity to decree the loss of an honest debt where the debt would be safe at law and that it would be very hard to put a mortgagee to follow the personal assets of Hugh Pomroy, the remainderman, for the payment of his debts, especially when the executor of Hugh, who is made a party, denies assets.

And as to the subsequent settlement, this cannot alter or prejudice the former security made by the first settlement for the portions.[1]

Lord Chancellor [LORD MACCLESFIELD]: It would be very material to know the yearly value of the premises charged with this portion that it might be known within what time the portion might be raised out of the annual profits. But, by the second settlement made by Roger Pomroy, which raises a term of ten years only, of the same premises for securing £1900 shows that the premises would in a reasonable time be a proper security for the raising this lesser portion of £1500.

HIS LORDSHIP took it as a rule that, where a trust of a term for raising portions for daughters does direct a particular method for raising portions, it implies a negative, that it shall not be raised any otherwise. And, where the trust of the term in the present case is to be raised, the portion by rents, issues, and profits as well by leasing for one, two, or three lives or for any term of years determinable on one, two, or three lives or for twenty-one years absolutely, it shall not be raised any other way. It is material that even this way by way of leasing, it could not be raised but by making such a lease upon which the old rent is reserved.

The natural meaning of raising a portion by rents, issues, and profits is by yearly profits. But to prevent an inconvenience, the word 'profits' has been extended to any profits which the land will yield, *viz.* by sale or mortgage. But, when there be subsequent words to explain and restrain it, *viz.* by leasing, I have not heard of any case which says that any other method should be used for the raising of it.

Here is as much the intent of the settlement to restrain the manner of raising this portion to leasing or to the annual profits as to secure any portion at all. And it would be a plain breach of trust to raise it any other way. And the mortgagee, who has notice of all this and in whose mortgage both settlements are recited, is necessary to the breach of trust.

And, at the time of the making of the settlement which was in 1651, I do not think that the word 'profits' was extended by any constructions before that time made to the profit that might be made of lands by sale or mortgage.

There is no time appointed for the raising of this portion, and, therefore, the portion in this case is due when the annual profit or profits by leasing can raise it. And it carried no interest. But, when the sum of £1500 is or might have been raised by annual profits or by leasing, the portion is due and the land is discharged as having borne its burden.

---

[1] persons *MS.*

The profits received by Hugh Pomroy are as received by the mortgagee Ivie, because it is said in the last clause of the mortgage deed that it should be lawful for Hugh Pomroy to take the rents without an account until default of payment, so that Mr. Hugh Pomroy by the clause [is] tenant at will to the mortgagee Ivie. And it is the same thing as if the mortgagee had let it to any other person at will. Therefore, this mortgage made to the plaintiff is not pursuant to the trust in regard the trust warrants only the raising of the portion by proportions of profits or by leasing.

And so much of the profits as have been received since the death of Roger Pomroy and his wife must go towards the payment and sinking of the portion only here, having been a power of leasing and the intention having been to charge the land as far as may be.

Let the Master see how far the land might have been charged by leasing and whether any lives were vacant. And I reserve the consideration how far the estate shall be chargeable thereby. And let the representative of Hugh Pomroy answer the profits by him received as far as his assets will extend.

Lincoln's Inn MS. Misc. 506, p. 65, pl. 1

Easter 8 George.

A term was given in trust to raise £1500. It was given for 120 years to trustees to raise the money out of rents and profits as well as by leases, except the mansion house and demesnes, not exceeding twenty-one years or three lives. The bill was to compel a sale for the raising of the £1500.

Lord Chancellor [Lord Macclesfield] dismissed the bill, for that the primary intention of the words 'rents and profits' does signify as they become due and so it has been held since the year 1651 when this deed was made, that now, however, they are construed to signify the lands themselves and, therefore, give the trustees the power to sell or mortgage, but then the reason of that construction is because the party's intention seems to be so, but, where the intention appears quite contrary, there is no reason to put such a construction on them, which is the case here, for it empowers the trustees to raise the money out of rents and profits as well as by leases, except the mansion house and demesnes, which leases are not to exceed twenty-one years or three lives so that it appears by the adding the power of leasing that he did not intend to give a power of selling or mortgaging, for then the power to make leases would be entirely useless nor is the power of leasing absolute, but, under certain restrictions as to the demesne lands, they are tied up from leasing them at all. Had there been a day fixed by which time the money was to be raised, as are the other cases, and the rents and profits would not raise the sum by that time, that would have varied the case because else the parties intention could not take effect. But here is no day fixed. Had there been no day fixed and the annual rents and profits would not raise the money in less than 100 years or the like, that might have been a reason to construe the words 'rents and profits' [as] a power to sell or mortgage because, otherwise, the party could never have the benefit of it. But that is not the case here.

The bill was dismissed.

British Library MS. Hargrave 83, pt. 2, f. 86

A man settles his estate to the use of himself for life, remainder to his first and every other son in tail and, if he should die without issue male, then to trustees for 120 years that they should raise out of the issues and profits as well by making leases reserving the accustomed rent as otherwise the sum of £1500, the remainder to his brother A. for life, with a remainder to his sons in tail, remainder to B. in tail, remainder to his own right heirs. He dies leaving issue a daughter. A. enters and takes the profits during his life, in which time the surviving trustee dying, the daughter took out administration to him. And she and A. mortgaged the term to the plaintiff for £1500. And A. gave his bond for a further security for the said sum and paid the interest of it and took the profits of the lands while he lived. The mortgagee, after the death of A., enters and brings a bill to foreclose against the executors of A. and the remainderman.

It was insisted on for the executors that, if a term be limited in trust to pay legacies, the trustees may mortgage it and the mortgage money shall not be paid by the tenants for life, but shall fall upon the inheritance, *quod fuit concessum*, that, if the whole burden was laid upon the tenant for life, it would be very hard.

But My Lord Chancellor [Lord Macclesfield] perceiving that it was mentioned in the deed that, if A. paid the £1500 in five years, he should hold it disencumbered and some other expressions whereby he conceived that the lands should be applied without delay to discharge that sum. He ordered the executors to account for what the testator had received. And it was decreed that, in this case, there being a particular method prescribed for discharging the £1500, the trustees could not mortgage the premises but are confined to that method, for every trust implies a negative. And whenever there is a sum mentioned to be raised, the trustees must not exceed that sum. And so it is when there is a method appointed to raise such a sum; they cannot raise it in another method, for which reason the trustees could not mortgage in this case, nor, of consequence, the daughter, who comes under them. The trustees should not have allowed the tenant for life to have received the profits, but should have applied them to the payment of the £1500.

The mortgagee shall have no interest for his money out of the profits of the estate coming in in the room of the daughter, who was to have none. But, if the profits which the tenant for life received do not on the account appear sufficient to discharge the principal sum of £1500, so much as they are deficient shall fall on the remainders and the mortgagee shall sue upon his security, which is the bond of the tenant for life, for his interest and costs. The executors must be accountable for the profits received by the tenant for life before the mortgage.

Consideration must also be had of the leases which fell in the life[time] of the tenant for life.

From this decree, there was an appeal to the House of Lords, where the decree was affirmed against the opinion of Lord Lechmere, who argued strongly against it.

[Other reports of this case: 2 Peere Williams 13, 24 E.R. 622, Precedents in Chancery 583, 24 E.R. 261, 2 Eq. Cas. Abr. 644, 645, 22 E.R. 540, 542.]

544

Hopson v. Trevor

(Ch. 1722)

A court of equity will specifically enforce a contract to make a marriage settlement.

1 Strange 533, 93 E.R. 683

The defendant, being the son of the late Master of the Rolls[1] and under the displeasure of his father, did upon the marriage of his daughter with the plaintiff enter into a bond of the penalty of £5000 conditioned to settle one-third of whatever estate in lands should come to him on the death of his father. The Master dying without a will, a very considerable estate descended to the defendant, his eldest son, who neglecting to make any settlement within the time limited, the plaintiff brought his bill in this court for a specific performance.

The defendant, by his answer, insists that he ought to be left to sue the penalty, having his remedy upon that at law.

But Lord Chancellor [Lord Macclesfield] decreed a specific performance, saying it was unreasonable to give an election to the defendant, when the plaintiff could have none, for, if the lands to be settled were not of the value of £5000, he could never resort to the penalty. And, on the other hand, if they exceeded that value, it was not just he should be left to it, neither would it answer the intent of the parties, which was to secure a provision for the wife and children by the settlement of the estate, because, if the plaintiff was to have the penalty, it must be as a debt due to himself, and this court would have no power to compel him to do anything out of it for their benefit.

[Other reports of this case: 10 Modern 507, 88 E.R. 829, 2 Peere Williams 191, 24 E.R. 695, 2 Eq. Cas. Abr. 21, 22 E.R. 17.]

[Related cases: Trevor v. Trevor (Ch. 1719), see above, Case No. 392.]

[1] K. Ellis, 'Trevor, Sir John (c. 1637–1717)', *Oxford Dictionary of National Biography*, vol. 55, pp. 362–363. Trevor was the Master of the Rolls from 1685 to 1717.

545

Peele v. Capel

(Ch. 1722)

Where a bond to resign from a rectory is misused, a court of equity will grant relief.

A contract between a patron and a rector for the rector to pay an annuity at the direction of the patron is simoniacal and unenforceable.

1 Strange 534, 93 E.R. 683

Capel, on presenting Peele to a living, took a bond from him to resign when the patron's nephew came of age, for whom the living was designed. When the nephew was of age, instead of requiring a resignation, it was agreed between them all that Peele should continue to hold the living, paying £30 *per annum* to the nephew. Peele makes the payment for seven years, but refusing to pay any more, the patron puts the bond in suit. And then, Peele comes into this court for an injunction and to have back his £30 *per annum*.

On the hearing, the Chancellor [Lord Macclesfield] granted the injunction, not, as he said, upon account of any defect in the bond itself, which he held good, but on account of the ill use that had been made of it. And, as to the money, it being paid upon a simoniacal contract, he left the plaintiff to go to law for it.

546

Hill v. Filkins

(Ch. 1722–1725)

A former Roman Catholic who takes the oaths of allegiance and supremacy can thereupon inherit, take, and hold land.

Lincoln's Inn MS. Misc. 506, p. 38

Easter 8 George.

Ann Stevenson, the grandmother of the plaintiff Hill and the defendant Frances, the wife of the defendant Filkins, by will, gave the estate in question to three trustees, two of them Papists, the third a Protestant, to sell for payment of her debts and legacies and the surplus of the money she devised to her granddaughter Frances at the age of twenty-one or marriage by the consent of the two Popish trustees, but, if she married without their consent or died under twenty-one, then, she gave the surplus to the plaintiff at the age of twenty-one and, in case he died under that age, then she gave it to the trustees to be disposed of to such uses as she should privately signify to them. Ann Stevenson, in her lifetime, had the care of her two grandchildren, their father not being able to maintain them, and, being herself a Papist, educated them in the Popish religion. After her death, the trustees continued their education in the same religion until about the year 1717, when the father, who was a Protestant, obtained an order by petition from the Lord Chancellor for their being placed out at Protestant schools. Soon after the execution of this order, Frances, who was then of the age of fifteen years, the plaintiff being much younger, by the consent of the two Popish trustees, married the defendant Filkins, a Protestant. Her marriage was first celebrated at her desire by a Popish priest at the Emperor's Envoy's Chapel, but, about a week afterwards, they were married a second time in the Fleet by a parson of the Church of England. When Frances came to the age of eighteen years, she took the oaths and subscribed the declaration appointed by the 11 & 12 Will. III, c. 4.[1]

The plaintiff is not only a remainderman under the devise, but likewise heir at law to the testatrix. The trustees never sold the lands, there being assets without it, but have received the profits ever since the death of the testatrix. The plaintiff brought a bill for an account and to have the trustees convey to him as being entitled on the disability of the defendant.

The case depends on that part of the Statute whereby it is enacted:

> That if any person educated in or possessing the Popish religion shall not within six months after the attaining the age of eighteen years, take the oath of allegiance and supremacy and subscribe the declaration mentioned in 30 Car. II, c. 1,[2] then such person shall in respect of him or herself only and not of their heirs, be disabled to inherit or take by devise or limitation in possession, reversion, or remainder any lands etc. and the next of kin of such person being a Protestant shall enjoy the lands during the life of such person or until such person shall take the said oath and subscribe the said declaration without being accountable for the profits.

And then a little after follows another clause:

> that every Papist or person making profession of the Popish religion, shall be disabled from purchasing lands and all estates, terms, or other interest in lands to be made, suffered, or done for the use of such person shall be utterly void.

The question in this case was whether the defendant Frances was by virtue of this Statute perpetually disabled from taking under the will of her grandmother. It was admitted on the authority of the case of Roper and Ratcliff, in Lord Cowper's time,[3] that the devise of a surplus of money arising out of the sale of

---

1 Stat. 11 Will. III, c. 4, s. 4 (*SR*, VII, 587).

2 Stat. 30 Car. II, stat. 2, c. 1 (*SR*, V, 894–896).

3 *Roper v. Radcliffe* (1712–1714), 9 Modern 167, 181, 88 E.R. 380, 387, 10 Modern 89, 230, 88 E.R. 639, 706, 5 Brown P.C. 360, 2 E.R. 731, 2 Eq. Cas. Abr. 508, 620, 621,

lands was to be considered as land and would be affected by the Statute. It was admitted also that the defendant was educated in the Popish religion both at the time of the devise and the death of the devisor, but whether she should be said to profess the Popish religion when she was but fifteen years of age was a little disputed.

But Lord Chancellor [LORD MACCLESFIELD] said that he thought it was clear she should from the beginning of the Statute, where a person before eighteen is supposed to profess the Popish religion and, though it may be hard to fix an exact age when a person may be said to be capable of understanding or professing a religion, yet there are times when one may affirm it with the greatest certainty, as in the present case, where she did knowingly do an act, one of the most solemn in that religion, i.e. marrying according to the Popish ceremonies by a Popish priest. So that the case rested chiefly on this, whether she was subject to the latter or only the former disability of the Statute.

The difficulty arose on this account, that these two sorts of disabilities seem intended for two distinct cases, whereas the present seems to fall within the description of both, for both affect persons professing the Popish religion and both affect estates by devise, the former mentioning 'devise' by name and the latter comprehending it under the general word 'purchase'.

It was insisted on for the plaintiff that this will was a mere contrivance to evade the Statute and, as such, within the general ground of the case of Roper and Ratcliff, which was so determined in order to prevent the effect of any such artifice to get estates into the hands of Papists contrary to the intent of the Statute, that the present case was within the words of the latter clause and precisely answered everything described in it. The defendant was a Papist at the time of the devise and at the death of the devisor and when the estate vested, *viz.* the time of her marriage so that she is plainly described by 'a person professing and the Popish religion.' The estate she is to take is by devise, not by descent as heir, which is an estate by purchase, the word used likewise in the latter clause. If the latter clause stood single, there could be no doubt, yet it is objected that there is another clause which takes in cases by devise, which inflicts only a temporal disability, but the primary intent of these different disabilities seems to have been to distinguish between those estates which came to Papists by descent from those they were to take by purchase. And the words 'devise or limitation' were added to prevent any attempt that might be made of evading that clause by devising to an heir so no case of devise or limitation is to be intended in the former clause. But where it is to an heir at law, that a devise is within the latter clause was determined in Roper's Case.

On the other side, for the defendant, it was insisted that there were two distinct disabilities inflicted by way of punishment and, therefore, must be intended

---

622, 625, 771, 22 E.R. 430, 520, 521, 525, 655, British Library MS. Add. 36651, f. 101, British Library MS. Hargrave 80, ff. 101v, 174v.

for two distinct cases and not that the same should be subjected to both. The case of the defendant is provided for by the first clause and in every respect answered by it, and, therefore, it is not to be taken within the meaning of the second. She was educated in the Popish religion and professed it under the age of eighteen and so was capable of the benefit of conformity. She did conform within the time of the Statute and, therefore, ought to have the advantage allowed by it. The Statute seems designed as much to encourage conformity to the Protestant religion as to disavow such as are obstinate in the Popish and, more especially, in the case of infants whose religion is owing only to the misfortune of their character. To lay those under a perpetual disability would be too great a punishment and frustrate the intent of the legislature by encouraging them in their errors rather than discouraging. The main view of the Statute in those two distinct clauses was to distinguish between active and passive purchasers where an estate is cast upon a person without his contrivance, as it always is in the case of infants. The legislative thought is too hard to take it away, but to stop the hands of purchasers who were adding new estates by their own purchase was the intent of the latter clause. And in that case, it is not so hard. The clauses are not reconcilable if taken in the full meaning of the words because the second clause would destroy the former, and, therefore, the first clause, being less general, must be taken as an exception out of the second, as, in the case of a will, where a man devises all his lands to A. and gives Blackacre to B., the general devise must be understood with an exception of Blackacre. So when the Statute in the second clause says 'all Papists', it must be understood with an exception of such Papists as had been comprehended under the first clause and, by that, subjected to a particular kind of disability, *viz.* infants under the age of eighteen to whom estates should descend or should come before that age. When that clause says, if they do not conform at that age, they shall be disabled to take, it must be understood that, if they do conform, then they shall not be disabled.

The Lord Chancellor [Lord Macclesfield] said that, to him, it seemed a very plain case, that the devise to the defendant was void. It is expressly within the words of the latter clause. Here is an interest in land conveyed to a person professing the Popish religion at the time of the making the will, at the time of the death of the testatrix, and at the time of the vesting of the estate which interest is in the express words made void by the Statute. It is said that, notwithstanding that, this present case is not within the meaning of it because it falls within the description of another clause wherein the disability is only a qualified one and, therefore, to be taken as a negative upon the second, like the devise of all and afterwards of part of those lands. But surely, this is a new notion. I have indeed heard that laws introductive of new matters imply a negative on everything not expressed. But I never heard that a disability by one clause shall take away disabilities in another. It only shows that the party shall not be disabled as to other cases by virtue of that clause. The general view of the legislature was to prevent estates from coming into the hands of Papists. The latter clause is general and disables all Papists or persons professing the Popish religion from purchasing estates and makes all estates made for their use or benefit. This clause extends to every case where one professing the Popish religion takes by purchase; it is to be taken in its full and largest meaning so as not to suffer any Papist to take any interest whatsoever by any kind of purchase. But still this clause though taken in its most comprehensive signification left out two sorts of cases which it equally concerned the legislature to provide against. Those are where persons professing the Popish religion take by descent and where persons educated in the Popish religion, but not professing it, were to take estates either by descent or purchase. To meet with both these cases, the first clause was inserted, but a disability of a lesser kind was inflicted. Estates by descent are taken in and persons educated in the Popish religion, though, by reason of their tender age, incapable of professing it, are made subject to that disability, so that there is a manifest difference as to the cases within the first and second clauses. The persons are different and the estates are different. If the words 'devise or limitation', which, in the first clause, are joined with 'descent', were left out, there would not be the least appearance of difficulty nor possibility of the two clauses interfering, there not being one case in the one that could be included within the words of the other. If, therefore, there be a proper use for those words without breaking in upon the second clause, there would be no difficulty as it stands at present.

Now, there are two uses of those words, the one to secure the effect of that clause as to descent, for the principal intent of that clause seems to be with regard to descents, for if the words 'devise or limitation' were left out, no estate should be left to descend, care would be taken that their heirs would have equal benefit under a devise or limitation, but should not receive it as heirs. The word 'limitation' seems particularly intended for those estates of Papists which, by being settled on first and other sons in tail etc., stop the course of descent. Indeed, where such 'devise or limitation' happens to fall on persons professing the Popish religion, the second clause will lay hold on them. But where there is no profession, but only an education, which will rise into an actual profession, no provision would be made were those words left out. And this is the other use of them that I would mention, *viz.* to subject children educated in but not yet capable of professing the Popish religion to that temporal disability of taking by devise or limitation, for this clause has been construed to extend to children to whom estates descend or are devised or limited before their age of eighteen so as to oblige them under the penalty of that disability to conform within six months after the age of eighteen. Should a devise be to an infant a year old or a remainder limited to the first son happen to fall when the son was of that age, this would be such a devise or limitation as is intended in the first clause, but plainly not included in the second. And I think no such devise or limitation was intended to be within the first clause which was comprehended in the second, but such only as were not provided for by the second. The objection taken from the word 'devise' being made use of in the first clause was made in the case of Roper and Ratcliff, but it was held notwithstanding that that case was within the second clause. The same rule may hold as to persons, for, suppose a person should fall within the description of both clauses, shall he, by that means, avoid the greater disability and incur only the less? There is another difference observable in the two clauses. The latter disability affects all purchases of lands when in possession, remainder, or reversion and makes them all void indifferently, but the first clause affects only estates in possession and not the vesting of remainders, for though the words 'in reversion or remainder' are inserted, yet that must signify such estates when they fall in possession because, during the time of nonconformity, the next Protestant kindred are to take the profits, which cannot be until the estate comes into possession.

[This was] to be reargued when the judges should be present. But, before that time, the Lord Chancellor [Lord Macclesfield] going out, it was heard before Lord Chancellor KING, who succeeded. And he was of opinion that the two clauses were to be taken together as one entire clause and, therefore, must have such a sense as may make them both quadrate and, consequently, whatever was included in the first should be exempt from and not intended to be included in the latter.

And so the bill was dismissed.

Lincoln's Inn MS. Misc. 384, p. 262

23 April.

Upon the Statute 11 & 12 Will. III, concerning Papists, the query was whether a devise of land to a Papist under eighteen, who, at that age, conforms, be good.

Lord Chancellor [LORD MACCLESFIELD]: [There is] a strong case for the plaintiff, the Protestant heir, within the express words of the second clause.

[It was] objected that the defendant has only a qualified disability within the first clause compared to a will, where two clauses are inconsistent. This is not so. The first clause [is] from 29 September 1700. If any person professing the Popish religion shall not within six months after eighteen take the oaths etc., he or she shall be disabled to take by descent or purchase etc. The Act supposes they may profess that religion before eighteen. It brings a disability unless they purge it. Does this clause prove that a further disability may not be contained in another clause? This clause is intended for estates descended. The second clause extends to the person who is a Papist at the time of the purchase and who professes the Popish religion. If an estate is devised to a Papist's child but of a year old, it is not within the second clause because he is not capable of possessing. In Roper v. Ratcliff, it was objected that the first was after disability and the second clause was a general one, therefore, that the first was an exception out of the second. But that would not hold because one penalty in the first does not hinder a further penalty in the second clause. If a person be professing the Popish religion at the time of the purchase is disabled by the second clause, though under eighteen, those that are not professing Popery at the time of the devise etc. are within the first clause. By the second clause, this is a perpetual disability [and] gives a right to the next Protestant remainderman.

[It was] objected that the first clause does not understand persons to profess the Popish religion under eighteen and that, therefore, the second clause extends only to persons above eighteen, but the words are 'professing', which a person may do under eighteen. [It is] difficult to fix the bounds exactly at what age a child is capable of professing any religion; that differs according to their capacity. But it is to be taken for granted that, at eighteen, they are capable of professing. The defendant's cause cannot be bettered by conforming at eighteen because it is by devise and she is a Papist at the time of the devise.

This will be a leading case. Therefore, I will have the assistance of the judges.

Lincoln's Inn MS. Misc. 384, p. 313, pl. 3

8 June.

[Upon a] construction of the Stat. 11 & 12 Will. III, the question was whether the defendant, who was an infant of eleven years old at the death of the devisor and educated in the Popish religion and married under eighteen and then turned Protestant is capable of taking by the devise.

Lord Chancellor [Lord King]: The Act only respects the qualification of the persons to take. The Lords determined all devises to be within the word 'purchase'. Otherwise, the Act might easily have been defeated. But they have not distinguished whether some devises may not be out of the Act. The words in the first clause are general. It refers to the age of eighteen. You must construe the second clause consistent with the first. The meaning must be that a devise to a person above eighteen is void. If a Protestant at the death of the testator professes before eighteen, he is within the Act. If that clause takes in all devises, it signifies nothing. I take it if a person professes the Popish religion at the time of the devise and before eighteen conforms, he may take. He may maintain an action of waste against the Protestant heir before conforming. [It is] not intended one part of the Act to contradict the other. Where a person was conformed in his religion within the Act, the age proper for that is fixed at eighteen. The testimony of the conformation is settled by the Act, the Test Act etc.

The defendant, having complied, is entitled to the devise. The bill is dismissed.

British Library MS. Hargrave 81, f. 165

Easter Term in the 8th year of King George [1722].

The case was this. The plaintiff Hill and the defendant Frances, being brother and sister, were educated by their grandmother, who was a Papist, in the Popish religion. But, by petition of their father to the Lord Chancellor, they were ordered to be taken from her and bred Protestants. And, accordingly, the plaintiff, being then about fourteen years of age, was sent to a Protestant school and educated in the Protestant religion. But the defendant Frances, when her father told her she must be a Protestant, said she would be torn limb from limb by wild horses before she would leave the true faith and become a heretic and used several other expressions which showed the principles of that religion were deeply rooted in her, so that she continued with the grandmother and a Papist. The grandmother, by her will, devises her real estate to three persons, two of whom were Papists, in trust to pay her debts and legacies and the residue for the defendant Frances, who was then a Papist and under the age of fifteen. And she died. And, in about five months after, the defendant Frances married the other defendant Philkin, a Protestant, and did herself before she attained her age of eighteen conform to the Protestant religion and did also take the oaths of allegiance and supremacy and subscribe the declaration.

And the plaintiff brings his bill as heir at law to be relived against this will as being a void devise by virtue of an Act of Parliament made against the growth of Popery in the 11th year of King William III,[1] the two clauses in which relating to this case are that:

> from and after the 29th September in the year of our Lord 1700, if any person educated in the Popish religion or professing the same shall not within six months after he or she shall attain the age of eighteen take the oaths of allegiance and supremacy and also subscribe the declaration set down and expressed in an Act of Parliament made in the third year of the reign of the late King Charles II,[2] entitled an Act for the More Effectual Preserving the King's Person and Government by Disabling Papists to Sit in Either House of Parliament to be by him or her made, repeated, and subscribed in the courts of Chancery, King's Bench, or Quarter Sessions of the county where such person shall reside, every such person shall in respect of him or herself only and to or in respect of any of his or her heirs or posterity to be disabled and made incapable to inherit or take by descent, devise, or limitation in possession, reversion, or remainder any land, tenements, or hereditaments within etc. and that during the life of such person or until he or she do take the said oaths and make, repeat, and subscribe the said declaration in manner aforesaid, the next of his or her kindred which shall be a Protestant shall have and enjoy the said lands etc. without being accountable for the profits by him or her received during such enjoyment thereof that, from and after the 10th of April which shall be in the year 1700, every Papist or person professing the Popish religion shall be disabled and is hereby made incapable to purchase either in his or her own name or in the name of any other person or persons to his or her use or in trust for him or her any manors, lands, etc. from and after the said 10th day of April and that every purchase to be made, suffered, or done to or for the use or behalf of any such person

[1] Stat. 11 Will. III, c. 4, s. 4 (*SR*, VII, 587).
[2] Stat. 30 Car. II, stat. 2, c. 1 (*SR*, V, 894–896).

or person or upon any trust or confidence, mediately or immediately, to or for the benefit or relief of any such person or persons shall be utterly void and of none effect to all intents, constructions, and purposes whatsoever.

It having been adjudged in the case of Roper and Ratcliffe that a devise was a purchase within the meaning of the second clause in the Act of Parliament on which this cause was founded, the single point here was whether this was a devise within the intent and meaning of the words in the first clause which disables any person educated in the Popish religion or professing the same to take any lands etc. by descent, devise, or limitation in case they do not comply with the terms therein mentioned to which this case cannot extend, the defendant having before her age of eighteen performed everything thereby required, or whether this devise was a purchase within the meaning of the second clause or so absolutely void, it was argued by the counsel for the plaintiff that this was a purchase by a person professing the Popish religion and so void to all intents and purposes by the express words of the second clause and that there was nothing in the first clause which exempted or took this case out of the general words of the second clause for, though there are the words 'devise or limitation' in the first clause, these words must not be construed to extend any farther than to answer the purposes they were there apparently intended for, for, if they are construed in the largest sense they will admit of, it must necessarily confound the two clauses and make them inconsistent one with the other, which ought not be admitted if any reasonable construction can be made that will make them consistent.

The intention of the Act was evidently from the whole tenor of it, first, to prevent all such landed interest as was then or should be at the time therein mentioned in the hands of Papists from being continued in such hands and, secondly, for preventing any addition or increase of such interest by any acquisition whatsoever. And the two clauses were contrived and adapted to answer these purposes, the first to prevent the continuation of such estates, for which purpose it was necessary to consider by what means estates might be continued according to the rules of law in order to make use of such words as would most fully and effectually answer that end. Estates are continued in families either by descent, which is the appointment of the law where the ancestor makes none, or by limitations in settlements, which is now the most usual way, or by devise of the ancestor by his last will and testament. And the intention of the first clause being to prevent the continuation of estates in Popish families, the words 'devise or limitation' there ought to be understood of such devises or limitations only as come in the places of descent. And the devise to the defendant Frances not being to one to whom the lands would descend is a devise not within the first clause, and, she being a person professing the Popish religion at the time the devise was made and a devise being adjudged to be a purchase within the meaning of the second clause, to her is therefore a purchase both within the words and meaning of that clause and consequently void.

Of the other side, for the defendant, it was said that the words in the first clause being that every person educated in the Popish religion or professing the same which should not comply with the terms therein mentioned should be disabled to take by devise, descent, or limitation did necessarily imply that every person educated in the Popish religion or professing the same who should comply with the said terms might take by devise, descent, or limitation and further that, in order to come within the second clause, she must be a person professing the Popish religion. And, as the law had not fixed any certain time when a person should be deemed capable of professing any religion, it was but a reasonable and equitable construction of the Statute that the same time should be allowed for professing themselves of any religion in the second clause as is allowed to excuse and exempt them from the disability in the first, which was until eighteen years old. And the defendant, having declared herself a Protestant in such manner as the law requires before that age, cannot reasonably be deemed a person within the description of that clause.

The Lord Chancellor PARKER, upon hearing the arguments of counsel on both sides, was of opinion for the plaintiff. He said he thought this was a very strong case in favor of the heir at law and that the devise to the defendant was a purchase both within the words and meaning of the second clause and consequently void. And he said he thought it was a strange inference which was made by the gentlemen who argued for the defendant that, because the words in the first clause are that every person educated in the Popish religion or professing the same who should not comply with the terms therein mentioned should be disabled to take by descent, purchase, or limitation, therefore, that every person educated in the Popish religion or professing the same who shall comply with the said terms might take by descent, purchase, or limitation, for surely it does not follow that, because such persons as comply with the terms in that clause mentioned are not disabled from taking by descent, devise, or limitation by that clause, therefore, they are not disabled to take by descent, devise, or limitation by any clause or law whatsoever, that is very far from a necessary consequence. But he said the words 'devise or limitation' in the first clause to him seemed clearly intended to mean such devise or limitation as came in the places of descent or such as are not by any other clause or law prohibited, that is devises or limitations to such persons educated in the Popish religion or professing the same to whom the estates devised or limited would have descended had not such limitation been made or devises or limitations to persons not disabled by the second clause or any other law, as to persons educated in the Popish religion and not capable of professing any, as to a child of six months old, which is certainly not within the second clause and plainly within the words of the first, for though there is no certain fixed time when a person is capable of professing a religion, there are some certain times in which we are certain they are not. And, in this case, it appears the defendant Frances had received very strong and deep impressions in favor of the Popish religion and may, therefore, very justly be said to be capable of professing it.

But he said, though he was very clear as to this point, yet as he believed it was a matter of too great consequence to that party to let it rest there, he would not make any decree until he had advised with some of the judges.

[Other copies of this report: British Library MS. Hargrave 82, f. 175, pl. 2.]

Lincoln's Inn MS. Misc. 11, p. 216, pl. 2

Michaelmas term 1722.

Ann Stevenson, the grandmother of the plaintiff and the defendant Frances, the wife of Filkins, by will gave the estate in question to three trustees, two of whom were Papists and the third a Protestant, to sell for the payment of debts and the surplus of the money she devised to her granddaughter Frances at her age of twenty-one or marriage with the consent of the two Popish trustees, but, if she married without their consent or died under twenty-one, then she gave the said surplus to the plaintiff at the age of twenty-one, and, in case he died under that age, then she gave it to the trustees to be disposed of to such uses as she should privately signify to them.

Ann Stevenson, in her lifetime, had the care of her two grandchildren, their father not being able to maintain them, and, being herself a Papist, she educated them in the Popish religion. After her death, the trustees continued their education in the same religion until about the year 1717 when their father, who was a Protestant, obtained an order by a petition to the Lord Chancellor for their being placed in Protestant schools.

Soon after the execution of this order, Frances, who was then of the age of fifteen years, the plaintiff being much younger, by the consent of the two Popish trustees, married the defendant Filkins, a Protestant. Her marriage was first, by her desire, celebrated by a Popish priest at the Emperor's envoy's chapel, but, about a week afterwards, they were married a second time in the Fleet by a parson of the Church of England. When Frances came to her age of eighteen, she took the oaths and subscribed the declaration appointed by the [Statute] 11 & 12 Will. III.

The plaintiff is not only a remainderman under the devise but heir at law also to the testatrix. The trustees never sold the land, there being assets without, but they have been in receipt of the profits ever since the testatrix's death.

This came out to be a case on a bill brought by the plaintiff as heir and remainderman to take advantage of the disability of the defendant Frances under the Statute 11 & 12 Will. III, c. 4.

The case depends on that part of the Statute by which it is enacted:

> That if any person educated in or possessing the Popish religion shall not within six months after the attaining the age of eighteen years, take the

> oath of allegiance and supremacy and subscribe the declaration [mentioned] in 30 Car. II, c. 1, then such person shall in respect of him or herself only and not of their heirs, be disabled to [inherit or] take by descent, devise, or limitation in possession, reversion, or reminder any lands, etc. and during the life of such person or until such conformity the next Protestant relation shall have the lands without accounting for the profits and that every Papist or person professing the Popish religion should be disabled and is hereby made incapable to purchase any manors, etc. and all estates, terms, and other interest in lands to be made, suffered, or done to or for the use or benefit of such person shall be utterly void.

The question was whether the defendant Frances was by virtue of this Statute perpetually disabled to take under the devise of her grandmother

It was admitted also that she was educated in the Popish religion both at the time of making of the devise and the death of the devisor. But whether she could be said to profess the Popish religion when she was but fifteen years old within the intent of the Statute was a little disputed, but it seems clear from the beginning of that part of the Statute where a person is supposed to profess the Popish religion before the age of eighteen.

And Lord Chancellor [LORD MACCLESFIELD] said, though it might be impossible to fix the exact age at which one may be said to be capable of understanding and professing a religion, yet there are cases in which one may affirm with the greatest certainty that a person is or is not capable of making such a profession, as, in the present case, when she did an act, one of the most solemn in that religion knowingly, *viz.* marriage according to the ceremonies of it, so that the case rested chiefly on this, whether she was to be considered as subject to the latter or the former disability created by the Statute.

The difficulty arose on this account, that these two sorts of disabilities seem intended for two distinct cases, whereas the present seems to fall within the description of both, for both are to affect persons professing the Popish religion, which the defendant did, and both affect estates by devise, the former mentioning devise by name and the latter comprehending it under the general word 'purchase'.

Lutwyche and *Talbot*, for the plaintiff, insisted that it appeared clearly that this will was a mere contrivance to evade the Statute and as such within the general ground of the Case of Roper and Ratcliff, which was determined in order to prevent the effect of any such artifice to get estates into the hands of Papists contrary to the intent of the Statute.

The present case was within the words of the latter clause and precisely answered everything described in it. The defendant was a Papist at the time of the devise and the death of the devisor and the vesting of the estate, that is at marriage, so that she was the person plainly described in it, one professing the Popish religion. The estate she is to take is by devise, not as heir or by descent, which is an estate by purchase, the word used in the Statute.

If this latter clause stood single, there could be no doubt. But there is another clause inflicting only a temporal disability, in which the word 'devise' is used. But the primary intent of these different disabilities seems to have been to distinguish between those estates which came to Papists by descent from those they were to take by purchase, and the words 'devise or limitation' were joined to 'descent' to prevent any attempt that might be made of evading that clause by devising to an heir at law. And so no case of a devise or limitation is to be intended in the former clause but where it is made to an heir at law.

That a devise is within the latter clause was determined in the Case of Roper and Ratcliff, which was a case of a devise.

Serjeant *Chesshyre*, *Cowper*, and *Peere Williams*, for the defendant, insisted that there were two distinct disabilities inflicted by way of punishment and, therefore, the legislature must intend two distinct cases for those disabilities and not that persons should be subject to both. The case of the defendant is provided for by the first clause and in every particular answered and, therefore, not to be taken within the meaning of the second. She was educated in the Popish religion. She professed it when under the age of eighteen and so was capable of the benefit of conformity. She did conform within the time of the Statute, and, therefore, she ought to have the advantage allowed by it.

The Statute seems to be designed as much to encourage conformity to the Protestant religion and, more especially, in the case of infants whose religion is owing to the misfortune of their education. To lay those under a perpetual disability would be too great a punishment and frustrate the intent of the legislature by strengthening them in their errors rather than encouraging them to leave them.

The main view of the Statute in those two distinct clauses was to distinguish between the cases of active and passive purchasers where an estate is cast upon a person without his contrivance, as it always is in the case of infants. The legislature thought it too hard to take it away. But to stop the hands of persons who are aiding, new estates by their own purchase is expressly within the words of the latter clause, and it is not so hard a punishment.

Peere Williams said the clauses were not reconcilable if they were to be taken in the full meaning of the words because the second clause would destroy the former; therefore, the first clause being left general, the second must be taken as an exception to the first, as it is in the case of a devise, where a man devises all his lands to A. and, in the same will, gives Black Acre to J.S., the general devise must be understood with an exception of Black Acre. So, when the Statute, in the second clause, says all Papists shall be disabled to purchase, it must be understood with an exception of those Papists who were comprehended in the former clause and subjected by that to a particular kind of disability, that is infants under the age of eighteen to whom estates should descend or come before that age and, therefore, when that clause says that, if they do not conform at that age, they shall be disabled to take it must be meant, if they do conform, they shall take.

Lord Chancellor [Lord Macclesfield]: It seems a very plain case that this devise to the defendant Frances is void by the Statute. It is expressly in the words of the latter clause. Here is an interest in lands conveyed to a person professing the Popish religion at the time of making the will, the death of the testatrix, and the vesting of the estate, which interest is in express words made void by the latter clause.

It is said, though this clause does relate to persons professing the Popish religion to whom any estate is made, yet the present case which falls within that description is not included because it comes within another clause wherein the penalty is only a qualified disability and, therefore, is to be considered as an exception out of the general words of the latter clause like the case of a devise of all and, afterwards, of part of those lands. But, surely, this is a new notion. I have indeed heard of laws introductive of new matters that imply a negative on everything not expressly mentioned, but I never heard that, because a person or case is declared to be within one clause and affected by the penalty thereby inflicted, that, therefore, he shall be excused from all other penalties which in any subsequent or other clause are as plainly laid upon it.

The meaning of those clauses in the Statute seems very much mistaken. The general intent of the legislature was to prevent any interests in land from coming into the hands of Papists. The latter clause is general and disables Papists or persons professing [that] religion to purchase estates and makes all estates etc. made for their use or benefit void. This clause extends to every case where one professing the Roman Catholic religion is to take by purchase. It is to be taken in its full and largest meaning so as not to suffer any Papist to take any interest whatsoever by any kind of purchase. But still, though taken in its most comprehensive signification, it leaves out two sorts of cases which it equally concerned the legislature to provide against. Those are where estates come by descent and where persons educated in the Popish religion but not professing it were to take estates, whether by descent or purchase.

To meet with both those cases, the first clause was inserted, a disability of a lesser kind inflicted on estates by descent are taken in and persons educated in the Popish religion, though, by reason of their tender years, incapable of professing it are made subject to that disability, so that here is a manifest distinction as to the cases within the first and second clauses, the persons are different and the estates are different.

If the words 'devise or limitation', which, in the first clause, are joined with 'descent', were left out, there would not be the least appearance of difficulty nor possibility of the two clauses interfering, there not being one case within the one that could be included within the words of the other. If, therefore, there is a proper use for those words without breaking in upon the second clause, there is no difficulty as it stands at present.

Now, there are two uses of those words, the one to secure the effect of that clause as to descents, for the principal intent of that clause seems to be with regard to estates by decent, for, if the words 'demise or limitation' were left out, no estates would ever be suffered to descend; care would be taken that their heirs should have equal benefit under a devise or limitation but should not receive it as heirs and the word 'limitation' seems particularly intended for those estates of Papists which by being settled on first and other sons in tail etc. stop the course of decent. Indeed, where such devises or limitations happen to fall on persons professing the Popish religion, the second clause will lay hold of them. But, where there is no profession but an education which will soon rise into actual profession, no provision would be made in this Statute were those words left out. And it is the other use of them that I would mention to subject children educated in, but not yet capable of professing, the Popish religion to that temporal disability of taking by devise or limitation, for this clause has been construed to extend to infants to whom estates descend or are devised or limited before their age of eighteen so as to oblige them under the penalty of that disability to conform within six months after their age of eighteen. Should a devise be to an infant of a year old or remainder limited to the first son happen to fall when the son was of that age, this would be such a devise or limitation as is intended in the first clause but plainly not included within the second. And I think no such devise or limitation was designed to be within the first clause which was comprehended in the second, but such only as were not provided for by the second.

This objection relating to the word 'devise' used in the first clause was made in the Case of Roper and Ratcliffe, but it was held that it was within the second clause and, though it should be true that a person might fall within the description of both clauses, one of which inflicts a lesser and the other a greater penalty, yet the coming under the lesser should not excuse him from the greater.

There is another difference observable in the second clause. The latter disability affects all purchases of interests and estates in land whether in possession, reversion, or remainder and makes them all void indifferently. But I take the first clause to affect only estates in possession and not to prevent the vesting of estates in reversion or remainder, for the words 'in possession, reversion, or remainder' are put in. Yet that must signify such estates when they fall into possession, because, during the time of non-conformity, the next Protestant kindred are to take the profits, which cannot be until the estates come in possession.

[Other reports of this case: 2 Peere Williams 6, 24 E.R. 619, Select Cases *tempore* King 22, 25 E.R. 200, 1 Cooper *tempore* Cottenham 428–443, 47 E.R. 933–941, 9 Modern 154, 167, 181, 88 E.R. 373, 380, 387, 10 Modern 89, 230, 481, 536, 88 E.R. 639, 706, 818, 841, 2 Eq. Cas. Abr. 508, 620, 621, 622, 624, 625, 771, 22 E.R. 520, 521, 522, 524, 525, 655, 4 Brown P.C. 640, 2 E.R. 436, 5 Brown P.C. 360, 2 E.R. 731.]

547

Countess of Coventry v. Earl of Coventry

(Ch. 1722–1724)

Where a written deed is intended to be signed and sealed but the accident of death intervenes, a court of equity will consider the deed to be completely executed.

Lincoln's Inn MS. Misc. 384, p. 257, pl. 2

17 April 1722.
24 March 1698[/99], Earl Thomas, by will, devises the premises to his son Gilbert for life etc., remainder to the defendant [William, earl of Coventry] for life with a power for the person in possession by any writing indented under hand and seal to limit and appoint any such manors or lordships, except Great and Little Milton, and any of the said messuages, lands, tenements, tithes, and hereditaments not exceeding in the whole £500 *per annum* to any wife for life for her jointure, she having an equitable portion.
5 June 1715, Earl Gilbert, then in possession, in consideration of a marriage with the plaintiff, the daughter of Sir Strensham Masters,[1] and of £10,000 portion, covenants that he or his heirs would at any time on request of Sir Strensham Masters according to the power or otherwise by good conveyance settle manors etc. of £500 *per annum* on the plaintiff for her jointure and that his heirs should also pay her £250 *per annum* additional jointure clear of taxes.

Earl Gilbert afterwards gives directions to have a proper part of the estate set out for the plaintiff's jointure, and, accordingly, deeds are prepared and engrossed. But, before they were examined, 27 October 1719, Earl Gilbert died, having the same day made his will. And thereby, he gives to the plaintiff besides what is settled on her by the marriage articles £3000 with all her dressing, plate, jewels, etc. The land, by limitation in the will of Earl Thomas, is come to the defendant, William, earl of Coventry.

The question is whether Earl Gilbert has well executed his power of appointing lands etc. of £500 *per annum* on the plaintiff for her jointure.

Serjeant *Chesshyre*, for the plaintiff, [cited] Smith v. Aston, 1 Ch. C. 264; Hale v. Hale, 2 ditto 29; Bath v. Montague, 69.[2] This is a favorable case. Earl Gilbert had a power to settle £500 *per annum*. The marriage articles had been a

[1] A. Grout, 'Masters, Sir Streynsham (1640–1724)', *Oxford Dictionary of National Biography*, vol. 37, pp. 247–248.

[2] *Smith v. Ashton* (1675), 1 Chancery Cases 263, 264, 22 E.R. 792, also 1 Freeman 308, 22 E.R. 1229, 89 E.R. 226, Reports *tempore* Finch 273, 23 E.R. 150, 3 Keble 551, 84 E.R. 874, 1 Eq. Cas. Abr. 345, 21 E.R. 1091, 73 Selden Soc. 191, 221; *Elliot v. Hele* (1680), 2 Chancery Cases 28, 87, 22 E.R. 831, 859, also 1 Vernon 406, 23 E.R. 547, 1 Eq. Cas. Abr. 345, 21 E.R. 1092, 79 Selden Soc. 816; *Earl of Bath v. Earl of Mountague* (1692–1693), 3 Chancery Cases 55, 103, 22 E.R. 963, 992, also *sub nom. Duchess of Albemarle v.*

good execution of the power if the particular lands had been specified. Accident is a head[1] of equity. What is agreed upon, a valuable consideration to be done, is considered in equity as done. Surrenders are supplied.

Mead: The marriage took effect on the faith [that] the then articles would be pursued. In equity, the covenant should be looked upon as an actual execution of the power; so, in covenants to lay out money in land, if there is a defective execution, it is proper to supply it here in favor of a purchaser or a child unprovided for. Parker v. Parker;[2] where the settlement could not be found, he misrecites his power and executes it in the presence of two witnesses instead of three, and he appoints £8000 for younger children instead of £7000; it was aided here.

The plaintiff, a purchaser, is relievable on the head of accident. Earl Gilbert intended to do justice. He took the opinion of counsel, who apprehended equity would relieve though the deeds were not executed, just delivered to Sir Strensham Masters. He mislaid them; the steward fell sick; the now steward was not acquainted with the estate. Where equity has denied supplying defective executions of powers, it has been where the plaintiffs were merely volunteers. Onions v. Tyrer, [. . .] on the head of accident, by Lord Cowper.[3]

Robins: In Bath v. Montague, a distinction was made between powers of [. . .] and to appoint jointures or portions. The first is construed strictly, being in the nature of conditions to defeat an estate; the latter are construed favorably.

Attorney General [*Raymond*], for Lady Carew,[4] the heir at law of Earl Gilbert and his executrix: If the £1500 *per annum* is not chargeable on the remainderman, it will fall on the executrix to make it good.

First, the intent of the donor was that the person in possession should take the estate clogged with that power. The reason why equity will not execute an agreement by a tenant in tail is because the donor intended the issue should not be bound.

Second, [there was] a continued resolution of Earl Gilbert for four years together to execute the power.

Third, what is the difference between undue execution and non-execution of powers where it is hindered by an accident; at law, undue executions are no executions.

Lutwyche: The plaintiff had an equivalent portion; she has a right to demand £500 *per annum* against the person in possession. The particular lands were

Earl of Bath, 2 Chancery Reports 417, 21 E.R. 704, Nelson 196, 21 E.R. 824, 2 Freeman 121, 193, 22 E.R. 1099, 1155, 2 Eq. Cas. Abr. 671, 22 E.R. 564.

1 I.e. jurisdiction.

2 *Parker v. Parker* (1714), Gilbert Rep. 168, 25 E.R. 118.

3 *Onions v. Tyrer* (1716), 1 Peere Williams 343, 24 E.R. 418, 1 Eq. Cas. Abr. 407, 21 E.R. 1138, 2 Vernon 741, 23 E.R. 1085, Precedents in Chancery 459, 24 E.R. 205, Gilbert Rep. 130, 25 E.R. 91, Lincoln's Inn MS. Misc. 12, p. 236.

4 Sic in MS.

reduced to a certainly by the engrossment. It happened to be locked up by the steward, which prevented the execution.

Peere Williams: A man covenants to convey lands to a purchaser, but, before he confesses judgment, it will not bind the purchaser. It was adjudged by Lord Cowper, in Finch v. Lord Winchelsea,[1] if a tenant covenants to make a lease, pursuant to the Statute,[2] the issue is bound though an infant. If Earl Gilbert had appointed more than £500 *per annum*, it had been good *pro tanto*, by Lord Somers. [In the case of] Sir Edward Barkham,[3] a power was not pursued as to the number of witnesses, yet he was decreed for a purchaser.

Cowper, for the defendant, the earl of Coventry: The plaintiffs are not relievable on the head of accident, for there was an opportunity of executing the power for four years together. There are no other circumstances of equity. Orby and Lord Mohun;[4] a defective execution of a power of leasing was not aided against the remainderman. The ancient rents were reserved generally without entertaining what those rents were. Powers which enlarge the estates of tenants for life are to be taken strictly. The plaintiff is relievable against the assets for breach of covenant. The power is not yet executed. There are cases where this court will not execute these powers. The circumstances must be strong to induce the court to do so. Piggott v. Penrice.[5] If the defendant had hindered the execution of the deeds, equity would have relieved. The defendant claims paramount, and not under the marriage articles. A plaintiff not unprovided for may have relief against the assets. If the plaintiff is relieved against the earl, it is in favor of the heir and executrix of Earl Gilbert.

Browne: The plaintiff is a creditor, not of the defendant, but of Earl Gilbert. There is no equity against the defendant.

Talbot: As to the defendant's claiming as a volunteer, it is indeed under a will, but that was made on a good consideration to support the dignity of the family. He is not a volunteer under the late earl, but under Earl Thomas, under whom the late earl claimed. He had the power to execute or not to execute. That is a contingency which the defendant ought to take the advantage of in this court as well as at law. Under the present circumstances of the estate, it is more agreeable to the support of the family not to execute the power, there being two jointures on the estate.

---

1 Perhaps *Finch v. Earl of Winchelsea* (Ch. 1719), see above, Case No. 408.

2 Stat. 29 Car. II, c. 3 (*SR*, V, 839–842).

3 *Brown v. Barkham* (1717), see above, Case No. 159.

4 *Orby v. Mohun* (1706), 2 Vernon 531, 542, 23 E.R. 944, 951, Precedents in Chancery 257, 24 E.R. 124, 3 Chancery Reports 102, 21 E.R. 741, Gilbert Rep. 45, 25 E.R. 32, 2 Freeman 291, 22 E.R. 1218, 1 Eq. Cas. Abr. 343, 21 E.R. 1090, British Library MS. Hargrave 80, f. 4v.

5 *Piggott v. Penrice* (Ch. 1717), see above, Case No. 167.

It is said the articles are an execution even at law. If so, why do they come here? The covenant is that he or his heirs would settle [the whole]; the whole intent was that it should either come out of the power or out of his own estate. If the heir had settled after his death, it had been a good execution. He did not intend to confine himself to his power. What is the plaintiff a purchaser of? No particular lands are mentioned in the covenant. She is the purchaser only of a right to a jointure of £500 *per annum*.

If there are assets to make good the personal covenant, they should be applied for that purpose.

As to the powers reserved to the party himself in voluntary settlements, they are construed favorably for the owner of the inheritance. This power was not reserved to Earl Thomas, but this is a power annexed to one man's estate to charge the estate of another, which should be taken strictly. There is no instance where the law is in favor of one to take it away for the benefit of another volunteer.

In cases of purchasers, creditors, or children unprovided for, equity will supply a defect of execution of powers. Arundell v. Phillpot,[1] in Bath v. Montague; the tender of a guinea was not supplied in equity. It is different from the present case. *Vide* Smith v. Aston.

First, the power is reserved to the original owner.

Second, the settlement is voluntary [for] a child unprovided for.

Third, there is not a total omission. There was a will made, not sealed.

Fourth, both claim under the same party.

In Hale v. Hale, no judgment was given in it. Lord Nottingham's distinction was that, if the power had been executed but not strictly, the court would supply it implies he would not unless it was attempted to be executed.

In Parker v. Parker, there was a mistaken execution. The deed was not with him. There were two witnesses instead of three in favor of children. The surrender of a copyhold was supplied for children etc. [not] against whomever, only against the heir at law.

In covenants to sell land, the vendor is a trustee for the purchaser. The case of an issue in tail making a mortgage is not carried against the issue. The tenant Gilbert died a tenant in tail for not suffering a recovery. Lower v. Weale; Lanyon v. Williams.[2]

The defendant is not bound by the covenant any more than an issue in tail. Assets are not marshalled in favor of a residuary legatee. Equity does no more

---

1 *Arundel v. Philpot* (1688), 3 Chancery Cases 70, 93, 22 E.R. 972, 986, 2 Freeman 102, 22 E.R. 1085, 2 Vernon 69, 23 E.R. 654, 2 Eq. Cas. Abr. 673, 22 E.R. 565, Lincoln's Inn MS. Misc. 498, p. 87, Lincoln's Inn MS. Misc. 503, p. 111, Lincoln's Inn MS. Misc. 504, p. 102.

2 *Weal v. Lower* (1673–1689), Pollexfen 54, 86 E.R. 509, 2 Freeman 107, 22 E.R. 1089, 1 Eq. Cas. Abr. 266, 21 E.R. 1035; *Lanyon v. Williams* (Ch. 1713), Lincoln's Inn MS. Coxe 89, vol. 3, pt. 2, p. 15.

than the creditors themselves might do. If the question is whether the plaintiff should have relief against a person bound by the covenant or one not bound, equity will determine in favor of the latter.

Solicitor General [*Yorke*], in reply: Unless the plaintiff can have satisfaction for her jointure against the earl, the assets will be exhausted and the plaintiff must lose part. The timber is worth £40,000, which Earl Gilbert might cut.

Objection: that the case have not been upon a non-execution of a power, but upon a defective execution, that the articles are not an execution because the particular lands are not specified. If more had been appointed, it were good *pro tanto*. Articles, in equity, are considered as a conveyance; the engrossment made by the direction of the earl was sufficient before the Statute of Frauds[1] to have amounted to a will, though not signed. The articles and engrossment are to be taken together.

Objection: that the articles are to settle pursuant to the power or otherwise, which may relate to the circumstances or manner of doing it or to the description of the power given by Earl Thomas's will or otherwise. What is the reason why equity should supply defects in executions and not non-executions when, at law, they are the same, for, at law, a defective execution is not an execution? The intention of the parties is the sole reason why equity supplies the one; [it is] the same reason for the other. The distinction is always allowed, where it is upon a valuable consideration and where otherwise.

As to the cases of copyholds, they are voluntary acts. This is a covenant upon a valuable consideration. Though this court will in the first place consider what other provision the party has, not in the latter. Prince v. Chandler in Smith v. Aston; that one reason why jointures are made good against the remainderman is because he claims under the same person who created the power. Orby v. Lord Mohun. Where the power is given to the heir, it is the same as if it were reserved to the ancestor. Where relief has been denied, it has always been where the party was merely a volunteer.

Covenants by tenants in tail are not executed against the issue because it is against the intent of the donor that he should alienate and also against the Statute *de Donis*.[2] There is no case where relief has been denied under the circumstances of this case. Lady Clifford v. Lord Burlington;[3] there was a power for Lord Clifford to settle £1000 *per annum*; he sent to his steward in Ireland to send a particular; it happened that it fell short £200 *per annum*; it was made good against the remainderman by Lord Keeper Wright.

---

1 Stat. 29 Car. II, c. 3 (*SR*, V, 839–842).

2 Stat. 13 Edw. I, Westminster II, c. 1 (*SR*, I, 71).

3 *Lady Clifford v. Earl of Burlington* (1700), 2 Vernon 379, 23 E.R. 841, Gilbert Rep. 167, 25 E.R. 117.

Chesshyre: The plaintiff is a purchaser of the execution of the power. The difficulty of the execution of this power arose from the settlement of the estate by Earl Thomas that the jointure should not be of lands in lease etc.

Lord Chancellor [LORD MACCLESFIELD]: The covenant is that he or his heirs would settle. How can you confine it to him singly? Could not his heirs execute it?

Mead [cited] Lassells v. Lord Cornwallis;[1] there was a power for Lord Cornwallis to charge £6000; he made an execution of the power, but it was by a mortgage for £3000 only, yet the whole was charged on the estate for creditors.

Lord Chancellor [LORD MACCLESFIELD]: The plaintiff has a strong a case as is possible to have her jointure of £500 *per annum*. But how she shall have it is the question. It does not appear whether the heir at law cannot literally perform this covenant. Then the question will be between the heir and the remainderman, which will make a quite different case. This is a case of so great consequence that I cannot be too cautious. I would have the assistance of the judges.

In the meantime, let there be an account of the assets. Then, it will be proper to consider whether the heir would be entitled to come into equity against the remainderman to make good this jointure in case my lady should bring an action against him upon the breach of covenant.

If she can have a satisfaction out of the assets, it will ease the case very much. If not, then the question will come in its full strength whether the plaintiff as a purchaser can affect the remainderman. I cannot effectually decree this estate to my lady but the issue of the defendant may call in question the decree. Therefore, it is better for the plaintiff to have a satisfaction out of the assets.

The great doubt with me is what was the intent of the articles, for there is a latitude for the earl either to execute his power or that his heirs shall make it good. Can the heir execute the power? No. But the other way, the covenant is complete that either he, according to his power, or otherwise his heirs should settle. Either way, the plaintiff could not complain, but the articles had been performed.

I will desire the assistance of the judges.

On 15 May 1724, the Lord Chancellor [LORD MACCLESFIELD], the Master of the Rolls [JEKYLL]. Baron PRICE, and Baron GILBERT were of opinion the power was well executed in equity and decreed the plaintiff to hold the lands according to the deed intended to be executed.

---

[1] *Lasselles v. Lord Cornwallis* (1704), Precedents in Chancery 232, 24 E.R. 113, 2 Vernon 456, 23 E.R. 898, 2 Freeman 279, 22 E.R. 1210, 1 Eq. Cas. Abr. 242, 21 E.R. 1019, 2 Eq. Cas. Abr. 467, 22 E.R. 397.

Lincoln's Inn MS. Misc. 12, p. 45

Thomas, Earl of Coventry, by will dated 24 March 1698[/99], devises lands to trustees and their heirs to the use of his first and other sons by his then wife in tail male, remainder to Thomas, Lord Deverhurst, his son by a former wife, and to his first and other sons in tail male, remainder to is son Gilbert in the like manner, with other remainders over, in which will was a proviso that it should be lawful for any person or persons who, by virtue thereof, should at any time after be seised of the premises by any writing or writings indented under his or their hands and seals to limit and appoint any part of the premises except etc. not exceeding £500 a year to any wife or wives, which such person or persons should marry for her or their respective life or lives for a jointure.

On 24th June 1715, Gilbert, Earl of Coventry, marries the plaintiff, who was the daughter of Sir Streynsham Masters. And, before the marriage, he enters into articles, whereby, in consideration of the marriage and a £10,000 portion, he covenants with Sir Streynsham Masters that he the said earl or his heirs according to the power given him by his father's will for that purpose or otherwise by a good conveyance would settle, limit, or appoint or cause to be settled, limited, or appointed manors, messuages, and lands of £500 a year upon the plaintiff for her jointure to commence in possession after his death if she survived him. And, by the articles, he further agrees that his heirs, after his death, should pay her £250 a year more for her life and that £5000 should be laid out in a purchase of lands and settled as an addition for her jointure.

Soon after the marriage, Earl Gilbert gives the articles to his steward, and he orders him to look into the rent rolls of his estate and see what part thereof might be most conveniently settled. Accordingly, a particular was drawn out and delivered to Sir Streynsham Masters, and he was desired to get a settlement drawn, which was done. But the draught being mislaid, a new one was drawn and engrossed. And it was by a lease and release dated 5 and 6 July 1720, wherein, reciting the will and the articles, the earl, in consideration of the portion, limits and confirms to Sir Streynsham Masters and one Leigh and their heirs divers lands therein particularly mentioned to the use of himself for life, then to the plaintiff, his wife, for life in part of her jointure, and, after her death, the deed is declared to be void.

Soon afterwards, the earl went to the Bath without executing the deed, and in a little time returned again very ill, and, soon afterwards, he died suddenly, having never executed the deed.

A little before his death, he made his will. And all in it which relates to the plaintiff is as follows: 'I give to my wife, besides what is settled on her by our marriage articles £3000.' And then he goes on and gives her several specific legacies, and he made his daughter, Lady Ann Carew, executrix.

The plaintiff now brought her bill to have her settlement made good to her according to her marriage articles. And the question was whether this court would make good the non-execution of a power.

For the plaintiff, it was said she was a purchaser, though not of any particular lands, yet of the execution of the power. The plaintiff purchased all that the earl could grant, and, though this court will not supply non-execution of powers or defective executions in favor of volunteers, yet this court will do it in favor of purchasers. Besides, the articles in a court of equity shall be considered as an execution of the power.

On the other side, it was said this court never does relieve in a case of the non-execution of powers. And, where they have relieved in a case of defective executions of powers, there have been some particular circumstances. The plaintiff is not without a remedy. The covenant in the articles is broken, and she may bring an action at law. Besides, she is not a person unprovided for. She has without the execution of the power a provision almost adequate to her jointure.

Where a man reserves a power to himself upon making a settlement, such a power is to be favorably expounded. But, where there is a power given to one man to charge the estate of another, such a power is always to be taken strictly.

In the Case of Smith and Asheton, cited on the other side, there was a voluntary settlement and the power was reserved to him who made the settlement. There was not in that case a total omission of the execution of the power, so that all that can be collected from that case is that this court has supplied a defective execution of a power in favor of younger children, who are considered in this court in the nature of purchasers or creditors, against one who was a volunteer and claimed under the same settlement. And this, it was said, was as far as the court had gone. In that case, there was an execution of the power by a will, but there wanted the ceremony of sealing.

It is true, where a man seised in fee covenants to sell or mortgages and makes a defective security and dies, this court will carry on the articles or make good the mortgage against the heir at law who claims under the mortgagor.

But, where a tenant in tail covenants to sell or mortgage and receives the money and covenants to suffer a recovery and dies before he does it, this court will never compel the issue in tail who claims *per formam doni* to suffer a recovery and convey to the purchaser or make good the mortgage. It was never done. And it was refused in the Case of Lanyon and Williams, where the tenant in tail lay in the Fleet [Prison] all his lifetime rather than perform a decree whereby he was ordered to suffer a recovery and convey according to his articles.

For the defendant were cited the following cases: Piggot and Penrice, *quod vide, liber* C, 88; Bath v. Mountague, the Duke of Albemarle had a power of revocation by a deed or writing under hand and seal in the presence of six witnesses, whereof three to be of the Privy Council. He makes a will and thereby revokes the settlement, and this will was executed in the presence of six witnesses, but none of them were Privy Councillors, the will being executed at Jamaica, where it was impossible to have such witnesses. It was decreed the revocation was not good.

[Other reports of this case: 2 Peere Williams 222, 24 E.R. 707, Gilbert Rep. 160, 25 E.R. 112, Lincoln's Inn MS. Coxe 89, vol. 3, pt. 2, pp. 9, 30, 1 Comyns 312, 92 E.R. 1088, 9 Modern 12, 88 E.R. 284, 10 Modern 463, 88 E.R. 811, Strange 596, 93 E.R. 722, 1 Eq. Cas. Abr. 348, 21 E.R. 1094, 2 Eq. Cas. Abr. 87, 660, 673, 22 E.R. 75, 555, 565.]

548

Awdley v. Trig

(Ch. 1722)

A court of equity will not order specific performance of a contract where the claimant has not acted in good faith.

Lincoln's Inn MS. Misc. 12, p. 39

27 April 1722.

The defendant lends the plaintiff's brother £800 on a mortgage. And, in the deed, was a covenant from the mortgagor that, if he or his heirs, at any time before the money was paid, should be minded to sell the premises, the defendant should have the first refusal thereof at such price as any other person should be willing to give.

The plaintiff, having contracted to sell the estate to another, brings his bill to redeem. And the defendant brings a cross-bill for a specific performance of the covenant.

Lord Chancellor [Lord Macclesfield] declared there was nothing in itself unreasonable in the covenant, but the defendant had made an ill use of it, as appeared by the proofs, for, though the plaintiff had no counterpart of the mortgage, yet the defendant would not give him a copy, nor did he give the plaintiff any notice of the covenant until he had actually contracted to sell the estate to another. And, besides, the defendant had sent several letters to the plaintiff wherein he offered to take in his money upon six month's notice. And, therefore, the court decreed a redemption.

549

Sherston v. Langworthy

(Ch. 1722)

In this case, under the terms of the settlement in issue, the daughter who was under age, though married, was entitled to receive a maintenance.

Lincoln's Inn MS. Misc. 12, p. 40

27 April 1722.

A term of years was limited by a settlement to trustees upon trust, by the rents and profits or by sale or mortgage, to raise daughters' portions, *viz.*, if but one, £1000 and, if two or more, £1500 to be paid at the age of twenty-one and, upon a further trust, then the trustees should pay and allow for the said daughter or daughters convenient and befitting maintenance suitable to their degree as to the trustees or the survivor should seem meet until such time as the said daughter or daughters should attain twenty-one or be married or her or their portion or portions be raised and paid.

The plaintiff married one of the daughters, and, before she was twenty-one, they bring their bill to have the portion raised. And they pray an allowance for maintenance from the time of the marriage.

Lord Chancellor [Lord Macclesfield] was of opinion the plaintiffs were entitled to have an allowance for maintenance until twenty-one notwithstanding the plaintiffs were married before the plaintiff's wife was twenty-one, for the provision in the settlement that the daughters should have a maintenance until they were twenty-one or married must be understood of a marriage after twenty-one. And the meaning is that maintenance is to be paid the daughters until they attain twenty-one and, afterwards, until the portions are paid unless they marry and, then, the maintenance is to cease.

550

Cocks v. Goodfellow

(Ch. 1722)

Trust assets are not liable for the debts of the trustee.

A debtor can prefer any creditor as to the payment of debts. Thus, an executor can pay to himself the debts the decedent owes to him.

Lincoln's Inn MS. Misc. 11, p. 223

5 May 1722. Cock and others, younger children of Peter Cock, deceased, plaintiffs; Charles Goodfellow *et al.* assignees under a commission awarded against Joanna Cock, the plaintiffs' mother, and the said Joanna and others, defendants.

Peter Cock, the plaintiffs' father, by his will dated 26 August 1712, gave two-thirds of the surplus of his personal estate amongst all his children equally and the remaining third to his wife. And he made his wife and two others executors, and he directed their children's shares to be placed out at interest. The wife only proved the will and possessed the personal estate.

After the testator's death, Mr. Vandermarsh, the plaintiffs' uncle, by his will gave the plaintiffs considerable legacies, and he made the plaintiffs' mother and two others executors. But she only proved that will.

On 25 December 1719, the plaintiffs' mother settled an account with some persons on the plaintiffs' behalf, upon which account it appeared that she was a debtor to the plaintiffs on account of what they were entitled to out of their father's estate and for the legacies given them by their uncle in near £6000 apiece.

The Plaintiffs' mother traded as a merchant for several years after her husband's death in the same manner as he had done, but she happened to fail and stopped payments on the 6th of December 1720. But some little time before she failed, *viz.* on the 17th of October 1720, she made a deed of trust between herself of the one part and the defendants Masham and Cowsmaker of the other part wherein [*blank*] reciting some articles made sometime before upon the marriage of her son, one of the plaintiffs, with Lord Trevor's daughter whereby she had agreed to pay £5000, which was to be laid out in lands with other moneys and settled for the benefit of the son and his wife and the issue of the marriage and reciting that the plaintiffs' mother, in order to make an improvement of the sums due to them had invested the same in the public stocks and other securities, that is to say £4730 Bank stock, £1000 India,[1] £4000 South Sea [Company], and other stocks therein mentioned amounting to £8000 and had subscribed annuities to the South Sea [Company] and that her name was used as trustee for her children and that she had on that day transferred the South Sea and India stock and had agreed to transfer the other stocks and annuities (when they could be transferred) to the said Masham and Cowsmaker in trust and for the benefit of the plaintiffs and for securing the said respective sums owing to them.

It is witnessed that the stocks so transferred and agreed to be transferred were upon trust for securing the moneys respectively due to the plaintiffs and the said £5000 agreed to be paid by the articles and to pay the remainder, if any, to the plaintiffs' mother. And, by the same indentures, there are other estates conveyed as a further security.

Note, before the making of this deed, one Vandermarsh, a merchant in Holland, the plaintiffs' uncle, with whom the plaintiffs' mother had great dealings, wanting money to keep up his credit, sent over his son to the plaintiffs' mother to credit him with £40,000, which she agreed to do. But he, afterwards, failed, which was the chief occasion of the failing of the plaintiffs' mother.

[1] I.e. the East India Company.

The plaintiffs brought their bill against the assignees and trustees to have an execution of the trusts and the benefit thereof.

It was insisted on by the assignees that this deed was made by the plaintiffs' mother but two month before her bankruptcy and at a time when she knew she could not stand and was made in fraud of her other creditors and, therefore, ought not to have the sanction of a court of equity, it being an act of bankruptcy itself within the Statute 1 *Jacobi.*[1]

Lord Chancellor [LORD MACCLESFIELD]: Whoever trusted the bankrupt must know she had only one-third of her husband's estate. The stock now in question, for anything that appears to the contrary, was stock subsisting at the death of the plaintiffs' father or has been placed in the room of stock then subsisting and since sold out.

The directions in the testator's will to place out the children's money at interest must be understood to place it in the funds and not in trade.

The law says a man may give a preference to one creditor before another. He may make a creditor executor, and that will give him a preference. And, if so, why may not a parent give a preference to his children? If they are creditors, are they in a worse condition for being children?

She was under the obligation of nature as well as justice to secure her children. And when she was going to credit her brother with £40,000, which was an act that would risk her estate, was it not reasonable, nay, was it not her duty to secure her children and not risk their fortunes? She had bought stock for her children and mixed it with her own and never declared the trust. But, when she was going to run a risk, she declares the trust. Was not this honest in her so to do? Was it not her duty to do that then which she should have done before?

It is said she knew her own circumstances and that she could not stand it long, and, therefore, she did this with a design to give an undue preference to her children.

I do not know but if a man does really see that he cannot stand and pays one creditor his whole debt but that he may justly do so. I see no injustice in this. It may fall out to be very reasonable to pay some particular creditors, though a man has not sufficient [assets] left to pay the rest.

Upon the whole, I think the deed of trust was very just, very honest, and very honorable.

As to the stock which was agreed to be transferred but was not transferred, the assignees can take this stock no otherwise than the bankrupt herself had it, that is as a trust for the plaintiffs. And, in a court of equity, it must be considered as the plaintiffs' stock.

---

[1] Stat. 1 Jac. I, c. 15 (*SR*, IV, 1031–1034).

The Case of Taylor and Wheeler,[1] cited by Mr. Talbot, where a man had articled for the sale of land and, afterwards, before he had conveyed it, confessed a judgment to a third person, and it was decreed the land was not affected with this judgment, is a very strong case for the plaintiffs. The commissioners [of bankrupts] can assign nothing but what the bankrupt might have assigned, nay, nothing but what the bankrupt could assign honestly. It is true Mrs. Cock might have assigned the legal estate of this stock after she had made the deed of trust. But she could not honestly have assigned it.

The trusts must be executed, and the assignees must transfer the trust stock to the defendants, the trustees, upon the trusts mentioned in Mrs. Cock's deed.

Lincoln's Inn MS. Misc. 506, p. 65, pl. 2

Easter 8 George.

The mother of the plaintiff, who was a trader and had money in her hands belonging to her children, a little before she becomes bankrupt, declares a trust of stock of the South Sea [Company] for the benefit of the children and covenants to transfer it when the books should be opened. But, before that time, she becomes a bankrupt. The bill was brought by the children to have a performance of the trust, which was opposed by the assignees of the Commissioners of Bankrupts, who claimed the stock as the effects of the bankrupt and insisted that the children should come in only as creditors *pro rata*.

Upon the hearing of the cause, the Lord Chancellor [Lord Macclesfield] decreed an execution of the trust. She was executrix of her husband and, by that means possessed of his estate, one-third whereof was given to her and the other two-thirds to the children. She was guardian of the children and, though there were others appointed executors and guardians, yet she was the only acting one. The husband had directed that they should put out the children's money to interest or other improvements upon good security until the children should come of age. Everybody must see that only one-third was her own. It appears that, by 'other improvements' must mean stock or such like and not trade or merchandise. It would not have been right to have employed it so without the consent of the guardians, for that was a risk of another kind. She carries on a great trade, but, at the same time, she had a great deal in the stocks she had in 1720. And, for what appears, it might be what she had before or, on changing the stock, what came in the room of it, it cannot be said that this was fraudulent to make a show of it because everybody must know that she was the guardian to her children and was possessed of what belonged to them. Then the uncle leaves several pecuniary legacies to the children, and she has from time to time answered the interest of them. On the marriage of the son, there is £5000 paid down to be laid out in

[1] *Taylor v. Wheeler* (1706–1709), 2 Salkeld 449, 91 E.R. 388, 2 Vernon 564, 23 E.R. 968, 1 Eq. Cas. Abr. 122, 312, 21 E.R. 928, 1068.

lands and she covenants to settle £100 *per annum* more. Then her brother in Holland comes into distress. His son comes over to borrow £40,000 pretending that, though he had not the money, yet he had effects sufficient. She gives credit to this and accepts her brother's notes to that value, from whence it is argued that, at the time of the declaration, she did not expect her brother would fail. However, though she was willing to risk her own, yet she thought she ought not to risk her children's money. And, therefore, she invests it in stock and declares that it is in trust for them. It happens that the thing does not succeed; her brother broke, and that ruined her. At this time, she transfers all she could and, reciting that she has stock, covenants to transfer the stock when the books should be opened. But, before she transfers the stock according to the covenants, she is a bankrupt. This is not a trust without a valuable consideration. The case of Taylor and Miller[1] was the same, only with this difference, that the money was advanced at the time of the deed and an inchoation of a legal estate, a surrender and no admittance, for the assignees must stand in the place of the bankrupt and take the land subject to the same conditions and charges, not because a surrender is a partial conveyance, for a partial conveyance is no conveyance at all, but it is only evidence of an agreement. What the bankrupt could not do, what he could not honestly do, the assignees cannot do. There was another case in Lord Cowper's time, Finch and Lord Winchester,[2] which received the same determination though no [there was] inchoation of a legal estate.

But it is insisted on that this deed of trust is not only fraudulent, but an act of bankruptcy itself. And it is founded on a clause in the Stat. of Jac. I, c. [*blank*].[3] But to bring it within that, it must be fraudulent and to defeat creditors of their just debts. Now this is to pay, not to defeat creditors. But it is said this is to prefer creditors and the preferring of some is the defeating of others. I do not know how this comes to be said. The law is contrary; by law, a man may make any of his creditors his executor and he may prefer himself. This the law does of itself so that to say this is unjust is to condemn the law. Nay, by law, the executor may prefer whom he will. It is true this court sometimes interposes by way of prevention because it may be an inlet to fraud, but, when once it is done, this court never interposes. This court never hinders an executor from paying himself because, the goods vesting in him immediately, it is an actual payment. Giving a security cannot be more a preference than actual payment. It is true, where a security is private and secret, it may be deemed fraudulent because it is probable that it may not be a just and fair debt.

But it is said these are her children. Is that an objection? Surely, the argument is the other way; their being children is a reason why they should be taken care of, but their having a double debt, both of nature and contract, ought not to

1 *Taylor v. Wheeler* (1706–1709), *ut supra*.

2 *Finch v. Earl of Winchelsea* (1719), see above, Case No. 408.

3 Stat. 1 Jac. I, c. 15 (*SR*, IV, 1031–1034).

hurt them. If a father devises copyhold lands to younger children, this court will decree the heir to surrender. They are called creditors and are upon an equal foot with the heir. It is true the court will not let the natural debt of children overrule that of creditors. But, when they stand on an equal foot of justice with others, surely their being children ought not to prejudice them. Suppose another person owed them money and was going to run a risk of his estate, would it not be the mother's duty to demand security for the children's debts at all events? And if it was her duty to demand it of another, was it wrong to do it herself? I do not know but there might be the same objection if she had done it upon going on a long voyage. Besides, to speak accurately, she has transferred over to the children not what was hers, but theirs, who are indeed creditors, but it is for their own estate. If she has paid her debts with it, she has done wrong and more than the creditors had reason to expect. If she really laid out the money in stock and intended it all along for them, though she had not declared it, yet she was but a trustee and it was what she ought to have done and the declaration of trust afterwards was only a declaration that she had not broken her trust before.

It is objected that the surplus is reserved for herself. That was right because the trust was not of land. It is objected that it is not said at what price she bought the stock; that is indeed a defect, but not such a one as to make the deed void. But, if a person did see that he cannot stand his ground, I do not see why he may not pay whom he will. There may or there may not be injustice. But surely there is no injustice when I pay a man whom I have made a creditor in spite of his teeth; he could not call upon me as another might. It is plain to me that she thought she could stand, else she would not have paid the £40,000 for him, but that she was persuaded, by the assistance thereof, her brother would stand. What she did was only prudent when she was going to run a risk.

The trustees were decreed to perform the trust.

[Other reports of this case: 10 Modern 489, 88 E.R. 822, 2 Eq. Cas. Abr. 100, 448, 22 E.R. 85, 382.]

[Related cases: Cocks' Case (Ch. 1723), see below, Case No. 584.]

551

Fielding v. Fielding

(Ch. 1722)

In this case, the custody of minor children was taken away from their father, who had come under the influence of his second wife, a Roman Catholic, who was attempting to convert her step-children away from Protestantism.

British Library MS. Hargrave 83, p. 21

Trinity term, 28 May 1722.

Colonel Fielding married a daughter of Justice Gould without his consent, but, afterwards, he was reconciled to the marriage and made a settlement for the benefit of his daughter and her children. The judge died, and his daughter died. Colonel Fielding married another wife, who was a Papist. My Lady Gould, grandmother of the children by the first venter, brought a bill in their behalf, the end of which was principally to have the children of the first marriage removed from under the influence of the Colonel's present wife, who was a Roman Catholic.

The proofs on the part of the plaintiffs were that the Colonel had expressed a favorable opinion of the manner in which children were educated in Roman Catholic countries, that since his marriage with this lady, he had left off the public rejoicings, which he used to make at his house in the country upon the king's birthday, and this was inferred to have been done by the influence of his wife. It was also in proof that the oldest son, who was about the age of fourteen and at Eton School, had used some suspicious expressions that looked as if he had been tampered with as to his religion. One instance was he put this question to one who talked to him of the Church of England where it was before the Reformation. This, My Lord said, was the very spirit of Popery and made this comparison to it. It is, says he, as if it should be asked where was the face before it was washed and shaved this morning.

There had likewise been an attempt to remove the young children, the daughters of the marriage, from Salisbury School to some place in Dorsetshire, which abounded with Roman Catholics, or at least they had been carried to make a visit in those parts.

The proofs for the defendant were in his answer declared that he was a Protestant and intended to continue so and to have his children bred up in that religion. It was proved that he had said that he would rather have their bones broken than that they should be Papists, that he had been a kind father to them, and that even the children of the second marriage had been christened by Protestant divines. It was argued that this suit was spirited up by Lady Gould and an aunt of the children because they were displeased at the second match and were angry the sole management and government of the Colonel's family was taken out of their hands since he married and that they had used very indecent words concerning the father to his own children, that it was time to take the daughters from school and introduce them to company, that the visit into Dorsetshire was not made upon the account that had been suggested, but was to some friends or relations that lived there, that the usual rejoicings upon public occasions were not omitted, but only the bonfire was removed to a greater distance from the house for the advantage of an higher eminence.

N.B. There was an offer made by the aunt of the children in court to settle £600 upon them, provided they might be removed from under the influence of their mother-in-law.

The counsel for the defendant touched very tenderly upon most parts of the defense and did not much press the paternal right.

My Lord Chancellor [Lord Macclesfield] observed that it was not decent that a commander of His Majesty's forces, a colonel of a regiment, should marry a Papist, and more indecent that, after he had made this false step, he should be averse to the securing of his children's education in the Protestant religion and should still insist to have them under the influence of his wife, an influence which it was plain was not little since it had induced him, though still in His Majesty's service, to omit, or at least to lessen and remove out of his wife's sight the rejoicings he used to make on public occasions. This, he thought, had an ill aspect, though he could not say public rejoicings with bonfires etc. was a duty incumbent upon all that were employed by the government, yet he thought them decent and respectful, but perhaps they were omitted by the Colonel for the sake of domestic peace. He urged it was plain that the sons had been tampered with and said he would not stay until the stroke was struck and the daughters removed into a nunnery. And therefore, he decreed that the children should for the present continue where they were at Eton and Salisbury, but should not go to their father's house at any time when their mother-in-law or any of her Roman Catholic servants were there.

The counsel proposed that some of the Colonel's relations of My Lord Radnor's family might take care of the children.

My Lord said, no doubt, the court would readily hearken to that if it should be offered but with restrictions as to their going home or being under the influence of their mother-in-law. Liberty was given to resort back for further directions.

552

Binks v. Metcalfe

(Ch. 1722)

In this case, an arbitral award was set aside and the defendant and the arbitrators were ordered to pay court costs.

British Library MS. Hargrave 83, p. 25

Trinity term 1722.

The plaintiff brought his bill to be relieved against an award made upon a bond of £10 in which he was bound to the defendant Metcalfe, and he made the arbitrators parties to his bill. It appeared upon the face of the award that the arbitrators had awarded £32 14s. for the £10 and interest due upon it for about two years, for the award was thus. First, they awarded that sum to be paid to the defendant by the plaintiff, and then they awarded that each party should bear his own costs and charges both at law and in equity in this court. It was also in proof that one of the arbitrators struck one of the plaintiff's witnesses.

The Master of the Rolls [JEKYLL] sitting in court decreed the award to be set aside and costs to be paid by the defendant Metcalfe and the arbitrators.

553

Douglass v. Douglass

(Ch. 1722)

A testator cannot bequeath his wife's paraphernalia.

Lincoln's Inn MS. Misc. 11, p. 222

22 June 1722.

Bley Douglass, by will, gave the defendant, his wife, all his plate and jewels for her life and, after her death, directed the same should go to the plaintiff, his only child, and, if the plaintiff died without issue, the jewels and plate should go to his brother, Robert Douglass, another defendant, whom he made executor.

It was decreed by Lord Chancellor [LORD MACCLESFIELD] that the wife should retain the paraphernalia to her own use.

Bley, by his will, did also devise all his real estate to his said brother after the death of the defendant, his wife, and the plaintiff without issue.

[There was] no estate to the wife by implication, but the whole rents were decreed to be brought before a Master and put out at interest for the plaintiff's benefit.

554

Milner v. Petit

(Ch. 1722)

Great-grandmothers and uncles are in equal degree of relationship to take by the Statute of Distributions.

Lincoln's Inn MS. Misc. 13, p. 9

27 June 1722.

After time was taken to consider of this case, SIR JOSEPH JEKYLL, Master of the Rolls, gave his opinion, having, as he said, taken the advice of a learned doctor of the civil law, *viz.* that upon the Statute of Distribution,[1] the great grandmother and the uncle are in equal degree to the intestate, *viz.* each three degrees from the intestate, that is to say, from the intestate to his father is one degree, from his father to his grandfather two degrees, and from the grandfather to the great grandmother three degrees. In like manner, from the intestate to his uncle

[1] Stat. 22 & 23 Car. II, c. 10 (*SR*, V, 719–720).

are three degrees, *viz.* from the intestate to his father is one degree, from the father to the grandfather two degrees, and from the grandfather to his son, the intestate's uncle, is three degrees, which proves that the great grandmother and the uncle are in equal degree and shall equally share the intestate's estate.

By the same way of reasoning, he said that the intestate's brother and his grandfather or grandmother are in equal degree, though he said this had not been determined.

Also he said there was no difference whether the grandfather or the grandmother were of the father's or the mother's side; they should both take equally; and also [he said] that the lineal descendants, though never so remote, shall be preferred before the ascendants, the descendants being from the loins of the intestate.

Lincoln's Inn MS. Misc. 11, p. 216, pl. 1

Between the seals after Trinity term 1722.

It was determined by the Master of the Rolls [Jekyll] after he had taken time to consider of it that a great-grandmother and an uncle were in equal degree to take by the Statute of Distributions.[1]

555

Lane v. Wroth

(Ch. 1722)

Where executors are given legacies, they are trustees for the next of kin and are not residuary legatees.

Lincoln's Inn MS. Misc. 107, f. 89

28 June 1722.

Mrs. Worley, the widow and relict of Humphrey Worley, by her will in August 1712 makes the defendants her executors and gives [them] £100 apiece for their care and trouble. And, at her death, which happened lately, there appeared to be about £900 surplus, which was not disposed of. And the question was whether this should go to the executors or whether it should be distributable.

It was said for the plaintiff that, if the executors were to have the surplus, then this £100 would be given them for their care and pains for themselves, which would be absurd.

And the defendants' counsel, after the late resolutions, said, unless they could distinguish this case from them, [they] had very little to offer.

[1] Stat. 22 & 23 Car. II, c. 10 (*SR*, V, 719–720).

And the distinctions they took being very immaterial, My Lord Chancellor [Lord Macclesfield] decreed the executors to account. And he said this case was rather stronger than any of the former, that the executors were to have only their £100 apiece, and he said it was directly within the case of Forster v. Munt[1] and other cases.

556

Dorison v. Westbrook

(Ch. 1722)

A court of equity will not give an equitable remedy to enforce a harsh contract.

2 Eq. Cas. Abr. 161, 22 E.R. 137

Trinity term 8 Geo.

Lord Macclesfield: [There was a] bill for a specific performance of a contract for £1000 York Buildings stock, at £105 percent. It was dismissed for that a court of equity will not carry these sorts of contracts into execution, but leave the parties to their remedy at law for the difference. But, no costs [were given] because the defendant's answer was falsified in several particulars.

557

Bluck v. Nicholls

(Ch. 1722)

In this case, the defendants were protected by an act of Parliament for investing their client's money in the South Sea Company.

Lincoln's Inn MS. Misc. 12, p. 72

Peter Bluck v. Nicholls, Fowler, and Wanley, goldsmiths and partners.

The plaintiff, in August 1718, left some lottery orders at the defendants' shop in order that the interest thereon might be received as it became due, and he took a receipt from a servant in the shop in the words following, *viz.* 'August 28, 1718, received of Mr. Peter Bluck £1020 princ. Lottery 1714 to account for on demand, for my master, G.W. etc. /s/ *E.W.*' And on the side of the receipt were written the numbers and courses of the several orders and the principal sums payable thereon. The interest was accordingly received and £50 principal on one of the orders which became due, all which was accounted for to the plaintiff 6 October 1719.

[1] *Foster v. Munt* (1689), 1 Vernon 473, 23 E.R. 598, 1 Eq. Cas. Abr. 243, 21 E.R. 1020, 2 Eq. Cas. Abr. 433, 443, 22 E.R. 368, 378, Dodd 78, Chancery Cases *tempore* Jac. II, 368.

On 4 August 1720, the defendants, without any order from the plaintiff, subscribed the orders into the South Sea [Company] stock in the plaintiff's name.

On 20 and 24 August 1720, the plaintiff was at the defendants' shop and received some running cash, but the defendants or any of their servants said nothing to the plaintiff then that his orders were subscribed.

The defendants, by answer, insist that they subscribed the orders pursuant to a late Act of Parliament[1] for the plaintiff's benefit and believe they had the plaintiff's orders for so doing (but of this there was no proof). And they insist that, as the orders were subscribed in the plaintiff's name, and, as he only could have had the benefit of the subscription, he ought to bear the loss.

There was no proof on the defendants' part when the plaintiff had first notice of the subscription. But there was a pretty strong proof on the plaintiff's part (as far as negative proof can go) that the plaintiff had no notice of the subscription until 25 January 1720[/21].

Upon the whole matter, the Master of Rolls [Jekyll], in the absence of the Lord Chancellor, was of the opinion that the defendants were trustees within the words of the late Act of Parliament which indemnifies trustees, guardians, etc. who should subscribe annuities etc. into the South Sea Company pursuant to the Act. And, therefore, he dismissed the plaintiff's bill, but without costs.

558

Taylor v. Hardman

(Ch. 1722 x 1725)

In this case, the court found that the bequest in issue was a gift to the widow, though subject to the payment of debts and legacies, and it was not a bare power to the executrix.

Lincoln's Inn MS. Misc. 12, p. 85

John Taylor, plaintiff; John Hardman *et al.*, defendants.

William Taylor makes his will dated 8 January 1712[/13] and, thereby, devises the land in question in the words following, *viz.*:

> Item, I give and devise unto Alice, my loving wife, and to her heirs forever all my lands and tenements in Normanton in the County of Nottingham to be sold, and my will is that the moneys to be raised by such sale to be assets in my executrix's hands and to come in aid of my personal [estate] towards the payment of my legacies above mentioned.

[1] Stat. 6 Geo. I, c. 4.

And then, he goes on and gives all the rest and residue of his goods, chattels, and personal estate whatsoever unto the said Alice, his wife. And he made her executrix.

The wife died soon after her husband and before she had proved the will. And the defendants took administration to the wife and administration *cum testamento annexo* to the husband.

The plaintiff is cousin and heir of the testator, and he brings his bill for an account of the personal estate and that the lands devised to the wife or so much as shall remain after payments of the legacies may be conveyed to him, he insisting that, after the payment of the legacies, there was a resulting or implied trust for the heir at law.

The defendants, by answer, admitted there were personal assets sufficient to pay all the debts and legacies, but they insisted that, the lands being by the will directed to be sold and to be assets in the hands of the executrix, it ought in a court of equity to be considered as personal estate and then it will belong to the defendants as the representatives of the wife. But, if it is considered as land, it will then belong to the defendant Hardman as heir at law of the testator's wife, it being by the will devised to her and her heirs.

The cause was heard by Baron GILBERT at the Rolls Chapel, who was of the opinion that, if this had been a bare power to sell for the payment of debts and legacies, the surplus of the lands, after the debts and legacies paid, would have belonged to the heir. But, here, the lands are expressly given to the wife and her heirs and there being no words in the will whereby it appears that it was the testator's intention his wife should not have the land after the legacies paid, he thought a court of equity ought not to take the land from the wife and give it to the heir. He decreed the bill to be dismissed.

559

Bucknall v. Hamond

(Ch. 1722)

Anyone is at liberty to bring a bill in the name of an infant as prochein ami*; however, where an infant is a defendant, he must defend by a guardian* ad litem *who must be admitted by the court.*

An infant when he or she comes of age or those who claim under him or her need not sue a bill of review to reverse a decree made during minority, but it can be impeached by an original bill.

Where a case in a court of equity is stated for the opinion of the common law judges or the common law judges are called into a court of equity to give their assistance on the arguing of a cause, the court of equity is not bound by the opinion of the judges.

Where a judgment has been given at common law by the common law judges in their own court, a court of equity is bound thereby as a matter of res judicata.

An heir at law should not be disinherited but by express words in a will or by a necessary implication.

A remainder must be supported by a particular estate.

A perpetuity is a void estate.

British Library MS. Hargrave 81, f. 176

Monday, 29 October 1722 in court before the Master of the Rolls [JEKYLL].

Thomas Kane, in pursuance of articles made on the marriage of Mary, his wife, in 1673, having laid out the sum of £1600, part of the sum of £2000, in the purchase of an estate in Woolwich in the County of Kent and settled the same to the use of himself for life, remainder to Mary, his wife, for her life, remainder to his own right heirs, does afterwards in 1676 make his last will and testament in writing wherein he devises in these words, 'as to my estate at Woolwich, my wife is to have it for her life and, after her death, it does of right go to my daughter Elizabeth [being his only child], provided she have heirs and, if she dies before her mother Mary and without heirs and my wife Mary should marry again and have an heir male, I give my said estate to such heir male and his heirs'. And he dies without laying out the residue of the money.

Mary, the widow, marries a second husband, by whom she has issue, the defendant, her son, in 1686. Mary, the mother, in her own right and as *prochein ami* to Elizabeth, her daughter, then an infant, brings her bill in this court to have the remaining £400 laid out in a purchase of lands and settled pursuant to the articles and will of Thomas Kane. And a decree was pronounced accordingly, and the Master was to settle the conveyance. And, thereupon, the lands in question lying in Essex were purchased and settled to the use of Mary for life, remainder to Elizabeth, the daughter, and the heirs of her body, remainder to the heirs male of the body of Mary, her mother, remainder to the right heirs of Thomas Kane in fee. After this purchase, Mary, the mother, dies. And, in 1717, Elizabeth, the daughter, dies without issue and unmarried. And the plaintiffs, being heirs at law to Elizabeth, brought their [action of] ejectment at law for the estate at Woolwich.

And, upon the trial, a case was made and stated for the opinion of the judges of the King's Bench, who, after two solemn arguments, did all unanimously give their opinions for the plaintiff as to the Woolwich estate, that the devise was not sufficient to pass any estate to the heirs male of the body of Mary or to Mary in tail male, first, for that there was no precedent estate to support it as a remainder, for that there was no estate before given to Mary or Elizabeth, but it was only a recital of what estates they had before by the settlement and no remainder can be without a particular estate to support it; secondly, this could not be good by way of executory devise, first, for that the first contingency on which it was to take place never happened, for Elizabeth did not die before her mother but survived her, and, as to the other, admitting the limitation were taken to be on the death of Elizabeth without heirs of her body, this was too remote to support or make it good as an executory devise because it was to take place after an estate tail, which by possibility might continue forever and, therefore, to construe it to be good that way would be to make it a direct perpetuity, which the law could not allow of. And, therefore, the Court of King's Bench gave their judgment unanimously that this was a void devise to Mary or the heirs male of her body and, consequently, that the lessors of the plaintiff in ejectment had a good title.

And now this bill was brought to have a conveyance of the other estate in Essex and an account of the profits from the death of Elizabeth and the deeds and writings to be delivered up to the plaintiffs. The defendant pleaded the settlement made pursuant to the decree in 1686 and that he claimed as heir male of the body of Mary.

And, upon arguing the plea, it was ordered to stand for an answer and the benefit thereof saved to the hearing.

And now, upon the hearing, it was insisted on for the defendant that there had been a decree already in this cause, that this was signed and enrolled, and that the settlement now in question was made in pursuance of that decree, and, therefore, if they would impeach it, they ought to have brought their bill of review, and that no attempt of this kind was ever yet made to impeach a decree by an original bill.

But, to this, it was answered and resolved by the court that this bill was brought by the plaintiffs who claimed as heirs at law to Elizabeth, the daughter, that Elizabeth, the daughter, was then an infant and the bill [was] brought by her mother as her *prochein ami*, that anyone was at liberty to bring a bill in the name of an infant as *prochein ami* though, where an infant was defendant, he must defend by guardian who must be admitted by the court, that bills of this kind might be brought by collusion and to the prejudice of the infant as it was plainly done in the present case, and, therefore, there was no need of a bill of review to reverse this decree but it might be impeached by an original bill by the infant herself when she came of age or by those who claimed under her, as the bill was brought by collusion to have such kind of relief, which relief was injurious to the infant, as it plainly was in the present case, and, therefore, several bills of this kind had been allowed without a bill of review.

And, as to the principal point, it was insisted on for the defendant that, notwithstanding the judgment in the King's Bench, this court was not bound to give the same judgment, that this court was to give judgment according to their own conscience and so did my Lord Chancellor Nottingham in the Duke of Norfolk's Case[1] against the opinion of the three chiefs, who assisted him, and so they might do where a case was sent to the judges for their opinion. Yet, if this

[1] *Howard v. Duke of Norfolk* (1681), 1 Vernon 163, 23 E.R. 388, 3 Chancery Cases 1, 22 E.R. 931, 2 Swanston 454, 36 E.R. 690, Pollexfen 223, 86 E.R. 568, 2 Chancery Reports 229, 21 E.R. 665, 2 Freeman 72, 80, 22 E.R. 1066, 1070, 79 Selden Soc. 904, 922, 999, Dodd 42, Oxford Bodleian Library MS. Rawlinson C.347.

court did not concur in the same opinion, they were not concluded by the opinion of the judges, that my Lord Chancellor had so declared. But, on Saturday last, where a case had been sent to the judges of the King's Bench for their opinion and though they were all unanimous in it, yet My Lord Chancellor, being of a different opinion, had ordered it to be spoken to and precedents to be searched how far he was bound by their opinion; so, in the present case, notwithstanding the judgment of the King's Bench, yet this court had pronounced a different decree that they were at liberty so to do and, therefore, the former decree and the settlement made in pursuance of it ought to stand, that this might be supported by very good reasons, for, if the estate to Mary for life with a remainder to Elizabeth in tail might be construed as new original devises, then there was a sufficient foundation whereon to support the remainder to the heirs male of the body of Mary, but, if these were only to be taken as a recital of those estates, then the devise to the heirs male of the body of Mary must be void for want of a particular estate to support it and as an executory devise for the remoteness of it that, therefore, the court would lay hold of that construction which would best support it rather than the will should be void. And so they had done in the present case. And, therefore, the decree ought to stand and the settlement made in pursuance of it.

But the Master of the Rolls [JEKYLL] was clearly of opinion that, though, where a case is stated for the opinion of the judges or the judges are called in to give their assistance on the arguing of a cause, this court is not bound by the opinion of the judges in either of those cases. Yet, where judgment has been given at law in their own courts, this court is not at liberty to alter the law as it has been so declared by the judges. But, in the present case, he said he was of the same opinion with the Court of King's Bench.

First, for that it was an undoubted maxim of law that the heir at law should not be disinherited but by express words or a necessary implication, that here were no express words for that purpose nor was there any necessary implication, for the first part of the will is only a narrative or declaration or a recital how the estate stood limited by the settlement and, therefore, no necessity to construe it to be a devise of those estates to his wife and daughter, that, though it is true, by reason of the fee simple in him, he might have made such devise, yet here appears no intention whatsoever to that purpose much less any such devises by necessary implication. Then, if this was nothing but a recital or narrative how the estate stood, the first original devise was to Mary, his wife, but that could not be good as a remainder for want of a particular estate to support it nor as an executory devise, because Elizabeth survived her mother or, if she had not yet for the remoteness of the contingency on which it was to take place being after a failure of heirs of the body of Elizabeth which possibly might never be and, therefore, to support such an executory devise would be a direct perpetuity, but, besides, he said the lands in the present case were not at all under the influence of the will, being not then purchased nor until long after his death and, therefore, they rested wholly upon the articles, not upon the will.

And so he decreed the defendants to execute a conveyance to the plaintiff. And it was observed as an instance of the collusion in obtaining the former decree and settlement that, by the will, the estate was to go to the heir male of the body of Mary and his heirs by way of purchase, whereas the settlement, as it was contrived, was to Mary and the heirs male of her body whereby she had given herself an estate tail, which was never intended.

[Other copies of this report: British Library MS. Hargrave 82, f. 187.]

560

Powell v. Hankey and Cox

(Ch. 1722)

Where a married woman consents to her husband's receiving the income from her separate estate, this is considered as a gift to him.

However, if the husband alienates the principal assets of his wife's separate estate, he or his personal representative must account for it.

British Library MS. Hargrave 81, f. 183

Wednesday, 31 October 1722, in court.

A widow, being seised of lands in her own right, upon her second marriage, with the consent of her intended husband, settles the same on trustees in trust to permit her to receive the rents and profits thereof to her own separate use during the coverture and wherewith her husband was to have no intermeddling power or control and that her receipts should be a sufficient discharge for the same. The marriage takes effect. And the husband, for ten years together, receives the rents and profits of this estate without any opposition from the wife or her trustees. And now, after his death, the widow brought this bill against his executors to have an account and satisfaction for the rents and profits of her estate so received by her husband upon the pretense, during his lifetime, she dared not interrupt him in the receipt thereof for fear of disobliging him and raising a quarrel between them.

But it was sworn and proved in the cause that they had lived well together from the time of the marriage to the husband's death, that he had never used any severity toward her, and, therefore, this silence or acquiescence of her was looked upon as a gift in law or a consent of the wife to her husband's receiving the same and she had the benefit thereof by being supported and maintained thereout by her husband and, whatever unwillingness she might be under to mention it herself to her husband, yet she might have complained thereof to the trustees and they would then have interposed therein and prevented or forbidden the husband to have received any more. But nothing of this kind appeared in the cause. And then, if a wife who has such a separate estate might sit still and let the husband receive the profits of it for ten or twenty years together without interrupting and afterwards call him or his executors to an account for the same, this might prove an utter ruin to them, for, though in respect of this separate estate, she is considered as a *feme sole*, yet, if she thinks fit to waive her power and suffer the husband to receive the profits of her estate, she is bound thereby and has had the benefit thereof by her being maintained and provided for by her husband. But as to any moneys raised by her husband on the sale of any part thereof for fines or admittance to copyhold estates part thereof, he and his representatives are accountable and must make her satisfaction for the same.

And accordingly, the decree was.

[Other copies of this report: British Library MS. Hargrave 82, f. 192.]

[Other reports of this case: 2 Peere Williams 82, 24 E.R. 649, 2 Eq. Cas. Abr. 151, 724, 22 E.R. 129, 610.]

561

Voughton v. Boley

(Ch. 1722)

A contract to purchase and settle lands does not create a lien on any land where the contract is not performed.

British Library MS. Hargrave 81, f. 185

Tuesday, 6 November, at the Rolls.

A man, upon the marriage of his daughter in 1681, entered into articles whereby he covenanted and agreed for himself, his executors, and administrators to pay to the father of the intended husband the sum of £3000 to be by him laid out in a purchase of lands to be settled to the use of the intended husband for life, remainder to the wife for life, remainder to the heirs of the body of the wife by the husband to be begotten, with the last remainder to the right heirs of the husband. The marriage takes effect, and they have issue, one son, named John. Then the husband dies. In 1684, the wife's father purchases the lands in question, which, as it was proved in the cause, cost him just £300. Afterwards, in 1685, the father makes a settlement of those lands by indenture whereby it is witnessed that, for settling and assuring of the lands and tenements after mentioned pursuant to articles made upon the marriage of Ann, his daughter, with Christopher Voughton, he grants and conveys the lands to the use of his said daughter, Ann, for her life without impeachment of waste, remainder to John, the son, and the heirs of his body, with the last remainder to the right heirs of the said Ann. After this, John, the son, dies an infant and without issue, and Ann, his mother, marries one Farmer, who, by fine or other conveyances, sold these lands to Cradock and Bacon, and they to others until, at last, they came to the defendants.

And this bill was brought by the plaintiff as cousin and heir at law to Christopher Voughton, the husband, in order to have a conveyance of these lands as heir at law to the husband in regard, by the articles, the last remainder was to have been limited to his right heirs. It appeared by the answers of some of the defendants [and] also by proofs in the cause that Farmer, before his joining in the sale to Cradock and Bacon, had with the assistance of some others got these articles and cut them to pieces, but the pieces were afterwards got together and sown with a needle and thread so that they were now produced in court and were legible. But Cradock and Bacon and all the other purchasers expressly swore that they never saw the articles nor had any other notice of them than as they were mentioned in the settlement in 1685, which the plaintiff's counsel insisted was notice sufficient that there were such articles, and, therefore, they, at their peril, were bound to have seen to the terms and limitations of these articles and consequently ought to be affected with them.

But the Master of the Rolls [Jekyll] said there was no color in the world for it, for here there was no agreement on the father's part to purchase these particular lands with the £300 so that there was no lien on these lands. Nay, there was no covenant by the father to purchase any lands at all with the £300, but he was to pay the £300 to the husband's father, who was therewith to purchase lands and make the settlement, so that he, not paying the money according to his covenant, was guilty of a breach of covenant only, for which his personal estate must answer, that he had not covenanted for himself and his heirs and, therefore, his real estate could not be bound or affected thereby, that this settlement, though it was recited to be in pursuance of the articles, yet being really different from them was no performance at all of the articles but must be looked upon as a voluntary settlement by him on his daughter, which he was at liberty to make notwithstanding the articles which he still stood bound to perform, that the covenant for payment of the £300 made no specific lien on the money, for money had no earmark whereby to be known, that, therefore, this settlement, not being pursuant to the articles, though it is expressly recited to be so, was no performance of his covenant but a voluntary settlement of so much more on his daughter and then, if the defendants, at the times of their several purchases, had actually seen and read over the articles, yet they might have safely proceeded in the purchase of these lands, which were not settled pursuant to the articles and, consequently, not at all bound or affected by the articles.

So he decreed an account to be taken of the personal estate of the wife's father against his representatives, who were likewise defendants, and that to be applied as far as it would go towards satisfying the plaintiff for this breach of covenant, the £300 having never been paid or laid out pursuant to the articles.

And the Master of the Rolls [Jekyll] was of opinion that, if this could have been called a settlement pursuant to the articles, that the purchaser would not at his peril have been bound to have seen the articles themselves but might very well have trusted to this settlement, which was said to be in pursuance of articles, and, if it should be otherwise, great inconvenience might happen by the loss of the articles etc. as they are not often times preserved with any great care when a settlement comes to be made.

[Other copies of this report: British Library MS. Hargrave 82, f. 194, Lincoln's Inn MS. Misc. 107, f. 91.]

562

Bruton v. Bruton

(Ch. 1722)

Court costs will not be awarded to an heir who contested a will and was thereupon ordered to join in a deed.

British Library MS. Hargrave 83, p. 26, pl. 1

Monday, 19 November 1722, or Tuesday, 20 November 1722, at the Rolls.

A. brought his bill and by it made his case such that it appeared by his own witnesses that there was very great reason to doubt whether a will under which he claimed a devise of lands was duly executed or not. The heir at law insisted to have a trial *devisavit vel non* as he had a right to do. And it was found a good will and well executed. And now the heir was decreed to join in a conveyance of the lands devised.

His counsel asked that he might have his costs at law as well as his costs in this court to which he is entitled by the course of the court if he joins in the conveyance.

His Honor [JEKYLL] said he had never known costs at law given but in one instance[1] when the heir at law contested the will and that was upon collateral circumstances and outside and it would be of very ill consequence to make more precedents of this kind and would induce every heir at law to contest every will that was made to his prejudice.

[1] [In margin:] I think it was the case of the Duke of Devonshire and Kent; query.

563

Vandepot v. Cock

(Ch. 1722)

Property in the hands of a factor cannot be reached by the creditors of the factor.

Lincoln's Inn MS. Misc. 11, p. 227, pl. 2

21 November 1722.

The plaintiff consigns whalebone from Holland to the defendant, Mrs. Cock, as his factor. She sells them upon credit and delivers bills of parcels in her own name. And before all the money was paid, she becomes a bankrupt. But, before her bankruptcy, she sends an account of sales to the plaintiff, wherein she charges him with a commission at 2 percent and makes him a debtor for the outstanding debts, which she says are upon his risk.

And the plaintiff brings his bill against the assignees [in bankruptcy] who claimed these debts and against the persons from whom they were owing.

It was agreed by the counsel for the assignees that, if there had been no other dealings between the plaintiff and Mrs. Cock, he would certainly have been entitled to these debts, but there were other dealings subsequent and an open account between them, and, after the sale of the whalebone, there was a time when, if the account was balanced, it would appear she had remitted to him near the amount of the outstanding debts. But it appearing likewise that, after that time, he had remitted to her several other sums of money so that, at the time of the bankruptcy, she was considerably in his debt, the plaintiff was decreed to have the money out of court, which the debtors had brought in upon a bill of interpleader, together with his costs to be paid out of the bankrupt's effects.

564

Hillier v. Hillier

(Ch. 1722)

A court of equity will not supply the want of a surrender of a copyhold in favor of younger children where the heir at law was wholly disinherited.

Lincoln's Inn MS. Misc. 11, p. 228

30 November 1722.

It was adjudged by the Master of the Rolls [Jekyll] that this court will not supply the want of a surrender in favor of younger children where the heir at law appears to be wholly disinherited. But he said, if there was any provision made for the eldest son, though it was less than what was given to the younger children, this court would supply the want of a surrender in that case and would not examine into the proportions or quantum of what was left to the children, for the parent was the best judge of that. But, where no provision at all was made for the eldest son, if this court should aid the want of a surrender, it would be to turn the eldest son abegging to help the other children.

565
Whitchurch v. Whitchurch

(Ch. 1722–1725)

A remainderman who has a vested interest is a necessary party to a suit relating to the grantor's estate.

A term of years attendant on the inheritance will not pass by a will unless the will be executed according to the requirements of the Statute of Frauds.

The intent of a testator cannot defeat the requirements of the Statute of Frauds.

British Library MS. Hargrave 81, f. 189

3 December 1722, at the Rolls.

In this case, the Master of the Rolls [JEKYLL] cited a case of Holt v. Holt,[1] in the time of My Lord Somers, where a man purchased an estate and took a conveyance of the inheritance to himself in fee and an assignment of a mortgage term to another in trust for himself, his executors, administrators, and assigns, yet this term was held to be attendant on the inheritance and, as such, not liable to simple contract debts.

And, in the principal case, a man was possessed of a term for 500 years, the remainder to another for 2000 years, with reversion to himself in fee. And by his will, he had devised those lands to one for life with remainder to another and the heirs of his body. But the will had but two witnesses so as not to be a good will for passing the inheritance. And, therefore, the question was upon the 500 years term, whether they had proper parties, for the tenant for life only was party and not the person to whom the remainder was limited in tail.

And this bill being for a discovery of writings in order to bring an [action of] ejectment at [common] law to impeach this will, the plaintiff being heir at law, the Master of the Rolls [JEKYLL] was of opinion that the remainderman ought to be a party, for that, in equity, this was looked upon as a fixed vested interest and the greater interest, he having the whole residue of the term in him and not a bare possibility and even at law, since the case of Matthew Manning, esquire, Co. 8,

[1] *Holt v. Holt* (1670), 1 Chancery Cases 190, 22 E.R. 756, 1 Eq. Cas. Abr. 85, 21 E.R. 897.

and Lampett's Case, Co. 10,[1] this was such an interest as would go to his executors or might be released. So, the plaintiffs were to amend their bill in that point.

[Other copies of this report: British Library MS. Hargrave 82, f. 197.]

Lincoln's Inn MS. Coxe 89, vol. 3, pt. 2, p. 7

4 February 1724[/25].[2] *Coram* GILBERT and RAYMOND, Commissioners [to Hold the Great Seal].

A. was seised of certain lands called B. in fee, and he mortgaged the same to C. for the term of 500 years. Afterwards, C. advanced more money upon these lands, and, for his security, the mortgagor granted the reversion for another term of 2000 years to D. in trust for C. to wait upon the inheritance and protect it. Afterwards, the mortgagor sold the equity of redemption and the reversion to E. in fee. E. sold the same to C., by which C. was now seised both of the terms and the inheritance. C., being thus seised, made his will and, thereby, devised all his said lands called B. to F. in fee. But this will was not executed by the devisor in the presence of three witnesses, as required by the Statute Car. II.

And the question was whether, notwithstanding the devise was void to pass the inheritance, the term for years did not pass.

It was insisted the Statute did not require so strict an execution of the will to pass a chattel and the devisor having a term in gross in him at the time of the devise, this will was sufficient to pass the term, for, by a devise of all his lands, a term for years will pass.

This cause was heard first before the Master of the Rolls [JEKYLL], who decreed that the devise was void to pass the term or any interest in lands to the devisee.

The devisee appealed from this decree to the Commissioners [to Hold the Great Seal]. And, upon the first hearing, GILBERT, Lord Commissioner, was clearly of opinion that the term did not pass. But RAYMOND doubted.

Afterward, on 10 February 1724[/25], RAYMOND, Justice, agreed with Baron GILBERT and confirmed the decree of the Master of the Rolls [JEKYLL]. They said [Statute of] 29 Car. II was made for the public good and was to be construed liberally in suppressing those frauds it was designed to remedy. They considered the intent of the devisor and to this purpose as one entire estate of inheritance and not as a distinct term in gross and a reversion expectant. [. . .] 2 Ch. Rep., Douse v. Percival,[3] when the lessee purchased the inheritance in trustees' names

---

1 *Clark v. Manning* (1609), 8 Coke Rep. 94, 77 E.R. 618; *Lampet's Case* (1612), 10 Coke Rep. 46b, 77 E.R. 994, *sub nom. Lampit v. Starkey*, 2 Brownlow & Goldesborough 172, 123 E.R. 880.

2 1727 *MS.*

3 *Dowse v. Percival* (1682–1684), 2 Chancery Reports 243, 21 E.R. 668, also 1 Vernon 104, 23 E.R. 345, 1 Eq. Cas. Abr. 151, 21 E.R. 951.

for him and his heirs and, afterwards, died intestate and his wife, taking out administration, claimed the lease as part of her personal estate, and the court decreed it to attend the inheritance.

Lincoln's Inn MS. Misc. 384, p. 311, pl. 3

6 February, Hilary [term] 1724[/25]. Lords Commissioners SIR JOSEPH JEKYLL, SIR ROBERT RAYMOND, SIR JEFFREY GILBERT. An appeal from the Rolls affirmed.

A term attendant on the inheritance will not pass by a will unless it be executed according to the Statute of Frauds and Perjuries[4] and not being expressly devised, but only all his land. [They] cited the Earl of Pembroke's Case; 2 Ch. Rep. 50, Tyffin v. T.; Cro. Ca. 109; and 1 Lev., Freeman, 1 Ven., Barns; 2 Ch. Ca. 156; Holt v. Holt, by Lord Somers, a trust of a term was declared to executors and administrators yet it was decreed to attend the inheritance.[5]

Lincoln's Inn MS. Misc. 380, pt. 2, p. 31

7 February 1724/25. GILBERT and RAYMOND, Commissioners, present.

Edward Whichurch purchased the estate in question of J.S. At the time of the purchase, the whole estate and interest in it consisted of two mortgage terms and the inheritance, which was vested in J.S. Edward Whitchurch took to himself an assignment of the first term, which was of 500 years, and had the second, which was of 2000 years, assigned over to B. in trust to attend the inheritance (both the mortgages being paid off) and had the inheritance conveyed to himself in fee. Edward Whitchurch, being so seised and entitled, in the year [*blank*], made his will and, thereby, devised all his estate called C., being the estate in question, which he purchased of J.S. to Edward Whitchurch, a relation of his, for life, remainder to his first and other sons in tail male, remainder to his right heirs. There were but two witnesses to the will so that it was not conformable to the Statute of Frauds and Perjuries with relation to devises of lands.

He died in [*blank*], and his heir at law brought this bill against the devisee in order to compel him to assign the term of 500 years to him, insisting that the

[4] Stat. 29 Car. II, c. 3, s. 5 (*SR*, V, 840).

[5] *Baden v. Earl of Pembroke* (1688–1690), 2 Vernon 52, 213, 23 E.R. 644, 739, Nelson 164, 21 E.R. 816, 3 Chancery Reports 217, 21 E.R. 771, 1 Eq. Cas. Abr. 241, 265, 21 E.R. 1019, 1035; *Tiffin v. Tiffin* (1681), 2 Chancery Cases 49, 55, 22 E.R. 840, 844, also 2 Freeman 66, 22 E.R. 1061, 1 Vernon 1, 23 E.R. 260, 1 Eq. Cas. Abr. 151, 241, 274, 21 E.R. 951, 1018, 1042, 2 Eq. Cas. Abr. 275, 22 E.R. 232, 79 Selden Soc. 872, 886, British Library MS. Stowe 406, f. 111; *Iseham v. Morrice* (1628), Croke Car. 109, 79 E.R. 696; *Freeman v. Barnes* (1670), 1 Levinz 270, 83 E.R. 401, 1 Ventris 55, 80, 86 E.R. 39, 56, also 1 Siderfin 458, 82 E.R. 1215, 2 Keble 597, 650, 84 E.R. 375, 409; *Anonymous v. Langton* (1683), 2 Chancery Cases 156, 22 E.R. 892; *Holt v. Holt* (1670), 1 Chancery Cases 190, 22 E.R. 756, 1 Eq. Cas. Abr. 85, 21 E.R. 897.

devise, by the Statute of Frauds and Perjuries, was void at law as to the inheritance and in this court as to the term for years.

The question was whether, in a court of equity, the formalities required by that Statute were necessary to the passing of the interest in this term of 500 years. It was admitted on both sides that, if this term was like a common term in gross, it would pass both legally and equitably by this devise of the land. It was likewise admitted that, as it is, it did pass the legal estate to the devisee.

What distinguishes it is that it is a term taken by the devisor for no other purpose but merely to protect his inheritance, and such terms are understood in a court of equity to partake of the nature of the inheritance, to go along with it, and to be subject to the same rules of alienation and liable to the same and no other charges and consequently seem to require the same formalities in the conveyance of it by devise as the inheritance itself.

The Attorney General [*Yorke*], Mr. *Lutwyche*, Serjeant *Hawkins*, *Peere Williams*, and *Talbot* were for the defendant. Solicitor General [*Wearg*], Mr. *Cowper*, Serjeant *Eyre*, and *Mead* were for the plaintiff.

For the defendant, it was admitted that a term in a trustee to attend the inheritance in the testator would not pass by such a will. But it was insisted that this case was different from that on these two accounts, that the legal estate of the term being in the testator, the will, in law, actually passed the estate in the term to the devisee and there is no equity to take it away from him when the law gives it to him, that this term of 500 years and the inheritance being both in the testator, the term cannot be said to be attendant on the inheritance.

As to the first, it was admitted on both sides that the will was sufficient in law to pass this term of 500 years so as to vest the legal estate in the devisee, the law not making any difference between terms in gross and such as attend on the inheritance, which is a distinction merely in equity and supported by no legal rules. It was, therefore, insisted that, though, where it is necessary to come into equity, the court will not assist a will to affect such a term unless it is attended with the necessary circumstances to pass the inheritance, yet, where there is no assistance required but the law itself gives this term, a court of equity will not interpose to prevent the effect of the law unless there are equitable circumstances to justify such interposition. The equitable circumstances are all on the side of the devisee. The intention of the testator is manifest that the devisee should have it, and it is the particular privilege of a will that both law and equity in general conspire to make the intention of it effectual and not to defeat that intention when it is known. If the law and equity will, therefore, strain the words sometimes *ut res magis valeat quam pereat*, how much less will they break through the rules of law in order to defeat that intention?

If the testator had taken particular notice of its being a term in himself and given it to the devisee expressly, it must certainly have passed to the devisee by this will. It is not so annexed to the inheritance but that the testator might have severed it if he pleased. He has shown his intent to give everything he could as much as if he had expressly mentioned the term. And it is impossible to render his devise of any effect but by making this severance.

The Case of My Lord Pembroke[1] was cited to this purpose. My Lord Pembroke, upon his marriage, agreed to settle a rent charge of £1500 for a jointure of his wife, and it was executed in this manner, by making a demise of all his estate to trustees for a term of ninety-nine years, who re-demised it to My Lord Pembroke himself for ninety-eight years rendering a rent of £1500 a year to the trustees for the use of his wife for life to commence from his own death. The wife died in his lifetime, after which, he died, leaving several simple contract debts. And he made his executors, in whom the term of ninety-eight years vested. The question was whether this term which, by the law, was in the executors should be assets to pay those debts or go to the heir at law, the only use and purpose of that term being satisfied upon the death of the wife. And it was there insisted that this was a term attendant on the inheritance and the intent of the term was fully satisfied and, therefore, it remained only for the benefit of the heir at law. But the court decreed it should be assets to pay simple contract creditors, and that decree was confirmed in the House of Lords. The foundation of that decree was that, the law giving that term to the executors, equity would not interpose to take it out of their hands to defeat honest creditors.

The next thing insisted on was that this was not properly a term attending on the inheritance since it was in the testator himself, who could not be said to be a trustee for himself.

For the plaintiff, it was insisted that the Statute of Frauds and Perjuries affected equitable as well as legal inheritances and, therefore, the chief thing to be considered in this case was what estate the testator had in him upon the principles of law and equity taken together, not distinctly, but as they both together make up the whole law of the land, the principles of equity being as much the law and as much regarded in conveyances as the strict rules of law themselves, that the estate which the testator had in him was the whole interest of the land or, in other words, an estate of inheritance, that the term was a term attending upon the inheritance, and such a term is always considered as partaking of the nature of the inheritance itself, that there could be no doubt whether this was a term attending on the inheritance, which does not depend on any particular trust declared for that purpose, but arises from the nature and use of the term itself where the interest in it belongs wholly to him who has the freehold and inheritance and subsists for no other purpose but for him in such a manner as to keep up his absolute power over the whole but to prevent some possible danger that might happen if they were merged, that almost all the great estates in the kingdom had terms of this kind subsisting upon them, and the courts of equity have wisely taken care of them that they should not prejudice the inheritance, as they

[1] *Baden v. Earl of Pembroke* (1688–1690), *ut supra.*

would certainly do if they were to go in a different channel by taking away the benefit of the estate from him who the law supposes has the chief interest in it, that, for this reason, it is that a devise not sufficient to convey the inheritance has been frequently held not sufficient to convey a term attending the inheritance. 2nd Chancery Cases 49, 55.[1] And for this reason, the term of 2000 years is not pretended by the defendant to belong to him.

[They argued] that the term of 500 years is of the same nature and subsisting for the same end and purpose and, therefore, must be supposed and considered in this court as equally attending upon the inheritance, that the term of 500 years being in the devisor makes no difference since, altogether, they make up but one estate of inheritance in the consideration of this court, that it would be of dangerous consequence to make a different determination as to the one or the other term, that it would tend to defeat the Statute of Frauds and Perjuries, which would seldom operate on any wills of lands because the intervening terms attending the inheritance would then pass though the inheritance itself would not, that the present case of a term in the devisor is very frequent though not so frequent as that of a term being in trustees, that, if reason is the same in both cases, equity must make one uniform determination and not suffer a naked, useless reversion to descend to the heir by the benefit of the Statute while the substance and effect of it is lost.

[They argued] that the objection that equity will not interpose to prevent the intention of the testator from taking effect is of no weight if the Statute is the rule of equity as well as law and it is of great consequence that it should govern in these cases, that this objection is equally strong against the case of a trust term attendant upon the inheritance, which it is admitted will not pass by such a will, when equity must necessarily interpose in the case of such a trust term to determine to whom it should belong, to the devisee or heir. It might be said with the same reason as in the present case that the devisee has the intention of the testator on his side. And why should not equity, since it must interpose one way or other, give the estate where the testator would give it since the Statute does not expressly require such circumstances in order to dispose of such a term. But the reason is plain in that and in the present case equally that the whole interest of the devisor is the thing to be considered and the Statute intends that such an interest shall not pass without those solemnities, that, therefore, if the testator had given the lands in express words, as a term of 500 years, it would not pass the term, being as part of the inheritance and no more to be severed by such a will than a term could be carved out of the legal inheritance by it, that the present case is much stronger because the testator does not consider it as a term but disposes of it as his whole estate and inheritance.

1 *Tiffin v. Tiffin* (1681), *ut supra.*

The LORDS COMMISSIONERS thought it a matter of a good deal of consequence and, therefore, took time to consider of it. And, afterwards, upon the 10th February, they decreed in favor of the plaintiff.

GILBERT said it was plain the testator's intention was to pass an estate of freehold for life and likewise an estate of inheritance by the form of the words in the devise. The Statute of Frauds and Perjuries makes all devises of lands and tenements void unless they pursue the particular directions of that Statute. The present devise is within the words of the Statute, but it is said that a term for years is not land within that Statute and, therefore, not affected by it. But the answer is plain and is the solution of this case, that, where a term will go to executors if undevised, a will deficient in the formalities required by the Statute may be sufficient to take it away from them. But, where it would go to the heirs if undevised, the will that passes it must be executed according to the Statute. Now, in this case, the term would not go to the executors in point of interest if it had been undevised.

But it is objected the will was intended to pass something to the devisee and, therefore, if it cannot pass the inheritance, it ought at least to pass the term. But that kind of reasoning is not good in this case because the testator understood his interest to be an inheritance and intended to pass it as such and to do it with the legal solemnities. Until those are performed, the will is not complete; it is only *in fieri* and the testator had an *animum deliberandi* until those solemnities were performed.

I do not think it is necessary to determine whether, if the testator had devised it expressly as a term, this will would have been sufficient because that is not the present case and, perhaps, it may be going too far to say that it should not pass it.

I think there are no arguments to be drawn in the present case from the absolute dominion the testator had over his estate and his intention because the intent must be executed according to the legal requisites or it shall not have any effect, the law destroying the instrument itself that is executed without those solemnities. I think, therefore, in this case, the term of 500 years ought to go to the plaintiff.

RAYMOND said he was entirely of the same opinion as to this particular case.

Lincoln's Inn MS. Misc. 12, p. 142

10 February 1724[/25].

One Biss, seised in fee of lands, mortgages them by an assignment of a term for 500 years which one Strode was possessed of in trust for Biss. The mortgage was afterwards assigned to A.B., who lends a further sum and takes a further mortgage for a term of 200 years in the name of a trustee and then purchases the equity of redemption and takes the conveyance in his own name.

After this, he makes his will all of his own handwriting, but it was not signed or sealed nor attested by any witnesses. And, by this will, he gives these lands to the defendant for life and to his first and other sons in tail with other remainders over, and he makes J.S. executor, who proves the will in common form and assents to the devise to the defendant.

The plaintiff, as heir at law of the testator, brings his bill against the devisee and also against the executor that he might assign the first term to him, insisting that, the lands being descended upon him as heir at law, the term which was attendant on the inheritance ought to be assigned in trust for him.

And so it was decreed by the Master of the Rolls [JEKYLL].

The defendant, the devisee, appealed from this decree, insisting that, though the will could not pass the inheritance, not being executed according to the Statute, yet it was sufficient to pass the term which the testator had in himself and, that term being vested in the defendant by the will and the assent of the executor and the plaintiff and the defendant being both volunteers, equity ought not to interpose and take away the law from the defendant.

But the Lords Commissioners, after they had taken time to consider of it, affirmed the decree.

Lord Commissioner GILBERT said, if the term had been devised, it could not have been separated from the inheritance and have gone to the executor. And, if it could not in such case have gone to the executor, it ought not to go to the devisee and defeat the heir unless the will had been executed according to the Statute.

Here is an estate of freehold devised and an inheritance intended to have passed by the will, but this intention was not perfected and whether he ever designed to complete that intention by executing his will as the law directs is uncertain.

Lord Commissioner RAYMOND said it did not appear to be the testator's intention to pass the term, but, on the contrary, it plainly appeared that he intended to devise an estate of inheritance. If he had intended to pass the term, that intention of his cannot take place, for, if the term was to pass, it would go to the next remainderman after the death of the tenant for life.

Note, when this case was first argued, Commissioner GILBERT seemed to think that the term and the inheritance were so connected together that, if the term had been expressly devised, it could not have passed unless the will had been executed according to the Statute. But, now, he seemed to retract that, and he said he had gone too far in what he said as to that matter. However, he said that was not the present case. When it came to be the case, it would be time enough to consider of that point then.

Note it was agreed on both sides by the counsel that, where a term is assigned in trust to attend the inheritance, the *cestui que trust* cannot devise the term but by a will executed according to the Statute.

Yale Univ. Taussig MS. 311, vol. 2, p. 775, pl. 1

Hilary term 1724/25. In Chancery upon an appeal from the Master of the Rolls.

A. takes an assignment of a mortgage of a term of 500 years and then agrees for the purchase of the inheritance and, finding an old term of 2000 years subsisting, has it conveyed to B. and C. in trust for himself to attend the inheritance and takes a conveyance to himself of the freehold and inheritance. And he makes his will and thereby devises the land to D. But the will had but two witnesses to it so as it would not pass the inheritance. Query whether it would pass the term.

[Before] Gilbert and Raymond [Lords Commissioners to Hold the Great Seal].

British Library MS. Add. 36651, f. 108v

Hilary [term] 11 Geo. I, 1724/25; heard before the Commissioners of the Great Seal.

Edward Whitchurch had a term of 500 years granted to him by one Seaman as a mortgage for securing a sum of money in certain lands in D. And the mortgagor granted a second term for 2000 years to J.S. by way of a mortgage in trust for the said Edward Whitchurch as a further security for the same sum. Afterwards, Edward Whitchurch purchased the equity of redemption and the inheritance of the said lands, which were conveyed to him accordingly.

Edward Whitchurch made his will in writing, but [it was] attested only by two witnesses, and he, thereby, devised all his lands purchased of Seaman to A. and his heirs male forever and died, B. being his heir at law.

B. brought this bill as heir at law, insisting that the will being attested by two witnesses only, the inheritance did not pass thereby, the Statute of Frauds[1] requiring three witnesses and the term of 500 years, being attendant on the inheritance, cannot be separated from it by this devise.

The defendant insisted that Edward Whitchurch, the testator, at the time of making the will and at his death, was possessed by virtue of the term for 500 years, which not being merged in the inheritance by reason of the intermediate term of 2000 years granted and remaining in J.S., his trustee, that, by the words of the will as well as the intent of the devisor, the term of 500 years did not pass by the will and, in the case of a devise of a term for years, three witnesses are not required by the Statute of Frauds, it being only a chattel and always held to be out of the Statute.

The principal question, therefore, was whether the testator in the eye of a court of equity shall be considered as seised of the fee and inheritance only or of a term of 500 years separate and distinct from the inheritance and not attendant thereon or whether all, i.e. the fee and the term as attendant thereon, shall be considered as one equitable inheritance and so not to pass by this will for want of those solemnities required by the Statute of Frauds.

[1] Stat. 29 Car. II, c. 3, s. 5 (*SR*, V, 840).

King's Inns Dublin MS. 92, p. 54

16 February. In Chancery upon appeal from His Honor.

A term for 500 years of Badcourt Lodge was in one Stroud. Edward Whitchurch advanced a sum of money upon it by way of a mortgage and had the term assigned to him. He, afterwards, advanced a further sum upon the security of the same estate and had a farther term of 2000 years created and assigned to Jonathan Whitchurch as a farther mortgage in trust for Edward. And, for securing both the sums, one Seman, afterwards, purchased the inheritance from the mortgagor. And Whitchurch, the mortgagee, purchased the inheritance from Seman so that Edward was seised of the land for the term of 500 years, remainder for 2000 years to his trustee, remainder in fee to himself. And, being thus seised, he made his will in writing and thereby devised the lands which he purchased of Seman to his younger brother, the defendant, for life and then in tail to his nephew and the heirs of his body forever. The will was prepared in this manner but not signed or published in the presence of witnesses. The defendant entered by virtue of this devise. The plaintiffs, daughters of an elder brother of the testator, as heirs at law, brought their bill against the defendant and against the executors of the testator and the trustee of the term to have the term of 500 years and the term of 2000 years assigned to attend the inheritance descended to them. The executor, by his answer, asserted that the term of 500 years should pass to the defendant, the devisee, if it might pass by the will.

The question in this case was whether, though the freehold or inheritance could not pass by this will, that which could pass by such a will, i.e. the term for 500 years did not pass by it and, if it did, whether there was any equity to take it from the defendant.

It was argued on the one side that it was a satisfied term by the mortgagee's purchase of the inheritance, that it was attendant, therefore, upon the inheritance, and that it was connected to it, that this will could not sever it by a favorable construction and was not a proper instrument for that purpose, that a testator could no more devise such a term so implicated with the fee and made part of it without the requisite formalities than he could devise the fee or freehold itself, and that it was never in the view of this testator to make such an advancement but that this intention was framed for him out of legal notions and not his own.

On the other side, it was urged that this was a term in possession in the testator, that, if it were not, yet he certainly had the power to separate it from the inheritance and to direct this one way and that another by express words, that, though he had not done it expressly, yet it being his intent to pass all his estate to the defendant, that which could pass by such a will ought to pass, that the term could and actually did pass to the defendant by the will, especially since the assent of the executor, that it having passed, and, the legal title being in him, there was no inducement to wrest it from him, both parties being volunteers.

My Lord Commissioner Gilbert seemed to be of the opinion that this was a term annexed to and partaking of the nature of a freehold and inheritance and that such a will was not a proper instrument to pass it.

My Lord Commissioner Raymond seemed to be of the opinion that, by express words, this term might be severed from the inheritance, either by deed or will. And he said it stuck with him whether the term passed in point of law or not and, if it did, what reason there was to take it from one volunteer to give it to the other.

Upon taking time to give their judgment, they did not think it necessary to determine the point in which they seemed to vary. But Lord Commissioner Gilbert gave the resolution in which they both agreed. Having stated the case, he said the question is upon this case, whether this will be a proper instrument to pass a freehold and inheritance and, if it be not, whether it can have any operation. The words of the Statute are 'all [etc. *qua vide*] otherwise shall be utterly void' so that the Statute vacates this instrument. It is true that the Statute does not reach terms, and the reason of that is plain and is the very solution of the case. A term undevised will go to executors, but an inheritance will not. And such a will as this may strip executors because it derogates only from them, but, where it derogates from the interest of the heir, it ought to have a strict execution according to the Statute. But, in this case, the term would not go to the executors. It is a property of inheritance, and the descent would carry it with it only as an appendix. But we need not go so far into this consideration. There is no occasion to determine that point now.

The main objection has been that the term did by this will pass to the devisee. The answer is that the will was *in fieri* and not perfect, that, until it was finished, the testator had an *animum deliberandi*, that it was plain he was endeavoring and intending to bring it up to the legal solemnity and preparing to pass the freehold and inheritance. That is the case before us. The term was not in the testator's view and ought not to be in ours. And we ought not to construe a will intending completely to pass a freehold and inheritance and being only *in fieri* to pass anything in the meantime before it comes up to the solemnities requisite for the purpose of the testator. I was properly retrenched by My Lord Commissioner Raymond the last time. The question whether a term attending an inheritance may pass by a will not executed according to the Statute is not now before us.

No argument is to be drawn in the case before us from the testator's dominion and intention because laws that appoint solemnities restrain dominion and intention and are always to be construed in the most liberal manner. Therefore, the Statute operates to destroy this very instrument as far as it concerns lands.

From the time of the Statute Hen. VIII,[1] it was an inconvenient power to devise without solemnities. Great frauds and abuses happened by it. Sir Matthew

---

1 Stat. 32 Hen. VIII, c. 1 (*SR*, III, 744–746).

Hale and Sir Lionel Jenkins, who had the drawing up of the Statute of Frauds, reformed that power upon the plan of the Roman law, which once required the solemnity of seven witnesses but reduced them to three by a Constitution of Leo.[1] The Statute takes place. The term still accompanies the inheritance and descends with it.

[Other reports of this case: 2 Peere Williams 236, 24 E.R. 712, Gilbert Rep. 168, 25 E.R. 118, 9 Modern 124, 88 E.R. 355, 1 Strange 619, 93 E.R. 737, 2 Eq. Cas. Abr. 517, 763, 22 E.R. 436, 647.]

566

Picant v. Jordan

(Ch. 1722)

Where a person makes a will bequeathing a mortgage or shares of stock and later calls in the secured debt or sells the stock, this is an ademption of the bequest.

British Library MS. Hargrave 81, f. 191, pl. 1

Thursday, 13 December 1722, at Lord Chancellor before the Master of the Rolls.

In this case, a difference was taken and agreed to by the court that, if a man has a sum of money out on a mortgage and, by his will, gives £100 or any other sum, part of £1000 etc. out upon such a mortgage and, afterwards, calls in the £1000 etc. and puts it out upon any other mortgage or keeps it in his own hands, that this is an ademption of the legacy. But, if the £1000 etc. had been paid in by the mortgagor on notice so that the mortgagee was forced to take in, this would be no ademption of the legacy, being not his own act.

So, in the principal case, where a man gave £100, part of his South Sea stock, and put out the money on Exchequer bills or other securities, this the court thought was an ademption of the legacy. But there were other words in the will which showed the testator's intention that the legacy of £100 should take place. However, the security was altered, and, therefore, it was accordingly decreed for the plaintiff.

[Other copies of this report: British Library MS. Hargrave 82, f. 198, Lincoln's Inn MS. Misc. 107, f. 94, pl. 1.]

[1] Constitution 41, S. P. Scott, ed., *The Civil Law*, vol. 17, pp. 244–245.

567
Snooke v. Snooke
(Ch. 1722)

A court of equity will grant relief on a bond that has been altered, since a plaintiff must 'draw equity from pure streams'.

Where a bond is given with a condition to do several things, the obligee can go into a court of equity to have specific performance of the agreement.

Lincoln's Inn MS. Misc. 11, p. 230, pl. 2

17 December 1722.

The defendant, upon her marriage, agreed that, in consideration of a settlement to be made upon her by her then intended husband of a copyhold estate of £40 *per annum*, she would, out of that estate, pay £10 a year to the plaintiffs during her widowhood if the marriage took effect. And she survived her husband. And she enters into a bond to her intended husband with a condition, reciting the marriage agreement to pay the £10 a year during her widowhood. The marriage took effect.

And, the husband being dead, the plaintiffs bring their bill for a specific performance of this agreement. And they insist that, by the bond, the annuity was to be paid during life.

The defendant, on the other hand, insisted that the agreement was only to pay it during widowhood and that the bond had been erased since her husband's death and the words 'during life' inserted instead of 'during widowhood'. And of this latter, there was some proof, though not positive and direct, by one witness. And, therefore, here having been a forgery, the plaintiffs ought not to have any assistance from a court of equity.

At first, the Master of the Rolls [Jekyll] seemed to be of opinion that, if the bond had been erased in a material part, yet it did not destroy the agreement in a court of equity, though it did at common law. But, upon further consideration, he said he had not known any case where the court had aided the party in such a case, for he that would have equity must draw it from pure streams.

But after much debate, he, at last, decreed the annuity to be paid the plaintiffs during the defendant's widowhood, the defendant's witness having not directly sworn that the erasure was made after the execution of the bond nor was there any proof that the plaintiffs were privy or consenting to the making of the erasure if it was made after the husband's death, which did not clearly appear, and though an erasure in a material part of a deed made it void at law and *non est factum* might be pleaded to an action brought upon it, yet it would be otherwise if done without the consent or privity of the party who would take advantage of the deed.

In the present case, he was of opinion that the bond in question, though given to the husband, was good even at law and was not extinguished by the marriage, it being not to do a thing during the coverture, but after the death of the husband, according to the resolution of Gage and Acton, 1 Salk. 325.[1] However, if it had been extinguished at law by the marriage, the court might set up the agreement.

He was also of opinion that, where a bond is given with a condition to do several things, though the obligee may maintain an action at law for the penalty, yet he may, if he thinks fit, come into equity to have a specific performance of the agreement.

568

Fisk v. Churchman

(Ch. 1722)

A resulting trust is not within the Statute of Frauds.

There cannot be a trust upon a trust.

British Library MS. Hargrave 81, f. 191, pl. 2

Mrs. Susan Fisk, in 1714, joined with one Mary King and others in putting out £430 upon a mortgage, which was taken in the name of Mary King, without any notice in the mortgage whose the money was. But Mrs. Susan Fisk, at the same time, draws up a minute in writing declaring that £200 thereof was the money of Mary King, £70 other part thereof the money of another, £10 thereof another, and £150 residue was her own money. And, in about a year after, she died. The defendant, having married her daughter, pays off Mary King and the rest and takes an assignment of this mortgage. But the £150 he did not pay, pretending that Mrs. Susan Fisk intended and had by word of mouth declared that she had put out £100 of it for Hester, one of his children, and £50 residue thereof for Alice, another of his children (and this was proved by his wife) and that the interest of this £150 had been applied accordingly for the benefit of the two children, Hester and Alice. The plaintiff was executor of Robert Fisk, who was the only son and heir and also executor and residuary legatee of the said Susan Fisk by her will made in 1704, so that the only question was whether the defendant was a trustee of this mortgage as to the £150 for the plaintiff as representative of Susan Fisk or for the children by virtue of the parol declaration, that is whether this parol declaration was sufficient to vest a trust for this £150 in the two children.

[1] *Gage v. Acton* (1700), 1 Salkeld 325, 91 E.R. 288, also 1 Comyns 67, 92 E.R. 962, 1 Lord Raymond 515, 91 E.R. 1244, 1 Freeman 512, 515, 89 E.R. 385, 387, Carthew 511, 90 E.R. 892, Holt K.B. 309, 90 E.R. 1071, 12 Modern 288, 88 E.R. 1327.

And the Master of the Rolls [JEKYLL] was of opinion after a good deal of debate that there would be no trust of it for the children as this case was, first, for that the resulting trust was plainly at first in Mrs. Fisk not only as the fact of paying the money by her was fully admitted and proved in the cause and, therefore, carried a resulting trust, which the Statute of Frauds and Perjuries[1] had expressly excepted, secondly, because this was declared in writing by the memorandum drawn up by herself and, if so, then there can be no other resulting trusts for any others without some writing of it, for that would let in all the mischiefs which the Statute of Frauds and Perjuries was intended to prevent and would be a trust upon a trust if this parol declaration of her for the children should be admitted to control both the written evidence and the construction of law of a resulting trust for herself and would also subvert her will, which was made in writing.

So the £150 was decreed to the plaintiff.

[Other copies of this report: British Library MS. Hargrave 82, f. 199, Lincoln's Inn MS. Misc. 107, f. 94, pl. 2.]

569

Brunnell v. Clavering

(Ch. 1722)

In this case, the equities were such that the equity court forbade the defendants from proving their title in any action at common law during the minority of the infant defendant.

British Library MS. Hargrave 81, f. 198

Michaelmas [term] 1722, in court.

Sir John Clavering, being tenant for life, with remainder to his son, the defendant, James, now Sir James, Clavering, who was then an infant of about two years old, of certain lands contiguous to the River Derwent and very necessary for the loading of coals from several pits thereabouts to the said river in order to be shipped off for London and other places, enters into articles with the plaintiffs for granting them a lease of a wagon way over the said lands for nineteen years, by which time, as he seems to have computed, his son, the defendant, would be of full age. And this lease was to be at a very considerable reserved rent and the plaintiffs, who, by the articles, were to be at the charges, had laid out several thousand pounds in making of wagon ways straightly and other things necessary in such cases and had for several years since paid the rent without any lease made to them and some years since. Sir John died, and the defendant, Sir James, his son, was now but about fourteen years of age.

[1] Stat. 29 Car. II, c. 3, s. 8 (*SR*, V, 840).

Sir John, by his will, had devised the guardianship of his said son until he should come to the age of twenty-one years to the defendant Lady Clavering, his mother and wife of the said Sir John. And it was admitted by the defendants Brunnell and others in the cross-cause, who were plaintiffs in the original cause, that they had notice that Sir John was but tenant for life of those lands but that, in respect of the necessity they were under of having a wagon way over the said lands and of the great advantage it was to the estate of Sir John and his son by reason of the rent and other great profits out of the coals, they were determined to run the hazard of Sir John's life for their term. But now, Sir John being dead, the defendant and his mother had pulled down a great part of the way, sunk pits in it, and threatened not only to make it entirely useless to the plaintiffs but also to bring their [action of] ejectment and turn the plaintiffs out of possession. It did not appear in the cause that any lease was made to the plaintiffs, but they held under the articles and had not only paid the reserved rent and been at such charges as aforesaid in the lifetime of Sir John but had also for some time after his death paid the said rent to the Lady Clavering. But being in a manner defeated of the way and threatened with ejectments, they brought this bill to be quieted in the enjoyment thereof from the nature and necessity of their case and the great benefit arising thereby to the estate of the Lady Clavering and her son.

In answer to which, all that seemed to be insisted on by the defendants was that they could have a much greater rent for the lands to be used as a wagon way and that other landowners thereabouts did make much more of their estates when leased out for such purposes and that Sir John being only tenant for life, if he had actually made a lease, it would have determined by his death and no acceptance of the rent after could have set it up again and that, if the defendants had the law on their side, a court of equity ought not to interpose to take it from them.

But My Lord Chancellor [Lord Macclesfield] said, though he could not decree the lease to be good, which was determined by the death of the tenant for life, nor decree the defendants to make a new lease, that he was of opinion that, as the father had power by the Statute[1] to devise the guardianship of his son until he was twenty-one years and he had in this case devised the guardianship to his mother until that age, this, in effect and consequence, gave him some power over his son's estate until that age since, otherwise, the guardianship would in effect be frustrated and defeated and the power of devising it given him by the Statute be in some sort eluded. Therefore, he said, though he could not establish the lease or articles, yet he would and did accordingly order that, if the defendants brought an [action of] ejectment, they should not be at liberty to give the settlement in evidence during the minority of Sir James whereby the estate was settled on his father for life with remainder to his son in tail.

---

[1] Stat. 12 Car. II, c. 24, s. 8 (*SR*, V, 260).

[Other copies of this report: British Library MS. Hargrave 82, f. 205, Lincoln's Inn MS. Misc. 107, f. 96.]

3 Swanston 690, 36 E.R. 1024

Sir John Clavering, being tenant for life, with remainder to his son, the defendant James, now Sir James Clavering, who was then an infant of about two years old, of certain lands contiguous to the River Darwent and very necessary for the landing of coal from several pits thereabout to the river in order to be shipped for London and other places, entered into articles with the plaintiffs for granting to them a lease of a wagon way over the said lands for nineteen years, by which time, as he seems to have computed, his son, the defendant, would be of full age. And this lease was to be at a very considerable reserved rent, and the plaintiffs, who by the articles were to be at the charges, had laid out several thousand pounds in making wagon ways, staiths, and other things necessary in such cases and had for several years paid the rent without any lease made to them. And, some years since, Sir John died. And the defendant, Sir James, his son, was now about fourteen years of age. Sir John by his will had devised the guardianship of his son until he should come to the age of twenty-one years to the defendant, the Lady Clavering, his mother and wife of Sir John. It was admitted by the defendants Brummell and others in the cross-cause, who were plaintiffs in the original cause, that they had notice that Sir John was but tenant for life of these lands, but that, in respect of the necessity they were under of having a wagon way over the said lands and of the great advantage it was to the estate of Sir John and his son by reason of the rent and other great profits out of the coal, they were determined to run the hazard of Sir John's life for their term. But now, Sir John being dead, the defendant and his mother had pulled down a great part of the way, sunk pits in it, and threatened not only to make it entirely useless to the plaintiffs, but also to bring their [writ of] ejectment and turn the plaintiffs out of possession. It did not appear in the cause that any lease was made to the plaintiffs, but they held under the articles, and had not only paid the reserved rent and been at such charges as aforesaid in the lifetime of Sir John, but had also for some time after his death paid the said rent to the Lady Clavering. But being in a manner defeated of the way and threatened with ejectment, they brought this bill to be quieted in the enjoyment thereof from the nature and necessity of their case and the great benefit arising thereby to the estate of the Lady Clavering and her son.

In answer to which, all that seemed to be insisted on by the defendants was that they could have a much greater rent for the lands to be used as a wagon way and that other landowners thereabout made much more of their estates when leased for such purposes and that Sir John being only tenant for life, if he had actually made a lease, it would have determined by his death and no acceptance of the rent after could have set it up again and that, if the defendants had the law on their side, a court of equity ought not to interpose to take it from them.

But the Lord Chancellor [Macclesfield] said, though he could not decree the lease to be good, which was determined by the death of the tenant for life, nor decree the defendants to make a new lease, yet he was of opinion that, as the father had power by the Statute to devise the guardianship of his son until he was twenty-one years and he had in this case devised the guardianship to his mother until that age, this, by consequence, gave him some power over his son's estate until that age, since, otherwise, the guardianship would in effect be frustrated and defeated and the power of devising it given to him by the Statute be in some sort eluded. Therefore, he said, though he could not establish the lease or articles, yet he would and did accordingly order that, if the defendants brought an [action of] ejectment, they should not be at liberty to give the settlement in evidence during the minority of Sir James, whereby the estate was settled on his father for life, with remainder to his son in tail.

At the hearing, the following decree was made, '7th November 1722, Whereupon etc. and whereas, upon arguing the plea [of the settlement under which he claimed] put in by the defendant Sir James Clavering to the said original bill, upon the 3d of August 1720 and the plaintiffs then consenting to pay, if this court should think fit, such advanced rent for the benefit of the defendant Sir James Clavering for the wagon way in, on, and over his ground for leading coal for such time past as well as to come as the court at this hearing should direct and to let the defendant Sir James Clavering make use of the way for leading coal without paying any rent, paying a proportion of the repairs of the way, it was ordered that the said plea should stand for an answer and that the benefit thereof should be saved to Sir James at the hearing, as by the said order now likewise read appears and the plaintiff Cotesworth now present in court, consenting that, if the old way-lease may be ratified, he will quit the 6s. 8d. per ton by the proposal agreed to be to him paid by Sir James Clavering and will quit the restraint on Sir James Clavering from leading more than the quantity of 800 tons, so as the like restriction may likewise be taken from him the said Cotesworth, and also offering, if the present term in the plaintiffs said way-lease shall be enlarged for a reasonable time after the defendant Sir James Clavering shall come of age, if Sir James shall within six months after he comes of age require the same and agree to enlarge his term for the same time, His Lordship does thereupon think fit and so order and decree that it be referred to Mr. Holford, one etc., to look into the new agreement mentioned in the said Sir James Clavering's bill to have been made in writing by some of his friends on his behalf with the said A., H., and B. and see whether the same can be made effectual or not and, if he shall find it can so be, then to see what advantages will accrue to Sir James Clavering thereby and also what disadvantages he may be liable to by reason thereof and what expense it has been or will be to him in making and finishing the said new way and staiths and other appurtenances belonging thereto, and the said Master is also to see whether the said old way be or can be made effectual or not, and, if the old lease should be ratified and confirmed consistently with what is now consented to and offered by Mr. Cotesworth, what advantage and what disadvantage it will be to Sir James Clavering and to state which of the said two ways is most to his advantage and the particulars wherein, and, if any difficulty shall arise before the said Master, he is to state the same specially for the farther direction of the court, and the said Master is also to consider what advanced rent, if any, is reasonable to be paid by the plaintiffs in the original cause to Sir James Clavering in respect of the said old ways lying over so much of Sir James Clavering's lands more than any of theirs or in respect of the situation of the said lands respectively. But His Lordship does reserve the consideration whether any and what allowance shall be made in respect thereof and likewise reserves all farther directions etc. with liberty to apply etc., but, in the meantime, the said Sir James Clavering is to be at liberty to make use of the said new ways to bring what coal he pleases from his collieries within his own grounds, Mr. Cotesworth now consenting thereto, and, if, in the meantime, any dispute shall arise or obstruction be made in the use or enjoyment of either of the said ways, either party is to be at liberty to resort to the court touching the same.' Reg. Lib. A 1722, ff. 333–336.

570

Wafer v. Mocato

(Ch. 1722–1724)

A court of equity will not grant relief against a forfeiture for the lessee's assigning a lease without the required consent of the lessor.

Lincoln's Inn MS. Misc. 11, p. 215, pl. 2

By the printed rules, if a defendant pleads a former suit depending, if the plaintiff is not satisfied with the plea, he is to get it referred to a Master and procure a report in a month or the bill is to stand dismissed with seven nobles costs.

The defendant in this case had pleaded a former suit depending in the Mayor's Court for the same matter as the now bill, which former suit was removed into this court by a *certiorari* bill.

The plaintiff, being advised the plea was good, within ten days after it came in and before any reference to the Master, moved as a motion of course to amend his bill on payment of 20s. costs, he being advised to take notice of the former proceedings, and to make his bill in the nature of a supplemental bill.

The plaintiff having an order to amend, the defendant moved to discharge this order, which was ordered *nisi*. And, on showing cause before the Master of the Rolls [Jekyll], it was made absolute. But, upon a motion before Lord Chancellor [Lord Macclesfield], he discharged the Master of the Rolls's order and gave the plaintiff leave to amend his bill, for the bill was not dismissed, and, though it was not right, it might be made so and, the plaintiff coming within time, there was no reason to discharge the order he had gotten for amending his bill.

Lincoln's Inn MS. Misc. 12, p. 123

30 October 1724.

The plaintiff, 12 August 1720, agrees to sell the defendant some houses which were held under a lease from the City for £150 South Sea [Company] stock, which was then agreed to be of the value of £1350. And one Captain Tratree, who was present at the time of the agreement, agreed to take the stock and to pay the plaintiff £1350 for it. And the stock was to be transferred at the opening of the books, which was the 22nd of August. But, in regard the lease was to be assigned the 16th of August and the stock could not then be transferred, the defendant was to give the plaintiff a note when he assigned the lease to transfer £150 stock to him at the opening, which note the defendant said would be the same as so much ready money in Exchange Alley.

At the time of this agreement, the plaintiff produced his lease, in which was a covenant that the plaintiff should not assign it over without a license from the City. The lease was read over by Mr. Dowse, the defendant's attorney, who made no objection in respect of the covenant, but he said the lease was a good lease and that the plaintiff had authority to assign it. And he promised to get the assignment ready by the 16th of August, the time agreed on for the execution.

Accordingly, the assignment was drawn and engrossed by the 16th of August, and the plaintiff then offered to execute the assignment. But Dowse refused to let him, pretending he must get a license from the City to assign. And, by this means, the plaintiff was put off until about the 17th of September. And then, after the plaintiff had used some endeavors to get a license, but could not, the defendant waived the objection as to the want of a license. And, on the 19th of September, he got the plaintiff to Dowse's house, and there the plaintiff executed the assignment, at which time, South Sea stock was about £400 percent. There being a blank left in the engrossment for the consideration, it was considered what sum should be inserted. And the plaintiff advised the defendant to put in no more than £600, that it might not appear when he came to renew with the City what he paid for the purchase. And, accordingly, that sum was put in. No stock was then transferred to the plaintiff nor any note given by the defendant to transfer £150 stock to him. But Dowse swears that it was then agreed that the defendant should transfer £150 stock to the plaintiff the next transfer day and that, in the meantime, the writings should remain in Dowse's hands.

The defendant, accordingly, on the 21st of September, transfers £150 stock to the plaintiff and leaves the receipt in Dowse's hands. And, upon the plaintiff's coming to him, he refused to deliver it to the plaintiff unless he would sign a writing, which Dowse had prepared, acknowledging that he accepted £150 stock in full satisfaction of the purchase money to be paid for the houses, which the plaintiff refusing, Dowse would not deliver him the receipt.

There were some variety of proofs in the cause. But, upon the whole matter, Lord Chancellor [Lord Macclesfield] thought, upon the circumstances in the case and from what appeared by the proofs in the cause, it was plain that the plaintiff did understand that he was to have the value of £1350 for his houses, and so he would have had if the defendant had performed his agreement. But he insisted after the time was past that the agreement should have been performed that the plaintiff should procure a license from the City, which the plaintiff was not obliged to do. But, if a license was necessary, the defendant ought to have procured it, the plaintiff having only agreed to assign the lease. And the defendant having delayed the execution of the agreement until the stock was fallen, by this pretense, he was of opinion that the plaintiff ought to be relieved.

But then he thought the plaintiff asked too much when he insisted by his bill to be paid the whole £1350, and, therefore, he decreed that the Master should compute the value of the houses as they were at the time of the agreement, reckoning them at six years and a half purchase, which was what the defendant's workmen valued them at when the defendant made the agreement, and that the plaintiff should take the stock at the price it was at when the assignment was executed with all the additions and dividends since and what the value of the houses should amount to more than the £150 stock should come to, computing it at the price it was at when the assignment was executed, should be paid by the defendant to the plaintiff. And, in regard the defendant had been in possession, he was to pay interest for the money which should be found due to the plaintiff, and the defendant was also to pay costs.

Note it was said the defendant had taken an opinion of counsel touching the lessee's assigning without a license and that counsel was of opinion that, though it was a forfeiture at law, the lessors' having a power to enter as well for breach of covenants as non-payment of the rent, yet that equity would relieve.

But Lord Chancellor [Lord Macclesfield] seemed to be of a contrary opinion, and he said, surely, a man might agree that no one should be his tenant but whom he approved of.

Note also the plaintiff, at first, brought his bill in the Mayor's Court and, by the mistake of the person who drew it, the plaintiff only demanded the £600, which was the consideration mentioned, and the mistake was not perceived until after the replication was filed and one witness was examined for the plaintiff, and then he gave notice for leave to withdraw his replication and amend his bill. But, before the motion was made, the defendant brought a *certiorari* bill and removed the proceedings out of the Mayor's Court into this court. The now plaintiff put in an answer to that bill and set out his case as it really was. And he took notice of the mistake in the proceedings below and then brought a cross-bill. But it was very improperly drawn, and the defendant pleaded the former proceedings and the pendency of the *certiorari* bill.

This being a good plea, the plaintiff moved for leave to amend the bill in the Mayor's Court, and he had an order for that purpose, but that order was discharged by Lord Chancellor [Lord Macclesfield] as being improper.

Then the plaintiff brought a bill in the nature of a supplemental bill, which I drew and therein set forth the substance of the bill in the Mayor's Court and of the defendant's answer and that a replication was filed and a witness examined and then took notice of the mistake and the steps taken to retrieve it and that the defendant brought a *certiorari* bill and that a writ of *certiorari* had issued and that the Mayor etc. in obedience thereto had certified and returned to this court the original bill and answer thereto and that the now plaintiff being served with process had appeared and put in his answer. And then I set forth the material parts of that answer. And then the bill goes on and says that the nature of the plaintiff's case, as set forth in the plaintiff's said answer, being very different from what it was by mistake represented to be in and by the plaintiff's said original bill and the said original bill and the proceedings thereon being now removed into this court by His Majesty's writ of *certiorari* before such bill was amended and set right as was designed and intended to have been done, the plaintiff, as he is advised, can have no decree made in his favor in this court any further than what is prayed by the plaintiff's said original bill in case the plaintiff by way of amendment thereof and addition thereto does not disclose the true circumstances of the plaintiff's case and, therefore, it has rendered it necessary for the plaintiff to exhibit this his bill of complaint by way of amendment or addition to the plaintiff's said original bill of complaint that the plaintiff may not be concluded by any mistakes in his former bill but that such mistakes may be rectified and the plaintiff's case brought before this court in such manner as the plaintiff may be relieved thereon. And in order thereto, the plaintiff does charge that the matters set forth in the plaintiff's said answer are true and Mocatto knows the same so to be and ought to discover the truth thereof. And the plaintiff prays that Mocatto may answer the same as if the aforesaid matters in the said answer contained were here again repeated.

And then the bill goes on and charges some facts set out in the now plaintiff's answer to the *certiorari* bill somewhat more fully than they are therein set forth and that the defendant takes advantage of the mistakes in the original bill and refuses to discover the truth of the premises and gives out he will plead the former bill and proceedings in the Mayor's Court and the removal thereof into this court in bar of any bill which shall be exhibited by the plaintiff in this court touching the matters contained in the bill in the Mayor's Court, though he knows the plaintiff's case is wholly mistaken therein and that the defendant and his solicitor exhibited the *certiorari* bill on purpose by removing the original bill to prevent the plaintiff's having an opportunity of rectifying such mistakes as the plaintiff intended to do, which, being an unfair proceeding in the defendant, he ought not to take advantage thereof and thereby defeat the plaintiff of that discovery and relief which the plaintiff would have been entitled to by amending his original bill in case he had not been prevented therein by such unfair contrivance.

And then the bill goes on in the usual manner, and all proper questions are asked, and it concludes as in other bills.

And, upon this bill, the defendant having answered and witnesses examined, it was that the cause was heard, it being revived by the executors of Wafer, who died before the cause came to a hearing. But, as to the *certiorari* bill, Mocatto had never revived it.

9 Modern 112, 88 E.R. 348

1724.

There was an agreement between the plaintiff and the defendant that the plaintiff, in consideration of £1300 to be paid to him by the defendant, should assign a term of years which he had in certain houses in London, which were leased to him by the City with a covenant that the lessee should not alien or assign the term without leave of the City under the penalty of forfeiting the said term. But the plaintiff having not yet gotten any licence from the City, the defendant would not take any assignment of this term for years until such licence should be procured, but he made over £150 South Sea [Company] stock to the plaintiff as a security to perform the agreement on his part.

Afterwards and before any licence was procured, the plaintiff assigned all his interest in this term to the defendant, who prevailed with the plaintiff that the consideration mentioned in the assignment should be £600, and no more, which was done because the true value might be concealed from the City, fearing that, when the defendant should renew the term, the City might raise the fine and the rent in proportion.

Now, it being plain that the plaintiff could have no remedy at law to recover any more than £600, that being the consideration mentioned in the assignment, and probably not that neither, because, having assigned the term without license from the City, it was a forfeiture thereof and, by that means and by color of an entry and eviction by the City, the plaintiff would be barred of his demands, therefore, this bill was brought to have the £1300 according to the agreement for the assignment of this term for years and to be relieved upon the whole matter set forth as aforesaid.

The defendant, by his answer, insists that he was to pay but £150 South Sea stock for the aforesaid assignment and that the houses were of little value and that the plaintiff had forfeited this term by making an assignment thereof without licence and, therefore, the assignment was void.

The court [Lord Macclesfield]: Where a man makes a lease for life or for years upon a condition of re-entry for a forfeiture or that the lease shall be void if the lessee assign or alien it without licence and, afterwards, the lessee assigns it without licence, this is a forfeiture and such a forfeiture against which this court cannot relieve, because it is unknown what shall be the measure of the damages, for this court never relieves but in such cases where it can give some compensation in damages and where there is some rule to be the measure of such damages to avoid being arbitrary.

[Other reports of this case: 2 Eq. Cas. Abr. 58, 22 E.R. 51.]

571

Anonymous

(Ch. 1723)

A deposition that was suppressed can be used to impeach the credibility of a subsequent deposition by the same witness.

British Library MS. Hargrave 83, p. 29, pl. 1

24 January 1722[/23].

My Lord Chancellor MACCLESFIELD suffered a deposition which had been suppressed to be now read to invalidate the testimony of the same deponent in a subsequent examination.

572

Weaver v. Fowler and Nicholls

(Ch. 1723)

Where trustees invested the corpus of a trust account in South Sea Company stock pursuant to an act of Parliament, the beneficiary of the trust has no cause of action at common law or in equity.

British Library MS. Hargrave 81, f. 173

The plaintiff delivered to the defendants, who were goldsmiths, some lottery orders and empowered them to receive the interest from time to time as the same became due. And, in the year 1720, the defendants, without any particular order or direction from the plaintiff, subscribed them into the South Sea Company in the plaintiff's name. And the plaintiff brings his bill to have a satisfaction from the defendants for the said lottery orders.

And it was argued by *Sir Robert Raymond*, Attorney General, for the plaintiff, that the Act of Parliament[1] which enabled the South Sea Company to take in the government securities therein mentioned empowered such persons only to subscribe the same as had an interest in their own right or in trust for others or as guardians to infants and the defendants here, not falling under any of these descriptions, had no manner of right to subscribe the said lottery orders and were, therefore, guilty of a breach of that trust which was reposed in them for a particular purpose, *viz.* to receive the interest only, and ought to answer for the ill consequences of it, and, since, by a subsequent Act of Parliament,[2] all subscriptions made to the South Sea Company, which, by the first Act, they were unable to

[1] Stat. 6 Geo. I, c. 4, s. 23.

[2] Stat. 7 Geo. I, stat. 1, c. 5.

take in, are made binding and conclusive upon the owners notwithstanding any defect in form or power by which the plaintiff is forever barred from coming at his said lottery orders and is, thereby, a great loser. He said he humbly hoped the plaintiff was very proper in applying to that court for satisfaction against the defendants notwithstanding it was by an Act of Parliament that he was barred since the Act of Parliament affected him only duly in consequence of the wrongful act done by the defendants in subscribing his said orders without any authority.

But of the other side, for the defendants, it was said that there was no color or foundation for the bill for that there was not any one ingredient in it which made it proper for a court of equity. It is not pretended that the defendants were guilty of any fraud, for, as they subscribed the said lottery orders in the name of the plaintiff, they could not propose any manner of advantage to themselves, but whatever benefit could have been had must have accrued to the plaintiff, the subscription being in his name so that, if the plaintiff has any right at all, his remedy is at law; it is a plain action of trover; but that there was no ground of complaint against the defendants either in law or equity, for as to part of the securities for which a satisfaction was sought, they were made payable to bearer. And, as to them, the defendants were authorized to subscribe them as trustees by the first Act of Parliament, the legal interest being in them by the very delivery and an equitable right only in the plaintiff. And, as to the residue that, in some sense, they may be said to be [. . .] trustees even for them. And, for that purpose, the case of a scrivener, which was said by Mr. Talbot to have been often adjudged in that court, was quoted, *viz.* that, if bonds or other securities to receive the interest from time to time as the same shall become due, the payment of the principal to such scrivener shall be deemed a good payment.

But supposing them to be such as they were not by the first Act of Parliament authorized to subscribe, yet certainly, by the second, they are excused from any manner of complaint, for, if they had no authority by the first Act, there was no injury done the plaintiff by the defendants' subscribing, for the subscription was void, and it is the second Act of Parliament which binds the plaintiff and not what was done by the defendants. And it is a very strange kind of equity to pray relief against the defendants for what an Act of Parliament has done, to which everybody in supposition of law is party, even the plaintiff himself, so that, in effect, it is praying to be relieved against this own act without any foundation of equity.

And there were two cases quoted wherein the court were of opinion that, in cases of subscribing without authority, if there was no circumstance of fraud, there was no foundation for relief against the subscribers. One was the Case of Bluck[1] against the present defendants heard before the Master of the Rolls, and the other was the case of one Marshall[2] against the same defendants, who, in an

---

1 *Bluck v. Nicholls* (Ch. 1722), see above, Case No. 557.

2 *Fowler v. Marshall* (Ch. 1724), see below, Case No. 659.

action of trover and conversion, obtained a verdict against the defendants, who brought their bill in this court to be relieved. And the matter being argued before Mr. Baron Price, who sat for the Lord Chancellor, he was of opinion that the plaintiffs in that bill were entitled to relief and, therefore, granted an injunction.

The Lord Chancellor [Lord Macclesfield] said he thought it would be a very hard case taking it upon the first Act only and supposing the defendants to have had no authority thereby to subscribe, but, in that case, the remedy would be at law and not in this court. And he was of opinion that, as to such of the securities as were payable to bearer, they were well subscribed by the first Act. But supposing none of them were well subscribed by the first Act, all the defendants did before the second Act give an election to the plaintiff whether he would confirm what they had done or take back his orders, which was so far from being an injury to the plaintiff that it was an advantage, and, certainly, then there was no ground of complaint. Then comes the second Act, which deprives the plaintiff of the benefit of election which the defendants left him and, in satisfaction thereof, gave a certain proportion of South Sea stock. This is no injury done him by the defendants so that the bill amounts to no more than this, the second Act has not made me a sufficient compensation, therefore, you must.

He said, if there were no authority, the action should have been at law, but he declared he thought there was no right in law or equity. And he dismissed the bill with costs.

[Other copies of this report: British Library MS. Hargrave 82, f. 183.]

573

Gregor v. Kemp

(Ch. 1723)

A marriage settlement to devise a certain part of the obligor's estate at death cannot be defeated by an inter vivos *gift by the obligor that renders his or her estate substantially less in order to defraud the obligee.*

British Library MS. Hargrave 81, f. 194

Tuesday, 29 January 1722[/23], in court.

Upon the plaintiff's marriage with one of the daughters and four children of Joan Kemp, widow, deceased, articles were entered into between the plaintiff and the said Joan whereby the plaintiff, in consideration of the portion or fortune he was to have with his intended wife, agreed to settle such and such lands upon her for life for her jointure. And, by the same articles, at the close thereof by way of an accumulative provision for the plaintiff and his wife, Joan Kemp, the mother, for herself, her executors, administrators, and assigns, covenants and agrees to leave to the plaintiff, his executors, and administrators either by deed or writing in her lifetime or by her last will and testament one full fourth part of all such personal estate as she should be possessed of or entitled unto at the time of her death. The marriage takes effect. And Joan Kemp, the mother, lives several years after, but, being taken ill of the sickness whereof she died, three days before her death, she sends for a friend of hers telling him that she had £1000 in bags lying at one Mr. Herle's, a banker's, hard by and directs him to draw up an instrument or authority in writing whereby she empowers him to give two of the bags containing £200 to one of her daughters, two other bags containing £200 more to another of her daughters, and the remaining £600 to such and such persons, whom she tells she had made trustees in her will, and this £600 was to be in trust for several of her grandchildren. Accordingly, an instrument or writing is prepared for the purposes aforesaid, and the £1000 is immediately and actually paid and delivered to the several persons to whom it was directed. And there was no pretense that this was revocable or was not to take place until after her death, but it was followed by an actual and immediate delivery of the money as aforesaid. And, by her will, she had given and devised all the residue and remainder of her goods, chattels, and personal estate to others of her children and made some of the defendants executors. And she died without leaving the plaintiff anything, either by will or otherwise, though, as it was proved in this cause, she died worth about £8000 so that this bill was brought, amongst other things, to set aside the said disposition as to the £1000 as made merely in fraud of the articles and to have an account of the personal estate of the said Joan Kemp and a fourth part according to the said articles.

And it was argued for the plaintiff that this was a disposition in fraud of the articles, that it was made in her last sickness and but just three days before she died, that it was at least a *donatio causa mortis* and would have been alterable by a will made after or in case she herself had recovered, that, if this was so, it was like the will of a freeman of London which never yet had been allowed to defeat or alter the customary shares of his widow or children after his death.

On the other side, it was argued that there could be no pretense in the world but that Joan Kemp notwithstanding those articles was at liberty in her lifetime to have disposed of her personal estate as she thought fit, that she might have invested it in a purchase or she might have lived upon the principal and, if she thought fit to spend or give it all away in her lifetime, the plaintiff must have been content and could have had no remedy, that this was not a *donatio causa mortis* but a *donatio inter vivos*, which is the opposite distinction taken in the civil law that this donation was followed by an actual delivery in her lifetime and could never after have been recalled or revoked, and, if she had recovered, that the £600 of this money was given to the same persons whom she had named trustees in her will yet that was only a description of the trustees she intended should take care of it for her grandchildren and did not make it any part of her will or in any sort dependent upon her will. And, therefore, the plaintiff had no color to impeach or call it in question.

But My Lord Chancellor [Lord Macclesfield] was clear of opinion that, as this case was, this is a disposition in fraud of the articles. But he agreed clearly that, notwithstanding the articles, Joan Kemp was at liberty to have made any disposition whatsoever of her personal estate but a disposition merely to elude the articles, that she might have given what part she thought fit in her lifetime to a daughter that had fallen to decay or as a portion or provision for a child that had wanted it or for any other purposes, but merely to subvert and destroy the articles, as this appears manifestly to be her intention in the present case, for it was made just when she was dying and past all hopes of recovery, it was not made to any that appeared to have any want of it and, therefore, could be made for no other end but to disappoint the articles. And, if it should prevail, such articles would signify just nothing at all. But as to the donees themselves, this was a good disposition. And, therefore, as against them, he decreed that the bill should be dismissed with costs. But he directed an account of the personal estate against the executors and they to pay the plaintiff a full fourth part of the personal estate which the said Joan Kemp had before the making of this disposition and also such costs as he should be obliged to pay to the other defendants.

[Other copies of this report: British Library MS. Hargrave 82, f. 201.]

3 Swanston 482, 36 E.R. 926

29 January 1722[/23].

Joan Kemp, mother of the defendant, on the marriage of her eldest son, John Kemp, with Mary, late wife of the present plaintiff, among other things, in consideration of the marriage, covenanted by her last will or otherwise to give, grant, or devise to John Kemp, his executors, or administrators, one full fourth part of all the real and personal estate she should be seised of or entitled to at the time of her death. The marriage took effect, but, afterwards, John Kemp and his daughter, the only issue of that marriage, both falling into a very bad state of health, the mother often declared her apprehensions that neither her son nor his child would long survive her and, therefore, appeared much dissatisfied at the covenant entered into, because so large a portion of the estate was likely to go into the hands of strangers. Three days before her death, she sent for a friend of hers, told him that she had £1000 in bags lying at Mr. Hearle's, a banker, hard by, and directed him to draw up an instrument or authority in writing, whereby she empowered him to give two of the bags, containing £200, to one of her daughters, two other bags, containing £200 more, to another of her daughters, and the remaining £600 to Hawes and Pearce, whom, she told him, she had made trustees in her will, and the £600 were to be in trust for several of her grandchildren. Accordingly, an instrument in writing was prepared for the purposes aforesaid, and, at the same time, she signed an order to Mr. Hearle to pay the said sums to Hawes and Pearce for the use of the children. Hearle delivered the money to Pearce in £100 bags, which Pearce sealed up and wrote upon them 'for Mrs. Hand, Mrs.

Tomkins, Mrs. N. Kemp', the three daughters, and then left them in the hands of Hearle to be delivered when called for. Three days after this transaction, Joan Kemp died, and, in a short time, John Kemp, the son, died, and, by his will, he devised to his wife all his goods and chattels, real and personal estate whatsoever, and made her executrix. His daughter died, and Mary, the widow, married the plaintiff, and died.

The plaintiff, as administrator of Mary and administrator *de bonis non* of John Kemp, filed a bill against N. Kemp to have an account of the estate of Joan Kemp and to have the full fourth part of her estate and that the £1000 disposed of as above might be charged upon the remaining three parts of the estate, insisting that the disposition was in fraud of the articles, that it was made in her last sickness and but just three days before she died, that it was at best a *donatio causa mortis* and would have been alterable by a will made after or in case she herself had recovered, that, if this was so, it was like the will of a freeman of London, which never had been allowed to defeat the customary shares of his widow or children after his death.

On the other side, it was argued that there could be no pretence that Joan Kemp, notwithstanding these articles, was not at liberty in her lifetime to have disposed of her personal estate as she thought fit, that she might have invested it in a purchase or might have lived upon the principal, and, if she had thought fit to spend and give it all away in her lifetime, the plaintiff must have been content and could have had no remedy, that this was not a *donatio causa mortis*, but a *donatio inter vivos*, that the donation was followed by an actual delivery in her lifetime and could never after have been recalled or revoked if she had recovered, that though £600 of the money were given to the same persons whom she had named trustees in her will, yet that was only a description of the trustees she intended to take care of it for her grandchildren and did not make it any part of her will or in any sort dependent upon her will, and, therefore, the plaintiff had no color to impeach or call it in question.

The Lord Chancellor [Lord Macclesfield] was of opinion that the disposition was in fraud of the articles. He agreed that, notwithstanding the articles, Mrs. Kemp was not restrained from disposing of her estate any way in her lifetime and had a full power over it, but with this single exception, *viz.* she was restrained from making a distribution on purpose to defeat the covenant, which it is here fully proved she did, for she was unwilling her estate should go to strangers; and the disposition is a plain fraud; it was the intent of the articles that it should be for strangers, for it is to him, his executors, etc. Therefore, if he should think proper to make his wife executrix, as he did, it was designed for her benefit. But supposing this disposition had not been with this avowed design to evade the articles, yet he should have thought it, as it is circumstanced, a *donatio mortis causa* and not good for, otherwise, articles of this nature will signify nothing if they are thus eluded by a disposition a day or two before death. And, in this case, she puts the greatest part of the money into the hands of the trustees named in her last will, so that it seems to have the air of a will. The plaintiff, therefore, must have the full fourth part of the estate after debts paid, but this disposition is good to affect the remaining three parts of her estate and must be satisfied out of it to the several defendants.

Whereupon, and upon long debate of the matter, etc. His Lordship [LORD MACCLESFIELD] declared that, although he was of opinion that the said Joan Kemp was not restrained in her lifetime from disposing her estate or doing anything which was not professedly in breach of the said articles made on the marriage of the said John Kemp, her son, yet it manifestly appearing that the said Joan Kemp's disposing the £1000 in the pleadings mentioned was not *bona fide* but purposely done that the articles might not take place; it was a fraud and ought not to stand against the plaintiff Gregor, and he does therefore order and decree that the defendants, the executors of the said Joan Kemp, and the other defendants to the plaintiff Gregor's bill do come to an account with the said plaintiff before Mr. Edwards, one etc., for what of the said Joan Kemp's estate came to their or either of their hands etc., and the said Master is also to take an account of the debts of the said Joan Kemp which remained unsatisfied at the time of her death and is to make an allowance thereof to the said defendants, the executors, out of the estate of the said testatrix and is also to make them all just allowances, and, for the better taking the account etc. and what, upon taking the said account, shall appear to be the personal estate of the said Joan Kemp after her debts satisfied and all other just allowances made to the said defendants, the executors, as aforesaid, it is ordered and decreed that the said defendants, the executors, do pay one-fourth part thereof to the plaintiff Gregor with interest for the same to be computed by the said Master from the end of the year after the death of the said testatrix and do likewise out of the three remaining fourths of the said Joan's estate pay unto the plaintiff Gregor £250, being a fourth part of the £1000 so disposed by the said Joan in fraud of the said articles; and do likewise pay interest for the said £250 from a year after the death of the said testatrix Joan Kemp; but, as to the other defendants to whom the said £1000 were given by the said Joan Kemp, His Lordship [LORD MACCLESFIELD] does order that the matter of the plaintiff Gregor's bill do stand dismissed out of this court with costs to be taxed etc., but such costs are to be repaid by the defendants, the executors, who are also to pay the plaintiff's own costs so to be taxed etc. Reg. Lib. A, 1722, ff. 267–269.

574
Thompson v. Thompson

(Ch. 1723)

A married woman cannot enter into an enforceable contract with her husband.

Lincoln's Inn MS. Misc. 11, p. 237

5 February 1722[/23].

The plaintiff's husband, upon his marriage, entered into articles to make a settlement upon the plaintiff and, thereby, covenanted to leave her £200 in money if she survived him or, if she died in his lifetime, that she might dispose of £100 to whom she thought fit by a writing under her hand and seal and that he would pay it.

The plaintiff had a niece, to whom, upon her marriage, the plaintiff's husband gave £150 as a portion. And the plaintiff, by a writing under her hand and seal, declared that, if she survived her husband, the £150 which had been paid for her niece's portion should be deducted out of the £200 which she would be entitled to by her marriage articles or, if she died in her husband's lifetime, that the £150 should be taken to be a satisfaction of the £100 which, in such case, she would have a right to dispose of.

The bill was brought against the executors of the husband to have a satisfaction of the £200. And the question was if this agreement should bind the wife.

The Master of the Rolls [Jekyll] was of opinion it should not, for she, being a married woman and *sub potestate viri*, could not discharge the marriage agreement or make any contract or agreement relating to the £200, and it might be of dangerous consequence to establish such agreements. And he decreed the £200 to the plaintiff.

Note it was not suggested that the plaintiff's husband had used any unfair or coercive means to prevail on her to sign this agreement.

575

Carteret v. Carteret

(Ch. 1723)

A fine or recovery by a beneficiary of a trust in tail binds in equity the issue or bar the remainders in the same manner as they would at law if he had had the legal estate in him.

Executory devises limited on fees which are circumscribed by lives in being are good.

British Library MS. Hargrave 81, f. 202

12 February 1722[/23]. In court.

In this case, it was held by My Lord Chancellor [Lord Macclesfield] that a fine or recovery by a *cestui que trust* in tail would in equity bind the issue or bar the remainders in the same manner as they would at law if he had had the legal estate in him and that so it had been oftentimes held in this court.

But the principal case was that Sir George Cartwright, being seised of the estate in question of about £300 *per annum* and having several children, who had been bred up in France in the Popish religion, devises this estate to trustees and their heirs in trust for one of his sons and his heirs provided he did within two years after his death become a Protestant and conform to the Church of England and, if not, then in trust for the defendant, who was his daughter, and her heirs provided she did within two years next after the expiration of the first two years or within six months after notice should be given her of this will become a Protestant and conform to the Church of England with several like limitations over. And he died. All the children at the death of the testator were above eighteen years of age. The son did not conform within the first two years, but the daughter did, within the time limited for her taking the estate, receive the Sacrament twice according to the rites of the Church of England but no other act of conformity whatever as appeared by the proofs in the cause nor had any of the other children conformed.

And this bill was brought by the next Protestant heir against the defendant and the trustees to have a conveyance of the estate and a discovery of deeds and writings upon the Statute 11 Will. III.[1] And it was urged for him, first, that the children being all above the age of eighteen years at the death of their father and being then Papists were incapable of taking; secondly, that being so, no conformity after will help them; thirdly, that, if it would, that this bare receiving the Sacrament twice was not a sufficient conformity within the words or meaning of this will.

But My Lord Chancellor [Lord Macclesfield] was clear of opinion that this case was entirely out of the Statute of Will. III, for, here, it was not a devise to them until they should become Protestants and conform to the Church of

[1] Stat. 11 Will. III, c. 14 (*SR*, VII, 586–587).

England, and, therefore, as Papists, they were not to take at all by the will and, when they become Protestants according to the terms of the will, all disabilities would then be removed. But he was very doubtful whether the defendant had sufficiently qualified herself within the words and meaning of this will to take the estate, for the words are in the conjunctive not in the disjunctive, become a Protestant and conform to the Church of England, and barely receiving the Sacrament twice was not a sufficient evidence of that, for it does not appear she was ever at church after or ever went to consult with any divine of the Church of England or ever made any renunciation of the errors of the Church of Rome, and several who have received the Sacrament to save their estates have been observed never to appear at church after.

But, because it was affirmed that the defendant was really a Protestant, the cause was ordered to stand over for a few days that the court might consider whether they should now let in the defendant to manifest her conformity and being a Protestant by any other acts being after the time allowed by the will for that purpose, as was said to have been done in the case of one Rawlinson, a Quaker, who had an estate given him upon the like terms, and the court let him in to manifest his conformity after the time prescribed by the will by other acts besides going to church, which was all he had proved to have done as evidence of his conformity within the time limited by the will.

And My Lord was clear of opinion that these executory devises being limited on fees which were circumscribed by lives in being were good.

[Other copies of this report: British Library MS. Hargrave 82, f. 208.]

Lincoln's Inn MS. Misc. 12, p. 4

25 May 1723. Elizabeth Carteret, plaintiff; Dame Mary Carteret, *vidua*, Edward, Philip, George, James, Elizabeth, Francis, and Anne Carteret, Sir Thomas Hardy, *et al.*, defendants.

Dame Elizabeth Carteret, the plaintiff's aunt, by will, devised a freehold estate at Hillindon in Middlesex to Sir Thomas Hardy and other trustees and their heirs upon trust out of the rents to pay several annuities to the plaintiff's father, Sir Charles Carteret [1667–1719], and the defendant, Dame Mary, his wife, and the defendants, her children, and, after the death of Sir Charles, the trustees were to stand seised subject to the annuities to the use of the eldest son of Sir Charles for two years and, if such eldest son should within two years after the death of the testator become a Protestant of the communion of the Church of England and receive the Sacrament according to the usage thereof is some cathedral or parish church in the presence of three credible witnesses, then to the use of such eldest son and the heirs male of his body being Protestants and so to the use of every son and sons of the said Sir Charles successively one after another and the heirs male of their bodies being Protestants, and, in case neither of the said sons should become a Protestant as aforesaid or should die without issue male, then to the use of the eldest daughter of Sir Charles as should then be living and be a Protestant as aforesaid and so to the use of every other daughter of Sir Charles successively one after another and the heirs male of their bodies lawfully begotten, being Protestants, and, in case neither of the said daughters should become a Protestant or should die without issue male, being Protestant, then to the use of the defendant Edward Hales and his heirs. And, by a codicil, she revokes the limitation of the remainder in fee and gives it to Sir Edward for life only and, afterwards, to his issue.

The testator died in March 1716, and Sir Charles Carteret died in July 1719. Sir Charles and the defendant Dame Mary, his wife, and all their children except the plaintiff were Papists. But the plaintiff, having conformed to the Church of England by receiving the Sacraments and having made an agreement with her mother and brother and sisters for their annuities, brought her bill against them and against the trustees and Sir Edward Hales and his sons that the trustees might join with her in suffering a recovery.

The first question was if the devise was not void by the Statute,[1] being a devise to Papists.

But, as to that Lord Chancellor [LORD MACCLESFIELD] declared the Act of Parliament cannot operate, the devise not being to a Papist but exclusive of such and being to such persons under the descriptions in the will as should become Protestants.

The next question was as to the plaintiff's conformity and she having only proved that she had received the Sacraments twice in the Church of England, Lord Chancellor [LORD MACCLESFIELD] was under some doubt whether that was a sufficient evidence of her being a Protestant in regard it did not appear that she had constantly frequented the service of the Church of England. And, therefore, the cause was ordered to stand over in order to give His Lordship further satisfaction.

And it now came on again. And it appeared by affidavits that, since the last hearing, that she had been several times at the service of the church and had received the Sacrament three several times and had also taken the oaths of allegiance and supremacy and subscribed the test.

This being satisfactory to the court, it was insisted by the defendant, Sir Edward Hales, that the trustees ought not to join with the plaintiff in suffering a recovery and barring the remainders for that it would be to do a thing contrary to the trust reposed in them.

Lord Chancellor [LORD MACCLESFIELD]: The *cestui que trust* has a right to come into this court and to pray that he may have the legal estate conveyed to him, that so he may have a power to bring actions. But, if an estate is devised to trustees upon trust out of the rents to pay an annuity to one for life and subject

1 Stat. 11 Will. III, c. 14 (*SR*, VII, 586–587).

to the annuity upon trust for A.B. or his heirs, in that case, though the annuitant has a power to distrain, yet, during the life of the annuitant, A.B. is not entitled to have the estate conveyed to him.

But, in the present case, the annuities being void as being given to Papists, His Lordship, at first, decreed the trustees to convey the estate in question to the plaintiff and the heirs male of her body with a remainder to Sir Edward Hales and his sons according to the codicil. But, afterwards, upon further consideration it not appearing what age the other daughters were at the death of the testator and, consequently, whether they might not if the remainder came to them conform when they came to the age of eighteen according to the Statute, the Master was ordered to enquire what ages the children were of at the death of the testator and then to come back to the court.

Note, when this cause was first heard, a case was cited for the plaintiff to show that the plaintiff's receiving the Sacrament was a sufficient evidence of her conformity, which was the Case of Rawlinson and the Archbishop of York, heard before Lord Cowper 2 May 1710,[1] and, as to that, the case was John Rawlinson, by will, devised land to trustees upon trust to pay some annuities and then to permit his niece Lowther and, after her death, his niece Aislabie to receive the rest of the rents until such time only as some son of his nephew, the defendant William Rawlinson, should conform to and profess the Protestant religion according to the doctrine of the Church of England as the same was then by law established and be confirmed by a bishop of the said church and, in case any such son should within seven years after the testator's death so conform and be confirmed, then to convey to such son in the manner therein mentioned. The plaintiff was the son of a Quaker, but, having been baptized and confirmed, he brought his bill to have the estate conveyed to him. Lord Cowper declared that the plaintiff by being baptized and confirmed by the bishop has so far conformed as to save a forfeiture but not so far as to have a conveyance and settlement until he should have received the Sacrament. And, therefore, he ordered the cause to stand over until the plaintiff could produce some evidence of that.

[Other reports of this case: 2 Peere Williams 132, 24 E.R. 670, 2 Eq. Cas. Abr. 622, 749, 22 E.R. 522, 635.]

[1] *Rawlinson v. Storeby* (Ch. 1711), British Library MS. Hargrave 80, f. 43, pl. 2, Chancery Cases *tempore* Harcourt, 105.

576

Beaumont v. Fell

(Ch. 1723)

Parol evidence is admissible to explain a mistaken identity of a specific legatee.

Where co-executors have a power to give a preference as to a legacy, they must act jointly, and if one dies before the power is exercised, the power fails.

Executors, in the case of a deficiency of the assets of the testator's estate, must pay all the legatees proportionally and cannot prefer one legatee to another.

British Library MS. Hargrave 81, f. 205

February 1722[/23], at the Rolls; Beaumont v. Lance.

A man, having a very great kindness and affection for one Mrs. Gertrude Yardley for several years and having frequently declared that he would leave her £500 at his death and that, if it did not appear by his will after his death that he had left her £500, that he would give everybody leave to say he did not die an honest man with several other like expressions of kindness towards her, as was fully proved in the cause, being taken ill, sends for the school master of the place where he lived to make his will and, among other legacies, he directs them to give £500 to Gatty or Kathy Arley, as the person who made the will apprehended. But not fully understanding whom he meant by it, he, several times, asked whom he meant or what he should call her. And he still explained it in such an obscure manner that the person who made the will could not understand it, upon which he asked him if he should write down her name Katherine Arley. And the testator agreed he should, adding that she was an acquaintance of Mr. English, as in truth Mrs. Yardley was, and down in the will it was written. And, when he had so done, he read it over to the testator, who approved it and, soon after, died. It was proved in the cause that the testator was an illiterate man, that he could neither write nor read, and that he sometimes called Gertrude Yardley Gatty, sometimes Katty, and sometimes Kitty, and that there was no other person whatsoever of his acquaintance named Katherine Ardley. And it appeared plainly to be a mistake for Gertrude Yardley.

And now, this bill was brought by the administrator of Gertrude Yardley to have an account of the personal estate and to be paid this legacy of £500. And the case of Keen v. Keen in My Lord Cowper's time, in Hilary Term 1709, was cited, where a man having several nephews gave the residue of his estate, which was above £20,000, to his nephew Christopher Ernest Keen of such a place and had no nephew named Christopher Ernest Keen at that place, his name being Randolph Keen, but then he had a nephew named Christopher Ernest Keen, but he lived at another place and not at the place named in the will, upon which proof was admitted to be read to explain his will, which of the nephews, who were brothers, he meant. And My Lord Cheney's Case, 5, 68, was cited, and the

Case of the Countess of Derby,[1] who living at Kew Green near Richmond had founded and endowed a school for poor boys and girls there and, by her will, gives £500 'for the augmentation of the maintenance of the poor boys and girls at [*blank*]' leaving a blank for the place. Yet parol proof was admitted to explain that she meant at Kew Green.

But the Master of the Rolls [JEKYLL] thought it too dangerous a point to establish against the Statute of Frauds and Perjuries,[2] this will being for above £30, *viz.* of a legacy of £500, and so required in the Statute to be in writing, that to admit parol proof would introduce uncertainty in wills and elude the Statute, and, therefore, he dismissed the bill as to this point.

But this was thought by everybody not to be right and that he ought to have admitted such proof in this case.

Another point [was] the testator had given legacies to several persons and makes two executors and empowers such executors to give preference in payment of the legacies to which of the legatees they thought fit, and one of the executors was dead. And whether this power should survive was the question.

And it was argued that it should, together with the office, and was a power annexed to the execution of their office as executors, which was to pay legacies.

But the Master of the Rolls [JEKYLL] was clear of opinion that it being a bare power not accoupled with an interest and that too against the duty and office of an executor, which was to pay all legatees in proportion, that it should not survive but was at an end by the death of one of the executors.

Note that, in the printed case, afterwards, the MASTER OF THE ROLLS, having taken time to consider of it, decreed the devise of the £500 to be good and cited Co. Litt. of a devise to Thomas, earl of Pembroke, etc., and Swinburn 389[3] etc.

[Other copies of this report: British Library MS. Hargrave 82, f. 211, Lincoln's Inn MS. Misc. 107, f. 98.]

Lincoln's Inn MS. Misc. 12, p. 13

Hilary term 1722[/23]. Beaumont v. Lance *et al.*

Benjamin Jackson, by will, amongst other legacies, gave to one Mrs. Catherine Erly £500, and he made the defendant Lance executor.

There was no such person as Catherine Erly to be found. But it was proved in the cause that the testator for several years before his death was well acquainted with one Gertrude Yardley, and he often declared he had a great value for her and that she was the woman in the world he admired and that he had married

---

1 *Lord Cheyney's Case* (1591), 5 Coke Rep. 68, 76 E.R. 158, also Moore K.B. 727, 72 E.R. 867; *Attorney General, ex rel. v. Earl of Arran* (Ch. 1719), see above, Case No. 394.

2 Stat. 29 Car. II, c. 3, s. 5 (*SR*, V, 840).

3 H. Swinburne, *Brief Treatise of Testaments and Last Wills.*

her but, hearing she was involved with her father's debts, said he durst not, but that, at his death, he would convince the world how great a share she had in his affections.

The same witness, Mr. English, proved that the testator, about two or three years before his death, frequently told him he, the testator, would leave her £500 and that the deponent should look into his will and, if he did not find it so, he should say Ben Jackson did not die an honest man. And he believed that, by Katherine Erly, the testator meant the said Gertrude Yardley. And he deposed further that the testator, about a year before he died hearing Sir Stephen Fox had left her but a small annuity, he often mentioned it with concern, and he declared that, at his death, he would do more for her than all her relations had done and that the testator usually called her Katty Erly.

Mr. Burroughs, who drew the will, deposed that, upon discourse with the testator about a legacy of £500 given to Kat Erly, he told him she was a friend of Mr. or Mrs. English and that they knew where she lived, that he put the testator's will into writing and read it over to him. He remembers that the testator, either through weakness or not being acquainted with the spelling of names, did pronounce the Christian name of the legatee so unintelligibly, the deponent several times asked him whether he said Gatty, Caty, or Kitty, whereupon he directed the deponent to write down her Christian name Katherine, which he did and read over the same to him, as well as the surname.

The Master of the Rolls [Jekyll], upon hearing this cause, was of opinion that the £500 legacy was not payable to the defendant Fenn, the executor of Gertrude Yardley, who died after the testator. But, afterwards, upon taking time to consider of the case, he decreed the legacy to be paid.

He said testamentary cases were to be governed by the rules of the canon and ecclesiastical law and not by the common law.

In the present case, there is no person that is called Kat Ernle and, therefore, no other rival. The defendant Fenn is the only person who claims the legacy, and the proofs are very strong that the testator by Katherine Erle meant Gertrude Yardley.

As to the objection of the Statute of Frauds, that is out of the case, for the defendant claims by a will in writing and not by a parol will.

In this case were cited the Case of Counden and Clerke, in Hobart;[1] Swinburne 396; Keen and Keen, a late case in this court; and the Case on Lady Derby's will, *quod vide, Lib.* C, 112.

Lincoln's Inn MS. Misc. 384, p. 227, pl. 1

30 May 1723, Rolls.

[1] *Counden v. Clerke* (1614), Hobart 29, 80 E.R. 180, also Moore K.B. 860, 72 E.R. 955, 1 Eq. Cas. Abr. 213, 22 E.R. 998.

There was a devise to Catherine Ernley of £500. Her real name was Gertrude Yardley. It was proved that the testator intended this person to take. There was no person called Catherine Ernley.

The decree was that the devise was good, the proof being clear and there being no other person to take. If any other could have taken, the devise had been void. Swinburn 389. If there was a devise to J.N., intending J.S., neither can take. J.N. cannot take because he was not meant; J.S. cannot because he was not named. Justinian, *de Testamentis*;[1] Co. Litt., to Thomas, earl of Pembroke, whereas his name was J., was good.

Lincoln's Inn MS. Misc. 384, p. 245

30 May 1723. Rolls.

A legacy of £500 was given to Catherine Ernley. Her name was Gertrude Yardley. In cases of grants, they are void where there is a mistake in name, especially in a Christian name, except it is helped by an addition. As to Thomas, earl of Pembroke, where his name was Henry, it was good because there was but one earl of Pembroke. Co. Litt. There may be several Sir Jameses but one Christian name. In the case of legacies, it is to be governed by the civil law.

Objection: The Statute of Frauds.[2] If she takes here, it must be by a nuncupative will.

Answer: She takes by a written will, and, as to the personal estate, it is no alter[ation] by the Statute. If, before the Statute, a legatee might show himself to be intended, so he may now, though there is an error in the name. Swinburn 389. [If there be an] error in the person, supposing an executor or legatee to be another person, [it is] void. If J.S. and J.N. are real persons and a legacy is given to J.N. intending J.S., neither can take, not J.N. because he was not intended, nor J.S. because he was not named. An error in name but not in person does not hurt except in certain cases, as where the testator is blind or mistaking the name of his own child lest [it be] taken as insanity.

The present case is an error in name only. There is no person named Catherine Ernly, *ergo*, there is nobody capable of [confusion][3] with Gertrude Yardley. In the present case, there is full proof that the testator intended Gertrude Yardley, professions of kindness and an intention to leave her something previous to the will. He used to call her Galey or Kaley, which sound alike. The testator, being asked whom he meant, referred to persons with whom she lived. There is no other person to whom the name agrees.

He decreed payment of the £500 legacy to her.

---

[1] Justinian, *Institutes*, 2, 10.

[2] Stat. 29 Car. II, c. 3 (*SR*, V, 839–842).

[3] controv. *MS*.

Lincoln's Inn MS. Misc. 12, p. 15

The testator, by his will, had directed that, in case the moneys arising by the sale of an estate, which he had ordered to be sold for the payment of his debts and legacies, should not be sufficient after the payment of his debts and funerals to pay all his legacies, then his executors should not make a dividend in proportion but should pay to such legatees only as they thought proper their full legacies as far as the moneys would go. One of the executors was dead. And the question was if the surviving executor, there being not sufficient [assets] to pay all the legacies, could prefer which of the legatees he thought fit.

The Master of the Rolls [Jekyll] was of opinion he could not. He said it was a bare naked power and not annexed to an estate, and, therefore, it did not survive, according to Co. Littleton, where two executors have a power to sell and one dies, the other cannot sell.

As to the objection that it is a power annexed to their office as executors, he said it was not a power annexed to their office, for the office of executors is in the case of a deficiency of the assets to pay all the legatees ratably and proportionally and not to prefer one legatee before another.

[Other reports of this case: 2 Peere Williams 141, 24 E.R. 673, 2 Eq. Cas. Abr. 366, 22 E.R. 311.]

577

Vernon v. Yalden

(Ch. 1723)

An administrator stands in the place of his decedent and cannot be in a better position.

Lincoln's Inn MS. Misc. 11, p. 238

14 February 1722[/23].

An obligee in a bond gives a declaration in trust declaring that his name was used in trust for A. And, afterwards, he assigns this bond for a valuable consideration to B., who has no notice of the declaration of trust. The obligee dies, and B. gets administration.

The plaintiff, who was the obligor, brings a bill of interpleader against A. and B., who both claimed the debt. And the question was to whom it belonged.

It was insisted for B. that, having taken administration to the obligee, he had both law and equity on his side and, therefore, was in a better condition than A., who had only equity, as where a man purchases and takes a conveyance in the name of a trustee and assigns his equitable interest to one and, afterwards, makes a second assignment of his equitable interest to another for a valuable consideration who has no notice of the first assignment and the second assignee gets in the legal estate from the trustee, he shall hold against the first assignee.

The Master of the Rolls [JEKYLL] was of opinion that B. had no right to the money due on the bond, for, although he was the administrator to the obligee and had by that means the legal interest of the bond in him, yet he could be in no better a condition than the intestate was and he could only stand in his place. And he was no other than a trustee for A., to whom he had given a deed of trust. And as to the subsequent assignment, nothing passed by that, for he had no equitable interest then remaining in him, having before executed a deed of trust. And, therefore, it differs from the case mentioned, where *a cestui que* trust, who has an equitable interest in him, makes a first and second assignment of that interest.

578

Anonymous

(Ch. c. 1723)

Where a debt due to a married woman accrued during the marriage but was not paid, the right to the money belongs to the husband or his next of kin.

Lincoln's Inn MS. Misc. 11, p. 239

This case was reported to me by Mr. Martin.

A woman, being the obligee in a bond, marries, and, before the debt is received, she dies. And, afterwards, the husband dies intestate, the bond still remaining due.

By Lord Chancellor PARKER, the next of kin of the husband and not of the wife, though the husband had not taken administration of the wife, are entitled to take administration to the wife and to have this debt. And, in case administration to the wife should be granted to the next of kin of the wife, they would be only trustees for the next of kin of the husband.

579

Reresby v. Newland

(Ch. 1723)

Where a daughter's portion is to begin at some future time, a court of equity cannot accelerate its vesting contrary to the terms of the deed no matter how hard that might be for the donee.

British Library MS. Hargrave 81, f. 209

Thursday, 21 February 1722[/23], at the Lord Chancellor's house.

On the defendant's marriage in 1688 with Mrs. Mary Gardiner, who had a portion of £2500, a settlement was made by the defendant to the use of himself for life, remainder to trustees during his life to support contingent remainders, remainder to his intended wife for her life for jointure, remainder to his first and other sons of that marriage in tail male successively, with remainder to trustees for a term of 500 years, remainder to the defendant's right heirs, and the terms of 500 years was declared to be in trust that, in case there were no issue male of that marriage or that all such issue male should die without issue male before they attained their respective ages of twenty-one years, then the trustees of the said term were by and out of the rents and profits of the said lands or by mortgage or sale thereof or of any part thereof to raise and pay the portions and maintenances following for the daughter or daughters of that marriage, that is to say, if but one daughter, then the sum of £3000 and, if two daughters, then the sum of £4000 between them and, if three or more such daughters, then the sum of £6000 equally between them, the said portion and portions to be paid and payable to such daughter and daughters at their respective ages of eighteen years or days of marriage, which should first happen, and, in the meantime, the sum of £35 apiece for the maintenance of such daughter or daughters to be paid and payable to her or them at the most usual feasts or days of payment in the year, that is to say, at the feast of St. Michael the Archangel and the Annunciation of the Blessed Virgin Mary, the first payment thereof to begin at such of the said feasts as should first happen next after the death of the defendant with a proviso that, after the portions and maintenance raised and paid or, if there should be no such daughter or daughters who should be living at the death of the defendant and that the said Mary Vincent should not be enceinte of any daughter or daughters at the time of the death of the defendant or, if the person or persons next in remainder or reversion should pay or give security for the said portion or portions, then and in all or any the said cases, the said term of 500 years was to cease, with a proviso that it should be lawful for the defendant at anytime during his natural life with the consent of the trustees or of the survivor of them and his heirs to revoke and make void all or any the uses and trusts in the said indenture mentioned.

The marriage takes effect. The wife dies about twenty-five years ago leaving issue only the plaintiff's wife, who attained her age of eighteen many years since and had been some years married to the plaintiff Reresby. But, as was proved in the cause, this was without the privity or consent of the defendant, her father, and, therefore, he refused to give her any portion, upon which this bill was brought to have the reversionary term of 500 years sold and the £3000 raised and paid.

It was proved in the cause that the defendant had been very unkind to the plaintiff, his daughter, not only in allowing her no maintenance but also in sending over for a foreigner who about eighteen years ago being here pretended to have married the daughter but had long since quitted all pretensions of that sort and returned to his own country, yet, upon the plaintiffs' intermarriage, the defendant sent over for this foreigner, treated him with great respect as his son-in-law and, upon his death, which happened not long since, buried him very pompously as his son-in-law. And he dying intestate, the defendant took out administration to him and thereby would have entitled himself to this £3000 as his daughter's portion belonging to the said foreigner, her husband.

But, on the other side, there was great proof to overthrow all this and a sentence in the spiritual court upon a suit there for jactitation of marriage against this pretended marriage. But there, proof by consent on both sides was wholly waived. And the defendants submitted to hear the cause upon the construction of the settlement whether the £3000 upon the several parts of this settlement could be raised in the father's lifetime or not.

My Lord Chancellor [Lord Macclesfield] very much condemned the defendant's behavior towards his daughter and said, if there had been any ground for the raising of this portion, he would have decreed it. But he was of opinion upon the whole settlement that it could not now be raised and, if the daughter should die before the defendant, her father, it would never be raisable at all. He said that this doctrine of raising portions in the lifetime of the father was against both reason and nature and would encourage the utmost undutifulness in children towards their parents, that it first began in a court of law in Greaves and Mattison's Case[1] and from thence came over to this court but, upon what ground or solid foundation it ever took place, he could not possibly discover, that it was the most monstrous thing in nature that, when the term was not to take place in possession until after the father's death, that this should be made a fund for raising it in his life, that it could never be raised without great loss and inconvenience to the family, for such a reversionary term would not sell for half the worth as it would do after the father's death when it came into possession. But since it had obtained that, in some cases, such portions should be raised even in the lifetime of the father, he would not now shake those cases, that however indifferent it were which way a point was settled at first, yet, when it once came to be settled, it would be the most dangerous thing in the world to overturn it, that it was striking a blow in the dark which whom it might murder or destroy no one living could tell, that the points which had been once settled were like ancient landmarks which ought never to be removed and therefore so far as the courts had already gone in this point, so far he would go but not a step further, and that, if he could distinguish this case from those which had been settled the other way, he would never decree the raising of the portion in the lifetime of the father how inconvenient soever it might prove to the plaintiffs. And he thought it might happen, if the father overlived his daughter, that the plaintiff would have no portion at all with his wife. And he said this case plainly differed from the other cases, for here, by all the parts of the settlement, it plainly appears that the portion was not to be raised until after the father's death, nay, that, if the father survived his

[1] *Greaves v. Mattison* (1682), T. Jones 201, 84 E.R. 1216, Skinner 38, 90 E.R. 19, 1 Eq. Cas. Abr. 336, 21 E.R. 1085.

daughter whatever age she was of or that she should leave several children, yet there was no help for it. That the maintenance was not to begin until after the father's death appears by an express clause, and yet that was to precede the raising of the portion, for, when the portion is raised, the maintenance ceases of course. But to raise the portion now is to make that precede the maintenance and so to invert the order of the settlement, that whatever inconveniences might arise to the children by this construction, as their not having their portions until they came to be fifty or sixty years of age and so to have no occasion for them or their loosing several good offers of marriage for want of their portion when they were young or such like, the same inconveniences would have happened if the mother had been living. And yet, in that case, there could have been no pretense to have demanded them in the lifetime of the father. But this is but beyond all possibility of doubt by the power of revocation which lasts during the father's life, that the father was a purchaser of this power of revocation as much as the mother was of her jointure or the children of their provision, that to say, when the daughter attained eighteen, the portion was in equity vested in her and, therefore, could not be defeated by a revocation was to make the power wholly useless, for so, if there had been a son, the estate would have vested in him at the instant of his birth and yet, by the father's executing his power of revocation, it would have again been divested, that perhaps this very power of revocation was the terms without which the marriage had never been. And, though he would not suffer the defendant idly or wantonly to destroy or revoke this settlement without very good reason, yet he would not say neither that he should not, for there might happen a case wherein it might be absolutely necessary as for the purpose if he had been ruined and undone in the South Sea [bubble] or by other inevitable accidents, surely, in such cases, he might revoke the settlement to preserve himself and his family. And, upon the whole, he said he could not help the plaintiffs and dismissed their bill.

[Other copies of this report: British Library MS. Hargrave 82, f. 212.]

[Other reports of this case: 2 Peere Williams 93, 24 E.R. 655, 6 Brown P.C. 75, 2 E.R. 942, 2 Eq. Cas. Abr. 644, 672, 746, 22 E.R. 540, 565, 633.]

580

Anonymous

(Ch. 1723)

Where several legacies are given out of specific funds and these funds are insufficient to pay them, there shall be an abatement among those legacies only.

8 Viner, Abr. 424

Hilary vacation 1723, Master of the Rolls.

Where several legacies are given out of bonds, securities, etc. and these fall deficient, there shall be an abatement among them only, and [it shall] not affect other legatees. Where there are several pecuniary legatees, they must abate in proportion, but no specific legatee, except in the case of his legacy.

581

Whitehead v. Newnham

(Ch. 1723)

Who a person's heir is cannot be known until that person's death.

There can be no devise over after a dying without issue.

The words 'for the default of such issue' refer to the time of the person's death.

Lincoln's Inn MS. Misc. 11, p. 240

1 March 1722[/23]. John Whitehead and Frances, his wife, plaintiffs; John Newnham *et al.*, defendants.

John Skinner, by will, gave a leasehold house to the defendants Gilbert and Mary in trust to permit Edith, the testator's wife to receive the rents during her life and, afterwards, to permit the plaintiff Frances and such child and children of her body as should be her heir or heirs at law and the heirs of the body and bodies of all and every such child or children to have and enjoy the said house and receive the rents to their own use for the remainder of the term then to come and, for default of such issue, that the said trustees should stand possessed of the said house for the then residue of the term in trust for the benefit of such minister for the time as should perform the offices of the Church of England there. And, after some legacies, he gave the residue of his personal estate to the said Gilbert and Mary in trust to permit his wife Edith to receive the interest thereof for her life and, afterwards, in trust for the only use of the plaintiff Frances and, in the case of her death, for the use of the surviving children of Thomas Newnham, equally to be divided. And he made Edith, his wife, executrix during her life, and, afterwards, he made Gilbert and Mary executors, requesting them to manage in the best manner they could what he had therein given to the plaintiff

Frances for her benefit and to pay over and deliver the same with the profit thereof at her day of marriage or age of twenty-one years which should first happen or at her first competent age of discharging them. The testator's wife was dead.

Lord Chancellor [LORD MACCLESFIELD]: The plaintiff Frances has only an estate for life in the house and her children have no interest therein during her life, for the devise is to such child or children as should be heir at law, which cannot be known until she dies; if she leaves any children, such as is her heir at law will then be entitled to the whole term, for there can be no devise over after a dying without issue. But, if there is no issue living at her death, then the charity will take place, for the words 'and for the default of such issue' must be restrained to the time of her death.

As to the surplus, the plaintiff Frances being married, she is become entitled to it, for this devise over in case of her death to the children of Robert Newnham must be understood in case of her death before she is twenty-one or marriage, it being directed by the will that the surplus should be delivered over to her at her age of twenty-one or marriage.

582

Anonymous

(Ch. 1723)

The Court of Chancery can protect the interests of an infant upon a mere petition without a pending lawsuit.

British Library MS. Hargrave 83, p. 26, pl. 2

Tuesday, 5 March 1722/23, third seal after Hilary term.

This case [Bertie and Falkner][1] was mentioned by the Solicitor General [*Yorke*] as a case where an infant was taken care of by the court upon a petition, though there was no cause in court to found the petition upon. This was in the time of Lord Somers, who then said that nothing had ever given him more concern than that, while he deliberated, while he could assist, without a cause in court, it became too late for him to assist.

[1] *Bertie v. Viscount Falkland* (1715), see above, Case No. 101.

583
Leigh v. Midwinter

(Ch. 1723)

Where London orphans are given legacies by their father, their legacies will be abated by their orphanage shares so far as they will go.

Lincoln's Inn MS. Misc. 12, p. 1, pl. 1

9 March 1722[/23].

Thomas Leigh, the plaintiff's husband, being a freeman of London, by will dated 25th of September 1701, gave to Thomas, his only child, £800 to be paid at twenty-one and £800 more to the child his wife was *enceinte* with to be paid, if a son, at twenty-one, if a daughter, at twenty-one or marriage and the interest to be paid to the plaintiff for their maintenance. And, if they died before their portions become payable, then he gave the interest to the plaintiff during her life and the principal after her death to such of his sister's children as should be then living. And he made the plaintiff, his wife, executrix.

After the testator's death, there was a child born, and both the children died infants. And the plaintiff took administration.

The testator having taken no notice of the custom in his will, but made a disposition of his whole personal estate without any regard to the custom, the question was whether the children at the death of their father were entitled to their legacies and their orphanage share too.

It was decreed by the Master of the Rolls [Jekyll] an account to be taken of the personal estate and that a distribution should be made according to the custom of the City of London and that the plaintiff should be paid one third part thereof and her widow's chamber and paraphernalia and the Master to see what the children's orphanage part of the said estate does amount to.

And the said children being since dead, the court decreed that, by the custom of the said City, the said children's customary parts of the said personal estate was to be deemed a satisfaction of the respective legacies given them by the will so far as the same would extend and that the surplus only of such legacies must be taken out of the testamentary part of the said testator's estate.

And, therefore, it was ordered that the Master, in making the said division, should deduct the legacies out of the said children's orphanage [part] and certify what would be remaining due for the said two legacies and what should be remaining should be brought into court and put out at interest and such interest to be paid the plaintiff during her life and the principal at her death to be divided according to the will.

584

Cocks' Case

(Ch. 1723)

Where the creditors of a bankrupt have received part payment of bills of exchange drawn by the bankrupt and accepted by another bankrupt, they can claim the full amounts of the bills because they are so liable to prior holders by their endorsements.

British Library MS. Hargrave 81, f. 217

Friday, 22 March 1722[/23], on petitions.

Mrs. Cocks, being a merchant in London and having very great dealings, drew bills for several thousand pounds on her brother, one Vandermarsh, a merchant in Holland, which he accepted. Before the bills were paid, a commission of bankruptcy issued out against Mrs. Cocks, and, about the same time, another commission was awarded against Vandermarsh. After these commissions of bankruptcy so sued out, Vandermarsh paid £40 percent upon the several bills of Mrs. Cocks which he had so accepted.

And the question before the Commissioners upon the commission against Mrs. Cocks was whether these creditors who had thus received £40 percent upon their bills should, notwithstanding, be let in as creditors for their whole debts or only for £60 percent, which was all that really remained due to them.

It was urged for the creditors that they ought to be let in for their whole debts, that, if there were twenty who had endorsed those bills one after another, every one of them was liable to the endorsee for the whole and that, if it were otherwise, it would be greatly discouraging to merchants, who always look upon their debts to be so much the better secured by the number of the endorsers, each of which was liable for the whole and for which several actions might be brought against every one of them at the same time, that it was like a bond given by two jointly and severally, each of which was liable for the whole and the obligee might sue both of them for the whole debt at the same time, that it was true he should recover but one satisfaction. But, until his whole debt was satisfied either by the one or the other or both, he might proceed for the whole against both. So, in the present case, they ought to be let in as creditors for the whole against Mrs. Cocks, that they might receive a satisfaction of their debts to the full if their distribution would admit of it, that, if it were otherwise, it would be no sort of advantage to have two or three bound or liable to a debt more than to have one single person only, that what Vandermarsh had paid was nothing to Mrs. Cocks nor could her creditors have any benefit of it.

On the other hand, it was insisted that, in case of a bond with a penalty or a judgment given for securing a lesser sum of money, the Statutes had expressly provided that these creditors should be let in for no more than was really due and owing to them, and, therefore, no more ought these creditors in the principal case, that, if it were otherwise, they might come in to receive £20, £30, or even £40 percent more than was really due and owing to them if Mrs. Cocks' effects should hold out to pay 15 or 20s. in the pound as for aught appeared they might do.

But Lord Chancellor [Lord Macclesfield held] they ought to be admitted for their whole debts and so in case of payment of any part by either of the obligors, for the payment by one is nothing to the other, they being all equally liable to the whole debt. But, in case the dividend should hold out more than remained due, these creditors will be trustees for such overplus for Vandermarsh, who paid the £40 percent, and so will the obligee in case the receiver's part upon a commission of bankruptcy against the surety and upon another commission against the principal obligor being let in creditor for the whole debt of his dividend against the principal comes to more than was really due including what he had before received of the surety, he shall be trustee as to the surplus so received for the surety. But in case Vandermarsh paid the £40 percent out of the effects of the said Mrs. Cocks, which he had in his hands, then this was a payment of so much by her and consequently her own debt as to the now petitioners will be so much lessened so that until it be inquired and seen what effects Vandermarsh had in his hands of Mrs. Cocks at the time of his payment of the £40 percent, it cannot be known whether the petitioners if their dividend upon being let in creditors for the whole £100 percent should be more than what with the £40 percent would satisfy their whole debts whether they shall be trustees as to such surplus for Vandermarsh or not, for, if the £40 percent should appear to be paid out of Mrs. Cocks' own effects, then their dividend upon the whole £100 percent must be so much less, as she will then appear to have paid them already £40 percent, so that this enquiry must first be made before any further directions can be given.

[Other copies of this report: British Library MS. Hargrave 82, f. 218, pl. 2, Lincoln's Inn MS. Misc. 107, f. 101.]

[Other reports of this case: *sub nom. Ex parte* Ryswicke, 2 Peere Williams 89, 24 E.R. 653, 2 Eq. Cas. Abr. 116, 22 E.R. 99.]

[Related cases: Cocks v. Goodfellow (Ch. 1722), see above, Case No. 550.]

585

Anonymous v. Lord Melsington

(Ch. 1723)

In this case, a purchaser of land was ordered either to pay the full purchase price agreed upon or to forfeit the deposit even though there had been severe fluctuations in the general economy.

British Library MS. Hargrave 83, p. 27

1 May 1723, Easter term.

Lord Melsington, in the South Sea year, was reported the best purchaser of the estate of Cobham for [*blank*]; the estate was under the yearly value of £2000. My Lord made a deposit before the master of £20,000. After the fall of South Sea [Company] stock,[1] he, like many others, was desirous to get off from the extravagant price which they had agreed to give for the purchase of estates. A bill was brought against him to compel him to complete his purchase. He insisted by his answer that the plaintiffs could not make him a good title to the estate. It was referred to a master to see whether a good title could be made, who overruled all the objections to the title and reported that it was good. Upon this, notice of a motion was given that Lord Melsington might go on with his purchase before the master, which was defended by his counsel, who argued that, in some late cases, one in Chancery and the other in the House of Lords, contracts for lands had been rescinded and set aside purely for the extravagance of the price agreed for in the time of infatuation and hoped this should be so and that without any terms of forfeiting the deposit, for nothing of that was contended in the notice. If it had, they should have been prepared to have given an answer to it.

The counsel on the other side insisted that the agreement or contract for the purchase of land had not been rescinded judicially in any one case purely on account of the extravagant price. There were other circumstances and ingredients in the two cases aimed at, and, upon them, one agreement was vacated here and the other in the House of Lords. As to the deposit, it was not their business to desire or accept of it as a deposit to be forfeited. It was for the advantage of their clients that it should be taken in part of payment and that Lord Melsington should go on and complete his purchase.

Lord Chancellor [Lord Macclesfield] said this case was different from the case of other contracts, for, in them, a party who had a remedy at law upon his covenant came into this court for to be aided farther and have a specific performance of the agreement. But, in this case, the argument really was with the court and the party had no remedy at law. He was fast and could not sell his estate to any other when a best purchaser was reported who had made a deposit, not as an

[1] I.e. the burst of the South Sea bubble in 1720.

earnest or penalty, but really as part of payment. Indeed, in these hard bargains, he had laid hold of the forfeiture of the deposit as the most equitable measure and handle for the court to release the extravagant bidders from their contract made with the court, but this was done at their request. If Lord Melsington would not apply to fare as others had done and forfeit his deposit and give up his right to the estate, he must [take] the other alternative and go on to complete his purchase.

586

Anonymous

(Ch. 1723)

A jointure or a contract to make a jointure will not defeat a London widow's customary share of her deceased husband's estate.

British Library MS. Hargrave 83, p. 29, pl. 2

8 May 1723.

In curiam, [it was] then said that any agreement by the husband to settle lands upon his wife or any settlement of lands is not a bar to the wife of her customary share of her husband's personal estate by the custom of the City of London and that this had been determined in a case which His Honor [JEKYLL] said he argued.[1]

587

Anonymous

(Ch. 1723)

A bail piece must be proved by an official copy of it and not by producing the judge's book.

British Library MS. Hargrave 83, p. 30, pl. 1

Eodem die [8 May 1723].

An objection was made to the reading of a witness for the plaintiff because he was bail to the action at law brought against the plaintiff upon the bond against which relief was now prayed. And to make good this objection, they offered to prove it by the judge's book, which they were ready to produce.

But Mr. *Lutwyche* insisted that was not sufficient, but they ought to prove their objection by a copy of the bail piece.

And so thought the Master of the Rolls [JEKYLL]. And they not being ready to do that, the witness was read.

---

[1] Perhaps *Atkyns v. Waterson* (Ch. 1715–1716), see above, Case No. 83.

588

Moor v. Barkham

(Ch. 1723)

Grandparents on both sides of an intestate's family take equally under the Statute of Distributions.

Lincoln's Inn MS. Misc. 13, p. 10

13 May 1723. Moor v. Banham.

One dies intestate, leaving a grandfather by the father's side and a grandmother on the mother's side. They shall take in equal moieties upon the Statute of Distribution,[1] as being in equal degree, for, though the grandfather on the father's side may in some respects be of the worthier blood, as being of the father's side, yet dignity of blood is not material upon the Statute, but the equality of the degree of kindred is the only thing to be regarded, as the degree of kindred must be equal. And the worthiness of blood is not material in regard the brother of the half blood shall take equally with the brother of the whole blood.

And the Master of the Rolls [JEKYLL] was so clear in this that he would not admit it to be debated.

[Other copies of this report: 1 Peere Williams 53, 24 E.R. 289.]

[Other reports of this case: 2 Eq. Cas. Abr. 441, 22 E.R. 376.]

589

Henriques v. Martin

(Ch. 1723)

Marriage contracts made between Jews in England are governed by the law of England.

Where property descends from a debtor to a creditor, this is a satisfaction of the debt.

Lincoln's Inn MS. Misc. 12, p. 2

23 May 1723.

The defendant had married a Jew. And, before such marriage, an agreement was drawn up in writing according to the Jewish form whereby, the defendant's husband taking notice that her portion was £1000, he agrees to add £500 more and that this should be her dowry and should be paid her out of the best of his goods and effects.

---

1 Stat. 22 & 23 Car. II, c. 10 (*SR*, V, 719–720).

The defendant's husband died intestate, and the defendant insisted to be paid this £1500 as a debt and her distributive share too.

On the other hand, it was insisted by the plaintiff that she could only have the £1500 and that this was to be in satisfaction of all she could claim out of her husband's estate. And they offered to read some witnesses to show what was the Jewish law in this case.

The Master of the Rolls [Jekyll]: The contract must be expounded according to the common law and not according to the Jewish law. And, therefore, it is to no purpose to read witnesses as to that matter.

The defendant cannot have both the £1500 and her distributive share too. But, if her distributive share is more than the £1500, it will be a satisfaction of the £1500. It is a matter that has been settled in this court. If a man enters into a bond to leave his wife £1000 at his death and he dies intestate, the condition of the bond at law is forfeited, but, in equity, it is a good performance of it that the wife's share by the Statute of Distributions[1] amounts to £1000.

This was said at the bar to have been the Case of one Wigmore,[2] which was heard before the late Master of the Rolls [Trevor] and so decreed, and, upon an appeal to Lord Cowper, the decree was affirmed.

The Master of the Rolls [Jekyll] cited a case where a man had covenanted to settle lands upon his son in tail and he left lands in fee simple to descend upon him; this was decreed to be a satisfaction of the covenant.

590

Dalston v. Coatsworth

(Ch. 1723)

A court of equity can establish a lost deed and will presume the contents against the person who destroyed it.

Lincoln's Inn MS. Misc. 384, p. 244

30 May 1723. At the Rolls.

A bill [was exhibited] to have the benefit of a deed destroyed by the defendant. The contents were set out imperfectly in the bill. The plaintiff claimed a remainder of a thousand years term subject to the defendant's life. The proof was strong that the defendant burned it. The witness was mistaken about the contents.

Curia [Jekyll]: The burning it is an evidence the deed was such as gave the plaintiff a title stronger than the witness's, a mistake of the word 'heirs' being in

[1] Stat. 22 & 23 Car. II, c. 10 (*SR*, V, 719–720).

[2] *Blandy v. Widmore* (1716), 2 Vernon 709, 23 E.R. 1066, 1 Peere Williams 324, 24 E.R. 408, 2 Eq. Cas. Abr. 352, 22 E.R. 300.

limitation of the term. I decree the defendant to assign the term to trustees for the defendant for life and to the plaintiff for the residue of the term [and] the defendant to pay costs.

He cited Hobart, Attorney General v. Lord Hunsdon,[1] a decree to hold until the defendant produced a deed which it was vehemently suspicious that the persons under whom the defendant claimed had suppressed. Sampson v. Romsey, 1705; the defendant had burned articles [and was] ordered to admit them as pursuant to the bill or stand committed; a cause agreed. Hamden v. Hamden, at the Rolls, 12 December 1707, reheard by Lord Cowper 8 December 1708, affirmed in the House of Lords;[2] proof of a will delivered to the defendant and by him suppressed; the contents were not proved [but] presumed against the defendant; the decree was the plaintiff was to hold against the defendant and his heirs. Woodroff v. Burton, by Lord Parker, 24 February 1719[/20];[3] a will was suppressed by the defendant; the contents were proved; the decree was the defendant was to convey to the plaintiff.

[Other reports of this case: 1 Peere Williams 731, 24 E.R. 589, 2 Eq. Cas. Abr. 287, 22 E.R. 241.]

591

Harris v. Bishop of Lincoln

(Ch. 1723)

Parol evidence is admissible to prove a testator's intention.

A devise of land to one's heir is a gift to the person who would take that land by the common law of descent.

Lincoln's Inn MS. Misc. 380, pt. 2, p. 9

Easter term, 9 Geo.

Talbot Barker, being seised of an estate in fee, by will, in 1719, gives it to trustees and their heirs in trust, out of the profits, to pay several annuities and, as for the remaining part of the rents and profits, he devises in these words, 'I give and devise the same to my right heirs forever on my mother's side.' The estate descended to the testator from his mother, to whom it had descended from her mother, who was the original purchaser. The plaintiff is the heir of his grandmother, from whom the estate originally descended; the defendants are the heirs of the grandfather on the mother's side. The question was whether this residue

---

1 *Rex v. Countess of Arundel* (1616), Hobart 109, 80 E.R. 258, also Moore K.B. 23, 72 E.R. 929, 2 Eq. Cas. Abr. 287, 22 E.R. 241.

2 *Hampden v. Hampden* (1708–1709), Dickens 26, 21 E.R. 176, 1 Peere Williams 733, 24 E.R. 590, 3 Brown P.C. 550, 1 E.R. 1492.

3 *Woodroffe v. Wood* (Ch. 1720), see above, Case No. 430.

of the rents and profits should go to the plaintiff or to the defendant by virtue of this devise.

It was agreed that, at law supposing it had not been the case of a trust and there had been no devise, it would have gone to the plaintiff from whose ancestors it descended. But the difficulty was whether the words of the devise did not describe another particular person.

In order to ascertain the more the plaintiff's right, some witnesses were read to show the testator's intention, who proved that, at the time of drawing the will, the testator being asked how he would have the residue to go, answered to his right heirs and being asked to what heirs, he said to those on the part of his mother because the estate came from them. This parol evidence was objected to for that the will ought to be construed according to what appears upon the face of it and not by any external evidence.

But Lord Chancellor MACCLESFIELD said he thought it very proper to be read since it was to determine the testator's meaning as to the person who was to take his estate. And he compared it to two persons having the same name. He likewise mentioned the case of Keen v. Keen, before the late Lord Cowper, where the case was that the testator devised his estate to his cousin Ernest Christian Keen in the service of the duke of Savoy. It appeared that he had two nephews, one of that name who lived in London and was not in the service of the duke of Savoy and another who was of a different name, but in the duke of Savoy's service. And Lord Cowper admitted parol evidence to be given as to the person meant in that devise. And upon evidence that the testator had frequently declared that he would give that nephew in London nothing and would never see him and that he would give his estate to his other nephew who was in the service of the duke of Savoy, it was decreed that the estate should go to him in the duke's service and not to the other.

As to the present case, *Lutwyche*, for the plaintiff, insisted that the words 'on his mother's side' must mean such heirs of his mother as were the proper heirs of that estate and that, if they did not signify that, they had no proper meaning at all since the testator had no heirs of his mother's side unless as they had a relation to this estate, that this was the construction even of more general words than these at law, as in 3 Lev. [*blank*],[1] where there was a limitation of an estate that descended to the conusor from his mother by a fine to the use of his right heirs. And it was there held that, by right heirs, in that case, were to be understood the right heirs on the mother's side, that there could be no foundation for the plaintiff to give this estate to his heirs on the part of his mother in so general a manner, but because the estate descended from his mother and, therefore, those heirs of his mother which would be entitled to the estate by descent from the mother must be meant by the testator in the present case.

1 *Godbold v. Freestone* (1694), 3 Levinz 406, 83 E.R. 753.

Sir Philip Yorke, for the defendant, insisted that the construction endeavored to be put upon these words by the plaintiff is such a one as would make the devise absolutely void since they would then do nothing more than what the law itself would do, that the words 'heirs on his mother's side' signify the same thing as the heirs of his mother and consequently must mean the heirs on the mother's father's side, which the law prefers before those on the mother's side. He cited the case of Counden against Clerk, in Hubbard,[1] where a distinction is taken between a grant of lands to J.S. and his heirs without declaring the use, in which case, the use shall go to the heirs of the grantor as the old original estate itself would go and, where the use is declared to the grantor and his heirs, in which case, it is there said that it shall go to the proper right heir of the grantor himself without regard to the original descent of it to himself.

The LORD CHANCELLOR said the case in Hubbard has been determined not to be [good] law in the Case of Abbot and Burton,[2] in which case, there was a limitation to such uses as he should declare and, if no declaration, then to his right heirs, and it was determined that the words 'right heirs' should in that case signify those on the part of the mother from whom the estate descended. He said he was very clear in the present case that it should go to the heir of the grandmother. The testator in this case manifestly intended to do no more than what the law would otherwise have done, but as he was disposing of the trusts of this estate after he had declared the particular purposes for which the trust was raised, it was necessary for him, in order to keep up an apparent consistency in his will, to declare how the residue should be disposed of and, when he says 'I give the residue to my heirs' etc., it is as much as to say 'I will not dispose of it, but it shall go according to the course of descent.' He said that his heirs on the part of the mother must signify such heir as is to inherit the estate which comes from his mother and consequently the heir on the part of the grandmother from whom the estate originally came, for, otherwise, the words would signify neither the general heirs of the devisor nor the special heir which is commonly meant by the words 'heirs on the part of the mother'. And he decreed accordingly.

[Other reports of this case: 2 Peere Williams 135, 24 E.R. 671, 1 Eq. Cas. Abr. 333, 367, 416, 499, 22 E.R. 284, 312, 353, 423.]

---

1 *Counden v. Clerke* (1614), Hobart 29, 31, 80 E.R. 180, 181, also Moore K.B. 860, 72 E.R. 955, 1 Eq. Cas. Abr. 213, 22 E.R. 998.

2 *Abbot v. Burton* (1708), 11 Modern 181, 88 E.R. 976, 2 Salkeld 590, 91 E.R. 494, 1 Comyns 160, 92 E.R. 1014.

592

Uvedale v. Halfpenny

(Ch. 1723)

Where a marriage settlement is so badly drafted as to defeat the intention of the parties, a court of equity will order the estate to be re-settled according to the true intentions of the settlor.

British Library MS. Hargrave 81, f. 221

29 June 1723, in Court before the Master of the Rolls.

Upon a marriage settlement, the estate was limited to trustees and their heirs to the use of the husband for life, remainder to trustees during his life to preserve contingent remainders, with remainder to the wife for life for her jointure, remainder to the first and other sons of that marriage successively in tail male, and, for want of such issue, to trustees for 500 years, with remainder to the right heirs of the husband. And it was thereby declared that the said term and estate for 500 years was so limited to the said trustees upon trust and to the intent and purpose that, if there should be any daughter or daughters of that marriage and one or more younger son or sons, that then the trustees should out of the rents and profits of the said premises after the death of the father or by mortgage or sale thereof or of so much as should be necessary for that purpose, raise and pay such and such sums to such daughter or daughters and younger son or sons at such times as are therein particularly mentioned for his, her, and their portion and portions together with interest for the same after the rate of £4 percent *per annum* for their maintenances in the meantime with a covenant to surrender several copyhold lands to the same trustees and their heirs upon trust to sell and dispose of the same in case there should be any deficiency in the said term of 500 years for the raising and making good of the said portions and maintenances. The marriage took effect, and there were several younger children, both sons and daughters, of this marriage. The father died.

And the younger children brought this bill to have their portions raised and placed out at interest for their benefit and to restrain the eldest son from barring this term by suffering a common recovery, which he threatened to do as soon as the jointure estate fell in and, as was said, had actually done since the bill [was] brought for a small part of the estate not comprehended in the jointure. This settlement was drawn by Mr. Webb, an eminent conveyancer, and he was a witness to it. But the absurdity in it was that this term which had been proper coming after the limitations to the first and other sons in tail male if it had been for raising portions for daughters only was likewise for raising portions for younger sons which so long as there were any sons at all were by the former limitations to take the estate itself in tail male and consequently as to them could not only never take place while there were any sons in being but was also barrable by a common recovery whenever the eldest son came of age and yet the portions, which were to be raised out of this term, which was not to take place until failure of issue male, were to be paid to younger sons, who were issue male, which, being an absurdity upon the face of the deed, the younger children brought this bill to have the term preferred and set before the limitations to the first and other sons, as it ought to have been and always is in settlements and would be idle and absurd if it were otherwise.

And several witnesses were examined to prove this to have been the intention of the parties.

The defendant, the eldest son, insisted upon the words of the settlement and that it was not an idle and altogether vain provision, for, if the sons all died without issue male, it would be a good fund for the raising of portions for daughters; besides, whatever became of this term with respect to the younger sons, yet the copyhold estate which was covenanted to be surrendered was to come in aid of raising the portions and, therefore, as far as that would extend, the younger sons would not be wholly unprovided for and, therefore, no assistance of this court ought to intervene for subverting the frame of the settlement. And, as for the parol proof, which the plaintiffs have made of the intention of the parties, this ought not to be admitted against the express words of the deed itself, which would be against the Statute of Frauds and Perjuries.[1]

But, on the other hand, it was urged that this court had several times transposed clauses in deeds to answer the intention of the parties, that this intention to raise portions for younger sons appeared plainly upon the face of the deed itself, and that the declaration of the trusts of the term were to raise them out of the rents and profits or by mortgage or sale of the term after the father's death and, therefore, the examining of witnesses to prove this was not to overthrow but to support the settlement and was consistent with the intention of the parties appearing upon the deed itself. And several cases were cited that this court had assisted the intention of the parties by transposing the several clauses of a settlement in order to support and make it good and intelligible, as the case of Taylor v. Lee, at the Rolls; the Case of Finch and the Earl of Winchelsea;[2] and several others. And, as to the pretense that the copyhold was clear of this objection and, therefore, the younger sons would not be without some provision, this was said to be a stronger way of reasoning, for the copyhold was only to come in aid and to be auxiliary to the provision intended by the term and, if the term itself were to be out of the case, the copyhold would be liable at least. If it were otherwise, that was no reason why this court should not support and subject the term, which was the principal and primary fund intended for the raising of these portions.

---

1 Stat. 29 Car. II, c. 3 (*SR*, V, 839–842).

2 *Taylor v. Lee* (Ch. 1713), British Library MS. Hargrave 80, f. 154, Chancery Cases *tempore* Harcourt, 388; *Finch v. Earl of Winchelsea* (Ch. 1719), see above, Case No. 408.

But the Master of the Rolls [JEKYLL] said there was no need at all of any parol proof in this case, for, upon the whole deed taken together, there was a plain agreement in writing for the raising of portions for younger children and that too payable to them at such and such ages after the death of the father and, therefore, it must be looked upon as a charge of these portions by agreement in writing upon the whole deed together and such an agreement, when it appeared in writing, this court might effectuate and carry into execution. And, since the term, as it stands placed in the settlement, labors with such an infirmity, the portions can never be raised out of that, a court of equity ought to regard the intention of the parties and endeavor to make it good. And, therefore, he decreed that the eldest son should suffer a common recovery of what still remained in him in tail and, to enable him thereto, the mother was to make a conditional surrender of her estate for life according to the usual course in such cases and, when the recovery was suffered and the uses declared to himself in fee, he was then to make a new settlement both of that estate and of the other whereof he had already suffered a common recovery to the very same uses with this settlement only preferring and setting the 500 years term before the limitations to the first and other sons and costs to come out of the estate.

And His Honor very much disliked the recovery which had been suffered of part *pendente lite* whatever power he had by law to do it. But he decreed that the copyhold as far as it would extend should be first sold and applied towards the raising of the portions and the residue to be made good out of this term of 500 years to be settled as aforesaid of the freehold.

[Other copies of this report: British Library MS. Hargrave 82, f. 222.]

Lincoln's Inn MS. Misc. 14, p. 152

29 June 1723. James Uvedale and his wife, one of the younger children of Bernard Halfpenny, and the other younger children of the said Bernard, plaintiffs; Sarah Halfpenny, widow of the said Bernard, and Bernard, their eldest son, and James Cotton, defendants.

After the marriage of Bernard Halfpenny, the plaintiff's father, with the defendant Sarah, the daughter of Charles Ballet, Thomas Halfpenny, father of Bernard, by lease and release, 4 & 5 January 1702[/03], in consideration of £3500 paid to Bernard by Ballet and £1000 more to be paid for the portion of the defendant Sarah and for settling a jointure upon her and making a provision for the younger children of the said marriage, conveys several manors and lands in the counties of Bedford and Hertford and Middlesex to trustees and their heirs, as to part, to Thomas Halfpenny for life and, after his death, as to the same lands and also as to all the rest of the premises to Bernard for life, remainder to trustees to preserve the contingent remainders, then, as to part, to the defendant Sarah for her jointure and, as to the jointure lands after her death and also, as to the rest of the premises, to the defendant Bernard, the eldest son of Bernard and Sarah, in tail male, remainder to their second and other sons in tail male, remainder to trustees for 500 years without [impeachment of] waste upon the trusts after mentioned and, after the determination of that the estate, to Bernard, the father, and his heirs.

The trusts of the term were declared to be that, if there should be any younger child or children of Bernard and his wife living at his death or born afterwards other than the eldest son of their two bodies begotten, then the trustees should after the death of Bernard, the father, by sale or mortgage of the term and with the rents in the meantime without prejudice to the jointure, raise any sum not exceeding £4000 for the portions of such younger children to be paid, share and share alike, to sons at twenty-one and to daughters at eighteen or marriage and until the portions became payable, the trustees, out of the rents of the premises such sums for maintenance as the interest of the portions amounted to at £4 percent. If any younger child died before his or her portion became payable or younger son became heir, then his or her portion to go to the survivors.

[There was] a covenant to surrender copyhold lands to the use of Thomas Halfpenny for life, remainder to Bernard, the father, for life, remainder to the use of trustees to permit Sarah to receive so much out of the rents as her jointure should fall short of £400 a year and then in trust for the better raising the portions and maintenance for the younger children and subject thereto.

Thomas and Bernard being both dead and Bernard having left the defendant Bernard, his eldest son, and the plaintiffs, his younger children, the defendant Bernard suffered a recovery of the lands not in jointure to the use of himself in fee and thereby barred the 500 years term and the trusts thereof.

The plaintiffs brought their bill against their mother and elder brother and against James Cotton, the surviving trustee of the term, that the said £4000 might be raised and that such of them as were of age or married might be paid their shares and that the shares of such as were infants might be put out at interest and the interest applied for their maintenance. And they insisted that the limiting of the term of 500 years after the limitation to the sons was contrary to the intention of the parties.

The defendant Bernard insisted on the settlement as it had been executed and upon his power to suffer the said recovery and that the said £4000 ought not to be raised.

Upon the hearing of this cause, the Master of the Rolls [Jekyll] was of opinion and so declared that it was plain that it was the intention of the parties that the term of 500 years should take place before the estate tail limited to the sons and that the said term was transposed in the settlement contrary to the intention of the parties. And he referred it to a Master to see how much of the copyhold estate was necessary to be set apart to make good the mother's jointure of £400 a year and, when that was done, the Master was to see so much of the residue sold as would be sufficient to raise the two children's portions, who were become entitled to the same, with interest for the same from the death of the father. If the money to arise thereby should not be sufficient to pay what was due to the plaintiffs, who were become entitled to their portions, then they might apply to the court for further directions.

He decreed the widow to make a conditional surrender of her estate and that a new settlement should be made to trustees for the term of 99 years if she lived so long and that, in such new settlement, the 500 years term for raising the younger children's portions was to be placed antecedent to the estate tail and the trustees were to be empowered to raise the portions as they became due with interest and the interest in the meantime to be applied for their maintenance. Costs [were] to be paid out of the estate. The Master [was] to settle the new conveyance.

[Other reports of this case: 2 Peere Williams 151, 24 E.R. 677, 2 Eq. Cas. Abr. 718, 22 E.R. 604.]

593

Parker v. Wilcocks

(Ch. 1723)

The question in this case was whether, by the terms of the will in issue, the testator's debts were a charge on his real estate.

British Library MS. Hargrave 81, f. 228

Saturday, 29 June 1723, in Court before the Master of the Rolls.

Mr. Wilcocks, the late High Bailiff of Westminster, made his will in writing in these words 'as to my worldly estate which it has pleased Almighty God to bestow upon me, I give and bequeath the same as follows: *imprimis*, I will that all my just debts and funerals be fully paid and satisfied.' And then he goes on and devises the several parts of his real estate chargeable with annuities and other out goings and devises the overplus of the rents and profits to his eldest son.

And the only question was whether the first part of the will amounted to a charge of his debts and funerals upon his real estate, there being a deficiency of personal assets to pay and satisfy the same.

And it was urged that it did. And a case of Troft v. Vernon, in My Lord Cowper's time, [was] cited to that purpose.

But the Master of Rolls [Jekyll], though he was of opinion it would have been so if the words had been 'I will that my just debts and funerals shall be in the first place paid and satisfied', yet he thought the words not sufficient in this case to charge the real estate because willing that his debts and funerals should be fully paid was saying no more than the law said without those words and also because he afterwards disposes of his real estate chargeable with such payments as he intended should take place thereout. And he decreed that the real estate was not chargeable.

But several at the bar thought this differed not from several cases which had been in this court where such words had been held to amount to a charge upon the real estate and the English of '*imprimis*' is 'in the first place' and, therefore, whether those words are placed at the beginning or middle of the clause makes no difference.

[Other copies of this report: British Library MS. Hargrave 82, f. 228, Lincoln's Inn MS. Misc. 107, f. 103.]

4 Viner, Abr. 463

Trinity 9 Geo. 1723. Barton v. Wilcocks.

'As touching all such worldly estate which God hath blessed me with, I dispose of the same as follows: Imprimis, I will that all my just debts be paid and satisfied.' It was argued that it is a general preface to make a general disposition of his real and personal estate as is mentioned after in the will, that it is an independent clause and means only an intention of a general disposition. He, after, devises his freehold and copyhold estate to his son and his heirs when he comes to twenty-one, paying his wife £100 a year for her dower in the meantime. After £100 *per annum* to his wife for dower, the rest of the profits are to be put out for the benefit of all his children, but he made no provision for debts. It was insisted that, if a man devises lands after debts paid, that is a charge.

But it was decreed that this is not a charge of debts upon the real estate.

[Other copies of this report: 2 Eq. Cas. Abr. 499, 22 E.R. 423.]

8 Viner, Abr. 439

Trinity 9 Geo. Master of the Rolls.

'As for concerning my estate with which God hath blessed me, I give as follows, imprimis, I will that all my debts and funeral charges be paid and satisfied.' And then he makes a particular disposition of the estate.

This was decreed no charge, as it would be when a testator says, 'I will my debts be paid in the first place', or where he gives away the estate after payment of debts and legacies, for here was a clause in the will that, after payment of legacies and funeral charges, the overplus was to go to such and such uses, which declare the intention to be that the same was to answer only legacies and funeral charges and not debts.

[Other copies of this report: 2 Eq. Cas. Abr. 371, 22 E.R. 316.]

594
Anonymous v. Woolaston
(Ch. 1723)

Courts of equity have jurisdiction over matters of fraud.

British Library MS. Hargrave 81, f. 230

Saturday, 29 June 1723, in Court before the Master of the Rolls.

He had obtained a patent for extracting oil out of a certain English vegetable, which afterwards was discovered to be out of the radishes, and in order to plant great quantities of land with radish seed, he bought 6000 acres of marsh land in the year 1720, divided his interest in this land into 3000 shares, which he sold for £20 a share, and gave printed receipts entitled land security with an oil patent, but, as appeared in the cause, though the land cost £31,000, yet, before giving out those receipts for shares, he had mortgaged it for £28,000 so that the adventurers had not above £3000 interest in the land for their security and consequently were to rest on the success of this project for the residue.

But this, amongst other projects of that memorable year,[1] coming to nothing, the plaintiffs, who had bought as many shares as came to £300, brought this bill to have their money back again. And they had a decree accordingly.

And the court said, though an [action of] *indebitatus assumpsit* lay at law for recovery back of the money in this and such like cases, yet, as the persons who advanced it were drawn in by fraud and that the whole was founded in a fraud, they might likewise bring a bill for it in this court, which, in such cases, had a concurrent jurisdiction by reason of the fraud with the common law.

And the Master of the Rolls [JEKYLL] said the obtaining of a patent in such cases gave no sort of sanction whatsoever to the project but that was left to the law to stand or fall just as it came out to be legal or illegal without any regard to the patent.

[Other copies of this report: British Library MS. Hargrave 82, f. 230, Lincoln's Inn MS. Misc. 107, f. 105, pl. 2.]

1 1720 was the year of the burst of the South Sea bubble.

595

Coant v. Dennett

(Ch. 1723)

A court of equity can give relief to a lessee for a forfeiture for non-payment of rent but not for non-performance of a valid land use agreement.

British Library MS. Hargrave 81, f. 232

Eodem die [29 June 1723].

The defendant made a lease of the lands in question to the plaintiff for eleven years at £3 10s. *per annum*, in which lease were several covenants on the part of the lessee and, amongst others, a covenant for payment of the rent at the times limited for payment thereof and also a covenant that he would keep the gates locked and would not suffer such a field, part of the leased premises, to be used as a way except only by such and such persons. Then comes a proviso that, if the lessee do not pay the rent and also perform all and singular the covenants, that it shall be lawful for the lessor to reenter. But the lessor having a mind afterwards to avoid this lease and there being half a year's rent in arrear, which was not tendered at the day, and the lessee having suffered this field to be made use of as a common highway and left open the gates, the lessor brought his [action of] ejectment. And the plaintiff, the lessee, brought this bill to stay his proceedings and to be relieved.

It was proved in the cause that there was and had been a way over this field for upwards of fifty years before and even time out of mind and that there was no other way to the church but over the field and that it had been likewise a way for coaches and carts. As to the rent, there was no manner of doubt but the court might give relief.

But, as to this collateral covenant, the court said they could set no value upon it or give any relief and that this had been the constant distinction in this court between payment of money for which the party may be recompensed, but a collateral covenant the court can set no value upon and, therefore, dismissed the bill with costs and said it had been so settled in the Case of the Duke of Somerset v. Sir Harry Peachy.[1]

But afterwards, the court said they would give the plaintiff leave to try the legality of this covenant and whether this way had been used as a common highway or not. And so it was done in the Duke of Somerset's Case.

[Other copies of this report: British Library MS. Hargrave 82, f. 231, Lincoln's Inn MS. Misc. 107, f. 106.]

---

1 *Peachy v. Duke of Somerset* (1721), see above, Case No. 515.

Lincoln's Inn MS. Misc. 12, p. 8, pl. 1

1 July 1723, Lescallet and Coant v. Dennet.

The defendant leased a piece of ground in Walthamstow to the plaintiff Coant pursuant to a covenant contained in a former lease made to the plaintiff Lescallet. And in the new lease is contained a covenant on the lessee's part that he should not during the term permit any person to make use of any part of the premises as a common way with carts, horses, etc. And the lessor covenanted to indemnify the lessee against all costs and charges he might be put to by his preventing the premises to be used as a common way. And in the lease is a proviso that the lessor might enter not only for the non-payment of the rent but for the breach of any of the covenants.

The plaintiff Coant having broken his covenant by willfully permitting several persons to make use of part of the premises as a common way to the church and there being half a year's rent in arrear, the defendant brought his [action of] ejectment, and the plaintiff brought his bill to be relieved.

Master of the Rolls [Jekyll]: The plaintiff is not entitled to be relieved against the breach of this covenant; if the defendant had entered for non-payment of rent only, the court would relieve, for, in that case, the court could have decreed the defendant an adequate satisfaction. But, in the present case, the covenant is of such a nature as that no satisfaction can be made the defendant for the breach of it. And the defendant having willfully broken this covenant, he ought not to have any relief, nor did this court ever relieve against the willful breach of such a covenant. And, therefore, he, at first, dismissed the bill with costs. But, afterwards, upon further consideration, he gave the plaintiff leave to try the matter at law touching the breach of the covenant and the defendant was to bring a new [action of] ejectment for that purpose.

596

Vandeput v. Betnam

(Ch. 1723)

In this case, a bona fide *purchaser for value of stolen securities was denied relief.*

Lincoln's Inn MS. Misc. 506, p. 68

Trinity 9 George.

One Monk, a widow, being possessed of divers Lottery annuities, employed one Rowe, a person at that time of very good repute, to receive the interest due on them, but never thought fit to trust him with the keeping of them. After this, Rowe came to her one day and, pretending there was some mistake in the entry of the annuities in the office and that he should need the annuities to correct them by, prevailed upon her to deliver them to him, which she did, wrapped up in a paper, and, the next day, he seemingly brought them to her again wrapped up in the same paper, which she never opened but locked up again. Soon after, there came one to Mrs. Monk to advise her not to trust Rowe, for that he was under a suspicion of foul practices. She replied that she was in no danger for he had nothing of hers and that she had her Lottery annuities safe back again. But afterwards, when she opened her papers, she found none of her annuities, but other papers in the room. These annuities had been sold by Rowe and came at last to the hands of the plaintiff Vandeput, who was sued at law by the defendant Betnam as executor of Monk, and Betnam had a verdict for the annuities.

The plaintiff brought a bill in this court for an injunction to stay the proceedings at law for that Monk did not acquaint him with this matter so soon as she knew it for fear of ruining Rowe's reputation, that she had got £100 from Rowe in part and was in hopes of getting the rest, though she had not yet, that Rowe was now gone to Holland so that the plaintiff could have no remedy against him.

The bill was dismissed.

597

Edwards v. Countess Dowager of Warwick

(Ch. 1723)

Where there is a will contest between the heir and the executor and the equities are equal, a court of equity always favors the heir.

Where money is due to a married woman, a court of equity will require it to be settled to her separate equitable use.

Lincoln's Inn MS. Misc. 506, p. 69

Trinity 9 George.

Upon the intermarriage of the father of the late earl of Warwick with the defendant, the manor of Kensington was settled upon the old earl for his life and upon the issue male in tail, remainder to the heirs of the old earl, and there was a covenant that £10,000 should be laid out in lands and settled in the same manner as Kensington. The earl, the son, levied a fine of the manor of Kensington and then died. The defendant is administratrix to her son. And the plaintiff is heir at law and brings a bill against the administratrix and the trustees to have a specific execution of the trust, *viz.* the £10,000 laid out in lands and settled to the uses as Kensington had been. This was opposed by the mother, who, as administratrix would be entitled to the money if not laid out in lands. It was agreed that the earl himself might have had either the money or the lands purchased for him in fee because he should not be put to a circuity of having it in tail and then suffering a common recovery.

It was insisted on that this money was the mother's portion, which she brought on the marriage, and that the heir was a very remote heir and not within the consideration of the covenant.

There were cited Nichols and Nichols,[1] where one who was entitled to a sum of money to be laid out in lands to the use of him and his heirs had a decree for the money itself.

Colwell and Shadwell,[2] an infant two years old entitled to money to be laid out in lands and settled on him in tail came to have the money decreed him, but it was denied because, though he might levy a fine when he was of age, yet here were a great number of years to interpose and to take away that chance from the remainderman would be very hard.

Witcomb and Witcomb;[3] one had purchased a considerable estate in Essex and had by his first wife two daughters and, afterwards, married a second; he made no disposition of his real estate, but, as he lay sick, being asked what he would do with it, he said it should go to his children as by law it ought. The second wife was enceinte and, after his death, was brought to bed of a son, who afterwards died at nine years of age. The daughters were but half-blood. A poor remote heir to the son brought a bill for a discovery [so] that he might bring an [action of] ejectment, but the court discouraged it, which prevailed on the heir to take a sum of money. This was mentioned to show how far the court will be influenced by the nearness of the relation.

Gilpin and Pigot; where an heir is not within the provision and consideration of the settlement, he is not entitled to the aid of a court of equity.

On the other hand, it was insisted on that this money could not now be called the countess's portion since she had purchased her jointure with it and would be liable to the earl's debts, that the insisting on the remoteness of the heir was contrary to the common rule that heirs are to be favored.

Chaplain and Horner;[4] the heir can have nothing to say if it were paid to the father, who was to have been tenant in fee in his lifetime, but, if not paid in the lifetime of the ancestor, it remains as land.

[It was argued] that all the uses are within the consideration, but, if they are not, yet that the plaintiff came properly against the trustees, which is not for relief but for the execution of the trust. As to what was said that it might be devised by a will with one witness, I believe it might. But the question is not whether it be to be considered as lands in all cases but whether it is not to be considered as such in this.

Lord Chancellor [LORD MACCLESFIELD] said that this case arose merely as the trustees are brought before the court to perform the trust so that the inquiry

[1] *Nichols v. Nichols* (1721), see above, Case No. 501.

[2] *Colwell v. Colwell* (*tempore* Cowper).

[3] *Whitcombe v. Whitcombe* (1709), Precedents in Chancery 280, 24 E.R. 135.

[4] *Chaplin v. Horner* (1718), see above, Case No. 315.

is why this trust should not be performed. The true question is what is the trust. And, therefore, how far the heir at law is within the consideration of the settlement is not now to be considered nor how far an heir or administratrix is to be favored in a court of equity. The trust is expressed in plain words to be laid out in lands to be settled to the same uses as Kensington, which was to the old earl for life, then to the issue male in tail and, for want of such, to the heirs of the old earl. Why should not this trust be performed? It is said the earl has shown his intention of disposing of his whole real estate. If this money be within that intention, then it is to be considered as land and must go to the heir. But I think the intention goes only to what was land at that time. A fine makes no alteration, for he could have disposed of his estate without a fine, for the remainder in fee was in him. The fine could operate only against the children. It is said that the defendant, the administratrix, is not a remote relation, as executors often are. The earl might have made this personal estate if he had pleased to have called for the money, for the remainder in fee was in him. And it is not like the case of Colwell and Shadwell, where there was a remainder over. I do not see indeed that the ceremony of a fine is to be waited for any more than a conveyance or sealing a deed. But then this is only a power of altering the trust so that the question is what method is necessary to vary the trust and whether he has done it. I do not know but he might have done it by parol. I am sure I should have showed it all the favor I could, but it does not appear to me that he has done any act to vary the trust. All that is said is that he was master of all the estate and that he would have the real go with the honor, but would dispose of the personal estate. Otherwise, the word 'dispose' implied he would give it otherwise than [how] it would go by law. But how he would dispose of it, whether to the heir or administrator, does not appear.

Where the contest is between the heir and the executor and they stand otherwise on an equal foot, this court always gives it in favor of the heir. This is a standing rule that I never knew departed from, as, where debts charge both, the executor shall discharge them.

Lord Scudamore's Case,[1] where money was given to trustees to be laid out in lands for the benefit of the Lady Scudamore in her lifetime and, after her death, that then it should go to her heirs, executors, and administrators, which I understood to mean that, if laid out in lands, it should go to the heir, but, if not laid out in her lifetime by reason of accident or want of time, then to the executors. In that case, though she were dead, the money not laid out, yet I decreed that it should be laid out in land and go to the heir because it was a breach of trust in not laying it out before; nay, there had been a decree for it and that decree was unperformed.

It was decreed that the trustees should lay out the £10,000 in lands and convey them to the plaintiff's heir at law and the interest of the money due in the

[1] *Scudamore v. Scudamore* (1721), see above, Case No. 483.

lifetime of Lord Warwick should be paid to the Lady Warwick as administratrix. But, because she was married since, that interest was decreed to be laid out in lands and settled upon her in fee.

[Other reports of this case: 2 Peere Williams 171, 24 E.R. 687, Dickens 51, 21 E.R. 186, 1 Brown P.C. 207, 1 E.R. 518, 1 Eq. Cas. Abr. 140, 21 E.R. 942, 2 Eq. Cas. Abr. 42, 52, 83, 22 E.R. 36, 46, 72.]

598

Cornelius v. Cornelius

(Ch. 1723)

Where a bequest of a mortgage fails because the mortgage debt was voluntarily repaid by the mortgagor, this is not an ademption and the amount of the mortgage debt will be paid to the legatee out of the decedent's estate.

Yale Univ. Taussig MS. 311, vol. 1, p. 565

In a cause heard before Sir Joseph Jekyll by consent, a grandfather makes his will and devises to A., B., and C., his grandchildren, pecuniary legacies and securities for money for so much more as made up the legacies, £800 apiece, and to D., his grandchild, he also gives a pecuniary legacy and a mortgage which made him exactly equal with the other grandchildren. But between the [time of the] will made and death, the mortgagor pays in the money upon the mortgage to D. And the Master decreed that the money paid in on the mortgage should be made good out of the executor's residue and held a diversity that, in case the testator had called in the money upon the mortgage, it had been otherwise. But the mortgagor's paying in shall not defeat the devise. And this, he said, was a distinction of the civil law.

By the relation of Mr. Morgan Owen, who was of counsel in the cause. The like had been decreed by Harcourt, Chancellor, in a case between [*blank*].

599

Russell v. Carlison

(Ch. 1723)

Where an executor is given a legacy specifically to compensate his services as such, that executor cannot take as the residuary legatee.

British Library MS. Hargrave 81, f. 229

2 July 1723, in Court before Mr. Justice Powys.

This was a case wherein Mr. Justice Powys had taken time to consider and search precedents, and it was this. A man, by his will, devises thus: 'I give to A.

£5 to B. £10 to C., the sole executor of this my will, £5 for his care in performing my will'. And he dies without disposing of the surplus or making C. executor in any other manner than as aforesaid.

And Mr. Justice POWYS was clearly of the opinion that, agreeable to the precedents of this court, the executor should have no more than his £5, which was given him for his care in performing the will, and that the surplus should be distributed amongst the next of kin. And so it is taken now to be the general course of equity though the next of kin have legacies as well as the executor.

[Other copies of this report: British Library MS. Hargrave 82, f. 229, Lincoln's Inn MS. Misc. 107, f. 105, pl. 1.]

Lincoln's Inn MS. Misc. 12, p. 8, pl. 2

2 July 1723. Rashley v. Carlessin. Judge Powys.

A.B., by will, after giving several legacies, makes the defendant executor, and she gives him £5 for his care in fulfilling her will. And she made no dispensation of the surplus of her personal estate. The question was if the executor was entitled to the surplus, having a legacy given him by the will.

The Judge [POWYS] took time to consider of it and now delivered his opinion. Foster and Mont[1] [is] the first case, in Lord Chancellor Jeffreys' time. And, there, [it was] decreed that giving a legacy to the executor excluded him of the surplus. The Commissioners [to Hold the Great Seal] who succeeded him reversed this decree. But, upon an appeal to the Lords, the Commissioners' decree was reversed.

Lord Cowper, in the Duchess of Beauford's Case,[2] decreed that the giving her the use of the plate for her life excluded her from the surplus, but the Lords reversed that decree and looked upon it that the devise of the use of the plate for life was an exception out of the surplus which otherwise she would have as executrix.

An executor in law is only a trustee, as it appears by this that, if he dies intestate, his administrators shall not have the goods of the testator, but administration *de bonis non* shall be granted to the next of kin of the testator.

Another reason to show he is only a trustee is, if a man marries an executrix and she dies, the husband shall not have the goods of the testator unadministered, but the next of kin of the testator shall take out administration *de bonis non* of the testator.

The House of Lords have admitted parol evidence to show the intention of the testator that the executor should have the surplus, but the reason is because

---

1 *Foster v. Munt* (1689), 1 Vernon 473, 23 E.R. 598, 1 Eq. Cas. Abr. 243, 21 E.R. 1020, 2 Eq. Cas. Abr. 433, 443, 22 E.R. 368, 378, Dodd 78, Chancery Cases *tempore* Jac. II, 368.

2 *Duke of Beaufort v. Lord Dundonald* (Ch. 1716–1717), see above, Case No. 131.

it is a proof that goes along with the law and, therefore, to be admitted. But I do not see why there may not be parol proof to show the contrary.

Now, in the present case, here are words which show that the executor was only a trustee; £5 is given for his care in fulfilling [her] will. There are some proofs in the present case of the intention of the testatrix, but I think such proof is a thing of a dangerous nature.

May v. Lewen *et ux.*, February 1720[/21],[1] on the will of one Mills, who gave £50 apiece to his two executors for their trouble and pains, there was in that case some considerable parol proof and a letter proved of the testator to one of his executors intimating his intentions that his executors should have the surplus. But, notwithstanding, Lord Chancellor [Lord Parker] decreed the surplus to the next of kin. This case comes very near to the present case.

I will not say that, in all cases, where a legacy is given to the executor without more words that shall exclude him of the surplus, there may be some strong proof to overthrow that implication, that, by giving an executor part, the testator intends to exclude him of the whole.

As to the present case, I am of opinion the executor is not entitled to the surplus. And, therefore, [it is] decreed the executor to account and that the surplus should be distributed between the plaintiffs, who were next of kin to the testatrix.

Lincoln's Inn MS. Coxe 89, vol. 3, pt. 2, p. 1, pl. 1

2 July Trinity 9 Geo. *Coram* Powys, Justice, in Chancery. Raphael v. Carlesin.

C. made his will and appointed the defendant his executor and devised to him £5 for his care in fulfilling the will, and he died possessed of a considerable estate in goods and chattels undisposed of by his will. The plaintiff brought his bill to compel the defendant to make distribution.

And it was insisted for the plaintiff that, when a specific legacy is given to an executor, there must be a distribution of the residue of the testator's personal estate according to the Statute,[2] for, by bequeathing a legacy, which is a gift in law, to the executor, it plainly shows the intent of the testator to be that the executor should have only that legacy and that nothing more should vest in him. The Duke of Beaufort's Case in Lord Cowper's time was cited,[3] where the testator devised to his executor the use of certain plate for his life and it was decreed there should be a distribution, but this decree was afterwards reversed in the House of Lords because, by the devise of the use of the plate only for life, the executor had not such a property in it as would empower him to dispose of it, and, therefore, it was that such a devise should not occasion a distribution. The Case of Littlebury

[1] *May v. Lewen* (Ch. 1721), see above, Case No. 489.

[2] Stat. 22 & 23 Car. II, c. 10 (*SR*, V, 719–720).

[3] *Duke of Beaufort v. Lord Dundonald* (Ch. 1716–1717), see above, Case No. 131.

v. Buckly[1] was cited, which was in the City Court before Lord Chief Justice King when he was the Recorder there, and, in that case, it was agreed that a legacy given to an executor barred him of the residue of the testator's personal estate.

It was insisted that, to many intents, an executor was but a trustee, for, if an executor dies without an executor, his administrator shall not have the goods which the executor had in the right of his executorship, but they shall go to the administrator *de bonis non*. So, if a man marries a widow executrix and she dies without a will, the personal estate shall not go to the husband but to the next of kin to the testator.

In questions of this kind, it has been usual to admit of collateral evidence in order to come at the intent of the testator. And, when a testator devises a certain thing to his executor for the doing some particular office for him, as the performing his will with care, this shows the testator thought the legacy a sufficient recompense for the trouble. And, indeed, it is a direct trust in the executor, for he shall not have the thing devised without performing the act for the doing of which it was devised.

It was said it had been held in some cases that even a devise of mourning [clothes] to an executor deprived him of his right to the residue of the personal estate.

The Case of May v. Lewin *et al.* was cited,[2] which was in this court 20 February 1720[/21]. In that case, there were two executors appointed and £5 apiece given them by the will with these words subjoined, *viz.* 'for their care and trouble'. And it was decreed the surplus of the estate should go to the next of kin.

It was insisted that, where a testator gives a legacy to his executor, it shall be taken by implication that no more was intended to the executor, and, in this case, a trust is created and the legacy given by way of satisfaction for that trouble.

Mr. Justice Powys, for these reasons, decreed that there should be a distribution and the next of kin should have the benefit of it.

600

Bosvil v. Streatfield

(Ch. 1723)

A trustee to preserve contingent remainders can be ordered to join with the life tenant and the first remainderman to suffer a recovery and defeat the entail.

Lincoln's Inn MS. Misc. 12, p. 151

4 July 1723.

---

[1] *Buckley v. Littlebury* (1711), 3 Brown P.C. 43, 1 E.R. 1165, 1 Eq. Cas. Abr. 245, 21 E.R. 1021, 2 Vernon 677, 23 E.R. 1040, Lincoln's Inn MS. Misc. 10, p. 86.

[2] *May v. Lewen* (Ch. 1721), see above, Case No. 489.

The plaintiff William Bosvil was tenant for ninety-nine years if he lived so long, remainder to trustees to preserve contingent remainders, remainder to his first and other sons in tail male, with other remainders over. The plaintiff Henry [Bosvil], being come of age, was willing to join with his father in suffering a recovery. And they applied to the defendant [Thomas] Streatfield, the surviving trustee for preserving contingent remainders, to join with them in making a tenant to the *praecipe*, which he refusing, they brought their bill for that purpose.

The defendant, in his answer, insisted that, by the settlement, the estate, in the case of a failer of issue of the plaintiff William [Bosvil], was limited to the defendant and other trustees for the benefit of several persons who were in poor and necessitous circumstances, which he looked upon to be in the nature of a charity.

But notwithstanding what was insisted on, the Master of the Rolls [JEKYLL] without any difficulty decreed the defendant to join with the plaintiffs in making a tenant to the *praecipe* in order to their suffering a common recovery of the estate.

601

Blois v. Betts

(Ch. 1723)

Where a man makes a contract to leave his wife money and to allow her to keep her jewels, upon his death, she is only a creditor of his estate.

An executrix of a decedent's will cannot retain any debts owing to her by her husband.

Upon the settlement of a decedent's estate, the creditors will take precedence over the legatees.

Lincoln's Inn MS. Misc. 12, p. 6

13 July 1723.

The defendant's husband, in his marriage settlement made before the marriage, declared that, in consideration of love and affection, he did voluntarily offer and agree that his then intended wife should retain[1] her jewels and rings if she survived him without rendering any account for the same.

The Master of the Rolls [JEKYLL] was of the opinion the property of the wife's jewels by the marriage settlement became vested in the husband and that, by virtue of this covenant, she could not retain them against the creditors, there being no sale of them to the trustees, but, the covenant being broken, she can only come in as a creditor for the damage she sustains by the non-performance of the covenant, the covenant being no specific lien on the jewels. But a precedent being mentioned by Mr. *Mead*, he said he would consider of it.

[1] detain *MS.*

So in like manner it was decreed that, Mr. Betts having covenanted with the wife's trustees to leave her £200 at his death, she must come in as a creditor for that £200, and, though she was the executrix, she could not retain out of the assets against the other creditors.

It was decreed also that, Mr. Betts having by his will devised lands to be sold for the payment of his debts and legacies, the creditors must have a preference before the legatees and that the legatees could not be paid *in pari passu* with the creditors.

Lincoln's Inn MS. Misc. 384, p. 246, pl. 1

13 July 1713.[1] At the Rolls.

Mr. H. Betts, on his marriage with the defendant, covenants to leave her £200 in case she survives him. He died indebted in bond. And the defendant was executrix. The defendant insists to retain the £200 in preference to the bond creditors.

Curia [Jekyll]: The rule for the executor's retaining does not hold in this case because the covenant is with trustees. The defendant must come in only in proportion with the other creditors of equal degree.

602

Wheelock v. Small

(Ch. 1723)

A debtor cannot prefer one creditor over another after he is bankrupt.

British Library MS. Hargrave 81, f. 233

Trinity vacation 1723, at the Rolls.

The two Norcotts in the Strand, bankers, being very much involved and encumbered, prevailed on the defendant Small to transfer to them £500 South Sea stock, which they sold for £1700. And being otherwise considerably indebted to Small and being possessed of two houses in York Buildings in the Strand for the residue of a term for years of which there were about thirty-five years to come let at the clear rent of £54 *per annum* above the ground rent and worth about £500 or £600 to be sold, they, in order to favor and prefer Small and in consideration of the £1700 lent them a little before on the 29th of September 1720, about five or six in the afternoon sent for one Brice, who had been bred to the law, and told him they were unable to support their credit any longer and that they intended to withdraw the next day and, therefore, desired him forthwith to prepare an assignment of these two houses to the defendant Small with a proviso to be void

[1] Sic in MS.

on their indemnifying and saving him harmless from a bond of £3000 penalty wherein they, together with Small, had entered into to the plaintiff for £1500 and interest and of which £1500 they had one moiety to their own use and Small the other moiety. Accordingly, Brice prepares the assignment, which was executed at the Norcotts' house about 11 or 12 o'clock of the same 29th of September. And, about three or four o'clock in the morning, the Norcotts removed most of their effects and goods and withdrew but left some money in the hands of John Stephens, their servant, with directions whom he should pay it to. And, accordingly, the next day, Stephens paid away the money in the shop as he was directed, paying some persons and refusing others. And, on the first of October 1720, the shop was shut up. And on the third of the same month, a commission of bankruptcy was sealed against the Norcotts. And the next day, being the fourth of October, an assignment [was] made by the commissioners of all their estate and effects to the defendant Mann in trust for himself and the rest of the creditors who should come in and contribute to the charges of suing out the commission. It was fully proved in the cause that, after this assignment thus made to Small, the Norcotts never appeared in their shop or publicly after, but they were never arrested. After these transactions, the plaintiff calling on Small for the whole £1500 and interest for which he together with the Norcotts had given a bond to the plaintiff, Small alleged that, by reason of the losses he had sustained by the Norcotts and otherwise, he was not able to pay the plaintiff but offered to assign over his security, which he had taken as aforesaid, of the two houses towards payment of what was due to the plaintiff, which the plaintiff agreed to accept. And, accordingly, on the 20th of December 1720, an assignment of these two houses was made by the defendant Small to the plaintiff.

But the defendant Mann, in behalf of himself and the rest of the Norcotts' creditors, insisting that the assignment to Small under the circumstances before mentioned was fraudulent and void and consequently that the plaintiff, who only stood in the place of Small, could be in no better condition than Small himself was, the plaintiff brought this bill to be satisfied his debt or to foreclose the equity of redemption upon the proviso in the assignment to Small. And the only question was whether this was a good assignment to Small, that is whether the Norcotts, under these circumstances, had power to give a preference to one creditor in exclusion of the rest.

But upon the opening of the case, the Master of the Rolls [JEKYLL] said he could do nothing in it, for would you have me try when the bankruptcy was. And, therefore, he sent it to an issue at law to try when they became bankrupts, whether before or after the assignment to the defendant Small.

[Other copies of this report: British Library MS. Hargrave 82, f. 233, Lincoln's Inn MS. Misc. 107, f. 107.]

[Related cases: Rex v. Mann (Ex. 1723–1727), Exch. Cases *tempore* Geo. I, vol. 1, p. 545.]

603

Walter v. Meliser

(Ch. 1723)

The question in this case was whether the creditors of a testator should be preferred over his legatees where the estate is insufficient to satisfy all of them.

British Library MS. Hargrave 81, f. 237

Trinity vacation at the Lord Chancellor's [house] on petitions.

One, being indebted in £500 on a mortgage etc., the plaintiffs, by bond and simple contract in considerable sums of money and being seised of some copyhold lands, surrenders the same to the use of his will and, afterwards, by his will, directs that this copyhold lands shall stand charged with the payment of all such just debts as he shall owe at the time of his decease and also with the several legacies after-mentioned. Then, he gives legacies to several of the defendants and then, taking notice that he had surrendered this copyhold lands to the use of his will, he now gives and devises the same to his son and his heirs chargeable with the payment of his just debts and the legacies before given and, of his will, makes his said son executor and dies. The son proves the will and, afterwards, became a bankrupt. And, an assignment being made of his real and personal estate to some of the defendants, this bill was brought against the assignees and legatees and the son for an account of the personal estate and to have the copyhold lands sold and the money applied towards payment and satisfaction of their debts.

Upon the hearing of the cause, it was decreed that an account should be taken and the copyhold lands sold and the moneys to be applied, first, for the payment of the mortgage, then the other creditors, and, afterwards, of the legatees, but, if there were a deficiency, the bond and simple contract creditors and the legatees to abate in proportion. Upon entering into the account, it appeared there would be a very great deficiency. And, therefore, before the account was gone through, this petition was preferred that, in case of a deficiency, the plaintiffs, the creditors, might be preferred before the legatees.

It was insisted on for the legatees that this copyhold being not otherwise subject to the payment of debts than as the testator had made it so by his will, that the creditors must take it as it was given, which was equally with the legatees, and, therefore, there ought to be no preference.

On the other side, it was urged that a man must be just before he is bountiful. And, therefore, if one owes a sum of money and, by his will, gives a legacy to the same person equal to the debt, this shall be applied in satisfaction of the debt.

And [they] cited 1 Chancery Cases 248, Hixon v. Wytham, and, 275, Whitton v. Loyd.[1]

But it being the last day of petitions and the point being likely to take up some time in debating, My Lord Chancellor [LORD MACCLESFIELD] said he would not enter into it now, but let the account go on and then apply to the court for directions upon the Master's report of the matter.

Specially note Mr. Talbot showed me a note of a case of Beke v. Bryen, Trinity 1712,[2] before Lord Harcourt, which was thus. The testator, before the Statute of Fraudulent Devises,[3] devises land to his second son subject to the payment of such debts as his personal estate should not be sufficient to satisfy and of a legacy of £500, makes his wife and his said son executors, and dies. The executors proved the will, and the debts appeared to be more than his personal estate. And the lands devised would extend to pay the son, [who] was likewise a creditor of his father for a considerable sum of money. And the first question was in what order the creditors should have satisfaction against the land. The son insisted that he being both creditor and executor ought to retain for his own debt preferably to any others. On the other side, it was insisted that the son, in this case, ought not to retain. And a distinction was taken between a devise to his executors by that name, for that implies an intention that the money should be applied in a course of administration, but a devise to a third person or to one by name, though he afterwards makes the same person executor, gives him no such preference. And the court decreed all debts to be paid equally. The second question was whether the legatees should come in equally with the creditors. And, for the legatees, it was insisted that the lands were liable only by the will and, by that being subject to both, both ought equally to be satisfied. And Sir John Churchill's Case was cited to that purpose. But the other side cited precedents to the contrary. Lord Keeper [Harcourt]: I will construe his meaning to be what it ought to have been and that he intended to be just before he was bountiful. And, therefore, he decreed the debts to be first paid.

And Mr. Talbot thought it a very good reason why the creditors should be preferred. Yet a court of equity will supply the want of a surrender for the sake of creditors, but not for the sake of legatees.

[Other copies of this report: British Library MS. Hargrave 82, f. 236, Lincoln's Inn MS. Misc. 107, f. 109.]

---

1 *Hixon v. Wytham* (1675), 1 Chancery Cases 248, 22 E.R. 784, also Reports *tempore* Finch 195, 23 E.R. 107, 1 Freeman 305, 22 E.R. 1226, 89 E.R. 222, 2 Eq. Cas. Abr. 369, 22 E.R. 314, 73 Selden Soc. 136, 152; *Whitton v. Lloyd* (1676), 1 Chancery Cases 275, 22 E.R. 798.

2 *Beake v. Brown* (Ch. 1712), British Library MS. Hargrave 80, f. 116, Chancery Cases *tempore* Harcourt, 276.

3 Stat. 3 Will. & Mar., c. 14 (*SR*, VI, 320–321).

604

Amherst v. Amherst

(Ch. c. 1723)

A counterpart of an ancient settlement is admissible evidence to prove that there was such a settlement.

Lincoln's Inn MS. Misc. 12, p. 1, pl. 2

A bill [was exhibited] for a discovery of a settlement made by the plaintiff's great-grandfather in October 1672. One of the defendants discovered in his answer a counterpart of this settlement.

The Master of the Rolls [JEKYLL] was of the opinion that, it being so ancient, it was an evidence there was such a settlement; at least, it was an evidence that the defendants had suppressed the original. And a decree was founded on this counterpart. But there was some proof that the original had been produced at a trial at law.

Note it was said that it was a question at law and never settled whether a counterpart of an ancient settlement was evidence that there was such a settlement.

605

Jackson v. Jennyns

(Ch. 1723)

Where a seller of land sues for specific performance of the contract and prays that the buyer defendant pay either the purchase price or the contractual penalty for non-performance, a court of equity will give the defendant that election.

Lincoln's Inn MS. Misc. 12, p. 38, pl. 1

Michaelmas term 1723.

The plaintiff's bill was to have a specific performance of articles for a purchase, in which there was a penalty of £2000. The plaintiff, very improperly, had prayed by his bill that the defendant might either perform the articles or pay the penalty.

Lord Chancellor [LORD MACCLESFIELD] would have decreed the articles to be performed, the defendant having by his answer made such a case as had entitled the plaintiff to have a decree against him though the estate was sold in the year 1720[1] at an extravagant price. But, in regard the plaintiff had given the defendant his option, My Lord Chancellor [LORD MACCLESFIELD] decreed that

[1] This was the year of the burst of the South Sea bubble.

the defendant should make his election whether he would take the purchase or pay the £2000 penalty.

But, afterwards, it being insisted that the title had been approved of by the defendant's counsel, the Master was directed to look into the title and that the defendant should make his election within a week after the Master's report.

606

Davis v. Gardiner

(Ch. 1723)

The realty of a testator is not charged with the payment of his debts by his will without express words to that purpose.

Lincoln's Inn MS. Misc. 12, p. 10

13 October 1723.

Upon the special matter of the Master's report, it appeared that A.B. made his will. And in the beginning of it were these words, 'as to such goods wherewith it has pleased God to bless me, after my debts and legacies [are] paid, I dispose thereof as follows'. And then the testator goes on with giving away several pecuniary and specific legacies. And then he devises his lands to his son upon a contingency. And there being a defect of personal assets to pay the legacies, the question was if the lands were charged with the legacies by the words in the beginning of the will.

Lord Chancellor [Lord Macclesfield] was of opinion the lands were not charged, there being nothing in the will that showed it was the intention of the testator to charge his lands, but the contrary, for, in the first place, he has given the lands to his son upon a contingency, which he would never have done if he had intended to charge those lands with the legacies for when and by whom shall they be paid. And, in the next place, when he comes to dispose of the surplus of his real and personal estate, he takes up the words again and says, 'after all my debts are paid, I devise the residue' etc., which makes it very plain he thought there would be a surplus of his personal estate and that, therefore, he could not think it necessary to charge his lands. Besides, the estate of an heir at law ought not to be charged but by plain and express words.

As to the words themselves, they are absurd, for the testator according to the letter of them is made to say that, after all his debts and legacies are paid, he gives such and such legacies.

[Other reports of this case: 1 Peere Williams 187, 24 E.R. 693, 2 Eq. Cas. Abr. 499, 22 E.R. 423.]

607

Hume v. de Barry

(Ch. 1723)

Where a third party's property is pledged and the pledgee has notice, neither the pledgee's creditors not the pledgor's creditors can reach this property.

Lincoln's Inn MS. Misc. 12, p. 41

Michaelmas term 1723. Robert Hume, plaintiff; David de Barry and the assignees under a commission of bankruptcy against Cox and Cleeve, defendants.

The plaintiff, being possessed of two long annuities, in May 1720, by a letter of attorney, empowers de Barry to subscribe these annuities into the South Sea [Company] or otherwise to sell and dispose of them for the plaintiff's benefit.

The bill is to have the orders delivered up and to have an account of the profits of these annuities.

It appears by the answer of the defendants that de Barry was indebted to Cox and Cleeve and that he deposited the annuity orders in their hands as a security for such debt. And they, afterwards, becoming bankrupts and a commission being taken out against them, the defendants, the assignees called upon de Barry for a satisfaction of what he owed the bankrupts. And he, being likewise become insolvent, assigned these orders to the assignees in satisfaction of such debt, who insisted on a title to the annuities under this assignment.

Lord Chancellor [Lord Macclesfield]: De Barry had only a letter of attorney to subscribe the annuities or dispose of them for the plaintiff's benefit. Cox and Cleeve must know that De Berry had no power to make a deposit of these securities as a security for any debt of his own. And the assignees, by taking an assignment of the orders after they had notice of the plaintiff's letter of attorney, were guilty of a breach of trust as well as the defendant and have thereby defeated the plaintiff of the benefit of having these annuities subscribed or sold.

He decreed, therefore, that the assignees should deliver up the orders to the plaintiff and pay costs and, the assignment to them not being registered at the Exchange, that was likewise ordered to be delivered up.

Lincoln's Inn MS. Misc. 384, p. 227, pl. 2

27 November 1723. Humes v. Assignees of Cox, Cleave, and Debarry.

The plaintiff empowered Debarry by a letter of attorney to receive interest on an annuity of £50 *per annum* and to dispose of them for the plaintiff's benefit. Debarry lodged them with Cox and Cleave to receive the interest. They being bankrupt and Debarry indebted to them, he assigns the annuity to the defendants, the assignees, Debarry being insolvent.

Mr. *Talbot* cited Crank v. Hooper *et ux.* and Drake, 1708. The plaintiff was a creditor of the testator for £100. Hooper's wife was executrix and residuary legatee. Hooper wasted the assets. Drake, a creditor of Hooper, bought a term of him, which was part of the testator's estate for £950, which he discovered, having notice of the plaintiff's debt. Hooper *et ux.* were bankrupt. A bill [was brought] for the £100. It was decreed against Drake because he was a party and privy to the devastavit.

Lord Chancellor [Lord Macclesfield]: These were the property of the plaintiff. The letter of attorney shows they were the plaintiff's. It was not made out that they were deposited in the hands of Cox and Cleve as a security but only to receive the interest for the plaintiff's use. In 1720, [there was] a new letter of attorney to empower Debarry to subscribe the annuity into the South Sea [Company]; nothing was done upon it. The defendants insist the Debarry might have sold them, but they are not sold, only assigned over without any new consideration. The defendants are trustees for the plaintiff.

608

Newland v. Shepard

(Ch. 1723–1724)

Where the child of a London freeman is given a marriage portion that is less than his or her orphanage share, that child can take his or her full orphanage share without any abatement for the portion.

Lincoln's Inn MS. Misc. 12, p. 43, pl. 2

24 October 1723.

In this case, a question arose touching the custom of the City of London, whether the plaintiff, who had married the daughter of Mr. Shephard, a druggist, and had received a portion with her, was fully advanced or not.

And in the arguing of this point; the Case of Dean and Lord Delaware was cited.[1] And Lord Chancellor [Lord Macclesfield] said what was settled in that case was, if a child was advanced in marriage with a portion less than the orphanage part, such child should be let in for her orphanage part upon bringing her portion into hotchpot, that is to say, if a man gives his daughter £9000 in marriage and the quantum of the portion appears by writing under his hand and he dies worth £30,000 and leaves no other child, the daughter shall come in and have a third of what was the value of her father's personal estate when he died, that is she shall have £10,000 out of her father's personal estate so that, in such case, she will have £19,000 in the whole. But, if her portion had been £11,000, which was more than a third of his personal estate, then she should be excluded.

[1] *Dean v. Lord Delaware* (1708), 2 Vernon 628, 23 E.R. 1011, 1 Eq. Cas. Abr. 156, 21 E.R. 955.

But query as to this, for, afterwards, the decree in Lord Delaware's Case was read, and, if I did not mistake, when it was read, what appeared thereby to be settled was this, *viz.*, if the portion of an advanced daughter appears by a writing under the father's hand and he dies leaving a wife and such daughter only and the portion given to the daughter does not amount to one full third of the personal estate which he dies possessed of, such daughter shall have one-third of what the personal estate together with her portion when added together amounts to, but, as to the widow, she shall have only a third of the personal estate which her husband left at his death.

Lincoln's Inn MS. Misc. 384, p. 314

12 June. Reheard.

The plaintiff married the daughter of Sheppard, a freeman of London. On the marriage, he gave her £6000 and a bond for £1000 on a contingency [?], which amounted to more than her orphanage share of what he left at his death, but not so much as her orphanage share of the estate if the £6000 were added to it.

Dean v. Lord Delaware is in point. [It was] certified, first, that the portion must be added to the estate at his death. Second, the certainty of the advancement appears under the freeman's hand; the child is not barred. Third, the portion not amounting to so much as the orphanage share, the daughter is to have both and not to bring the portion into hotchpot.

Lord Macclesfield decreed this case accordingly. Here, being only one child and a widow, there can be no hotchpot.

Lord Chancellor [Lord Macclesfield]: As to the £6000, it is the same case with Lord Delaware's, there being actual payment. But, as to the £1000 bond, that is not an actual advancement, but it is a debt. I was the Recorder when that certificate was made. There was a precedent in the City books, 14 Jac. I. There is no reason to vary the decree.

Lincoln's Inn MS. Misc. 12, p. 108

July 1724.

The plaintiff Newland married the daughter of Mr. Shephard, who gave with her a portion of £6000 and agreed to pay £1000 more upon a contingency, which has happened.

Mr. Shephard being a freeman of London and having made his will and the defendants executors, the plaintiffs bring their bill for the orphanage share of Mr. Shephard's personal estate, who had left issue only the plaintiff's wife.

It was insisted for the plaintiffs that the £6000 portion was less than one-third of the personal estate which Mr. Shephard died possessed of, for, as to the £1000, that was contingent and could not be reckoned as part of the portion, and that, therefore, the plaintiffs ought to be let into one-third of the personal estate without bringing the £6000 into hotchpot. And so it was said the custom was certified to be in the Lord Delaware's Case and that the decree was made upon that certificate. And, upon reading the decree, the case appeared to be exactly the same with the present case.

Lord Chancellor [Lord Macclesfield] said he was not satisfied with that decree. He thought it would be right for a child to have a third of the personal estate over and besides her portion if the portion was less than a third of the personal estate when added together because she had not been fully advanced. But, if a child has had more than one-third, she has then been fully advanced and has no reason to complain.

At a length after a pretty deal of agitation, he decreed the plaintiffs one-third of the personal estate exclusive of the portion, it appearing that the portion was less than one-third of the personal estate and the portion added together.

Note the quantum of the portion appeared by a writing under the father's hand.

Note this cause, upon the hearing, was sent to the Master to take an account of the personal estate, and the court reserved the consideration of the question touching the custom until after the account was taken. And now it came on upon the Master's report.

Lincoln's Inn MS. Misc. 13, p. 153

On the marriage of the plaintiff with Mr. Sheppard's daughter, Mr. Shephard agreed to give his daughter £6000 and £1000 more if his daughter or any issue of her body was living at the end of ten years after the marriage. Mr. Sheppard died before the ten years expired, leaving the defendant, his wife, and the plaintiff's wife, his only child, and being a freeman of London. The plaintiffs' bill was for an account of his personal estate and that the plaintiff's wife might have her orphanage share thereof.

Upon the hearing of the cause, it was referred to the Master to take an account of the personal estate. And the court reserved all further directions until after the account was taken.

The Master having reported the estate to amount to £18,500, Lord Macclesfield, when the cause came on upon the report, was of opinion that the £1000, being given upon a contingency, was not to be taken to be part of the portion of the plaintiff's wife. And, therefore, he decreed that she was not fully advanced and that she should come in for her orphanage [share] and that without bringing the portion into hotchpot, there being but one child and, consequently, no one who was entitled to have the portion.

The cause now came on to be reheard before the Lord King upon the defendant's petition, who insisted that, the plaintiff having now had £7000 for her portion, it was plain she was fully advanced, her portion being more than one-third of the personal estate, which her father left at his death, and, therefore, she was barred by the custom from claiming her orphanage part.

For the plaintiffs, it was insisted that, by the custom of London, if a child is advanced with a portion and the certainty of the advancement appears by a writing under the testator's hand and the portion does not amount to one-third of the personal estate left at his death and the portion added together, such child shall not be deemed fully advanced. And this was certified to be the custom in the Lord Delaware's Case, and, in that case as well as in this, there was but one child. And, consequently, there was no one with whom the portion was to be brought into hotchpot. And, therefore, the court there decreed the child her orphanage part without bringing the portion into hotchpot.

As to the plaintiff's portion, take it to be either £6000 or £7000, she has not had one-third of what the personal estate when the portion is added to it does amount to. And, therefore, she is a child not fully advanced within the custom, and, consequently, she must be let into her orphanage part.

Lord Chancellor [Lord King]: I was the Recorder when the certificate in the Lord Delaware's Case was made, and, as I remember, it was grounded upon a precedent in King James I's time. Take the case any way, it will come to the same thing. The decree must be affirmed.

9 Modern 467, 88 E.R. 579

A freeman of London had married his only child to Mr. Newland. And, by her marriage articles, he contracted to give her a portion of £7000, payable by installments of £1000 a time, the last of which was to be paid at the end of ten years if his daughter or any child of her was living at that time. Shepherd died before the expiration of the ten years, but the daughter lived to the end of them. And the question between her and the widow was whether she was fully advanced, for, if she was, she could claim no orphanage part.

And the court referred it to the Master to enquire what was the value of the estate. It was reported to be £18,000, which brought it to a very nice question, for, if the whole £7000 was considered as an advancement to the daughter, then she was fully advanced, having received her full third.

And Lord Macclesfield was of opinion that she was not fully advanced, but should be let into one clear third of the residue, as there can be no hotchpot between a child and the widow, that being only between the children themselves. And, in such case, the child comes in for an entire third of what is left. The ground of which opinion was that this sum of £1000, which was to be paid at the end of ten years if the daughter or any child of her should be then living, depending upon a contingency, was not an advancement at the death of the father.

And upon this point, the cause was reheard by Lord King, who was of the same opinion and affirmed the decree.

[Other reports of this case: 2 Peere Williams 194, 24 E.R. 696, 9 Modern 57, 88 E.R. 313, 2 Eq. Cas. Abr. 329, 22 E.R. 280.]

609

Walker v. Henwood

(Ch. 1723)

The Statute of Frauds does not require that the person who signs for another should have an authority in writing.

Lincoln's Inn MS. Misc. 12, p. 11

26 October 1723. Walker v. Henwood and Cox.

Upon an appeal from the decree of the Master of the Rolls [Jekyll], who decreed that the plaintiff should have a specific performance of articles which he had entered into with the defendant Henwood for the sale of an estate to him not only against the defendant Henwood but likewise against the defendant Cox, there being full proof in the cause that Henwood made this purchase for Cox and that by several subsequent declarations signified his approbation thereof. And it was further decreed that, if Henwood should be forced to pay the purchase money, then he should be at liberty to prosecute the decree against the defendant Cox in the plaintiff's name.

What was principally insisted on for Cox, who had appealed from this decree, was that Henwood had no authority from him in writing to contract for this purchase, and, therefore, he was not bound by the Statute of Frauds etc.[1]

Lord Chancellor [Lord Macclesfield]: A parol authority is sufficient, the words of the Act being that the agreement must be in writing signed by the party to be bound by it or some person by him authorized and it is not said authorized by writing. Therefore, it is not necessary that the person who signs for another should have an authority in writing. The decree is right and must be affirmed.

610

Anonymous

(Ch. 1723)

A case can be reheard after a final decree has been entered and enrolled where a party was betrayed by his solicitor.

British Library MS. Hargrave 83, p. 36, pl. 1

7 November 1723.

[It was] moved to have a cause reheard after a decree of dismission by default of the plaintiff, which decree was signed and enrolled, upon payment of the costs.

---

[1] Stat. 29 Car. II, c. 3 (*SR*, V, 839–842).

The plaintiffs had brought their bill against a parson to establish a *modus* for tithes. The solicitor whom they employed feed no counsel and had none to appear on the hearing, but went down into the country and told his clients that the cause was heard and the bill dismissed with costs. Upon this, they acquiesced. But coming afterwards to hear that this dismission was by default, they now made an affidavit of the whole matter.

My Lord Chancellor [Lord Macclesfield] made no order as to the rehearing this day. But a collusion being apprehended between the plaintiff's solicitor and the defendant, he ordered the solicitor to attend the last day of the term.

611

Atwood v. Whitehead

(Ch. 1723)

Where a defendant is physically removed from a court in order to be served with process, such act is a contempt of court.

British Library MS. Hargrave 83, p. 36, pl. 2

Eodem die [7 November 1723].

Atwood, the attorney, arrested another attorney, one Whitehead. It seemed by the proofs as if the bailiffs had first hustled Whitehead from within the Liberty of the Rolls to a place without it and then served their process. Atwood purged himself of its being done within the Liberty by his direction and would have had his costs, but His Honor [Jekyll] denied that and committed the bailiffs.

612

Anonymous

(Ch. 1723)

A preliminary injunction to stop a trial at common law can be extended where the defendant in equity does not answer only if the plaintiff's claim arises out of the substance of the defendant's answer.

British Library MS. Hargrave 83, p. 37, pl. 1

Eodem die [7 November 1723].

If you would have an injunction, for want of an answer or upon a *dedimus* [*potestatem*], extend to stay the trial, you must show from the nature of the bill that the defense at law is to arise out of the answer.

613
Waller v. Mackworth

(Ch. 1723)

Where a suit in equity was brought in complete good faith but later dismissed on the pleadings, the defendant will not receive court costs.

British Library MS. Hargrave 83, p. 35

26 November 1723. In Chancery.

In this case, My Lord Chancellor Macclesfield said that he remembered a case where a person, who loved to hear himself talk, had pretended to a very great intimacy with a gentleman, who died in the country, and had said that he was trusted by him in matters of moment and with several papers and valuable things, upon which some of the relations of the deceased, having occasion to bring a bill, made him a party and required a discovery of what he knew concerning the papers and affairs of the deceased. In his answer he fully denied any knowledge of his affairs or papers, yet he did not deny that he had given out what was charged by the bill.

The court upon this refused to give him his costs.

614
Ernle v. Ernle

(Ch. 1723)

The purchase of an advowson in order to present a specific person is simony.

A father may insist upon a child's allowing for his maintenance out of the interest of a legacy given to him.

Lincoln's Inn MS. Misc. 12, p. 24

26 November 1723.

Dame Martha Ernle gave the plaintiff £500, but no time was limited for the payment. And she made Walter Ernle, the plaintiff's and the defendant's father, executor. William Ernle died, and he made the defendant, his son, executor. The plaintiff's bill is to have a satisfaction of his legacy with interest.

The defendant insists his father gave the plaintiff a liberal education and maintained him at the University, where he studied divinity and went into orders and his father, afterwards, purchased the next presentation of a living at All Canings in Wiltshire worth £500 a year which cost £500 and, the incumbent dying, the plaintiff was presented to that living.

The defendant insists that the expenses of the plaintiff's education and what was paid for the purchase of the next presentation should be discounted out of the legacy.

Lord Chancellor [LORD MACCLESFIELD]: The laying out the £500 in the next presentation of the living could not be a satisfaction of the legacy. When it was bought, the son was not in orders and it was uncertain whether he would go into orders or no, and the living might have become void before he took orders. And, therefore, it could not be bought for him. And, if, after he had been presented, he had released the legacy, it would have been simony, for he would then have bought the living from[1] his father. And should I now decree it a satisfaction of the legacy, I should decree that which would make it simony and make his living void.

As to interest, a man may, if he pleases, insist upon a child's allowing for his maintenance out of the interest of a legacy given him. But, if the father does not insist on this but will give his son his maintenance, his executors shall not have an allowance for it. And, in the present case, it appears by the proofs the father did not intend to give his son his maintenance.

615

Lookes v. Briant

(Ch. 1723)

In this case, only the surviving children were the legatees, and they took as tenants in common.

Lincoln's Inn MS. Misc. 12, p. 16

2 December 1723.

The plaintiff's father, by his will, gave the interest of £1000 to his wife for her life, and, after her death, he declares his will to be that the £1000 should go to and be divided among his five children and 'to the survivors and survivor of them, each of them part and share alike'.

Three of the children died in the lifetime of their mother. And the two survivors bring their bill against the executors, the mother being dead, to be paid this legacy. And the question was if the five children were tenants in common or joint tenants.

The Master of the Rolls [JEKYLL] was of opinion that, if all the children had been living at the death of their mother, they would have been tenants in common by reason of the words to be divided among the five children. But, it being expressly given to the survivors, those words must be rejected if the representatives of the deceased children were to come in for a share of this legacy. And,

---

[1] for *MS.*

though the words 'each of them part and share alike' are added, those words will not overthrow and prevent the survivorship, they being applicable only to the surviving children and create a tenancy in common as between them.

It was objected that the representatives of the children that are dead ought to have been made parties that they might have contested this matter with the plaintiffs, the executors not being concerned in point of interest.

But it was said by the Master of the Rolls [JEKYLL] that, since the executors have made that objection, if they are overruled in it by the court, they will be indemnified in paying the £1000 under the decree to the plaintiffs though the representatives of the other children are no parties. And he being clear of opinion that the plaintiffs were entitled to the £1000, he thought there was no necessity of making those representatives parties. And he decreed the legacy to be paid to the plaintiffs.

616
Hort v. Baskerville

(Ch. 1723)

A court of equity will not take away any power given to trustees. However, if the trustees misuse their power, it is a breach of trust, and the court will then interpose.

Lincoln's Inn MS. Misc. 12, p. 17

Eodem die [2 December 1723].

Joseph Hort, the plaintiff's father, who was a Quaker in Bristol, makes his will, and he gives away his estate from the plaintiff, his eldest son. And, in the will, there is this proviso, *viz.* that, if the plaintiff should within seven years reform and return from his course and behavior by which he had incurred the testator's displeasure and which had occasioned the making of his will in the manner he had done and should behave himself continually for the space of two years together and that his trustees who should be then living or the survivors of them should by any writing under their hands certify and declare that they were in their consciences and judgments satisfied and do believe that his said son was reformed and reclaimed from such his ill courses, then, in such case after such behavior for two years and signing such certificate, it should be lawful for his trustees or the survivors of them to pay to his said son £200 to set him up in his trade or some other business, but, in this case, says the testator, 'I refer it wholly to the integrity and sincerity of my trustees to make such declaration and certificate not in the least doubting but they will be just.'

The plaintiff's bill was to be paid this £200 legacy.

The defendants, the executors and trustees, who were four, by their answer, say they believe the plaintiff has been so far from reforming that they do not think he has so much as begun to reform, but they do not mention any particular immoralities that he has been guilty of.

Several witnesses were examined on both sides touching the plaintiff's behavior, but none of them were very material.

It was much insisted on for the plaintiff that the court should interpose and, unless the defendants could show any immoralities the plaintiff had been guilty of, decree him his legacy.

The Master of the Rolls [Jekyll]: The testator has made his trustees judges, and, if this court should interpose and take away this power from the trustees, it would be to make a new will and to say that which is expressly contrary to what is said in the will.

If the trustees make an ill use of their power, it is a breach of trust, and the court will then interpose. But, otherwise, he said he never knew it had been done.

Then, it was insisted that the trustees had submitted that matter to the judgment of the court by their answer.

And, upon reading that part of the answer, the Master of the Rolls [Jekyll] said the defendants had entangled the matter by their submission, and, though, at first, he was inclinable to dismiss the bill, yet, after reading the answer, he said, if he should do so, the plaintiff, if he behaved himself well for two years, must bring a new bill. And, therefore, he sent it to a Master to enquire what the plaintiff's behavior for two years last past had been. And he ordered the defendants [to be paid] their costs.

617

Turner and Marks v. Crookshanks

(Ch. 1723)

A person does not have a cause of action where an act of negligence has not caused him any damage.

Lincoln's Inn MS. Misc. 506, p. 72

13 December 1723.

The plaintiffs had made several bargains for the defendant which were as yet unperformed and had in their custody a £1000 receipt of the plaintiffs in the South Sea [Company] subscription, as likewise two £500 receipts belonging to one Mitchell. The plaintiffs sold the receipts for £1000 intending to sell Mitchell's, but by mistake Crookshanks' £1000 was given, which the buyer took, one receipt being as good as another. The defendant gave orders for the sale of his receipt, but the plaintiffs told his agent that they could not sell it, not meeting with a chap, to which Rigsby, the agent, replied, 'If I sell it, will you deliver the receipt to the man I shall send to you with the money?' They said they would. Neither the defendant nor his agent ever sent any such person, but hearing that his receipt had been sold, he brings his action for the receipt and likewise for the money for which it was sold as for money had and received to his use. The plaintiffs pray an injunction.

Lord Chancellor [LORD MACCLESFIELD] decreed an injunction to the proceedings at law because, though it was the neglect of the plaintiffs, yet it was innocent and without any fraud or design, no benefit accruing to them thereby nor damage to the defendant that, if there had been any damage to the defendant though innocently done by the plaintiffs, yet, since it was by their neglect, the defendant should not suffer, as if one of the receipts had been lost or stolen and the defendant's No. 168 had not been lost, then he should not be compelled to bear his proportion as otherwise but he might say 'let whose will be lost, mine is safe'. But, in this case, one receipt is as good as another. If he had sold it and had sent the buyer to the plaintiffs, though they had not delivered No. 168, yet they would have delivered one of two of equal value, which would be all one to the purchaser. He would not have objected that it was not No. 168.

An injunction was decreed, but no costs.

[Affirmed on appeal: 7 Brown P.C. 255, 3 E.R. 166.]

618
Moreton v. Hicks

(Ch. 1723)

When a joint tenant suffers a common recovery, the tenancy becomes a tenancy in common and the right of the recoveree passes by the recovery.

Lincoln's Inn MS. Misc. 12, p. 22

16 December 1723.

Upon the special matter of the Master's report, which now came on to be heard. It appeared that, by a settlement made by Thomas Emes on the marriage of his son Benjamin, he had conveyed a messuage in Red Cross Street to trustees and their heirs to the use of his eldest son Joseph and the said Benjamin and, after the decease of one of them, to the use of A.B. and his heirs during the life of the survivor of them upon certain trusts therein mentioned and, after the death of his two sons and the survivor of them, to the use of the heirs of the body of Benjamin begotten on Mary, his intended wife, remainder to Thomas Emes and his heirs.

Benjamin, during the life of Joseph, suffered a common recovery of the whole house to the use of himself and his heirs.

The question was if the estate tail was barred by this recovery as to one moiety only of the house in Red Cross Street, for it was admitted that it was not good as to the whole, he and his brother being joint tenants of the freehold at the time of the recovery. But as to a moiety, it was said there was an estate tail executed in Benjamin and that the words 'heirs of the body of Benjamin' were words of limitation and not of purchase, according to Shelley's Case,[1] and, therefore, he might suffer a recovery of that moiety.

And of that opinion without any difficulty was Lord Chancellor [Lord Macclesfield]. He said Benjamin held *per my et per tout*, and, therefore, he had a freehold in the whole. But, by his conveyance, he had severed the joint tenancy, and, though he had conveyed the whole, yet it was by operation of law that a moiety only passed.

Another question arose upon the will of the said Thomas Emes, whereby he had devised five houses in Thames Street to William, another of his sons, and his heirs after the death of his, the testator's, wife, to whom he devised them for her life, and, afterwards, he declared his will to be that, if his son William should die without issue of his body then living or born in due time after his death, his son Benjamin or any issue of his body being then living, his will was that the said five houses should descend and come to his son Benjamin and his heirs, and, if both his sons William and Benjamin should die without issue, his son Joseph or any issue of his body then living, then he devised the said houses to his son Joseph and his heirs.

William died without issue, and, by will, he devised all his estate, real and personal, to his brother Joseph and his heirs.

Differences arising between Joseph and Benjamin about their father's estate, they came to an agreement [as to] what each should enjoy. And, inter alia, it was agreed William[2] should have the houses in Thames Street, and, accordingly, by the deed whereby it was agreed what each of them should have, Joseph grants, releases, and confirms to William[3] and his heirs all Joseph's right and title to these houses. The question was whether Joseph, having only a bare possibility or a contingent interest by the will of his father, could release it.

Lord Chancellor [Lord Macclesfield] said the release was good by way of extinguishment.

---

1 *Wolfe v. Shelley* (1581), 1 Coke Rep. 88, 76 E.R. 199, 1 Anderson 69, 123 E.R. 358, Moore K.B. 136, 72 E.R. 490, Jenkins 249, 145 E.R. 176, 3 Dyer 373, 73 E.R. 838.

2 Sic in MS. for Benjamin.

3 Sic in MS. for Benjamin.

619

Stent v. Baylis

(Ch. 1723–1724)

A contract is unenforceable where there is a failure of consideration.

The enforcement of a judgment at common law on a contract where there was a failure of consideration will be enjoined by a court of equity.

British Library MS. Hargrave 83, p. 37, pl. 2

The bill was brought to be relieved against a judgment recovered at law upon a contract in writing for transferring ten shares in the Lustring Company. And there was a memorial in writing endorsed on the contract that, although the books of the Company were not opened on the 6th of September, the time appointed, yet the plaintiff agreed to pay the money. An action at law was brought upon the contract, and, upon *non est factum* pleaded, judgment was recovered.

This cause being heard before the Master of the Rolls [JEKYLL] in court, he decreed that the plaintiff should be relieved because, if he paid his money, he could not have *quid pro quo*, the books of the Company not being opened to this day nor ever likely to open. And he decreed a perpetual injunction and satisfaction to be acknowledged upon the judgment.

N.B. There was a *scire facias* issued against this Company.

British Library MS. Hargrave 81, f. 271

Friday, 24 April 1724, at Westminster before the Master of the Rolls.

The plaintiff had bought ten shares of the defendant in September 1720 in the Lustrings Company at £58 per share, which came to upwards of £500, and had given a bond for the payment of the money. The defendant, on the other hand, had given a note for transferring of the shares at the next opening of the books, which were then shut.

But the book having never opened since nor being likely to open, the defendant brought this action upon the bond and, *non est factum* being pleaded to it, recovered a verdict, to be relieved against which this bill was brought, setting forth the nature of the case and the occasion of giving the bond.

The defendant by his answer admitted the case and insisted that he himself had bought these shares at a very great price, that he was ready whenever the books opened to transfer them to the plaintiff, and, therefore, insisted that, having obtained a verdict at law, a court of equity ought not to take away the benefit thereof from him and that he being only the defendant made it different from what it might have been if he had been the plaintiff and had wanted the assistance of a court of equity upon such a contract.

But the Master of the Rolls [JEKYLL] was clear of opinion that the plaintiff ought to be relieved against this verdict, that it was against conscience and natural justice that the plaintiff should be forced to pay for a thing which he could never have, and that, as the plaintiff could not have defended himself at law, he was proper to come into equity for relief. And, therefore, he decreed a perpetual injunction with liberty for the defendant to apply if ever the Lustrings Company's books opened.

[Other copies of this report: British Library MS. Hargrave 82, f. 262.]

[Other reports of this case: 2 Peere Williams 217, 24 E.R. 705, 2 Eq. Cas. Abr. 57, 689, 22 E.R. 50, 580.]

620

Mills v. Banks

(Ch. 1723–1724)

A trust to make payments out of 'rents, issues, and profits' gives the trustees the power to sell or mortgage the corpus of the trust only where it appears to be the settlor's intention they should have that power.

In this case, the settlor did not intend that the trust corpus could be sold or mortgaged.

The question in this case was whether an erroneous final decree should be reversed where a third party has justifiably relied upon it to his detriment.

The granting of a petition for a rehearing lies within the sound discretion of the court.

British Library MS. Hargrave 83, p. 38

A sum of money was advanced in confidence of a decree of the court. And by the order of the court with the approbation of a master, the money was laid out by the trustees of Sir George Rook and for his infant son. The rehearing now contended for was seventeen years after the original decree, and the petitioner had been an infant all that time. The decree was for a sale. The money advanced was by order in another cause and was by way of a mortgage. The decree being never enrolled, the rehearing was prayed, and the points upon which it was prayed were such that, if the petitioner prevailed, it might defeat the security.

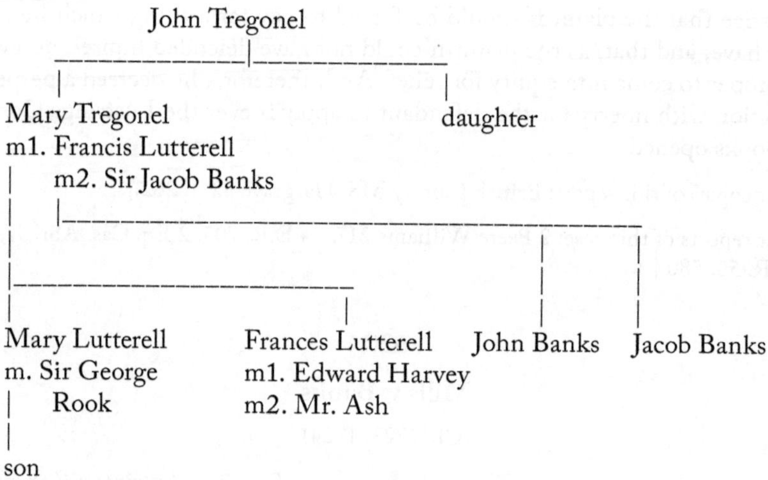

It was objected that this would not be for the honor of the court to weaken a security to which it has given a sanction and upon which it has laid out an infant's money, that a rehearing is discretionary and not *ex debito justitiae*, the party having another remedy by appeal, that if the decree should be altered there would be inconsistent and contradictory acts in the proceedings of the court.

It was answered that an infant's right could not be prejudiced in whom there was no laches after he had attained his age (though, in this case, there was no time given by the decree for him to show cause after he came of age, *quod nota*).

Curia advisari vult etc. Query.

Lincoln's Inn MS. Misc. 12, p. 287

3 August 1724. Samuel Mills, executor of Sir George Rooke, and Mr. Ash and his wife, plaintiffs; John Banks and Jacob Banks *et al.*, defendants.

Upon the marriage of Colonel Lutterell with Mary Tregonwell, a settlement was made and, therein, a term of 200 years is limited upon trust that, in case there should be issue of the marriage two or more children whereof one should be a son, the trustees should out of the rents of the lands comprised in the term or by granting leases for one, two, or three lives or for years determinable on one, two, or three lives of lands usually demised in possession, reversion, or remainder under the ancient rents or by granting estates by copy of court roll according to the custom of the manner raise and levy £10,000 for the child or children of the marriage, except the eldest son, to be paid to sons at twenty-one and to daughters at eighteen or marriage which should first happen or so soon as the same could or might be raised out of the premises as aforesaid, provided that, if there should be no issue male of the marriage or if there should be issue male and such issue should die without issue and there should be one or more daughters of the marriage, then the trustees should by and out of the rents and profits of the premises or by granting estates in the manner aforesaid raise and levy for such daughter or daughters the sum of £10,000 and, in case such child or children should die before the £10,000 or any part of it should be payable, then the £10,000 so raised for such child or children or so much thereof as should be raised should be paid to such person as should be seised of the inheritance of the premises and the term should be surrendered.

Mr. Lutterell died without issue male, leaving two daughters, one of which was married to Sir George Rooke and the other to Mr. Harvey. And Mrs. Lutterell married Sir Jacob Banks and had issue by him the two defendants.

Mr. Harvey and his wife brought their bill against the two defendants, who were entitled to the estate subject to the term, and against the trustees to have her moiety of the £10,000 raised and paid.

The cause was heard 6 December 5 Ann. [1706] before Lord Copwer, who declared that the rents and profits of the premises charged with the raising the £10,000 from the death of Lady Banks, she being then dead, ought to go towards raising the same and what such rents and profits should fall short of satisfying thereof ought to be made good and raised by the sale of so such of the premises as should be sufficient for that purpose. And he decreed the same accordingly and that the portions should carry interest from the time of the decree and that an account be taken of the rents received by Sir Jacob Banks since his lady's death and what on the account should fall short of the £10,000 it was ordered that so much of the premises as should be sufficient should be sold with the approbation of the Master and, until sold, the growing rents to be brought before the Master.

Mr. Harvey died, and his widow married the plaintiff, Mr. Ash, who, before such marriage made a settlement on his wife in consideration of her portion of £5000 to which she was entitled under the decree. And a mortgage was made by virtue of the decree for raising her £5000.

And the defendants John and Jacob Banks, who were infants at the time of the decree, being now come of age, petitioned for a rehearing of the case. And they complained of the decree for directing a sale and ordering interest to be paid.

Note the estate charged with the portions was something more than £700 a year.

Attorney General [*Yorke*], for the plaintiffs, insisted the decree was right.

By the first words, 'rents and profits', there is no doubt but there might be a sale. The rents and profits is the land itself. A grant of rents and profits is by law a grant of the land itself, and so a devise of rents and profits is a devise of the land. And this court has carried on that legal construction. And the question then is whether this court shall by the subsequent words restrain the generality of the first words.

In this exposition of this deed, the intent of the parties must be considered. Now, it is plain the parties could never intend that the portions should be raised by driblets. If, indeed, it did appear that the annual rents and profits would raise the portions in a little time, this court would not extend the words and decree a sale, but, where it appears that the portions cannot be raised in many years, as is the present case, it may reasonably be presumed that the parties could not intend the raising of them in this manner.

The Case of Ivy and Gilbert, which he said he expected to hear of from the other side, was very different from the present case, for, in that case, the rent and profits of the estate were sufficient to raise the portions in four or five years' time. And, besides, there was no time limited in the settlement for the payment of the portions. And he cited the Case of Trafford and Ashton, *quod vide*, L.C. 27.

As to interest, if the portions were to be raised by annual rents, they ought to carry interest from the time they became payable, for, otherwise, it signifies nothing to appoint a time when the portions are to be paid. And there have been several cases where a portion has carried interest though it could not be raised in one entire sum.

Mr. Solicitor General [*Wearg*], for the defendants: I must agree that, where there has been a trust to raise portions out of rents and profits, there are several precedents that the court has decreed them to be raised by a mortgage or sale, for money raised by sale is the profits of the estate, it not being material whether the profits are all raised at once or by degrees. But, in the present case, the portions are to be raised not only by rents and profits but by several other ways which are particularly prescribed. And he insisted on the Case of Ivy and Gilbert.

Then, as to interest, it was insisted that here was no time expressly limited when the portions shall be paid. They are not to be paid until they shall be raised by the rents and profits etc., for the words are that they shall be paid to sons at twenty-one and to daughter at eighteen or marriage or as soon after as the same could be raised out of the premises as aforesaid so that, until the portions can be raised, they are not payable, and consequently, no interest is due until that time.

Lord Chancellor [Lord Macclesfield] took notice that there was another settlement made at the same time that this settlement was made, whereby a provision is made for the daughters. And he thought that settlement might very properly be taken into consideration in expounding the present settlement. By the other settlement, the money to be raised for the daughters is called 'portions', which it is not in the present settlement, and maintenance is provided for them in the meantime. And, therefore, there being portions and maintenance provided for them another way, he thought the £10,000 was only as an additional bounty. Besides, he said, it was a material circumstance that here was no time limited when the money is to become payable.

He thought the present case did not materially differ from the Case of Ivy and Gilbert.

The trustees have only a power, and they cannot exceed it. They must execute the trusts in the manner prescribed by the deed and cannot go beyond it. If they could or if this court could empower trustees so to do, there would be an end of all trusts.

The primary import of the words 'rents and profits' is annual rents. But this court has extended those words when they stood singly to a mortgage or sale, which is an anticipation of the profits, when the circumstances of the case require it.

The subsequent words are not restrictive of the first words, but they show what the parties meant by the words 'rents and profits'.

But what decree can I make in this case, for all the parties who are interested in the estate are not before the court. A mortgage has been made under the decree, who is not before the court, and I cannot conclude him.

I think the proper method must be to bring a new bill and all persons interested made parties. But then they must consider what can be done in this case, for, if I reverse this decree, there will be inconsistent acts of the court in respect of this mortgage. I will neither reverse nor affirm.

Lincoln's Inn MS. Misc. 380, pt. 2, p. 15, pl. 2

3 and 4 August 1724.

John Tregonel, having two daughters, his co-heiresses, on the marriage of his daughter Mary with Francis Lutterell, settled part of his estate on her and her husband for their lives, remainder to trustees for a term of 2000 years, remainder to their first and other son in tail male, remainder to the first and every other son in tail male of his daughter Mary, remainder to the daughters of that marriage etc.

The trust of the 2000 years term was declared in this manner, *viz.* that, if Lutterell and his wife should have children, two or more, one of which should be a son, then the trustee should:

> out of the rents, issues, and profits or by granting estates by leases for one, two, or three lives of lands usually demisable in possession, reversion, or remainder under the ancient rent, or by granting estates by copy of court roll according to the custom of the manor raise and levy £10,000 to be paid to such child or children, other than the eldest son, if sons, at the age of twenty-one; if daughters, at the age of eighteen or marriage which should first happen or so soon after as the same can or may be raised out of the premises as aforesaid; and, if there shall be no son but only a daughter or daughters, then to raise and levy the same in the like manner and pay the same to such daughter or daughters.

The marriage took effect, and Francis, the husband, died leaving two daughters, Mary and Frances, and no son. Mary married Sir George Rook and died leaving a son. Frances married first Edward Harvey, since deceased, and is now married to one Ash. Mary Lutterell, the widow, married Sir Jacob Banks, by whom she had two sons, John and Jacob, and died. The bill was brought by Sir George Rook, as administrator to his wife, Mary, and by Edward Harvey and his wife, Frances, to have an execution of the trust of that term of 2000 years and to raise the £10,000 for the two daughters, to which bill Sir Jacob Banks and his two sons were parties, but both were infants. The 6th of December, the 5th Anne [1706], Lord Cowper, upon hearing the cause, decreed that the rent received from the death of Mary, the widow, should be applied towards raising the £10,000 and the residue should be raised by the sale of so much of the estate as was necessary for that purpose and interest be allowed from the death of the widow.

Sir George Rook afterwards died and left his son and heir an infant and made him by his will his residuary legatee of his personal estate. And his personal estate being ordered by a decree to be placed out at interest for the benefit of the infant, £4000 part of it was with the approbation of the Master placed out upon a mortgage of this trust estate. In 1719, Mills, the representative of Sir George Rook, revived the decree in this cause.

John Banks, the son of Sir Jacob Banks, being entitled to the trust estate subject to the £10,000, has obtained a rehearing, the decree not being signed and enrolled, and insists by his petition that the decree for the sale or mortgage of the estate is not warranted by the settlement and that the £10,000 is to be raised only by perception of the profits and making such leases as are specified in the declaration of the trust of the term. Upon this case, it now comes before the court.

The Attorney General [*Yorke*], *Lutwyche*, and *Peere Williams* were counsel for the plaintiff. The Solicitor General [*Wearg*], Serjeant *Chesshyre*, *Mead*, and *Talbot*, [were] for the defendant. Two questions were made: whether the decree itself was originally right; whether, supposing it was not, yet after this length of time and the proceedings that have been upon the decree, it is not too late now to rehear it.

As to the decree itself, it was argued for the plaintiff in favor of the decree that it has been the constant practice of this court to interpret a power given to trustees to raise money out of rents and profits to extend to the raising of it by sale or mortgage of the estate and this is agreeable to the common law itself, which construes a grant of the profits of the estate to convey the estate itself, that the former part of the declaration of the trust having given the trustees that power of raising it out of the rents and profits, it shall not be controlled or diminished by any subsequent words that give a less and inferior power to them.

And this is strengthened from the consideration of the smallness of the estate, it not being above £500 *per annum*, and of the use of the money when raised, it being for portions for daughters, which must be understood to be gross sums and not to come in by driblets, which would be to have a portion that could not be raised in less than twenty years, that daughters' portions have always been favored and such constructions put on the words of wills or deeds as may most effectually answer the intent of such a provision for them, that it appeared on the proofs that there were no part of the estate but what was let at a rack rent and, therefore, nothing could be expected to arise by means of fines on such leases on which the accustomed rent was reserved, that these words concerning 'the raising the money by leases' etc. seem to have been words put in by the person who drew the deed without direction not with an intent to restrain the general words preceding, but as a usual form that he had been wont to insert in trusts of this kind.

The Case of Traford v. Ashton[1] was cited, which was determined by the present Chancellor [Lord Macclesfield] upon the 23rd of May 1718, where, upon a marriage settlement, a portion of £8000 for younger children was to be raised by a trust of a term out of the rents and profits so soon as conveniently could or might be raised and this without mentioning any particular time when it was to be raised and yet it was decreed that it should be raised immediately by sale or mortgage and that interest should be paid until the portions were raised and paid.

For the defendants, it was argued that the intention of the parties was to govern in these cases and no arguments from the inconvenience of such portions that would come in by small parcels could be of any weight against the manifest intention of the parties who had full power over the estate, that all declarations of trust imply a negative upon everything or every power not expressly given. And it was so determined by the present Chancellor in the case of Butler v. Duncomb,[2] in the year 1719, in which case, a trust term was created in a settlement to raise portions for younger children and expressed to be out of the rents and profits and to be paid at the age of twenty-one or marriage and that, after the commencement of the term, the trustee might by sale or mortgage raise such portions; one of the younger children, being come of age in the lifetime of his father whose estate for life by the settlement was precedent to the commencement of the term, brought his bill in order to raise and pay his portion by sale or mortgage of the term in the lifetime of his father, but it was decreed that, though, if there had been no express power given to the trustee to raise the portions by sale or mortgage after the commencement of the term, they might by virtue of the words 'rents and profits' have sold or mortgaged the term in the life[time] of the father, yet, since there was an express power to raise them in that way after the commencement of the term, that carries a negative upon the doing of it before.

[It was argued] that, in the present case, the express power that is given to the trustees to raise the portions in a particular manner by granting estates by leases for one, two, or three lives etc. or by granting copyhold estates according to the custom and the particular mention of the reservation of the ancient rents of the estate showed that the intention of the parties was that the ancient estate itself should be preserved.

They cited a late case of Joy v. Gilbert,[3] which was decreed by the present Chancellor and affirmed by the House of Lords in an appeal, which was said to be exactly the same as the present case, and the only difference insisted on by the plaintiff's counsel was that, in that case, there was no particular time men-

---

1 *Trafford v. Ashton* (1718), see above, Case No. 249.

2 *Butler v. Duncomb* (1718–1719), see above, Case No. 282.

3 *Ivy v. Gilbert* (1722), see above, Case No. 543.

tioned when the portion would be payable. And the decree in that case was that the trustee could raise the portion only by the growing rents or profits and not by sale or mortgage.

They cited likewise the Case of Sir Willoughby Hickman v. Sir Stephen Anderson,[1] where the plaintiff having married the daughter of the defendant and it having been provided in the marriage settlement of the defendant that portions for daughters should be raised by trustees payable at the age of eighteen or day of marriage in case the father died leaving one or more daughters, the plaintiff brought his bill against the defendant, the father, and the trustees in order to have the portion of his wife raised, but Lord Cowper decreed that, though there was a time limited for the payment of the portions, to wit at the age of eighteen or marriage, yet the trust being declared to raise the portion for the daughters in case the father died leaving one or more daughters, it could not be raised until the father's death, it being uncertain whether the plaintiffs would be entitled to it or no.

The Lord Chancellor [Lord Macclesfield] said that it was true the words 'rents, issues, and profits' are extensive enough to give power to the trustees to sell or mortgage, but that is where it appears to be the party's intention they should have that power. He thought those words had been commonly carried further than what they properly signify, which took its rise from the common law's interpretation of them in grants or conveyances, where they have been held to mean a conveyance of the whole estate nothing remaining to give when the whole profits were disposed of, that, in the case of a trust for raising money out of rents and profits, they do not seem so naturally to signify a power of raising it by sale or mortgage, but only out of the growing and accruing profits and so to mean no more than a direction how the trustees shall apply those rents and profits as they arise. And a person that is not a lawyer must understand them in that sense and no other. But he agreed that this court has, and with reason, a little strained the meaning of those words in order to carry the main intent of the parties the more effectually into execution.

Where the words have been general and alone without any other to show a contrary intention and where the circumstances have been such as demand a speedy raising of the money which cannot be done in a reasonable time out of the growing profits, in such case, the court has usually extended those words to signify a power of disposing of the profits by way of anticipation. But if there are other words that show a contrary intention in the parties, there is no such room left for the court to strain the signification of those words beyond their proper and natural sense.

[He said] that, in the present case, when the parties expressly say this money may be raised by anticipation in a particular way as by leases for lives of twenty-

---

1 *Hickman v. Anderson* (1710), 2 Vernon 655, 23 E.R. 1027.

one years, reserving the ancient rents, etc., it plainly shows the parties intended no other method of anticipation and the particular method directed excludes all others, that if negative words 'and not otherwise' had been added to the words 'rents, issues, and profits', the case would not have been at all stronger than it is at present since, if the words 'rents, issues, and profits' were in themselves large enough to take in a sale or mortgage, the words 'not otherwise' could not exclude such sale or mortgage, that the subsequent words of 'by lease' etc. are not in the nature of a restriction of the former words 'issues and profits', but serve only to show the party's meaning in them.

[He said] that, for these reasons, he was clearly of opinion that the former decree was wrong and ought not to have been made. But he said he doubted very much whether as the circumstances of this case were, he was at liberty to reverse it upon this rehearing, not because of the length of time, because the petitioner was an infant at the time of the decree and but lately come of age and no laches could be imputed to an infant, but for these reasons, that a third person is now become interested in this decree and has lent money upon the credit of it and he is no party to this case nor has any opportunity of being heard in the defense of his title, that, by reversing this decree, the court will do an inconsistent act which will stand inconsistent upon the record of the court, for the mortgagee lent his money upon the credit of that decree and by virtue of the report of the Master, which states it as a proper security, and reversing this decree will not reverse that report or the proceedings in that cause, which is not the same with the present.

He said that a superior court indeed might reverse it, though he could not. And, if a superior court should, a bill might then properly be brought on the foundation of that reversal against the mortgagee in order to set aside his mortgage, that, on the other side, as he could not reverse the decree, so he could not tell how to affirm it.

He advised the parties to settle it in an amicable manner and, for that purpose, adjourned the petition of rehearing until the next term.

Upon the 7th of November 1724, the parties not having agreed it between themselves, it came on again before the court upon the single point whether, though the decree ought not at first to have been made, yet considering the circumstances of this case, it can now be reversed. The difficulty as to this arose upon these two heads, the length of time since the decree and the transactions that happened after it.

As to the length of time, the decree was made the 6th of December 1706, but the suit abated soon after by the death of Sir George Rook and was revived by Mills, his representative, in the year 1719. The petitioner was an infant until the year [*blank*], when he came of age, and, soon after, he exhibited this petition of rehearing.

As to the other transactions since the decree, there being a decree in another cause in which the son and residuary legatee of Sir George Rook, an infant, was plaintiff, that his personal estate should be placed out at interest by his trustees with the approbation of the Master, it was proposed to take a mortgage out of the estate of Banks for £4000 and the Master made his report that he approved the security, upon which the surviving trustees of the term of 2000 years assigned it to trustees for the infant Rook by way of a mortgage to be redeemable at a day four years after.

For the plaintiff, it was insisted that, after so long an acquiescence, it was too late to overturn the decree, that even writs of error at law are not to be had after twenty years, that the defendant's being an infant until about the time of the petition for rehearing does not answer this objection because the decree makes no reservation of any liberty for the infant to show cause when of age, as it is not usual in these kind of decrees for a sale or mortgage, which must be done presently, that the subsequent transactions in this cause make it still stronger, that an infant had lent his money upon the faith of this decree and upon the report of the Master, that the Master's approbation is the act of the court itself and the reversing of the decree will destroy that security which the court had before adjudged to be good and make the acts of the court directly inconsistent in determining that the mortgage is good by one act and by another that it is bad, both of which would in that case subsist at the same time, that the proper parties for making such a determination were not before the court, the trustees of the defendant Rook not being parties, that the court is not bound *ex debito justitiae* to grant a rehearing at all, which is a matter of discretion in the court whether from the circumstances of the case it is proper to take the decree into farther consideration. And for the same reason, the court may after the hearing of it again reject the petition as not judging it a fit matter to be reconsidered, that, where the circumstances of the case appear so hard after so long an acquiescence after the court has given the decree a second sanction by placing out an infant's money on the credit of it and considering the difficulty, if not impossibility, of putting all parties after the reversing the decree into the same condition as they were in before the making of it, the court may say as they have done in other cases, that they do not care to intermeddle themselves, but though they do not, another court may, and, since an appeal lies open to the House of Lords, there is no necessity for the court to interpose and favor so hard a case.

For the defendant, it was insisted that the objection from length of time is answered by the infancy of the petitioner until immediately before his petition, that this court never imputes any laches to an infant, that the use they would make of his infancy is not to reverse the decree for that reason, for it is acknowledged that there was no occasion in such a decree to reserve a liberty to the infant to show cause against it since of age, but only to answer the objection from the acquiescence for so long a time, which is an imputation of laches, that, as to subsequent transactions, they were no part of the present cause and, therefore, not proper to be read or taken notice of and will be no ways immediately or directly affected by reversing this decree, that the justice of the defendant's case was no ways altered by these transactions, that those who trusted the money on the deficient security must in this case, as in any other, suffer if no collateral satisfaction can be had, that there were some manifest oversights in the allowing of this as a proper security, that though the Master might not be supposed to dispute the justice of the decree which he had before him, yet he might object that it was not signed nor enrolled and that it was to sell the estate and not to mortgage it, which is very different in itself and a greater hardship on the persons entitled than a sale. The Master might also object that it was improper to make a mortgage not redeemable in less than four years when the reversioner, at the same time, has an equitable right to have the estate as soon as ever he should discharge the portions, that this mortgage is not properly the act of the court though approved by the Master, there being a great difference between a decree for the Master to sell and where the trustees are to sell with the approbation of the Master, this last being the act of the trustees only, but with an additional care which the court is pleased to take of the infant, that the court's discretion as to rehearings is no more than to judge whether it is proper to grant a rehearing or not, but, when once granted and the cause heard again, the same decree ought then to be made as if it was upon an original hearing, that the infant Rook is not without a remedy if the decree be varied, that it leaves the mortgage just as it was. The legal estate will still continue in the trustees of Rook, who can be dispossessed no way but by a bill in this court and, upon such bill, the court may consider whether it is proper to assist the defendant against one that has lent his money *bona fide* and upon a security under such circumstances, or an original bill may be brought for the infant Rook to assert his own interest in the estate.

And, as to what is said that the defendant, if this decree is affirmed, may bring his bill in the nature of a cross-bill against the mortgagee, the infant, and others, in order to take advantage of this construction of the words of the trust, the decree in the former cause would be pleadable to such a bill as soon as it is signed and enrolled.

The Lord Chancellor [Lord Macclesfield] said, it being a matter of great consequence and having a good deal of doubt how far he could take notice of these subsequent circumstances, he would take time to consider of it.

Lincoln's Inn MS. Misc. 107, p. 141

November 1724.

In this case, it was clearly held that, where there is a decree for the raising of portions or any sum of money which is directed to be paid at a certain time by sale or mortgage of an infant's estate, that the infant is bound by the decree and shall have no day to show cause after he comes of age, as he shall in ordinary cases. And, in the principal case, there was a term of 200 years vested in trustees by a settlement in trust out of the rents and profits to raise the sum of £5000 apiece for daughters' portions payable at twenty-one or marriage, which should first happen. And, on a bill brought against the heir at law, who was an infant, and the trustees so long since the year 1706, a decree was pronounced for the raising of those portions for two daughters, who were entitled to them, and the decree was that they should be raised by a sale of the term upon the notion which then prevailed and has since been established that, where the ordinary rents and profits of the estate will not raise the portions by the time they come to be wanted, then the word 'profits', by a liberal construction, shall be intended the profits arising by the sale or mortgage of that estate which are but the profits of it for so many years by way of anticipation. This decree being thus pronounced in another cause between other parties, there was a decree that the sum of £4000 should be placed out upon a security at interest with the approbation of the Master for the benefit of an infant who was entitled to it, upon which the parties concerned for this infant proposed to lend the £4000 upon an assignment of the 200 years term which was so decreed to be sold in the other cause. And, accordingly, an assignment was prepared, settled, and approved of by the Master and the money actually paid. The decree in the first cause had never been signed and enrolled, but stood open from the time of pronouncing it until about a year ago, when the first infant came of age, who then applied by a petition for a rehearing of the cause in order to bring on the question again whether these portions ought not to have been raised out of the ordinary rents and profits of the estate and not by a sale or mortgage and, consequently, if that should be the opinion of the court, then the former decree which directed them to be raised by a sale would be wrong.

My Lord Chancellor [Lord Macclesfield], upon all occasions of this nature, had declared himself in favor of raising such portions out of the ordinary rents and profits of the estate and seemed to be of opinion that no such sale or mortgage ought to be made and that it could not be inferred to be the intention of the parties to have them raised any other way than out of the ordinary rents and profits of the estate. But this question having been in peace for some years, he would not now shake it whatever his own opinion was. But now, upon this petition, if it should be granted for a rehearing, that point would become directly to be the question, and, if the court should reverse the former decree, one certain consequence would be that, instead of receiving the principal and interest due upon the mortgage, the party who advanced the money must have no interest at all for it and must be content to take his principal too as the ordinary rents and profits of the estate would raise it and that likewise in the case of an infant who, trusting to the faith and credit of the decree in the other cause, to which he was no party, had lent this £4000 upon it.

The case was very well and pretty fully spoken to on both sides. And it was thought to be a case of very great consequence since, on the one hand, if persons lending money or purchasing estates under decrees of this court where infants were concerned might be in danger of being defeated of their purchases and money too, nobody would ever after desire dealing in such cases, and, on the other hand, if the lending of money or purchasing of estates subsequent to such decrees were forever to bind and conclude infants from re-examining the justice thereof, they might be in danger of being greatly injured thereby. And, though it was agreed that, on the one hand, there was an acquiescence of eighteen years, yet, on the other hand, it must be admitted that the party lent his money under a decree not signed and enrolled. And, as no laches ought to be imputed to the infant who was entitled to the estate that he did not apply for a rehearing sooner by reason of his infancy, so, on the other hand, no laches ought to be imputed to the infant who was the lender of the money that he did not take care to get the decree signed and enrolled, he being an infant likewise and the rather because, if he had so done, yet even in that case, an appeal would have laid in Parliament, where the first decree might have been reversed and all the same consequences might have followed. And, therefore, as it was said in cases of this nature, some had been advised not to take any purchase or mortgage until an appeal had been brought and the case decreed in Parliament.

My Lord Chancellor [Lord Macclesfield] was inclinable to reject the petition. And he said he apprehended the consequences so great that, if he were not bound to receive it, as he thought he was not, he would not enter into the question again, which he said had been already settled, however different from his own opinion might be. And he said this petition for a rehearing was not like a writ of error, which was a writ of right, but this petition was discretionary in the court whether it should be granted or not. But it being of a very great consequence both ways, he would consider of it, especially since it was contended by some that, if the decree were reversed, all intermediate acts must fall and be void of course, as the reversal of a judgment upon a writ of error overreaches and defeats all intervening acts done in pursuance of the judgment.

And so no opinion was given [to] it at present.

From Mr. Cox's notes.

[Other reports of this case: 3 Peere Williams 1, 24 E.R. 943, 2 Eq. Cas. Abr. 491, 22 E.R. 417.]

621

Anonymous

(Ch. 1724)

A rehearing is based upon an alleged error, mistake, or omission in a decree, and, therefore, there should be no rehearing upon a decree by default.

British Library MS. Hargrave 83, p. 30, pl. 2

20 January 1723[/24].

At the seal this day, a motion was made to discharge an order for rehearing upon this case. The defendants had made default and had a day to show cause against the decree upon the common terms of paying costs. They showed no cause, but lay by. Subsequent to this, there were proceedings before the Master and a sequestration for costs, after which the defendants petitioned to rehear and had an order for it upon making the deposit.

My Lord Chancellor [Lord Macclesfield] said this was a new invention and, if it prevailed, there would be an end of showing cause upon the usual terms after a decree by default. And he would have discharged the order for rehearing or confined them only to the point of the regularity of the decree if they had not offered to pay the costs of the day and all other costs upon the doing of which the order was to stand. But My Lord directed it to be taken down that he would not in the like case ever hereafter make an order for rehearing because a rehearing was founded upon a possibility of error or mistake or omission in the decree, which counsel, being satisfied of, signed the petition to rehear. But, in such a case as this, there could be no grounds to rehear, for a decree by default was certainly right if regularly obtained and there was no room for bringing any other point but that before the court upon a rehearing.

622

Atkinson v. Swift

(Ch. 1724)

A pledge of a deed creates a lien on the land described in the pledged deed.

British Library MS. Hargrave 81, f. 247

Friday, 14 February 1723[/24], at the Rolls.

The plaintiff lent the defendant's testator the sum of £30; for securing the repayment thereof, the defendant's testator deposits with the plaintiff one of the title deeds belonging to his estate and writes on the back thereof to this effect 'I do acknowledge to have borrowed and received of Mr. Atkinson, [for] the repayment thereof, I have left this deed in his hands as a pawn. Witness my hand.' And he signs his name.

And this bill was brought against the defendants as executors and devisees of the estate to have an account of the personal estate and, if that be not sufficient, then to subject the lands comprised in the pledged deed to the payment of the debt and interest.

The Master of the Rolls [Jekyll] said this was perfectly a new case, and he had never known it before. But he thought it could never be imagined that the plaintiff lent £30 upon the parchment barely, but upon the estate or the lands comprised in the parchment, that a note has in this court been held sufficient to bind the lands and will be a lien thereon. And so it was held in the Case of the Earl of Kildare v. Kent[1] and in a case last term between Cooke and Sympson,

[1] *Earl of Kildare v. Kent* (1702), 2 Freeman 253, 22 E.R. 1192, *sub nom. Shepherd v. Kent,* Precedents in Chancery 190, 24 E.R. 92, 2 Vernon 435, 23 E.R. 879, 1 Eq. Cas.

where the defendant's testator, upon a composition for the purchase of South Sea [Company] stock at about £300 percent, which he had in the year 1720 contracted for at £1200 percent, gave a note under his hand that two houses which he had in Finch Lane, London, should be conveyed to the plaintiff towards payment and satisfaction of the money compounded for at such rates as the same should be valued and estimated at by two persons to be chosen one by himself and the other by the plaintiff, and he having the misfortune to be cast away in his voyage to Barbados with the Lord Belhaven before any conveyance or valuation made of the houses, on a bill brought against his heir and executor, it was held that this note was a specific lien upon the houses and, in case his personal estate was not sufficient, the two houses were decreed to be valued and conveyed accordingly.

And the Master of the Rolls [JEKYLL] in the present case was of opinion that the pledging of the deed was in equity an agreement to pledge the lands comprised in that deed and that the land was bound to answer the debt in case the personal estate was not sufficient. And he cited Lord Buckhurst's Case, 1 Co.,[1] that the deeds or charters belong to him who is to have or defend the title of the land.

[Other copies of this report: British Library MS. Hargrave 82, f. 245.]

4 Viner, Abr. 463

Hilary 10 Geo. I. 1723[/24].

The defendant was executor and devisee of the real estate of one Moore. The bill was to be paid £30, which the plaintiff had lent to Moore, either out of the personal estate, if sufficient, or, if not, then out of the real estate, for this reason, because, upon the lending of the money, the title deeds of the real estate were put into the hands of the plaintiff, and it was indorsed upon them that it was agreed that the deeds were so deposited as a security for the payment of so much money.

And the court declared the real estate in this case charged with the said debt.

[Other copies of this report: 2 Eq. Cas. Abr. 500, 22 E.R. 424.]

Abr. 142, 21 E.R. 944, Colles 253, 1 E.R. 273.

[1] *Lord Buckhurst v. Fenner* (1598), 1 Coke Rep. 1, 76 E.R. 1, also Moore K.B. 488, 72 E.R. 713, 2 Anderson 118, 123 E.R. 576, Tothill 141, 21 E.R. 148, 117 Selden Soc. 155, 221.

623

Jackson v. Jones

(Ch. 1724)

Executors can retain a legacy to a bankrupt to set off against a debt owed by the bankrupt to the testator.

British Library MS. Hargrave 81, f. 250

Eodem die [14 February 1724].

The plaintiffs were assignees of a commission of bankruptcy and brought this bill for a discovery and account of assets and to be paid a legacy of £100 devised by the defendant's testator to the bankrupt. The defendant insisted that the bankrupt was indebted to the testator at the time of his death in the sum of £190 by bond and that the legacy ought to be set off and he at liberty to retain the same towards payment of that debt.

For the plaintiff, it was urged that they, being assignees of a commission of bankruptcy, until the late Statute[1] was made, could not have been obliged to set off their demand even if it were a debt, but might have recovered the same at law and have put the defendant to his remedy at law for recovery of his debt, that, though the late Act of Parliament, where there are mutual dealings and debts and credits on each side, has obliged the commissioners to set one against the other and subjected only the balance to the bankrupt's creditors, yet this legacy was no such debt as could be set off by the defendant nor within the meaning of the Act and, therefore, ought to be paid without regard to the debt owing from the bankrupt.

On the other hand, it was argued that, without regard to this Statute, the plaintiff had no right to this legacy, but it ought to be set off and go towards satisfaction of the debt upon the common principle that he who asks equity must do equity, that, if the bankrupt himself had brought this bill, there could have been no question of it that the debt in his hands was part of the testator's assets, out of which his debts and legacies were to be paid, and, therefore, he ought to bring in those assets before he can recover his legacy, that he ought not to recover his legacy and then leave the executor to get in the debt from him as they could, that might tend to defeat both the debts and legacies of the testator, that the assignees stood in the place of the bankrupt and could have no other title than he had.

And the Master of the Rolls [Jekyll] was of the same opinion and dismissed the bill with costs.

[Other copies of this report: British Library MS. Hargrave 82, f. 247, Lincoln's Inn MS. Misc. 107, f. 126.]

---

1 Stat. 7 Geo. I, stat. 1, c. 31.

624

Damer v. Pitman

(Ch. 1724)

Where a devisee of a vested interest in a tenancy in common dies before it is payable, the money goes to his heirs or next of kin.

Lincoln's Inn MS. Misc. 380, pt. 2, p. 12

17 February 1723[/24]; at the Rolls.

Edward Damer, by his will, devises in the following manner, 'I give all the rest and residue of my personal estate to A. and B., my trustees, in trust for my three grandchildren, C., D., and E., to be divided between them when they shall come to their ages of twenty-one.' One of them died under twenty-one. And, upon a bill brought in order to have the personal estate distributed according to the will, it came to be a question who should have the estate of the deceased grandchild, whether his legal representative or the two surviving legatees.

It was insisted by Mr. *Mead* that this devise was of a joint estate until they came to the age of twenty-one and then the joint tenancy was to cease by the express words and not until then, since it was not to be divided until they came to their ages of twenty-one.

The Master of the Rolls [JEKYLL] was clear that this was only a tenancy in common from the beginning. The words 'to be divided between them' when they came to such an age signify not that it is not to be considered as divided until then, but, at that time, their respective shares shall be paid to them. It was a vested interest at first in each of them and to go to their respective representatives. And he decreed accordingly.

Lincoln's Inn MS. Misc. 12, p. 110

17 February 1723[/24]. Pitman v. Pitman *et al.*

Edward Damer, by will, gave the residue of his personal estate to trustees for the use and benefit of his three grandchildren, *viz.* the plaintiff, the defendant Thomas Pitman, and Edward Pitman, to be equally divided amongst them when they attained the age of twenty-one years.

Edward died under twenty-one and intestate and before any division was made. And the question was whether his administrator was entitled to his third part.

It was decreed by the Master of the Rolls [JEKYLL] for the administrator. He said it was an immediate gift and that one-third vested in Edward and ought to go to his administrator and, though the division was to be made when the grandchildren attained twenty-one, it was the same thing as though it had been to be divided at twenty-one, the words 'when' and 'at' being all one, and so it had been settled.

625

Attorney General, ex rel. Martin v. Hutcheson

(Ch. 1724)

In this case, the bequest in issue that was made for the benefit of Presbyterian ministers was upheld by the court.

Lincoln's Inn MS. Misc. 12, p. 78

24 February 1723/24. Attorney General, at the relation of Arthur Martyn and John Giniston v. Archibald Hutcheson and Dame Mary Gayer and Thomas Wooley, defendants.

Sir John Gayer, knight,[1] being about to return to England from Bombay in East India, of which place he was many years governor, made his will dated 5th October 1710, wherein is a legacy given in these words, *viz.*:

> Item, I dedicate and devote to God for the service of his Church £5000 to be disposed of by the persons after named to young students for the ministry and to such as are newly entered into that sacred office to furnish them with what is needful to make them most useful in the discharge of that great trust for which they are devoted to God, and it is my earnest desire that the persons amongst whom this sum shall be distributed may be men of sober, moderate principles, not inclined to domination nor to unnecessary separation, and, to express my mind more fully, I say, unto men of such principles as the late reverend and truly worthy Dr. Richard Baxter was, in whom the primitive spirit of holiness, love, and moderation did brightly shine, from whose works I have received great benefit how the persons I most earnestly require in conjunction with my wife and nephew, William Gayer, to undertake the distribution of what I have so solemnly devoted are Sir Henry Ashurst, baronet, and Mr. Thomas Woolley.

And of his said will, he made the defendant Dame Mary, his wife, executrix.

The testator soon after he made his will, returning to England, died. And his widow proved his will. And, afterwards, she married the defendant, Mr. Hutcheson.

The question was whether the £5000 should be applied for the benefit of students and ministers of the Church of England or of those of the Presbyterian persuasion.

It was decreed in favor of the latter, the Master of the Rolls [JEKYLL] being of opinion that the testator had fully declared that to be his meaning by saying that the persons who were to partake of that charity should be men of such

[1] G. Goodwin and A. Grout, 'Gayer, Sir John (d. 1711)', *Oxford Dictionary of National Biography*, vol. 21, pp. 680–681.

principles as Mr. Richard Baxter[1] was and it was proved that he was of the Presbyterian persuasion though he sometimes conformed to the Church of England.

626

Stanley v. Mortimer

(Ch. 1724)

A co-executor is accountable only for the assets of the estate that he himself received.

Lincoln's Inn MS. Misc. 12, p. 81

2 March 1723[/24]. Stanley v. Mortimer and Syer.

Upon the special matter of the Master's report, the case was that the defendants were executors of one Dorington, and they joined in the probate of the will and in exhibiting an inventory into the ecclesiastical court. Each of them received part of the assets of the testator. And the defendant Mortimer possessed a Class Lottery order, and he desired the defendant Syer to endorse his name upon the order to enable him, as he pretended, to receive the interest. But, instead of that, he sells the order for £126 and receives all the money. And he being likely to become insolvent, the question was if Syer should be charged with this money.

The Master of the Rolls [JEKYLL] was very clear he should not. He said both executors have the whole office of an executor in them. Each may release or discharge a debt, and even before probate. And, according to the method of accounting in this court, they are always charged with what comes to their respective hands and no more. And, as to the present case, it would be very hard and unreasonable to charge Syer, who never received one penny of the money. And he was of opinion that, if he had really joined in the sale and had not received the money, he ought not to be charged according to the Case of Fellow and Owen. *Vide* Churchill v. Hopson, 2 Salk. 318.[2]

But as to a sum of £40, which Syer had received and paid over to the other executor, he was ordered to stand charged with that, for, there, he trusts his co-executor.

Lincoln's Inn MS. Misc. 380, pt. 2, p. 13

Hilary term, 10th Geo.

---

[1] N. H. Keeble, 'Baxter, Richard (1615–1691)', *Oxford Dictionary of National Biography*, vol. 4, pp. 418–433.

[2] *Fellowes v. Owen* (1705), 2 Vernon 504, 23 E.R. 922, 2 Freeman 283, 286, 22 E.R. 1212, 1215; *Churchill v. Hopson* (1713), 1 Salkeld 318, 91 E.R. 280, also 1 Peere Williams 241, 24 E.R. 370, 1 Eq. Cas. Abr. 247, 21 E.R. 1023, British Library MS. Hargrave 80, f. 153, British Library MS. Hargrave 81, f. 81, Chancery Cases *tempore* Harcourt, 385.

A lottery order belonging to the estate of a testator, who had made two executors, both the executors signed a power for receiving the money at the Exchequer. One of them only received the money and, afterwards, broke without accounting for it.

On a bill brought against both, it was a question whether the executor who never received the money, but joined in signing the power for receiving it, should be accountable for it.

The Master of the Rolls [JEKYLL] held he should not since executors are accountable for no money but what comes to their respective hands. And he likened it to the Case of Fellows v. Owen, in this court, where two trustees joined in giving a receipt for a considerable sum of money, but divided the money between them, and [it was] decreed that each should be accountable only for the half which he received.

627
Goring v. Warner

(Ch. 1724)

A lease held by a bankrupt cannot be assigned contrary to a prohibition in the lease.

British Library MS. Hargrave 81, f. 252, pl. 1

Friday, 6 [March] 1723[/24], at the Rolls.

The bill was to be relieved against the forfeiture of a lease by having made an assignment thereof without the license of the lessor by writing under his hand contrary to a proviso in the lease for that purpose. And, though the assignment was made by the plaintiffs, who came to the interest in this lease as assignees under a commission of bankruptcy, yet the court said they could set no value upon the breach of these sort of conditions and, therefore, could not relieve against them. And the case of Sir Harry Peachy v. Duke of Somerset[3] was cited to that purpose.

[Other copies of this report: British Library MS. Hargrave 82, f. 248.]

Lincoln's Inn MS. Misc. 384, p. 311, pl. 2

14 November.

[There was a] proviso in a lease [that], if the lessee assigns without the consent of the lessor, the lessor is to re-enter. The lessee becomes bankrupt; the assignees assign over without consent. A bill [was filed] to be relieved against the forfeiture.

---

[3] *Peachy v. Duke of Somerset* (1721), see above, Case No. 515.

Curia [LORD MACCLESFIELD]: It is proper for relief here, and His Honor [JEKYLL] had directed a trial at law.

The decree was reversed.

7 Viner, Abr. 85

Michaelmas 11 Geo.

[There was an] appeal was from a decree of dismission at the Rolls upon this case. The defendant Warner made a lease of an inn to A. for years with a proviso in the lease that the lessee, his executor, or administrators should not assign the term to any person or persons without the consent of the lessor under his hand in writing first had and obtained with a power of re-entry in such case to the lessor and that the lease should be void. The lessee dies, and his executor enters and enjoys the premises and, afterwards, becomes a bankrupt. The commissioners assign this lease *inter alia* to the assignees chosen by the creditors. And, afterwards, in consideration of £50, they assign to the plaintiff Goring, who brought this bill to be relieved against this proviso and to stay proceedings in an [action of] ejectment brought by the lessor against him upon this proviso etc. The defendant Warner, by his answer, insists upon the forfeiture at law and that the proviso was reasonable and ought not to be set aside in equity.

Per MACCLESFIELD, Chancellor: I do not think this is a breach of the proviso or condition at law. But whether it be so or not, I think this is a proper case for relief in a court of equity. I think the assignment by the commissioners is clearly no breach of the proviso, for that is done by authority of a Statute,[1] which will supersede any private agreement between the parties inconsistent with it. And I am inclined to think the assignment over by the assignees is not a breach of a condition, for the first assignment by the commissioners is not a perfect and complete assignment within the meaning of the Statute and passes only the legal interest subject to a trust to be sold and disposed of for the benefit of the rest of the creditors and the disposition is not complete until sold by them for the benefit of the creditors. The first assignment is only formal and in ease of the commissioners and in order only to make a sale thereof for the benefit of the creditors, and their assignees stand in the place of the bankrupt and is in effect his assignee. And it is unjust and unreasonable that such a proviso should frustrate and overthrow the intent of a statute made in favor of honest creditors and deprive them of the advantage they may make of a beneficial lease. And, though it was insisted that the commissioners nor their assignees can be in no better a condition than the bankrupt himself and, consequently, cannot assign over without licence, I think, though that rule holds true generally, yet there may be some exceptions to it and that the present case is an exception out of that rule. And he decreed the plaintiff to hold and enjoy and an injunction to stay proceedings at law.

---

1 Stat. 5 Geo. I, c. 24.

2 Eq. Cas. Abr. 100, 22 E.R. 86

Michaelmas 11 Geo. 1 [1724]. On an appeal to Lord Macclesfield from a decree of dismission at the Rolls.

The defendant made a lease of an inn to A. for years with a proviso that the lessee, his executors, or administrators should not assign the term without the lessor's consent under his hand in writing with a power of re-entry in such case to the lessor and that the lease should be void. The lessee dies, and his executor enters and enjoys the premisses, and then he becomes a bankrupt. The commissioners assign this lease to the assignees chosen by the creditors, and, afterwards, in consideration of £50 they, the assignees, assigned it to the plaintiff, who brought this bill to be relieved against this proviso and to stay proceedings in an [action of] ejectment brought by the lessor against him upon this proviso. The defendant, by his answer, insists upon the forfeiture at law and that the proviso ought not to be set aside in equity.

Lord Chancellor [Lord Macclesfield] held clearly that the assignment by the commissioners, being done by authority of a statute, which will supersede any private agreement between even the parties, and the assignment over by the assignees was no breach of the condition. *Ergo*, he decreed the plaintiff to hold and enjoy and an injunction to stay proceedings at law.

628

Child v. Comber

(Ch. 1724)

In this case, there was a sufficient memorandum of a contract to sell land to satisfy the requirements of the Statute of Frauds.

Lincoln's Inn MS. Misc. 12, p. 81 [bis]

11 March 1723/24.

The plaintiff brought his bill to have an execution of a parol agreement for a lease, alleging that the defendant had by a letter under his hand acknowledged there was an agreement between him and the plaintiff and that the agreement had been in part executed, for that, in pursuance of the agreement, a lease had been drawn and perused and approved of by the defendant's counsel and was engrossed and ready to be executed.

The defendant pleaded the Statute of Frauds etc.[1] in bar to the relief and discovery.

[1] Stat. 29 Car. II, c. 3 (*SR*, V, 839–842).

It was insisted for the plaintiff that the agreement was in part executed and that, besides, here was a writing under the defendant's hand acknowledging the agreement which brought it out of the Statute.

But, to this, it was answered that the letter only acknowledged that there was an agreement, but it does not say what were the terms so that it does not appear by any writing signed by the party what were the terms of the agreement. And, if a bare acknowledgment of an agreement by a writing under hand is sufficient to bring it out of the Statute, then witnesses must be examined to prove what the agreement was, and this might let in that perjury which the Statute intended to prevent.

Lord Chancellor [Lord Macclesfield]: If the defendant will plead the Statute properly, he ought to support his plea by answering and denying, if he can, that there was any agreement at all made.

But now, the defendant pleads in bar to the discovery. And I cannot but think it reasonable the plaintiff should have a discovery whether any agreement was made or not. If the defendant should confess it, where will be the inconvenience of decreeing it to be performed? This will let in no perjuries which the Statute intended to prevent. If the defendant denies the agreement, it will be a question at the hearing whether the plaintiff shall make out the agreement by parol proof.

British Library MS. Hargrave 81, f. 252, pl. 2

Sir Caesar Child v. Comber. Wednesday, 10 March 1723[/24], at the Lord Chancellor's [house] on pleas and demurrers.

The defendant was possessed of the remainder of a lease for forty years from the Dean of St. Paul's, whereof about two years only were to come, of a very considerable estate consisting in houses and lands at Shadwell. And she was likewise seised or possessed of the market and profits of the market there, which were no part of the Dean's lease. The plaintiff comes to an agreement with her for the purchase of her tenant right in the Dean's lease in order to renew with the Dean and likewise of her right and interest in the market for £750, but this agreement was not in writing. But the plaintiff, in order to his being better recommended to treat with the Dean for a new lease, desires the defendant to give him a letter to the Dean for that purpose. And, thereupon, the plaintiff writes the letter, which the defendant signs, directed to Doctor Godolphin to this purpose:

> Sir, I have agreed with Sir Caesar Child for the purchase of all my right and interest in the lease which I hold of you for the remainder of the term [and] desire you will please to admit him to treat with you, which will oblige your humble servant, /s/ *Frances Comber.*

Upon this, the plaintiff goes to Dr. Godolphin, gives him the letter, and agrees with him for £152 0s. 0d. for a new lease for forty years on a surrender to be made to him of the old lease. And the Dean thereupon writes to Mr. Gilbert, his agent, acquainting him with the agreement he had made with the plaintiff and forbidding him to treat with any other person in the meantime. A draught was prepared for the defendant's assignment of the residue of her lease to the plaintiff. And, being left with the defendant's counsel, several alterations were made in it by the defendant's counsel, and, at length, the terms and draught were settled by counsel on both sides. And the plaintiff gave fifteen guineas to counsel on that occasion. But the defendant insisted and would have £250 more, in the whole £1000, before she would assign her interest to the plaintiff, which he was forced to comply with. And this was one of the alterations made in the draught, after which both the Dean and the defendant, being informed that their interest in the premises was much more valuable, refused to perform their agreement with the plaintiff, who had provided his money for that purpose, upon which the plaintiff brought two several bills, one against the Dean and the other against the now defendant, who has pleaded the Statute of Frauds and Perjuries and that there was no agreement in writing.

But the Dean's plea was overruled upon the letter he had sent to Mr. Gilbert, his agent, wherein he had taken notice of the agreement particularly and how much he was to have for the new lease. And, as to the defendant's plea, that was ordered to stand for an answer with liberty to except and the benefit of it saved to the hearing.

Both these being heard by the Master of the Rolls [Jekyll] in the absence of the Chancellor but the now defendant being dissatisfied, she petitioned for a rearguing of her plea, which now came on before the Chancellor [Lord Macclesfield].

The principal objection was that this letter not mentioning any of the terms of the agreement would make way for all that perjury which the Statute intended to remedy, that one might swear the agreement was for one thing, another for another, one that it was for so much money, another for less, and, here, it was the first agreement whatever; it was raised from £750 to £1000 and the draft and engrossment of the conveyance could be no way binding upon the parties to execute, that the agreement was not mutual and, if the plaintiff had refused to have gone on, the defendant could have had no remedy to have compelled him to it, that this letter was written by the plaintiff himself and, though the defendant signed it, yet it was only as a letter of recommendation to introduce him to treat with the Dean, that this £750 was to be paid for the interest in the market, which the Dean had nothing to do with, as well as for the remainder of the Dean's lease, and no notice was taken or any distinction made in the letter concerning it, that the plaintiff, being at liberty to except, would certainly except to the plea until they had an answer whether there was such agreement or not, and, if the defendant should be forced to own it, the court might decree a performance of it and so the benefit of the Statute be wholly taken away from the defendant.

On the other side, it was argued that letters written to third persons and not to the party himself had been frequently held to be a sufficient writing to take it out of the Statute, that, if the terms of the agreement had been certainly expressed, it would have been the same as the agreement itself and there would be then no difference between an agreement and a memorandum of an agreement, that its being written by the plaintiff was nothing to the purpose since the defendant had signed it, and the draught being settled by counsel on both sides, 15 guineas paid on that occasion, and the purchase money provided by the plaintiff were as much an execution of it on his part as where a man agrees by parol to let a lease and suffers the lessee to go on and build and then refuses to make the lease; this court has frequently assisted in that case.

Lord Chancellor [Lord Macclesfield]: This is barely a plea of the Statute of Frauds and Perjuries without any denial of the agreement. If, indeed, the plea had been as to so much as sought any discovery of an agreement that there was nothing reduced into writing and then had by answer denied the agreement, this had been directly a plea within the Statute. But, here, it is plain there was an agreement, and the plea only goes to the not being compelled to an execution or performance of it being not reduced into writing without any denial of the agreement. The primary intention of the Act and the principal object which the Parliament had in view was that no action at law should be brought upon agreements not reduced into writing because they would not suffer or give way to the variety of evidence which might be given at law in that case and, where an action will not lie at law, it is reasonable no bill should be allowed in this court.

But this is not a general rule as in a case where the agreement is performed in part on a contract for a building lease by parol though the agreement is denied, yet this court has admitted parol evidence to prove it on the head of the fraud, yet, there, the building does not in the least show what the terms of the agreement were, and, therefore, it lies as much open to fraud as the present case. But, where there is any fraud, this court interposes. And is it not strange to say I will not put it in issue whether any agreement or not but whether signed or in writing or not? But here is a note in writing owning that she had agreed and therefore no color to say that there was no agreement. But, if by her answer, she should deny that there was any agreement, it will then be proper to consider whether the plaintiff shall be admitted to give evidence of it. And here, the fees paid to the counsel, the drawing of the draughts and engrossing them, and the plaintiff's providing his purchase money are as much an execution of it on his part as the laying out money on the building was in the other case. And the circumstances of his agreement with the Dean in consequence [was] a proof of his agreement with the defendant, which, if she owns, where is the danger of perjury? Indeed, a note or memorandum of an agreement must mention the substance of the agreement in short; otherwise, no action can be brought upon it at law. But, where there is fraud, this court may interpose though the agreement be not reduced to such a certainty, and it is proper for the court to look into it.

And, therefore, he confirmed the order made by the Master of the Rolls. And My Lord said, though the defendant could have no remedy perhaps against the plaintiff on this agreement for want of his having signed some writing or memorandum, that was not material, for the Act does not say unless both parties or unless mutually signed, and, therefore, an action lies against the party who has signed.

[Other copies of this report: 3 Swanston 482, 36 E.R. 934, British Library MS. Hargrave 82, f. 249, Lincoln's Inn MS. Misc. 107, f. 127.]

[Other reports of this case: Dickens 39, 21 E.R. 181.]

629
Duke of Rutland v. Duchess of Rutland

(Ch. 1724)

There is a presumption that, where a testator gives a legacy to the executor of his will, the residuum of the estate will go to the next of kin and not to the executor.

In this case, the evidence was clear that the testatrix intended her executor to have the residuum of her estate.

British Library MS. Hargrave 81, f. 31

16 March 1723[/24], at the Lord Chancellor's house.

The Lady Rachel Manners, the duke's sister, being entitled to the sum of £10,000 secured to her upon the estate of the duke, her brother, by her last will and testament in writing, devised to her brother, the duke of Rutland, the sum of £500 and devised also to the rest of her brothers and sisters several specific legacies amounting in the whole to £5000 and made the duke her sole executor and died. The duke, among other things, brought his bill for the residuum of the £10,000 not specifically devised and insisted thereby that it was the intention of the testatrix that he should have the residuum and that it was to that end she made him executor. And in order to support that suggestion, he produced parol evidence to the effect following, *viz.*

Mr. Vernon, a clergyman who made the will, deposed that he did not know that the testatrix had made any express declaration that she intended the residuum for the duke but said he believed that was her intention for these reasons: first, for that, after she had given the several legacies in the will mentioned, he asked her if they were all the legacies she intended to give and she answered 'yes', upon which he replied 'then whom do you intend to make your executor?' she answered 'the duke of Rutland'; second, that, after the will was finished, she desired him to acquaint the duke that it was her desire that he would give £100 to a certain charitable use; and, lastly, that he would tell the duke that she hoped that he would not take it ill that she had given so much away from him by legacies.

The duchess of Devonshire, who was a subscribing witness, deposed that she came to the testatrix in her illness and that she being asked to whom she would leave the rest of her estate, to the best of her memory, answered 'to my brother, the duke of Rutland'.

And another person, who was either servant to the testatrix or the said duchess, swore positively that the testatrix, being asked to whom she would leave the residue of her estate, answered 'to the duke of Rutland'.

Upon this case, the questions were, first, whether parol evidence ought to be admitted and, next, in case it should, whether there were such plain and clear evidence in this case as to give the residuum to the executor and to deprive the persons who would be entitled to a distribution as the will stands without such parol evidence.

And the Earl of Macclesfield, Lord Chancellor, was of opinion that, as this case was circumstanced, the duke of Rutland was entitled to the residuum. He said it was a very mistaken notion that making a person executor was in law a gift of the personal estate anymore than the granting administration before the Statute of Distributions[1] was a grant of the intestate's [goods]. It indeed gave him a power over the estate but it was *in alieno jure*, for, if such an executor died intestate, the testator's estate shall not go to his administrator but there must be an administration *de bonis non* to which the relations of the testator is entitled and not those of the intestate, which could not be if the making him executor gave him a power in his own right. But before the Statute of Distribution, there being no person who by law had a right to demand an account from the executors of the testator's estate, it was the same in effect as an absolute gift. But now, since that Statute, there being persons appointed by law to take the residuum of an estate not devised, the reason is changed. However, that notion has so long prevailed that, if there be nothing in the will to show the contrary, the making a person executor is sufficient to carry the residuum. But, if, as in this case, there be a specific devise to the executor, it implies strongly that the testator did not intend him the residuum because, if he had, it had been needless to have particularly specified that part since it must have passed with the whole. And, therefore, the settled resolutions in such cases is that the residuum shall not pass to the executor, but be distributed according to the Statute.

But now, the question is whether parol evidence may be admitted in favor of the executor to destroy the presumption, which, by the specific legacies, is against him. And the Lord Chancellor said that the admitting parol evidence for the explaining of wills was of very dangerous consequence and might in time come to be the same as making parol wills if not kept within due bounds. Therefore, he would never carry it farther than the present settled resolutions had. In some cases, it is absolutely necessary, as where one devises certain goods or money to

[1] Stat. 22 & 23 Car. II, c. 10 (*SR*, V, 719–720).

his son John, having two sons of that name. It would be hard to defeat so plain an intention in the testator to give for the uncertainty of the person when it might be helped and explained by parol evidence. And in other cases, it has been admitted, as in the case of My Lady Lanesborough,[1] who directed the person who made her will to leave the residuum to her executor and he omitted it, parol evidence was admitted. And he said he thought it might here to explain what otherwise was very doubtful, there being one presumption against another, as the specific legacy induced a presumption against the duke. So his great quality and being head of the testatrix's family together with a general notion that making a person executor give them all the estate undevised makes it highly probable the testatrix meant something more by constituting such a person her executor than merely giving him trouble. And the evidence being very full and clear that she intended the duke [to have] the residuum, His Lordship decreed it accordingly.

[Other copies of this report: British Library MS. Hargrave 82, f. 27.]

British Library MS. Hargrave 81, f. 260

Monday, 16 March 1723[/24], at Lord Chancellor's [house].

The Lady Rachell Manners, sister to the present duke, being, by virtue of her father's marriage settlement, entitled to about £6000 and, by his will, to £4000, in all about £10,000, and, being indisposed, sent for one Mr. Richard Vernon, a clergyman, to make her will and, having several brothers and sisters, some of the whole blood and others of the half blood, she directs Mr. Vernon to give one £1000, two others £500 apiece, and to others of them £100 apiece, and to the present duke £500, and gives several other legacies to the amount of about £5000. And, accordingly, Mr. Vernon begins the will with a recital whereas she was possessed of £6000 under her father's marriage settlement and of £4000 by his will, 'now for the disposal of all my said fortune, I give and devise' and then gives the several legacies above mentioned, which took in all that would have been entitled under the Statute of Distributions, after which Mr. Vernon asked whom she would have her executor, to which she answered the present duke. And as was proved by the duchess of Devonshire and her woman, who came at that time to see her, being asked whether she intended the residue for the duke, she answered 'yes'. But Mr. Vernon did not remember that, but proved that he believed it was her intention to give the residue to the duke, that he himself understood it so and thought he had answered that intention by making the duke executor, which he accordingly did, and then the will was executed afterwards. The Lady Rachell desired one to speak to the duke that he would not take it amiss that she had given away so much from him and, at the same time, desired

[1] *Countess of Gainsborough v. Earl of Gainsborough* (1692), 2 Vernon 252, 23 E.R. 764, 2 Freeman 188, 22 E.R. 1152, 1 Eq. Cas. Abr. 230, 21 E.R. 1010

that he would give £100 in charity amongst the poor. And soon after, she died without making any disposition of the surplus.

And now, the cause being heard by consent, the only question was whether the duke, as executor upon the circumstances of this case, should have it or whether it should be distributed according to the Statute.

Lord Chancellor [Lord Macclesfield]: The common notion that, by a man's being made executor, he is entitled to the surplus is very strong, for it neither was so before the Statute of Distributions nor since, Before the Statute, the ecclesiastical courts never suffered the executor to go away with the surplus, but made him give a bond to distribute it amongst the next kin. And, whenever an executor would dispute it and refuse to give such bond, if they proceeded against him to compel him, the courts of common law, upon his application, would grant a [writ of] prohibition, which gave occasion to the making of the Statute. But the surplus was never looked upon to belong to the executor *in jure proprio* but *in jure alieno*. But, because nobody could claim a right as next of kin or force him to make a distribution, he, therefore, frequently went away with it unless where the ecclesiastical court, before any prohibition, had got him to give such bond. And, therefore, to put an end to these disputes between the ecclesiastical and temporal courts and fix a right in the next of kin was the Statute made. But neither before nor since had he the absolute right in it, for, if he died, he could not devise it, but it went to the administrator *de bonis non* of the first testator and not to his executor; if he died intestate, it was not distributable among his next of kin but among the next of kin of the first testator or suppose there was no executor named in the first will and thereupon administration with the will annexed was granted to one would this give him the surplus. And yet there is as much reason to say that he who is made executor by the court as he who is made by the party should have it to his own use, for the court in granting such administration does but supply the defect of making one by the will. And, if this be so, the question then will be whether the giving of legacies to all the next of kin in the present case can exclude them. If the legacies to all had been equal, there might be more color in it. But here, one has £1000, two others £500 apiece, and the rest but £100 apiece, and, therefore, there can be no pretense to exclude them in that respect. And the executor has likewise £500, and it would be absurd to give him a part if, by being made executor, he would have the whole where there is so great a surplus. Indeed, there may be cases where the intention of the testator in giving his executor a legacy may be that he may be sure of something as where there is no surplus and, therefore, he shall have his legacy in proportion with the rest. But this is not the present case. And, therefore, he can be considered but as a trustee for the next of kin upon the general reasoning on this head.

The next question is whether this parol evidence is to be admitted to explain the intention of the testator. It is in all cases extremely dangerous to admit of such proof, for, if the rule be broken into in one case, it may in another, which has one of the circumstances wanting that was in the former and so in another which wants two of those circumstances and so on until the rule comes to be laid wholly aside and broken into, which would destroy the Statute of Frauds and Perjuries,[1] that requires all wills to be in writing. And, therefore, in the Case of Litton v. Falkland,[2] where a man devised all his lands out of settlement and had some that never were comprised in any settlement and others that were but the uses of them were determined, yet the then Lord Chancellor, with the assistance of the judges, rejected parol evidence to prove his intention to pass the letter and, in no case whatsoever, shall any evidence be admitted to explain a will from subsequent declarations or expressions. But where the devise is to his son John and he has two sons of that name, there, parol evidence to explain which he meant is perfectly consistent with the will and it cannot be known what was his intention without such proof. But that differs exceedingly from the present case. But yet from expressions that are made use of and accompany the time of making the will, it may be reasonable in some cases to admit of parol evidence to explain the intention of the testator. And, therefore, in the case of the Lord Gainesborough v. Lady Gainesborough, where through the conceitedness of the person that drew the will, he refused to make an express devise of the residuum to the executor, urging that it was sufficient to make him executor and that would give him the whole, parol evidence of this was admitted to rebut the trust of equity that would otherwise arise for the next of kin. And, here, it is expressly proved by the duchess of Devonshire as to her remembrance and by her woman, Mrs. Stocks, positively that, upon the question asked whether she intended the residue for the duke, she answered 'yes' and, though Mr. Vernon, who drew the will, does not remember it, that might proceed from the notion he was full of, as he knows a good deal of the law, though not quite enough to know the construction this court has made of wills in the like cases and so to carry him through, that by making of the duke executor he would have the surplus and, therefore, might less regard what was said about it at that time. But it is plain he understood it would be sufficient to give the duke the residue. And, therefore, when the Lady Rachel was asked whether she would give any more legacies and answered 'no', he followed it with the question whom she would have made executor, which plainly shows that he thought that would carry the residue wholly to him in opposition to the particular legacies which she had before given to others and was to fulfill and make up what was wanting to make it a perfect and complete disposition of her estate. And so the very recital of the will shows her intention to be to dispose of her whole estate or fortune by that will, which, if the next of kin were to be let in, would be contradicted and defeated. And her request to the duke afterwards to give £100 away in charity proves that she apprehended he was to have the resi-

---

[1] Stat. 29 Car. II, c. 3, s. 5 (*SR*, V, 840).

[2] *Viscountess Falkland v. Lytton* (1709), 3 Brown P.C. 24, 1 E.R. 1152, 3 Chancery Reports 169, 21 E.R. 758, 2 Vernon 621, 23 E.R. 1008, 1 Eq. Cas. Abr. 210, 21 E.R. 996, British Library MS. Hargrave 80, f. 13v, Chancery Cases *tempore* Harcourt, 27.

due; otherwise, the request had been more proper to have been made to the next of kin, who were to have the residue and out of which the £100 was to come unless it could be supposed that she intended to take it out of his £500 legacy, which can never be supposed when, as it is fully proved, she desired him not to take it amiss she had given away so much from him. And, therefore, certainly, she never intended after that to take away more from him. And it is considerable that the duke was the head of the family and was to support the honor and dignity of it. And, therefore, she might be supposed to intend the residue for him on that account. And in the Case of Ball v. Smith,[1] it was a circumstance of a considerable weight that the executor was wife to the testator and, therefore, he might be supposed to intend her the whole for her own use.

And so upon the whole, he decreed in this case that the duke was to have the surplus to his own use not subject to distribution.

[Other copies of this report: British Library MS. Hargrave 82, f. 254.]

Lincoln's Inn MS. Misc. 12, p. 281

16 March 1723[/24].

The Lady Katherine Manners had made her will and the plaintiff executor and given him a legacy of £100 and made no disposition of the surplus. And the question was whether the plaintiff was entitled to it as executor.

Some parol proofs were read to show the testatrix intended the plaintiff should have the surplus. Edward Vernon deposed that the testatrix sent to him to make her will, which he did, and she executed it but did not then or at any other time in express words declare that she meant or intended to give the residue of her fortune, after debts and legacies paid, to the plaintiff. But he believed she supposed and understood at the time of signing her will that the surplus would go to the plaintiff and that she meant it should do so for the following reasons, *viz.* for that, when she gave instructions about her will, he, the witness, asked her if she would dispose of any more of her fortune, she answered 'no' and said she left her brother sole executor and, immediately after signing her will, she said she desired the poor should have £100 paid by her executor and that the deponent and her brother should consult about the distributing of it and, sometime after, she said she hoped her brother would not take it ill that she had given so much from him in legacies.

The duchess of Devonshire deposed that, after making the will, she was present when the will was read over, and the testatrix was asked if she intended her brother should have the remainder of her fortune; she said it should go to him.

---

[1] *Ball v. Smith* (1698–1711), 2 Vernon 633, 675, 23 E.R. 1014, 1039, 2 Freeman 230, 22 E.R. 1178, 1 Eq. Cas. Abr. 245, 21 E.R. 1022, 2 Eq. Cas. Abr. 133, 434, 22 E.R. 114, 369.

Another witness deposed to the same effect.

For the plaintiff, it was insisted that parol proof ought to be admitted in this case, for parol proof has been allowed when it is to support the legal construction of a will and to rebut that implication, which, by construction of equity, arises by giving a legacy to the executors. And, for this, was cited the Case of Littlebury and Buckley, in the House of Lords.

In the present case, not only the executor has a legacy, but all the other relations who can claim the surplus if it is to be distributed have legacies likewise. And, though there have been cases where some of the persons who have been entitled to a distribution have had legacies given them that it should not exclude them. But there has been no case where all the persons who have been entitled to a distribution have had legacies given to them that those legacies would not exclude them from the surplus.

On the other side, it was said that it was a matter of great consequence to admit of parol proof in the case of a will. It was expressly contrary to the Statute of Frauds. And, if such proof is to be admitted, it ought to be very clear and positive, which, in the present case, it was not.

Lord Chancellor [LORD MACCLESFIELD]: The general rule which has prevailed, *viz.* that, where an executor has a legacy given him and there be no disposition of the surplus by the will, the surplus shall be distributed, is founded upon right reason. The executor, in law, is a trustee, and the making a man executor is not by law a gift to him of the surplus. Indeed, since the Statute of Distributions, it has been so held. And the reason why he had it before was because no other could claim it. And so an administrator took the surplus before the Statute for the same reason. But it is plain that, in such case, if the executor or administrator had died, his representative should not have the surplus.

As to the proof that has been read, it is very strong.

Parol evidence is exceedingly dangerous in the case of a will. And one does not know what may be the consequence of allowing it. It has been admitted to allow parol evidence to oppose and rebut the equity arising by implication. And there is no inconvenience in it.

But I shall not allow parol proof in any other case nor in the present case any further than it has been allowed already. And I think the proof which has been read does not go further than has been allowed in other cases.

He decreed the surplus to the executor.

[Other reports of this case: 2 Peere Williams 210, 24 E.R. 703, 2 Eq. Cas. Abr. 416, 440, 22 E.R. 353, 375.]

630

Ex parte Vicary

(Ch. 1724)

Where a surety pays the debt of the principal debtor and takes an assignment of the debt, the surety cannot sue the principal debtor on the note in the name of the obligee-assignee, but he can offset it against his own debt to the principal and use it to put the principal into bankruptcy.

British Library MS. Hargrave 81, f. 268

Wednesday, 25 March 1724, on petitions at the Lord Chancellor's [house].

In this case, My Lord Chancellor [Lord Macclesfield] said that, before the Act for Amendment of the Law,[1] if two men were bound, the one as principal and the other as his surety, in a bond for the payment of £500 and interest on Midsummer Day next for the purpose and, on that very day, the surety pays the money and takes an assignment of the bond, if he puts it in suit in the name of the obligee against the principal, he might have pleaded *solvit ad diem* and given in evidence the payment by the surety and since the Act for Amendment of the Law, it is the same if the surety pays principal, interest, and costs at any time after the day. By that Act, the obligor is at liberty to plead *solvit ad diem* and he did not know in either of these cases that a court of equity had ever relived the surety or obliged the principal to make him satisfaction though it was said, upon an account directed before the Master between the principal and his surety, such payments by the surety had been always allowed to go in discount of his debt to the principal.

And, in this case, My Lord [Macclesfield] was likewise of opinion that, where such a surety having paid the money and had other debts owing to him from the same person that his taking an assignment of the bond or of any other specialty debts which he had been obliged to pay for the same person would so far unite and concur as one debt in him that, if they altogether amounted to £100 or upwards, he might take out a commission of bankruptcy against that person within the Statute 5 Anne[2] though his own proper debt or any of the other debts taken separately would not have qualified him within that Act to have taken out such a commission. And the reason he seemed to go upon was that all those debts were so far united in him that he made but one creditor in number for them all, not three or more according to the number of the debts taken in by him, and that, likewise, he was considered as a creditor in value for then all together as one debt not as several to answer the four-fifths in number and value necessary for the discharge of the bankrupt. But a case was cited in My Lord Harcourt's

[1] Stat. 4 & 5 Ann., c. 3, s. 13 (*SR*, VIII, 459).

[2] Stat. 4 & 5 Ann., c. 4 (*SR*, VIII, 461–465).

time [1710–1714] and seemed now to be agreed that, where a man goes and picks up several debts and gets an assignment of them only in order to take a statute against the debtor, that this is fraudulent and shall not be allowed within the Act of Parliament though they do amount to enough to entitle a real creditor to have taken out a commission of bankruptcy against him.

[Other copies of this report: British Library MS. Hargrave 82, f. 260, Lincoln's Inn MS. Misc. 107, f. 132.]

631

Ex parte Winch

(Ch. 1724)

Attorneys at law are not within the statutes relating to scriveners and stock brokers even though they have acted as such.

British Library MS. Hargrave 81, f. 270

Eodem die [25 March 1724].

He [Winch] was a sworn attorney but had practiced as a scrivener and stock jobber for about four or five years and had taken commission money and poundage on his buying and selling of stocks and putting out money on securities, yet My Lord [Chancellor LORD MACCLESFIELD] did not think him a scrivener or broker within any of the acts and, therefore, would not allow the certificate for his discharge.

[Other copies of this report: British Library MS. Hargrave 82, f. 261.]

632

Carpenter v. Bishop of Down and Connor

(Ch. 1724)

A devise to augment a marriage portion is a gift in fee.

Lincoln's Inn MS. Misc. 380, pt. 2, p. 14, pl. 1

23 April 1724.

William Carpenter, by will, in 1706, gives particular portions to his daughters and then devises a farm called Sherrington to his eldest son, John, and then goes on, 'but if he dies before he marries or has issue, then my will is that the said farm be divided between my said daughters to augment their portions'. The son died without marrying. The question was whether the daughters took the inheritance of that estate by virtue of the devise or only [for] their lives.

Lord Chancellor [LORD MACCLESFIELD] determined it to be a devise in fee because of the words 'to augment their portions'.

633

Burdett v. Young

(Ch. 1724)

In this case, the pecuniary legatees did not have to wait for the death of the residuary legatee before receiving their legacies.

Lincoln's Inn MS. Misc. 12, p. 82

25 April 1724.

A man, by his will, gives all his personal estate whatsoever to his wife for her life, and then he goes on and gives legacies, *viz.* to the plaintiff, his nephew, £1000 to be paid if he attained twenty-one or married and to his niece £1000 in like manner. He gives his nephew some specific goods after the death of his wife. He gives his wife a legacy for mourning [clothes], and he directs his executors to lay out a sum of money for a tombstone, and he gives 40s. to the minister that should preach is funeral sermon. He gives the surplus to the plaintiff.

The plaintiff, having attained twenty-one, brings his bill for his legacy. And, the testator's wife being living, the question was if it should be paid, the whole personal estate being given to the wife during her life.

It was decreed by Baron Price, in the absence of the Lord Chancellor, that the plaintiff's legacy was not payable during the wife's lifetime.

But upon an appeal to Lord Chancellor [Lord Macclesfield], he decreed the legacy to the plaintiff, there being nothing in the will to distinguish this legacy from the legacies for mourning [clothes] and for preaching his funeral sermon and the money to be laid out for a tombstone and, if the general bequest to the wife was to carry the whole personal estate to her for life, then those other sums could not be paid until after her death, which it is plain the testator could not intend. And he said such general clauses were not to be taken in so unrestrained a sense.

British Library MS. Hargrave 81, f. 273

Saturday, 25 April 1724, on appeal.

Thomas Sutton, the defendant's first husband, by his will 22 April 1714, gave and devised all his personal estate of what nature soever to his wife for her sole use during her life and also gave and bequeathed to his grandson, Thomas Roberts, and to his granddaughter, the plaintiff Frances, children of his son-in-law, George Roberts, £1000 apiece if they attained the age of twenty-one years or should be married, and he gave and bequeathed all his household goods, plate, and linen to his granddaughter, the plaintiff Frances, after the death of his wife. And all the residue of his estate of what nature or kind soever not thereby disposed of, he gave and bequeathed to his nephew, John Sutton, after the death of his said wife. And the only question was whether those legacies of £1000 apiece were payable when the grandson and granddaughter attained twenty-one or were married, which they had done in the wife's lifetime or whether they must not wait for them until after the wife's death, to whom the whole personal estate was given during her life.

This cause was heard before Mr. Baron PRICE, in the absence of the Chancellor, who was of opinion that the legacies were not payable until after the death of the wife, and, therefore, he decreed the defendants only to give security for them.

But now, on appeal to My Lord Chancellor [LORD MACCLESFIELD], he reversed that decree and was of opinion that they were payable as soon as the legatees attained twenty-one or were married and that the meaning of the devise of all to his wife for her life was only all that was not otherwise disposed of by his will and that, if they were to wait for their portions or legacies until the wife's death, they might come at a time when they might do them no good if the wife should live many years. And he said this was the stronger because the devise of the household goods, plate, and linen to Frances and of the rest of his personal estate to his nephew Sutton were expressly given after his wife's death and so would the legacies of £1000 apiece if that had been his intention. And he decreed accordingly.

But note there were some circumstances upon the whole will taken together which seemed not at all to favor this construction.

[Other copies of this report: British Library MS. Hargrave 82, f. 263.]

[Other reports of this case: 9 Modern 93, 88 E.R. 336, 5 Brown P.C. 54, 2 E.R. 529, 2 Eq. Cas. Abr. 557, 560, 22 E.R. 469, 472.]

634

Gifford v. Baldwin

(Ch. 1724)

A recovery by a life tenant constitutes a forfeiture of the estate, but a recovery by a tenant in tail bars the remaindermen.

British Library MS. Hargrave 81, f. 275

The last [day of] April 1724, in court.

Edward Baldwin, being seised of the estate in question, by his will, 2 October 1694, devises in these words:

> Item, I do hereby give and devise unto my kinsman William Baldwin and his assigns all my freehold, copyhold, and leasehold lands and tenements for and during the term of his natural life and, in case he happen to marry again and have issue by any other wife, then my will and meaning is and

> I do hereby give and devise all the said freehold, copyhold, and leasehold lands and tenements unto my said kinsman, William Baldwin, and to his heirs and assigns forever, and, for want of issue of any other wife, then my will is and I do hereby give and devise all my said freehold, copyhold, and leasehold lands and tenements to trustees and their heirs in trust to be sold and the money arising by such sale to be distributed to and amongst [the plaintiffs].

William Baldwin levies a fine and suffers a recovery and dies without ever being married again and without issue, his wife, who was living at the making of this will, surviving him.

And now this bill was against the trustees to have the estate sold and the money divided amongst the plaintiffs according to the will of Edward Baldwin. Some of the defendants were purchasers of part of the estate from William Baldwin and others claimed by devises under his will, but none of them pretended want of notice of the will of Edward Baldwin. And the single question in this case was what estate William Baldwin [had] and whether [it was] an estate in tail or only an estate for life, for, if his estate was but for life, then the recovery was a forfeiture of that estate, but then he being likewise heir at law to the testator, the forfeiture vested in himself. But, if he was tenant in tail, then the recovery was good and the plaintiffs [were] clearly barred.

[Other copies of this report: British Library MS. Hargrave 82, f. 264, Lincoln's Inn MS. Misc. 107, f. 133.]

635

Ord v. Smith

(Ch. 1724–1725)

There is a presumption of abandonment by a mortgagor where the mortgage has not been redeemed within twenty years.

However, this presumption against a mortgagor can be rebutted by the circumstances of the case, such as the absence and death beyond the seas of the mortgagor and the lack of knowledge in the mortgagor's heir.

Lincoln's Inn MS. Misc. 12, p. 115

5 May 1724. Martha Ord and Erasmus Ord, plaintiffs; Smith and others, defendants.

Christopher Ord, the plaintiff's brother, being seised in fee of the tithes of Soremerston in Durham, by indenture dated 16 June 1679, in consideration of £720, granted these tithes to Adam Smith and his heirs. And, by indenture dated 17th of the same month of June, reciting the said grant, Smith covenants that, if Ord, by himself or any by his authority, should pay £720 of his own proper money to Smith, his heirs, executors, or administrators at one payment on the 16th of November 1682 or the 16th November 1685 within the hours of ten and six and should give full six months' notice in writing of his intention to pay the same on the 16th of May in either of the said years to Smith or his heirs, then, upon payment of the said £720 of the said Ord's own money, the said Smith or his heirs should re-convey the tithes as by Ord or his counsel should be advised.

And it was thereby further agreed that, if Ord died before the respective days whereon the said £720 was to be paid or did not give notice to pay the same as aforesaid, the defeasance was to be void.

Ord or his heirs did not give notice to redeem within the times limited by the defeasance or at any time afterwards during Smith's life, and Smith died in 1704, having made his will 20 October 1702 and, thereby, devised the tithes to his children to be equally divided between them. And he declared that, if the tithes should be redeemed by Ord or any claiming under him, the money should be divided in like manner.

The plaintiffs' bill was for a redemption.

Lord Chancellor [Lord Macclesfield]: There is no covenant in the defeasance from Ord to pay the money so that Smith could not compel Ord to pay it. The defeasance is very particular. It confines the redemption to Ord's own person and to his own proper money. It seems to be nothing but a purchase with an agreement to let the vendor have it again if he thought fit in some reasonable time, but not at any time when he pleases. He has let the time agreed on slip. And I do not see any reason now to enlarge it. The value of money is now altered and so is the value of estates. And, if the estate is worth more now than it was in 1682 or 1685 and the defendants are to reconvey, they cannot have an adequate recompense.

As to the will, Lord Chancellor [Lord Macclesfield] thought it did not alter the case. Smith might not remember when he made his will what were the terms of the agreement or he might not know but that the estate was redeemable. He does not say it shall be redeemed but only that, in case it shall be redeemed, the money shall be divided between his children.

Upon the whole matter, Lord Chancellor [Lord Macclesfield] was of opinion the plaintiffs were not entitled to a redemption. And he dismissed the bill with costs.

Lincoln's Inn MS. Misc. 380, pt. 2, p. 5, pl. 3

28 April 1725.

The plaintiff's ancestors, in the year 1675, mortgaged an estate in tithes of the value of about £80 *per annum* to one, under whom the defendant claims, for £700. The method of making this mortgage was by conveying the inheritance to him in fee as an absolute purchase in one deed and, in another, the mortgagee's executing a defeasance at the same time by which he agreed that, if the mortgagor should in his own person out of his own money and during his own life repay that sum, then he would reconvey the estate to the mortgagor; otherwise, it should be absolute. Soon after the making of this mortgage, the mortgagor, being in distressed circumstances, was forced to go beyond the sea into the service of the army and there died in about ten years after. Upon his going away, the mortgagee entered into possession of the estate and continued so until 1704 without any interest paid him or any demand of account on the part of the mortgagor.

In 1704, the mortgagee made his will and, taking notice therein that this estate was a mortgage and redeemable, devises the same or the money in case it should be redeemed to the defendant and died soon after. The defendant goes into possession and continues so until the bringing of the bill without any interest paid to him or any demand on the part of the mortgagor's heir, who appeared to have been all along ignorant of this mortgage until lately when they brought their bill in order to redeem and thereby offered to waive the account of the profits and set them against the interest. The defendant, by his answer, insists upon the length of time since he and his predecessor had been in possession and that now it is too late to redeem.

This came first before the late Lord Chancellor Macclesfield, who dismissed the bill upon the account of the long possession of the mortgagee and the defendant.

It was now heard before Sir Joseph Jekyll and Sir Jeffrey Gilbert, two of the Lords Commissioners [to Hold the Great Seal], who decreed that, considering the circumstances of this case, the plaintiff should redeem on payment of the whole £700 without entering into the account of profits or interest unless the defendant himself insisted on it.

Sir Joseph Jekyll said that the rule that the equity of redemption should be barred by a neglect for twenty years to call the mortgagee in possession to account was a good general one, but he did not know that this court were so tied up by it as not to consider the circumstances of the case. On the contrary it was well known that this court constantly did permit redemptions after lengths of time in the cases of infancy, absence beyond the seas, coverture, etc., that the present case is varied from the common rule by its particular circumstances on two accounts: on account of the fraud and imposition that appears to have been [done] by the original mortgagee [and] on account of the peculiar circumstances that attend the length of time.

He said there was no time settled in this court to prescribe against relief in cases of fraud, and he thought there were strong circumstances of fraud and imposition in this case arising from the nature of the conveyances. The separating the defeasance from the deed of conveyance, by which means upon the face of it, it appears an absolute purchase carries something suspicious along with it. It at least opens a door for fraud. The defeasance itself is of a very extraordinary nature. It has so fettered and limited the power of redemption as makes it almost impossible for the mortgagor to comply with the terms of it. The conditions of the redemption are extremely uncommon, and, though this court will render them useless as to any effect they may have to prevent the redemption, yet they serve to terrify the mortgagor who cannot be supposed to know everything that a court of equity will do in his favor. When a mortgage once appears, this court never regards the particular terms relating to the manner of redemption, and with great reason since, if once they are to be of moment in a court of equity, the necessity of borrowers would give the lenders an opportunity of imposing any terms which they think fit, the borrowers being generally servants to the lenders and under their power.

But if it stood clear of fraud, yet there are circumstances to overrule the length of time. The mortgagor's absence and death beyond the sea excuses his neglect entirely. His heirs were ignorant of there being any such mortgage or any right of redemption, and the mortgagee himself, by his will, acknowledged it to be a mortgage. There can be no injury done to the mortgagee in making this decree because the length and intricacy of the account will be prevented by the setting of the interest against the profits unless he will run himself into it, and the value of the estate is greatly beyond the mortgage money.

Sir Jeffrey Gilbert said he thought the general rule of twenty years' neglect to bar the equity of redemption is very right and grounded on this supposition, that, after so long a neglect, the estate, being in the nature of a pledge, is supposed to be derelict by the mortgagor. But circumstances may be sufficient to prevent that supposition. And he thought the circumstances in the present case were of that kind, that no presumption could arise from the length of time of the mortgagor's intention to give up the estate.

Lincoln's Inn MS. Misc. 12, p. 161

28 April 1725.

This cause came on to be heard upon the plaintiff's appeal from the Lord Chancellor's decree, whereby the plaintiff's bill was dismissed. And, by the opinion of both Commissioners [to Hold the Great Seal, Jekyll and Gilbert], the decree was reversed and a redemption was decreed and for these reasons.

First, there was a fraud and imposition on the mortgagor in settling the equity of redemption in the manner he has done the defeasance. It is plain Ord was a necessitous person and was forced to submit to such terms of redemption as Smith would put upon him. And, if this court should give any countenance to things of this kind, equities of redemption may be so fettered and entangled that it may not be in the power of men to redeem their estates and their inheritances may be swallowed up by designing men.

Second, here being an imposition, the length of time, which was much insisted on, is out of the case, for length of time cannot be pleaded in bar of a fraud.

In the Case of Lord Warrington and Booth,[1] which was first heard in this court, it was determined in the House of Lords after consulting with the judges that the Statute of Limitations[2] could not be pleaded in bar to a fraud.

Third, but, however, the length of time is accounted for, for Ord went beyond the sea soon after the mortgage and died there, and the plaintiffs had no notice of the estate being only a mortgage until they saw Ord's will. And ignorance, in such a case, will excuse where it is not owing to any default of the party who would take advantage of it and especially where it does not turn to the prejudice of a third person.

Fourth, Smith has called it a mortgage in his will, which is a material circumstance. He was sensible he had imposed upon Ord in respect of imposing such terms of redemption upon him, and, therefore, when he came to make his will (and every man at such a time is presumed to speak true), he seems to own the estate was then redeemable.

Fifth, the conveyance was originally a mortgage and not intended to be a purchase.

Sixth, here can be no wrong done to the defendant by decreeing a redemption upon the terms offered by the plaintiffs, which is to pay the principal and to set the profits against the interest for the estate, which consists of tithes and so there are no repairs, is proved to be of greater yearly value than will pay the interest at £6 percent. And, if the defendant has interest for his money at 6 percent from 1679 down to this time, he will have no reason to complain.

Commissioner Gilbert said he thought it a good rule that there should be no redemption of a mortgage after twenty years possession, for it tended to the quieting of men's possessions and was agreeable to law, and the rule should be strictly kept to, for, if a man does not come to redeem in twenty years, it is presumed to be a dereliction of the pledge. But there may be circumstances to bring a case out of that rule, and this is such a case.

The plaintiff was decreed to redeem upon the terms he offered unless the defendant thought it more for his interest to go into the account of the profits as to which he was to signify his consent to the Register.

King's Inns Dublin MS. 92, p. 50

28 April 1725. Rehearing.

Ord, the plaintiff's ancestor, being in necessitous circumstances, made a mortgage to Smith, the defendant's ancestor, of some tithes forty-five years before the bill was brought. The mortgage money was £720. The mortgagor, by his deed, made an absolute conveyance to the mortgagee, from whom he had a deed of defeasance with clauses unusually restrictive, *viz.* that, if the mortgagor would

---

[1] *Earl of Warrington v. Booth* (H.L. 1714), 4 Brown P.C. 163, 2 E.R. 111, British Library MS. Hargrave 80, f. 175, Chancery Cases *tempore* Harcourt, 431.

[2] Stat. 21 Jac. I, c. 16 (*SR*, IV, 1222–1223).

redeem, it must be in his lifetime and he must bring the money himself and it must be his own proper money. The mortgagor, soon after, was obliged by his circumstances to go abroad. And he died in the service in the year 1702. Smith, the mortgagee, by his will, devised the legal estate of the tithes to the defendant with a proviso that, if it should be redeemed, then he devised the money. The plaintiff swore by [his] answer to a cross-bill brought unadvisedly by the defendant that this was the first notice he had etc. [and] discovery that he made of his title to redeem this estate. It was proved in the cause that the estate was above the value of the mortgage money.

The plaintiff, by his original bill, prayed upon his being admitted to redeem that the defendant might either set the profits against the interest of the mortgage, which bore 6 percent, or, upon payment of interest, account for the profits.

The question was whether, upon the circumstances of this case, the length of time should bar the redemption, which My Lord Macclesfield had decreed it should.

Lord Commissioner Jekyll: The difficulty that has been urged as an argument in this case why the account should be taken for such a length of time will be none without the defendant's own choice. He will have a very liberal allowance upon the redemption by an interest of 6 percent.

If a redemption is not decreed, we shall in effect establish a gross imposition and such a fraud as this court ought to relieve against, for, from the circumstances of a necessitous person, one who was flying the kingdom, advantage is taken to get a mortgage from him with such a restraint as to the redemption that it was not only improbable but almost impossible that this estate should ever be redeemed, as it was fettered with such conditions. And to color this the better, an absolute conveyance is first made. I think it is usual in the North to make mortgages in this manner and to have the defeasance in a separate deed. But it is always to be censured and suspected and is a great inlet to fraud and controversy. And, as for the terms that are put upon the redemption, this court might in justice reject them, for no injury is done to the lender if his money is sufficiently secured and repaid with interest. And this court will not endure that he shall grind the borrower, who is his servant, and fetter him with such terms that he can never be freed. If such restrictions were allowed, inheritances would be daily swallowed up by contrivances to defeat redemptions.

This, therefore, comes before the court not only as a case of redemption but as a case of imposition and hardship. And, where there is a fraud, no limitation of time takes place, as was resolved in the Case of Lord Warrington and Booth, in the House of Lords.

But I am also of opinion that there are circumstances in this case that, without the imposition and fraud, would entitle the plaintiff to relief. It is not true that only infancy, absence beyond the seas, and coverture are the cases where redemption shall be notwithstanding the length of time. There was a case before the late Master of the Rolls [Trevor] where a bill was brought to redeem after twenty years and it appearing that the mortgagee had brought a bill to foreclose within seven years after the mortgage was made, upon that redemption was decreed, and the decree was affirmed upon an appeal. And this case went upon the admission of the mortgagee. Is there not the strongest admission in this case? The sentiments of a man with the view of death upon him, when it is always to be presumed that he, at that time, entertains just and honorable thoughts when perhaps he was conscious that he had not done right in endeavoring to cover this estate from redemption, he, then, in his will, shows it to be redeemable. I think, therefore, that even the mortgagor himself might have been now entitled to redemption. But I am clear that, he dying abroad so long since, his representative, whose ignorance is not anyways imputable to him, especially that ignorance being accompanied with fraud and imposition in the person whom the defendant represents, the plaintiff ought to be relieved and admitted to redeem and that the defendant may have his choice whether he will set the interest against the rents and profits or go into an account of the rents and profits.

Lord Commissioner Gilbert: Length of time and limitation of actions ought for the sake of public quiet to be strictly observed. Equity, I find, followed the law in this respect in My Lord Nottingham's time, upon which My Lord Hale said that he was glad to see there could be a limitation of time in a court of equity. The estate mortgaged is a pledge deposited for the money lent. After twenty years, the legal title being barred, there is a destruction of the pledge. But, in this case, we cannot suppose such a dereliction, for the mortgagee himself, by the unusual clauses in his defeasance, has obscured the right of redemption, and they carry a fraudulent intent upon the face of them to defeat the mortgagor of his estate and to bind him up from redeeming it against the rules of equity so that it comes to be a question whether he shall be too hard for this court by his inventions and restrictions or whether this court shall pursue its equitable rules by breaking through them, for we must suppose that, if the mortgagor, under such circumstances, does not come to redeem, it is not a voluntary dereliction of his right.

The mortgagee, many years after the death of the mortgagor, which was in 1702, devises his legal estate and, if it be redeemed, then the money. This is really a devise of the estate subject to redemption upon the payment of the money. And, therefore, the mortgagor not having voluntarily by his own laches and acquiescence relinquished his right and the mortgagee not having considered the estate as belonging absolutely to him, it is equitable that this court should decree a redemption between their representatives.

[Other reports of this case: Select Cases *tempore* King 9, 25 E.R. 193, 2 Eq. Cas. Abr. 600, 22 E.R. 504.]

636

Squire v. Compton

(Ch. 1724)

The assignees of a bankrupt cannot defeat a right of dower by taking an assignment of a prior mortgage term.

Lincoln's Inn MS. Misc. 12, p. 148

5 May 1724. Mary Squire, administratrix of Rotham Squire v. Abraham Crompton.

The plaintiff's bill, *inter alia*, was to have her dower set out and a mortgaged term removed out of her way, which hindered her from going to law.

The defendant was an assignee under a commission of bankrupts awarded against the plaintiff's husband, who was since dead, and after his assignment, he agreed with the bankrupt to purchase the estate in question for £850, out of which he was to pay off a mortgage which was made before the plaintiff's marriage, and, over and above the £850, he was to discharge a second mortgage which was made to one in fee after the marriage.

The defendant pays £563 8s. 5d. in discharge of the first mortgage and takes an assignment of the term to A.B. in trust for himself. And, then, he takes a conveyance to himself from the second mortgagee, in whom the inheritance was vested, and the bankrupt. And this was in consideration of £655 paid the mortgagee and £194 2s. 7d. said to be paid (but not proved) to the bankrupt so that the whole which he had paid, supposing the £194 2s. 7d. paid amounted to £1412 11s., which was much short of the real value of the estate, the same being proved to be worth £1700.

The question was if the defendant was such a purchaser as that he should have the benefit of the mortgaged term to defend himself against the plaintiff's claim of dower.

Lord Chancellor [Lord Macclesfield]: The defendant is not properly a purchaser. He is both buyer and seller, for, as to the bankrupt, though he agreed to sell to the defendant and joined in the conveyance, yet he had no power to sell the estate, and, therefore, the defendant is to be considered only as an assignee under the commission. And, as such, he cannot after paying off the first mortgage keep it on foot to protect the estate against the plaintiff's dower.

And, therefore, let the Master set out a sufficient part of the estate to answer the interest of the money due on the first mortgage, and, then, the defendant must pay the plaintiff a third part of the remainder of the rents.

9 Viner, Abr. 227

Easter 10 Geo. I [1724].

The question was if assignees of commissioners of bankrupts, by taking an assignment of a mortgage term prior to the title of dower, shall protect their estate from dower.

It was insisted that creditors and assignees of commissioners of bankrupts stand only in the place of the bankrupt and, since such an assignment to the bankrupt himself or his heirs would not protect the estate from a title of dower in the hands of the heir, neither will it protect the estate in the hands of the creditors of the bankrupt or the assignees of the commissioners and this differs the present case from the Case of Lady Radnor and Vandebendy, in Dom. Proc.,[1] where it was held that such a prior term should protect the estate from dower in the hands of a purchaser.

(*Nota differentiam.*)

It was decreed that the plaintiff be let into her dower, keeping down the interest of a third part of the mortgage.

[Other copies of this report: 2 Eq. Cas. Abr. 387, 22 E.R. 330.]

637

Savage v. Forster

(Ch. 1724)

A person under a disability, such as coverture or infancy, will be estopped to deny the title of a bona fide *purchaser of land where he or she silently allowed that sale to proceed, the purchaser being unaware of the defective title.*

Married women and infants are accountable for their own fraud.

British Library MS. Hargrave 81, f. 277

Friday, 18 June 1724, in court.

The bill was that the plaintiff might have a decree to hold and enjoy against the defendant and his wife by reason of a fraud in suffering the plaintiff to purchase the estate in question without giving him notice of an estate for life the wife had in it, which she never discovered but was very forward in promoting the purchase in order raise money for her sister's portion wherewith the estate was charged.

And a decree was accordingly had and that the defendants, if they joined in a fine to extinguish their right before next Michaelmas term, were to be excused

---

1 *Countess of Radnor v. Vandebendy* (1683–1697), Shower P.C. 69, 1 E.R. 48, *sub nom. Lady Bodmin v. Vandenbendy*, 1 Vernon 179, 356, 23 E.R. 399, 520, 2 Chancery Cases 172, 22 E.R. 899, Chancery Cases *tempore* Jac. II, 156, *sub nom. Lady Radnor v. Rotheram*, 2 Freeman 211, 22 E.R. 1165, Precedents in Chancery 65, 24 E.R. 32, 1 Eq. Cas. Abr. 219, 21 E.R. 1002, 2 Eq. Cas. Abr. 383, 22 E.R. 326.

costs; otherwise, they were to pay the plaintiff his costs and fees. [He] said it was not necessary that the party should be active and instrumental in promoting the treaty, but, if he barely sat by and suffered it to go on without disclosing his will, it was such a fraud as would induce this court to decree him never to set up his title to defeat the purchase and that married women and infants of years of discretion would be affected by such frauds as much as other persons. And a case was cited of Watts v. Cresswell,[1] where an infant son, being tenant in tail in remainder after his father's death, was a witness to a deed made by his father for the sale of this estate without disclosing his title, and a decree was [made] against him for this fraud that the purchaser should hold and enjoy. So one Charles Clare's [Case], where an attorney's clerk having an encumbrance on his master's estate suffered his master to sell it and he engrossed the deeds without discovering his encumbrance, and the like decree was [made] against him.

[Other copies of this report: British Library MS. Hargrave 82, f. 265.]

Lincoln's Inn MS. Misc. 380, pt. 2, p. 3

19 June 1724.

The defendant had a right to the estate in question, but the plaintiff, believing that another person who was in possession and pretended to be the owner of the estate was the only person that had the right and knowing nothing of the defendant's title, treated with him about the purchase. The defendant was all the time acquainted with the treaty and suffered him to go on and complete his purchase and pay the purchase money without giving him any notice of her title.

Sometime after the purchase was completed, the defendant brought an [action of] ejectment in order to recover the land, upon which this bill was brought in order to be relieved against her title. The defendant was a married woman at the time of making the purchase and, by some circumstances, seemed to have promoted it, though that did not clearly appear. For the plaintiff, a case was cited of an attorney's clerk who had a mortgage of his master's estate and afterward actually engrossed and witnessed the execution of a deed by which his master conveyed and sold it to another without giving the purchaser any notice of the encumbrance, and, on a bill to be relieved, the court did establish the purchaser's title against the clerk's encumbrance, though he was an infant at the time of making the purchase.

The counsel for the defendant insisted on a distinction which they made between those cases where the party is merely guilty of an omission in not acquainting the purchaser with his title and where he is also guilty of actual fraud in assisting and contriving to draw him into the purchase. They likewise insisted that the defendant being a married woman at the time of this purchase could not

[1] *Watts v. Creswell* (1714), see above, Case No. 18.

by any act of her own without the proper solemnity which the law requires give away or destroy her own right.

Lord Chancellor Macclesfield said that the cases upon this head had hitherto gone so far as to relieve against the party's not giving him notice where it appears plainly that his not doing it must from the nature of the case arise from some evil design and it is not necessary to prove any fact of assisting to the drawing in the purchaser or recommending him to the purchase or being a party to the transaction, for it is manifestly against conscience when one has plain notice of another's intention to purchase an estate from a third person to which he himself has a title and knows he has so and has a fair opportunity and, much more, many opportunities of acquainting him with it [. . .] to conceal it and lie by until the purchase is completed and the money paid with his privity. In this case, there is no distinction to be made between a married woman, infants, and others, for though they are not accountable for their acts to their own prejudice, yet they shall for their fraud and knavery.

Everybody knows when he is dealing with an infant or a married woman, what he is to do in order to secure himself and that such and such proceedings are necessary, as a fine, etc. People then act with their eyes open. But in the present case, nobody can be aware of their fraud; there are no ceremonies required by the law as necessary to charge a man's self on account of fraud. A married woman and infant, when of years of discretion, are as capable of distinguishing plain honesty from cheating as other persons.

He, therefore, decreed that the purchaser should hold against the defendant's title and have a perpetual injunction and ordered the defendant to levy a fine in order to complete the plaintiff's title.

Lincoln's Inn MS. Misc. 12, p. 98

A bill [was exhibited] to be relieved against a fraud, which was that the defendants, knowing that the plaintiff was treating for the purchasing the estate in question, did not disclose her title and now sets it up at law.

In excuse for this, it was said that the defendant, when the plaintiff purchased, was a married woman.

In answer to which, it was said that, in the Case of Wats and Creswell, in Lord Cowper's time, where relief was had against an infant who had encouraged the plaintiff to lend money upon a mortgage of an estate which the infant had a title to and which title he concealed.

Lord Chancellor [Lord Macclesfield]: It is against all conscience to set up a title to an estate after what the defendant has done.

As to the objection that the defendant was a married woman, the case which has been cited is very strong. An infant cannot convey an estate; no laches shall be imputed to him. But he shall answer for a fraud. So, if a married woman will conceal her title to defraud a purchaser, this court will not suffer her to set it up afterwards, and she shall not screen herself under the pretense of being a married woman.

It has been said that the party against whom the relief is sought should be some way instrumental in drawing in a purchaser, I think, if he has concealed his title when he had a fair opportunity of disclosing it, it is a fraudulent concealment and ought to be relieved against.

He decreed the defendant to levy a fine to the plaintiff to extinguish her right and, if she submits so to do, to be excused costs, if not, to pay costs.

[Other reports of this case: 9 Modern 35, 88 E.R. 299.]

[Later proceedings in this case: Foster v. Savage (Ch. 1726), see below, Case No. 746.]

638
Billingsley v. Cobb

(Ch. 1724)

An accounting of a partnership will be enforced according to the terms of the agreement of the partners.

Lincoln's Inn MS. Misc. 12, p. 131, pl. 2

6 July 1724. Billingsley *et al.* v. Cobb and Cam, executors of A.B., the plaintiff's brother.

The defendant Cob and Arthur Billingsley, the plaintiff's brother, entered into articles of partnership and, amongst other agreements therein, it was agreed that the partners should on the first Monday of every month have the liberty to take out of the joint stock for defraying their particular occasions and charges of housekeeping, servants' wages, and other incidental charges relating to the said partnership the sum of £60, *viz.* Arthur Billingsley £45 and the defendant £15, which monthly sums should be entered in the partnership books and allowed in the next account. [They agreed] that a general account should be made up yearly and, if either died after an account made up, the surviving partner should have the whole partnership stock and effects and pay the executors or administrators of the deceased partner so much money as the share of the deceased amounted to at the time of the last account. The partners made up an account in December 1720 and died in July following, before any other account was made up.

The plaintiffs were legatees of Arthur Billingsley, and they brought their bill for an account of his share of the partnership estate and of the rest of his personal estate.

The testator had taken out two monthly sums of £45 each after the stated account. And the defendant Cob being by the articles, as surviving partner, to have all the partnership effects and to pay for it as it stood upon the last account, he insisted upon having an allowance in the account of those two sums of £45 each, which had been so taken out by the said Arthur Billingsley.

On the other hand, the plaintiffs insisted to have an allowance of so much of the monthly sums as became due after the stated account and before the death of Arthur Billingsley and was not received by him.

And Lord Chancellor [Lord Macclesfield] was of the opinion that the plaintiffs were entitled to such allowance, and he decreed accordingly, but they were to allow three-fourths of the servants' wages and all other expenses incident to the partnership.

639

Francklyn v. Williams

(Ch. 1724)

Where co-executors have a power, they must exercise the power jointly.

Lincoln's Inn MS. Misc. 12, p. 99

7 July 1724. Francklyn *et al.*; Williams, executrix of Williams, *et al.*

The plaintiffs are entitled to the surplus of their father's personal estate by virtue of his will, and the defendant's testatrix and the other defendant, are executors of such will.

Part of the estate consisted of £1000 South Sea [Company] bonds at the testator's death. The defendant Williams's testator sells the bonds and lays out the money in Lottery annuities, which he, afterwards, subscribes into the South Sea Company without the consent of the other executor, who, having notice thereof, blames Williams for what he had done, whereupon Williams agrees to take the subscription upon himself, and he promises to replace £1000 South Sea bonds to the estate.

The question was if Williams, the executor, was indemnified by the late Act of Parliament,[1] which enabled trustees and executors to subscribe into the South Sea Company, and that the defendant is not bound to make good the subscription.

For the defendant, it was insisted that this subscription was at first intended for the benefit of the plaintiffs, who were then infants, and, if it had proved a beneficial subscription, no agreement between the two executors could have precluded the infants from having the benefit of it.

Lord Chancellor [Lord Macclesfield]: By the will, both the executors were empowered to place the trust money out upon securities. And, therefore, one of them could not act in that respect without the other. And he swears he did

[1] Stat. 6 Geo. I, c. 4, s. 23.

not consent to the subscription. If he had agreed to it, it would have been a good subscription and have bound the infants.

What is said for the defendant, *viz.* that the agreement between the executors would not bind the infants is very material if that were so. But I think they would have been bound, for the subscription was not completed until the other executor had given his consent. And he not consenting to it and the other agreeing to take it to himself and to replace £1000 South Sea bonds in the room thereof, he ought so to do. And, accordingly, the defendant Williams, who was the executrix of Williams, the executor, was decreed the £1000 South Sea bonds which had been sold, but to pay no costs.

640
Anonymous
(Ch. 1724)

A bill of exceptions can be stricken on the ground of impertinence.

British Library MS. Hargrave 81, f. 164

9 July 1724. At the Lord Chancellor's.

Mr. Amarant moved to refer exceptions for impertinence. And the Master of the Rolls [Jekyll] then sitting for the Lord Chancellor doubted first whether that was proper to be done. But Mr. *Amarant* producing the copy of the exceptions, which were several sheets of paper, though there were but two exceptions, and acquainting the court that the whole bill and answer were recited therein, the Master of the Rolls, thereupon and upon being informed by the officers of the court that the late motion had been frequently granted, ordered it accordingly.

[Other copies of this report: British Library MS. Hargrave 82, f. 175, pl. 1.]

641
King v. Seys
(Ch. 1724)

The administrator of a deceased intestate's estate has a vested interest in the decedent's personal estate.

Lincoln's Inn MS. Misc. 12, p. 90

10 July 1724. Sir Peter King *et ux.* v. Seys *et al.*

Elizabeth Seys made her will, and she made the plaintiff Sir Peter King[1] executor, and she gave the surplus of her personal estate to her niece and nephew,

---

[1] D. Lemmings, 'King, Peter, first Baron King (1669–1734)', *Dictionary of National Biography*, vol. 31, pp. 655–659.

the Lady King and William Seys. William Seys died intestate. And Richard Seys, his father, took administration, and, having received part of William's share of the surplus, he died. And, before his death, he made his will and Evan, his son, executor.

Evan proved his will and took administration *de bonis non* of William, his brother, and he is since dead intestate. And the defendant Seys has taken administration *de bonis non* of William, administration *de bonis non cum testamento annexo* of Richard, and administration to Evan.

The other defendants together with the plaintiff, the Lady King, are next of kin of William.

The question was to whom William's share unreceived of Evan Seys' personal estate did belong, whether to the representative of Richard, the father, or to the next of kin of William.

Lord Chancellor [Lord Macclesfield] was clear of opinion it belonged to the representative of Richard, for he, being administrator to William, had such an interest vested in him in William's share of his aunt's personal estate as would go to his executor or administrator. And, as he was entitled to take administration as next of kin to his son and not subject to a distribution, if he had died before he had taken out administration, whoever afterwards had taken out administration would have been only a trustee for his representative.

642

Lord Lisburne v. Harris

(Ch. 1724)

Gifts made in exchange for an unlawful purpose, such as prostitution, can be rescinded and returned.

Lincoln's Inn MS. Misc. 380, pt. 2, p. 14, pl. 2

11 July 1724.

The plaintiff, soon after he came of age, fell into the company of the defendant Harris, the wife, who was at that time a common whore, who, after they had lived together for some time, prevailed upon him to settle an annuity of £200 a year upon her charged on his lands, which was mentioned in the deed to be in consideration of £1000 paid by her to him. He, likewise, gave her a diamond necklace and a gold watch. She, afterwards, married the defendant Harris, who brought his action against the plaintiff for the annuity.

The plaintiff brought his bill to be relieved as being granted without any consideration and, likewise, for the redelivery of the watch and the diamond necklace.

By her answer, she acknowledged that the £1000 mentioned to be the consideration was not paid nor intended to be paid, but that the true consideration of that grant was their correspondence and conversation together and the services that she had done him.

There was no proof of any fraud or any artifice or contrivance in obtaining this annuity or the jewels, but that they were free gifts.

The counsel for the plaintiff distinguished this case from other cases where gifts that have been considered as *praemia pudicitiae* have been held good in this court, that those have been where women have been first debauched by the men that made them those presents, but, in the present case, the defendant was a common whore about the town before the plaintiff had anything to do with her.

Lord Chancellor Macclesfield decreed the annuity to be delivered up and said, if the jewels had been still in the possession of the defendant, he would likewise have ordered them to be delivered, but, since that did not appear and it was likely they had been sold and disposed of, he did not think it proper to decree a recompense for them.

British Library MS. Hargrave 81, f. 278

Monday 13 July, in court.

The plaintiff, in his father's life[time], was drawn in by the defendant's wife before her marriage with the defendant to live in a very loose, dissolute manner with her and, as was proved in the cause, she conversed with other men and had been under a cure for a venereal distemper and was a common prostitute. The plaintiff, however, so far ensnared by her that, he, though he had a wife of his own, Sir John Bennett's daughter, from whom he had been parted a considerable time, lived with this other woman as his wife and gave out she was so and by many was thought to be his wife. During this commerce, the plaintiff made her several presents as a gold watch and a diamond necklace and laid out several sums of money upon her and, over and besides, made a settlement by way of a rent charge of £200 *per annum* on her for life to take place after his father's death. And this was mentioned to be in consideration of £1000 paid by her, though not a penny proved to be paid. After, this dispute happening between her and the plaintiff, they parted, and the defendant, in prospect of this £200 *per annum* married her. And this bill was brought to set aside this settlement, to have an account of what money she had had from the plaintiff, and to have back the watch and diamond necklace.

And My Lord Chancellor [Lord Macclesfield], without any difficulty, decreed the settlement to be set aside and the watch and the necklace delivered up if they were still in the defendant's custody, but not otherwise. But, as to an account of the moneys he had, that was spent and gone. And, therefore, he would not decree that and, as it was a great hardship on the defendant, the husband, to be thus defeated of the fortune he expected, he would not decree him to make satisfaction for the watch and necklace unless they were in the defendant's custody at the beginning of the bill. And His Lordship said that he would never take away a settlement or provision made for a woman who had been seduced and debauched by a man, but, here, it was proved she was a common prostitute both before and after and, therefore, should not profit by the settlement.

[Other copies of this report: British Library MS. Hargrave 82, f. 266, Lincoln's Inn MS. Misc. 107, f. 134.]

643

Lloyd v. Bartlet

(Ch. 1726)

The lord of a manor is the owner of any houses built on the waste ground of the manor.

Lincoln's Inn MS. Misc. 12, p. 231, pl. 1

13 July 1726.

The plaintiff was lord of the manor of Ewell in Surrey, and he brought his bill, claiming title to a house in Ewell built upon the waste.

It was said by Lord Chancellor [Lord King] that the lord of a manor is never said to be out of possession of what is built upon the waste and that whatever is built upon the waste is his, and that, upon a trial before Justice John Powell touching some cottages or tenements built on the waste, though the lord had not been in actual possession for sixty years and there had been several fines levied, by the opinion of the judge, the lord had a verdict.

[Other copies of this report: 6 Viner, Abr. 183, 2 Eq. Cas. Abr. 229, 22 E.R. 194.]

644

Wilcocks v. Wilcocks

(Ch. 1724)

A holographic will is valid to pass personal property but not to pass real property.

Copyhold lands surrendered to the use of a will pass to the heir at law where no valid will was ever made.

British Library MS. Hargrave 81, f. 280

Tuesday 14 July 1724, at Westminster, before the Lord Chancellor.

A man surrendered his copyhold land to the use of his will and, afterwards, makes his will whereby he gives and devises these copyhold lands to the plaintiff and his heirs. This will was all written with the testator's own hand but not attested by any one witness, which, though it was good enough as to his personal estate and had been accordingly proved in the spiritual court, yet it was not sufficient to pass any freehold lands within the Statute of Frauds and Perjuries[1] for want of three witnesses. And the question was whether it was sufficient to pass these copyholds which had before been surrendered to the use of his will, that is whether they passed by the will or by the surrender.

Mr. Lord Chancellor [LORD MACCLESFIELD] and the bar seemed to be clear of opinion that this was within all the mischiefs of that Statute and that, though it did not pass by the will, yet if no will were made, it would have descended to the heir at law notwithstanding the surrender and that, in the disposition of the lands to the disherison of his heir, the testator was as much liable to be imposed on as in a case of a devise from his heir of freehold lands.

Yet, because it was said the resolutions have been otherwise and also because it was merely triable at law whether a good will or not, an issue was directed to be tried for that purpose. And no judgment [was] given in it. And the Case of Dr. Johnson[2] was cited, that a will of lands to charitable uses which was not good as a will should not operate as an appointment, and a case of Jenner v. Harper, in Lord Harcourt's time,[3] that a parol devise of lands to a charity [was] not good, being not warranted by the Statute of Frauds and Perjuries, which being subsequent to the 43 Eliz.[4] was so far a repeal thereof.

[Other copies of this report: British Library MS. Hargrave 82, f. 268, Lincoln's Inn MS. Misc. 107, f. 136.]

---

1 Stat. 29 Car. II, c. 3, s. 5 (*SR*, V, 840).

2 *Attorney General v. Barnes* (1707), 2 Vernon 597, 23 E.R. 990, Precedents in Chancery 270, 24 E.R. 131, Gilbert Rep. 5, 25 E.R. 4, 3 Chancery Reports 150, 21 E.R. 753, 1 Eq. Cas. Abr. 97, 21 E.R. 908, British Library MS. Hargrave 80, f. 13, Chancery Cases *tempore* Harcourt, 25.

3 *Jenner v. Harper* (1714), 1 Peere Williams 247, 24 E.R. 374, Gilbert Rep. 44, 25 E.R. 31, Precedents in Chancery 389, 24 E.R. 175, 1 Salkeld 163, 91 E.R. 152, 2 Eq. Cas. Abr. 191, 22 E.R. 163, Chancery Cases *tempore* Harcourt, 432.

4 Stat. 43 Eliz. I, c. 4 (*SR*, IV, 968–970).

645

Paterson v. Cleveland

(Ch. 1724)

Interest for money not delivered is usurious.

A debtor can enforce in a court of equity a usurious contract by paying what is truly due and waiving the forfeiture of the Statute of Usury.

Lincoln's Inn MS. Misc. 12, p. 101

21 July 1724.

The plaintiff borrowed £11,000 of the defendant and deposited three South Sea subscriptions as a security. And, by his bill, he charges that £10,000 only was advanced by the defendant and that the defendant promised to advance the other £1000 but never did. And the plaintiff prays by his bill that an account may be taken of what is due upon the securities and that, upon payment thereof, they may be delivered up.

The defendant demurred for that the discovery sought by the bill will subject the defendant to the penalties of the Statute of Usury.[1]

Lord Chancellor [Lord Macclesfield]: The matter as laid in the bill is plainly usurious, for the whole money carried interest from the date of the securities, though part only is paid. The plaintiff ought by his bill to have waived all benefit of the Statute of Usury and have offered to pay what is really due, and, then, the court would not have suffered him after an answer put in to have dismissed his bill, but to go on to a hearing and, upon hearing the cause, the court would decree an account and compel him to pay what should be found due according to the offer in his bill.

But, as the bill now stands, if the defendant should answer and confess the fact as charged in the bill, the plaintiff might afterwards dismiss his own bill, and, if the defendant brought an action [at common law], the plaintiff might plead the usurious contract and give the answer in evidence.

The demurrer must be allowed, and the plaintiff must amend his bill.

---

[1] Stat. 13 Ann., c. 15 (*SR*, IX, 928).

646

Costyn v. Flower

(Ch. 1724)

The Statute of Frauds cannot be pleaded where the lessee has gone into possession of the premises and has made substantial improvements thereon.

Lincoln's Inn MS. Misc. 12, p. 102

21 July 1724.

A bill [was exhibited] for a specific performance of an agreement for a lease to be made for a term of seven years. And the plaintiff suggests he was put into possession and had continued in possession two years and had made great improvements on the said premises.

The defendant pleaded the Statute of Frauds,[1] and he averred there was no agreement in writing. And by his answer, he denied that any improvements had been made on the premises.

Lord Chancellor [LORD MACCLESFIELD] overruled the plea, for, if any improvements had been made and the plaintiff had stood by and would now take advantage of those improvements and turn the plaintiff out of possession, this was such a circumstance as would bring it out of the Statute and, though the defendant had denied this, yet the plaintiff ought to have an opportunity of making out his case by proofs. And it is proper the case should come before the court in all its circumstances. And, should the plea be allowed and the plaintiff reply to it, that would not bring the case before the court, for, then, the defendant would have nothing to do but to make out his plea.

And, therefore, he reserved the benefit of the plea until the hearing of the cause.

647

Twitty v. Anonymous

(Ch. 1724)

A gift of interest payments for life is proportionable between the life tenant and the remainderman, but a gift of a rent payment is not.

Lincoln's Inn MS. Misc. 380, pt. 2, p. 15, pl. 1

23 July 1724.

Lord Chancellor [LORD MACCLESFIELD], upon a motion for payment of interest, determined that, where a sum of money was put out at interest to be paid

---

[1] Stat. 29 Car. II, c. 3 (*SR*, V, 839–842).

to A. during life and then to B., if A. die between the usual times of payment of interest, that his executors should be entitled to the interest computed to the very day of his death. And he distinguished this from the case of a rent reserved upon a lease payable at certain times, in which case, the executors of the tenant for life are entitled to nothing but what became actually payable during his life and the remainderman will have the whole that becomes payable in his time because the rent, coming in lieu of the profits which arise only at certain times and cannot be distinguished by particular days, must follow the nature of those profits. But interest accrues for every day.

648

Clement v. Pope

(Ch. 1724)

A lawsuit cannot be revived against an executor of a decedent's will solely to collect court costs.

Lincoln's Inn MS. Misc. 12, p. 103, pl. 2

24 July 1724. Clement v. Pope, executor of Michael Pope, *et al.*

The defendant, who was the executor of the defendant Pope, came to show cause at the return of a subpoena scire facias why the decree against him should not be revived, by which decree the defendant Michael Pope was ordered to convey the estate in question to the plaintiffs and the defendant Michael Pope and the other defendants were to deliver up to the plaintiffs all the deeds and writings relating to the said estate in their custody and the defendant Michael Pope was to pay the plaintiff costs to be taxed by a Master.

The decree was signed and enrolled, and, before any proceedings were had thereon, Michael Pope died. And the plaintiffs brought a subpoena scire facias to revive the decree against the heir and also against the executor of Michael Pope.

The executor insisted that the costs not being taxed and there being nothing to be done by the executor but to pay the costs, the plaintiffs are not entitled to revive the decree as against him simply for costs.

And of that opinion was the Lord Chancellor [Lord Macclesfield], and he allowed the cause. And it being insisted on by the plaintiffs that the writings may be gotten into the executor's hands and, if so, then there will be something to be done by him and, therefore, the decree ought to be revived against him in order that he may deliver up the writings, but My Lord Chancellor [Lord Macclesfield] said the writings did not belong to the executor but to the heir and, if the executor had gotten them, the plaintiffs must exhibit a new bill against him.

649
Hamilton v. Pollard

(Ch. 1724)

Where a defendant is in default, a writ of sequestration to seize his property within the court's jurisdiction must precede such a writ against property in a foreign jurisdiction.

Lincoln's Inn MS. Misc. 12, p. 104

(Query if not Fuller v. Hamilton, *post* 138.[1])

A. brings a bill against B., and B. brings a cross-bill against A., and he being in Carolina, B. gets an order to serve the counsel in court of A. And A. being in contempt to a [writ of] sequestration, B. moves for a [writ of] sequestration directed to the Governor of Carolina to sequester the effects of A. there.

Lord Chancellor [Lord Macclesfield]: You are too early. You must get the [writ of] sequestration here returned and make an affidavit that you have endeavored to sequester A.'s effects here but can find none, and, then, the court will grant you a [writ of] sequestration directed to the Governor of Carolina to sequester the defendant's effects there.

650
Beaumont v. City of Norwich

(Ch. 1724)

A decree is enforceable as soon as it is made by the court and before it is drawn up and entered.

Lincoln's Inn MS. Misc. 12, p. 105

The defendants were decreed to prevent the butchers selling meat out of the Upper Market of the City during the continuance of the lease in question.

About two months after the hearing and before the decree was settled and passed, the lease expired, during which two months, the defendants suffered the butchers to sell meat contrary to the decree.

Lord Chancellor [Lord Macclesfield] declared a decree ought to be performed as soon as it is made and the parties know what the directions are, though in minutes not drawn up. And, therefore, he ordered the defendants to pay the damage sustained by the plaintiff betwixt the hearing and the expiration of the lease.

---

[1] See below the Case of *Fryer v. Vernon* (Ch. 1725), Case No. 678, for the identification of the parties.

651

Colchester v. Colchester

(Ch. 1724)

The daughter of a citizen of London is entitled to her customary share upon his death even though she has already received a marriage portion.

The doctrine of hotchpot applies among siblings but not children and parents.

British Library MS. Hargrave 81, f. 281

August 1724, at Westminster, after the seals, before the Lord Chancellor.

A freeman of London, having issue a daughter, his only child, gives her a portion of £6000 and the further sum of £1000 upon a contingency to happen ten months after his death. Some years after, he dies without any other issue, leaving a widow and £18,200 personal estate. And the only question in this case was whether the daughter should come in for any further share of her father's personal estate.

And my Lord Chancellor [Lord Macclesfield] was of opinion that she should have a full third part of what her father left at the time of his death without regard to what he had before given her, for the £6000 was not a full third part of what he left, though it wanted but little of it, and the other £1000 was contingent whether it would ever come to her or not. And, therefore, [it was] not a certain provision of a third part and so, not being provided for with a full third part of his personal estate, she must come in for her third of what he leaves at his death as if no provision at all had been made for her, not being fully provided for in his lifetime. And the £6000 she has already received cannot be brought into hotchpot for the sake of the widow, for hotchpot is only between the children. And His Lordship seemed to be of opinion that it would have been the same though she had been provided even with a full third part of what he left at his death, there being to be no hotchpot in the case, that is if she had had £7000 certain given her, which would have been more than a third of what [was] left at his death, though not a full third of the whole if that £7000 were to be thrown in. And he said that, in that case, he would at least have sent it to the City to certify what was the custom therein. But, in the principal case, he thought is so clear that no certificate of the custom was needful.

[Other copies of this report: British Library MS. Hargrave 82, f. 269, Lincoln's Inn MS. Misc. 107, f. 137.]

[Other reports of this case: Select Cases *tempore* King 13, 25 E.R. 196, 2 Eq. Cas. Abr. 281, 491, 22 E.R. 237, 417.]

652

Rowe v. Bassett

(Ch. 1724)

In this case, a mortgagor was allowed to redeem against a purchaser for value.

British Library MS. Hargrave 81, f. 283

10 October 1724, at the Lord Chancellor's [house].

The plaintiff, about twenty years ago, had made a mortgage of the estate in question and, by misfortune being reduced in his circumstances, could not continue to pay the interest as he had done for some time, upon which the mortgagee entered upon the estate about three years after the making of the mortgage. And, according to the usage of the selling of estates in Cornwall, where this estate lay, they called a public outcry for the sale of it to the best bidder. The mortgage money was £200 and some arrears of interest. It was proved in the cause that the plaintiff, the mortgagor, was present at the first bidding, but the money then bid for it being only £200, at the plaintiff's request, the outcry was adjourned for about a week to the defendant's house. And at the second bidding, as was proved in the cause, nobody was present but the defendant and another person, the plaintiff being gone to try to raise the money and pay off the mortgage from a person who had promised but had disappointed him of it, upon which the defendant was allowed the purchase for £200, nobody bidding more for it. And, thereupon, the defendant took a conveyance from the mortgagee without the mortgagor's joining or being a party to the suit and [had] been in possession under this title for about sixteen or seventeen years.

And now, this bill was brought for a redemption of the estate and an account of the rents and profits. The defendant insisted on his purchase, and the plaintiff consents to sell the estate as before. And there was likewise some proof that the plaintiff had before expressed his approbation for the purchase after it was made and that the adjournment of the outcry was at his request. But, as to his consent after, that was encountered by other proof on his part and that he was so far from consenting to sell it that he had used all means possible to raise the money in order pay off the mortgage and upon this case, though the estate did not appear to be of but very little value more than the money upon it.

Yet the court decreed a redemption to an account of the rents and profits and said, if the plaintiff was consenting to the sale, why did he not join in the conveyance, for the mortgagee could convey no more than he had, which was a redeemable estate, and the defendant had notice that it was but a mortgage and to extinguish the plaintiff's right of redemption by a parol proof of his consent is to let in all the mischiefs which the Statute of Frauds and Perjuries[1] was made

[1] Stat. 29 Car. II, c. 3 (*SR*, V, 839–842).

to prevent, which requires that all agreements for the sale or purchase of lands shall be in writing. Besides, the defendant here had not the purchase deeds to produce having as he pretended on a renewal of the lease, it being a leasehold estate, delivered up the deeds to the person that had the inheritance and who had granted him a new lease and, therefore, as the court said, for aught appeared he might have nothing but a bare assignment of it as a mortgage. And so he decreed a redemption.

[Other copies of this report: British Library MS. Hargrave 82, f. 270, Lincoln's Inn MS. Misc. 107, f. 138.]

653

Leigh v. Cutliff

(Ch. 1724)

Where a lessor can enter and recoup a debt out of the profits of the land, there can be no right to foreclose, but, if the right of entry is only in the nature of a penalty, there can be a foreclosure.

Lincoln's Inn MS. Misc. 12, p. 106

10 October 1724. Katherine Leigh, widow, plaintiff; Cutliff *et al.*, defendants.

The plaintiff being entitled as administratrix to her late husband to a lease of mills made by the Mayor etc. of Exeter for ninety-nine years if three lives, whereof the plaintiff's is one, should so long live at £13 10s. 0d. a year, she, by indenture 10 November 6 Will. & Mar. [1694] in consideration of £450 and an annuity of £150 a year for her life, assigned this lease to one Atkins for the remainder of the term. And Atkins covenanted to pay the £150 a year to the plaintiff for her life by quarterly payments and that, if it should be in arrear for the space of fourteen days after any of the days of payment, the plaintiff might distrain and, if in arrear twenty days, the plaintiff might enter into the premises and the same have again and keep until the annuity with the arrears thereof should be fully paid according to the true meaning of the indenture.

The annuity being in arrear, the defendants, who are entitled to this lease under the plaintiff's assignment, quietly delivered possession to the plaintiff, who now brings her bill that the defendants might pay her arrears or be debarred from all equity of redemption and that she might be quieted in the possession of the premises.

For the defendants, it was insisted they ought not to be foreclosed. The plaintiff has not the legal estate in her; she is only to hold and enjoy until she is paid all the arrears of her annuity out of the rents and profits, and, when that is done, there is an end of her estate and the defendants may then enter.

Lord Chancellor [LORD MACCLESFIELD]: The deed does not say the plaintiff shall enter and hold until she is paid out of the rents, but that she shall hold until she is paid. If it was to hold until she is paid out of the profits, there could be no foreclosure. A decree to foreclose would signify nothing, for, whenever the plaintiff is paid out of the profits, the defendants may enter notwithstanding the decree, which does not foreclose the legal estate but only the equitable interest.

But, if the liberty of entering and holding until paid is only collateral and by way of a penalty until the party who has covenanted to pay the annuity shall think fit to pay the arrears, the Lord Chancellor [LORD MACCLESFIELD] said he might in that case decree an account of what is due for the arrears and, if the defendants did not pay what should be found due by a time to be appointed by the Master, then the defendants should be foreclosed of all equity of redemption and the plaintiff should hold and enjoy until the end of the term

But he said he would not determine what construction should be put upon the deed but decree the defendants to be foreclosed of all equity of redemption if they did not pay what should be found due on the account by a time to be appointed by the Master. And, if the defendants should be foreclosed, they might afterwards enter if they thought they had a right by the deed so to do when the arrears were paid out of the profits and, then, the construction of the deed would properly come in question.

But, afterwards, he said he would reserve further directions until the account was taken, for, if it should appear that the arrears are so considerable that the surplus profits are not likely to pay them off during the continuance of the lease, he might decree the plaintiff in that case to hold and enjoy during the remainder of the lease.

Then, the plaintiff's counsel insisted that, in taking the account, she ought to have interest for the arrears, and of that opinion Lord Chancellor [LORD MACCLESFIELD] was at first, but, afterwards, he said he thought the plaintiff ought to have no interest, for, if the deed was so construed as that the plaintiff was to be paid out of profits, she could have no interest, there being no agreement in the deed for interest. However, he reserved the consideration of interest until the Master had made his report. And he directed the Master to state the circumstances of the estate and what improvements had been made thereon by the defendants, it being insisted by the defendants' counsel that they had built a new mill and laid out £250 in buildings. And which, if so, the Lord Chancellor [LORD MACCLESFIELD] said he thought it would be hard for a court of equity to give the plaintiff interest.

654

Sly v. Warner

(Ch. 1724)

A widow cannot have both her jointure and her dower.

However, a widow of a London freeman can have her dower and her customary rights.

The child of a London freeman must elect between a legacy and his customary share.

British Library MS. Hargrave 81, f. 286

Tuesday 13 October 1724, at the Lord Chancellor's [house].

The plaintiff's wife, the widow of Mr. Warner, the banker of Temple Bar, and upon a treaty of marriage with Mr. Warner, he being entitled to an estate of £87 *per annum* in reversion expectant on the death of his mother, before marriage, makes a settlement thereof to himself for life with remainder to his intended wife for life for her jointure and in full of her dower, with remainder to their first and other sons in tail male successively. The marriage takes effect. And, some years after, the mother dies. Mr. Warner, afterwards, took up his freedom of the City of London and grew very rich. And before his death, he made his will and thereby devised to his wife a one-third part of his personal estate upon condition she relinquished her dower or thirds of his real estate and, having two sons only, gave £2000 to the youngest and, all the rest of the two-thirds, he gave to his eldest son. And he died leaving about £400 *per annum* real estate and £30,000 personal estate. The widow, after his death, entered upon the estate settled on her before marriage and, afterwards, intermarried with the plaintiff, who, in her right, was still in possession thereof.

And this bill was brought to be let into the dower of the real estate or to have dower thereof assigned her upon the pretense that this jointure being only of a reversion was no bar of her dower within the [Statute of] 27 Hen. VIII,[1] and so it had been adjudged in Vernon's Case, Co. 4, 4.[2]

And My Lord Chancellor [Lord Macclesfield] was clear of this opinion so if she had not accepted her jointure, but, here, she had accepted it and is still in possession and, therefore, has made her election, and she cannot have a jointure and dower both.

Another part of the bill was to have an account of the personal estate and to have her customary share thereof, her paraphernalia, and widow's chamber. And as to this, the restrictive clause in the will was held of no force and that she was entitled notwithstanding her claim of dower to her full customary part and to

[1] Stat 27 Hen. VIII, c. 10, s. 4 (*SR*, III, 540–541).

[2] *Vernon v. Vernon* (1572), 4 Coke Rep. 1, 76 E.R. 845, also 3 Dyer 317, 73 E.R. 718, Benloe 210, 123 E.R. 147, 3 Leonard 28, 74 E.R. 519.

her paraphernalia and widow's chamber and that the jointure settled upon her in full of dower out of the real estate could be no bar of her customary share out of the personal estate no more than a settlement of personal estate would be a bar of dower out of the real estate. And for this was cited the Case of Atkins v. Waterson.[1] And so was the opinion of the court clearly, and an account was decreed accordingly.

And it was likewise held that the youngest son, by this will, could not be debarred of his customary share coming to him by the custom of London if it appeared to be better than the £2000 given him by the will, and, therefore, after the account taken, he was to make his election, and the other legacies were to be paid out of the dead man's third and the residue thereof to go to the eldest son according to the will.

Lincoln's Inn MS. Misc. 12, p. 204

The plaintiff's wife was the widow of Mr. Warner, the banker at Temple Bar, and, upon a treaty of marriage with Mr. Warner, he, being entitled to an estate of £87 *per annum* in reversion expectant on the death of his mother, before his marriage, makes a settlement thereof to himself for life with a remainder to his intended wife for her jointure and in full [satisfaction] of her dower, with a remainder to their first and other sons in tail male successively.

The marriage takes effect. And, some years after, the mother dies. Mr. Warner, afterwards, took up his freedom and grew very rich. And, before his death, he made his will and, thereby, devised to his wife one-third of his personal estate upon condition she relinquished her dower or thirds of his real estate. And, having two sons, he gave only £2000 to the youngest, and, all the rest of the two-thirds, he gave to his eldest son. And he died leaving about £400 *per annum* real estate and £30,000 personal estate.

The widow, after his death, entered upon the estate settled on her before marriage, and, afterwards, she intermarried with the plaintiff, who, in her right, was still in possession thereof.

And this bill was brought to be let into dower of the real estate. But she having accepted her jointure and being in possession thereof, it was decreed she had her election and could not have the jointure and dower both.

Another part of the bill was to have an account of the personal estate and to have her customary share thereof, her paraphernalia, and widow's chamber.

And as to this, the restrictive clause in the will was held of no force but that she was entitled thereto notwithstanding her claim of dower and that the jointure settled upon her in full [satisfaction] of dower out of the real estate could be no bar of her customary share out of the personal estate no more than a

[1] *Atkyns v. Waterson* (1715–1716), see above, Case No. 83.

settlement of a personal estate could be a bar of dower out of the real estate. And an account was decreed accordingly.

[Other copies of this report: British Library MS. Hargrave 82, f. 271, Lincoln's Inn MS. Misc. 107, f. 139.]

655

Societas pro Propaganda Fide v. Codrington

(Ch. 1724)

The word 'recommend' in a will is merely precatory and not disposing.

Lincoln's Inn MS. Misc. 12, p. 111

13 October 1724. Societas pro Propaganda Fide in Partibus Transmarinis, plaintiff; Sir William Codrington, defendant.

Christopher Codrington,[1] having granted an annuity of £140 to Mr. Cuningham for his life out of his plantations in Barbados and all other his estate in America with a clause of distress in all his lands whatsoever, makes his will. And he gives his plantations in Barbados to the plaintiffs, and other parts of his estate he gives to the defendant. And, taking notice of the grant of the annuity, he goes on and says <for> 'the due and constant payment whereof I earnestly and particularly recommend to the said William Codrington [the defendant] not only for the service he has done me but for his maintenance during his labors for the public good.' And he makes the defendant executor.

The question was if these words in the will would oblige the defendant to pay this annuity and to discharge the plaintiffs' plantations from the payment thereof, it being insisted on by the plaintiffs' counsel that a recommendation in a will was equivalent to a direction.

But the Lord Chancellor [Lord Macclesfield] was of opinion the words in the will were not sufficient to charge the defendant with the payment of the whole annuity, it being plain that the reason why the testator so earnestly recommended the payment of this annuity to the defendant was for what is mentioned in the last part of the clause and all the testator intended by it was that the defendant should see it paid out of the estate whereout it was issuing.

And, therefore, he decreed the defendant should only pay his share of the annuity in proportion to the value that his estate in America devised by the will bore to the plantations devised to the plaintiffs, but that the estate in England devised to the defendant, though it was liable to a distress in case of non-payment

---

[1] S. Mandelbrote, 'Codrington, Christopher (1668–1710)', *Oxford Dictionary of National Biography*, vol. 12, pp. 383–384.

of the annuity should not bear any proportion of this annuity, for the lands only out of which it was issuing ought to contribute towards the payment thereof.

656

Bass v. Burbidge

(Ch. 1724)

In this case, the London widow's marriage settlement in issue was not given as a composition for and a bar of her customary share of her deceased husband's estate.

Lincoln's Inn MS. Misc. 12, p. 114

16 October 1724.

In this case, it was insisted by the plaintiffs, who had brought their bill for an account of the personal estate of one Ford, the father of the plaintiff's wife, who was a freeman of London, and to be paid her orphanage part that the defendant, the widow, having a settlement made her of some Lottery orders, it was a composition by the custom and she was barred to claim her customary share and that, the husband being a purchaser of his wife's customary share, the estate ought to be divided in moieties, as though there had been no wife. And for this was cited the Case of Blundell v. Barker.[1]

But, by Lord Chancellor [Lord Macclesfield], this case is not like that. There, the husband had made a provision for his wife before marriage and she had agreed to accept it in satisfaction of her customary share and to release all claims to his executors after his death, which she could make to his personal estate, except what he should give her by his will. Now he might have given her notwithstanding her settlement her customary share by his will, but, having not done so, but having directed her to release to his executors, that was in effect a gift of her share to his executors and will go according to his will.

But that is not the present case. This settlement is not made in bar of the wife's customary share, and, therefore, though arising out of the personal estate, it will not bar the wife of her share by the custom.

[1] *Blunden v. Barker* (Ch. 1719–1720), see above, Case No. 381.

657

Osgood v. Strode

(Ch. 1724)

Courts of equity will enforce trusts, whether voluntary or upon consideration.

Lincoln's Inn MS. Misc. 13, p. 200

24 October 1724. John Osgood *et al.*, plaintiffs; James Strode and Mary, his wife, and John Coxwell, defendants.

By articles dated 29 May 1697 made on the marriage of Edward Head with Elizabeth Pocock, between Lawrence Head and the said Edward, his son and heir apparent, of the first part, Richard Spicer and Nathaniel Collins of the second part, and the said Elizabeth Pocock, of the third part, in consideration of the said marriage and £600 portion paid to Edward, Lawrence Head and his son covenant with Spicer and Collins, but not for their heirs, to settle, grant, and assure unto and upon the said Elizabeth for her life a rent charge of £60 a year to be issuing out of the manor and farm of Winterborn in Berkshire. And they did also covenant, but not for their heirs, in consideration of the marriage and for settling the manor and farm, to grant and convey the same to Spicer and Collins and their heirs in trust and for the uses following, *viz.* to the use of Edward for life and, afterwards, to be charged with the said rent charge of £60 a year and the premises to be immediately chargeable with £50 a year to Lawrence for life, after the death of Edward, to his first and other sons by Elizabeth chargeable with £600 for daughters' portions, remainder to Lawrence Head, the eldest son of Joseph Head, deceased, who was the youngest son of Lawrence, the father, in tail male chargeable with £100 to Eleanor Spicer, one of the daughters of Lawrence, senior, if then living, remainder to the plaintiff John Osgood, a grandson of Lawrence, senior, in tail male, chargeable with the payment of £100 to every other grandchild of Lawrence, senior, which should be then living, remainder to the plaintiff Robert Southby, another grandson, in tail male, chargeable in the same manner, remainder to the right heirs of Lawrence, senior.

After the marriage, Edward entered and enjoyed the premises during his life. Lawrence, the father, died in June 1697. Elizabeth, the wife of Edward, died without issue in 1716, and Edward, her husband, died October 1722. Lawrence, the remainderman, died without issue in the life of Edward, and Eleanor Spicer died also in the life of Edward.

The plaintiff Osgood, being entitled under the articles, and the three other plaintiffs, who were grandchildren of old Lawrence Head and claimed £100 apiece by virtue of the articles, brought their bill against the defendants, Strode and Mary, his wife, and Coxwell, the said Mary and Coxwell being heirs at law to both Lawrence, senior, and Edward, his son, no settlement having been made pursuant to the said articles, to stay proceedings upon an [action of] ejectment, which the defendants had brought to recover possession of the premises and that they might execute a conveyance to the plaintiff Osgood in tail male with remainders over according to the articles and to have the deeds and writings delivered up.

The defendants, by answer, set forth that Edward Head, by will, devised the premises to his wife for life, remainder as to one moiety to the defendant Mary, his niece, in tail male, remainder to the defendant Coxwell in tail male, with other remainders over. And he devised the other moiety to the defendant Coxwell in tail male, remainder to the defendant Mary in tail male with the like remainders over.

And they insisted that Lawrence and Edward, his son, had not bound their heirs by the articles and that the defendants ought not in a court of equity to be compelled to execute a conveyance of the premises in favor of the plaintiffs, who claimed merely as volunteers and not on any real or valuable consideration, they not claiming under the consideration of the said marriage and marriage portion.

Note it appeared by the proofs in the cause that Lawrence, the elder, in May 1676 after the death of Lawrence, his son, father of the defendant Mary Strode, settled the premises with a power of revocation charged with £1300 for the portions of the daughters of his son Lawrence. And old Lawrence, in February 1690, revoked the settlement except as to the said charge of £1300 and limited the estate to Edward and his heirs. And, in 1694, old Lawrence paid off the portions and, all along, continued in possession to the time of the articles.

For the plaintiffs, it was insisted that it was the intent of the articles to provide as well for the plaintiffs Osgood and Southby successively in remainder as for Edward and his wife in possession and for their issue male and that Lawrence and Edward were bound by the articles to make a conveyance to the uses therein mentioned and the defendants, who derived title to the premises as heirs of Edward by descent and now stand in his place, ought by virtue of his covenant, which is a lien on the estate, to execute the like conveyance as Edward should and ought to have done in his lifetime.

The plaintiffs are not strangers, but near relations, and, Lawrence having covenanted to settle to the use of his grandson, it has raised a trust. If it had been a covenant to stand seised, it would have raised a use. There is a natural obligation upon all men to provide for their family. And the consideration of the marriage and the marriage portion ran through all the uses in the articles. And for this was cited Hard. 395 and 1 Lev. 150, the same case.[1]

For the defendants, it was insisted that the plaintiffs were no parties and claimed merely as volunteers, the consideration of the articles not extending to them. The estate moved from Edward, the son, and, though his father joined in

[1] *Jenkins v. Keymish* (Ex. 1664–1666), Hardres 395, 145 E.R. 515, 1 Levinz 150, 83 E.R. 343, British Library MS. Hargrave 65, ff. 20v, 30v, Lincoln's Inn MS. Misc. 499, p. 209, British Library MS. Lansdowne 1109, f. 181v.

the covenant, yet he had no interest in the estate, he having before settled it upon Edward and his heirs.

If this had been a covenant to stand seised, no use could have arisen to the plaintiff Osgood, he not coming within the consideration. And for this was cited Cr. Ch. 529, Smith and Risley, and Ro. 2 Abr. 784.[1]

The articles being voluntary as to the plaintiffs, this court ought not to relieve them against the heir at law. An action at law upon a parol contract will not lie where there is no consideration, for it is a *nudum pactum* and the putting such a contract under hand and seal will not alter the nature of the contract. And, if there is no consideration, shall this court go further than the [common] law will?

Lord Chancellor [Lord Macclesfield]: The question is whether this agreement is such as will amount to a trust, for, if it does, it ought to be executed. Every trust, whether voluntary or not, shall be performed in this court.

I cannot say the articles are merely voluntary. The father, having paid off the £1300 for the portions, had an interest in the estate. And he might contract to settle the estate in what manner he thought proper. And both the father and the son, having an interest in the estate, might settle the same in the manner they have done.

He decreed the articles to be executed and the defendants to settle the estate accordingly.

[Other reports of this case: 2 Peere Williams 245, 24 E.R. 716, 10 Modern 533, 88 E.R. 839, 2 Eq. Cas. Abr. 25, 22 E.R. 21.]

658

Shuckburgh v. Eyles

(Ch. 1724)

In this case, the plaintiff was not defrauded as he alleged, but the fraud was committed against the general public.

Lincoln's Inn MS. Misc. 12, p. 118

24 October 1724. Shuckburgh v. Sir John Eyles *et al.*, trustees of the South Sea Company.

In December 1719, one Crisp, a broker, contracted with the plaintiff to give him 5s. percent premium for the refusal of the next Midsummer dividend upon £5000 South Sea stock at the rate of £3 percent. And, at the same time, he made the like contract with Moses Hart of £30,000 stock, Wymondsold on £10,000, Nunes £10,000, and Warner and Snow £5000. Crisp, going to France, desires

[1] *Smith v. Risley* (1639), Croke Car. 529, 79 E.R. 1058, 2 Rolle, Abr., *Uses*, pl. H, 4, p. 783, also W. Jones 418, 82 E.R. 219.

the defendant Poulter to get the contracts drawn and made in his own name and to receive the premiums from Sir John Blunt,[1] for whose benefit the contracts were then made, which Poulter accordingly does. And the contracts were executed and the premiums paid.

A dividend being made at Midsummer 1720 of £10 percent in stock and stock being about £1000 percent, Grigsby demands a performance of these contracts and a transfer of the dividend stock. And a meeting was had 15 July 1720 between Grigsby and Hart, Nunes, Snow, and the plaintiff. And Grigsby then proposed to adjust and make up the contracts at the rate of £25 percent, which Hart refused to comply with. And he said he would try the validity of the contracts at law. But Snow complied and paid £25 percent on his contract on Grigsby's promise that Snow should be on the same foot with Hart and Wymondsold. And, at the same time, the plaintiff agreed to give, and did give, his note to Grigsby to pay £1250, being £25 percent on the 25 August 1720 on condition that he should pay no more than in proportion to what Grigsby should receive from Hart and Wymondsold. And, thereupon, the plaintiff's contract was delivered up. And, at the same time, Nunes gave his note for the £25 percent on his contract. But previous to that meeting, Blunt had promised to deliver up to Nunes whatever note he should give, he having applied to Sir John Blunt, and, alleging poverty, he desired his contract might be delivered up.

The plaintiff's note being come to the hands of the trustees of the late directors' estates as part of Sir John Blunt's effects, they brought an action against the plaintiff on his note, who now brought his bill to be relieved against this action and to have his note delivered up.

And it was insisted for the plaintiff that the giving out 5s. premium for the refusal of the Midsummer dividend by Sir John Blunt was a fraud in him and has been so declared by the House of Lords that Sir John Blunt was the contriver of the South Sea scheme and, when the plaintiff and the rest of the parties had been drawn into these contracts, Sir John Blunt, by his influence over the Company, had gotten the Midsummer dividend to be made in stock, and, therefore, the whole transaction being a fraud in Sir John Blunt, the trustees, who stand in Sir John Blunt's place, cannot be in a better condition than he would have been.

Besides, there was a fraud in the composition, for Nunes was made to give his note in order to draw in the rest, and, the plaintiff's giving his note was conditional only, *viz.* that the plaintiff should pay no more in satisfaction of his note than what Hart and Wimondsold should pay.

But, for the defendants, it was insisted that, if there was a fraud, the persons for whom the defendants are trustees were cheated as well as the plaintiff. And, if so, shall the court relieve one of the parties cheated against the others, who are cheated too?

[1] H. Erskine-Hill, 'Blunt, Sir John (bap. 1665, d. 1733)', *Oxford Dictionary of National Biography*, vol. 6, pp. 353–354.

When the contracts were made, the Act of Parliament[1] for the South Sea scheme was not passed nor so much as brought into the House of Commons, and it was wholly uncertain whether the scheme would take place or no. And that depended entirely upon the Parliament.

As to the resolution of the House of Lords in declaring the giving out the 5s. premium for the refusal of the Midsummer dividend was a fraud, that was with respect to the public or to the Company, but not that it was a fraud upon the persons with whom such contracts were made.

And as to what is insisted on, that Nunes was made use of to draw in the rest, that appears by the proofs to be otherwise, for his note was not given until after the plaintiff had given his note and after Snow had paid his money.

And, as to the condition, which was said to be agreed on when the note was given, it was said that was parol, and, therefore, when an absolute note in writing was given, no parol condition could be tacked to it.

It was also insisted for the defendants that the plaintiff was improper to bring a bill in this court but ought to have made his claim before the trustees and proceeded in the method chalked out by the Act of Parliament,[2] for this note is part of Sir John Blunt's estate, and the plaintiff's bill is to have this note delivered up. And, therefore, it is a case properly within that clause in the Act of Parliament which directs how claims are to be prosecuted.

But, to this, it was said by the plaintiff's counsel that they claimed nothing out of Sir John Blunt's estate but insisted that this note ought not to have been put in suit, and, therefore, they might pray a perpetual injunction.

Lord Chancellor [Lord Macclesfield]: I make no doubt but the giving out premiums for the refusal of the Midsummer dividend in 1720 and then making a dividend of 10 percent in stock was a fraud. But who was this fraud upon? Not upon the plaintiff, but upon the public and upon the Company.

The plaintiff has had 5s. per cent for his dividend, more than, in strictness, he ought to have had. And all the rest of the dividend above the 3 percent was a fraud upon the Company, and the plaintiff has had the benefit of it, for he has gotten three-fourths of the stock. And he was indeed a purchaser of it, for he ought to have transferred the dividend stock pursuant to his contract. But, when the time came, he rather chose to pay 25 percent and keep the dividend, and now, he would keep the stock and pay nothing so that he would benefit himself by the fraud in making the dividend in stock and keep the three-fourths of the stock, and, at the same time, he would take away the other fourth from the Company, who are the parties injured.

As to the parol condition, I am not satisfied about it. The witnesses do not agree what the condition was. They differ in their depositions.

---

[1] Stat. 3 Geo. I, c. 9; Stat. 5 Geo. I, c. 19; Stat. 6 Geo. I, c. 4; Stat. 7 Geo. I, stat. 1, c. 5.

[2] Stat. 7 Geo. I, c. 28; Stat. 8 Geo. I, c. 23.

As to the plaintiff's coming here, I am not satisfied that this court has a jurisdiction in the present case.

However, upon the merits, he said he was of the opinion the plaintiff ought not to be relieved. And he dismissed the bill with costs.

659

Fowler v. Marshall

(Ch. 1724)

Where a person who holds securities for another exchanges them for other securities in the owner's name in good faith and for the latter's benefit though without the latter's consent, he will be relieved in equity against a common law judgment in trover.

Lincoln's Inn MS. Misc. 506, p. 73

Michaelmas 11 Geo.

The complainant had subscribed some lottery certificates into the South Sea Company belonging to the defendant without the defendant's authority or consent, upon which the defendant here had brought an action in the [Court of] Common Bench of trover for the certificates and had recovered full damages against the now plaintiff. And the defendant entered into a rule by consent that, upon the plaintiff's, the defendant at law, paying the money given by the verdict, he would transfer the stock that was put in his name in lieu of the Lottery certificates. This bill was brought by the defendant in the action to be relieved against this verdict as being against conscience, that he should be a loser for doing that which was intended for the benefit of the defendant and which, if the stock had risen, the defendant would have had the benefit of it, that he had done the same for the defendant as for himself, that there could be no fraud because it was subscribed in the defendant's own name, that no benefit was to accrue thereby to the complainant, and that, if there proved to be any loss to the defendant, it was not so designed by the complainant but on the contrary.

On the other side, it was insisted on that this subscription was a conversion and that, though the stock was subscribed in the defendant's name, yet he was but a trustee for the complainant, who, having converted the lottery certificates to his own use, was liable to answer the same in damages.

But the Lord Chancellor [LORD MACCLESFIELD] thought it very odd that a man should make another his trustee by doing him a tort. He said that, if the subscription was without authority, it was void and could be no prejudice to the defendant, who might have his certificates again, that it was the Act of Parliament[1] that bound down the defendant and imposed a loss on him, that, though the complainant had indeed by his means made it liable to the Act of Parliament,

[1] Stat. 7 Geo. I, st. 2; Stat. 8 Geo. I, cc. 20–22; Stat. 9 Geo. I, c. 6.

yet, that Act being made a good while after and not foreseen at that time, there could be no fraud in it and no benefit was intended for the complainant but for the defendant. He thought the plaintiff ought to be relieved and thus decreed a perpetual injunction.

Lincoln's Inn MS. Coxe 89, vol. 3, pt. 2, p. 8

Michaelmas 11 Geo. I.

The defendant Marshall brought [an action of] trover against Fowler for certain Lottery orders, and, upon the trial, the defendant produced a note under the plaintiff Fowler's hand acknowledging that he had certain Lottery orders belonging to the defendant Marshall, and Marshall likewise proved a demand and had a verdict and damages to the full value of the orders.

Fowler brings his bill in Chancery in order to be relieved against the verdict, and he sets forth that he had subscribed the said orders into the South Sea Company with an intent that it should be for the benefit of Marshall, and, therefore, he insisted that Marshall ought not to be allowed the produce of the subscription.

The defendant Marshall, in his answer, said the orders, if subscribed, were subscribed without his consent and without any authority from him for that purpose. And he insisted this subscription was void as to him or, if it should be good, the plaintiff ought to make good the deficiency and loss which the defendant has sustained by subscribing them.

It appeared in proof that the plaintiff had subscribed the orders without any authority from the defendant and that, when the defendant was told of the subscription, he immediately expressed his dislike of it, and, after, upon the fall of the stock, the defendant claimed his orders and arrested the plaintiff and obtained a verdict for them.

This case was heard before the Master of the Rolls [Jekyll], who decreed an injunction upon the plaintiff's transferring to the defendant such a proportion of stock as was allowed by Parliament for such orders as were subscribed. From this decree, the defendant appealed to Lord Chancellor [Lord Macclesfield] and prayed to be allowed the benefit of his verdict.

It appeared upon the depositions that the plaintiff, when he was arrested, proposed to the defendant that he would give other Lottery orders of equal value with those he had subscribed and in the same course of payment. And this was insisted on as a reason by the defendant why he should have the full value of his orders allowed him.

Lord Chancellor [Lord Macclesfield]: The action of trover was maintainable in this case, and the conversion was the plaintiff's subscribing the orders without authority. In actions of trespass, when a tort is committed, satisfaction cannot be given in evidence in mitigation of damages. But, in actions of *indebitatus assumpsit*, where no tort is said to be committed, payment which is a satisfaction is allowed to be given in evidence. In this case, the jury have given the whole in damages without any allowance to the plaintiff, which is a verdict without equity. The jury ought to have given damages only in proportion to the difference, and, if an action be brought for money and a receipt which is a satisfaction be lost, if, before the trial, there is a consent that it shall be allowed as evidence of a satisfaction, the jury shall find it as a satisfaction in proportion.

The present case is Lottery orders were put into the plaintiff's hands in order that he might receive the interest upon them at the Exchequer. Afterwards, when the South Sea [Company] stock was rising, the plaintiff, out of zeal to serve his customer, the defendant, subscribed his orders in his name intending it for his benefit and did as he did or would have done for himself. Nothing was meant by the plaintiff but the benefit of the defendant, for, if the stock had risen, the defendant would have had the benefit of the subscription. And it is not reasonable but that the defendant should now bear the loss, as the stock has fallen.

The Parliament has appointed a price for the orders subscribed. And I see no reason why the defendant should be allowed more than what the Parliament has thought proper. The Parliament has interposed and has given the defendant a satisfaction, and, though it is short of what the defendant before had a right to, yet there is no reason the plaintiff should make up the defendant's loss when it is plain the act he did was designed for the defendant's benefit.

And so he confirmed the decree of the Master of the Rolls [Jekyll].

Lincoln's Inn MS. Misc. 384, p. 311, pl. 1

31 October 1724.

Marshall, the defendant's testator, deposited Lottery annuities in the plaintiffs' hands as their cashiers to receive the interest. They subscribe them into the South Sea [Company], as they did their own. Marshall recovered in [an action of] trover. The bill was to be relieved, being justified by the Act of Parliament.

Lord Chancellor [Lord Macclesfield]: It is the Act of Parliament that made the conversion. If there had been any advantage, the defendant must have had it, and the plaintiffs could not hinder it. They intended a kindness. The verdict is against conscience. The plaintiff is relieved. The Master of the Rolls' decree is affirmed.

660

Wagstaff v. Bell

(Ch. 1724)

A devise to trustees must be executed according to the directions of the Statute of Frauds.

Lincoln's Inn MS. Misc. 12, p. 172

6 November 1724.

John Wagstaff, by a lease and release, conveys lands to the defendants [Bell and Edwards] and their heirs upon trust, by mortgage or sale, to raise several sums and to pay them to the persons therein named within six months after his death and that, in case his son Jasper should pay those sums, then the trustees were to convey the lands to Jasper and his heirs or to such person as he or they should appoint. Jasper pays the money charged on the lands and, before any conveyance was made to him, his dies, having made his will and devised the lands to his younger brother in tail with remainders over. But the will was executed in the presence of two witnesses only.

The plaintiff is the heir at law of Jasper. And he brings his bill against the trustees and the devisee to have the lands conveyed to him by the trustees, insisting that they did not pass by the will, it not being executed according to the Statute of Frauds and Perjuries.[1]

It was insisted for the devisee that, if the lands did not pass by way of devise, yet that they might by way of appointment and that the will might operate as an appointment, according to the resolution in the case of Sidney College and Dr. Johnson, in Lord Cowper's time.[2]

But the Lord Chancellor [LORD MACCLESFIELD] was clear of opinion that the lands did not pass by the will, for, if they passed at all, they must pass by way of devise. He said the words 'as he or they should appoint' signified nothing, for the trustees were to convey to him and his heirs.

---

[1] Stat. 29 Car. II, c. 3, s. 5 (*SR*, V, 840).

[2] *Attorney General v. Barnes* (1707), 2 Vernon 597, 23 E.R. 990, Precedents in Chancery 270, 24 E.R. 131, Gilbert Rep. 5, 25 E.R. 4, 3 Chancery Reports 150, 21 E.R. 753, 1 Eq. Cas. Abr. 97, 21 E.R. 908, British Library MS. Hargrave 80, f. 13, Lincoln's Inn MS. Coxe 89, vol. 3, pt. 2, p. 30, Chancery Cases *tempore* Harcourt, 25.

661

Hyde v. Skinner

(Ch. 1723)

In a lease with a covenant for renewal upon the same terms, the covenant for renewal cannot be continued indefinitely.

Lincoln's Inn MS. Misc. 12, p. 113

11 November 1723.

The defendant made a lease to William Hyde, the plaintiff's late husband, of a house in Enfield for seven years at £35 a year. And, therein, he covenants, inter alia, that he, his executors, administrators, or assigns should within twelve months before the end of the lease, if thereto required by the said William Hyde, execute to the said William Hyde a further lease of the premises under the like covenants and at the same rent as were therein contained for such further term as the said William Hyde should then desire.

Mr. Hyde died before the expiration of the lease, and the plaintiff, being his executrix, gave notice within the time limited by the lease that she would take a new lease for a further term of fifty years. And now, she brought her bill to have a specific execution of the covenants and a lease for fifty years pursuant thereunto.

The defendant insisted the covenant was personal only and that, Mr. Hyde being dead, the defendant was not obliged to make a new lease to his executrix.

But Lord Chancellor [Lord Macclesfield] was clear of opinion that the plaintiff was entitled to the benefit of the covenants. And he decreed the defendant to make a new lease to the plaintiff at the same rent and under the same covenants as were contained in the old lease, except the covenant for renewal, which was to be omitted. But this lease was to be made for twenty-one years only, for, though the covenant was general that a lease should be granted for such further term of years as Mr. Hyde should desire, yet that must have a reasonable construction.

[Other copies of this report: 4 Younge and Collyer Ex. 562, 160 E.R. 1131.]

[Other reports of this case: 2 Peere Williams 196, 24 E.R. 697.]

662

Osborne v. Macartney

(Ch. 1724)

A promoter of a company cannot enforce a bond by a subscriber for the purchase of shares of stock.

In this case, the court of equity granted relief against a common law judgment on such a bond.

Lincoln's Inn MS. Misc. 506, p. 74, pl. 1

Michaelmas 11 George.

This bill was brought to be relieved against some bonds entered into by the plaintiff conditioned for the delivering of shares in a co-partnership for lands in the Bahamas Islands.

Lord Chancellor [LORD MACCLESFIELD] declared that, in equity, the bonds ought not to be put in suit because the defendant, being a projector of this bubble himself, would be no loser if they were not and the plaintiff would be a great one if they were; otherwise if the defendant had been an innocent purchaser and had sold them again because there would be no reason why he should lose any more than the person who has purchased them of him.

He decreed the bonds to be given up.

Lincoln's Inn MS. Misc. 107, p. 144

11 November 1724.

The plaintiff had bought as many shares in the stock of the Bahamas Islands, which was one of the bubbles set up in the year 1720, as, at £350 per share, came to £1700 and gave a bond for it. It was proved in the cause that the defendant was one of the proprietors of this stock and concerned in the setting it up as one of the lessees of a forty year lease under the crown together with My Lord Londonderry and others. The plaintiff refusing to pay the money, the defendant had put it in suit and got judgment, [from] which this bill was brought for relief.

And MY LORD CHANCELLOR [MACCLESFIELD] decreed the bond to be delivered up and satisfaction to be acknowledged on the record of the judgment. And he took the difference where the seller was originally concerned in interest in setting the project on foot, as in this case, and where he only bought the shares at market and sold them again. And if that had been the case here, he would have given no relief, but the party must have paid the money.

From Mr. Cox's notes.

663

Anonymous

(Ch. 1724)

A father may use the income of his child to pay for the child's support, and he can use the child's capital for paying for an apprenticeship for the child.

Lincoln's Inn MS. Misc. 506, p. 74, pl. 2

Michaelmas 11 George.

The Master of the Rolls [JEKYLL] declared that, though a father cannot charge the principal of a legacy left to his child with maintenance, but can deduct only the interest, yet he may deduct out of the principal for putting him out as an apprentice or such like.

664

Anonymous

(Ch. 1724)

Where realty is devised, any liens upon it are to be paid off out of the decedent's personal estate.

Lincoln's Inn MS. Misc. 506, p. 74, pl. 3

Michaelmas 11 George.

It was decreed that, where there is a devise of the real estate, it must be understood so much as is clear after all debts be discharged to which it was subject, that, therefore, if there be particular sums bequeathed and there are specialties standing out which may affect the real estate, if the specialties be discharged out of the personal estate so that there be not sufficient to pay the legacies, the pecuniary legacies shall stand in their room; it is otherwise of specific legacies.

665

Anonymous

(Ch. 1724)

The Court of Chancery will not take jurisdiction over a matter where only a very small amount of money is in issue.

Lincoln's Inn MS. Misc. 506, p. 75, pl. 1

Michaelmas 11 George.

An action is brought at law upon a note for under £10. There is a verdict for the plaintiff which, together with the costs, amounts to £30. The defendant at law comes into equity to be relieved against the verdict suggesting that the note had really been satisfied, but there was no witness and, therefore, prays a discovery. But, because the original debt was under £10, the bill was dismissed.

666

Parthrick v. Friend

(Ch. 1724)

A gift causa mortis *must be expressly made in contemplation of immanent death.*

The delivery of a bond does not pass legal ownership.

Lincoln's Inn MS. Misc. 12, p. 133

16 November 1724.

Henry Parthrick, defendant's grandfather and plaintiff's grandfather, about a month before he died and when he lay ill of the sickness whereof he died, having fifteen East India bonds of £100 each in a tin box, upon the defendant's coming to see him, called for the tin box and delivered it to the defendant, saying, 'Take it and what is in it, and God bless you with it.' And, afterwards, he died intestate.

And upon a bill brought by the plaintiff for his distributive share of his grandfather's personal estate, that cause came to be heard. And the question being whether this gift to the [defendant] was a *donatio causa mortis*, it was sent to the Master to take an account of the personal estate, and the court reserved the determination of the matter relating to the bonds until after the Master should have made his report.

And now, it came upon the report, whereby it appears that eight of the bonds were made out in the intestate's name and not endorsed by him, and the rest were made out in other person's names and endorsed, and that the bonds were the whole personal estate, except about £150.

And, after great debate, the Master of the Rolls [JEKYLL] was of opinion that the defendant was not entitled to these bonds as *donatio causa mortis*. And he laid it down as a fundamental principle that, in every *donatio causa mortis*, two things are necessary, first, that the person who gives must actually deliver the thing given to the person to whom he gives it; second, that the person who gives must express or declare himself in such manner as that it may appear that he does it in view and contemplation of his death, which he expects to follow in some time after. Nothing of the latter appeared in the present case. And, partly for that reason and partly because the bonds were choses in action and the delivery thereof did not vest a legal property in the money, he decreed the bonds to be distributed with the rest of the intestate's personal estate.

There were some other circumstances in the case which likewise seemed to be inducements to incline His Honor to give this judgment, as that the defendant was a daughter who had been under her father's displeasure and the plaintiff was the son of his eldest son and his heir at law and unprovided for, and the bonds were near the whole of the personal estate.

[Other copies of this report: 2 Collyer 362, 63 E.R. 771.]

Lincoln's Inn MS. Misc. 384, p. 264, pl. 3

16 November. Partridge v. Friend. At the Rolls.

[The query was] whether East India [Company] bonds will pass by a *donatio causa mortis*, [which] the party brought three weeks before his death, having given the box in which they were with all in it, to the defendant, his daughter. The plaintiff is the grandchild. The East India bonds were almost all the estate, and several were not endorsed, so not transferrable. The wife was then living.

Curia [JEKYLL]: There is not sufficient evidence that he gave them in contemplation of death, which is requisite by the civil law. The donation is not good.

667

Anonymous

(Ch. 1724)

Where the unpaid principal and accrued interest on it is greater than the penalty of the bond to pay it, the entire amount due for principal and interest must be paid.

Lincoln's Inn MS. Misc. 380, pt. 2, p. 26

16 November 1724.

Upon an exception to the Master's report, the case was this. The testator was indebted by a bond in a penal sum conditioned for the payment of a less [sum] with interest. The interest was run so much behind that the principal and interest together amounted to more than the penalty of the bond. The bill was brought by the obligee against the executor of the obligor to discover assets and have satisfaction out of it for the principal and interest. The executor acknowledged assets. And it was referred to the Master to compute what was due for principal and interest. It now came to be a question whether this court should oblige the executor to pay out of assets more than the penalty of the bond since the testator himself would not have been obliged to it.

The Lord Chancellor [LORD MACCLESFIELD] ordered that the executor should pay the whole since he had assets and the whole was certainly justly and equitably due.

668

Theobalds v. Dufoy

(Ch. 1724)

A person who sells for the full value an interest in land can be required by a court of equity to convey the land even though the common law does not recognize such an interest as being a mere possibility.

A person under a disability can be estopped to deny his own conveyance where the full value was received and it was for his benefit.

Lincoln's Inn MS. Misc. 380, pt. 2, p. 27

16 November 1724.

A term for years was devised to one for life, the remainder to the defendant. The defendant being married, she and her husband, during the interest for life, sell their future interest in it for a full consideration in money. It was done by the consent of the wife and her relations, and she and her husband both joined in the deed of conveyance. After the husband's death and the death of the tenant for life, the wife brings an [action of] ejectment and recovers upon this point, that her interest at the time of the sale, being only a possibility, could not be assigned over. The plaintiff brings his bill to be relieved against this verdict.

Lord Chancellor [LORD MACCLESFIELD], having taken time to consider of this case, now gave his judgment. He said that it is true in law such an interest is not transferrable and it having been frequently so adjudged, he could not alter the law however unreasonable it seems to be.

The reason that is given for it is because it is not a certain interest but only a possibility. This seems exceeding strange to common sense that, where a person has a right to the residue of a term of 500 years after the death of another, it should be accounted merely a possible thing that the other should outlive that whole term, when an estate in fee being conveyed to one for life, remainder to another, that remainder is a certain vested interest.

He said it had been asked [of] him by persons conversant with the laws of other nations how it became a notion or maxim in our law that an estate for a man's life is accounted greater than a term for 500 years, that the answer he gave and which he apprehended the true one is that our law distinguishes between a greater and a longer estate, or rather takes notice of its being only a greater and not a longer estate. It is a greater estate because it was anciently a much less precarious, a more certain, secure, estate. And the reason was because, formerly, when lands were recovered chiefly in real actions, those actions could be brought against none but tenants of the freehold, that is tenants for life at least, and a termor for years could not falsify a recovery against a tenant for life, but must lose his term if the tenant for life lose his freehold. For this reason, terms for years were made chiefly upon a reservation of rents, which being pretty near the value of the estate, it was no great loss for the termor to lose his term because his rent ceased with it, and long terms were hardly ever made, but since long terms and upon small rents have grown more into use, acts of Parliament[1] have taken greater care to secure the interest of such terms.

Upon the foot of this notion of a term as an interest uncertain, capable of being easily destroyed, the law would not permit any remainder of a term to be limited after a life, but that being inconvenient, what could not be done under the notion of a remainder was allowed to be done as an executory devise, but the notion of its being a possibility was still kept up, and, upon that account, such a remainder was held not to be assignable.

And this rule, he said, should always so far stand by as it does not break in upon conscience, and, therefore, if a person purchase such a possibility for a sum of money and, afterwards, when the possibility falls into possession, another [person] without notice of the first for a valuable consideration purchase the term, I shall follow the law and let the second hold the term against the first.

But it is otherwise here. It is manifestly against conscience for one that has sold such a possibility afterwards when it comes *in esse* to say 'I could not grant it' and claim it himself contrary to his own honest contract; though it is not assignable in law, it is assignable in equity, as much as a bond is. And he would never suffer him to take advantage in a court of equity of that defect of legal title.

He said there was no difference between this and the present case in point of conscience. It is true this is a *feme covert* who, it is said, cannot bind herself and, therefore, she may take advantage of this legal defect, but she has done this without compulsion by the privity and consent of friends and relations. And great regard ought to be had to the act of a *feme covert* where it is done with the concurrence of her relations who thereby see that there is no imposition.

He said there was a Case of Sir Harry Every v. Lady Betty [*blank*].[2] The father of the defendant to whom she was heir made a mortgage of his estate to the plaintiff and died. The defendant [being] under age, it was necessary from the

---

[1] Stat. 6 Edw. I, Gloucester, c. 11 (*SR*, I, 49); Stat. 13 Edw. I, Westminster II, cc. 3, 4 (*SR*, I, 73–75); Stat. 11 Hen. VII, c. 20 (*SR*, II, 583).

[2] *Lady Betty Cromwell's Case*, 2 Eq. Cas. Abr. 517, 22 E.R. 436.

circumstances of the family that this mortgage should be continued and, by the consent of her mother and her nearest relations, it was agreed between the defendant, then an infant, and the plaintiff that the interest then owing should become principal and carry interest. It, afterwards, came to be a question in this court whether that agreement of the infant was binding, and the court established it upon the foundation of its being done with the concurrence of her relations and of the necessities of the family.

This was the case of an infant who is as much incapacitated as the wife. And yet the court had so great regard to an agreement made with the infant by the consent of her nearest relations that it was confirmed here. He, therefore, decreed this to be a good assignment to the plaintiff and ordered a perpetual injunction to stay proceedings upon the judgment and the plaintiff be quieted in possession.

Lincoln's Inn MS. Misc. 107, p. 147

17 November 1724.

This was a case which had long stood in the paper in order for the parties to agree it among themselves as the defendant was a poor woman and My Lord [Chancellor] was unwilling to decree against her, but she being obstinate as she thought she had the law on her side.

My Lord Chancellor [Lord Macclesfield] now pronounced his decree upon the case, which was this. Of a term for ninety-nine years of a house in Southwark, by his will he devised it to his wife for life with a power to her to make leases not exceeding twenty-one years, and, after her death, he devised it to his nephew and niece, William and Rebecca Rushley, and made his wife executrix, and he died. The wife proved the will. The niece married the defendant, who was an alien, and they, by an indenture for a valuable consideration, sold and assigned their moiety in the house to the plaintiff, after which, William Rushley, the nephew, dying, his moiety or interest in the said house was likewise [given] to the said Rebecca. And, thereupon, she and her husband, by another indenture for a valuable consideration, sold and assigned that moiety likewise to the plaintiff. And to secure the plaintiff's title the better, they renounced administration to the said William Rushley, which was thereupon granted to the plaintiff. The widow of the testator lived about eighteen years after the making of this will and, pursuant to her power, made a lease to the plaintiff for twenty-one years at £32 *per annum* rent which the plaintiff covenanted to pay. This sale by the defendant and his wife both of her own and her brother's moieties was made with the advice and consent of her friends and relations. And after the death of the widow, the plaintiff entered and laid out about £300 in repairs and held the possession quietly for several years. But the defendant's husband happening to die, she was advised, this sale and assignment being but of a mere possibility and she too a married woman at that time and moreover her husband [being] an alien, that they were not binding upon her as she had survived her husband. And she, thereupon, brought her action of covenant against the plaintiff for the reserved rent of £32 *per annum*, to be relieved against which and for a perpetual injunction, this bill was brought.

The case had been spoken to several times and, for the defendant, the two only things insisted on were, first, that her husband was an alien and therefore incapable of taking any interest otherwise than for his necessary habitation; secondly, that, if he were, that this was but a mere contingency, a mere possibility, for that the widow having an estate for life had all the interest in her and might outlive the term. And, therefore, this mere contingent possibility was not assignable according to Lampett's Case, Co. 10 Rep.[1] And, as the defendant had the law on her side, a court of equity ought not to take it from her.

The argument for the plaintiff I did not hear.

But My Lord Chancellor [Lord Macclesfield] now gave his opinion and awarded a perpetual injunction for a stay of the defendant's proceedings at law. He said he had been often asked by the civilians and those who were conversant in other laws how our law came to take up the notion that an estate for life was greater than an estate for years how long soever, which seemed a very great absurdity since nothing was plainer than that the tenant for life could not outlive these years, to which he said he had made that answer, which he thought was a true one, that an estate for life was in the eye of the law looked upon to be a greater estate than a term for years but a longer estate, for, at the common law and by the old books, it appears that a term for years was of very little regard and he who had the freehold or an estate for life was the only tenant to the *praecipe*, and, in those times when real actions were almost the only actions that were brought, the termor was entirely under the power of him who had the freehold and, if he suffered a recovery to be had against him, though by covin, the termor could not falsify or any ways help himself but he lost his term forever until some acts of Parliament were made for his relief which gave him power to falsify covinous recoveries. And this was little or no prejudice to him because his term was generally at a rack rent so that he lost nothing but the over-value of the land beyond his rent. And they knew nothing then of the terms for 500 or 1000 or 2000 years. Nay, My Lord Coke in his *Commentaries upon Littleton*[2] says that a lease for above forty years was then looked upon to be fraudulent and void. But to say that an estate for life is a longer estate than for 500 or 1000 years is absurd according to the course of human affairs. And, therefore, where is the difference in reason between a limitation to one for life with a remainder to another for life, that is good and a remainder actually vested. And a limitation of a term for 500 or 1000 years to one for life and, after his death, for so many years of that term as shall remain at the death of the first tenant, which it is almost certain he cannot outlive and though such a limitation is called a possibility or a contingency, yet

[1] *Lampet's Case* (1612), 10 Coke Rep. 46b, 77 E.R. 994, *sub nom. Lampit v. Starkey*, 2 Brownlow & Goldesborough 172, 123 E.R. 880.

[2] E. Coke, *First Institute* (1628), ff. 45–46.

it is such a one as most certainly will happen. And, therefore, though from the notice of law which has prevailed, such a contingency or possibility is not assignable. And, therefore, the party who makes it may after the death of the tenant for life bring his [action of] ejectment and recover it at law. Yet it is most certainly against conscience and equity that he should take another man's money for it and then set it aside and so have both the land and the money too. And a bond is no more assignable in law than such a contingency or possibility, yet it is every day made good in this court. And though, in this case, the defendant was a married woman, yet the husband who would have had the power over it if it had been a term in possession joining in the assignment and that too for a valuable consideration, his wife ought not to be at liberty to set it aside after[wards], especially as it was then thought to be for their benefit and she had renounced administration in order to let in the plaintiff to secure his possession. And an infant would be bound by acts done by his friends and relations for his benefit, as in the Case of Lady Betty Cromwell of interest made principal to keep the mortgagee from taking possession.

And as the husband's being an alien, nothing of that was proved, or, if it had, it would vest the interest in the crown.

And, therefore, a perpetual injunction was decreed to quiet the plaintiff in possession.

From Mr. Cox's notes.

[Other reports of this case: 9 Modern 102, 88 E.R. 342, 2 Eq. Cas. Abr. 88, 340, 22 E.R. 76, 290.]

669

Earl of Hindford v. De Costa

(Ch. 1724)

After making an election of remedies and suffering a nonsuit at common law, a plaintiff can file a bill of revivor in the equity court.

Lincoln's Inn MS. Misc. 12, p. 207

24 November 1724.

The plaintiff brought a bill against the defendant [De Paiba] for an account of several dealings relating to the buying and selling of stocks in the year 1720. And, after the defendant had put in an answer, the earl brought an action at law against the defendant for the same matters, upon which the defendant moved the court and obtained the common order for the plaintiff to make his election.

The plaintiff elected to proceed at law. And, accordingly, he brought on his cause for trial. And, being nonsuited, he then moved the Lord Chancellor

MACCLESFIELD that his bill might be retained, which was dismissed upon his electing to proceed at law.

And, accordingly, it was ordered that, upon paying the costs of the dismission out of the Purse and the costs of this motion and also the costs of the nonsuit, the bill should be retained, His Lordship [LORD MACCLESFIELD] declaring that the defendant having driven the plaintiff to law, it was but reasonable since he had failed there that he should be at liberty to resort back to this court.

Select Cases *tempore* King 4, 25 E.R. 191

10 December 1724.

The plaintiff brought a bill against the defendant for an account, and, after, he brought [an action of] assumpsit at law for part of what was included in the bill, so he was ordered to make an election on which he would proceed. He elected going to law and an injunction as to proceeding here. On the trial at law, it appeared by the witnesses that there were accounts between them. The counsel, finding they had mistaken the action, never controverted the defendant's proof, but suffered a nonsuit. So the plaintiff moves to have leave to revive, which was opposed by the defendant, in regard the plaintiff had made his election.

But the Chancellor [LORD MACCLESFIELD] gave leave to revive and declared the only end of the injunction was that he should not proceed on both together, not that choosing one, in which he miscarries, should preclude his right. It is not a favor, but *ex debito justitiae*; he might bring a new bill. And is it not of justice to make the coming at right as expeditious and as little expensive as possible, for, on a new bill, after much time and money spent, you would be but where you are on a bill of revivor.

The case of one Collett was quoted as in point.

670

Green v. Arundel

(Ch. 1724–1726)

A court of equity will not grant relief where a claim is barred by the Statute of Limitations or the Statute of Non-claim.

Lincoln's Inn MS. Misc. 384, p. 264, pl. 2

26 November. At the Rolls.

In 1690, when the plaintiff was an infant about two years old, the defendant's grandfather entered, and he died seised during the plaintiff's infancy. After his death, the defendant's father entered and levied a fine, and he died seised. The bill was for an account of the profits and to have possession delivered.

Curia [JEKYLL]: Whoever enters on an infant's estate, whether he claims title or not, is but a trustee and shall account for what he received, even after the infant came of [age]. He is not barred by the statutes of limitations or fines,[1] the bill being filed within five years, nor by a descent cast because the trustee died seised of the estate loaded with the account.

He decreed an account of the profits and to deliver possession. He cited Gallop's Case, by Lord Somers.

N.B. 7 July 1726, Lord Chancellor KING reversed this decree and dismissed the bill with costs.

Lincoln's Inn MS. Misc. 384, p. 248

7 July 1726. Appeal from the Rolls.

Solicitor General [TALBOT], for the defendant: The decree is for an account of the profits from 1690, though two descents past, because the entry was on an infant's estate. *Regula*: there is no remedy for possession in equity where the entry is barred at law. Where a man enters without declaring in what right, he may be deemed a trustee for the infant. But here, the defendant claimed title. The fine levied six years after the plaintiff came of age is barred by the Statute of Limitations. The defendant entered as guardian for another infant, not for the plaintiff. It is the entry of another infant. It is no release against a discontinuance.

Mr. *Lutwyche*: The plaintiff's title is barred by the statutes of non-claim and limitations. Equity cannot release against them. The plaintiff's title is merely as heir at law. There is no impediment to bringing [an action of] ejectment.

Lord Chancellor [LORD KING]: This decree is pulling up the whole common law. In November 1690, Gabriel Green enters; he dies in 1701; a descent is cast. Gabriel, Jr., continues in possession, and he levies a fine in 1717, and, afterward, he dies. Then, there is another descent cast. It is a pretty great stretch for [a court of] equity to decree possession where he is barred at law. What are the statutes made for? Are they not to quiet possession? This is to s*et al*l the statutes aside. Can equity repeal a statute? Did ever this court relieve against a discontinuance?

The decree was reversed. The bill was dismissed as to an account of the profits etc. He ordered a deed of settlement to be produced and the plaintiff at liberty to bring [an action of] ejectment. And, the bill being filed soon after the fine levied where the defendant at law should insist on the non-claim, he reserved the consideration of it.

[1] Stat. 21 Jac. I, c. 16 (*SR*, IV, 1222–1223); Stat. 23 Eliz. I, c. 3 (*SR*, IV, 661–663).

671
Betlanjun's Creditors v. Graham

(Ch. 1724)

Where an estate is burdened with an equity and the owner sells it for a valuable consideration without notice, the bona fide *purchaser shall hold the estate clear of the equity, and the person entitled to the equity can have a remedy only against the vendor.*

Lincoln's Inn MS. Coxe 89, vol. 3, pt. 2, p. 4

28 November 1724.

One Betlanjun was seised in fee of the manors of A. and B. And he becoming greatly indebted, a bill in Chancery was brought against him by his several creditors. And such trees as were then timber growing on the said manors of A. and B. were decreed to be cut down and the money arising by the sale to be disposed of for the payment of his debts. Afterwards, Betlanjam sold the said manors to Mr. Graham, and, in the conveyance to Mr. Graham, the said timber trees were expected. About six years afterwards, Mr. Graham sold the said manors to Lady Lonsdale together with the woods, underwoods, etc. thereunto belonging. This sale appeared to be made in 1712 and, as appears from the depositions in the cause, without any express notice to the purchaser of the charge on the timber. And, from the evidence on both sides, there was little more than a bare probability that the purchaser had any notice of this encumbrance at all. Lady Lonsdale died, and her son and heir, the Lord Lonsdale, entered and enjoyed he said premises under the purchase. And, in 1722, the creditors of Betlanjun and their representatives brought their bill in Chancery against Mr. Graham and Lord Lonsdale and prayed the execution of the former decree and that the said timber might be cut down for their benefit.

Master of the Rolls [Jekyll]: If an estate be loaded with an equity and the owner of such estate sells it for a valuable consideration without notice, the purchaser shall hold the estate clear and the person entitled to equity shall have his remedy only against the vendor. This is a constant rule in equity, and there are multitudes of precedents founded upon it. He cited Cherry's Case,[1] where an equitable lien on an estate shall never affect a fair purchaser without notice. But suppose a tenant in fee simple makes a bill of sale of the timber on his estate and, afterwards, sells the same estate to a purchaser without notice; in that case, the vendee of the timber shall have it against the purchaser, for, by the sale, which is different from an equitable lien, the wood became a chattel and was severed from the land.

---

[1] *Ferrars v. Cherry* (1700), 2 Vernon 383, 23 E.R. 845, 1 Eq. Cas. Abr. 3, 331, 21 E.R. 830, 1081, British Library MS. Hargrave 80, f. 89, Chancery Cases *tempore* Harcourt, 211.

In this case, if it had been clearly proved that the Lady Lonsdale purchased without notice of the encumbrance, there could have been no doubt but she should have held the land discharged. But seeing there is no express proof given that she purchased without notice, it is reasonable that the value of the estate at the time of the purchase should be considered and that this point should be determined by the price given for the estate. From the evidence, it appears that the manor and appurtenances when sold exclusive of the timber were very near equal to the price paid for the estate and, if it can be proved the estate exclusive of the timber was worth the purchase money, it will be clear that it was not intended that the purchaser should have the timber. But as the value of the timber at the time of the purchase by Lady Lonsdale does not appear on the present proofs, it will be proper it should be enquired into by a jury.

And, accordingly, he decreed an issue to be tried of what value the timber exclusive of the rest of the manor was at the time of the purchase by Lady Lonsdale and another of what value the estate itself was at that time exclusive of the timber.

Note this was thought a hard decree, for, by this, the purchaser was put to prove a negative, *viz.* that he had not notice of the encumbrance, which is contrary to the other cases of this kind, where the rule has been that the other party should prove he had notice, and the reason upon which the decree is founded would extend to endanger all purchasers who have had cheap bargains.

N.B. Upon a rehearing before Lord Chancellor King, he directed another issue to be tried whether Lady Lonsdale purchased with or without notice of this encumbrance.

672

Birch v. Baker

(Ch. 1724)

The question in this case was whether the legacies in issue were revoked by a subsequent partition entered into by the testator of the subject of the legacy.

Lincoln's Inn MS. Misc. 12, p. 211

Michaelmas term 1724.

Penelope Baker, by will, gave all her share of the personal estate of her late brother, Thomas Lockington, to trustees upon trust to apply £200 for the use of her grandson Thomas Birch and, if residue of the money arising out of her share of the personal estate of the said Thomas Lockington, it was to be placed out at interest by the trustees for the benefit of her granddaughter, Elizabeth Birch, to be paid to her at twenty-one or marriage.

The bill was to have an execution of the trusts in the will. It happened that, after the making of the will, the parties entitled to Lockington's estate made a division between themselves, and the testatrix received in the greatest part of her share.

At the hearing, it being a question whether the legacies were revoked, it was sent to the Master to state what the share of Penelope Baker amounted to and when and in what manner it was paid in and to state the whole circumstances.

On the report, it appeared a division had been made and the testatrix had received £200 East India [Company] bonds, a £100 Exchequer bill, and £21 17s. 0d. in money, total £321 17s. 0d., and by orphan's stock, Bank stock, and [East] India [Company] stock £936 8s. 8d. transferred to her.

[Other reports of this case: Mosely 373, 25 E.R. 447.]

673

Hudson v. Wanley

(Ch. 1724)

A writ of ne exeat regno *lies to force a defendant to make discovery to a judgment creditor of the location of his property.*

Lincoln's Inn MS. Misc. 12, p. 135

19 December 1724.

The plaintiff [Sir Roger Hudson] having obtained a verdict against the defendant upon a contract for stock at £600 percent and the defendant having brought a writ of error, which was expired, and threatening to go beyond the sea, the plaintiff brought his bill suggesting this matter and the [defendant] had made over his estate to trustees on purpose to prevent the plaintiff's taking out a [writ of] *elegit* and the plaintiff's having obtained a [writ of] *ne exeat regno* and taken the defendant upon it, the defendant now moved to discharge the *ne exeat*, it being never known that this writ had been granted in a case of this nature, for, though the bill prayed relief, yet no equity was suggested and the bill, in effect, was to pervert the course of the law, for, at law, the plaintiff could not take the body in execution and then extend the land. But, if this method was to prevail, the body, in effect, would be taken in execution and the land notwithstanding might be extended.

But Lord Chancellor [Lord Macclesfield] would not discharge the writ but continued it until the answer and further order. He said, if the defendant had made over his estate, it might be extended. However, if the defendant was going beyond the sea, he thought it reasonable that he should discover where his estate was, the plaintiff being entitled to have that discovery from him.

674

Anonymous

(Ch. 1724)

Exceptions to a Master's report taxing court costs can be made without leave of court.

Lincoln's Inn MS. Misc. 12, p. 136

Eodem die [19 December 1724].

Upon a motion to discharge exceptions to a Master's report which had taxed costs, the Register informed the court that an order had been made that no exceptions should be put in to such a report without leave of the court.

Lord Chancellor [Lord Macclesfield] would not discharge the exceptions but ordered the party to pay all the money at which the bill was taxed, except what was included in the exceptions.

675

Kinaston v. Delahay

(Ch. 1725)

Pending a dispute over a decedent's estate, the Court of Chancery can order the assets of the estate to be paid into the Chancery for safekeeping.

Lincoln's Inn MS. Misc. 380, pt. 2, p. 29

12 January 1724/25. *Coram* Sir Joseph Jekyll, Baron Gilbert, and Judge Raymond, Commissioners of the Great Seal.

A motion was made in behalf of the plaintiff that the defendants might bring into court the whole personal estate and securities of Delahay, deceased, who was the husband of the defendant Delahay. The plaintiff, by his bill and also by an affidavit to support the motion, set forth that, on the balance of an account between him and the deceased, who died intestate, there was due to himself upwards of £14,000.

The widow Delahay upon his death, immediately took possession of his personal estate and securities and endeavored to get letters of administration, but was opposed by the plaintiff as the chief creditor of the intestate. And the question concerning the administration is still depending in the spiritual court.

The defendant had put in her answer and acknowledged considerable effects were come to her hands, but insisted that, by the papers and writings of the intestate, she could not find that anything was due to the plaintiff, that it appeared by divers receipts under the hand of the plaintiff, which she found among her husband's papers, that the plaintiff had received on account many sums of money from the intestate amounting to upward of £70,000, but the account being not liquidated, she could not set forth what was due of either side and insisted that she was a widow and, as such, entitled to the administration and, therefore, to retain the effects in her hand in order to pay the intestate's debts.

The COMMISSIONERS were all of opinion that the estate ought to be brought into court to be secured for such persons as should be entitled. And the Case of Powis v. Andrews[1] was cited, where, pending a suit in the spiritual court concerning the validity of the will, a bill was brought in this court in order to compel the executors, who had got the personal estate into their hands, to bring it into this court for security, there being no power in the spiritual court to lay hold of and secure it during the suit, and so it was ordered by Lord Chancellor Parker and confirmed by the House of Lords on appeal upon 7th February 1723/24.

676

Mills v. Toll

(Ch. 1724 x 1725)

A legacy to an infant must be paid directly to the infant and not to his father.

British Library MS. Hargrave 83, p. 39

An executor pays an infant's legacy to his father. By the Master of the Rolls [JEKYLL], payment of a legacy to an infant is good, if to his own hands, but not good to his father. Between Michaelmas and Hilary terms 1724.

677

Holt v. Tyrrell

(Ch. 1725)

Where a demurrer is sustained upon a reason not alleged in the written demurrer, the demurrant will not be awarded court costs.

British Library MS. Hargrave 83, p. 40

Monday, 25 January, at the Rolls, SIR JOSEPH JEKYLL sitting alone upon pleas and demurrers.

Tyrrell brought an original bill to set aside a voluntary settlement made by Mrs. Brewton in which she had reserved a power to revoke the uses by the consent of Sir Cloberry Holt and Colonel Tyrrell. She, without their consent, cancelled one part of the settlement. Upon this, Colonel Tyrrell brought his bill *inter alia* to have the counterpart delivered up. Holt brought his cross-bill against

[1] *Andrews v. Powys* (1724), 2 Brown P.C. 504, 1 E.R. 1094, 2 Eq. Cas. Abr. 377, 421, 22 E.R. 321, 358, note also 1 Lee 242, 161 E.R. 90.

Tyrrell and one Aldworth, a niece of Mrs. Brewton, suggesting that she persuaded Mrs. Brewton to cancel that part of the settlement and to make a will in favor of Tyrrell but showing that both by the will and by the settlement Mrs. Aldworth was to have the same benefit, *viz.* £200 *per annum* for life or thereabouts. To this bill, Aldworth demurred and showed for cause of demurrer that she was not a party concerned in interest and might be examined upon the hearing of the cause. The matter was strenuously debated by many counsel.

My Lord Commissioner [Sir Joseph Jekyll] allowed the demurer, but not for the cause assigned. And therefore, he made the defendant who demurred pay costs according to the printed rules. The cause for which he allowed the demurer as cause assigned *ore tenus* was because the plaintiff had no equity to pray relief upon against Aldworth, for the cancelling of one part of the settlement was no manner of prejudice. And though it was urged that this contrivance and fraud of the defendant Aldworth was the cause and foundation of the original bill and that this was so gross upon the circumstances of this case and the condition of Mrs. Brewton, who was then struck with a palsy and had lost the use of her speech, that she might for her contrivance be decreed to pay costs upon the hearing. But this not being charged in the cross-bill as the cause of the suit, he said he would not take notice of it as such and said, as to any discovery of fraud, that might be had by examining her upon interrogatories.

[Other reports of this case: 1 Barnardiston K.B. 12, 94 E.R. 8.]

678

Fryar v. Vernon

(Ch. 1725)

The Court of Chancery cannot grant a writ of sequestration to be executed outside of its own geographical jurisdiction.

British Library MS. Hargrave 83, p. 41

Thursday, 28 January 1724[/25]. In Chancery, before Sir Joseph Jekyll and Sir Robert Raymond, Lords Commissioners.

Serjeant *Chesshyre* moved for a [writ of] sequestration into Ireland for want of an answer. He urged the admiralty case where a judgment was given in Friesland[1] and the governor there requested execution here. And likewise the case where a sequestration was moved for here against one in the plantations, which was under the deliberation of Lord Macclesfield when he left the seals.

1 [In margin:] The Serjeant's mistake for Ireland.

The two Lords Commissioners denied the motion and said that the case of the Lord Arglass[1] in King Charles II's time might perhaps lead the serjeant's client into the hopes of obtaining this sequestration. But that was a case of an extraordinary kind and there was the king's letter to the Lord Lieutenant to compel the party to come in upon the process. And those cases which stand upon the law of nations, as the Ireland case, are not to be compared to this, and it is a matter that would require very mature deliberation, whether the process of this court ought to be enforced in the plantations. They have been of great advantage to this nation as they are a kind of asylum to indigent persons. Besides, the sovereignty of the king and council over them would be concerned in such a proceeding, and that case was never determined by the late Lord Chancellor.

Lincoln's Inn MS. Misc. 380, pt. 2, p. 30

28 January 1724/25. Sir John Fryar v. Vernon.

The defendant not having put in his answer and all the process to a sequestration being gone through, upon an affidavit that the defendant had no goods nor estate in England but had considerable effects in Ireland, Serjeant *Chesshyre* moved for a [writ of] sequestration to Ireland against him and cited a case where Lord Chancellor Parker did grant a sequestration to North Carolina upon an affidavit of that kind.

Sir Joseph Jekyll, First Commissioner, said he did not see what authority this court had to send sequestrations to Ireland. There were courts of justice and a Chancellor there, and he did not know how a sequestration could be executed there under the authority of this court. He said that it had been attempted to get sequestrations to the plantations, but he thought they could not be justified upon several accounts, that it was the policy of our government to let the plantations be a kind of asylum for insolvent persons here, that courts of justice were there as well as here, and the law was open, and the plaintiff might have the benefit of it there, that to grant such sequestrations seemed to be most inconsistent with that sovereignty which the king in council has over the plantations in hearing and determining the causes that come from thence by appeal, that a bill was some time ago brought into the House of Commons in order to subject the plantations to processes from England, but it was thought so disadvantageous and unpolitic that it was thrown out.

Judge Raymond, another Commissioner, was of the same opinion.

And the motion was denied.

---

[1] *Earl of Arglasse v. Muschamp* (1682), 1 Vernon 135, 23 E.R. 369, 1 Eq. Cas. Abr. 133, 21 E.R. 937, note also 1 Vernon 75, 237, 23 E.R. 322, 438, 2 Chancery Reports 266, 21 E.R. 675.

Lincoln's Inn MS. Misc. 12, p. 138

Serjeant *Chesshyre* moved for a [writ of] sequestration into Ireland against the defendant, who was in contempt for not answering, to sequester his real and personal estate in that kingdom. And he cited the Case of Fuller and Hamilton, *quod vide ante* 104.[1] But, upon the Lords Commissioners enquiring of the Register what My Lord Chancellor did in that case, he said that the Lord Chancellor said he would consider of it, and the sequestration in the present case was denied.

Commissioner JEKYLL said that, in Ireland, they have laws and courts of their own. And he believed no court at law here would make a rule to execute a judgment of that court in Ireland.

To what purpose is a motion made when a plaintiff who brings a bill here appears to be in Ireland that he may give security to answer costs unless it is because he is not amenable by the process of this court.

As to the case that has been cited, the Register says My Lord Chancellor would not grant a [writ of] sequestration to the Governor of Carolina, but he said he would consider of it. And, indeed, it is a matter which deserves consideration. The king in council has a sovereign jurisdiction in all the plantations, and, if this court should send sequestrations to the governors there, I do not know whether it would not be an infringement of His Majesty's jurisdiction.

Select Cases *tempore* King 5, 25 E.R. 191

A motion was made for a particular sequestration against the defendant's lands in Ireland, she having stood out the process of contempt here. And he relied on the case of Hamilton and Pollard, in July or October last,[2] where, on like motion for a particular sequestration to North Carolina, the Chancellor said it might be right, but the method should be well considered, as its being to be a precedent. And he inclined it should be to sequestrators.

But the *Register*, on being asked, said, that sequestration never went.

Master of the Rolls [JEKYLL]: What leads you into this motion was the case of the Earl of Arglasse v. Muschamp, 1 Vern. 75, where it was denied by the court; but after application was made to the king and a letter was sent to the Governor of Ireland, but never heard of anything else of that sort. It would be very odd that the process of this court should have anything to assist it. I remember that a bill was brought into Parliament to extend judgments to the plantations, but it was rejected. But, as to the plantations, it is particularly odd as it affects the king's sovereignty in Council over them. But what makes it clear to demonstration that it should not go is this, where a defendant to a bill, whose usual residence is in Ireland, happens to be here, he is obliged to give security,

---

1 *Hamilton v. Pollard* (Ch. 1724), see above, Case No. 649.

2 *Hamilton v. Pollard* (Ch. 1724), see above, Case No. 649.

which makes it plain he is not amenable to this court, for, if he was, that precaution would be unnecessary.

So a particular sequestration was denied, but a general one of course was granted.

[Other reports of this case: 9 Modern 124, 88 E.R. 355, *sub nom.* Fryer v. Bernard, 2 Peere Williams 261, 24 E.R. 722, 2 Eq. Cas. Abr. 82, 711, 22 E.R. 71, 597.]

679

Skurray v. Web

(Ch. 1725)

Interest does not accrue until the principal money is payable.

In the administration of a decedent's estate, a legatee has priority over an executor who is entitled to receive court costs.

Lincoln's Inn MS. Misc. 12, p. 141

3 February 1724[/25].

[The argument was] upon a special report of the Master, to whom it was referred by an interlocutory order to state what was due to one Elizabeth Singer, a legatee in the will of Henry Bodeley for £500 for principal and interest, which legacy was given to Elizabeth, who was the granddaughter of the testator, to be paid immediately after the death of Mary Singer, her mother, if she survived her mother and attained the age of twenty-one years and, if she died before, the legacy is given over. And, in the will, there is a direction that Mary Singer, the mother, should receive the interest of the £500 during her life to her own use.

And, she dying in 1702 and Elizabeth, her daughter, not attaining twenty-one until 1714, the question was from what time the interest should commence, whether from the death of the mother or from the time that Elizabeth attained twenty-one.

And the Master of the Rolls [JEKYLL] was of the opinion the interest could not commence but from the time it became payable.

Note the bill was brought by the residuary legatee against the executor, and an account was decreed. And £1330, which were all the assets, was brought before the Master. And, upon the hearing, costs were reserved, and it was insisted that the plaintiff, who was the executor of the residuary legatee and had revived the suit, ought to have his costs out of the £1330 preferable to the payment of the legacy, Elizabeth Singer being no party to the suit and the residuary legatee having been at all the expense of recovering the money from the executor.

But *per curiam* [JEKYLL], the legatee must be paid in the first place. Had she brought her bill, she would have been decreed her legacy with costs.

680

Anonymous

(Ch. 1725)

Where a bill to redeem a mortgage is dismissed in favor of the defendant-creditor, it, being res judicata, *is the equivalent of a foreclosure of the mortgage.*

Lincoln's Inn MS. Misc. 380, pt. 2, p. 5, pl. 1

4 February 1724/25. Upon a motion.

Sir Joseph Jekyll, Master of the Rolls, said that a dismission of a bill to redeem was by operation of law a foreclosure.

I suppose he meant that, in case a new bill to redeem was brought, the former dismission might be pleaded in bar.

681

Anonymous

(Ch. 1725)

A creditor can sue in equity to foreclose a mortgage and sue at common law to recover the debt at the same time.

Lincoln's Inn MS. Misc. 380, pt. 2, p. 5, pl. 2

Eodem die [4 February 1724/25].

The plaintiff's bill was to foreclose. And he, at the same time, brought an action of covenant for the mortgage money, upon which the defendant moved for an injunction to stop the proceedings upon the action of covenant for that the plaintiff ought not to proceed both at law and in this court. And he offered to consent to give possession of the land to the plaintiff as soon as a decree upon the hearing should be made for him. But the Master of the Rolls [Jekyll] said the plaintiff might proceed in both and he would not take away the remedy which the law gave him, and he denied the motion.

682

Adams v. Meyrick

(Ch. 1725)

Normally, a decedent's debts are paid out of the decedent's personal estate. However, in this case, it was expressly devised that the debts be paid out of the real estate.

Lincoln's Inn MS. Misc. 12, p. 145

19 February 1724/25.

A.B., by will, gives several pecuniary legacies, and then he devises lands to trustees and their heirs upon trust that they 'do and shall' by sale or mortgage of the lands pay all his debts and his said legacies. Then, he proceeds and gives all his goods and chattels at his house in B. to his wife. And he gives all the residue of his personal estate to the defendant.

The question was whether the residuary legatee should have the personal estate exempt from the payment of the debts and legacies or not.

It was insisted that, though here is a fund provided for the payment of debts etc., yet that was only intended as a provision in case the personal estate should happen to be deficient, that by the residue of his personal estate must be understood the residue after payment of debts and legacies, that here were no negative words to exempt the personal estate, and, therefore, the personal estate ought to be liable according to the Case of Garraway and Christ's Hospital.[1]

But notwithstanding what was insisted on, it was decreed the debts and legacies should be paid out of the land.

The Master of the Rolls [JEKYLL] said there was something in this case different from the former cases. Here is an express direction that the trustees shall mortgage or sell for the payment of his debts and legacies. The words 'do and shall' are imperative and mandatory and such stronger than when lands by a will are only charged or made liable to the payment of debts or legacies. Why, then, when he has made this provision for the payment of his debts and legacies, he goes on to dispose of his personal estate and gives some specific goods to his wife and then immediately follows the devise of the residue, by which it seemed plain the testator meant the residue of all his personal estate besides what he had given to his wife.

Lincoln's Inn MS. Misc. 380, pt. 2, p. 38, pl. 1

19 February 1724/25. At the Rolls.

A. makes her will and gives several particular legacies, one after another, and then goes on, 'I devise my estate in F. to B. and C. and their heirs in trust by sale or mortgage to pay all my debts, legacies, and funeral expenses. And what

---

1 *Christ's Hospital v. Gallway* (Ch. c. 1714), see above, Case No. 5.

shall remain I give to D.' She goes on, 'I give all my goods, chattels, and household stuff which shall be at my dwelling house at the time of my death to E. and all the rest and residue of my personal estate, I give to G., whom I make my executor.'

It was a question at the hearing whether the personal estate should be first applied to the payment of her debts and legacies or whether they should be discharged wholly out of the real estate devised.

The Master of the Rolls [JEKYLL] said, where debts and legacies are charged upon a real estate, if it is by way of a charge only, the personal estate shall be applied in the first place to pay them unless there are express negative words that they shall not because such a charge is only in the nature of a further security. But, in this case, the devise is more than a charge. It is an express giving away of the estate to trustees and declaring the trust of it to be to pay all her debts and legacies, which shows a particular intention that the real estate should be appropriated to that purpose. It is an express command of the trustees to pay the debts and legacies. And there is nothing in the manner of giving the personal estate that shows an intention that it should be likewise chargeable with them, for the words 'rest and residue', though relative in themselves, yet they appear here plainly to relate to the precedent disposition of her household goods. And he decreed accordingly.

[Other reports of this case: 1 Eq. Cas. Abr. 271, 21 E.R. 1040.]

683

Wilmot v. Brand

(Ch. 1725)

Depositions taken in the lifetime of a testator are not admissible in evidence against his executor where the lawsuit was revived against the executor.

Lincoln's Inn MS. Misc. 12, p. 146

22 February 1724/25.

It was insisted by the counsel for one of the defendants, and so agreed by the court, that his testator having put in an answer to the original bill and dying after a replication filed and before publication passed and after passing publication the cause is revived against the executor and heard as against him upon the bill and answer, no depositions taken in the cause could be read against him or his testator.

684

Duke of Buckinghamshire v. Ward

(Ch. 1725)

Evidence of matters not in issue will be disregarded.

1 Cooper *tempore* Cottenham 533, 47 E.R. 986

March 1724[/25]. Edmund, duke of Buckinghamshire and Normanby, an infant, by his guardian, and David, earl of Portmore, Charles, earl of Orrery, George, lord Willoughby de Brooke, Thomas, lord Trevor, Allan, lord Bathurst, and Patrick Garden v. John Ward.

John, duke of Buckinghamshire and Normanby, in 1706, demised to the defendant a certain estate and alum mines and bargained and sold to him all the stock of alum then upon the premises. But there was an exception of certain quantities of alum in the storehouses ready to be shipped, which, if the same should come into the defendant's possession when he entered upon the premises, were to be immediately delivered to the duke's agent. There were numerous covenants in the lease, and amongst them was a covenant that the lessee should, at the end of the lease, deliver to the duke or his heirs various quantities of alum. And there was a reference to a schedule for ascertaining the quantities.

The Duke John being dead, the suit was instituted by his infant heir and the trustees and executors under his will for a performance of different covenants contained in the lease, including the covenant aforesaid. And it was insisted that the quantity of 315 tons of alum, being one of the quantities mentioned in the schedule, was one of the quantities to be delivered by the lessee at the end of the lease.

The defendant, by his answer, admitted the lease and the schedule, but he contended that, according to the true construction thereof, the quantity of 315 tons of alum was not one of the quantities that he was bound to deliver at the end of the lease.

The cause came on to be heard before the Lords Commissioners of the Great Seal, Sir Geoffrey Gilbert and Sir Robert Raymond, on the 2d of March 1724[/25], when the defendant produced in evidence a certificate of one Newton dated 11th April 1706 and an order of the late duke endorsed on such certificate dated 30th April 1706, by which it appeared that the 315 tons of alum mentioned in the schedule was one of the quantities of alum in the storehouse ready to be shipped and was part of the alum excepted as above mentioned and that such alum having as was anticipated come into the possession of the defendant at the time when he entered upon the premises, it was, as it had been agreed, immediately after delivered to the duke's agent. It was said that the certificate and order were not insisted upon by the defendant in his answer, the same having been lost and not discovered until after his answer was put in and the commission for the examination of witnesses was executed and the defendant having but an imperfect memory of the same.

The counsel for the plaintiffs objected that such certificate and order had not been put in issue by the defendant in his answer and suggested that, if, as was alleged, the same was not discovered until the answer was put in and witnesses were examined, of which allegation, however, there was no proof, the defendant ought to have applied to be at liberty to put the certificate and order in issue, either by amending his answer stating such certificate and order or by some other mode so as to give the plaintiffs notice thereof. And the plaintiffs' counsel said that the pretense of the quantity of alum in question having been delivered to the duke so many years ago, which was only to be delivered at the expiration of the lease, was a very great surprise upon the plaintiffs.

The LORDS COMMISSIONERS, having inspected the certificate and order, observed that it seemed to be erased in several places. And they said that it was impossible that the defendant could, as was suggested, have forgotten the delivery of this quantity of alum, supposing that the certificate and order had been lost. And yet nothing was insisted upon by the answer touching the delivery of this quantity of alum, but, on the contrary, it was insisted that it never was intended to be delivered. No regard ought under the circumstances to be had to the order and certificate. The defendant was decreed, at the expiration of the lease, to leave upon the premises 315 tons of alum, the quantity aforesaid.

The certificate and order, or at least the latter, turned out to be a forgery.[1] Although the Lords Commissioners said that no regard ought to be paid to the certificate and order, yet it appears on reference to the Registrar's book to be included in the exhibits that were read at the hearing of the cause. Reg. Lib. 1724 A, f. 191.

There was an appeal from this decree to the House of Lords. It was heard on the 4th May 1725, when the decree was affirmed.

[Affirmed on appeal: 3 Brown P.C. 581, 1 E.R. 1511.]

---

1 *Rex v. Ward* (1727), 1 Barnardiston K.B. 10, 94 E.R. 7, 2 Strange 747, 93 E.R. 824, 2 Lord Raymond 1461, 92 E.R. 451, 3 Lord Raymond 358, 92 E.R. 732.

685

Le Bass v. Green

(Ch. 1725)

Where a legacy for a specific purpose is partially performed before the testator's death, the partial payment is an ademption pro tanto.

Lincoln's Inn MS. Misc. 12, p. 147, pl. 1

4 March 1724/25. Master of the Rolls [JEKYLL].

Charles Le Bass, the plaintiff's cousin, gave to the plaintiff £200 to put him out to some business or employment, and, about a year and half after the making of his will, the testator put the plaintiff out an apprentice to a woolen draper and gave £80 with him.

It was decreed this £80 was to be a satisfaction *pro tanto* of the legacy.

686

Russell v. De la Rose

(Ch. 1725)

A court-ordered partition of land will bind an infant.

A court-ordered partition of land will be enforced by an order for mutual conveyances.

Lincoln's Inn MS. Misc. 12, p. 147, pl. 2

Eodem die [4 March 1725].

The bill was for a partition and that a commission might issue to set out each parties' share and that, afterwards, they might convey to each other. And one of the defendants interested in the estate was an infant.

The Master of the Rolls [JEKYLL] was of the opinion that the partition would bind the infant and that, therefore, he was not to be allowed six months after he came of age to show cause against the partition.

But then he doubted at first whether he should decree the parties to convey to each other after the lands were set out and divided by the commissioners, he thinking it not necessary. But, upon further consideration, he changed his opinion, for that a partition in equity would not vest a legal estate in the respective parties.

And, there being a question between the defendants whether the infant or Mr. De la Rose and his wife were entitled to a moiety of the estate and there being a suit depending to settle the right, he ordered that the infant, when of age, if he had the right, should convey to the plaintiffs what should be set out for them and, if not, that the other defendants should convey to them.

687

Ex parte Harward

(Ch. 1725)

The Court of Chancery can direct that a lunatic's money be invested in real estate and that such real estate shall be treated as personal property upon the lunatic's death.

Lincoln's Inn MS. Misc. 380, pt. 2, p. 38, pl. 2

17 March 1724/25.

Dr. Harward, having married the daughter of a lunatic, who had a considerable sum of money undisposed of, and, being made the committee of the lunatic, petitioned the court that the money might be laid out in the purchase of certain lands which he proposed for that purpose. The court having referred the consideration of it to the Master, who reported that the purchase of it would be for the interest of the lunatic's estate, it was now upon this report and a petition for that purpose ordered that the money should be so laid out in the name of Harward and that the estate so purchased should go in case of the death of the lunatic in the same manner as the personal estate would go.

688

Anonymous

(Ch. 1725)

A court of equity can set aside a commission of bankruptcy that was wrongfully taken out.

Lincoln's Inn MS. Misc. 380, pt. 2, p. 39

17 March 1724/25.

Upon a petition to supersede a commission of bankruptcy on account that the person was no bankrupt and the creditor taking out the commission was not a creditor for so much money as the Statute[1] requires, the court ordered an issue at law to try whether the commission was rightly sued out.

---

[1] Stat. 5 Geo. I, c. 24.

689

Yorke v. Lakeward

(Ch. 1725)

The statute that allows a sheriff to charge a fee for receiving money does not apply to other officers.

Lincoln's Inn MS. Misc. 12, p. 150

17 March 1724[/25].

The defendant, being decreed to pay a sum of money, was taken up upon a [writ of] attachment for not performing the decree. And he paid the money into the hands of Mr. Benson, the Secondary of the P. Compter. And, thereupon, he was discharged out of custody.

The plaintiff applies to Mr. Benson for the money, and, he refusing to pay it unless the plaintiff would allow him poundage, the plaintiff, thereupon, carries on the process against the defendant, who complains thereof to the court.

And the court was of the opinion the plaintiff was regular in his proceedings, for he was not bound to go to the sheriff, but only to call for a return of the writ.

Upon this, the defendant pays the money to the plaintiff and then petitions that Mr. Benson might re-pay him the money which he had paid into his hands. Mr. Benson insisting on poundage, the late Lord Chancellor [LORD MACCLESFIELD] ordered precedents to be searched. And now it came on again before the Lords Commissioners [to Hold the Great Seal].

Mr. Benson could produce no precedent where poundage had ever been allowed the sheriff upon any process issuing out of this court. However, it was insisted that a [writ of] attachment after a decree in equity was in the nature of an execution upon a judgment at law and, though it was not within the letter, yet it was within the reason and equity of the Statute[1] which gives the sheriff poundage.

On the other hand, the plaintiff produced a precedent out of the Court of Exchequer where that court in a like case had declared that Mr. Benson, who now insists on the same allowance here, was not entitled to poundage.

And of that opinion were the LORDS COMMISSIONERS, and they ordered Mr. Benson to re-pay the money with costs to be taxed by the Master.

---

1 Stat. 29 Eliz. I, c. 4 (*SR*, IV, 769).

690

Stephens v. Colton

(Ch. 1725)

In this case, it was clearly not the intent of the testator that the plaintiff's legacy should be forfeited for marrying without permission, she not being related to the testator, but being his former housekeeper.

Where there is a gift over in cases of legacies out of real estate upon a condition of not marrying without consent, such condition is always held good.

Lincoln's Inn MS. Misc. 12, p. 152

26 March 1725. Stephens *et ux.* v. Colton and Harle, executors of Richard Fountaine *et al.*

Richard Fountaine, by a will dated 15 July 1721, amongst many other legacies, gave to the plaintiff's wife, [who was] then living with him, £630 and £20 more to buy her mourning in recompense of her great care of him and his wife. And he made the defendants executors. And he gave the residuum of his estate equally between the plaintiff's wife and a great number of other persons, relations of the testator, in all thirty-three, in which will, there was a proviso that, if the plaintiff's wife, during the testator's life, married, she should not have any part of the surplus or be deemed as one of the residuary legatees. And he declared his will to be that, if any of his residuary legatees should happen to marry before a dividend was made of the remainder of his estate without the consent and approbation of his executors first had, then the share or shares of those so marrying should be divided amongst the rest, share and share alike, and that, if any of the female legatees married without having a jointure equivalent to the legacy given, unless with the executors consent and approbation, such legacy, if not before paid, should go to his residuary legatees, share and share alike.

The plaintiff is a freeman of London and, by trade, a mercer at Enfield, where the testator lived. And, in the testator's lifetime, he made his address to his wife at the testator's invitation. And, after the testator's death, the plaintiffs applied to the defendant Harle for his consent, who approved of the match, but said, in regard the plaintiff was a man in trade, no settlement could be expected from him, but he thought it reasonable the fortune should be settled for her benefit. And he believed the other executor would consent on those terms, to which the plaintiff made answer he thought it sufficient only to settle so much of the fortune as should arise out of the residuum, for, he being a freeman, his wife and children, if any, would have a provision out of his personal estate, and he desired the defendant Harle to write to the other executor and acquaint him with the proposals made by the plaintiff, which the defendant accordingly did on the 15th March 1721[/22], Colton living in York. And the same day, he paid the plaintiff's wife £50 in part of her legacy. And, on the 17th of March, the defendant received a letter from Colton, wherein he insisted all the fortune should be settled, without which he did not think that he and the defendant Harle performed their trust. But before this letter was received, the plaintiffs married without any other consent of the executors than as aforesaid.

The plaintiffs' bill was to be paid the legacy and the share of the surplus.

The defendants, by their answer, say they never gave their consent in any other manner than as aforesaid and that, if the plaintiff will consent to settle the whole fortune, they still approve of the marriage.

The question was if the legacy and the share of the surplus bequeathed to the plaintiff's wife or either of them is forfeited or not.

For the plaintiffs, it was insisted that the plaintiff Christian was thirty years of age at the time when the will was made and she was in no manner of degree related to the testator and that the conditions in the will were not intended nor ought to be construed to extend to her, but only to such of the female legatees and residuary legatees as were related to the testator and were under age and the rather for that the testator, on the plaintiff's making his addresses at first, did not insist on any settlement.

The Master of the Rolls [Jekyll] took time to consider of this cause. And this day [26 March 1725], he gave his opinion that neither the legacy nor the share of the surplus bequeathed to the plaintiff Christian was forfeited. He said, among the particular legatees, one is a widow, some are married women, one in doubt whether married or not. There is a conditional consent if the whole fortune was settled. These terms [are] such the court may impose on a husband when he comes for the fortune.

I incline to think that might make it a sufficient consent. But supposing that one or both executors had not consented, yet I am of the opinion that the particular legacy is not forfeited. It is impossible to annex the condition to all the legacies; one a widow, several married, one doubtful. Married women must necessarily be excepted. The plaintiff was above twenty-one. The testator had some imagination of her marrying in his lifetime.

The £650 is given for a just recompense for her services. The proviso about her marrying in his lifetime shows his desire that she should continue with him until death, and it is not to be presumed that he intended to cease to be just to her if she married after, though without the consent of his executors.

The proviso [is], 'if any of my female legatees' etc., it shall go to the residuaries, i.e. it shall sink into the surplus, which is no more than the law says, and, therefore, the legacy in this case is not given over.

If a creditor came here for a debt out of assets, this court might as well judge of that debt differently from the courts of common law, as in cases of a legacy out of the personal estate. It could determine differently from the spiritual courts, who have the like original jurisdiction in testamentary cases.

In the civil law, there is no distinction in cases of conditions annexed to legacies relating to marriage, whether given over or not, except in one case, when given to a religious house.

These conditions, though of use to particular families, yet are hurtful to the public. And on that reason, the rescriptions of the [Roman] emperors are founded.

In cases of legacies out of real estate upon a condition of not marrying without consent, if given over, this court has always held such conditions good, because it is as much the intention of the testator that the person to whom [it is] given over should have it if the condition is broken as the first legatee if [it is] performed.

The £650 comes out of the personal estate and is not forfeited. Her share of the residuum is not forfeited. The condition annexed to her share of not marrying in his lifetime is not broken.

The general proviso relating to the residuary legatees could not relate to all, some married, some of age, others infants. The testator intended to comprehend infants only under this proviso.

No time is appointed by the will for the payment of particular legacies or of the residuum, except in cases of infants, who are not to have their share until twenty-one. As to the others, no time is appointed, but they are to take their shares immediately.

Before a dividend be made is before their legacies become payable. A dividend ought to be made to them that are of age immediately; to infants, not until twenty-one.

691

Rider v. Wager

(Ch. 1725)

A legacy of a debt due to the testator is revoked when the testator later receives the payment of the debt in his lifetime.

Lincoln's Inn MS. Misc. 12, p. 208

5 April 1725. Sir Barnham Rider and Dame Susannah, his wife, plaintiffs; Sir Charles Wager *et al.*, defendants.

James Littleton, by will, gives to his godson James Masters £500, part of the money owing by Sir Harcourt Masters, and he gives the rest of the money so owing him amongst the rest of Sir Harcourt's children, share and share alike, the whole to remain in his hands for the benefit of his said godson and the rest of Sir Harcourt's children until they should be capable of receiving and discharging the same. And the legacies and shares of any of them dying before such time were to go to the survivors equally. And, by a codicil, he gives to his brother, James Batson, the money owing by him.

When the will was made, it was proved in the cause, there was £1121 16s. 3d. due to the testator from Sir Harcourt Masters. And he swears in his deposition that, after the making of the will, there were separate accounts settled, and, upon the last of those accounts, which was settled in June 1722 (and the will was made 13 June 1716), there was a balance of £558 13s. 2d. due from him, which he paid to the testator at his desire and request.

James Masters, the godson, died in the testator's lifetime.

At the time of the codicil, there was due from the defendant Batson to the testator upwards of £200, being the remainder of a debt of £300 due on bond, and, after the making of the codicil, the defendant (as was proved in the cause) had voluntary paid in the whole debt to the testator's receiver. But the testator, when he gave the receiver the bond, told him that, if the defendant paid in the money, he should take no interest.

The question was whether the receiving in of these debts was an ademption of the legacies.

For the plaintiffs, it was admitted that the £500 given to James Masters being a particular sum given out of a debt if he had survived the testator, the legacy would have subsisted though the whole debt was paid in. But, as to the residue of the debt, it was a different case, for the debt being paid in, there was nothing due at the testator's death and, consequently, nothing could pass to the other children.

To this, it was answered that there was no difference between giving the whole debt to one or giving part of a debt to one and the residue to another, and, if, in the first case, the receiving in the whole debt was no evidence of the testator's intention to revoke the legacy, the reason was as strong that it could not be so in the other.

But the Lord Chancellor [Lord King] was of opinion that the legacy of the residue of the debt given to the other children, the debt being paid in at the testator's desire, was extinguished, for the testator having directed that the whole should remain in Sir Harcourt Master's hands for the benefit of the godson and the rest of the children until they should be capable of receiving and discharging the same and, he having called in the money, it was an evidence of his intention to revoke the legacy.

As to what was insisted on, that the children were entitled to the whole debt, in regard that James Masters died in the testator's lifetime and the testator had directed that the legacies and shares of any of them dying before they were capable of discharging the same should go to the survivors equally, Lord Chancellor [Lord King] said what never vested could not go over. And he thought, if a legacy is given to A., another to B., and another to C. and there is a direction that, if any of them die under twenty-one, his legacy shall go to the survivors and one of them dies in the testator's lifetime, his legacy is lapsed and shall not go over, for it never vested in the legatee.

As to the debt given to Batson, Lord Chancellor [Lord King] was of the opinion that his legacy was also extinguished, for, he being the debtor, the giving him the debt was in the nature of a release. And it would be so if these were assets. It is true it is not so in respect of creditors if there are not assets sufficient to pay the debts, but, otherwise, it is if there are assets.

He decreed the legacies both to the children and the defendant Batson to be extinct.

In this case were cited Pawlet's Case in Raymond; Smith v. Orme, Vernon's reports; and Birch v. Baker, which was heard at the Rolls.[1]

In the principal case, Mr. Littleton had by his will given to his two daughters, Susan and Jane, and their heirs six houses in London. After the will, Mr. Littleton married his daughter Susan to the plaintiff and, by articles before that marriage, covenanted to settle a moiety of those houses to the use of himself for life, then to the plaintiffs for their lives, remainder for the benefit of the younger children of their two bodies. The testator died before any settlement was made. And the question was whether the articles were not a revocation of that moiety of the houses which were given to the plaintiff Susan by the will or whether she should have an equal share with her sister in the other moiety of the houses.

Lord Chancellor [Lord King]: The articles are no revocation in law, but they are so in equity. And so far as the articles are not inconsistent with the will, the will must stand.

If a man, by will, devises lands to A. and his heirs and, afterwards, grants those lands to B. for life, it is a revocation *pro tanto* only. And, therefore, since the testator has agreed to settle a moiety of the houses by the articles, so the plaintiffs must have a moiety according to the articles and half of the other moiety by the will.

And, accordingly, it was so decreed.

British Library MS. Hargrave 83, p. 45, pl. 2

Sir Barnham Rider v. Sir Charles Wager.

A will in which infants were concerned was not admitted to be proved in court, but the cause was ordered to stand over that the plaintiff might forthwith reply and that there might be a subpoena to rejoin returnable immediate and that service on the defendant's clerk in court might be good service and publication might pass the first seal after Christmas.

N.B. This process was held necessary though in a cause by consent, an infant being concerned.

---

[1] *Pawlet's Case* (1679), T. Raymond 335, 83 E.R. 174; *Orm v. Smith* (1711), 2 Vernon 681, 23 E.R. 1042, also Gilbert Rep. 82, 25 E.R. 58, 1 Eq. Cas. Abr. 302, 21 E.R. 1061, British Library MS. Hargrave 80, f. 78, pl. 3, Chancery Cases *tempore* Harcourt, 186; *Birch v. Baker* (1724), see above, Case No. 672.

[Other reports of this case: 2 Peere Williams 328, 24 E.R. 751, 2 Eq. Cas. Abr. 569, 773, 22 E.R. 480, 657.]

692
Cox v. Belitha

(Ch. 1725)

The child of a citizen of London can make a contract to receive a sum of money or an annuity in lieu of his or her orphanage share.

A contract will not be set aside where there is some consideration.

Lincoln's Inn MS. Misc. 12, p. 156

20 April 1725. Samuel Cox and Hannah, his wife, and Elizabeth Belitha, which Hannah and Elizabeth were the daughters of Edward Belitha, plaintiffs; William Belitha, defendant.

About thirteen years after the marriage of the plaintiffs Cox and his wife, Edward Belitha settles freehold and leasehold lands which cost £2400 for the separate use of the plaintiff Hannah for life and, after her death, for the benefit of his children. And, by this deed, the plaintiff Cox and his wife acknowledge the premises cost £2400 and that they had before received £1600, making together £4000, and they agree to accept it in full satisfaction of the orphanage share of the personal estate of Edward Belitha, which the plaintiff Hannah might be entitled to at his death. And, by a deed poll bearing date with the settlement, they make the like declaration, and the plaintiff Samuel covenants with Edward Belitha to execute a release after his death to his executors or administrators of all claims touching the premises by virtue of the custom of London or otherwise, except what he should leave them by his will or otherwise.

The plaintiffs Cox and his wife bring their bill against the defendant, the executor of their father, for the plaintiff Hannah's orphanage share. And the plaintiff Cox insists he was imposed upon and that no estimate of the personal estate was laid before him when he executed these deeds.

But the court [Lords Commissioners Jekyll and Gilbert], without any difficulty, dismissed the bill. And the defendant having brought a cross-bill to have a specific execution of the covenant, Samuel Cox was decreed to execute a release according to his covenant.

As to the plaintiff Elizabeth Belitha, the case was thus. The father, by his will, gave the plaintiff Elizabeth, his daughter, £3500. And, after his death, she came to an agreement with the defendant, her brother, to accept of an annuity of £250 a year for her life. And, accordingly, he made a mortgage to four persons in trust for her for securing this annuity, and, in consideration thereof, she executed a release, whereby she released her legacy and likewise all claim to the personal estate of her father by the custom of the City of London.

And, as to the plaintiff Elizabeth, the bill was to set aside this release, suggesting she had been imposed on, that she did not understand the purport of the release and that no account was laid before her of the value of the personal estate, so that she did not know what her share was nor what she released, and that, if she was entitled to no more than her legacy, yet £250 a year for her life was not an adequate satisfaction for £3500.

It was proved in the cause and much insisted on by Elizabeth's counsel that she was a very weak woman, and it was not denied by the defendant's counsel, and it was likewise insisted that she was entitled not only to her legacy but to her customary share, which was very considerable and she was made to release that as well as her legacy and without any consideration.

But as to that, it was insisted by the defendant's counsel that the testator having by his will taken upon himself to dispose of his whole personal estate without any regard to the custom, the plaintiff could not claim by the will and the custom too but must either renounce her legacy or her customary share.

And of that opinion was the court without any difficulty.

As to the manner of obtaining this release, it was said by the defendant's counsel that he had sworn in his answer that his father, after the making of his will and a little before his death, had desired him to give his sister an annuity of £250 a year in lieu of her legacy and, though there was no proof of this and, therefore, it was objected the answer could not be read, yet that fact being recited in the articles between the plaintiff and defendant and sworn to be true in the defendant's answer and nothing suggested in the bill to the contrary, it should now be taken to be true.

As to what was said of the imposition on the plaintiff, it was proved that the annuity was agreed to be paid the plaintiff with the approbation of her friends, who thought an annuity more proper for her than money in her circumstances and that the release was read over to her trustees and approved of by them. And the plaintiff Samuel, who has joined his sister with him in this bill, was a witness to the release so that, if it was a fraud, he was privy to it. And besides, there had been an acquiescence for six or seven years under this agreement without any complaint made until the filing the bill.

And, as to the objection that £250 a year was not an adequate consideration for £3500, supposing she was entitled to no more, much less was it a consideration for her orphanage part, which was much more than her legacy, which it was agreed she might have insisted on, it was answered that she had waived the custom by accepting an equivalent for her legacy and she might possibly be induced to acquiesce under the will out of a pious regard to her father. And, though £250 a year for life might not be a sufficient consideration for releasing £3500, yet it being between a brother and sister, the consideration was not strictly to be measured. And besides, there was the consideration of blood, and the plaintiff, if she pleased, might give away the whole or any part of her fortune to her brother. And £250 a year was an ample provision for her and more than she had occasion for.

And, for these reasons, the court dismissed the bill.

And it was said further by the Lord Commissioner Jekyll that here was no fraud, either apparent or proved. There was neither *suppressio veri* nor *suggestio falsi*, and deeds ought not to be set aside unless there was fraud used in obtaining them. He said he never knew a deed set aside barely for a defect in the consideration. If that was to be the rule, it would render men's properties very precarious.

The plaintiff Cox was ordered to pay the costs of dismissing the bill, he having tacked his sister's case to his own in hopes to make his own case, which had nothing in it, appear better, and, besides, it was endeavoring to impeach a deed as fraudulent, to which he himself was privy and a witness.

[Other reports of this case: 2 Peere Williams 272, 24 E.R. 727, 2 Eq. Cas. Abr. 269, 270, 22 E.R. 227, 228.]

693

Caius College, Cambridge v. Mallom

(Ch. 1725)

Where a recovery has barred remainders and trusts to preserve remainders that constituted a perpetuity, a court of equity will order specific performance of a contract to sell an advowson.

Lincoln's Inn MS. Misc. 12, p. 168, pl. 2

21 April 1725.

The defendant John Mallom, by a lease and release, 1 and 2 August 1692, upon his marriage with Elizabeth, his now wife, settled, *inter alia*, the advowson of Stratton in Norfolk to the use of himself for life, then to trustees to preserve contingent remainders, then to his wife for her jointure, remainder to trustees for 500 years, remainder to the first and other sons of the marriage in tail male, remainder to the defendant and his heirs. The trusts of the term were declared to be that, in case there should be a failer of issue male, the trustees, by sale or mortgage, should raise £1050 for daughters' portions. The plaintiffs contracted with the defendant for the purchase of this advowson, and he and his son, who was come of age, in order to make a good title, suffered a recovery to the use of the father and his heirs.

The plaintiffs' bill was to have the purchase completed and that the trustees of the term might assign that term to protect the purchase, it being apprehended that, though the legal estate of the term, it being precedent to the limitation to the son's, was not barred by the recovery, yet that the trusts of it were. The son and also the daughters, one of whom was an infant, were made defendants, as well as the trustees.

The cause was first heard by consent before the Master of the Rolls [JEKYLL], but he would make no decree, believing that the limiting of the term before the limitation to the sons was not a blunder of the drawer of the settlement but was done with a design to prevent the eldest son, when he should come of age, from the barring of his sisters.

And, thereupon, the cause was set down and heard before Lord Macclesfield, who referred it to a Master to see what was the value of the estate over and above the advowson and what it was worth to be sold and to state the matters to the court.

The Master having made his report, it now came on for further directions.

And Lord Commissioner GILBERT was of opinion that the trusts of the term were barred by the recovery, for, otherwise, there would be a perpetuity. And he seemed to wonder the trustees were not decreed to assign the term without sending it to a Master to enquire into the value of the estate.

And it was ordered that the defendant Mallom and his son and two daughters, who were of age, should join in conveying the advowson to the plaintiff and the trustees were to assign the term to attend the inheritance.

694

Dews v. Brandt

(Ch. 1725)

A contract can be set aside in a court of equity on the ground of overreaching.

Lincoln's Inn MS. Misc. 506, p. 75, pl. 2

Easter 11 George.

The plaintiff, being entitled to a remainder in tail after the death of his father, did in the lifetime of his father article to sell the same to the defendant for £1300. The estate was £375 *per annum* with taxes and outgoings. It was done with the father's privity, who was in the Mint and very poor. But the son not being able to make a tenant to the *praecipe*, there could be no conveyance because the father might outlive the son. Thus, the money was not to be paid until the father's death and then to be paid with interest from the date of the articles. There were other articles afterwards made somewhat more to the disadvantage of the plaintiff, as that interest should not be paid for £300.

The Master of the Rolls [JEKYLL] had decreed that the plaintiff should be relieved against the articles.

The Lords Commissioners [to Hold the Great Seal], on an appeal, affirmed the decree because of the great disproportion of the price. They agreed that there was no general rule that a remainder sold by heirs should be void, but each case must stand on its own particular circumstances, as where there is a great inequality in the price, not a small inequality, e.g. where it is for half or so or where there are circumstances of fraud or imposition or where a young heir is wheedled by the allowance of money to nurse his prodigalities. There was cited the case of [*blank*] and Griffith,[1] where there was this circumstance, that the purchaser drew the son from his father's house and advised him not to sell his remainder to his father.

The articles were set aside.

[Other reports of this case: Select Cases *tempore* King 7, 25 E.R. 192, 2 Eq. Cas. Abr. 510, 679, 22 E.R. 432, 570.]

695

Boothby v. Vernon

(Ch. 1725)

The widower of a life tenant cannot be a tenant by the curtesy.

Lincoln's Inn MS. Hill 29, p. 78

Easter 11 Geo. I. In Chancery. *Coram* Gilbert and Raymond, Lords Commissioners.

Sir Henry Boothby [1682–1710], seised in fee, by will, devises lands to his only sister and heir at law, Ann Boothby, and her assigns for and during the term of her natural life and, in case his said sister should happen to marry and leave issue male living of her body lawfully begotten at the time of her death, then to such issue male of his said sister and his heirs males forever, but, in case she should leave no issue male of her body lawfully begotten at the time of her death, then to George Boothby and his heirs forever, under whom the plaintiff claims.

Sir Henry Boothby died without issue. Ann, his sister, enters and was possessed and then married Matthew Vernon and had issue one son, Henry. Ann died in 1712, then her son Henry died in 1719, being about nine years of age. During the life of Henry, the defendant, Matthew Vernon, by the fraud of some concerned for him, procured a conveyance from the heirs of the part of the father and mother of his son Henry. And, on application to the court, a decree was made in favor of the plaintiff. And the defendant was directed by the decree to convey to the plaintiff all his estate in the said lands in general terms.

The plaintiff, apprehending himself to be injured therein, now petitions the court for a rehearing forasmuch as he is advised that he is tenant by the curtesy in the said lands and, therefore, conveying all his estate in general terms would be to convey away his right of tenancy by the curtesy.

This petition setting forth the whole matter as above and also that the point in law had been referred to the judges of the Common Pleas, *viz.* whether the

---

[1] *Twistleton v. Griffith* (Ch. 1716–1721), see above, Case No. 118.

remainder to the defendant's son was a contingent remainder or not, and whether the reversion in fee did not in the meantime until the contingency happened descend to Ann, the defendant's wife, in such a manner to entitle the defendant to be tenant by the curtesy and that the judges of the Common Bench certified their opinions that the defendant was not by the curtesy of England entitled to the premises during his life, but that there was now another doubt, *viz.* whether Ann had not by the will an estate tail, which was not argued before the judges, and, consequently, the defendant thereby entitled to be tenant by the curtesy. The case was now argued on the petition. But the point of the estate tail in Ann was little insisted on by the counsel for the petitioner.

The Lords Commissioners soon determined that it was only an estate for life to Ann and an estate tail to the son by the will, but, forasmuch as the reversion of the inheritance was in Ann during her life and the plaintiff claims as heir at law to Ann, it was argued whether the defendant should not be tenant by the curtesy. And the cases cited in the argument were Plunkett v. Holmes, 1 Lev. 11, 1 Sid. 47; Purefoy v. Sanders, 1 Sand.; Carter v. Barnardiston; Archer's Case; Lord Bowles' Case.[1]

Gilbert and Raymond, Lords Commissioners, said they thought the defendant could not be tenant by the curtesy and relied a great deal on the case of Plunket v. Holmes.

Gilbert said particularly that it was formerly a principle of the old law that an estate should not be in abeyance and the reason was because the lord would then be deprived of an homager, but, that reason being now destroyed by the alteration of the tenure of estates,[2] I do not know why we might not make an estate in abeyance, which is indeed the sense of the case of Plunket v. Holmes, though they do not say so openly, but [it is] one court to construe it as a reversionary interest, which is the case here, for it was not the devisor's intention to give Ann the fee simple, for he gives it her but for life. There was indeed a fee simple to arise at her death, but he does not certainly design to have her the dominion over it as a person having the inheritance. Would it not be strange then if, by the operation of law, she should have such an estate as he never designed her? And, as the son was to have the estate by the will immediately after the death of the mother, I think it unjust to allow a tenancy by the curtesy, which would be to alter the will

---

1 *Plunket v. Holmes* (1661), 1 Levinz 11, 83 E.R. 271, 1 Siderfin 47, 82 E.R. 961, also T. Raymond 28, 83 E.R. 15, 1 Keble 29, 119, 83 E.R. 792, 848; *Purefoy v. Rogers* (1671), 2 Williams Saunders 380, 85 E.R. 1181, also 2 Levinz 39, 83 E.R. 443, 3 Keble 11, 84 E.R. 566, 1 Eq. Cas. Abr. 189, 21 E.R. 980, Lincoln's Inn MS. Misc. 500, ff. 192, 194b; *Carter v. Barnardiston* (Ch. 1718–1719), see above, Case No. 283; *Baldwin v. Smith* (1597), 1 Coke Rep. 63, 76 E.R. 139, Croke Eliz. 453, 78 E.R. 692, 2 Anderson 37, 123 E.R. 533; *Bowles v. Bury* (1615), 11 Coke Rep. 79, 77 E.R. 1253, 1 Rolle Rep. 177, 81 E.R. 413.

2 Stat. 12 Car. II, c. 24 (*SR*, V, 259–266).

of the testator. And supposing the inheritance descend to Ann during her estate for life and that there is a hiatus so that the estate is not in abeyance, yet, at the very instant she dies, which is the time when the tenancy by the curtesy would consummate, she has no more than an estate for life (because she leaves a son) out of which estate a tenancy by the curtesy cannot spring.

Lincoln's Inn MS. Misc. 506, p. 76

Easter 11 George.

Sir Henry Boothby devised his lands to his sister Ann Boothby, who was his heir at law, during her natural life and, after her death, then to her eldest son, which she should have living at the time of her death and his heirs male etc., but, if she had no son living at the time of her death, then to the plaintiff George Boothby and his heirs forever. The testator dies, and his sister married the defendant, by whom she has issue, a son and a daughter. The daughter died; then the mother died, and, half a year after the mother's death, the son died an infant. George Boothby takes possession of the land, but Vernon knowing the plaintiff had the right colludes with one Young, who, under pretense of being empowered to bring an [action of] ejectment against the plaintiff, prevails with the plaintiff to convey the estate for 50 guineas to the defendant by a deed of feoffment and a letter of attorney to Young to make livery and seisin, who accordingly did so.

The bill was to be relieved against the feoffment obtained by fraud and to have a re-conveyance. The feoffment was set aside and a re-conveyance was decreed by the Master of the Rolls [Jekyll].

It came now before the court upon a point reserved, which was whether the defendant in the re-conveyance should not except a right of tenant by the curtesy. It was insisted on for him that his wife was seised of the fee simple in possession along with the estate for life, which was not merged, but kept separate to let in the executory devise to the son and George Boothby, that there was a coalescence until the contingency happened and then it opened to let in the contingent estate, when which was expired it closed again. Plunket and Holmes, in 1 Sid. 47 and 1 Lev. 11; it had been made a case of and sent to the judges of the Common Bench, who were unanimous there could be no tenant by the curtesy for that he, not having a right at his wife's death, could not have it afterwards and that, if there were a coalescence, yet, at the time of the wife's death, the estates were parted and she was then but tenant for life and that being the time of the consummation of the husband's right, if she had not the fee simple in possession then and he could not be tenant by the curtesy.

So the re-conveyance was decreed to be executed without that exception.

Lincoln's Inn MS. Misc. 384, p. 312, pl. 1

24 April 1725.

Sir Henry Boothby devises to Ann, his sister and heir, for life, and, if she has issue male of her body living at her death, then to such issue male and his heirs male forever, but if she leave no issue male at her death, then to George Boothby in fee. Ann marries and leaves issue male. Query whether the husband of Ann shall be tenant by the curtesy.

His Honor [JEKYLL] sent it as a case to the judges of the [Court of] Common Pleas, who were of opinion that the husband was not entitled to be tenant by the curtesy.

Lord Commissioner GILBERT [was] of the same opinion.

RAYMOND [was] of the same opinion.

The chief case relied on by the other side is Plunket v. Holmes. The old law was that, where a remainder was in contingency, it was in abeyance. Carter v. Bernardiston; where, by the same conveyance, there will be an opening, but where by another, it will be merged. Lewis Bowles, Co.; Harrison and Belt, Ventris; no inheritance [was] joined with the freehold.[1]

Lincoln's Inn MS. Coxe 89, vol. 3, pt. 2, p. 1, pl. 2

Easter 11 Geo. *Coram* Raymond and Gilbert, Lords Commissioners.

A bill was brought to oblige the defendant to deliver up or cancel a feoffment which he had obtained by fraud of the plaintiff. And the case was thus. Sir Henry Boothby was seised in fee of certain lands, and, by his will, he devised them to Anne, who was his sister and heir at law, for life, and, if she died leaving issue male at the time of her death, then to such issue male and his heirs male forever and, if she died without leaving issue male, then the remainder to [George] Boothby and his heirs. Sir Henry Boothby died, and Anne, his sister, married the defendant, Mr. Vernon, and had issue a son, and she died leaving that son. Afterwards, the son died, and [George] Boothby entered as in his remainder. And the defendant, claiming to be tenant by the curtesy of his wife's estate, brought an [action of] ejectment against [George] Boothby. And to strengthen his title, he procured by fraud a conveyance from the plaintiff, who was the heir at law to Sir Henry Boothby. It appeared that this conveyance was obtained from the plaintiff for a very trifling consideration and before the plaintiff had any knowledge of his title, upon which circumstances, the plaintiff brought his bill to be relieved against this conveyance. And he prayed that it might be cancelled or delivered up or that he might have a re-conveyance from the defendant Mr. Vernon.

Upon the hearing, it appeared plainly that the conveyance was obtained from the plaintiff by fraud, and the court decreed a re-conveyance to be made to him by the defendant. But it being insisted upon that the defendant should

[1] *Bowles v. Bury* (1615), *ut supra*; *Harrison v. Belsey* (1680), 1 Ventris 345, 86 E.R. 222, also T. Raymond 413, 83 E.R. 216, Pollexfen 573, 86 E.R. 650, T. Jones 136, 84 E.R. 1185, Dodd 32, *sub nom. Harrison v. Belcher*, 1 Freeman 484, 89 E.R. 364, *sub nom. Harris v. Belchey*, 2 Shower K.B. 91, 89 E.R. 814.

not re-convey absolutely to the plaintiff in respect of his title to be tenant by the curtesy, it was urged for the defendant that the re-conveyance ought to be with a particular reservation of his particular estate. And upon this arose a question whether Anne, the wife of Mr. Vernon, had such an estate in her as would entitle the husband to be tenant by the curtesy. And it was agreed that, if Mr. Vernon was entitled to be tenant by the curtesy, that then the re-conveyance must be with a reservation of that right and, if he was entitled etc., then it must be absolute.

A case was made of this point of law for the opinion of the judges of the [Court of] Common Bench, who certified their opinion that Mrs. Vernon had not any estate in her as would entitle the defendant to be tenant by the curtesy.

And now, upon the petition of the plaintiff to have a re-conveyance made to him, the merits of the case were argued in this court.

The counsel for the plaintiff argued that the defendant's wife had only an estate for life and not such an estate as would entitle the husband to be tenant etc., for the wife must be seised in fee simple or tail. Co. Litt. 29.[1] It must be of an estate of inheritance in possession. And, therefore, if land is given to two sisters and to the heirs of their bodies, by which they have a joint estate for life with several inheritances and the one takes a husband, who has issue by her, and then she dies, the husband shall not be tenant by the curtesy, for the jointure was not severed by their having issue. 2 R.A. 90.[2]

By this devise, the wife has an estate for life expressly limited to her, and, therefore, though the inheritance did descend to her as heir at law, yet there was no union of the two estates. But there was an opening left for the interposition of the remainders when they should happen. Archer's Case, Co. 64. But the case which comes nearest the present is that of Plunkett v. Holmes, 1 Lev. 11, 1 Sid. 47, Raym. 30, 3 Lev. 434, s.c., cited, which case was thus. J.S., being seised in fee, devised his lands to his eldest son J. for life and, if he died without issue living at the time of his death, then to L., another son, and his heirs, but, if J. has issue at the time of his death, then the fee shall remain to the right heirs of J. forever, and it was resolved that J. took only an estate for life by the will, remainder to his heirs unexecuted and, though he was the heir to whom the reversion descended, yet the estate for life was not merged against the will of the devisor but left an opening for the remainder to vest when it happened. It was said the present case would be determined by this authority and that the wife's estate for life should be kept distinct and separate from the fee and that the instant she died leaving issue male, the remainder vested in such issue male and her estate was become then merely as an estate for life.

As to the opening of the fee to let in remainders, Lewis Bowles' Case, 11 Coke 79, explains it in the best manner. In that case, an estate for life was made

1 E. Coke, *First Institute* (1628), f. 29.

2 2 Rolle, Abr., *Jointenants*, pl. I, p. 90.

to A. and B., the remainder to their first son that they should have in tail, remainder to A. and B. in tail. In this case, it was held that an estate tail was executed in A. and B. until a son was born and then their estates are immediately divided and A. and B. become tenants for life, remainder to the issue male in tail, remainder to A. and B. in tail, and the estate for their heirs was not absolutely merged, but with this implied limitation until they have issue male. Vent. 306, 344; 2 Saund. 336, 7. So, in the present case, the inheritance which descended upon Anne shall be severed from the estate for life upon her leaving issue at the time of her death, and, at that instant, the inheritance shall open to let in the remainder.

It was argued for the defendant that, if he must re-convey, it ought to be with a reservation of this particular estate, for the wife having the inheritance in her during the coverture and dying possessed thereof, the husband was entitled to be tenant by the curtesy. It was insisted that the reversion descended to the wife, the estate for life was merged in it, as in Cro. Ja. 260, Wood and Ingersole, where the reversion descending on the devisee for life drowns the particular estate. And a distinction was taken where the reversion comes to the particular estate by limitation in the same deed and where it comes by descent or any other conveyance. And it was said that, where a particular estate for life and a reversion over is appointed in the same conveyance to the same person, there the reversion shall not drown the particular estate, but, when the reversion comes by a different conveyance or by descent, there the particular estate is drowned, as in 2 Co. 60, Wiscott's Case, as if a man makes an estate to three and the heirs of one of them, though the one has a fee, yet the jointure continues, for all is but one entire estate created at one time and, therefore, the fee cannot drown the jointure. But, if there are two joint tenants for life and one of them purchases the fee or the fee descends to him, there, the estate for life is drowned by it, for the estate for life was *in esse* before and might be surrendered or drowned. So, by an acquisition of a reversion in the present case by descent and at a different time, the estate for life is drowned.

It was also insisted on for the defendant that there should be no re-conveyance because it having been decreed that the conveyance was procured by fraud, it was as if there had been no conveyance at all and, therefore, a re-conveyance was unnecessary.

Gilbert, Lord Commissioner: The defendant has put himself under a necessity of re-conveying for he has gained an interest from the plaintiff by fraud which he must restore to him. But, though the defendant has gained the plaintiff's interest by fraud, yet, if the defendant has a prior right, it must be reserved to him in the re-conveyance. Therefore, the question will be if he has any prior right, which will depend upon what estate his wife had in the said lands. And, as to this point, I am clearly of opinion with the judges of the Common Bench that the wife had not such an estate as would entitle the husband to be tenant by the curtesy and for these reasons.

First, a tenancy by curtesy is consummated by the death of the wife. And, in this case, the very instant the wife died, her estate was only for life, for the inheritance, at that instant, went from her and vested by way of remainder in her son. It must be admitted the inheritance did descend to the wife upon the death of the devisor. But then, it did not vest in her absolutely but a remainder only in her until the contingency of her dying and leaving issue male happened. By this descent of the inheritance to the wife, there was no union or coalescence of estates, but they were kept separate to answer the contingent remainders and, upon her dying leaving issue male, the two estates opened and let in the issue into his remainder, which was then executed. Plunket v. Holmes, Raym. etc. comes up to the present case, for, there, the reversion descended on the devisee for life, and yet it was held there was no union of estates but that there should be an opening to admit the remainder limited by the testator.

In the old law, abeyances used to be abhorred, and they would never construe any estate to be in abeyance when they could construe the inheritance to be in any[one], and the reason of this was because, by the old law, estates were held by homage or other services and, if the estate had been allowed to be in no particular person, then the homage and other services had been lost. But tenures have been so much altered by late statutes[1] that I think that old way of reasoning cannot now be made use of.

Secondly, the intent of the testator ought to determine this question. It appears by the will that here is an estate for life expressly given to the wife and a contingent remainder is expressly appointed to take place upon her death. The devisor who had power over his estate has limited it to his daughter for life only and never intended she should have any greater estate. But, if we construe this an inheritance in the wife, we should then by construction of law give the defendant, who is a third person and a stranger to the testator an interest in his estate which he never intended and such an interest as will interfere with the estate which the devisor has appointed to take place at the instant of the wife's death. Therefore, if this estate by curtesy should be allowed of, it would make the construction and operation of law supplant the plain intent of the testator.

RAYMOND, Lord Commissioner: The judges at common law have determined the question, and their opinion is sufficient to direct our consciences unless we are greatly dissatisfied with it. He said that, when the reversion comes to a particular estate for life by a different conveyance, it closes with the particular estate, and there is a coalescence. But, when it comes by the same conveyance, it is otherwise. He cited to this point Harrison v. Belsay, 1 Vent. 306, Raym. 413. He agreed with the judges of the Common Bench.

And *per curiam*, the defendant was decreed to re-convey absolutely without any saving of his estate by curtesy.

---

[1] Stat. 12 Car. II, c. 24 (*SR*, V, 259–266).

Lincoln's Inn MS. Misc. 13, p. 175

25 April 1725.

Sir Henry Boothby, by will, devised the lands in question to his sister, Anne Boothby, for her life, and, in case she married and left issue male living at her death, then he devised the lands to such issue male and his heirs male forever. But, in case his said sister should happen to leave no issue male living at her death, then he devised the said lands to George Boothby and his heirs forever. After the testator's death, Anne married the defendant, and she died leaving issue by him, a son and a daughter. Three months after her death, the daughter died, and the son died soon after the death of his sister.

The question was if the defendant was tenant by the curtesy, it being insisted for the defendant that the limitation to the issue male was a contingent limitation and that there being no disposition of the reversion in fee, it descended upon Anne, the testator's sister, as heiress at law to him, and, therefore, she having the inheritance until the contingency happened, the defendant, her husband, ought to be tenant by the curtesy.

Upon the hearing of the cause, Lord Chancellor Macclesfield sent the case to the judges of the [Court of] Common Pleas for their opinion, who certified that they were of opinion that the defendant was not tenant by the curtesy.

And when the cause came on to be heard on the equity reserved, it was decreed that the defendant, who had got a conveyance from the plaintiff, and against which the plaintiff had brought his bill to be relieved, as being gained by fraud, should re-convey the estate to the plaintiff. And, now, it came on before the Lords Commissioners [to Hold the Great Seal] upon the defendant's petition for a rehearing, who insisted, first, that he was tenant by the curtesy, second, supposing he was not so, yet there was no reason to decree him to convey all his interest in the estate. It was sufficient to set aside the conveyance, which was all that was prayed by the bill.

As to the point of law, it was insisted for the defendant that the fee simple upon the testator's death was not in abeyance, but it did descend upon the defendant's wife, but not so as to confound the will, but only sub modo so as to let in the contingent remainders when they should happen. In the case of Purefoy and Rogers, Judge Hale would not suffer that point to be spoken to, whether the fee did not descend in the meantime until the contingency happened. And, therefore, if the defendant's wife had an estate in fee during the marriage, the defendant consequently must be tenant by the curtesy. And the case of Plunkett and Holmes, in Lev., was much insisted on.

As to the other matter, it was said that, if the defendant has a case in which there is any probability, he ought not to be precluded of his right, as he will be if he executes a conveyance. And, although the conveyance was obtained by fraud, yet the defendant was no party to the fraud. It was transacted by another without his privity.

Gilbert: If the defendant was a party to the fraud and has got a conveyance of the inheritance, his estate for life is merged.

Raymond: There is no doubt but his estate for life is merged. But I would put this case. Suppose a man is tenant for life and gets a conveyance of the inheritance by fraud. Shall he lose his estate for life in this court? Surely, no.

As to the point in law, Gilbert was very clear that the defendant could not be tenant by the curtesy, for, if so, it would be to make a construction upon the words of the will contrary to the plain intention of the testator. He says that his sister shall be tenant for life and, if she leaves a son, that he shall have the estate. No, says the defendant's counsel, the son shall not have it until after the death of his father. He said he was satisfied in the resolution of Plunket and Holmes, but not in the reason of it.

Supposing there was a coalition of the estate for life and the reversion in fee and that would make the defendant tenant by the curtesy. Yet, when the testator's sister dies leaving a son, she was then at that instant only tenant for life. And if a married woman has a conditional fee simple, whenever that estate is determined, whether in her lifetime or at her death, the tenancy by the curtesy will determine.

Raymond: As to the case of Plunket and Holmes, it was the first case where it has been adjudged that a fee simple could be limited after the limitation of a fee upon a contingency. I think the resolution of that case is right. But the judges did not think that the reversion closed, for, if it had, the contingent remainder would have been destroyed.

It has been settled that, where an estate for life is limited and, by the same deed, a remainder is limited upon a contingency with a remainder in fee to the right heirs of the tenant for life, the remainder in fee is not so united with the estate for life but that, when the contingency happens, it shall open and let in the contingent remainder. He cited the Case of Harrison and Belsey, in 1 Ventris 345.[1]

As to the other matter, both sides seemed to agree that the defendant ought not to do any act whereby he might prejudice any right that he may have. But the difficulty was how to frame a conveyance whereby the defendant should convey to the plaintiff without giving up his own interest.

Serjeant *Comyns* insisted that the deed executed by the plaintiff was a feoffment with livery of seisin and, being fraudulent, was void. And so it is resolved in Hobart. And, besides, it is void for this reason. The plaintiff was not in possession when he executed the deed and, therefore, being out of possession, the feoffment is void.

---

[1] *Harrison v. Belsey* (1680), 1 Ventris 345, 86 E.R. 222, also T. Raymond 413, 83 E.R. 216, Pollexfen 573, 86 E.R. 650, T. Jones 136, 84 E.R. 1185, Dodd 32, *sub nom. Harrison v. Belcher*, 1 Freeman 484, 89 E.R. 364, *sub nom. Harris v. Belchey*, 2 Shower K.B. 91, 89 E.R. 814.

And it was insisted by Mr. *Acherley* that, if the plaintiff would have executed a legal conveyance, he should have gone upon the land or given a letter of attorney to some person to go upon the land and seal the deed there and deliver seisin, as is done in the common case where an [action of] ejectment is to be brought and there is no tenant in possession; the party goes upon the land and seals a lease there or gives a letter of attorney to another to seal a lease for him upon the land.

Attorney General [*Yorke*], for the plaintiff, said that, if a man is not in possession when he executes a feoffment, yet, if he is in possession when livery is made or enters before he makes livery and seisin, it is a good conveyance, for the estate passes by the livery and seisin.

And it was said by the court that there being livery of seisin, the feoffment was not void, and, as to the case in Hobart, it was upon the Statute of Elizabeth and the deed was void by that Statute. But the case is different where a conveyance is set aside in this court as fraudulent.

Then, it was insisted for the defendant that the delivering up and cancelling the deed would be sufficient, for, if anyone would set up a title at law under a deed, he must produce the deed.

But, in answer to this, it was said by Mr. *Fazakerley* that, though a man has not the deed in his possession under which he makes a title, yet, if he can prove that it is in the hands of the other party and he will not produce it, the court will let the plaintiff give the contents of the deed in evidence. And so it was done in Sir Edward Seymour's Case.[1]

[Other reports of this case: 9 Modern 147, 88 E.R. 368, 2 Eq. Cas. Abr. 727, 22 E.R. 612.]

696

Anonymous

(Ch. 1725)

Where a plaintiff sues for an account, the defendant can plead a release, but, if the defendant recites the release in his answer, he must also give an account.

Lincoln's Inn MS. Misc. 506, p. 77, pl. 1

Easter 11 George.

If a bill be brought for an account and there be a release thereof from the plaintiff to the defendant, yet, if the defendant sets forth the release in his answer without setting out the account, his answer may be excepted to and will be insufficient though, upon the hearing, a decree would be for the defendant because

1 *Heywood v. Smith* (1612), 10 Coke Rep. 95, 77 E.R. 1070, 1 Bulstrode 162, 80 E.R. 853.

there may arise some equity out of the nature of the items. But, if the defendant would take advantage of the release without setting out the account, he ought to plead it.

697

Marriot v. Lucas

(Ch. 1725)

The time period of the Statute of Limitations for an account starts to run upon the last promise to come to an account.

Lincoln's Inn MS. Misc. 12, p. 163

4 May 1725.

A bill [was exhibited] for an account of a partnership between the plaintiff and the defendant's husband, to which the defendant had pleaded the Statute of Limitations.[1] And the plea having been allowed and the plaintiff having replied to the plea and answer, it now came on to be heard.

And it appearing by the proofs that frequent applications had been made to the defendant's husband within six years before the filing the bill to come to an account and that he had promised so to do, the court decreed an account.

698

Besse v. Haringold

(Ch. 1724)

A court of equity will not decree a forfeiture of an estate.

An affidavit is not admissible in evidence.

Lincoln's Inn MS. Misc. 12, p. 139

4 May 1724.

The plaintiff's bill was to have an account of the rents of the estate of William Windsor, her uncle, which she claimed as the next Protestant heir, she being a daughter of one of Mr. Windsor's three sisters. And the defendants were the other two sisters and were said to be Papists. The plaintiff had been brought up in a Popish seminary beyond the sea, but it was said she was become a convert to the Protestant[2] religion and had taken the oaths of allegiance and supremacy and received the Sacrament according to the rites of the Church of England. And, for proof of this, she produced the record.

---

[1] Stat. 21 Jac. I, c. 16 (*SR*, IV, 1222–1223).

[2] Popish *MS*.

Lord Chancellor [Lord Macclesfield]: The plaintiff's bill is improper in this court. She comes for a forfeiture, which is a matter of law. If she had recovered at law, I would have decreed an account of the profits.

The plaintiff has made no proof that Mr. Windsor was a person professing the Popish religion, which she ought to have done, one of the defendants claiming a title under a settlement made by Mr. Windsor. All the proof which the plaintiff has made is only the record of the conviction of Mr. Windsor of his being a Popish recusant on the Statute 1 *Jacobi.*[1] Now, that is no proof of his being a person professing the Popish religion, for a non-juror may be convicted for not taking the oaths and so be in the condition of a Popish recusant convict.

In the next place, the plaintiff has not made sufficient proof that she is a Protestant, for the certificate from the minister and churchwardens is no evidence of her having received the Sacrament, for though the certificate is never received without an affidavit, yet that is no evidence, for the affidavit cannot be received as evidence in regard the other side has no opportunity of cross-examining the witness.

Besides, the plaintiff has not proved the identity of the person. The record produced is only that one of the same name with the plaintiff took the oaths such a day. She ought to have proved that she was that very person.

The plaintiff has made out no case, and the bill must be dismissed with costs.

699

Ashton v. Dawson

(Ch. 1725)

A gift causa mortis *is not a legacy, and it is not within the jurisdiction of a court of probate.*

A gift causa mortis *is not complete without a delivery.*

Lincoln's Inn MS. Misc. 12, p. 164

5 May 1725.

A.B. being ill of the sickness whereof he died, about four days before his death, he called the defendant to him and said, 'Here, my dear Ann, take these [*viz.*, a Bank note and a Sword Blade Company bond], they are yours; but, if I live, you must give them to me again.'

The testator had made a will and the plaintiff executor, who had brought his bill and controverted this gift to the defendant.

Upon the hearing of the cause before the Lord Chancellor Macclesfield, he had directed an issue to try whether the Bank note and Sword Blade [Company] bond were delivered to the defendant for her own use.

[1] Stat. 1 Jac. I, c. 4 (*SR*, IV, 1020–1022).

And now, the cause came on to be reheard before the Lords Commissioners, Jekyll and Gilbert, who were of opinion this was a *donatio causa mortis* and as such is of a testamentary nature and not triable in the common law courts and that no issue ought to have been directed in this case, for that, in effect, is to send it to [the common] law to try what is a *donatio causa mortis*, which is a matter of ecclesiastical cognizance and, as this court has a concurrent jurisdiction, they ought to have determined the matter upon the proofs. And, accordingly, being very clear that this was a *donatio causa mortis* and it being proved that the plaintiff himself had assented to the gift, the bill was dismissed with costs.

Note a *donatio causa mortis* differs from a legacy in this respect, a legacy is an absolute gift to take place after the testator's death; a donation *causa mortis* is conditional and must be redelivered to the donor if he recovers whether it is so expressed or not at the time of the delivery.

[Other copies of this report: 2 Collyer 363, 63 E.R. 772.]

Select Cases *tempore* King 14, 25 E.R. 196

5 May 1725. Ashton v. Dawson and Vincent.

One Cowper, after making his will, three or four days before his death, gave Mrs. Dawson some bank notes to her own use if he died, else to be returned. On his death, Ashton, who was his executor, on inquiring into the affair, said he was very well pleased that they were given her. She desired Mr. Ashton to keep the notes for her and employ them to the best advantage for her. He took them and gave her a note for them. She having after married contrary to his inclination, he refused to deliver up the notes, on which an action was brought on his note and a recovery and damages. A bill was brought here to be relieved, but relief was denied.

Curia. You come here to be relieved against the note, which cannot be but on the foot of fraud. At the time of giving it, the whole affair was examined. It is not a legacy, nor is there any occasion for the executor's assent to it. It is not a gift at common law but in view of death. Here are express words, but, if he had used no words and had been near death, it had been looked on as a donation *mortis causa*. It is a testamentary legacy, of which the common law takes notice, but it is not provable in the ecclesiastical court. It is only questionable here. And the executor's assent is not necessary because he might die intestate. This further differs from a legacy, which depends solely on the disposing words. But in a *donatio mortis causa*, there must be a delivery, which is something more. So the bill was dismissed with costs.

This cause was reheard before Lord Chancellor King, 6 August 1725, and he affirmed the decree, but only altered it in respect of the defendants' costs, who, being trustees, should have it out of the estate. But he inclined to have ordered a trial at law had Mr. Ashton not given a note.

Lincoln's Inn MS. Misc. 12, p. 230, pl. 2

6 August 1725.

Upon a petition of the plaintiff to rehear this cause, the decree of the Lords Commissioners was affirmed with this variation only, that the costs to be paid by the defendant should be paid out of the testator's estate.

700

Feltham v. Feltham

(Ch. 1725)

In this case, the legacies in issue were charged by the testator's will on his real estate.

If a legatee dies, his executors or administrators shall not receive the legacy before the deceased himself might have.

Lincoln's Inn MS. Misc. 12, p. 165

7 May 1725.

Mr. Feltham, the plaintiff and the defendant's father, makes his will. And he begins it thus, as to what estate, either personal or real, he was possessed of, he gave as follows, *viz.* his debts being paid, he gives to the plaintiff £2500 to be paid at her age of twenty-two years or day of marriage, which should first happen. And then, he goes on and gives legacies to his other daughters to be paid in the same manner, and, then, he gives to the defendant, his only son, all the rest and remainder of his estate, as well personal as real, whatsoever, no real estate being before given, over and above what was thereby disposed of, paid, and satisfied. And he made the defendant executor.

The question was if the legacies were charged upon the real estate.

Curia [Jekyll and Gilbert] were clear of opinion they were, the words being very strong and plain to show that the testator intended to give nothing more to his son than the surplus of his estate over and above what he had before taken out of it.

There was another question which arose upon a clause in the will, whereby the testator declared that, if any of the daughters died under the age of twenty-two and before marriage, the portions of the daughters so dying should be divided amongst the survivors of his daughters, share and share alike. One of the daughters died before her portion became payable. And the question was when her portion should become payable and from what time the plaintiff should have interest for her share of that portion, there being no time mentioned in the will when the portion of any daughter dying under twenty-two and unmarried should be paid to the survivors.

Commissioner Jekyll, at first, was of the opinion it should be paid to the surviving daughters at the time when they respectively became entitled to receive their original portions.

But Commissioner Gilbert said he thought it was the intention of the testator that the portion of any daughter so dying should be all paid at one and the same time. And, therefore, he was of the opinion that it should not be paid until such time as the deceased daughter, if she had lived, would have attained twenty-two.

And, accordingly, it was so decreed.

2 Peere Williams 271, 24 E.R. 726

One, having several daughters and being seised in fee of lands, by will, charges the premises with the payment of his daughters' portions, £1000 apiece to each daughter at her age of twenty-two years or marriage, which should first happen, and, if any of his said daughters should die before her portion became payable, the share of her so dying to go to the survivors. One of the daughters dies before twenty-two or marriage, and another of the daughters attains twenty-two years of age.

It was insisted that, there being no time appointed when the portion accruing by survivorship should be paid, it ought to be paid presently.

Lords Jekyll and Gilbert: This portion arises out of lands, and it would be a hardship on the heir, whom equity favors, to make it payable before the time it was intended.

Now there can be no reason to make the additional portion payable before the original one, wherefore, as the heir is to suffer by the raising of these portions, it may reasonably be presumed in favor of him that the testator might compute within what time they might be paid, so that this additional portion shall not be paid before such time as the daughter to whom it was given should have come to the age of twenty-two years if she had lived. (*Vide* Laundy v. Williams, *post*, 480.[1])

And, as I understood, the court also declared that the other daughters should not have their shares of the portion so accruing by survivorship until they respectively should have attained their age of twenty-two or be married, it not being the intention of the testator to trust any of his daughters with their portions until twenty-two or marriage.

Select Cases *tempore* King 15, 25 E.R. 197

7 May 1725.

---

[1] *Laundy v. Williams* (1728), 2 Peere Williams 478, 24 E.R. 823, also 1 Eq. Cas. Abr. 299, 21 E.R. 1060, 2 Eq. Cas. Abr. 561, 22 E.R. 472.

A person charged his lands with the payment of certain portions to his children. And he appointed that, if any of his children should die before the age of twenty-two or marriage, such child's portion should be divided equally among the survivors. One of the children died before the age of twenty-two unmarried.

The question was whether the survivors should receive their proportion of it when they received their own portions or not until this portion of the deceased would have become due.

The court [JEKYLL and GILBERT] was of opinion it should be paid when the deceased would have received it, because else would be so many several divisions of it as each person's title to it accrued, whereas it was designed to be one entire payment. If a legatee dies, his executors or administrators shall not receive the legacy before the deceased himself might have done it, for it is absurd that an accident of death of a legatee should vary a time of payment appointed by another person. And this is particularly strong being to charge a real estate. The devisor might perhaps have made a computation and considered how and at what time his estate would bear such a charge, and, if the part of the deceased should be paid at the time that the survivor's portion was payable, it might be charging the estate sooner than the devisor intended it should.

[Other reports of this case: 2 Eq. Cas. Abr. 646, 22 E.R. 542.]

701

Barker v. Giles

(Ch. 1725)

The mention of survivorship in a devise makes it a devise of a joint tenancy.

Lincoln's Inn MS. Hill 29, p. 82

Trinity 11 Geo. I.

J. Barker, by will, devises all his real estate to his executors to be sold and directs that (after some other provisions were made) the surplus of the money arising by the sale thereof together with that of his personal estate be laid out in the purchase of other lands to be settled:

> to the use of and in trust for Jerome and Robert Barker, the sons of my brother Sir W. Barker, the survivor or survivors of them, their heirs, and assigns forever to be equally divided between them, share and share alike.

Jerome, one of the devisees, dies in the lifetime of the testator.

Robert, the other devisee, now brings his bill against the executors and the heir at law of the devisor for an account and conveyance of the estate to be purchased to the use of him and his heirs. And he insists that the words of the will create a joint tenancy and, therefore, the whole ought to be conveyed to him as the survivor.

The defendant, the heir at law, insists that, by the will, Jerome and the plaintiff were tenants in common and, Jerome dying before the testator, one moiety was undevised and he is entitled to it as heir at law, so that whether the words of the will create a joint tenancy or a tenancy in common was the point debated.

This question was twice argued in this term, once before Gilbert and Raymond, two of the Lords Commissioners for the Custody of the Great Seal, who did not determine it. And a few days afterwards, it was heard before Lord King, Lord High Chancellor of Great Britain.

The plaintiff's counsel urged that it evidently appears the testator designed to disinherit his heir at law, that a devise to two men and their heirs implies a joint tenancy, but here is not a bare implication, but he gives it expressly to the survivor of them, and, if it were construed a tenancy in common, the word 'survivor' must be quite struck out.

As to the words 'equally to be divided' etc., they will not now make a tenancy in common in a deed and there was a time when it was doubted whether they would make a tenancy in common in a will, Dyer 25; Ratcliffe's Case, 3 Rep.,[1] so that they are not terms of art necessarily implying *vi termini* a tenancy in common but have been of late construed to imply as much. But then can it be said that words barely implying a tenancy in common shall overrule express words for a joint tenancy?

Mr. *Lutwyche* quoted the case of Fisher v. Weaks, in Lord Holt's time,[2] which was this, a surrender of a copyhold estate to the use of two equally to be divided between and to their respective heirs and assigns; the court were equally divided in opinion whether it was a joint tenancy or a tenancy in common, but Holt was for the joint tenancy and said that 'equally to be divided' does not necessarily imply a tenancy in common, for that does not make several freeholds; but the proper way was *habendum* one moiety to one and his heirs, the other moiety to the other and his heirs. So in 2 Rol. Abr. 90; Sty. 211, Hurd v. Lenthall.[3] A devise to two daughters equally to be divided and to the survivor of them and to the heirs of the body of the survivor of them [was] resolved to make a joint ten-

---

[1] *Anonymous* (1537), 1 Dyer 25, 73 E.R. 53; *Norton, ex dem. Ratcliff v. Rowland* (1592), 3 Coke Rep. 37, 76 E.R. 713.

[2] *Fisher v. Wigg* (1700), 1 Peere Williams 14, 24 E.R. 275, Holt K.B. 369, 90 E.R. 1104, 1 Salkeld 391, 91 E.R. 339, 3 Salkeld 206, 91 E.R. 779, 1 Lord Raymond 622, 91 E.R. 1316, 1 Comyns 88, 92, 92 E.R. 974, 976, 12 Modern 296, 88 E.R. 1332, 1 Eq. Cas. Abr. 291, 21 E.R. 1053, 2 Eq. Cas. Abr. 535, 22 E.R. 451.

[3] *Furse v. Weekes* (1650), 1 Rolle, Abr., *Jointenants*, pl. G, 5, p. 90; *Hurd v. Lenthall* (1650), Style 211, 82 E.R. 653.

ancy by reason of the express word 'survivor'. Tuckerman v. Jefferys, 6 Ann.[1] A devise to two daughters, equally to be divided between them during their natural lives, and, after the death of them two, to the right heirs of one of them, though there was no express limitation to the survivor, yet, because the limitation over was not to take place until after the death of the other, the words 'equally to be divided' would lose their force, and [it was] adjudged a joint tenancy so that, when the words 'equally to be divided' come in competition with a necessary implication or an express limitation, they have been overruled and the construction has been for a joint tenancy.

As to the case quoted by the other side, Bissett v. Cranwell, in 3 Lev. 373 and Salk. 206,[2] the words 'to them and their heirs, equally to be divided' seem to have guided the revolution and make the case different from this. And so stress was laid also on the words 'after my wife's death'.

The counsel for the defendant [said], though the words are never expressed against an heir at law, yet, if the estate is not taken from him, he must have it. A joint tenancy or a title by survivorship is not favored, especially in a court of equity, for it is a title depending only on the strength of a man's constitution or his care of himself.

There are many cases where the words 'equally to be divided' have been construed a tenancy in common. 2 Vent. 365; the like case in Cro. Eliz. 729 and Moor 667.[3]

The case of Bissett v. Cranwell is in point for us; so Draper's Case, in 2 Ch. Case; Sty. 434.[4] In the case of Fisher v. Weaks, the court was equally divided and the cases in Styles and Tuckerman v. Jeffryes were governed by the words 'after the death of' etc. If this is a joint tenancy, many more words must be rejected than must if it be construed a tenancy in common.

King, Lord Chancellor: It must be agreed that the construction of this point is the same as if it were of a real estate actually the same. In the construction of wills, the intent of the testator is to be considered. That intention must appear from the will itself and not out of the will. In the construction of wills, every word must be made to agree as far as possible, and, unless inconsistent or nuga-

---

1 *Tuckerman v. Jeffries* (1707), 11 Modern 108, 88 E.R. 930, also Holt K.B. 370, 90 E.R. 1104.

2 *Blisset v. Cranwell* (1693), 3 Levinz 373, 83 E.R. 736, 1 Salkeld 226, 91 E.R. 201, also Comberbach 256, 90 E.R. 463.

3 *Earl of Salisbury v. Bennet* (1685–1691), 2 Ventris 365, 86 E.R. 489, also Nelson 170, 21 E.R. 818, 2 Vernon 223, 23 E.R. 744, Skinner 285, 90 E.R. 129, 1 Eq. Cas. Abr. 109, 21 E.R. 917; *Shaw v. Sherwood* (1599), Croke Eliz. 729, 78 E.R. 962, *sub nom. Shaw v. Norwood*, Moore K.B. 667, 72 E.R. 827, also Owen 127, 74 E.R. 949.

4 *Draper's Case* (1681), 2 Chancery Cases 64, 22 E.R. 848; *Torret v, Frampton* (1653), Style 434, 82 E.R. 840.

tory and useless, no word should be rejected, as, in this case, the words 'or survivors' are certainly absurd and, therefore, must be rejected.

In this case, the devisor certainly intended to disinherit his heir, and yet the heir will have whatever is not devised. In like manner, he as certainly intended that one should not have the whole. The word 'survivor' implies a joint tenancy and 'equally to be divided between them, share and share alike' implies a tenancy in common and, if any interpretation can be made so as to make these words consistent, we should admit it.

Therefore, I think the only one that can allow force to all the words is that he intended a joint tenancy during their lives with several inheritances afterwards, and, therefore, let the conveyance be to the plaintiff of the whole during his life and, after his death, one moiety to the heir at law and his heirs, the other to the plaintiff and his heirs.

Lincoln's Inn MS. Misc. 506, p. 77, pl. 2

Trinity 11 George. Blake v. Barker.

A man devises lands in trust for A. and B., his two nephews, and the survivor or survivors of them and their heirs forever to be equally divided, share and share alike. A. dies in the life[time] of the testator. The question was whether B. should have any more than a moiety and that which was given to A. should be looked on as a lapsed legacy or whether the whole should go to B., which depended on this question, whether the estate devised to A. and B. was a joint tenancy or a tenancy in common. It was insisted on that the word 'survivors' showed it to be a joint tenancy in fee. On the other side, [it was insisted] that the words 'to be equally divided' and 'share and share alike' showed it to be a tenancy in common.

The Commissioners Gilbert and Raymond had been divided in opinion.

But Lord Chancellor King decreed it to be a joint tenancy for life with several inheritances and that the word 'survivors' seemed to him to be added without any meaning, but only of course, but that the word 'survivor' made it a joint tenancy for life. And so he decreed an execution of the trust of the whole to B. for his life with an inheritance in one moiety and, after B.'s death, the other moiety to descend to the heir of the testator.

Lincoln's Inn MS. Misc. 384, p. 313, pl. 2

31 May. Gilbert and Raymond.

B. devises the surplus of his personal estate to the defendant's trustees to be laid out in land and settled to the use of the plaintiff and Jeremy, his brother, and the survivor and survivors of them, their heirs, and assigns forever to be equally divided between them, share and share alike. Jeremy died in the life of the testator. Query whether the whole or only half belongs to the plaintiff.

Talbot, for the plaintiff: The heir is intended to be totally disinherited. The whole estate is given to trustees. The word 'survivor' is to be entirely rejected.

Trinity 6 Ann., King's Bench, Tuckerman v. Jefferies; a devisee to two daughters, Jane and Elizabeth, to be equally divided between them during their lives and to the heirs of Jane was adjudged a joint tenancy.

Peere Williams, for the defendant: If both had survived the testator, they had been tenants in common. The death of one cannot alter it. He cited Blissett v. Cranwell, 3 Lev. 373, in point; Boucher v. Cook, on Sir Owen Buckingham's will; Scattergood v. Edge, Salk. 229.

No decree [was made].

Lincoln's Inn MS. Misc. 384, p. 313, pl. 1

4 June 1725.

It was decreed that the plaintiff and Jeremy, his brother, were joint tenants for life and tenants in common of the inheritance and the fee simple.

702

Jones v. Henrick

(Ch. 1725)

A final decree in equity is res judicata.

Lincoln's Inn MS. Hill 29, p. 89

Trinity 11 Geo. I.

A. mortgages lands in 1683, which mortgage comes to Cranmer in 1691, whose representative the defendant is. In 1702, a decree was made for foreclosure of A., who dies in 1710. His heir, an infant, who being now come of age in 1724, brings an original bill to be let into the redemption, suggesting that the estate was of double the value of the money due on it, that his ancestor was in prison at the time of the former decree, that himself was but lately come of age, and that there were several errors in the former decree.

The defendant pleads the former decree and answers over. The earl of Macclesfield, late Lord Chancellor, overruled the plea.

And now the cause came to a hearing before King, Lord Chancellor, who said that the defendant's plea though overruled, yet the substance of it, as it stood in the answer, he would consider. He said he thought there was an error in the decree in 1702, but, as it stands as a decree of the court, he must take it to be a good decree. Now, if the decree subsists, it would be absurd to allow an original bill and make a decree contrary to a former decree now in the court.

It would be of dangerous consequence to admit mortgagors in to redeem after a decree such a great number of years ago. This would take away the security a purchaser has under the decree of the court.

When a mortgagee has applied to the court to have his money or that the mortgagor may be foreclosed and the mortgagor has notice of this [and] is brought before the court and chooses rather to part with the estate than pay the money, shall he be allowed afterwards to come and pay a redemption? I think the ancestor could not within the eight years that he lived after the decree of foreclosure have brought his original bill to redeem, but, if there was error in the decree, he should have brought a bill of review, and the heir cannot be in a better case than his ancestor was.

Therefore, let the plaintiff's bill be dismissed without costs.

703

Lorimer v. Harris

(Ch. 1725)

A bill of review for new matter discovered since the decree cannot be filed without leave of the court.

Lincoln's Inn MS. Misc. 12, p. 168, pl. 1

3 June 1725.

Upon a motion to dismiss a bill of review because it was brought without leave of the court, being grounded upon new matter discovered since the decree, it was certified by the Register to the court that the bringing of a bill of review where it was for new matter discovered since the decree without leave of the court was irregular notwithstanding the plaintiff had deposited £50.

[Other copies of this report: 2 Cooper *tempore* Cottenham 443, 47 E.R. 1240.]

[Other reports of this case: 2 Peere Williams 283, 24 E.R. 731.]

704

Pocock v. Pocock

(Ch. 1725)

Where land devised is subject to a lien, the lien is to be discharged out of the personal estate of the decedent even though the lien was created after the making of the devise.

As the mortgage is considered as a debt, it must always be first discharged out of the personal estate before the legacies are paid, unless there is something particular to make it otherwise.

In the case of an heir, equity gives the preference to the legatees because the testator has declared by his will in their favor, which can be fulfilled no other way but by leaving the bond or mortgage chargeable on the heir's estate when the personal estate is not sufficient to answer both.

Lincoln's Inn MS. Misc. 380, pt. 2, p. 8

8 June 1725.

One seised of an estate in fee makes his will and thereby devises it to the plaintiff and his heirs and gives several personal legacies and makes the defendant his executor. Afterwards, he mortgages the same estate for a term of years and dies without redeeming it. The executor proved the will and continued for some years in the execution of it and paid several of the legacies. The plaintiff now brings his bill in order to have the estate devised to him redeemed out of the personal estate. The executor, by his answer, insisted that it ought not to be disencumbered out of the real estate and that he has not sufficient [assets] of the testator's estate remaining in his hands over and above the legacies which he had paid for that purpose. It now came to be heard.

And Mr. *Talbot*, for the executor, insisted that, though the common rule was that a mortgage both in the hands of the devisee and of the heir should be discharged out of the personal estate, yet, in the present case, the mortgage being after the devise ought to be considered as a revocation *pro tanto*, or at least that the personal legacies ought to be first discharged. He said this was agreeable to the usual equity of this court where there are bond debts and likewise debts upon simple contracts and legacies given by the will but [there is] not sufficient personal estate to satisfy them all, this court will so order and marshal the payment of the debts that the personal estate shall go first in discharge of the simple contracts and the bond debts be discharged out of the real in the hands of the heir in order to leave sufficient [assets] to satisfy the legacies.

Sir Joseph Jekyll, Master of the Rolls, said, as to the first question, that a mortgage was always considered in this court as a personal charge and as such to be always discharged in the first place out of the personal estate and this though there was no covenant in the mortgage deed for the payment of the money and that, therefore, it was the constant practice of this court to make the personal estate discharge it as well for the benefit of the devisee as of the heir at law and its being made after the devise does not render it less a personal debt than it would have been if it had been made before.

As to the question concerning the legatee, he said he was clear that the devisee's estate should be the first disencumbered out of the personal assets before the legatee should be entitled to anything.

As the mortgage is considered as a debt, it must always be first discharged out of the personal estate before the legacies are paid unless there is something particular to make it otherwise; in the case of the heir, equity gives the preference to the legatees on account of the manifest intention of the testator declared by his will in their favor, which can be fulfilled no other way but by leaving the bond or mortgage chargeable on the heir's estate when the personal estate is not sufficient to answer both. And this contradicts no other intention of the testator because he has given nothing to the heir. But in the case of the devisee, where the mortgage upon his estate and the legacy cannot be both satisfied, the intention of the testator with regard to them both, cannot be fully complied with and there is no reason to imagine that the testator intended his devise of the land should give way to the pecuniary legacies. And, therefore, since the mortgage in its own nature is a personal debt and a lien in the first place on the personal estate, it is agreeable to the rule of the court in like cases to discharge it out of that and let the loss fall upon those bequests which are to be satisfied out of that fund.

And it is the stronger in this case since the estate was devised to him before it was mortgaged, and the intent of the testator thereby [is] manifest that the devisee should have the whole estate. And he decreed accordingly.

Lincoln's Inn MS. Misc. 12, p. 170

18 June 1725.

Robert Pocock, by will, gives a house and land to his nephew, Joel Pocock, and Robert, his son, and their heirs. And he gave several pecuniary legacies and made A.B. executor. And, after making this will, he mortgaged the estate for £1000, and then he died.

The executor dying in the testator's lifetime, the defendant took administration *cum testamento* annexo and paid the legacies. Robert, the devisee, died in the lifetime of his father, and then the father died, having first made his will. And he gave the premises to the plaintiff, his wife, for her life and then to his son Joel and his heirs. And she and her son bring their bill against the administrator *cum testamento* annexo and the mortgagee to have an account of the personal estate and that it might be applied to pay off the mortgage.

It was insisted for the administrator that he has paid the legatees and that, if the personal estate was applied to discharge the mortgage, the legacies would be defeated and that it was as much the intention of the testator that the legacies should be paid as that the devisee should have the land and, though the mortgagee may take his satisfaction out of the personal estate, yet, as between the devisee and the legatees, the personal estate shall not be applied to exonerate the real estate when it will defeat the legacies.

But, to this, it was answered by the Master of the Rolls [Jekyll] that there being a covenant in the mortgage to pay the money, it is a debt upon the personal estate and the personal estate is the primary fund to pay the debts and the legatees are not entitled to their legacies until the debts are paid. And, though, where lands descend, as between the heir at law and the legatees, the heir at law is not entitled to have the personal estate applied to exonerate the real whereby to defeat the legacies. Yet it is otherwise where the land is specifically devised.

And he decreed an account of the personal estate and the administrator to pay off the mortgage so far as he shall appear to have assets.

705

Angel v. Brown

(Ch. 1725)

In a suit to perpetuate testimony, the defendant is entitled to receive court costs even where he cross-examines a witness.

Lincoln's Inn MS. Misc. 12, p. 174, pl. 1

Trinity term 1725.

The bill was brought to perpetuate the testimony of witnesses to a will against the defendant, the heir at law. And the witnesses having been examined and publication passed and it not being intended to proceed any further in the cause, no relief being prayed, the defendant now moved for his costs, which was opposed by the plaintiff's counsel, who said the defendant had cross-examined one of the plaintiff's witnesses and, therefore, was not entitled to his costs.

But, notwithstanding that, the court ordered the plaintiff to pay the defendant's costs.

706

Drayton v. Nash

(Ch. 1725)

If an executor wastes his testator's assets and dies, a legatee can only come in as a simple contract creditor upon his estate.

The Statute of Frauds requires all declarations of trusts to be in made writing.

Creditors and legatees cannot trace the assets of the decedent's estate when they have been used to buy land by the executor.

It is much better that one person should suffer a loss than that the court should introduce a general inconvenience and uncertainty into the law.

Lincoln's Inn MS. Misc. 12, p. 174, pl. 2

20 August 1725.

An executor had laid out a great part of his testator's personal estate in a purchase of lands and had devised those lands to the defendants. And he died without leaving personal assets sufficient to pay an annuity to the plaintiff, which the first testator had directed to be paid out of his personal estate.

And the plaintiff's bill was that she might follow the lands and be paid her annuity out of the rents thereof, they having been bought with the personal assets.

Lord Chancellor [Lord Macclesfield]: I believe from the proofs that the land was bought and paid for out of the personal estate of the first testator but, if

I was never so well satisfied of that, yet it is not in my power to charge the lands. If I should decree the land to satisfy the annuity, I must alter the law and tear up the Statute of Frauds[1] by the roots. The law says, if an executor wastes his testator's assets and dies, a legatee can only come in as a simple contract creditor upon his estate. And can I say otherwise?

Then, as to the Statute, that says all declarations of trusts shall be in writing. Can I, therefore, say that an heir or devisee of the real estate is a trustee for the creditors or legatees of the first testator when there is no writing declaring any such trust.

It is a hard case, but it is not in my power to help it. It is much better that one person should suffer than introduce a general inconvenience and uncertainty in men's estates, as would follow if creditors or legatees might follow the assets when turned into land by the executor.

Another thing prayed by the plaintiff was that the Master might set out her dower, which she was entitled to in the lands devised by the will to the infants.

But, to this, it was said by the infants' counsel that, though they thought it would be for the interest of the infants to have the dower set out by the Master, yet they could not consent to it, in regard it had never been allowed that a woman might bring a bill in equity to have her dower set out. Indeed, if a woman entitled to dower is in possession of the whole estate and a bill is brought against her to account for the rents, the court will direct the Master to see of what lands she is dowable and make her an allowance accordingly. But the court will not allow a bill to be brought to have dower set out.

And of that opinion was Lord Chancellor [Lord Macclesfield]. But he said he would remove all impediments out of the way whereby a doweress was hindered from bringing a writ of dower at common law.

And, as to the plaintiff, he said she should go to [common] law and ascertain her dower and she might come back and he would then direct an account to be taken of the rents of the lands from the death of the husband, which had been received by the executors in trust for the infant, for the arrears of the dower from the husband's death would not be allowed in damages upon the judgment in dower.

Another matter mentioned in this cause was that a bond creditor should be turned upon the real estate that a legatee might have a satisfaction out of the personal estate, which was said to be the settled rule of this court.

But the Chancellor [Lord Macclesfield] seemed much surprised at it. And he seemed to intimate that he should not do it.

---

1 Stat. 29 Car. II, c. 3 (*SR*, V, 839–842).

707

Clavering v. York

(Ch. 1725)

A gift causa mortis *should be included in the inventory of a decedent's estate because it is liable for the payment of the decedent's debts.*

Lincoln's Inn MS. Misc. 506, p. 78, pl. 1

Michaelmas 12 George.

The bill was brought for an account of the personal estate of the defendant's intestate and to have a distribution according to the Statute.[1] The defendant, who was the mother and administratrix of the intestate, had formerly given her daughter £500 and, when her daughter lay sick a little before her death, she took out of her daughter's trunk two papers and holding them out in her hand, asked her daughter if she gave them to her 'freely'. The daughter answered 'yes'. There was proof that there was some discourse about a bond and a note. And one of the witnesses swore that he judged it to be a bond and a note. There were no other securities proved to be among the daughter's effects but the bond for £150 and a note for £500, which were the bond and note insisted on by the defendant to be given her by her daughter. It was objected by the plaintiff that the defendant had inserted them into the inventory and that there was not sufficient proof that they were the papers given by the daughter.

The Master of the Rolls [Jekyll] thought that there was and that it was a *donatio mortis causa* and ought to be inserted in the inventory because [they are] liable to debts. But he would not allow the mother for the maintenance of her daughter who lived with her, which was £120, but he took the *donatio mortis causa* to be a legatory disposition and, being more than the maintenance, should be supposed to be in satisfaction of it and, though the word 'freely' was added, that imported only that the act was voluntary and without constraint and not with respect to its operation.

2 Collyer 363, 63 E.R. 772

15 October 1725.

A young woman who had lived with her mother five years and had never paid anything for her board, a little before her death, gave her mother a bond for £500 and a note for £100, which were debts owing to her from other persons.

The Master of the Rolls [Jekyll], in the first instance, decreed that this gift should be a satisfaction of the debt owing for the board. But he, afterwards, expressed his opinion that, supposing anything to be due for the board (as to which there appeared some doubt), the bond and note were not a satisfaction of the

---

[1] Stat. 22 & 23 Car. II, c. 10 (*SR*, V, 719–720).

debt, for one debt could not be a satisfaction of another debt, and, as this was so in the case of a will, it would be the same in the case of a *donatio mortis causa*, which was of the same nature as a legacy.

Lincoln's Inn MS. Misc. 12, p. 178

25 October 1725.

[It was] agreed by the Master of the Rolls [JEKYLL] that a donatio causa mortis would operate upon a debt though a debt could not be delivered over to the donee.

And, in this case, a young woman, who had lived with her mother five years and had never paid anything for her board, a little before her death, gave her mother a bond for £500 and a note for £100, which were debts owning to her from other persons.

And it was decreed that this gift should be a satisfaction of the debt owing for [?] the board, for a *donatio causa mortis* was a testamentary disposition and as a legacy given by a will to one to whom the testator is indebted when the legacy is more than the debt is a satisfaction of the debt, it ought to be much rather so in the case of a *donatio causa mortis*.

The next day after this cause was heard, the Master of the Rolls [JEKYLL] took occasion to mention this case again. And he said that, being a new case, he had considered further of it and was still of opinion that the mother ought to have no allowance for the board of the daughter in regard there was no agreement that mother should be paid anything for the board nor did she, though her daughter lived five years with her, ever demand anything and, besides, the daughter was of age and she had her fortune in her own hands and the mother was not accountable to the daughter for any profits of the fortune.

And, as to the question whether the bond and note should be a satisfaction of the board, supposing anything was due for it, upon further consideration, he was of opinion it was not, for one debt cannot be a satisfaction of another debt, it being uncertain whether the debt would ever be received or not. It would not be so in case a debt was given by a will to one to whom the testator owed a debt and, therefore, not so in the case of a *donatio causa mortis*, which is of the same nature as a legacy.

708

Hinton v. Scott

(Ch. 1725–1730)

Where a settlement is made upon a wife out of her own personal estate by her husband, the creditors of the husband cannot reach this settlement.

Lincoln's Inn MS. Misc. 12, p. 176, pl. 2

21 October 1725. At the Temple Hall.

The plaintiffs, who are creditors by bond and simple contract of A.B., bring their bill against him and his wife and against the defendant Scott, the widow and executor of Robert Scott, to have an account of the personal estate of Robert Scott, who was a freeman of London and the father of the defendant, the wife of A.B., and to be paid their respective debts out of the customary share of the estate of Robert Scott, which A.B. was entitled to in the right of his wife.

The defendant pleaded that A.B., after the death of Robert Scott, assigned over his wife's customary share to trustees upon trust for the separate use of the wife during her life and then for her children and that, afterwards, the goods of A.B. being taken in execution, he made another assignment to two of his creditors of all his household goods and also of his wife's customary share of her father's estate for the satisfaction of the several creditors mentioned in a schedule.

The defendant being advised that the first assignment would be void against the second, she paid off the schedule debts, and then the trustees in the last assignment, by the direction of the schedule creditors and of A.B., in consideration of the defendant's having paid off the schedule debts, assign and release the said goods and also the said customary share to the defendant. And the wife of A.B. has since obtained a sentence of divorce *propter saevitiam* in the ecclesiastical court. And she and her children were wholly maintained by the defendant.

And, for the defendant, it was insisted, first, that the plaintiff's bill was improper, the plaintiffs having no lien upon the wife's customary share, for they have no judgment against A.B., but they come here at the first instance to have a satisfaction of their debts, and, if such bills should be allowed, any man, who has had any dealings with another, may be brought into this court.

Secondly, it was insisted that, supposing the bill to be proper, yet the plea was a good bar, for, though the first assignment was voluntary and might be fraudulent as against the second, yet the last assignment was made upon a good consideration and the defendant thereby became a purchaser of the wife's share and, as such, entitled to hold it against the plaintiffs.

Lord Chancellor [Lord King] inclined to think the bill improper. But, however, he said he would not allow nor disallow the plea but let it stand for an answer without liberty to except and save the benefit of it until the hearing.

Mosely 336, 25 E.R. 426

Tuesday, 2 June [1730].

Mr. Reynoldson, the defendant, married the defendant Mrs. Reynoldson, the daughter of Mr. Scot, a freeman of London. Mr. Scot died, and the husband, who had a considerable portion with his wife on the marriage and had never made any provision for her, assigned over her orphanage part to trustees for her sole and separate use during life and, after her decease, for her children. The creditors of the husband file this bill against the executors of Mr. Scot the husband, wife, children, and trustees to have this money paid to them as fraudulently assigned.

Master of the Rolls [Jekyll]: I shall suppose the plaintiffs to be creditors prior to the assignment, though they have not clearly proved it. The husband by law is entitled to the estate of his wife, but, if he wants the aid of this court to recover it, he must make a provision for his wife before the court will decree it to be paid to him. And he could not recover this chose in action without a subpoena. And, at law, if he sues for a chose in action in the right of his wife, he must join her in the action. And, if he dies before he reduces it into possession, the action survives to her. And the court imposes terms on the husband on that principle, that he who would have equity must do equity. So there only remains to be considered whether the plaintiffs are not entitled to the interest during the life of the husband. The husband has no title to it, because he has assigned it for the separate use of the wife. Then, if I decree it to the plaintiffs, I must break through a settlement I think a very reasonable one, for, where the husband is indigent and the wife in a starving condition, the court has often obliged him to settle the portion on the wife for her own separate use. So the bill must be dismissed.

Lincoln's Inn MS. Misc. 384, p. 294, pl. 1

2 June 1730. At the Rolls.

The defendant's wife was an orphan of London. The plaintiffs are creditors of the husband. The bill was to set aside a settlement, which the husband had voluntarily made on his wife of her orphanage share for her separate use. There was cited Richmond v. Taileur; Jacobson v. Peere Williams, that the creditors cannot be in a better case than the husband and, he not having settled any estate of his own upon her, this court would have directed this part of her fortune to be settled on her for her separate use. It appears that the husband was insolvent. He dismissed the bill with costs.

709

Green v. Sparrow

(Ch. 1725)

Fraud is a good ground of jurisdiction in a court of equity.

3 Swanston 408, 36 E.R. 927

25 October 1725.

The plaintiff, in the year 1721, leased to the defendant some coal mines, reserving a rent of £600 *per annum*, the first quarter's rent to be paid at the next feast after the lessee should have dug 1000 stacks of coal; the lessee covenanted that he would dig or cause to be dug the said 1000 stacks of coal without delay and in a reasonable time. And it was further covenanted between the parties that the defendant might upon six months' notice determine and quit the said lease, paying all the rents due and performing all the covenants contained in the lease. The lessee entered, and, in 1723, gave six months' notice, according to the agreement, whereby he insisted that the lease was determined at Christmas 1723. The plaintiff preferred his bill and set forth that the defendant, after entering into the lands at Christmas 1721, wrought in the mines and, having dug the 1000 stacks of coal about a week before quarter day, wanting only a small quantity, employed his workmen in other works, telling some of them that he was not such a fool as to pay a quarter's rent for a few days' work, by which means the 1000 stacks of coal were not dug until after Lady Day [25 March], whereas they might have been dug before, had not the defendant himself prevented it. And he insisted that the first quarter's rent therefore ought to have been paid upon Lady Day 1721 and prayed that the defendant might be obliged specifically to perform his covenants and continue the lease for the twenty-one years; for not having performed his covenants, he insisted he could not determine it, for that the power to determine by notice was conditional, *viz.* on paying the rent and performing the covenants, by one of which he was obliged to dig the pits in a workman-like manner and to level the pits with the gin pits, *viz.* the pit where the engine is to carry away the water, which he had not done, whereby the pits were overflowed with water and become of no service to the plaintiff.

It was said for the plaintiff that the plaintiff's application was very proper in this court, for the defendant had made use of fraud and contrivance to prevent the commencement of the rent and that he was entitled to insist on a specific performance of the defendant's covenant and continuance of the lease, for, though there might be an action of law for breach of covenants if he had not performed them, yet it is more just and reasonable in a court of equity to oblige the defendant specifically to perform his covenants than to drive the plaintiff to an action of law to recover damages only for the breach of them.

For the defendant, it was said that the bill ought to be dismissed, because the plaintiff, if injured, might have his remedy at law, for, if the defendant had prevented the digging of the 1000 stacks of coal by design, an action of covenant would lie against him at common law, since he covenanted that he would dig them without delay etc. And, as to the second point, if he has not performed his covenants, he cannot determine the lease, and then it still continues without the assistance of this court. If he has performed them, he may determine it, and this is a proper fact for a jury to decide, and not for this court.

King, Lord Chancellor, agreed that, as to the second point, it is proper to be tried at law and in an action of debt, for, if the defendant has not performed his covenants, he cannot then determine the lease and, if that is still subsisting, which is a fact for a jury to try, an action lies for the rent. But, as to the first point, though he might indeed have a remedy by an action of covenant upon the collateral covenant to dig the coal without delay etc., yet here was fraud in preventing the digging before the quarter day in order that the rent might not commence so soon, and this fraud requires the interposition of the court. He decreed, therefore, the defendant must pay the first quarter's rent due at Lady Day 1721 and account and pay the rent to Christmas 1723 until which time he allows the lease continued and the plaintiff to have the costs against the defendant so far as he has prevailed. And, as to the other point, whether the lease is determined or no, it is properly cognizable at common law, and the bill must be dismissed as to that, and the defendant, as to that matter, so far must have his costs.

The following is the entry in the register relative to the question noticed in the preceding report: 'Upon debate etc., His Lordship declared that the said George Sparrow fraudulently delayed the getting the 1000 stacks of coal until after the quarter day on purpose to keep off the commencement of the rent, and he does, therefore, think fit to order and decree that the defendant Sparrow do pay to the plaintiff Green the first quarter's rent for the said colliery works as due at Lady Day 1721 and do continue to pay the rent for the same from Lady Day 1721 to Christmas 1723' etc. Reg. Lib. A 1725, ff. 120–124.

710

Baldwin v. Baldwin

(Ch. 1725)

A court of equity can enforce a decree for the payment of alimony.

Lincoln's Inn MS. Misc. 12, p. 206, pl. 2

Michaelmas term 1725.

The plaintiff, as administratrix of her brother, Mr. Player, a surgeon, being entitled to some leasehold houses in Castle Yard in Holborn, married the defendant, who proved an ill husband, leaving her and lived with another woman, whereupon she brought a suit in the spiritual court for a divorce. And she obtained a sentence for a divorce *a mensa et thoro* and that he should allow her £50 a year for alimony. Which he refusing to pay and standing excommunicated for non-payment, the plaintiff brought her bill by her next friend to enjoin the defendant from selling these houses and that the £50 a year might be paid to her out of the rents.

And, accordingly, it was decreed the alimony of £50 a year decreed the plaintiff should be established and that the Master should settle a proper conveyance for securing the payment of the £50 a year to the plaintiff out of the houses according to the sentence in the spiritual court.

711

Gibson v. Hudson's Bay Company

(Ch. 1725)

Where the bylaws of a company allow a shareholder's stock to be seized to satisfy the shareholder's debt to the company, this is a matter of mutual accounts for the purpose of a bankruptcy liquidation of the shareholder.

Lincoln's Inn MS. Misc. 506, p. 78, pl. 2

Michaelmas 12 Geo.

The bill was brought by the assignees of a commission of bankruptcy taken out against Sir Stephen Evans[1] against the Hudson's Bay Company to transfer the stock which Sir Stephen had in their books. The Company, by their answer, insisted that Sir Stephen was indebted to them in £824, that there was a bylaw of the Company which empowered them to distrain and impound the stock of every proprietor for debts due from him to the Company, that Sir Stephen had been a Governor of the Company and was a party to the bylaw, that they were ready to transfer the surplus or balance after the debt due to the Company should be first discharged.

It was insisted on by the assignees that the Company ought to transfer the whole stock and come in only *pro rata* with the other creditors, that this was not a mutual accounts because stock was one thing and money another, that the bylaw was void as overturning the common law of the land in prescribing a different method of execution and giving a preference where the law does not, that if it were good, yet it could not bind the assignees, who were strangers to it, that they had not pursued the bylaw nor executed their power for that they had not distrained nor impounded the stock.

---

[1] H. Lancaster, 'Evance, Sir Stephen (1654/5–1712)', *Oxford Dictionary of National Biography*, vol. 18, p. 660.

Chief Justice Raymond and Baron Price thought it a good bylaw for that it was to encourage the credit of the Company, which the court ought to countenance, that things ran now in another channel from what they did formerly when companies were erected only for the government of particular places, that now companies were usually erected for the better carrying on the trade to particular places and ought to be supported in such bylaws as were made for the encouraging of trade and merchandise, which is by maintaining the credit of the Company, that the bankrupt himself was bound by the bylaw and assignees must stand in his place. (Two cases were cited: one where the assignees were decreed to perfect a prior agreement of the bankrupt for the sale of his lands; another where the assignees who brought a bill for a legacy left to the wife of the bankrupt were obliged upon taking the legacy to make an answerable settlement on the wife as the bankrupt must have done if she had sued for it.) They said the Company had executed the power of the bylaw for that the denial to transfer the stock was impounding it, being all the impounding such things were capable of.

Lord Chancellor [Lord King] seemed to waver about these things.

But the whole court agreed that these were mutual accounts within the Act of Parliament,[1] that stock was credit on one side, that money lent was credit on the other side, that, therefore, here were mutual accounts of debtor and creditor, and thus the company should be answerable only for the balance. There had formerly been a case between a sugar baker and a tobacco merchant where the one had sent the other in sugar and the other had sent him in tobacco and they were allowed to be mutual accounts within the Act. And it is but reasonable it should be so because credit is often given with a view to that security. The Company thus were decreed to transfer only the surplus after the debt of £824 due to the Company should be first deducted.

Lincoln's Inn MS. Misc. 384, p. 265, pl. 1

3 November 1725. Lord Chancellor [Lord King], Chief Justice Raymond, Baron Price.

The plaintiff, as assignee of Sir Stephen Evance, brought a bill, to compel the defendants to transfer £2000 of their stock.

The defendants insisted that the bankrupt [Evance] was indebted to them for £800 and that, by a bylaw in 1679, they might distrain the stock of any member for a debt due to the Company.

The judges [Raymond and Price] attended to give their opinion as to the validity of the bylaw.

Lord Chancellor [Lord King] [was] of opinion the bylaw was not good, that it was contrary to the law to give a preference to a creditor by a simple contract, even to a judgment, and without legal process.

---

[1] Stat. 5 Geo. I, c. 24.

Both of the judges were to the contrary, that it was good by way of contract, that any man might agree that his stock should be a pledge, [and] that it was for the benefit of trade.

N.B. When the Lord Chancellor found the judges to differ in opinion with him, he put it on another point and considered it on the Statute of Bankrupts, and he was of opinion that the stock was to be looked upon as money and, there being a mutual account, the balance only was to be paid to the plaintiff.

Lincoln's Inn MS. Hill 29, p. 91

Michaelmas 12 Geo. I. In Chancery.

A bill was brought by the plaintiffs as assignees under a commission of bankruptcy against Sir John Evans praying that the defendants might be decreed to admit the plaintiffs to transfer some stock of the bankrupt in the said Company.

The defendants, by answer, set forth that the bankrupt was at the time he became bankrupt greatly indebted to the Company for monies he had received for them as their cashier, and that, in 1676, a by-law of the Company was made to this effect, that every adventurer's stock in the said Company should be liable to answer the debts due to the said Company from the said respective adventurers in the said Company.

Lord Chancellor KING called to his assistance SIR ROBERT RAYMOND, Chief Justice of the King's Bench, and Price BARON of the Exchequer. And it was much debated at the bar whether this by-law was good or at least could bind an assignee under the Statute of Bankrupts.[1]

And [it was said] by RAYMOND and PRICE it is good so as to bind the plaintiffs, which the Lord Chancellor [KING] seemed to doubt, but he said he apprehended that that point was not necessary to be determined on this case for that the bankrupt being indebted to the said Company and the Company having effects in their hands, the one debt should be set against the other, which RAYMOND and PRICE agreed to. And [it was] so decreed.

1 Strange 645, 93 E.R. 755

In Chancery. *Assistentibus* RAYMOND and PRICE.

The plaintiff, as assignee of the effects of Sir Stephen Evance, a bankrupt, brings his bill against the Company to oblige them to suffer him to transfer stock. The Company insist that Sir Stephen Evance was their banker and greatly indebted to them and that, upon the clause in the Bankrupts Act, which directs the commissioners to state the account between mutual dealers, they shall be allowed to hold the stock and account only for the balance, if any shall appear against them.

And of this opinion was the court, and [it was] decreed accordingly. Query.

---

[1] Stat. 5 Geo. I, c. 24.

Indiana University, Lilly Library,
MS. 'Cases in the Exch., vol. 5,' p. 78
(Price's reports)

3 November 1725. The assignees of the estate and effects of Sir Stephen Evans, a bankrupt, against the Hudson's Bay Company. Lord Chancellor King assisted by Chief Justice Raymond and Baron Price.

Sir Stephen Evans had, in 1711, £1700 stock in the Hudson's Bay Company, which grew to £5100, and the dividends ever since were £2500. Sir Stephen Evans owed the Company £884, which was lent him by Potter, secretary and servant to the Company.

There was a bylaw made in the Company in 1679 that, where [there was] an adventurer in any stock of the Company, his stock should be obliged to pay all such debts as he owed the Company and that he shall not transfer his stock until all such debts [be] paid and that the Company and committee might distrain his stock for the same. The charter has been confirmed by an act of Parliament.[1]

The questions were whether the bylaw made by the Company was good and binding to the plaintiffs; second, if the Statute about bankrupts, 5 Anne, where the commissioners are to allow the assignees but the balance of the account between the parties where there was mutual credit [applies].

As to the first point, Lord Chancellor [King] was of the opinion that the bylaw was not good to give a priority of payment to those who had shares in the stock before others the Company's creditors, for that would postpone the king's debt and others and take place of judgments as well as the assignees of the courts of bankrupts.

On the other side, the two judges were of the opinion that the bylaw was good and that Sir Stephen Evans's contract and submission to the bylaw bound him and what bound him would bind those who claimed under him and that the plaintiffs can have no better right than he had therein, that the bylaw was for the benefit of trade and the good of the Company and for the promotion of the credit of the Company and, consequently, of any adventurer or sharer in the stock and all claiming under them, as it appears that £1700 begot £5100 and £2500 in dividends and all the stock and money advanced in the stock is for promoting trade and commerce and taking it that, by the agreement or bylaw, the stock was a pledge to pay what was due to the Company, the plaintiffs are subject to it. And it is usual in these companies to have calls towards protecting the stock and goods.

Second, the Lord Chancellor [King] and the judges [Raymond and Price] agreed they were within the Statute 5 Anne[2] to be allowed the defendant's debt on account and so the plaintiff ought to allow the defendants the said £884 due to them in the said account.

[Other reports of this case: 2 Eq. Cas. Abr. 122, 22 E.R. 104.]

---

1 Private act of 2 Will. & Mar. (*SR*, VI, 179).

2 Stat. 4 & 5 Ann., c. 4, s. 12 (*SR*, VIII, 463).

712

Thomas v. Pendlebury

(Ch. 1725)

Where a government security is mortgaged, upon a decree for a redemption, the mortgagee must return a like government security of equal value regardless of any decline in value in the meantime.

Lincoln's Inn MS. Misc. 13, p. 150

9 November 1725.

An annuity payable at the Exchequer is by marriage articles agreed to be purchased and assigned to the husband of the plaintiff for his life, then to the plaintiff for her life, remainder for the benefit of the issue of the marriage, subject to a power for the husband to raise £300. The husband borrows £300 of the defendant, and the annuity is assigned to him as a security. And, in the assignment, the defendant covenants, upon payment of the principal and interest, to reassign the annuity. After the mortgage was become forfeited, the defendant in pursuance of the South Sea [Company] Act, 6 *Georgii*,[1] subscribes the annuity into the South Sea [Company] stock. The husband dies, and the plaintiff and her children bring their bill to redeem the mortgage.

The question was where the loss arising from the subscription should fall.

Lord Chancellor [Lord King] was of opinion the mortgagee was not a trustee within the Act of Parliament. He has only the estate as a security for his money and has covenanted, upon payment of the principal and interest, to reassign the annuity upon the same trusts as it was then subject to. And, therefore, it was decreed that the defendant should procure an annuity of the like value and account for what might have been received out of the annuity mortgaged to him and, upon payment of what is due for principal, interest, and costs, discounting what he might have so received, he is to assign the annuity, which he is to procure, upon the trusts in the marriage articles.

[Other reports of this case: 2 Eq. Cas. Abr. 601, 22 E.R. 505.]

[1] Stat. 6 Geo. I, c. 4, s. 23.

713

Hodges v. Escourt

(Ch. 1725)

In this case, the intent of the testator was that his debts should be paid out of the income from his land and not out of his personal estate alone.

Lincoln's Inn MS. Misc. 13, p. 151

Eodem die [9 November 1725].

Lands are devised to J.S. for two years upon trust out of the profits to pay debts, legacies, and funeral expenses. And after bequeathing some legacies, the residue of the personal estate is given to J.S., who is made executor, for his own use.

It was insisted by the plaintiff, to whom the lands were devised after the two years, that the personal estate ought to be applied in the first place to pay the debts etc. in ease of the land and, if anything remained of the rents of the lands during the two years after the debts etc. were paid, the same ought to be paid to him as devisee of the estate.

Lord Chancellor [Lord King]: It is plain the intention of the testator was that the profits of the lands during the said two years should be added to the personal estate and go to the payment of the debts and legacies and that, if anything remained, it should belong to the executor. And accordingly, it was so decreed.

714

Richardson v. Mitchell

(Ch. 1725)

In a suit for an account of rents and profits, the defendant cannot avoid making the account by alleging that the plaintiff has no right to any account in the first place.

British Library MS. Hargrave 83, p. 40

10 November 1725. Upon exceptions in Chancery.

An account was prayed by the bill of the rents and profits of a plantation. The defendant, by answer, sets forth her purchase made in the year 1710 and insists that she is a purchaser for a valuable consideration and that, therefore, she should not be obliged to set forth an account of the rents and profits. And she swears by her answer that she is not able to set forth an account of the rents and profits by reason of casualties. Exceptions were taken to this answer, and the answer was reported insufficient generally. An exception taken to this report was now overruled, and, without going through any of the other exceptions to the answer but that relating to the account of the rents and profits, the defendant was ordered to answer *de novo*.

In this case was cited the case of Stevens and Stevens, where the plaintiff brought his bill and laid claim under the same will by which the defendant claimed the estate of the testator, and his bill was to have his share of that estate by virtue of the will; the defendant, by his answer, insisted that the plaintiff had no right to anything by the will of the testator; an exception was taken to this answer for not setting forth an account of the testator's estate; upon arguing the exception, it was insisted for the defendant that it might appear to the court by the will set forth in the answer that the plaintiff had no right to an account of the testator's estate; Lord Macclesfield said he would not determine this point upon the exception, but, since the defendant had submitted to answer, he ought to answer and give an account of the estate. And Edwards and Freeman[1] was then cited by My Lord Chancellor King, where the defendant insisted by his answer that the plaintiff's wife was by a provision made by her father barred of her distributive share and, therefore, had no right to an account of the testator's estate. The exception to the answer was held good.

Select Cases *tempore* King 51, 25 E.R. 217

10 November.

A bill was brought to set aside a purchase and to have a discovery of the site and profits of the estate.

The defendant, by answer, insists that he is a purchaser and that he is not obliged to make a discovery, to which an exception was taken for not answering. And that exception was allowed.

In support of the exception, the case of Stephens v. Stephens, before Lord Macclesfield, [was cited]; a bill was brought for a discovery of the rents and profits of an estate, which he claimed by will from a common ancestor; the defendant says he is entitled to the estate and, therefore, until the right is determined, he was not obliged to give account of rents and profits. Lord Macclesfield said this might have been good by way of plea, but, having answered, he must answer the charge of the bill. So lately the Case of Edwards v Freeman; a bill was brought for an account; the defendant controverted the right and said he was not obliged to give an account before that was settled; and Your Lordship was of opinion that, having answered, the charge of the bill must be answered.

It was so resolved here.

[Other reports of this case: 2 Eq. Cas. Abr. 67, 378, 22 E.R. 58, 322.]

---

[1] *Edwards v. Freeman* (Ch. 1726–1728), see below, Case No. 753.

715

Webber v. Taylor

(Ch. 1725)

A modus decimandi *to pay tithes in kind or not at the election of the parson is invalid.*

Select Cases *tempore* King 52, 25 E.R. 218

15 November 1725.

A bill was brought to establish a *modus*, which was laid thus, for payment of such a sum of money, but, if in the hands of any other person, to pay tithe in kind or the money at the election of the parson.

A *modus* is not to be established without trial, if desired. Lord Chancellor [Lord King]: I will never establish a *modus* against a parson without a trial at law if he desires it, but this *modus* is clearly ill, for a *modus* cannot be desultory.

[Other copies of this report: 2 Eq. Cas. Abr. 734, 22 E.R. 622, 1 Rayner 215, 2 Gwillim 656, 1 Eagle & Younge 802.]

716

Tilney v. Wheeler

(Ch. c. 1725)

The question in this case was whether an executor might retain a legacy given to himself against the other legatees and not be obliged to abate in proportion with them in case of a deficiency of assets.

A bequest of a sum of money to be raised in a certain manner is a pecuniary legacy.

Lincoln's Inn MS. Misc. 12, p. 181

In this case, Lord Chancellor [Lord Macclesfield] seemed to be pretty clear of opinion that an executor might retain a legacy given to himself against the other legatees and not be obliged to abate in proportion with them in case of a deficiency of assets. And he grounded his opinion upon the law which allows an executor to retain for his own debt and to pay himself in the first place before other creditors of equal nature. And he thought it was more reasonable he should do so in the case of a legacy in regard he had the trouble of the executorship and the legatees none.

He asked the bar if they ever knew any determination otherwise, and no one could say it had ever been determined one way or the other. However, he did not determine the question, the case turning upon another point, *viz.* a legacy of £100 given out of some East India [Company] bonds was a specific or a pecuniary legacy. And it was urged that it was a specific legacy, it being the same thing to give a sum of money out of an [East] India bond as to give a moiety or any other particular part of such a bond.

But Lord Chancellor [Lord Macclesfield] was of opinion that it was a pecuniary legacy as appeared from this, that, if a man gives a sum of money out of any particular thing and he really has no such thing, yet the legacy subsists and shall be paid out of the personal estate according to the case in Raymond 335.[1]

717

Colt v. Nettervill

(Ch. 1725)

A court of equity can decree specific performance of a contract for the sale of stock in a company.

Lincoln's Inn MS. Misc. 12, p. 182

17 November 1725.

A bill was [exhibited] for a specific performance of two contracts for sale of York Buildings stock, and the plaintiff charges that he paid the defendant the sum of [*blank*] in part of payment of the money which was agreed to be paid for the stock.

As to one of the contracts, the defendant pleaded the Statute of Frauds and Perjuries,[2] and he avers that he accepted no money in part of payment.

And, as to the other contract, he demurred because the plaintiff had a proper remedy by action at law.

Lord Chancellor [Lord King] said he would not determine the question whether a contract for stock was within the Statute of Frauds, the judges having been divided in their opinions about it and those who were of opinion that it was not within the Statute laid great stress upon the Act of Parliament passed soon after the Restoration for reversing the proceedings against Sir John Westenholme,[3] who had been declared a trader and bankrupt for having bought and sold East India [Company] stock, so that, in the opinion of the Parliament, stock was neither wares nor merchandises.

But, as to the plea itself, it was not good for want of a proper averment, for the plaintiff has charged that he paid the defendant some money in part of payment and the defendant only avers that he did not accept any money in part of satisfaction. Now *quicquid solvitur solvitur in modum solventis*, and, therefore, if anything was paid in part, it matters not whether the defendant accepted it as such.

---

1 *Pawlet's Case* (1679), T. Raymond 335, 83 E.R. 174.

2 Stat. 29 Car. II, c. 3 (*SR*, V, 839–842).

3 Stat. 14 Car. II, c. 24, ss. 3, 4 (*SR*, V, 420).

As to the demurrer, the Case of Cudd and Rutter[1] was insisted on for the plaintiff, in which case the Master of the Rolls decreed a specific performance of a contract for the sale of South Sea stock and, upon an appeal to Lord Macclesfield, he did not dismiss the bill but only varied it so far as, instead of decreeing a specific performance, he decreed the difference. And, therefore, the plaintiff had very properly laid the prayer in the bill in the disjunctive, either that the defendant might transfer the stock or pay the difference.

Lord Chancellor [Lord King] seemed to think the court might properly decree a specific performance of a contract for the sale of stock and, if a man has two remedies, he thought equity ought not to take away one of them. And, therefore, he overruled the demurrer.

For the defendant, as to the plea, was cited the Case of Nunes v. Hill, *Liber* C, 16.[2]

[Other reports of this case: 2 Peere Williams 304, 24 E.R. 741, 2 Eq. Cas. Abr. 95, 22 E.R. 81.]

718

Huet v. Lord Say and Seal

(Ch. 1725)

Where a plaintiff dies pendente lite *and his successor in interest is both a devisee and an executor, the suit can be revived by a bill partly a bill of revivor and partly a bill in the nature of a bill of revivor.*

Lincoln's Inn MS. Misc. 12, p. 183

Eodem die [17 November 1725].

Three tenants in common bring a bill against the defendant, who was the other tenant in common, for a partition and that he might account for the rents which he had received. One of the plaintiffs dies and makes his will and devises his fourth part to J.S. and makes him executor. J.S. and the two surviving plaintiffs bring a bill of revivor against the defendant, who demurred because a devisee could not bring a bill of revivor, but he ought to bring a bill in the nature of a bill of revivor.

It was admitted for the plaintiff that a devisee could not bring a bill of revivor, but, here, the devisee was also the executor and the original bill being not only for a partition but for an account of the rents and, as to the arrears of rent incurred in the life of the testator, his share thereof now belonged to his executor and, therefore, the executor might properly revive the suit as to them and, as he

---

1 *Cud v. Rutter* (Ch. 1719–1720), see above, Case No. 410.

2 *Nunnes v. Hill* (Ch. 1716), see above, Case No. 161.

was proper to revive in one capacity, he might very well be joined with the others in a bill of revivor though he was only a devisee.

After long debate of the matter, it was agreed that the most proper way would be to make the bill partly a bill of revivor and partly a bill in the nature of a bill of revivor as to the devisee. And, thereupon, the demurrer was allowed, and the plaintiffs had leave to amend their bill.

Select Cases *tempore* King 53, 25 E.R. 219

A bill of partition was brought by several persons; one dies, who devises his part to a co-plaintiff, and he makes him executor.

He brings a bill of revivor, to which it was demurred.

It was said that bills of revivor and bills in nature of bills of revivor are very different. A bill of revivor can only be by the heir, as to the realty, and by an executor or administrator, as to the personalty. On a bill of revivor, the estate continues the same as before the abatement, but here, in the case of a devisee, who is a purchaser, the estate is altered, and a purchaser can never revive. 1 Ch. Ca. 174.[1] And an answer must be put in and publication pass, though possibly it may have the benefit of orders etc.

The demurrer was allowed. But leave was given to amend the bill and revive as executor. And an original bill in nature of a bill of revivor as devisee was thought the most proper method.

719

Paxton v. Meller

(Ch. 1725)

A court of equity will not require an interrogatory to be answered where the answer might lead to a penalty.

Lincoln's Inn MS. Misc. 12, p. 260

17 November 12 Geo. [1725].

The matter upon the demurrer put in by John Meller, Esq., formerly one of the Masters of this court, to part of the third interrogatory exhibited by the said Paxton, administrator of John Borrett, deceased, on behalf of the suitors of this court in pursuance of an order of the twenty-first day of June last made upon the petition of the said Paxton whereby it was ordered that the said Mr. Meller should be examined upon interrogatories touching all the money and effects of the suitors delivered over by him to the said Mr. Borrett or by him retained at the time of his surrendering his said office to the said Mr. Borrett and whether any

[1] *Backhouse v. Middleton* (1670), 1 Chancery Cases 173, 208, 22 E.R. 748, 765, also 3 Chancery Reports 39, 21 E.R. 722, 2 Freeman 132, 22 E.R. 1108.

and what sum of money belonging to the suitors besides the £632 8s. 9d. therein mentioned does still remain in his hands unaccounted for to the suitors coming this present day to be argued before this Rt. Hon. the Lord High Chancellor of Great Britain [Lord King] in the presence of counsel learned on both sides, as to such part of the said third interrogatory as required him the said Meller to set forth or discover whether the said John Borrett before or at or after his the said Meller's surrender of his said office gave unto him the said Meller a note under his hand or any other and what security for payment of the sum of £9000 or any other and what sum of money and whether there was any and what consideration for the said note and what was become of the said note or security, if any such there was, or which seeks any discovery touching the said John Borrett's payment of the sum of £9000 or any part thereof to him the said Meller or the manner of such payment, if any such there was, he the said Meller did demur in law to the said part of the third interrogatory for that the selling any office which touches or concerns the administration of justice and the receiving, having, or taking any money, fee, reward, or any other profit directly or indirectly for any such office or to the intent that any person should have, exercise, or enjoy any such office and the taking any promise, agreement, covenant, bond, or any assurance to receive or have any money, fee, reward, or other profit, directly or indirectly, for any such office being prohibited or made illegal by the laws and statutes of this realm, he, therefore, insisted that he is not obliged to discover or set forth any of the facts enquired after by the said part of the third interrogatory, which, if the same were true, might tend to show that he had acted contrary to the said laws and might subject him to the penalties consequential thereto, for that neither the suitors of the court nor the said Paxton on their behalf is or are entitled to the discovery of any contract or agreement made between the said Borrett and him, if any such there was, or of money paid or security given by the said Borrett to him, if any there were, other than of money paid to him the said Meller out of the moneys, securities, or effects belonging to the suitors of this court or of securities given to him or paid out of the moneys, effects, or securities of the said suitors, if any such there had been, and for that the said Paxton, as administrator to the said Borrett, could not be entitled to have any such discovery from him by the aid of this court upon a bill exhibited by him against the said Meller and was much less entitled to demand it in a summary way upon a petition, whereupon and upon debate of the matter and hearing what was alleged on both sides, His Lordship [Lord King] held the said demurrer to be good as to the discovery whether there was any and what consideration for giving such note or other security and did therefore order that the said demurrer be so far allowed. But, as to all other the matters demurred to, he did order that the same be overruled.

Select Cases *tempore* King 53, 25 E.R. 219

17 November 1725.

If a man gives a general answer and a particular question be asked which is included in the general, yet he must answer it particularly, else it may be demurred to, for that may be a matter of judgment.

A man is not obliged to answer any question which may subject him to a penalty; anything else material he must.

[Other copies of this report: 2 Eq. Cas. Abr. 67, 22 E.R. 58.]

720

Collins v. Griffith

(Ch. 1725)

Where a debt is joint and several, the creditor can sue any one of the debtors alone.

Lincoln's Inn MS. Misc. 12, p. 184

26 November 1725.

The defendant was the executor of A., who was bound in a bond together with B. and C. jointly and severally to the plaintiff for the payment of £100 with interest. And the plaintiff had brought his bill against the defendant only for a discovery of assets and a satisfaction of the debt.

The defendant demurred because the plaintiff had not made the other two obligors parties, who, if they were before the court, might show the debt was satisfied.

Lord Chancellor [Lord King] overruled the demurrer for, the bond being joint and several, any one of them may be sued alone, and, if it should be allowed otherwise in this court, it would be to alter the law.

[Other reports of this case: 2 Peere Williams 313, 24 E.R. 745, 2 Eq. Cas. Abr. 168, 188, 22 E.R. 143, 162.]

721

Richards v. Richards

(Ch. 1725)

An infant heir cannot sue for an account of the decedent's estate without making the decedent's administrator a party.

Lincoln's Inn MS. Misc. 12, p. 185

Eodem die [26 November 1725].

The plaintiff made a title to some lands as heir at law to George Richards, his father, who died intestate. And he suggested that the defendant, who was the nephew to George Richards claimed title as heir at law and threatened to bring [an action of] ejectment and disturb the plaintiff in his possession, pretending the plaintiff was not the legitimate son of George Richards. And so he prayed a discovery and account of the personal estate and to be quieted in the possession and the deeds and writings delivered to him and an injunction to stay the defendant's proceedings at [common] law and to be relieved.

As to so much of the bill as seeks an account of the personal estate or any relief touching the same, the defendant demurred because it appeared by the bill that George Richards died intestate and the plaintiff had not made the administrator a party.

And, as to so much of the bill as seeks to impeach the defendant's title to the lands in the bill or from proceeding at law for recovering possession thereof or to have the deeds and writings relating thereto delivered or any relief touching the said real estate, the defendant demurs for that the only title which the plaintiff pretends to set up to the said lands is as heir at law to the said George Richards, which is a title tryable at law and not in a court of equity and the plaintiff has not suggested that he is under any incapacity of trying such his title at law nor shown any matter of equity whereby this court ought to enjoin the defendant from asserting his title at law or from recovering possession of the premises nor ought the complainant to have any aid of this court for obtaining possession of the deeds and writings relating to the estate until he has established his title at a proper trial at law.

And, as to the discovery, the defendant answered.

Mr. Solicitor [General, *Wearg*], for the plaintiff, insisted that, though, as to the personal estate, the plaintiff indeed was not proper to have an account without having the representative of the intestate before the court, yet they were proper to have a discovery and the demurrer went to both.

But, for the defendant, it was said, and of that opinion was the Lord Chancellor [LORD KING], that the plaintiff was entitled to neither unless he made the representative a party, for, otherwise, he might be doubly harassed.

As to the other part of the demurrer, Mr. Solicitor [*Wearg*] insisted that the plaintiff was an infant and, though a man of full age could not bring a bill for an account of profits until he had established his title at law, yet an infant might and the court, if it was necessary, would direct a proper trial at law.

Sed non allocatur. And the demurrer was allowed as to both parts of it.

722

Waldie v. Wharton

(Ch. 1725)

A defendant in a suit in equity can rejoin voluntarily without being served with a subpoena to rejoin.

British Library MS. Hargrave 83, p. 44, pl. 2

15 December 1725. At the Lord Chancellor's house.

The bill was brought against an executor for an account of the testator's estate. The defendant said by his answer that he had laid out part of the testator's money in South Sea annuities at a time when he likewise purchased annuities for himself, which annuities he subscribed into the South Sea [Company] in 1720. To this answer, the plaintiff replied but never served the defendant with a subpoena to rejoin, by which means, as it was said, the defendant had no opportunity to examine witnesses.

But by the counsel and Lord Chancellor [King], the defendant might have rejoined himself voluntarily. But, however, this appearing to be a hard case that the defendant should bear the loss of this subscription if he had acted bona fide and given any notice of his employing the estate in this manner to any friends of the infant, for whom the bill was brought, or to the co-executor, My Lord King directed the master to inquire into the matter and state all the circumstances.

723

Reeve v. Whiting

(Ch. 1725)

That a will was duly executed by the testator and duly witnessed can be proved by a single witness.

British Library MS. Hargrave 83, p. 45, pl. 1

Thursday, 16 December 1725. At the Lord Chancellor's house.

A will charging land was proved only by two of the subscribing witnesses. The third was alive and not examined.

Mr. *Cowper* objected to the proof of the will.

Lord Chancellor [King] said that one witness proving that he saw the others subscribe was good at law. And he remembered a case where two witnesses being dead and the third, who survived, being a legatee, Sir Edward Northey said they would not have come here to have proved the will if either of the other witnesses had been alive.

The will was now read as well proved.

724

Hasket v. Strong

(Ch. 1726)

Where the holder of a third mortgage buys the first mortgage, he has priority over the holder of the second mortgage for his entire debt.

2 Strange 689, 93 E.R. 786

At the Rolls.

Mr. How made a mortgage for 500 years dated 9 June 1720 to Neal. He, afterwards, made a mortgage in fee to the plaintiff. And Neal assigned to the defendant, who, afterwards, advancing more money took a conveyance of the inheritance with an agreement that the term should be kept on foot as an additional security. The term was never assigned over to a third person. And, on the question touching priority, it was agreed that, if the term had been regularly kept on foot, the defendant would have been in the common case of a third mortgagee taking in the first encumbrance to protect himself, by which he would have had the law on his side; whereas, here, the term was merged upon the grant of the inheritance, and, therefore, at law, it would be with the plaintiff, who had the first mortgage in fee.

To which it was answered and decreed by the court that the plaintiff's conveyance of the inheritance interposing between the term and the defendant's grant, the grant of the defendant was void in law, the grantor having nothing in him, and, then, the term could not be merged in a void grant of the inheritance, and the defendant must be first paid his whole money.

Strange, for the defendant.

[Other reports of this case: 2 Eq. Cas. Abr. 613, 22 E.R. 515.]

725

Anonymous

(Ch. 1726)

In a suit to perpetuate testimony, the defendant is not entitled to receive court costs where he examines a witness in chief.

Lincoln's Inn MS. Misc. 12, p. 206, pl. 1

Hilary term 1725[/26].

The plaintiff having brought his bill to perpetuate the testimony of the witnesses to a will against the defendant, the heir at law, and the cause being at issue, witnesses were examined and publication passed. And the plaintiff, designing to proceed no further, [the defendant] moved for his costs.

Whereupon, I showed that the defendant had not only cross-examined the plaintiff's witnesses which he brought to prove the will but had examined another witness of his own against the will. And, for this last reason, Lord Chancellor [Lord King] was of the opinion the defendant was not entitled to his costs. And he denied the motion.

726

Sikes v. Lister

(Ch. 1726)

Where a seller of land dies before executing a conveyance, a court of equity will order the seller's executor, devisee, and heir to make the conveyance.

5 Viner, Abr. 541

Hilary 12 Geo.

A bill [was exhibited] for the execution of articles for the sale of lands against the executor and devisees of land for life and the infant heir of the vendor.

Mr. *Lutwyche*, for the plaintiff: Though these articles for the sale of this estate were made and executed by the vendor after the making of his will, which he thought was a revocation of the devise of those lands in equity, yet the legal estate for life, he apprehended, was in the executor and devisees. And, therefore, he prayed a conveyance from the devisees and an injunction for quiet enjoyment against the infant heir at law etc. But he did not pray an immediate conveyance from the infant heir because he did think him a trustee within the meaning of the Stat. 7 Ann., cap. 19,[1] so as to be able to make a good conveyance by virtue of that Act, for, though the vendor after a contract for sale of his lands is considered in equity as a trustee for the purchaser, yet he is only a trustee by implication and not an express trustee, as where lands are conveyed to A. in trust for B. and these express trusts only are within the Stat. 7 Ann., cap. 19.

King, Chancellor, decreed, that the articles be carried into execution and the plaintiff Sikes, upon paying the purchase money to the executor, to be let into possession at Lady Day [25 March] next, and the defendants, the executors and devisees, to make a conveyance to the plaintiff and his heirs at the costs of the plaintiff, and the plaintiff to hold and enjoy the premises against the infant heir, and the heir, when he comes of full age, to convey to the plaintiff and his heirs, unless the infant heir, within six months after he comes of full age, shows cause to the contrary.

---

1 Stat. 7 Ann., c. 19 (*SR*, IX, 89).

2 Eq. Cas. Abr. 25, 22 E.R. 22

A bill [was exhibited] for the execution of articles for the sale of lands against the executors and devisees of land for life and the infant heir of the vendor.

[It was] decreed that the articles be carried into execution and the plaintiff Sikes, upon paying the purchase money to the executors, to be let into possession at Lady Day next, and the executors and devisees to make a conveyance in fee to the plaintiff at his costs, and the plaintiff to hold the premises against the infant heir, who, when of full age, was to convey to the plaintiff and his heirs unless within six months after he comes of age he shows cause to the contrary.

727
Anonymous
(Ch. 1726)

Where there is a lien upon a fund out of which court costs are payable, the court costs can be taxed upon a petition without a bill of revivor.

British Library MS. Hargrave 83, p. 46, pl. 1

22 January 1725[/26].

Though it be a rule that you cannot revive for costs only, yet, where there is a lien by the decree upon any particular fund out of which costs are to be paid, the party entitled to them need not revive in order to have them, and, if he does, it is superfluous. And this the Master of the Rolls, Sir Joseph Jekyll, declared upon a petition to have costs taxed and paid.

728
Anonymous
(Ch. 1726)

A bill of exceptions should include all exceptions to be made, and those exceptions not included are deemed to have been waived.

British Library MS. Hargrave 83, p. 46, pl. 2

Eodem die [22 January 1726].

The plaintiff took one exception to the defendant's answer which was allowed, and then he amended his bill and took several other exceptions not only as to the answer to the amended bill but also as to matters charged in the original bill and not answered. The defendant attended the master upon the exceptions. And now, before the master had gone through all the exceptions, he petitioned to discharge those that related to the charges in the original bill. And though it was insisted that the original and amended bills were but one bill in record, which appeared by the subpoena taken out upon the amendment and likewise that the defendant had waived his objection to these exceptions by going before the master upon them, His Honor [Jekyll] discharged the exceptions.

729

In re Petition of Wright

(Ch. 1726)

The Court of Chancery can order a commission of review of a case in an ecclesiastical court to be filed in the Court of Chancery so that new parties can intervene.

British Library MS. Hargrave 83, p. 47

A commission of review had been granted by Their Excellencies, the Lords Justices, upon the petition of A., B., C., etc. in a cause that had been before the [Court of] Delegates concerning the will of one Rhodes. And now the counsel of one Thomas Wright were to show cause why the commission should not be amended.

The cause was thus. A final sentence had been given by the Delegates establishing the will of Rhodes, and, afterwards, it appearing that there had been great fraud and collusion and false swearing in this cause, the Lords Justices were applied to to grant a commission of review. It bore great debate and was long deliberated whether such a commission could issue. At length, it was resolved that it should. The petitioners that applied for this commission were A., B., C., etc. and one Thomas Wright. It appeared that Thomas Wright lived here in town and had negotiated this cause for his mother who lived in the country in Lancashire. His mother was party to the suit in the ecclesiastical court and before the Delegates and was next of kin to the testator Rhodes, whose will she sought to impeach. But Thomas Wright had joined in the petition in his own name without taking notice that he was agent for her. She died and made Gilbert Wright her executor, who proved her will. A., B., C., etc. and Thomas Wright, upon whose petition the commission has issued and who had possession of it, agreed with the person who claimed under the pretended will and kept the commission in their custody so that there were no proceedings upon it. By this means, Gilbert, the representative and executor of his mother, could have no benefit of the commission. And upon this whole matter, it was now moved that Gilbert's name might be inserted in the commission instead of the name of Thomas and the commission might be brought into court for that purpose.

My Lord Chancellor King refused to amend the commission, for he said that the testatrix of Gilbert, his mother, was not a party to this petition and had not joined in it, that Thomas Wright had presented the petition in his own name and not as agent to her.

But Dr. *Henchman* of the [Doctors'] Commons, who attended with other civilians upon this occasion, having laid it down that, by the rules and practice of their courts, such a commission being granted was in the nature of an appeal and opened the cause, so that a person who had an interest, though not a party in the cause before, might come in and have the benefit of proceeding upon this commission.

My Lord [Lord King], upon Gilbert's payment of the commission to be taxed, ordered that the commission should be brought into court for Gilbert to have liberty to make use of it and proceed upon it as he could by the rules of the ecclesiastical court.

730

Anonymous

(Ch. 1726)

The question in this case was whether a separate creditor can participate in bankruptcy proceedings against joint debtors.

Lincoln's Inn MS. Misc. 506, p. 80, pl. 1

Post Hilary 12 Geo.

Upon a petition to Lord Chancellor [Lord King], the question was whether, on a commission of bankruptcy against two partners, a creditor who had lent one of the partners money upon his bond only, though applied to the use of the joint trade, should be admitted to his share of the effects, paying his contribution money. It was said that it was not a settled point whether a separate creditor might not come in along with the joint creditors, it having received different determinations.

But as this case was, the Lord Chancellor thought him a joint creditor and directed he should come in along with the others.

731

Beak v. Friend

(Ch. 1726)

The validity of a dead person's deed can be proved by proving his signature alone without proving the signatures of the attesting witnesses to the deed who cannot be found.

British Library MS. Hargrave 83, p. 49

30 March 1726. At the Lord Chancellor's house among the causes by consent.

Henry Partridge, upon his marriage with Mary, his wife, in the year 1708, made a settlement, in which he covenanted that a moiety of a mortgage of £1200 and £800 to which she was entitled should be vested in trustees and should be in her power to dispose of either by deed or will. She, by her will reciting this deed, disposes of the money. A deed was now produced, in which the name of Mary, then Mary Hunt, was erased, but the name of her husband Henry Partridge's remained. This induced some suspicion of foul practice, though it was of no effect, for the name of Henry Partridge, the covenantor, remained unaltered. The defendant, who was the administratrix of Henry Partridge, by her answer, denied that she knew of any such settlement. And now, upon the proof of the deed of settlement, this was the point.

One witness swore that he had made a diligent search and inquiry after the two attesting witnesses, that he had been informed that one of them was a distiller in Holborn and long since dead, that, as to the other, he had been informed that a person of that name, who lived near Gray's Inn, used to associate much with Henry Partridge, but what was become of him he could not learn though he had inquired at the place where he lived.

To this proof, it was objected by Mr. *Lutwyche* that evidence here ought to be the same as at law, that it was the constant experience of the circuit that, if a witness was dead, it was necessary to prove his hand, which they had not done in this case, that it was not sufficient to prove the covenantor's hand subscribed, but the hand of the witness to the execution of the deed must be proved.

But My Lord Chancellor [Lord King] said that it had been sometimes one way and sometimes another and was not a constant rule. And he admitted a witness to be examined *viva voce*, for which they had an order, to prove the hand of Henry Partridge subscribed to the deed. And upon this deed thus proved, he chiefly founded his decree.

732

Somner v. Hooker

(Ch. 1726)

Where a testator gives legacies to his executor and all the next of kin, the undisposed of residuum goes to the executor.

Lincoln's Inn MS. Misc. 12, p. 229

1 April 1726.

William Evelyn, seised of real and possessed of a considerable personal estate, 1 August 1722, makes his will and devises to the defendant, whom he makes executor, his household goods and furniture and his house and lands in Hammersmith for life, remainder to Edward, his son, in fee. He gives his executor all his South Sea [Company] stock, paying £200 a year to the plaintiff, one of his next of kin, for life. He gives to A.B. his house in the Minories for life, remainder to his executor. He gives legacies to others of his next of kin and makes no disposition of the surplus.

The question was to whom the surplus belonged.

Lord Chancellor [Lord King]: In point of construction, here is exclusion against exclusion. Must not then the law prevail? Without entering into the question whether the executor, when he has a legacy and there is no disposition of the surplus, is a trustee for the next of kin. I think, there being particular legacies given to the next of kin as well as to the executor, they are as much excluded by those particular legacies as the executor and then the law should prevail and the executor must take the surplus.

Lincoln's Inn MS. Misc. 506, p. 80, pl. 2

Post Hilary 12 Geo.

Upon a will wherein specific legacies were devised, some to his executor, others to his nearest of kin, the question was whether the residuum, which was undevised, should go to the executor or be distributed among the nearest of kind.

Lord Chancellor [Lord King] decreed it to the executor. He said he would not determine how it might be in case there had been no particular legacies to the next of kin, but, as to any implication which might be made of the legacies left to the executor, as if no more was intended him, both he and the next of kin were *pari gradu*, and, as the executor had the law of his side, it ought to go to him.

Afterwards in Easter 12 Geo. [1726] upon the like case, only that the testator died leaving his will unfinished, the Lord Chancellor [Lord King] decreed a distribution upon a presumption that, if he had lived to finish his will, he might have given the residuum away from the executor.

[Other reports of this case: 2 Peere Williams 338, 24 E.R. 756, 2 Eq. Cas. Abr. 425, 441, 22 E.R. 361, 376.]

733

Attorney General v. Hooker

(Ch. 1726)

A legacy to be paid out of a particular fund must be paid out of the general personal estate of the testator if the particular fund no longer exists.

Lincoln's Inn MS. Misc. 12, p. 230, pl. 1

Eodem die [1 April 1726].

Mr. Evelyn, by will, gave to the poor seamen of Greenwich Hospital £2000 out of his Bank stock; the remainder thereof he gave to the defendant, whom he made executor. The testator, when he made his will, had £3000 Bank stock, but, afterwards, he sold £2000 of it.

It was decreed the legacy to be made good out of the rest of the personal estate, according to the difference taken in Pawlet's Case, Raymond 335.[1]

[Other reports of this case: 2 Peere Williams 338, 24 E.R. 756.]

734

Feast v. Feast

(Ch. 1726)

Money due to a child pursuant to a marriage settlement is a debt and not an advancement or a payment of a customary share.

1 Eq. Cas. Abr. 250, 21 E.R. 1026

3 April 1726.

On a marriage treaty, Sir Felix Feast covenanted to leave his wife £2000 at his death, £2000 to his eldest son, and £1000 apiece to his younger children. And, afterwards, being a freeman of London, he died, leaving several younger children. And it was held in that case, that the £1000 apiece to the younger children, being due only by a covenant, was a debt on the personal estate, and, not being to be paid until after the father's death, it was no provision or advancement, either within the Statute of Distributions[2] or the custom of London, to bar them of their customary or distributory shares of their father's personal estate, which were greatly advanced at the time of his death.

Lincoln's Inn MS. Misc. 384, p. 319, pl. 3

5 April.

Sir Felix Feast, by marriage articles, settled £2000 among his younger children.

The defendants insisted it was an advancement to bar them of the customary share. That was overruled. They then insisted it ought to be brought into hotchpot by the Statute of Distributions. That, likewise, was overruled, it being by purchase.

9 Modern 468, 88 E.R. 579

5 April 1726.

Sir Felix Feast, a freeman of London, upon his marriage, agreed to leave his wife if she survived him having one or more children £2000, his eldest son £2000, and £1000 apiece to his younger children, and, if his eldest son died before twenty-one, the £2000 to be paid to the next son, and, in case any of the

---

1 *Pawlet's Case* (1679), T. Raymond 335, 83 E.R. 174

2 Stat. 22 & 23 Car. II, c. 10 (*SR*, V, 719–720).

younger children died before that age, the £1000 to be equally divided amongst the other younger children. The provision made for the wife was by the articles agreed to be in bar of her dower and claim by the custom of London. But nothing is said as to the children. Sir Felix Feast died intestate, leaving a widow and an eldest son, a daughter married and advanced, and two or three younger children. The eldest son insisted he was entitled to his £2000 in the nature of a debt out of his father's personal estate and also, under the custom, to an equal share with his brothers without bringing anything into hotchpot.

And it was decreed by Lord King that the £2000 which Lady Feast claimed by the marriage articles, the £2000 claimed by the eldest son, and the £1000 claimed by the younger children were a debt on the personal estate and should be paid with interest from the father's death and the surplus to be divided in moieties, one whereof to go according to the custom amongst all the children and the other according to the Statute of Distributions, without any direction for bringing into hotchpot. This was the Lord King's opinion, who had been Recorder of London.

735

Richardson v. Hamilton

(Ch. 1726)

A plaintiff who files a scandalous and impertinent bill of complaint must pay court costs.

Lincoln's Inn MS. Misc. 12, p. 231, pl. 2

April 1726.

The plaintiff's bill was reported scandalous and impertinent, and the costs were taxed at £82 1s. 0d. But he being a merchant in Pennsylvania and making an oath that he had not effects here to the value of that sum, Lord Chancellor [Lord King] referred it back to the Master to review his report. And he moderated and reduced the costs to £62 1s. 0d.

736

Gambier v. Leheup

(Ch. 1726)

An amended bill of complaint is a new bill, and the defendant may respond to the whole bill.

Lincoln's Inn MS. Misc. 12, p. 213

20 April 1726.

The bill was for an account of the estate of one Devarenne, to whom the plaintiff was executor, which had come to the hands of the defendant.

The defendant put in an answer and set forth an account of the dealings which had been between him and the testator. And he insisted on a stated account.

And exceptions being taken to that answer and it being reported insufficient, he put in a second answer. And, afterwards, the plaintiff amended his bill and prayed a further discovery than he had done before as to some matters relating to the account.

To this amended bill, the defendant put in a plea and set forth the same matters as he had done in his answer. And he insisted on the stated account in bar of any account to that time. And this plea going to the whole matter, the plaintiff now moved to discharge the plea as being irregular, for, though it was admitted that, when a bill is amended, a defendant may plead to those amendments, yet he cannot plead to any matter which he has before answered to.

But Lord Chancellor [Lord King] was of opinion, when a bill was amended, it was a new bill and that the defendant may plead to the whole bill. And, besides, he thought it was improper to discharge the plea upon a motion, but it ought to be set down to be argued.

Dickens 44, 21 E.R. 183

20 April 1726.

The defendant put in his answer. The plaintiff, afterwards, amended his bill. The defendant then put in a plea to the whole bill. On the above day, the plaintiff invoked to discharge the plea, because it was to the whole bill.

But the court denied the motion.

737

Newell v. Parker

(Ch. 1726)

Where the executor of a will is given a legacy, the undisposed of residuum of the decedent's estate goes to the decedent's next of kin.

Lincoln's Inn MS. Misc. 12, p. 214, pl. 2

28 April 1726.

Philip Gardner makes his will in these words, *viz.*, after the preamble, he goes on thus, 'I desire Mr. Lawrence Parker and Mr. John Nurse to be my executors. I leave to my sister Sarah Newell [who is the plaintiff's wife] £400. I leave to my cousin Anne Ayloff £5. I leave to Elizabeth Penny £10. I leave to her daughter Elizabeth £10. I leave to my two executors £10 each. I leave to my servant Ralph Anthony £10 to buy him mourning to assist my executors in gathering in my debts.' And then he goes on and gives some other small legacies. But he does not finish his will, but breaks off thus, 'I leave to Brian Dolben.'

The plaintiff and his wife brought their bill for an account of the testator's personal estate, and they insisted that, the surplus not being disposed of, the testator was dead intestate as to that and that it was distributable according to the Statute of Distributions.[1]

And the question was whether, in regard the executors had a legacy given them and the will was not perfected, the surplus belonged to the executors or was distributable amongst the next of kin according to the Statute.

Lord Chancellor [Lord King], having taken time to consider of the case, this day, gave his opinion. And he said this case stood upon a different foot from former cases where the surplus had been decreed from the executors when a legacy had been given them and the surplus not disposed of by the will, for, here, the testator has not finished his will and it is very plain he intended to make a further disposition of his estate. But it is wholly uncertain what he intended to do with the surplus. And, therefore, he thought he might go so far in conformity with former resolutions, which he seemed not very well to like, as to decree the surplus to the next of kin. And, accordingly, it was so decreed.

[1] Stat. 22 & 23 Car. II, c. 10 (*SR*, V, 719–720).

738

Turner v. Turner

(Ch. 1726)

An infant's next friend is liable for court costs, but not the infant.
Court costs cannot be collected from a dead person.

British Library MS. Hargrave 83, p. 50

14 May 1726.

An infant brought his bill by his next friend for an estate, the whole of which he claimed by virtue of a will if the will was good; if not, he was entitled to a share of the estate by descent. The will appeared to be cancelled, and, when the cause came to be heard, the court directed an issue to try whether it was cancelled before or after the death of the testator. It happened upon the day of trial that the infant's *prochein ami* died. And the infant's counsel not being able to make out that the will was cancelled after the death of the testator, he was nonsuited. There were no farther proceedings until the infant came of age. The trial, which was at the bar, was in Easter term 1723, and the infant came of age the March after. The defendant then brought on the cause upon the equity reserved, and the infant appeared by his counsel, but made no farther opposition, and the bill was dismissed with costs generally.

Upon the rehearing of this cause as to the matter of costs, My Lord Chancellor King took time to consider.

And the cause standing for judgment this day, it was argued by Mr. *Talbot* and Mr. *Cowper* for the plaintiff, that, by the course of the court, if an infant's bill is dismissed generally with costs, when the decree is executed, no subpoena is ever made out against the infant for the costs, but it is always made out against his *prochein ami*, that any person, whether a relation or not, may take up the cause of an infant and bring a bill as his next friend, and, if the defendant complains that the next friend is not sufficient to answer the costs, upon that, the court always refers it to a master to see whether the next friend be sufficient, that any person may without the privity and against the will of an infant bring a bill as his next friend and herein consists the difference between an infant and a married woman, that the infant during his infancy cannot disavow the bill brought by his next friend, but the married woman may during her coverture, but unless the infant does some act after he attains his age to avow the suit, costs shall not be given against him.

And these points are confirmed by experience, for upon search in the Subpoena Office, no instance could be found of a subpoena against an infant for costs. And this was agreed to by the Register, of whom My Lord now asked whether this that was alleged was so.

For the defendants, by Mr. *Lutwyche*, *Mead*, and *Kettleby*, it was argued that, by the death of the next friend, the defendant would be remediless for his costs unless he could have them from the plaintiff though the suit was never so unreasonable, that the plaintiff since he was of age had so far avowed this suit as to appear by his counsel when the cause came on upon the equity reserved, that equity ought to proceed upon reason at least as much as law. At law, the infant is the plaintiff and liable to costs and the judgment is against the infant. Here, both the infant and the *prochein ami* are liable, the infant principally and the *prochein ami* as surety. As to the costs that have been at law, there can be no reason or equity from precluding the defendant from having them as he is entitled to have them by law whatever the judgment may be as to the costs in this court.

Lord Chancellor [Lord King]: It has been said that costs are given at law against the infant. But I asked whether there was any authority for that because I have some authorities to the contrary. At common law, there were no costs, but only pledges found to prosecute and then there was an amercement *pro falso clamore*. But an infant never found pledges nor was ever amerced *pro falso clamore*.

The Statute of Gloucester[1] giving costs against defendants, the infant's guardian, by whom he defended, was liable to costs and, at common law, could neither sue nor defend but by a guardian, who has a different consideration from a next friend, as he is now a guardian receiving the profits of the infant's estate. But however the next friend is now, as it were substituted in his place, Westminster I[2] introduced the next friend to sue for the infant in some particular cases. Westminster II[3] enlarged it to all. And it is observable upon those statutes that both the next friend to sue and the guardian to defend ought to be particularly admitted for those several purposes by the court whatever the practice may be now, which shows that the court has a concern in these cases to take care that proper responsible persons sue in behalf of the infants, the course of this court imitates the common law. And if it has proceeded in the manner that has been certified and granted no subpoena against an infant for costs, I do not see any reason now to subject the plaintiff to costs. That infants are not subject at law to costs, there are two authorities, 3 Cro. 410, Smith v. Smith; and 1 Bulst.[4]

I was of another opinion before, but the course of the court being as it has been represented and there being these two authorities and no authority produced to show that an infant is liable to costs at law, as has been urged, I have changed my opinion.

---

1 Stat. 6 Edw. I, c. 1 (*SR*, I, 47).

2 Stat. 3 Edw. I, Westminster I, c. 48 (*SR*, I, 38).

3 Stat. 13 Edw. I, Westminster II, c. 15 (*SR*, I, 82).

4 *Smith v. Smith* (1635), Croke Car. 410, 79 E.R. 956; perhaps *Hamlen v. Hamlen* (1612), 1 Bulstrode 189, 80 E.R. 877.

The bill was dismissed without costs, but without prejudice to the defendant's getting his costs at law if he is entitled to them there. The plaintiff is to have back his deposit.

Lincoln's Inn MS. Misc. 384, p. 319, pl. 2

14 May.

The bill of an infant by a *prochein ami* was dismissed with costs. The *prochein ami dies*. Query whether the infant is liable to pay costs.

Acherly: The subpoena for costs is always taken out against a prochein ami. If the *prochein* is not sufficient, the court will order a new *prochein*.

Mead: That may be as well for the benefit of the infant as of the defendant. The suit was not abated by his death. [Upon a] trial at law against the plaintiff, the defendant brings it on upon the equity reserved after the infant comes of age.

Lord Chancellor [Lord King]: At common law, [there were] no costs of either side; [they] only found pledges; infant plaintiffs did not; [there was] no amercement against them. When the Statute of Gloucester gave costs against defendants, if a guardian loses an infant's lands, he had a writ of deceit against him, by the Statute of Westminster II, plaintiffs may sue a *prochein ami*, who is admitted by the court. This is upon the plaintiff's bill [being] dismissed. 3 Cr. 33, Grave v. Grave; an infant nonsuited shall not pay costs; Bulstr. 109, Hamilton v. Bucks; an infant appeared by an attorney.[1] I do not know of any other book case in the course of this court agreeable to law. It is hard as to the defendant. The reason of this court's naming a good *prochein ami* is to secure the defendant's costs. If he dies, the costs are gone. The defendant may proceed at law to get his costs there as he can. The bill here is dismissed without costs.

[Other reports of this case: 2 Peere Williams 297, 24 E.R. 737, Select Cases *tempore* King 49, 25 E.R. 216, 2 Strange 708, 93 E.R. 798, 2 Eq. Cas. Abr. 238, 22 E.R. 203.]

[1] *Grave v. Grave* (1584), Croke Eliz. 33, 78 E.R. 298; perhaps *Hamlen v. Hamlen* (1612), 1 Bulstrode 189, 80 E.R. 877.

739
Farrington v. Becket

(Ch. c. 1726)

Where an executor mortgages lands devised to someone other than himself, the devisee can claim the land and rents from the mortgagee and court costs from the executor or his representative.

Lincoln's Inn MS. Misc. 12, p. 215, pl. 2

One Pen, a stationer in the Temple, by his will, gave to one Bowdler a house in Essex Street, which was held under a lease from Dr. Barbon for his life and, after his death, to the plaintiff's wife. And he made Bowdler executor and residuary legatee, who proved the will. But he never assented to the bequest but mortgaged the house to the defendant Becket for £100.

And Bowdler being dead, the plaintiff and his wife bring their bill against Becket, who was in possession, he having a legal title under the executor, who had never assented to the devise, that he might deliver up the deeds and writings and also against the tenant who rented the house that he might attorn and pay his rent to the plaintiffs.

The question on the hearing was whether, Bowdler being executor as well as devisee for life of the house, the mortgage by him made to Becket was not good, for *non constat* but he might borrow the money to pay debts and legacies, and it was insisted that it was not incumbent upon the mortgagee to inquire for what purpose the £100 was borrowed or to see how it was applied.

But the Master of the Rolls [JEKYLL] sent it to the Master to enquire whether the testator left assets exclusive of this house to pay his debts and legacies, and, if he did, then the deeds and writings were to be delivered up and the rents paid to the plaintiffs. But, if not and there was any deficiency, then so far as there should appear to be a deficiency, the defendant Becket was to stand in the place of the executor and have a satisfaction of the principal and interest out of the house.

The Master found there was no deficiency of assets. And it now came on upon the Master's report as to costs, which were reserved, and the plaintiffs were ordered to have their costs from the representative of Bowdler, who was made a defendant.

740

Keilway v. Keilway

(Ch. 1726)

Where a man dies intestate without a wife or where he dies without children, the mother takes in equal proportion with the brothers and sisters.

Lincoln's Inn MS. Misc. 12, p. 217

19 May 1726.

Mr. Kelway, the surgeon, died intestate, leaving a wife and no child and also leaving a mother and some brothers and sisters. The wife being entitled to one moiety of the personal estate, the question was between the mother and brothers and sisters as to the other moiety, whether she should have the whole of such moiety or whether it should be equally divided between her and her children according to the Statute of the first [year] of Jac. II, c. 17,[1] which says that, if, after the death of a father, any of his children should die intestate without wife or children in the lifetime of the mother, every brother and sister and the representatives of them shall have an equal share with her. And, in the principal case, there was a wife but no children.

It was decreed the intestate's brothers and sisters should take an equal share with the mother in a moiety of the personal estate by the Stat. 4 Jac. II, the other moiety belonging to the wife by the Statute of King Charles II.[2]

Yale Univ. Taussig MS. 311, vol. 2, p. 904

Easter term 1726.

Robert Keilway, the surgeon, died intestate leaving a wife, but no children, a mother and brother and sisters and nephews. And the question was whether his mother should have one moiety of his personal estate or should only come in for an equal share with the brother and sisters for that moiety.

And by King, Chancellor: The Statute is where a man dies without wife or children, that is where he dies without a wife or where he dies without children, the mother shall come in in equal proportion with the brothers and sisters. And so he decreed in this case that, as to one moiety, the mother and brothers and sisters should divide it equally, the nephews to have their father's share.

This was determined Thursday, being Ascension Day 1725, on which, notwithstanding it was a holiday, the Chancellor heard causes by consent and this cause was heard by consent.

[Other reports of this case: 2 Strange 710, 93 E.R. 800, 2 Peere Williams 344, 24 E.R. 758, Gilbert Rep. 189, 25 E.R. 133, 2 Eq. Cas. Abr. 441, 442, 22 E.R. 376.]

---

1 Stat. 1 Jac. II, c. 17, s. 7 (*SR*, VI, 19).

2 Stat. 22 & 23 Car. II, c. 10 (*SR*, V, 719–720).

741

Baynes v. Hare

(Ch. 1726)

An executor must pay simple contract debts before specialties where those specialties are securely payable out of the real estate.

Lincoln's Inn MS. Misc. 506, p. 85, pl. 1

Easter 12 George.

The defendant, being executor to one who was indebted by simple contract as well as by specialties and a mortgage which might affect the land, was decreed to account for all that came to his hands 'not paid away in a due course of administration'.

Upon a rehearing the Lord Chancellor [Lord King] varied the decree with respect to the words 'not paid away in due course of administration' because that would mean legal administration and, by law, bond debts would be satisfied before simple contracts, but, in equity, the court will oblige him to pay simple contract debts before specialties if those specialties are otherwise secure out of the real estate, else, by paying the specialties, the simple contract creditors might go quite unsatisfied; therefore, when an executor had paid debts or legacies, though not according to a due course of legal administration, yet in such manner as a court of equity would have ordered, it is fitting the court should support him in it. Instead of those words, it was ordered it should be inserted as follows 'not paid upon account of debts, legacies, or funeral expenses'.

742

Duke of Bedford v. Lord Russell

(Ch. 1726)

Land held by descent is liable to the payment of a decedent's debts before his widow's paraphernalia is.

Lincoln's Inn MS. Misc. 12, p. 218, pl. 1

25 May 1726.

The question in this case touching the paraphernalia of the wife, whether they should be applied towards the satisfaction of the debts of the husband, he having not left personal assets sufficient for that purpose and having devised a real estate to be sold for the payment of his debts, it being insisted by Mr. *Williams* that, although the wife should retain her paraphernalia against the heir at law where real assets were descended, yet it was otherwise where lands were devised for the payment of debts and the personal estate was not sufficient to pay the debts.

But this distinction was exploded, and the paraphernalia was decreed to the wife.

743

Davis v. The Tailors' Company

(Ch. 1726)

A term in a lease for a renewal upon the same terms as the present lease is unenforceable because it would give the lessee an interest in fee.

Lincoln's Inn MS. Misc. 12, p. 218, pl. 2

Eodem die [25 May 1726].

In a lease made by the defendants to the plaintiff's testator of a house for twenty-one years, there was a covenant that the defendants, at the end of the first seven years, would upon the surrender of that lease make a new lease for the term of twenty-one years at the same rent and with the same covenants as were reserved and contained in the old lease.

The bill was for a specific performance of this covenant. And the question was if the covenant for renewal should be inserted in the new lease.

The Master of the Rolls [JEKYLL] was of opinion it should not, there being no words to show that it was the intention of the parties that the lease should be renewed *toties quoties*, for that, in effect, would be to give the plaintiff a fee. And, therefore, he decreed the defendant to make a new lease, but without that covenant for renewal.

744

Webster v. Webster

(Ch. 1726)

Where the residue of a personal estate is given to the children and one of them dies after the testator and before any division is made, his share survives to the other children as being a joint devise.

Lincoln's Inn MS. Misc. 12, p. 219, pl. 1

Eodem die [25 May 1726].

This cause standing for judgment, it was again spoken to. And the question was whether the residue of a personal estate being given to the children of Sir Thomas Webster and one of them dying after the testator and before any division made, his share should survive to the other children as being a joint devise.

And the Attorney General [*Yorke*], who argued that there should be no survivorships in the case of a legacy, cited the Case of Taylor v. Lady Shore, T. Jones 161.[1]

And Mr. *Lutwyche*, on the other side, cited the Case of Bastard and Stukely, in the same book, fo. 130.[2]

The Master of the Rolls [JEKYLL] took further time to consider of it, and, as Mr. Mead informed me, afterwards, decreed the share of the child that died to the surviving children.

[Other reports of this case: 2 Peere Williams 347, 24 E.R. 759, 2 Eq. Cas. Abr. 572, 22 E.R. 482.]

745
Nightingale v. Sitwell

(Ch. c. 1726)

When the plaintiff and the defendant have together committed an act to which a penalty might be imposed, there is no privilege from discovery on the ground that it might result in a penalty.

Lincoln's Inn MS. Misc. 12, p. 219, pl. 2

The plaintiff's bill being for an account of several cargoes of goods which were sent to the East Indies by Sir Robert Nightingale and the defendants in partnership between them and had been disposed of there, the defendant pleaded the acts of the 9th of King William and the two acts 6 Ann.,[3] which give the East India Company the sole trade to the Indies and lay penalties on those who trade thither without a license from the Company. And he says that Sir Robert Nightingale or any person on his account never had, as the defendant is advised and insists, any license, permission, or authority from the East India Company to send any ship or merchandises to the East Indies, either on his own account or jointly with any other person, neither did Sir Robert or any person on his account never had, as the defendant is advised and insists, any license, permission, or authority from the East India Company to send any ship or merchandises to the East Indies, either on his own account or jointly with any other person, neither did Sir Robert or any person on his account, as the defendant is advised and

[1] *Taylor v. Lady Shore* (1681), T. Jones 161, 84 E.R. 1197.

[2] *Bastard v. Stukeley* (1675–1679), T. Jones 130, 84 E.R. 1181, also 2 Levinz 209, 83 E.R. 522, 3 Keble 440, 458, 490, 613, 676, 686, 755, 828, 84 E.R. 811, 822, 838, 910, 947, 952, 993, 1036, 1 Eq. Cas. Abr. 242, 21 E.R. 1019, *sub nom. Bastard v. Stockwell*, 2 Shower K.B. 50, 89 E.R. 785.

[3] Stat. 9 Will. III, c. 44, s. 71 (*SR*, VII, 444–445); Stat. 6 Ann., c. 71 (*SR*, VIII, 824–829).

insists, ever give the security required by the said acts for any goods sent by him or on his account thither, wherefore and forasmuch as if the facts charged upon the defendant were true, of which a discovery is sought by the bill, and the defendant should be compelled to answer the same upon his oath, the defendant would thereby subject himself to the respective forfeitures and penalties in the said acts of Parliament or some of them. And, therefore, they plead the said acts of Parliament and the forfeitures and penalties therein in bar of a discovery and account of the goods and effects in the bill mentioned or of the sale or produce thereof.

It was much insisted on that this was a good plea, for that no rule was more established in this court than that a man should not be obliged to discover anything that will subject him to any penalty of forfeiture and there was the less reason to oblige the defendant to do it in the present case, for that it was plain the plaintiff was seeking an account of a clandestine trade carried on contrary to law, and, therefore, he ought to have no assistance from a court of equity.

To which it was answered by the plaintiff's counsel that, generally speaking, the rule was as the *Solicitor General* has laid down, but, in the present case, the defendant has gone too far, for he pleaded the acts of Parliament not only in bar of a discovery but in bar of relief, for it was in bar of an account, which was the relief sought by the bill. And, besides, the defendant had not brought the present case within the acts of Parliament for want of a sufficient averment, for he had only said he was advised and insisted that Sir Robert Nightingale had no license to trade etc.

And of that opinion was the Lord Chancellor, and he overruled the plea and said, though there was no occasion to go into the merits, yet he thought the case very different from what it would be if the Company came for a discovery of a clandestine trade. And when two people carry on such a trade jointly, they are supposed to agree to waive as between themselves all benefit of insisting upon a plea of this nature.

746

Foster v. Savage

(Ch. 1726)

A bill of review lies only for error appearing upon the face of the record or for new matter arisen since the decree.

Lincoln's Inn MS. Misc. 12, p. 222

28 May 1726. Foster v. Savage, Browne, *et al.*

The defendant Browne, before her marriage with her first husband, settled several houses so as that the same, after her death, were to come to the issue of that marriage. The defendant's first husband died leaving issue, one child only, who afterwards married with the plaintiff. The defendant Brown, afterwards, married one Brown, her second husband, by whom she had issue, a son and a daughter. And, upon the marriage of the daughter, Brown and his wife, by a fine, conveyed these houses to the husband and his heirs as a portion with his wife. And he, afterwards, sold the houses to the defendant Savage for a valuable consideration.

After the defendant's purchase, the plaintiff and his wife set up a title under the first settlement and brought their [action of] ejectment, insisting on a forfeiture of the estate for the life of Brown's wife by the fine, and, thereupon, the defendant Savage brought his bill to be relieved.

It was proved in the cause that the plaintiff's wife was privy to the marriage of her sister-in-law and to the terms on which that match was agreed and that she then knew of the settlement under which she claimed and of her title under that settlement and that she never disclosed of it. And this was insisted on to be a great fraud and such as in a court of equity ought to preclude her from setting up a title under a settlement which was concealed against a purchaser for a valuable consideration.

The cause was heard before My Lord Macclesfield, and, notwithstanding the now plaintiff's wife was a married woman and might not understand the nature of limitations in deeds and that what was insisted on by the other side was to bar her and her issue of her inheritance, who, by law, could not be barred but by a fine, yet His Lordship relieved the plaintiff and decreed a perpetual injunction and that the now plaintiffs should levy a fine to the use of the then plaintiff and his heirs and, if they did so, they should be excused costs, but, if not, should pay costs.[1]

This decree being signed and enrolled, the now plaintiffs brought a bill of review and assigned for error that it did not sufficiently appear by the proofs in the original cause that the plaintiff's wife knew of her title under the settlement or of the terms on which her sister's marriage was had.

The defendant Savage put in the usual demurrer.

And, upon the arguing of this demurrer before the present Lord Chancellor [LORD KING], he allowed the demurrer and said he could not enter into the proofs, but he must judge upon the record, for, by the rules of the court, a bill of review would only lie for error appearing upon the face of the decree or for new matter arisen since the decree, of which etc.

[Other copies of this report: 2 Cooper *tempore* Cottenham 418, 47 E.R. 1226.]

[1] *Savage v. Foster* (Ch. 1724), see above, Case No. 637.

747

Lepidge v. Shorey

(Ch. 1726)

A debt has priority of payment over an unpaid inter vivos *gift, but such a gift has priority over a legacy.*

Lincoln's Inn MS. Misc. 12, p. 225, pl. 1

14 June 1726.

The plaintiff married the daughter of John Shorey, the defendant's father. And he received a portion of £400 with his wife. Sometime after the marriage, John Shorey agreed to make his daughter's fortune up £1000, and, accordingly, he paid the plaintiff £200 and gave him a bond that his executors should pay him £400 more within a month after his death.

The plaintiff insisted that this bond ought to be paid out of assets preferable to debts by simple contract.

But it was decreed by Lord Chancellor [Lord King] that, it being a voluntary bond and given without any valuable consideration, it shall be paid after debts by simple contract but preferable to any legacies.

748

Bingham's Case

(Ch. 1726)

An infant cannot be a bankrupt.

Lincoln's Inn MS. Misc. 12, p. 225, pl. 2

25 June 1726.

Bingham having been a trader and committed acts of bankruptcy, a commission was sued out against him. And he now petitioned that the commission might be superseded in regard he was an infant. And, accordingly, the commission was ordered to be superseded, Lord Chancellor [Lord King] being of the opinion an infant could not be a bankrupt.

749

Underwood v. Phillips

(Ch. 1726)

If a legatee die before his legacy becomes due and payable, his administrator cannot receive it before such time as the legatee would have received it.

Lincoln's Inn MS. Misc. 12, p. 226, pl. 2

Eodem die [27 June 1726].

One Crow gave legacies to the defendants, his nieces, to be paid at twenty-one or marriage, and he made the plaintiff the residuary legatee. The legatees being infants, the question was whether they should have interest in the meantime until their legacies became payable, the legacies being vested.

It was decreed by the Master of the Rolls [JEKYLL] they should not have interest, but, otherwise, he said, it would have been if the legatees had been the children of the testator.

And he said, if one of the legatees should die before his legacy should become due, his administrator would not be entitled to receive the legacy until such time as the legatee would have attained the age of twenty-one.

And so the Solicitor General [*Talbot*] told me it was lately determined by the opinion of the Master of the Rolls [JEKYLL] and the two chief justices upon an appeal to the [Privy] Council from one of the plantations upon that single point.

Lincoln's Inn MS. Misc. 384, p. 247, pl. 1

27 June 1726. At the Rolls.

Mr. *Mead* cited the case of Harrison *contra* Buckler, where His Honor decreed that the administrator of an infant should not have interest for a legacy given to the infant to be paid at twenty-one before such time as the infant, if he had lived, would have attained that age. He said it to be contrary to former resolutions.

750

Overy v. Pope

(Ch. 1726)

The question in this case was whether the Court of Chancery can determine the validity of a marriage.

British Library MS. Hargrave 83, p. 54

27 June 1726.

A bill was brought by executors against a husband and wife. The wife, before her marriage with this husband, having been the widow of a citizen, the bill was to compel her to make her election whether she would claim under her former husband's will, who had given her a legacy, or would chose her customary share. It appeared by the proofs in the cause that the wife both before and after her marriage with this husband was *non compos* [*mentis*]. Indeed, the witnesses said that, at the time of her marriage, she was something better or pretty well.

My Lord Chancellor [Lord King] said he would do nothing in it until it appeared whether it was a good marriage or not, and he was for directing an issue to try whether the marriage was good or not, for, if she was a lunatic, it was nullity. But the Attorney General [*Yorke*] objecting that His Lordship could not direct an issue to try the validity or nullity of a marriage, My Lord directed notice to be given to the next of kin to the wife and that the next of kin might be at liberty within a time fixed to take out a commission of lunacy if they thought fit and proceed to contest the validity of this marriage. But if a commission were not taken out within the time fixed, then His Lordship would consider farther of the case.

[Related cases: Overy v. Pope (Ch. 1714), see above, Case No. 44.]

751

Hazard v. Dixon

(Ch. 1726)

After a final judgment on a bond at common law, a court of equity will not set aside the bond on the ground of fraud.

British Library MS. Hargrave 83, p. 55

27 June 1726.

The bill was brought against an executor and against the heir of a testator to have an account of personal and real assets. The executor insisted upon a bond and judgment obtained upon it, which, if paid, would exhaust the personal assets. The bond was for £200, and it was given by the testator two hours before his marriage and was intended as a provision for the younger children of the marriage. But in case there were no younger children, then it was to be for the benefit of the wife. The contingency happened, and the, wife being entitled to the bond, obtained judgment at law upon it against the executor, no defense being made. But the bill sought to set it aside.

Lord Chancellor [LORD KING]: Do you think that, after you have had an opportunity at law to try whether this bond was fraudulent or not, I will after a judgment set it aside in this court though I do not much like the bond and the circumstances under which it was given?

As to the real assets, the [party] must demur in equity as at law where the bill seeks to charge an infant with assets by descent.

N.B. In this cause, the bond produced and in question was not duly stamped, but upon the undertaking of the solicitor in the cause to pay the stamp duty, My Lord suffered it to be read.

The Attorney [General *Yorke*] said he did not know whether he, who was concerned for the king, ought to suffer it. But My Lord [LORD KING] saying, if he insisted, the cause must stand over, he did not farther oppose.

Lincoln's Inn MS. Misc. 12, p. 226, pl. 1

27 June 1726. Hazard v. Dickenson.

Upon a bill by a bond creditor to be paid out of personal and real assets, the defendant, the heir, being an infant, it was ordered that the parol should demur and that the proceedings as to the infant should stay until he came of age.

9 Viner, Abr. 418

Trinity term 12 Geo.

A bill [was brought] by a bond creditor against the heir and the executor of the obligor to have a satisfaction of a debt due upon a bond out of personal and real assets. The heir insists that, as to him, the parol ought to demur, for that he is an infant and the bill seeks to charge his inheritance, which came to him by descent from the obligor. The parol shall demur until the defendant comes to his full age, as well in this court as at law, which was not denied by the Attorney General [*Yorke*], counsel for the plaintiff.

By KING, Chancellor, [it was] ordered that the cause should stand in statu quo until the infant heir come to full age. But, as to the other defendant, the executor, [he was] decreed to account and make a satisfaction out of the personal assets as far as they would go.

[Other copies of this report: 2 Eq. Cas. Abr. 518, 22 E.R. 437.]

752

Foot v. Hobart

(Ch. 1726)

A court of equity will order an issue out of Chancery for a jury verdict only where there is some doubt about the case.

In this case, the lease in issue was not subject to any power to lease.

Lincoln's Inn MS. Misc. 384, p. 247, pl. 2

28 June. Rolls.

Attorney General [*Raymond*], for the plaintiff, cited 2 Rol. Ab. 262, quoted in 5 Mod. 378,[1] where a power was for the tenant for life to let leases reserving former rents, part was in lease, part not, it is sufficient to reserve the former rent on that part which was in lease. Sir John Maynard's Will [Case];[2] there was a power for the person in possession to lease for four lives reserving the now rents now in being.

Solicitor General [*Yorke*]: The lease in question was made by Lady Stafford, one of the co-heirs of T.M. [It was] objected the barton of B. or the land now let was not let before; I answer the power is to l*et al*l or any part. Suppose Lady Stafford had l*et al*l reserving the whole rent; it had been within the words.

Mr. *Lutwyche*: The reason of coming into equity to set a mortgage out of the way [is the] general power to l*et al*l. If part is not let, it is not necessary to reserve any rent. Cumberford's Case, 2 Rol. Ab.; a reserved rent which was two years before; part was not then let, he need not reserve any. 2 C. 150; 1 Ven. 294;[3] an estate consisted of land and a rectory and tithes; a power so as such a sum was reserved for every acre; the rectory was let without reserving any rent [was] good.

Serjeant *Carter*, for the defendant: This is proper to be tried at law.

Curia [JEKYLL]: Where this court sends it to law, it must be where there is some doubt. But here is none. In Cumberland's Case,[4] the power covered the whole land. A man may restrain it to such part as was then in lease. In the other

---

[1] *Cumberford's Case* (1634), 2 Rolle, Abr., *Powers*, pl. A, 15, p. 262; *Winter v. Loveday* (1697), 5 Modern 244, 378, 87 E.R. 635, 717, also 1 Freeman 507, 89 E.R. 382, Holt K.B. 414, 90 E.R. 1128, 1 Comyns 37, 92 E.R. 947, Carthew 427, 90 E.R. 847, 1 Lord Raymond 267, 91 E.R. 1075, Comberbach 371, 90 E.R. 534, 2 Salkeld 537, 91 E.R. 456, 12 Modern 147, 88 E.R. 1225.

[2] *Hobart v. Countess of Suffolk* (1709), 2 Vernon 644, 23 E.R. 1020, 1 Eq. Cas. Abr. 272, 21 E.R. 1040, *sub nom. Earl of Stamford v. Hobart* (1710), 3 Brown P.C. 31, 1 E.R. 1157, note also *In re Maynard's Will* (1691), Dodd 101.

[3] *Throckmerton v. Tracy* (1555), 1 Plowden 145, 150, 75 E.R. 222, 229, also 2 Dyer 124, 73 E.R. 272, 124 Selden Soc. 93; *Walker v. Wakeman* (1676), 1 Ventris 294, 86 E.R. 189.

[4] *Cumberford's Case* (1634), *ut supra*.

case, the rectory consisted only of tithes, out of which no rent could be reserved; therefore, the power of leasing the rectory must have been void if there must have been a rent reserved. Those lands were not held of the manor of B., but part of the demesnes, whereas the power is only of what was held of the manor. So this is not within the power.

The bill was dismissed.

753
Edwards v. Freeman
(Ch. 1726–1728)

Where specific lands are contracted to be settled, a debt is not created.

The intent of the Statute of Distributions is to make the shares of all of the decedent's children to be equal.

Where a father dies intestate not having paid an agreed upon portion and the daughter sues for both the portion and her distributive share, the portion will go into hotchpot.

A person who claims a distributory share of an intestate's estate must bring a into hotchpot any contingent interest in real estate that was an advancement.

The doctrine of hotchpot does not include payments already made for support or education.

Lincoln's Inn MS. Misc. 13, p. 143

27 June 1726.

Richard Freeman, esquire, late Lord Chancellor of Ireland,[1] deceased, by articles on his marriage with Elizabeth Keck, one of the daughters of Sir Anthony Keck, dated the 19th of February 1693, in consideration of the marriage and £4000, the marriage portion, covenants for himself, his heirs, executors, and administrators with the said Sir Anthony Keck that he, the said Richard Freeman, his heirs, or assigns would within six months after a request made by the said Sir Anthony Keck convey all his lands in the County of Gloucester to the use of himself for life without impeachment of waste, remainder to trustees to preserve contingent remainders, then to the use of the said Elizabeth Keck for her life for her jointure, remainder to the first and other sons of the marriage in tail male, remainder to trustees for 500 years in trust to raise portions for the daughters of the said Richard Freeman and Elizabeth Keck, *viz.*, if but one daughter, the sum of £5000 and, if more than one daughter, the sum of £6000 equally to

[1] Richard Freeman (1646–1710), the law reporter, was Lord Chancellor of Ireland from 1707 to 1710; O. J. Burke, *History of the Lord Chancellors of Ireland* (1879), pp. 109–111; S. Handley, 'Keck, Sir Anthony (bap. 1630, d. 1695)', *Oxford Dictionary of National Biography*, vol. 31, p. 9.

be divided, payable at their respective ages of eighteen years or days of marriage, which should first happen, and also maintenance for such daughter or daughters in the meantime particularly mentioned in the articles. And, after such portions should be raised or paid or if there should be no such daughter or daughters, the said term of 500 years to cease and, from and after the determination of the said term, to the use of the right heirs of the said Richard Freemen forever. And the said Richard Freeman covenants that the said premises agreed to be settled were of the clear yearly value of £500 above all reprises, public taxes excepted, and that he had full right and power to settle and convey the same subject to the charges aforesaid free from all other encumbrances. The said Mr. Freeman, at the same time, gave a bond of the penalty of £8000 conditioned for the performance of the covenants in the said articles.

The marriage took effect, and the said Mr. Freeman had issue by the said Elizabeth, his wife, only one daughter, named Mary, who was under the age of twelve years at the death of her father. But having afterwards attained the age of eighteen years, she became entitled to the said £5000 secured by the said articles. And she has since intermarried with the plaintiff, Walter Edwards. The said Elizabeth, the wife of the said Richard Freeman dying, the said Mr. Freeman soon after married Mrs. Anne Marshall, by whom he had issue, the defendants Richard and Anne, on which marriage he made a settlement of a considerable part of the lands contained in the said articles, but not of the whole, there being sufficient or very near sufficient of those lands omitted to satisfy the said £5000.

The said Richard Freeman never made any settlement in pursuance of the above articles, but, being Lord Chancellor of Ireland, he died in that kingdom on the 20th of November 1710 intestate, leaving a considerable personal estate. His widow, Anna Freeman, soon after, took out administration to her late husband and possessed herself of his personal estate.

The plaintiffs brought their bill against the said Anna Freeman, his widow and administratrix, and also against her son and daughter, the other defendants, Richard and Anna, to have an account and a distributory share of the intestate's personal estate, according to the Statute of Distributions.[1] And the said Anna Freeman dying, the plaintiff Mary took administration *de bonis non* of Richard Freeman and the defendant Richard took administration to his mother, and the cause was thereupon revived.

The points in dispute were two:

First, whether the £5000 secured by the said articles and which depended on the contingency of the plaintiff Mrs. Edwards's attaining the age of eighteen or being married and did not become due until several years after the death of her father should be looked on as an advancement by the father within the meaning

[1] Stat. 22 & 23 Car. II, c. 10, s. 3 (*SR*, V, 720).

of the Statute of Distributions and be brought into hotchpot in the distribution of the personal estate;

Second, whether the said £5000 should be esteemed in equity only as a charge on the real estate mentioned in the articles as it would have been in case the settlement had been made pursuant thereunto or whether it should be looked on as a personal charge so as to be deducted out of the personal estate.

For the plaintiff, it was insisted that this portion was not to be paid by the father in his lifetime nor to be paid out of his personal estate, but it was a charge upon the land and to be paid after his death. And the articles are to be considered as carried into execution, for, in a court of equity, they are considered as though they were actually executed. And the Case of the Countess of Coventry[1] is a very strong case as to this point. The Case of Feast and Feast[2] was cited, which was heard the 5th of April last. Sir Felix Feast, by articles on his marriage, covenanted to leave his wife £2000, the like sum to his eldest son, and £1000 apiece to all his younger children. He died intestate and left his wife and several children. It was decreed the sums to which the children were entitled under the articles were no advancement within the custom of London nor any advancement within the Statute of Distributions.

The plaintiff's wife is a purchaser under her father's marriage articles, and what is to be brought into hotchpot upon the Statute of Distributions must be a voluntary provision or bounty of the father and not what comes in consideration of marriage and the marriage portion.

But what will put this case out of question is that the plaintiff's wife was an infant of eleven years of age at the death of her father, and it was uncertain whether she would have lived until she came to the age of eighteen. And, if she had died before her portion became due, it could not be raised for the benefit of an administrator, according to Lady Paulet's Case.[3]

Suppose, therefore, she had brought a bill by her *prochein ami* immediately after the death of her father and before her portion became due. Could the administrator have set up these articles in bar of so much of her distributive share? Or suppose she had died soon after her father and her administrator had brought a bill for her distributive share. Could it be said that there was a provision made for her by articles which never took affect?

The intention of the Statute is that the estate is to be distributed as it stands at the death of the intestate, and then it is to be considered what provision each child has had. But now, according to the construction the defendants would put upon the Statute, the distribution could not be made in the present case in any

---

1 *Countess of Coventry v. Earl of Coventry* (1722–1724), see above, Case No. 547.

2 *Feast v. Feast* (Ch. 1726), see above, Case No. 734.

3 *Lady Pawlett v. Lord Pawlett* (1685), 1 Vernon 204, 321, 23 E.R. 415, 496, also 2 Freeman 93, 22 E.R. 1079, 2 Chancery Reports 286, 21 E.R. 680, 2 Ventris 366, 86 E.R. 489, 1 Eq. Cas. Abr. 267, 21 E.R. 1036, Lincoln's Inn MS. Misc. 498, p. 14.

little time after the father's death, but it must wait six or seven years until it could be seen whether the plaintiff's portion would become due or not.

For the defendants, it was said that, true it is, articles are considered in many cases in a court of equity as carried into execution. But that is in respect only of those who claim under the person who was bound by the articles. It has been objected that there is no covenant in the articles to pay the portions. The answer [is] there is a covenant to raise a term and Mr. Freeman has broken his covenant by making a settlement on his second marriage, for, thereby, he disabled himself from settling those lands for raising the £5000 and, since the covenant is broken, can anyone say that the £5000 must not be paid out of the personal estate?

As to the other point, it was said that whatever provision is made by a father for his child, be it out of real or out of personal estate, it shall be brought in upon the distribution. And whether the provision is made voluntarily or upon a consideration, it is all one. The Statute has made no distinction. The intention of the Act was that all the children should be made equal. But now, if the plaintiffs are to prevail, there will be a great inequality.

This being a case of difficulty, the Lord Chancellor [Lord King] said it should be spoken to again, and he would have the assistance of some judges.
6 March 1727[/28].

Accordingly, the Lord Chancellor [Lord King] was assisted by the Lord Chief Justice Raymond, the Master of the Rolls [Jekyll], and Mr. Justice Price, and the case having been argued before them and they having taken time to consider thereof, it now came on for judgment in the absence of Mr. Justice Price, who was indisposed.

The Master of the Rolls [Jekyll] was of the opinion the £5000 was a charge upon the lands and not a debt upon the personal estate of Mr. Freeman. The articles in the present case must be considered as carried into execution, and the settlement must be taken to be made.

As to the other question, which was the principle point, *viz.* whether the plaintiff's portion is to be brought into hotchpot upon the distribution, he said he was of opinion it ought to be brought in and collated to the personal estate of the intestate.

The Statute of Distribution of Intestates' Estates appears to be intended to make the estate of the children equal, and the design of the Act is to supply the want of the intestate's care of his children. It is *providentia legis* to do what a prudent parent would have done, *viz.* to make an equal distribution of his estate among his children. And this equality must not extend to such estate only as the father had power to dispose of, nor to such provisions only as are made by voluntary settlements. But this equality must extend to all sorts of provisions. He said he did not mean a provision by a will, for that is not a provision which takes place in the life of the father. A will is of no effect until after the testator's death.

Now, a child may be provided for by land or an annuity out of land or by money or stock, and these provisions may be made to take place at the age of twenty-one or at marriage or upon a contingency according as the circumstances of the parent may be. And, therefore, as there might be a great variety of provisions for children, the Act could not take notice of them all, but it intended to take in all sorts of provisions made by the father in his lifetime, which excludes a provision by a will, for a man may make a will and yet die intestate as to all or to part of his personal estate, as where he makes no executor or makes a will only of his real estate.

This Act must receive its exposition from the rules of the civil law, and of that opinion was Lord North in the Case of Carter and Crawley, Raym. 496,[1] in which case, a good account is given of the reason of making this Statute.

The Act is a direction to the ecclesiastical courts. And though the temporal courts have a right to expound all statutes and are not presumed to be cognizant of the civil law, yet, if the legislature intended the Act should be expounded according to the civil law, the judges must so expound it. The civil law makes no distinction between real and personal estate. That is a distinction of the common law.

Lady Paulet's Case was the first case where a portion provided by a settlement for a child who died before it became due should not be raised in favor of an administrator. And this case has made all the difficulty.

Lord Chief Justice Raymond said he agreed entirely with the Master of the Rolls [Jekyll] that the £5000 portion ought to be brought into hotchpot. The design of the Act is to make a disposition of such part of the estate of the father as by remissness or otherwise he has made no disposition of and to do it in such a manner as a parent not influenced by partial affection would or ought to have done. If a child is provided for, he is to enjoy that provision which has been made for him. But, if he is not fully provided for and comes to take away what is left for the other children, he must bring in the provision which he has had.

It has been said that the settlement intended by the Act must be a voluntary settlement and not a settlement made on a valuable consideration, as marriage and a marriage portion. The Act is general. There is nothing in it which looks as if it was intended to make a distinction between voluntary settlements and settlements in consideration of marriage. Suppose a father had made a provision by a settlement on his marriage for raising £5000 for his eldest daughter and, afterwards, died intestate and left but £2000 and several children. If he was to have made a will, he would have given the £2000 to those children. What in reason a parent would have done in such a case, the Act must be intended to have done.

As to the objection that the provision for the plaintiff was contingent and it was uncertain whether it would ever take place, it is no provision until the contingency happens.

---

[1] *Carter v. Crawley* (1683), T. Raymond 496, 83 E.R. 259, also 1 Freeman 296, 297, 298, 89 E.R. 215, 216.

Suppose a father covenants that his executors shall pay a child a sum of money within three months after his death if such child is then living. This is not a provision within the Act until the contingency happens. And so it would be if it was to be paid at any future day within a reasonable time and was not a very remote contingency.

The words in the Act, *viz*. 'shall be advanced by the intestate in his lifetime', were purposely inserted to exclude provision by will, for that is given to the child and the Act makes only a disposition of what the father dies intestate.

If a contingent portion is within the intent and meaning of the Act, as I think it is, the portion is to be brought in when the contingency happens.

However, the distribution is not to wait in the meantime. If a child brings a bill for his distributive share of his father's personal estate, the court must decree a distribution to be made. But, if it is made and the contingency afterwards happens, why may not the other children have a bill for a share of this contingent portion as to so much, as the child entitled to that portion has gone away with more than he should have had.

Lord Chancellor [Lord King]: Judge Price has signified his opinion to me by a letter, which agrees with the opinion of the Chief Justice and the Master of the Rolls. And I am of the same opinion upon considering the whole Act together.

The intent of the Statute was to put an end to a long controverted point between the ecclesiastical and temporal courts. After the Reformation, the ecclesiastical courts took bonds upon granting administrations to make a distribution amongst the next of kin. And the temporal courts thought the administrator ought to have the personal estate and was not obliged to make a distribution. And, therefore, when actions were brought on these bonds, they adjudged them to be illegal. Hughes v. Hughes, Carter 125 and 1 Lev. 233.[1] That case was a hard case and was the reason of making the Act of Distributions.

Before the Act, by the ecclesiastical law, a provision by law or out of land was not to come into the *collatio bonorum*. And, therefore, the Act must intend by inserting the word 'settlement' to intend all settlements and that a settlement of land or out of land should be brought into the collation.

But then it is objected that this is a future contingent provision. Call this what you will, it is an interest, and, though contingent, it was such a contingency as must happen within a short time if at all.

If the contingency is very remote, it may admit of another consideration. Whenever a distribution is made, there must be a reservation of something or other that is contingent. A contingent interest may be valued. But, however, there is no need to give any opinion as to that, for now the contingency has

[1] *Hughes v. Hughes* (1666), Carter 125, 124 E.R. 867, 1 Levinz 233, 83 E.R. 384.

happened before the distribution is made. And, therefore, I am of opinion that the £5000 is to be brought in.

But then, another question will arise, whether the maintenance is to be brought in. And I am of opinion it ought not, for, by the civil law, the maintenance of the children was not to be collated.

And of that opinion also were the Chief Justice and the Master of the Rolls.

And, therefore, Lord Chancellor [Lord King] declared that the £5000 provided for the plaintiff by the marriage articles was within the Act, and, if the plaintiffs will come in for a distributive share, they must bring in the £5000. And in order thereunto, he decreed an account of the personal estate.

But then another question arose, whether the interest of the £5000 since it became due should not be brought in as well as the principal sum, for, in the distribution, the plaintiffs will have a share of the interest, which has been made of the personal estate.

But to this, it was said by the counsel for the plaintiff that by the custom of London, when a portion is to be brought into hotchpot, the interest of the portion is never brought in.

The Master of the Rolls [Jekyll]: The court being of opinion that the distribution is to be made before the contingency happens, whenever the contingency happens and the portion becomes due, then the collation is to be made and, when the collation is to be made, from that time, the interest of the money to be brought in must be brought in too.

And after some litigation of the counsel, it was at length decreed as it were by consent, that the defendants should take £5000 apiece out of the estate and have the interest which had been made thereof and the plaintiff to have her portion and all the interest since it became due.

Lincoln's Inn MS. Misc. 384, p. 319, pl. 3

28 June 1726.

Attorney General [*Yorke*], for the plaintiff: A bill [was exhibited] for the distributive share of Lord Chancellor Freeman's personal estate of the value of £20,000 to three children. 19 February 1693, articles [were made] on the marriage of the plaintiff's father and mother, if [there be] no issue male, [for] a 500 years term [to] trustees to raise £5000 for the daughter payable at eighteen or marriage, which the defendants insist is an advancement and bar to the plaintiff's distributive share. The plaintiff insists it is not an advancement within the Statute. Here, it is not payable in the father's lifetime. The settlement mentioned in the Statute must be understood of a voluntary settlement. Here, it is by way of purchase. 5 April, Feast v. Feast; Sir Felix Feast, by marriage articles, settled £2000 among his younger children; the defendants insisted it was an advancement to bar them of the customary share; that was overruled; they then insisted it ought to be brought into hotchpot by the Statute of Distributions; that likewise was overruled, it being by purchase. This could not be called a certain provision at the death of the plaintiff's father. If the plaintiff had brought a bill on the death of her father, these articles could not have barred her, it being uncertain whether she would ever attain eighteen or be married. So, if she had died, her administrator would have been entitled to her distributive share. This is not a debt on the personal estate but a charge on the real estate. The articles are looked upon as a settlement. The plaintiff was twelve years old at her father's death in 1710. Lady Coventry v. Lord Coventry.

Mr. *Lutwyche*: The Statute directs how the estate shall be distributed at the intestate's death. This trust term is subsequent to an estate tail. If there had been a son of this marriage, there had been no provision. If the plaintiff had died before eighteen or marriage, the portion had sunk into the estate. Lord Pawlett's Case, Vern. Reports.

The words of the Statute are the surplus to be distributed among the children 'other than such . . . children not being heir at law as shall have an estate by the settlement of the intestate or . . . advanced by the intestate in his lifetime by . . . portions equal to their share.'[1]

Mead: If the estate had been distributed at the death of her father, could she have been compelled to refund when she became entitled to her portion?

Mr. Solicitor General [*Talbot*], for the defendant: What is contended for is unreasonable. We differ as to the consequence drawn from the marriage articles to be looked upon as carried into execution only as to those who claim under the parties or by voluntary conveyances. As to purchasers with notice, equity will not carry them into execution. Lord Coventry's Case is quite different. He was entitled to a remainder subject to a power [and] intended to execute it. Here, Mr. Freeman settled the lands subject to his charge on the second marriage. Whether this portion is a charge on the real or on the personal estate, [there is] no covenant to pay money but to make a security for the payment out of the land which he has settled on the second marriage. A breach of a covenant is to be made good out of the personal estate; the real estate settled is not liable so that this portion will be a charge on the personal estate. On the Statute of Distributions, the general intent is that there shall be a distribution equally made. The plaintiffs insist the word 'settlement' is only of land. The intent of the Statute is to take in all sorts of advancements. It appears by the second clause that the child who has only a partial advancement shall have it made equal to the rest.

[It was] objected the £5000 was not an advancement by the father, it being no more than the mother's portion. The answer is but the Statute has made no distinction between voluntary provisions and [those] on a valuable consideration. Equality is intended.

[It was] objected this was not a certain provision. The answer is but here is a certain maintenance and a certain portion when she can want it. It will not

---

[1] Stat. 22 & 23 Car. II, c. 10, s. 3 (*SR*, V, 720).

distinguish it out of the Statute. It does not say it shall be paid in the father's life[time]. A settlement of a revocation or a contingent interest is of some value. There is a necessity to have regard to contingent interests. If considered as a contingent debt on the personal estate, could the whole be divided with regard to this debt? It would not postpone the distribution, but sufficient [funds] must be set aside to answer it when the contingency happens. Here, the inequ[ality] will be £5000.

Curia [Lord King]: This will be considered as a charge on land as to the parties, not as to the petitioners, who claim under the second settlement. Both questions should be before me at the same time. Here, the question as to the portion is not before me. The bill is only for the distributive share.

Mr. *Cowper*: There is no case yet determined like this. It is hard to say, if it was payable in six months after the intestate's death, yet that it is not a settlement within the Statute. If the personal estate had been but £6000, it would have been hard to have claimed £5000 under the articles and the distributive share too.

Lord Chancellor [Lord King]: Query what the law is; equity must follow it. There are several difficult questions on the construction of the Act: whether this settlement is such a one as was intended by the Statute, whether it should be an estate at the time of the distribution, and further whether [it is] a contingent estate, what value is to be set on it. If this settlement be not within the Statute, it is strange no such case should have happened before. I will have the judges' assistance.

Lincoln's Inn MS. Misc. 384, p. 322, pl. 1

15 July. Lord Chancellor [Lord King], Mr. Baron Price, Mr. Justice Fortescue.

Mr. Solicitor [General *Talbot*], for the defendant, cited Copley v. Copley and Kemys v. Thomas,[1] not two provisions; Lord Pawlett's Case, where [it was] charged on land, if she died before payment, it is to sink. This is a portion, a charge on the personal estate at the death of the intestate. There must be a regard to contingent debts.

Curia: [This is] a new case. [We will] consider of it until next term.

Lincoln's Inn MS. Misc. 384, p. 334

6 March 1727/28. Lord Chancellor [Lord King], Lord Chief Justice Raymond, the Master of the Rolls [Jekyll]; Mr. Justice Price [was] sick.

Master of the Rolls [Jekyll]: Mr. Freeman, in consideration of a £4000 portion, covenanted, within six months after a request by Sir Anthony Keck, to

[1] *Copley v. Copley* (1711) 1 Peere Williams 147, 24 E.R. 333, 2 Eq. Cas. Abr. 639, 22 E.R. 536, British Library MS. Hargrave 80, f. 48, Lincoln's Inn MS. Misc. 383, p. 94; *Thomas v. Kemeys* (1696), 2 Vernon 348, 23 E.R. 821, 2 Freeman 207, 22 E.R. 1163, Colles 112, 1 E.R. 206, 1 Eq. Cas. Abr. 269, 21 E.R. 1037.

settle on himself for life, remainder to trustees for 500 years to raise £5000 for one daughter payable at eighteen or marriage and maintenance in the meantime, then the term to cease, remainder in fee to his right heirs; at the same time, a bond [was given] of £8000 penalty to perform the covenants. The wife died. The plaintiff is the only issue. Mr. Freeman married a second wife, by whom he had the defendant. Before any request to settle, Mr. Freeman died intestate. The plaintiff was then twelve years old. A bill [was exhibited] for the £5000 portion and a distributory share. The defendant insists, first, it is a debt; secondly, it is an advancement and to be brought into hotchpot. First, it is not a debt in point of law. The bond is only to perform covenants. In the articles, there are no covenants to settle but upon request, and no request was made. But that will not vary the case. Though the covenants were broken, yet any person claiming under it cannot concern the personal estate first, but it is on the land. The articles are a settlement of the land in equity. It is different from a mortgage. Though he might by payment exonerate the land, for there the land is only pledged as a security. Here it is charged on the land. Lady Coventry's Case is stronger to go against the land; there the covenant was by virtue of the power or otherwise, and it was insisted he might have settled other lands, there being no lien on particular lands; but the court was of opinion she had a specific lien on the lands comprised in the power. Here, particular lands are covenanted to be settled.

Second, whether the plaintiff's portion of £5000 shall be brought into hotchpot [by the] Statute of 22 Car. II, for distributions, the intent of the Statute was to make the shares of all the children equal. [He was] of opinion that this portion ought to be collated to the personal estate of her father. Consider it as if she were under eighteen, the Act was to supply the intestate's care for his children and to do that which a prudent father would have done. This equality is not to be confined to voluntary provisions. I do not speak of provisions by a will, but by settlements. The equality is designed to be with regard to all sorts of provisions made by the father in his lifetime and to those charged on the land as well as the land itself and also though given on a contingency if other children besides the eldest son are provided for, though they must bring it into hotchpot. Children may be provided for either out of land or money. And as to the time when they may take place, either on marriage or at a certain age, and with an infinite variety, it is impossible for the legislature to specify all the cases. But it is necessary to lay down some general rule which might extend to all cases. To imagine they designed to take in provision by the land itself and not to take in a charge or portion out of land would be a strange construction. If the provision is equal to his share, he is totally excluded. Then comes the case of a child not totally excluded. The words are 'and in case any other child than the heir at law' shall have an estate by a settlement of the intestate etc. Here, the trustee having the term in him makes the plaintiff within the words of the Statute. The occasion of the Statute [was] Carter and Crawley, at the end of Raymond's reports, 497. Lord North consulted the judges [as to the] difference between the ecclesiastical and the common law as to the distribution of intestates' estates. The child must be advanced by the father in his lifetime, which excludes the will, and it must be by some act completed in his lifetime. Writ *de rationabile parte bonorum*, Register 142; by the custom of the Province of York; Swinburne [*Testaments*] 200. If a father in his lifetime bestows an annuity on a child, then it is not to take effect until after his death; yet it is an advancement, which shows that future provisions are taken into consideration. Lady Pawlet and Lord Pawlet, Easter 1 Jac. II, Vern. 321. At the time of the making of this Statute, anyone would think such a portion as this was a bare possibility; therefore, it is not a *debitum in praesenti*. It does not arise until the contingency of the father's dying without issue male. Consider it by the rules of the civil law. The Act is directory to the ecclesiastical courts. It intended to restore the ecclesiastical jurisdiction where, before, the courts of common law would send [writs of] prohibition. Vaug. 208; lib. 37, tit. 7, *Corpus Juris Civilis, viz. Si sub conditione pater vel extraneus [dotem] promiserit, cautione opus erit, ut tunc conferat mulier dotem, cum dotata esse coeperit.*[1] By their law, such a provision as this ought to be collated. The Statute does not say when the distribution shall be made but only when it shall not be made, that is not before a year after the death. Were it a right indeed vested at the death of the father, part of the estate may depend on a contingency. A present distribution may be made of what is certain and a future one of what is uncertain. It must be brought into hotchpot.

Lord Chief Justice Raymond: The general question is whether this £5000 shall be considered either as an advancement or a provision made by the father in his lifetime. [He was] of the same opinion that it must be brought into hotchpot. The distribution is to be made according to reason and equity, and the Statute has made a Parliamentary will for him. The rule of equality is most agreeable to nature. That is the intent of the Statute. If the children are unprovided for, then the residue is to be equally divided. If they are partially provided for, then they are to have so much as to make them all equal. If they are fully provided for, then they are to have no more. This is the manifest intent of the Act. Therefore, the most favorable construction must be to fulfill the intent. Plow. 467.[2]

[It was] objected from the words of the Act, not from the intent, that of a settlement, whether it meant only voluntary here is a co[. . .] and the plaintiff is a purchaser, as if the child purchased part of his father's estate, not like this case. There is nothing in the Act to distinguish between marriage settlements and others. The words are general. The marriage portion is looked upon as the consideration of the whole settlement. Suppose the father has left other children and but a £2000 personal estate. [It would be] very hard to take that away when such a plentiful provision was made for the eldest. If he had made a will, would he be supposed to give away this £2000 from his younger children?

---

[1] *Harrison v. Burwell* (1668), Vaughan 206, 208, 124 E.R. 1039, 1040, also 2 Ventris 9, 86 E.R. 278; *Digesta*, 37, 7, 7.

[2] *Eyston v. Studd* (1574), 2 Plowden 459, 467, 75 E.R. 688, 698.

The second objection was the estate by the settlement is only land. This is not land nor a portion advanced in the lifetime of the father. [It is] admitted that any estate in land must be valued. It is very odd that, when the Statute intends all to be equal and that even land shall be brought in, yet that part of the personal estate should not.

[He was] of opinion, if the plaintiff is provided for by a portion, it is within the last clause. If the father covenants to pay a portion to a daughter when [she becomes] eighteen, there is no difference whether she attains eighteen in her father's lifetime or soon after his death. It is different where it depends on a contingency and when it is payable at a time certain. If there is a bond to pay within three months after his death if the daughter be then living, it is a portion when the contingency happens; it shall not be brought into hotchpot before, but then it shall. The reason is the same if, within a reasonable time, as in a limitation of terms, a parent would consider such a child provided for. The Act does not say the portion is to be paid in the father's lifetime; it is sufficient if it is secured in his lifetime. It is only meant in contradiction to wills, that what is given by a will shall not be brought in. A different construction would overthrow the intent of the Act.

[It was] objected [that it was] uncertain whether this would ever happen. I do not think a contingency can be valued. But this is not to be considered as a portion until the contingency happens. Contingencies being within the Act, the other children are entitled to have it brought in when the contingency happens; there is no necessity to distribute the estate at the death of the intestate. Whenever a contingent part falls in, the distribution of that part may be made. When an executor pays a legacy on compulsion and after[wards] a debt is discovered, the legatee must refund.

[It was] objected there is no precedent of a contingency being brought in. The answer is it may be it was never questioned, but acquiesced in.

This is not a debt because there was no covenant to pay the money.

Lord Chancellor [Lord King]: Mr. Justice Price, being indisposed, has signified his opinion to the same effect.

As to my own opinion, considering every part of the Statute, I think this £5000 must be brought into hotchpot. The lands in the second settlement are first liable, being part of the trust term, and the rest to come out of the personal estate. Hughes v. Hughes, Carter 125, 1 Levinz 233. The son as administrator took the whole personal estate [which] would give nothing to his sister gave occasion to the Statute of Distributions, which revived the method of the spiritual courts and took away the power which the administrator had of keeping the whole estate. When the civilians found this Statute, they left out the word 'land', which was added by Lord Chief Justice Hale – so by Justice Price. Land is as much a provision as money, but the spiritual courts could not meddle with it, for a [writ of] prohibition would lie. *Collatio bonorum* only extended to the personal estate. Here, the Act had in view all provisions usually made for younger children by settlements and makes it a collatable estate. The child cannot be a creditor because she was not in being when the settlement was made. The father is not strictly a debtor for this. The Statute intended to bring in all provisions made by the father in his lifetime.

[It was] objected this was a future, contingent interest and the plaintiff's right to the distributive share accrued on the death of her father. But this is still an interest and one to happen within a reasonable time and must be certain at the death of the intestate. It was valuable and a present interest in the trustees as to maintenance. If they are future debts, by the Statute, the person entitled to a distribution shall give a bond to refund. If there are debts owing to the intestate, they cannot be distributed until gotten in. Here, the contingency has happened before the distribution was made. If the plaintiff has less than her share, it must be made equal and the plaintiff must bring this £5000 into hotchpot. As to the £80 *per annum* maintenance, it is not to be brought in. By the civil law, if one child was better entertained or more was laid out in the education, yet it was not to be brought in. Stair's *Institutes* 499.[1]

Lincoln's Inn MS. Misc. 506, p. 86

6 March 1727[/28], 1 George II.

The plaintiff's father, on his marriage with his first wife, the plaintiff's mother, did in consideration of the said marriage and of a £4000 marriage portion article to settle certain lands on himself for life, on his said wife for life, then on trustees during the lives of him and his wife to support contingent remainders, then to the trustees for a term of years to raise portions for daughters and younger children, which, in case of only one child, was to be £5000, and then on the eldest son, and so on to the second, third, etc. His first wife dies leaving issue, only one daughter married to the plaintiff Edwards. The father marries a second wife, by whom he has issue, the defendants, and dies intestate. The £5000, to which the plaintiff is entitled by the marriage articles, was payable after the father's death and then not unless the plaintiff arrived at the age of eighteen or marriage, with a provision for maintenance in the meanwhile so that it was not only a future, but a contingent, interest. The plaintiff did not arrive at the age of eighteen until many years after her father's death, at which time, her portion of £5000 was paid her, and, over and above that, she demanded an equal share with the other children in the two-thirds of her father's personal estate.

The defendants insisted on her collating the £5000 if she insisted on a rateable share of her father's estate according to the Statute of Distributions.

On the other hand, the plaintiff insisted that the £5000 was a debt, that it was purchased by her mother's marriage and the marriage portion, as being the consideration of the settlement, that it was both a future and an uncertain

[1] J. Dalrymple, viscount Stair, *The Institutions of the Law of Scotland.*

interest as depending on a contingency that might never happen and so not within the clause of the Act that requires a collation.

Upon this question, the Lord Chancellor [Lord King] called to his assistance the Master of the Rolls [Jekyll], Lord Chief Justice Raymond, and Baron Price, who, upon taking time to consider, were unanimously of opinion that the £5000 ought to be collated if the plaintiff made a demand on the personal estate of the intestate, but that there ought to be no consideration had of the allowance of maintenance because that could in no sense be called an advancement, being only a subsistence until she came of proper age to be advanced, that this was a collatable interest though not to be collated until the contingency happens, for though a contingent interest may have some sort of value set upon it, yet that is not what a court of equity will compel a sale of. It is an advancement and an advancement in the lifetime of the intestate, for, though the contingency does not happen in his lifetime, yet it is a portion provided for in his lifetime. The Act makes no difference between marriage settlements and other provisions or settlements where a child buys an estate of the parent; that is not properly a settlement, but a purchase. And though the mother may be a purchaser, yet, *quoad* the child, it is a voluntary provision. An equality among all the children was what the Act principally aimed at. And, as to the difficulty in making a distribution, there was nothing in that because the estate of the intestate, which it is collated to, may happen to be of the same nature and the distribution is not to be made until the contingency happens. They said they would not extend the rule to all remote possibilities, but only to such as must happen in a reasonable time and such a time as is allowed for the limitation of a term of years. A legacy left by a will (for a man may make a will as to part and die intestate as to the rest) is a different case and not to be brought into hotchpot because there is a plain design of a preference and it is not in his lifetime, for the gift is not completed until death. This Act is directory to the ecclesiastical courts and to be put in execution by ecclesiastical censures and, therefore, ought to be expounded by the *juris civilis* and, by that law, such a provision as this is collatable. Swinburne, [*Testaments*]; Customs of York; Ver. 321; Raym. 498; Vaugh. 208; Cart. 125, 1 Lev. 233, Hughes v. Hughes.[1] By the same law, maintenance is not to be collated how different soever the same may be, for the intestate is the best judge of the children's qualifications and thus may make them what allowance he pleases.

It was thus decreed that the plaintiff should have a distribution, but that it should be upon condition of collating the £5000, that the interest which had been made of the personal estate should go to the increase of it.

It was then urged that the plaintiff should bring the interest of the £5000 into hotchpot.

---

[1] *Lady Pawlett v. Lord Pawlett* (1685), *ut supra*; *Carter v. Crawley* (1683), *ut supra*; *Harrison v. Burwell* (1668), *ut supra*; *Hughes v. Hughes* (1666), *ut supra*.

As to that, the court ordered that it should be at her election to bring it in or not, only that, if she did not bring it in but chose the interest which had been made of that specific sum, it should be counted as a retainer of so much of her share and she should not be allowed the interest of that part of her share, but only until the time as she received the said £5000.

British Library MS. Lansdowne 588, f. 105

Freeman, on his marriage with the plaintiff's mother, in consideration of marriage and a £4000 portion, covenanted to settle lands to the use of himself for life, then to his heirs male, then to trustees for 500 years to raise £5000 if he should leave only one daughter payable on the day of marriage or age of eighteen with a provision for other contingencies that are out of the present case, and, if he left no daughter, then the term was to cease. Then, Freeman gave a bond of £8000 for the performance of the covenants.

The plaintiff, Mrs. Edwards, was the only issue of this marriage. Freeman died intestate leaving the plaintiff under twelve years of age and a second wife and a son and a daughter by her.

The plaintiff brings her bill for a distribut[ion] of the personal estate and demands the £5000 portion besides to be levied on the real estate or, if not levied on the real estate, yet that it shall charge the personal estate as a debt to be satisfied before distribution and that the portion ought not to be brought into hotchpot.

Opinion [Sir Joseph Jekyll, Master of the Rolls]: The £5000 is not a debt owing by Freeman. It is not a debt in [common] law. The covenant is not absolute, but only to pay on request, and there was no request. So the covenant is not broken in point of law.

First point, this portion will charge the real estate first. If that is not sufficient, it will charge the personal estate for the residue. The articles are a settlement in equity. This differs from the case of a mortgage, to which it was compared. In the case of a mortgage, the original intention is to repay the money, for which the land is designed only [as] a security. But here, the original intention was to raise the money out of the lands.

I admit that Freeman might have exonerated the lands. He had a liberty to pay the portion in discharge of the lands. But he was under no lien to do it. Countess Dowager and Earl of Coventry. In the case there was a covenant to settle lands for a jointure with a power to raise money for the payment etc., it was insisted that he, the earl, might have executed his power or might settle the lands and that the countess had no specific lien on the land but might charge the assets. But Lord Macclesfield held that it was a specific lien to the value of £5000 *per annum* because the original intention was to raise the money out of the land.

The present case is stronger. Here is a covenant to settle particular lands. It is to be construed as a settlement.

Second point, the portion must be brought into hotchpot or, to speak more properly, it must be collated to the personal estate. The intent of the Statute 22

Car. II was to make the estate of all the children as nearly equal as can be estimated. This equality must be the rule to judge by in this case. The Statute intended to supply the intestate's will. It is in a manner a Parliamentary will.

Edwards is now married and above the age of eighteen so that the contingency now has happened. Yet I admit that it must be considered *in statu quo fuit* at the time of Freeman's death, when she was under the age of eighteen and unmarried, at which time the contingency had not happened.

The equality intended by the Statute is not confined to such estates as the father might settle voluntarily. The Statute must be intended to take in settlements on considerations, for those settlements are most common. *Ad ea quae frequentius accidunt, jura adaptantur.* The Statute extends to contingent portions, and it is intended to take in all manner of advancements. The Statute did not intend to enumerate all the several kinds of advancements to which it did extend, for there is a great variety in the subject matter as well as in the time of the provisions intended by the Statute.

The Statute mentioned settlements of lands to give the spiritual court jurisdiction, for without this expression in the Statute, the spiritual court would not have taken notice of such settlements in computing the estate of the intestate on a distribution.

Any estate by a settlement of the intestate means any estate, either personal or real, for the Statute chiefly concerns personal estates. If the advancement is not equal to the share of the personal estate, then it may be collated. The plaintiff has an estate in lands in the Statute, for she is the owner of the term in equity so far as to raise her portion out of it.

Lord North, in the end of Raymond's reports, in the Case of Garter v. Prawling,[1] gives the history of the occasion of the making of this Statute. It was occasioned by a long contest that there had been between the courts temporal and spiritual. The intent of the Statute was to make all the children's estate equal by collation agreeable to the civil law, which makes no difference between estates real and personal. The words of the Statute 'advancement in the lifetime of the father' are intended in opposition to an advancement by a will, which is not to be collated. An advancement by a will does not exclude from a share of the personal estate. If, where a father makes a will of part of his estate and dies intestate as to the residue, Reg. 142; Swinb. 200,[2] it is an advancement by the custom of the province of York, though it is not to take place until after his death because it is a settlement made in his lifetime. By the custom of the province of York, he that takes anything as heir is excluded, yet he takes not in the lifetime of the intestate. Future provisions bar a distribution.

---

1 *Carter v. Crawley* (1683), *ut supra*.

2 *Registrum Brevium*; H. Swinburne, *Brief Treatise of Testaments and Last Wills.*

The first case on the Statute was Lady Pawlett v. Lord Pawlett, Easter 1 Jac. II, Vern. 321. If a child dies before a portion is payable, it sinks for the benefit of the heir.

It has been objected that the plaintiff has only a contingent interest, it is a debt or portion that does not exist until a future contingency has happened; therefore, it is not a *debitum in praesenti*. The term arises on the father's death, but it is no trust for the plaintiff until the contingency has happened. Therefore, it ought not to be collated. The portion is not *in esse* at the time of the father's death. I add the child has only a possibility.

The portion may be collated though it is contingent; it may be collated when the contingency happens. This obviates all the difficulties that have been objected.

It must be determined by the rules of the civil law. The Statute was made for the direction of the spiritual court. So says Lord North in Raym. 497. On the Reformation, the spiritual court distributed according to the rules of the civil law. Raym. 504. This distribution was despised and rejected by the temporal courts, and the scope of the Act was to make it legal.

It is objected that the exposition of acts of Parliament belongs to the temporal [courts]. This objection is called spurious and empty in Vaughan 208. A contingent portion may be collated by the rules of the civil law. *Digesta*, lib. 37, tit. 7, l. 1; [*blank*] *Codex* [*blank*]; *Si sub conditione pater vel extraneus dotem promisserit, cautione opus erit ut tum conferat mulier cum dotata esse caperit.*

The Statute appoints no time when the distribution shall be made. It is only said that it shall not be until after a year.

The personal [estate] may consist of sums payable *in futuro*, which, therefore, cannot be distributed *instanter*. Therefore, a portion contingent may be collated since it is of the same nature with the estate of the intestate.

There may be a present distribution of the substance in possession and a future distribution of the contingencies.

Lord Chief Justice Raymond, *ad idem*: This portion may be collated. The design of the Statute was to make a disposition of the substance of which he had not disposed according to justice and equity in such manner as he ought to have done. The children's estate is to be as nearly equal as possible. The equality is to be the rule.

There are many cases, Plowd. 460, where statutes have been construed contrary to the letter to comply with the intent. Here, the intent is plain.

It is objected that the Statute means only voluntary settlements but that this is on a valuable consideration, that, therefore, the plaintiff is a purchaser and is in the same condition as if the child or a stranger for him had purchased, that, therefore, it is not to be collated.

I answer that these cases differ, *viz.* where a child or a stranger purchase for the child, these are purchases not settlements. The Statute makes no difference between settlements voluntary or on a valuable consideration. Many difficulties would arise should we enter into a consideration of that point, whether the settlement moves from the father. I admit that the portion of £4000 given on the marriage is a valuable consideration for all the uses in the settlement.

But this matter may be waived, for the Statute makes no distinction of settlements. I think a marriage[1] settlement is in the Statute.

Suppose here had been only a surplus of £2000. Could it be imagined that the legislators intended that a child that had a portion of £5000 by a settlement on marriage should have a share on this without collation? This would not answer the intent of the Statute, which was to make an equality. When the Statute speaks of estates, it means personal as well as real, for personal estates are the subject of the Statute. Where the Statute says land, it drops the personal, yet land is only mentioned as an instance. Personal may as well be implied as rents.

It was objected that contingent portions are not in the Statute, which says 'in his lifetime'.

I answer that a portion made payable to a son three years after the father's death if the son is then living is as much contingent as the present case. The remoteness of the contingency does not alter the case. Yet it was never doubted whether such a portion ought to be collated. It is a portion when the contingency happens, and it must then be collated.

The Statute says 'advanced in the lifetime'. It is not said that it shall take effect in the lifetime. It means the same as if it had been said secured in the lifetime. It is used in contradiction to wills, for an advancement by a will is no advancement in a lifetime to bar a distributory share.

A different construction would overturn the design of the Act. A court of equity will not compute the present value of the contingency according to the rules of chances. But the distribution of that which is contingent waits until the contingency happens.

Lord Chancellor [Lord King]: I am of the same opinion, and so is Justice Price, who cannot attend but has certified his opinion that the portion ought to be collated if the plaintiff receives a distributory share.

The only question now is whether this portion ought to be collated. The intent of the Statute 22 Car. II, c. 10, was to end a dispute between the spiritual and temporal courts. Before the Reformation, the spiritual court disposed of the personal estates of intestates to pious uses for the good of their souls. But, afterwards, when this pretense was taken away, they distributed the personal [estate] according to the rules of the civil law. But this being contrary to the law of the temporal courts, which gave the surplus to the administrator, they prohibited the spiritual courts from distributing the personal [estate] according to the civil law. To evade this, the spiritual court, upon granting administration, compelled the administrator to give a bond to distribute the surplus according to their law. But

[1] mortgage *MS*.

on a suit on such a bond in the temporal court, the bond was held to be void. Not long before the Statute, a case happened which occasioned the making of the Statute, *viz.* Trinity [term] 18 Car. II, Hughes v. Hughes, Carter 125, 1 Lev. 235; a father died intestate leaving a son and a daughter. The son took out administration and carried all the estate from his sister, and the temporal courts adjudged all to him. This occasioned the Statute.

This Statute restored and regulated the method of the spiritual court and made it legal. Before this Statute, the spiritual court sometimes preferred one, sometimes another. Civilians drew the bill and omitted the settlement of land in the computation of the estates to be collated because the spiritual court had no jurisdiction in a case of lands. The words 'settlements of lands' etc. were added by Lord Chief Justice Hale. Without this clause, [writs of] prohibition had lain if they had taken notice of freeholds.

Collatio bonorum in the civil law, as practiced in England, did not relate to lands. But now, lands are collateable. Money out of lands is a settlement of lands.

It is objected that the father is a debtor; so the settlement is not voluntary.

I admit that it is not voluntary, but that it is for a valuable consideration. But the Statute makes no difference of settlements. The plaintiff was not in being at the time of the settlement; therefore, she is not to be esteemed to be a purchaser. The portion is provided for the child only out of the tenderness of the parents. Therefore, he is not strictly a debtor.

Dr. Strahan's translation of Domat[1] [shows] our law is different from the civil law. By the civil law, the children advanced were forced to collate. (Query, vide Dig., l. 17, tit. 7, leg. 9.) It must be considered as it was at the time of the father's death.

This contingent interest is not remote. A contingent portion may be collated.

On a distribution, the Statute gives bonds to refund if new debts appear.

This contingency now has happened before a distribution; so there is no difficulty. If Edwards claims a distributory share, she must collate £5000.

Edward had by the settlement a maintenance of £80 *per annum*. This is not to be collated. Only the pecuniary interest is to be collated, not the entertainment or expenses of education. L. Stair's *Inst.* 499. Expenses of education are not to be collated.

The £5000 must be made equal to the distributory share of the other children. An account must be taken of the whole.

Talbot: The interest of the £5000 ought to be brought into hotchpot.

Sir Philip Yorke: By the custom of London, only the principal sum, not the fruits, are collated. So it is in the civil law; the *usufructus* is never collated.

Lord Chancellor [Lord King]: The principal only is collated by the custom of London.

[1] J. Domat, *Civil Law in its Natural Order* (W. Strahan, trans., 1722).

Master of the Rolls [Jekyll]: The opinion of the court is that the portion ought to be collated when payable. Therefore, when Edwards claims a distributory share, she lets in the other children to claim a share of her portion. Therefore, the interest from the time that is payable ought to be collated.

Lord Chancellor [Lord King]: If no interest was made of the £5000, the plaintiff ought not to account for the interest.

By the civil law, the advanced child may either collate or *minus tanto accipere*.

Curia: The decree [was] let an account be taken of the interest that has been made of the personal estate and of the £5000 since the time that it became payable. And distribution shall be made of the principal and interest.

[Other reports of this case: 2 Peere Williams 435, 24 E.R. 803, 1 Eq. Cas. Abr. 249, 267, 21 E.R. 1025, 1036, 2 Eq. Cas. Abr. 442, 443, 446, 447, 22 E.R. 377, 378, 380, 381.]

754

Pierce v. England

(Ch. 1726)

A gift made by a woman after her engagement but before marriage and without the consent of her fiancé is fraudulent as to him and will be set aside upon his suit.

Lincoln's Inn MS. Misc. 12, p. 245

29 June 1726. Peirce, administrator of Anne, his late wife, plaintiff; John England *et al.*, defendants.

The plaintiff's late wife was entitled to a legacy of £1100 under the will of John England, her father, who directed the legacy to be paid when she came to the age of twenty-one years or when she married, provided she married a man that could or did make her a jointure of £60 a year and by the consent of her mother and overseers. But, if she married without such consent and without having such jointure, then she was to have only the interest of the £1100 for her life, and, after her death, the principal was to be divided between her two brothers in case she had no children and, if she had, then her portion was to go to them.

The daughter, having attained twenty-one, married the plaintiff without the consent of her mother or the overseers and without having any settlement made upon her. And, during the courtship, she made a deed of appointment without the plaintiff's privity how the £1100 should go after her death. And she being now dead and the plaintiff having taken administration to her, he brought his bill to set aside his wife's deed of appointment and to be paid the legacy.

Curia [Jekyll] declared that the £1100 became due to the plaintiff's wife when she attained twenty-one.

And, as to the deed of appointment, the plaintiff not being privy thereto, the same was fraudulent as to him. And, therefore, he decreed it to be delivered up and cancelled.

As to the £1100, the plaintiff being present and consenting, the interest was to be paid to him during his life and, after his death, the principal was to go to a child that his wife had left by him.

755

Palmer v. Jennings

(Ch. 1726)

A Roman Catholic cannot receive an annuity charged on land.

Lincoln's Inn MS. Misc. 12, p. 229

8 July 1726.

The plaintiff's bill was for the payment of an annuity of £25 a year payable for the plaintiff's life and charged upon the defendant's estate by a settlement made in the year 1672.

The defendant insisted that the plaintiff, when she was twelve years of age, was sent beyond the sea to be educated in the Popish religion and that she was now in a nunnery at Liege and had been there for several years and that, therefore, she was incapable to hold this annuity by the Statute of King James I, ca. 4.[1]

There was some proof made of the plaintiff's being sent abroad and the general opinion of the family that she was sent to a nunnery. But what was principally relied on by the defendant was what was sworn by one witness, who said she lately saw her in a nunnery at Liege and in a nun's habit, one who owned her name to be Phoebe Palmer and the sister of Sir [*blank*] Palmer, which the plaintiff was, and that she was in a nun's habit and owned she was a nun and had been in the nunnery several years.

And though it was objected that what this witness swore was not sufficient, especially upon a penal statute where the party is to forfeit his estate, yet Lord Chancellor [Lord King] was of the opinion that, since this matter was put in issue by the answer of the defendant and the plaintiff, though a witness was examined to prove she was living, had not proved as she might have done, the fact had been so that she was not a nun nor professed the Popish religion, the evidence on the defendant's part was sufficient to bring the plaintiff within the Act of the first [year] of King James. And, therefore, he dismissed the bill, saying that the court must take the law as it is and act accordingly how hard soever it may fall out to be in some particular cases.

---

[1] Stat. 1 Jac. I, c. 4 (*SR*, IV, 1020–1022).

Note it was agreed in the arguing of this case that the Statute of King Charles II[1] as to convictions did not alter the disability by the Statute of King James I and that so was the opinion of all the judges in the Duke of Hamilton's Case.[2]

756

Staniford v. Caswall

(Ch. 1726)

A person is bound by the acts of his servants and agents.

Where a person takes several distinct securities for securing distinct sums of money and there is no agreement to tack them together, he may redeem one without the other.

Lincoln's Inn MS. Misc. 12, p. 226 [bis]

11 July 1726.

The plaintiffs having in the year 1718 entrusted some Bank annuities in the hands of Riley and Mitton, they, in the year 1720, pawned them to the defendant Caswell and Company as a security for £1200 and interest, who had no notice that the annuities belonged to the plaintiff.

Riley and Mitton pay off the £1200 and interest and take a note from Caswell's servant promising to transfer those annuities to them or order on demand, which note they endorse over to the plaintiff.

About a month after paying the £1200, Riley and Mitton borrow £1000 of the defendant and Company and pawn South Sea [Company] stock as a security. And about [*blank*] after that, they borrow £1000 more upon the security of other South Sea stock.

The plaintiff's bill is that the £1200 Bank annuities may be transferred to him.

The defendant insisted that the plaintiff is not entitled to redeem the annuities without paying what was due upon the whole account from Riley and Mitton. And, for the defendant was cited the Case of Demainbray v. Metcalfe, L.C. 23.[3] And it was insisted that the defendant having no notice that the annuities were the plaintiff's, the plaintiff could be in no better condition than Riley and Mitton would have been and whatever equity the defendant would have been entitled to against Riley and Mitton he will be entitled to have against the plaintiff. And, if Riley and Mitton had brought their bill to redeem the annuities, the court would not have admitted them to redeem without paying what was due upon the whole account.

---

1 Stat. 30 Car. II, stat. 2, c. 1 (*SR*, V, 894–896).

2 *Thornby v. Fleetwood* (1721), 5 Brown P.C. 374, 2 E.R. 740.

3 *Demainbray v. Metcalf* (Ch. 1715), see above, Case No. 105.

Lord Chancellor [Lord King]: The plaintiff can be in no better case than Riley and Mitton would have been. However, I think the plaintiff is entitled to redeem the annuities without paying off what may be due on the other securities. The money lent on the two last was after the £1200 was paid and after a note was given by the defendant's servant to transfer the annuities. And the defendant, in this case, is bound by the act of the servant.

He decreed the annuities to be transferred to the plaintiff, but without costs.

And Lord Chancellor [Lord King] seemed to be of the opinion that, where a man takes three distinct securities, though of personal things, for securing three distinct sums and there is no agreement to tack them together, he may redeem one without the other.

757

Moor v. Carent

(Ch. 1726)

Upon a suit to redeem a mortgage, the mortgagee is to be paid for capital improvements that he made to the premises.

Lincoln's Inn MS. Misc. 12, p. 243, pl. 1

18 July 1726.

The defendant, being seised in fee of houses in Covent Garden subject to a mortgage for £2500, married William Carent, who, after his marriage, paid off the mortgage and took an assignment to trustees for himself. And, during the marriage, he received the rents, and then he died. And the plaintiff's wife has taken administration and brought a bill to foreclose the equity of redemption.

The Master of the Rolls [Jekyll] was of the opinion and so decreed that the plaintiff should only be allowed interest on the mortgage from the last quarter day before the death of William Carent, after which time, no rents were received, for, during the time he received the rents, he was bound to keep down the interest on the mortgage. But in taking the account of what was due on the mortgage, the Master was to make the plaintiffs an allowance of what William Carent had laid out for lasting improvements.

758

East India Company v. Jennings

(Ch. 1726)

A court of equity can retain a suit for discovery and grant common law relief also.

Lincoln's Inn MS. Misc. 12, p. 232

August 1726.

The plaintiffs brought their bill suggesting that the defendants Elwick and Jennings (one of them had been the Governor at Fort St. George and the other at Fort St. David's in the East Indies) had acted contrary to their trust and, particularly, that they had sent home great quantities of salempores and long clothes, which did not come up to the musters, either as to quantity or quality, which musters are patterns that are kept at the said forts and according to which all the salempores and long clothes which are sent home ought to be made, and that the said defendants had not taken a due care in sorting the said goods and returning back to the black merchants of whom they were bought such of them as did not come up to the muster and that such goods as the said defendants had sent home to the plaintiffs had been sold at their public sales to great loss and for much less than the like goods sent home, as well before as since the time that the said defendants were governors at the said forts had sold for, and that, by reason of the badness of the goods sent home by the defendants, the plaintiffs had been damaged to the amount of £100,000 and charging a combination between the defendants and the black merchants to defraud the plaintiffs with respect to the measures and qualities of the said goods and an agreement between them that they should provide goods of less value than had been formerly done and yet have the same prices and that the black merchants made the defendants presents equivalent to the gains the merchants had by these practices and praying that the defendants may pay the plaintiffs the difference of the price between the goods sent home by them and such as they ought to have sent and may otherwise recompense the plaintiffs for the fraud and abuse of trust committed by the defendants in the premises and that the plaintiffs may have a commission to examine their witnesses abroad and otherwise [be] relieved.

As to so much of the bill as sought any relief or satisfaction from the defendant Elwick for or on account of any damages pretended to be sustained by the plaintiffs by reason of the defect of any goods sent by the defendant from Fort St. George to the plaintiffs or for or by reason of any neglect or mismanagement which the plaintiffs, by their bill, pretend the defendant has been guilty of in the execution of his office or place of Governor of Fort St. George or by reason of the defendant's having not observed or acted contrary to the orders or directions of the plaintiffs or their court of directors, which the defendant in no sort admitted, the defendant demurred in law and assigned for cause of demurrer that, if the plaintiffs had sustained any damage as by the bill was pretended, they ought to seek satisfaction for the same by a proper action at law, wherein such damages are properly to be assessed if the plaintiffs are entitled to recover any damages against the defendant and there was nothing suggested in the bill whereby to entitle the plaintiffs to have any relief in this court against the defendant touching any such damages. And, as to the discovery, the defendant put in an answer.

The defendant Jennings put in the like demurrer and answer.

Lord Chancellor [Lord King] was of the opinion the cause was proper to proceed to a hearing and, when it was seen how it came out upon the proofs, it would then be proper to determine whether the plaintiffs should be sent to law or not. And, therefore, he overruled the demurrer but reserved a liberty to the defendants to insist upon the same matters at the hearing as they have done by their demurrers.

759

Taylor v. Austin

(Ch. 1726)

Where a person has perpetrated a fraud, he cannot use the Statute of Frauds as a defense to a suit in equity for relief against the fraud.

Lincoln's Inn MS. Misc. 12, p. 250

Trinity vacation 1726. Samuel Taylor, plaintiff; John Austin and Elizabeth West, defendants.

The plaintiff and his father before him having rented a farm in Drayton in Oxfordshire under the defendant West, in October 1722, the defendant West agreed to let him a lease for forty-one years at £20 a year and a £20 fine. And, thereupon, the plaintiff employed Austin, who was an attorney, to prepare the lease, which he, accordingly, did. But he discouraged the defendant West from executing the same by representing the plaintiff to be a person in bad circumstances. And, on the other hand, he prevailed on the plaintiff to let the lease be made in his, the defendant's name, promising he would only be a trustee therein for the plaintiff. And, accordingly, the lease was made in Austin's name with the plaintiff's consent, and Austin paid the fine. But no deed of trust was executed by Austin. And, after he had gotten the lease made in his own name, he set up for himself and brought [actions of] ejectment and turned the plaintiff out of possession, who now brought his bill to be relieved and that Austin might assign the lease to the plaintiff.

Austin, by answer, admitted the agreement to make the plaintiff a lease and that he was employed to draw the lease, but that, the defendant West coming afterwards into the country and finding the premises out of repair, she insisted on security for the performance of the covenants, which the plaintiff not being able to do she refused to execute the lease and, afterwards, made a lease to the defendant Austin for forty-one years at the same rent and fine. And he utterly denied any trust for the plaintiff.

At the hearing, the Statute of Frauds[1] was much insisted on for the defendant, here being no deed of trust in writing.

But it being fully proved by Mrs. West that Austin, after he had prepared the lease, discouraged her from executing it by representing the plaintiff [to be] in bad circumstances and that it would be better to have the lease made in the name of a third person and proposed himself as such third person and that she would not agree to it until the plaintiff had consented the lease should be made to Austin and that Austin declared the plaintiff should not be turned out of possession and that he would give a bond of £500 penalty for his quiet enjoyment of it and that he only desired to secure the fine, which he was to lay down, and that, when she executed the lease to Austin, she looked upon it to be only made in trust for the plaintiff.

Lord Chancellor [Lord King] decreed the defendant Austin to assign the lease to the plaintiff and deliver up the possession and account for the mesne profits. And he said the Statute was never intended to establish frauds but to prevent them.

Now, where a man takes a lease upon an agreement to execute a bond that another shall hold the premises or that he will execute a deed of trust and when he has gotten the lease refuses to do either, will anyone say this is within the Statute? If it was, the Statute would establish frauds instead of preventing them.

760

Blakeway v. Earl of Strafford

(Ch. 1726)

A debt that was barred by the Statute of Limitations can be affirmed and revived by a provision in the debtor's will.

British Library MS. Hargrave 83, p. 56

19 October 1726. Pleas and demurrers at the Lord Chancellor's house.

A debt was due from Sir Henry Johnson to a tradesman for sailcloth in 1696; in 1714, part of this debt, *viz.* £50, was paid. In 1719, Sir Henry Johnson having by his will provided a fund for the payment of his debts and legacies, a bill was brought for this debt, to which the defendant demurred, the debt being as he insisted and which he showed for cause of demurrer extinguished by the Statute of Limitations.[2]

---

[1] Stat. 29 Car. II, c. 3 (*SR*, V, 839–842).

[2] Stat. 21 Jac. I, c. 16 (*SR*, IV, 1222–1223).

The demurrer was overruled. And My Lord Chancellor [Lord King] said that the debt was not extinguished by the Statute, but that the creditor was barred of his remedy. But in this case, the debtor having provided a particular fund and willed that his debts should be paid, this gave a new remedy and included all just and honest debts, especially upon the circumstances of this case, part of the debt, though of so long standing, having been paid in 1714 and by that and the subsequent devise, the debt was revived.

Dickens 48, 21 E.R. 185

19 October 1726.

A bill [was filed] to be paid a debt of twenty years standing due from Sir Thomas Johnson. By his will, he directed his personal estate to be applied in payment of his debts and, if the personal estate should not be sufficient, then his real estate to be subject to his debts.

The defendant pleaded the Statute of Limitations.

The plea, on argument, was overruled, the will directing his debts to be paid, taking the case out of the Statute.

[Other reports of this case: 2 Peere Williams 373, 24 E.R. 772, Select Cases *tempore* King 57, 25 E.R. 221, 2 Eq. Cas. Abr. 579, 22 E.R. 487, 6 Brown P.C. 630, 2 E.R. 1312.]

761

Henriques v. Rodrigues

(Ch. 1726)

Where an executor of a decedent's estate is outside the jurisdiction of the court and is in contempt of court, the debtors of the decedent are liable to make discovery of the decedent's assets that they may have in their hands.

Lincoln's Inn MS. Misc. 12, p. 237

19 October 1726.

The plaintiff brought his bill setting forth that, in the year 1710, he had made contracts with David Mesquita for the refusal of stock and that there became due to him for the difference on account of those contracts a considerable sum and that David Mesquita was dead and had made the defendant J.M. executor and that J.M. had paid over the stock and effects of the testator into the hands of the other defendants in order to prevent the plaintiff from having a satisfaction of his demands and, being in Holland, set the plaintiff at defiance and that the defendants A. and B., in whose hands these effects were, threatened to assign them over to the defendant M. And, therefore, to have a discovery of these effects and that they might not be paid over to the defendant M. and that M. might come to an account was the end of the bill.

As to so much of the bill as sought a discovery and account of the stock and effects belonging to the defendant M. in his own right, the defendant Rodrigues demurred, for that the plaintiff's demands against the defendant M. were only as he was the executor of his father and the plaintiff had not suggested any matter whereby he was entitled to any discovery or relief touching any effects belonging to the defendant M. in his own right, which might be in the hands of the defendant Rodrigues and for that the bill is in the nature of a foreign attachment, which was not to be countenanced by the rules of this court.

And, as to so much of the bill as sought a discovery and account of the stock and effects of the testator, the defendant demurred for that such a discovery would tend to lay open the nature of the defendant's dealings in the way of his trade, which might be very prejudicial to him, and for that the plaintiff is not entitled to have any discovery from the defendant of the testator's effects until it appeared there was something due to him from the testator and that the defendant M. had not assets to satisfy the same.

And, as to so much of the bill as sought to restrain the defendant from transferring any stock in his name belonging to the testator's estate, the defendant Rodrigues demurred for that he is accountable for such stock to the proper representative of the testator and must when demanded transfer the same to him or be subject to actions.

Upon arguing this demurrer, Lord Chancellor [Lord King] was of the opinion that, in the common case where a man dies indebted, the creditor shall not bring a bill against the executor and make anyone who is a debtor to the testator a party to have a discovery from him what money he owed the testator or what effects of his he had in his hands. But the present case was different, for, here, the executor is beyond the sea out of the jurisdiction of this court and his effects are here in the hands of other persons and he himself stands in contempt and will not answer (as it appeared he did).

And, as to the effects belonging to the defendant M. in his own right, it being charged that he had sold the testator's effects and laid out the money in stock in his own name and that such stock was come to the defendant Rodrigues, Lord Chancellor [Lord King] was of the opinion that the demurrer ought to be overruled unless the executor would give security to abide the order on the hearing. And a month's time was allowed to give an answer. And, in the meantime, the judgment on the demurrer was to be suspended and the defendant Rodrigues to be enjoined from transferring the stock.

Lincoln's Inn MS. Misc. 384, p. 249, pl. 2

19 October 1726.

The bill was by a creditor of A., making the executor and several debtors of A. defendants and praying that the debtors may be enjoined from paying anything to the executor, but they may pay the debts to the plaintiff. The debtors demur.

The Attorney General [*Yorke*] cited Sir Matthew Decher v. Ryswick. The plaintiff was a creditor of Ryswick, who lived in Holland and had effects in the hands of Mrs. Cock, a bankrupt. An injunction was granted to attach the effects.

Curia: In common cases, it is not reasonable for the creditors of A. to make all his debtors parties, but, here, the executor lives in Holland and stands in contempt to a sequestration. Therefore, there is a necessity to attach the effects until he appears. I overrule the demurrer.

762
Holbech v. Gamberini

(Ch. 1726)

Where no lien has been perfected, a judgment creditor cannot get discovery of the judgment debtor's assets from third parties.

Lincoln's Inn MS. Misc. 12, p. 240

Eodem die [19 October 1726]. Holbech *et al.* v. Charles Gamberini and Manuel Valencini *et al.*

The plaintiffs were bail for the defendant Gamberini in two actions brought by the defendants A. and B., who had recovered a judgment but, before the judgment was recovered, Gamberini went beyond the sea and left goods in the hands of the defendant Valencini. And it was charged that Gamberini was not returned or, if he was, he was concealed by Valencini and that A. and B. refused to take the goods in the hands of Valencini in execution and, therefore, that Valencini might discover these goods and deliver them up to the plaintiffs that they might be applied in satisfaction of judgments was the bill.

As to the discovery of these goods or any relief touching the same, the defendant Valencini demurred for that it does not appear by the bill that the plaintiffs have any lien upon any of the goods of the defendant Gamberini or any right to a discovery or account concerning such goods nor is there any equity suggested in the bill whereby the plaintiffs are entitled to any discovery or relief as against the defendant for any of the matters in the bill.

Curia [Lord King]: The demurrer must be allowed.

Note for the defendant was cited the Case of Angell v. Draper, Vernon's Rep., 1 vol., fo. [*blank*].[1]

[1] *Angell v. Draper* (1686), 1 Vernon 399, 23 E.R. 543, also 1 Eq. Cas. Abr. 77, 21 E.R. 890.

763

Badcock v. Stanhope

(Ch. 1726)

Where the wife of a London freeman accepts a settlement, she is barred from her statutory distributive share as well as her customary share.

7 Viner, Abr. 211

Michaelmas 13 Geo. in Chancery.

A settlement was [made] on the wife of a citizen of part of the personal estate of the husband in bar and satisfaction of all her claim and demand out of his personal estate by the custom or otherwise. The husband died intestate. The wife is barred of her distributive share of her husband's estate by the Statute of Distributions[1] by force of the words 'or otherwise', for they can extend to nothing else. And it was said to be twice so adjudged by Cowper, Chancellor, in the cases of Pit v. Lee and Davila v. Davila.[2]

And it was decreed accordingly by King, Chancellor.

[Other copies of this report: 2 Eq. Cas. Abr. 277, 22 E.R. 234.]

Lincoln's Inn MS. Misc. 384, p. 322, pl. 2

25 October 1726.

A settlement by a freeman on his wife in bar of her customary share or otherwise bars her claim of the distributory share under the Statute. Pett v. Lee; Devila v. Devila.

Lincoln's Inn MS. Misc. 12, p. 241

25 November 1726. Lovell Badcock, an infant son of Richard Badcock, deceased, plaintiff; Jane Badcock, widow and administratrix of Richard Badcock, *et al.*, defendants.

On the marriage of Richard Badcock with the defendant Jane, it was agreed that £4000 Bank stock and £1000 South Sea [Company] stock should be vested in trustees upon trust to pay the dividends to Richard Badcock for his life, then to the defendant, his wife, for her life, then in trust for the issue of the marriage, and Richard Badcock agrees that his wife might dispose of her jewels and that, if she survived him, his executors should pay her £500 in six months after his death. And there is a clause in the articles whereby it was agreed that, if Jane survived Richard Badcock, she might waive the provisions thereby made and have such share as belonged to her of Richard's personal estate by the custom of

[1] Stat. 22 & 23 Car. II, c. 10 (*SR*, V, 719–720).

[2] *Pett v. Lee* (Ch. 1714–1715), see above, Case No. 46; *Davila v. Davila* (Ch. 1716), see above, Case No. 119.

London or otherwise without the benefit of this settlement so as such waiving the settlement and demanding such customary or other part be made in writing under her hand and attested by two witnesses and delivered to Richard Badcock's executors in six months after the probate of his will or granting letters of administration. And, in case she should waive the settlement and demand her customary or other part, then she was to have no benefit by the settlement, but, if she did not waive the settlement, then she should be debarred of any share of the said personal estate by virtue of the custom or otherwise than what would belong to her by the said settlement and by Richard Badcock's last will.

Richard Badcock died intestate, and the defendant Jane took administration. The bill was for an account of the intestate's personal estate and that the defendant Jane might make her election whether she would waive or abide by the provisions made for her by the settlement.

The defendant put in her answer and thereby said that she waived any part of her said husband's personal estate by the custom of London and made her election to take the provision made for her by the deed of settlement.

The question was whether, after having made this election, she was barred not only of her customary share but also of her share under the Statute of Distributions.

And Lord Chancellor [Lord King] after talking with the Master of the Rolls [Jekyll], who was present in court, was of the opinion that the words 'or otherwise' extended to bar the defendant of her share of the personal estate under the Statute.

The Case of Pett and Lee was cited for the plaintiff.

764

Teasdale v. Teasdale

(Ch. 1726)

A person who has a reversion will be estopped to claim it where he knowingly did not assert it when the tenant for life made a settlement claiming the entire fee.

Lincoln's Inn MS. Misc. 12, p. 243, pl. 2

26 October 1726.

The defendant, upon the marriage of his son, the plaintiff's husband, was privy to an agreement made by the son for settling a jointure on the plaintiff. And he was a witness to the settlement but did not treat the match. And, after the son's death, the defendant set up a title and said his son was only tenant for life and that the reversion was then in the defendant. And he had brought his [action of] ejectment and recovered at [common] law. And the plaintiff brought her bill to be relieved and that the defendant might confirm the settlement.

And Lord Chancellor [LORD KING] was clear of opinion the plaintiff was entitled to relief.

But, then, the question was in what manner the settlement should be confirmed, for the settlement was made in an unusual manner, the estate being limited to the wife for life without impeachment of waste and then to the husband for his life but not without impeachment of waste.

And it was insisted that, since there was no fraud in the defendant, for he had sworn in his answer that her did not know but his son was seised in fee, for, by the will of the grandfather, who had given the estate to the son, it was devised to him by the name of all his lands, tenements, and hereditaments, but the defendant did not know that that was only a devise for life, that, therefore, the defendant ought only to make a reasonable settlement, for, if the plaintiff comes for equity, he must do equity.

And, therefore, he decreed an injunction to quiet the plaintiff in the possession during her life but subject to impeachment for waste.

N.B. It was confessed by the defendant's answer that he knew of the match and saw a draft of the settlement and heard it read over after it was engrossed. But he said he was ignorant of his title.

And the Solicitor General [*Talbot*] insisted that this relieving the plaintiff was going further than any cause have yet done, for all the cases have gone upon fraud.

But Lord Chancellor [LORD KING] said, if a father will let a son settle an estate on his marriage and is privy to the agreement and a witness to the settlement, he shall not after that come and say that he had a title but did not know it.

Note the Case of Watts and Creswell was cited for the plaintiff, *ante* 98.[1]

[Other reports of this case: Select Cases *tempore* King 59, 25 E.R. 222, 2 Eq. Cas. Abr. 391, 22 E.R. 334.]

765

Pigot v. Bolen

(Ch. 1726)

A legacy to be paid for the legatee's best advantage will be ordered to be invested until the legatee comes of age and then to be paid to him or her.

Lincoln's Inn MS. Misc. 12, p. 341

27 October 1726. Ann Pigot, an infant by prochein ami, plaintiff; Andrew Bolen, defendant. Master of the Rolls [JEKYLL].

---

[1] *Watts v. Creswell* (Ch. 1714), see above, Case No. 18.

Joan Bolen, the plaintiff's grandmother, by will, gave the plaintiff after the death of Dorothy Portman, the plaintiff's aunt, £50 to be paid by the defendant at such time and manner as he should think most for the plaintiff's advantage. And she made the defendant her executor.

Dorothy Portman being dead, the plaintiff's bill was to be paid her legacy with interest.

The defendant insisted he was not liable to pay interest nor yet the principal until the plaintiff should be in some way of trade or business or in some likelihood of being advanced in marriage.

The decree was the Master to compute what is due for the £50 and interest from the death of Dorothy Portman and what shall be reported due to be paid into the Bank and placed out on security to be approved by the Master for the benefit of the plaintiff until she attains twenty-one and then to be paid her.

766

Bettesworth v. Dean of St. Paul's

(Ch. 1726–1727)

Where a long term lease is in violation of a statutory time limit, a court of equity will not enforce the lease at all rather than reduce the period of the lease to what is permissible.

Lincoln's Inn MS. Misc. 12, loose sheet

16 November 1726. Chief Justice RAYMOND and Justice PRICE and the Master of the Rolls [JEKYLL] present.

In <time of Philip and Mary> 2d February 10th [year] of Queen Elizabeth, 1567, the dean and chapter made a lease of Doctors' Commons for ninety-nine years at £5 8s. 0d. a year at £20 fine with a covenant to renew for the like time and at the same rent and fine.

A bill [was exhibited] for a performance so far as the defendants were able by the Statute of Queen Elizabeth, *viz.* for forty years at the same rent and fine.

Attorney General [*Yorke*], for the defendants: If the defendants are disabled from making such a lease as they have covenanted to make, the court will not decree them to make a lease, for it would be void as soon as it was made [by the] provision in the Statute of 13 Eliz. [It was] objected that the Statute of 14 Eliz. has repealed the Statute 13 Eliz. as to houses in corporate and market towns.[1] The Statute 14 [Eliz.] does not repeal the proviso. 1 Vent. 244.[2] By the Statute 13

[1] Stat. 13 Eliz. I, c. 10, s. 2 (*SR*, IV, 544–545); Stat. 14 Eliz. I, c. 11 (*SR*, IV, 601–602).

[2] *Bayly v. Murin* (1673), 1 Ventris 244, 86 E.R. 164, also 2 Levinz 61, 83 E.R. 450, 3 Keble 46, 107, 193, 84 E.R. 586, 620, 671.

& 14 [Eliz.], the dean and chapter are disabled from making such a lease as they have covenanted; the covenant is rescinded. 1 Salk. 198.[1]

The plaintiffs do admit the defendants cannot make such a lease to bind their successors as they have covenanted to make. The covenant in the lease is that they would make a new lease at and under the same rents and covenants, and they would have a lease for forty years with a covenant to renew for forty years and so to a perpetuity. But this covenant could not be in the new lease if the Act is out of the case. Besides, such a covenant would be as much against the Act of Parliament as a lease for more years than the Act allows.

They put a case on the other side, where a man has a power to lease for twenty-one years and he makes a lease for thirty-one years, equity will make it good for twenty-one years. I agree if it is made upon a valuable consideration, but not if it is voluntary.

Williams, same side, [cited] 1 Jo. 235; 7 Co. 47;[2] in all acts of Parliament.

Objection: Though the covenant is discharged as to the whole, yet [it is] in *esse* in part.

Answer: The covenant is entire, and, if discharged by the Act of Parliament, it is discharged *in toto.*

British Library MS. Lansdowne 587, p. 49

Michaelmas term 13 Geo. Doctors' Commons v. Dean and Chapter of St. Paul's and Trinity Hall in Cambridge.

Talbot, Solicitor General: [Upon a] bill for specific performance of covenants, the case [was], before the Statute of Elizabeth, the dean and chapter of St. Paul's leased to the Doctors' Commons for a long term with covenants of renewal for ninety-nine years with like covenants, paying a fine of £20 and rent £5 8s. Then were made the statutes 13, 14, and 18 Eliz.[3]

The doctors had enjoyed the lands by virtue of the old lease for about 149 years. The old lease being now within four years of its expiration, the doctors bring a bill to compel the dean and chapter of St. Paul's to grant to the doctors leases for forty years with the like covenants as before, which is all they can do since the statutes of Elizabeth, by which they are disabled to lease for more [than] forty years.

---

1 *Brewster v. Kidgell* (1698), 1 Salkeld 198, 91 E.R. 177, also 2 Salkeld 615, 91 E.R. 521, 3 Salkeld 340, 91 E.R. 860, Carthew 438, 90 E.R. 853, Holt K.B. 175, 669, 90 E.R. 995, 1270, 1 Lord Raymond 317, 91 E.R. 1108, 5 Modern 368, 87 E.R. 711, 12 Modern 166, 88 E.R. 1239, Comberbach 424, 466, 90 E.R. 424, 466.

2 *Fawlkner v. Bellingham* (1631), W. Jones 233, 235, 82 E.R. 122, 123, also Croke Car. 80, 214, 79 E.R. 671, 787, Hetley 28, 36, 124 E.R. 315, 323, Littleton 42, 124 E.R. 127; *Playne's Case* (1586), Croke Eliz. 47, 78 E.R. 310.

3 Stat. 18 Eliz. I, c. 11 (*SR*, IV, 622–623).

Littl., sect. 352;[1] where covenants cannot be literally performed, they shall be performed as near as possible. The dean and chapter ought to lease for forty years, which is the utmost they can do subject to the same qualities etc. Since they are disabled by the statutes to perform their covenants completely, they ought to perform them as nearly as they can.

Lutwyche: The Statute 13 Eliz. recites that, lately, unreasonable leases have been made etc., therefore, no lease is to be made for more than twenty-one years or three lives, reserving the yearly accustomed rents, proviso that this extends not to leases made on the surrender of old ones. The Statute is not to be taken strictly, for leases for a less number of years are not void on this Statute.

By the Statute 14 Eliz., leases shall not exceed forty years in corporate towns or market towns. The Statute 13 Eliz. extends not to leases in market towns, but they may lawfully make grants, which extend not to the inheritance as if the said Statute had not been made, provided [they are] not to extend to leases in reversion or whereon the usual rent is not reserved or if they are without a clause of reparation or, if the alienation is without an equivalent in lands etc. So it may be alienated under these reflections.

Thus, houses in market towns are out of the Statute 13 Eliz. A lease for forty years will answer the intent of the Statute, which is that such a lease is reasonable. The old rent and more is reserved.

If one that has a power to lease for twenty-one years leases for thirty-one years, this lease is void after his death that made it and does not bind the successor. Yet a court of equity will make it good for the term for which he had a power to lease, *viz.* for twenty-one years. 1 Ch. R. 23.[2] So it has been often settled. One covenants to assign over a term of ninety-nine years, having only a term of fifty years; this court will compel him to lease such time as he can.

Cases were cited of covenants that became totally unlawful and impossible to be performed in any part, as in covenants to export corn etc. But here, they have a power to perform the covenants in part and to lease for forty years, which is all [that is] required by the bill. The Statute is mentioning bonds, covenants, and sales [?], which shall be hereafter made. Thus, they extend only to future covenants that shall be hereafter made.

Also the [Statute] 43 Eliz.[3] extends only to a judgment which shall hereafter be had, a method having been invented to evade the former statute by a judgment.

Alius, ad idem: Statutes for the encouraging of learning are to be expounded liberally. Porter's Case.[4] This lease was made 149 years ago. It is the only case of

---

[1] T. Littleton, *Tenures*, sect. 352.

[2] *Pawcy v. Bowen* (1663), 1 Chancery Cases 23, 22 E.R. 674, also 3 Chancery Reports 11, 21 E.R. 713, 1 Eq. Cas. Abr. 342, 21 E.R. 1089.

[3] Stat. 43 Eliz. I, c. 9, s. 1 (*SR*, IV, 973).

[4] *Attorney General v. Porter* (Ex. 1592), 1 Coke Rep. 16, 76 E.R. 36.

that kind that can happen. And it cannot affect the whole ecclesiastical body in its consequences. 1 Roll 378, Long v. Rosewell; a lease to the king, who assigned to Long; he was relieved. Plowd. [*blank*]; 1 Vent. 245; Hob. 296;[1] 14 Eliz. is called a restraining statute; 18 Eliz. does not restrain us. It was objected that this covenant is entire, but an entire covenant may be lessened or altered by the consent of the parties.

Mead and *Fazackerley*, for Trinity Hall, consented to the arguments for the plaintiffs.

Sir Philip Yorke, Attorney General, for the dean and chapter of St. Paul's: The lease was [made] on the 10th of Eliz. A court of equity will not decree a specific performance of a covenant where it is not on a valuable consideration or where it is a prejudice to the party. Trinity Hall [are] the lessees; Doctors' Commons [are] the trustees. The fine is not an adequate compensation. There is also a covenant to give advice *gratis*, but this they have never performed, but have taken the usual fees for advice.

The value of lands may alter and have altered. Therefore, it is most [in]equitable to decree a specific performance in this case.

The Statute 13 Eliz. that makes void leases extends to covenants then subsisting. The Statute is, if a covenant is to [?] surrender and renew, such renewed lease etc. shall be void if etc. The covenant is bad, against equity, even without the Statute 13 Eliz.

It is objected that it is in the Statute 14 Eliz., which, as to towns corporate, excepts this case out of the Statute 13 Eliz. Yet, under the Statute 14 Eliz., there is the same inconsistency with this covenant and there is the same disability to lease according to the covenant for ninety-nine years.

The Statute 14 Eliz. says that the [Statute] 13 Eliz. shall not extend to houses in towns corporate. This is only that the branch concerning ecclesiastical persons shall not extend etc., which extends not to the clause of bonds. 1 Vent. 244. The Statute 14 Eliz. is an appendix to the [Statute] 13 Eliz. and does not repeal it but *sub modo*.

The statutes of leases are all to be coupled together in their construction. The disabling clause amounts to a dispensation. Salk. 198; covenants not to do an act which is lawful and then a statute makes it lawful, the covenant is repeated; the statute repeals the covenants. A covenant to make a new lease with the same covenants must be intended only as to rents, repairs, etc., not to have a new clause of renewal.

Equity, as well as law, will esteem the rights of all parties (to the statute) to be bound. Bills in equity are always for a specific performance, granting which is the foundation of the jurisdiction of this court.

---

[1] *Long v. Roswell* (1618), 1 Rolle, Abr., *Chancerie*, pl. S, 1, p. 378; *Bayly v. Murin* (1673), *ut supra*; *Crane v. Taylor* (1616), Hobart 269, 80 E.R. 415.

It is as inconsistent with the Statute to make leases for forty years with perpetual clauses of renewal as to make a lease for ninety-nine years since it binds the body forever.

Where one has a power to lease for twenty-one years and he makes a voluntary lease for thirty-one years, this court will not make it good for twenty-one years. Where a statute makes leases for ninety-nine years void, if such a lease is made for ninety-nine years, this court cannot make it good for part of the term.

Peere Williams: The Statute amounts to a release of the covenant, the plaintiffs' being parties to the Statute. 1 Jon. 235; 1 Cro. 47. The covenant is entire and not apportionable. This covenant is in the mischief of the Statute recited, and it affects the revenues of the church. The estate is worth £500 *per annum*, and the rent is only worth £5 8s. Therefore, the plaintiffs have no equitable right.

Alius, ad idem: The interest of the Statute is to make void the covenants as well as the leases. 1 Inst. 207; 8 Co. 137; Hob. 256;[1] Dy. [*blank*]. (There is no difference as to this point between bonds and covenants.) If the dean covenants to lease for ninety-nine years, though possibly this court, during his life, might compel a lease of forty years, yet they will not compel his successor. It is not unconscionable that the dean and chapter should refuse to make these leases. They rather acted against conscience that first covenanted to make such leases to the prejudice of the church and their successors. And it is not like the case of executors or an heir that claim under the testator. The present dean and [chapter] do not claim under these that made the covenants, but by a title paramount. The plaintiffs have not an equitable right. *Anno* 1656, a decree was made between Doctors' Commons and Trinity Hall, in which this court was of opinion that this was a subsistant covenant. But this does not affect the dean and chapter of St. Paul's, who were not parties.

Sir Philip Yorke cited Salk. 198; 1 Vent. 244; 1 Inst. 207; 8 Co. 137; Hob. 256.

Hilary vacation, March the 13th, 1726/27, before the Lord Chancellor [LORD KING], the Master of the Rolls [JEKYLL], the two chief justices [RAYMOND and EYRE], and Justice PRICE. The Master of the Rolls [JEKYLL] thought that the dean and chapter of St. Paul's ought to grant a lease for forty years. But the other four were of opinion that the covenant was defeated by the Statute and that the doctors had no right to have their lease renewed at all by virtue of the covenants. And it was determined against Doctors' Commons.

[Other reports of this case: Select Cases *tempore* King 66, 25 E.R. 226, 2 Eq. Cas. Abr. 15, 26, 22 E.R. 13, 23, 1 Brown P.C. 240, 1 E.R. 541.]

---

[1] E. Coke, *First Institute* (1628), f. 207b; *Chalke v. Peter* (1610), 8 Coke Rep. 136, 77 E.R. 681, also Godbolt 167, 78 E.R. 102, 2 Brownlow & Goldesborough 289, 322, 123 E.R. 947, 966, 1 Rolle Rep. [137], 81 E.R. 385; *Duncombe v. Wingfield* (1617), Hobart 254, 80 E.R. 400, also 2 Rolle Rep. 447, 81 E.R. 908.

767

Burroughs v. Gemineau

(Ch. 1726)

A foreign judgment is enforceable in a court of equity.

Lincoln's Inn MS. Misc. 12, p. 246

22 November 1726.

A., a merchant in London, draws a bill of exchange on the defendant, his correspondent at Leghorn, payable to B., a merchant also in London. B. endorses it over, and it is negotiated through Venice and Genoa and then comes to Leghorn where it is presented to the defendant, who accepts it. A., at that time, had failed, but the defendant did not know it. But, before the bill became due, he had notice of it and, thereupon, refused to pay the bill. And the defendant was sued in the proper court at Leghorn upon the said bill of exchange, which he had so accepted.

And the court was of the opinion the defendant was not liable to made good the bill, for, by the laws of Leghorn, if a man accepts a bill drawn upon him by his correspondent in any foreign country and, before the bill is accepted, the drawer fails and afterwards, the drawee accepts the bill without notice that the drawer is become insolvent, in such case, he is not liable to pay the bill, notwithstanding his acceptance of it any further than he has effects of the drawer in his hands.

The defendant happening afterwards to come over into England, the plaintiff brought his bill against him upon the said bill of exchange, praying that he might pay the money for which the same was drawn, he having accepted it.

The defendant insisted on the sentence in the court at Leghorn which had determined that he was not liable.

Lord Chancellor [Lord King]: The matter arising beyond the seas and having been determined by a court there which had the proper cognizance of it, it must conclude all parties, and this court ought not to meddle in it. And such decree of a foreign court might have been given in evidence upon *non assumpsit* pleaded to an action at [common] law, for, he said, it was the opinion of My Lord Chief Justice Holt that, whatever went to discharge or destroy the promise may be given in evidence on *non assumpsit* pleaded.

And, as to the principal matter, that the courts at Westminster Hall are tied up by determinations in foreign courts that have proper cognizance, he mentioned the case in Charles II's time of one who had killed a man in Portugal, where he was tried and acquitted, and he, afterwards, coming over into England, a commission issued to try him here, and he pleaded the trial and acquittal in Portugal. And the judges were of the opinion it was a good plea.[1]

Note Mr. *Mead* mentioned the Case of Goodine and Stoneham, where a man having brought a suit in the Court of Admiralty for his wages at sea and recovered and, afterwards, brought a bill in this court for his wages pretending he had not recovered all that was due to him, and the Master of the Rolls dismissed his bill.

Lincoln's Inn MS. Misc. 506, p. 85, pl. 2

Michaelmas 13 George.

This was a bill brought for a perpetual injunction to stay proceedings on an action brought by the defendant here against the now plaintiff. The case was one Skinner, a merchant in London, drew a bill for 1500 pieces of eight on the plaintiff Burroughs, payable at two usances, three months each, to a merchant at Venice, who endorses it to the defendant Gemineau, a merchant at Leghorn, where Burroughs resided. Burroughs accepts the bill six days before the bill became payable. Skinner becomes insolvent. Burroughs apprehending it, refused payment, upon which he was sued before the court at Leghorn by Gemineau. In the meanwhile, he receives an account of the failure of Skinner, which he pleads in bar of the suit by Gemineau and had a sentence for him, and the money which he had deposited to answer the suit was returned to him, it being the law and the custom of merchants at Leghorn that the acceptor is not bound by his acceptance if the drawer fail within the time that the bill becomes due and have not effects in his hands to answer it. When Burroughs was returned to England, Gemineau brings an action in the [Court of] King's Bench here upon the bill of exchange, upon which Burroughs brings this bill for an injunction.

It was urged that the courts could not take notice of the laws or decrees of foreign courts, that, by our law, the acceptor was chargeable and, if it might be taken notice of, yet there was no equity in the bill because it might be given in evidence on the general issue.

Lord Chancellor [Lord King] said that, if he were to try the cause, he would allow it to be given in evidence, but he could not tell what opinion other judges might be of, that he thought we ought to take notice of the laws and sentences of foreign nations where the party and the transaction was within the limits of their jurisdiction. And, therefore, he decreed a perpetual injunction.

Dickens 48, 21 E.R. 185

22 November 1726.

[1] *Rex v. Hutchinson* (1677), 3 Keble 785, 84 E.R. 1011, also cited in *Beak v. Thyrwhit* (1688), 3 Modern 194, 87 E.R. 124.

The bill was to be relieved against two actions brought upon two bills of exchange, the drawer having failed before the bills were accepted. And, by the custom of Leghorn, the acceptance is void if it be after the drawer becomes a bankrupt. And so it was determined in the present case in the proper court of Leghorn, in which a decree had been made for setting aside the acceptance.

Upon hearing this cause, the court allowed the said decree to be read and said this matter has been judicially determined at Leghorn and this court will not overrule what was determined in a proper court where the action was brought. Therefore, let the injunction granted in this cause be perpetual, and let the defendant, at the plaintiff's expense, acknowledge satisfaction on the record of the judgment.

[Other reports of this case: Select Cases *tempore* King 69, 25 E.R. 228, Mosely 1, 25 E.R. 235, 2 Strange 733, 93 E.R. 815, 2 Eq. Cas. Abr. 476, 524, 22 E.R. 405, 443.]

768

Townsend v. Lawton

(Ch. 1726)

Trustees to preserve contingent remainders will not be compelled to join in the destruction of contingent remainders unless the land will remain in the settlor's family.

Lincoln's Inn MS. Misc. 12, p. 249

22 November 1726. Townsend v. John Lawton, senior, Edward Lawton, John Lawton, junior, and Mr. Mountague.

By a settlement on the marriage of the defendant Lawton, senior, lands were settled to the use of Lawton, senior, for ninety-nine years if he should live so long, remainder to the defendant Mountague and another trustee for preserving contingent remainders, remainder to the wife for life, remainder to the first and other sons in tail, with remainders over. The wife was dead, and the defendants John, junior, and Edward were the only issue of the marriage.

The defendant John, the father, having mortgaged the estate to the plaintiff and the defendant Edward, the son, being come of age, he and his father entered into articles with the plaintiff and covenanted that they would suffer a recovery and procure Mr. Mountague, who was the surviving trustee, to join therein.

Mountague refusing to join in making a tenant to the *praecipe*, the plaintiff brought his bill for a performance of the covenants and that Mr. Mountague might join in suffering the recovery.

Mr. Mountague, by answer, submitted to do as the count should direct.

John, the younger son, being made a defendant, Lord Chancellor [Lord King] asked if he would consent that the trustee should join in making a tenant to the *praecipe*, and, being told no, he said then he should not decree the trustee to join, for he would not take away any man's right.

It was then insisted for the plaintiff that the court had done it in the Case of Mr. Winnington,[1] where his eldest son being come of age and about to marry and a settlement was agreed to be made on the son's marriage, the trustees for preserving contingent remainders refused to join, in regard there was a possibility that there might be other sons of Mr. Winnington, and the court, in that case, decreed the trustees to join with Mr. Winnington and his son in suffering a recovery.

Lord Chancellor [LORD KING]: So shall I too when that comes to be the case when the estate is to be settled on the eldest son in marriage and to be kept in the family, but not when it is to enable the father to alien the estate.

And, therefore, he dismissed the bill against Mr. Mountague and the younger son with costs. But he directed the defendants John, the father, and Edward, the son, specifically to perform their covenants with the plaintiff.

[Other reports of this case: 2 Peere Williams 379, 24 E.R. 775, Select Cases *tempore* King 71, 25 E.R. 229, 2 Eq. Cas. Abr. 749, 22 E.R. 635.]

769

Dod v. Dickenson

(Ch. 1726)

A grant of a life estate of a term gives the entire interest in it such that there cannot be a remainder.

Lincoln's Inn MS. Misc. 12, p. 252

26 November 1726.

A.B., by will, devises some long Exchequer annuities to trustees upon trust to permit the plaintiff Dod to receive the annuities during so many years of the ninety-nine years terms as she should live and, after her death, to permit the other two plaintiffs to receive the same for so long of the terms as they or the survivor should live and, after the death of the survivor, upon trust for the heirs of their two bodies lawfully begotten for and during the residue of the term and, for default of such issue, to the defendant Dickens, his executors, and administrators.

The annuities were subscribed into the South Sea [Company] and the plaintiffs, having agreed between themselves about dividing the stock, which was allowed by the Company in lieu of the annuities, bring their bill against the trust-

[1] *Winnington v. Foley* (Ch. 1719), see above, Case No. 348.

ees and the person in remainder that the stock should be sold and the money divided between the plaintiffs according to their agreement.

Accordingly, it was so decreed, for a limitation to a man and the heirs of his body of a term does vest the whole interest in him and a devise over for want of such issue is void.

8 Viner, Abr. 451

Joseph Aunge, by will dated 28 April 1708, gave several long annuities for ninety-nine years in the Exchequer amounting to £320 *per annum* to trustees for the residue of the term in trust for Elizabeth Dod for so many years of the said term as she should live and, afterwards, for the plaintiffs, his godsons, for so many years of the said term as they or the survivor of them should live and, after the decease of the survivor, in trust for the heirs of their bodies lawfully to be begotten for all the residue of the said term of ninety-nine years and, for default of such issue, in trust for his nephews, the defendants, Joseph and Richard Dickenson. These annuities were subscribed into the South Sea Company in the year 1720. And the bill was to have the South Sea stock and annuities, the produce thereof, sold and the money raised by sale thereof to be paid to the plaintiffs, who were the godsons and devisees for life, with remainder to the heirs of their bodies etc.

Cases cited for the plaintiffs were 3 Lev. 22, Gibbons v. Somers; 1 Lev. 290, Love v. Windham *et al.*; cited *contra*, Pinbery v. Elkins, *tempore* Macclesfield, C.; Peacock v. Spooner, in the House of Lords.[1]

Lord Chancellor King said, where a term is devised to a man and his heirs or to the heirs of his body, the whole term vests in the devisee, and any remainder over is void. And so it was held in the House of Lords the last sessions, in the Case of Sir John Rushout.[2] The remainder in the present case is void, being after a limitation in tail. He decreed that the stock and annuities be sold, and the money thereby raised to be paid to the plaintiffs.

[Other copies of this report: 2 Eq. Cas. Abr. 325, 348, 22 E.R. 277, 296.]

[1] *Gibbons v. Summers* (1681), 3 Levinz 22, 83 E.R. 557; *Love v. Windham* (1670), 1 Levinz 290, 83 E.R. 412, also 1 Siderfin 450, 82 E.R. 1211, 2 Chancery Reports 14, 21 E.R. 602, 2 Keble 637, 84 E.R. 401, 1 Ventris 79, 86 E.R. 55, 1 Modern 50, 86 E.R. 724, 1 Eq. Cas. Abr. 191, 21 E.R. 982; *Pinbury v. Elkin* (Ch. 1719), see above, Case No. 404; *Peacock v. Spooner* (1688–1690), 2 Vernon 43, 195, 23 E.R. 638, 727, 2 Freeman 114, 22 E.R. 1094, 1 Eq. Cas. Abr. 362, 21 E.R. 1104.

[2] *Rushout v. Rushout* (1725), 6 Brown P.C. 89, 2 E.R. 952, 2 Eq. Cas. Abr. 655, 22 E.R. 550.

770

Lord Grimston v. Bridgman

(Ch. 1726)

Where there have been mutual dealings and mutual credit given, one debt can be set off against the other.

Lincoln's Inn MS. Misc. 12, p. 253

30 November 1726.

The plaintiff sold timber to the defendant's intestate and, afterwards, employed him to do carpentry work, which came to more than the timber. And, before any account was settled, the intestate died. And the defendant took administration and brought an action against the plaintiff for the work done.

And the plaintiff brought his bill to be relieved and that one debt might be set against the other and that he might pay the balance only.

It was proved that, a little before the intestate's death, he was applied to to settle the account and that he said there was no haste for that he would take the debt due from himself as so much cash paid him. And it was insisted for the plaintiff that the setting one debt against another was highly just and equitable and that a very little matter would be a sufficient reason in a court of equity to decree it should be so.

On the other hand, it was said that, if it should be so decreed in the present case, the creditors would be defeated, for, without this debt which is due from the plaintiff, there would not be assets to pay the creditors 12d. in the pound, that as to what was proved if there was such a promise by the intestate as the witness swears, it might be given in evidence at law and would be a good discharge of so much of the debt as was due from him and then he had no occasion to come into equity.

The Master of the Rolls [Jekyll] said this was a very plain case for relief upon the intestate's promise and, though possibly it might be given in evidence at [common] law, yet the plaintiff was proper to come into equity for an account, and it was every day's practice that, where there is an account depending between two persons, goods sold on one side and money paid on the other, bills are brought for an account and to stay actions at law for the goods sold. And he said he had never know it otherwise than that, where there have been mutual dealings and mutual credit given, this court has set one debt against the other.

And, it being admitted that, if the debt from the intestate was to go in discharge of the plaintiff's debt, there would be but £31 due from the plaintiff, he was decreed to pay that sum only to the defendant without costs.

The Case of Dowman v. Matthews was cited for the plaintiff, *quod vide ante* 28.[1]

---

[1] *Downam v. Mathews* (Ch. 1722), see above, Case No. 535.

771

Napier v. Lady Effingham

(Ch. 1726–1727)

After a final decree in equity against an infant, the infant can reopen the case upon attaining his majority and re-plead defensively but not affirmatively.

Anyone may bring a bill in the name of an infant; no judicial assignment of a next friend is necessary.

British Library MS. Hargrave 83, p. 33, pl. 2

This was cited as a precedent in the case of Sir John Napper and Lady Effingham, Westeram and Dolphin or Western and Tonkin (2 May 31 or 35 Eliz.);[1] by the decree made in this case upon a bill brought by an infant, special leave was given by the decree for the infant to bring a new bill when he came of age.

Fountain v. Cave, Trinity term 1718,[2] cited in the same case and confirmed by Sir Joseph Jekyll then present; Jephs, the purchaser of the estate in question, apprehending he could not buy it safely without the decree of the court, an infant being concerned, a bill was brought and a decree made for the sale with liberty for the infant to show cause against the decree within six months after he should come of age. A motion was made for the infant to be at liberty to put in a new answer. But the counsel not being prepared to support the motion by precedents, His Honor, Sir Joseph Jekyll, took time to consider, and, upon the view of precedents, where such orders were made by Sir J. Trevor upon petitions *ex parte*, he gave the infant liberty to put in a new answer.

Tallman v. Plunkett;[3] upon a petition *ex parte*, an order was made by Sir J. Trevor, Master of the Rolls, that the infant might be at liberty to take his former answer off the file and put in a new answer. This was done, and the infant so much bettered his case by the new answer that a decree was made for him. Against this decree, there was an appeal, and, in the petition of appeal, this order was *inter alia* complained of. But Lord Harcourt reversed the decree upon the merits, and this matter did not come in question before him.

Richmond v. Tailleur;[4] there was an absolute decree against an infant in the case of a personal estate. The infant, when he came of age, brought an original bill suggesting fraud in obtaining the decree. The decree was pleaded in bar. Lord

1 *Western v. Tolpitt* (1595), Tothill 108, 21 E.R. 138, 117 Selden Soc. 203, 249.

2 *Fountain v. Caine* (1718), 1 Peere Williams 504, 24 E.R. 491, 2 Eq. Cas. Abr. 516, 22 E.R. 435.

3 *Talman v. Plukenett* (Ch. 1712), British Library MS. Hargrave 80, f. 132, Lincoln's Inn MS. Misc. 383, p. 234, Lincoln's Inn MS. Misc. 106, p. 197, note also *Talman v. Pluckenett* (1719), Lincoln's Inn MS. Misc. 11, p. 113, pl. 1, Chancery Cases *tempore* Harcourt, 322.

4 *Richmond v. Tayleur* (1721), see above, Case No. 502.

Macclesfield overruled the plea, and the court declared that, in a case [where] fraud was suggested in obtaining the decree, this was a proper method of showing cause to avoid the decree and that, even in the case of a personal estate, an infant should have time to show cause and might avoid the decree either by a bill of review, original bill, rehearing, or putting in a new answer or any other method by which he may come at the justice of his case.

Lincoln's Inn MS. Misc. 12, p. 274

26 January 1726[/27].

The defendant, Lady Napier, brought a bill against the now plaintiff [Sir John Napier], then an infant, who put in an answer by his guardian and then brought a cross-bill. The causes were both heard together. And the Lady Effingham obtained a decree, and the infant's cross-bill was dismissed.

The infant appealed to the House of Lords because there was no day given him to show cause against the decree when he came of age. And, thereupon, the House of Lords ordered he should be at liberty to show cause within six months after he came to the age of twenty-one.

The plaintiff being now come of age, he petitioned the Lord Chancellor that he might have leave to bring a new or supplemental bill and also amend his answer to the original bill. And if he should do so was now the question.

It was insisted for the plaintiff, the petitioner, that an infant here is not in a worse case than he would be at law. If an action is brought against him, the parol shall demur. And though it shall not demur where he is the plaintiff at law, yet, if it shall appear to the court that an improper action is brought by an infant, the court will stay the proceedings in the action.

It was agreed that an infant, where he has time to show cause, cannot bring a new or supplemental bill where there has been only a neglect or omission in those concerned for him without leave of the court. But where there has been fraud, leave of the court is not necessary for bringing a new bill to be relieved upon the head of fraud.

The precedents cited for the plaintiff were one in Queen Elizabeth's time, where there was a decree for quiet enjoyment until the infant came of age and that then he should be at liberty to bring a new bill.

Richmond v. Taylor, 1720, [there was] a decree against an infant and no day was given him to show cause. He brought an original bill when he came of age to be relieved against the decree upon the head of fraud. The decree was pleaded, and the plea was overruled.

Fountain v. Caine, 1718, liberty was given to the infant to amend his answer when he came to show cause against the decree. And the like was done in the Case of Talman v. Pluncket, in 1712.

A case in Lord Macclesfield's time [was cited], where a cause by consent was heard against an infant and his interest was given up, and, upon an original bill brought by him when of age, he was relieved. And there was a like case before the Lords Commissioners.

Note it was said that, in the Case of Richmond and Tayleur, the defendant pleaded the former decree, but, it being suggested in the bill that the decree was obtained by fraud, the plea was overruled. And the court said, if there was fraud, the infant might bring an original bill and that not only where a real estate but also where a personal estate was also in question and that, in the Case of Fountain v. Caine, when the infant moved for leave to put in a new answer, the Master of the Rolls said he had seen a precedent where the late Master of the Rolls, upon a petition *ex parte*, had given an infant leave to put in a new answer.

For the defendant, it seemed to be admitted that, where an infant, by a decree, has a day given him to show cause when he comes of age, he may with leave of the court put in a new answer and that, without leave of the court, he may bring an original bill to be relieved against a decree where he was the defendant upon the head of fraud.

But it was said there was no precedent where an infant was the plaintiff that he has been allowed to make a new case when he came of age by amending his bill or bringing a new one merely because there has been a neglect or mismanagement in those who managed for the infant, which is all that is pretended in the present case.

The Master of the Rolls [Jekyll]: I am of the opinion that an infant shall have liberty when he comes of age where he is a defendant and has a day given to him to show cause against the decree either to amend his answer or put in a new one. And this proceeds from that care and superintendency which the common law has lodged in this court of infants and their estates.

In the Case of Talman and Pluncket, which has been mentioned, the late Master of the Rolls made a decree upon a new answer put in by the infant, and, though, upon an appeal to My Lord Harcourt, that decree was reversed, yet that was not because a new answer was put in by the infant, but Lord Harcourt's decree was grounded upon the case as made by the new answer.

Upon the case mentioned by Mr. *Williams* wherein I was moved that the infant might put in a new answer, I was not then apprised of the practice of the court, but, upon enquiry, I found that the practice was so, that an infant may amend his answer or put in a new one, and this without giving any reason, for that may in some cases turn to his prejudice.

As to the order of the House of Lords, it will not alter the case, for, by giving the infant leave to show cause must be understood to show cause according to the course of this court.

And, therefore, I am of opinion that the plaintiff ought to have leave to amend his answer or put in a new one or do both and make new proofs if necessary to make out his case.

As to the plaintiff's amending his bill, for it is dismissed by the order of the House of Lords, I am of opinion he ought to have leave to do that likewise.

Anyone may bring a bill in the name of an infant, for the court does not name the *prochein ami*. And there is no inconvenience in this, for, if the infant's bill is dismissed, the *prochein ami* pays the costs. Nay, two persons may each bring a bill in the infant's name for the same matter and against the same persons. But, in that case, though the defendants cannot plead to the latter bill the pendency of the former, yet the court will not suffer both suits to proceed but, upon the defendant's application, will consider which of the suits is most for the infant's advantage and stay the other.

When an infant's bill is dismissed, he has no day given him when he comes of age to show cause. And the reason of this is because, when he comes of age, he may bring a new bill and the decree of dismission cannot be pleaded in bar to such bill.

Lord Chancellor [Lord King]: The order in the House of Lords for dismissing the infant's bill is unless the infant shall show cause within six months after he comes of age. Now, the cause to be shown must be shown in this court and, therefore, must be according to the course of this court.

And it seems to me to be the course of the court that an infant, when he comes of age and is to show cause against a decree, may amend his answer or put in a new one.

But there is no instance, where an infant's bill is dismissed, that a day is given him to show cause against that dismission. And, since there is no instance, I must take it that, by the course of the court, an infant, where he is the plaintiff, cannot amend his bill when he comes of age. And, therefore, the House of Lords having given the infant leave to show cause when he should come of age against the dismission of his bill, it must be understood that he must show cause according to the course of this court, that is upon the bill as it now stands. And, though he cannot amend his bill, yet he may apply to rehear his cause. And, if he amends his answer and enters into new proofs, which may vary the decree of dismission, the court, upon application, will respite the rehearing until the cross-cause can be brought on and will then judge upon the whole matter.

It was ordered that the plaintiff should have leave to amend his answer or put in a new one but not amend his bill.

Lincoln's Inn MS. Misc. 384, p. 323

26 and 27 January.

The plaintiff comes to show cause within six months after [becoming] twenty-one against a decree. He moves for leave to exhibit a supplemental bill, there being several material things omitted in the former cause. Talman v. Plunket, 1712.

Solicitor General [*Talbot*]: [There are] several cases where the interest of an infant was given up [and] leave was given to bring a new bill. At law, the parol demurs. An infant is as much favored here. If there was fraud, he might bring a new bill with leave. If [there was an] improper defense, he must apply for leave.

Peere Williams, for the plaintiff, cited Fountain v. Caine, Trinity 1718. The decree was the estate was to be sold. The Master was to look into the articles, the heir [being] an infant. [There was a] motion for the heir to put in a further answer. A precedent for leave given on a petition *ex parte* by Sir J. Trevor is Richmond v. Tayleur, Hilary 1720. An infant, when of age, brings an original bill, [and a] decree during infancy was pleaded [and] overruled. The court declared, if there were any fraud, it is proper for an original bill to set it aside, even for a personal estate. Here the infant's inheritance is concerned. If this be allowed, any infant may lose his estate.

Mr. *Wills*, for the defendant, insisted that, by a decree of the House of Lords, no leave is given to bring a bill which ought to be or apply there for leave.

The Solicitor General [*Talbot*], in reply: Leave is given to show cause, i.e. sufficiently, not imperfectly, the same as if such liberty were given by this court adm[. . .] that then the infant might put in a new answer [upon the] same reason for bringing a new bill of necessity that this court must put a construction on the meaning of the House of Lords.

Master of the Rolls [Jekyll]: The plaintiff's petition prays he may amend the answer to the cross-bill or bring a new bill. [There are] two questions as to amending the answer. By the course of the court, he may and he may put in a new one. Infants, always in the answer, pray that the court will take care of their interests. The court is bound to do so. All decrees wherein infants are concerned are *nisi causa* when he comes of age. Talman v. Plunket, in 1712; leave to put in another answer [was granted] by the Master of the Rolls. Richmond v. Tayleur; [there was a] new bill for fraud. Fountain v. Caine. I enquired into the course of the court [whether] an infant may amend an answer or may show cause on an old pleading. He need not open the merits to the court in order to obtain leave to amend his case. The court will do it of course. The infant may put in a better answer during his infancy. Leave given by the House of Lords to show cause must be according to the course of the court. Otherwise, such leave would signify little.

The second question is whether an infant plaintiff may not amend his case. If he may not in this case, the trustees would retain the estate to their own use, which is absurd. As to the course of the court, any person may bring a bill in the name of an infant. No person is assigned a guardian or *prochein ami*. There have been different bills brought by different *prochein amis*. The defendant cannot plead the pendency of two bills, but must apply to the court, who will order that bill to proceed which is most for his benefit. A bill brought by an infant cannot be pleaded against him. If he brings a new bill after he comes of age, if he wants to bring new matter in issue, he may by amending his bill. Whether this is precluded by the House of Lords, I think it was their intent that the infant might make the best of his case, as well where he is plaintiff as where defendant.

Lord Chancellor [Lord King]: The question is on the order of the House of Peers. The cause to be shown is in the Court of Chancery, which brings in the question what is the course of the court whether an infant shall only rehear the cause or may make a new cause. Now, considering the care the court takes of infants, it should be something more. If [there is] a decree of forfeiture and after[wards] he finds a settlement whereby his ancestor had no power, he cannot otherwise be relieved. By the precedent of 37 Eliz., he may amend his answer. As to an amended bill, if [there was a] decree of dismission, [there is] no instance of his having time to show cause against it or amending the bill. By an order of the House of Lords, leave was given to show cause why the bill should not be dismissed. How must that be by the course of this court? It must be by a rehearing only. I shall be very cautious of introducing new practices. Sir John Napier may amend the answer, but he may not amend the bill.

[This was] reversed by the House of Lords.[1]

British Library MS. Hargrave 83, p. 57

26 and 27 February 1726[/27].

A settlement was made by Sir John Napper upon the defendant, his Lady. In that settlement, a particular tenement was settled and then the manor of Shitlington and then another tenement in the occupation of a particular tenant named in the deed. Sir John Napper, an infant, by his *prochein ami*, brought his bill to set aside this conveyance upon this and other circumstances. And Lady Napper brought her cross-bill to establish the settlement, to which Sir John Napper, by his guardian, put in an answer. Upon hearing this cause and some circumstances of obtaining a report in it, which it was contrived that the infant should move to confirm, though it was alleged to be to his prejudice, an order was made that the infant should be at liberty to bring a new or supplemental bill. And a decree was made absolutely without giving the infant the usual time after he came of age to show cause against it. Upon this, there was an appeal to the House of Lords, who reversed part of the decree and affirmed another part of it unless the infant should show cause within six months after he came of age. The order that the infant might be at liberty to bring a new or supplemental bill was included in that part of the decree which was reserved.

Sir John Napper, being now of age, came within the six months to show cause and alleged that several matters had not been brought before the court in the former pleadings which would have been beneficial for him, and he petitioned that he might be at liberty to amend his former bill or bring a new one or both and to amend his former answer or put in a new one or both.

N.B. Before they proceeded to argue the points of the petition, it was said by the court and admitted that, Sir John Napper having come within the six months

[1] *Lady Effingham v. Napier* (1727), 4 Brown P.C. 340, 2 E.R. 230, 5 Brown P.C. 221, 2 E.R. 640.

to show cause, no advantage could be taken of his not actually doing that which the court might judge him at liberty to do for showing cause within six months.

It was argued for the petitioner by Mr. *Talbot*, the Solicitor General, that Sir John Napper is both plaintiff and defendant in this suit before the court and entitled to the privileges that belong to infancy in both respects and, though this court, in a suit where an infant is concerned, permits the [*prochein*], which would have demurred at law, to go farther here and suffers a decree to be obtained, yet it takes care that the decree shall be without prejudice to the infant and he, at his age, may come and show for cause that a proper defense was not made for him and may pray to be admitted to amend his former answer or put in a new or supplemental answer and that this is the course of the court.

The cases of Fountain v. Cave and Richmond v. Tailleur are authorities in point. If this be established, it is as reasonable and equitable that he should likewise be at liberty to bring a new bill or a supplemental bill, for he may be as much prejudiced by an improvident bill as by an improvident answer. And, in the case of Weston and Tonkin, 2 May 31 Eliz., a liberty was given to the infant to bring a new bill. The decree of the House of Lords does not abridge any privilege the infant may have here in this matter or in the matter of his showing cause, for as part of the complaint of the appeal was that time was not given as usual after he came of age and that complaint was thought just, he now comes before the court as if he had such time originally given him by the decree and the cause he is to show ought not to be upon a fruitless bill or answer, for then it would be vain and, if he is to be bound by his former bill or answer, that may be the consequence, for the bill was to set aside a conveyance made to the defendant and, if it should only appear on the proceedings had on the answer to the cross-bill and not upon the original bill that the conveyance was not duly obtained, that would not make out a case to entitle him to relief upon his original bill, but the estate must remain in the trustees and neither plaintiff nor defendant could come at it or the profits. Therefore, the course of the court being clear in the case of an infant's answer and as reasonable and not unprecedented in the case of his bill and necessary for the infant to come at justice, all the prayer of the petition is proper.

Attorney General [*Yorke*] and *Wills*, *contra*, for the defendant: No one instance is produced where, by the course or leave of the court, a new original bill has been brought by an infant. In this, equity follows the law, for, where an infant is the demandant, the *prochein* shall not demur and the infant has no privilege of age. In the precedent of Weston v. Tonkin (or Western v. Dolphin) in 31 (or 35) Eliz., there, the liberty to bring a new bill is by the special penning of the decree and it is not upon a decree giving time to show cause generally after attaining age. In the case of Griffin v. [*blank*] and of Richmond v. Tailleur, the decree was founded upon answers collusively to the infant's prejudice. And laying these precedents out of the case, there is nothing to warrant what is alleged to be the course of the court with respect to an infant's putting in a new answer. In the case of Tallman v. Plunkett, upon the appeal to Lord Harcourt, this was indeed objected and urged, but the opinion of the court was not upon this point. If the words of the House of Lords are dubious in their order upon the appeal, this petition is not a proper method for determining that point, but a bill ought to be brought to bring the matter in judgment before the court or the House of Lords may be applied to by petition to explain their order upon the appeal.

Master of the Rolls, Sir Joseph Jekyll: The merits of the cause are not now under consideration, but only the course of the court. And I take it that, by that, the infant now he is come of age may amend the former answer put in by his guardian or make a new answer. This course of the court proceeds from its care of infants and from the claim they usually, by their answer, put in to have the care of the court and which the court *ex officio* is obliged to take of them from the general superintendency which the common law vested in this court with regard to infants and which still remains here to this day in good measure.

In the case of Westeram (or Weston) v. Dolphin (Takin) 35 (31) Eliz., the court, taking special notice that a new bill was necessary, made special provision for it upon the circumstances before them, but that case does not shape with the common course of the court.

In the case of Tallman v. Plunkett, the late Master of the Rolls [Sir John Trevor] (1712), upon a petition, gave liberty for the infant, after he had attained his age, to put in a new answer, and the infant by his answer so much bettered his case that the decree was for him. Upon this, there was an appeal to Lord Harcourt, who varied the decree upon the merits. The point of giving liberty to put in the new answer could not come before him in judgment, for the appellant should have applied to discharge that order before hearing, and, though it was thrown into the petition of appeal, it could be no ingredient in reversing the decree. The case of Richmond v. Talleur went upon the fraud. Therefore, those precedents may be laid out of the case.

In Trinity vacation 1718, in the case of Fountain v. Cave,[1] it was moved by counsel not fully instructed that the infant might be at liberty to put in another answer, applications having been but vain for infants to show cause, and it has seldomer happened that they have insisted upon varying their defense after they have come of age. In that case, I took time to consider of it and then apprehended upon the best judgment I could make that the course of the court was that an infant might amend his answer or put in another answer or apply to hear the cause again upon the merits within six months after he came of age and that without stating his case in the petition as to the merits of his cause because the setting down of his case and obtaining the order upon the merits might prejudice the judgment of the court. But application and leave is necessary in order to make a connection of the proceedings.

[1] *Fountain v. Caine* (1718), *ut supra.*

An infant may before he comes of age apply to have his answer taken off the file and that he may put in a better answer. And that was done and ordered in the case of Lord Colraine v. Gregg. And, if he may do it during nonage, he may at full age when, in the eye of the law, he is in another stated capacity. I take it that the order of the House of Lords is relative to the course of this court. The question then seems to result to this, whether, when the court always takes care that an infant shall not be prejudiced upon what comes before them, he shall not have liberty to amend his bill as he is plaintiff as well as he has to amend his answer as a defendant.

Anyone may bring a bill in the name of an infant. No assignment of a *prochein ami* is necessary. He does it at his own peril. Two or three suits may be brought by two or three *prochein amis*, different persons, for the same matter. I have known them brought so. But to this, an objection arises that it is a vexation to the defendant, who cannot plead against the infant pendency of a former suit. But in that case, the court will itself consider which bill is most beneficial for the infant and order that to be proceeded on and the proceedings on the others to be stayed.

If a bill be brought generally, and I believe always in the case of an infant, it is absolutely dismissed, and not *nisi causa* [be shown]. And the reason of it is because such dismission in the case of an infant, like dismissions before hearing, is not pleadable in bar to another bill. This shows that the court takes care of the infant in respect of the bills brought by him as well as with regard to his answer. And, if in this case by his answer to the cross-bill, he should bar the defendant's equity by new matter put in issue and yet should be concluded by his original bill standing as it is so that he could not have relief upon it, the trustees must retain the ownership of this estate. Nay, they may go farther; they may enter and receive the rents and profits. This is a consequence that may happen unless the court gives leave to the plaintiff to amend his bill.

I, therefore, am of opinion that, where it may be necessary that he should amend his bill as well as his answer to better his case, he ought to be at liberty to do both. And I apprehend the House of Lords intended him all the benefit that he could have by any method of showing cause consistent with the rules of the court.

Lord Chancellor King: The question is upon the order of the House of Lords and the meaning of that. The cause to be shown is in this court and, consequently, according to the course of it. The court in its care of infants who had put in an answer considered something more than the bare rehearing of the cause, as, where a bill is brought against an infant to foreclose, the infant puts in an answer [and] acknowledges payment, there is a common decree for foreclosure *nisi causa* etc. by the time the infant comes of age; he discovers that the estate was in settlement and could not be mortgaged. Which way can he show cause to have justice done but by insisting on new matter?

He may, by the course of the court, therefore, in this and other instances, amend his answer. But I do not see that it is the course of the court for him to have respite until he comes of age to amend a bill that is dismissed generally and without any regard to his infancy, as in the case of another person. The way then he can only have redress by the course of the court upon this bill is by a rehearing, and that rehearing ought to be respited until the cause may come to be heard upon the new or amended answer. And then there need be no defect of justice, the trustees being before the court and under its control so that here is no necessity, no urgent occasion to break in upon the course of the court. And, therefore, I shall be cautious of making a new precedent not supported by any one parallel case. Sir John Napper may amend his answer or put in a new one. But this bill must stand as it was at the time of the decree made.

British Library MS. Lansdowne 587, p. 130

Hilary [term] 13 Geo. I [1727].

Lutwyche: Sir J. Napier, being an infant, brought a bill in Chancery against the defendant, and she brought a cross-bill against him. Upon an appeal, a decree was made in the House of Lords against the infant with liberty to show cause to the contrary in Chancery in six months after he came of age.

Query if, by virtue of this clause to show cause, he may amend his answer or bring a new original bill or a new supplemental bill? Showing cause means to lay his whole cause before the court.

Fountain v. Cave, Trinity 1718; Cave, seised in fee devised to his wife to pay debts and left an infant heir. A. articled to buy the estate, and he brought a bill against the creditors and the infant. And he obtained a decree to have the estate sold. But the infant had time to show cause in six months after he came of age. On a motion for the infant defendant to put in a new answer, it was granted without hearing the other party as a matter of course.

Richmond v. Tebure, Hilary 1720[/21], before Lord Macclesfield; fraud being suggested by an infant on a decree against him, he may give a new answer or bring a supplemental bill or a new original bill.

The infant has a privilege to be relieved etc. The intent of the rule to show cause is that the infant should not be prejudiced, which cannot be unless the whole merits are laid before the court. Otherwise, he might be easily excluded and barred of his right.

Sir Philip Yorke: The query is what is the course of the court when an infant is to show cause. The merits were fully determined. The infant prays to amend his answer and his original bill and to bring a new supplemental bill. An infant plaintiff, at common law, has no more privilege than other persons but, when he is defendant, the parol demurs.

Weston v. Talkin; [there was a] bill to set aside a conveyance under which an infant claimed.

In the present case, the decree is particular to show cause, not by the course of the court, but by a special reservation.

Tiffin v. Tiffin; Richmond v. Telure; these cases are not like the present case. In these cases, the infant was permitted to bring a new bill because there was fraud. But here is a special reservation to the infant to show cause.

Query, is it by the course of the court on such a reservation the infant may bring a new bill without suggesting matter of fraud?

Talman v. Plunkett; the Master of the Rolls gave liberty to bring a new bill, and the Lord Chancellor reversed it generally. And the Court insisted that it was irregular. Therefore, this is no authority for bringing a new bill.

New bills are permitted only where there is a gross collusion or negligence of the guardian, but not on a special reservation to show cause by the course of the court. The intention of the Lords' decree to show cause was only on the proofs and pleadings in the cause. The infant may bring a new bill without asking leave if there were fraud.

Lord Chancellor [Lord King]: The infant having commenced a suit to show cause before the six months are expired may continue after the six months. It is to be looked on as one continual act.

Afterwards, in this cause, the infant was admitted to amend his answer but not to bring a new bill nor a supplemental bill.

[Other reports of this case: 2 Peere Williams 401, 24 E.R. 786, 2 Eq. Cas. Abr. 59, 22 E.R. 52.]

772

Betham v. Gunter

(Ch. 1726)

A bill in equity will be dismissed on account of the plaintiff's laches.

Lincoln's Inn MS. Misc. 12, p. 257

2 December 1726. Betham *et al.* v. Alice Gunter and John Smith.

John Gunter, the defendant's husband, by his will, gave an estate called Willoxbridge to his brother and heir, Peter Gunter, and his heirs upon the condition he paid off the mortgage thereon and released to the defendant Alice Gunter, the testator's wife, and the defendant John Smith all his right to a leasehold estate which he devised to them, and, in case he did not pay off the mortgage and indemnify the defendants, whom he made his executors, therefrom and execute a release and permit the defendant Alice quietly to enjoy her jointure, then he devised the said estate called Willoxbridge to the defendants and their heirs.

Peter Gunter entered on the said estate, but he refused to execute a release and did not pay off the mortgage. And he brought [actions of] ejectment for the jointure estate, in which he failed, and then he brought a bill in Chancery, which was dismissed for want of prosecution. And, thereupon having broken the condition, the defendants brought an [action of] ejectment and recovered the estate. And, after he had acquiesced under that recovery about six years, he died in 1711.

And the plaintiffs, who were his heirs at law, now brought their bill, offering to release and confirm the jointure and praying to be relieved against the forfeiture and that the title deeds relating to the jointure might be delivered up to them.

Upon the hearing of this cause, the Master of the Rolls [JEKYLL] dismissed the bill without any difficulty. And now it came on again before him upon a petition to rehear the cause, and the length of time since Peter died was excused. However, His Honor [JEKYLL] continued his former opinion and said, if relief was to be given in such a case, no man could tell how to make his will.

It was insisted that Peter was an infant when his brother died though, in truth, the suits by him brought were after he came of age, to which it was answered by the Master of the Rolls [JEKYLL] that an infant was bound by the condition.

As to the writings, though one of the plaintiffs was an infant, yet it was now ordered that, when he came of age and confirmed the jointure together with the other plaintiffs, the writings should be delivered up to the plaintiffs.

773

Barnardiston v. Simpson

(Ch. 1726)

A marriage settlement made in consideration of dismissing a suit for divorce and alimony is made upon a valuable consideration and is not a voluntary conveyance that can be set aside by the settlor's creditors.

Lincoln's Inn MS. Misc. 12, p. 255

3 December 1726.

The defendant Simpson having used his wife with great cruelty and turned her out of doors, she libeled against him in the spiritual court for a divorce for cruelty and adultery, upon which he, being sensible of his fault, employs a friend to mediate a reconciliation. And several meetings were had for that purpose between him and some friends of the wife, who insisted that a settlement should be made upon her, which he agreed to. And, accordingly, he transferred £1200 South Sea [Company] annuities to trustees upon trust to permit the wife to receive the dividends during her life for her separate use, which trust was declared by a deed in writing.

Upon these terms, the wife surceases her suit in the spiritual court and agrees to cohabit again with her husband, which she, accordingly does. And, during such cohabitation, the defendant borrows money of the plaintiff and confesses a judgment for securing it, and the wife had solicited the plaintiff to lend her husband the money. And, to induce the plaintiff so to do, she told him her husband had an estate in Jamaica but took no notice of the settlement of the annuities.

After this, the defendant falls out again with his wife, uses her ill, and turns her out of doors a second time, upon which she brings a new suit for a separation and obtains a sentence accordingly.

The plaintiff's bill was to charge the annuities with his judgment and to have a satisfaction thereout of his debt.

The consideration mentioned in the deed of trust was only that of a marriage had and of love and affection of the defendant towards his wife. And, though it was not mentioned to be for divers other good causes etc., yet the defendant, the wife, was allowed to read proofs to show the annuities were transferred upon another consideration besides what was mentioned in the deed, which being fully proved, the Master of the Rolls [Jekyll], though it was insisted for the plaintiff that, if the wife had proceeded in her suit, she could only have obtained a sentence for separation and alimony, which alimony would have ceased upon their cohabiting together again and the settlement came only in the room of alimony, was clear of opinion that the settlement was made upon a good consideration and was not fraudulent as against the plaintiff. And, therefore, he dismissed bill with costs.

774

Hungerford v. Hungerford

(Ch. 1727)

A fine at common law levied by a tenant in tail in possession makes a discontinuance of the estate.

Lincoln's Inn MS. Misc. 12, p. 263, pl. 1

18 January 1726[/27].

It was agreed in this case that, if a fine is pleaded and it is not said to be with proclamations, it must be taken to be a fine at common law only. A fine at common law levied by a tenant in tail in possession will work a discontinuance, but not if it is levied of an estate tail in remainder or reversion.

775
Burnaby's Case
(Ch. 1727)

A judgment creditor who has taken out a writ of execution cannot put his judgment debtor into bankruptcy.

Lincoln's Inn MS. Misc. 12, p. 263, pl. 2

Hilary term 1726[/27].

A commission of bankruptcy was taken out against Mr. Burnaby, a brewer, and, afterwards, it was superseded by Lord Chancellor King because the creditor who sued out the commission had taken out execution against the bankrupt and had him in custody when the commission was taken out.

776
Blunt's Case
(Ch. 1727)

Where a creditor's debtor in execution is later forced into bankruptcy, the creditor can either join in the bankruptcy proceedings and discharge his writ of execution or enforce the execution and oppose the discharge in bankruptcy of his debtor.

Lincoln's Inn MS. Misc. 12, p. 264

Hilary term 1726[/27].

A commission of bankruptcy being taken out against Blunt,[1] one of his creditors who had judgments against him, having taken him in execution and come in as a creditor under the Statute, he petitions to be discharged. And the question was whether the creditor should not make his election either to abide by his execution and waive all benefit under the commission [of bankruptcy] or to come in as a creditor under the Statute[2] and discharge the execution.

Lord Chancellor [Lord King] was of the opinion that the execution ought to be discharged if the plaintiff in the action came in under the commission so as to receive any benefit therefrom. But he seemed to think that, notwithstanding the execution, the plaintiff might so far come in as a creditor under the Statute as to oppose the bankrupt's having his certificate [of discharge], for otherwise it would be in the power of the other creditors to defeat him of all the benefit of his execution, for as soon as the certificate is allowed, the bankrupt must be discharged by the late Act of Parliament by the court where the execution is sued out.

---

[1] H. Erskine-Hill, 'Blunt, Sir John (bap. 1665, d. 1733)', *Oxford Dictionary of National Biography*, vol. 6, pp. 353–354.

[2] Stat. 5 Geo. I, c. 24.

777

Ex parte Burrough

(Ch. 1727)

The question in this case was whether a legacy, which comes to a bankrupt's wife after the commission of bankruptcy has been sued out, is liable to the husband's debts.

Lincoln's Inn MS. Misc. 12, p. 265, pl. 1

[Hilary term 1727].

Upon a petition, the question was whether a legacy, which came to the bankrupt's wife after the commission was sued out, could be assigned by the commissioners.

And it was said by the Attorney [General *Yorke*] and the Solicitor General [*Talbot*] that it had been determined by the Lord Macclesfield that the choses in action of the wife of a bankrupt are assignable by the commissioners.

But Lord Chancellor [Lord King] gave no opinion, but he said the assignees might bring an action [at law].

778

Dews v. Norton

(Ch. 1727)

A contract to convey land in the future when the owner of the remainder should come into possession will be set aside by a court of equity.

British Library MS. Hargrave 83, p. 31

25 January 1726[/27].

These [cases] were cited by Mr. *Talbot* in the case of Jeremy Dews v. Norton, *quod vide*.

Twisleton v. Griffith;[1] the father of the plaintiff Twisleton was tenant for life, remainder to the plaintiff in tail with a remainder over. The plaintiff, being in want of money, applied to the defendant to get him some upon the sale of his remainder. The plaintiff was then no very young man, for he had a daughter fifteen years old or thereabouts as appeared in the cause. It was also proved that the defendant advanced the plaintiff more money than others offered. The defendant gave after the rate of seven years purchase, and the money was actually paid, and a fine was levied by the plaintiff and a covenant to suffer a recovery. After the death of the plaintiff's father, the defendant applied to the plaintiff to perfect the conveyance and suffer a recovery. Upon his insisting, the plaintiff brought his bill

[1] *Twisleton v. Griffith* (Ch. 1716–1721), see above, Case No. 118.

to be relieved upon payment of what was due for principal and interest. My Lord Cowper took time to consider of the case and was attended by precedents. But the precedent of Nott and Hill, in Mr. Vernon's reports,[1] was not laid before him, for I believe Mr. Vernon only had it and he was of the other side. Lord Cowper, when he made the decree, said that he had some vibration in his mind (that was his expression), but thought it of worse consequence that such contracts should stand than to relieve against them, and he relieved upon payment of what was due for principal, interest, and costs.

The same day, and in the same cause, this case was likewise cited by Mr. Solicitor General [*Talbot*], Berney and Pitt;[2] the defendant lent the plaintiff £1000 in the lifetime of his father and the plaintiff gave the defendant a recognizance to repay £2500 in case he survived his father, if not, the £1000 was to be lost. The bill was brought by Berney after the death of his father. Lord Nottingham would not relieve, but Lord Jeffreys upon rehearing did.

779

Cross v. Cross

(Ch. 1727)

Where a decedent's personal estate is insufficient to pay off his debts, the legacies will abate to that purpose before his real estate.

Lincoln's Inn MS. Misc. 12, p. 265, pl. 2

31 January 1726[/27].

Thomas Cross, by his will, gave several legacies to the plaintiffs and also devised several parts of his real estate to other persons and all the rest and residue of his real and personal estate to trustees for building an almshouse.

The personal estate falling short to pay the legacies, the plaintiffs brought their bill insisting that the surplus of the real estate was charged with the legacies and praying it might be sold for the payment thereof, for that, by the devise of the residue must be understood the residue of his estate which shall remain after the payment of his debts and legacies.

But Lord Chancellor [Lord King] dismissed the bill with costs, saying the court had never gone so far as was attempted by this bill.

---

[1] *Nott v. Hill* (1683), 1 Vernon 167, 23 E.R. 391, also 2 Chancery Cases 120, 22 E.R. 875, 1 Eq. Cas. Abr. 275, 21 E.R. 1042.

[2] *Berney v. Pitt* (1686), 2 Chancery Reports 395, 21 E.R. 697, 2 Vernon 14, 23 E.R. 620.

780

Gray v. Walker

(Ch. 1727)

Where a debtor in a usurious contract offers to repay the principal and legal interest in a suit in equity, the creditor-defendant can get an order of the court to that purpose with a deduction for court costs.

Lincoln's Inn MS. Misc. 12, p. 266

9 February 1726[/27].

The plaintiff gave a bond to the defendant for the payment of £100, but, in truth, he received £80, the defendant being to have £20 for advancing the money. Afterwards, the defendant brought an action at [common] law against the plaintiff upon the bond, who pleaded the usurious contract, but, not being able to prove it, he brought his bill for a discovery and to stay the proceedings in the action, and he offered to pay what was due for principal and interest of the money really lent.

The defendant, by answer, confessed the usurious contract and now moved that the plaintiff, according to the offer in his bill might pay the money really lent and the interest. And it was said that the defendant had no other way to come at the money, for the plaintiff, notwithstanding the offer in his bill might dismiss his own bill and then give the defendant's answer in evidence upon a trial at law and the defendant could not make the plaintiff bring his cause on to a hearing, whether he would or no, nor could the defendant set down the cause by proviso, there being no issue joined.

The Master of the Rolls [Jekyll] said this was a new case. And, at first, he was for denying the motion. And he said the defendant might set down it by proviso. But, afterwards, he changed his opinion as to that and, at length, ordered the plaintiff should pay the money according to the offer in his bill.

And the plaintiff having given a cross-notice that the defendant might pay the costs at [common] law and in this court, His Honor [Jekyll] was of the opinion that the defendant having made a usurious contract, which was against the law and void in itself and on which the defendant, if the contract could have been proved, would have recovered nothing, and, therefore, he was of the opinion that the defendant ought to pay costs. And, accordingly, he ordered the plaintiff should deduct the costs at law and in this court out of the money he offered to pay by his bill.

Note, upon this motion, was cited the Case of Pattison v. Cleveland, before Lord Macclesfield,[1] were the plaintiff brought his bill for a usurious contract, the defendant demurred, and the demurrer was allowed. Afterwards, the plaintiff

---

[1] *Paterson v. Cleveland* (Ch. 1724), see above, Case No. 645.

amended his bill and offered to pay what was really due for principal and interest, and, then, the defendant demurred again. And the demurrer was overruled, for the plaintiff having offered to pay what was really due, the defendant is bound to discover what the contract really was.

Mr. Solicitor General [*Talbot*], though not in the motion, stood up and said he remembered the case very well.

781
Parker v. Spendlow

(Ch. 1727)

A witness whose deposition is suppressed as impertinent is not liable to pay court costs.

Lincoln's Inn MS. Misc. 12, p. 268, pl. 1

13 February 1726[/27].

The depositions of one A.B., a witness for the defendant, taken by commission being reported scandalous and impertinent, the plaintiff obtained an order to suppress the depositions and that the witness should pay the costs of the scandal and impertinence. But, upon my motion to discharge that part of the order, which ordered the witness to pay the costs, Lord Chancellor [Lord King], having first consulted the Master of the Rolls [Jekyll], who was then in court, discharged it, it being the fault of the commissioners to take down any depositions which were either scandalous or impertinent. And he said it would be very hard if a witness, who is bound to come and give his evidence and [who is] not a proper judge of what is or is not pertinent to the matter in question, should be made to pay costs in such a case.

Note the depositions complained of were taken to the last general interrogatory.

782
Anonymous

(Ch. c. 1727)

A will that creates a charity must be executed according to the Statute of Frauds.

Lincoln's Inn MS. Misc. 12, p. 268, pl. 2

Note, in another cause, the Case of Sidney College v. Johnson, in Lord Cowper's time,[1] was cited by the Solicitor General [*Talbot*], who said it was there decreed that, if an appointment is made by a will for a charity within the Statute of

[1] *Attorney General v. Barnes* (1707), 2 Vernon 597, 23 E.R. 990, Precedents in Chancery 270, 24 E.R. 131, Gilbert Rep. 5, 25 E.R. 4, 3 Chancery Reports 150, 21 E.R.

Queen Elizabeth,[1] the will must be executed according to the Statute of Frauds and Perjuries.[2]

783

Henley v. Bertie

(Ch. 1727)

A contract is enforceable against the estate of the obligor.

Lincoln's Inn MS. Misc. 12, p. 269, pl. 1

17 February 1726[/27].

Sir Robert Henley made his will and My Lady Henley, his wife, and the defendant Bromfield executors. And he gave the defendant £10 a year for his pains. The executors proved the will. And then, at the desire of Mr. Anthony Henley, the eldest son, they assigned over to him the executorship and all the personal estate, and he thereby covenanted to pay Mr. Bromfield his annuity according to the will. Anthony Henley, accordingly, paid this annuity until his death, which was about thirteen years. And, upon the Master's special report, the question was if this annuity was still subsisting.

The Master of the Rolls [Jekyll] was very clear of the opinion that Mr. Bromfield was entitled to this annuity for his life. And he ordered the arrears and growing payments to be paid to him.

784

Yates v. Wallis

(Ch. 1727)

Where a debt is bequeathed, where the debt is paid in voluntarily, it is not an ademption of the bequest.

Lincoln's Inn MS. Misc. 384, p. 250, pl. 1

26 January 1726[/27]. At the Rolls.

Where a testator devises such a sum, which is out on such a particular security to A., and, after making the will, the money or part of it is paid in to the testator, if it is paid in voluntarily, it is not an ademption of the legacy, but otherwise

---

753, 1 Eq. Cas. Abr. 97, 21 E.R. 908, British Library MS. Hargrave 80, f. 13, Lincoln's Inn MS. Coxe 89, vol. 3, pt. 2, p. 30, Chancery Cases *tempore* Harcourt, 25.

1 Stat. 43 Eliz. I, c. 4 (*SR*, IV, 968–970).

2 Stat. 29 Car. II, c. 3 (*SR*, V, 839–842).

it is if it is paid in by compulsion. Lord Pawlet's Case, Raymond 335; Rider v. Wager; Swinburn.

Lincoln's Inn MS. Misc. 12, p. 269, pl. 2

Eodem die [17 February 1727].

Elizabeth Bawler, by will, gave to her executors two bonds, one for £250 and the other for £150, in trust for her grandson, the plaintiff Joseph. After the making of this will, the testatrix received in the money due on the £250 bond and £20, part of the principal due on the other. And she lived some years afterwards and died without making any alteration in her will.

And this being stated specially by the Master's report for the judgment of the court, the question was whether the receiving in of the money was not an ademption of the legacy. And it not being stated by the report whether the money was paid in voluntarily or not, the Master of the Rolls [JEKYLL] sent it back to the Master to certify how and in what manner the money was paid.

And now, it came on again upon the Master's further report whereby he had certified that the £250 bond was paid off voluntarily by the obligors a few days before it became due. And, as to the £20 paid on the other bond, it was paid at two payment and the obligor made an affidavit that he believed that he was called upon or sent to to pay the money.

The Master of the Rolls [JEKYLL] was clear of opinion that the legacy was still subsisting, for the distinction in the civil law is that, where the debt is paid in voluntarily, it is no ademption of the legacy, but, where it is paid in by compulsion, it is. And though the obligor in the latter bond says he believed he was called upon to pay the second, yet he speaks only as to his belief, and that is not evidence.

785

Oxton v. Oxton

(Ch. 1727)

After a sale of land equitable conversion does not occur before the buyer pays or tenders the purchase price.

Lincoln's Inn MS. Misc. 12, p. 271

20 February 1726[/27].

A. sells an estate to B., his son, for £150. The conveyance is executed, and a receipt is given for the consideration money, but no money is paid, A. having taken a bond for the payment of it within three months after demand. And A. continues in the possession and dies without having demanded the money. And B., likewise, dies, and his heir brings an [action of] ejectment. And, thereupon, the plaintiff, who is both heir and executor of A., brings his bill against the heir of B. for an injunction and to be paid the money due on the bond without making any previous demand in writing as he should have done, for, until three months after such demand, the bond was not due. And he makes the administratrix of B. a party.

And, for the plaintiff, it was insisted that the purchase money having never been paid, it was against conscience for the heir of B. to bring an [action of] ejectment and that the plaintiff ought not to be turned out of possession until the purchase money was paid and that either the heir or the administratrix of B. ought to pay it.

For the defendant, the administratrix, it was insisted the bill was brought before any debt was due, the plaintiff having never made any demand in writing, and, besides, if the debt was due, it ought to be paid by the defendant, the heir, the bond being given for the purchase money and was a lien upon the estate. And he ought not to have the estate without paying the consideration money.

On the other hand, the heir, by his answer, insisted that the estate was discharged, the vendor having taken a bond for the money, which was payment, and, therefore, it ought to be paid out of the personal assets.

The Master of the Rolls [JEKYLL] was of the opinion the plaintiff could not bring his bill against the administratrix until the bond was due. And he said it never could be due from her.

When an estate is sold, there is a resulting trust to the grantor until the purchase money is paid. And, when the purchase money is paid, then and not before, it becomes the estate of the vendee, both in law and equity.

If the vendor dies before the money is paid, the resulting trust descends to his heir and cannot be taken out of him without paying the purchase money. Now, the vendee not having paid the money and the legal estate being descended upon his heir, if he would defeat the resulting trust, he must pay the purchase money and not the administratrix.

And, therefore, he dismissed the bill as against the administratrix with costs and decreed the plaintiff to hold the land until the £150 was paid and an injunction in the meantime.

786

Rastall v. Jenison

(Ch. 1727)

The Statute of Frauds cannot be pleaded in order to support a fraud.

Lincoln's Inn MS. Misc. 12, p. 273 [bis]

Hilary term 1726[/27]. Rastall v. Jenison and Hutchinson.

The plaintiff, being minded to purchase a house in Newark belonging to the defendant Sir Matthew Jenison, employed the defendant Hutchinson to treat for the same and to purchase it for the plaintiff. And it was agreed between them that, if Hutchinson could purchase it, he should have a lease of it at the rent of 1s. a year for every 20s. he paid for the purchase.

Hutchinson agrees with Sir Matthew to purchase the house for £35, and he pays the same and has a conveyance made to him. But, afterwards, he refused to convey to the plaintiff. And, thereupon, the plaintiff brought his bill, and, after the bill was brought, Hutchinson re-conveys the house to Sir Matthew Jenison, upon which the plaintiff files his supplemented bill against the defendants, suggesting that this was a contrivance to defeat the plaintiff of the benefit of the purchase.

The agreement between the plaintiff and the defendant Hutchinson being by parol only and there being no declaration of a trust in writing, the defendant Hutchinson pleaded the Statute of Frauds.[1]

But it being insisted on for the plaintiff that Hutchinson had acted in a fraudulent manner and that the Statute was made for the preventing of frauds and not for the support of them, Lord Chancellor [Lord King] saved the benefit of the plea until the hearing with liberty to except.

787

Anonymous

(Ch. 1727)

The corporation courts of the Cinque Ports have jurisdiction to try actions of ejectment.

British Library MS. Hargrave 83, p. 66

Tuesday, 7 March 1726/27.

Fazakerly moved to quash a [writ of] *supersedeas quia improvide emanavit.* It was directed to one of the corporation courts within the jurisdiction of the Cinque Ports and was to stay their proceedings in an [action of] ejectment. He produced a printed copy of their charter whereby a power was granted this inferior court to hold pleas of all actions real, personal, and mixed, actions of trespass, assize, novel disseisin, and mort d'ancestor. The common *supersedeas* in the Register was taken out from the Cursitor. The authority given by the charter was insisted on and that this *supersedeas* tended entirely to overthrow it.

On the other side, *Lutwyche* insisted from the words of the writ that the common law inferior courts could not hold a plea in ejectment, that in the Case of the Mayor of Bewdley, lately before My Lord Chancellor [Lord King], a *supersedeas* was granted and, upon a motion to discharge it and time taken by My Lord to consider of it, My Lord refused to discharge the *supersedeas* though the charter had the same words with this only that the general words of real, personal,

[1] Stat. 29 Car. II, c. 3 (*SR*, V, 839–842).

and mixed were followed with this restriction, so that it did not exceed a certain sum. And this was the very last seal. And, in considering this case, a precedent was produced which was in the year 1702, where a *supersedeas* was granted to the Court of the Honour of Windsor, which has a very great and extensive jurisdiction and as large words to support it in their charter as are in the present case, that upon this and other instances mentioned in that precedent, My Lord Chancellor [Wright] refused indeed to discharge the *supersedeas*, but said, if they were not satisfied, they might put it in a way of trial and, if they proceeded, an attachment being then to issue, they might have the direction of the court for them to declare upon the attachment as in prohibition.

To this *Fazakerly* replied that they should be without a remedy in this case, for there was no instance or precedent of a declaration in an attachment upon such a case.

The Master of the Rolls [JEKYLL] distinguished this case from others because the Cinque Ports, he said, and their jurisdiction was well known to the law and taken notice of in the books. The king's writ did run within the other jurisdictions where the cases cited arose, but, within the jurisdiction of the Cinque Ports, the king's writ did not run. But if they proceeded without authority in an inferior court within that jurisdiction, there was the Court of the Castle of Dover which had the supreme jurisdiction and to that court an application to restrain them would be proper, but not here.

Lutwyche urged that prohibitions went from the courts of Westminster to courts within the counties palatine, and he remembered instances in Cheshire and Lancashire, which the Master of the Rolls and Lutwyche did not admit that the king's writ did never run within the Cinque Ports, but argued that it might as well go there as in the counties palatine, of which there were many instances.

Fazakerly did agree that, where it was an action *in personam* or where it was the king's suit in respect of his prerogative, his writs did run into the counties palatine, but never where it was otherwise *in rem*. Many instances in cases of *quo minuses* and *latitat*s he had known, but, in all his experience, he did not remember any one instance of an ejectment out of the King's Bench or the Common Bench for all proceedings *in rem* by ejectment or real action out of the proper jurisdiction are void. Anyone that executed process on such proceedings on the land would be a trespasser. And he compared it to the case of a fine levied in the King's Bench of lands in ancient demesne. And he insisted that the reason on which the Lord Chancellor went in the Case of Bewdly was the restrictive words by which it was made doubtful whether the charter intended that court should have jurisdiction in the case then before him.

His Honor [JEKYLL] said it was true that the writs of *quo minus* and *latitat* had gone into the most ancient counties palatine and such as were before the time of prescription, *viz.* Chester and Durham. Lancaster is upon a different foundation being by charter and confirmed by an Act of Parliament, but that the writ of *latitat* never ran in the counties palatine until since the Restoration. And he would not prognosticate how soon *capias*es might get in too and grow as common there. If it were *res integra* to grant prohibitions to inferior courts within the jurisdiction of the counties palatine, he should think it unreasonable. [He said] that he knew no instance of such a prohibition to an inferior court in Wales.

(N.B. An instance was mentioned of a case depending where, by the King's Bench, a prohibition was granted to the Grand Sessions itself in the case of one Vaughan, which Cowper, the Chief Justice of Chester, present now in court, *concessit.*)

He concluded that the jurisdiction of the Cinque Ports was as ancient as the common law itself, that this method would overthrow all inferior jurisdictions, and, therefore, he quashed the *supersedeas.*

788

Harvey v. Woodhouse

(Ch. 1727)

After a bond to release an attachment against a defendant for contempt of court was put in suit at common law and then the contempt was purged, court costs in equity and common law will be taxed to the defendant.

Lincoln's Inn MS. Misc. 12, p. 302

19 April 1727.

The defendant was arrested on an attachment for want of her answer, and she gave a bail bond to the sheriff in the penalty of £40. But not putting in her answer in time, the bond was put in suit against her and also against her bail, and judgment was recovered in both actions. And exceptions being taken out, the bond was paid, the £40 recovered in the action against the defendant as well as the penalty recovered in the other action. And the defendant having put in her answer, she and her bail now moved that it might be referred to the Master to tax the costs at law and in this court and, after deduction of the costs so to be taxed out of the money recovered at law, the remainder might be paid to the defendant.

The Lord Chancellor [Lord King], after consulting with the Master of the Rolls [Jekyll], ordered the Master should tax the costs at law and in this court touching the contempt. And he reserved the consideration how the surplus should be disposed of until it appeared whether the defendant had put in a full answer to the bill.

789

Meredith v. Browning

(Ch. 1727)

A court of equity will not order specific performance of a contract in a lease to repair the premises where the premises are more valuable at the end of the lease than at the beginning.

Lincoln's Inn MS. Misc. 12, p. 303

20 April 1727.

A.B., being seised in fee, leases a house to J.S. for years, and the lessee covenants to keep the premises in good repair and so to leave them at the end of that term. Part of the premises being burnt down, the same were in part rebuilt, but not wholly, by the defendant, who was an assignee of the lease.

The reversion being come to the plaintiff Meredith for life with remainder in fee to the other plaintiff and the lease being expired, they bring their bill against the defendant for a specific performance of the covenant for leaving the premises in good repair.

And it was insisted on for the plaintiffs that such a bill was proper, for the remainderman could not maintain an action at law upon the covenant nor could he join in such action with the tenant for life and, if the tenant for life brought an action, he could only recover damages in proportion to his interest in the estate.

Lord Chancellor [LORD KING] asked the plaintiffs' counsel if they knew of any case where the court had decreed a specific performance of a covenant to repair. But they could not produce any. He said it was not like a covenant to do a thing in certain.

And, after some proofs whereby it appeared that, by the buildings the defendant had made, the premises were of more value than when the defendant first entered, Lord Chancellor [LORD KING] dismissed the bill with costs, saying the matter lay in damages only and was proper at law.

790

Page v. Page

(Ch. 1727–1728)

Where one joint devisee dies in the lifetime of the testator, his part survives to the other devisees.

A devise of 'all my real estate' passes a fee.

Lincoln's Inn MS. Misc. 12, p. 325

21 April 1727.

Joseph Wilkins, by will, devises in these words, *viz.*:

> I give to my cousin A., my cousin B., my cousin C., my cousin D., my cousin E., and my cousin F. all my lands and houses whatsoever and wheresoever belonging to me and all my personal estate, mortgages, judgments, bonds, notes, bills, debts, and everything belonging unto me in the world whatsoever in trust only and upon this express condition and not otherwise that they or some or one of them shall pay and discharge, fulfill, and accomplish in every part without fraud but honestly according to the true intent and meaning and at all times appointed all my legacies and all my orders in this my will that all my lands and whole estate whatsoever are and shall be security for the same and not otherwise and that then, after all these things discharged, the remainder shall be equally divided between them, share and share alike, to all the six, i.e. to my cousin A. his equal share, to my cousin B. his equal share, out of which I give to his sister J.S. the income or yearly rent of £3 a year to be paid her half yearly and so continue paying as long as she lives and then to return to him again, and to my cousin C. his equal share.

And so he names the rest in the same manner, and he makes them executors of his will. Then, there comes this clause:

> and I do further give them this my charge that they will everyone of them distribute at their decease or sooner as need shall require to all their children respectively, shares and shares alike, as I have done to them and as I have given considerable competencies to them to do the same leaving it as this my order at their discretions.

First question: Whether an estate for life or in fee passed in the real estate.

Second: One of the devisees having died in the life of the testator, whether his part belonged to his heir at law or survived to the other devisees.

It was agreed on both sides that there were personal assets sufficient to pay all the debts and legacies; so there was no possibility of loss.

Lord Chancellor [Lord King]: It is a joint devise of the legal estate, and, one devisee dying in the life of the testator, his part survived to the other devisees. Then, the question it is what estate passes. It has been adjudged that a devise of 'all my real estate' passes a fee. Why here, he gives a real estate and gives a personal estate, and then there are these words 'and everything I have in the world', which must pass his whole interest in his estate as well as the estate itself. And then, when the following words are considered, it is plainer still, for, where an estate is given upon trust to pay, it carries a fee, and it is not to be considered whether there may be a loss or not.

2 Peere Williams 489, 24 E.R. 828

One devised the residue of his personal estate to six persons, to each of them a sixth part, and he made them executors. But one of these six executors and residuary legatees died in the lifetime of the testator.

Lord Chancellor [Lord King]: This is a lapsed legacy as to one-sixth, and it is undisposed of by the will, the residuary legatees being tenants in common and not joint tenants. And, therefore, the legacy shall not survive, but go to the testator's next of kin, according to the Statute of Distribution.[1]

2 Strange 820, 93 E.R. 871

A. devises to his six relations, C., D., E., F., G., H. all his lands etc. and all his personal estate in trust to perform his will, and, after all these things discharged, he directed that the remainder should be equally divided amongst them, share and share alike, and made his said six relations executors.

C., one of the legatees, died, and then A., the testator, died. Query whether the share of C., dying in the lifetime of the testator, should go to the surviving residuary legatees as part of the residuum or whether, in this case, it should go to the next of kin of the testator, as so much of his estate undisposed of.

Mr. Solicitor General [*Talbot*] argued that, where there is a lapsed legacy, it falls into the residuum of the personal estate generally. But here, a part of the residuum itself is the lapsed legacy and, consequently, undisposed of and ought to go to the next of kin of the testator, for the executors are to take nothing as executors, but as residuary legatees, and, C. dying in the lifetime of the testator, his share must go according to the Statute of Distributions, as undisposed of.

And so it was decreed.

[Other reports of this case: Mosely 42, 25 E.R. 259.]

---

[1] Stat. 22 & 23 Car. II, c. 10 (*SR*, V, 719–720).

791

Vernon v. Young

(Ch. 1727)

A judgment creditor has priority over a bond creditor.

Lincoln's Inn MS. Misc. 12, p. 215, pl. 1

2 May 1727, Mr. Justice REYNOLDS.

The plaintiff having obtained a decree for the payment of a sum certain by the defendant's testator, it was now decreed the plaintiff should be paid that sum out of the assets preferable to the bond creditors.

Lincoln's Inn MS. Misc. 384, p. 319, pl. 1

2 May. Mr. Justice REYNOLDS.

There was a decree for the payment of a sum certain equal to a judgment. The defendant administrator cannot retain for a bond debt, though it was objected by Mr. Solicitor [General, *Talbot*] that, at law, the defendant could not plead a decree in bar to an action on a bond.

792

Brome v. Berkeley

(Ch. 1727–1728)

In this case, the plaintiff's portion was not payable at the time of the lawsuit according to the terms of the settlement.

Arguments based on public policy are not relevant where the words of a contract or statute are unambiguous.

Lincoln's Inn MS. Misc. 384, p. 327, pl. 3

10 May 1727.

A bill [was exhibited] to have £2500 raised for the plaintiff's portion, it being payable at twenty-one or marriage. The mother, who is tenant for life, is living.

Mr. Solicitor General [*Talbot*], for the plaintiff, cited Sands v. Sands, by Lord Macclesfield, 16 January 1721; Greaves v. Mattison, Jon. 201; Corbet and Maidwell, Salk.; Staniforth v. Staniforth.[1]

---

[1] *Sandys v. Sandys* (Ch. 1722), see above, Case No. 536; *Greaves v. Mattison* (1682), T. Jones 201, 84 E.R. 1216, also Skinner 38, 90 E.R. 19, 1 Eq. Cas. Abr. 336, 21 E.R. 1085; *Corbett v. Maidwell* (1709–1710), 1 Salkeld 159, 91 E.R. 147, also 3 Chancery Reports 190, 21 E.R. 764, 2 Vernon 640, 655, 23 E.R. 1019, 1027, 1 Eq. Cas. Abr. 337, 21

Mr. Attorney General [*Yorke*], for the defendant: The intent of the parties it that the portion should not be raised until the trust term came into possession. In the same clause, maintenance is provided of £100 *per annum* out of the profits when in possession. The maintenance is in lieu of interest. Of the portions, the former cases have gone too far. Thus [see] further Reresby v. Newland, 21 February 1722[/23], by Lord Macclesfield, affirmed in the House of Lords.[1] The first payment of the maintenance was to be paid at such a feast as should happen after the death of the father. Butler v. Duncomb;[2] trustees from and after the commencement of the term to raise the portions.

N.B. By an endorsement, there is a power to charge £2000 if there be no issue male by that marriage but by a second wife and that was not to be raised during the life of the mother.

Mr. Solicitor [General *Talbot*] in reply: First, the portion is to be raised presently; second, interest is due from the time it became payable. In Reresby v. Newland, there was a contingency which could not happen until the death of the father. Therefore, the portion could not be raised in his lifetime. Corbett v. Maidwell; if a daughter was unmarried at the father's death or then unprovided for, which cannot be known during his life. Butler v. Duncombe; trustees from and after the commencement of the term were to raise the portions. Those cases are materially different. In this, there is no difference from the common cases.

Mr. Attorney [General *Yorke*]: As to interest, there was no demand before filing the bill though the plaintiff was of age in 1712. It is very hard to load the estate with fourteen years interest. It was decided in Sands v. Sands.

Curia: Portions payable at a time certain may be raised by a sale of the reversionary interest so settled. Here, it is to trustees in fee on the failure of issue male. If the father die without sons and leaving one daughter, then the trustees, out of rents or by sale or otherwise, are to raise £2500 for her portion and pay the same to her at twenty-one or the day of marriage which shall first happen, and to pay £100 *per annum* for her maintenance, the first payment to be at the first feast as should happen after the trust should take effect in possession. There are two ways to raise the portion and also two ways to raise the maintenance. I will see the Case of Sands v. Sands.

N.B. Afterwards, the bill was dismissed by the Lord Chancellor [Lord King] and the Master of the Rolls [Jekyll], and the plaintiff appealed to the House of Lords, where the decree was affirmed.

Lincoln's Inn MS. Misc. 384, p. 349

13 November. Lord Chancellor [Lord King], Master of the Rolls [Jekyll].

E.R. 1086; *Staniforth v. Staniforth* (1703), 2 Vernon 460, 23 E.R. 895, 1 Eq. Cas. Abr. 337, 21 E.R. 1086, see also above, Case No. 362.

[1] *Reresby v. Newland* (Ch. 1723), see above, Case No. 579.

[2] *Butler v. Duncomb* (Ch. 1718–1719), see above, Case No. 282.

28 January 1689, there was a settlement on the marriage of the plaintiff's father and mother to the use of George Berkeley for life without [impeachment of] waste, then to trustees, then to Jane for life, then to the first son in tail, then to trustees for years in trust if no son and one or more daughters by the rents and profits etc. or otherwise to raise, if one daughter, £2500 and to pay it to her at twenty-one and £100 maintenance until the portion should become due and payable. The first payment was to be at the first feast day which should happen next after the estate limited to the trustees should take effect in possession. George, the husband, died in 1694; the mother is still living. The plaintiff is the only issue of the marriage. The plaintiff married and brought a bill to have the estate sold in the life[time] of the jointress to pay the portion and interest. The defendants insist the plaintiffs are not entitled during the life of the mother.

The Master of the Rolls [Jekyll]: The question is whether it ought to be raised in the life[time] of the jointress. I am of the opinion that it ought not [to be raised] until the estate limited to the trustees takes effect in possession. There have been different opinions as to the raising of portions. I admit, if the term be limited to trustees which is vested, the daughter shall not wait until the death of her mother but have it at marriage etc. Sands v. Sands, 26 January 8 Geo., by Lord Macclesfield; a limitation to the plaintiff's father for life, then to the first son in tail male, then to trustees for 500 years in trust if no son who should attain twenty-one, then to raise £5000 for a daughter to be paid at twenty-one or marriage. The mother died leaving only a daughter who married. He decreed the portion to be raised immediately. The term was vested. Corbett v. Maidwell, Trinity, Sal. 159, Lord Cowper. If a term is not vested or depends on a condition precedent, if *res integra*, [I] would not do it. Why may not a father direct it to be raised after his death and why should a court of equity control it? The daughter was to be unmarried at the death of her father, which was contingent. The maintenance was not to arise until after the death of the father, and that must proceed the raising of the portion. Jones v. Hilliar;[1] the term was vested. Gerard v. Gerard, 2 Vern. 458;[2] the contingency on which the term was to arise had happened, so as such daughter does not marry without consent of the parent or grandparent if living, which implies the marriage might be before the mother's death. This is omitted in Vernon's reports. Staniforth v. Staniforth, 2 Vern. 460, does not prove that the court should decree a sale of the term where the condition has not completely happened. Schuldham v. Schuldham, 321.[3] The opinion of three judges of the King's Bench, in Graves v. Mattison, 2 Jon. 201; Jones was of another opinion; his reasons are stronger than those of the other three.

---

1 *Hellier v. Jones* (1689), 1 Eq. Cas. Abr. 337, 21 E.R. 1085.

2 *Gerrard v. Gerrard* (1704), 2 Vernon 458, 23 E.R. 894, also 2 Freeman 271, 22 E.R. 1204, 1 Eq. Cas. Abr. 337, 21 E.R. 1086.

3 *Shouldham v. Shouldham* (1694), 2 Vernon 321, 23 E.R. 807, also 2 Eq. Cas. Abr. 337, 21 E.R. 1086.

The two first cases are not to the purpose. Lord Cowper was plainly of another opinion; he was not bound to follow those cases. One or two precedents are not sufficient. Therefore, this point is still open for the court to consider whether the term ought to be sold before the death of the mother. There are but two reasons for it, first, all that is contingent has happened. That reason is not sufficient. The execution of the trust of the term is the same as the commencement of the term. Until the death of the mother, it is executory. The second reason is, if a daughter is to stay until the death of the father and mother, she may be so old as not to want a portion. But that may be prevented by the parent's frugality. Though here it is an inconvenience, yet a much greater one will happen to families by a sale of such a reversionary term. A large estate may for a small sum be sold away from a family.

If only one daughter married and then another, there must be different sales and [it would] tear the estate to pieces. Arguments *ab inconvenienti* ought only to have place where the words are ambiguous. Dyer 5a; Lord Falkland v. Bertloe, 2 Vern. 303.[1] Deeds are private laws which men make to themselves and ought not to be altered by any court. In the present case, admitting the contingency on which the execution of the trust is to take effect has happened, but the settlement has provided a maintenance and postponed it to the estate's taking effect. Therefore, the portion must wait too; until it takes effect in possession, the raising the maintenance must precede the raising the portion. Southwell v. Earl of Chesterfield, 29 March 1720, by Lord Macclesfield; to trustees to raise after the commencement of the term, the reversion was not charged with the interest before. Butler v. Duncomb, 2 Vern. 760; Lord Macclesfield took time to consider of it [and] declared it could not affect the reversion until the term commenced. Here, the plaintiff never demanded the maintenance; though she came of age in 1712, she did not bring a bill until 1724, though her father died in 1694. The bill ought to be dismissed. The portion is not to be raised until after the term commenced.

Lord Chancellor [Lord King]: There is very little left for me to say first. All men's deeds must be construed according to their meaning. If these cases had not been adjudged, I should have thought otherwise. If the father were to be asked whether he intended it should be in his lifetime, he would say no. This case stands clear of all the resol[utions]. The maintenance is in the meantime until the portion be raised. So it must precede. And, by this deed, it is not to be until after the estate comes into possession. The bill is brought too soon and must be dismissed.

[This was] affirmed in the House of Lords.

---

[1] *Anonymous* (1533), 1 Dyer 5a, 73 E.R. 12; *Viscount Falkland v. Bertie* (1696), 2 Vernon 333, 23 E.R. 814, also 1 Salkeld 231, 91 E.R. 205, 3 Chancery Cases 129, 22 E.R. 1008, 2 Freeman 220, 22 E.R. 1171, 12 Modern 182, 88 E.R. 1248, Holt K.B. 230, 90 E.R. 1026, Colles 10, 1 E.R. 155, Dickens 25, 21 E.R. 176, 1 Eq. Cas. Abr. 110, 21 E.R. 917, Chancery Cases *tempore* Harcourt, 17.

Lincoln's Inn MS. Misc. 506, p. 89

Michaelmas 2 Geo. II, 1728.

This case stood for the resolution of the court.

Master of the Rolls, Sir Joseph Jekyll: On the marriage of the plaintiff's father and mother, there were indentures of lease and release dated 28 February 1689 whereby, in consideration of marriage and of a £2000 marriage portion, the manor and rectory of [*blank*] were conveyed to George Berkley, the husband, for life, remainders to Jane Cole, the wife, for her life, remainder to trustees to support contingent remainders remainder to the first and every other son in tail male etc., and, in default of issue male, to William Smith and Harry Cole and their heirs on trust that, in case there be no son but only daughters, then, if but one daughter, to raise by sale or otherwise the sum of £2500 to be paid at the age of twenty-one or marriage, the which shall first happen and the yearly sum of £100 for maintenance until the portion should become due and payable to be paid half yearly on Lady Day and Michaelmas, the first payment to be made on the first of those days which should happen after the estate limited to the trustees should take effect in possession etc., etc., other portions in case of more daughters than one. George Berkley died 1694. Jane, the wife, is still living. The plaintiff Elizabeth is the only issue of the marriage. She married the plaintiff Broom, and they two bring a bill against the trustees and the persons entitled to the benefit of the trust in remainder to have the remainder in fee sold during the life of the jointress to raise the £2500 with interest from the time that she came of age. Henry and George Berkley, by their answer, insist that the money cannot be raised until the death of the jointress, when the estate will come to the trustees in possession.

William Smith and Henry Cole, they admit the settlement in the manner set out in the plaintiff's bill and submit to do as the court shall direct.

Upon the whole, the question is whether this portion of £2500 may be raised in the life[time] of the jointress or must stay until after her death. I am of opinion that it ought not to be raised until her death, but to wait until the remainder in fee to Cole and Smith takes place in possession. I think this case very different from the common case by reason of a necessary implication of the words declaring the trust. I admit that, where a term of years or other estate is limited to trustees for raising a portion payable to the daughter at a day certain, if the time of payment be come and the interest is vested, the daughter is not obliged to expect the death of her father or mother until she receive her portion unless it appears from the words declaring the trust that there is an intent to defer it.

Sands v. Sands, 26 January 8 Geo. I, goes no farther than what I have already admitted. There, the limitation was to the father for life, remainder to the first and every other son in tail male, and, in default of issue male, to the trustees for 500 years on trust, that, in case there should be no son and one daughter, to raise £5000 to be paid at twenty-one or marriage, the which shall first happen. The mother died, leaving but one child, a daughter, who was married. She and the husband brought a bill to have the portion raised in the life[time] of the father. It was decreed it should be forthwith raised. Here, the term was vested and the precedent condition had happened.

Corbet and Maidwell, Trinity, 9 Ann. I have a fuller report of that case than is in Salkeld. In that case, Lord Cowper admitted that, if the term did not vest but on a condition or was absolutely vested and the like condition annexed to the payment, there, when the condition for the payment had happened, the term might be sold to raise the portion. But then, he went on and said, 'If this were *res integra*, I should not adjudge it so. And I go into this only by way of concession because one of the cases produced was so. I do not see why the father cannot agree to charge his estate in such manner as shall not take place until after his death. And, if he does, I know no reason why this court should overrule it.' He said that, in that case, the deed went on and made it plainer, for the maintenance is to be raised out of the profits, which profits cannot arise until the death of the father and, therefore, must postpone the payment of the portion, for the maintenance must precede the portion.

Jones and Hilyard was then cited. But the Lord Chancellor [Lord King] observed it was nothing to the purpose.

Gerrard and Gerrard, 2 Vern. 458. The book ought to have said without issue male of that marriage, for so the case was. Here, the contingency had happened. Indeed, the declaration of trust is when the daughter shall marry or arrive at the age of twenty-one after the decease of the father and mother. But to this, it was objected that, if it were not to be payable until the daughter should marry or arrive at twenty-one after the death of the mother, it might never be payable, for the daughter might marry and arrive at twenty-one in the lifetime of the mother. The deed goes on, so as such daughter do not marry before eighteen without the consent of the parent or grandparent if then living; hence, it was argued it might be payable in the life[time] of the mother because her consent to the marriage is required. The Lord Keeper decreed the portion to be raised in the life[time] of the mother.

Stannyforth and Stannyforth. There is reason to think from the report of that case in 2 Vern. 460 that the court did not look upon the condition as a condition not happened, for it is founded on such precedents as would not otherwise warrant it. Sholdam and Sholdam, 2 Vern. 321. But suppose Staniforth's Case were a precedent, it is a single one and unsupported.

Greaves and Matison, 2 Jo. 301; there it was an opinion of three judges against one. In that case, the judges of the King's Bench acted as mediators. I think the reason of the one judge outweighed the reason of the other three. I see no occasion they had to give their opinion upon that point. And though Lord Cowper, in the Case of Corbet, said he would have decreed a sale if the case had come up to that, yet he sufficiently and repeatedly declared his own opinion otherwise, whose opinion I may oppose to that of Trevor, the Master of the Rolls, in

Stannyforth's Case, for I do not think one or two judgments are enough to bind down the opinion of the court.

The arguments for raising the portion are two: first, that all that is contingent has happened; second, that women would not otherwise have their portions at a proper time of life when they most want them.

First, I answer that, where the death of the father or mother is a condition precedent to the term or the execution of it, there the death of the father or mother is inserted to denote the time when it shall be lawful to raise the portion and, until then, the trust is but executory and all that is contingent has not happened, for, though it be certain that all men must die, yet nothing is more uncertain than the time of death.

Second, as to the inconveniences that may follow, they may in great measure be prevented by the care and frugality of the parent. And that is the case here, for it appears in proof that there are considerable other provisions. On the other hand, there may be considerable inconveniences that befall families by these sales, for it is a future interest and but a term when it shall fall out. At this rate, a large estate may for a small sum be sold away from a family and the subsequent limitations disappointed, for, if there be never so many daughters, they have all an equal right as they marry or come of age and so the estate will be mangled and torn in pieces. But great as these inconveniences are, I must admit that they are not to be objected where the words will allow that meaning. But where the sense is plainly otherwise, they ought to prevail to support it. The intent of the parties ought to be the only rule in these cases. I admit that, here, the remainder in fee is a vested estate and that the precedent contingency has happened and, if there were no more in the case, the plaintiff would be entitled to a decree for an immediate sale. But, since, by the clause which provides for a maintenance, the maintenance is not to be raised until the trust estate takes place in possession and that cannot be until the mother's death, it appears to me that the portion cannot be raised until the mother's death, for the maintenance must certainly precede the portion. And Lord Cowper relies on that reason in the case of Corbet and Maidwell.

Tudwell v. Earl of Chesterfield, 29 March 1728. Vice Chamberlain Coke, on his marriage with Mary Stanhope, settled the lands to the common uses with a trust of a term to raise a portion of £5000 at any time after the term should take place, in possession, to be paid when the daughter should marry or attain the age of twenty-one. The wife dies leaving only one daughter. A bill is brought for raising the portion in the life[time] of the father. There, though the Vice Chamberlain submitted to raise it and undertook to keep down the interest, yet the court took care that, in the mortgage, no greater charge should affect the reversion than if it had not been raised until after the father's death.

Butler and Duncomb; there was a proposition to keep down the interest and the husband, being a trader and needing the money, though, by the deed, the portion was not to be raised until after the commencement of the term, the court did go so far as to allow a moiety, but the court declared that the portion was not payable until the death of the jointress nor would it carry interest until then.

It is plain in this case that the plaintiff never thought she had a right to this portion until just before the filing of her bill. The father died in 1694. She was then underage and unmarried [and] never demanded any maintenance. She came of age [in] 1712, married about a year after, and never filed a bill until Trinity vacation 1724.

Lord Chancellor KING: All deeds are to be construed according to the intent of the parties; whether wise or not is not to be considered. Had it not been for the cases that have been, I should have doubted whether, in any case, it ought to be raised in the life[time] of the parent, for, where a sum of money is to be raised by profits or mortgage or sale, one would think it should be when the trustees have a power to receive the profits, mortgage, or sell, but, though that point has been settled otherwise in the cases which have been mentioned, the question is whether this case does not stand clear of those other cases. The maintenance in this case is expressly not to be raised until the trustees come into possession, which cannot be until after the mother's death, and it is evident the maintenance is to be raised before the portion. I think it has been carried far enough already.

The bill was dismissed.

[Other reports of this case: 2 Peere Williams 484, 24 E.R. 826, 6 Brown P.C. 108, 2 E.R. 965, 1 Eq. Cas. Abr. 340, 21 E.R. 1088, 2 Eq. Cas. Abr. 649, 22 E.R. 545.]

793

Waller v. Waller

(Ch. c. 1727)

Where a vendor defrauds a purchaser as to encumbrances on the land sold, a court of equity will grant relief to the purchaser.

Lincoln's Inn MS. Misc. 12, p. 304, pl. 2

A purchase deed being lost, in which was a covenant from the vendor against encumbrances and, after the purchase, it was discovered the estate was subject to an annuity, the plaintiff brought his bill against the heir and executor of the vendor to have satisfaction for this annuity.

The draft by which the conveyance was engrossed was fully proved, but there was not a sufficient proof of the execution of the conveyance, and, though it was admitted that the plaintiff did really purchase the estate, yet it was not admitted that there was such a covenant.

However, the Master of the Rolls [JEKYLL] decreed the plaintiff a satisfaction of what he had paid or should pay in discharge of the annuity out of the personal assets, for, he said, though the proof that there was a covenant against encumbrances was not sufficient and, therefore, the heir could not be affected with the plaintiff's demand, yet, if there really had been no covenant at all against encumbrances, the vendor would be liable in equity to make satisfaction for any encumbrance which was upon the estate at the time of the sale and which was concealed from the vendee where the sale is for a full and valuable consideration.

794
Collingwood v. Wallis
(Ch. 1727)

In this case, the devise in issue was valid and passed the estate in issue to the plaintiff.

Lincoln's Inn MS. Misc. 12, p. 305

13 May 1727.

Collingwood and his wife conveyed lands to the plaintiff and B. and their heirs on trust that they should or might with the consent of him and his wife sell and dispose thereof for the raising of so much money as should be sufficient to pay off the proper debts as well of the said C. charged on his estate at D. as also all the debts of J.S. which should be allowed by C. and his wife to be due and all interest that should become due until payment and, if, after the sale of all and every the premises and after payment of all of the said debts and interest, there should remain any money in the hands of the trustees, then they or the survivor should forthwith pay such surplus to C. and his wife or to such person as they, by writing, should appoint.

The trustees sold the greatest part of the estate and paid the debts. C. survived his wife and, by will, gave part of the lands unsold to the plaintiff and his heirs.

The plaintiff brought his bill against the surviving trustee and the heir at law of the wife that the trustee might convey the estate so devised to the plaintiff, to him, and his heirs. It was admitted that the estate in question was originally the estate of the wife.

For the defendant, the heir at law, it was insisted that the intention of the parties was only to provide for the payment of the debts and to sell no more than was necessary for that purpose and, that end being satisfied by the payment of the debts, there was a resulting trust to the heir at law of the wife whose estate this originally was.

Lord Chancellor [Lord King]: There is no difficulty in this case. The words are that all and every part shall be sold and C., having survived his wife, by the express words of the settlement became entitled to the surplus. If the wife had survived her husband, she would have had it. C. might have considered the surplus either as real or personal estate. At his death, it was real estate, and he has devised it accordingly.

It appearing there were some debts unpaid, the estate devised to the plaintiff was decreed to be sold and the surplus, after the debts paid, was ordered to be paid to the plaintiff.

[Other reports of this case: 1 Eq. Cas. Abr. 395, 21 E.R. 1128.]

795

Berners v. Berners

(Ch. 1727)

A posthumous child is a living child of his deceased father.

Lincoln's Inn MS. Misc. 12, p. 307

17 May 1727.

By a settlement made on the marriage of William Berners with Elizabeth Raworth, the plaintiff's father and mother, a term of 1000 years was limited to trustees precedent to the limitations to the first and other sons of the marriage upon trust that, in case the said William Berners should have one or more younger child or children, whether male or female, begotten on the body of the said Elizabeth which should be living at the time of the death of the said William Berners, then the trustees should after his death or in his lifetime with his consent by the rents and profits or by the sale or mortgage raise the sums thereinafter mentioned for the portions and maintenances of such younger child or children in such parts and proportions as the said William Berners should appoint and, for want of such appointment, as follows, *viz.* if but one younger child, to raise £3000, if two £4000, if three or more £5000 to be paid to sons at twenty-one and to daughters at twenty-one or marriage, if either died, the share of such child to go to the survivors but no one child to have more than £3000, and £40 a year apiece was provided for the maintenance of the younger children.

Sometime after the marriage, William Berners, by his will, reciting the settlement and taking notice that he had but [one] younger son and that his wife was then with child, he appoints, if his wife should have another child in his lifetime or after his death and such child should be a son, his younger son then born and such other son should have £4000 between them. William Berners died, leaving two sons, Robert and the defendant William, and his wife *enceinte* with the plaintiff, who was born about three months after the death of his father. Robert, the eldest son, died under age after his father.

And the plaintiff, being now the only younger child, brings his bill for his portion of £3000.

And he being a posthumous son, the question was if he was entitled, the trusts of the term being to raise portions for such younger child or children as should be living at the death of the father.

The Master of the Rolls [JEKYLL] was clear of opinion that the plaintiff, though born after, was a child living at the death of the father and within the provision of the settlement. And, without any difficulty, he decreed the plaintiff the £3000 portion and maintenance in the meantime.

796

Anonymous

(Ch. 1727)

In this case, the question was whether a bond to keep the peace should be discharged after five years of good behavior.

British Library MS. Hargrave 83, p. 69

Trinity term, 4 June 1727.

Upon a motion to vacate a recognizance entered into upon a *supplicavit*, five years being elapsed since, as was suggested, and no cause since given for continuing the recognizance by any misbehavior of the conusor, Lord Chancellor [LORD KING] had referred it to a master to state in what manner recognizances had been usually given upon a *supplicavit* and how vacated. And now, this motion came on upon the master's report, which was to this effect, that of late, recognizances had been usually given indefinitely without any limited time, that, formerly, they were given sometimes for a year and a day, and, at other times, generally, that the method of discharging them had been either by consent or upon certification of the party's good behavior for a considerable time.

It was now urged that it was unreasonable that a person should lie in prison or under the penalty of such a recognizance for life, that it was the course of the King's Bench to take such recognizances only for a year and a day and then they were discharged of course upon motion, that this was the ancient usage of this court and there ought to be uniformity in the proceedings of both courts as to the same matter, that there had now been a long space of time elapsed and no complaint made and, therefore, the recognizance ought to be vacated, that besides it had been taken irregularly, for it was upon the affirmation of a Quaker against her husband that she had tried to obtain this upon articles in the King's Bench, but the court there took it to be a criminal proceeding and so not within the Statute that indulges a Quaker's affirmation.[1]

It was answered that persons come into this court on *supplicavits* only for enormous offenses and upon such attempts as made it necessary to have a rod hang over the person who had discovered such a malicious intention, that they had an affidavit which showed that the threats and outrages of the person who

[1] Stat. 7 & 8 Will. III, c. 34, s. 1 (*SR*, VII, 152).

gave the recognizance had been such that it was by no means fit to vacate it, which they desired might be read.

But My Lord [KING] referred it to the master to examine the matter and certainty whether the party's behavior had been such that it was fit to vacate the recognizance. But he said he would not consider the matter of the affirmation or whether it had been taken regularly in that respect.

797

Downes v. Baines

(Ch. 1727)

Part performance of a contract is sufficient proof thereof to take it out of the Statute of Frauds.

Lincoln's Inn MS. Misc. 12, p. 309

5 June 1727. At Westminster.

In this case, the Master of the Rolls [JEKYLL] was of opinion that A.B., under whom the plaintiff claimed, having taken a mortgage in the name of another person in the year 1682 for £150 and there was no receipt upon the deed for the consideration but [it was] only mentioned to be paid to the person to whom the mortgage was made and a bond was given to the same person, nor was there any proof of actual payment but only a proof that the mortgagor acknowledged the money was paid by the *cestui que trust* and the person to whom the mortgage was made, though he had executed no declaration of trust, had in an answer to a bill formerly brought against him by the defendant, who had a second mortgage, acknowledged that he did not pay the £150 nor knew anything of the mortgage when it was made and claimed no interest therein in his own right, that all this taken together was sufficient to take this case out of the Statute of Frauds[1] and to make it a resulting trust.

He said that, if the mortgage had been a late transaction, it would be necessary to bring it out of the Statute and to make it a resulting trust, that there should be proof of some fact. But, in the present case, after so great a length of time, it was not reasonable to expect proof of an actual payment, and, though there was no receipt upon the back of the deed, yet there was a bond, which was as good, if not better, than a receipt, for it was a distinct instrument, so that here was a proof of a fact, *viz.* the execution of the bond, and, although the bond as well as the mortgage was made in the name of a third person, yet he had disclaimed, and, besides, he took notice that the mortgage and bond were in the hands of the plaintiff and it was highly improbable the plaintiff should have them

---

[1] Stat. 29 Car. II, c. 3 (*SR*, V, 839–842).

unless the person under whom he claimed had paid the money. And this was a circumstance which he very much relied on.

798
Lord Castlehaven v. Page

(Ch. 1727)

The question in this case was whether a contract can be set aside as harsh where there is a gross inadequacy of consideration.

Another question in this case was whether acts of Parliament can be proved by the printed version only without resort to the records of Parliament.

British Library MS. Hargrave 83, p. 71

10 June 1727. At the Lord Chancellor's house.

The bill was for a specific performance of articles entered into in October 1720 after the fall of South Sea [Company] stock for the purchase of lands. There was some proof in the cause that the lands were not worth above £80 *per annum*, but that proof was not full. The purchase money was to be £3500.

My Lord Chancellor [Lord King] inclined to decree for the plaintiff, but gave time to the defendant until next Monday to offer a composition.

In this case, there was nothing insisted on but the exorbitant price. And yet the Solicitor General [*Talbot*] seemed to be very strong in his opinion against My Lord, though the Chancellor observed that this was after the fall of stock and when the delusion was pretty well over.

In this case, there was a struggle whether an inventory given in upon oath by one of the South Sea directors pursuant to the Act of Parliament[1] and printed by order of the House of Commons should be read, the Attorney General [*Yorke*] insisting it was not evidence and could not. And My Lord inclining to that opinion, however, he looked into it himself, but it was not a point upon which the case turned.

The counsel that would have had it read compared it to a printed act of Parliament and to the printed accounts of the deficient Masters in Chancery.[2]

On the other side, it was argued that printed acts of Parliament had but of late come in to be read as evidence, and still it was only such as were printed by the King's Printer and that privately printed acts were not yet admitted in evidence, but there must be a copy compared with the record and proved to be a true copy.

And in the case of the Masters, their accounts were printed by order of the court and consequently were an act of the court and part of its proceedings.

1 Stat. 7 Geo. I, stat. 1, c. 1.
2 Stat. 12 Geo. I, cc. 32, 33.

The Attorney General [*Yorke*] said that a printed proclamation could not be given in evidence, but that there must be a proved copy of the record, which My Lord Chancellor [King] agreed in criminal cases.

Query whether printed acts of Parliament be not read at the Old Bailey?

Index of Names of Persons and Places

[References are to case numbers, not page numbers.]

Subject Index

[These references are to case numbers, not page numbers.]